GATEWAYS
TO DEMOCRACY

AN INTRODUCTION TO AMERICAN GOVERNMENT

JOHN G.
GEER
VANDERBILT UNIVERSITY

WENDY J.
SCHILLER
BROWN UNIVERSITY

JEFFREY A.
SEGAL
STONY BROOK UNIVERSITY

 **WADSWORTH**
CENGAGE Learning™

Australia • Brazil • Japan • Korea • Mexico • Singapore • Spain • United Kingdom • United States

WADSWORTH
CENGAGE Learning™

Gateways to Democracy: An Introduction to American Government
John G. Geer, Wendy J. Schiller, and Jeffrey A. Segal

Publisher: Suzanne Jeans

Executive Editor: Carolyn Merrill

Managing Development Editor:
    Jeffrey Greene

Developmental Editor: Ann Hofstra Grogg

Assistant Editor: Laura Ross

Editorial Assistant: Nina Wasserman

Media Editor: Laura Hildebrand

Marketing Manager: Lydia LeStar

Marketing Communications Manager:
    Heather Baxley

Production Manager: Suzanne St. Clair

Art Director: Linda Helcher

Print Buyer: Fola Orekoya

Printer: RRD Menasha

Rights Acquisition Specialist, Image:
    Jennifer Meyer Dare

Rights Acquisition Specialist, Text:
    Katie Huha

Photo Researcher: Stacey Dong

Text Researcher: Sarah D'Stair

Production Service: MPS Limited,
    a Macmillan Company

Copy Editor: Sybil Sosin

Cover and Interior Designer: RHDG

Cover Images:
    Front Cover: © Marjorie Kamys Cotera;
    Kenn Stilger/Shutterstock; Photo
    courtesy of George Tarbay, University
    Relations, Northern Illinois University;
    Courtesy of the University Science and
    Arts of Oklahoma; Courtesy of the
    College of the Redwoods, Eureka
    Back Cover (Student Edition): © 2010
    Carlos Gotay/Getty Images;
    DianeRicePhotos.com; © Bob Kalmbach/
    University of Michigan Photo Services—
    ALL RIGHTS RESERVED

Compositor: MPS Limited,
    a Macmillan Company

Library of Congress Control Number: 2010935367

Student Edition:

ISBN-13: 978-0-618-90695-6

ISBN-10: 0-618-90695-9

Wadsworth
20 Channel Center Street
Boston, MA 02210
USA

Cengage Learning is a leading provider of customized learning solutions with office locations around the globe, including Singapore, the United Kingdom, Australia, Mexico, Brazil, and Japan. Locate your local office at **www.cengage.com/global**.

Cengage Learning products are represented in Canada by Nelson Education, Ltd.

To learn more about Wadsworth, visit **www.cengage.com/Wadsworth**.

Purchase any of our products at your local college store or at our preferred online store **www.cengagebrain.com**.

Printed in the United States of America
2 3 4 5 14 13 12 11

BRIEF CONTENTS

FEATURES

Supreme Court Cases

Policy Coverage

Other Places

CONTENTS

PART II   Citizen Gateways in a Democracy

6 PUBLIC OPINION 174

7 THE NEWS MEDIA AND THE INTERNET 208

8 INTEREST GROUPS 244

9 POLITICAL PARTIES 280

15 THE JUDICIARY 520

16 THE UNITED STATES AS A GLOBAL PARTNER 558

PREFACE

Our book begins with a simple question: How does anyone exert political influence in a country of more than 308 million people? We know that students in American government classrooms across the country are grappling with this question as they develop an appreciation of their role in American public life. In our own classrooms, students ask us, What is my responsibility? Can I make a difference? Does my participation matter? How can I get my opinions represented? These are gateway questions that probe the opportunities and limits on citizen involvement in a democracy.

Although the size and complexity of the American constitutional system is daunting, it is imperative to prepare students for the demands of democratic citizenship. As teachers and scholars of American government, we have come together to write a textbook that explains the theoretical and structural foundations of American democracy and the resulting political process that demands an active and informed citizenry. To help students understand American democracy and see how they can be involved in their government, we peel back the layers of the political system to expose its inner workings and to examine how competing interests can both facilitate and block the people's will. In doing so, we use the conceptual framework of gateways. We contend that there are gates—formal and informal—that present obstacles to participation and empowerment. But there are also gateways that give students a chance to influence the process and to overcome the obstacles.

The gateways framework helps students conceptualize participation and civic engagement—even democracy itself—with reference to access. Our book is both realistic and optimistic, contending that the American system can be open to the influence of students and responsive to their hopes and dreams—if they have information about how the system works. But we avoid cheerleading by also pointing out the many gates that undermine the workings of government.

We use the gateways theme to encourage students to develop critical thinking skills. We employ concrete examples of political activism and engagement, from a teenager to the president of the United States, inviting students to enter a conversation about the workings of American democracy. This textbook digs below the surface of standard descriptions of democracy by asking students to consider how democratic we are as a nation. We pose questions: Does equality require an equal process, or does it require equal outcomes? How responsive and accountable is American government? And we challenge students to figure out their own standards for the society in which they want to live in the twenty-first century. Questions like these encourage students to think about the meaning of self-government, and they constitute a sustained analytical component of this textbook.

Organization of the Textbook

We begin and end with student engagement. Chapter 1 describes the demands of democratic citizenship, and Chapter 17 asks students to judge American democracy. In the three parts in between, we examine the foundations of the American constitutional system, the means of citizen access and influence in a democratic society, and the institutions of American government.

Chapter 1, Gateways to American Democracy, provides the rationale and road map for citizen engagement in self-government. We describe the Constitution as a gatekeeper, protecting liberty and order but also facilitating representation. The dimensions of representation are set forth as ideological, economic, and partisan. The chapter's overall goal is to establish the nature of democracy, the need for an informed citizenry, and the framework we employ on this intellectual journey.

We include in this chapter a special section that describes the policy-making process as a foundation for policy coverage throughout the book. We view policy as central to understanding American democracy. As a result, we do not isolate the discussion of policy in chapters at the end of the book. Instead, we integrate policy into each of the substantive chapters, situating it as a central part of understanding American politics. By so doing, we underscore the importance of the topic and give students a better understanding of American government.

Part I, Building a System of Government, includes chapters on the Constitution, federalism, civil liberties, and civil rights that discuss the major issues the Framers confronted when they created a representative government. This section examines why the Framers made particular choices and what the intended and unintended consequences of their decisions have been over time. Students will understand that the ideals expressed in the Declaration of Independence have only slowly been realized and are still evolving. This section of the textbook provides basic information about the operation of American government—the separation of powers, unitary president, lifetime appointments for judges, staggered elections, divided legislature, state and local government, and geographic apportionment—and helps students assess whether the foundations of American government ensure responsiveness and equality.

Part II, Citizen Gateways in a Democracy, includes chapters on public opinion, the news media, interest groups, political parties, campaigns and elections, and voting and participation. Together these chapters address the question of how a single individual's opinions are formed, expressed, and included in the policy-making process at all levels of government. These matters are essential to our approach. If students are to be part of the political process, they need to understand how to make the best use of the avenues for representation that exist in the American political system. We begin with basic data about how much people know about American government, where they get their information, whom they listen to, and to what extent their opinions change over time. By starting with individual opinion, we help students assess their own opinions about politics and analyze the sources of those opinions.

We continue with the nature of communication among citizens by addressing the impact of the news media on American politics. The news media are important sources of information for the public, politicians, and policy elites. They do more than just report the news; they frequently construct the news. We talk about the role of the news media not only historically but also in the context of the rise of cable news networks, the growth of the Internet, the decline of newspapers, and the potential of social networking. Does the immediacy of the modern media environment have an empowering or a detrimental effect on our democratic system? Does the intense and sometimes intrusive media scrutiny enhance or restrict government's responsiveness to the needs of its citizenry? These are the kinds of questions we address to get students thinking about the political environment in which twenty-first-century government has to function.

We then turn to interest groups as a means by which individual opinions are aggregated and given voice in a democracy, but in markedly different ways and to varying degrees of success. Community or grassroots efforts, from environmental movements to religious organizations to public interest groups, are often a satisfying and empowering form of civic participation. The conventional wisdom is that powerful "special interests" can trounce small citizens' groups when competing for government benefits, but we counter that the increasing number of interest groups means that more people are represented in the formulation of public policy and that improved communication has given small citizens' groups a new gateway for influence.

We next examine how political parties evolved and their crucial and controversial roles in the functioning of government. From the first debates over the ratification of the Constitution to the recent Tea Party movement, this chapter delves into the reasons why the United States remains a predominantly two-party political system. We also address the nature of partisan identification, realignment, modern party organizations, and the nature of party accountability in government. A fundamental theme of the chapter is whether parties have the potential to serve as instruments for engaging and channeling citizens' efforts to elicit responsiveness from government.

The last two chapters in this part look directly at the most basic form of participation in a democracy—elections, campaigns, and voting. When politicians seek elective office, they strive to appear as responsive as possible. Can voters make informed decisions and hold their elected officials accountable? We grapple with the difficult question of whether or how much campaigns as political institutions shape our government. Campaigns tend to be associated with "dirty politics" and candidates who are willing to say anything to get elected. But such perceptions miss the fact that campaigns are also gateways connecting the public and politicians. We argue that political campaigns provide voters with the information they need to make good choices and to hold public officials accountable. We also provide comprehensive analyses of the accuracy and type of information presented in campaigns, the financing of campaigns, the strategic framing of campaign issues, and the factors that ultimately determine the outcomes of elections.

Voting is, of course, the most straightforward and least costly form of participation in American democracy. It is also the simplest way for individuals to influence their elected officials. But students are often skeptical about the power of the vote. Given the size of the country, do all votes even count? If they do, are they counted equally? The election of 2000 serves as a sharp illustration of why and how individual votes can matter, and we look also at the 2008 election that sparked great interest and attention. We discuss other types of civic participation such as membership in religious and community-based organizations, not-for-profit organizations, and Internet blogging. We use this chapter in part to illustrate how the gateways to involvement in twenty-first-century American life are wider and more direct than they have been in the past.

Part III, The Institutions of American Government, provides an in-depth description and explanation of Congress, the presidency, the bureaucracy, and the judiciary. In the Institutions chapters, we describe the fundamental components of Congress, the presidency, and the judiciary as well as the ways each interacts with the other two. We ask students to examine the behavior and outputs of government by responsiveness and equality. For example, does having term limits weaken the president relative to Congress, which does not have term limits? Does the bicameral structure of Congress give the legislative branch an advantage when dealing with the executive branch? We also focus students' attention on how party politics creates a governing dynamic that changes depending on the balance of control of these branches. For the judicial branch, we contend that the courts provide an important gateway for influencing the process and also for advancing the cause of equality. Yet courts are not electorally accountable to citizens, and federal judges hold life tenure. Do the courts mete out equal justice to all citizens, regardless of race and income? If they do not, are there means beyond elections by which Congress and the president can help hold courts accountable?

In the chapter on the bureaucracy, our aim is to show students how policy making and the bureaucracy affect day-to-day life. We examine the layers of bureaucratic decision making to demonstrate that the decisions made at each level of an agency or cabinet department can have a profound impact on how laws affect individuals. We discuss decision making in the areas of economic policy, budget policy, entitlement spending for the elderly and the disadvantaged, health care policy, education policy, and environmental policy, all in the context of the dynamics of policy implementation within agencies and the departments that oversee them. In these discussions, we highlight the areas of public policy that students may experience firsthand.

We have two concluding chapters. The first—**Chapter 16, The United States as a Global Partner**—examines how the United States will navigate the changing global economic and political environment of the twenty-first century. In it we look at the compatibility of American democratic ideals, values, and institutions with other forms of government and ask whether the United States can forge working relationships with governments that are different from it. This chapter looks at the global footprint of the United States in the areas of trade and economic development, arms control and human rights, and health, energy consumption, and climate change.

The final chapter—**Chapter 17, Judging the Democratic Experiment**—encourages students to synthesize the book's content and assess how they might navigate the gateways we have examined to become effective citizens. In doing so, we want to provide students with tools and incentives to assess the quality of their current political institutions. We point out that how one assesses the American political system depends very much on where one sits. Further, the standards one brings to bear shape the answers one develops. There will always be a gap between the ideals and the realities of government, but that is a good thing, for it provides the reason to improve government and bring the nation closer to its ideals. In short, this textbook offers students the information they need to answer gateway questions thoughtfully. Their participation in your classroom will be an important step toward engaging the demands of twenty-first-century public life.

Special Instructional Features

Special instructional features facilitate a comprehensive introduction to American government that also takes the demands of citizenship seriously.

Participation. A goal of the book is to encourage participation in public life by helping students recognize their own self-interest and a broader civic interest. The book makes the case that democracies demand citizen participation and that citizenship is a serious responsibility.

Critical thinking. We also want to facilitate critical thinking by asking students to evaluate American democracy through the measures of government responsiveness and citizen equality. This emphasis sharpens students' analytical skills and gives them greater competence and additional confidence to become involved in public life. We devote special sections in each chapter to fundamental types of information that we believe students need to navigate the political process. We also add pedagogical tools to help both instructors and students identify key concepts and terms.

Constitutional and legal setting. For instructors, the book provides strong support for the institutional foundations of American government. The first section of every chapter is an overview of the constitutional and legal setting of the chapter's subject. This essential basic information helps ensure that students are equipped with what they need to know to understand the process, limits, and safeguards of democracy.

Public policy. We believe public policy is much too important to be relegated to separate chapters at the back of the book. Students cannot take their place as active citizens in American democracy unless they understand how the policy process works. We bring policy applications into our consideration of every aspect of American government by incorporating the policy process and specific policy examples in a dedicated section in every chapter. Attention to a series of specific issues in a variety of contexts helps students understand the political process. And, indeed, specific policies are often the best incentives for getting them engaged.

Student engagement. In the opening of every chapter we focus on people who were young when they got their start in political and civic life, to encourage students and show them reasons and ways to become involved.

Comparative feature. A box in each chapter examines a particular topic with reference to political practice in other countries.

Supreme Court feature. To buttress the book's attention to the legal and constitutional context in which American government operates, each chapter features a relevant Supreme Court case, stating the facts and the decision, with an analysis of its impact.

Pedagogical Tools for Conceptual Reinforcement

An array of pedagogical tools supports the textbook's purpose and aids in student learning.

Focus questions. Focus questions at the beginning of each chapter encourage students to think about the chapter topic in terms of government's responsiveness, the people's equality, and the gates and gateways to access. These questions are revisited in the chapter's final section, where we offer interpretive responses.

Margin questions and cues. Brief questions in the margins provoke students to think about the big issues even as they are reading about the details of American government. These questions keep students thinking critically about the information they are absorbing, serve as prompts for class discussions, and aid in chapter review.

Key terms. Terms important to know for an understanding of American government are boldfaced in the text and defined on the page for ease of understanding and review.

Gateways to Learning. A special "Gateways to Learning" section at the end of each chapter includes a ten-point list of main ideas for review and learning. Lists of key terms, timelines, exercises, review questions, and resources are also included in this section and on the book's website.

To access additional course materials and companion resources, please visit www.cengagebrain.com/shop/ISBN/0618906959 or visit www.cengagebrain.com and search on the ISBN of this book.

Supplements

For ordering information, see www.cengage.com/community/gatewaystodemocracy.

PowerLecture DVD with JoinIn™ and ExamView®
ISBN-10: 0495913405 | ISBN-13: 9780495913405

This DVD includes two sets of PowerPoint® slides—a book-specific set and a media-enhanced set—a Test Bank in both Microsoft® Word and ExamView formats, an Instructor's Manual, JoinIn clicker questions, and a Resource Integration Guide.

- **Interactive book-specific PowerPoint lectures** make it easy for you to assemble, edit, publish, and present book-specific lectures for your course. You will have access to outlines specific to each chapter of the text as well as to photos, figures, and tables found in the text.
- **Media-enhanced PowerPoint slides** can be used on their own or easily integrated with the book-specific PowerPoint outlines. Look for audio and video clips depicting both historic and current day events; animated learning modules illustrating key concepts; tables, statistical charts, and graphs; and photos from the book as well as from outside sources.
- **Test bank in Microsoft Word and ExamView computerized testing** offers a large array of well-crafted multiple-choice and essay questions, along with their answers and page references.
- **Instructor's Manual** includes learning objectives, chapter outlines, discussion questions, suggestions for stimulating class activities and projects, tips on integrating media into your class (including step-by-step instructions on how to create your own podcasts), suggested readings and web resources, and a section specially designed to help teaching assistants and adjunct instructors.
- **JoinIn "clicker" questions** test and track student comprehension of key concepts.
- **The Resource Integration Guide** outlines the rich collection of resources available to instructors and students within the chapter-by-chapter framework of the book, suggesting how and when each supplement can be used to optimize learning.

CourseMate
ISBN-10: 0538498986 | ISBN-13: 9780538498982

The media-rich CourseMate website offers a variety of rich online learning resources designed to enhance the student learning experience. These resources include video activities, audio summaries, critical thinking exercises, simulations, animated learning modules, interactive timelines, primary source quizzes, flashcards, learning objectives, glossaries, and crossword puzzles. Chapter resources are correlated to key chapter learning concepts, and users can browse or search for content in a variety of ways.

NewsNow is a new asset available in CourseMate. It is a combination of weekly new stories from the Associated Press and videos and images that bring current events to life for the student. For instructors, NewsNow includes an additional set of multimedia-rich PowerPoint slides posted each week to the password-protected area of the text's instructor companion website. Instructors may use these slides to take a class poll or trigger a lively debate about the events that are shaping the world right now.

The **Engagement Tracker** assesses student preparation and engagement. Use the tracking tools to see progress for the class as a whole or for individual students. Identify students at risk early in the course. Uncover which concepts are most difficult for your class. Monitor time on task. Keep your students engaged.

CourseMate also features an **interactive eBook** that has highlighting and search capabilities along with links to simulations, animated PowerPoint slides that illustrate concepts, interactive timelines, video activities, primary source quizzes, and flashcards.

Go to www.cengagebrain.com/shop/ISBN/6018906959 to access your Political Science CourseMate resources.

American Government CourseReader: Politics in Context

CourseReader Printed Access Card: ISBN-10: 111147995X | ISBN-13: 9781111479954

The CourseReader allows instructors to create a customized reader using a database of hundreds of documents, readings, and videos. Instructors can search by various criteria or browse the collection to preview and then select a customized collection to assign their students. The sources are edited to an appropriate length and include pedagogical support—a headnote describing the document, and critical-thinking and multiple-choice questions to verify that the student has read and understood the selection. Students can take notes, highlight, and print content. The CourseReader allows the instructor to select exactly what students will be assigned with an easy-to-use interface and also provides an easily used assessment tool. The sources can be delivered online or in print format.

Aplia (available for Fall 2011 classes)

Text + Aplia Printed Access Card: ISBN-10: 1111300801 | ISBN-13: 9781111300807

Aplia is dedicated to improving students' learning by increasing their engagement with your American government course through premium, automatically graded assignments. Aplia saves instructors valuable time they would otherwise spend on routine grading while giving students an easy way to stay on top of coursework with regularly scheduled assignments.

Assignments are organized by specific chapters of the students' textbook, and the students receive immediate, detailed explanations for every answer they input. Grades are automatically recorded in the instructor's Aplia gradebook.

Instructor Companion Website

The instructor companion site includes the Instructor's Manual; text-specific PowerPoint slides containing lecture outlines, photos, and figures; and NewsNow PowerPoint slides.

WebTutor™ on WebCT or Blackboard

**Printed Text + WebCT Printed Access Card: ISBN-10: 0538474718 |
ISBN-13: 9780538474719**

**Printed Text + Blackboard Printed Access Card: ISBN-10: 0618906401 |
ISBN-13: 9780618906406**

Rich with content for your American government course, this web-based teaching and learning tool includes course management, study/mastery, and communication tools. Use WebTutor to provide virtual office hours, post your syllabus, and track student progress with WebTutor's quizzing material.

CourseCare

Available exclusively to Cengage Learning, CourseCare is a revolutionary program designed to provide you and your students with an unparalleled user experience with your Cengage Learning digital solution.

CourseCare connects you with a team of training, service, and support experts to help you implement your Cengage Learning Digital Solution. Real people are dedicated to you, your students, and your course from the first day of class through final exams.

Political Theatre 2.0

ISBN-10: 0495793604 | ISBN-13: 9780495793601

Bring politics home to students with Political Theatre 2.0, up-to-date through the 2008 election season. This second edition of the three-DVD series includes real video clips that illustrate American political thought throughout the public sector. Clips include both classic and contemporary political advertisements, speeches, interviews, and more.

JoinIn on Turning Point® for Political Theatre

ISBN-10: 0495798290 | ISBN-13: 9780495798293

For even more interaction, combine Political Theatre with the innovative teaching tool of a classroom response system through JoinIn. Poll your students with questions created for you, or create your own questions.

The Wadsworth News Videos for American Government 2012 DVD

ISBN-10: 1111346143 | ISBN-13: 9781111346140

This collection of three- to six-minute video clips on relevant political issues serves as a great lecture or discussion launcher.

Great Speeches Collection

Throughout the ages, great orators have stepped up to the podium and used their communication skills to persuade, inform, and inspire their audiences. Studying these speeches can provide tremendous insight into historical, political, and cultural events. The Great Speeches Collection includes the full text of over sixty memorable orations for you to incorporate into your course. Speeches can be collated in a printed reader to supplement your existing course materials or bound into a core textbook.

ABC Video: Speeches by President Barack Obama

ISBN-10: 1439082472 | ISBN-13: 9781439082478

This DVD of nine famous speeches by President Barack Obama includes his speech at the 2004 Democratic National Convention; his 2008 speech on race, "A More Perfect Union"; and his 2009 inaugural address. Speeches are divided into short video segments for easy, time-efficient viewing. This instructor supplement also features critical-thinking questions and answers for each speech, designed to spark classroom discussion.

Election 2010: An American Government Supplement

Text + Election 2010 supplement: ISBN-10: 1111341788 | ISBN-13: 9781111341787

Written by John Clark and Brian Schaffner, this booklet addresses the 2010 congressional and gubernatorial races, with both real-time analysis and references.

The Obama Presidency—Year One Supplement

ISBN-10: 0495908371 | ISBN-13: 9780495908371

Kenneth Janda–Northwestern University
Jeffrey M. Berry–Tufts University
Jerry Goldman–Northwestern University

Much happens in the first year of a presidency, especially a historic one like that of Barack Obama. This sixteen-page full-color supplement by Kenneth Janda, Jeffrey Berry, and Jerry Goldman analyzes such issues as health care reform, the economy and the stimulus package, changes in the U.S. Supreme Court, and the effect of Obama policy on global affairs.

Instructor's Guide to YouTube for Political Science

Instructors have access to the Instructor's Guide to YouTube, which directs American government instructors to the locations of Internet videos that can be used as learning tools in class. Organized by fifteen topics, the guide follows the sequence of an American government course and includes a preface with tips on how to use Internet videos in class.

Acknowledgments

Writing the first edition of an introductory textbook requires a dedicated and professional publishing team, and we were extremely fortunate to work with a number of excellent people at Wadsworth Publishing/Cengage Learning. Our development editor, Ann Hofstra Grogg, has been outstanding; she was an essential part of translating our ideas about encouraging students to participate in American politics into an organized and comprehensive textbook. Although our sponsoring editor, Edwin Hill, did not see this project to its completion, he was an integral part of it, and we thank him for all his guidance. We thank Matthew DiGangi for his time and energy. We want to extend a special note of thanks to Carolyn Merrill, who has been so supportive of this project. Joshua Allen, Stacey Dong, Jeffrey Greene, Suzanne Jeans, Monica Ohlinger, and Sybil Sosin all provided key support on format, photos, and production of this book. We also would like to thank Amy Whitaker, Lydia LeStar, and the entire sales force at Wadsworth Publishing for their tireless efforts to promote the book. In addition, we thank Traci Mueller for her early support of this project.

By definition, an American politics textbook is a sweeping endeavor, and it was not possible to succeed without our reviewers. They provided truly constructive input throughout the writing process. We list their names below, and we are grateful to them for their contributions to the development of this textbook.

Each of us would also like to thank the individuals who supported us throughout the project.

John G. Geer: I wish to thank Corey Bike and Mason Moseley for able research assistance. I also want to express deep appreciation to my daughter, Megan Geer, and my cousin, William Geer Masalehdan, for reading early drafts of my chapters and providing helpful comments. A special note of thanks goes to Cyndi Keen, who twenty years ago recommended that I write a textbook; I hope that this text was worth the wait. Finally, I want to thank my coauthors, Wendy and Jeff. When I pulled this team together, I knew that Jeff and Wendy were good people and gifted scholars. Having worked with them over the last few years, I now realize that judgment underestimated their many talents. It has been an honor for me to be part of this collaboration.

Wendy J. Schiller: I would also like to express my appreciation for the opportunity to work with John and Jeff—two excellent scholars and supportive colleagues. I would like to thank Mary Jane April, Ilene Berman, Matthew Corritore, Lucy Drotning, Helen Guler, Curtis Kelley, Fiona McGillivray, Molly Phee, Marsha Pripstein Posusney, Jessica Breese Schiller, Jordana Schwartz, Alastair Smith, Tiffany Trigg, Miriam Wugmeister, and Alan Zuckerman for all their support and assistance with this project. A special thanks goes to Roger Cobb, with whom I teach introduction to American politics at Brown, for all his help. Lastly, I would like to thank my husband, Robert Kalunian, who provided an endless supply of patience, support, and perspective.

Jeffrey A. Segal: I would like to thank my family—Christine, Michelle, and Paul—for allowing me the time to work on this project as needed. I also have special gratitude for my coauthors, who made working on the book as pleasant as possible. Writing the book coincided with difficult medical news, and John, Wendy, and everyone involved at Wadsworth/Cengage stepped up, no questions asked. I cannot overstate my appreciation on this score. I also thank several people for research assistance, including Nasser Javaid, Roland Kappe, Ellen Key, Magen Knuth, Maxwell Mak, Andrew O'Geen, Christopher Parker, and Shannon Stagman, plus my colleagues in the Department of Political Science at Stony Brook University, who readily answered the questions I asked them. It is nearly impossible to imagine a more supportive work environment.

Reviewers and Contributors

We would like to thank the following faculty for leading us through the many gateways we encountered in creating this new textbook. Some participated in focus groups, others answered surveys, and still others provided valuable feedback on the drafts of the manuscript. The people whose names are in boldface reviewed the manuscript.

Yishaiya Abosch, California State University–Fresno

Martin Adamian, California State University Los Angeles

Grace Adams-Square, Towson University

Noe Alexander Aguado, University of North Alabama

Gary Aguiar, South Dakota State University

Philip Aka, Chicago State University

Craig W. Allin, Cornell College

Davida Alperin, University of Wisconsin–River Falls

Rodney Anderson, California State University Fresno

Warren Anderson, North Harris College

Louis Andolino, Monroe Community College

Steve Anthony, Georgia State University

Andrew Aoki, Augsburg College

Phillip Ardoin, Appalachian State University

Leighton Armitage, College of San Mateo

Ruth Arnell, Idaho State University

Ross Baker, Rutgers University

Thomas Baldino, Wilkes University

Evelyn Ballard, Houston Community College Southeast

Jodi Balma, Fullerton College

Chris Banks, Kent State

Michael Baranowski, Northern Kentucky University

Lance Bardsley, Gainesville State College

Kedron Bardwell, Simpson College

Mary Barnes-Tilley, Blinn College

Tim Barnett, Jacksonville State University

Joyce Baugh, Central Michigan University

Chris Baxter, University of Tennessee at Martin

Kris Beck, Gordon College

Jenna Bednar, University of Michigan

James Belpedio, Becker College

Robert E. Bence, Massachusetts College of Liberal Arts

Philip Benesch, Lebanon Valley College

John Berg, Suffolk University

Justin Bezis, West Hills College

Amanda Bigelow, Illinois Valley Community College

Robert Bilodeau, South Plains College, Levelland

Richard Bilsker, College of Southern Maryland

William Binning, Youngstown State University

Bethany Blackstone, University of North Texas

Ted Blair, Diablo Valley College

John Blakeman, University of Wisconsin–Stevens Point

Jeff Blankenship, University of South Alabama

Leon Blevins, El Paso Community College

Richard Blisker, College of Southern Maryland

Julio Borquez, University of Michigan–Dearborn

Janet M. Box-Steffensmeier, Ohio State University

Matthew Bradley, Indiana University-Kokomo

Todd Bradley, Indiana University-Kokomo

Stephen Bragaw, Sweet Briar College

Lynn Brink, North Lake College

Andreas Broscheid, James Madison University

Lee Brown, Reedley College

Ronald Brown, Wayne State University–Detroit

Martin Brownstein, Ithaca College

Jane Bryant, John A. Logan College

Richard Buckner, Santa Fe Community College, Gainesville

Laurie Buonnano, Buffalo State College, SUNY

Randi Buslik, Northeastern Illinois University

Jennifer Byrne, James Madison University

Rachel Bzostek, California State University Bakersfield

Joseph Cammarano, Providence College

Michelle Camou, College of Wooster

Mary Caravelis, Barry University

James Carlson, Providence College

Jamie Carson, The University of Georgia

Monica Carter, Chaffey College

Terrence Casey, Rose-Hulman Institute of Technology

Marn Cha, California State University–Fresno

James Chalmers, Wayne State University

Van Chaney, El Camino College

Elsa Chen, Santa Clara University

Alade Chester, San Bernardino Valley College

Wendy Cho, University of Illinois

John Clark, Western Michigan University

Michael Clark, St. Xavier University

Kurt Cline, California State University–Fresno

Jean Clouatre, Manchester Community College

Michael Cobb, North Carolina State University

Carolyn Cocca, SUNY College at Old Westbury

Jeff Colbert, Elon University

Annie Cole, Los Angeles City College

Kathleen Colihan, American River College

Paul Collins, University of North Texas

Todd Collins, Western Carolina University

Frank Colucci, Purdue University–Calumet

David Connelly, Utah Valley University

George Connor, Missouri State University–Springfield

Joseph Corrado, Clayton College and State University

Thomas Costa, Florida Community College–Jacksonville

Michael Coulter, Grove City College

Albert Cover, Stony Brook University

Leland Coxe, University of Texas at Brownsville

Robert Craig, The College of St. Scholastica

William Cunion, Mount Union College

Dyron Keith Dabney, Albion College

Alison Dagnes, Shippensburg University

Nicholas D'Arecca, Temple University

Peter Davies, California State University–Sacramento

Paul Davis, Truckee Meadows Community College

Wartyna Davis, William Paterson University

Derek Davis, Austin Community College

Frank De Caria, West Virginia Northern Community College

Laura De La Cruz, El Paso Community College

Robert DeLuna, St. Phillips College

Iva Deutchman, Hobart and William Smith Colleges

Jeff Diamond, Skyline College

Brian Dillie, Odessa College

Richardson Dilworth, Drexel University

Thomas Dolan, Columbus State University

Jay Dow, University of Missouri–Columbia

Alan Draper, St. Lawrence University

Mary Drinan, Palomar College

Bryan Dubin, Oakland Community College

Patricia Dunham, Duquesne University

Cecile Durish, Austin Community College

Diana Dwyre, California State University–Chico

Joshua Dyck, University of Buffalo–SUNY

Stanley Dyck, Colorado Christian University

Victor Edo-Aikhionbare, Palm Beach State College

Kathryn Edwards, Ashland Community and Technical College

Sheryl Edwards, University of Michigan–Dearborn

Matthew Eshbaugh-Soha, University of North Texas

Andrew Ewoh, Kennesaw State University

Hyacinth Ezeamii, Albany State University

Vallye Ezell, Richland College

Traci Fahimi, Irvine Valley College

Frank Fato, Westchester Community College–SUNY

Henry Fearnley, College of Marin

William Felix, Rutgers University

Therese Filicko, Ohio State University–Newark Campus

Glen Findley, Odessa College

Mark Fish, Dallas Christian College

Patrick Fisher, Seton Hall University

Sam Fisher, University of South Alabama

Michael Fisher, John Jay College of Criminal Justice–CUNY

Richard Flanagan, College of Staten Island–CUNY

Brian Fletcher, Truckeee Meadows Community College

Julianne Flowers, DePaul University

Michael Frank, Anderson University

Steve Frank, St. Cloud State University

Bill Franklin, San Bernardino Valley College

Rodd Freitag, University of Wisconsin–Eau Claire

Barry Friedman, North Georgia College and University

George Gallo, Albertus Magnus College

Hoyt Gardner, Columbia State Community College

Steve Garrison, Midwestern State University

Yolanda Garza-Hake, South Texas College

Michael Gattis, Gulf Coast Community College

Eddie Genna, Phoenix College

Mitch Gerber, Southeast Missouri University

Jeffrey Gerson, University of Massachusetts–Lowell

Chris Gilbert, Gustavus Adolphus College

James Gleason, Purdue University

Dana Glencross, Oklahoma City Community College

Herbert Gooch, California Lutheran University

Martha Good, Miami University (Ohio)

Robert Green, St. Phillips College

Steven Greene, North Carolina State University

Gloria Guevara, Oxnard College / California State University Northridge

Max Guirguis, Shepherd University

Rhonda Gunter, Maryland Community College

Jose Angel Gutierrez, University of Texas–Arlington

Michael A. Haas, University of North Carolina–Wilmington

Anna Liesl Haas, California State University–Long Beach

Lori Han, Chapman University

Roger Handberg, University of Central Florida

Cathy Hanks, University of Nevada–Las Vegas

Sally Hansen, Daytona State

Richard Harris, Rutgers University

Edward Hasecke, Wittenberg University

Lori Hausegger, Boise State University

David Head, John Tyler Community College

Stacy Hunter Hecht, Bethel University

Robert Heineman, Alfred University

Diane Heith, St. John's University

Joann Hendricks, City College of San Francisco

John Hermann, Trinity University

Jeffrey Hernandez, East Los Angeles College

Richard Herrera, Arizona State University

John Heyrman, Berea College

Kenneth Hicks, Rogers State University

Marti Hill, Southwest Texas Junior College–Uvalde

Jefferey Hill, Northeastern Illinois University

James Hite, Portland State University and Mt. Hood Community College

John Hitt, North Lake College

James Holland, University of Akron

Suzanne Homer, City College of San Francisco

Jennifer Hora, Valparaiso University

Randolph Horn, Samford University

Melody Huckaby, Cameron University

Elizabeth Huffman, Consumnes River College

Scott Huffmon, Winthrop University

Patrick Hughes, Camden Community College

Gregg Ivers, American University

David Jackson, Bowling Green State University

Robert Jackson, Florida State University

Winsome Jackson, Sierra College

Lloyd Jansen, Green River Community College / University of Washington

Amy Jasperson, University of Texas at San Antonio

Mark Jendrysik, University of North Dakota

Terri Jett, Butler University

Alana Jeydel, American River College

Richard Johnson, Oklahoma City University

Scott Johnson, Frostburg State University

Susan Johnson, University of Wisconsin–Whitewater

Jean-Gabriel Jolivet, Southwestern College

Oliver Jones, Palo Alto College

Rebecca Jones, Widener University

James Joseph, Fresno City College

Andrew Karch, University of Texas at Austin

Mary Kazmierczak, Marquette University

Gina Keel, SUNY College at Oneonta

Michael Kelley, Pittsburg State University

Sean Kelly, California State University–Channel Islands

John Kemanski, Oakland University

Alyson Kennedy, University of Mississippi

Linda Kennedy, Lassen Community College

Stephen Kerbow, Southwest Texas Junior College

Brian Kessel, Columbia College

Jeffery Key, Hardin-Simmons University

Soleiman Kiasatpour, Western Kentucky University

Richard Kiefer, Wabaunsee Community College

Bill Klein, St. Petersburg College

Daniel Klinghard, College of the Holy Cross

Elizabeth Kloss, Oklahoma State University

Helen Knowles, SUNY Oswego

Katie Knutson, Gustavus Adolphus College

Jonathan Krasno, Binghamton University

Stephen Krason, Franciscan University

Dina Krois, Lansing Community College

William Kubik, Hanover College

Ashlyn Kuersten, Western Michigan University

Brian Kupfer, Tallahassee Community College

John Kuzenski, North Carolina Central University

Jeffrey Lantis, College of Wooster

Roger Larocca, Oakland University

Maria Perez Laubhan, Lake County

Lisa Laverty, Eastern Michigan University

Russell Lawson, Bacone College

Celeste Lay, Tulane University

Roger D. Lee, Salt Lake Community College

Wayne Lesperance, New England College

Tal Levy, Marygrove College

Angela Lewis, University of Alabama

Steven Lichtman, Shippensburg University

Nancy Lind, Illinois State University

Matt Lindstrom, St. John's University

John Lipinski, Robert Morris University

Brad Lockerbie, East Carolina University

Fred Lokken, Truckee Meadows Community College

Kenneth Long, Saint Joseph College

Claude Louishomme, University of Nebraska at Kearney

James Lutz, Indiana University Purdue

Edy Macdonald, University of Central Florida

Shari MacLachlan, Palm Beach State College

Donald Mac-Thompson, Winston Salem State University

Tony Madonna, University of Georgia

Richard Maiman, University of Southern Maine

Gary Lee Malecha, University of Portland

Lorie Maltby, Henderson Community College

Joseph Mancos, Lenoir-Rhyne University

William Mangun, East Carolina University

David Mann, College of Charleston

Magdaleno Manzanarez, Western New Mexico University

Nancy Marion, University of Akron

Bobby Martinez, Northwest Vista College

Nancy Martorano, University of Dayton

Asher Matathias, St. John's University (Queens Campus)

Derek Maxfield, Capital Community College

Terry Mays, The Citadel

Colette Mazzucelli, Molloy College

Heather Mbaye, University of West Georgia

Scott Mcclurg, Southern Illinois University

Tera McCown, University of Charleston

Adam McGlynn, The University of Texas-Pan American

Patrick McKinlay, Morningside College

Bryan McQuide, University of Idaho

R. Michael Mcsweeney, Bunker Hill Community College

Scott R. Meinke, Bucknell University

Nathan Melton, Utah Valley University

Joseph Melusky, Saint Francis University

John Mercurio, San Diego State University, San Diego City College, Grossmont College

Mark Milewicz, Gordon College

Melissa Miller, Bowling Green State University

Alexander Moon, Ithaca College

Martin Morales, Consumnes River College

Lucas Morel, Washington and Lee University

Eric Moskowitz, College of Wooster

Joanna Mosser, Drake University

Benjamin Muego, Bowling Green State University

Melinda Mueller, Eastern Illinois University

Lanette Mullins, Ivy Tech Community College

Philip Mundo, Drew University

Leah Murray, Weber State University

Mark Robert Murray, South Texas College

Christopher Muste, University of Montana

Jason Mycoff, University of Delaware

Carolyn Myers, Southwestern Illinois College

Trevor Nakagawa, Merritt College

Blaine Nelson, El Paso Community College

Steven E. Nelson, Northern Michigan University

James Newman, Idaho State University–Pocatello

William L. Niemi, Western State College of Colorado

Douglas Nilson, Idaho State University–Pocatello

Barbara Norrander, University of Arizona

Timothy O' Neill, Southwestern University

Al Ortiz, San Joaquin Delta College

James Owens, Oakton Community College

Richard Pacelle, Georgia Southern University

Steven Parker, University of Nevada–Las Vegas

David Penna, Gallaudet University

Mark Peplowski, Southern Nevada Community College

Gerhard Peters, Citrus College

Geoff Peterson, University of Wisconsin–Eau Claire

Joyce Pigge, Bethany College

Jamie Pimlott, Niagara University

Daniel Ponder, Drury University

Barbara Poole, Eastern Illinois University

Robert Porter, Ventura College

David Price, Santa Fe Community College

Narges Rabii, Santiago Canyon College / Orange Coast College / Saddleback College

Chapman Rackaway, Fort Hays State University

Daniel Reagan, Ball State University

Renford Reese, Cal Poly Pomona

Keith Reeves, Swarthmore College

B. Jeffrey Reno, College of the Holy Cross

Tim Reynolds, Alvin Community College

Patricia Bayer Richard, Ohio University

Christopher Riley, Big Bend Community College

Delbert Ringquist, Central Michigan University

Hank Rischel, Macomb Community College Center Campus

Kent Rissmiller, Worcester Polytechnic Institute

Chase Ritenauer, University of Akron

Laurie Robertstad, Navarro College

John Robey, University of Texas–Brownsville

Karin Robinson, Hood College

Rob Robinson, University of Alabama–Birmingham

Richard Robyn, Kent State

Sheri Rogers, Calvin College

Joe Romance, Drew University

Tom Rotnem, Southern Polytechnic State University

Donald Roy, Ferris State University

Ted Rueter, University of Wisconsin–Oshkosh

Mark Rush, Washington and Lee University

Patricia Ryan, Fairmont State University

Robert C. Sahr, Oregon State University

Bart Salisbury, Green River Community College

William Salka, Eastern Connecticut State University

Arthur Sanders, Drake University

Eric Sands, Berry College

Stephanie Sapiie, Suffolk Community College

Robert Saunders, Farmingdale State College

Todd M. Schaefer, Central Washington University

Michael Scheib, Lewis University

Steven E. Schier, Carleton College

Diane Schmidt, California State University–Chico

Michael Schnall, Pace University

Monica Schneider, Miami University (Ohio)

B. Schrader, Rowan University

Deron Schreck, Moraine Valley Community College

Ronnee Schrieber, San Diego State University

Vann Scott, Snead State Community College

Margaret Scranton, University of Arkansas at Little Rock

Michael Semler, Oxnard College / California State University Northridge

Stanley Serwatka, El Paso Community College

Allen Settle, Cal Polytechnic

Mark Setzler, High Point University

William Shafer, Purdue University

David Shafie, Chapman University

Edward Sharkey, Columbia College

Maurice Sheppard, Madison Area Technical College

John Shively, Longview Community College

Chris Shortell, Portland State University

Stephen Shulman, Southern Illinois Carbondale

Sanford Silverburg, Catawba College

Leigh Sink, University of North Carolina–Greensboro

Michael Slattery, Campbell University

Candy Stevens Smith, Texarkana College

James Smith, Indiana University

Karl Smith, Delaware Technical and Community College

Keith Smith, University of the Pacific

Ron Smith, Hanover College

Sandra Smith, Indiana University Northwest

Udi Sommer, University at Albany–SUNY

David Sousa, University of Puget Sound

Jeff Spanbauer, Illinois Valley Community College

June Sager Speakman, Roger Williams University

Scott Spitzer, California State University Bakersfield

John Squibb, Lincoln Land Community College

Marcus Stadelman, University of Texas at Tyler

Barry Steiner, California State University–Long Beach

Robert Sterken, University of Texas–Tyler

Janet Stevens, Madison Area Technical College

Willard Stouffer, Southwest Texas State University

Ginny Stowitts-Traina, Palo Alto College
Mark Stratton, Indiana University–Purdue
Ryane Straus, College of Saint Rose
Robert A. Strong, Washington and Lee University
Tamir Sukkary, American River College
Julie A. Sullivan, San Diego State University
John Swain, Governors State University
Regina Swopes, College of DuPage
John Szmer, University of North Carolina–Charlotte
Tressa Tabares, American River College
Barry Tadlock, Ohio University
Edwin Taylor, Portland State University
Jami Taylor, Ohio State University
Dange Tedla, Sacramento City College
Frank Thames, Texas Tech
John Theilman, Converse College
Michael Thompson, William and Patterson University
Alec Thomson, Schoolcraft College
Trevor Thrall, University of Michigan Dearborn
Jim Thurman, Central Wyoming College
Daniel Tichenor, University of Oregon
Terri Towner, Oakland University
Joe Trachtenberg, Clayton College and State University
Cathy Trecek, Iowa Western Community College
Margaret Tseng, Marymount University
David Tully, De Anza College
Bill Turini, Reedley College
Cindi Unmack, American River College
Richard Valelly, Swarthmore College
Jeff VanDerWerff, Northwestern College
Pamela Van Zwaluwenburg, Modesto Junior College
John Vento, Antelope Valley College
William Vogele, Pine Manor College
Mathis Waddell, Galveston College
Kevin Wagner, Florida Atlantic University
Scott Wallace, Indiana University–Perdue
Dana Waller, Front Range College
George Waller, University of Wisconsin–Fox Valley
Howard Warshawsky, Roanoke College
Andrew Jackson Waskey, Dalton State College
Rick Whisonant, York Technical College
Eric Whitaker, Western Washington University
Lois Duke Whitaker, Georgia Southern University
James A. White, Concord University
Elizabeth Williams, Santa Fe College

Kenneth Williams, Michigan State University

Jon Winburn, University of Mississippi

Michael Wiseman, Ashford University

Tony Wohlers, Cameron University

Christina Wolbrecht, University of Notre Dame

Robert (Bo) Wood, University of North Dakota

Gordon Vurusic, Grand Rapids Community College

Peter Yacobucci, Walsh University

Brad Young, Ocean Community College

Melanie Young, University of Nevada Las Vegas

Jay Zarowitz, Muskegon Community College

Noah Zerbe, Humboldt State University

Martha Zingo, Oakland University

1

GATEWAYS TO AMERICAN DEMOCRACY

▲ **University of Virginia, Charlottesville**

> *Being there is half the battle. What can happen from there is because you are involved in the process.*

CourseMate

Visit http://www.cengagebrain.com/shop/ISBN/0618906959 for interactive tools including:

- Quizzes
- Flashcards
- Videos
- Animated PowerPoint slides, Podcast summaries, and more

On a hot August day in 2006 a 20-year-old college student was doing the summer job he had volunteered to do. Working for the Senate campaign of Democrat Jim Webb, S. R. ("Sid") Sidarth was videotaping Webb's Republican opponent, Senator George Allen, who was seeking reelection in what was assumed would be an easy win. Allen, who had solid conservative credentials, had been a popular governor of Virginia. In his first Senate race he had beaten longtime Virginia Senator Chuck Robb. Some observers were comparing Allen to former President Ronald Reagan, and he seemed to be on his way not only to winning his second Senate race but also to running for president in 2008.

Sidarth, a computer engineering and American government major at the University of Virginia, had long been interested in politics—a family tradition. He had been an intern on Capitol Hill and a volunteer in John Kerry's presidential campaign and in the Virginia governor's race. The summer before his senior year in college he had volunteered for Webb. At first he worked behind the scenes at Webb's campaign headquarters in Arlington, helping set up field offices around the state and doing odd jobs. Then, on August 7 the campaign gave him a digital camcorder and asked him to follow Allen on his "Listening Tour" of Virginia, taping the candidate's appearances in a routine campaign practice known as tracking. Sidarth drove off alone. The work was mostly solitary. At campaign stops he chatted with Allen's aides, and once the senator had walked up to him, shook his hand, and asked his name. "I'm following you around," said Sidarth, and he knew Allen understood what that meant.

On August 11 the Allen campaign held a meet-and-greet picnic at Breaks Interstate Park in far southwest Virginia, near the Kentucky border. Allen picked up his microphone and Sidarth picked up his camcorder. During the speech, however, Allen paused and pointed: "This fellow here, over here with the yellow shirt, macaca, or whatever his name is. He's with my opponent. He's following us everywhere." As his supporters began to laugh, Allen continued, "Let's give a welcome to macaca, here. Welcome to America and the real world of Virginia."

Sidarth recorded it all. The episode, posted on YouTube, led to a furor. Within a week, more than two hundred thousand people had watched

S. R. Sidarth ▶

the clip, and major newspapers across the country were picking up the story. Allen's campaign was in trouble. He had poked fun at Sidarth by using a pejorative term with strong racial overtones. "The kid has a name," said Webb communications director Kristian Denny Todd. "This is trying to demean him, to minimize him as a person." The irony was that Allen, born and raised in California, had first come to Virginia as a college student, and Sidarth had been a Virginian all his life. It was Allen who appeared out of touch with the increasing diversity of the state he was representing.

Allen's lead disappeared, and on election day, out of more than 2.3 million ballots cast in Virginia, he lost by just over seven thousand votes. With this narrow defeat, Allen's presidential hopes died as well.

When asked about his role in this dramatic turn of events, Sidarth chose his words carefully. "I was just doing my job, and I got sort of pulled into this," he said. "I was the only person of color there, and it was useful for him [Allen] in inciting his audience. I was annoyed that he would use my race in a political context." Later, after the election, Sidarth wrote in the *Washington Post,* "I am proud to be a second-generation Indian American and a practicing Hindu," but "I would not wish the scrutiny on anyone." Still, he reflected, "Webb's victory last week gives me hope that Virginia will not tolerate playing the race card. . . . The politics of division just don't work anymore. Nothing made me happier on election night than finding out the results from Dickenson County, where Allen and I had our encounter. Webb won there, in what I can only hope was a vote to deal the race card out of American politics once and for all."[1]

It does not often happen that a summer volunteer alters political careers and changes the composition of the U.S. Senate, but that it happened points to the power of the individual in a democracy. In a democracy, citizens have the right, and the responsibility, to be involved in the public sphere and to take part in governing themselves. In this case, the impact of Sidarth's story was magnified by the Internet, but the ability of citizens to influence the political process does not depend on new technologies. Since the nation's beginnings more than 230 years ago, the actions of citizens have shaped the country's development. We open each chapter of this textbook with the story of one of those citizens. Some of them are ordinary, some are extraordinary; most are college students. Each used one of the many gateways to participation in government that American democracy provides because, at its core, American government is about individuals and self-governance. These young people have worked to get out the vote and have run for office themselves. They have joined with others to promote causes they care about on campus, in state legislatures, and in the halls of Congress. They have used their skills in statistics, music, and writing to communicate their messages to others. They have challenged laws they thought were wrong through peaceful protests and through lawsuits that went all the way to the Supreme Court. They have worked with political parties and served in government agencies and in the military. Any one of them could be you.

Even though the size of American government is daunting, individuals can make real changes. What often appear to be small and localized efforts can produce big shifts. Elections, for example, offer the chance to transform the system. Citizens can hold government accountable by voting legislators and presidents in and out of office. They can make their opinions known more directly because the right to speak out and to join with others in promoting causes is protected by the Constitution. A free press and the Internet allow information and opinion to be widely spread and shared. Courts hear cases brought by citizens, and citizen juries determine the outcome. Citizens can change—and they have changed—the Constitution through amendments. Elections, protest marches, blogs, the courts, and the constitutional amendment process are all gateways of influence. So are interest groups and political parties, and even Congress itself, for they represent the views of citizens, especially those who are active and engaged.

This textbook, *Gateways to Democracy*, explains how citizen involvement has expanded American democracy and how each of you, too, can influence the political system. We call the avenues of influence "gateways." This book serves as kind of a handbook for democratic citizenship by peeling back the layers of American government to reveal the ways you can get involved and to explain the reasons you should do so. The American political system is complicated, is large, and can be frustrating. As the term *gateways* implies, there are also gates—obstacles to influence, institutional controls that limit access, powerful interests that seem to block the people's will. We describe these as well, because to be a productive and influential member of American society, you need to understand how American government and politics work.

AP Photo/Bill Haber

Through citizen involvement, American democracy has achieved many successes:

- The nation and its institutions are amazingly stable. The United States has the oldest written constitution in the world.
- The government has weathered severe economic crises, a civil war, and two world wars; yet it still maintains peaceful transitions of power from one set of leaders to the next.
- Citizens are able to petition the government and to criticize it. They can assemble and protest the government's policies.
- Americans enjoy substantial freedom and are protected from the abuse of power by the government.
- The American economy has created an excellent standard of living, among the highest in the world.
- Americans exhibit more commitment to civic duty than do citizens in nearly all other major democracies.[2]
- Americans show a great deal more tolerance for wide-ranging political views than do citizens in other major democracies.[3]

Four out of five young people do volunteer work in high school and college, and, according to the Harvard University Institute of Politics, 94 percent believe that volunteer service is an effective way to deal with challenges in their local communities. In 2008, college students from around the country spent their spring break as volunteers in New Orleans, painting houses that had been damaged in Hurricane Katrina.

John Moore/Getty Images

Social scientists have been measuring the gap between the rich and the poor since the 1930s, and in the past few decades that gap has grown. Reports in 2007 indicated that the top 300,000 Americans enjoyed the same total income as the bottom 150 million Americans. Following job losses in the 2008 recession, this Wilmington, Ohio, family is living in a homeless shelter.

These successes do not mean that there are not problems:

- Inequality persists, and government is sometimes slow to respond.

- Even with the election of President Barack Obama in 2008, racial tensions continue to haunt the country.

- The imbalance of wealth in this country continues to grow, with increasing numbers of people living in poverty.[4]

- The public's trust in the institutions of government has eroded in recent years.[5]

- The rate of turnout in elections is among the lowest of the major democracies.

- Despite a high level of religious tolerance, there is also persistent distrust of some religious minorities, such as Muslims.[6]

- Political polarization is now so extensive that members of Congress often attack one another on personal as well as political grounds. Some members have even taken to yelling at the president.

- The American military is stretched thin by major military commitments in Afghanistan and Iraq while waging a global war against terrorism.

To solve these and other problems and achieve the "more perfect Union" promised in the Constitution, the nation's citizens must be vigilant and engaged. We have framed our book with the goal of demonstrating the demands and rewards of democratic citizenship. As we explore the American political system, we place special emphasis on the multiple and varied connections among citizenship, participation, institutions, and public policy. Our focus is on the following gateway questions:

- How can you get yourself and your opinions represented in government?
- How can you make government more responsive, and responsible, to citizens?
- How can you make American democracy better?

Democracy and the American Constitutional System

Today democracy is presumed to be a good form of government, and some would say the best form. It is the kind of government to which the people of many nations aspire. But it has not always been so. Only in the last two centuries—partly through the example of the United States—has democracy gained favor. Let us sketch some of the fundamental aspects of American democracy.

Liberty and Order

democracy: *System of government in which the supreme power is vested in the people and exercised by them either directly or indirectly through elected representatives.*

self-government: *Goal of democracy, whereby average people have control of the institutions of government.*

majority rule: *Idea that a numerical majority of a group should hold the power to make decisions binding on the whole group; a simple majority.*

Literally and most simply, **democracy** is rule by the people, or **self-government**. In a democracy, the citizens hold political authority, and they develop the means to govern themselves.

In practice, that means rule by the majority, and in the years before American independence, **majority rule** had little appeal. In 1644 John Cotton, a leading clergyman of the colonial period, declared democracy "the meanest and worst of all forms of government."[7] Even after American independence, Edmund Burke, a British political philosopher and politician, wrote that a "perfect democracy is . . . the most shameless thing in the world."[8] At the time democracy was associated with **mob rule**, and mobs were large, passionate, ignorant, and dangerous. If the mob ruled, the people would suffer. There would be no **liberty** or safety; there would be no **order**. Eighteenth-century mobs destroyed private property, burned effigies of leaders they detested, tarred and feathered their enemies, and threatened people who disagreed with them. In fact, such events occurred in the protests against British rule in the American colonies, and they were fresh in the minds of those who wrote the Declaration of Independence and the Constitution.

John Adams, a signer of the Declaration of Independence and later the nation's second president (1797–1801), was not a champion of this kind of democracy. "Democracy," he wrote, "while it lasts is more bloody than either aristocracy or monarchy. Remember, democracy never lasts long. It soon wastes, exhausts, and murders itself. There is never a democracy that did not commit suicide."[9] Adams knew about mobs and their effects firsthand. As a young lawyer before the Revolution, he agreed to defend British soldiers who had been charged with murder for firing on protesters in the streets of Boston. The soldiers' cause was unpopular, for the people of Boston detested the British military presence. But Adams believed that, following British law, the soldiers had a right to counsel (a lawyer to defend them) and to a fair trial. In later years, he considered his defense of these British soldiers "one of the best pieces of service I ever rendered my country."[10]

Why? In defending the soldiers, Adams was standing up for the **rule of law**, the principle that could prevent mob rule and keep a political or popular majority under control so it could not trample on **minority rights**. An ancient British legal principle, the rule of law holds that all people are equal before the law, all are subject to the law, and no one is above it. Adams and the others who wrote America's founding documents believed in a **constitutional system** in which the people set up and agree on the basic rules and procedures that will govern them. A constitutional system is a government of laws, not of men. Without a constitution and rule of law, an unchecked majority could act to promote the welfare of some over the welfare of others, and society would be torn apart.

The American constitutional system, therefore, serves to protect both liberty and order. The Constitution sets up a governmental structure with built-in constraints on power (gates) and multiple points of access to power (gateways). It also has a built-in means for altering the basic rules and procedures of governance through amendments. As you might expect, the procedure for passing amendments comes with its own set of gates and gateways.

The Constitution as Gatekeeper

"If men were angels," wrote James Madison, a leading author of the Constitution and later the nation's fourth president (1809–17), "no government would be necessary. . . . In framing a

The Granger Collection, New York

Paul Revere printed this famous engraving of the Boston Massacre in 1770. Emphasizing the shedding of innocent blood—five colonists died—it rallied Bostonians to resist British tyranny. Evidence at the trial of the soldiers indicated that they were provoked by the mob with taunts, clubs, and stones. Lawyer John Adams argued for the defense.

mob rule: *Government by a mob or mass of people with no formal authority whatsoever.*

liberty: *Political value that cherishes freedom from an arbitrary exercise of power that constricts individual choice.*

order: *Political value in which the rule of law is followed and does not permit actions that infringe on the well-being of others.*

rule of law: *Legal system with known rules that are enforced equally against all people.*

minority rights: *Idea that majority should not be able to take certain fundamental rights away from those in the minority.*

constitutional system: *System of government in which people set up and agree on the basic rules and procedures that will govern them.*

Framers: *The people who were involved in writing the Constitution.*

Founders: *The people who were involved in establishing the United States, whether at the time of the Declaration of Independence or the writing of the Constitution.*

social contract: *Theory that government has only the authority accorded it by the consent of the governed.*

natural (unalienable) rights: *Rights that every individual has and that government cannot legitimately take away.*

direct democracy: *Form of democracy in which political power is exercised directly by citizens.*

representative democracy: *Form of democracy in which citizens elect public officials to make political decisions and formulate laws on their behalf.*

republic: *Form of government in which power derives from citizens, but public officials make policy and govern according to existing law.*

faction: *Defined by Madison as any group that places its own interests above the aggregate interests of society.*

government which is to be administered by men over men," he continued, "the great difficulty lies in this: You must first enable the government to control the governed; and in the next place oblige it to control itself" (see *Federalist* 51 in the Appendix). Madison and the other **Framers** of the Constitution recognized that the government they were designing had to be strong enough to rule but not strong enough to take away the people's rights. In other words, the Constitution had to serve as a gatekeeper, allowing and limiting access to power at the same time.

James Madison, Thomas Jefferson, John Adams, and the other **Founders** had read many of the great political theorists. They drew, for example, on the ideas of the British political philosophers Thomas Hobbes and John Locke in perceiving the relationship between government and the governed as a **social contract**. If people lived in what these philosophers called a state of nature, without the rule of law, conflict would be unending and the strong would destroy the weak. To secure order and safety, individuals come together to form a government and agree to live by its rules. In return, the government agrees to protect life, liberty, and property. The right to life, liberty, and property, said Locke, are **natural** or **unalienable rights**, rights so fundamental that government cannot take them away.

But these ideas about government as a social contract were just theories when Madison and others began to write the Constitution. The closest actual model for self-government was ancient Athens, where the people had governed themselves in a **direct democracy**. In Athens, citizens had met together to debate and to vote. That was possible because only property-owning males were citizens, and they were few in number and had similar interests and concerns.[11]

But the new United States was nothing like the old city-state of Athens. It was an alliance of thirteen states—former colonies—with nearly 4 million people spread across some 360,000 square miles. Direct democracy was impractical for such a large and diverse country, so those who wrote the Constitution created a **representative democracy** in which the people elect representatives who govern in their name. Some observers, including the Framers, call this arrangement a **republic**, a form of government in which power derives from the citizens but their representatives make policy and govern according to existing law.

Could a republic work? No one knew, certainly not the Framers. The government they instituted was something of an experiment, and they developed their own theories about how it would work. Madison, for example, rejected the conventional view that a democracy had to be small and homogeneous so as to minimize conflict. He argued that size and diversity were assets because competing interests in a large county would balance and control—or check—one another and prevent abuse of power. Madison called these competing interests **factions**, and he believed that the most enduring source of faction was "the various and unequal distribution of property. Those who hold and those who are without property, have ever formed distinct interests in society," he wrote. "Those who are creditors, and those who are debtors, fall under a like discrimination. A landed interest, a manufacturing interest, a mercantile interest, a monied interest, with many lesser interests, grow up of necessity in civilized nations, and divide them into different classes, actuated by different sentiments and views" (see *Federalist* 10 in the Appendix).

In a pure democracy, where the people ruled directly, Madison expected that passions would outweigh judgments about the common good. Each individual would look out for himself, for his self-interest, and not necessarily for the interests of society as a whole, what we might call civic interest. In a republic, however, the people's representatives would of necessity have a broader view. Moreover, they would, Madison assumed, come from the better educated, a natural elite. The larger the republic, the larger the districts from which the representatives would be chosen, and thus the more likely that they would be civic-minded leaders of the highest quality. More important, in a large republic it would be less likely that any one faction could form a majority. In a small seaside republic, for example, it would be possible for fishing interests to form a majority that could pass laws to the detriment of non-fishing interests. In another small republic, a religious sect could form a majority. But in a large and diverse republic, such narrow-minded majorities would not be possible. Interests would balance each other out, and selfish interests would actually be checked by majority rule.

Balance, control, order—these values were as important to the Framers as liberty. So while the Constitution vested political authority in the people, it also set up a governing system designed to prevent any set of individuals, any political majority, or even the government itself from becoming too powerful. The Framers purposely set up barriers and gates that blocked the excesses associated with mob rule.

Consequently, although the ultimate power lies with the people, the Constitution divides power both vertically and horizontally. Within the federal government, power is channeled into three different branches—the **legislature** (Congress), which makes the laws; the **executive** (the president and the government departments, or bureaucracy), which executes the laws; and the **judiciary** (the Supreme Court and the federal courts), which interprets the laws (see Figure 1.1). This vertical division of power is referred to as the **separation of powers**. To minimize the chance that one branch will become so strong that it can abuse its power and harm the citizenry, each branch has some power over the other two in a system known as **checks and balances**. The Constitution also divides power horizontally, into layers, between the national government and the state governments. This arrangement is known as **federalism**. In a further division of powers, state governments create local governments.

The American constitutional system thus simultaneously provides gateways for access and gates that limit access. The people govern themselves, but indirectly and through a system that disperses power among many competing interests. This textbook explores both the gateways and the gates that channel and block the influence of citizens.

American Political Culture

As an experiment, the American republic has been open to change in the course of the nation's history. Despite their theorizing, the Framers could not have anticipated exactly how it would develop. Madison was right, however, about the enduring influence of factions. The people quickly divided themselves into competing interests and shortly into competing **political parties**, groups organized to win elections. The process by which competing interests determine who gets what, when, and how is what we call **politics**.[12]

separation of powers: *Government structure in which authority is divided among branches (executive, legislative, and judicial), with each holding separate and independent powers and areas of responsibility.*

checks and balances: *Government structure that authorizes each branch of government (executive, legislative, and judicial) to share powers with the other branches, thereby holding some scrutiny of and control over the other branches.*

federalism: *System of government in which sovereignty is constitutionally divided between national and state governments.*

political parties: *Broad coalitions of interests organized to win elections in order to enact a commonly supported set of public policies.*

politics: *Process by which people make decisions about who gets what, when, and how.*

Legislative Branch	Executive Branch	Judicial Branch

Makes the laws	Executes the laws	Interprets the laws

FIGURE 1.1 The Three Branches of Government.

political ideology: *Set of consistent political beliefs.*

liberals: *Individuals who have faith in government to improve people's lives, believing that private efforts are insufficient. In the social sphere, liberals usually support diverse lifestyles and tend to oppose any government action that seeks to shape personal choices.*

conservatives: *Individuals who distrust government, believing that private efforts are more likely to improve people's lives. In the social sphere, conservatives usually support traditional lifestyles and tend to believe that government can play a valuable role in shaping personal choices.*

moderates: *Individuals who are in the middle of the ideological spectrum and do not hold consistently strong views about whether government should be involved in people's lives.*

libertarians: *Those who generally believe that government should refrain from acting to regulate either the economy or moral values.*

populists: *Those who oppose concentrated wealth and adhere to traditional moral values.*

political culture: *Set of beliefs common to a group of people.*

individualism: *Set of beliefs holding that people, and not government, are responsible for their own well-being.*

capitalism: *Economic system in which businesses and key industries are privately owned and in which individuals, acting on their own or with others, are free to create businesses.*

socialism: *Economic system in which the government owns major industries.*

egalitarianism: *Belief in human equality that disdains inherited titles of nobility and inherited wealth.*

Madison was right, too, about the sources of division, which are often centered in the unequal distribution of property and competing ideas about how far government should go to reduce inequality. Public opinion about such matters is sometimes described as falling on a scale that ranges from left to right, and when people have a fairly consistent set of views over a range of policy choices, they are said to have a **political ideology**. On the left end of the scale are **liberals** who favor government efforts to increase equality, including higher taxes on the wealthy than on the poor and greater provision of social benefits, such as health care, unemployment insurance, and welfare payments to support the poor. **Conservatives**, on the right, believe that lower taxes will prompt greater economic growth that will ultimately benefit everyone, including the poor. Thus, liberals support a large and active government that will regulate the economy, while conservatives fear that such a government will suppress individual liberty and create a dependency that actually harms those it aims to help.

The left–right division is not just about economics, however. For social issues, liberals generally favor less government interference, while conservatives favor rules that will uphold traditional moral values (see Figure 1.2). Conservatives are, therefore, more likely to support laws that ban abortion and same-sex marriage, while liberals are more likely to favor a woman's right to make decisions over private matters as well as the right of same-sex couples to wed.

Although terms such as *conservative* and *liberal* are often used to label American political attitudes, most Americans are not very ideological in their orientation to politics. They are likely to take independent positions on various issues, leaning left on some, right on others. In fact, most Americans are **moderates**, not seeing themselves on one end of the scale or the other. A sizable number of Americans also describe themselves as **libertarians**, believing that government should not interfere in either economic matters or social matters. Others take a **populist** perspective, opposing concentrated wealth and adhering to traditional moral values.

Despite its many perspectives, American **political culture** as a whole generally favors **individualism** over communal approaches to property and poverty, especially in comparison to the industrialized democracies of Europe and elsewhere in the world (see Other Places: Social Welfare and Free Enterprise). The United States spends less on government programs to help the less-well-off than many other countries, and it has historically refrained from assuming control of business enterprises, such as railroads and banks, except in times of crisis. The United States tends to favor **capitalism**, an economic system in which business enterprises and key industries are privately owned, as opposed to **socialism**, in which they are owned by government. Yet, to prevent the worst abuses of capitalism, which can arise as businesses pursue profit to the detriment of citizens, Congress has passed laws that regulate privately owned businesses and industries. Government monitors banks and financial markets, for example, ensures airline safety, and protects workers from injury on the job.

These regulations tend to moderate vast inequalities in wealth as well. Though prizing individualism, American political culture also has a long-standing **egalitarian** tradition. Americans rejected kings in the Revolution and titles of nobility in the Constitution. They also rejected British inheritance laws, which gave virtually all property to the eldest male.

FIGURE 1.2 American Political Ideology.

Political ideology has been described in many ways. In one version, political thought is plotted on a continuum between left (liberal) and right (conservative). The terms left and right derive from the seating arrangements for political parties in the Assembly during the French Revolution.

LEFT (LIBERAL):
Greater faith in a large and active government to promote equality.

RIGHT (CONSERVATIVE):
Greater preference for a small and limited government to encourage economic growth.

But this version is somewhat simplistic. A more fully developed version plots a graph that shows where liberals and conservatives stand on both economic and social issues. Liberals favor government regulation of the economy; conservatives do not. Conservatives favor government regulation of traditional moral values; liberals do not.

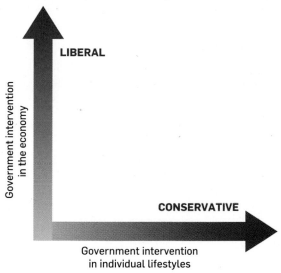

In a third version, the ideological spectrum is further complicated by the inclusion of libertarians, who favor no government intervention in either the economy or society, and populists, who favor government intervention in both the economy and society.

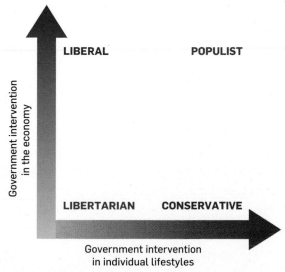

The truth is, however, that Americans are not really very ideological. Most Americans describe themselves as moderates or as independent thinkers who might lean left on some issues and right on others. Americans generally look to government to be active in some areas of life, but they differ on which areas.

otherplaces

Social Welfare and Free Enterprise

Throughout this book we look at American democracy from a more global perspective, comparing aspects of the U.S. government and civic life to those elsewhere in the world. Often comparisons highlight other democracies, especially the United Kingdom, India, Israel, Mexico, and South Africa. We chose these five countries to capture some of the diversity in the many democracies around the world. We begin with two related items: the extent to which the United States and other countries provide social welfare benefits, and the extent to which the economies of the United States and other countries are controlled by the government.

The first table shows that the United States allocates a smaller percentage of its budget to social welfare programs than do most other industrial democracies. The social democracies of western Europe provide the highest social welfare expenditures (with higher tax rates to pay for such benefits), whereas democracies in Asia, North America, and eastern Europe generally provide lower levels of benefits.

The second table, scoring governmental control over the economies, indicates that the governments of North Korea, Libya, Cuba, and Zimbabwe exercise the most control. None of these countries is politically democratic. On the other end of the scale, the countries with the least governmental control over their economies are Singapore and New Zealand. Singapore is not a democratic nation, but New Zealand is. Although nations with capitalist economies have been either democratic or nondemocratic, as have nations with mixed capitalist and socialist economies, there are no examples of nations that have exercised complete or nearly complete control over economic matters that have not simultaneously exercised complete or nearly complete control over political matters. Also note that nations with extensive social welfare systems can be both politically democratic and free-market oriented.

Public Social Expenditures as a Percentage of Gross Domestic Product, 2005

Country	Percent of Budget for Social Welfare
Sweden	29.4
France	29.2
Austria	27.2
Denmark	26.9
Germany	26.7
Belgium	26.4
Finland	26.1
Italy	25.0
Luxembourg	23.2
Portugal	23.1
Hungary	22.5
Norway	21.6
United Kingdom	**21.3**
Spain	21.2
Poland	21.0
Netherlands	20.9
Greece	20.5
Switzerland	20.3
Czech Republic	19.5
Japan	18.6
New Zealand	18.5
Australia	17.1
Iceland	16.9
Ireland	16.7
Slovak Republic	16.6
Canada	16.5
United States	**15.9**
Turkey	13.7
Mexico	**7.0**
South Korea	6.9

Source: Organisation for Economic Co-Operation and Development, "Society at a Glance 2009—OECD Social Indicators," www.oecd.org/els/social/indicators/SAG.

Degree of Free Enterprise among Various Nations

Rank of Country	Economic Freedom Score, Lowest (0.0) to Highest (100.0)
1. North Korea	4.4
2. Libya	31.8
3. Cuba	32.0
4. Zimbabwe	33.9
40. China	51.1
44. India	**51.5**
93. France	60.5
106. Mexico	**63.7**
108. Israel	**63.9**
116. South Africa	**65.9**
128. Austria	68.8
136. Sweden	72.8
144. Denmark	76.3
149. United Kingdom	**77.8**
150. United States	**77.8**
154. New Zealand	82.0
155. Singapore	88.6

Source: Jan Teorell, Sören Holmberg, and Bo Rothstein, *The Quality of Government Dataset 2008* (May 15, 2008). University of Gothenburg: The Quality of Government Institute, Economic Freedom Index Score, www.qog.pol.gu.se.

- **Why do countries that have free market economies also tend to be democratic?**

- **What do these data suggest to you about how the United States compares to other countries, especially other democracies?**

With estates divided more equally, and with a vast frontier that allowed land ownership to spread broadly, property in the United States was never as concentrated in the hands of a few as it had been in Europe. This greater equality, in turn, produced a political culture that values each individual's ability to achieve wealth and social status through hard work, not inheritance, and supports a free enterprise economic system, within limits. These observations were first made by Alexis de Tocqueville, one of the many Europeans who traveled to the United States in the nineteenth century to investigate the American experiment. His *Democracy in America* (1835) is a classic study of American institutions and culture. It remains insightful today for its thoughtful observations about American politics and character.

Réunion des Musées Nationaux/Art Resource, NY

Alexis de Tocqueville (1805–59), a French political writer, was sent to America by his government to investigate prisons in the early 1830s. But what fascinated him was American democracy, then a half-century old, especially the ways American society differed from aristocratic Europe. Tocqueville noted Americans' allegiance to equality and their belief in hard work. We call on his insights in subsequent chapters.

Public Policy under a Constitutional System

public policy: *Intentional actions of government designed to achieve a goal.*

The laws that regulate the American economy, as well as the tax rates, exemptions, and subsidies that help direct it, are examples of **public policy**—the intentional action by government to achieve a goal. It is in the arena of public policy—in determining who gets what, when, and how, and with what result—that we can see whether the constitutional system created by Madison and the Framers really works. Can the people pursue policies that advance their own interests? Can the people's representatives, while pursuing policies that advance their constituents' interests, produce a nation that looks out for the civic interest generally, for the common good, and for the welfare of all the people?

With a government deliberately designed to constrain power and the popular will, and a citizenry divided into factions and prizing individualism, the development of public policy has never been easy. In some ways, it has tended to cycle. One argument gains favor, driving policy in one direction. But new problems arise, calling for a redirection of policy. In the early years of the American republic, for example, Congress raised tariffs (taxes on imports) to help support new manufacturing enterprises, which could then undersell foreign competitors. But when agricultural interests complained about having to pay high prices for foreign goods, Congress lowered tariffs. Banking policies were similarly adjusted, sometimes to favor debtors, other times to favor creditors.

Government policy is just one cause of decay in Detroit. The decline of the auto industry is a major explanation for the condition of this city, which has lost half its population since the 1950s. Policy makers are now developing plans to turn some of its forty square miles of abandoned properties into farms.

JEFF HAYNES/AFP/Getty Images

The development of good public policy is always difficult and complex. A policy, for example, of providing tax benefits to homeowners to spur home ownership sounds like a good thing. It would help homeowners, support the home construction industry, and create jobs, building more stable communities. But what sounds simple rarely is that simple, because there are usually unintended consequences. A policy of tax benefits for homeowners can also encourage sprawl that turns agricultural land into suburbs, thus decreasing crop yields and altering food production, while leaving cities with vacant housing and declining tax bases. Subsequently, government responds to these new problems by developing additional policies to revitalize both agriculture and urban infrastructure.

With so many competing interests and the high potential for unintended negative consequences, government seeks to pursue policy making that maximizes benefits and minimizes costs. This is not easy. Political scientists—those who study politics and the processes of government—have categorized the steps in policy making to make the process more understandable.

The first step is **identification** of the problem. For example, constituents might complain to members of Congress that the cost of college is too high. The second step is for the issue of the cost of higher education to make it to the agenda of policy makers.[13] Of all the problems that government might be able to solve, only a small fraction can receive attention at any one time. Those that get on the **policy agenda** get the attention of Congress, the president, the executive branch agency that deals with the issue, the courts, political parties, **interest groups**, and interested citizens. These **stakeholders** attempt to **formulate** a policy that will solve the problem (see Figure 1.3). In the example of the high cost of college, which got on the policy agenda in 2009, the stakeholder network considered direct federal loans to college students, promoting private loans by paying banks the interest on student loans while the student is in college, and guaranteeing the loans if students are unable to repay them. In a fourth step, **policy enactment**, the legislative branch passes a law that enacts one or more of those proposals, as Congress did regarding student loans in 2010. Following passage, the legislature grants an executive branch department the authority to **implement** the program. In this case, the Department of Education was given the authority to direct the student loan program. In a few years, Congress might revisit the new student loan program to see if it is producing the outcomes that were intended. Following this **policy evaluation**, the cycle of policy making might begin again, with new legislation to adjust the program to make it work better (see Figure 1.4).

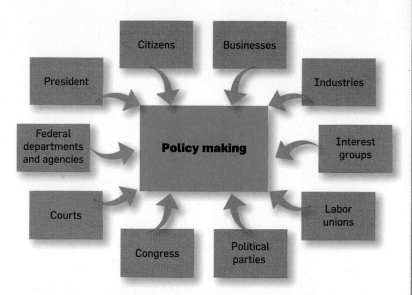

FIGURE 1.3 Stakeholders in the Policy-Making Process. One reason policy making is difficult and complex in the United States is that so many citizens, businesses, industries, labor unions, and interest groups as well as the political parties, Congress, the president, federal agencies, the courts, and others have a stake in policy outcomes. For emphasis, we repeat this figure in discussions of policy making throughout this textbook, with the various stakeholders identified.

In a republic, policy making should reflect the will of the people expressed through their elected representatives and interest groups. Madison envisioned that the people's representatives managing the policy-making process would be an elite—well-educated people of "merit." But if the people divided into different classes, as Madison also envisioned, there is a danger to democracy if the people's representatives are an elite who represent only their own interests, and not civic-minded leaders who consider the common good. In the 1950s the sociologist C. Wright Mills in fact wrote of a narrow **power elite** made up of leaders from corporations, government, and the military that controlled the gates and gateways to power. But in the 1960s the political scientist Robert Dahl took issue with Mills and argued that policy making has a more **pluralist** basis, with authority held by different groups in different areas. In this view, coal companies, as stakeholders, have a large say in coal policy, and farmers, as stakeholders, have a large say in farm policy, rather than a single power elite controlling both policy areas. While it is true, for example, that the coal industry pursues its interests vigorously, so do other industries. Elected representatives seek to balance these various interests even as they seek to do what is best for their constituents. The fact that no one group has a monopoly on power suggests that a more **majoritarian** policy-making process is in the making, in which those with a numerical majority hold the authority.

interest groups: *Groups of citizens who share a common Interest—a political opinion, a religious or ideological belief, a social goal, or an economic characteristic—and try to influence public policy to benefit themselves.*

stakeholders: *Participants in the policy-making system who seek to influence the content and direction of legislation.*

power elite: *Small handful of decision makers who hold authority over a large set of issues.*

pluralism: *System of policy making in which competing interests hold authority over issues most important to them.*

majoritarian: *System of policy making in which those with a numerical majority hold authority.*

FIGURE 1.4 The Policy Making Process.

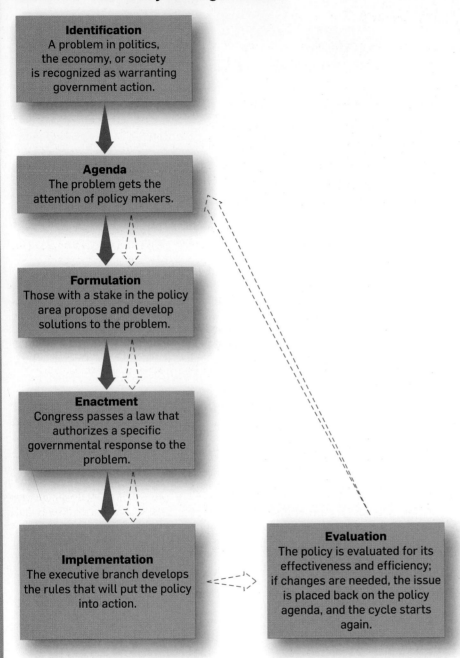

Identification
A problem in politics, the economy, or society is recognized as warranting government action.

Agenda
The problem gets the attention of policy makers.

Formulation
Those with a stake in the policy area propose and develop solutions to the problem.

Enactment
Congress passes a law that authorizes a specific governmental response to the problem.

Implementation
The executive branch develops the rules that will put the policy into action.

Evaluation
The policy is evaluated for its effectiveness and efficiency; if changes are needed, the issue is placed back on the policy agenda, and the cycle starts again.

Although presidents and members of Congress formally appear to be in command of the policy-making process, they have to navigate a maze of gates imposed by competing centers of power. Sometimes it is a short trip from idea to the law of the land, but more often the journey is long and complicated. In 2009, for example, Congress, facing a steep economic downturn, quickly passed President Barack Obama's (2009–) nearly $800 billion stimulus proposal. Given that over 90 percent of the public thought that the state of the economy was "fairly" or "very" bad, it is no surprise that the bill passed so quickly.[14] Even though this bill sped through Congress, its implementation by the executive branch was uneven. Many observers complained that the stimulus money had not yet reached the local level, raising concerns about bureaucratic efficiency.[15]

In clear contrast to the quick passage of the stimulus bill, Congress failed to enact immigration reform during President George W. Bush's (2001–2009) second term. The large percentage of Americans who thought the immigration system was not working well put immigration reform on the policy agenda; the divisiveness and complexity of the issue were among the gates that prevented reform. Some Americans favored citizenship for illegal aliens; others wanted to secure the borders to prevent more immigrants from illegally entering. Compromises that would have done both failed to get through either chamber of Congress in 2005, made it through the Senate but not the House in 2006, and again failed to make it through either chamber in 2007. By the time 2007 rolled into 2008, the ongoing battles between the Democratic and Republican Parties in an election year were added to the mix, and the divisiveness surrounding this controversial issue kept any law from being passed. In the spring and summer of 2010 immigration reform was back on the national policy agenda, following passage of a controversial Arizona law regarding illegal aliens.

Responsiveness and Equality: Does American Democracy Work?

Does American democracy work? That is a question we will be asking in every chapter of this book, and we invite you to start working on an answer. As citizens, you have both a right and a responsibility to judge the government—because it is your government.

To guide your thinking, we focus on two basic themes, **responsiveness** and **equality**. Is government responsive to the needs of its citizens? Do all citizens have an equal chance to make their voices heard? We ask you to keep these themes in mind as you learn about the U.S. political system. To give you a basis for making a judgment, we inform you of the findings of political scientists who have been asking and answering these questions for decades. Throughout this textbook, we present the latest data that speak to these broad issues. It is important to remember that we are not offering our opinions about government; instead, we are putting forward the most important evidence and theories, from a variety of perspectives, over the last fifty or so years. It is up to you to consider them and form your own conclusions.

One way to begin to evaluate American democracy, and to appreciate it, is to look briefly at alternative models of government. In **autocracy**, **oligarchy**, and **monarchy**, a single person or a small elite rules society. Such rulers have little need to be responsive to the people. They hold most of the power and are not generally accountable to those they rule. They may try to satisfy the people with programs that meet basic needs for food and safety, but they do so to ensure submission. These rulers have a low regard for the people and do not want them to be engaged in public life. In these systems, the rulers are excessively wealthy, and the people are likely to be impoverished. To maintain order, the rulers typically rely on a strong army or a secret police force to keep the people in line through fear and intimidation. Rulers in such systems are overthrown when dissatisfaction rises to a level at which citizens are willing to risk their lives in open revolt, or when the army or police conspire to replace one ruler with another.

In contrast, a democracy asks the citizens to be actively engaged in their own governance, for the benefit of all. As the preamble to the Constitution states, the people create government (agree to a social contract) to "establish Justice, insure domestic Tranquility, provide for the common defence, promote the general Welfare, and secure the Blessings of Liberty to ourselves and our Posterity." The American system of government fundamentally provides protection from foreign enemies and from internal disorder; it also strives to meet the common needs of all citizens.

To promote the general welfare, the government develops public policy, as we have seen. Through incentives, it can alter the actions of individuals that lead collectively to bad outcomes. Consider the following example. If everyone drives to work, pollution increases and more resources are consumed. If a few people then decide to take the bus, those decisions, while admirable, do not yield a cleaner environment or save many resources. But if government incentives, such as a tax on cars, encourage many people to take the bus, the result is a cleaner environment and a saving of resources.

The government often has a stake in pursuing what economists call **public goods**: goods that everyone benefits from. The core idea is that no one can be excluded. We all get the benefits of clean air, even if we have been driving cars and not taking buses. **Private goods**, by contrast, can be extended to some individuals and denied to others. When a government

responsiveness: *Idea that government should implement laws and policies that reflect the wishes of the public and any changes in those wishes.*

equality: *Idea that all individuals are equal in their moral worth and so must be equal in treatment under the law and have equal access to the decision-making process.*

autocracy: *System of government in which the power to govern is concentrated in the hands of an individual ruler.*

oligarchy: *System of government in which the power to govern is concentrated in the hands of a powerful few, usually wealthy individuals.*

monarchy: *System of government that assigns power to a single person who inherits that position and rules until death.*

public goods: *Goods or benefits provided by government from which everyone benefits and from which no one can be excluded.*

private goods: *Goods or benefits provided by government in which most of the benefit falls to the individuals, families, or companies receiving them.*

© Richard T. Nowitz/Corbis

Pittsburgh was once a city in decline, suffering huge losses as the steel industry left town. The smokestacks are now gone, and new industries and green spaces have taken their place. In 2009 and 2010 it was named the nation's Most Livable City. The Sixth Street Bridge, pictured here, is closed to vehicular traffic when the Pirates and Steelers have home games.

trustee: *Idea of representation that says elected officials should do what they think best, even if the public disagrees, and that elections allow the public to render a judgment on their decisions.*

delegate: *Idea of representation that says elected officials should do what the public wants and not exercise independent judgment.*

political equality: *The idea that people should have equal amounts of influence in the political system.*

awards a contract to build a new library, the firm that wins the contract gets private goods (that is, money) from the government. The firms that lost the bid are denied that chance.

Who determines what goods, whether private or public, the government should provide, at what levels, and how to pay for them? These are core public policy problems. There are competing interests at every point in determining who gets what, when, and how. Politics is the process by which the people determine how government will respond. And it is in evaluating the basic fairness of government's response, and the basic equality of the people's general welfare that is thus secured, that we see whether American democracy is working.

For a representative democracy to succeed, there must be a constant interaction between the people and the government. But should representatives act as **trustees** who exercise independent judgment about what they believe is best for the people, or should they act as **delegates** who do exactly as the people wish? This question has been long debated. In the end, the government must be responsive to the needs and opinions of the people, and the people must find ways to hold government accountable. Those who are unresponsive to the people need to be removed from office. Elections provide the most common way to remove elected officials and are the primary mechanism for forging responsiveness. But unelected officials are also responsive to the public. Supreme Court justices are appointed by the president, with the advice and consent of the Senate, and they generally issue judgments that are consistent with public opinion. The bureaucrats who are hired to work in government departments carry out laws that the people's representatives have passed and the president has signed. In addition, work in government is always subject to review and investigation by other branches of government, by the media, and by citizen watchdog groups.

For a government to respond fairly to citizens, all citizens must have an equal opportunity to participate in it. Each citizen must have a chance to have his or her voice heard, either by voting or by participating in the political process and public life. These ideas form the basis of **political equality**. If citizens are not treated equally, with the same degree of fairness, then the foundation of democratic government is weakened. The notion of equality was enshrined in the Declaration of Independence: "We hold these truths to be self-evident: That all men are created equal, that they are endowed by their Creator with certain unalienable rights, that among these are life, liberty and the pursuit of happiness." But this ringing statement did not announce an enforceable right, and government under the Constitution has in the course of the nation's history involved profound inequalities, most notably permitting slavery and a severe restriction of the civil rights of the African American minority for nearly two centuries. The American constitutional system was nearly a century and a half old before it guaranteed women the right to vote. Other racial and ethnic minorities have had to challenge the system to secure their rights, and, as the next chapters demonstrate, civil rights are still evolving. One way to evaluate American democracy is to evaluate the degree to which political equality has been achieved.

There are other aspects of equality. **Equality of opportunity** is one aspect—the expectation that citizens will be treated equally before the law and have an equal opportunity to participate in government. Does equality of opportunity also mean that citizens have an equal opportunity to participate in the economy (to get a job, to get rich) and in social life (to join a club, to eat at a restaurant)? And what about **equality of outcome**, the expectation that incomes will level out or that standards of living will be roughly the same for all citizens? In the United States, equality of outcome, or results, might entail the proportional representation of groups that have experienced discrimination in the past; that is, for full equality of outcome in Congress or on corporate boards, the number of African Americans would have to be equal to their proportion in the overall population, about 13 percent. What can, or should, government do to ensure equality of opportunity, or equality of outcome? These questions are hotly contested, especially efforts to forge equality of outcome. We return to these issues in the final section of this introductory chapter.

equality of opportunity:
Expectation that citizens may not be discriminated against on account of race, gender, or national background, and that every citizen should have an equal chance to succeed in life.

equality of outcome:
Expectation that equality is achieved if results are comparable for all citizens regardless of race, gender, or national background, or that such groups are proportionally represented in measures of success in life.

One way to think further about equality is to contrast American democracy with European democracies, which, as we have seen, have more communal approaches to property and poverty than does the United States and spend more on social programs. European democratic socialism, particularly as it exists in the Scandinavian countries, limits extreme wealth through tax policies, and the result is greater income equality than in the United States. But the political culture of these nations does not prize individualism as

AP Photo/Senior Master Sgt. Thomas Meneguin, Department of Defense/US

When Barack Obama took the presidential oath of office on the steps of the Capitol on January 20, 2009, a record crowd turned out to see this historic transition of power.

highly as does the political culture of the United States, and the equality of results valued in democratic-socialist systems is nothing like American egalitarianism, which prizes individual effort and rejects Europe's rigid class divisions and inherited titles and wealth.

If the Declaration of Independence announced equality as a natural right of humankind, then the American democratic experiment has taken a long time to work out what that equality means. There have been gains and setbacks. We recently witnessed one of the gains.

Regardless of one's partisan leanings, the election of Barack Obama as president is significant achievement for American equality. Many observers thought it would be decades before the country elected an African American president.[16] That view reflected the long history of discrimination in this country. But Obama's win was a strong statement about equality in America.

"I stand here today humbled by the task before us," said President Obama as he began his inaugural address in January 2009, "grateful for the trust you have bestowed, mindful of the sacrifices borne by our ancestors." Those ancestors include the millions of Americans who over more than two centuries have worked to make American democracy more responsive and to make America more equal. We challenge you to join them. This textbook will give you the information you need to understand the way American government works, to recognize the gates and the gateways. We also invite you to think critically about American democracy, to engage in a class-wide and nationwide conversation about how well it is working, to offer ideas for making it work better, to influence the decision makers who make public policy, and even to become one of them.

The Demands of Democratic Citizenship

If you were born in the United States or have been naturalized, you are a citizen, and it is important for you to know what that entails. Citizenship is not a spectator sport. It does not mean choosing sides and rooting for your team from the sidelines, or from the comfort of your living room. It requires more than being a fan; you need to get into the game. But politics is more than a game. It shapes your life on a day-to-day basis. Citizenship, as a result, carries with it both rights and responsibilities. While the specific reasons to be involved in public life may vary, the need to participate does not.

Self-Interest and Civic Interest

self-interest: *Concern for one's own advantage and well-being.*

The first reason to be involved is **self-interest**. You want government to serve your needs. Those needs, of course, range widely, depending on your stage of life, personal circumstances, and values. Some citizens prefer that the government stay out of people's lives as much as possible, and others prefer governmental assistance for the causes they hold dear. As a student, you may want the government to invest more in higher education and job creation; as a parent, you may want more aid for child care and school construction; as a working person, you may view job security as the most important government responsibility. Whatever way you define your self-interest, by getting involved you send signals to elected officials, and if enough people agree with you, the government will likely act.

civic interest: *Concern for the well-being of society and the nation as a whole.*

civil society: *Voluntary organizations that allow communities to flourish.*

The second reason, what we call **civic interest**, is more complex. The idea is that citizens get involved in the process because they want to be part of the voluntary organizations that make up the **civil society** that enables communities to flourish. They want to help others, improve their neighborhoods, and create an even better country. Groups of interested people can accomplish things that individuals acting alone cannot. Sometimes these activities supplement governmental action; for example, neighborhood watch groups keep communities safe, and soup kitchens feed the hungry. Sometimes the activities aim at getting more out of government—more environmental protections or more funding for the arts, for example. By working together, people can encourage greater responsiveness from government. In so doing, they become better citizens and are better able to communicate their needs to a government that thus becomes more responsive.

As gains in civic interest lead to broader public involvement, they also advance equality. In a democracy, the power of individual acts can be amplified, as Sidarth's actions demonstrate. Sometimes this amplification takes place through the courts; lawsuits arising from an alleged injustice experienced by one person can result in broad rulings that affect a great many. There are spillover effects to citizen activism that can benefit everyone. One example comes from the civil rights movement (see Supreme Court Cases: *Garner v. Louisiana*).

You are more likely to be civic-minded than college students in previous generations. If you were born between 1982 and 2003, you are part of the generation that social science researchers have identified as the **Millennials**. In reaction to the idealistic and ideological baby boomer generation born between 1946 and 1964, and the cynical Generation X born between 1964 and 1982, Millennials are more likely to be optimistic and practical, to value consensus and community building, to solve problems through compromise, to be committed to political involvement, to be concerned for the welfare of others, and to want to strengthen the political system.[17]

Participation in the public sphere serves the larger civic interest. Voting is the most obvious political act. In addition, people express their views and ideas to public officials by volunteering in political campaigns, attending rallies, writing letters, and organizing meetings. E-mail, websites, blogs, social networking, text messages, and uploading of videos on YouTube offer additional means of joining the debate about politics and having an influence on government. Those who control the levers of power need to know your views so they can respond. With all the new technologies, the interface between people and politicians is now easier than ever.

When terrorists hijacked planes and crashed them into the World Trade Towers in New York City on September 11, 2001, most Americans said their lives changed forever. The nation seemed vulnerable; a very few people intent on harming the United States could do a great deal of damage, and the victims were innocents. How can the government protect the nation against such attacks?

Millennials: *Generation born between 1982 and 2003.*

Politics and the Public Sphere

Your generation has the power to shape the future in which you will live. The following five issues are a small sample of the concerns that confront this nation, and they are reason enough to take part in the nation's civic life.

Terrorism and Civil Liberties.
U.S. efforts to defeat terrorism involve a long-term military and ideological commitment against an opponent than defies traditional state boundaries. In response to the danger of international terrorism, and specifically to the attacks on the United States on September 11, 2001, Congress and the president curtailed basic civil liberties to help protect the nation's borders. So, for example, the Federal

supremecourtcases

Garner v. Louisiana (1961)

QUESTION: Can Louisiana use "disturbing the peace" laws to convict peaceful sit-in protesters who refuse to leave the dining establishment?

ORAL ARGUMENT: October 18–19, 1961 (listen at www.oyez.org/cases)

DECISION: December 11, 1961 (read at www.findlaw.com/casecode/supreme.html)

OUTCOME: No, overturning the conviction (9–0)

Following sit-in demonstrations by students in Greensboro, North Carolina, who sought to desegregate lunch counters, two black students from Southern University in Baton Rouge, Louisiana, took seats at the lunch counter at Sitman's drugstore and remained there quietly despite being ordered to leave. The police arrested them and charged them with disturbing the peace on the grounds that such behavior could reasonably and foreseeably result in a breach of the peace.

Following a conviction in Louisiana's trial court, the Louisiana Supreme Court denied the defendants' appeal, but the U.S. Supreme Court decided to hear their case. The National Association for the Advancement of Colored People (NAACP), a leading civil rights organization, defended the students. Among the attorneys was Thurgood Marshall, who had successfully argued the *Brown v. Board of Education* (1954) school desegregation case and would later become the first African American to serve on the Supreme Court. The students also had the backing of the John F. Kennedy (1961–63) administration's Justice Department, which filed a legal brief on their behalf.

The U.S. Supreme Court ruled unanimously that there was no evidence whatsoever to back the state's claim that the students had acted in a manner that could have foreseeably led to a disturbance of the peace. To convict the students under such circumstances denied them due process of law, as guaranteed by the Fourteenth Amendment.

Following this decision, southern states found another way to arrest sit-in protesters, charging them under laws prohibiting trespass. Many of these cases reached the Supreme Court, but the Warren Court (1953–69), famously sympathetic to civil rights, always found technical reasons, or legal loopholes, to dismiss the convictions. Ten days after the last of the sit-in case decisions, Congress passed the Civil Rights Act of 1964, which, among other things, made it illegal to refuse service to anyone on account of race, color, religion, or national origin.

- **Was this case about disturbing the peace or about the right of citizens to be served in places of public accommodation?**

- **Do you know of any other Supreme Court cases in which small and localized actions, taken to the courts, had a nationwide impact?**

Bureau of Investigation (FBI) can more easily tap phones than it was able to prior to 9/11. The FBI and other intelligence agencies have argued that access to private phone conversations will help prevent another terrorist attack. That seems important. But given that the 9/11 attackers were Muslims, government wiretaps have more frequently targeted Muslims than non-Muslims. Such action does not treat all citizens equally. If the Constitution protects freedom of religion, should people who worship differently be treated differently? The answer, it turns out, is not simple. There is often an inverse relationship between liberty and order. At times, protecting the safety of the public requires that the civil liberties of some people be curtailed. On the issue of terrorism and civil liberties, some say curtailment is essential; others that it has gone too far. We do not take a position on this matter. Instead, in the following chapters, we discuss the implications of these developments. It is your responsibility to forge informed opinions on such matters and to create the kind of society in which you want to live.

Chip Somodevilla/Getty Images

Congressman Joe Wilson (R-S.C.) shouted "You lie!" during President Barack Obama's address on health care to a joint session of Congress on September 9, 2009. Tensions over health care proposals were high following acrimonious town hall meetings on the issue during the summer. Wilson's outburst followed a statement by the president that the proposed plan would not cover illegal immigrants.

Political Polarization and the Media.   Over the past few decades, the U.S. political system has become highly polarized, as the gulf between the Democratic and Republican Parties has widened. This polarization plays out not only in the halls of Congress but also on the streets of Middle America. Politicians question each other in harsh and nasty tones, and people describe one another with labels that can be equally harsh and nasty. The outburst by Congressman Joe Wilson (R-S.C.) during President Obama's speech on health care in September 2009— "You lie!"—is an example of this current partisan conflict.

Many believe the news media have intensified this polarization as a result of the decline of newspapers and the growth of cable TV and blogging. Certainly, individuals with extreme views now have many more opportunities to broadcast them widely. The news media are no longer centralized and hierarchal, and their transformation has given rise to the citizen-journalist, someone like Sidarth who posts videos on the web to provide firsthand reports of what public officials are doing and saying. The Internet now enables information to move from the bottom up as well as from the top down, and it is available 24-7. The new media promote equality, but do they promote responsiveness in government? Is there too much information? Is it now too easy for biased assessments to circulate and distort information? The Internet is certainly a gateway to citizen involvement in a democracy, but it may be creating new gates as well.

Social Security and Entitlement Programs.   As a nation, we are aging. As Figure 1.5 shows, by 2040 citizens over 65 will constitute 20 percent of the population, double the percentage of just twenty-five years earlier. This graying of America affects the kinds of policies the nation pursues because older citizens tend to vote in great numbers and thus get the attention of elected officials. They want to protect their Social Security payments and the Medicare program, which pays for part of their medical bills. Given that they have contributed to these funds their whole lives, one can hardly blame them. But these entitlements are so costly that they will determine what else can and cannot be done with the federal budget (see Figure 1.6). Over the next twenty-five years, the cost of Social Security benefits will

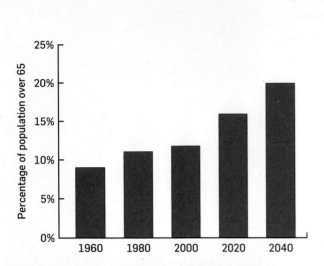

FIGURE 1.5 The Graying of America.
Source: Data from U.S. Census.

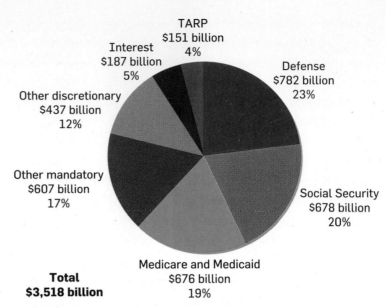

FIGURE 1.6 U.S. Budget, FY 2009. Social Security payments accounted for 20 percent of U.S. federal spending in 2009, and Medicare accounted for 13 percent (shown here in combination with Medicaid, the program that provides medical benefits to the poor). That means that about one-third of all federal spending goes for benefits to senior citizens.
Source: OMB, 2011 Budget.

increase at a rate greater than economic growth, saddling the nation with a greater burden that has implications for you.[18] Your tax dollars will support these programs for the elderly.

This example underscores how politics can often affect your self-interest in direct and tangible terms, but it also directly affects the lives of older members of your family. Imagine that you had to support your parents or elderly relatives and pay for their medical care as they aged. That, too, would have important implications for you. This issue is more than just self-interest. It also involves civic interest. How does a government respond fairly to secure the welfare of all the people and treat them equally? Should all people, regardless of age, have access to a decent standard of living? These are tough questions with no easy answers.

Immigration and Diversity. Another policy that matters is immigration, not only the rise of undocumented workers, but the larger pattern of legal immigration as well. This development has a major effect on the nation. The data in Figure 1.7 show that within thirty or so years the Hispanic population will approach 25 percent. The proportion of Asian Americans will triple in this time frame. These gains mean that the relative proportion of the Anglo population is declining, while the African American community is holding steady at about 13 percent of the population. The United States is indeed becoming more and more diverse, and diversity will have implications for elections, political parties, and the policies they produce. The question for students of American politics in the twenty-first century is how to manage all the competing interests from these different sectors of society.

You may have your own questions: How much does ethnic background matter to you personally, or to politics generally? As Americans, are we becoming more diverse, or more integrated? Do you see your future as determined by competition among groups for government response, or by a decline in the importance of racial and ethnic categories? Is diversity making America more or less equal?

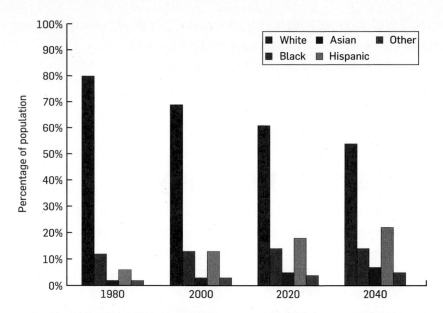

FIGURE 1.7 The Changing Ethnic Composition of America.
Source: Data from U.S. Census.

Education.　Education policy is another, surely more immediate, concern. Each of you, for example, knows that the cost of college is rising faster than the general rate of inflation (see Figure 1.8). Beyond your own ability to pay for your education, what impact will decreased access to education have for American democracy as a whole? Is education an equalizer? Does education offer equality of opportunity? Can it ensure equality of outcome? Do American schools make Americans more or less equal? What should and will government do to respond to problems in education? These are serious questions that warrant careful debate. Yet Americans do not hear much discussion about education in the news media. A recent study by the Brookings Institution indicates that only 1.4 percent of coverage by

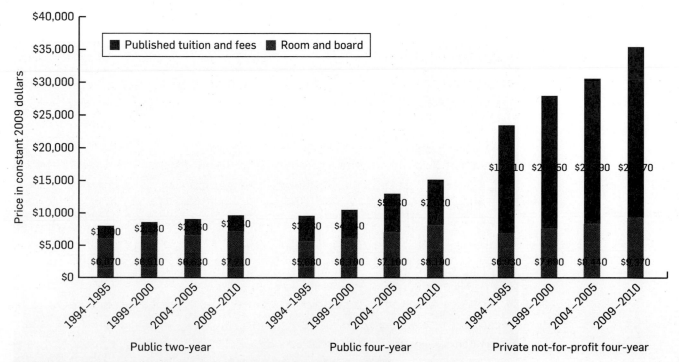

FIGURE 1.8 Increasing Costs of Education, 1994–2010.
Source: The College Board, *Trends in College Pricing*, 2009, fig. 7. Reprinted by permission.

television, websites, and radio in 2009 dealt with education.[19] This lack of attention poses additional barriers to forging a helpful solution to this pressing problem.

These five issues are a small sample of the many problems that confront America. How you and your fellow citizens choose to participate will affect their resolution.

A Gateway to American Democracy

James Madison, whom we have quoted extensively in this introductory chapter, offers one final thought: "Knowledge will forever govern ignorance; and a people who mean to be their own governors, must arm themselves with the power which knowledge gives."[20] To govern yourself, you will need to understand your government, to be informed about issues you care about, to participate in politics, and to be engaged in the nation's civic life. As Madison and all those who wrote the nation's founding documents understood, an engaged public is the best check on excesses of power that threaten fair and just government. If the people do not meet the demands of democratic citizenship, if they do not fulfill their responsibilities, they will lose the freedoms they cherish.

We have written this book to give you the information you need to understand your government—its gates and gateways. We hope it will also push you to evaluate whether government is working for you and for all the nation's citizens. How democratic are we? How can we be better? One thing is certain: We will not be better unless you are involved. The only way to make American democracy more responsive and more equal is by participating.

We, therefore, invite you—actually, we urge you—to enter the gateways to democracy. These gateways are open to you as an American. They empower you, as a citizen, to play an important role in American civic life, and they enable you to experience the amazing arena of American politics. We look forward to sharing the journey with you.

Bob Daemmrich/Photo Edit

GATEWAYS TO LEARNING

Each chapter concludes with review materials that will help you study and learn. For this chapter, we offer a ten-point summary, review questions, and a list of key terms. In other chapters there also will be timelines and exercises to help you apply what you have learned in the classroom to American civic life. Visit the book's website—www.cengagebrain.com/shop/ISBN/0618906959—for more.

To help you get started thinking about whether American democracy works, for Chapter 1 we also include advance questions to keep in mind as you read the book. They will help you judge the democratic experiment when you get to the last chapter.

Top Ten to Take Away

1. American democracy offers many gateways to participation because, at its core, American government is about individuals and self-governance. (pp. 4–6)

2. There are also gates against public participation—obstacles to influence, institutional controls that limit access, powerful interests that seem to block the people's will. (pp. 5–6)

3. To be an engaged and productive citizen, you need to take advantage of the gateways but also know how to navigate around the gates. (pp. 5–6, 20–21)

4. Democracy is self-government. In the American constitutional system, the people set up and agree on the basic rules and procedures that will govern them. (pp. 6–7)

5. The American constitutional system works to protect both liberty and order. The Constitution sets up a governmental structure with built-in constraints on power (gates) and multiple points of access to power (gateways). (pp. 7–9)

6. Power in American government is divided among three branches (executive, legislative, and judicial) and between the national government and the states. (p. 9)

7. American political culture favors individualism, and the U.S. economic system favors capitalism. (pp. 9–13)

8. American citizens may lean conservative or liberal, but most are moderates. (pp. 10–11, 13)

9. With a government designed to constrain power and the popular will, and a citizenry divided into different perspectives and prizing individualism, the development of public policy is difficult and complex. (pp. 14–26)

10. One way to evaluate whether public policy is serving the people of the United States and to judge whether American democracy is working is to measure government responsiveness and citizen equality. (pp. 17–20)

A full narrative summary of the chapter is on the book's website.

Ten to Test Yourself

1. What did the nation's Founders think about democracy?

2. How is government thought of as a social contract?

3. What is the difference between a direct democracy and a representative democracy?

4. How do checks and balances and the separation of powers work?

5. What are the most important American political values?

6. What are the stages in the making of public policy?

7. How should public policy be evaluated?

8. What are various meanings of equality?

9. How can citizens hold government accountable? How can citizens make government responsive?

10. What does it mean to be a citizen?

More review questions and answers and chapter quizzes are on the book's website.

GATEWAYS LEARNING

Terms to Know and Use

autocracy (p. 17)
capitalism (p. 10)
checks and balances (p. 9)
civic interest (p. 20)
civil society (p. 20)
conservatives (p. 10)
constitutional system (p. 7)
delegate (p. 18)
democracy (p. 6)
direct democracy (p. 8)
egalitarianism (p. 10)
equality (p. 17)
equality of opportunity (p. 19)
equality of outcome (p. 19)
executive branch (p. 9)
faction (p. 8)
federalism (p. 9)

Founders (p. 8)
Framers (p. 8)
individualism (p. 10)
interest groups (p. 15)
judicial branch (p. 9)
legislative branch (p. 9)
liberals (p. 10)
libertarians (p. 10)
liberty (p. 7)
majoritarian (p. 15)
majority rule (pp. 6, 7)
Millennials (p. 21)
minority rights (p. 7)
mob rule (p. 7)
moderates (p. 10)
monarchy (p. 17)
natural (unalienable) rights (p. 8)

oligarchy (p. 17)
order (p. 7)
pluralism (p. 15)
policy agenda (pp. 15, 16)
policy enactment (pp. 15, 16)
policy evaluation (pp. 15, 16)
policy formulation (pp. 15, 16)
policy implementation
  (pp. 15, 16)
political culture (p. 10)
political equality (p. 18)
political ideology (p. 10)
political parties (p. 9)
politics (p. 9)
populists (p. 10)
power elite (p. 15)
private goods (p. 17)

problem identification
  (pp. 15, 16)
public goods (p. 17)
public policy (p. 14)
representative
  democracy (p. 8)
republic (p. 8)
responsiveness (p. 17)
rule of law (p. 7)
self-government (p. 6)
self-interest (p. 20)
separation of powers (p. 9)
social contract (p. 8)
socialism (p. 10)
stakeholders (p. 15)
trustee (p. 18)

Advance Questions

Use these questions to guide your reading of this textbook and your learning in this course. How would you answer them now? They will be repeated in the book's final chapter. When you get there, your answers may be different. They will undoubtedly be fuller.

1. Does American democracy work? How can you evaluate it?

2. How democratic was the constitutional system of 1787? How democratic is the United States today?

3. What are the pros and cons of a system in which state governments and a national government share power?

4. What should be the balance between liberty and order? How has the U.S. government balanced the two? What liberty versus order questions do citizens face today?

5. Why is equality important in a democracy? What role does, or should, government play in ensuring equality? What kinds of equality can, or should, government ensure? What should be the balance between equality and liberty?

6. What role does public opinion play in government responsiveness? How responsive should government officials be to public opinion?

7. Describe the role of the press, or more generally the media, in a democracy. Are the media today working to make government better or to make governing more difficult?

8. What is the role of interest groups in a democracy? How do interest groups serve citizens? Are they working today to make government better or to make governing more difficult?

9. What is the role of political parties in the American electorate? In government? Are they working today to make government better or to make governing more difficult?

10. Why are elections important? Are they fair? Do political campaigns ensure that voters' ideas and wishes are represented?

11. Voting is the most fundamental action a citizen can take. Does voting matter? Is voting fair? What ways other than by voting can citizens influence public policy?

12. The Framers thought that Congress would be the most powerful branch of government. Is it? How effective is Congress as a legislative body? What gates limit its effectiveness?

13. The presidency grew in power over the last one hundred years. Is it too powerful now? What are the checks on presidential power? What are the necessities for presidential power?

14. The bureaucracy is often under attack for inefficiency and unresponsiveness. Describe the purpose of the bureaucracy. Which parts of it function well? Which do not? Why?

15. The pediment above the main entrance to the Supreme Court proclaims "Equal Justice under Law." What does that mean? How do the courts ensure equality? Is the judiciary responsive?

16. How has the U.S. role in the world changed in your lifetime? What are the prospects for global partnerships? For global conflict?

17. How do you judge the American democratic experiment?

18. What are the dangers to democratic government in the twenty-first century?

19. Why do you think the United States has survived as a representative democracy for more than two centuries? What has been the experience of other democracies?

20. How easy or hard is it to influence public policy? What types of people have had the greatest influence—politicians, corporate executives, military leaders, grassroots organizers?

21. How do cultural similarity and diversity work to help or impede the operations of American democracy?

22. How can you get yourself and your opinions represented in government?

23. How can you make government more responsive and responsible to its citizens?

24. How equal are America's citizens? How equal should they be? What kinds of opportunities do American citizens have? Are the outcomes equitable?

25. What can you do, as an active citizen, to make American democracy better?

2 THE CONSTITUTION

▲ **University of Texas at Austin**

> *An active and engaged citizen must have the ability to pressure politicians for a long period of time and have plenty of resources available.*

CourseMate

Visit http://www.cengagebrain .com/shop/ISBN/0618906959 for interactive tools including:

- Quizzes
- Flashcards
- Videos
- Animated PowerPoint slides, Podcast summaries, and more

Gregory Watson, a sophomore economics major at the University of Texas at Austin, had a term paper to write for a government class. It was 1982, the year in which the proposed Equal Rights Amendment to the U.S. Constitution, which would have prevented any state or the United States from denying equality of rights on account of sex, would expire unless three more states ratified it. Congress had proposed the amendment in 1972, setting a seven-year time frame for ratification by the states, following the two-step course established in the Constitution for the passage of amendments. The proposed amendment got off to a quick start, with twenty-two of the thirty-eight states necessary to pass the amendment approving it. Momentum slowed, however, as opposition to the amendment mobilized, and even though Congress extended the deadline for three more years, no more states ratified the amendment. It was the legality of this extension—an "odd process," Watson called it, that fascinated him, and he decided to investigate the failure of the amendment.

While researching that issue, Watson discovered another unratified amendment, one that dated back to 1789. This amendment, proposed by James Madison, would prohibit any congressional pay raise from taking effect until after an ensuing election. In essence, it prevented members of Congress from awarding themselves pay raises within sessions; if they did vote an increase, they would have to stand for election before it went into effect. Six states ratified this amendment between 1789 and 1791, but no other state approved it until Ohio did so in 1873. Then, in 1978, Wyoming approved it. By that time, it would have needed the approval of thirty-eight states to go into effect, but it seems there was no deadline. Watson switched the topic of his paper to argue that the Constitution does not put time limits on ratification, that the congressional pay raise amendment was still pending, and that it should be passed, for it would help protect members of Congress against charges of corruption.

Gregory Watson ▶

Watson got a C on the paper. "The professor told me this amendment could not pass. I was disgusted," he later told *USA Today*, and he set out to prove her wrong. Using $6,000 of his own money and voter anger over congressional pay raises, he launched a letter-writing campaign to targeted states. In 1983 Maine ratified the amendment, and other states followed. In 1992 Alabama became the thirty-eighth state to approve the amendment, and on May 14 of that year the archivist of the United States declared it the Twenty-Seventh Amendment. It states: "No law, varying the compensation for the services of the senators and representatives, shall take effect, until an election of representatives shall have intervened."

Watson's professor never changed his grade, but Watson pursued his interest in politics as an aide in the Texas legislature and continued to research the status of other amendments. When he discovered that Mississippi had never ratified the Thirteenth Amendment, abolishing slavery, he launched another letter-writing campaign that also brought success. In 1995 Mississippi officially approved the amendment.[1]

The amendment process that so interested Watson is the means by which the U.S. Constitution, the fundamental law undergirding the structure of American government, can be formally changed over time. Although the basic foundations of government remain essentially as they were established in the 1787 Constitution, amendments to the Constitution have provided guarantees of essential rights and liberties. They have outlawed slavery and guaranteed equality under the law. They have removed gates that limited voting. No constitution can remain impermeable to change if it is to regulate a society that continues to change. Gregory Watson used the gateway of citizen lobbying, in this case a letter-writing campaign, to bring about a change to the nation's fundamental law that had been two hundred years in the making.

In this chapter, we examine the governing documents prior to the Constitution, particularly the Articles of Confederation and its deficiencies. We also track the debates at the Constitutional Convention and afterward, as the people of the United States decided whether to ratify the new Constitution. They did ratify it, but almost immediately they amended it. After we examine the structure and philosophy behind the new Constitution, we consider its responsiveness, through both amendment and less formal procedures, to changing times.

FOCUS QUESTIONS

- In what ways did the Constitution ensure that government would be responsive to the people? How has government become more responsive since 1787?

- In what ways did the Constitution seek to control the popular will and ensure order?

- In what ways did the Constitution seek to control government itself?

- In what ways did the nation's founding documents promote equality? In what ways did they fail to promote equality?

- Is the Constitution a gate or a gateway to American democracy? Is it a gatekeeper? Explain.

Before the Constitution

From the beginning, Great Britain accorded the American colonists, as British subjects, a certain amount of self-rule. When the colonists perceived that Parliament and the king were blocking their participation in government, they moved toward independence from Britain. They established a new national government under documents that included state constitutions and a national Articles of Confederation. In this section, we trace that process.

What Is a Constitution?

A **constitution** is the fundamental law undergirding the structure of government. In a modern democracy, a constitution sets forth the basic rules and procedures for how the people shall be governed, including the powers and structure of the government, as well as the rights retained by the people. The British constitution is not a single document but rather a series of documents, beginning with the Magna Carta in 1215, that define the rights of the people and limit the powers of the king, as well as a series of customs and precedents. Following the so-called Glorious Revolution of 1688–89, Parliament asserted its supremacy over the monarch. Thereafter, the monarch was forbidden to suspend the law, to levy taxes, and to maintain a standing army. These powers passed to Parliament, the legislature representing the people, and King William III acknowledged that he ruled not by divine right but by right of contract with his subjects. By the eighteenth century British subjects believed that the British constitution guaranteed them certain rights, including the right not to be taxed without their consent and the right to be tried by a jury of their peers.

constitution: *Document or set of documents that establish the basic rules and procedures for how a society shall be governed.*

What rights do you think you have as an American? When was the last time you thought about those rights?

Toward Independence

The American colonists believed they had all the rights of British subjects. Thus they objected when, following the French and Indian War (1754–63), Great Britain tried to recoup some of the costs of defending the colonies by imposing regulations and taxes on them. The Sugar Act of 1764 set forth a long list of items that could be exported only to Great Britain, limiting competition for the colonists' goods. The Stamp Act of 1765 established a tax on virtually all forms of paper used by the colonists. Although Britain had previously levied import and export taxes on the colonies, this was the first direct tax by Britain on the colonists for products made and sold in America.

The colonists reacted angrily, forming trade associations to boycott, or refuse to buy, British goods. They also published pamphlets denouncing the loss of liberty. Led by Patrick Henry, they challenged not just the taxes themselves, but Parliament's authority to pass such measures. "Give me liberty," proclaimed Henry in the Virginia House of Burgesses, "or give me death." Soon enough, riots broke out against Stamp Act collectors, making enforcement impossible.

Britain repealed the Stamp Act in 1766, replacing it with the Townshend Acts, which imposed taxes on various imports. Having successfully fought off the direct internal taxes on paper, colonists mobilized against the new external (importation) taxes. Led by Samuel Adams, the Massachusetts legislature issued a letter declaring the Townshend Acts unconstitutional because they violated the principle of "no taxation without representation." The colonists thus began to insist that they had the right to participate in the political decisions that affected them, a right they believed they held as British subjects.

The British had a more limited view of both participation and representation. At the time, only about one in six British adult males had the right to vote for Parliament, whereas two-thirds of free American adult males could vote for their colonial representatives.[2] Women and children could not vote anywhere; males, as heads of the family, were assumed to be able to represent them. Moreover, while most British cities did have representation in Parliament, some—just like the colonies—did not. Rather, representation in Parliament was based on historic population centers, so large new cities such as Manchester and Birmingham sent no

The Granger Collection, New York

Samuel Adams (1722–1803) was born in Boston. Like his cousin John Adams, he was a leader in the American Revolution. He organized the Stamp Act protests and, as a member of the Massachusetts legislature, drafted a letter on the Townshend Acts that was circulated throughout the colonies.

representatives to Parliament, while the town of Dunwich continued to send a representative even though storms and erosion had swept it into the North Sea centuries earlier.

As for cities such as Manchester and Birmingham, the British justified their lack of representation by claiming that all English citizens were virtually represented by all members of Parliament, who purportedly acted in the common good. As Edmund Burke wrote, "Parliament is a *deliberative* assembly of *one* nation, with *one* interest, that of the whole."[3] The colonists, however, rejected the views that their interests were one with Britain's and that Parliament could represent those interests.

How does the American view of representation differ from the British view?

Aggrieved by taxation without representation, the colonists continued to resist the Townshend Acts. Britain responded by dissolving the Massachusetts legislature and seizing a ship belonging to John Hancock, one of the leaders of the resistance. Britain also sent troops to quell the resistance, but the presence of soldiers during peacetime aggravated tensions. British soldiers fired on a threatening crowd in 1770, killing five colonists and wounding six others in what became known as the Boston Massacre. With boycotts of British goods costing Britain far more than the taxes raised, Parliament rescinded all the Townshend Act taxes except the one on tea. In 1773 Parliament granted the East India Company the exclusive right to sell tea to the colonies, which then granted local monopolies in the colonies. Angered by both the tax and the monopoly, colonists once again took action. Disguised as Indians, they dumped a shipload of tea in Boston Harbor. In 1774 Britain responded to the **Boston Tea Party** with the Coercive Acts, which, among other things, gave the royal governor the right to select the upper house of the Massachusetts legislature. The Coercive Acts also denied Massachusetts the right to try British officials charged with capital offenses. The Quartering Acts required colonists to quarter British soldiers in their private homes, even during times of peace.[4] These acts convinced many colonists that their liberty was at stake, and that rebellion and independence were the only alternatives to British tyranny.

Boston Tea Party: *Protest in 1773 in which colonists dressed as Indians boarded vessels in Boston Harbor and threw chests of tea overboard to express anger at Britain's tax policies and commercial regulations.*

What do the Tea Party protests that began in 2009 have in common with the Boston Tea Party?

In an attempt to present a united front about colonial grievances, Benjamin Franklin proposed a **Continental Congress**. The First Congress, with delegates chosen by the colonial legislatures, met in Philadelphia in 1774. It rejected a reconciliation plan with England and instead sent King George III a list of grievances. It also adopted a very successful compact among the colonies not to import any English goods. Finally, it agreed to meet again as the Second Continental Congress in May 1775. This Second Continental Congress acted as the common government of the states between 1775 and 1781.

Continental Congress: *Initial governing authority over the Revolutionary War and other common affairs of the thirteen independent states. The first Congress met in 1774, and the second in 1775–81.*

In April 1775, following skirmishes with British troops in Lexington and Concord, outside of Boston, the Second Continental Congress named George Washington commander of a new Continental Army. In 1776, with battles raging throughout the colonies, Thomas Paine penned his influential pamphlet *Common Sense*, which called for independence from Britain. "There is something very absurd in supposing a continent to be perpetually governed by an island," he argued.[5] *Common Sense* was the most widely distributed pamphlet of its time, and it helped convince many Americans that independence was the only way they could secure their right to self-government.

Was the American Revolution really about taxation, or was it about something else?

The Declaration of Independence

In June 1776 the Continental Congress debated an independence resolution, but postponed a vote until July. Meanwhile, it instructed Thomas Jefferson and others to draft a **Declaration of Independence**. Congress approved the Declaration of Independence on July 4. Jefferson's Declaration relied in part on the writings of John Locke in asserting that people had certain natural (or unalienable) rights that government could not take away, including the right to life and liberty (see Chapter 1, Gateways to American Democracy). For Locke's reference to property, Jefferson substituted "the pursuit of Happiness."

Declaration of Independence: *1776 document declaring American independence from Great Britain and calling for equality, human rights, and citizen participation.*

The Declaration that Jefferson penned was a radical document. It declared the right of the people to alter or abolish governments that do not meet the needs of the people; it declared the colonies independent from Britain; it contained a stirring call for equality, human rights, and public participation in government that, though not at the time legally enforceable, has inspired generations of Americans seeking to make these ideas a reality.

What has the Declaration of Independence's statement on equality meant to Americans? How are Americans equal, and not equal, today?

> *We hold these truths to be self evident: That all men are created equal, that they are endowed by their Creator with certain unalienable Rights, that among these are life, liberty, and the pursuit of happiness; that, to secure these rights, governments are instituted among men, deriving their just powers from the consent of the governed; that whenever any form of government becomes destructive of these ends, it is the right of the people to alter or to abolish it, and to institute new government, laying its foundation on such principles and organizing its powers in such form, as to them shall seem most likely to effect their safety and happiness.*

The Declaration went on to list grievances against King George III, including suspending popularly elected colonial legislatures, imposing taxes without representation, and conducting trials without juries. It then declared the united colonies to be thirteen "free and independent states." (The full text of the Declaration of Independence is in this book's Appendix.)

Even before the Declaration, the Continental Congress advised the colonies to adopt new constitutions "under the authority of the people." Reacting against the limitation on rights imposed by the British monarch and by royal governors in the colonies, these new state constitutions severely limited executive power but barely limited legislative authority. At the same time, Americans made little effort to establish a national political authority, as most Americans considered themselves primarily citizens of the states in which they lived. Nevertheless, the Continental Congress needed legal authority for its actions and proposed the **Articles of Confederation** in 1777.

© Francis G. Mayer/CORBIS

Members of the Second Continental Congress voted to approve the Declaration of Independence on July 4, 1776, though only John Hancock, president of the Congress, signed it that day.

Articles of Confederation: *Initial governing authority of the United States, 1781–88.*

The Articles of Confederation

The Articles required unanimous consent of the states for adoption, which did not occur until 1781, just a few months before American victory in the Revolutionary War. They formally established "the United States of America," in contrast to the Declaration, which was a pronouncement of "Thirteen United States of America." According to the Declaration, each of the thirteen independent states had the authority to do all "acts and things which independent states may of right do," such as waging war, establishing alliances, and concluding peace. These were thirteen independent states united in a war of independence. With the

Articles, the states became one nation with centralized control over making war and foreign affairs. But due to the belief that Great Britain had violated fundamental liberties, the Articles emphasized freedom from national authority at the expense of order. Thus the states retained all powers not expressly granted to Congress under the Articles.

Moreover, those expressly granted powers were extremely limited. Congress had full authority over foreign, military, and Indian affairs. It could decide boundary and other disputes between the states, coin money, and establish post offices. But Congress did not have the authority to regulate commerce or, indeed, any authority to operate directly over citizens of the United States. For example, Congress could not tax citizens or products (such as imports) directly; it could only request (but not command) revenues from the states.

In addition to limiting powers, the Articles made governing difficult. Each state had one vote in Congress, with the consent of nine of the thirteen required for most important matters, including borrowing and spending money. Amending the Articles required the unanimous consent of the states. In 1781 tiny Rhode Island, blocking an amendment that would have set a 5 percent tax on imports, denied the whole nation desperately needed revenue. Moreover, the Articles established no judicial branch, with the minor exception that Congress could establish judicial panels on an ad hoc basis to hear appeals involving disputes between states and to hear cases involving crimes on the high seas. There was no separate executive branch, but Congress had the authority to establish an executive committee along with a rotating president who would manage the general affairs of the United States when Congress was not in session.[6]

These deficiencies led to predictable problems. With insufficient funds, the nation's debts went unpaid, hampering its credit. Even obligations to pay salaries owed to the Revolutionary War troops went unfulfilled. Without a centralized authority to regulate commerce, states taxed imports from other states, stunting economic growth. Lack of military power allowed Spain to block commercial access to the Mississippi River. Barbary pirates off the shores of Tripoli captured American ships and held their crews for ransom.

While the government of the United States suffered from too little authority, James Madison, Thomas Jefferson, and others came to believe that the governments of the states possessed too much authority. Popularly elected legislatures with virtually no checks on their authority passed laws rescinding private debts and creating trade barriers against other states. They also began taking over both judicial and executive functions. As Jefferson declared, this aggregation of power was no more acceptable if done by a plural legislature than if done by a unitary executive: "173 despots would surely be as oppressive as one." Though the legislature was chosen by the people, "An *elective despotism* was not the government we fought for."[7]

With the United States in desperate financial straits, James Madison proposed a convention of states to consider granting the national government the power to tax and to regulate trade. Only five states showed up at this 1786 Annapolis Convention, preventing it from accomplishing anything.

Why didn't the Articles of Confederation work as a governing document?

Daniel Shays led a protest movement of debt-ridden farmers facing foreclosures on their homes and farms. Demanding lower taxes and the issuance of paper money, they engaged in mob violence to force the Massachusetts courts to close.

© Bettmann/CORBIS

As the Annapolis Convention took place, word spread of a revolt in western Massachusetts that made the weakness of the national government all too clear. Revolutionary War hero Daniel Shays and several thousand distressed farmers forced courts to close and threatened federal arsenals. Not until February 1787 did Massachusetts put down **Shays's Rebellion**. The revolt helped convince the states that, on top of the Articles' other problems, there was too much freedom and not enough order, which neither the federal nor the state governments could ensure. The Annapolis Convention thus issued an invitation to all thirteen states to meet in Philadelphia in May 1787 to consider revising the Articles of Confederation. Only Rhode Island declined the invitation.

Shays's Rebellion: *Revolt in 1786–87 by Massachusetts farmers against heavy debts; it helped convince states that neither the federal nor state governments were functioning properly.*

The Constitutional Convention

The delegates chosen for the Constitutional Convention were charged with amending the Articles of Confederation so that the national government could work more effectively. Almost immediately, however, they moved beyond that charge and began debating a brand new constitution. To complete that newly proposed constitution, the delegates needed to reach compromises between large and small states over representation, between northern and southern states over issues related to slavery, and between those who favored a strong national government and those who favored strong state governments in the balance of power between the two. The document they created, which was then sent to the states for ratification, is, with subsequent amendments, the same Constitution Americans live by today. (The full text of the Constitution of the United States is in this book's Appendix.)

Were the delegates to the Constitutional Convention more concerned about liberty or about order?

The Delegates

The fifty-five delegates to the **Constitutional Convention** of 1787 represented large (Virginia) and small (Delaware) states. They represented states in the south with large slave populations (South Carolina, 43 percent of total population), states in the north with small slave populations (Connecticut, 1 percent of population), but only one state (Massachusetts) with no slaves.[8] Not all the delegates were rich, but none were poor. All were white, and all were male. Most were in their thirties or forties, and a majority had legal training.[9] Not surprisingly, the delegates' behavior at the Convention substantially reflected their interests and the statewide interests they represented.[10] The delegates included James Madison, who would draft much of the Constitution; George Washington, the former commander of the Continental Army who presided over the Convention; and Benjamin Franklin, the scientist, inventor, diplomat, and revered elder statesman. (see Figure 2.1).

Constitutional Convention: *Meeting in 1787 by twelve states to revise the Articles of Confederation, which ended up proposing an entirely new Constitution.*

The Convention's rules granted each state one vote, regardless of the size of the state or the number of delegates it sent. To secure the assent of all states represented at the Convention, compromises had to be reached that would satisfy the various interests represented there. To keep the gateways to compromise open, the delegates voted to keep their deliberations secret until they completed their work. This decision also created a gate that limited popular influence.

What compromises made the Constitution possible? Is compromise, as a political strategy, good or bad for democracy? Do politicians use compromise as a strategy today?

Large versus Small States

Upon the opening of the Philadelphia Convention in May 1787, Edmund Randolph of Virginia presented the delegates with James Madison's radical proposal for a new government. Known as the **Virginia Plan**, Madison's proposal included a strong central government that could operate directly on the citizens of the United States without the states acting

Virginia Plan: *Madison's proposal at the Constitutional Convention to radically strengthen the national government.*

FRAMERS

FOUNDERS

John Jay (1745–1829)	John Adams (1735–1826)	Thomas Jefferson (1743–1826)	Benjamin Franklin (1706–90)	James Madison (1751–1836)	George Washington (1732–99)	Alexander Hamilton (1755–1804)
of New York was a delegate to the First Continental Congress and president of the Second, though he was not present when the Declaration of Independence was signed. He was U.S. minister to Spain from 1780 to 1782 and a negotiator of the peace treaty with Britain in 1783. He was an author of the *Federalist Papers* and the first chief justice of the Supreme Court. *The Granger Collection, New York*	of Massachusetts was a delegate to the First and Second Continental Congresses and, with his cousin Samuel, a Signer of the Declaration of Independence. He was a diplomat to France in 1778–79, a negotiator of the peace treaty with Britain in 1783, and U.S. minister to Britain in 1785–88. He was vice president under George Washington and president from 1797 to 1801. *Réunion des Musées Nationaux / Art Resource, NY*	of Virginia, was a delegate to the Second Continental Congress and drafted the Declaration of Independence. He was U.S. minister to France in 1785–89, vice president under John Adams, and president from 1801 to 1809. *© Corbis*	was born in Boston but moved to Philadelphia. He was a delegate to the Second Continental Congress and helped draft the Declaration of Independence. He was a diplomat to France in 1776–85 and a negotiator of the peace treaty with Britain in 1783. He was a member of the Constitutional Convention. *National Portrait Gallery, Smithsonian Institution / Art Resource, NY*	of Virginia was a delegate to the Second Continental Congress. He was an influential member of the Constitutional Convention and author of the *Federalist Papers,* and he was instrumental in drafting the Bill of Rights. He was president from 1809 to 1817. *The White House Historical Association (White House Collection)*	of Virginia was a delegate to the First and Second Continental Congresses and was commander of the Continental Army. He presided over the Constitutional Convention and was president from 1789 to 1797. *© Bequest of Mrs. Benjamin Ogle Tayloe; Collection of The Corcoran Gallery of Art*	who was born in the West Indies but attended college in New York, served on General Washington's staff during the Revolution. At the Constitutional Convention, he advocated a strong central government. He was an author of the *Federalist Papers* and the first secretary of the treasury. *The Granger Collection, New York.*

FIGURE 2.1 Founders and Framers. The Founders were the leaders of the American Revolution and the new United States. The Framers were those who wrote the Constitution. All Framers were Founders, but not all Founders were Framers. Only some of the Founders were Signers, the people who signed the Declaration of Independence.

proportional representation: *Used by the Framers to signify a system of legislative districting in which larger states receive more representatives than smaller states; today an electoral system that assigns party delegates according to vote share in a presidential primary election or that assigns seats in the legislature according to vote share in a general election.*

New Jersey Plan: *Counterproposal to the Virginia Plan aimed at strengthening the Articles of Confederation but leaving the basic workings of the Articles intact.*

Connecticut Compromise: *Compromise on legislative representation whereby the lower chamber is based on population and the upper chamber provides equal representation to the states.*

as intermediaries. The legislative branch would consist of two chambers: a lower chamber elected by the people, and an upper chamber elected by the lower chamber. Each chamber would have **proportional representation**, representation proportional to the populations of the states: the larger the population, the more representatives a state would have. The legislature would have general authority to pass laws that would "promote the harmony" of the United States and could veto laws passed by the states. The Virginia Plan proposed a national executive and a national judiciary, both chosen by the legislature. A council of revision, composed of the executive and judicial members, would have final approval over all legislative acts.

Madison's proposals astonished many of the delegates from the smaller states, and some from the larger states as well. To counter them, on June 15 William Paterson of New Jersey presented the Convention with the so-called **New Jersey Plan**, which strengthened the Articles by providing Congress with the authority to regulate commerce and to directly tax imports and paper items. It also proposed a national executive chosen by the legislature and a national judiciary chosen by the executive.[11] Each state would retain equal representation in Congress.

The convention debated these measures, with the question of proportional or equal representation generating enormous controversy. Madison insisted that proportional representation for both chambers was the only fair system, and the small states insisted that they would walk out if they lost their equal vote. Roger Sherman of Connecticut proposed what became known as the **Connecticut Compromise**. The makeup of the lower chamber, the

House of Representatives, would be proportional to population, but the upper chamber, the Senate, would represent each state equally.

Nation versus State

While the question of representation threatened the Convention, there was substantial agreement over the nationalist platform that Madison supported. The delegates rejected the New Jersey Plan, which would have continued government under the Articles, by a 7 to 3 vote, with Maryland divided and New Hampshire absent.

The delegates did not approve the Virginia Plan in full, but it substantially influenced the proposed Constitution. Under the new Constitution, the government had the authority to operate directly on the citizens of the United States. Congress was not granted general legislative power, but rather **enumerated powers**, that is, a list of powers it could employ. Among its enumerated powers were the authority to tax to provide for the general welfare; to regulate commerce among the states and with foreign nations; to borrow money; to declare war, raise armies, and maintain a navy; and to make all laws "necessary and proper for carrying into Execution the foregoing Powers." The tax and commerce powers were among those missing from the Articles.

Congress did not receive the authority to veto state laws, but the Constitution declared that national law would be supreme over state law, bound state judges to that decision, and created a national judiciary that would help ensure such rulings. Moreover, the Convention set explicit limits on state authority, prohibiting the states from carrying on foreign relations, coining money, and impairing certain rights. Finally, the Convention approved a national executive (that is, the president) who could serve as a unifying force throughout the land. Table 2.1 presents the components of the Virginia Plan, the New Jersey Plan, and the proposed Constitution.

enumerated powers: *Powers of Congress listed in Article I, Section 8 of the Constitution, such as regulating commerce and coining money.*

TABLE 2.1 The Virginia and New Jersey Plans Compared to the Constitution

Issue	Virginia Plan	New Jersey Plan	Constitution
Operation	Directly on people	Through the states	Directly on people
Legislative structure	Bicameral and proportional	Unicameral and equal	Bicameral, with lower chamber proportional and upper chamber equal
Legislative authority	General: power to promote the harmony of the United States	Strict enumerated powers of the Articles of Confederation, plus power to regulate commerce and limited power to tax	Broad enumerated powers
Check on legislative authority	Council of revision	None	Presidential veto, with possibility of a two-thirds override
Executive	Unitary national executive chosen by legislature	Plural national executive chosen by legislature	Unitary national executive chosen by Electoral College
Judiciary	National judiciary chosen by legislature	National judiciary chosen by executive	National judiciary chosen by president with advice and consent of Senate

North versus South

Resolving the question of nation versus state proved less difficult than resolving the question of representation. More difficult still were questions related to slavery. Although slavery existed in every state except Massachusetts, the overwhelming majority of slaves, nearly 95 percent, were in the southern states, from Maryland to Georgia.[12] As Madison put it, "The States were divided into different interests not by their difference of size, but principally from their having or not having slaves."[13] Not all northern delegates at the Convention opposed slavery, but those who were abolitionists wanted an immediate ban on importing slaves from Africa, prohibitions against the expansion of slavery into the western territories, and the adoption of a plan for the gradual freeing of slaves. Delegates from Georgia and South Carolina, whose states would never accept the Constitution on these terms, wanted guaranteed protections for slavery and the slave trade, and no restrictions on slavery in the territories. To secure a Constitution, compromises were necessary.

Many supporters of slavery recognized the horrors of the foreign slave trade, and by 1779 all states except North Carolina, South Carolina, and Georgia had banned it. Leaving the authority to regulate the foreign slave trade to Congress would inevitably have resulted in its being banned everywhere and probably would have kept those three states from joining the union. Thus, a slave trade compromise prohibited Congress from stopping the slave trade until 1808. This compromise also resulted in a ban on taxing exports, a substantial benefit to the export-driven economies of the southern states.

A second compromise involved how slaves should be counted when calculating population for purposes of representation. Madison's Virginia Plan based representation on the number of free inhabitants of each state, whereas the southernmost slave states wanted slaves to be fully counted for purposes of representation. Delegates from the northern states, on the other hand, argued that slave states, which by definition denied the humanity of slaves, should not benefit by receiving extra representation based on the number of slaves that they had. Under the Articles, taxes requested of the states were based on the population of each state, with five slaves counting as three people. The Convention agreed to use this **three-fifths** formula not just for representation, but also for whatever direct or population taxes the national government might choose to levy. This compromise had a significant impact on representation in the House of Representatives,[14] as Figure 2.2 demonstrates.

A third compromise involved slavery in the western territories, and it came not from the Convention but from the government under the Articles, which passed the Northwest Ordinance in July 1787. This ordinance, which established the means for governing the western lands north of the Ohio River (eventually the states of Ohio, Indiana, Illinois, Michigan, and Wisconsin, and parts of Minnesota), prohibited slavery in this territory, but also provided that fugitive slaves who escaped to the territory would be returned to their owners. The Constitution repeated these provisions.

Were the delegates right or wrong to compromise on slavery?

three-fifths compromise: *Compromise over slavery at the Constitutional Convention that granted states extra representation in the House of Representatives based on their number of slaves at the ratio of three-fifths.*

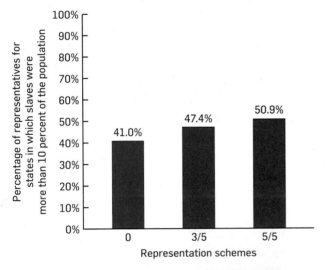

FIGURE 2.2 The Impact of Counting Slaves for Purposes of Representation. If slaves counted fully for purposes of representation (5 slaves = 5 people), the interests of slaveholding states would have been magnified substantially. If slaves did not count at all for purposes of representation (slaves = 0 people), the interests of slaveholding states would have been diluted. The three-fifths compromise provided some representation in the House based on the number of slaves in each state.
Source: Data from the 1790 Census.

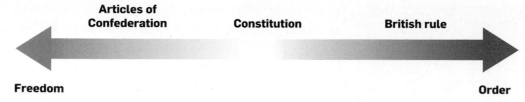

Articles of Confederation   **Constitution**   **British rule**

Freedom   **Order**

FIGURE 2.3 Relative Balance of Freedom and Order.

With the precedent of prohibiting slavery in the Northwest Territory established in the Northwest Ordinance, the Convention gave Congress the right to regulate the territories of the United States without mentioning whether slavery could be allowed or prohibited. Silences such as this often allow compromises to be reached in instances where explicit statements would force one side or the other to object.

Gates against Popular Influence

Compared to the British constitutional system, the 1787 Constitution provided direct and indirect gateways for popular involvement (see Figure 2.3). Nevertheless, the Framers did not trust the people to have complete control over choosing the government. In two important ways—the election of the president and the election of the Senate—the Constitution limited popular control. One of these gates against the people's participation—the election of the president through the **Electoral College**—remains in effect today.

Rather than directly electing the president through a popular vote, the Constitution established an Electoral College, in which electors actually choose the president. Each state receives a number of electors equal to its number of representatives plus senators, and each state legislature chooses the manner for selecting the electors from its state—by popular vote, legislative selection, or some other mechanism. Today, each state legislature allows the people of the state to choose that state's electors, but in the early days of the **republic**, many state legislatures kept that right for themselves. See Chapter 10 (Elections and Campaigns) for a full discussion of the Electoral College and its consequences for presidential elections and campaigns.

State legislatures also selected U.S. senators. The Framers feared that a Congress elected directly by the people would be too responsive to the popular will. Popularly elected state legislatures often passed unjust and confusing laws. What Madison called "a spirit of *locality*" often superseded the common interest, allowing single-chamber legislatures to yield to sudden and violent passions that swept the nation.[15] Others shared Madison's fear. To make the point, George Washington used an analogy. "Why do you pour that coffee into your saucer," he asked Thomas Jefferson. "To cool it," replied Jefferson. "Even so," said Washington, "we pour legislation into the senatorial saucer to cool it."[16] The indirect election of senators was thus intended to serve as a check on the popular will. In 1913 the Seventeenth Amendment granted the people the right to elect senators directly.

The Ratification Process

With agreements reached on representation in Congress, federal or national power, and slavery, the delegates made a few final decisions. First, despite the urging of George Mason of Virginia, the delegates chose not to include a **Bill of Rights**—a listing of rights retained

Electoral College: *The presidential electors, selected to represent the votes of their respective states, who meet every four years to cast the electoral votes for president and vice president.*

Why did the delegates set up gates against citizen participation? Whose participation did they not consider at all?

republic: *Form of government in which power derives from citizens, but public officials make policy and govern according to existing law.*

Did the delegates trust the people?

Bill of Rights: *First ten amendments to the Constitution, which provide basic political rights.*

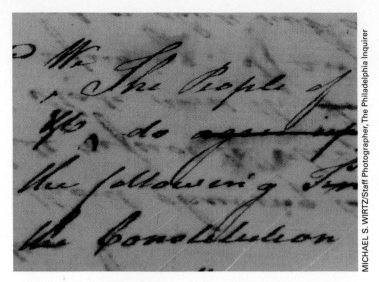

This draft of the Constitution, written by Pennsylvania delegate James Wilson, was rediscovered in 2010 in Wilson's papers in Philadelphia. At the start of the Constitutional Convention, the delegates adopted a rule of secrecy that has limited access to their thoughts and daily deliberations ever since. Researchers are still uncovering the history of the Convention.

Do the people today retain the right to institute new government?

Why did the delegates establish three branches of government?

by the people that Congress did not have the authority to take away, such as freedom of speech and freedom of religion. Because Congress had enumerated powers only, and because the authority to regulate speech, religion, and other freedoms were not among the powers granted to Congress, delegates believed there was no need to prohibit Congress from abridging such rights.

Second, the delegates needed a method for ratifying, or granting final approval of, the Constitution. Fortunately, the states had already established a precedent for ratifying constitutions. In the early years of independence, state legislatures passed bills that established what were essentially state constitutions, setting up the branches of the state government or declaring the fundamental rights that their state citizens possessed. But with no special mechanism for approving such fundamental laws, what one legislature passed, another could simply repeal. Giving relative permanence to these fundamental laws required an extra step. Thus many states had moved to have their constitutions approved and enshrined in state ratifying conventions. The people's representatives at these conventions therefore had the exclusive authority to establish constitutions.

Similarly, the delegates at the Philadelphia Convention chose to send the proposed Constitution to the states for approval via special ratifying conventions to be chosen by the people. The Constitution would take effect among those states approving it when ratified by nine of the thirteen states. The Articles had required unanimity of state delegations for amendment, but the Constitutional Convention sought approval from a higher authority: the people of the United States. This process for ratification followed the statement in the Declaration of Independence that "it is the right of the people . . . to institute new government." Hence, the Constitution's preamble establishes the Constitution in the name of "We the People of the United States."

In September 1787, with these final steps taken, the Convention voted on the final document. Some of the delegates had left by September, but thirty-nine signed the document, with only three refusing to do so. Crucially, given Convention rules, a majority of the delegates from each of the states voted yes.

Government under the Constitution

The final document sent to the states for ratification laid out a structure of democratic government and proposed mechanisms whereby the Constitution could be amended. It also reflected the Framers' attempt to establish a government powerful enough to ensure public order yet containing enough gateways to guarantee individual liberty.

The Structure of Government

The Constitution established three branches of government: the legislative, the executive, and the judicial.

The Legislative Branch. The legislative branch, as explained in Chapter 1, makes the laws. The Constitution established a **bicameral** Congress, consisting of two chambers. The lower chamber, the House of Representatives, is proportioned by population (until the Civil War, the slave population was added to the free population according to the three-fifths formula described above). Members of the House are elected for two-year terms directly by the people, with voting eligibility determined by each state. Representatives have to be at least 25 years old, residents of the state they serve, and U.S. citizens for at least the previous seven years.

The upper chamber, the Senate, consists of two senators from each state, regardless of size. Designed to serve as a check on the popular will, which would be expressed in the House of Representatives, state legislatures chose senators until the Seventeenth Amendment granted the people of each state the exclusive right to do so. A six-year term also serves to limit responsiveness to popular whims, and an age minimum of 30 presumably provides more mature and levelheaded thinking. Senators also have to be residents of the state in which they serve and U.S. citizens for nine years or more.

Bills to levy taxes have to originate in the House, but other bills may originate in either chamber. To become law, a bill has to pass each chamber in identical form. It is then presented to the president for his signature. If the president signs the bill, it becomes law, but if he disapproves, he can **veto** the bill. Congress can then **override** the veto by a two-thirds majority in each chamber.

Article I, Section 8 of the Constitution limits Congress's authority to an eighteen-paragraph list, or enumeration, of certain powers. The first paragraph grants Congress the authority "to collect Taxes . . . to pay the Debts and provide for the common Defence and general Welfare of the United States." Paragraphs 2 through 17 grant additional powers such as borrowing and coining money, regulating commerce, and raising an army. Then paragraph 18 grants Congress the authority to pass all laws "necessary and proper for carrying into Execution the foregoing Powers."

Additionally, the Constitution gives the House the authority to **impeach**—to bring charges against—the president and other federal officials. The Senate has the sole authority to try cases of impeachment, with a two-thirds vote required for removal from office. The Senate also has the sole authority to ratify treaties, which also requires a two-thirds vote, and to confirm executive and judicial branch appointments by majority vote.

The Executive Branch. The executive branch of government consists of a unitary president, chosen for a four-year term by an Electoral College. The Electoral College itself is chosen in a manner set by the legislature of each state. Eventually, every state gave the people the power to vote for its electors. Each state receives the number of electors equal to its number of representatives plus senators. If no person receives a majority of the Electoral College vote, the election goes to the House of Representatives, where each state gets one vote. The Electoral College also chooses a vice president who presides over the Senate, casting votes in case of a tie. The vice president becomes president following the death, resignation, removal, or disability of the president.

A president must be at least 35 years of age, a resident of the United States for the previous fourteen years, and either a natural-born citizen of the United States or a citizen of the United States at the time of the adoption of the Constitution.

Because the Framers believed that the legislative branch would naturally be stronger than the executive branch, they did not feel the need to enumerate the executive powers

bicameral: *Two-chamber legislature, such as the U.S. House of Representatives and Senate.*

veto: *Authority of the president to block legislation passed by Congress. Congress can override a veto by a two-thirds majority in each chamber.*

override: *Congress's power to overturn a presidential veto with a two-thirds vote in each chamber.*

impeach: *Authority of the House of Representatives to bring charges against the president and other federal officials.*

as they did the legislative powers. Recall that Congress does not have a general legislative authority, but only those legislative powers granted under the Constitution. In contrast, the Constitution provides the president with a general grant of "the executive power" and certain specific powers, including the right to veto legislation and grant pardons. The president also is commander in chief of the armed forces. With the advice and consent of the Senate, the president makes treaties and appoints ambassadors, judges, and other public officials. The president leads the executive branch of government, being charged with taking care that the laws are faithfully executed.

The Judicial Branch.

The Constitution vests the judicial authority of the United States in one Supreme Court and other inferior courts that Congress might choose to establish. The president appoints judges with the advice and consent of the Senate. They serve during "good Behaviour," which, short of impeachment, means a life term.

The Constitution extends the authority of the federal courts to hear cases involving certain classes of parties to a suit—cases involving the United States, ambassadors, and other public ministers; suits between two or more states or citizens from different states—and certain classes of cases, most notably cases arising under the Constitution, laws, and treaties of the United States. In the historic case *Marbury v. Madison* (1803), the Supreme Court took this authority to hear cases arising under the Constitution of the United States to establish the power of **judicial review**, the authority of the Court to strike down any law passed by Congress when the Court believes the law violates the Constitution (see Supreme Court Cases: *Marbury v. Madison*).[17]

judicial review: *Authority of courts to declare laws passed by Congress and acts of the executive branch to be unconstitutional.*

amendment: *Formal process of changing the Constitution.*

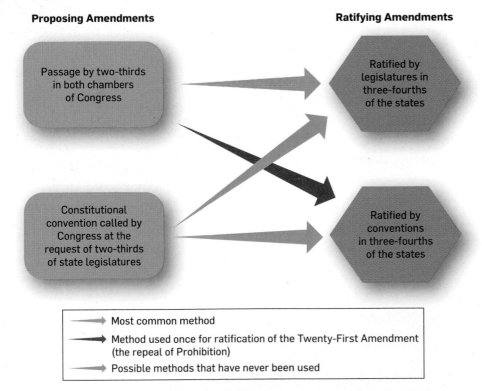

FIGURE 2.4 **Amending the Constitution.** An amendment can be proposed by two-thirds of each chamber of Congress or by a constitutional convention called by two-thirds of state legislatures. Either way, ratification requires three-quarters of the states to approve the amendment. Why do you think the methods indicated by the blue arrows have never been used?

The Amendment Process

The Constitution provides two paths for changing the constitution, or **amendment**. The first path requires a two-thirds vote in each chamber of Congress, followed by the approval of three-fourths of the states. That statewide approval can be attained either through the state legislatures or through state ratifying conventions, as directed by Congress. The second path allows two-thirds of the states to request a national constitutional convention that could propose amendments that would go into effect when approved by three-fourths of the states (see Figure 2.4). Again, this approval could be obtained through state legislatures or through state ratifying

supremecourtcases

Marbury v. Madison (1803)

QUESTION: Does Congress have the authority to expand the Supreme Court's original jurisdiction beyond that granted by the Constitution?

ORAL ARGUMENT: February 10, 1803

DECISION: February 23, 1803 (read at www.findlaw .com/casecode/supreme.html)

OUTCOME: No, thus establishing the power of judicial review (4–0)

It is hard to imagine a more momentous decision resulting from what the historian John A. Garraty called this "trivial squabble over a few petty political plums."* In the closing days of President John Adams's administration, the Federalist Adams nominated William Marbury to the position of justice of the peace for the District of Columbia, and the Federalist Senate confirmed the nomination. But in the hectic final hours of Adams's administration, Secretary of State John Marshall forgot to deliver the commission. When Democratic-Republican Thomas Jefferson became president, his new secretary of state, James Madison, refused to deliver the commission, thus keeping Marbury from assuming his office.

Marbury filed suit at the Supreme Court, believing that the Judiciary Act of 1789 expanded the Court's original jurisdiction to give the Court the authority to hear cases involving writs of *mandamus* (orders to government officials to undertake specific acts) as an original matter, that is, as a trial, and not just as an appeal.

The Supreme Court declared that, because the Constitution precisely specified which types of cases the Supreme Court could hear as an original matter, the section of the Judiciary Act that expanded the Court's original jurisdiction conflicted with the Constitution. Moreover, if a law conflicts with the Constitution, either the law is supreme over the Constitution, or the Constitution is supreme over the law. The Court ruled that it must be the case that the Constitution is supreme over the law. Finally, the Court declared that the judiciary would decide such issues. "It is emphatically the province and duty of the judicial department to say what the law is," wrote Marshall, who in the closing days of the Adams' administration had been nominated and confirmed as chief justice of the United States.

The Court thus granted itself the momentous authority of judicial review, the power to strike down laws passed by Congress on the grounds that those laws violate the Constitution. Though the Court did not frequently use this power in the early days of the republic, citizens filing lawsuits would later use it to get the Court to strike down, among other things, segregation in District of Columbia public schools (1954), discrimination on account of sex in military benefits (1973), and limits on campaign contributions in congressional races (2003).

- **How does judicial review provide a gateway to participation in the political system?**
- **Why is it the judiciary's job to determine whether a law is unconstitutional?**

* John A. Garraty, "*Marbury v. Madison:* The Case of the 'Missing' Commissions," in *Quarrels That Have Shaped the Constitution,* ed. John Garraty (New York: Harper and Row, 1964), 13.

conventions. Additionally, the Constitution prohibits amendments that would deny any state an equal vote in the Senate, or any amendment that would have allowed a banning of the foreign slave trade prior to 1808.

Both paths for amending the Constitution are complex and difficult, and that has kept the Constitution from being modified over popular but short-lived issues. Recently, these have included proposed amendments that would require a balanced federal budget, allow the federal or state governments to prosecute those who burn the American flag, and prohibit states from recognizing same-sex marriages. In 1919 Congress proposed and the states ratified the temporarily popular Prohibition amendment (the Eighteenth Amendment), which banned the manufacture, sale, and transportation of alcohol, only to have it repealed in 1933 (Twenty-First Amendment) in the face of massive civil disobedience.

The states have never called a constitutional convention to amend the 1787 Constitution, but Congress has sent thirty-three proposed amendments to the states for ratification. Other than the Twenty-First Amendment (the repeal of Prohibition), which Congress sent to state ratifying conventions, all other proposed amendments went directly to the state legislatures. Of the thirty-three amendments that Congress proposed, twenty-seven have received the required assent of three-fourths of the states. These include the Bill of Rights (the First through the Tenth Amendments), which passed within two years of the adoption of the Constitution, and three Civil War amendments (the Thirteenth through the Fifteenth Amendments) that abolished slavery and attempted to protect the rights of former slaves. The Equal Rights Amendment that interested Gregory Watson did not pass, nor did a proposed 1978 amendment granting the District of Columbia representation in Congress, but the Twenty-Seventh Amendment, which Watson revived, did. We further discuss these and other amendments to the Constitution later in this chapter.

The Partition of Power

Why does the Constitution divide and separate power?

federalism: *System of government in which sovereignty is constitutionally divided between national and state governments.*

separation of powers: *Government structure in which authority is divided among branches (executive, legislative, and judicial), with each holding separate and independent powers and areas of responsibility.*

checks and balances: *Government structure that authorizes each branch of government (executive, legislative, and judicial) to share powers with the other branches, thereby holding some scrutiny of and control over the other branches.*

In attempting to explain and justify the constitutional structure, James Madison wrote of "the necessary partition of power among the several departments as laid down in the constitution" (see *Federalist* 51 in the Appendix). He acknowledged that "a dependence on the people is no doubt the primary control on the government," and thus elections serve as the primary means of ensuring that the government is responsive to the wishes of the people. If it is not, the people can vote for a new government. Under the Constitution, the people have direct authority to elect the House of Representatives. But to prevent the majority from imposing oppressive laws on the minority, the rest of the government was chosen indirectly: the Senate by the state legislatures, the president by the Electoral College, and judges by the president, with the advice and consent of the Senate.

Lest the people not be sufficient to keep government under control, however, the Constitution had built in "auxiliary precautions," as Madison called them, to make sure government could not concentrate power. Thus, **federalism** splits power between nation and state, **separation of powers** divides the powers that remained with the national government among the three branches of government, and **checks and balances** give each branch some authority over the powers of the other branches. Even after all this, the Constitution places additional limits on both federal and state powers.

Federalism.   The first means of preventing a concentration of power was to divide authority between the national and state governments. Rather than provide Congress with a general power to legislate in the national interest, the Constitution granted Congress enumerated powers. All powers not granted to Congress remained with the states. This division of power is made explicit in the Tenth Amendment to the Constitution: "The powers not delegated to the United States by the Constitution, nor prohibited by it to the States, are reserved to the States respectively, or to the people."

Has the division of power between the national government and the states hindered or advanced democracy?

Separation of Powers.

Madison believed that "the accumulation of all powers, legislative, executive, and judiciary, in the same hands, whether of one, a few, or many, and whether hereditary, self-appointed, or elective, may justly be pronounced the very definition of tyranny."[18] Thus, after dividing power between the national and state governments, the Constitution separates those powers that it grants to the national government among the three branches. Under the Constitution, all legislative powers granted belong to Congress, the executive power vests in the president of the United States, and the judicial authority resides in a Supreme Court, plus any lower courts Congress might choose to establish. Moreover, because the "legislative authority . . . necessarily predominates" in a republican government (*Federalist* 51), legislative power was further separated into two distinct chambers—a House and a Senate—each with different manners of election and terms of office. This separation of powers followed the recommendations of the eighteenth-century French philosopher Charles, Baron de Montesquieu, who believed that a government in which powers were separated and balanced was the best guarantee of freedom of the individual.

Checks and Balances.

Under the Constitution, balance among the branches was achieved by giving each one some authority to counteract, or check, the authority of the other two (see Figure 2.5). Thus the president has the authority to propose legislation to Congress and to veto bills passed by Congress; Congress can override that veto by a two-thirds majority of each chamber. The president has the authority to pardon people convicted of crimes. The president also nominates federal judges, subject to the advice and consent of the Senate. The Senate also advises and consents to high-ranking executive branch appointments, such as ambassadors and cabinet officials. The House can impeach executive and judicial appointees, and the Senate can convict and remove impeached officials from office by a two-thirds majority. Congress, subject to presidential veto, has the authority to establish lower courts and set their jurisdiction (decide what cases they can hear). It also has the authority to set the Supreme Court's appellate jurisdiction. The appellate jurisdiction is the Supreme Court's authority to hear cases on appeal from lower courts and is the heart of the Supreme Court's judicial power. Congress has this authority over the courts; the courts, on the other hand, can decide the constitutionality of laws passed by Congress. While this power of judicial review is not explicitly granted courts by the Constitution, it has been largely unchallenged since announced by the Supreme Court in *Marbury v. Madison*. The courts also have the authority to review the legality of actions taken by executive branch officials.

What is the purpose of checks and balances?

Limits on Powers.

The delegation of powers to Congress, and the reservation of all remaining powers to the states, would have given states the same authority to pass oppressive laws they had under the Articles. To prevent that, the Constitution limits state authority in several ways. First, it makes federal law supreme over state law. Second, it guarantees that the states provide a republican form of government. Third, the Constitution sets limits on the sort of legislation states can pass. Not only are states prohibited from coining money

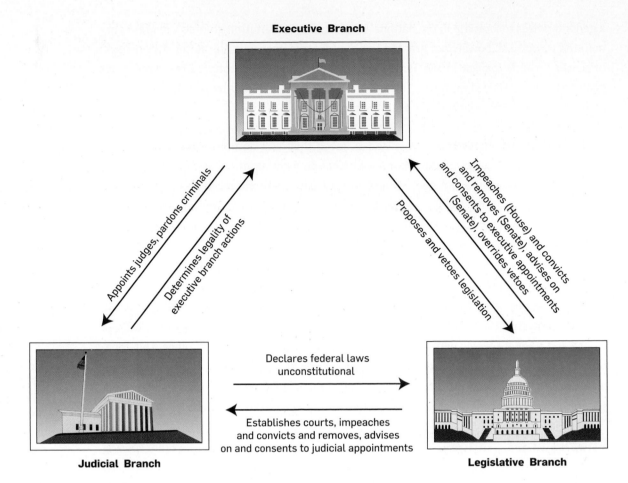

Executive Branch

Appoints judges, pardons criminals

Determines legality of executive branch actions

Impeaches (House) and convicts and removes (Senate), advises on and consents to executive appointments (Senate), overrides vetoes

Proposes and vetoes legislation

Declares federal laws unconstitutional

Establishes courts, impeaches and convicts and removes, advises on and consents to judicial appointments

Judicial Branch

Legislative Branch

FIGURE 2.5 Checks and Balances.

bills of attainder: *Legislative acts that declare individuals guilty of a crime.*

ex post facto laws: *Law that make an act a crime after the act is committed.*

writ of habeas corpus: *Right of individuals who have been arrested and jailed to go before a judge who determines whether their imprisonment is legal.*

or engaging in foreign affairs, but they also cannot pass **bills of attainder** (legislative acts declaring people guilty of crimes) or prosecute individuals under **ex post facto laws**, which make behavior illegal after individuals have engaged in it. In a provision indicative of American egalitarianism, the Constitution denies states the power to grant titles of nobility. While not embracing the notion of equality announced in the Declaration of Independence, the Framers did make it clear that they rejected the British system of inherited social status. The Constitution also prohibits states from passing laws that would allow individuals to disregard the obligation of contracts, such as laws negating debts.

The Constitution also expressly limits the authority of Congress. Like the states, Congress can pass neither bills of attainder nor *ex post facto* laws. It also cannot suspend the **writ of habeas corpus**—a guarantee that incarcerated people can go before a judge to have the legality of their confinement determined—except in cases of invasion or rebellion. Also like the states, Congress cannot grant titles of nobility.

The Ratification Debates

With the proposed Constitution to be accepted or rejected by the people of the various states, the state ratification debates largely ignored the question of representation that led to the Connecticut Compromise. So too, little debate took place about the questions involving slavery. Instead, most of the debate concerned the extent of national power under the Constitution, including a feared consolidation of federal authority over the states, the scope of executive and legislative power, and the lack of a bill of rights.

Federalists and Antifederalists

By the time the state ratifying conventions started meeting, two distinct camps had formed. Those who supported the Constitution cleverly named themselves **Federalists**, even though they were really more nationalist than federalist. ("Federal," according to Madison, meant "a confederacy of sovereign states,"[19] which better described the Articles of Confederation, or even the New Jersey Plan, than the new Constitution.) Those who opposed the Constitution, whose leaders included the outspoken Revolutionary leader Patrick Henry of Virginia, became known as the **Antifederalists**.

Madison, along with John Jay, who later became the first chief justice of the United States, and Alexander Hamilton, who later founded the Federalist Party and served as the first secretary of the treasury, wrote eighty-five essays, today known as the ***Federalist Papers***, that attempted to convince the citizens of New York to ratify the Constitution. They wrote anonymously under the pen name "Publius," taken from an early leader in the ancient Roman Republic. Madison's essays, especially, are still read today as a leading source for understanding the Constitution. We quoted from them earlier in this chapter and in Chapter 1, and two of the most famous essays, numbers **10** and **51**, are in this book's Appendix. The Antifederalists published their attacks under anonymous pen names as well, most notably "Brutus"—another leader of the ancient Roman Republic—and "Old Whig," named after the English political party that opposed the monarchy.

Consolidation of Federal Authority

The Antifederalists found much to disapprove of in the proposed Constitution. They argued that the Constitutional Convention had violated the Articles by moving beyond mere amendment and proposing a new government, one that did not require the unanimous consent of the states. They worried that because sovereignty, the ultimate lawmaking authority, could not be split, and because national law was supreme over state law, a national government under the Constitution would inevitably consolidate its authority over the state governments.

The Federalists answered both of these charges by claiming that sovereignty rested not in the legislature, as had typically been believed, but in the people, as the preamble to the Constitution suggested. Therefore the people could propose any new form of government they wished. And if the people were sovereign, they could split their grant of lawmaking authority between the national and state governments as they saw fit.

The Scope of Executive Authority

Other concerns centered on the scope of executive authority. With no term limits on the executive in the original Constitution, the Antifederalists feared that the president would turn into a monarch. George Mason, who attended the Convention but was one of three delegates not to sign the proposed Constitution, also worried that "the President of the United States has the unrestrained Power of granting Pardon," which could be used to instigate crimes and

Federalists: *Initially, those who supported the Constitution during the ratification period; later, the name of the political party established by supporters of Alexander Hamilton.*

Antifederalists: *Those who opposed the new proposed Constitution during the ratification period.*

Were the Antifederalists more concerned about liberty or about order?

Federalist Papers: *Series of essays written by James Madison, Alexander Hamilton, and John Jay arguing for the ratification of the Constitution; today a leading source for understanding the Constitution.*

Federalist 10: *Written by James Madison, argues that in a large republic diverse interests will prevent any faction from gaining a majority.*

Federalist 51: *Written by James Madison, discusses the needs for checks and balances in government.*

then cover them up by pardoning his criminal partners. Alexander Hamilton responded in *Federalist* 69 with an explanation of the limits on the executive: elections, whereby the president could be voted out of office; impeachment, whereby the president could be removed from office for "high crimes and misdemeanors"; and the limited veto power, which could be overridden. The president of the United States, Hamilton concluded, was much closer in power to the governor of New York than to the king of England.

Why were the Antifederalists opposed to a strong executive?

The Scope of Legislative Authority

Two provisions in Article I, Section 8 of the Constitution, which specified the powers of Congress, particularly alarmed the Antifederalists: the **general welfare clause** and the **necessary and proper clause**. This section of the Constitution begins by stating that "Congress shall have Power to lay and Collect Taxes . . . to . . . provide for the . . . general Welfare of the United States." It concludes by stating that Congress has the power "to make all Laws which shall be necessary and proper for carrying into Execution the foregoing Powers." Antifederalist Brutus contended that "the legislature under this constitution may pass any law which they may think proper."[20] Brutus further wrote that the necessary and proper clause, labeled "the sweeping clause" by the Antifederalists, granted the government "absolute and uncontroulable power, legislative, executive and judicial." James Monroe, who would later serve as the fifth president (1817–25), told the Virginia ratifying convention that the sweeping clause gave Congress "a general power . . . to make all laws that will enable them to carry their powers into effect. There are no limits pointed out. They are not restrained or controlled from making any law, however oppressive in its operation, which they may think necessary to carry their powers into effect."[21]

general welfare clause: *Gives Congress the power to tax to provide for the general welfare (Article I, Section 8).*

necessary and proper clause: *Gives Congress the power to pass all laws necessary and proper to the powers enumerated in Section 8 (Article I, Section 8).*

What elements of the Antifederalist argument do you detect in political arguments today?

Madison responded in *Federalist* 41 that the power to tax "to provide for the general welfare" was not a general grant of power to tax for any purpose whatsoever but, rather, a power to tax for the enumerated powers that followed. "Nothing is more natural nor common than first to use a general phrase, and then to explain and qualify it by a recital of particulars."[22] To Madison, when Article I, Section 8 granted the right to tax to provide for the general welfare, and then listed various other powers, those other powers defined the scope of the general welfare clause.

Similarly, the Federalists argued that the necessary and proper clause was not a general grant of authority to pass all laws that were necessary and proper, but rather, as the clause explicitly stated, the authority to pass all laws that were "necessary and proper for carrying into Execution the foregoing [that is, previously listed] Powers." Thus, if a law is necessary and proper for borrowing money, or raising an army, or establishing a post office, Congress may do so, for those powers are among the "foregoing Powers" granted Congress. This explicit restriction of the necessary and proper clause to the other powers was absent, however, in the general welfare clause. To Madison, the restriction was obviously implied; to the Antifederalists, it was a threat to limited government.

Nevertheless, to clarify that the Constitution did not provide general powers to Congress, the Federalists agreed to an amendment to the Constitution that declared that "The powers not delegated to the United States by the Constitution, nor prohibited by it to the States, are reserved to the States respectively, or to the people." Interestingly, the amendment parallels a similar provision from the Articles that declared that the states retained all powers not "expressly delegated" to the national government. By limiting congressional authority to those powers delegated to it, rather than the stricter standard of those powers expressly delegated to it, the Constitution creates a somewhat greater authority for **implied powers**.

The Lack of a Bill of Rights

The most serious charge against the Constitution was that it did not contain a bill of rights. Patrick Henry, who had famously proclaimed "Give me liberty or give me death" in 1765, told the Virginia ratifying convention in 1788 that, if the state gives up its powers "without a bill of rights, you will exhibit the most absurd thing to mankind that ever the world saw—[state] government that has abandoned all its powers—the powers of direct taxation, the sword, and the purse. You have disposed of them to Congress, without a bill of rights—without check, limitation, or control."[23]

In contrast, the Federalists argued that a bill of rights was not necessary because Congress had only those powers granted by the Constitution. If Congress was not granted the authority to, say, abridge freedom of the press, it was unnecessary to say that Congress could not abridge freedom of the press. The Federalists went further to claim that a bill of rights could be dangerous because listing some rights but not others could imply that the rights not listed could be abridged.

Consider two documents. The first one states that Congress has the right to regulate commerce between the states, to tax to provide for the general welfare, and to raise armies. Under this document, does Congress have the right to abridge the right to assemble? The Federalist answer was no, because Congress has enumerated powers only, and the right to limit freedom of assembly is not one of them. The Antifederalist answer was yes, because the power was not prohibited.

Now consider a second document that states that Congress has the right to regulate commerce between the states, to tax to provide for the general welfare, and to raise armies. In addition, it states that Congress may not abridge freedom of the press. May Congress abridge the right to assemble? The Federalists argued that the potential for Congress to regulate the right to assemble is greater in the second document than in the first. That is, in the second case, Congress could say "we are prohibited from abridging freedom of the press, but we are not prohibited from abridging the right to assemble, so we are allowed to do that." By listing certain rights, the Constitution could be interpreted as allowing Congress to limit those freedoms not listed.

It is hard to imagine people concluding from the Federalist argument that rights would be safer without a bill of rights. Not only is this is a complicated argument, but combining the necessary and proper clause with the broad powers granted Congress under the Constitution—such as regulating interstate commerce and taxing to provide for the general welfare—probably means that Congress could have found ways to pass laws abridging freedom of assembly, freedom of speech, and other freedoms. The Federalists eventually gave in to the Antifederalist argument, agreeing that amending the Constitution to provide a bill of rights would be among the first items of business under a newly ratified Constitution. To prevent the listing of certain rights to create an assumption that Congress could abridge other rights

The Granger Collection, New York

Although he is best known for his declaration "Give me liberty or give me death," Henry was a prominent Antifederalist. He was instrumental in forcing the adoption of the Bill of Rights to amend the new Constitution.

Was the Bill of Rights necessary in 1787? Is it necessary today?

not listed, the Bill of Rights included the Ninth Amendment: "The enumeration in the Constitution, of certain rights, shall not be construed to deny or disparage others retained by the people."

Despite the Antifederalist arguments about excessive national power, the lack of a bill of rights, and a too-powerful executive, states began ratifying the new Constitution. Government under the Articles was simply not an acceptable alternative. Just two months after the Convention sent the proposed Constitution to the states, Delaware became the first state to ratify. In quick succession, New Jersey, Pennsylvania, Georgia, and Connecticut followed. Other states acted more slowly, with some states suggesting proposed rights to be added by amendment and ratifying only after promises that amendments to protect fundamental rights would be offered once the first Congress under the Constitution met. By June 1788 ten states had ratified, one more than needed to establish the new Constitution. New York then followed, but North Carolina and Rhode Island did not ratify until after George Washington was elected president.

What would have happened if the Constitution had not been ratified?

The Responsive Constitution

The government the Framers devised has lasted more than two hundred years. As in 1787 it still has three branches of government, Congress still consists of two chambers, and the Electoral College still chooses the president. But other parts of the U.S. constitutional system have changed substantially, some to fix flaws and some to respond to new circumstances and developing ideas about the nature of equality. Some of these changes, such as the Bill

After more than two hundred years, Americans love the Constitution and are interested in learning about it. The original is in a sealed case at the National Archives in Washington, D.C., but visitors to the National Constitution Center in Philadelphia enjoy the multimedia exhibits that tell the story of the Constitution, and its contemporary relevance.

William Thomas Cain/Getty Images

of Rights, came through the formal amendment process. Others were the result of changing interpretation by the Supreme Court about what the Constitution means. Still others are what some call "extraconstitutional." That is, they affect the way the constitutional system operates even though the Constitution itself has not been amended to reflect them. Most prominent is the development of political parties (see Chapter 9, Political Parties).

The Bill of Rights

As part of the fight over ratification, the Federalists agreed that they would propose a Bill of Rights once the new Constitution was ratified, and some state ratifying conventions forwarded proposals for specific amendments. Madison, elected as a member of Congress from Virginia, quickly selected twelve proposed amendments, among them the congressional pay raise amendment that Gregory Watson revived nearly two hundred years later. The states then ratified ten of the amendments in 1791 as a Bill of Rights that became part of the Constitution. Many of these amendments stated rights that had been guaranteed under British law or had been abridged by the British during the decade before the Revolution, causing the Americans to demand independence (see Other Places: The English Bill of Rights).

The First Amendment guarantees major political rights including freedom of speech, press, and assembly and the free exercise of religion. It also prohibits establishing a national religion or, more precisely, any law "respecting an establishment of religion." The Second Amendment protects the right to bear arms; the Third Amendment prohibits the quartering of soldiers in one's home in times of peace. The Fourth, Fifth, Sixth, and Eighth Amendments protect rights relating to criminal procedure, including the right at trial to the assistance of an attorney and the right to a trial by jury (Sixth). (The Seventh Amendment protects the right to a trial by jury in civil cases over $20.) The criminal procedure amendments also prohibit unreasonable searches and seizures (Fourth), compulsory self-incrimination (Fifth), double jeopardy, or being tried a second time for a crime after one is found not guilty (Fifth), and cruel or unusual punishments (Eighth). The Fifth Amendment also prohibits deprivations of life, liberty, or property without due process of law, and it prohibits the government from seizing private property for a public use without fair or "just" compensation. We examine the meanings of these amendments in Chapter 4 (Civil Liberties).

The Civil War Amendments

Following the Civil War, Congress proposed and the states ratified three amendments. The Thirteenth Amendment (1865) prohibits slavery. The Fourteenth Amendment, (1868) aimed at protecting the newly emancipated slaves, makes all people born in the United States citizens of the United States. It also prohibits states from denying anyone due process of law, the equal protection of the law, and the privileges or immunities of citizens of the United States. The Fifteenth Amendment (1870) prohibits states from denying anyone the right to vote on account of race or prior status as slaves. All three amendments give Congress the authority to enforce the measures by appropriate legislation, thus adding to Congress's enumerated powers. These amendments radically changed the structure of the federal government by giving the national government authority over internal matters of the states. We deal with these civil rights more extensively in Chapter 5 (Civil Rights).

The Articles of Confederation, once ratified, did not last a decade. Why has the Constitution lasted for more than two centuries?

How has the Constitution changed, and why?

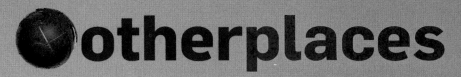

The English Bill of Rights

In 1689 Parliament won the long power struggle with the monarch by making the acceptance of a written Declaration of Rights a condition for ascending the throne. King William III and Queen Mary agreed. They became lawful sovereigns, and the English people—including those who lived in Britain's colonies—were confirmed in their belief that they possessed "undoubted Rights and Liberties." These rights, recorded on parchment, included the following:

- That levying money for or to the use of the Crowne by pretence of Prerogative without Grant of Parliament for longer time or in other manner than the same is or shall be granted is illegal

- That it is the right of the Subjects to petition the King and all Commitments and prosecutions for such petitioning are illegal

- That the raising or keeping a Standing Army within the Kingdome in time of Peace unless it be with Consent of Parliament is against Law

- That the Subjects which are Protestants may have Armes for their defence suitable to their Conditions and as allowed by Law

- That the Freedome of Speech and Debates or Proceedings in Parliament ought not to be impeached or questioned in any Court or Place out of Parliament

- That excessive Bayle ought not to be required nor excessive Fines imposed nor cruell and unusuall Punishments inflicted

- That Jurors ought to be duely impannelled and returned and Jurors which passe upon men in Tryalls for high Treason ought to be Freeholders

Read this list of rights carefully. They were written almost exactly a century before the American Bill of Rights. The language and spelling are certainly different, but the content is familiar.

The English Bill of Rights is preserved at Britain's National Archives in London.

- **Which of these rights did the American colonists believe the British had violated before the Revolution?**

- **Which of these rights did the citizens of the new United States write into their Bill of Rights?**

UK National Archives

54

Amendments That Expand Public Participation

Other amendments have further extended the gateways to public participation in government by giving the people the right to vote for their senators directly (Seventeenth, 1913), guaranteeing women the right to vote (Nineteenth, 1920), allowing residents of the District of Columbia to vote in presidential elections (Twenty-Third, 1961), prohibiting states from setting poll taxes as a requirement of voting in federal elections (Twenty-Fourth, 1964), and guaranteeing the right to vote for those age 18 or older (Twenty-Sixth, 1971). For a summary of all the amendments, see Figure 2.6.

Constitutional Interpretation

The Constitution has also changed through interpretation by the Supreme Court. Following the explicit establishment of judicial review in *Marbury v. Madison,* the Court has exercised the authority to determine what the Constitution means. Under that authority, the powers of Congress have grown enormously. During the Great Depression of the 1930s, the Court began to interpret Congress's power to tax to provide for the general welfare as extending beyond the enumerated powers. Rather, in line with the interpretation of the general welfare clause that the Antifederalists feared, the Court now holds that Congress can tax and spend for virtually any purpose that is not expressly prohibited.

What is the significance of judicial review?

Additionally, Congress's authority to regulate commerce between the states is now so grand that it covers virtually all commercial activity. In one case, the Court ruled that Congress's authority to regulate commerce between the states was so broad that Congress could regulate wheat grown by a farmer for consumption by livestock on that farmer's land because of the effect that all similarly situated wheat could have on national grain markets (see Supreme Court Cases: *Wickard v. Filburn* in Chapter 12, Congress). This is an authority that even the Federalists hardly could have imagined.

This growth of national authority confirms that the Antifederalists were correct to insist on a Bill of Rights. Although Congress has not been granted the explicit right to abridge freedom of speech or freedom of the press, it would have the authority to do so under current readings of the commerce, taxing, and various other clauses, were it not for the Bill of Rights.

AP Photo/Jacquelyn Martin

I Demand the Vote

Future Amendments

Many of the formal changes in the Constitution since the Bill of Rights have centered on greater direct participation: direct voting for senators; no poll taxes; no abridgements of rights to vote on account of race, sex, or age so long as one is 18; and no exclusion of residents of the District of Columbia from voting for president. District residents do not have representation in Congress, however, because the Constitution declares that "The House of Representatives shall be composed of Members chosen every second Year by the People of the several States," and the District of Columbia is not a state. District residents are always hopeful that a constitutional amendment will give them representation. As they overwhelmingly vote for Democrats, the Democratic Party supports such an amendment, but Republicans oppose it. It is unlikely that three-quarters of the states would approve, given the partisan consequences of such a change.

Eleanor Holmes Norton is now in her eleventh term as nonvoting delegate to Congress from the District of Columbia. The Constitution gives Congress authority over the District of Columbia, and residents were not able to vote for president until 1961. The position Norton holds as a nonvoting delegate has been permanent only since 1971.

FIGURE 2.6 The Amendments to the Constitution. Following the specific protections of the first eight amendments to the Constitution, many subsequent amendments have corrected structural problems in the operation of government. Others have expanded participation and equality.

Color Code :
Criminal procedure   Participation   Equality   Structure   Miscellaneous

First (1791): Prohibits abridging freedoms of religion, speech, press, assembly, and petition

Second (1791): Prohibits abridging the right to bear arms

Third (1791): Prohibits involuntary quartering of soldiers in one's home during peacetime

Fourth (1791): Prohibits unreasonable searches and seizures

Fifth (1791): Affirms the right to indictment by a grand jury and the right to due process; protects against double jeopardy, self-incrimination, and taking of property without just compensation

Sixth (1791): Affirms rights to speedy and public trial, to confront witnesses, and to counsel

Seventh (1791): Affirms right to jury trials in civil suits over $20

Eighth (1791): Prohibits excessive bail, excessive fines, and cruel and unusual punishments

Ninth (1791): Declares that the enumeration of certain rights does not limit other rights retained by the people

Tenth (1791): Reserves the powers not granted to the national government to the states or to the people

Eleventh (1798): Prevents citizens from one state from suing another state in federal court

Twelfth (1804): Requires that electors cast separate votes for president and vice president and specifies requirements for vice presidential candidates

Thirteenth (1865): Prohibits slavery in the United States

Fourteenth (1868): Makes all persons born in the United States citizens of the United States, and prohibits states from denying persons within its jurisdiction the privileges or immunities of citizens, the due process of law, and equal protection of the laws; apportionment by whole persons

Fifteenth (1870): Prohibits states from denying the right to vote on account of race

Sixteenth (1913): Grants Congress the power to tax income derived from any source

Seventeenth (1913): Gives the people (instead of state legislatures) the right to choose U.S. senators directly

Eighteenth (1919): Prohibits the manufacture, sale, or transportation of intoxicating liquors

Nineteenth (1920): Guarantees women the right to vote

Twentieth (1933): Declares that the presidential term begins on January 20 (instead of March 4)

Twenty-First (1933): Repeals the Eighteenth Amendment

Twenty-Second (1951): Limits presidents to two terms

Twenty-Third (1961): Grants Electoral College votes to residents of the District of Columbia

Twenty-Fourth (1964): Prohibits poll taxes

Twenty-Fifth (1967): Specifies replacement of the vice president and establishes the position of acting president during a president's disability

Twenty-Sixth (1971): Guarantees 18-year-olds the right to vote

Twenty-Seventh (1992): Sets limits on congressional pay raises

Another perennial suggestion is the replacement of the Electoral College with some form of popular vote. Calls for this reform by Democrats revived after George W. Bush became president in 2000 despite losing the popular vote. Bush was not the first to win the electoral vote without winning a popular majority. John Quincy Adams in 1824, Rutherford B. Hayes in 1876, and Benjamin Harrison in 1888 won the presidency without popular majorities, and the election of 1960 was so close that John F. Kennedy, too, might have become president despite losing the popular vote.[24] Nevertheless, expanding participation through the direct election of the president remains unlikely given the difficulties of amending the Constitution and the influence of small states.

One occasional proposal would limit a controversial form of protest. Following Supreme Court rulings that the First Amendment protects the burning of the American flag, members of Congress have proposed an amendment that would allow Congress and the state governments to prohibit this practice. To date, the proposed amendment has obtained strong majorities in Congress, but not the two-thirds majority that the Constitution requires to send an amendment to the states.

What new amendments to the Constitution would you like to see passed?

Other Changes

Not all changes to the Constitution occur via amendment or interpretation. Fundamental changes to the U.S. constitutional system have occurred through the establishment of new institutions, most notably **political parties**. They began to emerge during Washington's first term as president. When Secretary of the Treasury Alexander Hamilton pushed for aggressive use of the sweeping clause to allow the national government to regulate the economy, James Madison and Thomas Jefferson rose in opposition (see Chapter 9, Political Parties). These early divisions between political elites laid the groundwork for the emergence of the first set of opposing political parties.

political parties: *Broad coalitions of interests organized to win elections in order to enact a commonly supported set of public policies.*

The rise of political parties has meant that the president and vice president run as members of a political party, not as individuals. In Congress, representatives and senators organize themselves by parties, with members of the majority party having most of the power. The struggle that James Madison envisioned between the different branches of government, with Congress and the president checking each other, really exists only when the president and the majority party in Congress represent different parties, a situation known as **divided government**. When Congress and the president are of the same party, checks by Congress are curtailed. Members of the president's party in Congress are more likely to be loyal to the president than they are to their own branch of government.[25]

divided government: *Situation when one party controls the executive branch and the other party controls the legislative branch.*

Political parties also allow for greater responsiveness of politicians to the national welfare. In the early pre-party days of the United States, a representative had little incentive to care about national conditions. A voter could decide whether he (virtually all voters were male then) liked or disliked the job that his representative was doing for his district and could vote accordingly, but he had little way of knowing whether the representative was responsible for the state of the nation. With political parties, however, voters can hold a representative of the party in power accountable not just for the job that the representative is doing for the district, but also for the job that the government is doing for the nation. Thus the representatives of the people are more likely to be responsive to the interests of the people.

Policy Making in a Constitutional System: The Death Penalty

The decisions the Framers made in constructing the constitutional system have profound implications for public policy making. The U.S. constitutional system imposes separation of powers, but that separation is limited by a system of checks and balances that adds complexity to the policy-making process. Additionally, the federalism component adds a level of inconsistency by allowing each state, within the bounds of the Constitution, to pursue its own policies. This inconsistency generates an inequality in the application of the death penalty, which we examine as an example.

Checks and Balances

Although the separation of powers established under the Constitution means that it is generally true that the legislature makes laws, the executive enforces laws, and the judiciary interprets laws, the checks and balances established in the Constitution complicate the process, granting all three branches a say in policy making. The president can set the legislative agenda and veto legislation. If the legislation passes, implementing the law is up to the executive branch, and because laws cannot cover every circumstance, the executive branch usually uses discretion in carrying them out. For example, if state or federal law allows for the death penalty in certain types of cases, state or federal prosecutors in their respective executive branches must decide whether to seek the death penalty in an appropriate case. When the executive branch has little discretion in carrying out a law, such as deciding the amount paid to Social Security recipients, it does little policy making. But where discretion is substantial, such as regarding the death penalty, the executive branch becomes a key player in policy making.

Another notable feature of checks and balances is that the judiciary can strike laws passed by the legislative branch if it believes that those laws violate the Constitution. The judiciary can also strike actions the executive branch takes if those actions violate constitutional provisions. Thus, under the U.S. constitutional system, all three branches of government can have a say in policy making.

Federalism

The fact that each state has its own separate government and set of laws further complicates the policy-making process. The Constitution, particularly as interpreted by the Supreme Court, leaves some policies in exclusive federal control, some (though as Chapter 3, Federalism, shows, a shrinking number) under exclusive state control, and many others under both state and federal control. States, for example, may generally establish their own criminal justice systems, but those systems must abide by guarantees found in the Constitution.

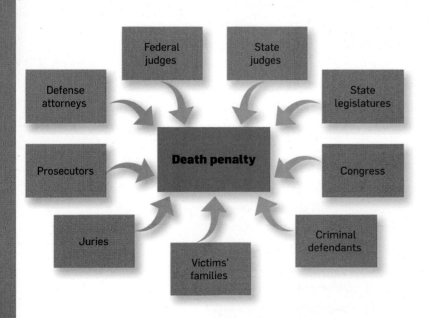

Does the federal system make government more or less responsive? Does it make citizens more or less equal?

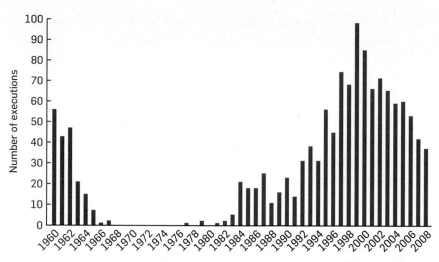

FIGURE 2.7 Annual Executions in the United States, 1960–2008. Annual executions dropped significantly in the years prior to the Supreme Court's temporary halt of capital punishment in 1972, but public support for capital punishment remained high. After the Court reinstituted capital punishment in 1976, the number of executions rose. The number later dipped, as DNA evidence revealing that some death row inmates had been wrongly convicted made the public wary about the death penalty.
Source: Death Penalty Information Center.

The Death Penalty

This balancing act among the branches of the federal government and between the nation and the states affects a wide range of policy issues, including the imposition of the death penalty, also known as capital punishment. The Constitution contains some degree of ambiguity about the death penalty. In several places, it seems to allow capital punishment. The Fourteenth Amendment's due process clause says that states may not deprive people of life, liberty, or property without due process of law, thus suggesting that life, liberty, and property may be taken so long as the states follow due process. Similarly, the Fifth Amendment's declarations that no person shall be held for a capital crime without indictment by a grand jury similarly suggests that a person can be held for a capital crime when indicted by a grand jury.

Alternatively, the Eighth Amendment prohibits "cruel and unusual" punishments. The Supreme Court interprets that clause to mean that the constitutionality of punishment is to be subject to evolving standards of justice and that the death penalty might violate those standards.

Before 1972, most states allowed capital punishment and did so by declaring crimes for which capital punishment could be imposed (usually murder, but sometimes also rape) and then leaving it up to the jury to decide whether capital punishment should be inflicted in a specific case. In 1972 the Supreme Court put a temporary halt to capital punishment, declaring that the process of complete jury discretion was cruel and unusual in that it led to an arbitrary and unequal imposition of the death penalty.[26] According to one justice in this sharply divided case, who received the death penalty and who did not was as arbitrary as who gets hit by lightning. (Figure 2.7 shows the fluctuations in the number of executions per year.)

Various states responded to this decision by requiring juries to follow certain guidelines before imposing the death penalty. In 1976 the Supreme Court ruled 7–2 that the death penalty with such guidelines did not constitute cruel and unusual punishment under the

Constitution.[27] Currently, thirty-five states permit capital punishment.[28] Given strong public approval for the death penalty, Congress allows it for certain federal crimes, including terrorist acts that result in death, murder for hire, kidnappings that result in murder, and running large-scale illegal drug enterprises.[29] The federal death penalty can be imposed throughout the country, even in states that do not allow the death penalty for violations of state law.

Though the Supreme Court has attempted to limit the unequal application of the death penalty, one clear finding from studies is the effect of the race of the victim: Juries are far more likely to impose the death penalty when the victim is white than when the victim is black.[30] The Supreme Court has ruled that, even if this were the case overall, someone challenging a death sentence based on such statistics would have to prove that the jury intentionally discriminated in the particular case.[31]

The Supreme Court has put limits on who can be sentenced to death. Offenders who were under the age of 18 when their crimes were committed and those convicted of rape, even the rape of a child, cannot receive the death penalty.[32]

Some states have begun to limit their own use of this punishment. The Innocence Project, a group dedicated to reversing convictions of people who were innocent, reports 218 death penalty cases in which DNA testing demonstrated that the wrong person was convicted of the crime.[33] This finding has led many states to reduce the number of death penalty sentences. It has also led many, but not all, states to allow convicted criminals access to DNA evidence, though the Supreme Court does not require them to do so.[34] Illinois was the first state to suspend the use of the death penalty because the evidence in several death penalty cases was shown to be insufficient in establishing guilt and the newest scientific methods using DNA exonerated several death row inmates. Nevertheless, the Illinois legislature has not removed the death penalty from the criminal statutes.

In considering how well policy making works in the constitutional system, it is worth noting the inconsistent use of the death penalty across states. If two individuals commit the same crime in different states, one criminal might be put to death, and the other might be allowed to live. Should states have their own policies on capital punishment, or should the federal government impose a uniform policy on them? The inconsistent use of the death penalty raises questions about equality under the constitutional system and serves as one of the most important examples of the unintended consequences of constitutional design.

Do you think the death penalty is constitutional?

The Constitution and Democracy

Government under the 1787 Constitution would today be considered severely lacking in both democracy and equality. The government allowed some of the people, mostly white males with property, to choose one chamber of the legislative branch of their government but did not grant the people a direct vote for the other chamber of the legislature or for the chief executive. And a government that allowed slavery would be a pariah, an outcast, among the nations of the world.

Moreover, in 1787 states regulated the right to vote. Slaves were not allowed to vote, but states differed as to whether free blacks, women, and men without property could vote. In 1790 Georgia, South Carolina, and Virginia prohibited free blacks from voting. South Carolina required voters to believe in God, heaven, and hell. Only New Jersey granted women the right to vote, a right that lasted only until 1807. Every state except Vermont required some form of tax payment for voter eligibility.[35]

Yet, compared to the despots and monarchs who had long ruled other countries, the government of 1787 allowed for a remarkable degree of participation by the common person. By giving voters a direct say in their state legislatures and at least indirect influence in all branches of the national government, the 1787 Constitution was a striking break with the past, even if it did not live up to the Declaration's statement that "all men are created equal."

Today participation is much more widespread than in 1787. Although the Electoral College continues to play its role every four years, each state allows the people to choose their electors. And those electors exert no independent influence on who shall be president. Aside from the rare faithless elector, they vote for the candidate chosen by the people of the state. In addition, amendments to the Constitution have widened the gateways to democracy. Due to the Seventeenth Amendment, the people today directly choose their senators, making that body directly responsive to public wishes. Moreover, voting equality is guaranteed in various ways: Poll taxes are illegal (Twenty-Fourth Amendment), and voting rights, which are now guaranteed to those 18 years old and older (Twenty-Sixth Amendment), may not be abridged on account of race (Fifteenth Amendment) or sex (Nineteenth Amendment).

Although the 1787 Constitution allowed the national government to exercise direct control over the citizenry, the tiny size of the national government left the people with far more control over their daily lives than they have today. But it is also the case that today the people have more control over the government. In addition to new constitutional gateways, opportunities for participation are greater than ever, with the Internet relaying information virtually instantly. It is much easier for representatives to be responsive to their constituents' desires when they can easily learn what their constituents believe, and constituents can readily learn what their representatives have done.

FOCUS QUESTIONS

- In what ways did the Constitution ensure that government would be responsive to the people? How has government become more responsive since 1787?

- In what ways did the Constitution seek to control the popular will and ensure order?

- In what ways did the Constitution seek to control government itself?

- In what ways did the nation's founding documents promote equality? In what ways did they fail to promote equality?

- Is the Constitution a gate or a gateway to American democracy? Is it a gatekeeper? Explain.

GATEWAYS TO LEARNING

Top Ten to Take Away

1. The colonists declared independence from Britain because they believed that the British Parliament and king were denying their rights as British subjects. (pp. 32–35)

2. Congress's powers under the Articles of Confederation were limited, and the structure the Articles established made governing difficult. (pp. 35–37)

3. In 1787 delegates from twelve states met in Philadelphia to amend the Articles; instead, they wrote a new Constitution. (pp. 37–42)

4. To secure the assent of all states represented at the Constitutional Convention, the delegates reached compromises between large and small states over representation, between northern and southern states over issues related to slavery, and between those who favored a strong national government and those who favored strong state governments in the balance of power between the two. (pp. 37–41)

5. This newly proposed Constitution was then sent to the states for ratification, and it is, with subsequent amendments, the same Constitution Americans live by today. (pp. 49–57)

6. The Constitution lays out the structure of democratic government and the means by which the Constitution can be amended. It reflects the Framers' attempt to establish a government powerful enough to ensure public order yet restrained enough to guarantee individual liberty. (pp. 42–48)

7. Debates over the ratification of the Constitution centered on a fear of consolidated federal authority over the states, the scope of executive and legislative power, and the lack of a bill of rights. (pp. 49–52)

8. To achieve ratification, the Federalists gave in to Antifederalist demands for a bill of rights, passing one as the first ten amendments to the Constitution. (pp. 51–53)

9. Subsequent amendments ended slavery, protected the rights of African Americans, and generally extended public participation in government while also expanding federal authority over the states. (pp. 53, 55)

10. The constitutional system established in 1787 has also been changed by constitutional interpretation and its operation altered by the development of political parties. (pp. 55–57)

A full narrative summary of the chapter is on the book's website.

Ten to Test Yourself

1. How did English and colonial notions of representation differ?

2. What were the deficiencies of the Articles of Confederation?

3. Overall, how did pro-slavery and antislavery interests fare at the Constitutional Convention?

4. In what ways did the proposed Constitution more closely resemble the Virginia Plan, and in what ways did it more closely resemble the New Jersey Plan?

5. In what ways was power divided under the Constitution?

6. What powers did the legislative, executive, and judicial branches receive from the 1787 Constitution?

Timeline to Keep Things in Order

First Continental Congress marks the beginning of coordinated resistance by the colonies to British policies.

Second Continental Congress acts as the common government of the states until 1781.

Congress instructs Thomas Jefferson and others to write a Declaration of Independence, which it approves.

The Articles of Confederation are proposed; adopted in 1781, they are in effect until 1788.

1774 • • • • 1775 • • • • 1776 • • • • 1777 • • • •

7. What are the checks that each branch has over the other branches?

8. How has the extent of public participation expanded since colonial times?

9. What were the Antifederalists' fears about the Constitution? How justified were these fears?

10. Describe the complications (gates) to policy making in the U.S. constitutional system.

More review questions and answers and chapter quizzes are on the book's website.

Terms to Know and Use

amendment (p. 44)
Antifederalists (p. 49)
Articles of Confederation (p. 35)
bicameral (p. 43)
Bill of Rights (p. 41)
bills of attainder (p. 48)
Boston Tea Party (p. 34)
checks and balances (p. 46)
Connecticut Compromise (p. 38)

constitution (p. 33)
Constitutional Convention (p. 37)
Continental Congress (p. 34)
Declaration of Independence (p. 34)
divided government (p. 57)
Electoral College (p. 41)
enumerated powers (p. 39)
ex post facto laws (p. 48)
federalism (p. 46)

Federalist 10 (p. 49)
Federalist 51 (p. 49)
Federalist Papers (p. 49)
Federalists (p. 49)
general welfare clause (p. 50)
impeach (p. 43)
implied powers (p. 51)
judicial review (p. 44)
necessary and proper clause (p. 50)
New Jersey Plan (p. 38)

override (p. 43)
political parties (p. 57)
proportional representation (p. 38)
republic (p. 41)
separation of powers (p. 46)
Shays's Rebellion (p. 37)
three-fifths compromise (p. 40)
veto (p. 43)
Virginia Plan (p. 37)
writ of *habeas corpus* (p. 48)

Use the vocabulary flashcards on the book's website.

Learning That Works

WHAT YOU NEED...

TO KNOW	TO DO
The causes of the American Revolution	Appreciate American political culture today
How the three branches of government check and balance each other	Evaluate whether government moves too slowly
How federalism works	Perceive sources of inequalities in public policy
How the Constitution balances liberty and order	Understand why American government has survived
How the Constitution can be amended	Recognize why it has rarely been amended
Ways that American government has changed	Consider whether it has been responsive to its citizens
How American government works	Be an active citizen

Shays's Rebellion helps convince the new nation's leaders that the Articles are not operating successfully.

1786

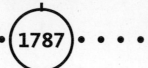
The Constitutional Convention proposes a new Constitution with a more powerful national government and with balanced legislative, executive, and judicial branches.

1787

Nine states ratify the Constitution, and it goes into effect.

1788

George Washington is elected president.

1789

The first ten amendments to the Constitution are ratified as the Bill of Rights.

1791

3 FEDERALISM

> *As I grew up, my mom and dad taught me the values that attracted them to this country, and they instilled in me an immigrant's wonder at the greatness of America.*

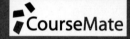

Visit http://www.cengagebrain
.com/shop/ISBN/0618906959

for interactive tools including:

* Quizzes

* Flashcards

* Videos

* Animated PowerPoint slides,
   Podcast summaries, and more

In 1992, when Bobby Jindal was a senior at Brown University in Rhode Island, he had a lot of choices to make. As an honors student in biology and public policy, he had been accepted to law school and medical school at both Harvard and Yale. He was also selected as a Rhodes Scholar, and he decided to accept the scholarship to study politics at Oxford. In England he contemplated joining the priesthood. Though raised as a Hindu by parents who immigrated to the United States from India before he was born, he had converted to Catholicism as a teenager. But his interest in politics was too strong to commit to a career in the church. At Brown, his conservative views had put him in the minority, and he had founded the university's first Republican Club, later serving as its president and as president of the Rhode Island College Republican chapters. Once Jindal decided on a career in politics, his rise was meteoric. By 2007 he was governor of Louisiana. Though swift, his career path was a zigzag, not a straight line, reflecting the separate and overlapping state and national authorities built into America's federal system.

Following study at Oxford, Jindal returned to his native Louisiana and got his crucial start in politics, at age 24, as head of the Louisiana Health and Hospitals Department. State hospital administration in Louisiana, as in all fifty states, is a mix of both national and state monies and regulations. The department is among the most important in Louisiana, accounting for about 40 percent of the state budget. Its responsibilities include programs such as Medicaid, a joint state–federal program that provides free health care to poor people. When Jindal took over in 1996, the department was running a $400 million deficit. Jindal wiped out the deficit and returned a substantial surplus to the state.

In 1997, when Congress created the National Bipartisan Commission on the Future of Medicare, a federal program that provides health care to senior citizens, Jindal was named executive director. Two years later he was working for the state of Louisiana again, appointed president of the Louisiana university system. The university system is largely free of federal regulations, but it does receive grants from the federal government

Bobby Jindal

that come with federal requirements. Two years later, Jindal moved to Washington to become an assistant secretary in the U.S. Department of Health and Human Services.

Again after two years, Jindal, now age 32, resigned his federal position and went back to Louisiana to run for governor. He lost that 2003 race but then quickly decided to run for a House seat in Louisiana's First Congressional District. Jindal received the Republican Party endorsement in the conservative district and won the 2004 race with 78 percent of the vote. Back in Washington, Jindal served on House committees that worked with national issues (Homeland Security) and traditionally local issues (Resources and Education). He won reelection in November 2006, but in January 2007 he announced that he would again run for governor. This time, against three other candidates, Jindal won with 54 percent of the vote. At age 36 he became the nation's youngest governor and the nation's first governor with South Asian heritage.[1]

In political systems where nearly all power is wielded at the national level, the main gateway to higher office is through the national system. But in systems where both national and state governments wield power, state governments offer a second gateway to office. Jindal's career not only demonstrates the state government gateway to a political career in a federal system; it also demonstrates the modern interplay between state and federal policies. State higher education systems receive federal money but, beyond guarantees of equal rights, are largely free of federal regulation. Health care, on the other hand, is heavily regulated by both the state and the federal governments, and heavily subsidized by them. Jindal's expertise in health care administration allowed him to move seamlessly between important positions in the state and national governments and to establish himself as a serious candidate for elected office.

In this chapter, we examine the federal system of government, including the authority of the national and state governments, how that authority has shifted over time, and how federalism can both enhance and detract from American democracy.

FOCUS QUESTIONS

- How does federalism affect government's responsiveness? To what and to whom are federal systems accountable?

- What does it mean for citizen equality when different states are allowed to have different laws on certain subjects?

- How does a federal system make it easier for citizens to have an influence in government?

- What has been the relationship between federalism and the push for equality in the United States?

- Is federalism a gate or a gateway to democracy? Explain.

Why Federalism?

The delegates to the 1787 constitutional convention in Philadelphia recognized that the system of government established by the Articles of Confederation was failing. Congress did not have the authority to regulate commerce or to raise money by taxing citizens or imports; it could only request revenues from the states. Thus, the nation's debts went unpaid, and its credit was sinking. Moreover, trade barriers erected by states against other states impeded commerce. Something had to be done. If the delegates were not able to fix the problems caused by the Articles, James Madison and others feared, the union could disintegrate.[2] All the steps taken toward union since 1774 would be reversed (see Chapter 2, The Constitution).

Why Unify?

The original colonies took their first step toward union when they sent delegates to meet as the First Continental Congress in 1774. The Second Continental Congress approved the Declaration of Independence, which declared the colonies to be united. The Articles of Confederation further declared that the union "shall be perpetual." Finally, the Constitution established itself in the name of "We the People of the United States." In these actions, the colonies—now states—chose to unify. They need not have taken this path. Federalism presupposes some form of union, so the answer to the question "why federalism?" first requires an answer to the question "why unify?"

The primary answer is that some form of union allows smaller political entities to pool their resources to fight a common enemy. The colonists could not have won the Revolutionary War if they had not banded together to fight the British. Benjamin Franklin published his famous cartoon "Join or Die" to represent the need for the colonists to stick together in military battles in the French and Indian War (1754–63).[3] By the late 1760s, though, the cartoon had come to symbolize the need for united action against British rule. After the Revolution, common threats remained not only from England, but also from France and various Indian tribes.

Beyond military necessity, the colonists considered themselves to be part of a common nation with Americans in the other states. A **nation** exists when people in a country have a sense of common identity due to a common origin, history, or ancestry, all of which the colonists shared. This sense of common identity made some form of union not only a military necessity but also a political advantage. The American people, however, also had strong loyalties to their states, an attachment that would have made eliminating states politically impossible. How strong the national government would be was the subject of heated debate at the Constitutional Convention.

The Granger Collection, New York

JOIN, or DIE.

Benjamin Franklin published this political cartoon in his *Pennsylvania Gazette* on May 9, 1754, shortly after hostilities began in the French and Indian War. The earliest depiction of the need for union among Britain's American colonies, it shows New England as one segment, and leaves out Delaware and Georgia altogether. Later, during the Revolution, it was a powerful symbol of American unity.

Today the people of the United States no longer share a common origin, history, or ancestry. Does it matter?

nation: *Political unit whose people share a sense of common identity.*

Confederal, Unitary, and Federal Systems

Because splitting up was an unattractive option, one of the forms of union available to the colonists was to continue, but strengthen, the **confederal system** that existed under the Articles of Confederation. In a confederal system, independent states grant powers to a national government to rule for the common good in certain limited areas such as defense. The independent states that make up the confederation usually have an equal vote, and the confederation might require unanimous consent or other supermajorities (for example, two-thirds or three-quarters) to pass legislation. The confederal organization usually acts through the states that constitute it rather than acting directly on the citizens of those states.

But the Framers who met in Philadelphia in 1787 were not inclined to continue the confederal system. A majority of the delegates believed that the New Jersey Plan, which would have strengthened the Articles but still granted each state one vote and still required a supermajority to pass most important issues, did not go far enough. They knew that the United States needed a stronger national government.

confederal system: *System of government in which ultimate authority rests with the regional (for example, state) governments.*

Ronald Martinez/Getty Images

Although bitter rivalries exist between some state universities, fans of both teams consider themselves Americans first. At the 2006 Cotton Bowl, rival Texas Longhorns and Oklahoma Sooners stand at attention during the singing of the national anthem.

unitary system: *System of government in which ultimate authority rests with the national government.*

federalism: *System of government in which sovereignty is constitutionally divided between national and state governments.*

Which government has the biggest impact on you—the federal government or your state government?

self-government: *Rule by the people.*

If a confederal system gives hardly any power to the national government, a **unitary system** of government gives it virtually every power. State or regional governments might still exist under a unitary system, but their powers and, in fact, their very existence are entirely up to the national government. The authority of a state or regional government in a pure unitary system is similar to the relationship between a state government today and the cities and counties that exist under the state's jurisdiction. Counties can make local decisions, but they exist only because their state established them, and a county has only the authority the state grants to it. Madison's original Virginia Plan did not propose a pure unitary system— Congress could not eliminate the states—but by giving Congress a complete veto over laws passed by the states and by granting Congress the general authority to pass laws that would "promote the harmony" of the United States, it would have moved the United States in that direction.

A confederal system was too weak for the United States, and an overly strong central government would pose its own set of problems. The Framers particularly feared that too much power in any government could lead to tyranny. Freedom would be better guaranteed by dividing governmental powers, rather than by concentrating them in a central government.

The Framers thus established a new system of government, **federalism**. A federal system, like that of the United States, mixes features of confederal and unitary governments. The Constitution created one legislative chamber chosen by the people and based on population and another chosen by the states and based on equal representation. Within the states' areas of authority—those areas not granted to the national government—their decisions are final and cannot be overturned by the national government. Moreover, the existence of states in a federal system does not depend on the national government; rather, the states derive their authority directly from the people. Nevertheless, within areas of authority granted to the national government, or areas of authority shared by the states and the national government, the national government reigns supreme. The political scientist William Riker defines federalism as a system of government in which there exists "a government of the federation [that is, a national government] and a set of governments of the member units [that is, the states] in which both kinds of governments rule over the same territory and people and each kind has the authority to make some decisions independently of the other" (see Figure 3.1).[4]

A federal system, besides lessening the risks of tyranny, promotes self-government. While any representative democracy involves **self-government**, or government by the

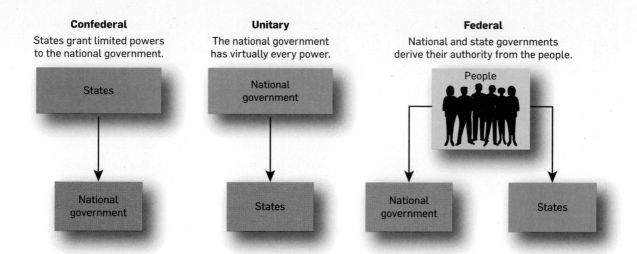

FIGURE 3.1 Confederal, Unitary, and Federal Systems of Government.

people, self-government is enhanced when the decisions that affect the citizens' lives are made by representatives who are local, closer to them, and more similar to them, rather than by representatives who live far away and are dissimilar. Thus self-government is enhanced when people in Massachusetts, to the extent possible, make rules for the people who live in Massachusetts, while people in Georgia make rules for the people who live in Georgia.

The Framers' choice of a federal system of government was innovative, as virtually all the world's governments at the time were either unitary or confederal. The American system was an experiment, and its evolution has been shaped by the tensions, even conflicts, inherent in a system in which power is both divided and shared. Since 1787 about two dozen other nations have ordered themselves as federal systems (see Other Places: Federal Political Systems).

In addition to federalism, in what other ways was the Constitution of 1787 innovative, even experimental?

Constitutional Framework

The Constitution lays out the framework of the U.S. federal system in a variety of ways. First, the Constitution grants specified powers to the national government, reserving all remaining powers to the states or the people. Second, the Constitution sets limits on both the powers granted the federal government and the powers reserved to the states. Third, the Constitution lays out the relationships among the several states as well as between the states and the federal government.

Grants of Power

The Constitution lists the grants of power to Congress in Article I, Section 8. These **enumerated powers** include several powers that could only lie in a national government. These are raising armies, declaring war, and establishing rules for citizenship. The enumerated powers also grant powers that the central government under the Articles of Confederation did not have, including the power to tax to provide for the general welfare, to borrow money, and to regulate interstate and foreign commerce. To the list of powers in Article I, Section 8, the Framers added one final power that would substantially strengthen the national government: the power to make all laws that are "necessary and proper" for carrying out the enumerated powers.

enumerated powers: *Powers expressly granted to Congress by the Constitution.*

otherplaces

Federal Political Systems

Only a small percentage of the world's nations are federalist systems, but the tendency of larger nations to rely on federalism means that they cover a vast majority of the world's landmass. Of the world's largest countries—Russia, Canada, the United States, China, Australia, and Brazil—only China is not federalist. Of the world's most populous countries—China, India, the United States, Indonesia, and Brazil—all but China and Indonesia are federalist. Note that federalism does not necessarily mean democratic (as in Russia), and democratic does not necessarily mean federalist (as in the United Kingdom).

With the recent devolution of power to Scotland, Wales, and Northern Ireland, however, the United Kingdom is not quite as unitary as it once was. India, a multilingual nation, has a federal system with twenty-eight states and seven territories. Its federal system has a stronger national government as compared with the government of the United States, with reserve powers belonging to the national government and the states' powers enumerated. South Africa is another multilingual nation with a federal system. The constitution divides the country into nine provinces and delegates certain powers to the national government, others to the provincial governments. Unlike the United States, the provinces do not retain reserve powers. Mexico is a federal system with thirty-one states plus a federal district. The Mexican constitution limits the form of those state governments in ways that the U.S. Constitution does not. In short, within federal political systems as a type, there are many variations, as multilingual and multiethnic nations around the globe feel a greater need to provide the local autonomy that comes with federalism.

- **Why have certain nations chosen a federal system?**

- **Why have most nations not chosen a federal system?**

Countries with Federal Political Systems.

Source: Forum of Federations, "Federalism by Country."

FIGURE 3.2 Constitutional Amendments That Pertain to Federalism.

Color Code :
Criminal procedure | Participation | Equality | Structure | Miscellaneous

Fifth (1791): Affirms the right to indictment by a grand jury and right to due process; protects against double jeopardy, self-incrimination, and taking of property without just compensation

Tenth (1791): Reserves the powers not granted to the national government to the states or to the people

Eleventh (1798): Prevents citizens from one state from suing another state in federal court

Thirteenth (1865): Prohibits slavery in the United States

Fourteenth (1868): Makes all persons born in the United States citizens of the United States, and prohibits states from denying persons within its jurisdiction the privileges or immunities of citizens, the due process of law, and equal protection of the laws; apportionment by whole persons

Fifteenth (1870): Prohibits states from denying the right to vote on account of race

Sixteenth (1913): Grants Congress the power to tax income derived from any source

Seventeenth (1913): Gives the people (instead of state legislatures) the right to choose U.S. senators directly

Although the Antifederalists who opposed the ratification of the Constitution claimed otherwise, this **necessary and proper clause** does not grant Congress the authority to pass any law that it desires. Rather, the clause requires that the law be necessary and proper to one of the listed powers, such as collecting taxes or regulating commerce.

The original Constitution does not list the powers of the state governments, as the states retained all powers that were not prohibited by the Constitution. But to ease the concerns of the Antifederalists who wanted this relationship spelled out in the Constitution, the Tenth Amendment declares that "the powers not delegated to the United States by the Constitution, nor prohibited by it to the States, are reserved to the States respectively, or to the people" (see Figure 3.2 for the amendments that pertain to federalism). The **reserve powers** of the states, sometimes referred to as the **police powers**, include powers to protect the safety, health, and welfare of their citizens, though the federal government now regulates many of these activities. However, marriage and divorce laws, insurance regulations, and professional licensing (of teachers and electricians, for example) remain almost exclusively within state authority. States have authority to define and prosecute most crimes, but the federal government may do so too, with the most prominent examples including federal laws relating to guns, drugs, and terrorism.

Many powers belong to both the state and national governments. These **concurrent powers** include taxing, borrowing and spending money, making and enforcing laws, establishing court systems, and regulating elections. Many areas that were once exclusively within state authority, such as health care and education, are now regulated by both the state and the federal governments (see Figure 3.3).

Limits on Power

The Constitution grants only specified powers to the national government, but even those powers are limited. The Constitution prohibits Congress from suspending the **writ of habeas corpus**, the right of individuals who have been arrested and jailed to go before a judge who

necessary and proper clause: *Gives Congress the power to pass all laws necessary and proper to the powers enumerated in Section 8 (Article I, Section 8).*

reserve powers: *Powers retained by the states under the Constitution.*

police powers: *Authority of the states to protect the health, safety, and welfare of their citizens.*

Are there any state powers you think the federal government should have? Are there any federal powers you think should belong to the states?

concurrent powers: *Powers held by both the national and state governments in a federal system.*

writ of habeas corpus: *Right of individuals who have been arrested and jailed to go before a judge who determines whether their imprisonment is legal.*

National
Regulating interstate commerce
Raising armies
Declaring war
Coining money

Shared
Taxing
Borrowing
Spending
Regulating health*
Regulating education*
Setting time, place, and manner
    of congressional elections*

State
Regulating intrastate commerce
Regulating family law
Licensing
Handling most criminal law

*These were once reserved powers of the states, but the growth of federal authority means that they are now regulated by both.

FIGURE 3.3 Examples of National, State, and Shared Powers.

determines whether their imprisonment is legal. Also prohibited are the passage of any law that declares an individual guilty of a crime (a bill of attainder) and any law that make an act illegal after the fact (an *ex post facto* law). The Constitution also protected slavery, including the right of states to import slaves, preventing Congress from prohibiting the foreign slave trade until 1808.

Following concerns expressed by Antifederalists during the state ratification debates that the proposed Constitution granted the national government too much power, one of the first orders of business for the First Congress was a proposed bill of rights. The first ten amendments to the Constitution created associational freedoms (speech, press, assembly, and religion) that Congress could not abridge; limited the authority of governmental prosecutions against alleged criminals by restricting searches and seizures and guaranteeing the right to counsel and to public trials; and protected certain additional rights, including the right to bear arms and the right to jury trials in civil suits over $20 (see Chapter 4, Civil Liberties, for more details on these rights). The Bill of Rights originally applied only to the national government, not to the states.

The Constitution contains its own set of limits on the state governments. Like the national government, states cannot pass bills of attainder or *ex post facto* laws, or create titles of nobility. Moreover, states cannot enter into treaties or alliances with foreign nations. The Constitution also limits the authority of states to tax imports and exports.

The **guarantee clause** of the Constitution (Article IV, Section 4) guarantees that states shall have a "Republican Form of Government," meaning that a state cannot establish a pure **direct democracy** (although New England towns sometimes run along these lines), a monarchy, or a dictatorship (here the term *republican* has nothing to do with the Republican Party but refers to representative democracy). In *Federalist* 39, Madison defined a republican form of government as one that "derives all its powers directly or indirectly from the great body of the people; and is administered by persons holding their offices during pleasure, for a limited period, or during good behavior."[5] That is, as long as the people who run the government are selected directly (as in the House of Representatives) or indirectly (as in the Electoral

guarantee clause: *Provides a federal government guarantee that the states will have a republican form of government (Article IV, Section 4).*

direct democracy: *Form of democracy in which political power is exercised directly by citizens.*

College) by the people, and those officeholders either have limited terms of office (as do the president and members of Congress) or can be removed for not meeting the standards of "good behavior" (as in the judiciary), the government can be considered republican.

The Supreme Court has declared that the question of whether a state has a republican form of government is one that Congress must decide, not the federal courts.[6] It thus rejected the authority to rule whether state use of citizen-oriented procedures such as **recall** (the right of citizens to vote to remove elected officials before their terms expire), **initiative** (a citizen petition for particular laws), or **referendum** (an up or down vote by the people before a law goes into effect) violate the guarantee clause because they are closer in form to a direct democracy than to a republican or representative government. Congress could make such a decision, but given the popularity of these procedures, there is little reason for Congress to act against states that use them. They are discussed in more detail later in the chapter.

The Fourteenth (1868) and Fifteenth Amendments (1870), however, limit state authority. The Fourteenth Amendment prohibits the states from denying "any person" due process of law and the equal protection of the laws, and the Fifteenth Amendment prohibits states from denying voting rights on account of race, color, or previous condition of servitude. The Supreme Court later used the **due process clause** of the Fourteenth Amendment to require the states to follow most of the provisions of the Bill of Rights (see Chapter 4). Thus states must protect the same liberties as the federal government, resulting in a nationalizing of the nation's most basic rights. Both the Supreme Court and Congress have used the Fifteenth Amendment to protect equal voting rights in the states and the **equal protection clause** of the Fourteenth Amendment to protect other civil rights (see Chapter 5, Civil Rights).

Groundwork for Relationships

In the U.S. federal system, where both the states and the federal governments have the final say over different matters, the Constitution lays out not only the powers of the national government and restrictions on the powers of both the national and the state governments, but also the groundwork for the relationship between the national government and the state governments, and for relationships among the state governments.

Relationships between the Nation and the States.

The Constitution regulates the relationship between the national government and the states through three main clauses: the supremacy clause, the Tenth Amendment, and the sovereign immunity provision of the Eleventh Amendment. The **supremacy clause** (Article VI) makes the Constitution of the United States, plus all laws and treaties made under the Constitution, supreme over state law. Thus, if federal law conflicts with state law, the federal law (assuming it is within the powers of Congress) is supreme. Moreover, because state and federal courts might differ about whether state and federal law actually conflict in a particular case, the ultimate decision rests with the U.S. Supreme Court.[7]

The supremacy clause also allows for the **preemption** of state laws. If Congress and the states both seek to regulate an area of concurrent authority, such as pollution control or the minimum wage, the supremacy clause requires states to meet national standards if national standards are higher than state standards. Thus, if a state sets a $7 per hour minimum wage but Congress sets an $8 minimum wage, businesses in the state must abide by the higher

recall: *Process whereby citizens can remove an elected state official prior to the end of the term of office.*

initiative: *Process by which citizens place proposed laws on the ballot for public approval.*

referendum: *Process by which public approval is required before a state can pass certain laws.*

due process clause: *Prevents the federal government (Fifth Amendment) and the state governments (Fourteenth Amendment) from denying any person due process of law.*

equal protection clause: *Prevents the states from denying any person the equal protection of the law (Fourteenth Amendment).*

supremacy clause: *Makes federal law supreme over state laws (Article VI).*

preemption: *Doctrine by which extensive federal regulation can prevent regulation by the states.*

national standard. On the other hand, states are usually able to set higher standards than the national government. So if Congress sets a minimum wage of $7 per hour but the state sets a minimum wage of $8, businesses in the state must pay the higher state rate. But there are two exceptions. First, Congress can declare that it has preempted state legislation in that area, meaning only Congress can legislate on the topic. For example, Congress preempted state regulation of warnings on cigarette packages, prohibiting the states from adding their own warnings. Second, even if Congress has not explicitly declared that it has preempted state activity, the Supreme Court can rule that Congress's regulation is so thorough that Congress must have intended to "occupy the field," thus disallowing state regulations. The Supreme Court struck down state regulations of Communist activities under this exception.[8]

As noted above, the Tenth Amendment states that all powers not delegated to the national government under the Constitution are reserved to the states or to the people. The Articles of Confederation had a similar clause, but it included the word *expressly* before the word *delegated*. Because the Tenth Amendment omits the word *expressly*, the implication is that the national government retains the sort of **implied powers** granted by the necessary and proper clause.

If the government illegally harms an individual or seizes the person's property, that person might be inclined to sue the government. The doctrine of **sovereign immunity**, however, means that a government cannot be sued without its permission. For example, a state might choose to allow suits against it for racial discrimination, but might choose to prohibit suits based on the hours or wages of state employees. In a federal system with both state and federal courts, however, a state can prevent suits against itself in its own courts simply by passing a law preventing such suits. It cannot necessarily prevent lawsuits against it in federal court. Thus in 1793 the Supreme Court allowed the lawsuit of a South Carolina man against the state of Georgia.[9] Following this decision, Congress proposed and the states quickly ratified the Eleventh Amendment, which prohibits federal courts from hearing suits against a state by citizens of another state. The Eleventh Amendment is not absolute: Congress can allow suits based on provisions in constitutional amendments passed after the Eleventh, such as the due process and equal protection clauses of the Fourteenth Amendment.

Relationships among the States. One of the many problems of governance under the Articles of Confederation was that the states could establish trade barriers against one another, thus limiting economic growth. Therefore, in the **commerce clause** (Article I, Section 8) the Constitution established Congress's exclusive authority to regulate commerce among the states. Thus states may not establish trade barriers against goods from other states. A state may tax goods from other states equal to the amount that it taxes goods produced in its own state, but it cannot charge extra taxes to goods that are made out of state. Congress cannot establish trade barriers in interstate commerce either, because Article I, Section 9 prohibits Congress from taxing exports from any state.

The Constitution also requires agreements between two or more states to receive the approval of Congress. States that share rivers, lakes, or other natural resources frequently make agreements over the use of their shared resources so that no one state overuses or overpollutes those resources.[10]

Article IV of the Constitution establishes additional rules that guide relationships among the states. The **full faith and credit clause** generally requires states to accept court decisions

Should the state or the national government set the minimum wage? Should the minimum wage vary with local conditions?

implied powers: *Powers not expressly granted to Congress but added through the necessary and proper clause.*

sovereign immunity: *Doctrine holding that states cannot be sued without their permission.*

commerce clause: *Gives Congress the power to regulate commerce with foreign nations, with Indian tribes, and among the various states (Article I, Section 8).*

full faith and credit clause: *Requires states to accept civil proceedings from other states (Article IV, Section 1).*

made in other states. Couples who are married (or divorced) in Las Vegas, Nevada, are married (or divorced) throughout the United States. This seemingly simple constitutional rule has recently become controversial, as some states have recognized same-sex marriages as valid. Under the full faith and credit clause, same-sex marriage performed in Massachusetts would presumably be valid throughout the nation. But the clause allows Congress to create exceptions. Congress passed and President William Jefferson (Bill) Clinton (1993–2001) signed one such exception into law with the Defense of Marriage Act (1996), which relieves states of the obligation of accepting the validity of same-sex marriages performed in other states. Another general exception to the full faith and credit clause concerns child custody decisions. Because the best interests of a child may change over time, when a child is moved from one state to another the courts in the new state need not accept the child custody determinations made by the previous state.

Justin Sullivan/Getty Images

Through its **privileges and immunities clause**, Article IV also requires states to treat people from other states equally to their own residents. Thus a state may not limit the right to practice law to residents, nor may it require people to live in the state for a set amount of time to receive welfare benefits. The courts, however, have allowed certain exceptions to this constitutional guarantee, the most notable being the higher tuition that out-of-state residents pay at state universities.

The Changing Nature of American Federalism

The ratification of the Constitution pitted the state-centered Antifederalists against the nation-centered Federalists, and pro-state and pro-nation interests have contested the relative balance between the two ever since. Because a federal system presupposes separate states with guaranteed rights, tension between the layers of government is built-in and inevitable. People who believe in relatively more national power contend that the national government does not derive its powers from the states, but from the people. They cite as evidence the statement in the Preamble that the Constitution was established by "We, the People of the United States." Others believe in greater state power, a view that considers the national government to be an agreement by thirteen independent states (the original colonies) to delegate certain limited powers that they had held to a national government.

From the origins of a two-party system during George Washington's presidency (1789–97) through the expansion of national authority over health care under Barack Obama (2009–), politicians and citizens have fought over the proper role of the national and state governments. Different eras show a dominance of one view over the other, but even when one side dominates, the other side pushes back. Overall, however, the nation began with a period of nationalization that lasted until around 1835, followed by the movement toward

Same-sex marriage is a contentious issue related to federalism. Regulating family law has been a state power, and some states have approved same-sex marriage. The federal Defense of Marriage Act (1996) affirms that other states do not have to recognize these marriages. A challenge regarding the status of same-sex marriage is likely to reach the Supreme Court.

Should all states be required to recognize same-sex marriages that are valid in one state?

privileges and immunities clause: *Requires states to treat nonresidents equally to residents (Article IV, Section 2).*

Should out-of-state students pay higher tuition at state universities? Why?

secession and civil war. Following the Civil War, the states and the federal government had clearly separate powers. In the era following the Great Depression and the election of Franklin Delano Roosevelt (1933–45) in 1932, national power grew enormously, only to retreat slightly following the election of Richard M. Nixon (1969–74) in 1968. Throughout these eras, as we shall see, a recurring substantive theme in the federalism debate has involved slavery, race, and equality.

Americans might have sincere preferences about the relative authority of the national and the state governments, but it is also the case that politicians can use federalism arguments to mask substantive concerns. For example, while Republicans in recent years have generally supported state authority more often than Democrats, Democrats will support state authority when states support liberal policies, and Republicans will be particularly supportive of state authority when states support conservative policies.

Nationalization in the Founding Generation

In the 1789 and 1792 elections, every elector cast a vote for George Washington. Washington did not run as the candidate of any political party, and his administration had no organized opposition. Within his administration, however, divisions over the extent of the authority of the national government split Secretary of the Treasury Alexander Hamilton and his allies from Secretary of State Thomas Jefferson and his allies. Hamilton favored a **nation-centered federalism**. He sought expansive federal power and in 1790 proposed that Congress establish the National Bank of the United States under a broad reading of the necessary and proper clause. Jefferson, who favored a **state-centered federalism**, unsuccessfully opposed the bank, which Congress created with a twenty-year charter. Jefferson's allies, however, were able to limit Hamilton's plan to promote manufacturing through subsidies to producers and taxes on imports. The split between Hamilton and Jefferson over federal authority and other issues led to the development of the first party system in the United States, with the pro-national Hamiltonians labeling themselves the Federalist Party and the Jeffersonian supporters of **states' rights** labeling themselves the Democratic-Republicans (see Chapter 9, Political Parties).

In 1798, when the Federalist administration of John Adams (1797–1801) passed the **Sedition Act** (see Chapter 4), making criticism of the government illegal, Jefferson wrote a resolution adopted by the Kentucky legislature that declared the act void, claiming that states could decide for themselves which national laws to obey. James Madison authored a similar resolution that the Virginia legislature passed. Known as the Virginia and Kentucky Resolutions, these acts argued for **nullification**, the right of states to nullify, or reject, national laws that went beyond the powers granted in the Constitution. Though the Virginia and Kentucky Resolutions met with little approval outside their home states, the doctrine of nullification has reappeared when pro-state forces have questioned national authority.

The debate over national authority to establish a bank resurfaced after the first National Bank charter expired and Congress chartered a Second National Bank. The Supreme Court resolved this issue in **McCulloch v. Maryland** (1819) in an opinion written by Federalist Chief Justice John Marshall.[11] Marshall noted that Congress had the explicit authority to coin money and collect taxes, and declared that the creation of a bank helped reach those goals. Thus creating a bank was an implied power that fell within the scope of authority granted by the necessary and proper clause (see Supreme Court Cases: *McCulloch v. Maryland*).

nation-centered federalism: *View that the Constitution and the federal government derive from the people, not from the states.*

state-centered federalism: *View that the states created the Constitution and the federal government.*

states' rights: *View that states have strong independent authority to resist federal rules under the Constitution.*

What do supporters of states' rights think states should have the right to do?

Sedition Act: *1798 act that made it a crime to criticize the government; later repealed.*

nullification: *Right of states to invalidate acts of Congress they believe to be illegal.*

McCulloch v. Maryland: *1819 Supreme Court decision upholding the right of Congress to create a bank.*

supremecourtcases

McCulloch v. Maryland (1819)

QUESTION: May the federal government establish a bank? If so, does a state have the right to tax that bank?

ORAL ARGUMENT: February 22, 1819

DECISION: March 6, 1819 (read at www.findlaw.com/casecode/supreme.html)

OUTCOME: Yes, the bank is constitutional, and no, Maryland may not tax it (6–0).

Following the decision of Congress to establish the Second National Bank, the state of Maryland imposed a tax on the Maryland branch. The bank manager, James McCulloch, refused to pay the tax, and Maryland brought suit. The Maryland Supreme Court ruled that the bank was unconstitutional because the Constitution does not grant Congress the specific authority to create a bank. McCulloch appealed to the Supreme Court.

Attorney Daniel Webster, who had served in the House and would later serve in the Senate and as secretary of state, represented McCulloch before the Supreme Court. Among the most famed litigators of his day, Webster also represented the nationalist position before the Supreme Court in a District of Columbia lottery case and the New York steamboat case.

The Supreme Court's decision, written by Chief Justice John Marshall, began by accepting the nation-centered view of the Constitution's founding: Rather than a compact of states, the government established by the Constitution "proceeds directly from the people; is 'ordained and established,' in the name of the people."

Regarding the power to establish a bank, Marshall noted that while the Constitution makes no reference to a bank, it does provide for coining and borrowing money, paying government debts, and levying taxes. It also allows Congress to pass all laws that are "necessary and proper" to any of the enumerated powers. Declaring that "necessary and proper" does not mean "absolutely necessary," Marshall read the necessary and proper clause to mean "ordinary and appropriate."

In explaining the scope of the necessary and proper clause, Marshall declared, "Let the end be legitimate, let it be within the scope of the constitution, and all means which are appropriate, which are plainly adapted to that end, which are not prohibited, but consist with the letter and spirit of the constitution, are constitutional." Thus, creating a bank was an appropriate means of legitimate ends: regulating money and collecting taxes.

As for state taxation of the bank, Marshall based his response on the supremacy clause, observing that "the power to tax involves the power to destroy." Because states cannot destroy creations of the federal government, neither can they tax them.

The *McCulloch* decision created a broad scope for implied powers under the Constitution, powers that are not explicitly in the Constitution but are related to powers that are. Without this broad set of implied powers, Congress could not establish criminal laws for offenses, investigate executive wrongdoing, provide student loans, establish administrative agencies, or conduct many of the other activities it routinely engages in today.

- **If Congress does not have the express authority to establish a national bank, by what authority may it do so?**

- **What is the harm to federalism if a state can tax a national bank?**

broad construction: *Interpretation of the Constitution that goes beyond the plain meaning of the specific words used.*

Gibbons v. Ogden: *1824 Supreme Court decision giving broad latitude to Congress under the commerce clause.*

Five years later the Court, in another opinion by Marshall, established a **broad construction**, or interpretation, of Congress's enumerated power to regulate interstate commerce. In **Gibbons v. Ogden** (1824) the Court ruled that Congress's authority to regulate commerce among the states gave it, rather than the states, the authority to manage the licensing of steamboats traveling between New York and New Jersey. Marshall further declared that the authority of Congress to regulate commerce between the states did not begin or end at state boundaries, but necessarily included commercial activities interior to each state.[12] Between the decisions in *McCulloch* and *Gibbons*, the Supreme Court under Marshall supported the Federalist Party position of a strong national government with expansive powers.

The Revolt against National Authority: Nullification, Slavery, and the Civil War

As Marshall's Supreme Court pushed the United States in a national direction, the precedent set by the Virginia and Kentucky Resolutions led various states to claim the right to disregard national laws that they believed were unconstitutional or merely unwise. Several New England states threatened to ignore the Embargo Act of 1807, and in 1828 Vice President John C. Calhoun insisted on South Carolina's right to nullify a federal tariff. As the union was merely a compact among the states, Calhoun argued, dissenting states even had the right to **secede**. Against such claims, Senator Daniel Webster insisted that the union was not a compact of states, but a compact among the people of the United States. In opposition to secession, he declared, "liberty *and* Union, now and forever, one and inseparable." At a Jefferson Day dinner a few months later, President Andrew Jackson (1829–37) reinforced Webster's argument in offering this toast: "Our Union. It must be preserved." Whereupon Calhoun rose to counter Jackson: "The Union, next to our liberty, most dear."[13]

secession: *Act of seceding, or formally withdrawing, from a nation-state.*

Though disagreements over federal tariff rates proved an insufficient instigation to secede, federal authority to regulate slavery eventually led to secession. Slavery concessions at the Constitutional Convention included the **fugitive slave clause** of Article IV, requiring states to return runaway slaves. Congress passed a Fugitive Slave Law in 1793 that established procedures for the return of slaves. But in 1826 Pennsylvania passed a "personal liberty" law that prohibited any runaway slave from being forcibly removed from the state. Under this law, in 1839 Pennsylvania convicted a slave catcher named Edward Prigg who had forcibly abducted a woman who had lived free but had not been formally freed. Prigg appealed to the Supreme Court, which ruled in **Prigg v. Pennsylvania** (1842) that the Pennsylvania law that made it a felony to abduct runaway slaves was unconstitutional, in that it contradicted the fugitive slave clause of Article IV, and that it was in violation of the supremacy clause due to its conflict with the Fugitive Slave Law of 1793. In 1850, as part of the last compromise over slavery, Congress strengthened the national authority over runaways by actually forcing states to aid in their return. The act prohibited jury trials for alleged runaway slaves and paid the newly hired commissioners who heard the cases $10 if they ruled for the slave owner but only $5 if they ruled for the alleged slave.[14]

fugitive slave clause: *Required states to return runaway slaves; negated by the Thirteenth Amendment (Article IV, Section 2).*

Prigg v. Pennsylvania: *1842 Supreme Court decision declaring that the Pennsylvania law prohibiting the abduction of runaway slaves was unconstitutional.*

Because nothing in the Constitution suggested that Congress had the power to limit slavery in the states, the most heated contests over congressional authority to regulate slavery involved the territories. This debate split abolitionists who wanted to ban slavery in the territories, states' rights supporters such as John C. Calhoun who thought that slave owners had the right to take their slaves into any territory, and those who favored compromises that would allow slavery in some territories but not in others. In 1857 the Supreme Court sided with the states' rights supporters, declaring in **Dred Scott v. Sandford** that Congress had no authority to regulate slavery in the territories (see Chapter 4).[15]

When Abraham Lincoln (1861–65), who favored federal efforts to prohibit slavery in the territories, won the presidential election of 1860, South Carolina seceded. The 1860 South Carolina Declaration of the Causes of Secession affirmed that "the frequent violations of the Constitution of the United States by the Federal Government, and its encroachments upon the reserved rights of the States," justified secession.[16] Other southern states followed, and they soon established their own constitution. The Confederate Constitution followed the U.S. Constitution in most respects, with two significant differences. It specifically protected the right to hold slaves, and its preamble suggested a more state-centered federalism, declaring "We, the people of the Confederate States, each State acting in its sovereign and independent character." On the other hand, the Confederate Constitution contained both a supremacy clause and a necessary and proper clause, suggesting that a national government with too much power was not a primary worry of the Confederate states.

During the Civil War, Lincoln used his power as commander in chief to issue the Emancipation Proclamation, which prohibited slavery in states under rebellion, as slave labor was an asset to the Confederate army. Even during the war, few believed that the national government could end slavery in the four slave states—the so-called border states of Delaware, Kentucky, Maryland, and Missouri—that had remained in the union. Slavery in some of these states did not end until the states ratified the Thirteenth Amendment (1865), which prohibited slavery throughout the nation.

The Congresses that followed the Civil War tried to exert federal power over the states to promote equality between freedmen and whites, but President Andrew Johnson (1865–69) vetoed a civil rights bill, claiming it represented a trend toward "centralization and the concentration of all legislative power in the National Government."[17] The bill granted former slaves the rights to make contracts, sue, and give evidence and to inherit, purchase, lease, and convey real and personal property. In 1866 Congress passed it over Johnson's veto. But as part of the effort to ensure that all such laws would be constitutional, Congress proposed and the states ratified the Fourteenth Amendment (1868) and the Fifteenth Amendment (1870). These greatly expanded the authority of the national government over the states. The Fourteenth Amendment requires states to provide each person due process of law (see Chapter 4) and the equal protection of the laws (see Chapter 5). The Fifteenth Amendment prevents states from abridging the right to vote on account of race. Like the Thirteenth Amendment, the Fourteenth and Fifteenth Amendments granted Congress the authority to enforce their provisions by appropriate legislation, thus adding to Congress's enumerated powers.

In 1883, however, the Supreme Court decided in the **Civil Rights Cases** to keep Congress's powers within the words of the amendments: Congress could prevent states from denying people equality, but it could not prevent private businesses or individuals from doing so, for example, by refusing to hire former slaves or to serve them at inns or restaurants. The Court thus invalidated Congress's Civil Rights Act of 1875, which had prohibited this type of private discrimination. This era, covering the period before and after the Civil War, saw the defeat of the most strident (secessionist) state-centered views, but with the Supreme Court's interpretation of the Civil War amendments, state authority remained strong.

Dred Scott v. Sandford: *1857 Supreme Court decision declaring that blacks could not be citizens and Congress could not ban slavery in the territories.*

What was the primary cause of the Civil War—slavery, states' rights, something else?

Civil Rights Cases: *1883 Supreme Court decision that limited congressional authority to prohibit private discrimination under the Fourteenth Amendment.*

Dual Federalism

Although the supporters of state-centered federalism lost the Civil War, the viewpoint of a national government with limited powers did not disappear. A new viewpoint, **dual federalism**, recognized that, while the national government was supreme in some spheres, the state governments remained supreme in others, with layers of authority separate from one another, an arrangement that political scientists later compared to a "layer cake" (see Figure 3.4).[18] Thus the national government would be supreme over issues such as foreign affairs and interstate commerce, and the states would be supreme in matters concerning intrastate commerce and police powers.

Given that the Constitution does not specifically define the difference between interstate commerce and intrastate commerce, this division worked out well so long as Congress made little effort to regulate any form of commerce. In fact, for more than a decade following its 1875 attempt to prevent discrimination at inns and other places of public accommodation, Congress left the regulation of the economy to the states. With an increase in the industrialization at the end of the nineteenth century, however, came increases in economic inequality, with calls for Congress to help those who were harmed by the increasing concentration of wealth. Congress responded with the Interstate Commerce Act of 1887, which established the first federal regulatory agency, the **Interstate Commerce Commission**. The act charged the commission with making sure that railroads charged fair rates to farmers and other shippers.

Because concentrations of wealth and power were not limited to the railroads, Congress passed the Sherman Antitrust Act of 1890, an antimonopoly law that prohibits all contracts and combinations in restraint of trade. The United States went to court using the law to break up the Sugar Trust, a monopoly that controlled 98 percent of the nation's sugar refining. In 1895 the Supreme Court conceded in *United States v. E.C. Knight Co.* that the Sugar Trust was a monopoly and recognized that it conducted business throughout the United States. The Court nevertheless declared that Congress had no authority to regulate that monopoly because manufacturing was a subject of intrastate commerce only, even when the company in question manufactured its product in several states.[19] Here the Court used the Tenth Amendment as a gate protecting state powers against federal encroachment, declaring that it is up to the states to regulate the harms caused by monopolies. As in the *Civil Rights Cases*, the Supreme Court limited national authority that Congress had claimed over areas that states' rights supporters thought belonged to the states.

Layer cake   Marble cake

FIGURE 3.4 Dual Federalism and Cooperative Federalism. Dual federalism has been likened to a layer cake (left), and cooperative federalism has been likened to a marble cake (right). © Cengage Learning, *Source:* LAITS, University of Texas College of Liberal Arts

Beyond monopolies, Congress tried to limit child labor by barring the shipment of goods across state lines if the manufacturer used child labor. According to the Court, this too was a regulation of manufacturing, not a regulation of interstate commerce, and thus went beyond Congress's powers. When Congress alternatively tried to discourage child labor by placing a tax on goods made by children under the age of 14, the Supreme Court struck down that law too, claiming the fee was not a "tax" but rather a "penalty" that Congress did not have the right to impose. Again, under the Tenth Amendment, the authority to regulate social harms fell to the states.

This period of dual federalism left the national government and the states supreme in their respective spheres, but granted Congress only a very narrow sphere. Regulations of manufacturing and mining remained under the control of the states, even if the goods later crossed state lines and entered interstate commerce. But a countertrend was emerging. In 1913 Congress passed and the states ratified the Sixteenth Amendment, which granted Congress the power to tax income from whatever source derived, giving the national government access to millions

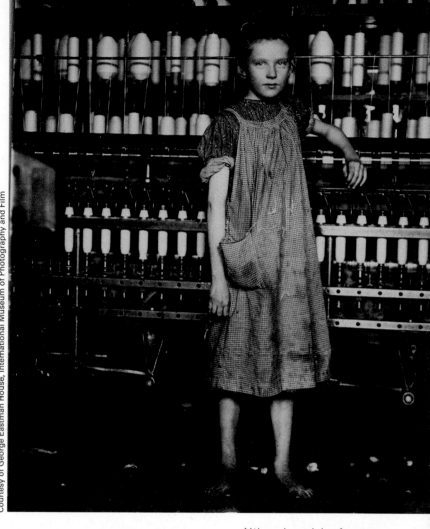

Courtesy of George Eastman House, International Museum of Photography and Film

(and later billions and even trillions) of dollars in revenue. The increase in federal authority over areas once left to the states was aided that same year by the ratification of the Seventeenth Amendment, which took the selection of U.S. senators out of the hands of state legislatures and required that they be directly elected by the people of each state. Prior to 1914 state legislatures hoped senators would be responsive to the needs of the states, but with direct elections, senators had to be responsive to the needs of the people.[20]

Cooperative Federalism: The New Deal and Civil Rights

With the onset of the Great Depression following the stock market crash of 1929, the people wanted national action to aid the economy, and the nation-centered federalism signaled by the Sixteenth and Seventeenth Amendments strengthened considerably. In 1932 voters elected Franklin Roosevelt as president. During his campaign, Roosevelt had promised a "New Deal" to Americans who had lost their jobs, their homes, and their savings. Following his inauguration, Congress passed a series of laws designed to lift the ailing economy. As before, Congress asserted its authority under the commerce clause to regulate American industry. As before, the Supreme Court rejected such legislation, claiming in one case that

Although social reformers, including Lewis Hine, who took this famous photograph, advocated for a national law prohibiting child labor, many states resisted, and the Supreme Court twice overturned child labor laws passed by Congress. Not until the Fair Labor Standards Act of 1938 was the employment of children under 16 prohibited in manufacturing and mining.

Why do citizens look to the federal government in times of crisis?

the mining of coal by a company with operations in several states was production and not interstate commerce.[21]

Given that the power to tax for a given purpose also grants the power to spend for that purpose, Congress alternatively attempted to regulate industry through the taxing clause—Congress's power to "lay and Collect Taxes" to "provide . . . for the general Welfare" (Article I, Section 8). Again the Supreme Court said no, declaring in one case that the taxing and spending provisions in a farm bill, whether for the general welfare or not, violated the Tenth Amendment.[22]

Despite vast support from Congress and the American people for his New Deal policies, Roosevelt saw the Supreme Court strike down one law after another, often by 5–4 or 6–3 votes. In response, Roosevelt proposed in 1937 to increase the number of justices on the Supreme Court. He would then be able to pack the Court with his own appointees. This controversial **Court-packing plan** met with fierce opposition in Congress. The Supreme Court, however, made passage of the plan unnecessary, for shortly after Roosevelt's proposal, the Court reversed itself and started accepting the broad authority of Congress to regulate the economy.

On taxing and spending, the Court accepted the view that virtually any taxing or spending plan that Congress believed supported the general welfare would be acceptable. Today, for example, although Congress has no direct authority to set drinking ages, it effectively does so by denying federal highway funds to states that set the drinking age under 21; for a variety of reasons, including low voting rates by younger Americans, no states do.

On commerce, the Court began by accepting the regulation of a giant steel company with operations throughout the United States as an appropriate regulation of interstate commerce.[23] Congress could also use the commerce clause to regulate employment conditions, said the Court, rejecting the Tenth Amendment as a limit on federal power.[24] The Court's definition of what constituted interstate commerce grew to include anything that affected interstate commerce, whether over several states or confined to one state. According to the Court, this included wheat grown on a farm that was consumed on that farm, due to the effect that such wheat plus all the similarly used wheat grown by other farmers would have on the market (see Supreme Court Cases: *Wickard v. Filburn*, in Chapter 12, Congress). With federal intervention in manufacturing, farming, and other areas traditionally governed by the states, Roosevelt's nation-centered federalism was said by political scientists to more closely resemble a "marble cake," with specific powers under both national and state authority, than the layer-cake structure of dual federalism.[25]

Nation-centered federalism continued to dominate dual federalism through World War II and beyond. President Lyndon Baines Johnson's (1963–69) Great Society program expanded national authority even further, with federal aid to public schools—traditionally a state duty—and health care coverage to the poor (Medicaid) and elderly (Medicare). The Johnson administration also expanded national power to ensure greater equality, pushing for passage of the **Civil Rights Act** (1964), which prohibited job discrimination and segregation in public

Court-packing plan: *President Franklin Roosevelt's proposal to add new justices to the Supreme Court so that the Court would uphold his policies.*

Should the drinking age be 21 or 18? Who should decide?

Columbus (Ohio) Dispatch 10 Feb 1937, Basil O'Connor Collection

Civil Rights Act: *Prohibits discrimination in employment, education, and places of public accommodation (1964).*

accommodations, and the **Voting Rights Act** (1965), which regulated voting rules that had largely been left to the states since the adoption of the Constitution (see Chapter 5).

State-centered federalism gained some traction, though, in opposition to the push toward equality and civil rights. Following President Harry S. Truman's (1945–53) expressed support for national protections of civil rights, southern segregationists formed the States' Rights Democratic Party and ran South Carolina Governor Strom Thurmond for president in 1948. Then, in 1954 in *Brown v. Board of Education*, the Supreme Court struck down school segregation, which had been legally mandated or permitted in twenty states plus the District of Columbia.[26] The Supreme Court decision helped put the federal government at the forefront of the fight for equality. In response to this decision, seven states passed "interposition resolutions" that asserted the right to nullify the Supreme Court decision. Such resolutions have no legal validity. In one of the last challenges to integration, segregationist Governor George Wallace of Alabama ran for president in 1968. His party, the American Independent Party, condemned what it considered to be the unconstitutional use of federal power to desegregate schools and enforce voting rights.[27] Wallace received more than 9 million votes and won the electoral vote of five states.

The New Federalism

Although Wallace lost the race, the strength of his campaign signaled a degree of wariness among voters about the powers of the national government. Other politicians, starting with Richard Nixon, the winner of the 1968 election, responded to these concerns.[28]

Presidents, Congress, and the New Federalism.

The Nixon administration (1969–74) began the trend, labeled **New Federalism**, of shifting powers back to the states.[29] While the Democratic Johnson administration gave money to the states in **categorical grants**, that is, money for the states to use on what the national government wanted, the Republican Nixon administration began a general revenue sharing program that gave the states greater leeway about how the funds could be spent. The main idea behind Nixon's federalism was that states could more efficiently spend governmental resources than the enormous federal bureaucracy could.

Republican President Ronald Reagan (1981–89) sought to reduce the power of government in general and, as an avid supporter of the New Federalism, of the federal government in particular. In his first inaugural address, he declared, "Government is not the solution to our problem; government is the problem."[30] He thus cut back on categorical grants, replacing them with fewer, more flexible **block grants**, which set fewer restrictions on how the money could be spent. He also eliminated **general revenue sharing** (see Table 3.1).

President Bill Clinton did not have strong views on federalism, but one of his early proposals was a plan for national health insurance for all Americans, traditionally an area that had been left to private parties, such as businesses and individuals, and to the states. Opposition to Clinton's plan led both to the plan's defeat and a Republican platform in the 1994 congressional elections called the **Contract with America** that included limits on the powers of the federal government. Voters that year chose Republican majorities in both the House and the Senate, believing, by 47 percent to 6 percent, that the federal government had too much power as compared to the state governments.[31] Similarly, in 2010 the Republicans' Pledge to America, calling for a repeal of federal health care legislation, helped them regain the House.

Voting Rights Act: *Gives the federal government the right to prevent discrimination in voting rights (1965).*

Was the Johnson administration right to use federal power to ensure equality?

New Federalism: *Shifting of power back to the states that began in the Nixon administration.*

categorical grants: *Money from Congress to the states that had to be spent in specific categories.*

block grants: *Money from Congress to the states that had to be spent in broad, rather than specific, categories.*

general revenue sharing: *Money from Congress to the states that could be spent any way the states wanted.*

Was Reagan right in stating that "government is the problem"?

Contract with America: *Campaign proposal containing ten legislative initiatives used by Republicans running for the House of Representatives in 1994.*

TABLE 3.1 Annual Percent Change in Federal Aid to State and Local Governments, in Constant Dollars

President	Percent Change
Lyndon Baines Johnson (1963–69)	11.7%
Richard M. Nixon (1969–74)	9.0%
Gerald R. Ford (1974–77)	8.7%
Jimmy Carter (1977–81)	–1.0%
Ronald Reagan (1981–89)	–1.3%
George H. W. Bush (1989–93)	8.4%
William J. Clinton (1993–2001)	4.2%
George W. Bush (2001–2009)	3.9%
Barack Obama (2009–)	18.5%*

*2009–2010 only. This increase is largely due to added stimulus spending to address the 2008–2009 recession.

Source: GPO Access, U.S. Budget for Fiscal Year 2009, 2010, Historical Tables, Table 12.1.

devolution: *Shifting of power from the national government to the states.*

mandates: *Congressional requirements on the states to undertake particular activities; states object particularly to unfunded mandates.*

Following the Republican victories, Clinton shifted gears and worked with the Republicans on a **devolution** of power from the national government to the states, declaring that "The era of big government is over."[32] During the Clinton administration, Congress moved to shift the balance of power toward the states in several ways. First, it limited unfunded **mandates**—legal requirements Congress imposes on the states (for example, to provide clean air, disability access, or health benefits to poor people under Medicaid) without supplying the resources to accomplish those activities. Congress did not eliminate such mandates, but it did make them harder to impose. Second, Clinton and Congress overhauled the federal welfare system, ending the federal guarantee of welfare to poor families with children. Third, Congress abandoned national speed limits that had been established at the time of the 1973 Arab oil embargo and allowed states to set whatever speed limits they desired.

While President Clinton supported these initiatives, common ground eroded in the winter of 1995–96 over Republican plans for more spending cuts than Clinton was willing to accept. This stalemate led to a temporary shutdown of nonessential government agencies and furloughs for hundreds of thousands of federal workers. A majority of Americans opposed the shutdown and, by a substantial margin, thought the Republicans were more to blame than the Democrats (see Figure 3.5). Much as Clinton suffered the political consequences of pushing to expand the national government too much in 1994, the Republicans suffered the political consequences of pushing to contract the national government too much in 1996. President Clinton rallied from very low approval ratings to win that year's presidential election.

Although Republicans have typically supported state authority over that of the national government since the New Deal, President George W. Bush oversaw an administration that strengthened national authority, sometimes at the expense of the states.[33] His most prominent actions in this regard included the No Child Left Behind Act (2002), which increased federal

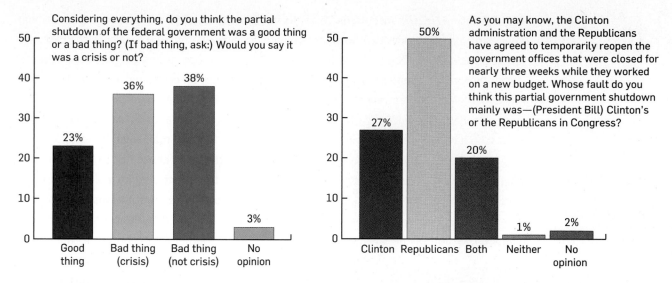

FIGURE 3.5 Public Opinion on the Government Shutdown in 1996. By a 74–23 percent margin, Americans thought the shutdown of government during the Clinton administration was a bad idea. By a 50–27 percent margin, the public blamed the Republicans in Congress rather than Clinton.
Source: ABC News/Washington Post poll, January 6–7, 1996, based on telephone interviews with a national adult sample of 852.

involvement in public education, and his prescription drug plan for Medicare.[34] The Bush administration went to court along with the auto industry in an attempt to preempt California's fuel economy and emission standards for cars, which were stricter than national standards (see Chapter 14, The Bureaucracy).[35] Following the terrorist attacks of September 11, 2001, Congress and the Bush administration expanded national power in various ways, including the establishment of national standards for driver's licenses. Though Bush was a Republican and a former governor—two factors that might ordinarily indicate greater support for the states over the federal government—his administration was, conclude two political scientists, "routinely dismissive of federalism concerns."[36]

On the other hand, two early decisions by the Obama administration signal support for state-centered federalism, at least where the policies support Democratic Party positions: support for permitting states to set higher standards than the federal government on fuel economy and tailpipe emissions and a reversal of the Bush administration's crackdown on state medical marijuana programs.[37] Additionally, the stimulus package of 2009 directed more than $100 billion in federal revenue to the states.[38] Some Republican governors, however, with Louisiana Governor Bobby Jindal among them, refused some of the stimulus funds that were earmarked for unemployment insurance because accepting them would have required expanded unemployment coverage once the federal stimulus funds ran out.

Do you tend to support nation-centered federalism or state-centered federalism? Which is more responsive? Which ensures citizen equality?

The Supreme Court and the New Federalism.   President Reagan was supportive of state-centered federalism. By nominating William Rehnquist to be chief justice in 1986, Reagan hoped to move the Court toward greater judicial respect for the states. He was not disappointed. As an associate justice (1971–86), Rehnquist had pressed, often alone on the Court, for what the Supreme Court once labeled "Our Federalism."[39] As chief justice (1986–2005), he further advanced New Federalism, now aided by a Republican bloc that grew to include seven justices. The Rehnquist Court put together pro-state majorities in two series of decisions: interstate commerce and sovereign immunity.

Concerning interstate commerce, for the first time since 1937 the Court rejected national laws as beyond Congress's authority to regulate under the commerce clause. In one case, the Court struck down congressional legislation banning the possession of guns near schools, declaring that the possession of a gun near a school is not an economic activity.[40] Similarly, the Court rejected a central provision of the Violence against Women Act, which gave victims of gender-based violence the right to sue their attackers in federal court. A Virginia Tech student who had allegedly been raped by members of the football team sued her attacker and Virginia Tech, a state university, in federal court after the state chose not to bring criminal charges. The Court rejected congressional findings on the effect of such violence on commerce, and it ruled that the section of the act that allowed the lawsuits was beyond Congress's authority either under the commerce clause or under its authority to enforce the equal protection of the laws under the Fourteenth Amendment.[41] According to the Court,

Should guns be allowed near or in schools? Who should decide?

AP Photo/Reed Saxon

The La Brea Collective medical marijuana dispensary in Los Angeles displays varieties of marijuana in canning jars. Fourteen states including California have legalized medical marijuana. Elsewhere in the United States, marijuana cannot be sold or used for medical purposes, although cancer patients report that it relieves nausea and vomiting during chemotherapy, and others claim a variety of additional medical benefits. In November 2010 Californians rejected an initiative to legalize marijuana use for any purpose.

"Gender-motivated crimes of violence are not, in any sense of the phrase, economic activity." In essence, the Court was saying that to allow Congress to regulate noneconomic activity because of the effect it might have on economic activity would allow the national government to regulate virtually everything.

The Rehnquist Court also limited national authority over the states through the doctrine of sovereign immunity. Although the Eleventh Amendment prevents citizens of one state from suing a different state in federal court, the Court ruled that the amendment limits the rights of citizens to sue their own states in federal court. The Court thus prevented citizens from suing their own states for violations of federal labor law,[42] for harm to businesses by unfair competition and for infringements of patents or copyrights by state universities,[43] and for otherwise illegal discrimination against a breast cancer victim by her employer, the Alabama State University system. According to the Court in the Alabama State University case, "the ultimate guarantee of the Eleventh Amendment is that nonconsenting States may not be sued by private individuals in federal court."[44]

While these decisions stand in contrast to the decidedly pro-national decisions of the Court since the New Deal, most questions of federal authority still are decided in favor of the national government. The Court, for example, did not permit states to allow medical marijuana.[45] Indeed, it routinely continues to uphold Congress's authority to regulate commercial activity; there has been no return to the pre-New Deal distinction between commerce and manufacturing.

Summing Up: Were the Antifederalists Correct?

The people of the United States ratified the Constitution over the protests of Antifederalists, who claimed that the Constitution gave virtually unlimited powers to the national government. Nevertheless, until the New Deal, either because of congressional inaction or Supreme Court reaction when Congress did act, the powers exercised by the national government were clearly limited. Today, however, between the popular belief in the need to regulate a complex economy and the Supreme Court's interpretation of the Constitution, Congress has vast powers. The fact that Congress can regulate, through the commerce clause, a farmer's production of wheat even when that wheat is consumed on that farm, that Congress can spend money on virtually anything as long as it is not specifically prohibited by the Constitution, and that the necessary and proper clause means "ordinary and appropriate," leads to the conclusion that, as far as the powers of the national government are concerned, the Antifederalists were correct: The federal government's powers have few limits. But as the 1994 elections demonstrate, if the people believe that the national government has too much power, they can vote for candidates who wish to limit that power. The Republican takeover of the House of Representatives in the 2010 midterm elections was in part a reaction against federal power and the health care act that the Democrats in Congress had passed earlier that year.

Were the Antifederalists right to fear the power of the national government?

State and Local Governments

The Constitution requires that the states maintain a republican form of government, and all have done so by patterning their structure after the national government, with separate legislative, judicial, and executive branches. With the exception of procedures that allow citizens to place proposed laws directly on the ballot, state governments look remarkably similar to the federal government. Local governments, however, use a greater range of organizational options.

State Governments

All fifty states have separate legislative and executive branches, and all fifty states choose the head of the executive branch by direct election. Most states have four-year gubernatorial terms, limit their governors to two consecutive terms, and provide for succession by the lieutenant governor. Figure 3.6 presents the states that use different rules.

The governors of all fifty states have the authority to veto laws subject to override by the state legislatures. Most states further grant their governors a **line-item veto**, the ability to veto certain parts of a spending bill without vetoing the entire bill. The president does not have this power, so when Congress passes spending bills, it usually does so by combining tens of thousands of separate spending items in an **omnibus bill**. The president's choice is to sign the entire bill or to veto it; he cannot veto only the appropriations he disfavors. Governors in forty-two states do have that authority, however, giving them a much stronger tool to control spending than the president has.

Of those forty-two states, twenty-six allow governors to veto not just appropriations, but also language in appropriations bills.[46] Wisconsin's veto authority, known as the "Frankenstein" veto, allows the governor to create entirely new language by crossing out words and numbers throughout a bill, leaving behind new language that could radically change the meaning of the law. For example, when the state created a five-person Minority Business Development Board that gave other individuals the authority to appoint three of the five members, the governor vetoed the words of the law that delegated those three appointments to others, thus taking the authority to appoint all five members. A state constitutional amendment approved by the voters in 2008 retained the governor's authority to change the meaning of laws by crossing out particular words or numbers (eliminating "not" from a sentence can have enormous consequences!), but the governor can no longer stitch together new sentences from two or more previous sentences.[47]

line-item veto: *Power given to some governors to veto parts of appropriations bills.*

omnibus bill: *One very large bill that encompasses many separate bills combined to help ensure passage.*

What would happen if the president had a line-item veto?

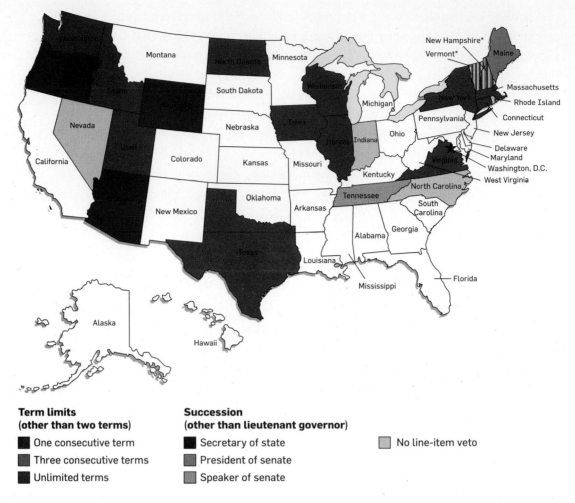

**Term limits
(other than two terms)**

■ One consecutive term

■ Three consecutive terms

■ Unlimited terms

**Succession
(other than lieutenant governor)**

■ Secretary of state

■ President of senate

■ Speaker of senate

□ No line-item veto

FIGURE 3.6 Exceptions to Typical Gubernatorial Authority.

Source: Council of State Governments, *The Book of the States.*

In addition to the line-item veto, some states grant governors special budgetary authority to limit spending. West Virginia's constitution does not allow the legislature to increase spending on any item over the amount proposed by the governor. New York's governor has sole authority over the language in spending bills. The legislature can increase or decrease the amounts, but it cannot add provisions excluded from the governor's budget, nor can it change formulas for distributing aid contained in spending bills.[48] Every state except Vermont requires a balanced budget. Unlike the federal government, which can borrow money to pay for spending programs, popular spending increases in the states typically have to be matched by typically unpopular tax increases. The governor generally seeks less spending than legislators, especially a governor who is facing a tough reelection campaign.[49]

On the legislative side, forty-nine of the fifty states have bicameral (two-chamber) legislative branches; Nebraska has only a single chamber. Nebraska also has nonpartisan elections, meaning that candidates for election are not listed under a party banner. Most states have four-year terms for their upper chambers and two-year terms for their lower chambers. Figure 3.7 presents the exceptions. While there are no term limits for members of Congress, fifteen states mandate term limits for state legislators, with limits ranging between six and twelve years. Such limits spread power more equally throughout government, preventing a given legislator from amassing too much power over time.

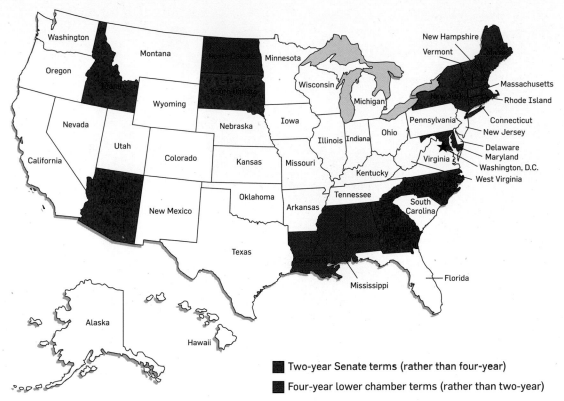

■ Two-year Senate terms (rather than four-year)

■ Four-year lower chamber terms (rather than two-year)

FIGURE 3.7 Exceptions to Typical State Legislature Terms.
Source: Council of State Governments, *The Book of the States.*

The greatest differences between the national and the state governments appear at the judicial level. Federal judges are nominated by the president and confirmed by the Senate. States have various procedures for selecting judges: nearly half use an appointment process for judges on their highest court, while the rest use elections (see Figure 3.8). For states that use appointments, most grant the governor the right to make appointments (usually with the consent of the state senate).

While federal judges serve during good behavior, which essentially means life terms, only Rhode Island does that at the state level, with Massachusetts and New Hampshire judges serving until age 70. In the rest of the states, judges have set terms. For example, in the widely copied **Missouri Plan** for selecting judges, also know as the merit plan, a board of experts recommends candidates to the governor, who selects judges from the list. The selected judges are then subject to **retention elections**: When a judge's term expires, voters get to vote yes or no on retaining the judge. Although judges overwhelmingly win retention elections, being unresponsive to voter preferences on important issues can cost them their seats. Such was the case when California voters rejected the retention of California Chief Justice Rose Bird and a majority of the judges of the California Supreme Court over their frequent votes against the death penalty. Because voters are more likely to be upset by judges who are too lenient—rather than too harsh—on criminals, many judges are more likely to approve death sentences or longer prison terms as their elections draw near.[50]

Election of state judges obviously means election campaigns. States have tried to prohibit judicial candidates from making campaign promises about how they would rule if

What effect do judicial elections have on judges' decisions? What effects should they have?

Missouri Plan: *Process for selecting state judges whereby the original nomination is by appointment and subsequent retention is by a retention election.*

retention election: *Election in which voters determine whether a state judge, originally appointed under a merit plan, should be retained in the state court system.*

Nonpartisan elections*

Partisan elections†

Missouri (Merit) Plan‡

Legislative election

Gubernatorial appointment††

Exceptions to fixed terms** and gubernatorial appointment††

*The ballot does not list the political party of the candidates.
†The ballot lists the political party of the candidates.
‡Some form of appointment to office followed by retention elections.

**Massachusetts and New Hampshire: until age 70; Rhode Island: "good behavior."
††Usually with consent of legislature.

FIGURE 3.8 Judicial Selection to State Supreme Courts.
Source: American Judicature Society, "Methods of Judicial Selection."

certain issues came before their court; the parties in such cases have a right to come before judges who have not committed to ruling a certain way before the trial or appeal has even started. The Supreme Court, however, ruled that the First Amendment's right to freedom of speech protects the right of judicial candidates, including their right to discuss their views on relevant issues.[51]

Judicial campaigns also mean campaign contributions, and these are most likely to come from people who might have business before the judges in question. In Texas, for example, where the state supreme court, like the U.S. Supreme Court, chooses whether to hear cases appealed to it, people who contributed to the campaigns of the justices of the supreme court were nine times more likely to have their cases heard than people who did not.[52] This situation arguably violates the common view of how the judiciary should run. As expressed in the judicial oath that federal judges take (state oaths vary), judges must "administer justice without respect to persons, and do equal right to the poor and to the rich." This type of "pay to play" gives substantial advantages to those who have money.

In West Virginia the president of a coal company appealing a $50 million jury verdict spent $3 million to defeat an incumbent state supreme court justice and elect a challenger who would be friendlier to the company. After the newly elected justice joined a 3–2 majority overturning the award, the U.S. Supreme Court declared that the state court justice could not rightfully participate in the case, given the risk of bias.[53] More of these cases will undoubtedly come before the federal courts. Generally, state courts can conduct their affairs free of federal court interference unless a federal law, a treaty, or the U.S. Constitution is under consideration. The broad terms in the Constitution and the broad scope of congressional lawmaking mean, however, that the Supreme Court often has the ability to review state court decisions.

Local Governments

Local governments are far more diverse in function and design than state governments. First, there can be several different layers of local governments, with residents regulated by villages, cities, and towns or townships at the most local level, and by counties above that. Some local governments run all local services, including police, schools, and sanitation. Many states, however, delegate specialized activities to special jurisdiction governments, such as school boards, water districts, fire districts, library districts, and sewer districts. Overall in the United States, there are tens of thousands of special jurisdiction governments and about five hundred thousand local elected officials, plus another one hundred thousand who serve on school boards.[54] These local governments provide a ready gateway for citizen involvement in public affairs.

Second, local governments, unlike state governments, do not necessarily consist of three separate branches. One reason is that criminal and civil trials are usually handled in state courts, leaving little need for a local community to have its own judicial branch. Many local governments have elected leaders of the executive branch—mayors for villages and cities, county executives for counties, and supervisors for townships—but many use a **city-manager system** in which the legislative branch appoints a professional administrator to run the executive branch.

The most distinctive form of local government in the United States is the **New England town meeting**, in which the adult population of the town meets at least once a year to adopt the budget and vote on any legislation being considered. While this gateway to civic involvement is open to all, only about 20 percent of eligible citizens show up at such meetings; as many as 70 percent show up in the smallest towns, but as few as 10 percent in the larger ones.[55] This form of direct democracy eliminates concerns about whether the policies pursued by the town legislators are responsive to the wishes of the people; the legislators are the people. But it can work only in small towns.

Direct Democracy

New England town meetings are not the only direct gateways to democracy in American federalism; recall, initiative, and referendum are other examples (see Figure 3.9). Recall allows citizens who gather enough petition signatures to force a special vote to remove state or

> What impact does your local government have on you?

> **city-manager system:** *Local government system in which the legislative branch hires a manager to run the executive branch.*

> Why are town meetings used primarily in New England?

> **New England town meeting:** *Local government arrangement used in some New England towns in which all adults act as the town council.*

local elected officials before their terms expire. Permitted in eighteen states, recall allowed California voters to remove unpopular Governor Gray Davis in 2003; voters then replaced him with actor Arnold Schwarzenegger in a special election. Initiative is a process that allows citizens who collect the required number of petition signatures to place proposed laws directly on the ballot for the state's citizens to vote on. Referendum allows legislatures to put certain issues on the ballot for citizen approval and requires legislatures to seek citizen approval for certain actions. Depending on the state, these actions could be proposals to borrow money, increase taxes, or approve constitutional amendments. All fifty states require referenda on some issues. Only twenty-four states allow initiatives.[56] Both procedures allow well-organized citizens to bypass the elected representatives in their state. The U.S. Constitution, in setting specific terms for senators, representatives, and presidents, prohibits recall of federal officials, and in granting all legislative powers to Congress, it similarly prohibits initiative and referendum at the national level.

The New England town meeting, like this one in Strong, Maine, is an example of direct democracy at the local level. New England town meetings allow residents to vote directly on budgets and taxes without the election of representatives as intermediaries.

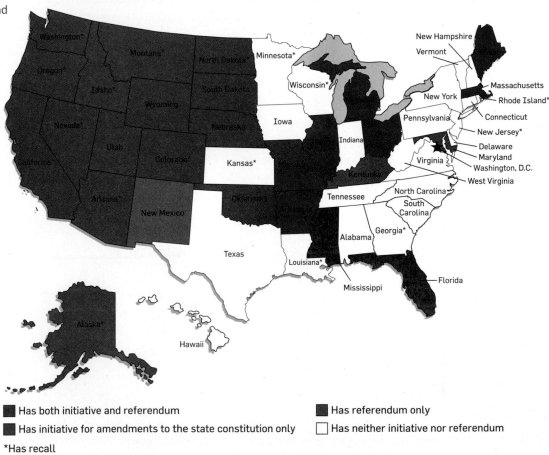

- ■ Has both initiative and referendum
- ■ Has initiative for amendments to the state constitution only
- ■ Has referendum only
- □ Has neither initiative nor referendum

*Has recall

FIGURE 3.9 States That Allow Recall, Initiative, and Referendum.
Source: Council of State Governments, *The Book of the States.*

The idea of the initiative came from admittedly radical groups that believed power in state legislatures was effectively in the hands of business and corporate interests. The Socialist Labor Party and the Populist Party of the 1890s were the first to endorse the initiative and referendum. South Dakota first established its initiative process in 1898, and other states eventually followed.

The number and importance of initiatives have grown in more recent years. California's Proposition 13 famously slashed property taxes in 1978. Ward Connerly, chair of the American Civil Rights Institute, has put initiatives banning **affirmative action** (the use of racial preferences in hiring and university admissions) on the ballot in California, Michigan, Colorado, and Nebraska, with bans passing in California, Michigan, and Nebraska (see Chapter 15, The Judiciary). In 2008 voters across the United States voted on fifty-nine initiatives, approving twenty-four of them, including bans on gay marriage in Arizona, California, and Florida.[57]

Direct democracy is not without its critics. As are other aspects of American government, initiatives are heavily influenced by money. Although socialists and populists originally pushed for direct democracy to expand the influence of ordinary citizens, the cost of gathering enough signatures to get on the ballot means that initiatives are limited largely to those with great financial resources. In 1998, for example, California Indian tribes spent $66 million in support of a successful California proposition that would allow them to expand casino gambling on Indian reservations. Fearful of losing business, Las Vegas casinos spent $26 million in opposition to the proposal. In the 2008 California vote banning gay marriage, contributions totaled over $72 million, with the money nearly evenly split between the supporters and opponents of the successful ban (see Figure 3.10).

The last time you voted, were there any initiatives or referenda on the ballot? Were you well enough informed about them to make a choice?

affirmative action: *Policies that grant racial or gender preferences in hiring, education, or contracting.*

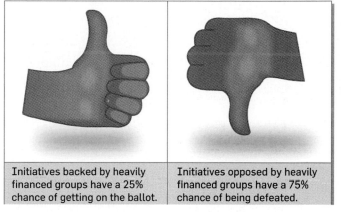

| Initiatives backed by heavily financed groups have a 25% chance of getting on the ballot. | Initiatives opposed by heavily financed groups have a 75% chance of being defeated. |

FIGURE 3.10 Initiative Spending. Large interest groups with abundant funds powerfully influence initiatives. Most initiatives have no chance of getting on the ballot, but money makes a difference. The influence of money in initiatives calls into question their reputation as direct democracy.
Source: Thomas E. Cronin, *Direct Democracy: The Politics of Initiative, Referendum, and Recall* (Cambridge, Mass.: Harvard University Press, 1989).

Federalism and Public Policy: Education

The structure of the federal system has a profound effect on public policy. It allows states to copy policies from one another but sometimes forces them into competition with one another. Many state policies involve issues in which the national government does not get involved, whereas in other areas, such as welfare policies, federal mandates and incentives push the states to do what the federal government wants. In this section, we examine education policy as an example.

Federal Aid to the States

Through the supremacy clause, Congress has the final say on many issues, but an **intergovernmental lobby**, made up of groups such as the National Governors Association (NGA), the National Conference of State Legislatures, and the National League of Cities, pressures Congress to limit mandates and provide funding for state and local needs.

intergovernmental lobby: *Set of lobbies that represent the interests of state and local governments.*

Federal aid to the states is influenced by a large number of factors, including equal representation in the Senate.[58] The fact that small states have the same number of senators as large states means that small states receive a disproportionate amount of federal aid. For example, in 2007 Wyoming and Alaska received the most aid per capita.[59] These states even get more antiterrorism aid per capita than do terrorist targets such as New York.[60] As the president is particularly responsive to the people and party who elected him, it is hardly surprising that states that heavily supported the incumbent president in the previous election, and states whose governors are of the same party as the president, get more federal aid than other states.[61]

Where does your state rank in the amount of federal aid it receives?

Policy Diffusion

In a 1932 opinion Supreme Court Justice Louis Brandeis wrote, "It is one of the happy incidents of the federal system that a single courageous State may, if its citizens choose, serve as a laboratory; and try novel social and economic experiments without risk to the rest of the country."[62] As far back as the Revolutionary era, New Jersey experimented with women's suffrage, as did several western states at the end of the nineteenth century. Nebraska has experimented with a unicameral legislature, Wisconsin experimented with an unemployment insurance program in the 1920s, and Oregon is currently experimenting with the nation's only physician-assisted suicide law. Perhaps, as occurred with a unicameral legislature, other states will reject physician-assisted suicide. Or perhaps, as with unemployment insurance, states or the federal government will see the benefits of such laws.

policy diffusion: *Process by which policy ideas and programs initiated by one state spread to other states.*

The main benefit of states serving as laboratories of change is that other states can learn about successful programs and copy them, or likewise learn what not to do if an experimental program fails. This takes place through a process known as **policy diffusion**, and it typically starts with states that border one another. Examples are numerous, including the Children's Health Insurance Program,[63] school choice plans (allowing students to choose which school in a district to attend),[64] health care reform,[65] and Indian gambling casinos.[66] States learn not only from neighboring states but also from their local governments. Such was the case with antismoking ordinances, which cities and towns successfully adopted before states did.[67]

The Race to the Bottom

race to the bottom: *Situation in which states compete with one another to lower protections and services below the level they might otherwise prefer.*

If diffusion is the good side of policy making in a federal system, the **race to the bottom** can, depending on one's point of view, potentially involve negative consequences. A race to the bottom exists when states compete against each other to reduce taxes, environmental protections, or welfare benefits in order to create incentives for businesses to come to the state or disincentives for poor people to come. For example, lower tax rates draw people to a state, yet to keep people there, the state cannot raise taxes even when the public might desire more spending.[68] When states are economic competitors with one another, if one state decreases environmental enforcement, a neighboring state may be forced to do so as well.[69] In terms of welfare benefits, individuals seeking benefits move to the most generous states. This situation led states to establish residency requirements for welfare. The Supreme Court, however, prohibits such residency requirements.[70] Consequently, states that want to increase welfare benefits for their own citizens hesitate to do so unless neighboring states also do so, lest they attract an overload of recipients from those other states.[71] Alternately, the Obama administration established a "race to the top" in education, whereby states that implement education reforms, such as increasing the number of charter schools, receive more federal aid. This action coincides with increasing federal involvement in education over the past fifty years.

Education Policy

The Founders considered an educated citizenry essential to the survival of the democracy. John Adams wrote that "Wherever a general knowledge and sensibility have prevailed among the people, arbitrary government and every kind of oppression have lessened and disappeared in proportion."[72] In other words, an educated people will be able to hold their leaders accountable and will pay attention to the overall responsiveness of their government.

Despite the fact that federally elected politicians talk frequently about the importance of education, the federal government itself funds only 8 percent of all elementary and secondary education spending.[73] The primary reason for this minimal funding is the federal structure. With education among the reserved powers left to the states, state and local governments developed the responsibility for educating the populace. Originally, states set education policy that local communities then implemented through locally elected school boards, or what one book called "ten thousand democracies."[74] Depending on the state, local school boards had differing amounts of power to establish the curriculum, support extracurricular activities, hire and fire teachers, negotiate salaries for school district employees, and set standards for graduation. Over time, funding for elementary and secondary education became based on local property taxes, with some additional assistance from state governments. Just as the overall wealth of local communities and states varies, so does the amount of funding available for education. As a result, there are vast disparities in the quality of education provided by elementary and secondary schools across the country. In addition, the legacy of racial segregation and other forms of discrimination has compounded regional inequalities in education.

Congress originally played almost no role in public school (K–12) education, but as with health care and many other areas, Congress's role increased after World War II. In 1944 Congress passed the GI Bill, which provided educational benefits for veterans. Then in 1958 it passed the National Defense Education Act, which provided grant money for increased math and science education in elementary and secondary schools. In 1965 it passed the Elementary and Secondary Education Act and the Higher Education Act.[75] Each of these programs widened the gateway of access to quality education by increasing federal responsibility to fund specific programs ranging from remedial reading and writing for elementary school children to subsidized loan programs for students in college and graduate school. Each of these programs is reauthorized by Congress about every five years, so Congress and the president have a chance to revise them according to changing needs.

Should the federal government make sure funding for public education is equal, with the same amount per child in every state?

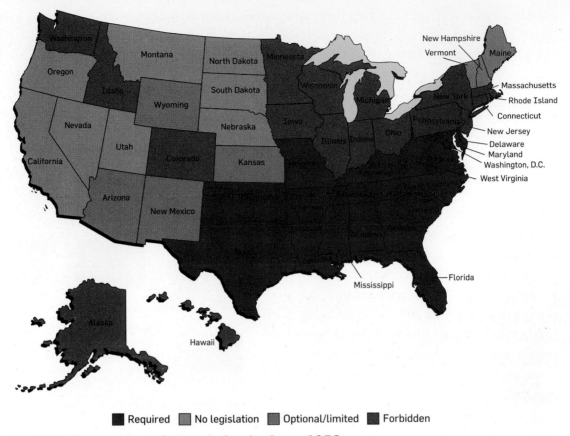

■ Required ■ No legislation ■ Optional/limited ■ Forbidden

FIGURE 3.11 School Segregation by Law, 1950.
Source: Gerald Rosenberg, *The Hollow Hope (*Chicago: University of Chicago Press, 1991), 42.

As with the general trends on federalism covered in this chapter, part of the initial impetus for federal regulation came because of the denial of equality of educational opportunity by the states. Many southern states and a few border states had separate education facilities for whites and blacks (see Figure 3.11). The practice was legitimized by the Supreme Court's 1896 decision in *Plessy v. Ferguson* upholding separate-but-equal railroad facilities for whites and blacks, although facilities for blacks were rarely equal, nor was the quality of education.[76] Even after the 1954 *Brown v. Board of Education* decision banning segregated schools, southern school districts were slow to desegregate, and one year later the Supreme Court ambiguously told schools to desegregate "with all deliberate speed," allowing desegregation to proceed (or not) based on local conditions.[77] This standard allowed local judges to rule that special conditions in their districts made desegregation impossible.

The Civil Rights Act of 1964 put Congress in the role of regulating education. Title IV of the act grants the attorney general the authority to file suits on behalf of the United States to end school segregation. Title VI prohibits schools that receive federal funds from discriminating on the basis of race. The act left enforcement to the Department of Health, Education, and Welfare (HEW; today there is a separate Department of Education). The importance of the funding provision increased when the Elementary and Secondary Education Act of 1965 vastly increased federal spending on education. This act gave HEW a powerful tool to fight segregation. According to one analysis of school desegregation, "Districts under HEW enforcement were significantly less segregated than court-ordered districts."[78]

Today the federal government has numerous programs to provide equal access to education across income level, race, and level of disability. These programs are under the jurisdiction of a variety of agencies. For example, the Department of Health and Human Services (HHS) oversees the Head Start and Early Head Start programs for low-income children, while the Department of Education has programs for homeless children and remedial education for disadvantaged children, and it also implements programs for children with disabilities under the

LUKE SHARRETT/The New York Times/Redux Pictures

On March 30, 2010, President Obama approved the Student Aid and Fiscal Responsibility Act at Northern Virginia Community College in Alexandria. He was introduced by Dr. Jill Biden, (far left), the vice president's wife, who teaches English on the campus. In her remarks, Biden said, "I have seen the power of community colleges to change lives and serve as a gateway to opportunity for students at all stages of their lives and careers."

Individuals with Disabilities Education Act (IDEA). All these programs serve those who have historically not had access to high-quality education because of low income or disability.[79] They remain the foundation of the federal role in education policy, albeit in different forms from the original programs. For example, most people know the Elementary and Secondary Education Act as No Child Left Behind, President George W. Bush's effort to revamp the program to impose stricter performance and accountability standards for education. One controversy related to this program is that the federal government mandated a number of changes for states and localities to implement without providing the federal funds necessary to accomplish these goals. President Barack Obama seeks to change the No Child Left Behind program by setting higher standards that will measure U.S. students against their peers worldwide but also to allow states and schools to have more flexibility in achieving goals.[80]

At the higher education level, a number of federally funded financial aid programs are available to undergraduate and graduate students. These programs include need-based grants, need-based loans, subsidized and unsubsidized loans, and work-study programs.[81] Under the previous loan system, the federal government contracted with banks and private lenders, which would then lend money to students, and the government paid the interest on loans while the students were in school. In March 2010 Congress passed the Student Aid and Fiscal Responsibility Act (SAFRA) as part of the Health Care and Education Reconciliation Act. SAFRA ended the federally guaranteed student loan program and created a new program that authorizes the federal government to do 100 percent of the lending for student loan programs directly.[82] The new arrangement means that students applying for loans now deal directly with the federal government instead of with banks. In addition, SAFRA increased spending for Pell Grants, increased funding for community colleges by $2 billion dollars over four years, and increased spending for historically black colleges.[83] SAFRA represents a major extension of the role of the federal government in financing higher education and in expanding equality of educational opportunity. Despite the stronger federal role, however, education under a federal system still permits inequality by allowing a vast disparity in how much states and local communities choose to spend on it.

Federalism and Democracy

A federal system has more gateways to influence than a confederal or unitary system. In confederal systems, citizens can influence their local governments, but there is little value in influencing the national government given its limited scope. Alternatively, in unitary systems, the national level has a lot of authority, but citizens cannot work their way through more localized structures to influence it. Although federal systems create multiple gateways to influence, they also make it less clear who is responsible if policies are not well run. If health care in Governor Jindal's Louisiana falters, for example, is that the fault of the national government or the state government?

FOCUS QUESTIONS

- How does federalism affect government's responsiveness? To what and to whom are federal systems accountable?

- What does it mean for citizen equality when different states are allowed to have different laws on certain subjects?

- How does a federal system make it easier for citizens to have an influence in government?

- What has been the relationship between federalism and the push for equality in the United States?

- Is federalism a gate or a gateway to democracy? Explain.

conformity costs: *Cost of democracy borne by people in the minority, who on one or more issues live under the rules set by the majority.*

Under a unitary system, there is little doubt who is responsible if a policy fails. A unitary system also means that diverse state laws would be replaced with one set of laws on issues such as medical marijuana, gay marriage, divorce, and gun control. Given that Americans have different views on these issues, the strength of a federal system is that it allows people in, say, Arizona, to live under laws created by other people in Arizona, rather than by people throughout the United States.

A unitary system also increases **conformity costs** by increasing the number of people who disagree with the policies of the government. These costs are not financial; they represent the dissatisfaction that people feel when they live under laws they do not like. Consider medical marijuana, for example. Under a unitary system, the nation would have a single set of medical marijuana laws. Either medical marijuana supporters or opponents would not get their way regardless of local public opinion. With federalism, each state gets to choose for itself whether to allow the use of medical marijuana. Federalism does not eliminate conformity costs, but it does lower them. Overall, federalism allows the people who live in the most conservative states to have local rules that favor conservative values, and those who live in the most liberal states to choose local rules that favor liberal values.

Citizens in states with conservative majorities can obtain conservative government by electing conservative representatives, and citizens in states with liberal majorities can elect liberal representatives. These citizens can also obtain results they desire through direct governing procedures such as the initiative and referendum. Although initiative procedures presumably provide for greater democratic responsiveness than does filtering preferences through elected representatives, initiatives may be too responsive to citizen desires. Madison, though not referring to the initiative itself, feared direct democracy, believing that citizens were prone to factions that would put self-interest over the best interests of society. Thus Madison and the Framers preferred a large-scale republic over local democracies, fearful that local majorities would infringe the rights of local minorities (see *Federalist* 10 in the Appendix). One disadvantage of federalism in the United States has been that people opposed to equality for blacks have used arguments about states' rights to protect slavery and limit civil rights. Alternatively, the nation-centric view of federalism has been used to create a more equal society for minorities subject to discrimination.

Overall, though, federalism enhances democracy by enabling more people to live under laws that are made locally, rather than forcing everyone in the nation to live under all of the same rules. State experiments with direct democracy procedures such as the initiative and referendum give citizens a gateway to influence that they do not have with the national government.

GATEWAYS TO LEARNING

Top Ten to Take Away

1. The American colonies joined together as a nation to pool their resources in fighting for their independence from Britain, but they also shared a common identity based on origin, history, and ancestry. (pp. 66–67)

2. In writing a new Constitution in 1787, the Framers established a new system of government—federalism—in which state and national governments share power. (pp. 67–69)

3. The Constitution grants specified powers to the national government, reserving all remaining powers to the states and to the people. It also limits both federal and state powers and lays out the relationships among the states and between the states and the federal government. (pp. 69–75)

4. The American system was an experiment, and its evolution has been shaped by the tensions, even conflicts, inherent in a system in which power is both divided and shared. From the beginning, nation- and state-centered interests have been pitted against each other. (pp. 75–76)

5. One recurring substantive theme in the federalism debate has involved slavery, race, and equality, with nation-centered federalism used generally to advance equality for minorities subject to discrimination. (pp. 78–79)

6. Over the years nation-centered federalism has generally expanded through legislation and court interpretation, though there have been eras in which the Court held Congress back and elections in which the people indicated that they thought the national government had too much power. (pp. 76–87)

7. All fifty states have separate legislative, executive, and judicial branches that look remarkably similar to those of the federal government, while local governments use a greater range of organizational options. (pp. 87–93)

8. The structure of the federal system has a profound effect on public policy, allowing states to learn from each other, but sometimes forcing them into competition with each other. (pp. 93–95)

9. The federal system also allows for vast disparities among the states, particularly in the quality of elementary and secondary education. (pp. 95–97)

10. Benefits of federalism include multiple gateways to influence, including methods of direct democracy such as the initiative and referendum. Federalism also enhances democracy by enabling more people to live under laws that are made locally, rather than forcing nationwide conformity. (pp. 98–99)

A full narrative summary of the chapter is on the book's website.

Ten to Test Yourself

1. What distinguishes confederal, unitary, and federal systems?
2. What are the advantages and disadvantages of each?
3. By what authority did Congress create a national bank?
4. What is nullification?
5. What are the different types of aid that Congress provides to the states?
6. What is the New Federalism?
7. How have states served as laboratories of change?
8. How do state governments differ from the federal government?
9. How do local governments differ from the federal and state governments?
10. Describe the concurrent powers over education.

More review questions and answers and chapter quizzes are on the book's website.

Timeline to Keep Things in Order

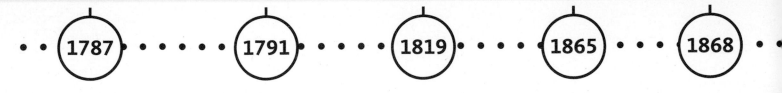

Constitution establishes a federal system of government; ratified 1788.	Tenth Amendment reserves powers not delegated to the United States to the states or to the people.	*McCulloch v. Maryland* broadens the scope of Congress's powers.	Union victory in the Civil War ends the threat of secession.	Fourteenth Amendment expands national authority over the states.
1787	**1791**	**1819**	**1865**	**1868**

Terms to Know and Use

affirmative action (p. 93)
block grants (p. 83)
broad construction (p. 78)
categorical grants (p. 83)
city-manager system (p. 91)
Civil Rights Act (p. 82)
Civil Rights Cases (p. 79)
commerce clause (p. 74)
concurrent powers (p. 71)
confederal system (p. 67)
conformity costs (p. 98)
Contract with America (p. 83)
Court-packing plan (p. 82)
devolution (p. 84)
direct democracy (p. 72)
Dred Scott v. Sandford (p. 79)
dual federalism (p. 80)

due process clause (p. 73)
enumerated powers (p. 69)
equal protection clause (p. 73)
federalism (p. 68)
fugitive slave clause (p. 78)
full faith and credit clause (p. 74)
general revenue sharing (p. 83)
Gibbons v. Ogden (p. 78)
guarantee clause (p. 72)
implied powers (p. 74)
initiative (p. 73)
intergovernmental lobby (p. 93)
Interstate Commerce
  Commission (p. 80)
line-item veto (p. 87)
mandates (p. 84)
McCulloch v. Maryland (p. 76)

Missouri Plan (p. 89)
nation (p. 67)
nation-centered federalism
  (p. 76)
necessary and proper clause
  (p. 71)
New England town meeting
  (p. 91)
New Federalism (p. 83)
nullification (p. 76)
omnibus bill (p. 87)
police powers (p. 71)
policy diffusion (p. 94)
preemption (p. 73)
Prigg v. Pennsylvania (p. 78)
privileges and immunities
  clause (p. 75)

race to the bottom (p. 94)
recall (p. 73)
referendum (p. 73)
reserve powers (p. 71)
retention election (p. 89)
secession (p. 78)
Sedition Act (p. 76)
self-government (p. 68)
sovereign immunity (p. 74)
state-centered federalism
  (p. 76)
states' rights (p. 76)
supremacy clause (p. 73)
unitary system (p. 68)
Voting Rights Act (p. 83)
writ of *habeas corpus* (p. 71)

Use the vocabulary flash cards on the book's website.

Learning That Works

WHAT YOU NEED . . .

TO KNOW

How federalism works

The way federal power has grown

The reasons state power has declined

The powers that states have

The scope of federal powers

The balance between federal and state
  powers

TO DO

Appreciate why you are a citizen of the nation and of a state

Evaluate whether the federal government is responsive or too powerful

Assess whether state governments are responsive or too narrow

Understand how it can be that in some areas citizens are not equal

Recognize the role of federal power in equality

Determine whether you should push the federal government to use its
  power to ensure equality of education

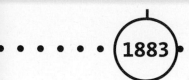

Civil Rights Cases limits
Congress's power under the
Fourteenth Amendment.

1883

New Deal legislation
expands Congress's
power to regulate the
economy.

1933-39

*Brown v. Board of
Education* strikes down
school segregation.

1954

Civil rights legislation
expands Congress's
power to regulate
society.

1964-65

Richard Nixon begins
shifting power back to
the states.

1969

4 CIVIL LIBERTIES

▲ **Theodore Roosevelt High School, Des Moines, Iowa**

> *It's not only important for citizens to stand up for what they believe in, but it makes life really interesting and meaningful.*

In November 1965 Mary Beth Tinker, age 13, listened intently to the stories she heard from her mother and older brother John on their return from a peace march in Washington, D.C. Her father was a Methodist minister "who put the values of love, brotherhood, and democracy into action," she later recalled, and "showed us that being a citizen-activist could be a good way of life." These family values, together with images of the Vietnam War on television—of "children and soldiers being burned and killed," Mary Beth said—convinced her and her brother that they should do something in Des Moines to continue to stand up for peace. With their friend Chris Eckhardt, who had also been at the Washington peace march, they decided to wear black armbands to school. As word of their planned protest got out, the school administrators banned the wearing of armbands, perhaps because they believed that the armbands would disrupt educational activities, or more likely because they opposed antiwar activities. As the school board president declared, "Our leaders have decided on a course of action and we should support them."

Despite the prohibition Mary Beth and Chris wore the armbands, leading the district to suspend them. The Iowa Civil Liberties Union, an interest group that supports civil rights and liberties, brought suit against the school board on behalf of the Tinkers and Eckhardt, claiming that students are equal to other Americans and retain freedom of speech rights granted by the First Amendment. The federal trial court ruled in favor of the school board, and the court of appeals upheld the trial court. The students then appealed to the Supreme Court, which agreed to hear their case, *Tinker v. Des Moines School District.*

Mary Beth Tinker and John Tinker

© Bettmann/CORBIS

Ikonix Studio

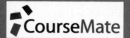
CourseMate

Visit http://www.cengagebrain.com/shop/ISBN/0618906959 for interactive tools including:

• Quizzes

• Flashcards

• Videos

• Animated PowerPoint slides, Podcast summaries, and more

At the Supreme Court, the Des Moines School Board claimed that it banned the armbands due to fear of disruption, but no disruption in fact occurred. Because the board allowed students to wear other political symbols, such as the German iron cross, the Supreme Court concluded that the board's main reason for opposing the armbands was the antiwar message they conveyed. This or other forms of "viewpoint discrimination" are not sufficient justification for limiting speech, declared the Court, creating a landmark decision guaranteeing First Amendment rights to students in schools. The Court ruled that the gates that keep unwanted intruders away from schools cannot also be used to keep out unwanted ideas: "It can hardly be argued that either students or teachers shed their constitutional rights to freedom of speech or expression at the schoolhouse gate."[1]

Today Mary Beth Tinker is a registered nurse, but she regularly gives invited lectures about freedom of speech, urging ordinary citizens like her to "speak up, shake things up and create change that makes the world a better place."[2] Students today have the right to express their viewpoints because of the Tinkers. They and their lawyers used the gateway of the courts to secure this right. In recent years, lower courts have upheld the right of a student to wear a T-shirt making fun of President George W. Bush, the right of a student to give a speech critical of homosexuality, and the right of students who wore black armbands—as had the Tinkers—to protest the school's dress code.[3]

Disagreements about politics, particularly in wartime, test people's willingness to tolerate differences in opinion. Even outside of wartime, the tension between liberty, the desire to say or do what one wants, and order, the need for rules necessary for society to function, divide society. Americans want their homes to be secure against police intrusions, but they also want the police to be able to find evidence of crimes committed by others. They want freedom to follow their personal religious beliefs, but they do not want illegal practices to be allowed just because one religion might endorse them. In this chapter, we examine the balance and tension between liberty and order, with particular attention to the liberties guaranteed in the U.S. Constitution.

FOCUS QUESTIONS

- What is government's role with regard to civil liberties? How responsive can or should it be to the people's will?

- What is the proper balance between liberty and order?

- Under what circumstances should civil liberties be restrained?

- What happens when rights clash? Are restrictions of civil liberties justified if they promote equality?

- In what ways does the guarantee of civil liberties promote democracy? Or does it pose challenges for democratic government that can be considered gates?

What Are Civil Liberties?

In 1787 the most powerful argument of the Antifederalists against the proposed constitution was that it did not protect fundamental liberties. The Antifederalist who wrote under the name Brutus declared that these liberties, including the rights of conscience and the right of accused criminals to hear the charges against them, needed to be explicitly stated.[4] As we saw in Chapter 2, the Federalists eventually agreed and, to secure ratification of the Constitution, promised to amend it immediately.

Civil Liberties and Civil Rights

The **civil liberties** that were then written into the Constitution as the first ten amendments, or **Bill of Rights**, were freedoms that Americans held to be so fundamental that government may not legitimately take them away. This placed into law some of the **natural** or **unalienable rights** that Jefferson spoke about in the Declaration of Independence. These include, among others, freedom of speech and religious belief. As Supreme Court Justice Robert Jackson wrote in 1943, in a case striking down a state requirement that children salute the flag in school, "If there is any fixed star in our constitutional constellation, it is that no official, high or petty, can prescribe what shall be orthodox in politics, nationalism, religion, or other matters of opinion or force citizens to confess by word or act their faith therein."[5] By this, Jackson meant that the Constitution prohibits the government from interfering in what individuals say or think. Civil liberties are outside government's authority, whereas **civil rights** are rights that government is obliged to protect. These are based on the expectation of equality under the law and relate to the duties of citizenship and to opportunities for full participation in civic life (see Figure 4.1). They are the subject of the next chapter.

Balancing Liberty and Order

The protection of civil liberties requires a governmental system designed to do so. James Madison noted in *Federalist* 10 (see the Appendix) that a representative democracy will be able to keep a minority from abridging the rights of others but may not be able to hold back a majority. Yet civil liberties, by their very nature, are so basic that they cannot be taken away regardless of whether it is a minority or a majority that might wish to do so. Thus if a majority wishes to abridge rights, it often falls to the judiciary, which is not designed to be responsive to public desires, to protect those rights. During debate in the First Congress over the proposed bill of rights to the Constitution, Madison, then a representative from Virginia, argued that if the bill of rights were approved, the judiciary would consider itself the special guardians of those rights and would naturally resist any effort by the legislative or executive branches to limit them.[6] Thus the system of separation of powers and of checks and balances would help ensure the rights of all.

civil liberties: *Those rights, such as freedom of speech and religion, that are so fundamental that they are outside the authority of government to regulate.*

Bill of Rights: *First ten amendments to the Constitution, which provide basic political rights.*

natural (unalienable) rights: *Rights that every individual has and that government cannot legitimately take away.*

civil rights: *Set of rights centered around the concept of equal treatment that government is obliged to protect.*

What freedoms do you have as an American citizen that government cannot take away?

Civil liberties   Civil rights

FIGURE 4.1 Distinction between Civil Liberties and Civil Rights. Civil liberties provide a gate or barrier that protects people against interference by the government in fundamental liberties, such as freedom of speech or religion. Civil rights often require active involvement of the government in opening gateways to full civic participation by all, regardless of race, gender, or religion.

While maximizing individual liberty might seem like a great idea, complete liberty could lead to a breakdown of order. As Supreme Court Justice Oliver Wendell Holmes wrote in a World War I speech case, *Schenck v. United States*, freedom of speech does not mean that an individual has the right to falsely shout "Fire!" in a crowded theater, and cause a panic.[7] Nor can liberty completely protect people from police investigations when criminal activity is suspected. Too much freedom can lead to **anarchy**, a state in which everyone does as he or she chooses without regard to others. Alternatively, too much order can lead to **tyranny**, a state in which the people are not free to make decisions about the private aspects of their lives. Protecting civil liberties thus requires a balance between individual liberty and public order.

The freedom obtained through civil liberties can conflict not only with order, but with equality as well. In fact, civil liberties and civil rights sometimes conflict with each other. As we shall see in Chapter 5, government's attempts to ensure the equality of some people can limit the freedoms of others. For example, civil rights laws that forbid businesses to refuse to serve customers because of their race limit freedom of association and infringe on property rights. Efforts at colleges to create an equal environment for all students have led to speech codes that restrict what students can say on campus. Society must decide how to strike such balances, and often that decision is a difficult one. In the case of businesses serving all customers, the nation, through its elected representatives in Congress, decided that the restriction on liberty was well worth the gain in equality. In the case of campus speech codes, students have successfully pressured many universities to rescind speech codes, and where the universities have kept the codes, students have used the gateway of the judicial system to bring lawsuits against their schools. The courts have consistently ruled that speech codes violate the First Amendment.

Constitutional Rights

The main sources of civil liberties are the Constitution and the Bill of Rights. The Constitution protects the right of *habeas corpus*, the right of individuals to be brought before a judge to have the legality of their imprisonment determined. It also prohibits *ex post facto* **laws**, which make an act a crime after the act is committed, and **bills of attainder**, legislative acts that declare individuals guilty of a crime. The Constitution also guarantees the right to a trial by jury.

The Bill of Rights, ratified in 1791, protects various rights surrounding freedom of expression and criminal procedure, plus a few additional rights (see Figure 4.2). The expression-based freedoms are included in the First Amendment; they are freedom of speech, freedom of the press, freedom of assembly, freedom to petition the government, and the free exercise of religion. The criminal justice provisions of the Bill of Rights protect individuals accused of crimes by directing how the government may investigate crimes (Fourth and Fifth Amendments), conduct trials (Fifth and Sixth Amendments), and punish those convicted (Eighth Amendment). The Fifth Amendment also protects certain economic and property rights: individuals cannot be deprived of their property without due process of law, and if the government takes private property for public purposes, such as to build a highway or park, it must provide just compensation. The Second Amendment protects a very particular property right: the right to keep and bear arms. Finally, starting in the 1960s the Supreme Court has interpreted the Ninth Amendment to include a very general right, the right to privacy.

anarchy: *State of society without governmental authority in which people do as they please.*

tyranny: *Government that severely limits liberty.*

Which is more important to you, liberty or order?

Which is more important to you, liberty or equality?

writ of *habeas corpus*: *Right of individuals who have been arrested and jailed to go before a judge, who determines whether their detention is legal.*

***ex post facto* laws:** *Laws that make an act a crime after the act is committed.*

bills of attainder: *Legislative acts that declare individuals guilty of a crime.*

FIGURE 4.2 Constitutional Amendments That Pertain to Civil Liberties.

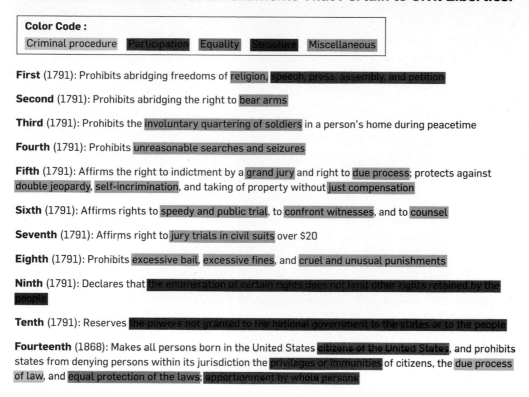

Color Code:

Criminal procedure   Participation   Equality   Structure   Miscellaneous

First (1791): Prohibits abridging freedoms of religion, speech, press, assembly, and petition

Second (1791): Prohibits abridging the right to bear arms

Third (1791): Prohibits the involuntary quartering of soldiers in a person's home during peacetime

Fourth (1791): Prohibits unreasonable searches and seizures

Fifth (1791): Affirms the right to indictment by a grand jury and right to due process; protects against double jeopardy, self-incrimination, and taking of property without just compensation

Sixth (1791): Affirms rights to speedy and public trial, to confront witnesses, and to counsel

Seventh (1791): Affirms right to jury trials in civil suits over $20

Eighth (1791): Prohibits excessive bail, excessive fines, and cruel and unusual punishments

Ninth (1791): Declares that the enumeration of certain rights does not limit other rights retained by the people

Tenth (1791): Reserves the powers not granted to the national government to the states or to the people

Fourteenth (1868): Makes all persons born in the United States citizens of the United States, and prohibits states from denying persons within its jurisdiction the privileges or immunities of citizens, the due process of law, and equal protection of the laws; apportionment by whole persons

The Bill of Rights and the States

As originally written, the Bill of Rights limited the activities of the national government, not the state governments. Only at the end of the nineteenth century did the Supreme Court slowly begin to apply, or **incorporate**, the provisions of the Bill of Rights to the states.

The First Amendment is explicit about its application to the national government as it forbids certain actions by Congress. But other amendments are not explicitly tied to the national government. Thus the Fifth Amendment prohibits taking private property without just compensation. Was this a protection of citizens only against actions by the federal government, or against their state governments as well?

The original answer, given by the Supreme Court in ***Barron v. Baltimore*** (1833), was that the Bill of Rights applied to the national government only. Under the *Barron* decision, state governments could abridge freedom of speech, the press, and religion, could conduct unreasonable searches and seizures, and more without violating the Constitution. State constitutions might protect such rights, but often they did not. During World War I one citizen of Minnesota was convicted and sentenced to prison for stating that the war was a plot to protect Wall Street investments, another for stating that America needed to be made more democratic.[8] And in 1920, when a Montana farmer spoke ill of the American flag and refused to kiss it, he was sentenced to ten to twenty years of hard labor for violating a state law that prohibited bringing the flag into disrepute.[9]

The potential for the application of the Bill of Rights to the states began with the passage of the Fourteenth Amendment (1868), which adds several restrictions on what the states can do. One section declares, "No State shall make or enforce any law which shall abridge the privileges or immunities of citizens of the United States; nor shall any State deprive any

incorporate: *Process of applying provisions of the Bill of Rights to the states.*

Which government are citizens more likely to need a gate against—national or state?

Barron v. Baltimore: *1833 Supreme Court decision declaring that the Bill of Rights was not binding on the states, slowly reversed in the twentieth century.*

What laws, if any, should protect the American flag?

AP Photo/The Salt Lake Tribune, Scott Sommerdorf

person of life, liberty, or property, without due process of law." Some of those who wrote this amendment stated that one of its purposes was to overturn the *Barron v. Baltimore* decision and make the entire Bill of Rights applicable to the states.[10]

The Supreme Court never agreed with this position, known as **total incorporation**. But beginning in 1897 it slowly began to use the protection of "life, liberty, or property" in the Fourteenth Amendment's **due process clause** to incorporate some of the provisions of the Bill of Rights as binding on the states. In the 1897 case the Court used this clause to hold that states could not deprive a railroad of its property without just compensation, a right similarly protected by the Fifth Amendment.[11] In 1925 the Court assumed that the protection of liberty in the due process clause prevented states from abridging freedom of speech, a right similarly protected by the First Amendment.[12] By 1937 the Court had settled on a process of **selective incorporation**, using the due process clause to bind the states to those provisions of the Bill of Rights that it deems to be **fundamental rights**.[13] This process helps equalize the protection of rights across the United States.

Today, almost all of the provisions of the First, Second, Fourth, Fifth, Sixth, and Eighth Amendments have been incorporated, with the exception of grand jury indictment and excessive bail (see Table 4.1). Thus, states can indict people, or bring them up on charges, through the decision of judges, though charges in federal courts need the approval of a **grand jury**, a special jury whose sole duty is to determine whether an individual should be put on trial. The Third Amendment's protection against the quartering of soldiers in one's home during peacetime, a practice that angered the colonists, has not been incorporated but is not likely to be used today. Nor are states required, as the Seventh Amendment commands, to provide jury trials in civil suits over $20.

The fact that a right has been incorporated does not answer how the Court will determine whether that right has been violated. Generally speaking, rather than rule on each case purely on its own, the Court adopts a **test** to guide its decision and applies the test to the case at hand to determine whether a particular limitation of rights is acceptable. For the political rights in the Bill of Rights, such as freedom of speech, the Court most commonly uses variations of the **compelling interest test**. Under the compelling interest test, the federal government or a state can limit rights only if the Supreme Court decides that (1) the government has a compelling interest in passing the law (for example, the law is necessary for the functioning of government), and (2) the law is narrowly drawn to meet that interest.

Recent Tea Party protesters have adopted a flag bearing a coiled snake and the slogan "Don't Tread on Me" that was first used by patriots during the Revolutionary War. Here Tea Party activists rally outside the state capitol in Salt Lake City, Utah, on "tax day"— April 15, 2010—to signal their opposition to high taxes and high government debt.

total incorporation: *View, rejected by the Supreme Court, that the Fourteenth Amendment makes all of the provisions of the Bill of Rights binding on the states.*

due process clause: *Prevents the federal government (Fifth Amendment) and the state governments (Fourteenth Amendment) from denying any person due process of law.*

selective incorporation: *Doctrine used by the Supreme Court to make those provisions of the Bill of Rights that are fundamental rights binding on the states.*

TABLE 4.1 Incorporated and Not Incorporated Provisions of the First through Eighth Amendments

Amendment	Incorporated Provisions	Provisions Not Incorporated
First	Religion, speech, press, assembly, petition	
Second	Keep and bear arms	
Third		Quarter soldiers
Fourth	No unreasonable searches and seizures	
Fifth	Double jeopardy, self-incrimination, due process, taking of property without just compensation	Grand jury indictment
Sixth	Speedy and public trial, right to confront witnesses, right to counsel	
Seventh		Jury trials in civil suits over $20
Eighth	Cruel and unusual punishments, excessive fines	Excessive bail

In the *Tinker* case, the Des Moines School Board did not convince the Court that there was sufficient justification for suppression of nondisruptive speech, even during wartime. The extent of these and other rights have been fought over throughout American history.

Civil Liberties in Times of Crisis

In some regard, the effort to censor the Tinkers fits a pattern in American politics: Attempts to limit civil liberties are more frequent in wartime or during other threats, given the government's increased concern for order and citizens' increased concerns about security. This pattern has existed from the earliest days of the republic; it continued during the Civil War, the two world wars, and the Cold War, and following the terrorist attacks of September 11, 2001. Popular support for civil liberties usually rebounds once the crisis ends.

From Revolution to Civil War

In the aftermath of the 1789 French Revolution, while Britain and France were at war, the United States engaged in a limited and undeclared war with France over trade issues. In 1798, as part of the war effort, the Federalist-dominated Congress passed the **Sedition Act**, which, among other things, made it illegal to "write, print, utter, or publish" any "false, scandalous, and malicious writing" about the federal government, either house of Congress, or the president. The Federalist administration of John Adams (1797–1801) used the act to try opposition (Democratic-Republican) officeholders and newspaper owners, and lower courts upheld

fundamental rights: *Those rights deemed by the Court to be essential to liberty.*

grand jury: *Special jury charged with determining whether people should be put on trial.*

test: *Standard used by courts to determine whether a law or a right has been violated across a range of cases.*

compelling interest test: *Standard frequently used by the Supreme Court in civil liberties cases to determine whether a state has a compelling interest for infringing on a right and whether the law is narrowly drawn to meet that interest.*

Sedition Acts: *Laws passed in 1798 and 1918 (and later repealed) that made criticizing the government a crime.*

What civil liberties are you willing to give up to ensure more protection against terrorist attacks?

the act against claims that the convictions violated the freedoms of speech and press as guaranteed by the First Amendment. When Thomas Jefferson (1801–1809) and the Democratic-Republicans took power following the election of 1800, they pardoned those convicted under the act, which had by then expired, and refunded the fines they had paid.

During the Civil War, President Abraham Lincoln (1861–65) suspended the writ of *habeas corpus*, thus allowing southern sympathizers in border states—slave states located between the North and South that did not secede from the Union—to be tried by **military tribunals** rather than by civilian courts. Military tribunals contain fewer procedural safeguards for defendants than do criminal trials, with a two-thirds vote rather than unanimity required for conviction, lesser standards of evidence, and no *habeas corpus* protections. Given the threat the Civil War posed to the United States, Lincoln thought that a restriction on *habeas corpus* was justified. He famously asked, "Are all the laws but one to go unexecuted and the Government itself go to pieces lest that one be violated?"[14] Because the authority to suspend *habeas corpus* presumably rests with Congress, Congress subsequently affirmed Lincoln's order. Later, Lambdin Milligan, a civilian, was accused of aiding the Confederacy and was sentenced to hang by a military tribunal in Indiana. Because civilian courts were operating in Indiana, the Court declared in 1866 (after the war and the threat of secession ended) that the government had no authority to deprive Milligan of his right to a trial by jury.[15]

In 1868 the Supreme Court prepared to hear the appeal of journalist William McCardle, a former Confederate soldier who had been convicted of writing "incendiary and libelous articles" about the war. The pro-Union Congress, angry about the *Milligan* decision and concerned about the *McCardle* case, removed the Supreme Court's appellate jurisdiction over *habeas* petitions. As the Constitution explicitly grants Congress the authority to regulate the Court's appellate jurisdiction, the Court, backing away from a confrontation with Congress, dismissed McCardle's appeal.[16]

The World Wars

During World War I Congress passed the Espionage Act of 1917, which made it a crime to obstruct military recruiting, and amendments known as the Sedition Act of 1918, which banned "disloyal, profane, scurrilous or abusive language" about the Constitution or the government of the United States, as well as speech that interfered with the war effort. Subsequently, juries convicted antiwar activist Charles Schenck for circulating a flyer to draftees that compared the draft to the involuntary servitude prohibited by the Thirteenth Amendment, and Socialist presidential candidate Eugene V. Debs for giving a speech criticizing the war. The Supreme Court upheld both convictions, noting that greater restrictions on speech could be allowed in wartime.[17] The Court also upheld the conviction of Jacob Abrams, an anarchist and immigrant from Russia who had dropped leaflets in Yiddish and English from his New York City tenement calling for a strike to protest sending American troops into Russia.[18] Russia, engulfed by the Communist revolution, had withdrawn from the war, and the United States had sent troops to aid anti-Communist forces. In a forceful dissent, Justice Oliver Wendell Holmes, who had written the opinion of the Court in the *Schenck* and *Debs* cases, voted this time to overturn the conviction, arguing that the First Amendment protected the **marketplace of ideas**. Under this concept, the best test of the validity of an argument, similar to the best test of the value of a commercial product, is to put it forth to see if people accept it.

military tribunal: *Specially created court that determines the innocence or guilt of enemy combatants.*

How free should you be to criticize the government? Should you be less free in wartime? Following 9/11?

marketplace of ideas: *Idea that the government should not restrict the expression of ideas because the people are capable of accepting good ideas and rejecting bad ones.*

Can you trust the people to decide whether an idea has merit? Do good ideas survive and bad ideas fade away?

After the war Congress repealed the Sedition Act and President Warren G. Harding (1921–23) pardoned Debs. The government also released Abrams from prison but deported him to Russia. Fears that Communism would spread to the United States had led to a crackdown on socialists, Communists, and other radicals. This **Red Scare** peaked after radicals exploded eight bombs, including one at the house of U.S. Attorney General A. Mitchell Palmer. Following the bombings, the government arrested thousands of Americans, some merely for their speech or associations.[19] Given the atmosphere of fear, the *Washington Post* declared "There is no time to waste on hairsplitting over infringement of liberty."[20] But when Palmer's warning that radicals would attempt to overthrow the government on May 1, 1920, proved incorrect, the scare began to subside. In no subsequent wars has the government restricted speech as it did with the Sedition Acts of 1798 and 1918.

Other liberties, however, continue to be restricted during wartime. One event during World War II raised the question of procedural rights for enemy combatants, an issue that is also relevant in the post–September 11 world. In the summer of 1942 teams of German saboteurs landed at Amagansett, New York, and Ponte Vedra, Florida. President Franklin Delano Roosevelt (1933–45) ordered that they be tried by military tribunals rather than in criminal courts. The accused saboteurs nevertheless filed *habeas corpus* petitions. The Supreme Court agreed to review the case, but according to Justice Owen Roberts, Roosevelt's attorney general told him before the Supreme Court hearing that, with the nation at war, Roosevelt planned to have the saboteurs executed no matter what the Court ruled.[21] The Supreme Court eventually denied the *habeas* petitions, and the government eventually executed several of the saboteurs. Unlike antiwar speech, where views soften after the crisis has passed, invasions of and planned attacks on American soil generally do not meet with later forgiveness.

The Cold War and Vietnam

The fear of Communism that had led to a suppression of civil liberties following World War I recurred following World War II. As the Soviet Union installed Communist dictatorships throughout eastern Europe, Americans worried that Communism would spread further. Though the United States never fought the Soviet Union directly during this period, frosty relations led to the so-called Cold War.

With allegations, convictions, and at least one confession that Communist spies in the United States gave the Soviets secrets about how to build atomic bombs,[22] Senator Joseph McCarthy (R-Wis.) began indiscriminately charging Americans with being "card-carrying" members of Communist organizations or with being sympathetic "fellow travelers" of such groups. The **McCarthy era** was similar to the Red Scare in its agitated suspicion that opposition to the government was Communist-inspired. Congress banned the Communist Party and membership therein, and held hearings investigating individual citizens' political views and personal associations. Hollywood studios began **blacklisting** screenwriters with left-wing sympathies, while state governments and school districts fired teachers and other state

Speaking in Canton, Ohio, on June 16, 1918, Eugene V. Debs, labor organizer and three-time Socialist candidate for president, criticized the government for restricting free speech during wartime and declared, "If war is right let it be declared by the people." Charged with sedition, he was convicted and sentenced to prison. While in jail, he ran for president once again and received more than 900,000 votes about 3.4 percent of all votes cast.

Red Scare: *Period following World War I during which a fear of domestic radicals led to infringements on liberty.*

Should enemy combatants have the same procedural safeguards as American citizens? What if the enemy combatant is an American citizen?

McCarthy era: *Period following World War II during which a fear of domestic Communists lead to infringements on liberty.*

blacklisting: *Act of denying people work because of their political views.*

Should government imprison people for their political views? Or should views, such as belief in Communism, be allowed to be tested in the marketplace of ideas?

workers suspected of such beliefs. The Supreme Court originally set strict limits on these investigations,[23] but following the introduction of several bills that would have limited its authority, the Court backed down and accepted them.[24]

During the McCarthy era, the government imprisoned hundreds of individuals for their political views, and thousands more lost their jobs.[25] McCarthy himself began losing support before his movement did. During the televised 1954 Army-McCarthy hearings over alleged Communist infiltration of the Army, Americans witnessed the recklessness with which McCarthy attacked people's reputations. Edward R. Murrow, host of the TV program *See It Now*, produced a special show on McCarthy using McCarthy's own speeches to demonstrate the extent to which he had been dishonest in his charges. The public reacted overwhelmingly favorably to Murrow's broadcast. A free press—in this case, television—allowed the marketplace of ideas to flourish and led to McCarthy's downfall. In December 1954 the Senate voted 67–22 to censure McCarthy.

But suspicion of people who criticized the government rose again during the Vietnam War. In the mid-1960s **COINTELPRO**, the counterintelligence program of the Federal Bureau of Investigation (FBI), infiltrated and disrupted groups that expressed opposition to mainline American policies, including antiwar, civil rights, left-wing, and white supremacy groups. Later, a Senate investigation into the legality of COINTELPRO revealed that the FBI's activities had included illegal wiretapping, inciting violence, and encouraging Internal Revenue Service audits of suspects. The FBI had targeted even nonviolent antiwar organizations because of a potential for violence, and nonviolent citizens who opposed the war because "they gave 'aid and comfort' to violent demonstrators by lending respectability to their cause."[26] Congress reacted by putting restrictions on surveillance of political organizations, including limits on the sharing of information between the Central Intelligence Agency (CIA) and the FBI.

Senator Joseph McCarthy gave his name to an era noted for fear of Communism and the use of fear tactics to suppress freedom of speech and belief. Here, during the 1954 Army-McCarthy hearings, he testifies on Communist Party organizations in the United States with the aid of a huge map. His dishonesty and abusive treatment of witnesses during these hearings turned both the Senate and the public against him.

COINTELPRO: *Counterintelligence program of the FBI designed to disrupt domestic political groups that favored civil rights or opposed the war in Vietnam.*

Should government have access to your phone calls and e-mail messages?

The War on Terror

After the terrorist attacks of September 11, 2001, Congress passed the USA PATRIOT Act, which overturned many of the COINTELPRO reforms, blamed by some for intelligence failures prior to the attacks. The act allowed greater sharing of intelligence information and enhancement of law enforcement's ability to tap telephone and e-mail communications. It also regulated financial transactions with overseas entities and eased the process of deporting immigrants suspected of terrorist activities. Beyond the act, President George W. Bush (2001–2009) claimed the right, as commander in chief, to indefinitely detain alleged enemy combatants, whether U.S. citizens or foreign nationals. Thus Bush declared Jose Padilla, an American allegedly involved in a plan to detonate a radioactive bomb in the United States, an "enemy combatant" and transferred him from civilian to military authority, where he would have few, if any, procedural rights. The government kept Padilla in complete isolation for more than three and a half years. Unique among those declared enemy combatants, Padilla had not been captured on the field of battle but on American soil, and, having been born in Brooklyn, he was an American citizen. Thus his claims of procedural legal protections were stronger than those of two other American citizens, Yaser Hamdi and John Walker Lindh, who were captured while allegedly fighting American forces in Afghanistan, and of the thousands of foreigners captured during the war in Afghanistan.

In June 2004, when the Supreme Court ruled that Hamdi could not be held indefinitely as an enemy combatant, it became clear that Padilla could not either. So, in November 2005 the Justice Department removed Padilla from military custody and charged him under federal criminal law with providing material support to terrorist organizations. The government did not charge him with attempting to detonate a radioactive bomb in the United States or with conspiring to commit terrorist acts in the United States, suggesting that the original claims against him might not have held up in a court of law. His trial in Miami, with the full set of constitutional rights, required that Padilla be represented by counsel, that he be allowed to cross-examine witnesses, and that the government prove its case beyond a reasonable doubt. The government proved its case, and a jury quickly determined that Padilla was guilty of conspiring to kill people overseas. The judge then sentenced him to seventeen years in prison.

Although fewer rights exist for enemy combatants who are not U.S. citizens,[27] the Supreme Court has ruled that Congress must authorize hearings to determine the legality of the detention of even foreign enemy combatants. Such hearings must be consistent with the 1949 **Geneva Conventions**, an international treaty that protects the rights of prisoners of war (see Chapter 16, The United States as a Global Partner).[28]

Beyond the enemy combatant cases, President Bush ordered warrantless wiretapping of conversations and interception of e-mail between American citizens and suspected foreign terrorists; normally, wiretapping requires a **warrant** signed by a judge or magistrate backed by **probable cause** that a crime is being committed. No court decisions exist on the wiretapping, though Congress did endorse aspects of the president's plan after the *New York Times* published stories about the then-secret program. The Obama administration has not made public a decision to continue or discontinue the program, but in 2009 it moved on national security grounds to block a lawsuit over the wiretapping.[29] The executive branch, with the most direct responsibility over national security, is more likely to support restrictions on civil liberties during times of crisis than is either the legislative or judicial branch.

Civil Liberties and American Values

As these examples have demonstrated, in times of crisis Congress and the president limit civil liberties to secure order, often with public support. The courts, however, being less responsive to public pressure, can push back against these efforts. Thus, the courts forced the government to try Padilla in civilian courts, knowing that if the evidence fell short of the "guilty beyond a reasonable doubt" standard required for conviction, an alleged terrorist could have been freed. The courts have also blocked efforts to censor newspapers even when the government has believed that the publication of certain reports would benefit wartime enemies. Nevertheless, in wartime or other times of crisis, concerns about order are at their highest, and protections for civil liberties by national and state governments

Are alleged terrorists enemy combatants?

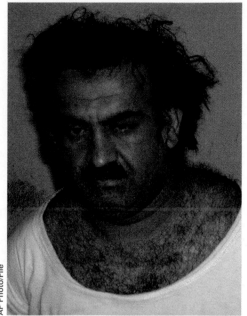

AP Photo/File

This widely circulated photograph of Khalid Sheikh Mohammed was taken on March 1, 2003, shortly after his capture during a raid in Pakistan. He is accused of masterminding the September 11, 2001, terrorist attacks on the United States and is being held at Guantanamo Bay, Cuba, awaiting trial.

Geneva Conventions: *Set of treaties that define lawful military combat and protect the rights of prisoners of war.*

Should the United States obey the Geneva Conventions?

warrant: *Legal document authorizing a search or a seizure.*

probable cause: *Determination by a neutral official that specific evidence is likely to be found in a place to be searched, or that an individual to be seized has likely committed a crime.*

typically decline. Following the emergency, a political culture that favors freedom means that public support for civil liberties, as well as the government's protections of those liberties, generally rebounds.

The First Amendment and Freedom of Expression

The civil liberties most at risk during times of crisis are those protected by the First Amendment—freedom of speech, freedom of the press, and freedom of association. In this section, we examine each of these freedoms of expression individually. Their scope has expanded over time, despite occasional ratcheting back during wartime.

Freedom of Speech

While the First Amendment declares that "Congress shall make no law . . . abridging the freedom of speech," the Court has never taken the phrase "no law" literally. Prohibitions on speech once included blasphemy (inappropriate references to God) and defamation (speaking ill of others). States have since rescinded such laws, either legislatively or judicially. Today the Court allows limits on advocacy of unlawful activities, the use of fighting words, symbolic speech, and campaign spending.

clear and present danger test: *First Amendment test that requires the state to prove that there is a high likelihood that the speech in question would lead to a danger that Congress has a right to prevent.*

Brandenburg v. Ohio: *1969 Supreme Court decision requiring imminent lawless action before speech can be banned.*

Given terrorist attacks against the United States, should the government have to wait until violence is imminent (about to happen) before criminalizing advocacy of violence?

fighting words doctrine: *Doctrine allowing speech to be banned if the likely response would be a punch.*

How can you distinguish between fighting words and hate speech?

hate speech: *Speech that attacks or demeans a group, rather than a particular individual.*

Advocacy of Unlawful Activities.   When Justice Holmes wrote in the opinion in the case of Charles Schenck that free speech does not mean that a person can falsely shout fire in a theater, he went on to explain that words spoken in wartime may have a different impact than they would in peacetime. "The question in every case," he continued, "is whether the words used are used in such circumstances and are of such a nature as to create a clear and present danger that they will bring about the substantive evils that Congress has a right to prevent." From this statement, the Court adopted the **clear and present danger test**. The Court shifted standards in subsequent decades, at one point allowing states to limit speech that merely had a tendency to cause unlawful acts. But in 1969 the Court moved back toward a stricter protection of civil liberties, ruling in **Brandenburg v. Ohio** (see Supreme Court Cases) that speech cannot be banned unless it leads to "imminent lawless action."

Fighting Words and Hate Speech.   Besides speech that imminently incites unlawful activities, the Supreme Court also allows restrictions on the basis of the **fighting words doctrine**. "Fighting words" are phrases that might lead the individual to whom they are directed to respond with a punch. Today, hateful racial epithets are the leading examples of fighting words, but when the Supreme Court first developed the doctrine, many milder types of words offended people. Thus, in 1942 the Court used the fighting words doctrine to uphold the conviction of a defendant for calling a town marshal a "God-damned racketeer" and a "damned Fascist."[30]

Related to fighting words is **hate speech**, which attacks or demeans a group rather than a particular individual. Over the past thirty years, as we noted earlier, more than 350 public colleges and universities have attempted to provide equal, nonhostile educational environments through speech codes that tell students what they are and are not allowed

supremecourtcases

Brandenburg v. Ohio (1969)

QUESTION: Can states prevent racist speech that advocates illegal action but falls short of inciting a riot?

ORAL ARGUMENT: February 27, 1969 (listen at www.oyez.org/cases/)

DECISION: June 9, 1969 (read at www.findlaw.com/casecode/supreme.html)

OUTCOME: No, Brandenburg's conviction is overturned, establishing a broad right to freedom of speech (8–0).

Clarence Brandenburg headed an Ohio branch of the Ku Klux Klan. The Klan, formed following the Civil War, was an avowedly racist organization that revived and grew in the 1920s, when it opposed Catholic immigration to the United States, and in the 1950s and 1960s, when it opposed the civil rights movement. Seeking publicity for his group, Brandenburg invited a Cincinnati reporter and camera crew to film his speeches. At one speech, he threatened, "We're not a revengent organization, but if our President, our Congress, our Supreme Court, continues to suppress the white, Caucasian race, it's possible there might have to be some revengeance taken." In another speech, he declared, "Personally I believe the n–* should be returned to Africa, and the Jew returned to Israel." The state of Ohio tried and convicted Brandenburg for violating its criminal syndicalism law, which made it a crime to advocate "the duty, necessity, or propriety of crime, sabotage, violence, or unlawful methods of terrorism as a means of accomplishing . . . political reform."

The Supreme Court unanimously reversed Brandenburg's conviction, declaring that the First Amendment protection of freedom of speech means that states cannot prohibit speech advocating the use of force "except where such advocacy is directed to inciting or producing imminent lawless action and is likely to incite or produce such action." Because Brandenburg's speech may have been "mere advocacy" of lawless action, as opposed to the "incitement of imminent lawless action," it was protected by the First Amendment.

- **Does hate speech deserve the same constitutional protection as other forms of speech?**

- **Should the government have the right to ban speech that advocates violence even if the violence would not be imminent (immediate)?**

*Offensive epithet deleted.

EQUAL·JUSTICE·UNDER·LAW·

California State University, Long Beach, posts a sign designating its free-speech zone, now official renamed the "Speaker's Platform."

Does your college have a speech code? Should your college regulate what you can and cannot say?

What is more important, freedom of speech or an equal and nonhostile educational environment?

Should the Tinkers have been suspended for wearing armbands to school to protest the Vietnam War?

symbolic speech: *Expressive communication, such as wearing armbands, that is not verbally communicated.*

content-neutral: *Free speech doctrine that allows certain types of regulation of speech, as long as the restriction does not favor one side or another of a controversy.*

to say.[31] For example, the University of Wisconsin prohibited speech that created "an intimidating, hostile, or demeaning environment for education (or) university-related work."[32] The University of Connecticut's speech code banned "inappropriately directed laughter" and purposefully excluding people from conversations.[33] Tufts University established three separate free speech zones: public areas, where speech could not be prohibited; classrooms and libraries, where derogatory and demeaning speech could be punished; and dorms, where the university placed the strictest restrictions on speech. Whereas students at many universities accepted speech codes, students at Tufts debated the issue, held public forums about freedom of speech, and physically marked off "free speech" from "non–free speech" zones.[34] Under this pressure, Tufts, a private university not legally bound by the Bill of Rights, rescinded the code.

The University of Michigan's speech code prohibited any speech that "stigmatizes or victimizes individuals or groups on the basis of race, ethnicity, religion, sex, sexual orientation, creed, national origin, ancestry, age, marital status, handicap, or Vietnam-era veteran status." In addition to the regulations, the university created guidelines that gave examples of actionable conduct. The examples included stating in class that women are not as good as men in a particular field, not inviting someone to a party because she is a lesbian, excluding someone from a study group because of race or sex, displaying a Confederate flag, telling jokes about gays or lesbians, laughing at jokes about people who stutter, and commenting in a derogatory way about a particular person's physical appearance.[35]

A graduate student in psychology was concerned that Michigan's code would prevent class discussions of theories that claimed the existence of biological differences between sexes and races, and he brought suit against the code in federal court. The court struck down the code as violating the First Amendment.[36] Two years later, a federal court struck down the University of Wisconsin's speech code.[37] Thus the courts have made it clear that while state universities may encourage the goal of equality, they cannot do so by limiting First Amendment rights. Note that the First Amendment applies to these schools because they are state universities. The Bill of Rights limits the national government and, through the selective incorporation doctrine, also limits state governments and thus state universities. Private colleges, though subject to certain federal regulations, are not subject to the Bill of Rights.

Symbolic Speech. The armbands that Mary Beth and John Tinker wore to protest the Vietnam War were not pure speech; the Tinkers voiced no opinions while wearing them. Rather, the armbands were considered **symbolic speech**, like other nonverbal activities that convey a political message, such as saluting the flag, burning the flag, or burning draft cards—the latter two actions also undertaken by anti–Vietnam War protesters.

The Court has allowed prohibitions on the burning of draft cards, because Congress has a **content-neutral** justification for requiring draft-eligible citizens to be in possession of their draft cards. That is, draft cards are essential to the smooth running of the draft,[38] and prohibiting their destruction is not intended to suppress the views of those who burn them. States also have a neutral justification for banning cross burning, a terrorist tactic historically used

David McNew/Getty Images

by the white supremacist Ku Klux Klan to intimidate African Americans.[39] But the Court has overturned laws that require saluting the flag, as such laws do intend to instill a political viewpoint.[40] Similarly, the Court has overturned laws prohibiting flag burning, as they are based almost entirely on opposition to the idea being delivered by flag burning.[41] Of course, flag burners can be arrested on charges that would apply to anyone who starts a fire in public. On the other hand, the content-neutral rule, like most constitutional rules, is not absolute. Some messages can be regulated solely because of opposition to the message, as when the Supreme Court upheld a student's suspension for unfurling a banner at a parade that declared "Bong Hits 4 Jesus" because of the banner's promotion of drug use.[42] It is easy for the Court to formulate simple rules, such as a prohibition on content-based regulations, but harder for the Court to apply those rules consistently in the unusual cases that come before it.

Clay Good/ZUMA

In 2002 high school student Joseph Frederick unfurled this banner while his class watched the Olympic Torch relay pass through Juneau, Alaska. When the principal suspended Frederick for the banner's message about drugs, Frederick sued, saying that his free speech rights had been violated. The court of appeals, relying on the *Tinker* case, reversed the suspension, but in 2007 the Supreme Court upheld it, saying a student's free speech rights did not extend to the promotion of illegal drugs.

Campaign Finance.   Another attempt to advance equality by restricting expression involves laws that try to level the playing field in elections by limiting campaign contributions. Supporters of campaign finance reform claim that the wealthy will have a disproportionate influence on elections without such limits. Nevertheless, the Supreme Court has consistently ruled that campaign contributions are a form of speech protected by the First Amendment and that laws restricting campaign contributions or campaign activities must pass the compelling interest test (see Chapters 8, Interest Groups, and 10, Elections and Campaigns).

Time, Place, and Manner Regulations.   The fact that the First Amendment protects freedom of speech does not mean that there is a right to speak wherever one wants, whenever one wants. Regulations of the time, place, and manner of speech, such as when or where protests may take place, are generally valid as long as they are neutral or equal, that is, they do not favor one side or another of a controversy. Thus states can prohibit protests near school grounds that interfere with school activities as there is no indication that such bans favor one side of any controversy over any other side.[43] Alternatively, the American Nazi Party, with backing from the pro–free speech **American Civil Liberties Union**, won the right to protest in the heavily Jewish Chicago suburb of Skokie because the main reason

Should Americans be required to salute the flag? Should they be prevented from burning the flag?

American Civil Liberties Union: *Interest group devoted to freedom of expression, criminal due process, civil rights, and reproductive rights.*

Should the American Nazi Party, the Ku Klux Klan, or the Communist Party be allowed to march in public streets? Should their ideas be suppressed, or should they be allowed to be tested in the marketplace of ideas?

that Skokie sought to block the march was opposition to the Nazis' views.[44] Nevertheless, the Court has upheld bans on protests near abortion clinics, even though the protesters are almost always against abortion, given concerns over the safety of women seeking abortions.[45]

Freedom of the Press

Thomas Jefferson, among other Founders, thought freedom of the press crucial to a free society because the press keeps the public informed about the government's activities. When the Bill of Rights was written, "the press" meant newspapers; today the term covers not only the large companies that own television and radio stations but also individually run blogs and Internet sites that anyone can create. While freedom of the press once belonged to those who owned one, today it belongs to everyone.

prior restraint: *Government restrictions on freedom of the press that prevent material from being published.*

Like freedom of speech, however, freedom of the press is not absolute. In extraordinarily extreme cases, the government can censor items before they are published. This practice is known as **prior restraint**. In other situations, the government can punish people after the fact for what they publish.

Prior Restraint.   Following English law, freedom of the press in the colonies and in the early years of the United States meant freedom from prior censorship;[46] today, an extraordinary burden of proof of imminent harm is needed before the courts will shut down a newspaper before a story is printed. Even when the *New York Times* began publishing excerpts from a top-secret Pentagon analysis of U.S. involvement in the Vietnam War, the courts refused to stop the presses. The story of this case, *New York Times v. United States* (1971),[47] is told in more detail in Chapter 7 (The News Media and the Internet). One case in which the courts said that the government had met the extraordinary burden standard involved the publication of instructions on how to build a hydrogen bomb,[48] but generally, court approval of censorship by prior restraint has been so difficult to achieve that the federal government has not sought it since the 1970s.

First Amendment law protects the Internet and blogs from government censorship in much the same way that it protects newspapers, but the technology of the Internet makes censorship far more difficult. This was the lesson learned in 2008 by a federal judge who tried to censor the Wikileaks website,[49] which specializes in publishing confidential documents from government, business, and religious organizations. Though the judge ordered the Wikileaks.org domain name disabled, Wikileaks already had mirror sites set up all over the world. Facing a barrage of criticism from bloggers and mainstream media groups, and given the ineffectiveness of his original decision, the judge reversed himself. But while many people support the right of Wikileaks to publish allegations of money laundering by a Swiss bank, as in this case, what happens when Wikileaks publishes, as it has, a diagram of the first atomic bomb or secret documents about the war in Afghanistan?[50]

What information on the web should the government censor?

Subsequent Punishment.   In certain instances, the government can engage in **subsequent punishment**, fining and/or imprisoning writers and publishers after the fact for what they publish. Examples here include penalties for libel and for publishing obscenity, incitement to acts of violence, and secret military information.

subsequent punishment: *Restrictions on freedom of the press that occur after material is published.*

libel: *Publishing false and damaging statements about another person.*

The standards for convicting in a case of **libel**—the publishing of false and damaging statements about another person—vary according to whether that person is a public figure. The Supreme Court has made it harder for public figures to sue for libel than for ordinary individuals, because public figures have access to the media and can more readily defend themselves without lawsuits. For public figures to sue, the materials must be false and damaging, and the writer or publisher must have acted with **actual malice**, that is, with knowledge that the material was false or with reckless disregard of whether it was true or false (see Supreme Court Cases: *New York Times v. Sullivan* in Chapter 7). Further, satire is largely exempt from libel laws. Such was in the case in *Hustler Magazine's* spoof on the "first time" for the Reverend Jerry Falwell, the founder of the conservative Christian group, Moral Majority.[51] For private figures to sue for libel, the material must be false and damaging, and there must be some degree of negligence, but the actual malice test does not apply.

Prior to the development of the World Wide Web, only those who published printed materials could libel someone, but even then, the damage would largely be limited to those who subscribed to the publication. With the Internet, anyone can libel anyone else, and the whole world can see it. At Yale University, for example, anonymous contributors to a popular law school message board wrote derogatory comments about several female law students, including fabricated statements about their mental capacity and sexual activities. Because anyone, including potential employers, can see such statements, the potential for harm is enormous.[52] Given the anonymous nature of the posts, identifying and prosecuting the source of the statements can be difficult, if not impossible. Since freedom of speech is a fundamental right, there is no easy solution to protecting privacy in the Internet age.

The term **seditious libel** refers to the criticizing of government officials, regardless of whether the criticism is true, false, or just a matter of opinion. During the colonial era the 1735 New York trial and acquittal of John Peter Zenger established that seditious libel is not a reason for punishment, though, as we have seen, Congress twice made sedition a crime during wartime. The *Zenger* case is regarded as a landmark in freedom of the press and is discussed in more detail in Chapter 7.

Today, the government can seek subsequent punishment against individuals who publish military secrets or obscene materials. Pornographic material is not necessarily obscene, and pornography that falls short of the legal definition of *obscenity* receives First Amendment protection. Specifically, for materials to be obscene, they must pass all three parts of what has become known as the *Miller* **test**: (1) to the average person, applying contemporary community standards as established by the relevant state, the work, taken as a whole (not just isolated passages), appeals to the prurient (sexual) interest; (2) the work depicts in an offensive way sexual conduct specifically defined by the state law; and (3) the work lacks serious literary, artistic, political, or scientific value.[53]

Under the *Miller* test, only "hard-core" materials could be banned.[54] The government has much greater leeway to prohibit "kiddie porn" that uses actual children,[55] but not "virtual child pornography," which uses computer-simulated children.[56] Nor can the government's desire to protect children from indecent materials be used as a justification for prohibiting pornography that does not reach the level of obscenity from the Internet.[57] The *Miller* test reversed a trend toward greater protection of pornography that the liberal Warren Court (1954–69) had instituted and opposed the general trend of greater rights of the press to publish without fear of prosecution by the state.

actual malice test: *Supreme Court test for libel of a public figure, in which the plaintiff must prove that the publisher knew the material was false or acted with reckless disregard of whether it was true or false.*

How can you protect yourself from what others may say about you on the web?

seditious libel: *Conduct or language that incites rebellion against the authority of a state.*

***Miller* test:** *Supreme Court test for determining whether material is obscene.*

Should pornography be submitted to the marketplace of ideas?

The Right of Association

The First Amendment's protections include the right of the people to peaceably assemble. This means the right to associate with whom one wants, as well as the right not to associate with those with whom one does not want to associate. As we observed earlier, here a civil liberty can conflict with a civil right, as when a restaurant owner might choose, for example, not to serve people of a certain race. This dilemma was resolved by the Civil Rights Act and subsequent court challenges in the 1960s so far as businesses that serve the public are concerned (see Chapter 5, Civil Rights). But if a group's expressed beliefs reject association with people of certain groups, such as Boy Scouts rejecting homosexuals and the Ku Klux Klan rejecting blacks and Jews, the group has a **right of association** that overrides state laws banning discrimination.

If a group discriminates for no apparent purpose, however, state laws can limit the right of association. Thus the Court declared that Minnesota has the right to prevent the Jaycees from discriminating against women because the presence of women does not violate any of the expressive interests of the Jaycees.[58] On the other hand, New Jersey's law prohibiting private groups from discriminating against homosexuals did not override the Boy Scouts' stated belief that homosexuality is inconsistent with the group's values. The Court thus allowed the Scouts to prohibit homosexuals from being members.[59]

Religious Freedom

The First Amendment sets forth two distinct protections about religion. Congress and now the states generally may not prevent people from practicing their religious beliefs. They also cannot pass laws that establish an official religion or even favor one religion over another.

Free Exercise

Many of the first settlers in the American colonies came because of restrictions on their religious beliefs in England, where the Anglican Church was established as the official religion. When these settlers first arrived, they did not establish general freedom of religion, but rather freedom for their religion. In 1635, for example, the Massachusetts Puritans banished Roger Williams for his disagreements with the church. Williams established a colony in what would become Rhode Island that was the first to grant religious "liberty of conscience." Other colonies followed. Maryland's Toleration Act (1649) guaranteed freedom of worship to all Christians, including Catholics, who often faced persecution in Protestant Europe. British colonists in Flushing, New Amsterdam (now Queens, New York), fought for the religious freedom of others, protesting Dutch Governor Peter Stuyvesant's persecution of Quakers. The Flushing Remonstrance (1657), a historic demand for religious freedom, called on the governor to let "every man stand or fall to his own Master."[60]

Victories for religious freedom, though significant, were rare in the colonial period. In 1786, however, the Virginia General Assembly passed Thomas Jefferson's Statute for Religious Freedom, which declared freedom of religious conscience to be a natural right of mankind that governments could not abridge. Five years later, this right was affirmed in the **free exercise clause** of the Bill of Rights. While religious freedom is taken for granted by Americans today, it is still not protected throughout much of the world (see Other Places: Civil Liberties).

Like all the provisions of the Bill of Rights, however, the free exercise clause originally protected individuals only against the national government, and at the time only two

right of association: *Right to freely associate with others and form groups, protected by the First Amendment.*

Which is more important to you, freedom of association or laws banning discrimination?

Should all religions get equal treatment?

free exercise clause: *First Amendment clause protecting the free exercise of religion.*

Otherplaces

Civil Liberties

Freedom House, an independent nongovernmental organization that supports the expansion of freedom worldwide, ranks the amount of freedom in every country on a scale of 1 to 7, with 1 representing the most freedom and 7 the least. The United States has a ranking of 1 due in part to its free and diverse press, made even more diverse by the growing role of Internet journalism. It also has "a long tradition of religious freedom." Freedom House notes complaints that the criminal justice system is excessively harsh, particularly toward members of minority groups.

The rankings of the nations we often look at in these Other Places features are as follows: United Kingdom, 1; India, 3; Israel, 2; Mexico, 3; and South Africa, 2.

- **Is the Internet likely to increase or decrease freedom of the press in other countries?**

- **Do constitutional guarantees of rights such as freedom of religion mean that those rights will be protected?**

■ Free
■ Partly Free
Not Free

Freedom Status	Country Breakdown	Population Breakdown
Free	89 (46%)	3,088,704,000 (46%)
Partly free	58 (30%)	1,367,440,000 (20%)
Not free	47 (24%)	2,333,869,000 (34%)
Total	194	6,790,013,000

Map of Freedom, 2010. The Map of Freedom reflects the findings of Freedom House's Freedom in the World 2010 survey, which rates the level of political rights and civil liberties in 194 countries and 14 related and disputed territories during 2009. Based on these ratings, countries are divided into three categories: free, partly free, and not free. A free country is one where there is broad scope for open political competition, a climate of respect for civil liberties, significant independent civic life, and independent media. Partly free countries are characterized by some restrictions on political rights and civil liberties, often in a context of corruption, weak rule of law, ethnic strife, or civil war. A not free country is one where basic political rights are absent, and basic civil liberties are widely and systematically denied.

Source: Freedom House, Map of Freedom 2010. Reprinted by permission.

During the Vietnam War heavyweight boxer Muhammad Ali refused military induction, claiming membership in the Nation of Islam gave him conscientious objector status. His draft board did not agree. In 1971 the Supreme Court ruled in Ali's favor. Here he reacts to learning of the Court's decision.

valid secular purpose: *Supreme Court test that allows states to ban activities that infringe on religious practices as long as the state has a nonreligious rationale for prohibiting the behavior.*

establishment clause: *First Amendment clause prohibiting governmental establishment of religion.*

Lemon test: *Test for determining whether aid to religion violates the establishment clause.*

separationists: *Those who believe that the establishment clause requires a wall of separation between church and state.*

accommodationists: *Those who believe that as long as the government does not favor one religion over another, it may generally support religious practices.*

states—Virginia and Rhode Island—had unqualified religious freedom. Maryland demanded belief in Christianity; Delaware and North Carolina required belief in the divinity of the Bible; Pennsylvania and South Carolina required belief in the divinity of the Bible plus heaven and hell; and Connecticut, Maryland, Massachusetts, New Hampshire, and South Carolina limited civil office to Christians or Protestants.[61] So ingrained was state authority to regulate religion that when James Madison proposed an amendment that would have limited such authority, Congress rejected it.[62] Today, however, with the incorporation of the Bill of Rights, the right of individuals to the free exercise of religion is also outside of state authority to regulate.

Under the First Amendment, the government cannot criminalize an individual's private religious beliefs. Nor can the government ban specific religious activities just because they are based on religious beliefs. For example, the Supreme Court struck down a ban on religious-based animal sacrifices because killing animals for other reasons was not prohibited.[63] But not all religious-based activities are protected, and states are generally free to pass laws that restrict religious practices as long as such laws have a **valid secular** (nonreligious) **purpose**. For example, states can ban polygamy, even though marriage with multiple wives is a central belief in some religions.[64] In the 1960s, however, the Court ruled that states must have a compelling interest before they could abridge people's religious practices, even if the law had a valid secular purpose. Thus even though the government has a valid secular purpose in conducting a military draft, members of religious groups that oppose warfare, such as Quakers, may be exempt. In the case of Muslim boxing champion Muhammad Ali, who argued that he could only fight wars declared by Allah or the Prophet, the Court overturned a conviction for draft evasion.[65]

One case that demonstrates the contest between the branches of government over what constitutes free exercise concerns the use of the hallucinogenic drug peyote in religious rituals. In 1990, when two Native American drug counselors who used peyote were fired from their jobs and denied unemployment compensation, the Supreme Court used the valid secular purpose test to uphold Oregon's decision to deny this compensation. Members of Congress overwhelmingly disapproved, however, and passed legislation stating that the Supreme Court must use the compelling interest test in deciding free exercise cases. The Supreme Court responded by declaring that law unconstitutional, repeating the statement from *Marbury v. Madison* that the province of the judicial branch is "to say what the law is." Congress does have the authority, however, to declare the religious use of peyote to be legal, and it has done so. But generally, states need only have a valid secular purpose to pass laws that also happen to restrict religious practices.

The Establishment of Religion

The **establishment clause** of the First Amendment prevents Congress from recognizing one church as the nation's official church, as Britain had done with the Anglican (Episcopal) Church. Originally, states were free to establish state religions if they chose to, and when the Constitution was adopted nearly half the states had done so.[66] The antiestablishment movement began in Virginia, where between 1784 and 1785 James Madison fought tax assessments used to support Christian religious teachers, and Thomas Jefferson secured passage of the

Disestablishment Bill in 1786, which ended Virginia's official establishment of the Anglican Church. In an 1802 letter to the Baptists of Danbury, Connecticut, Jefferson called for a "wall of separation" between church and state. The Supreme Court adopted that phrase in 1947, but declared that using taxpayer funds to provide public transportation to parochial schools did not breach the wall.[67]

The establishment clause literally prohibits not just the establishment of religion, but also any law "respecting an establishment of religion." The Supreme Court has taken this phrase to mean that steps by the government that favor one religion over another, or even religion over no religion, cannot be taken, even if those steps fall far short of an official establishment of religion.

The Supreme Court's test for determining whether laws violate the establishment clause is known as the **Lemon test**, named after a litigant in a 1971 case.[68] Under this test, a challenged law must be shown to have a secular (nonreligious) legislative purpose and a primary effect that neither advances nor inhibits religion. The law must also avoid an excessive entanglement between church and state, such as a strict monitoring of church activities. Using these standards, the Supreme Court has banned organized school prayers (*Engel v. Vitale*) and devotional Bible readings (*Abington School District v. Schempp*).[69] The Bible can be read as part of a comparative religion course, however, and students can pray silently. The Supreme Court has also used this test to strike down laws that prohibited the teaching of evolution[70] as well as laws granting equal time for creation science—the position that evidence supports the biblical view of creation—if evolution is taught.[71] In 2005 a district court judge in Pennsylvania ruled that "intelligent design"—a view that claims that the world is too complex to have resulted from evolution and that thus there must have been a purposeful designer of the universe (that is, God)—was nothing more than renamed creation science. Whether doctrines are called creation science or intelligent design, courts have ruled that they are religious doctrines that cannot be taught as part of the science curriculum in public schools.

It is often difficult to understand why some activities violate the establishment clause and others do not. **Separationists** believe, with Jefferson, that there should be a strict wall between church and state. **Accommodationists**, on the other hand, believe that as long as the state does not favor one religion over another, it can generally pass laws that support religion. The Supreme Court's decisions on these grounds have been mixed, with conservative justices typically supporting the accommodationist position and liberal justices typically supporting the separationist view (see Chapter 15, The Judiciary, on ideology and the Supreme Court). The end result has been confusion: The Court allows short religious prayers by clergy at high school graduation ceremonies as

Monticello/photograph by Mary Porter

Toward the end of his life, Thomas Jefferson wrote an inscription for his tombstone highlighting, of all his many accomplishments, the three that were most important to him. Note that "author of the Statue of Virginia for Religious Freedom" was one of them.

Universal Press Syndicate, Tom Toles The Washington Post 3-3-05

Should prayers be allowed in school? Under what circumstances? What types of prayers? Is saying a prayer the same as wearing an armband?

long as students are not compelled to participate,[72] but not by students at high school football games.[73] States may provide textbooks for secular subjects in parochial schools,[74] but not instructional aids like charts and maps.[75]

The Right to Keep and Bear Arms

What are the arguments for and against gun control? What is your position?

While many if not most Americans agree about the fundamental aims of the various First Amendment rights, no such agreement exists about the fundamental aims of the Second Amendment. The amendment declares, "A well regulated Militia, being necessary to the security of a free State, the right of the people to keep and bear Arms, shall not be infringed." Supporters of gun rights view the amendment as providing an individual right to keep and bear arms, while opponents view the "well regulated Militia" clause as limiting this right to those in organized militias.

At the time of the amendment's passage, the term *militia* meant all free, able-bodied adult males, who could be called upon to protect their states or communities from external military threats. The Founders favored citizen militias, which could be called on in moments of crisis, over standing armies, which could pose a threat to liberty.

Not until the 1934 National Firearms Act did the federal government attempt to regulate gun ownership. In 1939 the Supreme Court upheld a conviction under the act for possession of a sawed-off shotgun against a Second Amendment challenge, unanimously ruling that as such weapons had never been used by any militia, they did not receive Second Amendment protection.

Gerald Martineau/The Washington Post/Getty Images

In 2008 the Supreme Court heard a challenge to a 1975 District of Columbia law banning handguns, claiming that the Second Amendment's right to bear arms superseded the local law of a federal enclave, which, as the seat of government, the District is. Here D.C. Mayor Adrian Fenty comments outside the Court following oral arguments. Against objections by Fenty and gun control advocates, the Court struck down the D.C. law.

The Court sidestepped the question about whether there was an individual right to bear arms.

The Supreme Court finally decided that issue in 2008, ruling that there is an individual right to possess a gun, at least for self-defense in one's home.[76] The case involved a law prohibiting the private possession of firearms by the District of Columbia, which is a "federal enclave" and, for constitutional purposes, is considered part of the federal government rather than a state. The Court's 5–4 decision split along ideological lines, with the five most conservative justices supporting an individual right to keep and bear arms for self-defense, indicating that the right can be regulated but not denied. The four most liberal justices dissented, arguing that the well-regulated militia clause limits whatever right of gun ownership exists to military purposes.

The conclusion that the Second Amendment protects an individual right to bear arms does not answer the question of whether that amendment is also binding on the states. The Supreme Court answered that question in 2010, declaring that the right is incorporated.[77]

Criminal Procedure

Provisions in the Fourth, Fifth, Sixth, and Eighth Amendments contain the heart of the protections afforded people against arbitrary police and law enforcement tactics. They protect the manner in which the police conduct investigations, the procedures used at trial, and the punishments that may be given following conviction. The liberal Warren Court greatly expanded the rights of accused criminals, but since then more conservative courts have trimmed those rights.

Investigations

The major limits on investigating crimes involve the authority to search for physical evidence and the warnings that must be given prior to questioning a suspect.

Searches and Seizures.   The English practice of issuing writs of assistance, general warrants that allow searches of any person or place with no expiration until the death of the king, was among the causes that led to the American Revolution. Thus, the Fourth Amendment prohibits unreasonable searches and seizures. Though the amendment does not specify what makes a search unreasonable, it does specify that warrants must be backed by probable cause.

The Supreme Court has never interpreted the amendment to require warrants for all searches or seizures. If the police see illegal goods in plain view, they may seize them without a warrant. Similarly, if they observe a crime, they do not have to get a warrant before they arrest the individual. The Supreme Court has also established a broad right to search the person and the area within his or her control following an arrest and incident to it.

The areas over which individuals have Fourth Amendment protections are those in which there is an **expectation of privacy**. According to the Supreme Court, there are no Fourth Amendment rights in areas over which there is no expectation of privacy, such as discarded garbage, someone else's home, a hotel room once one has checked out, or an international border. The Supreme Court has not ruled on the issue, but several state supreme courts have upheld the right of schools to search lockers used by students, because students have a diminished expectation of privacy over their lockers. While students at public universities do have an expectation of privacy in their college dorm rooms, many schools require them to waive their Fourth Amendment rights when they sign their dorm contracts. (Like the First Amendment, the Fourth Amendment does not limit private parties, such as private universities.) More generally, people waive their Fourth Amendment rights whenever they grant permission for the police to search, as long as the police request is not coercive.[78]

For areas over which there is an expectation of privacy, the degree of Fourth Amendment protection depends on the level of that expectation, as determined by the Supreme Court. For example, the Court has ruled that individuals have the highest expectation of privacy in their homes, nearly as much in their places of business, but substantially less in their cars.[79] There is no expectation of privacy in what is exposed in plain view, even if, like a marijuana patch on private property, it requires a low-flying plane to view it.[80] There is no expectation of privacy over smells, allowing police to use drug-sniffing dogs to establish probable cause. There is, however, an expectation of privacy over the thermal (heat) signals given off by homes, thus prohibiting the police from using heat monitors to establish probable cause for indoor marijuana growing.[81]

Searches of homes almost always require a warrant (and thus probable cause). Searches of businesses usually do, but the Court allows warrantless searches of businesses that are subject to health, safety, or administrative regulations, such as restaurants, construction sites, and banks. For example, a restaurant kitchen suspected of health violations may be searched without a warrant. The police may establish, without probable cause, roadblocks to

expectation of privacy test: *Supreme Court test for whether Fourth Amendment protections apply.*

Where would you draw the line in searches? Should the government be allowed to search your home? Your car? Your bank account? Under what conditions?

stop all cars on a road to check for licenses and registration, or for drunk drivers. They may, of course, pull over any car for an observed violation, and they may search the car incident to arrest if they choose to arrest the person for that violation.[82] The Court also allows drug testing without probable cause in "special needs" cases, such as student athletes and people applying for jobs at the U.S. Customs Office, but not of politicians seeking elective office.[83]

If the police conduct a search that is later found to be in violation of the Fourth Amendment, the **exclusionary rule** holds that the evidence cannot be used in trial. Originally established by the Supreme Court in 1914, the doctrine was made binding on state and local governments, where most law enforcement takes place, by means of selective incorporation in **Mapp v. Ohio** (1961).[84] Defenders support the rule, which is not explicitly in the Constitution, as the only means of making sure that the police follow the Fourth Amendment. Police will have less incentive to violate the Fourth Amendment if they know that the evidence from illegal searches cannot be used in court. Critics complain that excluding such evidence allows guilty people to go free simply because the police made a mistake.[85] The Supreme Court has backtracked a bit on the rule, establishing a **good faith exception**, which allows evidence to be used if the police obtain a warrant but the warrant is later found to lack probable cause.

Interrogations.

The Fifth Amendment protects the right against **self-incrimination**, being forced to give testimony against oneself during criminal investigations or at criminal trials. The Supreme Court originally interpreted the self-incrimination clause to prohibit coerced confessions because they are inherently unreliable. But in the famous 1966 decision *Miranda v. Arizona*, the Court declared that the right against self-incrimination would be protected regardless of whether there was any evidence of coercion.[86] Rather, prior to police interrogation of subjects who are in custody, the subjects must be told that (1) they have the right to remain silent, (2) anything they say may be used against them, and (3) they have the right to an attorney, free if they cannot afford one. Police strenuously objected to these requirements at first, fearing that they would drastically curtail legitimate confessions. But, in 2000 the Court upheld the *Miranda* decision, noting that its requirements had become so embedded in routine police practice that they had become part of the national culture.[87]

MIRANDA WARNING

1. YOU HAVE THE RIGHT TO REMAIN SILENT.
2. ANYTHING YOU SAY CAN AND WILL BE USED AGAINST YOU IN A COURT OF LAW.
3. YOU HAVE THE RIGHT TO TALK TO A LAWYER AND HAVE HIM PRESENT WITH YOU WHILE YOU ARE BEING QUESTIONED.
4. IF YOU CANNOT AFFORD TO HIRE A LAWYER, ONE WILL BE APPOINTED TO REPRESENT YOU BEFORE ANY QUESTIONING IF YOU WISH.
5. YOU CAN DECIDE AT ANY TIME TO EXERCISE THESE RIGHTS AND NOT ANSWER ANY QUESTIONS OR MAKE ANY STATEMENTS.

WAIVER

DO YOU UNDERSTAND EACH OF THESE RIGHTS I HAVE EXPLAINED TO YOU? HAVING THESE RIGHTS IN MIND, DO YOU WISH TO TALK TO US NOW?

The Miranda rights statement is so famous that almost everyone who watches police shows on TV can recite it, although law enforcement officers generally read it to those under arrest.

Trial Procedures

The trial protections of the Bill of Rights include the right to indictment by a grand jury (Fifth Amendment), the **right to counsel** and an impartial jury (both Sixth Amendment), and the right against self-incrimination (Fifth Amendment), which, as noted, applies to trials as well as investigations.

To prevent the government from bringing people to trial without sufficient cause, the Fifth Amendment requires indictment by a grand jury, which indicts by majority vote. This right has not been incorporated so it applies to the federal government only, which prosecutes only a small percentage of total criminal cases, as criminal law is mostly under the authority of the states.

The Sixth Amendment's right to counsel originally meant that defendants could have an attorney represent them if they could afford one. In ***Powell v. Alabama*** (1932), a case involving undoubtedly false allegations of rape filed against several black youths, the Supreme Court ruled that, in death penalty cases where the defendants were ignorant, illiterate, or the like, the government must provide an attorney if defendants cannot afford one.[88] In 1942 the Supreme Court chose not to guarantee poor people a right to counsel in all felony cases, usually defined as crimes where possible imprisonment exceeds one year.[89] In 1963 the Court, recognizing how crucial counsel is in even simple cases, overruled the 1942 decision in the landmark ***Gideon v. Wainwright*** case.[90] Today, the rule applies to any case in which a defendant could receive even one day of jail time.[91]

The Sixth Amendment also guarantees the right to a trial by an impartial jury. Originally, a jury trial meant twelve people deciding unanimously, but the Court now allows juries as small as six people, and twelve-person juries need not decide unanimously.[92] The *impartial* part of the clause grants the defense and prosecutor unlimited rights to challenge potential jurors for cause. Examples include knowing other people in the case, having been a victim of a similar crime, and not having an open mind on the issue. These challenges must be approved by the trial judge. State rules also grant prosecutors and defense counsel a limited number of peremptory challenges, or challenges without cause. The substantive limit on peremptory challenges is that neither side may use the potential juror's race or gender as a reason for the challenge.[93]

The application of the self-incrimination clause to trials means that defendants cannot be compelled to be witnesses against themselves. That is, they have an absolute right not to testify, and the prosecution cannot even tell the jury that the defendant chose not to testify.

Verdict and Punishment

At the end of a trial, the jury must decide whether to convict or acquit the defendant. Following conviction, the judge imposes a sentence, unless it is a death penalty case, in which case the jury decides.

Double Jeopardy. If the jury acquits the defendant, the **double jeopardy clause** prevents the person from being tried again for the same offense. But if the jury cannot reach a verdict, the government can retry the defendant. Also, if the defendant is found guilty at trial but the conviction is overturned on appeal, the defendant may be tried again. The Supreme Court does allow a defendant to be tried separately for the same offense by the state government and the federal government, even if the defendant was found not guilty at the state or federal trial that was held first. Because most crimes are either state offenses or federal offenses, this form of double jeopardy does not often occur.

The main exception concerns a trial for the federal crime of violating someone's civil rights, which is occasionally prosecuted after a state acquittal on the specific offense (such as murder or assault). For example, in 1993 the Los Angeles police officers acquitted in 1992 on state charges for the infamous videotaped beating of Rodney King were convicted in federal courts of violating King's civil rights. Double jeopardy also does not prevent private civil suits following criminal acquittals. So in 1997 a civil jury found O. J. Simpson liable for the

Why did the First Congress write so many protections regarding criminal procedure into the Bill of Rights?

Powell v. Alabama: *1932 Supreme Court decision creating a right to appointed counsel in exceptional cases.*

Gideon v. Wainwright: *1963 Supreme Court decision creating a right to appointed counsel in all felony cases.*

double jeopardy clause: *Prevents the government from retrying someone for a crime after an initial acquittal (Fifth Amendment).*

MAR. 3 1991

CNN via Getty Images

In 1991 Los Angeles police were videotaped beating Rodney King, a drunk driving suspect, following a high-speed chase. The incident raised tensions between police and the black community, and in 1992, when an overwhelmingly white jury acquitted the four police officers in a state court for use of excessive force, riots broke out. The federal government later tried the officers for civil rights violations, and two were found guilty.

Is the U.S. criminal justice system too harsh? Is it biased against minority groups?

death of Ron Goldman following Simpson's acquittal in 1995 on criminal charges of murdering his wife and Goldman, allowing Goldman's family to recover damages from Simpson.

Sentencing. Following a guilty verdict, the judge determines the sentence, except in death penalty cases, where the jury makes the determination. Sentences must not violate the Eighth Amendment's prohibition on cruel and unusual punishment. The concern of the Framers undoubtedly grew out of English punishments that included torture.[94] The phrase itself, however, is highly ambiguous, leaving courts with a fair amount of discretion about whether punishments are unconstitutional.

As for the length of the sentence imposed, the Supreme Court grants great leeway to the states. In 1980 the Court upheld the sentencing to a life term with the possibility of parole of a defendant who had committed his third felony. The first felony was fraudulent use of a credit card for an $80 purchase, the second a forged check for $28.36, and the third accepting payment of $120.75 to fix an air conditioner that he never fixed.[95] As the defendant found out, the Supreme Court rarely finds constitutional violation in the length of a sentence.

On the death penalty, however, the Supreme Court ruled in 1972 that the complete discretion given to juries as to which people are convicted of capital crimes was so arbitrary as to constitute cruel and unusual punishment.[96] Then, in 1976 the Court ruled mandatory death sentences to be unconstitutional, but allowed states to impose the death penalty provided they give jurors specific guidelines to consider, such as the brutality of the crime or whether the crime was murder for hire.[97]

The Right to Privacy

Although a number of constitutional provisions bear on privacy, such as search and seizure, self-incrimination, and First Amendment freedoms, none explicitly grants a general right to privacy. Nevertheless, the Ninth Amendment demands that the listing of certain rights, such as speech and religion, should not be understood as invalidating rights not listed. Since 1965 the Supreme Court has used the Ninth Amendment, the due process clause of the Fourteenth Amendment, and other privacy-related amendments to establish a general right to privacy. Subsequently the Court has faced decisions about whether to expand this privacy right to include abortion, homosexual behavior, and the right to die.

Birth Control and Abortion

In 1873 Anthony Comstock, a crusader for traditional morality, lobbied Congress to pass a law prohibiting the transportation in interstate commerce of both pornography and birth control. Many states, including Connecticut, passed their own Comstock Laws, which prohibited the use of birth control, even by married couples. In 1961 Estelle Griswold, executive director of the Planned Parenthood League of Connecticut, opened a birth control clinic in order to get arrested or fined so that she could challenge the constitutionality of the law. Her $100 fine, upheld by the Connecticut Supreme Court, allowed her to appeal to the U.S. Supreme Court.

No Soldier shall, in time of peace be quartered in any house, without the consent of the Owner. . . .

Third Amendment

Congress shall make no law . . . abridging . . . the right of the people peaceably to assemble. . . .

First Amendment

The right of the people to be secure in their persons, houses, papers, and effects, against unreasonable searches and seizures, shall not be violated. . . .

Fourth Amendment

The enumeration in the Constitution, of certain rights, shall not be construed to deny or disparage others retained by the people.

Ninth Amendment

No person . . . shall be compelled in any criminal case to be a witness against himself. . . .

Fifth Amendment

. . . nor shall any State deprive any person of life, liberty, or property, without due process of law. . . .

Fourteenth Amendment (section 1)

In 1965, in *Griswold v. Connecticut*, the Supreme Court overturned a Connecticut law that made it a crime for any person, including married couples, to use birth control. This landmark case drew on guarantees in the First, Third, Fourth, Fifth, Ninth, and Fourteenth Amendments to establish a general right to privacy. These guarantees are the right of association, the prohibition against quartering soldiers, the protection against unreasonable searches, the protection against self-incrimination, the rights retained by the people, and the due process of law. Justice William O. Douglas, who wrote the opinion, explained the justification with reference to "penumbras," or "zones": "Specific guarantees in the Bill of Rights have penumbras formed by emanations from those guarantees that help give them life and substance." He also stated the justification more bluntly: "Would we allow the police to search the sacred precincts of marital bedrooms for the tell-tale signs of the use of contraceptives? The very idea is repulsive."

FIGURE 4.3 The Right to Privacy.

In **Griswold v. Connecticut** (1965), the Court voided what one justice called "an uncommonly silly law."[98] The case established a **right to privacy** (see Figure 4.3), and the Court soon expanded this decision to cover the right of unmarried people to use birth control.[99]

Prior to the middle of the nineteenth century, most states followed the English practice of making abortion illegal only after "quickening," that is, noticeable movement by the fetus, usually around the sixteenth to eighteenth week of pregnancy. By the end of the nineteenth century, most states had eliminated the quickening distinction, making abortion illegal throughout pregnancy. By the 1950s every state but Alabama banned abortion except to save the life of the mother; Alabama's broader exception included preserving the mother's health.

Following a substantial increase in birth defects caused by the sedative thalidomide (1957–61) and a German measles epidemic (1962–65), deaths from illegal abortion, and the resurgence of the women's rights movement, interest groups such as the National Association for the Reform of Abortion Laws (NARAL) organized for the loosening of anti-abortion laws. Between 1967 and 1969 ten states passed laws allowing abortion if there was a "substantial risk" that the child would be born with a "grave physical or mental defect," that continuing the pregnancy would "gravely impair the physical or mental health of the

Griswold v. Connecticut: *1965 Supreme Court case establishing the right to privacy.*

right to privacy: *Constitutional right inferred by the Court that has been used to protect unlisted rights such as sexual privacy and reproductive rights, plus the right to end life-sustaining medical treatment.*

Roe v. Wade: *1973 Supreme Court case extending the right to privacy to abortion.*

undue burden: *Current test used by the Court to determine whether abortion regulations are allowable.*

mother," and in cases of rape or incest.[100] In 1970 three states legalized pre-viability abortions, those performed before the sixth month of pregnancy, when the fetus could not survive on its own.

Then, in 1973 the Supreme Court decided ***Roe v. Wade***, which established a national right to abortion.[101] Using the compelling interest test, the Court declared that states had a compelling interest in preventing abortion in the third trimester, when the fetus could live on its own, and a compelling interest in regulating abortion during the second trimester to protect the health of the woman seeking the procedure. The state had no interest in regulating or preventing abortion in the first trimester. The Court's ruling took the issue out of state politics, where it had been located, and situated it in national politics, where it has become a perennial controversy, with presidential candidates regularly vowing to nominate Supreme Court justices who would either uphold or strike down *Roe v. Wade*. Since that time, states have sought to regulate and limit the procedure, and in the past twenty years abortion rates have slowly declined.

Following years of debate about *Roe v. Wade*, the Court reconsidered the decision in 1992.[102] That decision upheld the basic right to abortion established in *Roe v. Wade*, but replaced the compelling interest/trimester framework, declaring that states could regulate abortion prior to viability as long as those regulations did not constitute an **undue burden** on a woman's right to terminate her pregnancy. According to the Court, spousal notification constitutes an undue burden, but requiring doctors to provide the woman with information about the risks of abortion and a twenty-four-hour waiting period does not. Parental consent for minors is not an undue burden as long as the minor has an option of seeking a judge's approval if she cannot obtain a parent's consent.

Perhaps the most controversial abortion procedures are those conducted late in a pregnancy. The Supreme Court struck down Nebraska's ban of these so-called partial-birth abortions in 2000 in a 5–4 decision because the state law did not contain an exception for the woman's health. Congress responded with national legislation banning late-term abortions, and the Court upheld the statute by a 5–4 vote in 2007. The difference was the replacement of Justice Sandra Day O'Connor, who voted to strike the statute in 2000, by Justice Samuel Alito, who voted to uphold the statute in 2007.

AP Photo/Topeka Capital-Journal, Anthony S. Bush, file

What happens when rights clash? In 2009 the Supreme Court agreed to hear a case involving the Westboro Church of Topeka and Albert Snyder of York, Pennsylvania. Westboro members claim that freedom of speech permits them to protest at military funerals, which they do to assert that the deaths of military personnel are God's punishment for the tolerance of homosexuality. Snyder claims that their protest at his son's funeral was an invasion of privacy causing emotional distress. Here Westboro members protest at the funeral of an Albany, New York, soldier in 2005.

Abortion remains a salient issue in national politics, with the Supreme Court's role front and center. At confirmation hearings for Supreme Court nominees (see Chapter 15), senators ask more questions about *Roe v. Wade* than about any other case.[103]

Homosexual Behavior

As of 1961 every state had laws prohibiting sodomy, and these laws were broad enough to cover virtually all sexual conduct between people of the same sex. In the next decades some states decriminalized sodomy, and by 1986 only twenty-four states continued to outlaw sodomy between consenting adults. Georgia, one of the states that continued such laws, authorized twenty-four years of imprisonment for a single act of consensual sexual behavior that fell under its sodomy laws. In a case challenging this law, the Supreme Court declared that the right to privacy did not cover homosexual behavior.[104] At the time, more than 80 percent of Americans thought that homosexual behavior was "always" or "almost always" wrong.[105] But by 2003, with the percentage of Americans with this belief down more than 20 percentage points, the Supreme Court reversed itself, declaring in **Lawrence v. Texas** that "the liberty protected by the Constitution allows homosexual persons the right to choose to enter upon relationships in the confines of their homes and their own private lives."[106]

What are the arguments for and against the right of privacy in relation to abortion? What is your opinion? Are you "pro-life" or "pro-choice"?

Lawrence v. Texas: 2003 *Supreme Court case extending the right to privacy to homosexual behavior.*

The Right to Die

As part of the right to privacy, the Supreme Court has held that that people who make their wishes clearly known have a constitutional right to terminate life-sustaining care, such as artificial feeding or insertion of breathing tubes.[107] This right does not, however, include the right to assisted suicide, when physicians or family members provide ill people with pills or other means of ending life.[108]

Student Housing

The Supreme Court rejected the use of the right to privacy to strike down laws that ban more than two unrelated unmarried people from living together in the same house or apartment. Instead, it declared that states have a legitimate interest in passing land use legislation.[109]

Does government have a right to say whether two unrelated unmarried persons can live in the same house or apartment?

Civil Liberties and Public Policy: Private Property and Public Use

Civil liberties include not only political rights but also economic rights, particularly the right of property, which is explicitly protected in the Constitution. While the Fifth and Fourteenth Amendments, respectively, prevent the federal and state governments from denying people life, liberty, or property without due process of law, the strongest protection of private property is the Fifth Amendment's **takings clause**, which prohibits the government from using its power of **eminent domain**, the taking of private property for public use, without providing **just compensation**. The takings clause requires compensation not just for wholesale seizures of private property but also for changes in economic regulations that severely limit the economic value of private property.

David Lucas, who purchased beachfront property in South Carolina with the intent of building homes similar to those nearby, sued the state after it passed new regulations

takings clause: *Requires just compensation when the government seizes private property for a public purpose (Fifth Amendment).*

eminent domain: *Right of the government to seize private property for public use.*

just compensation: *Payment by the government of fair market value for seized property.*

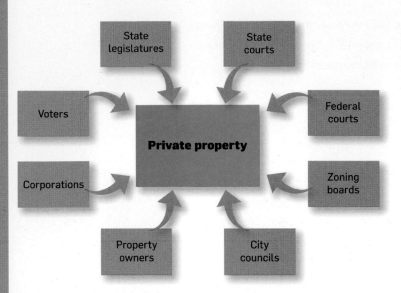

public use: *Requirement of the takings clause that once meant that the use of seized property had to be beneficial to all citizens, such as the building of roads or parks, and not just to private parties.*

Susette Kelo had always wanted a home overlooking the water, and in 1997 she purchased this little pink house on Long Island Sound. When the Supreme Court ruled in *Kelo v. New London* (2005) that New London could seize her property for public use, defined as economic development, she, her neighbors, and homeowners across the country were outraged.

prohibiting construction in that area. While the state did not technically take Lucas's property, his inability to build on it made the land essentially worthless. Because South Carolina denied Lucas all economically beneficial use of the property, the Supreme Court ordered South Carolina to pay just compensation.[110]

The Framers respected private property, but they also understood that society sometimes needs to seize land to build roads or establish harbors. Thus takings under the Fifth Amendment must be for **public use**. This once meant building public parks or highways that would be available to all residents of a community,[111] but the Supreme Court has recently expanded this definition. In 2000 the city of New London, Connecticut, approved a private development plan that would use eminent domain to seize dozens of homes and use the land for a research facility for the Pfizer pharmaceutical company plus a hotel, a marina, and high-end housing units. Proponents argued that the development would have a public benefit because it would create more than a thousand jobs and increase tax revenues. But Wilhelmina Dery stood to lose the home in which she had been born in 1918 and had lived in all her life. She, Susette Kelo, and seven other homeowners brought suit against New London, arguing that taking their homes and giving them to private developers violated their constitutional rights because the taking was not for a truly public use. But the Supreme Court declared in *Kelo v. New London* (2005) that the public use requirement means only a "public benefit," and that the taking of the petitioners' homes would in fact produce a public benefit.[112] The *Kelo v. New London* decision led to angry reactions from homeowners throughout the country, and many states responded by explicitly limiting the situations under which eminent domain could be exercised.

Moreover, even though the homeowners lost their case with the city, this conflict between individual rights and public benefit did not result in very much public benefit. In 2009 Pfizer announced that it was pulling out of the New London facility as a cost-cutting measure, taking 1,400 jobs with it. The developer never constructed the hotels, stores, and condominiums that were supposed to be built there, and the land on which the seized houses existed remains vacant.[113]

Civil Liberties and Democracy

At the beginning of the chapter, we quoted Justice Jackson's opinion from the flag salute case that no government official can declare what shall be required in terms of basic beliefs and values. But what if elected officials do so anyway? Jackson responded that it was then the Court's job to protect such rights: "The very purpose of a Bill of Rights was to withdraw certain subjects from . . . political controversy, to place them beyond the reach of majorities and officials and to establish them as legal principles to be applied by the courts. One's . . . fundamental rights may not be submitted to vote; they depend on the outcome of no elections."[114]

Judicial decisions do not exist in a vacuum. Over the long run, if the Court is unresponsive to the people, new presidents will appoint new judges who better represent the people's preferences.[115] And while the Supreme Court is not accountable to the electorate in the same way that Congress and the president are, Congress and the president do have ways to try to hold the Court accountable. For example, in 1937 President Franklin Roosevelt threatened to pack the Court as a result of the Court's decisions on economic policy. In the 1950s Congress threatened to take away the Court's authority to hear certain types of cases in the wake of Court decisions about congressional investigations of Communists. In recent years, members of Congress have threatened to impeach justices over Court decisions with which they disagreed.

These attempts failed, the older ones largely because the Court proved responsive to the threats and backed away from its original positions. This outcome suggests that one way or another, the Court cannot stand alone in protecting civil liberties if popular support is not behind it. One of the difficulties in protecting civil liberties in a democracy is that although it is easy to feel sympathy for teenagers who wear black armbands to protest war, most litigants whose cases set precedents that protect all the nation's freedoms are not as wholesome, and the causes they espouse may be racist, sexist, or violent.[116]

Unlimited liberties can also harm social order, particularly in times of crisis. Note, however, that in the period following September 11, 2001, Congress made no attempt to criminalize antiwar speech, as it had during World War I; there was little public demand for such restrictions, as tolerance of opposing viewpoints among Americans has increased dramatically over the years. **Political tolerance**, the willingness of people to put up with ideas with which they disagree, is essential to both the marketplace of ideas and democratic stability.[117]

Consider the willingness of Americans to allow Communists to give speeches in their community. This willingness has increased, as has tolerance toward atheists and militarists (see Figure 4.4). If the people are tolerant, elected politicians will be tolerant also.

Similarly, the appointment process furthers responsiveness. Although critics have attacked the Supreme Court for establishing a right to privacy that is not explicitly in the Constitution, this decision remains highly popular, with 98 percent of Americans considering the right essential or important.[118] In 1986, when Supreme Court nominee Robert Bork stated that he rejected the validity of this right, the Senate rejected his appointment. But if the public loses its concern over civil liberties, sooner or later, the Supreme Court will as well.

FOCUS QUESTIONS

- What is government's role with regard to civil liberties? How responsive can or should it be to the people's will?

- What is the proper balance between liberty and order?

- Under what circumstances should civil liberties be restrained?

- What happens when rights clash? Are restrictions of civil liberties justified if they promote equality?

- In what ways does the guarantee of civil liberties promote democracy? Or does it pose challenges for democratic government that can be considered gates?

When the people disagree with a Supreme Court decision, what can they do about it?

political tolerance:
Willingness of people to put up with ideas with which they disagree.

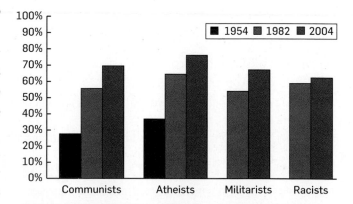

FIGURE 4.4 Percent Allowing Speeches by Members of Disfavored Groups, 1954–2004.
The willingness of Americans to allow Communists, atheists, and militarists (those who would do away with elections and have the military run the government) to give speeches has increased over the past sixty years. Tolerance toward racists, on the other hand, has not increased.
Source: General Social Survey, various years.

GATEWAYS TO LEARNING

Top Ten to Take Away

1. Civil liberties are freedoms so fundamental that they are outside the authority of government to regulate. It often falls to the judiciary to protect them. (pp. 104–6)

2. They include, among others, rights surrounding freedom of expression and criminal procedure, and they were written into the Constitution in 1791 as the first ten amendments, or Bill of Rights. (pp. 106–7)

3. Although these protections of individual freedoms at first applied only to the federal government, Supreme Court decisions have gradually applied many of them to the states as well. (pp. 107–9)

4. Attempts to limit civil liberties are more frequent in wartime and during other threats, given increased government need for order and increased citizen concern about security. But support for the protection of civil liberties usually rebounds after the crisis ends. (pp. 109–14)

5. The scope of First Amendment freedoms of expression has generally expanded, although during wartime they are likely to be curtailed. (pp. 114–17)

6. Even in wartime, the courts have almost always protected the press from government censorship, but the government can prosecute newspapers for publishing obscenity, secret military information, and articles that incite violence. (pp. 118–20)

7. The First Amendment also protects freedom of religious practice and prevents the government from establishing one religion over all the others. (pp. 120–24)

8. Provisions in the Fourth, Fifth, Sixth, and Eighth Amendments protect individuals accused of crimes in police investigations and regulate trial procedures and types of punishments. (pp. 125–26)

9. Although the Constitution and its amendments do not explicitly grant a general right to privacy, the Supreme Court has used various constitutional provisions to establish this right, creating one of the most contentious areas of constitutional law and interpretation. (pp. 128–31)

10. While in the short run the Supreme Court can protect liberties without public approval, in the long run procedures relating to the presidential appointment and Senate approval of justices keep the Court responsive to the people. (pp. 132–33)

A full narrative summary is on the book's website.

Ten to Test Yourself

1. How have civil liberties fared during times of war and other crises?

2. Why does it fall to the judicial branch to protect civil liberties?

3. What is the selective incorporation doctrine?

4. What is the compelling interest test?

5. What types of speech receive more and less protection by the Supreme Court?

6. In what ways is the concept of neutrality important to First Amendment rights?

7. How has the Supreme Court applied the *Lemon* test?

8. What constitutional rights do criminal defendants have during investigations? At trial? During sentencing?

9. What is the constitutional basis for the right to privacy?

10. What rights related to private property are protected by the Constitution?

More review questions and answers and chapter quizzes are on the book's website.

Timeline to Keep Things in Order

Bill of Rights protects inalienable rights from infringement by the national government.

1791

Fourteenth Amendment restricts what states can do and later allows the Court to bind protections of fundamental rights on the states.

1868

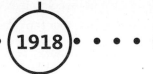
Woodrow Wilson's Sedition Act prohibits language critical of the United States.

1918

Schenck v. United States sets a standard for restricting speech.

1919

Earl Warren is named chief justice, and the Court begins to expand civil liberties.

1953

Terms to Know and Use

accommodationists
(pp. 122, 123)

actual malice test (p. 119)

American Civil Liberties
Union (p. 117)

anarchy (p. 106)

Barron v. Baltimore (p. 107)

Bill of Rights (p. 105)

bills of attainder (p. 106)

blacklisting (p. 111)

Brandenburg v. Ohio (p. 114)

civil liberties (p. 105)

civil rights (p. 105)

clear and present danger test
(p. 114)

COINTELPRO (p. 112)

compelling interest test
(pp. 108, 109)

content-neutral (p. 116)

double jeopardy clause (p. 127)

due process clause (p. 108)

eminent domain (p. 131)

establishment clause (p. 122)

ex post facto laws (p. 106)

exclusionary rule (p. 126)

expectation of privacy test
(p. 125)

fighting words doctrine (p. 114)

free exercise clause (p. 120)

fundamental rights
(pp. 108, 109)

Geneva Conventions (p. 113)

Gideon v. Wainwright (p. 127)

good faith exception
(p. 126)

grand jury (pp. 108, 109)

Griswold v. Connecticut (p. 129)

hate speech (p. 114)

incorporate (p. 107)

just compensation (p. 131)

Lawrence v. Texas (p. 131)

Lemon test (pp. 122, 123)

libel (p. 118)

Mapp v. Ohio (p. 126)

marketplace of ideas
(p. 110)

McCarthy era (p. 111)

military tribunal (p. 110)

Miller test (p. 119)

Miranda v. Arizona (p. 126)

natural (unalienable) rights
(p. 105)

political tolerance (p. 133)

Powell v. Alabama (p. 127)

prior restraint (p. 118)

probable cause (p. 113)

public use (p. 132)

Red Scare (p. 111)

right of association (p. 120)

right to counsel (p. 126)

right to privacy (p. 129)

Roe v. Wade (p. 130)

Sedition Acts (p. 109)

seditious libel (p. 119)

selective incorporation
(p. 108)

self-incrimination (p. 126)

separationists (pp. 122, 123)

subsequent punishment
(p. 118)

symbolic speech (p. 116)

takings clause (p. 131)

test (pp. 108, 109)

total incorporation (p. 108)

tyranny (p. 106)

undue burden (p. 130)

valid secular purpose
(p. 122)

warrant (p. 113)

writ of *habeas corpus* (p. 106)

Use the vocabulary flash cards on the book's website.

Learning That Works

WHAT YOU NEED . . .

TO KNOW

What civil liberties are

What the Bill of Rights protects

Court rulings on free speech

Criminal procedure protections and the right to privacy

The relationship between government and religion

The limits on government

The limits on private property

TO DO

Recognize the restraints on what government can do

Appreciate the freedoms you have

Question whether your university's speech code is constitutional

Decide whether government should have access to your and everyone else's e-mail, health records, financial records, and social networking pages

Evaluate restrictions on religious practice: Are all religions equal? Should they be treated equally?

Understand whether government does or does not protect you, and if so, from what

Know how secure your home and possessions are from search, seizure, and taking

---

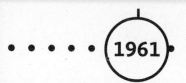

Mapp v. Ohio is the first in a series of modern decisions expanding the rights of people accused of crimes.

1961

Griswold v. Connecticut establishes a right to privacy.

1965

Brandenburg v. Ohio refines the standard for restricting speech.

1969

Roe v. Wade extends the right to privacy to abortion.

1973

Lawrence v. Texas extends the right to privacy to homosexual behavior.

2003

5 CIVIL RIGHTS

Fisk University, Nashville, Tennessee

> *I think it's really important to realize that each individual shoulders a great deal of responsibility, and that's the way the movement in the 1960s was accomplished.*

In 1956, when Diane Nash went to college, she first chose Howard University in Washington, D.C., where she enrolled as an English major. But she soon transferred to Fisk University in Nashville, Tennessee. Attending school in the segregated South was something of a shock for the Chicago native. "I understood the facts," she later recalled, but "when I went south and saw the signs that said 'white' and 'colored,' and I actually could not drink out of that water fountain or go to that ladies' room, I had a real emotional reaction." Nashville was more of a shock than Washington, and humiliation turned to outrage.

But the ethic of service that Howard and Fisk promoted in African American students was familiar to Nash, who had grown up in a Catholic family and considered becoming a nun. Instead, while at Fisk, she began attending workshops on social change and Christian nonviolence led by John Lawson, a graduate student in theology at nearby Vanderbilt University, and she also attended workshops at the Highlander Folk School, where civil rights leaders such as Rosa Parks and Martin Luther King had received training. When four African American college students in Greensboro, North Carolina, launched a sit-in movement to integrate lunch counters in February 1960, Diane Nash was ready.

Quickly, Nash organized and trained local students to carry out nonviolent protests at downtown lunch counters. When she was arrested, she spoke eloquently of injustice to the judge. Confronting the mayor of Nashville, she turned his plea for praying together into a case for eating together, and the mayor caved in. After the lunch counters were desegregated, Nash organized college students to replace Freedom Riders who had been beaten while testing the enforcement of desegregation orders on buses and in bus stations across the South. A founding member of the Student Nonviolent

Diane Nash

Jack Corn/The Tennessean

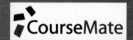

Visit http://www.cengagebrain
.com/shop/ISBN/0618906959 for interactive tools including:

- Quizzes
- Flashcards
- Videos
- Animated PowerPoint slides, Podcast summaries, and more

Coordinating Committee (SNCC), she left Fisk to become a full-time activist, leading civic education and voting rights campaigns in Mississippi and Alabama.

Twenty years later, reflecting on her role in the civil rights movement, Nash was astonished at her own courage. "I remember realizing that with what we were doing, trying to abolish segregation, we were coming up against governors of seven states, judges, politicians, businessmen, and I remember thinking, 'I'm only 22 years old. What do I know? What am I doing?'" But she also felt "the power of an idea whose time had come." "The movement had a way of reaching inside me and bringing out things that I never knew were there," she continued. "Like courage, and love for people." "I think it's really important," she concluded, "that young people today understand that the movement of the sixties was really a people's movement. . . . Young people should realize that it was people just like them, their age, that formulated the goals and strategies, and actually developed the movement. When they look around now, and see things that need to be changed, they should say: 'What can I do? What can my roommate and I do to effect that change?'"[1]

Fifty years after Nash and young people throughout the South risked their lives for the right to drink at a water fountain, to eat at a lunch counter, and to vote and participate in American civic life, Barack Hussein Obama, the child of a white mother and an African father, was elected president of the United States. An African American president could scarcely have been imagined at the time, but the gateways that civil rights activists like Nash forced open changed American law and politics forever. Yet the road from slavery to segregation, and from segregation to Obama, was long, and the struggle for equality was led not only by African Americans but by women, immigrants, and other groups who were blocked from participation in America's civic life. In this chapter, we examine the changing concept of equality from exclusive to inclusive and track the changing responses and responsibilities of government.

FOCUS QUESTIONS

- What is the meaning of equality? How has its meaning changed since the Constitution was written in 1787?

- What role has government played with regard to equality in the past? What role does it assume today?

- What means have various groups used to secure their civil rights? What means has government used to respond?

- What is the effect on a democracy if some of its people lack civil rights?

- Are civil rights a gate or a gateway to democracy? Explain.

What Are Civil Rights?

Although the Declaration of Independence declared that "All men are created equal," the 1787 Constitution had little to say about equality, at least as the concept is understood today. The Antifederalists insisted on a Bill of Rights that would protect fundamental liberties, but they did not argue for equality. Today equality is a hallowed principle of American political culture, but the notion and the reality evolved slowly over two centuries.

Civil Rights and Civil Liberties

civil rights: *Set of rights centered around the concept of equal treatment that government is obliged to protect.*

Civil rights are rights related to the duties of citizenship and the opportunities for participation in civic life that the government is obliged to protect. These rights are based on the expectation of equality under the law. The most important is the right to vote. In contrast to civil rights are **civil liberties**, freedoms so fundamental that government may not legitimately take them away. They are the subject of Chapter 4 (Civil Liberties).

Civil rights also differ from civil liberties in that while government is the only authority that could suppress liberties, for example by suppressing freedom of speech or forbidding a certain religious belief, both government and individuals have the capacity to engage in **discrimination** by treating people unequally: the government through laws that discriminate, and individuals or businesses through actions that discriminate.

The government can therefore take three different roles when it comes to civil rights. It can engage in state-sponsored or **public discrimination** by actively discriminating against people. It can treat people equally but permit **private discrimination** by allowing individuals or businesses to discriminate. Finally, it can try, as the U.S. government has since the 1960s, both to treat people equally and to prevent individuals or businesses from discriminating. Thus it falls to government to protect individuals against unequal treatment and to citizens to ensure that the government itself is not discriminating against individuals or groups. In a democracy, the majority rules, but the gateways for minorities must also be kept open.

The Constitution and Civil Rights

Despite the statement on equality in the Declaration of Independence, the role of the government with regard to ensuring equality was not written into the Constitution, and the United States has a bleak history on civil rights. The Founders were not much concerned with equality as it is understood today. Many of them owned slaves, and they did not see a contradiction between doing so and the Declaration's statement on equality. Though the Constitution does not use the words *slave* and *slavery*, it endorsed the slave system by requiring states to return runaway slaves and by prohibiting a ban on importing slaves from Africa until 1808. The Constitution also gave the states authority over voting, and most states restricted the right to vote to free males with a certain amount of property. Slaves could not vote, and in a few states free African Americans could not either. Neither could women (except in New Jersey), Native Americans, and in many states men without property.[2] During the nation's first century and even thereafter, state laws and the national government actively discriminated against people on the basis of race, gender, and ethnic background.

Following the Civil War, the Thirteenth Amendment ended slavery, and the Fourteenth Amendment forbade states to deny any person "the equal protection of the laws." Nevertheless, the equality of African Americans was not thereby guaranteed. Some of the members of Congress who wrote the Fourteenth Amendment believed that equality was limited to "the right to go and come; the right to enforce contracts; the right to convey his property; the right to buy property" and little more.[3] The courts agreed, and the federal government made little effort to ensure equal treatment during the nation's second century.

During these years, however, women won the right to vote (1920) but not the right to full participation in public life. Native Americans became citizens (1924), but not until the civil rights and women's movements of the 1950s and 1960s did legal discrimination against African Americans, women, and ethnic minorities end. Today, the government actively aims to treat individuals and groups as equals before the law and to use its authority to prevent state and local governments, and individuals and businesses, from discriminating.

In the last half-century, the meaning of "all men are created equal" has been expanded to include women and all people subject to the jurisdiction of the United States. Americans

civil liberties: *Those rights, such as freedom of speech and religion, that are so fundamental that they are outside the authority of government to regulate.*

discrimination: *Favoring one person over another, usually on irrelevant grounds such as race or gender.*

Why would a government discriminate?

public discrimination: *Discrimination by national, state, or local governments.*

private discrimination: *Discrimination by private individuals or businesses.*

What did equality mean to the Founders?

now look to the government to protect equality and enforce equal treatment under the law. But they still debate the meaning of *equality*. Should, or can, the government ensure **equality of opportunity** for all people? Should, or can, it engineer **equality of outcome**? That is, is it enough for society to provide equality of opportunity by prohibiting discrimination? What if that still leaves members of groups that have historically been discriminated against, such as women and minorities, with fewer advanced degrees and lower incomes? As it has throughout the course of the nation's history, the meaning of equality continues to evolve.

In the next sections, we see how, as the idea of equality expanded, the federal government moved from actively treating different groups unequally under the law, to asserting equality under the law but doing little to protect it, to actively enforcing it. Equality of rights is now a central feature of the Constitution and the Court's interpretation of it.[4]

Legal Restrictions on Civil Rights

Slavery split the United States from the founding of the nation through the Civil War. After the Civil War the Constitution prohibited slavery. It also prohibited the states from denying equality, but many states continued to discriminate. Both Congress and the Supreme Court had the authority to enforce equality, but neither took action. Women as well as African Americans suffered under unequal laws, with denial of the right to vote and laws that limited their full participation in labor markets, professions, and public life. Discriminatory laws also affected Asians, prohibiting those who were not born in the United States from becoming citizens and later preventing them from immigrating to the United States altogether. As exemplified by the internment of Japanese Americans during World War II, government restrictions on the civil rights of ethnic minorities are far more likely during wartime.

Slavery

Slavery came to the colonies in 1619 when a Virginian purchased Africans from a Dutch shipper. Colonial Africans originally were servants, largely indistinct from indentured servants of other races who bound themselves to service for a limited number of years in return for free passage to Britain's American colonies. But African slavery soon became established in colonial law. In 1664 Maryland passed legislation declaring that all "Negroes or other slaves hereafter imported shall serve" for life.[5] The law also made slaves of the children of slaves.

The compromises made at the Constitutional Convention allowed the United States to form, but they also allowed slavery to grow and spread. By 1808, when Congress banned the further importation of slaves from Africa, the slave population had reached 1 million, and it continued growing through natural increase thereafter. With neither slave nor free forces dominant politically, Congress continued to compromise. The **Missouri Compromise** (1820) banned slavery in the territories north of the southern border of Missouri, thus keeping most of the vast lands of the Louisiana Purchase free. The Compromise of 1850 allowed territories captured in the Mexican War to decide for themselves whether to be free or slave and denied alleged fugitive slaves the right to a jury trial. The Kansas-Nebraska Act (1854) undid the

Missouri Compromise by allowing each territory to vote on whether to allow slavery. The Supreme Court further extended the reach of slavery in **Dred Scott v. Sandford** (1857).[6]

Dred Scott, a slave who had moved with his master from the slave state of Missouri to the free Wisconsin Territory and then back to Missouri, sued in federal court for his freedom based on his extended stay in free territory. The Supreme Court's decision in the case, written by Chief Justice Roger Taney, a former slave owner, declared (1) that no black—slave or free—could be an American citizen, and thus that no black could sue in a federal court; (2) that blacks were "beings of an inferior order" who had "no rights which the white man was bound to respect"; (3) that the Declaration's statement that "all men are created equal" did not include men of African heritage; (4) that Congress's authority to "make all needful Rules and Regulations respecting the Territory . . . [of] the United States" did not include the right to prohibit slavery in those territories; and (5) that slaves were the property of their owners, so freeing Scott would violate his owner's Fifth Amendment right against being deprived of his property without due process of law. With this decision, the regulation of slavery in the territories was moved from the national hands of Congress into the local hands of those territories.

The 1860 election of Abraham Lincoln (1861–65), who opposed the extension of slavery, prompted southern states to secede from the union. During the ensuing Civil War, Lincoln issued the **Emancipation Proclamation**, which made slavery illegal in those states in rebellion as of January 1, 1863. Slavery was finally ended in the United States following Union victory and ratification of the Thirteenth Amendment in 1865 (see Figure 5.1).

Racial Segregation and Discrimination

The end of slavery did not make former slaves equal citizens. Immediately after the war, southern states wrote new constitutions that severely limited the civil and political rights of the freedmen. These so-called **black codes** prevented them from voting, owning land, and leaving their plantations. Congress responded with the Civil Rights Act of 1866, which guaranteed the right of freedmen to make contracts, sue in court if those contracts were violated, and own property. Congress also established military rule over the former Confederate

Library of Congress

FIGURE 5.1 Constitutional Amendments That Pertain to Civil Rights.

Color Code :
Criminal procedure   Participation   Equality

Thirteenth (1865): Prohibits slavery in the United States

Fourteenth (1868): Makes all persons born in the United States citizens of the United States, and prohibits states from denying persons within its jurisdiction the privileges or immunities of citizens, the due process of law, and equal protection of the laws; apportionment by whole persons

Fifteenth (1870): Prohibits states from denying the right to vote on account of race

Nineteenth (1920): Guarantees women the right to vote

Twenty-Fourth (1964): Prohibits poll taxes

In 1846 Dred Scott, a black slave pictured here with his family, sued for his freedom, claiming that since his owner had taken him to a free territory, he should be free. The Supreme Court said no, and went further to say that Scott, as an African American, had no standing to sue, and that Congress could not prohibit slavery in any territory. The 1857 ruling pleased southerners but infuriated northerners.

Emancipation Proclamation: *Lincoln's 1863 order ending slavery in states in rebellion.*

black codes: *Southern laws that prohibited freedmen from voting, owning land, and leaving their plantations.*

Reconstruction: *The period from 1865 to 1877 in which the former Confederate states gained readmission to the Union and the federal government passed laws to help the emancipated slaves.*

equal protection clause: *Prevents states from denying any person the equal protection of the laws (Fourteenth Amendment).*

After ratification of the Fifteenth Amendment, who could not vote?

Ku Klux Klan: *White supremacist terrorist organization.*

poll taxes: *Tax on voting; prohibited by the Twenty-Fourth Amendment (1964).*

white primary: *Election rules that prohibited blacks from voting in Democratic primaries.*

literacy tests: *Tests requiring reading and interpretation skills in order to vote.*

grandfather clauses: *Election rules that exempted people from difficult literacy and interpretation tests for voting if their grandfathers had been eligible to vote.*

Jim Crow laws: *Southern laws that established strict segregation of the races.*

Plessy v. Ferguson: *1896 Supreme Court case that upheld the validity of segregation.*

separate-but-equal doctrine: *Supreme Court doctrine that upheld segregation as long as there were equivalent facilities for blacks.*

If some people are blocked from voting, what is the effect on government?

states, which would end in a state when it passed a new state constitution that guaranteed black suffrage and when it ratified the Fourteenth Amendment. With former Confederates barred from voting, blacks constituted a majority of the electorate in several states, and more than six hundred freedmen served in state legislatures during **Reconstruction**, as this era was called.

The Fourteenth Amendment (1868), in addition to guaranteeing that no state shall deny any person due process of law (see Chapter 4), prohibits states from denying any person the **equal protection** of the law. It also makes all people born in the United States citizens of the United States, overturning the Supreme Court's ruling in the *Dred Scott* case that blacks could not be U.S. citizens. In an attempt to prevent states from rescinding the right of black suffrage, the Fifteenth Amendment (1870) declared that the right to vote could not be abridged on account of race.

Opponents of freedmen rights turned to violence. In 1866 Confederate veterans formed the **Ku Klux Klan** (KKK), a terrorist organization aimed at restoring white supremacy. In 1873 white supremacists massacred more than a hundred blacks in Colfax, Louisiana, as part of an ongoing election dispute. The federal government brought charges against three of the perpetrators, but the Supreme Court reversed their conviction, arguing that the Fourteenth Amendment gave Congress the authority to act only against states that violated civil rights (public discrimination), not against individuals who did so (private discrimination).[7]

Reconstruction ended with a deal over the 1876 election. A close and contested race between Republican Rutherford B. Hayes and Democrat Samuel Tilden was resolved when southern Democrats in Congress agreed to allow Hayes to become president in return for the withdrawal of federal troops from the South. Freed from military rule, white supremacist groups such as the Klan embarked on a campaign of lynching and other forms of terrorism against blacks.

State governments were not responsive to the victims because, despite the Fifteenth Amendment, southern politicians established a set of rules that kept blacks from voting. **Poll taxes** limited the voting of poor blacks (as well as of poor whites). The **white primary** took advantage of the fact that, with the Republican Party negatively associated with Lincoln and the Civil War, the Democratic Party completely dominated southern politics. Therefore whoever won the local Democratic primary for an office was sure to win in the general election. Excluding blacks from voting in Democratic primaries meant that blacks had no effective vote at all. Even so, states used **literacy tests** to disqualify voters. These involved reading and interpreting difficult passages. To avoid thereby disqualifying white voters as well, **grandfather clauses** gave exemptions to men whose grandfathers had been eligible to vote. The men who received these exemptions were, of course, always white (see Chapter 11, Voting and Participation, for further discussion of these techniques and an example of a literacy test).

These legal strategies effectively disfranchised black men. In addition, state and local **Jim Crow laws** enforced segregation of whites and blacks in all public places. When a New Orleans civil rights organization challenged a Louisiana law requiring segregated railway cars by having Homer Plessy, who was one-eighth black, sit in the whites-only section, the Supreme Court upheld the segregation.[8] ***Plessy v. Ferguson*** (1896) established the **separate-but-equal doctrine**, which held that states could segregate the races without violating the equal protection clause of the Fourteenth Amendment as long as the separate facilities were equal.[9] Southern states segregated schools, libraries, and other public institutions and required the segregation of restaurants, inns, and other places of public accommodation. The facilities were almost never equal. African Americans in northern states often experienced discrimination in hiring, housing, hotels, and restaurants, though segregation was not enforced by law. African Americans could serve in the military, but generally in segregated units under white officers. During the late nineteenth and early twentieth centuries discrimination was state-sponsored in the South; elsewhere in the nation, people engaged in private discrimination without challenge.

Other ethnic groups besides blacks also suffered discrimination. California's 1879 constitution prohibited Chinese from voting and from employment in state and local government. Three years later, Congress passed the **Chinese Exclusion Act**, which prohibited Chinese immigration. In 1913 California prohibited Japanese immigrants from purchasing farmland.[10]

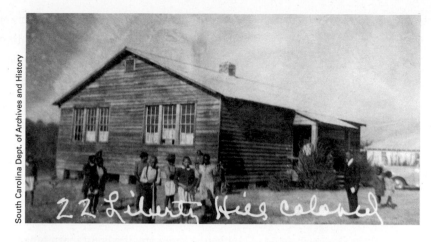

South Carolina Dept. of Archives and History

South Carolina Dept. of Archives and History

Segregation in the South often placed Hispanics in the same position as African Americans. Segregation also existed in the West. Phoenix, Arizona, ran separate schools for blacks, Indians, and Mexicans.[11] California ran separate schools for Asians as well as Mexicans,[12] while Texas kept Mexican Americans in separate classrooms[13] (see Figure 3.11 in Chapter 3, Federalism, for a map of states with school systems that were segregated as of 1950).

Women's Suffrage

By law and by custom, women were also excluded from public life from the earliest days of the nation. In 1776 Abigail Adams had urged her husband, John Adams, to "remember the ladies" in drafting the nation's founding documents. In language similar to that later used by Jefferson in the Declaration, she warned, "if particular care and attention is not paid to the ladies, we are determined to foment a rebellion, and will not hold ourselves bound by any laws in which we have no voice or representation."[14] Nevertheless, neither the Declaration nor the Constitution made any provision for women's rights. Rather, the states continued the English policy of **coverture**, which granted married women no rights independent of their husbands. They could not own property, keep their own wages, or sign contracts. As for voting, each state set its own rules. In 1789 only New Jersey allowed women the right to vote (provided the women met the state's property requirements), a right it rescinded in 1807.[15]

In 1848 leaders of the **women's suffrage** movement met in Seneca Falls, New York, to organize for the right to vote. They prepared a "Declaration of Sentiments" that used the language of the Declaration of Independence to assert that "all men and women are

In segregated school systems, the schools for black children and the schools for white children were almost never equal. These insurance photographs show Liberty Hill Colored School and Summerton Graded School in Clarendon County, South Carolina, in 1948. They were used as evidence in *Briggs v. Elliott*, one of the school segregation cases decided with *Brown v. Board of Education* (1954).

Chinese Exclusion Act: *1882 act barring immigration of Chinese to America.*

Do members of Congress represent all the people in their district or state, or only those who voted for them?

coverture: *Legal doctrine that grants married women no rights independent of their husbands.*

women's suffrage: *Movement to grant women the right to vote.*

Were Anthony and Stanton right or wrong to lobby against the Fifteenth Amendment?

created equal," but few results came from this meeting. Then, in 1869 Susan B. Anthony and Elizabeth Cady Stanton formed the National Woman Suffrage Association (NWSA), which lobbied for the right of women to vote and unsuccessfully opposed the Fifteenth Amendment unless it was changed to include women's suffrage. With the NWSA focused on gaining national suffrage through constitutional amendment, an alternative organization, the American Woman Suffrage Association (AWSA), formed to press for state-by-state suffrage rights.

In 1872 a Missouri voting registrar prohibited suffragist Virginia Minor from registering to vote. Minor sued, alleging that the privileges of citizenship, as guaranteed by the Fourteenth Amendment, include the right to vote. The Supreme Court ruled, however, that citizenship does not imply a right to vote.[16]

That same year the Court ruled that the right to practice law was not a privilege or immunity guaranteed by the Fourteenth Amendment, allowing Illinois to keep law a male-only profession. Representing common views at the time, one justice wrote, "The paramount destiny and mission of women are to fulfill the noble and benign offices of wife and mother. This is the law of the Creator."[17] States passed various types of so-called **protective legislation** that limited the jobs women could work at and/or the number of hours they could work. These laws had the express purpose of protecting women because of their status as wives and mothers, but their main impact was to put women at a disadvantage in the employment market.[18]

protective legislation:
Laws that limited women's participation in the workforce.

Why was there such strong resistance to women's suffrage?

Although women's rights advocates typically opposed protective legislation, they focused their attention on the right to vote. With the courts rejecting a gateway to voting through the Fourteenth Amendment, suffragists focused on the legislative arena. Anthony presented the 1887 Congress with ten thousand petition signatures demanding women's suffrage. In 1894 suffragists presented the New York legislature with six hundred thousand signatures. The suffragist movement, though, was not universally admired; many people opposed voting equality for women because it threatened their notions of appropriate gender roles. In 1913 a mob attacked a suffrage parade in Washington, D.C. Suffragist protests outside the White House in 1917 led to hundreds of arrests.

Library of Congress

During World War I members of the National Woman's Party picketed the White House. Wearing banners announcing their colleges, they challenged President Woodrow Wilson to bring home the concern for liberty that he expressed for Europe. More than 150 women were arrested, and about 100 were sentenced to federal prisons, where some went on hunger strikes and were force-fed.

While state control of voting gave southern states the power to disfranchise blacks, it also gave western states the power to experiment with women's suffrage. The territory of Wyoming granted women's suffrage in 1869, and continued it upon statehood in 1890. Males in Colorado voted for women's suffrage in 1893. Utah granted women the right to vote in 1895. In 1913 Illinois granted women the right to vote for president, but not for other national offices. In 1916 the people of Montana elected the first woman to serve in the U.S. House of Representatives, Jeannette Rankin (see Figure 5.2).

Suffragist amendments failed numerous times in Congress before receiving the necessary two-thirds vote in both chambers in 1919.[19] By August 1920, with effective lobbying by suffragist groups, three-quarters of the states ratified the Nineteenth Amendment, guaranteeing women the right to vote in the November 1920 presidential election (see also

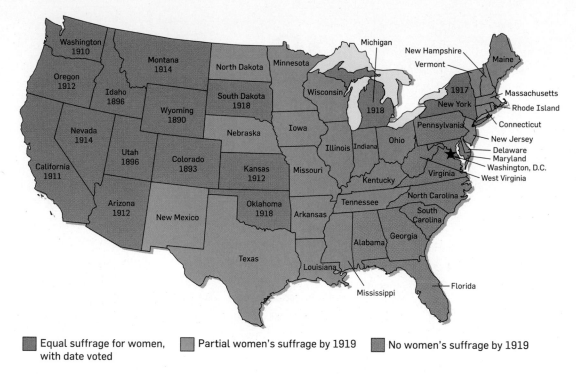

■ Equal suffrage for women, with date voted   ■ Partial women's suffrage by 1919   ■ No women's suffrage by 1919

FIGURE 5.2 Women's Suffrage by States, 1890–1919. Because states control voting laws, women's suffrage advocates campaigned at the state level, and before the Nineteenth Amendment was ratified in 1920 women could vote in some elections in most states. The Nineteenth Amendment superseded state law, stating that the right to vote could not be denied or abridged by the United States, or by any state, on account of sex.
Source: Sandra Opdycke, *The Routledge Historical Atlas of Women* (New York: Routledge, 2000), 82.

Chapter 11; for information on women's suffrage elsewhere in the world, see Other Places: Equal Treatment of Women).

Continued Gender Discrimination

Nevertheless, public law and private attitudes continued to block women from full participation in the nation's public life. Radical feminists pushed for an equal rights amendment, which would have overturned protective legislation and other laws that treated men and women differently, but though introduced in Congress in 1923 and every year thereafter, it was not taken seriously. Even in 1945, only a minority of white males thought that women should be able to take jobs outside the home.[20]

Not surprisingly, the federal and state governments were responsive to these sorts of views. As late as 1972 eleven states continued to enforce coverture laws.[21] Louisiana law, for example, gave a husband "as 'head and master' of property jointly owned with his wife," the complete right to dispose of such property without his wife's consent.[22] Teachers were commonly forced to retire if they got married.[23] Outside of coverture laws, Social Security provided survivors' benefits for children if their working fathers died, but not if their working mothers died. It similarly provided unemployment benefits to children of unemployed fathers, but not to children of unemployed mothers. Males in the military received benefits for their dependents that females in the military did not receive. Idaho gave preferences to men over women in determining who would administer a dead relative's estate. Utah required parents to support sons until age 21, but daughters only until age 18. A woman could not work as a bartender in Michigan unless she was the wife or daughter of the bar's owner.[24]

Should women be protected by an equal rights amendment?

otherplaces

Equal Treatment of Women

Virtually all nations formally protect equality under the law, but the degree to which women actually obtain equal treatment varies enormously. Freedom House and the State Department have reported the following about women's equality in other democracies.

Great Britain. Women receive equal treatment under the law but are underrepresented at the top levels of business. Immigrant women have decidedly lower standards of living.

India. Females suffer from legal and societal discrimination, including forced prostitution, prisoner rape, and the murder of female babies. The murder of women for bringing dishonor to their families, or their husbands' families, continues despite laws to the contrary. *Sati*, the custom in which a widow kills herself on the funeral pyre of her husband, also continues, despite the Sati Prevention Act of 1987. Dowry, the exchange of money or goods from the bride's family to the groom's, is also illegal, yet the press regularly reports on dowry disputes that have led to the murder of the bride.

Israel. Israel's Declaration of Independence guarantees equality on account of sex, and equality is largely the case in secular society. Military service is compulsory for men and women. The nation's fourth prime minister was a woman—Golda Meir. Religious courts, on the other hand, prevent women from obtaining divorces without the consent of their husbands.

South Africa. South Africa's constitution prohibits discrimination on account of sex, but there is pervasive violence and discrimination against women in South Africa, including violence by the military.

Source: Freedom House; United States Department of State.

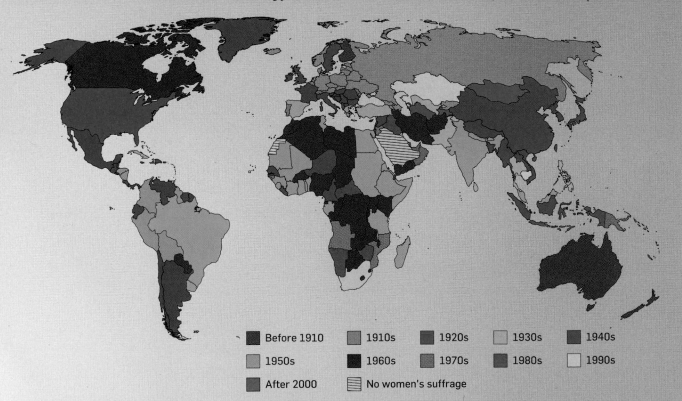

Legend:
- Before 1910
- 1910s
- 1920s
- 1930s
- 1940s
- 1950s
- 1960s
- 1970s
- 1980s
- 1990s
- After 2000
- No women's suffrage

Decades in Which Women Achieved the Right to Vote. This map shows when women gained the right to vote in countries around the world. Many of the countries, such as China, do not have meaningful elections, so granting women the vote is not substantively important.
Source: "Historical Atlas of the 20th Century," users.erols.com, with additions; Jone Johnson Lewis, International Woman Suffrage Timeline, about.com.

Because women were treated differently than men under the law, many laws also discriminated against men. Colorado allowed females to drink beer at age 18; males had to wait until they turned 21. California, like many states, made it a crime for males of any age to have sexual relations with females under the age of 18, but had no corresponding penalty for females having sexual relations with underage males. Alabama, like many states, imposed alimony obligations on men only. New York allowed unwed mothers, but not unwed fathers, to block the adoption of their children. Florida provided property tax relief to widows, but not to widowers. Only males had to register for the military draft.[25] Many of these laws were based on an implicit assumption that women, viewed as the weaker sex, needed special protection by the government.[26] As late as 1961 the Supreme Court exempted women from jury duty because they were "the center of home and family life."[27]

Restrictions on Citizenship

In the case of both African Americans and women, the status of **citizenship** did not guarantee the right to vote or serve on juries. Yet on the basis of ethnic background, some groups were denied even the status of citizenship and the privileges it entailed, such as protection, under the Fourteenth Amendment's **privileges or immunities clause**, from state laws that curtail rights that other citizens hold.

citizenship: *Full-fledged membership in a nation.*

privileges or immunities clause: *Prohibits states from abridging certain fundamental rights (Fourteenth Amendment).*

Citizenship in the Constitution.

The Constitution was not explicit on birthright citizenship, but the clause requiring that presidents be **natural-born citizens** seemingly implies that people born in the United States are citizens.[28] But the *Dred Scott* ruling, until overturned by the Fourteenth Amendment, belied that assumption, as did the status of Native Americans.

natural-born citizens: *People who are citizens in a nation from birth, usually by being born there.*

In 1823 the Supreme Court declared that Native Americans were merely inhabitants, "an inferior race of people, without the privileges of citizens."[29] The Fourteenth Amendment's citizenship clause did not remedy this situation: The Court ruled in 1884 that the clause did not provide citizenship to Native Americans born on reservations because reservations are not fully under the jurisdiction of the United States.[30] Not until the Indian Citizenship Act of 1924 did Congress provide natural-born citizenship to Native Americans born on reservations.

Should all citizens have the right to vote? Are there any citizens who should not have this right?

Naturalization.

The Constitution explicitly allows people not born in the United States to become citizens through **naturalization** by granting Congress the authority "to establish a uniform rule of naturalization." Congress's first such law, the Naturalization Act of 1790, restricted citizenship to "free white persons" who had lived in the United States for two years, swore allegiance to the United States, and had "good character." Though restrictive on race, the act allowed Catholics, Jews, and other "free white persons" to become naturalized citizens, rights that most European nations did not allow. The act also declared people born overseas to parents who were U.S. citizens to be natural-born citizens.

naturalization: *Acquired citizenship through formal application procedures.*

Congress first allowed nonwhites to become naturalized citizens in 1870, when it extended naturalization to "persons of African descent." Asians, however, still could not become naturalized citizens. Indeed, fear of Chinese immigrants led to an 1882 prohibition on the immigration of Chinese to America. That ban was the first significant restriction on immigration to the United States. Congress extended this ban to all Asians in 1921. The ban stayed in effect until 1943, when Congress allowed an annual quota of

105 immigrants from China, a World War II ally. The 1943 act also allowed Chinese to become naturalized citizens, but did not allow other Asians to do so. Congress ended this restriction on Asian naturalization in 1952, but kept strict limits on the number of Asian immigrants until 1965.

Congress also used immigration laws to keep out undesirables, including "idiots," insane people, paupers, felons, polygamists, anarchists, and people coming for "immoral purposes."[31] Immigration officials used the morality clauses to keep homosexuals from entering.[32]

In the early twentieth century, as immigration soared, the Ku Klux Klan resurfaced, now targeting immigrants, Catholics, and Jews as well as blacks. With nearly 5 million members and chapters throughout the country, the Klan joined others with less violent supremacist beliefs to pressure Congress to limit immigration.[33] The Immigration Act of 1924 based quotas for ethnic groups on the proportion of Americans from each nationality resident in 1890, thereby severely limiting the number of whites considered to be of "lower race," that is, those from southern and eastern Europe.[34] Under the act, the quota for Italy, for example, dropped more than 90 percent.[35]

In 1952 President Harry S. Truman (1945–53), claiming that such quotas were un-American, vetoed a bill that continued the national quota system, but Congress overrode his veto. With the Immigration and Nationality Act of 1965, Congress rescinded the quota system and the especially severe restrictions on Asian immigration. Today, to apply for citizenship, one must have had legal permanent residence for five years, or three years if married to a U.S. citizen. Applicants also must be of good moral character and must be able to pass a test on questions such as "who elects the president?" (Table 5.1; see if you can pass the test).

Restraints during Wartime

As noted in Chapter 4, civil liberties suffer during wartime because the balance between freedom and order tilts toward order when survival is at stake. When the wartime enemy is racially or ethnically distinct from the majority of the American people, civil rights are also likely to suffer.

Two months after the Japanese attack on Pearl Harbor, President Franklin Delano Roosevelt (1933–45) issued an executive order for the evacuation of all 110,000 people of Japanese ancestry who resided west of the Rocky Mountains—whether citizen (most of them) or not—and their placement in relocation camps. Congress ratified the president's order, and in 1944 the Supreme Court endorsed it in **Korematsu v. United States**, ruling that the authority for relocation was within the war power of the United States.[36]

Although the government justified the program on the grounds of military necessity rather than racial animosity, it did not attempt wholesale roundups of German Americans despite the existence of the German American Bund, a pro-Nazi association with about twenty thousand members before the war. That the government even rounded up Japanese American children from orphanages suggests that racial animosity was more important

Who should be a citizen?

What restrictions, if any, should there be on immigration?

Korematsu v. United States: *1944 Supreme Court decision upholding the detention of Japanese Americans during World War II.*

AP Photo/Dennis Cook

On January 15, 1998, President William J. Clinton presented Fred Korematsu with the Presidential Medal of Freedom in a ceremony at the White House. Korematsu had been the plaintiff in a case challenging the legality of the internment of Japanese Americans during World War II. The Court decided against him in 1944, but in 1988 Congress officially apologized for the violation of the civil rights of American citizens.

TABLE 5.1 Questions on the Citizenship Test

The U.S. Citizenship and Immigration Service administers a citizenship text to applicants for naturalization. Following is a sampling of the questions from the American Government section of the test. There are also American History and Integrated Civics sections.

1. What is the supreme law of the land?

2. What does the Constitution do?

3. The idea of self-government is in the first three words of the Constitution. What are these words?

4. What is an amendment?

5. What do we call the first ten amendments to the Constitution?

6. What is <u>one</u> right or freedom from the First Amendment?

7. How many amendments does the Constitution have?

8. What did the Declaration of Independence do?

9. What are two rights in the Declaration of Independence?

10. What is freedom of religion?

11. What is the economic system in the United States?

12. What is the "rule of law"?

13. Name <u>one</u> branch or part of the government.

14. What stops one branch of government from becoming too powerful?

15. Who is in charge of the executive branch?

16. Who makes federal laws?

17. What are the two parts of the U.S. Congress?

18. How many U.S. senators are there?

19. We elect a U.S. senator for how many years?

20. Who is one of your state's U.S. senators?

21. The House of representatives has how many voting members?

22. We elect a U.S. representative for how many years?

23. Name your U.S. representative.

24. Who does a U.S. senator represent?

25. Why do some states have more representatives than other states?

Source: More questions plus the answers at about.com.usgovinfo.

than security concerns.[37] The program remained in effect through the war years, although the government filed no charges of disloyalty or subversion against any person of Japanese ancestry. Many Japanese Americans valiantly served the United States in segregated military units during the war.

After the terrorist attacks of September 11, 2001, which were carried out by Muslim Arabs, other Arabs and Muslims in the United States came under suspicion. The government immediately rounded up and detained more than five thousand immigrants, most

Does military necessity overrule civil rights? If so, under what circumstances?

from Muslim or Middle Eastern countries. Of these detainees, three were convicted of terrorism-related crimes unrelated to 9/11, and two of those had their convictions overturned.[38] None of the other detainees had terrorism-related charges brought against them (see also Chapter 4).

The Expansion of Equal Protection

Today the public discrimination documented in the previous section has been ended by acts of Congress, constitutional amendments, and court decisions, and no clause has been as powerful in this effort as the equal protection clause of the Fourteenth Amendment, which prohibits states from denying any person the equal protection of the law. The amendment gives Congress the authority to enforce its provisions by appropriate legislation, adding to Congress's enumerated powers by allowing the passage of laws that prevent states from discriminating. Additionally, the Supreme Court, through the power of judicial review, retains the authority to strike state laws that violate equal protection. Thus the federal government has a crucial role in the push for equality. This section examines equal protection before we continue the account of how the U.S. government shifted from engaging in discrimination to protecting against it.

The Changing Meaning of Equality

Equality had a very different meaning in 1776 than it does today. At the time of the Declaration of Independence, Thomas Jefferson saw nothing inconsistent about owning slaves, on the one hand, and declaring that "all men are created equal" on the other. The Civil War and the Thirteenth Amendment ended slavery, with the Fourteenth Amendment guaranteeing every person equal protection under the law. This constitutional protection did little to stop the massive inequalities imposed on black people by Jim Crow laws that denied them basic political and civil rights. The civil rights movement following World War II pushed to end state-sponsored segregation and private discrimination in businesses and public accommodations. The equality of opportunity goal of that era has been superseded, among civil rights activists, by the goal of equality of outcome, wherein economic well-being should be roughly equal and employment in various professions should be roughly proportional to each group's proportion of the population.

Who should ensure citizen equality? State governments? The federal government? The president? Congress? The courts? Citizens?

State Action

Shortly after the passage of the Fourteenth Amendment, Congress tried to ban private discrimination at inns, public conveyances, theaters, and other public places. The Supreme Court rejected congressional authority to do so in the ***Civil Rights Cases*** (1883), ruling that the Fourteenth Amendment prohibited public discrimination by the states only, not private discrimination by business or individuals. From the 1880s until the 1940s the federal government remained passive with regard to discrimination, allowing states and locales to require segregation of the races and permitting public and private institutions to make their own rules regarding it.

Civil Rights Cases:
1883 decision that limited congressional authority to prohibit private discrimination under the Fourteenth Amendment.

In 1948, however, the Court ruled that private discrimination can be prohibited if it involves significant **state action**. The case involved housing. A group of homeowners signed a contract pledging never to sell their homes to blacks, but one of the homeowners did so. The neighbors sued to prevent the new owners from taking possession of the house, and the state supreme court ruled in favor of the neighbors. The U.S. Supreme Court reversed the state supreme court, ruling that judicial enforcement of the discriminatory private contract constitutes state action and thus is prohibited by the Fourteenth Amendment.[39]

Judicial Review

While the state-action doctrine allowed the Supreme Court to prohibit limited types of private discrimination, the equal protection clause of the Fourteenth Amendment is better suited to fighting public discrimination. In the next two decades, the Supreme Court actively applied the equal protection clause of the Fourteenth Amendment to do so. Congress also has the authority to enforce the equal protection clause, but democratically elected legislatures and executives are not necessarily designed to be responsive to minority groups, for they are chosen by a majority of voters. Thus civil rights organizations such as the **National Association for the Advancement of Colored People (NAACP)** turned to the judiciary, whose members are not elected and so do not directly depend on majority support, for assistance in establishing legal equality. Congress later wrote protections of civil rights into law.

As with civil liberties issues, for which the Court uses the standard of **compelling interest** (see Chapter 4), in civil rights cases the Court has constructed **tests** to determine whether laws violate the equal protection clause. Depending upon the group whose right has been violated, the Court sets different standards of how closely it will scrutinize the law alleged to violate equal protection. There are at least three levels. The Court reserves the toughest standard of review, **strict scrutiny**, for laws alleged to discriminate on account of race, ethnicity, religion, or status as an alien. It uses mid-level or **heightened scrutiny** for laws that discriminate on account of sex, and the lowest level of scrutiny, **rational basis**, for general claims of discrimination (see Table 5.2).

We now turn to an examination of how grassroots racial, ethnic, and gender-based movements pressured the courts to protect civil rights and how Congress enforced court

state action: *Action by a state, as opposed to a private person, that constitutes discrimination and therefore is an equal protection violation.*

National Association for the Advancement of Colored People (NAACP): *Civil rights organization dedicated to helping African Americans.*

compelling interest test: *Standard frequently used by the Supreme Court in civil rights cases to determine whether a state has a sufficient justification for making distinctions on account of race, ethnicity, religion, or citizenship status.*

test: *Standard used by the courts to determine whether a law or a right has been violated across a range of cases.*

strict scrutiny: *Toughest standard of review, used when laws discriminate on account of race, ethnicity, religion, or alien status.*

heightened scrutiny: *Standard of review used when laws discriminate on account of sex.*

rational basis: *Lowest standard of review, used when laws discriminate against groups that do not receive strict or heightened scrutiny.*

TABLE 5.2 Supreme Court Scrutiny in Equal Protection Cases

Claim of Discrimination	Standard of Review	Test
Unprotected category	Lowest	Rational basis to achieve a legitimate governmental objective
Sex	Heightened	Exceedingly persuasive justification; use of sex as a governmental category must be substantially related to important governmental objectives
Race, ethnicity, religion, and alien status	Strict	Most rigid scrutiny; use of race as a governmental category must be precisely tailored to meet a compelling governmental interest

If equality was not explicitly protected in the 1787 Constitution, how did it get to be so important today?

rulings with legislation. As with civil liberties (see Chapter 4), however, finding the right balance of rights for minority groups frequently divides members of society from one another, and democratically responsive legislatures from lifetime-appointed judges.

The End of Legal Restrictions on Civil Rights

What gateways did citizens use to end segregation?

The events that brought about the government's shift from enforcing discrimination to protecting against it did not begin with the government. It began with pressure from groups that were discriminated against that mobilized on their own behalf. This gateway of public pressure generally involves the use of civil liberties such as freedom of speech and of assembly to engage in protests and other activities aside from voting, because minority groups, by definition, do not have the numbers to change policies through the ballot box alone.

Brown v. Board of Education: *1954 Supreme Court decision striking down segregated schools.*

Carl Iwasaki/Time Life Pictures/Getty Images

The African American soldiers and sailors who fought for freedom in World War II against totalitarian regimes in Nazi Germany, fascist Italy, and imperial Japan often returned uneasily to hometowns, particularly in the South, where segregation remained the law. The three largest legal barriers African Americans faced in the post–World War II era were state-sponsored segregation of supposedly separate-but-equal public facilities, such as schools and buses; the legal right of private businesses to discriminate, that is, the right not to serve customers or hire people on account of race; and effective prohibitions on the right to vote, such as discriminatorily enforced literacy tests. These gates blocking full civic participation existed throughout the United States, but most prevalently in the former slave states. After we trace the African American struggle for equal rights, we turn to the women's movement, which likewise pressured the government to dismantle gender-based discrimination.

Dismantling Public Discrimination Based on Race

Among the most consequential forms of segregation from the Jim Crow era was the mandatory separation of schools for whites and blacks. Beginning in 1935 the NAACP's Legal Defense Fund embarked on a legal campaign—led by Thurgood Marshall, who would later become the first African American to serve on the Supreme Court—to dismantle the system of separate-but-equal schools in southern and border states that were always separate but rarely equal. After a series of cases in which the Supreme Court struck down specific segregated schools because they were not equal,[40] the Court ruled more generally in **Brown v. Board of Education** (1954) that separate schools were inherently unequal, even should facilities be essentially similar (see Supreme Court Cases: *Brown v. Board of Education*). Segregation in schools violated the equal protection clause of the Fourteenth Amendment. The Fourteenth Amendment only requires that states provide equal protection of the laws, but on the same day as the *Brown* decision, the Supreme Court used the due process clause of the Fifth Amendment to prohibit the national government from denying equal protection.[41]

In 1950, when Linda Brown was entering third grade, her father Oliver Brown tried to enroll her in the Sumner School. The 10-year-old had been going to Monroe School, walking between train tracks and along streets without sidewalks to get there. But Sumner, though closer, was for white students, and when Oliver Brown was told Linda could not attend, he took his case to the NAACP. Here the family stands in front of their home; Linda is on the left.

supremecourtcases

Brown v. Board of Education (1954)

QUESTION: Can states provide segregated schools for black and white schoolchildren?

ORAL ARGUMENT: December 7–9, 1953

DECISION: May 17, 1954 (read at www.findlaw.com/casecode/supreme.html)

OUTCOME: No, separate educational facilities are inherently unequal (9–0).

When Linda Brown was in third grade, her father, with the help of the NAACP, brought a suit against the Topeka school board for refusing to allow her to attend the local school that white children in their neighborhood attended.

In *Plessy v. Ferguson* (1896), the Supreme Court had ruled that the equal protection clause of the Fourteenth Amendment did not prohibit the states from establishing separate-but-equal facilities for whites and blacks. The Court did not really begin to look at whether the facilities were equal or not until 1938, when it held that Missouri's paying for blacks to go to law school out of state was not the same as providing facilities within the state that were equal to its white law school.[*] A pair of 1950 cases declared, first, that admitting a black to an all-white school but forcing him to sit in a separate row and dine at a separate table was unconstitutional,[†] and second, that the equality of separate schools had to be compared on both objective factors that could be measured, such as the number of faculty members, and subjective factors that could not be measured, such as the reputation of the faculty.[‡]

The *Brown* case came to the Supreme Court with similar desegregation cases from South Carolina, Virginia, Delaware, and Washington, D.C. Thurgood Marshall, who was in charge of legal strategy for the NAACP and would later become the first African American to serve on the Supreme Court, argued the *Brown* case. He readily admitted that the schools in Linda Brown's case were roughly equal in objective characteristics but argued that segregation in and of itself denied black students the equal protection of the laws by creating a feeling of inferiority among them.

The Supreme Court's preliminary vote following the arguments showed a majority favoring striking segregation, with two or three dissenters. Chief Justice Earl Warren, however, thought that a decision that was bound to be met with resistance in the South should be unanimous if at all possible. Following several months of bargaining and persuasion, he eventually got every member of the Court to agree that the Court should strike down school segregation.

- **Can separate schools ever be equal?**
- **Why were the courts more likely to be responsive to the problems of segregated schools than the legislature?**

[*] *Missouri ex rel. Gaines v. Canada*, 305 U.S. 337 (1938).

[†] *McLaurin v. Oklahoma*, 339 U.S. 637 (1950).

[‡] *Sweatt v. Painter*, 339 U.S. 629 (1950).

AP Photo/Montgomery County Sheriff's office

Rosa Parks was often described as being too tired to stand up and give her seat to a white man on the day she was arrested. But in fact she was a civil rights activist—secretary of the Montgomery NAACP and participant in a workshop on resisting segregation at the Highlander Folk School in Tennessee.

Chapter 3 asked this question: What has been the relationship between federalism and the push for equality in the United States? What was your answer?

What are terrorists? Were the people who bombed King's house terrorists?

As historic as the *Brown* decision was, the case by itself did little to desegregate southern schools. Part of the problem was that the Court allowed local circumstances to influence the rate of integration, ambiguously requiring that local districts desegregate "with all deliberate speed."[42] Further, southern segregationists launched a massive resistance to the *Brown* decision. This campaign included "The Southern Manifesto," a document signed by 101 southern members of Congress deploring the *Brown* decision; the denial of state funds to any integrated school; and tuition grants for white students to attend segregated private schools. In addition, unruly segregationist mobs threatened black students seeking to integrate previously white schools. While neither the Supreme Court nor the Dwight D. Eisenhower administration (1953–61) could prevent every school disruption by segregationist mobs, both intervened in Little Rock, Arkansas. Eisenhower federalized the Arkansas National Guard and sent in the 101st Airborne to protect the black students seeking to integrate Central High School, while the Supreme Court, declaring that it had the final say on what the Constitution means, rejected the threat of violence as a justification for delaying integration (see Chapter 15, The Judiciary, for more on the Little Rock case).[43]

For desegregation at the college level, President John F. Kennedy (1961–63) had to send 25,000 federal troops to ensure the enrollment of one black man, James Meredith, at the University of Mississippi in 1962. The following year, segregationist Governor George Wallace of Alabama famously "stood at the schoolhouse door" to prevent two black students from registering at the University of Alabama. He stepped aside only when Kennedy again sent troops to enforce integration.

Nevertheless, with few blacks able to vote, there was little need for southern politicians or school board officials to be responsive to their concerns, especially given massive opposition to desegregation by those who could vote. Only when the federal government took action did states respond. After Congress cut off federal aid to segregated schools in 1964, many districts began to integrate.[44] The rate of integration increased further in the late 1960s when the Supreme Court ended the "all deliberate speed" era and required an immediate end to segregated schools, thus pushing open the gateways to greater equality.[45]

Outside of schools, civil rights activists fought segregation in public facilities. The first grassroots action to receive nationwide attention was a bus boycott in Montgomery, Alabama. On December 1, 1955, police arrested Rosa Parks, a 42-year-old black seamstress and an active member of the NAACP, for refusing to give her seat to a white person. In response, the black community, led by a 26-year-old Baptist minister, Martin Luther King Jr., launched a boycott of city buses. Blacks walked, bicycled, and shared rides to avoid using the Montgomery bus system. Although the city arrested boycotters and violent segregationists terrorists firebombed King's home, the boycotters held firm for over a year. The Supreme Court then declared Montgomery's segregated bus system uncon-stitutional.[46] A new ordinance allowing blacks to sit anywhere on any bus ended the boycott. King became one of the national leaders of the emerging **civil rights movement**, and Rosa Parks its first heroine.

With the *Brown* precedent in hand, the Supreme Court struck down state-mandated segregation not only in public transportation but also in other public facili-ties, such as beaches and city auditoriums. Given the massive opposition to the *Brown* decision, however, the Court refused to hear the appeal by a black woman sen-tenced to prison for the crime of marrying a white man.[47] As one justice reportedly said when the Court rejected another interracial marriage case, "One bombshell at a time is enough."[48] Not until 1967 in *Loving v. Virginia* did the Court strike down **miscegenation**, finding no compelling interest in a law that prohibited interracial marriage.[49]

© Bettmann/CORBIS

Childhood sweethearts Mildred and Richard Loving married in Washington, D.C., because they could not marry in Virginia, where they lived. One month later, police burst into their bedroom and arrested them for violating Virginia's Racial Integrity Act. The couple eventually sued Virginia with legal assistance from the American Civil Liberties Union. In 1967 the Supreme Court struck down Virginia's law.

Dismantling Private Discrimination Based on Race

The decisions of businesses about whether to serve customers or hire workers on account of their race (or sex) were largely beyond judicial authority because the Four-teenth Amendment's equal protection clause only prevents states from discriminating; it does not bar private discrimination. Thus, if a restaurant chose not to serve blacks or an employer chose not to hire them, there was little a court could do unless Congress passed legislation forbidding such actions. The effort to dismantle private discrimination thus took two tracks: protests to pressure businesses into serving blacks, and lobbying to pressure Congress into passing legislation that would make private discrimination in commercial matters illegal.

The grassroots protests began when four African American freshmen at North Carolina Agricultural and Technical College sat down at the whites-only counter at Woolworth's, asked for coffee, and refused to leave when not served. Within weeks the sit-ins spread to dozens of other cities, with Diane Nash leading Nashville's protests. Tens of thousands of people par-ticipated in the sit-ins, and thousands were arrested.[50] Nash and other young participants in these protests formed the Student Nonviolent Coordinating Committee (SNCC), which along with the Congress of Racial Equality (CORE) served as the more activist "younger brothers" of the NAACP.

In 1961 CORE organized **freedom rides**, trips on interstate buses into the segregated South, where the integrated buses were legal under federal law even though they violated local segregation rules. Mobs attacked the buses—firebombing one of them—and beat the riders. Under pressure from the federal government, including protection of the riders by federal marshals, the states eventually agreed not to interfere with interstate travelers.[51]

civil rights movement: *Movement after World War II to gain equal rights for African Americans, later expanded to end discrimination on account of race, gender, sexual orientation, and disability status.*

Loving v. Virginia: *1967 Supreme Court case striking down laws that prohibited racial intermarriage.*

miscegenation: *Interracial marriage and/or sexual intercourse, often forbidden by state law until* Loving v. Virginia.

freedom rides: *Integrated bus trips into the segregated South in 1961.*

What is more important, equality or freedom of association?

Jack Corn/The Tennessean

In the spring of 1963 Martin Luther King Jr.'s Southern Christian Leadership Conference (SCLC) led demonstrations in Birmingham, Alabama, to bring about the integration of downtown businesses. The police met demonstrators with fire hoses, police dogs, and cattle prods. Police arrested hundreds of protesters, including King. When white clergymen questioned why King, an outsider, had come to Birmingham, King answered in his famous "Letter from Birmingham Jail": "I am in Birmingham because injustice is here."[52] Rejecting violence, King insisted that peaceful **civil disobedience** was the only gateway to negotiation. The negotiations took place and ended with Birmingham businesses agreeing to integrate lunch counters and hire more blacks. Nevertheless, or perhaps because of this, members of the KKK exploded a bomb at a local black church on a Sunday morning, murdering four young girls.

On April 19, 1960, following a wave of sit-in protests, Diane Nash and 3,000 others promoting integration marched to the courthouse square in Nashville. On the way, some of them sang "We Shall Overcome," a gospel song that became the anthem of the civil rights movement. Confronting the mayor on the courthouse steps, the protesters forced him to admit that segregation was morally wrong.

civil disobedience: *Peaceful protests in violation of a law believed to be unjust or immoral.*

If a law is immoral, are you right or wrong to disobey it? What is the remedy?

Civil Rights Act: *Prohibits discrimination in employment, education, and places of public accommodation (1964).*

Which branch of government has been most powerful in ensuring equality? Why?

Earlier that summer, King had led two hundred thousand protesters at the March on Washington. It was there that King delivered his historic "I Have a Dream" speech, in which he declared:

> *I have a dream that one day this nation will rise up and live out the true meaning of its creed: "We hold these truths to be self-evident: that all men are created equal." I have a dream that one day on the red hills of Georgia the sons of former slaves and the sons of former slave owners will be able to sit down together at the table of brotherhood. I have a dream that one day even the state of Mississippi, a state sweltering with the heat of injustice, sweltering with the heat of oppression, will be transformed into an oasis of freedom and justice. I have a dream that my four little children will one day live in a nation where they will not be judged by the color of their skin but by the content of their character.*[53]

President Kennedy proposed a civil rights bill that would have banned discrimination in public accommodations, such as restaurants and hotels. Five days after Kennedy's assassination in November 1963, President Lyndon Baines Johnson (1963–69) told Congress that nothing could better honor Kennedy than passage of this bill. The next year, Congress passed the **Civil Rights Act**, which significantly strengthened Kennedy's original bill by also prohibiting employment discrimination on account of "race, color, religion, sex, or national origin."

Because the Fourteenth Amendment's equal protection clause applies only to state-sponsored discrimination, the Supreme Court upheld Congress's authority to ban private discrimination under the interstate commerce clause. Given the Court's broad interpretation of interstate commerce (see Chapter 3), the Court ruled that even small inns and restaurants had to abide by the act.[54]

In 1971 the Supreme Court interpreted the Civil Rights Act to limit job quali- fication requirements that had a **disparate impact** on whites and blacks.[55] For example, if more whites receive high school diplo- mas than blacks, requiring a high school diploma for a job would be more harmful to blacks than to whites. A business seeking to establish job requirements that have a disparate impact would have to prove that the require- ment is necessary to the

AP Photo/File

On August 28, 1963, more than 200,000 people gathered on the Washington Mall in a March for Jobs and Freedom. Among them were seventy- five members of Congress who were working to pass a civil rights bill that had President Kennedy's support. Folk singer Joan Baez led the crowd in singing "We Shall Overcome," but the day belonged to Martin Luther King Jr., whose "I Have a Dream" speech still challenges Americans to work for equality.

job. In the late 1970s and through the 1980s, a more conservative Supreme Court reached a series of decisions that restricted civil rights protections, for example, making disparate impact more difficult to prove and ruling that discrimination against pregnant women was not a form of sex discrimination under the Civil Rights Act.[56] Passing new laws, Congress overturned these Court decisions plus several others, thus demonstrating widespread sup- port for the continued protection of civil rights. The new rules, for example, make it easier to find that job tests have a disparate impact, but leave it to the courts to determine whether disparate impact, by taking race into account, conflicts with the equal treatment obligation of the Civil Rights Act.[57]

Dismantling Voting Barriers Based on Race

As noted previously, the end of Reconstruction left black men in the South with a consti- tutional right to vote, but a hostile social and legal environment that made it extremely difficult for them to do so. The Supreme Court pushed things along, striking down grandfather clauses (1915) and white primaries (1944), the latter in a suit filed by the NAACP.[58] Congress and the states pushed things along further, outlawing poll taxes with the Twenty-Fourth Amendment (1964). Martin Luther King Jr. identified four gates that kept blacks from voting: white terrorist control of local governments and sheriffs departments; arrests on trumped-up charges of those seeking to vote; the discretion given to registrars, where "the latitude for discrimination is almost endless"; and the arbitrary nature of literacy tests.[59]

During the summer of 1964 voting rights supporters from around the country, many of them college students, moved south to help with **voter registration** drives. Klansmen

disparate impact: *Job tests that differentially affect minority groups, even if there is no intent to discriminate.*

What restrictions, should be placed on voting?

voter registration: *Enrollment required prior to voting to establish eligibility.*

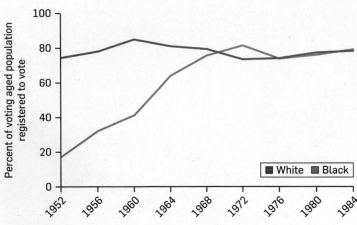

FIGURE 5.3 White and Black Southern Voter Registration, 1952–1984. Dramatic increases in black voter registration preceded passage of the Voting Rights Act in 1965, but substantial equality between whites and blacks did not occur until after its passage.
Source: Data from Harold W. Stanley, *Voter Mobilization and the Politics of Race* (New York: Praeger, 1987), Appendix A.

Voting Rights Act: *Gives the federal government the power to prevent discrimination in voting rights (1965).*

The Feminine Mystique: *1963 book by Betty Friedan considered by many to have launched the modern feminist movement.*

Equal Pay Act: *Prohibits different pay for males and females for the same work (1963).*

Why, in U.S. history, do women's rights movements follow, rather than precede, movements to remove racial barriers?

National Organization for Women (NOW): *Organized interest group devoted to securing equal rights for women.*

Equal Rights Amendment (ERA): *Proposed amendment that would have banned the federal and state governments from discriminating on account of sex.*

murdered three of the volunteers in Philadelphia, Mississippi, that June. In March 1965 King organized a voting rights march from Selma to Montgomery, Alabama. With national news media on hand, Alabama police, under the authority of Governor George Wallace, beat the marchers with whips, nightsticks, and cattle prods. Selma natives murdered two more voting rights activists.

A week later President Johnson addressed a joint session of Congress, calling for passage of the strictest possible voting rights legislation. He ended the speech by adopting a line from the civil rights movement, telling Congress and the nation, "we shall overcome."[60] Congress responded by passing the **Voting Rights Act** in August 1965. The act banned literacy, interpretation, and other such tests for voting. It required states with low voter registration levels, essentially seven southern states plus Alaska, to receive Justice Department approval for any changes to its voting laws. It also established new criminal penalties for those who sought to keep people from voting on account of race. The law was an enormous success. By 2008 blacks and whites voted at essentially the same rate nationwide,[61] and at slightly higher rates in some southern states[62] (see Figure 5.3).

Dismantling Discrimination Based on Gender

The success of the civil rights movement inspired other groups, most notably women, to put pressure on the political system to obtain equal rights under the law. Women active in the civil rights movement easily shifted the movement's strategies to promoting rights for women, particularly after the publication of Betty Friedan's **The Feminine Mystique** (1963), a book considered by many to have launched the modern American feminist movement. Based on a survey Friedan sent to her Smith College classmates in advance of their fifteenth reunion, the book broadcast the dissatisfaction that many American women felt in their roles as wives and mothers. About the same time, the Kennedy administration's President's Commission on the Status of Women, charged with making recommendations for overcoming sex discrimination, urged passage of the **Equal Pay Act**. Passed by Congress in 1963, the act prohibits employers from paying different wages for the same job on account of sex. Although the act did not prohibit discrimination in the hiring of male and female workers, that prohibition came with the Civil Rights Act of 1964.

Following passage of the Civil Rights Act, Friedan helped found the **National Organization for Women (NOW)**, which advocated for women's rights through education and litigation. NOW protested airline policies that forced stewardesses to retire at marriage or age 32 and help-wanted ads that listed jobs by gender, as well as protective legislation. NOW also supported abortion rights and a proposed **Equal Rights Amendment (ERA)**, which would have prohibited the federal government and the states from discriminating on account of sex.

In 1972 the American Civil Liberties Union (ACLU) established the Women's Rights Project, which worked to eliminate discriminatory laws. The first project director, future Supreme Court Justice Ruth Bader Ginsburg, developed a litigation strategy for ending gender-based discrimination. Prior to Ginsburg's work, the Court had rejected equal protection claims for women. Ginsburg first persuaded the Court to strike laws based on the rational-basis standard, and then got the Court to approve a heightened-scrutiny standard. This is a step below the strict scrutiny used in cases discriminating on account of race, but the standard is tough enough that the Court usually strikes laws that discriminate according to sex.

Meanwhile, the ERA, passed by Congress and sent to the states for ratification in 1972, began to falter. An anti-ERA movement led by political activist Phyllis Schlafly reversed the momentum by arguing that the amendment would remove special privileges women enjoyed with regard to protective legislation, Society Security benefits, and exemption from the draft . Ironically, another argument against the ERA was that it was unnecessary because the Supreme Court was striking down most laws that discriminated on account of sex. Despite an extension of the deadline to 1982, the ERA ultimately fell three states short of the three-quarters majority needed to pass an amendment (see Figure 5.4).

By the 1980s the civil rights era was over and the nation had taken a conservative turn. But like African Americans whose officeholding and participation in civic life generally increased after passage of the Voting Rights Act, women were increasingly taking public roles. In 1984, two years after the ERA failed, only 17 percent of Americans thought that the United States was ready to elect a woman president. In 2008 the Democratic presidential primary campaign of New York Senator Hillary Clinton and the Republican nomination of Alaska Governor Sarah Palin for vice president were evidence that the nation was ready.

© Bettmann/CORBIS

In 1960, when Columbia law student Ruth Bader Ginsburg applied for a Supreme Court clerkship, Justice Felix Frankfurter chose not to interview her. Ginsburg went on to a distinguished career as a professor of law and chief litigator for the American Civil Liberties Union, eventually arguing cases before the Court, which she joined in 1993 as the second female associate justice. She is pictured here in 1977.

How has expansion of the right to vote affected citizen participation? How has it affected public policy?

Frontiers in Civil Rights

Many of the civil rights battles against legal discrimination have been won: Governments cannot discriminate on account of race or sex, and businesses cannot discriminate in whom they hire as employees or serve as customers. But the expanded notion of equality promoted by the civil rights and women's rights movements inspired other groups, such as homosexuals and the disabled, to demand full access to equality. At the same time, as the fight over the ERA made clear, the extension of rights for some may involve a loss of privileges for others, and sometimes rights clash. Congress and the courts have sought to define the meaning and limits of rights as new areas of conflict emerge over such issues as racial and religious profiling, the voting rights of felons, and the civil rights of illegal immigrants. Whatever the new issues, however, the trend in the United States has been for a broader meaning of equality and greater support for civil rights.

Is the era of civil rights over? Have all the battles been fought and won?

Sexual Orientation and Same-Sex Marriage

The movement to protect the rights of homosexuals first received widespread public attention in 1969 when a police raid on the Stonewall Inn, a gay bar in New York City,

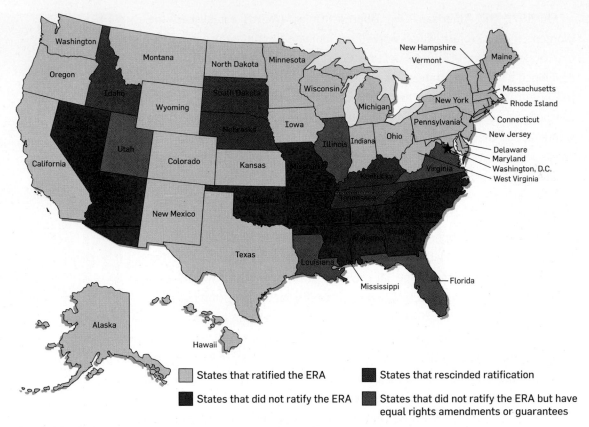

FIGURE 5.4 States Approving the Equal Rights Amendment. Passed by Congress in 1972 and sent to the states for ratification, the Equal Rights Amendment got a quick start, then faltered as opposition materialized and grew. In 1979 Congress extended the deadline for ratification to 1982, but in 1982 the amendment expired. Thirty-five states (of the thirty-eight needed) had voted to ratify it, and five states had voted to rescind ratification.

Legend:
- States that ratified the ERA
- States that rescinded ratification
- States that did not ratify the ERA
- States that did not ratify the ERA but have equal rights amendments or guarantees

Stonewall riots: *Street protest in 1969 by gay patrons against a police raid of a gay bar in New York that is credited with launching the gay rights movement.*

turned into a riot by the bar's patrons and gay rights supporters living in the area. The **Stonewall riots** became the signature event of a growing gay rights movement. Activists soon formed the Gay Liberation Front, which established branch organizations around the world. By the 1990s the movement had expanded into a broader LGBT movement that sought to protect the rights of lesbians, gays, bisexuals, and transgendered persons.

At the time of the Stonewall riots, all states banned sodomy, which would include virtually all sexual activity between same-sex couples.[63] In the following years several states decriminalized homosexual activity, but as noted in Chapter 4 the Supreme Court ruled in 1986 that homosexual activity was not a fundamental right, so states could still keep homosexuality illegal if they so chose. Colorado went further, passing an amendment to its state constitution that prohibited the state, or any city or town in the state, from passing laws that granted civil rights protections on account of sexual orientation. The Supreme Court struck this law in 1996, claiming that it was born of dislike toward gays.[64] Then, in *Lawrence v. Texas* (2003), the Supreme Court reversed the 1986 decision and declared that states could not prohibit sexual activity between people of the same sex.[65]

Nevertheless, a majority of Americans continue to believe that homosexual conduct is always or almost always wrong,[66] and issues related to homosexual rights have been

Library of Congress

Justin Sullivan/Getty Images

fraught with conflict. Under President William Jefferson (Bill) Clinton (1993–2001), Congress enacted a **don't ask, don't tell** policy for the military. Prior to the implementation of this policy, simply having homosexual tendencies, without any evidence of homosexual activities, was sufficient grounds for discharge. Under the policy, sexual orientation alone is not a ground for discharge, but lesbians, gays, and bisexuals can be discharged for engaging in homosexual relationships or for discussing their sexual orientation. President Obama has asked Congress to change the policy so that lesbians, gays, and bisexuals can serve openly, while a lawsuit on its constitutionality is working its way through the federal judiciary.

Thousands of citizens in same-sex partnerships want to be married but are not eligible for that legally recognized status, which brings advantages with regard to the right to make health care decisions for a spouse, inheritance rights, and tax benefits. The issue of same-sex marriage is highly controversial. State laws typically govern family matters, including marriage, divorce, child custody, and wills, and in most states marriage is limited to one man and one woman. While each state can set its own rules, the full faith and credit clause of the Constitution generally requires each state to accept the status granted by other states. Thus, opposite-sex couples who get married in Las Vegas under Nevada law are recognized as married throughout the United States.

When the Hawaii Supreme Court ruled in 1993 that, under the state constitution, Hawaii would have to show a compelling interest in its prohibition of same-sex marriages, opponents feared that same-sex marriages performed in Hawaii would have legal recognition throughout the United States. In 1996 Congress passed and President Clinton signed the **Defense of Marriage Act**, which defines marriage, for the purpose of federal law, as between a man and a woman and declares that states do not have to recognize same-sex marriages performed in other states. Later that year, the Hawaii Supreme Court ruled that the state did not have a compelling interest in prohibiting same-sex marriages, but voters then approved a state constitutional amendment allowing the state legislature to ban same-sex marriage. Since that time, courts, legislatures, and citizen initiatives have battled over same-sex marriage, with judicial protection sometimes overridden by popular opposition, as in California (2009)

Has discrimination ended? While restaurants are no longer segregated as was the Farmers Cafe Quick Lunch in Durham, North Carolina, in 1940, Denny's restaurant chain was sued for racial bias in the early 1990s. Plaintiffs reported that black customers had been refused service, required to pay cover charges, subjected to derogatory remarks, and forcibly removed, primarily from restaurants in California. In a settlement, Denny's agreed to end the practices in question and train employees to treat all customers fairly.

don't ask, don't tell: *Policy allowing gays to serve in the military if they do not discuss their sexual orientation.*

Do court decisions follow public opinion? Do they lead public opinion? What should be the relationship?

Defense of Marriage Act: *1996 federal law exempting states from any requirement to recognize same-sex marriages performed in other states.*

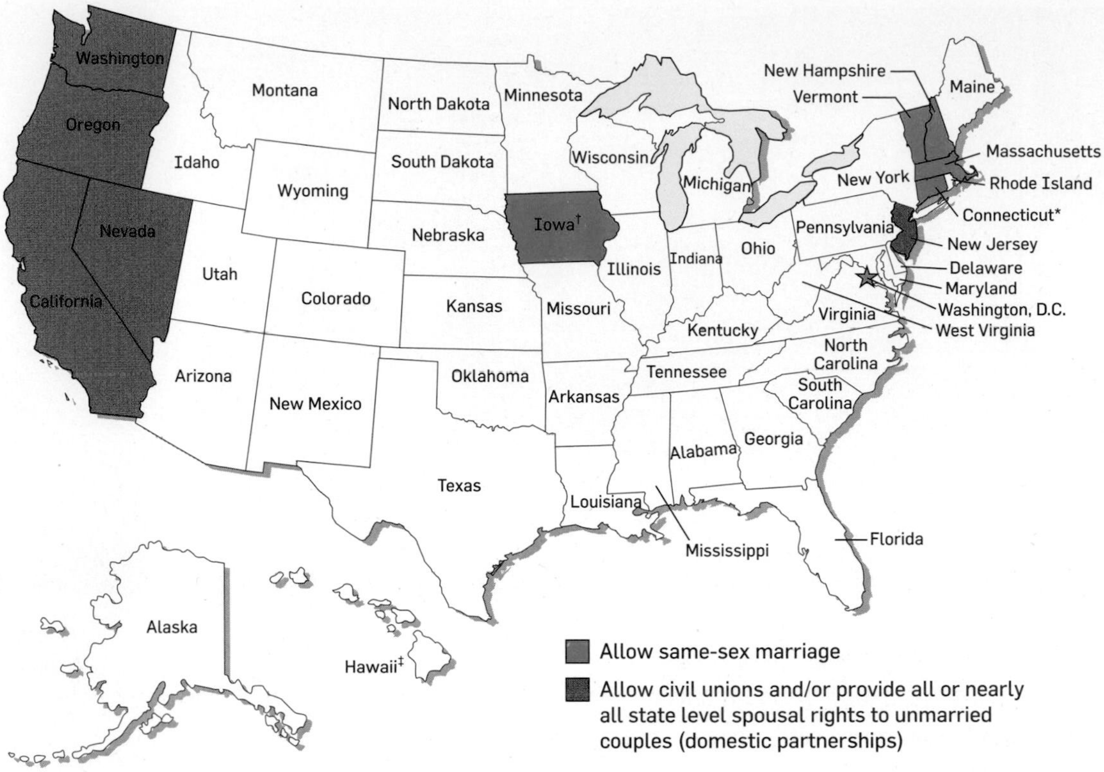
Washington
Oregon
California
Nevada
Idaho
Montana
Wyoming
Utah
Arizona
Colorado
New Mexico
North Dakota
South Dakota
Nebraska
Kansas
Oklahoma
Texas
Minnesota
Iowa†
Missouri
Arkansas
Louisiana
Wisconsin
Illinois
Michigan
Indiana
Ohio
Kentucky
Tennessee
Mississippi
Alabama
Georgia
Florida
South Carolina
North Carolina
Virginia
Pennsylvania
New York
New Hampshire
Vermont
Maine
Massachusetts
Rhode Island
Connecticut*
New Jersey
Delaware
Maryland
Washington, D.C.
West Virginia
Alaska
Hawaii‡
Allow same-sex marriage
Allow civil unions and/or provide all or nearly all state level spousal rights to unmarried couples (domestic partnerships)

*In October 2008 the Connecticut Supreme Court invalidated the state statute banning same-sex marriage.
†In April 2009 the Iowa Supreme Court invalidated the state statute banning same sex marriage.
‡Hawaii's constitution was amended in 1998 to read "The Legislature shall have the power to reserve marriage to opposite-sex couples." The Hawaii legislature subsequently passed a law prohibiting marriage for same-sex couples.

FIGURE 5.5 States Approving Same Sex Marriage, 2010.
Source: Data from National Conference of State Legislatures.

What government (state or federal) or branch of government (executive, legislative, or judicial) should have the power to decide whether same-sex marriage is legal?

and Maine (2009) (see Figure 5.5). In 2010, a federal district court ruled that the California initiative banning same-sex marriage violated the equal protection clause, but the court of appeals temporarily blocked enforcement of that decision. Whatever decision the appeals court ultimately makes will almost certainly be appealed to the Supreme Court.

civil unions: *State laws that provide the benefits of marriage to same-sex couples without using the term* marriage.

National public opinion remains mixed on the matter of same-sex marriage (see Figure 5.6). While a majority of Americans favor some form of legal recognition for same-sex couples,[67] only five states and the District of Columbia have legally recognized same-sex marriage; another five recognize **civil unions**. The major political parties are internally divided on the issue; while Democrats are typically more supportive of same-sex marriage than Republicans, President Barack Obama, a Democrat, opposes federal recognition of same-sex marriage, and Republican former Vice President Dick Cheney supports it. Because support for same-sex marriage is much greater among younger Americans than among older Americans, the legality of same-sex marriage may increase over time.

Affirmative Action

affirmative action: *Policies that grant racial or gender preferences in hiring, education, or contracting.*

Almost as controversial as gay rights are remedies for overcoming the effects of centuries-long discrimination. Known as **affirmative action**, these programs grant preferences to African Americans, other minorities, and/or women in employment, education, or

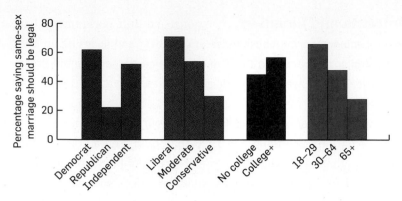

FIGURE 5.6 Views on Same-Sex Marriage, 2009.
Source: Jennifer Agiesta, "Behind the Numbers: On Gay Marriage, a New Even Split," *Washington Post,* April 30, 2009.

contracting. They not only aim to ensure equality of opportunity but also to promote equality of outcome.

President Johnson first stated the rationale for affirmative action: "You do not take a man who for years has been hobbled by chains, liberate him, bring him to the starting line of a race, saying, 'you are free to compete with all the others,' and still justly believe you have been completely fair."[68] And while Martin Luther King Jr., as noted earlier, dreamed that one day his children would live in a nation where they would be judged "not by the color of their skin, but by the content of their character," he also stated that "A society that has done something special against the Negro for hundreds of years must now do something special for the Negro."[69]

But do the effects of unequal treatment in the past justify potentially unequal treatment in the present? Is fear of causing inequality in the present sufficiently compelling to not correct the inequalities of the past? The Supreme Court has struggled to find the right balance between these positions. Today affirmative action programs by private businesses must comport with the Supreme Court's interpretation of the nondiscrimination clauses of the Civil Rights Act; affirmative action programs by national, state, and local governments also must comport with constitutional requirements of equal protection.

Private Business.   The Supreme Court has ruled that businesses and unions can agree to establish voluntary affirmative action programs where there has been a substantial racial imbalance in the workforce. In one case, white steelworker Brian Weber was turned down for a promotion to craft worker because in a workforce that was 39 percent black, fewer than 2 percent of the skilled craft workers were black, and Kaiser Aluminum and the United Steelworkers had agreed that 50 percent of future promotions would go to blacks, even if that bypassed whites with higher seniority. Weber sued, but the Supreme Court upheld the affirmative action plan.[70] On the other hand, the Court ruled that seniority cannot be overridden when it comes to layoffs: Whites with higher seniority cannot be laid off ahead of minorities with lower seniority, even if seniority-based layoffs will harm racial balance and even if minorities had less seniority because original hiring practices discriminated against them.[71]

Why are rules and decisions regarding affirmative action murky and contested?

Government Contracts and Licenses.   National and state governments have established preferences for minority-owned businesses in contracts and licensing. In 1987 the Court upheld a plan, similar to the one in the Steelworkers case, that granted preferences to women.[72] A 1980 decision allowed the federal government to require 10 percent of its grants to state and local governments for public works projects to go to minority-owned businesses.[73] Nine years later, however, a more conservative Court prohibited the city of Richmond, Virginia, from doing the same thing.[74] In 1990 the Court used an intermediate level of scrutiny to uphold the granting of radio license preferences to minority broadcasters; six years later, the Court reversed that decision and reestablished strict scrutiny for all racial categorizations.[75]

Higher Education.   As colleges and universities actively sought racial and gender balances in their student bodies, several controversial cases arose. The Supreme Court first confronted college affirmative action plans in 1978. The medical school at the University of California, Davis, had eighty-four seats in each entering class for which anyone could apply and sixteen seats set aside for minority candidates only. Allan Bakke, a white male, was denied admission although he had a 3.5 grade point average (GPA) and a Medical College Admission Test (MCAT) score in the 90th percentile, whereas the average scores for the sixteen minority seats were a 2.6 GPA and an MCAT score in the 20th percentile. Bakke sued, and a split Court decreed in **Bakke v. California** that this sort of quota system violated the Civil Rights Act. Nevertheless, the Court held that affirmative action plans in which race is a "plus" in an applicant's overall file did meet the state's compelling interest in establishing a diverse student body.[76]

Bakke v. California: 1978 Supreme Court decision upholding affirmative action at colleges as long as there are no quotas.

The Supreme Court revisited the *Bakke* decision in a pair of 2003 cases that are discussed more extensively in Chapter 15. In one case the Supreme Court upheld the affirmative action program at the University of Michigan Law School because the law school considered race as one part of an entire file.[77] In the other case the Court struck down the program at the University of Michigan's undergraduate college in which race automatically created a set number of points toward admission without individualized consideration of how particular applicants who were minorities might contribute to the school's diversity.[78]

In the law school case, Justice Sandra Day O'Connor, the first woman to serve on the Court, expressed the belief that the Constitution required affirmative action programs to be temporary solutions only, and the hope that by 2028 they would no longer be necessary. Opponents of affirmative action, such as Ward Connerly, chair of the American Civil Rights Institute, hope that such plans will not last that long. Connerly has launched state-level referenda in California, Washington, Michigan, Nebraska, and Colorado to let voters decide whether such programs should be allowed. Voters rejected affirmative action in all those states except Colorado.

Should race or sex be a factor in college admissions?

Disability Rights

Americans with Disabilities Act: *Requires businesses and government to make reasonable accommodations for employees with known physical or mental limitations (1990).*

Advocates for the rights of the disabled, encouraged by the civil rights, women's rights, and other movements, successfully lobbied for the Rehabilitation Act of 1973, which prohibits discrimination against disabled individuals by any federal agency or by any private program or activity that receives federal funds. The landmark **Americans with Disabilities Act** (ADA) passed in 1990 goes further, requiring public and private employers to make "reasonable accommodations" to known physical and mental limitations of employees with disabilities and, if possible, to modify performance standards to accommodate an employee's disability.

To comply with the act, public transportation authorities have made buses and trains accessible to people in wheelchairs. Public accommodations, such as restaurants, hotels, movie theaters, and doctors' offices must also meet ADA accessibility standards, within reason removing barriers from existing structures. Related legislation, the Individuals with Disabilities Education Act (IDEA; 1990, updated 2004) requires states to provide free public education to all children with disabilities in the least restrictive environment appropriate to their particular needs.

Congress does not provide a full list of disabilities covered under the ADA, but rather covers any disability that "substantially limits a major life activity." Thus, a trucking company need not make accommodations for a driver who can see clearly out of only one eye because the disability does not substantially limit a major life activity. On the other hand, the ADA does protect people who have HIV or AIDS. It even protects people with drug and alcohol problems, provided the drug use in question is not illegal.[79]

Many organized interests support the rights of the disabled. While prejudice against people of different races, religions, sexual orientation, and country of origin might lead responsive representatives to oppose the rights of minorities, there are few if any votes to be had by lobbying against the rights of the disabled.

Racial and Religious Profiling

Profiling, the use by police of certain racial, ethnic, or religious characteristics in determining whom to investigate for particular kinds of crimes, has become controversial because of increasing evidence that profiling entails unequal treatment under the law. For example, along the I-95 corridor north of Baltimore, a team of observers found that about 17 percent of cars had black drivers and nearly 76 percent had white drivers, and that the drivers observed traffic laws in similar proportions. Nevertheless, over 80 percent of the cars stopped and searched by the Maryland State Police were driven by blacks and Hispanics, while cars driven by whites constituted fewer than 20 percent of the searches.[80] So much more likely were blacks to be pulled over than whites that the phrase "driving while black" came to signify African American drivers' feeling that they risked being treated as criminals on the roads. In 2008 the Maryland State Police agreed to pay more than $400,000 to settle racial profiling suits, and litigation continues in eight other states.[81] State and federal courts have specifically prohibited the use of race as a factor in "drug courier profiles."[82]

Following the terrorist attacks of 9/11, profiling of Arabs and Muslims increased, particularly in matters of airline security. In efforts to identify potential terrorists, mistakes are often made. In 2007, for example, police detained six Arabs, some of whom were American citizens returning from teaching Marines about Iraqi culture, when an airline passenger became worried after hearing the men speak in Arabic. Where issues of security are at stake, profiling is especially controversial.

National Park Service

Ramps on sidewalks and wheelchair lifts on public buses have become familiar aspects of urban life since the passage of the Americans with Disabilities Act in 1990. Less familiar, but equally welcomed, are efforts by the National Park Service to provide access to trails for people in wheelchairs. At Gulf Islands National Seashore, a boardwalk makes a trip to the beach possible for everyone.

profiling: *Practice of using racial or ethnic characteristics to determine whether to investigate.*

Should profiling be used to protect American citizens against terrorist plots?

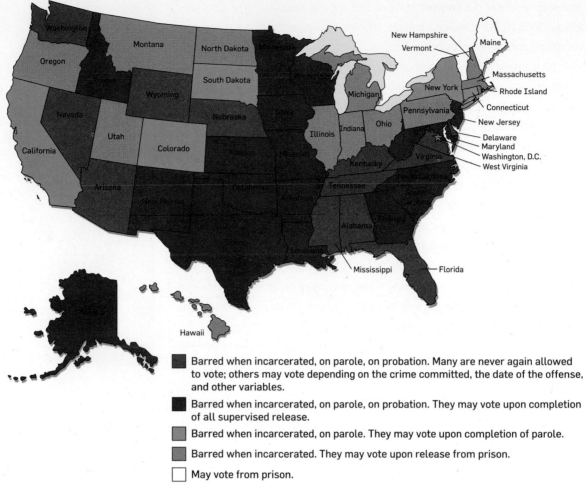

Barred when incarcerated, on parole, on probation. Many are never again allowed to vote; others may vote depending on the crime committed, the date of the offense, and other variables.

Barred when incarcerated, on parole, on probation. They may vote upon completion of all supervised release.

Barred when incarcerated, on parole. They may vote upon completion of parole.

Barred when incarcerated. They may vote upon release from prison.

May vote from prison.

FIGURE 5.7 Voting Rights for Felons.
Source: Data from Procon.org.

Voting Rights for Felons

Since passage of the Civil Rights Act of 1964 and the Voting Rights Act of 1965, voting rights have been scrupulously protected, even as stricter requirements for voter identification have been enforced to prevent fraud (see Chapter 11). But there remains a persistent inequality regarding whether felons have the right to vote, with each state making its own determinations (see Figure 5.7). At one end of the spectrum, Maine and Vermont allow prison inmates to vote. Thirteen states and the District of Columbia allow felons to vote upon release from prison, and twenty-three more allow them to vote upon completion of probation or parole.[83] Twelve states do not automatically restore voting rights, with the specifics of restoration varying among them. With over 4 million released felons living in the United States, such laws markedly influence close elections because felons are more likely than the general population to be poor and poor people are more likely to vote Democratic.[84]

Should being convicted of a felony mean forfeiting the right to vote? Forever? While in prison? Until completion of probation or parole?

Illegal Immigrants

The Fourteenth Amendment's equal protection clause prohibits states from denying to any person—in other words, not just citizens—equal protection under the law. Thus even illegal immigrants receive some degree of legal protection in the United States. The level of that protection is deeply controversial, especially as the number of illegal immigrants, estimated to be about 12 million, has skyrocketed in recent years (see Chapter 8, Interest Groups, for further discussion of immigration policy).

Congress has been considering a number of actions, including creating easier paths to citizenship for illegal immigrants or, alternatively, denying natural-born citizenship to U.S.-born children of illegal immigrants. By a 49 percent to 45 percent margin, Americans do not believe such children should automatically become citizens, but the constitutionality of a law that would deny them citizenship, given the Fourteenth Amendment's citizenship clause, remains unclear.[85]

While the Court reviews laws that discriminate against legal immigrants under its strictest level of scrutiny, it reviews laws that discriminate against illegal immigrants under the easier rational-basis standard. Yet, the Court has held that states may not deny public education to illegal immigrants,[86] and federal law requires hospitals to provide emergency care to illegal immigrants through Medicaid, the federal program that supports health care to poor people. The growth of civil rights to cover illegal immigrants is surely one of the most controversial of the frontiers we have examined.

Should children of illegal immigrants who are born on American soil be U.S. citizens?

Civil Rights and Public Policy: Workplace Equality

Although national legislation and constitutional amendments define civil rights policy and the Supreme Court interprets such laws—deciding whether they are constitutional and, if so, what they mean—the day-to-day protection of civil rights now falls to two separate executive branch agencies. One is the Civil Rights Division of the Department of Justice, with sections on educational opportunity, employment, housing, voting, and disability rights. The other is the Equal Employment Opportunity Commission, which protects against sexual harassment in the workplace and promotes gender equity.

The Equal Employment Opportunity Commission

The **Equal Employment Opportunity Commission (EEOC)** is an independent agency with commissioners selected for five-year fixed terms. Unlike the heads of government departments, EEOC commissioners cannot be removed by the president. They are thus thought to

Equal Employment Opportunity Commission (EEOC): *Independent federal agency charged with protecting equal employment rights.*

be shielded from political pressures, but fixed terms also limit responsiveness to the president, who is the chief executive of the United States.

Congress established the EEOC as part of the Civil Rights Act of 1964. The original EEOC could receive and investigate complaints of discrimination on the basis of race, sex, religion, and national origin (Congress later added age and disability status). As one of the compromises that allowed the act to pass, the EEOC originally had no enforcement power. Rather, it could refer cases in which there were patterns or practices of discrimination to the Justice Department. In 1972 Congress provided the commission with the right to file lawsuits against companies that discriminate.

Although Congress passed the basic law declaring discrimination based on race or sex to be illegal, the EEOC established the guidelines that prohibited discrimination against hiring married women, pregnant women, and mothers. The commission also allowed companies that had previously engaged in discriminatory practices to establish affirmative action plans with quotas for hiring and promoting women and minorities.

Sexual Harassment

The problem of discrimination on account of sex can take many forms, and one of the most prevalent in the workplace is sexual harassment. Survey data reveal that nearly 60 percent of women report having experienced potentially harassing behaviors at work.[87] The EEOC receives more than twelve thousand sexual harassment complaints per year.[88]

The commission first set regulations against sexual harassment in 1980, stating that such harassment was a form of sex discrimination prohibited by the Civil Rights Act. The Supreme Court agreed with the EEOC's interpretation of the act in 1986, upholding the lawsuit of a woman who claimed that her boss coerced her into having sex with him and then fired her.[89] (See Chapter 15 on the sexual harassment allegation against Supreme Court nominee and former EEOC chair Clarence Thomas.)

The Supreme Court recognizes two distinct types of sexual harassment. Some harassment takes quid pro quo form in which supervisors link the benefits of employment to sexual favors. But to be harassment behavior does not have to be linked to benefits or threats. Sexual harassment takes place whenever one or more employees establish, on account of sex, a hostile work environment, one that interferes with a worker's ability to do his or her job.

Gender Equality in the Workplace

From a policy standpoint, the underlying principle of equal pay is that two people who are employed in the same job and do the same quality of work should be paid the same wage. Achieving gender equality in the workplace means that there are no barriers to advancement or hiring based on gender, and that gender plays no role in how employees

Should laws regarding the behavior of women in the workplace be different from laws regarding the behavior of men? Do women need or warrant added protection?

are treated and compensated. Unfortunately, true pay equity has not been achieved in the American workplace. Census statistics from 2008 show that women earned only 77.8 percent of what men earned in 2007. For African American and Latina women, this percentage was even lower: African American women earned only 68.7 percent, and Latinas earned only 59 percent, of what men made.[90]

LILLY LEDBETTER
ALABAMA

Mark Wilson/Getty Images

Though the Equal Pay Act is supposed to guarantee equal pay for the same work, and the Civil Rights Act aims to protect against any form of employment discrimination on account of sex, the judicial branch has also played a pivotal role. A recent set of Supreme Court decisions has prompted changes in the laws governing discrimination, harassment, and pay equity in the workplace. In one case, the Supreme Court ruled in favor of a woman who was suspended without pay for more than a month and was reassigned to a less desirable position after she claimed sex discrimination in the workplace. The Court decided that an indefinite suspension without pay is retaliation that would reasonably deter any employee from making a discrimination complaint, and that it was therefore illegal.[91]

But the Court's 2007 ruling in *Ledbetter v. Goodyear Tire and Rubber Co.* had the greatest impact on public policy.[92] In 1998 Lilly Ledbetter filed a complaint with the EEOC that she had consistently received poor job performance evaluations because of her gender, and that over the nineteen years she had worked at the Goodyear Tire plant she had fallen well below her male colleagues who did the same type of job. Her employer countered that, even if that had been true in the past, she did not file her complaint within the 180 days required by the Civil Rights Act. The Court ruled in favor of Goodyear, stating that her claims alleging sex discrimination were time-barred because the discriminatory decisions relating to pay had been made more than 180 days prior to the day she filed the charge with the EEOC. In her dissent, Justice Ruth Bader Ginsburg wrote that the effect of this ruling would allow "any annual pay decision not contested immediately (within 180 days) . . . [to become] grandfathered, a *fiat accompli* beyond the province of Title VII ever to repair."[93] Basically, a company could pay a woman less on the basis of gender, and as long as she did not contest the discriminatory wage within 180 days, the discriminatory wage could not be challenged in federal court.

In 2009 Congress reversed the Court's ruling by passing the Lilly Ledbetter Fair Pay Act, which President Obama signed into law. The act restarts the clock each time an employee receives a paycheck that has been compromised by discriminatory practices.[94] Many equal pay advocates think that this new law will be helpful, but not nearly helpful enough to close the salary gap between men and women.

Lilly Ledbetter's pay discrimination suit went all the way to the Supreme Court. After the Court ruled against her, Ledbetter spoke at the 2008 Democratic National Convention. "How fitting," she said, "that I speak to you on Women's Equality Day, when we celebrate ratification of the amendment that gave women the right to vote. Even as we celebrate, let's also remind ourselves: the fight for equality is not over." The next year Congress reversed the impact of the decision by passing the Lilly Ledbetter Fair Pay Act.

Why do women still earn less than men for performing the same job? Do women warrant equality of opportunity or equality of results?

Civil Rights and Democracy

The core demand of civil rights is equal opportunity under the law. When laws discriminate or allow discrimination, people are effectively excluded from civic life. The demands for equal opportunity are often made to government, which alone has the authority to prohibit discrimination.

While a democratic system of government works to be responsive to its citizens, responsiveness to minorities is harder to obtain when majorities seek to limit minority rights. As noted in Chapter 2, The Constitution, James Madison saw a large republic with varied interests as a cure for the mischiefs of faction. But when factions form on the basis of majority group versus minority group, such as white versus black, heterosexual versus gay and lesbian, or native-born versus immigrant, responsiveness to minority preferences has been achieved through the gateways of lawsuits, protests, and other forms of civic engagement by the minority group. In response, the government has struck laws that discriminated and passed laws that prevented other people from discriminating.

Out of all the activities by groups seeking equal rights, voting might be key. With the vote, declared Martin Luther King Jr. in 1965, comes accountability. Blacks could "vote out of office public officials who bar the doorway to decent housing, public safety, jobs, and decent integrated education. It is now obvious that the basic elements so vital to Negro advancement can only be achieved by seeking redress from government. . . . To do this, the vote is essential."[95]

While voting rights provide accountability by allowing citizens to "throw the bums out," they also provide responsiveness. A minority group's elected opponents are not as forceful once a group has the right to vote. George Wallace is an example. As Alabama governor in 1963, he personally blocked the schoolhouse gates to prevent two African Americans from enrolling at the University of Alabama. When first inaugurated as governor, Wallace declared "segregation now, segregation tomorrow, and segregation forever." In 1968 Wallace ran for president as a third-party candidate on an avowedly segregationist platform. But because the Voting Rights Act increased the number of black voters in Alabama, Wallace moderated his views. By the 1980s blacks constituted more than 20 percent of registered voters, too large a population to ignore in what was no longer a solidly Democratic state. In Wallace's final campaign for governor, he admitted that he had been wrong on segregation, received strong support from blacks at the polls, and appointed many blacks to state offices after his election. (For more on Wallace and the effect of African American votes on his views, see Chapter 11, Voting and Participation.)

More generally, the voting patterns of southern House and Senate members on issues related to civil rights have moderated over the past forty years, proving that King was certainly correct about the value of the ballot.[96] While members of Congress representing southern states once voted in lockstep opposition to civil rights issues, their votes on such issues now differ only slightly from those of representatives of other states.[97]

These changes are part of a larger evolution in the idea of equality that has proceeded over the course of the nation's more than 230 years. Americans once

FOCUS QUESTIONS

- What is the meaning of equality? How has its meaning changed since the Constitution was written in 1787?

- What role has government played with regard to equality in the past? What role does it assume today?

- What means have various groups used to secure their civil rights? What means has government used to respond?

- What is the effect on a democracy if some of its people lack civil rights?

- Are civil rights a gate or a gateway to democracy? Explain.

believed that slaveholding was not inconsistent with demands for equality; today African Americans, women, and others once discriminated against have achieved full participation in the nation's civic life. But the frontiers of civil rights will continue to evolve. Some Americans believe that equal opportunity is not enough, that the government must take stronger measures to ensure greater equality of outcome. Because there is no constitutional right to equal results, the battle over this meaning of equality will be fought not in the courts, but in democratically elected legislatures.

GATEWAYS TO LEARNING

Top Ten to Take Away

1. Civil rights relate to the duties of citizenship and opportunities for civic participation that the government is obliged to protect. They are based on the expectation of equality under the law. The most important is the right to vote. (pp. 138–39, 170)

2. With regard to civil rights, the government can engage in state-sponsored or public discrimination; treat people equally but permit private discrimination; or try, as it has since the 1960s, both to treat people equally and to prevent individuals or businesses from discriminating. (pp. 139–40)

3. It falls to government to protect individuals against unequal treatment and to citizens to ensure that government does not discriminate against individuals or groups. (p. 139)

4. During the nation's first century, and even thereafter, state laws and the national government actively discriminated against people on the basis of race, gender, and ethnic background. (pp. 139–50)

5. During the nation's second century, discrimination was state-sponsored in the South; elsewhere private

discrimination was practiced without challenge. (pp. 139–50)

6. Today public discrimination has been ended by constitutional amendments and the courts, largely through the Fourteenth Amendment's equal protection clause. (pp. 150–52)

7. Beginning in the 1950s litigation and grassroots protests led the federal government to end segregation and secure voting rights for African Americans and to end limits to women's full participation in public life. (pp. 152–59, 162–64, 167–69)

8. The expanded notion of equality promoted by the civil rights and women's rights movements inspired other groups, such as homosexuals and the disabled, to demand full access to equality. (pp. 159–62, 164–65)

9. The extension of rights for some may involve a loss of privileges for others, and sometimes rights clash. Congress and the courts seek to define the meaning and limits of rights in new areas of contention. (pp. 165–67)

10. The trend has always been for a broader meaning of equality and greater support for civil rights. (pp. 170–71)

A full narrative summary of the chapter is on the book's website.

Ten to Test Yourself

1. What are civil rights?
2. What did the *Dred Scott* case decide?
3. What rights are protected by the Thirteenth, Fourteenth, and Fifteenth Amendments?
4. Why is the distinction between public (governmental) and private (individual and business) discrimination important?
5. How have immigration and naturalization laws been tied to the public mood?
6. In what ways were women second-class citizens?
7. What are the tests the Supreme Court uses to determine the validity of laws alleged to discriminate?
8. What laws protect civil rights?
9. What is the difference between equality of opportunity and equality of outcome?
10. How does government try to ensure workplace equality?

More review questions and answers and chapter quizzes are on the book's website.

Timeline to Keep Things in Order

 The Constitution endorses slavery and makes no provision for the rights of women.

 The women's suffrage movement is launched in Seneca Falls, New York.

 Union victory in the Civil War and the Thirteenth Amendment end slavery.

 The Fourteenth Amendment guarantees equal protection of the laws.

 Plessy v. Ferguson upholds segregation.

1787 · **1848** · **1865** · **1868** · **1896**

Terms to Know and Use

affirmative action (p. 162)
Americans with Disabilities Act (p. 164)
Bakke v. California (p. 164)
black codes (p. 141)
Brown v. Board of Education (p. 152)
Chinese Exclusion Act (p. 143)
citizenship (p. 147)
civil disobedience (p. 156)
civil liberties (p. 139)
civil rights (p. 138)
Civil Rights Act (p. 156)
Civil Rights Cases (p. 150)
civil rights movement (p. 155)
civil unions (p. 162)
compelling interest test (p. 151)
coverture (p. 143)
Defense of Marriage Act (p. 161)

discrimination (p. 139)
disparate impact (p. 157)
don't ask, don't tell (p. 161)
Dred Scott v. Sandford (p. 141)
Emancipation Proclamation (p. 141)
Equal Employment Opportunity Commission (EEOC) (p. 167)
equality of opportunity (p. 140)
equality of outcome (p. 140)
Equal Pay Act (p. 158)
equal protection clause (p. 142)
Equal Rights Amendment (ERA) (p. 158)
The Feminine Mystique (p. 158)
freedom rides (p. 155)
grandfather clauses (p. 142)
heightened scrutiny (p. 151)

Jim Crow laws (p. 142)
Korematsu v. United States (p. 148)
Ku Klux Klan (p. 142)
literacy tests (p. 142)
Loving v. Virginia (p. 155)
miscegenation (p. 155)
Missouri Compromise (p. 140)
National Association for the Advancement of Colored People (NAACP) (p. 151)
National Organization for Women (NOW) (p. 158)
natural-born citizens (p. 147)
naturalization (p. 147)
Plessy v. Ferguson (p. 142)
poll taxes (p. 142)
private discrimination (p. 139)

privileges or immunities clause (p. 147)
profiling (p. 165)
protective legislation (p. 144)
public discrimination (p. 139)
rational basis (p. 151)
Reconstruction (p. 142)
separate-but-equal doctrine (p. 142)
state action (p. 151)
Stonewall riots (p. 160)
strict scrutiny (p. 151)
test (p. 151)
voter registration (p. 157)
Voting Rights Act (p. 158)
white primary (p. 142)
women's suffrage (p. 143)

Use the vocabulary flash cards on the book's website.

Learning That Works

WHAT YOU NEED...

TO KNOW

What civil rights are

The U.S. record on civil rights

The way civil rights have been expanded

The nature of discrimination

The meanings of equality

Where to turn for remedies to civil rights violations

TO DO

Recognize which of your rights government is obligated to protect

Understand the basis for affirmative action and assess its value

Appreciate the impact active citizens can have on government

Determine whether you think all the civil rights battles have been won

Track how the meanings have changed and decide whether we are all equal now

Protect or expand civil rights

The Nineteenth Amendment gives women the right to vote.
1920

Brown v. Board of Education holds that segregated schools violate equal protection.
1954

The Civil Rights Act prohibits discrimination.
1964

The Voting Rights Act prohibits discrimination in voting.
1965

The Americans with Disabilities Act protects the disabled.
1990

6 PUBLIC OPINION

> *Entire states may change hands as a result of motivating the youth vote, particularly in the South . . . and the West . . . where young voters are abundant.*

CourseMate

Visit http://www.cengagebrain.com/shop/ISBN/0618906959 for interactive tools including:

- Quizzes
- Flashcards
- Videos
- Animated PowerPoint slides, Podcast summaries, and more

At the University of Chicago Nate Silver was an economics major. He might have studied math or statistics, given his love of numbers. His father recalls that Nate would start counting when they dropped him off at preschool. "When we picked him up two and a half hours later, he was 'Two thousand one hundred and twenty-two, two thousand one hundred and twenty-three . . . .'" By kindergarten Nate was multiplying two-digit numbers in his head, and by age 11 he was using advanced statistics to determine whether there was a relationship between the size of a baseball stadium and attendance. Growing up in Michigan, he was a Detroit Tigers fan, and his love of baseball was almost as great as his love of numbers. He also liked to write, and in college he wrote for the *Chicago Weekly News* and the *Chicago Maroon.* He spent his junior year studying abroad at the London School of Economics.

After graduation Silver worked as an economic consultant for an accounting firm in Chicago. But the work was boring. For fun he started a website called the Burrito Bracket, rating Mexican restaurants in Wicker Park. Now adopting the Chicago White Sox and Cubs as his home teams, he began using statistics to predict player performance. His system generated a huge amount of attention within the baseball world. In 2004 he sold his PECOTA projection system to Baseball Prospectus and joined its staff, writing books and articles forecasting team and player performance.

Three years later Silver turned his forecasting skills to politics. He began by writing a political blog for Daily Kos under the pseudonym "Poblano." Frustrated by sloppy polling and reporting, in March 2008 he established his own blog, FiveThirtyEight (the total number of electoral votes in a presidential election), which tracked and predicted the outcome of presidential primaries so accurately that it got attention from pundits and commentators. Silver sliced and diced the political polls in a way that made them easy for the public to grasp. Sometimes he dismissed the results of a new poll, telling why he did not trust it. At other times he was able to show important trends in public opinion that warranted close attention.

FiveThirtyEight became a daily staple of political junkies and political observers of all stripes. During the course of the campaign, stories in the *New York Times,*

Nate Silver ▶

Beth Rooney/The New York Times/Redux

© Bob Krist/Corbis

the *Wall Street Journal, Newsweek,* and *New York Magazine* focused on this new prophet. He appeared on Keith Olbermann's show on MSNBC and *The Colbert Report* on Comedy Central. On election night he was in Washington, at a studio in the Newseum, serving as an on-air analyst for *Dan Rather Reports*. At 9:46 P.M., on FiveThirty Eight, he called the election for Barack Obama, whom he had forecast as the winner way back in March. Silver's rise "from obscurity to quotable authority" was compared to Obama's, the candidate he had supported all along. "Not only," said *Vanity Fair,* "did his disciplined models and microfine data mining command respect, his prognostications hit the Zen mark on Election Day."[1]

Nate Silver's gateway to participation in the American political system came by doing what he loved—working with numbers—and applying those skills to politics. He still runs FiveThirtyEight and now writes a monthly column of political analysis for *Esquire.* He speaks with authority because his work has made political polling more useful and understandable to the public. It has also highlighted the importance of public opinion in a democracy. In fact, without the expression of the public will, there would be no democracy. For politicians, knowing which way the public leans or what citizens think is an avenue to power. For citizens, being able to express opinion and know it is being heard is a gateway to influence. But reading public opinion correctly is not easy. Polls are a great help, but they can be flawed. Even if well measured, public opinion does not always produce a sound direction for the country. A sound direction requires an informed citizenry. In this chapter, we investigate the contours, sources, and impact of public opinion.

FOCUS QUESTIONS

- How does public opinion influence public policy?

- In what ways are elected officials responsive to public opinion? How responsive should they be?

- Is every citizen's voice equal, or are some people more influential? Why?

- How well does polling capture public opinion? Should polls direct public policy?

- Does public opinion provide a gateway or a gate to democracy?

The Power of Public Opinion

"Our government rests on public opinion," claimed Abraham Lincoln (1861–65). "Public sentiment is everything. With public sentiment, nothing can fail. Without it, nothing can succeed."[2] The nation's sixteenth president was, of course, the great champion of "government of the people, by the people, and for the people," as he expressed it in his Gettysburg Address. He understood that democratic government must be responsive to the will of the people. The hope in a democracy is that each citizen has an equal voice and that those voices, collectively, will be heard by government officials and will guide their actions. Knowing what the public is thinking and having public support are a powerful combination. Writing more than one hundred years ago, James Bryce, a famous observer of U.S. politics, contended that public opinion is "the greatest source of power" in the United States, more important than the power of presidents, Congress, and political parties.[3]

The Power of Presidential Approval

Perhaps no one appreciates the power of public opinion more keenly than former President George W. Bush (2001–2009). He came to office in 2001, following a contested election in which more than half the electorate had voted against him. However, following the terrorist attacks on September 11 of that year, the country rallied to his side.[4] President Bush enjoyed the approval of 90 percent of the public. No president had ever scored higher—not Ronald Reagan (1981–89), not John F. Kennedy (1961–63), not Franklin Delano Roosevelt (1933–45). With this unprecedented level of public support, Bush was able to get Congress to agree to nearly everything he wanted. It passed the Patriot Act, which expanded the powers of the federal government in the area of national security, and it approved his call for a new cabinet-level Department of Homeland Security.

When President Bush launched the Iraq War in March 2003, his **approval rating** was above 70 percent. Then it began to drift downward (see Figure 6.1). In 2004 he won reelection in a tight race, but the increasing unpopularity of the Iraq War undermined his support among the American

Eric Draper/White House/Getty Images

Standing on the rubble of the World Trade Center in New York City, President George W. Bush commends firefighters and police for their response to the terrorist attacks of September 11, 2001. For his own response to the attacks, the president enjoyed near unanimous public approval.

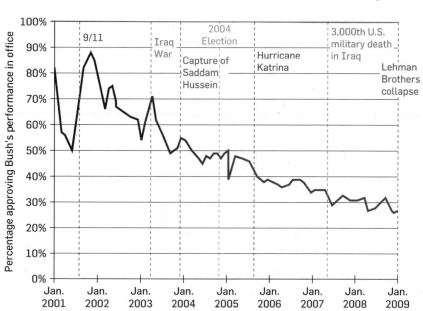

FIGURE 6.1 Approval Ratings of President George W. Bush, 2001–2009. President George W. Bush's approval ratings went from an all-time high to an all-time low. Presidents' approval ratings generally decline during their time in office, but Bush's popularity was hard hit by an increasingly unpopular war in Iraq, an inadequate federal response to Hurricane Katrina, and a severe downturn in the economy.
Source: NBC/*Wall Street Journal.*

approval rating: *Job performance evaluation for the president, Congress, or other public official or institution that is generated by public opinion polls and is typically reported as a percentage.*

How did public opinion
influence public policy
during the George W. Bush
administration?

Were President Bush's
policies responsive to public
opinion?

people and his influence with Congress. Even on the heels of his successful reelection, he could not convince Congress to reform Social Security. Then the inadequate federal response to Hurricane Katrina, which devastated the Gulf Coast, further eroded Bush's standing with the public. By 2007 Bush's public approval rating hovered around 35 percent, and he faced a Democratic Congress—the consequence of the "thumping," as he put it, that the Republicans took in the 2006 midterm elections.

In 2007, when the immigration reform bill he backed was defeated, President Bush visited Congress personally in an effort to revive the legislation, but even this unusual move had little effect. In fact, Bush was rebuked by his own party when Senator Jeff Sessions (R-Ala.) stated that the president "needs to back off."[5] By the time of Barack Obama's (2009–) election in November 2008, Bush's approval stood in the mid-20s, and the CBS/*New York Times* poll suggested that he had become the most unpopular president since the start of scientific polling in the 1930s.[6]

President Bush's political roller coaster reveals the power of the public. The views of average citizens can humble the most experienced statesman and elevate a novice to great influence. The example of Bush is not unique. Harry S. Truman (1945–53) began his presidency with widespread support and left office with approval ratings around 30 percent. During 2009 President Obama started out with high ratings from the public; by mid-2010, his approval rating had sunk below 50 percent. Like Bush, Obama faced a struggling economy and an unpopular war—in this case in Afghanistan.[7]

What Is Public Opinion?

Public opinion is recognized for its power, but it is ever changing, hard to measure, harder to predict, and nearly impossible to control. **Public opinion** is the aggregate of individual attitudes or beliefs about certain issues or officials, and it is the foundation of any democracy.

public opinion: *Aggregate of individual attitudes or beliefs about certain issues or officials.*

Of course, the electorate expresses its opinion primarily through voting, and elections are the most visible means by which citizens hold elected officials accountable. But a system that claims to be democratic should not rely just on elections to ensure that politicians are doing the people's will. Elections are not held very often. Further, elections give signals, but not directions. For example, the electoral success of the Democrats in the 2006 midterm elections was hailed as a sign that the public was unhappy with the conduct of the Iraq War. But what should be done? Did the people want an immediate pullout? A slower disengagement? Election results do not say. Voters can indicate only whether they like one candidate more than the other; they cannot convey the reasons for their vote. So legislators and elected executives who want to stay in power expend considerable energy trying to find out what the public wishes and to respond accordingly. Because public opinion plays such an important role in forging responsiveness, it is central to understanding U.S. politics.

polls: *Methods for measuring public opinion.*

Today surveys of public opinion, or **polls**, are the most reliable indicators of what the public is thinking, and a whole industry and science have grown up around measuring opinion on everything from presidents to toothpaste. Polls are not the only sources of public opinion. In one recent Supreme Court case, the justices sought to gauge public opinion on what constituted "cruel and unusual punishment" by looking at laws passed by state legislatures (see Supreme Court Cases: *Roper v. Simmons*). Other sources of public opinion are the size of rallies and protests, the tone of letters sent to elected officials or newspapers, the amount

supremecourtcases

Roper v. Simmons (2005)

QUESTION: Does the cruel and unusual punishment clause of the Constitution prevent states from executing people who were minors at the time of their crime?

ORAL ARGUMENT: October 13, 2004 (listen at http://www.oyez.org/cases/)

DECISION: March 1, 2005 (read at http://www.findlaw.com/casecode/supreme.html)

OUTCOME: States may not execute people who were minors at the time of their crimes (5–4).

While only 17 years of age, Christopher Simmons plotted a murder, believing he could get away with it because he was a minor. Simmons and another minor burglarized the house of Shirley Cook, tied her up, and threw her off a bridge into a river. A jury found Simmons guilty of first-degree murder and sentenced him to death. Simmons challenged the death sentence on the grounds that executing a person who is a minor at the time of the crime constitutes cruel and unusual punishment, which is prohibited by the Eighth Amendment.

U.S. Supreme Court decisions on the Eighth Amendment consider sentences to be cruel and unusual if they violate society's "evolving standards of decency." This makes the Court's Eighth Amendment decisions, alone among constitutional clauses, explicitly dependent on public opinion.

The Court's use of public opinion, however, is not based on public opinion polls but rather on the actions of the states' democratically elected legislative branches. The Court assumes that the legislatures are responsive to the wishes of the people. They thus represent the "clearest and most reliable objective evidence of contemporary values."

In 1989 the Supreme Court declared in a 5–4 decision that executing minors did not violate evolving standards of decency because twenty-five of the thirty-seven states that allowed the death penalty allowed the execution of 17-year-olds, and twenty-two of those states allowed the execution of 16-year-olds.

By the time the Simmons case reached the U.S. Supreme Court, the states had shifted away from the execution of minors, with four more state legislatures prohibiting the practice. Although recognizing that this change was not dramatic, it was enough to tip the Court majority against allowing the execution of minors.

Polls of public opinion, which the Court finds to be a less reliable indicator of public values than legislative decisions, show that a majority of Americans do in fact oppose the death penalty for those who were minors when they committed the crimes. Typically, the percentage of people opposed falls in the mid-50s, whereas the percentage of supporters is in the mid-30s.

- **Which branch of government is most likely to be responsive to "evolving standards of decency"? Which would be least responsive? Why?**

- **Do different state standards on the death penalty violate democratic principles of equality? Explain.**

of money given to particular causes or candidates, the content of newspaper editorials, and information gleaned from day-to-day conversations with average Americans.

The Public's Support of Government

The health and stability of a democracy rest with the public. Just as government must respond to what the people want, so citizens must view the system as legitimate and want to be part of it. If the public withdraws its support, the government collapses. For these reasons, political scientists have sought to measure the public's faith in the political system. Two of the most common efforts involve assessing whether the people trust their government and whether they believe their participation in government matters. Political scientists call the latter **efficacy**—the extent to which people believe their actions affect the course of government. **Political trust** is the extent to which people believe the government acts in their best interests. Political trust has generally declined over the last fifty years, with a steeper decline since the Iraq War began in 2003 and the financial collapse began in 2008. One estimate in February 2010 suggested that just 19 percent of the public trusted "the government in Washington to do what is right."[8] This is a very low rating by historical standards.[9]

Efficacy has also declined. It stood at over 70 percent in 1960; by 1994 it had fallen by half. In other words, only one-third of Americans felt that their opinions mattered to government. The figure rebounded to 60 percent by 2002, but then declined again during the Iraq War and financial crisis. There is little doubt, as President Barack Obama said in his 2009 inaugural address, that there has been a "sapping of confidence across our land."

Public trust and efficacy react to changes in government and whether the nation is experiencing good or bad times. Yet, through it all, Americans' commitment to the country and its core institutions has remained strong. Patriotism, for example, shows little decline. In 2008 only 5 percent of Americans viewed themselves as unpatriotic.[10] Almost no one in the country favors overthrowing the government.[11]

Public Opinion Polls

Polls make it possible to gauge the public's thinking on a variety of issues or officials, but they have been scientifically conducted only since the 1930s. Even today, a poorly designed or executed poll can produce misleading results. Moreover, there is so much information available from surveys that it is important to know which findings warrant attention and which warrant caution. Poll results can be biased, contradictory, and confusing, which is why Nate Silver's clear assessments of them during the 2008 presidential race were so popular.

Gauging Public Opinion in the Past

In the eighteenth and nineteenth centuries, the contents of letters, the sizes of crowds at rallies, and people's willingness to sign petitions were used to gauge public opinion. They were crude indicators. Politicians had to go to great lengths to secure information about the public mood. George Washington (1789–97) was so frustrated with not being able to sense what voters thought about his policies as president that he literally mounted his horse and rode into the countryside to talk to the people. Abraham Lincoln held public meetings at the White House "to renew in me a clearer and more vivid image of that great popular assemblage out of which I sprung," he said, and he called these receptions his "public opinion baths."[12] President William

efficacy: *Extent to which people believe their actions can affect public affairs and the actions of government.*

political trust: *Extent to which people believe the government acts in their best interests.*

What does a decline in efficacy and public trust mean for American democracy?

How do public officials learn what citizens think?

McKinley (1897–1901) had his staff clip newspaper articles and put the clippings in a folder at night so he could read them to gauge the public's thinking.[13] President Franklin Roosevelt also paid close attention to newspapers. And both Lincoln and Roosevelt, presidents in times of crisis, learned what the people thought through the many letters that citizens wrote to them. Even in the twenty-first century, citizens still write to the president. President Barack Obama receives about forty thousand letters a day, and his staff selects ten, which are delivered to him when he arrives at the Oval Office in the morning. He reads them, individually, throughout the day.[14]

Yet none of these sources of "public sentiment," as President Lincoln called it, gave very precise indicators. Lincoln once said that he wanted to "get done . . . what the people desire to have done," but the problem was that he did not know what they desired.[15] Because public opinion was so difficult to determine, there were many disagreements about its shape and direction. Moreover, because it was based on the content of newspapers and letters, on petitions, and on conversations with political observers, it was really **elite opinion**.[16] In other words, the most activist and literate elements of society were defining public opinion. Those who could write letters, for example, and would take the time to do so were the ones whose voices were heard. Thus politicians had biased readings of public opinion, because the views they heard tended not to represent the people as a whole.

Scientific Polling and the Growth of Survey Research

In the 1800s newspapers and other organizations polled the people to assess public opinion, but these polls were of limited help because it was unclear who was being surveyed. So-called **straw polls**, for example, sought to predict the outcome of elections. During the presidential campaign of 1824, the *Harrisburg Pennsylvanian* canvassed the opinion of newspaper readers and concluded that Andrew Jackson would get 63 percent of the vote and win easily.[17] As it turned out, Jackson received only about 40 percent of the popular vote.

Though straw polls were often inaccurate, newspapers and magazines continued to poll readers' opinions well into the twentieth century. During the 1936 presidential campaign, the *Literary Digest* conducted a poll that predicted Republican Alf Landon would win the election by 57 percent over President Franklin Roosevelt. The reverse happened: Roosevelt won with a landslide 61 percent of the vote. Why did the *Literary Digest* get it so wrong? It had sent out 10 million ballots. But it had sent them to names drawn from automobile registration lists and telephone books and asked recipients to mail the ballots back. The sample, as a result, was biased. First, in 1936 those who owned automobiles and had telephones were wealthier than average Americans, and were more likely to be Republicans. Less wealthy Americans, responding favorably to Roosevelt's actions to end the Great Depression, were increasingly aligning themselves with the Democrats. Second, the poll asked respondents to mail in their ballots, introducing additional bias. Those who would take the time to do so would likely be better off, further increasing the Republican bias of the sample. Even though 2 million ballots were returned, the poll did not offer a very sound basis on which to make a prediction.

Arizona Republic and Phoenix Gazette, September 27, 1941

elite opinion: *Political opinion of the most active and wealthy members of a political community.*

straw polls: *Ballot polls by nineteenth-century newspapers to predict the outcome of elections.*

In the 1930s George Gallup developed a scientific approach to polling, greatly increasing its accuracy and authority.

random sample: *Method of selection that gives everyone who might be selected to participate in a poll an equal chance to be included.*

Gallup Poll: *Best-known and perhaps most respected polling firm in the United States, founded by George Gallup.*

scientific polling: *Method of polling that provides a fairly precise reading of public opinion by using random sampling.*

But George Gallup, who had founded the American Institute of Public Opinion in 1935, correctly predicted the outcome of the 1936 election by using a **random sample** to generate a way to select people to participate in surveys. He made his sample representative of the American public by giving, in effect, every American an equal chance to be part of it. The end product was a sample of five thousand, which was far smaller than the *Literary Digest*'s sample but far more representative of average Americans. As a result of his innovative approach, Gallup is often considered the father of modern polling, and the best-known name in polling today remains the **Gallup Poll**. His **scientific polling** and survey research techniques have been refined over the years.

The advent of scientific polling made it possible to assess the opinions of the public with some degree of ease and accuracy. V. O. Key, a leading scholar of public opinion, described its impact this way: "In an earlier day public opinion seemed to be pictured as a mysterious vapor that emanated from the undifferentiated citizenry and in some ways or another enveloped the apparatus of government to bring it into conformity with the public will. These weird conceptions . . . passed out of style as the technique of the sample survey permitted the determination, with some accuracy, of the opinions within the population."[18] Scientific polling also permitted greater equality in assessing public opinion, because the polls had the ability to tap the opinions of all Americans. George Gallup understood this aspect of polling—that scientific polls democratized the measurement of public opinion.[19]

By the early 1940s the federal government began to see the value of survey research, too, and in October 1941 the U.S. Army conducted a survey to understand the opinions of enlisted men and officers. Today, the federal government continues to undertake a wide variety of polls, ranging from surveys about health issues to tapping the public's thinking on the economy. Polls are undertaken by other organizations as well. After the end of World War II, the University of Michigan founded the Survey Research Center, now the academic center for all sorts of polling.[20] By the 1960s John Kennedy was making use of pollsters, and both Lyndon Baines Johnson (1963–69) and Richard M. Nixon (1969–74) followed his lead.[21] The news media also saw the value of information about the public's thinking. By the 1980s all the major television networks had polling operations in conjunction with major newspapers or news services.

President Lyndon Johnson was obsessed with the news and public opinion. He had three televisions installed in the Oval Office so he could watch several networks at once, all the time.

Today, Americans are regularly surveyed on a wide range of things other than politics. Polls ask about sexual practices, television viewing preferences, car purchases, and how often we go bowling. Because of extensive polling, we know what proportion of the nation believes in UFOs, what kind of soap people buy, and at what age children stop believing in Santa Claus. In December 2009 the Pew Research Center asked Americans whether they were paying more attention to golfer Tiger Woods's marital infidelity, to President Obama's decision to send more troops to Afghanistan, or to congressional legislation on health care reform. You may be relieved to learn that only 10 percent of respondents rated the Tiger Woods story as the one they followed most closely. A vast majority of the public was focusing on issues such as health care, the economy, and the war in Afghanistan.[22]

Are polls the best way to find out what the public thinks?

Types of Polls

In a nation of more than 200 million adults, gathering opinions from everyone is not practical. Even the U.S. **census**, a count of the population required by the Constitution every ten years, has trouble reaching every adult.[23] So polls draw a **sample** from a larger population. But first the **population** must be defined. It might be all adults over age 18, or only voters, or only voters who contributed to Republican candidates in 2008.

The typical size of a sample survey is one thousand people, though it can vary between five hundred and about fifteen hundred. Size does not matter as much as whether the sample is representative of the population being assessed. Having a **representative sample** means, in effect, that everyone in that population has an equal chance of being asked to participate in the poll. If a random one thousand people are asked to be part of the survey, they should be representative of the population generally—in, say, wealth, ethnicity, or educational attainment. The key to a representative sample is the randomness. It should be much like drawing numbered balls for a lottery: each ball has the same chance of being chosen.

There are various ways to collect the information being sought. For in-person interviews, survey researchers send interviewers into neighborhoods and communities to ask questions in person. This was long the favored method, but it became increasingly expensive. With the near universal presence of telephones by the 1970s, calling people became a more viable and much less expensive option. Telephone polls have dominated survey research over the last thirty years and continue to be used much of the time. The latest platform for polling is the Internet. Internet polls have much potential, but the fact that older and poorer Americans may lack access to computers introduces bias. As with telephones in the past century, however, more and more people are using computers and the web, so in the future Internet polling will likely become the dominant platform for survey research.

Call-in polls or write-in polls are other means of securing a sample. For the former, a telephone number is posted on the television screen, for example, and people are asked to call to register their views. In the latter, a newspaper publishes an appeal for subscribers to write letters offering their opinions. Such approaches can yield a large number of participants, but the size of the sample can be misleading, for those who are willing to call or write are different

census: *Constitutionally mandated count of the population every ten years.*

sample: *Subset of a population from which information is collected and analyzed to learn more about the population as a whole. The norm for an accurate sample size is around one thousand people.*

population: *Group the poll is to represent.*

representative sample: *Polling sample that is not biased, in which all members of the population have an equal chance of being included.*

Richard G. Bingham II/BinghamPhotography.com

In-person interviews were long considered the best method for polling the people; despite the expense, they are still occasionally used.

from those who are not. The samples yielded in these polls are not representative and, thus, are highly suspect.

Consider the following example of a call-in poll. The Miss America Beauty Pageant had long used a swimsuit competition to help decide who would win the much-coveted crown. However, critics demanded the elimination of the swimsuit segment because they believed it exploited women as sexual objects. Yet those who ran the contest knew that the swimsuit competition was very popular. The managers of the pageant decided to "let the public decide" by having a call-in poll asking whether the swimsuit competition should continue. The results were "clear": 87 percent voted to retain the swimsuit portion.[24] But did the public really speak here? Because the telephone number was posted only during the airing of the pageant, the respondents were people already watching the pageant and therefore were likely to be favorable to it. Those opposed to the swimsuit segment were more likely to be doing something else.

Presidential elections are awash in polls. In the heat of the fall campaign, nightly polls gauge changes in voters' preferences for the major contenders. These surveys are called **tracking polls**. Another type of survey involving elections is the **exit poll**, conducted as voters leave the polling booth. The goal here is to learn about the reasoning behind the votes citizens just cast, but, more important, to predict the outcome of the election before all the ballots are formally counted.

The most famous and consequential exit poll took place in Florida during the 2000 presidential elections, fueling one of the most controversial electoral struggles of all time. The major networks used an exit poll to predict that the Sunshine State would go to Vice President

tracking polls: *Polls that seek to gauge changes of opinion of the same sample size over a period of time, common during the closing months of presidential elections.*

exit polls: *Polls that survey a sample of voters immediately after exiting the voting booth to predict the outcome of the election before the ballots are officially counted.*

Sequential editions of the *Orlando Sentinel* following election day 2000 testify to the confusion wrought by news media's calling the election on the basis of exit polls and early returns, which in this case were misleading.

Albert Gore Jr. (1993–2001). Florida's electoral votes would put Gore over the 270 needed, making him the apparent winner of the presidency. These predictions started to roll in at 8 P.M. on election night. The campaign of Republican George W. Bush protested, saying it was too early to call the state and that the race was still too close to know who won. By 10 P.M. the earlier forecast was withdrawn, and the outcome of the presidential election was again unclear. By 2 A.M. the next morning, Fox News called the election for Bush, with the other major networks soon following. Just two hours later, however, the call was retracted. There followed a thirty-six-day legal battle over which candidate actually won in Florida. It was not settled until the U.S. Supreme Court halted the Florida recount in mid-December, giving Bush the presidency (see Supreme Court Cases: *Bush v. Gore*, in Chapter 10, Elections and Campaigns).

Many have wanted to blame exit polls for the confusion that election night, but the polls were not as big a problem as the news media's use of them. The networks feel real pressure to make early calls, and that pressure sometimes leads them to go beyond what the data support. So while CBS was making that first call around 8 P.M., its polling experts behind the scene were urging caution.[25]

A final kind of election poll is actually a campaign strategy. **Push polls** are conducted by interest groups or candidates who try to affect the opinions of respondents by priming them with biased information. During the 2000 presidential primary in South Carolina, for example, Arizona Senator John McCain claimed that George W. Bush ran a push poll against him. Interviewers had called people to ask if they knew that McCain was a "cheat" and a "liar." The question was not designed to get information but to turn people against McCain.[26] Such polls seek to shift public opinion, not to measure it.

Error in Polls

Pollsters do everything they can to ensure that their samples are representative. Even if the sample is drawn properly, however, there is still a chance of error. To capture this uncertainty, all poll numbers come with a **confidence interval** that captures the likely range 95 percent of the time. The poll produces a single estimate of the public's thinking, but the best way to think of that estimate is as a range of possible estimates. For a sample of six hundred respondents, the **sampling error** is ± 4 percent. That 4 percent generates the confidence interval. Assume, for example, that 65 percent of those sampled support the efforts of Congress to reform the campaign finance laws. With a sampling error of 4 percent, the best way to think of the proportion is that, with 95 percent certainty, the actual amount of public support is somewhere between 61 percent and 69 percent. This range is the confidence interval. Note, however, that there is still a one in twenty chance (5 percent) that the true proportion is above or below that 8-point confidence interval. Hence, caution is always required when interpreting poll data.

In addition to sampling error, the wording of the question can introduce bias. The controversial issue of abortion offers a vivid example. What the public thinks about this issue depends a great deal on the way the question is asked. In November 2003 an NBC News/ *Wall Street Journal* poll asked a representative sample of Americans the following question: "Which of the following best represents your views about abortion—the choice on abortion should be left up to the woman and her doctor, abortion should be legal only in cases which pregnancy results from rape or incest or when the life of the woman is at risk, or abortion should be illegal in all circumstances?"

Have you ever looked at a poll and questioned its validity? If so, did you do more research on the issue?

Do polls make sure the people's voices are heard?

push polls: *Polls that are designed to manipulate the opinions of those being polled.*

confidence interval: *Statistical range, with a given probability, that takes random error into account.*

sampling error: *Measure of the accuracy of a public opinion poll reported as a percentage.*

YOU DECIDE

U.S. officials say Iran is about a year from being nuclear-bomb capable, a timeline that has been predicted for 10 years. What should the U.S. do now?

○ Nothing. Israel will deal with it.

○ Use our own missiles to bring an end to the program

○ Work on tougher sanctions with the U.N. and other nations

○ Overthrow the Islamic regime by helping democratic forces on the ground

[**Vote**]   View Results

Screencapture courtesy of FOXnews.com

Quick vote

Was the Supreme Court right to overturn the ban on animal cruelty videos?

○ Yes   ○ No

[VOTE] or view results

Screen capture courtesy of cnn.com

Many websites, especially of news organizations, invite participation in polls. How reliable do you think the results are?

Do all Americans have an equal chance of being included in polls?

The answers show that 53 percent of the public felt that abortion was a decision best left to the woman and her doctor. Only 15 percent of Americans felt it should be illegal in all circumstances, with 29 percent wanting to have exceptions. In short, a majority of the public appeared to support abortion rights for women. That is an important finding.

But is it true? Consider the following question asked earlier that year, in July, by Fox News/Opinion Dynamics: "Once a woman is pregnant, do you believe the unborn baby or fetus should have all the same rights as a newborn baby?" The answers tell a different story. Nearly 60 percent of the public said yes, the unborn fetus should have the same rights as a newborn baby. Only 26 percent said no. According to this poll, a strong majority wants to protect the rights of the unborn and, therefore, to limit abortion rights for women.

So what is American public opinion on abortion? Clearly, the answer depends on the wording of the question, specifically on whether respondents are asked to focus on the rights of women or the rights of the unborn. This same dynamic applies to other controversial issues, such as attitudes toward homosexuality and race. Because of America's long and tortured history of race relations, people often try to give socially acceptable responses so as to suggest they are tolerant and not bigots or racists. Although interviewers are trained to be neutral in their questioning, respondents sometimes try to give responses that they think the questioner wants to hear. Another source of error in polls involves what political scientists call **nonattitudes**. When asked, many people feel compelled to answer, even if they do not have opinions or know much about the question. They do not want to seem uninformed, but their responses create error in the survey.

The Future of Polls

Despite all the concerns about potential errors in polls, surveys are powerful tools, and pollsters learn from their mistakes. If done correctly, surveys open a valuable window on the public's thinking. Even in the controversial election of 2000, the Zogby organization predicted the outcome for each state accurately. In 2004 the polls were again accurate, correctly anticipating a narrow win by President George W. Bush over Massachusetts Senator John Kerry. An average of the nine national polls conducted just before the 2008 elections predicted that Obama would win with 52 percent. The actual vote was 52.9 percent, suggesting once again that surveys remain good indicators of the public's thinking.

Today polling is facing a transition. Representative sampling in telephone surveys is increasingly affected by the growing number of cell phones, as many pollsters do not have access to cell phone exchanges and many cell phone users, especially young people, do not have landlines, which are used in telephones polls. At this point, there is not a lot of evidence to suggest that people without landlines vote differently from those with them, but the shift from landlines to cell phones continues.[27] Perhaps more important is the widespread use of caller ID and answering machines. By 2003 half of the public had answering machines at home,[28] which means that today more and more Americans can screen their calls and refuse to participate in surveys. In fact, there is a general "polling fatigue" among the public. People are asked to participate not only in political polls but also in surveys for insurance companies, health care providers, and an endless array of products. Automobile dealers call customers to see if they are satisfied with their most recent visit; banks make similar calls. The result is that fewer people are willing to participate in telephone surveys. The declining

response rate is lessening the ability of pollsters to capture public opinion accurately. In the 1990s the rate of response was nearly 40 percent, and now it is about 25 percent.[29]

With telephone surveys in trouble, Internet polls represent the future for measuring public opinion. Through the Internet, polls can be done quickly and cheaply, but respondents may not be representative of the population. Once statisticians develop reliable ways to correct for bias, the web will become an even more powerful tool than it is now to measure the public's thinking. As more people gain access to the web, the amount of bias will decline. Such trends suggest that the future of survey research lies with the Internet.

response rate: *Proportion of the public that responds to inquiries from pollsters to participate in surveys.*

What Drives Public Opinion?

Where does public opinion come from? If it is the aggregate of citizen attitudes and beliefs, it starts with individuals. In this section, we examine the major forces that shape political thinking on a personal level, including the social and political environment in which one grows up and the generation and family into which one is born. Self-interest also affects political attitudes, as do the ideas of opinion leaders such as journalists, political observers, policy makers, and experts.

socialization: *Impact and influence of one's social environment on the views and attitudes one carries in life, a primary source of political attitudes.*

Independents: *Individuals who do not affiliate with either of the major political parties.*

Social and Political Environment

Political attitudes are shaped by environment—the kind of place one grows up in and lives in. Someone who grew up in a small town in Alabama centered around the local Baptist church would be influenced by that setting, and would be different from someone who grew up in, say, Seattle, Washington, in a family that was not religious. Attendance at a suburban private high school would yield differing influences than attendance at an urban public school. Each of us is a product of our family, friends, and community. We call the process by which our attitudes are shaped **socialization**.

The way we live our lives, the kinds of foods we eat, the types of vacations we enjoy, and the houses of worship we attend—all shape how we are socialized. Our political attitudes are no different. The clearest embodiment of political socialization is partisanship, and evidence shows that parents pass their partisan views along to their children. If parents are Democrats, there is a two-thirds chance that their children will identify themselves as Democrats. They might identify as **Independents**, but there is just a 10 percent chance they will be Republicans. The impact of socialization depends, of course, on whether the parents identify with the same party. If the parents are split on partisanship, the chance of the children being Independents rises considerably.[30]

High divorce rates have changed family structure in recent years, but there is no evidence that they have interfered with the passing along of political values, even when children are exposed to many more potential influences. Recent research concludes that "despite [the] transformation in the political environment and the character of family life over the last thirty years, our findings about youth coming of age in the 1990s strongly parallel those based on youth socialization in the 1960s."[31]

AFP/Getty Images

Parents generally pass political attitudes, including party identification, on to their children.

How do individuals form their opinions?

It may be that political values are passed on in families by genes as well as by socialization. Recent research offers some tantalizing hints that genetics may shape political views.[32] Political scientists have been slow to embrace the possibility, but it warrants close consideration. That some people are more outgoing and more willing to build social networks appears to have a basis in one's genes.[33] If so, such a tendency could explain a willingness to become involved in politics, and it may even shape political views. Studies of twins are particularly revealing. Data collected from sets of twins indicate that identical twins, who share their entire genetic code, expressed more similar political attitudes than did fraternal twins, who are no more similar than any set of siblings. Such data are not conclusive, but they are suggestive. Admittedly, some political attitudes are less likely to have a genetic component, and partisanship appears to be shaped by family and friends. But ideological leanings—whether one is more or less open to change—may be shaped in part by genetics.[34] This new area of research offers fascinating possibilities for understanding the sources of public opinion.[35]

Whether through family socialization or genes, parents have the biggest impact during a child's early life, but starting in the teenage years, friends also influence attitudes and behavior, as do schools and communities. Communities that are homogeneous, in which most people share many of the same views and opinions, are likely to reinforce the attitudes of parents. Colleges, too, influence attitudes, and college attendance often offers students a chance to break out of the homogeneous settings of their early years. Students meet people from different states or communities, people with different backgrounds and attitudes. College classes and experiences can also shape political leanings.

Have your political opinions ever changed? If so, what led to the change?

Socialization does not end at college graduation, however. It continues as young people pursue careers and chose where and how they will live. Consider people who live in San Francisco versus those who live in Dallas. Those different environments will surely have different effects on residents. Of course, those who choose to live in San Francisco may have different attitudes to begin with from those who move to Texas.

Generational Effects

Major events can change an entire generation's thinking about politics. The Great Depression, for example, which started in 1929 with the crash of the stock market, shaped the attitudes of millions of Americans. It was an economic calamity that even the severe economic downturn of 2008–2009 did not match. Millions lost their savings and their homes. In 1932 one of every four Americans was out of work, and incomes had declined by 50 percent. One consequence was that the public blamed the party in power, the Republicans, and switched party allegiance. The Democrats, as a result, became the majority party for the first time in generations.

The terrorist attacks of September 11, 2001, were another defining event that caused Americans to change their views, this time on national security. Quite suddenly, many were willing to give up some personal freedom to reduce the threat of terrorism (see Figure 6.2). Searing events, such as the Great Depression and the terrorist attacks, can have long-term effects on public opinion, especially if the generation that experienced them most acutely reacts as a bloc.

generational effects: *Effects on opinion from the era in which one lives.*

Generational effects need not be limited to life-altering events, however. They can also be affected by the era in which is one is young and first active as a citizen. Those who were young during the term of Republican President Ronald Reagan are likely to think of politics differently than those who are young during the term of Democratic President Barack Obama. The former will naturally think more favorably about Republicans, the latter more favorably about Democrats. Exit polls from 2008 indicated that 66 percent of all 18- to 29-year-old voters supported Obama.[36] By historical standards, this level of support was quite high. Although it remains to be seen whether being a member of what may be called the "Obama generation" will have an enduring effect on partisan identification and politics, America's **Millennial** generation does seem distinctive. Millennials seem to be more trusting of government than previous generations. There is also evidence to suggest that this group is less religious than previous generations.[37]

Self-Interest and Rationality

Forming political opinion is much more than just a psychological process tied to socialization, however. People also respond to the context in which they find themselves. That is, to a certain extent people are "rational" in that they act in a way that is consistent with their **self-interest**. For example, as income rises, the chance of someone being a Republican increases. Why? The Republicans have pursued tax policies that protect individual wealth, while the Democrats pursue tax policies that tax the wealthy at higher rates to pay for social programs that benefit the less wealthy. In fact, one could argue that although the transmission of partisanship reflects socialization, the reason it sticks is that it is in one's self-interest.

Examples of **rationality** and self-interest abound. Couples with school-age children get interested in education policy. Homeowners become more focused on issues tied to property taxes than do individuals who rent. As citizens approach retirement age, they become protective of Social Security and Medicare benefits. Recently young people, too, have been concerned about these benefits, but in ways that reflect their self-interest. They wonder if the entitlement programs will be bankrupt before they are of age to receive the benefits, and they have engaged in the debate about whether the federal government should privatize Social Security, allowing people to invest the Social Security taxes they pay while they are working directly in the stock market. The prospect seems attractive when the market is doing well, but when it fluctuates and falls, there is evidence that citizens "update their opinions about Social Security reform . . . particularly when movements in the markets remind citizens of the risks inherent in investing."[38] Such evidence suggests the public is rational and that people act in ways consistent with their self-interest.

Self-interest clearly shapes political attitudes, but that does not mean that people are selfish. It means that they are trying to advance and protect their own interests, and that in itself is encouraging. Since a democracy rests on the sound judgments of the electorate, it is good to know that there is some evidence that citizens act rationally.

Elites

One of the big questions in the field of public opinion is what role **elites**—leaders of opinion—play in shaping citizens' thinking. A democracy is supposed to be a system in which the average person has a say in government and the people's preferences drive public policy. Yet some people

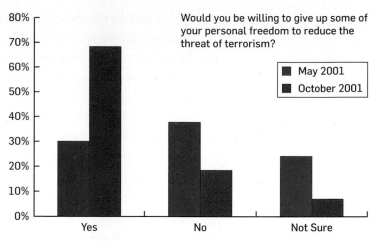

Would you be willing to give up some of your personal freedom to reduce the threat of terrorism?

■ May 2001
■ October 2001

FIGURE 6.2 Shift in Public Opinion following the Terrorist Attacks of September 11, 2001. The terrorist attacks of September 11, 2001, are likely to have a long-term effect on public opinion. The graph shows before-and-after responses to the question about being willing to give up personal freedom. When the question was asked again in May 2006, 56 percent answered yes, a 17-point decline from October 2001, but still well above the levels registered before September 11, 2001.
Source: Fox News/Opinion Dynamic Poll, October 2001, May 2001, and May 2006.

Millennials: *Generation born between 1982 and 2003.*

self-interest: *Concern for one's own advantage and well-being.*

rationality: *Acting in a way that is consistent with one's self-interest.*

What are the sources of public opinion?

elites: *Group of people who may lead public opinion, such as journalists, politicians, and policy makers.*

elite theory: *Idea that public opinion is shaped by discourse among elites and is a top-to-bottom process.*

Does every citizen have an equal chance to be heard?

worry that experts, policy makers, political observers, journalists, and others in the news media have an undue influence in shaping public opinion. If elites shape public opinion, can the United States be a democratic nation? One way to approach the question of what political scientists call **elite theory** is to recognize, first, that it is not so simple a matter as elites offering an opinion and the public swallowing it. That assumption attributes far too much influence to elites and far too little credit to the people. Instead, it appears that elites can influence citizens if two conditions are met: first, citizens must be exposed to the message, and, second, they must be open to it.[39]

Let's assume that scientists find clear evidence that being gay is completely genetic. Such evidence does not exist, but if it did, that would mean that sexual orientation is fixed, just as eye color is fixed. If true, the public's attitudes toward homosexuality would surely change, as it is harder to justify discrimination against homosexuals if sexual orientation is an inborn characteristic. Yet some citizens, when learning this new information, would be resistant to the idea due to their moral beliefs. Social conservatives, for example, would on average be far less likely than social liberals to accept this information. The prior beliefs of social conservatives would serve as a check on accepting it. By comparison, social liberals would have preexisting views that would fit better with the new information. They would be open to it.

This theory of who changes opinions and who does not has a number of implications. First, massive change in public opinion is not likely because the public is not made up of puppets. Second, elites' ability to change public opinion is a product of the intensity and consistency of the message. Disagreement among elites on a new issue will decrease the potential for change. The public, for example, remained divided on global warming in the 1990s. Liberals were more willing to believe that climate change was caused by human activity. Conservatives had more doubts. As the scientific evidence mounted and more elites embraced the notion, however, the public began to shift its thinking. In 1997, 60 percent of the public felt that more research about global warming was needed to be sure of its effects, and only 28 percent felt that it was a serious problem. Ten years later, only 25 percent felt that more research was needed, and 64 percent felt that action needed to be taken to deal with climate change.[40]

Elites do influence public opinion, but they are not members of a monolithic group seeking to advance its own interests; in fact, elites often disagree among themselves. When there is agreement among elites, however, that is probably a sign of the merits of the idea. Second, people respond only to ideas that they find appealing and that fit with their own values and opinions. As a model for how people change opinions in response to events, acting out of both self-interest and rationality, we can look at how Americans are viewed by others (see Other Places: The Rise and Fall of Anti-Americanism).

The Shape of Public Opinion

To understand public opinion, it is essential to appreciate the ways it is shaped by partisanship and ideology. These two variables can, to a large extent, explain the opinions of citizens. Although not everyone is partisan or ideological, these forces provide useful frameworks for understanding the public's thinking on issues. With a firm understanding of partisanship and ideology in place, we can address two major questions about public opinion: How informed is the public? And is the public polarized?

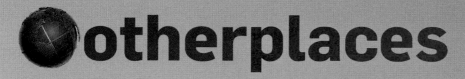

otherplaces

The Rise and Fall of Anti-Americanism

Following the terrorist attacks of September 11, 2001, the world rallied to support the United States. There was an outpouring of good will and cooperation. More than forty countries joined the United States in providing military assistance to rid Afghanistan of the Taliban, hoping to root out a major source of terrorism. But this support started to erode as the United States deemphasized cooperation to pursue independent policies. The U.S. attack on Iraq in 2003 and the subsequent war caused global public opinion to turn against the United States. The figure below shows a downward trend in the image of the United States held by four democracies. Israel's image of the United States remains stable, reflecting long-standing ties.

This trend is now reversing itself. The election of Barack Obama was hailed across much of the world and has signaled a new tone of cooperation. As a result, the U.S. image abroad has begun to improve. In Europe, there has been an across-the-board upturn. Between 2008 and 2009 ratings from the United Kingdom increased from a little over 50 percent to nearly 70 percent. Ratings from Germany doubled—from about 30 percent to over 60 percent. The same is true for countries in other parts of the world, such as Indonesia and Nigeria. Ratings in India increased from 60 percent to 75 percent.

The rise and the fall of anti-Americanism are not unusual. Anti-Americanism has generally increased when the United States has been at war, as it did also during the Vietnam War. Each time that America has fallen out of favor, there has also been a rebound. Public opinion around the world is a product of self-interest and rationality.

- **How closely does the world's opinion of the United States coordinate with what Americans think about their country?**

- **Should American government be responsive to world opinion?**

Favorable Image of the United States, 2000–2007.

Source: Pew Research; Giacomo Chiozza, *Anti-Americanism and the American World Order* (Baltimore: Johns Hopkins University Press, 2009); Giacomo Chiozza, Report to the APSA Task Force, APSA annual meeting, 2009.

Partisanship

party identification:
Attachment or allegiance to a political party; partisanship.

perceptual lens: *Ideological framework that shapes the way partisans view the political world and process information.*

Does party loyalty shape public opinion?

Party identification, or partisanship, is central to understanding how people think politically. Party identification represents an individual's allegiance to a political party. This psychological attachment usually forms when an individual is young. The attachment, through what is called the **perceptual lens**, shapes the way partisans view the political world and process information. The perceptual lenses of partisans act like prisms that bend light. Democrats have prisms that bend light in one direction; Republicans' prisms bend it in another direction. The result, for example, is that a Republican would be slower to turn against the Iraq War, initiated by a Republican president, than would a Democrat. Conversely, a Republican would be less sympathetic to Barack Obama's reform of health care than would a Democrat.[41]

By knowing party identification, political scientists can predict—with considerable accuracy—attitudes on a range of issues. Republicans, for example, are less likely than Democrats to support government spending to help the poor and elderly. Republicans are not opposed to helping such people, but they want to do so through private charities and individual initiative. More generally, Republicans are less supportive of an activist federal government, while Democrats are more open to giving government an active role in the lives of citizens.

An easy indicator of the power of partisanship is the public's approval of President Barack Obama. In February 2010 about 53 percent of Americans approved of the job Obama was doing as president, but that proportion hides a much more powerful finding about partisanship. Among Democrats, around 80 percent approved of his performance in the Oval Office. By contrast, just over 20 percent of Republicans supported the president—a gap of 60 percentage points.[42] President George W. Bush experienced the same kind of gap in public opinion, with Republicans approving of his performance at far higher rates than Democrats.

Although partisanship shapes how an individual thinks about politics, it can subside in times of national crisis. Following the September 11 terrorist attacks, Americans put aside partisan differences. In late September 2001 over 98 percent of Republicans and more than 80 percent (up from 25 percent) of Democrats approved of the job President Bush was doing.[43] Partisanship returned the next year, however, with the 2002 midterm elections.

Because party identification is central to understanding public opinion, pollsters have been asking about partisanship since the 1940s. The American National Elections Studies, a premier academic survey organization, has been asking the same question since 1952: "Generally speaking, do you usually think of yourself as a Republican, a Democrat, an Independent, or what?"[44] This question asks respondents how they think about themselves in order to capture political identification and the general tendency, or the perceptual lens, of their thinking. The theoretical underpinnings are psychological. Partisanship can also be likened to loyalty, like the loyalty to sports teams or to friends that lasts through ups and downs. Partisanship can change over a person's life, but it tends to be stable, especially when compared to other political attitudes.

In the last few years, there has been much discussion in the press about Independents, with claims that they are the "largest group in the electorate."[45] With the rise of the so-called Tea Party movement, their numbers are increasing. The view that Americans are mostly Independents is, however, a myth.[46] It is true that many citizens claim to be Independents, but they actually behave like partisans. That is, most Independents lean toward one party or the other. Figure 6.3 charts changes in the share of "pure Independents" as contrasted with "Independent leaners" since the 1950s. The number of those of the pure variety has been pretty much flat during these six decades. The growth has been in the leaners, and that growth has been substantial. But such individuals vote consistently for one party and are very much partisans, despite self-professed labels. Their behavior is testimony to the strength of partisanship in the United States.

Ideology

Political ideology has a complex relationship with partisanship. **Liberals** tend to be Democrats, and **conservatives** tend to be Republicans, but ideology speaks to both political and social values. Conservatives view a good society as one that allows individuals to pursue their economic interests in an unfettered fashion. Liberals worry that, without some governmental regulation to curb abuse and moderate economic cycles, the rich will get very rich and the poor will get very poor. This concern leads liberals to believe that government can improve

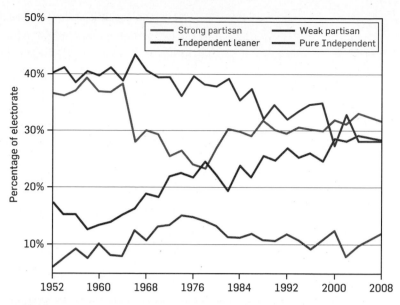

FIGURE 6.3 Independents in the Electorate, 1952–2008. These data show that pure Independents constitute a small part of the American electorate, and that their proportion that has remained about the same for the last fifty years. Such data are important in understanding the continuing importance of partisanship in America. *Source:* John Sides, George Washington University.

people's lives and prevent inequalities that harm society and the economy as a whole. Conservatives are much more leery of government and view it as a problem in and of itself. They contend that less government interference will give the poor the opportunity to improve their lives by themselves. On social issues, the tables are turned. That is, liberals tend to believe that people should be able to make personal choices free from government interference. Conservatives, by contrast, value more traditional lifestyles and want government, at times, to enforce such choices.

Not all citizens think of themselves as liberals or conservatives. Depending on the wording of the question, about 40 percent of Americans views themselves as ideological **moderates**, about 25 percent as liberals, and the remaining 35 percent as conservatives.[47] But there is also a debate among political scientists about whether citizens think ideologically at all. That is, do people have coherent views about politics? One famous effort to measure the ideological foundations, or **levels of conceptualization**, of the public's thinking found little evidence of such organized opinions. Data from the 1950s indicated that only about 12 percent of the public viewed the political parties in ideological terms, whereas over 40 percent judged the parties by the groups (such as social classes or racial and ethnic groups) they were thought to represent rather than the policies they pursued. About 25 percent evaluated the parties by "the nature of the times": Is the economy doing well? Are we embroiled in a war? The remainder—just over 20 percent—did not think about issues at all when evaluating the parties and candidates; this part of the public showed "no issue content."[48]

Over the last fifty years, there have been some changes in the sizes of these four groups, but not major ones. Using data from 2000, about 20 percent of citizens can be thought of as being ideological thinkers, 28 percent focus on groups, another 28 percent is driven by the nature of the times, and 24 percent have no issue content in their political thinking.[49] Even in 2011 it would be hard to argue that a majority of the public has a coherent, ideologically driven view of politics.

political ideology: *Set of consistent political beliefs.*

liberals: *Individuals who have faith in government to improve people's lives, believing that private efforts are insufficient. In the social sphere, liberals usually support diverse lifestyles and tend to oppose any government action that seeks to shape personal choices.*

conservatives: *Individuals who distrust government, believing that private efforts are more likely to improve people's lives. In the social sphere, conservatives usually support traditional lifestyles and tend to believe that government can play a valuable role in shaping personal choices.*

moderates: *Individuals who are in the middle of the ideological spectrum and do not hold consistently strong views about whether government should be involved in people's lives.*

levels of conceptualization: *Measure of how ideologically coherent individuals are in their political evaluations.*

How does party identification relate to ideology?

How coherent is public opinion?

Nevertheless, it is still worth looking at the public's ideological mood. Is the public, collectively, becoming more liberal or more conservative? Such changes should aid understanding of the general direction of the country. Figure 6.4 maps changes in the public's ideological thinking between 1937 and 2009.

This seventy-year time period reveals some interesting trends. The liberal nature of public opinion was apparent between 1937 and 1964—an era dominated by the Democrats. In the mid-1960s, with the unpopularity of the Vietnam War and growing concerns about civil rights, crime, and excessive government involvement in the economy, conservatism grew—and grew quickly. The pattern since the 1960s has been back and forth, with liberalism on the rise of late. Even with the recent gains, however, the share of liberals in the population generally is still far less than in the time of Presidents Franklin Roosevelt, Harry Truman, and John Kennedy.

Is the public becoming more liberal or more conservative? How can you tell?

Is public opinion worth listening to? How does it influence your opinion?

Is the Public Informed?

A democracy depends on having an engaged and well-informed electorate. Otherwise, how can the public make good choices? If the power is to rest with the people, the people need to be knowledgeable about the issues of the day and the candidates who compete for public office.

The Framers were definitely concerned about the public's capacity to be informed and make good choices, especially because only 10 percent of Americans at the time were literate.[50] These concerns were one of the driving forces behind the gates and gateways in the Constitution, a document that sought to represent the public's views but also to establish institutions that would, according to James Madison, "refine and enlarge" them (see *Federalist* 10 in the Appendix). By that Madison meant that elected officials would react to public sentiment, but not be a slave to it. Instead, they would debate it in a way that would improve it and allow for better government. Over time, the amount of input by citizens has increased; now senators are voted into office by direct election, not by state legislatures. Literacy in 2010 stands at about 99 percent,[51] suggesting that citizens are better able today than in the eighteenth century to meet the demands of being "informed."

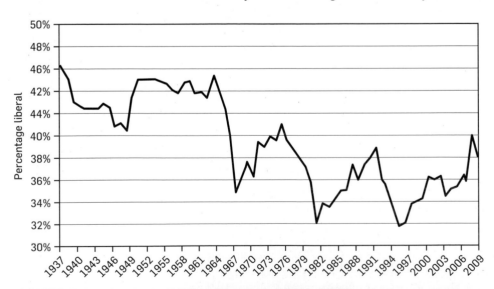

FIGURE 6.4 Liberal Self-Identification, 1937–2009. Liberal self-identification has declined since highs in the mid-1930s and early 1960s, but now appears to be on the rise. *Source:* Christopher Ellis and James A. Stimson, "On Symbolic Conservatism in America," paper presented at the 2007 annual meeting of the American Political Science Association; data updated by Ellis and Stimson.

But are they? When survey research began in the 1940s, it became possible to gather systematic information on the public's knowledge about politics. The early evidence was not encouraging. In a detailed study of the 1940 presidential campaign, scholars from Columbia University assumed that voters were like consumers and would look for the best deal, and that the campaign would be an important source of information as they made their choices. But the data told a different tale. Instead, most voters made up their minds before the campaign, and their choices were driven by where they lived and whom they knew.[52] In a subsequent study, the Columbia researchers went so far as to argue that low turnout in elections might actually be a good thing, because the uninformed would not be choosing the nation's leaders.[53] This argument has strong elitist overtones and certainly strays far from the assumptions about government responsiveness and citizen equality on which American democracy rests. Together with previous findings about levels of conceptualization,[54] the argument suggested that the public may not be capable of meeting its democratic responsibilities. What ensued was a debate over the accuracy and interpretation of these core findings.

Political scientists went, in effect, in search of the "informed voter," and they learned that citizens do not know many details about politics. Only 10 percent of the public knows the name of the Speaker of the House. Only about a third can name one U.S. Supreme Court justice. Only about half of Americans know which party controls Congress, and fewer than half know the name of their own congressional representative.[55] These facts suggest that average citizens do not possess the detailed information necessary to hold their government accountable.

Should these data be taken as evidence that the public is not able to meet its democratic responsibilities? Let us consider some findings that give reason for optimism. First, the public, collectively, seems to make reasonable choices. For example, when the economy is doing poorly, the party in power suffers. Voters hold presidents and legislators accountable; failures are punished and successes are rewarded. Further, Americans do not favor long wars, and they tend to reward candidates who pursue peace.[56]

AP Photo/Morry Gash

Second, although individuals do not know all the details about candidates' views on all the issues, they do tend to know candidates' views on the issues that are **salient** to them. Hunters know candidates' views on gun control; college students know candidates' views on student loans. One study estimates that when an issue is salient to an individual, that individual knows candidates' views on that issue correctly more than 90 percent of the time.[57]

Third, the public can learn quickly if an issue is salient enough to them and receives attention in the news media. The public quickly learned about AIDS when it started to become a public health crisis in the 1980s. Following the terrorist attacks of September 11, 2001, the public understood the need to consider some curtailment of civil liberties to ensure security.

Fourth, public opinion is more stable than is suggested by the shifting answers people give to the same question just a few months apart. The instability reflected in polls does not speak to a fickle or poorly informed public. Instead, it appears that polls themselves may be at fault.[58] That is, survey questions and the normal error associated with these questions make people's attitudes appear more unstable than they really are. Further, most issues are complex and leave many people genuinely conflicted. Being conflicted is not a sign of lack of information, but perhaps a realization that some problems are thorny and not easily answered. The following is one example:

Tonight Show host Jay Leno finds humor in stopping people on the street to ask what they know about current news and American politics. In one famous segment he asked, "Do you know the three branches of our government?" No one answered correctly.

salient: *Indication of importance and relevance of an issue to an individual.*

Can the public be trusted?

Courtesy Gerald R. Ford Library

Campaigning in 1976, President Gerald Ford visited Texas and, as politicians almost always do, sampled the local food. When he bit into a tamale with the husk still on, it was more than a humorous incident. Many interpreted the gaffe as indicating that Ford did not understand the people he claimed, as president, to represent.

low information rationality: *Idea that people do not need to have lots of information to make good decisions.*

polarization: *Condition in which differences between parties and/or the public are so stark that disagreement breaks out, fueling attacks and controversy.*

Does a polarized public prevent good policy making?

depolarized: *Political system in which the parties adopt the same positions on issues and choice is limited, leading citizens to feel less compelled to participate in elections.*

Vincent Sartori cannot decide whether or not the government should guarantee incomes, because he cannot decide how much weight to give the value of productivity. He believes that the rich are mostly undeserving and . . . yet he is angry at "welfare cheats" who refuse to work. . . . Caught between his desire for equality and his knowledge of existing injustice, on the one hand, and his fear that a guaranteed income will benefit even shirkers, on the other, he remains ambivalent about policies toward the poor.[59]

So Sartori could easily give different answers to the same survey question, depending on what he is thinking about at the time. But different answers say more about the issue's complexity than about his inability to make up his mind.

Fifth and finally, personal decision making is not always based on complete information, so why should political decision making be expected to conform to rational models that scholars use? Individuals often rely on cues and instincts to make decisions, rather than on analyses of detailed information. Scholars have termed such thinking **low information rationality**.[60] There are two famous examples from presidential campaigns. In 1976, President Gerald R. Ford (1974–77), campaigning in Texas, bit into a tamale with the husk still on, a gaffe suggesting that he knew little about the foods and habits of the people he hoped would vote for him. In 1992, President George H. W. Bush (1989–93) asked what milk cost in grocery stores. His admission that he did not know suggested that he was out of touch with ordinary Americans, who do their own shopping. His competitor, William Jefferson (Bill) Clinton (1993–2001), knew the price of milk and other items, such as jeans. Simple things like not knowing how to eat a tamale or what groceries cost turned some voters against Ford and Bush. These individuals concluded that the candidates were not like them and were not likely to understand their problems. Small bits of information can be informative.

It is easy to make any member of the public—even a president!—look uninformed, and of course it would be better if the public knew more about politics. But individuals do appear to learn about the issues that matter to them. Gaining information is a gateway to influence because, individually, people learn what they need to know to advance their interests, and collectively voters do hold government officials accountable.

Is the Public Polarized?

The engaged and informed citizens of a democracy cannot be expected to agree on everything. They will naturally have different views on issues. When the differences become stark, however, the danger is that **polarization** will fuel controversy and personal attacks to the point that compromise and consensus become impossible. Congress has clearly become more polarized over the last thirty years. Figure 6.5 tries to capture the idea of polarization on a simple left–right continuum. In the 1970s the parties adopted positions that were closer to the middle; thirty years later, their positions are more at the extremes. In fact, Democrats and Republicans disagree on more issues now than at any time since the end of the Civil War.[61]

In the 1970s there were numerous liberal Republicans and conservative Democrats. By 2008 these two groups were nearly extinct. In 2009, for example, Pennsylvania Senator Arlen Specter, one of the few moderate Republicans in Congress at the time, bolted the Republican Party and became a Democrat. He switched parties because of what he saw as a swing to the right by the Republicans. The differences between the parties have grown.[62] What is less clear is whether the public, too, is polarized.

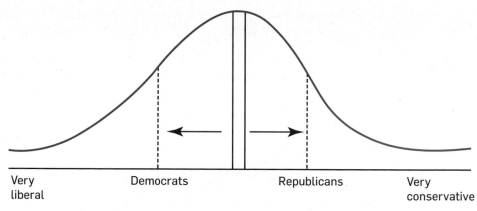

Very liberal   Democrats   Republicans   Very conservative

FIGURE 6.5 Political Polarization in the United States. When the parties are polarized they move toward the tail of these distributions. When parties are depolarized they adopt positions near each other. Currently the parties are polarized, but that was not the case in the 1970s.
Source: The authors

Some scholars have argued that the public has polarized along with parties, but there is also evidence that the public is more moderate, even though the choices the parties offer them are not.[63] For example, according to a series of surveys conducted by the Pew Center between 1987 and 2007, "the average difference between Republican and Democratic identifiers on forty political and social issues increased from 10 to 14 percent, a surprisingly small difference."[64] These data suggest that the public is more moderate than the choices that are laid before them in elections would suggest.[65]

Many observers worry that one effect of polarization will be more personal attacks on political figures and greater incivility in politics. Others argue, however, that increasing polarization indicates that people's interest in elections has increased and that they care more about who wins. In fact, the share of the public that cares about which party wins the presidential election has increased since 1988. Interest in elections, generally, also seems to be on the rise. In 1988, 44 percent of the public paid "a lot" of attention to the presidential campaign. In 2000, the proportion stood at 53 percent, a notable gain. By 2008, the percentage was a whopping 72 percent.[66] The 2008 increase surely reflects the response to the candidacy of Barack Obama, but it is also true that the differences between the candidates in recent elections have been stark enough to prompt lots of interest.

Having a clear choice engages people and gives them a stake in an election outcome. If the system became **depolarized** (see Figure 6.5), the public would lack a choice. It would no longer matter whether Democrats or Republicans won, because they would do the same thing once in office. For these reasons, many scholars in the 1950s called for **responsible parties** that would offer the public a real choice (see Chapter 9, Political Parties). Citizens, under such conditions, can more effectively hold officials accountable for misdeeds and reward successes.

Do political parties influence public opinion, or is it the other way around?

responsible parties: *Parties that take responsibility for offering the electorate a distinct range of policies and programs, thus providing a clear choice.*

TIM SLOAN/AFP/Getty Images

At town hall meetings held on health care proposals during the summer of 2009, opponents were vocal. Such vocal discussions occasionally turn hostile, highlighting the consequences of the continued polarization of the American political system.

Group Differences

Public opinion is shaped by partisanship and ideology. Social scientists find that demographics also matter—that is, the tendency for certain groups within the American population to hold similar views. These breakdowns by group are the microfoundations of public opinion. In this section, we look at the ways that socioeconomic status, religion, gender, race and ethnicity, and education tend to organize public opinion.

Socioeconomic Status

socioeconomic status: *Combined measure of occupation, education, income, wealth, and relative social standing or lifestyle.*

Socioeconomic status is a combined measure of occupation, education, income, wealth, and relative social standing or lifestyle. It influences where one lives, what kind of work one does, whom one knows, the kinds of schools one attends, and the kind of opportunities one can take advantage of. These matters inevitably mold political attitudes. Working-class people are more likely than wealthier people to favor more government programs to help the poor and provide child care, more funding for public education, and more protection for Social Security. Around 70 percent of Americans earning between $15,000 and $35,000 support spending by government on such social services. Among those earning between $75,000 and $105,000, the proportion drops to about 55 percent.[67]

Part of the reason for the strong differences in opinion among different income groups is that political parties have a class bias. Republicans draw far more support from those who come from higher socioeconomic status than do Democrats. Starting in the 1980s, however, Republicans also began to draw support from working-class people who supported a conservative social agenda and a decreased role for government in the economy. These so-called **Reagan Democrats** were central to Republican success in the ensuing decades.

Reagan Democrats: *Voters traditionally affiliated with the Democratic Party based on their working-class status who voted for Ronald Reagan in the 1980s because of his conservative message on social issues, emphasis on national security, and call for limited government.*

Does being a member of a demographic group shape opinion?

Age

Age also influences opinions on issues, because the stage of one's life affects how one thinks about issues. For instance, 70 percent of people under 30 years of age favor increased spending on student loans. That drops to 42 percent among those over 55. This gap makes sense because younger people are more likely to need student loans. Younger people are much more likely to favor making marijuana legal than older people. Those under 30 also are more supportive of gay marriage than people over 55. In general, older citizens are more socially conservative than younger citizens,[68] and there is evidence that people tend to become more conservative as they age.

Religion

Religious affiliation is another indicator of opinion. Overall, for example, Protestants are more conservative than Catholics or Jews. Only 12 percent of Jews describe themselves as conservative, compared to 36 percent of Protestants. On some issues, Muslims have been found to be more liberal than the general population and significantly more liberal than Protestants and Catholics. For example, 70 percent of Muslims favor an activist government, whereas just 43 percent of the public as a whole subscribes to that view. On social issues, however, Muslims show a much more conservative tendency. When asked "Which comes closer to your view? Homosexuality is a way of life that should be accepted by society or homosexuality is a way of life that should be discouraged by society," 61 percent of Muslims said that homosexual lifestyles should be discouraged. Only 38 percent of all Americans gave that response.[69]

Recent studies of religion and public opinion have focused on differences within denominations, particularly with the rise of evangelical Christianity among Protestants. Starting in the 1970s, and especially after the *Roe v. Wade* Supreme Court decision made abortion legal under some conditions in 1973, evangelicals became more active in politics. They also strongly oppose gay rights and support school prayer. On the issue of abortion, in 2004 only 11 percent of evangelical Protestants described themselves as pro-choice. Among more secular Protestants, nearly 60 percent advocated pro-choice positions. The same pattern holds for supporting same-sex marriage. Secular Protestants were six times more likely than evangelical Protestants to favor same-sex marriage.[70]

Table 6.1 explores differences among Protestants on the issue of immigration. White evangelical Protestants take a much less favorable view of immigrants than do "mainline" Protestants (those belonging to older denominations such as the Presbyterian and Episcopal churches) and those who describe themselves as secular, that is, without religious affiliation. Among evangelicals, 63 percent see "newcomers" as threats to "traditional American customs and values." Only 39 percent of seculars hold that opinion. A near majority of seculars (45 percent) believe that immigrants "strengthen our country with their hard work and talents." Fewer than 30 percent of white evangelicals agree. These kinds of differences underscore the importance of looking within denominations for patterns in U.S. public opinion.

TABLE 6.1 Religious Tradition and Views on Immigrants

	All	White Evangelical Protestant	White Mainline Protestant	White Non-Hispanic Catholic	Secular
The growing number of newcomers from other countries . . .					
Threatens traditional American customs and values	48%	63%	51%	48%	39%
Strengthens American society	45%	32%	44%	47%	54%
Don't know/Refused	7%	5%	5%	5%	7%
	100%	100%	100%	100%	100%
Immigrants today . . .					
Are a burden because they take our jobs, housing, and health care	52%	64%	52%	56%	46%
Strengthen our country with their hard work and talents	41%	29%	42%	41%	45%
Don't know/Refused	7%	7%	6%	3%	9%
	100%	100%	100%	100%	100%

Source: Gregory Smith, "Attitudes toward Immigration: In the Pulpit and the Pew," Pew Research Center, April 2006.

Gender

Starting in 1980 a **gender gap** emerged in U.S. politics. Before 1980 the differences in political attitudes among men and women were not large and did not draw much attention. However, in elections since Ronald Reagan's 1980 victory over Jimmy Carter (1977–81), women have been generally more supportive of Democrats than of Republicans. In 1980 the gap was 8 percentage points: 54 percent of men backed Reagan and only 46 percent of women. The gap has varied from 4 percent in 1992 to 11 percent in 1996. Barack Obama secured 56 percent of the female vote and just 49 percent of the male vote. The differences are such that, if only women were allowed to vote, the Democrats might have won every presidential election since 1980 save for Reagan's landslide against Walter Mondale in 1984.[71]

In general, women are more liberal than men, and gender gaps are also evident on specific issues. Women were less supportive of the Iraq War, believing in larger numbers in 2004 that the war "was not worth fighting." Women favor more spending on social programs than men. In 2000, 67 percent of women favored more spending on child care, whereas 58 percent of men held this view. Men are much more likely to support the death penalty than are women (62 percent versus 38 percent). This gap is not nearly as wide when it comes to abortion. In 2009, 50 percent of women and 44 percent of men thought abortion should be legal.[72]

Taylor Jones/Getty Images

In the summer of 2005 Cindy Sheehan, whose son Casey had been killed in the Iraq War, held a month-long vigil a few miles from President George W. Bush's Texas ranch. Her protest attracted media attention, and she became known as "Peace Mom."

Is your political opinion shaped by your social class, age, religion, gender, race and ethnicity, and/or education level?

Race and Ethnicity

Another divide in public opinion involves race and ethnicity. The issue of slavery tore the nation apart, and more than one hundred years after the Civil War, Americans remained divided about issues involving race. In 1964 African Americans overwhelmingly endorsed desegregation, whereas white Americans were split on the issue. In 1974 only 25 percent of white Americans felt "government should help blacks," whereas 63 percent of African Americans believed that government should take that role.[73] Similar gaps exist in regard to support for **affirmative action** policies that grant preferences to people (not only African Americans but also women) who have suffered discrimination in the past in job hiring, school admissions, and contracting. In 2004 only 11 percent of whites favored "preferences for hiring blacks." Four times as many African Americans favored affirmative action.[74]

The term *Latino* is used to describe a broad array of groups that do not necessarily share common experiences, so opinion among Latinos tends to be divided. Some Latino families have lived in the Southwest for centuries, since before the area became part of the United States in 1848. Others came to the United States within the last few years from homelands throughout Central and South America. Cuban immigrants, who left their homeland following the rise of Fidel Castro and the Communists in the late 1950s, tend to be much more conservative than Puerto Ricans and Mexican Americans. According to one study, about 60 percent of Cuban Americans are Republican identifiers, compared to only about 15 percent of Mexican

Americans.[75] Latinos are divided in other ways as well. According to one group of prominent scholars:

> On many key domestic issues, significant majorities of each [Latino] group take the liberal position. On other issues, there is no consensus and, depending on the issue, Mexicans may be on the right, while Cubans and many Puerto Ricans are on the left of the nation's current political spectrum. Thus, labels such as liberal or conservative do not adequately describe the complexity of any one group's political views.[76]

Thus, both parties compete for the support of the Latino community. In 2004 Latino support for President George W. Bush helped him defeat John Kerry. In 2008, however, Barack Obama gained two-thirds of the Latino vote, a shift partly owing to actions by Republicans in Congress to block immigration reform. As a group, Latinos support bilingual education and policies that favor immigration more than do Anglos. These differences surely reflect the fact that the issues are more salient to them.[77]

Asian American public opinion has not drawn the same level of attention as that of other groups. Asian Americans are, however, a growing segment of the population and constitute a sizable part of the population of some states, especially California. In general, Asians are a bit more liberal than white Americans. In 2004, for example, about 60 percent of Asian Americans supported John Kerry, whereas only 44 percent of white Americans did so. Their disapproval of the Iraq War was stronger than that of white Americans, but not nearly as strong as that of African Americans.[78] Like Latinos, Asian Americans are diverse, including people from Korea, Vietnam, Japan, and China.

Education

One important change in the American population is the increasing level of education. Figure 6.6 charts the share of Americans who had attended college for at least a year over the last sixty years. The pattern is striking. In 1948 about one in seven Americans had gone to college for at least one year. By 2008 more than one in two Americans had attended college. The upward trend has been continuous since the end of World War II in 1945. There are two key reasons for this trend. The first is that more young people have access to a college education. The second is what is called "generational replacement." That is, older, less-educated citizens have passed on, and the average level of education of the American public has thus increased.

That people in the United States are more educated matters. In broad strokes, there is a long-standing belief that a democracy is best able to endure when its citizens are engaged and informed. With more education, the public should be more aware of politics and better able to find ways to ensure that government responds to them. In the language of this book, a better-educated public should be in better position to travel through the gateways of influence and find ways around the many gates in the American political system.

Education level is also connected to public opinion. Views on the controversial issue of immigration reform

Think again: does being a member of a demographic group shape opinion?

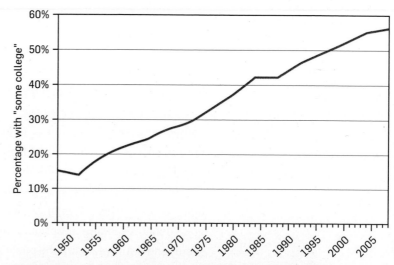

FIGURE 6.6 Percentage with "Some College" Education, 1948–2008. Since the end of World War II, education levels have steadily increased. Level of education is a factor affecting public opinion on a range of specific issues. *Source:* American National Election Studies.

offer an instructive example. Among college graduates in April 2009, 75 percent favored making it possible for those here illegally to become citizens (providing they pass background checks, pay relevant fines, and have jobs). Among those with a high school education or less, the proportion falls to 56 percent.[79] The 20 percentage point gap is significant. Individuals with higher education generally take a more liberal position on a variety of social and economic issues ranging from government spending to defense policy to gay marriage.[80]

Public Opinion and Public Policy: Military Action and Antiterrorism

To see how public opinion affects the policies pursued by government, we examine foreign policy, focusing on military action and antiterrorism measures. The relationship between public opinion and domestic policy is taken for granted, but with continuing terrorist attacks around the world and a war in Afghanistan, it is important to consider their relationship. Public opinion exerts a different type of influence on each.

Military Action

The president, as commander in chief, has always made the decision to engage in military action. Although Congress has formally declared war only five times, U.S. troops have been sent into conflicts and potential conflicts about 250 times since the beginning of the nation.[81] Today, in making the decision to engage in military action, the president is heavily influenced by the recommendations of the secretary of defense, the national security adviser, and the director of the Central Intelligence Agency. For military missions that are publicized, not secret, a president usually enjoys widespread support if the mission can be clearly tied to preserving national security. In cases in which the United States is attacked on its own soil, support for a military response is even higher. This so-called **rally-around-the-flag effect** is a surge in patriotic sentiment that translates into presidential popularity.[82] For example, when President George H. W. Bush commenced the first Gulf War, his approval ratings shot up to 89 percent.[83] His son, President George W. Bush, experienced a similar spike in popularity after the terrorist attacks of September 11, 2001; his job approval ratings went from 52 percent to 90 percent, and they remained above 70 percent for almost an entire year.[84]

rally-around-the-flag effect: *Surge of public support for the president in times of international crisis.*

Should public opinion influence foreign or defense policy when military secrets are withheld from the public?

The public's influence on the president's decision to engage in military action is always limited because the amount of information available to the public is purposely restricted, both to ensure the safety of the troops involved and to preserve military advantages in conflict. Simply put, the president and his military advisers have access to far greater amounts of information than the average citizen, and in turn, the average citizen expects the president to act on this information in a way that preserves national security. Even when Congress debates sending troops or funding military action, most classified information is held in secret and not revealed to the public. The fundamental imbalance of information held by the government and what the general public understands poses a major problem for the assumptions of a democracy because the people cannot hold the government fully accountable if they are not fully informed. Nevertheless, when a president decides to send troops, he has to anticipate public reaction and hope that the public maintains its trust and confidence in his decision to take such action.

As the rally-around-the-flag effect fades over time, public support for extended military engagements also declines, as the polls reveal. Americans do not like war, and this core value drives public opinion and U.S. defense policy. The fundamental problem for the American public is that once the United States enters into a military conflict, there are few ways for the public to effectively change military strategy or troop levels. Only when public opinion turns against a war effort is there any real pressure on the president and Congress to take steps to end it.

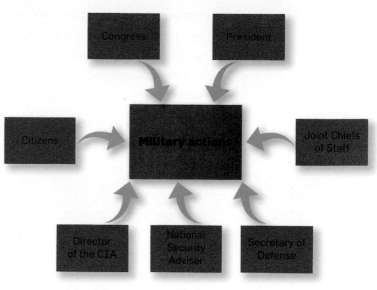

For example, Figure 6.7 tracks public opinion on two major conflicts, the Vietnam War and the Iraq War. At the beginning of each, there was considerable public support; only 25 percent of the public thought it was a mistake to go into the conflict. However, as time progressed and the number of American troops killed and wounded grew, public apprehension about the war also grew. From 1965 to 1968 the percentage of the public that thought the Vietnam War was a mistake more than doubled, and it became a major issue in the 1968 presidential campaign. Richard Nixon, the Republican presidential candidate, sensed a change in the public's attitude toward the war and pledged to end the U.S. involvement in Vietnam by promising "peace with honor." As president, Nixon did end the war, but it took him five years to do so.

In the case of the Iraq War, there is even stronger evidence that the number of casualties directly affects public support for military conflict. For example, in the 2006 House elections, voters punished Republican candidates in districts with higher casualty rates.[85] It also appears that the public's support for conflict is a product of calculations involving the likely winner, the upward or downward trend in casualties, and the possible payoff from the conflict.[86] From 2003 to 2008 the portion of the public that thought the Iraq War was a mistake grew from 25 percent to 60 percent, and in 2008 the Democratic nominee Barack Obama promised to withdraw the majority of American troops from Iraq within two years. President Obama kept that promise, withdrawing the last of American combat troops from Iraq on August 31, 2010. But he did decide to send thirty thousand more

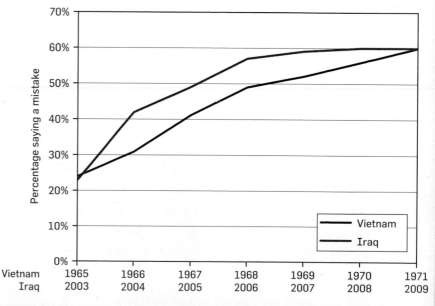

FIGURE 6.7 Percentage Who Thought Sending Troops to Vietnam and Iraq a Mistake. While only about 25 percent of Americans thought it was a mistake to send troops to Vietnam and to Iraq at the beginning of these conflicts, within three years more than 50 percent of the public saw the conflicts as mistakes, and the percentages continued to grow. *Source:* Gallup Poll.

troops to Afghanistan. The public was uncomfortable about such a move, given the problems in Iraq, but Obama nevertheless sought to secure public support.[87] Although the power of public opinion is slow-moving, when a majority of the Americans oppose a military conflict, elected leaders recognize that they either must change course or find a way to rally the public to their side.

Antiterrorism Measures

The terrorist attacks of September 11, 2001, prompted a huge increase in government's efforts to stop future terrorism against U.S. citizens at home and abroad. In general, public opinion was highly supportive of the steps that President George W. Bush claimed were necessary to fight terrorism. These steps were taken with advice from the same units that handle military policy, with the important addition of the Federal Bureau of Investigation and the Department of Justice. The Bush administration authorized the detention of suspects, whether U.S. citizens or not, without charges or trials, and wiretapping (eavesdropping) without a warrant. With the onset of the war in Iraq, the measures employed in the name of antiterror security increased. Then, in 2004 CBS News and the *New Yorker* magazine broke the story about the Abu Ghraib facility in Iraq, where Iraqi prisoners were subject to activities that violated international norms of treatment and might be considered torture.[88] Subsequently, it was revealed that the U.S. interrogators used waterboarding, a near-drowning technique, as a means of getting information from prisoners about potential terrorist plots. The international community considers waterboarding to be torture, and many Americans also objected. The issue of treatment of detainees became a major issue in the 2008 presidential campaign. After he took office, President Obama declared that the United States would no longer engage in any practice that violated international norms. The president also announced that the Guantánamo Bay facility located in Cuba, which was being used to detain and question suspected terrorists outside of the United States, would be closed. Despite an early consensus in the White House to close this controversial facility, deciding what to do with existing detainees and how best to handle others who may be engaged in terrorism has proven difficult.[89]

Americans remain conflicted about the type of force necessary to preserve national security. As of 2009 a Gallup Poll reported majority support for the use of harsh interrogation techniques on suspected terrorists (see Figure 6.8). The same poll revealed, however, that 51 percent of the respondents favored an investigation into how these techniques were used. Here is the same dilemma the public faces with military action: by their very nature, antiterrorism policies must remain secret to be effective, and the only opportunity the public has to register an opinion about government action is after that action has been taken. If it can be shown that harsh interrogation techniques saved American lives by uncovering and then preventing a terrorist attack, the public will support the use of the techniques; otherwise, the public will want to limit their use. However,

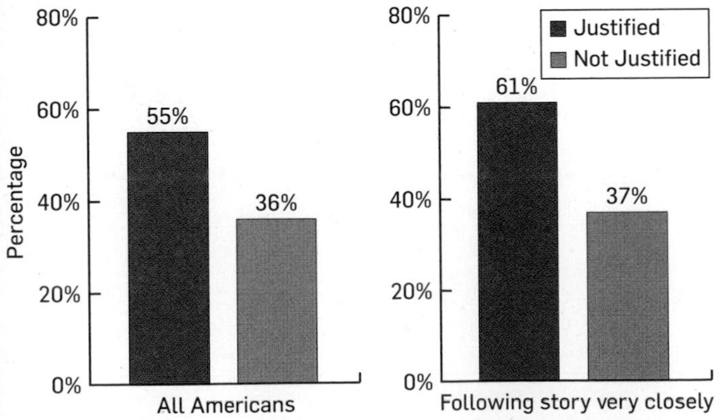

FIGURE 6.8 Support for Harsh Interrogation Techniques, 2009. A majority of the public supports the use of harsh interrogation techniques on terrorism suspects, and the more closely a person follows the story of the treatment of terrorism suspects, the more likely that person is to support the techniques.
Source: Gallup Poll daily tracking, April 24–25, 2009.

as the nature and shape of potential terrorist attacks are constantly changing, it is unlikely that the American public will ever seriously limit support for broad government flexibility ensuring national security.

Public Opinion and Democracy

For a country to be considered democratic, the views of the public must affect the course of government. For this reason, the public must be sufficiently well informed to be able to make good decisions and to ensure that politicians act in a way consistent with public preferences. Average Americans do not know a lot of details about politics, but the nation's many successes indicate that the public is equal to the task of self-government. As Key observed nearly fifty years ago, "Voters are not fools."[90] In 2008, when most people thought the country was on the wrong track, they voted for change and put Barack Obama in office. By supporting Obama, the public signaled a desire for a clear break from the policies of the Bush administration.

Elections are one means by which the public expresses its will, but on a year-to-year, even day-to-day, basis, public officials can stay in touch with what the public thinks through public opinion polls. Scientific polling permits researchers to measure people's thinking with considerable accuracy and gives average Americans a chance to speak out on policy and contribute to policy making. Scientific polling, introduced in the 1930s, not only created greater equality but also provided the gateways through which the public could affect the course of government. Polls are not perfect, but they do open up the democratic process.

Although it is clear that public officials are generally responsive to public opinion,[91] there are legitimate questions about how responsive American government actually is. Some observers suggest that the connection between opinion and policy is weak. Others point out that the public has mixed feelings on many issues and does not have concrete opinions about some of the toughest questions, and can thus offer little guidance. Still others argue that politicians use policy to manipulate public opinion. That interaction is troubling and not the way a democratic system in which the government is accountable to the people should work. These concerns are why it is so instructive to look at the general patterns and the nation's general successes.

It is also important to recognize that, in a democracy, politicians know the kinds of issues the public will respond to and rebel against, and so they adopt views that will not arouse the electorate's anger. They are aware, in other words, of what political scientists call **latent public opinion**,[92] and this awareness makes them responsive and accountable. The ability to anticipate public opinion is an invaluable skill, helping officials avoid quagmires and stress issues that hit a responsive chord with the public. Thus the power of public opinion in a democracy is both direct and indirect. It is also imperfect in that there are both gates and gateways that shape how the public directs the course of government.

FOCUS QUESTIONS

- How does public opinion influence public policy?

- In what ways are elected officials responsive to public opinion? How responsive should they be?

- Is every citizen's voice equal, or are some people more influential? Why?

- How well does polling capture public opinion? Should polls direct public policy?

- Does public opinion provide a gateway or a gate to democracy?

latent public opinion: *Underlying opinions and attitudes of the public that are not always captured in public opinion data but are recognized by public officials and influential in policy making.*

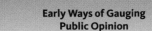

GATEWAYS TO LEARNING

Top Ten to Take Away

1. Public opinion—the aggregate of citizen attitudes—is essential to the workings of a democracy. (pp. 176–80)

2. Scientific polling enables public officials to gauge public opinion with some degree of confidence, though polls can be in error. (pp. 180–87)

3. Citizens' opinions and attitudes are shaped by environment, political socialization, generational effects, and self-interest. (pp. 187–89)

4. Elites do drive public opinion, but only to the extent that citizens are exposed and open to their message. (pp. 189–90)

5. Party identification can help predict individual attitudes, and liberal or conservative leanings shape views on political and social issues. Generally, the

public has been becoming less liberal, although there has been a recent uptick. (pp. 190–94)

6. People generally know what advances their interests and hold government accountable. (pp. 194–96)

7. Although parties have grown more polarized in recent years, the electorate is more moderate than party choices allow. (pp. 196–97)

8. Political opinion also differs among demographic groups. (pp. 198–202)

9. In recent years, efficacy and public trust in government have fallen. (p. 180)

10. In national security issues, the public is often deliberately not informed, and public officials have to work hard to maintain public trust, especially as the American public has a strong preference for peace. (pp. 202–5)

A full narrative summary of the chapter is on the book's website.

Ten to Test Yourself

1. How was public opinion gauged before scientific polling?

2. Describe how polls may be in error.

3. How does environment shape political attitudes?

4. What other factors shape political attitudes?

5. Is the public rational? How do you know? What are some examples?

6. What is the relationship between partisanship and ideology?

7. What do liberals generally believe? What do conservatives generally believe?

8. How well informed, or uninformed, is the American public? Does it matter?

9. What are the effects of political polarization?

10. In what way does public opinion affect military action and antiterrorism policy?

More review questions and answers and chapter quizzes are on the book's website.

Timeline to Get Things in Order

Early Ways of Gauging Public Opinion

George Washington rides into the country-side to learn what the people think.

Newspapers conduct straw polls to learn what the people think.

Abraham Lincoln holds White House receptions to learn what the people think.

Franklin Roosevelt reads newspapers to learn what the people think.

 **1790s**

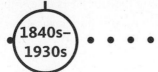 **1840s–1930s**

 1860s

 **1930s**

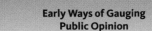

Terms to Know and Use

affirmative action (p. 200)
approval rating (p. 177)
census (p. 183)
confidence interval (p. 185)
conservatives (p. 193)
depolarized (pp. 196, 197)
efficacy (p. 180)
elite opinion (p. 181)
elites (p. 189)
elite theory (p. 190)
exit polls (p. 184)
Gallup Poll (p. 182)
gender gap (p. 200)

generational effects (p. 188)
Independents (p. 187)
latent public opinion (p. 205)
levels of conceptualization
 (p. 193)
liberals (p. 193)
low information rationality
 (p. 196)
Millennials (p. 189)
moderates (p. 193)
nonattitudes (p. 186)
party identification (p. 192)
perceptual lens (p. 192)

polarization (p. 196)
political ideology (p. 193)
political trust (p. 180)
polls (p. 178)
population (p. 183)
public opinion (p. 178)
push polls (p. 185)
rally-around-the-flag effect
 (p. 202)
random sample (p. 182)
rationality (p. 189)
Reagan Democrats (p. 198)
representative sample (p. 183)

response rate (p. 187)
responsible parties (p. 197)
salient (p. 195)
sample (p. 183)
sampling error (p. 185)
scientific polling (p. 182)
self-interest (p. 189)
socialization (p. 187)
socioeconomic status (p. 198)
straw polls (p. 181)
tracking polls (p. 184)

Use the vocabulary flash cards on the book's website.

Learning That Works

WHAT YOU NEED...

TO KNOW

How polls can be in error

What polls can reveal

The sources of public opinion

The role of partisanship and ideology

The relationship between demographics and public opinion

How public opinion affects policy

TO DO

Evaluate the validity of polls

Determine whether politicians are responsive, fickle, or manipulative

Recognize where your attitudes come from

Consider whether the public makes rational choices

Understand divisions in public opinion

Assess citizen influence in a democracy

The Rise of Scientific Polling

The *Literary Digest* misses in predicting the outcome of the presidential election.
George Gallup correctly predicts the outcome and introduces scientific polling.

1936

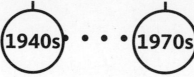

Survey research develops and expands.

1940s

Telephone polls dominate.

1970s

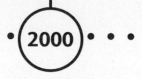

News networks cause confusion by calling the presidential election sooner than exit poll data support the call.

Internet polls are on the rise.

2000

7 THE NEWS MEDIA AND THE INTERNET

▲ Northern Illinois University, DeKalb

> *I didn't have the pedigree to be 'heard,' and the media and political gatekeepers worked to marginalize me and my new allies in the nascent but growing netroots. But it didn't matter. The floodgates were open, and technology allowed us to easily (and gleefully) crash those gates.*

CourseMate

Visit http://www.cengagebrain .com/shop/ISBN/0618906959 for interactive tools including:

- Quizzes
- Flashcards
- Videos and more

In 1992 Markos ("Kos") Moulitsas Zúniga started taking classes at Northern Illinois University. He approached college a bit differently from many students, for he had just finished a three-year tour with the U.S. Army, trained as a 13P, a specialist in the multiple launch rocket system (MLRS). Kos did not experience combat, but he knew something of war from his childhood. Born in Chicago in 1971 to a Salvadoran mother and a Greek father, he had spent his formative years in El Salvador, where he saw firsthand the ravages of the Salvadoran civil war.

Kos was a little older than most college students, and his military training had accustomed him to a demanding schedule. It had also forged his interest in politics. With his background and interests, he sought to earn two bachelor's degrees, majoring in philosophy, journalism, and political science and minoring in German. But Kos did much more than just take a demanding set of courses. By his senior year, he was editor of the Northern Illinois student newspaper, the *Northern Star*. Following graduation in 1996, Kos went straight to law school at Boston University, but he did not want to be a lawyer. Law school provided training that would further his interest in politics.

Kos had been a Republican when he joined the army. But his time in the army and college shifted his attention to liberal causes. In May 2002 he launched the Daily Kos, a blog through which he voiced his opinions, particularly his frustration with the presidency of George W. Bush. Blogging was still relatively new at the time, and Kos had no sense of what would unfold. But his blog coincided with the partisan battles that raged

Markos ("Kos") Moulitsas Zúniga ▶

once the shock of the terrorist attacks of September 11, 2001, had subsided. Americans' concerns about terrorism and how to combat it were reshaping political life. Kos's commentary drew a large audience, and his blog became a forum for criticism of Bush and of the Iraq War, which began in 2003. He tapped into the anger surrounding the war, and his support for Howard Dean's presidential run in 2004 made him a powerful player in Democratic Party politics. In recent years prominent politicians such as Nancy Pelosi, Harry Reid, and Barack Obama have posted regularly on Daily Kos. For Kos, blogging has been a gateway to influence. In 2007 he was named one of the fifty most important people on the web by *PC World*. *Forbes* magazine listed him as the third most influential person on the web in the same year. Today Daily Kos announces itself as "the premier online political community with 2.5 million unique visitors per month and 215,000 registered users. It is at once a news organization, community, and activist hub." As of January 2010 Daily Kos was the seventeenth most popular blog in the nation.[1]

Kos's gateway to influence involved more than just blogging. The title of a book Kos coauthored—*Crashing the Gate: Netroots, Grassroots, and the Rise of People-Powered Politics*—suggests how the Internet is transforming the way Americans learn and share news about politics. The Internet provides a new platform to distribute the news. Rather than passively learning about events from professional journalists, citizens now take active roles in communicating news and opinion and in shaping political debate about issues that are important to them. Political information flows from the bottom up, not just from the top down. The Internet is a gateway that makes it possible for more Americans to participate in the political process. The transformation of the news media from print to digital has had costs as well. Not everyone has equal access to the Internet, generating a digital divide that potentially fosters inequality. In this chapter, we examine and assess the critical role that the news media play in a democracy. We analyze the functions and impact of the press, survey its history, and describe and evaluate the new forms of communication in the twenty-first century.

FOCUS QUESTIONS

- How do the mass media help make government accountable to the people?

- How has the rise of the Internet increased or decreased the ability of the public to hold government accountable?

- How does the bottom-up approach of twenty-first-century mass media affect citizen participation and equality? What are its other effects?

- When, and under what conditions, should government regulate the media?

- In what ways do the mass media offer gateways to American democracy? In what ways do the modern media establish new gates?

The Political News

In a democracy such as the United States, citizens are supposed to be the ultimate source of power. The decisions made by the public shape the course of government. The public, therefore, needs information about politics to make good choices. Most people cannot directly observe political events, so they rely on the mass media for information about politics and government.

What Are the Mass Media?

The **mass media** represent the vast array of sources of information that are available to the public. These sources include newspapers, television, radio, blogs, online sources, cell phones, and social networks like Facebook. The **news media** (also called the **press**) are a subset of the mass media that have traditionally provided the news of the day, gathered and reported by journalists. But, with all the new technologies of the twenty-first century, the news media are changing; now the average citizen is able to report on politics through blogs such as Daily Kos and websites such as YouTube. These new media have recast journalism by providing a proliferation of news outlets without a monolithic entity that shapes and defines political reporting. In this chapter, we use the term *mass media* to describe the many ways citizens learn about government and politics.

One aspect of the mass media today is speedy communication. What used to take days, weeks, and sometimes months now takes seconds. For example, it took up to four days for some Americans to learn about the assassination of President Abraham Lincoln (1861–65) in April 1865. But no longer: A click of the mouse brings up news as it is happening, day and night; there is no need to wait for the evening news on TV. Most young people today (the **Millennials** born between 1982 and 2003) grew up with the 24-7 news cycle, an information world that is very different from that of their parents (and their professors). This chapter takes those changes into account.

Access to information is important because an enduring and effective democracy demands a knowledgeable public.[2] For the people to be informed, the press needs to be able to do its job free from government interference, and journalists must feel free to be critical of the government. This **watchdog** role of the press lies at the very heart of a democracy. In 1787 Thomas Jefferson observed, "Were it left to me to decide whether we should have a government without newspapers, or newspapers without a government, I should not hesitate a moment to prefer the latter."[3] What Jefferson meant is that only a well-informed public is capable of self-governing. Freedom of the press is intertwined with the very idea of democratic government, and the First Amendment to the Constitution protects it.

The Functions of the News

The mass media help ensure government accountability and responsiveness by performing three important tasks: informing, investigating, and interpreting the news.

Informing.   Journalists, simply put, inform. Coverage of the war in Afghanistan, for example, might include stories about casualties or about intense fighting in various locales. Coverage of a political campaign might include information about candidates' previous experience, their personal temperaments, or their views on important issues. If there is a crisis in the economy, journalists provide information about the problem, explain the solutions being proposed, and indicate what can be expected in the future. In August 2008—just a month before a financial crisis rocked the nation—about 5 percent of news stories dealt with the economy. In September that proportion soared to nearly 30 percent.[4] A quick scan of any newspaper or network news website can inform readers about a wide range of topics.

mass media: *News sources, including newspapers, television, radio, and the Internet, whose purpose is to provide a large audience with information about the nation and the world.*

news media: *Subset of the mass media that provide the news of the day, gathered and reported by journalists.*

How do you get your news?

press: *Another term for the news media or journalists, both of which provide information to the public about political events.*

Millennials: *Generation born between 1982 and 2003.*

How often do you consume the news?

watchdog: *Role of the press in monitoring government actions.*

Does the news inform you about American government and politics?

Investigating.   The media can also make news by researching and revealing information about events. The **Watergate scandal**, uncovered by two reporters from the *Washington Post*, revealed questionable activities in the Richard M. Nixon administration (1969–74) (see also Chapter 13, The Presidency). Bob Woodward and Carl Bernstein played the ultimate role of watchdog, creating a news story that gripped the country for more than a year. The episode ended with Nixon's resignation on August 9, 1974, the only time a U.S. president has resigned. This scandal would never have been uncovered without the tireless efforts of the *Post's* investigative reporters.[5] Their work was the high point of investigative journalism.

Politicians often court the press, but they want favorable coverage. They want journalists to advertise their accomplishments to voters. Yet journalists and politicians are usually in an adversarial relationship because journalists want to report new stories on topics of interest to the public. So reporters love to unearth scandals—something that politicians want to avoid. Scandals are fresh and exciting, and uncovering them gives journalists real influence. The investigative function not only allows the press to fulfill its role as the watchdog of democracy; it makes reporters' jobs exciting and important. Also, scandals sell newspapers, and the profit motive is a central part of the process.

Ken Feil/The Washington Post/Getty Images

Washington Post reporters Bob Woodward and Carl Bernstein became legends for their work in following up on a news story about what seemed to be a routine break-in. But it was the Democratic campaign headquarters that was broken into on June 17, 1972, and the trail they picked up led to the White House. Certain to be impeached, President Richard M. Nixon resigned on August 9, 1974.

Why is the relationship between the press and politicians adversarial?

Interpreting.   When the media inform, they also interpret the news. Just giving one story front-page coverage and relegating another to an inside page involves interpreting what is more and less important. The role of interpretation has taken on even greater significance in the last few decades. In 1960, for example, journalists covered presidential campaigns in a very descriptive fashion. About 90 percent of campaign stories focused on describing what happened in the campaign that day. But in the following decades, journalists started to interpret events more frequently, assessing why something happened. By the 1990s more than 80 percent of campaign stories were interpretive.[6]

The Law and the Free Press

The First Amendment to the Constitution states that "Congress shall make no law . . . abridging the freedom . . . of the press." This protection is not unlimited. During times of war (or threat of war), national security concerns may require that the press not publish a story.

The government, however, is often too eager to stop publication of controversial stories, whereas the press may be too willing to report on controversial stories that will boost sales. This conflict plays out in debates over **prior restraint**—government's ability to restrict the publication of sensitive material (see Chapter 4, Civil Liberties). When can government invoke prior restraint? At what point does prior restraint become censorship and thus undermine the ability of the press to be a watchdog?

Answers to these difficult questions have been shaped by Supreme Court decisions. In the early 1930s, for example, the state of Minnesota stopped a small newspaper from publishing controversial claims about the mayor of Minneapolis and convicted the publisher, Jay Near, under state libel laws. Near appealed the conviction all the way to the Supreme Court. The Court ruled in ***Near v. Minnesota*** (1931) that only in exceptionally rare cases could the government stop the printing of a story, overturning Near's conviction and invalidating the Minnesota law that led to his conviction. The Court has also reinforced the protections of press freedom in a **libel** case, ***New York Times v. Sullivan*** (1964), which also set a very high standard—proof of **actual malice**—to convict in a libel suit. Justice William J. Brennan wrote, "We consider this case against the background of a profound national commitment to the principle that debate on public issues should be uninhibited, robust, and wide open, and that it may well include vehement, caustic, and sometimes unpleasantly sharp attacks on government and public officials" (see Supreme Court Cases: *New York Times v. Sullivan*).

The landmark modern case on the freedom of the press was the ***Pentagon Papers* case** (1971). During the Vietnam War, the *New York Times* secured a copy of a top secret Department of Defense analysis detailing U.S. involvement in Vietnam and began publishing it, believing that the information, some of which contradicted official statements, was essential to public understanding of government policy. Citing national security, the Nixon administration secured a court injunction forcing the *Times* to cease publication, but the newspaper appealed, and the case quickly went to the Supreme Court. While not denying the possibility that censorship can be warranted, the Court in this instance rejected the government's argument that national security took precedence over the right to publish documents embarrassing to the government. The government, said the Court, had not met the extraordinary burden of proof needed for prior restraint.

In general, the courts have tended to give the edge to the press in the belief that, in the long run, it is better to protect press freedoms so that the press can, in turn, help inform the public, which can then hold elected officials accountable. Consistent with this general predisposition, there are very few laws that constrain the print media, such as newspapers and magazines. The electronic media, however, are more heavily regulated by government. As early as the 1920s Congress sought to regulate radio to ensure it would serve the public interest. It was a new medium, and Congress wanted to guard against its being used in a way that might undermine equality and fairness. In 1934 Congress created the **Federal Communications Commission** (FCC), now a powerful agency that regulates all forms of electronic media, including radio, broadcast television, cable television, cell phones, and even wireless networks. Anyone can start a newspaper, but starting a radio station requires a license from the FCC.

The FCC monitors media ownership as well. For a long time, the FCC worked to ensure that ownership of the news media was not concentrated in just a few hands, concerned that a monopoly would undermine the ability of the media to be fair and able to perform its

---

prior restraint: *Government restrictions on freedom of the press that prevent material from being published.*

Near v. Minnesota:
1931 Supreme Court case that declared that only in exceptionally rare cases can the government prevent the printing of a news story.

libel: *Publishing false and damaging statements about another person.*

New York Times v. Sullivan:
1964 Supreme Court case establishing that proof of actual malice is required to convict in a libel suit.

actual malice: *Supreme Court test for libel of a public figure, in which the plaintiff must prove that the publisher knew the material was false or acted with reckless disregard of whether it was true or false.*

***Pentagon Papers* case:** *1971 Supreme Court case (New York Times v. United States) permitting publication of classified documents on the Vietnam War and thus favoring freedom of the press over the executive authority of the president.*

Should the standard for press freedom be the same in cases of terrorism as in wartime?

Federal Communications Commission: *Executive branch agency charged with regulating and overseeing radio, television, and electronic broadcasting.*

supremecourtcases

New York Times v. Sullivan (1964)

QUESTION: What level of negligence must be found when public officials sue newspapers for libel?

ORAL ARGUMENT: January 6–7, 1964 (listen at www.oyez.org/cases/)

DECISION: March 9, 1964 (read at www.findlaw.com/casecode/supreme.html)

OUTCOME: Actual malice must be found to convict for libel, thus overturning the libel conviction of the *New York Times* (9–0).

Libel is the publication of false and damaging information about someone. Prior to libel laws, the defamed person often responded to libel by challenging the libeler to a duel, as when Vice President Aaron Burr challenged *Federalist* author and former Treasury Secretary Alexander Hamilton to a duel and killed him. To prevent such acts, various states made libel a criminal act. Today libel is almost exclusively a question for a civil suit, in which one person sues another for damages.

The *Sullivan* case derived from an advertisement placed in the March 29, 1960, *New York Times* by an ad hoc group of civil rights supporters called the Committee to Defend Martin Luther King. The ad condemned the "wave of terror" against nonviolent civil rights activists by unnamed "southern violators." Because some of the actions against King included arresting him, the chief of the Montgomery, Alabama, police department claimed that all of the allegations were about him and that he had been libeled.

Under Alabama law, once damaging statements are found, the only defense is for the publication to prove that all the particulars are true. The ad in this case was not true in all the particulars. For example, it claimed that protesting students sang "My Country 'Tis of Thee" when they actually sang "The Star-Spangled Banner." The jury thus found against the *Times*, awarding the police chief $500,000 in damages.

The Supreme Court reversed the verdict, declaring that a law holding a newspaper liable for criticism of a public official only if the paper could prove that every statement in the article was true would lead to massive self-censorship by the press. Instead, the Court declared that libel against a public official required a finding of actual malice, that is, knowledge that the statement was false or reckless disregard of whether it was true or false. Under this standard, the Court found that the ad was substantially true, but even if it had not been substantially true, there was no evidence that the *Times* acted with malice.

This decision has made it much easier for newspapers to criticize public officials. The Court has expanded the ruling to cover public figures as well. When a supermarket tabloid trashes a popular actor or singer, the individual thus harmed has to prove actual malice to win a suit for libel.

- **What would happen if the media were held legally responsible for any false statement they made?**
- **Should the burden of proof for proving libel of public officials be treated equally to the burden of proof for libel of private people?**

watchdog function. The Telecommunications Act of 1996 eased the rules concerning multiple ownership, and the FCC has started to relax this standard. As a result, there has been a trend toward greater concentration of media ownership in the last decade. In 1995 major companies generally owned around ten television stations each; ten years later that number stood at nearly forty. The ownership of radio has also changed. Clear Channel Communications owned 520 radio stations in 1999. By 2008 the number stood at 833.[7]

This recent concentration of media ownership is not unique. Concerns about the consequences of control of the news by just a few people date to the late nineteenth century, when individuals such as William Randolph Hearst controlled major news organizations. Without genuine competition, the press, some fear, will become lapdogs, not watchdogs. But even the changes of the last few years have not eliminated competition. It is true that newspapers are now dominated by seven major chains; Gannett alone controls more than a hundred daily newspapers. But that is still only about 6 percent of all newspapers in this country.[8] With so many outlets for news in the twenty-first century, one person or company will likely be unable to control it all.

Any effort to monopolize the press or curtail its freedom is met by strong protests from people fearing a trend toward **authoritarian** rule. A government that limits press freedom seeks to insulate itself from criticism, thereby decreasing the chance for the public to hold leaders accountable. The absence of a robust press means that government will no longer be responsive, but that it will instead pursue policies that advance the interests of the few rather than the many. In this situation, greater inequality arises between those in power and those out of power. It is for all these reasons that an evaluation of how democratic a nation is rests on how much freedom its press enjoys (see Other Places: Freedom of the Press).

What are the newspapers in your city or town? Who owns them?

authoritarianism: *Form of government in which citizens are subjected to the complete power of one individual or a select few, usually through some oppressive measure.*

The History of the Press in America

The press in America has always been dynamic. Newspapers have developed from occasional pamphlets in the early 1700s, to comprehensive daily publications that aimed for objective reporting of political news, to today's online enterprises filled with a mix of news and entertainment. By the 1900s journalism emerged as a profession with a commitment to objectivity. In the twentieth century radio and then television changed how Americans received the news and how they reacted to it. Throughout, the press has at times supported government and elected officials and at times assumed an adversarial role as it has given citizens the information they need to make government accountable and responsive.

The Colonial Era, 1620 to 1750

In the early colonial period newspapers were not widely available, and there were few printing presses. *Public Occurrences,* which began publication in Boston in 1690, had only a few pages and was more a pamphlet than a newspaper. Circulation was small, usually less than two thousand copies.[9] Newspaper publication was more of a hobby for publishers than anything else, and the notion that the press had the right to criticize government was not widely accepted. Colonial governments in fact feared that harsh criticism would incite the public and create instability, so publishers who attacked those in power could be thrown into jail and their printing presses confiscated.

otherplaces

Freedom of the Press

Freedom House gathers data to rate the freedom of the press in thirty different nations. To rate each nation, the organization gauges such things as the amount of government censorship of the press, whether the press is corrupt, and whether big financial interests control the press. The lower the score, the more freedom of the press enjoyed in the country.

The United States fares well on this scale, having a free press. Russia, by contrast, fares poorly, and that is one of the main reasons why observers do not consider the country democratic. As noted by Freedomhouse.org, "Although the constitution provides for freedom of speech and of the press, the Kremlin used the country's politicized and corrupt criminal justice system to harass and prosecute independent journalists." Mexico and India are viewed as having partially free presses. Mexican journalists are not only denied access to information but often face government intimidation. In 2004 four Mexican journalists were killed, creating an environment that is not conducive to a free press and democratic government. In India, the government has also sought to limit journalists' access to information, but reporters have not faced violence.

- **Why is the United States rated lower than such countries as Finland and Belgium?**

- **Do democracies create a free press, or does a free press create a democracy?**

Freedom of the Press Worldwide, 2007

Country	Freedom House Scores	Overall
Finland	9	Free
Belgium	11	Free
Sweden	11	Free
New Zealand	13	Free
Germany	16	Free
United States	16	Free
Canada	17	Free
United Kingdom	19	Free
Australia	21	Free
France	21	Free
Japan	21	Free
South Africa	28	Free
Israel	29	Free
Italy	29	Free
Chile	30	Free
South Korea	30	Free
India	35	Partly Free
Brazil	42	Partly Free
Philippines	46	Partly Free
Mexico	48	Partly Free
Argentina	49	Partly Free
Turkey	49	Partly Free
Indonesia	54	Partly Free
Colombia	57	Partly Free
Egypt	62	Not Free
Pakistan	63	Not Free
Venezuela	74	Not Free
Russia	75	Not Free
Saudi Arabia	82	Not Free
China	84	Not Free

Source: Freedom House.

In 1734 John Peter Zenger was jailed for criticizing the colonial governor of New York in his *New York Weekly Journal*. When his case came to trial the next year, his lawyer, Andrew Hamilton of Philadelphia, decided on a bold strategy. Zenger would admit guilt—he had published the critical statements—and then argue that the jury should find him not guilty because the statements were true. The press, in other words, had a fundamental right to criticize government, and a free press was more important than the law against **seditious libel** that had put Zenger behind bars. Much to the surprise of the governor and his supporters, the jury agreed and freed Zenger. The case is a landmark in advancing the idea of a free press.

In the same decade, in Philadelphia, Benjamin Franklin was laying the groundwork for the press as a viable institution in America with his *Philadelphia Gazette*. The paper would set the standard for American news with its ability to present news accounts in an interesting and enlightening manner. Franklin had a gift for writing and a flair for satire and parody. His accounts of government and stories of personal interest, including crime, sex, violence, and mysteries, became the foundation for modern American news coverage. He is considered by many to be one of America's first sensationalist journalists. But Franklin was much more than just trying to pique the interest of readers. He also believed that the news was critical to educating the public. His "An Apology for Printers" (1731) defended objectivity in journalism. Though it contradicted the prevailing view at the time, it helped set the standard for the future of American journalism.[10]

seditious libel: *Conduct or language that incites rebellion against the authority of a state.*

Why was freedom of the press so important to the colonists and members of the Founding generation?

The Founding Era, 1750 to 1790

As tensions between the colonies and Britain increased, interest in politics grew as well, and the press responded. The circulation of newspapers grew twice as fast as the population between 1760 and 1776.[11] That year, when Thomas Paine published *Common Sense*, a pamphlet attacking King George, it sold 150,000 copies, far more than the 2,000 copies political documents normally sold.[12] Given that there were only 2.5 million people in the colonies, that is the equivalent of 18 million copies today.

The press helped spread the idea of independence because newspapers served as networks for sharing information. They reached not only subscribers but also many people who could not read, for they were read aloud in taverns and town squares. Newspapers were also shared in places of business. Information was a valuable commodity, and people sought it. Newspapers in this era did not try to be objective; rather, they explicitly supported partisan causes. During the Revolution, some papers backed independence; others supported the British Crown.[13]

Partisanship in the press carried over to the battle for ratification of the Constitution, and newspapers provided a vital forum for debate. The Antifederalists waged a fierce campaign against the Constitution,[14] and those supporting the Constitution responded, most famously in a series of essays published in New York newspapers. These essays, by Alexander Hamilton, James Madison, and John Jay, are today known as the ***Federalist Papers*** and are still regarded as a leading source for understanding the Constitution. At the time, the essays helped to lay the groundwork for ratification of the Constitution by the state of New York—a state absolutely critical for making the new government a reality. It is also worth noting that the Antifederalists' criticisms led to the adoption of the Bill of Rights (see Chapter 2, The Constitution, and the Appendix, where *Federalist* 10 and *Federalist* 51 are reprinted).

Federalist Papers: *Series of essays written by James Madison, Alexander Hamilton, and John Jay arguing for the ratification of the Constitution; today a leading source for understanding the Constitution.*

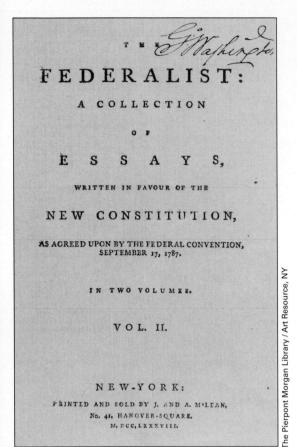

The Pierpont Morgan Library / Art Resource, NY

The Federalist Papers are an early example of the power of the press in America. Writing as "Publius," James Madison, Alexander Hamilton, and John Jay published seventy-seven essays in New York newspapers arguing for the ratification of the Constitution. In 1788 these and eight other essays were republished in two volumes. They are still read today for insights into the interpretation of the Constitution and the Framers' vision for a republic.

Sedition Act: *1798 act that made it a crime to criticize the government; later repealed.*

In the standoff between Adams and Jefferson over the Sedition Act, who do you think was right?

penny press: *Newspapers sold for a penny, initiating an era in which the press began to rely on circulation and advertising for income, and not on political parties.*

The Partisan Era, 1790 to 1900

Following the adoption of the Constitution, most newspapers allied themselves with the Federalists or with the newly emerging Jeffersonian party. Their writers made no effort to adjudicate between the claims and ideas of competing parties. Consequently, rhetoric was often harsh. George Washington was attacked constantly by the Jeffersonian press during his time in office. After the signing of Jay's Treaty (1794), which many thought was too favorable to Britain, Washington was hung in effigy (as was John Jay) in towns around the country. For most of his career Washington had been able to rise above partisan squabbles, and these attacks were difficult for him to accept.

Even worse criticism was leveled at the second president, John Adams (1797–1801), who was not as universally admired as Washington. Adams was called a liar and feebleminded, among other things.[15] His administration's **Sedition Act** (1798) made it illegal to print or publish any "false, scandalous, and malicious writing" about the federal government, either house of Congress, or the president. At the time, the United States was engaged in a limited and undeclared war with France over trade issues, and the Federalists believed that attacks on Adams and the government were ripping the new nation, barely a decade old, apart. The Articles of Confederation had not even lasted ten years; might not the same fate await the Constitution? But the Jeffersonians were equally adamant that laws suppressing criticism of the government violated the Constitution. Jeffersonian publishers did not cease their attacks, and some went to jail and paid fines. After he and his party won the 1800 presidential election, Thomas Jefferson (1801–09) pardoned all publishers convicted under the act, and Congress refunded their fines.

Now it was Jefferson and his party's turn to be attacked. The Federalist opposition was very critical of Jefferson, calling him the "anti-Christ."[16] While Jefferson had long been a proponent of a free press and had severely criticized the Sedition Act, the attacks he endured were so vicious that he began to question the merits of this partisan press. In 1807 he conceded, "The man who never looks into a newspaper is better informed than he who reads them."[17] This was quite a change for a man who, twenty years earlier, had argued that newspapers were more important than the institutions of republican government itself. Jefferson's dilemma reveals a core issue about the press. The media do inform, playing a vital function. But informing almost always carries some bias, and when informing is deliberately intended to manipulate public opinion, the public responds with distrust.

Newspapers continued to have close alliances with political parties in the next decades of the nineteenth century. They not only served to attack the opposition but also provided a way for presidents and party leaders to express their opinions on the issues of the day. Some presidents, such as James K. Polk (1845–49), even started their own newspapers to get out their message.[18]

During the 1830s and 1840s new steam presses reduced the cost of publishing newspapers. In 1833 Benjamin Day sold his *New York Sun* for a penny an issue, initiating the era of the **penny press**. At the same time literacy throughout the nation was growing, and newspaper owners began to realize that they could make higher profits through circulation and advertising than as arms of political parties.[19] They also saw that partisanship drove away customers who did not share their political views. So to increase circulation, newspapers began to move toward sensationalism, printing news of crimes and scandals and stories about personalities, much as tabloids do today and as Ben Franklin did in the 1700s. In 1870, for example, only about 13 percent of all newspapers were independent of a political party. By 1900 that proportion had swelled to nearly 50 percent.[20]

The circulation of newspapers rose from about 1.4 million in 1870 to over 8 million within the next thirty years. The quest for market share led to competition over which newspaper could grab the most attention with sensational headlines and stories. Known as **yellow journalism**, this form of news reporting distorted the presentation of events and could mislead the public, all in the interest of boosting sales. Joseph Pulitzer and William Randolph Hearst, the most famous newspaper publishers at the time, used large type, provocative headlines, pictures, and color to attract readers. Hearst introduced comics as a way to sell more papers. The competition became particularly fierce over American relations with Spain, as stories of Spanish atrocities in Cuba inflamed the public. When the USS *Maine* sank in Havana Harbor, the newspapers quickly blamed Spain, and Congress declared war on Spain on April 25, 1898. Many observers credit these sensational newspaper stories with fueling the start of the Spanish-American War.[21]

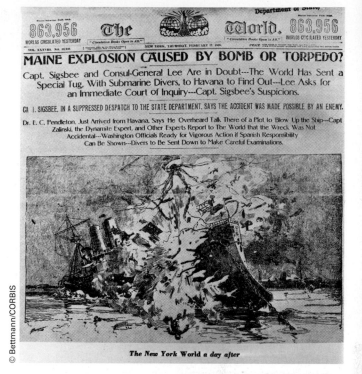

The Professional Era, 1900 to 1950

The development of mass circulation newspapers also led journalism to develop into a serious profession with an ethic of objective reporting. Pulitzer, despite his role in advancing yellow journalism, was a key figure in this transition, believing that a vibrant independent press was essential for a democracy to endure. In 1904 he observed that "our Republic and its press will rise or fall together. An able, disinterested, public-spirited press . . . can preserve that public virtue without which popular government is a sham and a mockery."[22] Pulitzer stood behind these words and endowed the Columbia School of Journalism and the Pulitzer Prize for excellence in journalism.[23] Other schools of journalism followed, and they continue to train journalists today.

The idea of a public-spirited press was increasingly realized in efforts to investigate wrongdoing in government, business, and industry. Adolph Ochs purchased the *New York Times* in 1896 with the goal of pursuing objective reporting. Such commitments led journalists, with the backing of people like Ochs and Pulitzer, to expose corruption and encourage genuine reform. Though President Theodore Roosevelt (1901–1909) labeled such efforts as **muckraking**—after a character in *Pilgrim's Progress* who rakes "muck," looking for the worst rather than the best—he came to appreciate the service these investigative journalists provided. Perhaps the most famous example was Upton Sinclair's *The Jungle* (1906), a novel that exposed the horrors of the meatpacking industry. Roosevelt, who had read an advance copy of the book, called for government regulation of the food industry.[24] In response, Congress passed the Pure Food and Drug Act and the Meat Inspection Act to help ensure food safety.

William Randolph Hearst's *New York Journal* and Joseph Pulitzer's *New York World* competed for circulation with sensational news and screaming headlines. The frenzy they stirred up over the sinking of the USS *Maine* in Havana Harbor in February 1898 helped lead to war with Spain. It is now generally believed that the explosion on the *Maine* was not caused by a Spanish bomb or torpedo but was accidental, a spontaneous combustion in inadequately vented coal bunkers.

What are the advantages and disadvantages of partisan control of the press?

What are examples of sensationalized news stories today?

yellow journalism: *Style of journalism in the late nineteenth century characterized by sensationalism intended to capture readers' attention and increase circulation.*

muckraking: *Journalistic practice of investigative reporting that seeks to uncover corruption and wrongdoing.*

Give other examples of investigative journalism that has made government responsive.

the scoop: *Colloquial expression for journalists' goal of breaking a news story, providing original and important information to the public.*

off the record: *Information a journalist acquires from interviews that, though not intended for publication, can be useful in setting a context for important news reports.*

background: *Information journalists gather from individuals that provides valuable context for a story.*

Should the press expose the personal lives of politicians? Why or why not?

Is it better for Americans to have a single source of trusted news or many sources, some of which may be less trustworthy?

Muckraking gave politicians an additional reason to pursue good public policy: to avoid bad press. It is overly simplistic (and optimistic) to claim that muckraking single-handedly led to a fundamental change in politicians' behavior, but investigative journalism has helped hold public officials accountable, even as it has transformed the press into an institution that seeks to advance the public interest.

The rise of professional journalism is also tied to an ethic of objectivity. The goal of being impartial and unbiased in reporting became part of the journalist's creed, especially as taught in new schools of journalism. The American Society of Newspaper Editors adopted a set of principles that declared that "news reports should be free from opinion or bias of any kind."[25] Reporters were trained to present facts, not personal opinions, and to describe, not judge.

The muckraking impulses faded by about 1916 or so, but the press's role as a watchdog did not. Now a key goal became to get **the scoop**—to write a story that presented the public with new and important information that was well researched and carefully documented. Journalists sought to cultivate politicians for access to news and stories, and this cultivation led to a different dynamic between politicians and the press. It remained adversarial, but both sides knew they needed each other. As the press and politicians formed closer relationships, the potential for conflicts of interest increased. To retain the relationship, politicians made certain statements **off the record**, with the understanding that journalists would not use them in a story except as **background**, information that could help set the context and provide a broader understanding for the story. As a result, journalists have a strong ethic about not revealing confidential sources.

The press took some topics off the table, including the personal lives of politicians. For example, few Americans realized that President Franklin Delano Roosevelt (1933–45) was paralyzed from polio; the press chose not to cover his handicap and rarely photographed him being carried from his car. Journalists did not deem Roosevelt's condition relevant to governing, and his handicap did not interfere with his performance as president, seemingly justifying the press's decision.

This practice did have costs, however. Using the same example, one could argue that the press relinquished its role of watchdog in not covering Roosevelt's health, especially as it declined. Roosevelt died in April 1945, three months after taking the oath of office for his fourth term. There were clear signs that he was ill, but the press chose not to report them.[26]

The Television Era, 1950 to 2000

The rise of television in the 1950s recast the news media and the information available to the public. By the 1960s the three major networks—ABC, CBS, and NBC—had a near monopoly on television news. The *New York Times* was the most influential newspaper and clearly the leader in American journalism. The *Los Angeles Times* and the *Washington Post* were gaining in importance, but they still lagged behind. Radio stations broadcast news summaries—usually five minutes of news, weather, and sports on the hour.

TV news was shaped by a handful of "anchormen." Walter Cronkite, anchor of CBS *Evening News,* was an icon. Not only was he famous, but he was also widely admired and trusted. In 1973 Americans rated him "the most trusted man in America."[27] Cronkite represented both the height of what might be called "objective" journalism and the dominance of TV network news. Most Americans assumed that Cronkite provided the facts and did not let partisanship shape his reporting. He closed his evening news show by saying "and that's the way it is," and viewers agreed that that was the way it was.

Prior to the advent of television in the 1950s, newspapers and radio had been Americans' main sources of information about their political leaders. By the 1960s people started to rely more on television news programs than on newspapers for their political information.[28] Television's visuals, especially, redefined the news and even political events. Politicians now aimed to look good on television because viewers could detect nervousness and judge body language.

The 1960 presidential campaign is a well-known example of the new emphasis on the visual side of politics. Most viewers of the televised presidential debates between Senator John Kennedy and Vice President Richard Nixon thought that Kennedy performed better.[29] He looked tanned and rested; in fact, he had spent a few days prior to the debate resting on a beach. Nixon, by contrast, had kept campaigning and had spent time in the hospital for a very sore leg. He was tired and in pain. He also refused to wear makeup. Nixon was not at his best, while Kennedy looked presidential. People who listened to the debate on the radio, however, thought that Nixon had won, further suggesting the power of visuals. Many commentators attribute Kennedy's razor-thin victory in the election to his performance in the debates.[30]

CBS /Landov

From 1961 to 1981 Walter Cronkite was the anchor of CBS *Evening News* and one of the most trusted men in America. Usually calm and objective, he broke down when announcing that President John F. Kennedy, shot in Dallas on November 22, 1963, had died. His emotions on the air exemplified the feelings of all Americans.

The Mass Media in the Twenty-First Century

The media have always been a dynamic institution, but the speed of changes in the last few decades is truly staggering. The impact of television, for example, changed further with the rise of cable television from the 1970s to the 1990s. It was now possible to bring news to the public any time of day, reshaping the American news environment. Recent advances in technology have opened up additional avenues of communication—nearly all at the same time. The pace and the depth of these changes make the information environment of the twenty-first century different from those that preceded it.

The Changing Media Environment

The options open to Americans for gathering information about politics have constantly expanded. Figure 7.1 displays the changing **media environment** and suggests two main

media environment:
Structure and design of media through which people obtain information about politics or other current events.

lessons. First, Americans adopt new media quickly. In the early 1920s there were only five radio stations, and few households owned radios. By 1927 there were seven hundred stations, and ownership was rapidly increasing.[31] By the end of the 1930s almost everyone in the United States had access to a radio. Television caught on even more quickly. Only 10 percent of Americans had TV sets in their homes in the early 1950s; by 1960 the figure was 90 percent. Today, nearly all American households have not one television set but often two or three. Internet access also shows a steep upward trend, from few households in the mid-1990s to more than 70 percent of Americans in 2007.[32] The speed by which these new media have entered the marketplace itself increases. It took television thirteen years to reach 50 million users. In just three years on the market, more than 50 million iPods were sold, and when the iPad was released in 2010, about 3 million were sold in eighty days. Facebook added 100 million users in just nine months![33]

Second, there are more options for news than ever before. In the 1930s newspapers and radio were the main sources. In the 1950s television was a new option, but there were only

Television proved its importance as a source for political information when the NBC board chair invited the 1960 presidential candidates to debate the issues on television. John F. Kennedy accepted first, saying "I believe you are performing a notable public service in giving the American people a chance to see the candidates of the two major parties face to face." More than 70 million Americans watched the Kennedy-Nixon debates, and today presidential debates are fixtures of the fall campaign.

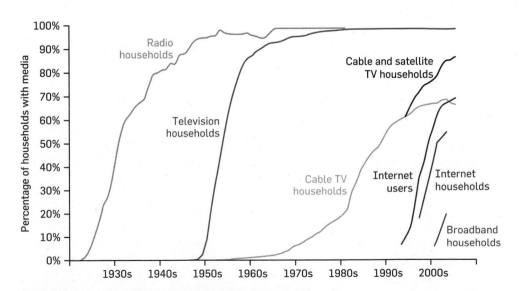

FIGURE 7.1 The Changing Media Environment.
Source: Markus Prior, *Post Broadcast Democracy* (New York: Cambridge University Press, 2007).

three networks, and they broadcast the news only in the evening. Now cable television, satellite TV, and the Internet make news available night and day.

The Decline of Newspapers

Traditional printed newspapers are in decline. The number of daily papers dropped from about 1,600 in 1990 to just over 1,400 in 2007.[34] In 2009 alone two major newspapers—*Seattle Post-Intelligencer* and *Rocky Mountain News*—shut down. Ann Arbor, Michigan, a medium-size city with a big university, no longer has a newspaper. Rumors were rampant that the *Boston Globe* would cease publication in 2009. The paper survived, but others face similar difficulties, and the future of newspapers is by no means certain.

Clearly, newspaper readership is declining. Figure 7.2 shows the plunge in circulation in the last decade. This pattern is part of a long-term trend. In 1977 about 70 percent of the public read newspapers; the figure is now below 50 percent.

The decline of newspapers raises concerns because newspapers tend to contain more **hard news**, more fact-based stories as opposed to interpretive narratives, than is reported on TV. In 2009 Alex Jones, one of the leading observers of the press, indicated that 85 percent of hard news comes from newspapers rather than from TV.[35] Will the decline of newspapers deprive Americans of hard news, of the facts they need to hold government accountable?

Some observers counter that readers are simply migrating from the printed newspapers to online versions. In January 2004 online newspapers had about 41 million visitors; by 2008 the number had jumped to 67 million.[36] Although the move from the printed to online versions may offer some hope about the continued significance of the newspaper industry, it has not solved the industry's financial difficulties. Fewer readers of print newspapers mean fewer advertisers buying space and lower rates being charged for the space; online advertising has not been able to make up the difference.[37] Not only commercial ad revenue has been lost. The number of want ads has shrunk has well, as potential buyers and sellers turn more often to Craigslist and other specialty websites that share information without charge. With

What newspapers do you read? Print or online?

hard news: *Political news coverage, traditionally found in the printed press, that is more fact-based, opposed to more interpretive narratives and commentary.*

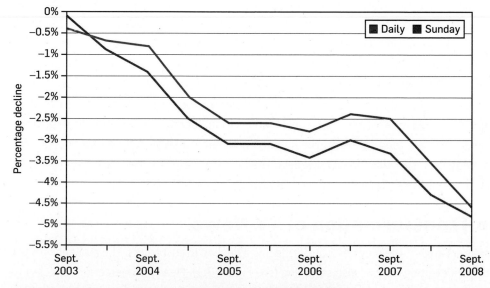

FIGURE 7.2 Newspaper Circulation, 2003–2008.
Source: Nielsen Media Research, State of the News Media, 2009.

revenue plummeting, newspapers survive only by cutting staff. The *Boston Globe* once had journalists overseas reporting on international events. That is no longer true.[38] The *Los Angeles Times* has seen its newsroom decline from 1,200 to 850 reporters.[39] Fewer reporters, editors, and other journalists mean that newspapers have less ability to inform and investigate. If the press cannot perform its watchdog role, the people stand to lose the means by which they hold government accountable.[40]

Are the newspapers in your town struggling? How can you tell?

Despite these serious concerns, Americans want the news and continue to seek it out, so newspaper owners have an incentive to develop new ways to make a profit.[41] Moreover, today's leading newspapers, such as the *New York Times,* have been powerful for only about 70 years, whereas American democracy has survived for 230 years. In fact, worries about the health of the newspaper industry are not new. In 1944 Oswald Garrison Villard's book *The Disappearing Daily* opened with this statement: "The outstanding fact in any survey of the American press is the steady and alarming decrease in the number of dailies."[42] Concerns about newspapers may indicate how much Americans depend on the press to hold government accountable. Any change in the means by which news is delivered raises fears that democracy itself may be weakened.

The Durability of Radio

In many ways, radio is underappreciated as a medium of communication; current debates center on newspapers, television, and the Internet. But radio remains important, especially considering how often Americans listen to the radio in their cars. The percentage of Americans who listen to the radio has remained unchanged in the last decade. In 1998, 95 percent of the American public tuned into an AM or FM station at least once a week; in 2007, 94 percent had listened to the radio in the previous seven days. Radio is expanding its reach by means of satellite radio and streaming audio on desktop and laptop computers. In fact, it is possible that "radio" is becoming "audio," reflecting advances in digital technology.[43]

political talk radio:
Media format dominated by conservative commentators that has become a vital gateway in disseminating political issues and events to millions.

Political talk radio, a medium dominated largely by conservatives, is increasingly popular. In 2008 nearly 50 million Americans listened to talk radio,[44] most to conservative programs. According to one estimate, conservatives hosted 91 percent of programming hours in 2007, and liberals just 9 percent. Over 90 percent of stations do not even broadcast progressive (that is, liberal) talk radio.[45] Of the conservative commentators, Rush Limbaugh is by far the best known and the most controversial. Liberals sought to make inroads with the now-defunct Air America, but had no success. The reasons for this lack of success are unclear. Perhaps it is because there are more conservatives than liberals in the United States. Moreover, conservatives tend to live in the suburbs and rural areas and therefore spend more time driving their cars than do city dwellers. Their greater opportunities for listening may be another reason for the dominance of conservative programming.[46]

The Transformation of TV News

Newspapers are not the only news outlets facing a decline in customers. The audience for the TV network evening news is also shrinking (see Figure 7.3). Nearly 25 percent of Americans watched the evening news in 1980; by 2010 that figure was just 8 percent.[47] The downward trend is likely to continue because older Americans make up the current audience for TV news. Young people, who represent the future audience, are not big consumers of network

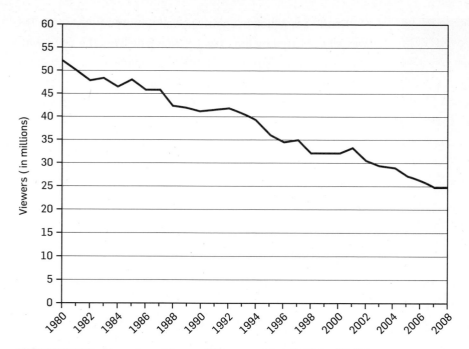

FIGURE 7.3 Evening News Viewership, 1980–2008.
Source: Nielsen Media Research, State of the News Media, 2009.

news. Their habits are not likely to change, painting a bleak picture for the industry in the coming years.

This decline, like that of newspapers, generates concern about how well informed the public is about politics. But these concerns are counterbalanced by the rise of cable news, which has become increasingly available since 1980. Households are now watching two or three hours a week of cable news, a rate of viewership higher than that for network news in the 1980s. Of the cable networks, Fox has the largest audience, more than CNN and MSNBC combined. Bill O'Reilly has become exceptionally popular, though not nearly as popular as Walter Cronkite once was. Even so, his show has a substantial following.

Cable news is not like the evening news shows of the 1970s, which were thirty-minute broadcasts around dinnertime. Cable news is available twenty-four hours a day. Events are covered live, transforming the news cycle. No longer do politicians time public appearances to appear on the evening news. News now comes at viewers at a rapid-fire rate, and cable news networks include interpretation in their constant programming. MSNBC's *Hardball with Chris Matthews* and *The Rachel Maddow Show* and Fox's *The Beltway Boys* are examples. Cable news has taken the interpretive function of the news media to a whole new level.

Of course, the web offers yet another platform for gathering news, one that seems to be on the rise. In 2008 msnbc.com, foxnews.com, and cnn.com all registered significant gains in the number of visitors.[48] Overall, the sources for news have increased. We examine the impact of these developments later in the chapter.

Infotainment

Television viewers also get political news through talk shows, such as *The Oprah Winfrey Show*, the *Late Show with David Letterman,* and *Jimmy Kimmel Live.* These sources offer what is called **infotainment** or **soft news**, news with fewer hard facts of the kind newspapers generally report and with more emphasis on personal stories that engage (or shock) the public and often appeal to the emotions rather than the intellect.

Which cable news station do you watch? Do you think the presentation of the news is fair?

infotainment: *Sources of news geared toward a less politically attentive audience, offering less substantive and more entertaining coverage than hard news.*

soft news: *News stories focused less on facts and policies than on sensationalizing secondary issues or on less serious subjects of the entertainment world.*

Would you describe the news you seek as hard or soft?

Bill O'Reilly and Rachel Maddow are highly visible news anchors in the media environment of the twenty-first century. Unlike Walter Cronkite, each conveys the news with a clear ideological edge.

Have you ever written a blog? What inspired you?

Nearly 1.5 million people, especially young adults, watch *The Daily Show* hosted by Jon Stewart, which delivers the news with humor and satire four days a week.[49] With Stewart's tough questions and hard-hitting reporting, it would be misleading to suggest that the news the show provides is "soft," but events like the murder of students and faculty at Virginia Tech in 2007 drew little mention on *The Daily Show*, though it dominated more traditional outlets. Nor is Stewart a liberal who goes after Republicans only, as he seemed to be when President George W. Bush (2001–2009) was in office. He attacks whoever is in power; now President Barack Obama (2009–) is subject to his rapier wit. The guests who appear on *The Daily Show* cover the full ideological spectrum, indicating at least some desire for balance.[50]

Blogs

A **blog** is a website that provides a forum for bottom-up commentary, descriptions of events, video postings, and general conversation. Through blogs, average citizens are able to express their opinions to a wider audience, and they offer a gateway for people to influence politics. There are all kinds of blogs, with political blogs representing a subset. Of the twenty-five most popular blogs in 2009, four are political. The Daily Kos remains popular, with nearly six hundred thousand visitors per month in 2009.[51] During the 2008 presidential campaign, interest in liberal blogs was very high, but their appeal has declined since the election of Barack Obama. With the Democrats now occupying the White House, conservative blogs are becoming a popular way for people to express their unhappiness with the Obama administration.

In many ways, blogging symbolizes the modern transformation of the mass media. Blogs capture the interest of people of all ages, and some observers hope that they will provide a forum for more participation and deliberation. While there is some evidence that blogs do foster participation, they do not seem to foster deliberation. Liberals read liberal blogs, and conservatives read conservative blogs: In fact, 94 percent of people read blogs that share their ideological viewpoint. These data suggest that blogs reinforce existing preferences and do not provide opportunities to hear the other side.[52] Moreover, blogs are usually strong in their ideological leanings. Daily Kos is a liberal blog, as is the Huffington Post.[53] Conservative blogs include those of Matt Drudge and Rush Limbaugh.[54]

Blogs also have the potential to spread false information. Because no one checks the accuracy of a posting, individuals—some call them trolls—can say outrageous things merely to get attention without penalty.[55] In contrast, the traditional press has a well-established set of norms for vetting the accuracy of information; when false statements do get through, the journalists are likely to pay a heavy penalty. Trolls, on the other hand, often gain notoriety for lying.

The importance of blogs appears to be on the rise. In early 2004 fewer than 20 percent of Internet users claimed to be visiting blogs. Two years later that figure had doubled. Blogs can have powerful effects. In 2004, when former Senator Trent Lott (R-Miss.) made favorable comments about Strom Thurmond's 1948 presidential candidacy, which advocated racial segregation, the mainstream media did not pick up the story, but it got play in the **blogosphere**. The comments raised such a public outcry that the mainstream media had to cover the story and Lott had to resign his leadership of the U.S. Senate.

Politicians increasingly understand the power of blogs as sources of news. Former Massachusetts Governor Mitt Romney established the Five Brothers blog as part of his 2008 presidential campaign. The intent was to have his five sons write about their father and life on the campaign trail. The blog provided a way for the public to get a close look at Romney's children and gain an understanding of his family life. This information was valuable because Romney's family was a real strength of his candidacy.[56] Other candidates have also used blogs to communicate with followers and potential supporters.

Blogs have given rise to **citizen journalists**, who clearly influenced the political debate during the 2008 presidential campaign. One example is Mayhill Fowler, who reported on huffingtonpost.com that Barack Obama had said that working-class people were "clinging" to their "guns and religion" because they were "bitter."[57] Obama made those comments at a private fundraiser, and he did not know he was being recorded. But once the comments were posted, the Obama campaign faced a firestorm of protest. Fowler did not intend to become a media sensation, but her actions indicate how easy it is for citizens to become part of the process of holding politicians accountable. The new media have opened more gateways for conveying news than were available in the previous century.

Social Networking

The Internet has also enabled new social networks for sharing information. Just as personal conversations are important sources of information, social networking websites are increasingly important ways to spread political news. The leading website is Facebook, which is especially popular among college students. It calls itself "a social utility that connects people with friends and others who work, study, and live around them. People use Facebook to keep up with friends, upload an unlimited number of photos, share links and videos, and learn more about the people they meet." Mark Zuckerberg started the so-called utility from his Harvard dorm room in February 2004 as a social networking service limited to the Harvard campus. By the end of March the service was extended to Stanford, Columbia, and Yale universities. By the end of the year the network had more than 1 million users, and it reached 5.5 million by the end of 2005 as it was extended to all universities and high schools in the United States and Canada. Today, if Facebook were a country, it would be the world's fourth largest, between the United States and Indonesia.[58]

Facebook is a worldwide phenomenon with launches in more than fifteen different languages. According to Student Monitor's Lifestyle and Media Study in 2006, 71 percent of college students had Facebook accounts, tying "drinking beer" for second place among the "in-things" to do on campus (having an iPod was number 1, with 73 percent).[59] Currently, according to the web information company Alexa, Facebook ranks fourth among the most trafficked sites on the Internet.

Just as politicians began to use blogs to communicate with the public, so have they begun to use social networks. A recent study found that 32 percent of 2006 senatorial candidates and 13 percent of 2006 congressional candidates posted information on their Facebook profiles (which the company created for every candidate that year). In total, about 1.5 million people (13 percent of the user base at the time) were connected to either a candidate or an issue group.[60]

blog: *Short for weblog, a website where people post news, commentary, pictures, video, and other information to share with other users.*

blogosphere: *Collective term for political and nonpolitical blogs that can be used to gauge public opinion on many political issues.*

citizen journalists: *Ordinary individuals independent of news organizations and with no formal journalistic training who play active roles in reporting the news or commenting on current events, primarily through the Internet and weblogs.*

How could you be a citizen journalist?

Do you use Facebook? If so, is it a source of political news or action for you?

With its exponential growth, Facebook has become a vital medium of political communication, especially for young people. In December 2007 Facebook teamed up with ABC News to create a presidential campaign application entitled "U.S. Politics," allowing users to get involved in political discussions in a variety of ways, such as by subscribing to the profiles of reporters on the campaign trail and writing their own reactions, and by starting discussion groups based on press reports.

The social network offered a variety of other software applications for its users to engage in the 2008 presidential election. The *Economist* and the *Washington Post,* as well as private individuals, sponsored applications that provided campaign and election information. Once an application is added to an individual's account, he or she can post comments on articles or create discussion groups to debate topics or issues.

Aside from offering a forum for U.S. politics, Facebook also teamed up with ABC News to sponsor Democratic and Republican debates on January 5, 2008. After the four hour-long debates, users could go to the website and discuss the issues and positions of the candidates. The partnership was the 2008 version of MTV's Rock the Vote, which had been launched more than a decade earlier to encourage young people to get involved in politics. According to Facebook vice president Dan Rose, "The goal [was] to extend the debate from being a one-hour session that happens on television to a dialogue that can take place before, after and now during the debate between voters."[61]

Facebook has become a valuable means whereby candidates reach out to a younger generation of voters both to convey their messages and to raise money. Candidates can list biographical details, post advertisements and other Internet feeds, provide links for donations, and create discussion groups. Users are, in turn, able to become candidates' supporters with access to all posted information. Private individuals have also used Facebook to campaign for candidates on their own. It is a new gateway for volunteering that is less costly and may reach more voters.

Another development in social networking is the rise of Twitter. One can communicate with a large number of people through Internet-based messages ("tweets"). Politicians, actors, sports figures, and other celebrities are using this technology to share information, and it has spread rapidly around the world. In June 2009 Iranians used Twitter to organize people to attend rallies protesting the outcome of Iran's presidential election.[62] It is far from clear that Twitter had any real impact on the outcome,[63] but its growth is phenomenal (see Figure 7.4).

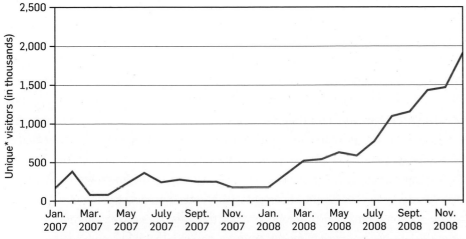

*"Unique" means that each person counts only once, so multiple visits by the same person are counted as one.

FIGURE 7.4 Twitter Audience, 2007–2008.
Source: Nielsen Media Research, State of the News Media, 2009.

In just ten months during 2008, there was a tenfold increase in Twitter use. Once again, new technologies have opened gateways for individuals to become involved in the political arena.

Cell phones have made possible yet another means of communication—text messaging, which is replacing e-mail for many people, especially young people. In the United States over 60 percent of cell phone users engage in text messaging. The percentage is even higher elsewhere: In Germany it is 90 percent, and in Britain 85 percent.[64] About 10 percent of text messages contain some kind of political information.[65] Politicians and political parties have also started to use this medium to communicate with supporters. Presidential candidate Obama, for example, informed his supporters about the selection of Joe Biden as his vice presidential nominee via a text message (as well as e-mail). Supporters can also send messages to various political organizations. Text messaging is yet another gateway, and the increasing popularity of iPhones and other advanced cellular devices promises new means of communicating and sharing information in the future.

Jae C. Hong, File/Associated Press

People in today's media environment expect immediate news and instantaneous communication. When campaigning for president, Barack Obama relied heavily on his BlackBerry smart phone. Many observers thought he would have to give it up when he became president, but he has managed to keep it while ensuring that there would be no security breaches by someone trying to hack into his e-mail.

What is the future of political communication?

The News and the Millennials

The changes in the media environment do not affect all citizens equally. For example, the Millennial generation consumes news differently from the way older Americans do. Americans over 40 years old read the newspaper more often, watch TV news more often, and tune into the radio with greater frequency than do those under 40. By contrast, young people rely more on Internet news. Further, when younger Americans read a newspaper or listen to a radio program, they do so for a much shorter period of time than do those over 40.[66] The youth seem to do more channel surfing, while older Americans are more likely to sit down and watch an entire news program. These habits may reflect differences in lifestyles between, for example, college students and adults with full-time jobs and families.[67] It may also be that older adults are more cautious about new technology, whereas younger people embrace it. When the public began to rely on TV news instead of newspapers, commentators worried that people would be less informed and that television would somehow cheapen the information available. Change always generates uncertainty, and with the increasingly rapid rate of technological change, worry increases as well.

Conventional wisdom has always said that young people are less interested in politics than older Americans are. But Millennials appear to be more interested in politics at this point in their lives than were previous generations. This interest is not gauged by whether they watch the evening news or read newspapers, but by the ways they use new media to share information and learn about and express interest in politics.[68] Young adults tend to reject the top-down approach to learning about politics in which the news is filtered by professional journalists and trusted news anchors such as Cronkite. Instead, they seem much more interested in the bottom-up approach made possible by the wide-open availability of new media for citizen participation.

These changes are going to become more important over time as more Millennials become eligible to vote and older generations pass on. Technological change continues to spread, making the Internet and all its information increasingly available to more Americans. The United States is in the midst of a major transformation in the media environment, and observers are only beginning to understand the changes in how Americans transmit and consume the news.

Which do you trust more— bottom-up or top-down journalism?

The Impact of the News Media on the Public

The press provides information, investigation, and interpretation of the news. The news media, both old and new, make decisions about what to cover, what not to cover, and how to cover it. How does the public respond to this information? This section looks at several models ranging between two extremes: that the mass media have no effect on the public and that the mass media dominate the public's thinking.

The Propaganda Model

Few people believe that the media have no influence on citizens. To hold such a view, one must either believe that the public ignores the media or that citizens learn about politics by observing the events themselves. Neither is true. We can confidently label this the "naïve model" and dismiss it.

propaganda model: *Extreme view of the media's role in society, arguing that the press serves the interest of the government only, driving what the public thinks about important issues.*

The polar opposite has been called the **propaganda model**. This approach is exemplified by the Nazi dictatorship in Germany in the 1930s and 1940s. The Nazi Party controlled the content of newspapers and radio. It dictated the information available to citizens, affecting the direction and shape of public opinion. Through controlled programming, the German people often heard about the greatness of Adolf Hitler and the dangers of racial impurity. By holding a monopoly on information, the government could easily marshal public support. This is a dangerous model, and it is also inconsistent with how the press works in open societies. In the United States media sources control programming, and they compete for audience share; the government does not control the flow of information. The Constitution guarantees a free press.

The Minimal Effects Model

Toward the end of World War II, having seen the powerful effects of propaganda in Nazi Germany, scholars in the United States began to study public opinion and the influence of the media on it. Paul Lazarsfeld and others examined the media's influence on voting in the

1940 presidential election. The results were surprising: The researchers discovered that people had made up their minds prior to the campaign, and new information altered only a handful of people's choices.[69] Lazarsfeld's study gave rise to what has been called the **minimal effects model**. Lazarsfeld and his colleagues contended that the news media had only marginal influence on the public's thinking about politics. The public did not have much information about politics, and attitudes were shaped by long-standing forces such as partisanship or the neighborhood in which people lived.

According to this model, in a process described as **selective exposure**, people secured information from sources that agreed with them, leading to the reinforcement of beliefs, not to a change of beliefs. The minimal effects model was also based on a complementary process called **selective perception**—a concept developed in a study of the American voter published by Angus Campbell and three coauthors in 1960.[70] Selective perception describes partisans as interpreting the same information differently. In other words, partisanship involves a perceptual lens (see Chapter 6, Public Opinion) that shapes how outside events are viewed. So, for example, 70 percent of Democrats supported Obama's economic stimulus package in February 2009, whereas only 24 percent of Republicans did.[71]

The Not-So-Minimal Effects Model

The minimal effects model dominated the field of political science for about forty years. Then, starting in the 1970s, scholars began to reassess it.[72] This reassessment took place at two levels. First, rather than looking at whether the news media shifted citizens' opinions about an issue, scholars examined the more subtle effects that might arise from how the press covered politics (more will be said about this later). Second, they started to gather better data that could more effectively test for the impact of the news media. This next generation of research produced the **not-so-minimal effects model**. While not overstating the power of the news media, the model acknowledges that the coverage of politics by the press matters in subtle and important ways. In particular, there are three kinds of media effects: agenda setting, priming, and framing.

Agenda Setting.
By stressing certain issues, the media influence what the American public views as the most pressing concerns. This effect is called **agenda setting**. Given that on any particular day there are literally hundreds of stories that could be reported, journalists' decisions about which stories to cover (and which story to lead with, and which to bury inside the paper or at the end of a newscast) matter considerably. Politicians and their advisers make a huge effort to convince the media to cover some stories and ignore others. Should the news lead with a story about casualties in the war in Afghanistan or about growing problems in the nation's public education system? As one scholar explains, the media "may not be successful most of the time telling people what to think, but it is stunningly successful in telling its readers what to think about."[73] The evidence is compelling. If the media talk about crime, the public starts to care about it. If the press starts paying additional attention to the federal budget deficit, the issue becomes more salient to citizens. Since only about 1 percent of news coverage is dedicated to the topic of education, it is not surprising that education policy rarely rises to the top of politicians' agendas.[74]

minimal effects model: *View of the media's impact as marginal, since most people seek news reports to reinforce beliefs already held rather than to develop new ones.*

selective exposure: *Process whereby people secure information from sources that agree with them, thus reinforcing their beliefs.*

selective perception: *Process whereby partisans interpret the same information differently.*

not-so-minimal effects model: *View of the media's impact as substantial, occurring by agenda setting, framing, and priming.*

Have the news media changed your mind about a political issue or figure?

agenda setting: *Ability of the media to affect the way people view issues, people, or events by controlling which stories are shown and which are not.*

What issues are the media putting on the political agenda right now?

AP Photo/Matt York

Priming. An extension of agenda setting is **priming**. The media can alter the criteria that citizens use when evaluating political leaders, and this priming affects the vote. In the 2008 campaign, the Republican candidate John McCain hoped the public would vote on the basis of national security, believing that a majority would vote for him on that criterion. The Obama team wanted the focus to be on the economy. By priming the public to think about gas prices and the housing crisis, the news media could give the public more reason to vote for Obama. Such effects are real. Following the terrorist attacks on September 11, 2001, for instance, the news media's coverage of terrorism was the most powerful force shaping President Bush's popularity.[75] The public gave Bush credit for dealing effectively with these tragic events. So when terrorism was the focus, Bush prospered. But when the topic shifted to the economy, for example, the public was less supportive of the president.

Media attention to an Arizona law passed in April 2010 put immigration reform back on the political agenda. The law, which requires police officers to detain people they suspect are illegal immigrants, sparked protests all over the country, especially for its potential for racial profiling. In Phoenix on May 1 a protester suggests that the Arizona law raises constitutional issues.

priming: *Process whereby the media influence how the public views politicians by emphasizing criteria that make them look either good or bad.*

framing: *Ability of the media to influence public perception of issues by constructing the issue or discussion of a subject in a certain way.*

Framing. **Framing** is the ability of the media to alter the public's view on an issue by presenting it in a particular way. If the battles waged in the Middle East are framed as an issue of fighting terrorism, the public thinks about the war in a much more favorable light than if these conflicts are framed by the casualties incurred. Framing can have a very powerful effect, actually changing public opinion on an issue.

Perhaps the most famous example of framing comes from the work of Amos Tversky and Daniel Kahneman.[76] In an experiment, they told research subjects that the United States was preparing for the outbreak of an unusual disease, which was expected to kill six hundred people, and asked which program should be implemented to deal with the disease. If program A was adopted, two hundred people would be saved; if program B was adopted, there was a one-third probability that six hundred people would be saved, and a two-thirds probability that no one would be saved. Of those surveyed, 72 percent favored program A, and 28 percent favored program B. Such a strong result suggests that the government should adopt program A. But another group of subjects was also given a choice between two different programs. The options were described as follows: If program C was adopted, four hundred people will die. If program D was adopted, there was a one-third probability that nobody would die, and a two-thirds probability that six hundred people would die. Here, 22 percent of subjects favored program C, and 78 percent favored program D.

There is a 50 percentage point difference in people's willingness to support program A versus program C. Yet the programs yield the exact same policy outcome: Two hundred people live, and four hundred people die. The only difference is that the description of program A stressed saving people, while the description of program C stressed the deaths of people. This experiment underscores the power of framing—that the public reacts to a news event or a policy depending on how it is presented.

Evaluating the News Media

"The American Press is in crisis," wrote Lance Bennett and his colleagues in their 2007 book, *When the Press Fails*.[77] Concerns about the modern news media are widespread. In 2003 a book called *The Nightly News Nightmare* appeared. In 1996 James Fallows subtitled his book *How the Media Undermine American Democracy*. Thomas Patterson sounded an early warning in 1993, publishing a highly influential book titled *Out of Order*.[78]

Worries about the news media often center on two general concerns. One is that the media are biased and do not present objective information. The second, which is related, focuses on the general quality of information available to the public. The emphasis on soft news, for example, worries observers who do not think the public has enough exposure to more substantive hard news. Without enough hard news, these observers fear, the public will not be well enough informed to hold elected officials accountable.

Whether these concerns are valid or not (we examine them later), it is clear that the public's faith in the press has declined (see Table 7.1). In the early 1970s around 15 percent of the public did not have much confidence in the press; by 2004 the percentage had nearly tripled to about 45 percent. The share of the public that thinks the press gets the facts "straight" has declined over the last twenty years. In 1985, 55 percent of the public thought the press got the facts right. By 2007 that had shrunk to 39 percent. In November 2001, following

TABLE 7.1 Persistent Criticisms of the Press, 1985–2007

	Percentage of Survey Respondents							
	July 1985	Feb. 1999	Sept. 2001	Nov. 2001	July 2002	July 2003	June 2005	July 2007
News organizations . . .								
Are moral	54%	40%	40%	53%	39%	45%	43%	46%
Are immoral	13%	38%	34%	23%	36%	32%	35%	32%
Protect democracy	54%	45%	46%	60%	50%	52%	47%	44%
Hurt democracy	23%	38%	32%	19%	29%	28%	33%	36%
Get facts straight	55%	37%	—	46%	35%	36%	36%	39%
Stories often inaccurate	34%	58%	—	45%	56%	56%	56%	53%
Are careful to avoid bias	36%	31%	26%	35%	26%	29%	28%	31%
Are politically biased	45%	56%	59%	47%	59%	53%	60%	55%
Are highly professional	72%	52%	54%	73%	49%	62%	59%	66%
Are not professional	11%	32%	27%	12%	31%	24%	25%	22%

Source: Pew Research Center for the People and the Press, "Views of Press Values and Performance: 1985–2007," August 9, 2007. These survey questions were not repeated in 2008.

Do you trust the news media? What source, if any, gets it right?

the terrorist attacks of September 11, 60 percent of the public felt that the press protected democracy. Now, less than half of the public holds that belief.[79]

Is there reason to worry about the media? Are the mass media of the twenty-first century less able to fulfill their watchdog role? This section looks at media bias, the quality of information, and the implications of the Internet and media choice.

Are the Media Biased?

The press claims to be objective, and professional journalists subscribe to an ethic of neutrality. Yet, given that even the selection of which stories to cover influences public opinion, bias may be inevitable. Nevertheless, it need not be evil or ideological. David Broder, a well-known columnist for the *Washington Post*, attributes bias to the speed with which journalists have to act. "The process of selecting what the reader reads involves not just objective facts but subjective judgments, personal values, and, yes, prejudices," he confesses. Broder points out that "the newspaper that drops on your doorstep is a partial, hasty, incomplete, inevitably somewhat flawed and inaccurate rendering of some of the things we have heard about in the past 24 hours—distorted, despite our best efforts to eliminate bias, by the very process of compression that makes it possible for you to lift it from the doorstep and read it in about an hour."[80]

With the rise of the 24-7 news cycle, bias in selecting what to cover becomes even more evident. For example, during the 2008 presidential campaign, three candidates—John McCain, already the Republican nominee, and Barack Obama and Hillary Clinton, still contending for the Democratic nomination—were scheduled to give speeches on the evening of June 2. McCain spoke first, and all the major cable networks covered his speech. During the middle of the speech, however, Obama secured the few extra delegates that officially gave him the presidential nomination. MSNBC broke away from McCain's speech to announce this important development. Fox News did not. It flashed the information on the lower part of the screen, but continued to cover McCain's speech. Both networks were informing the public, but they were making different choices about what was most newsworthy and what was not. Insofar as MSNBC's choice seemed to support a liberal outlook and Fox's choice a conservative outlook, they might be described as biased.

Do you think the news media are too liberal?

A broader point is that, for many years, conservative commentators have claimed that the news media are liberal. Accuracy in Media, a conservative watchdog organization, contends that over 80 percent of mainstream journalists support the Democratic Party. Such partisan loyalties, according to critics, drive the liberal bias.[81] Yet the people who own the most major media outlets—such as Rupert Murdoch, whose media properties include the *Wall Street Journal* and Fox News—are conservative. Should one assume that because most news outlets are owned by conservatives the media are really conservative? It is far from clear whether the media are liberal or conservative.

If you think a media source is biased, do you ever listen to or view it? How can you evaluate it?

Yet, complaints about a liberal press seem to resonate with the public. Gallup Poll data measuring the public's belief about ideological bias in the news media indicate that about half the public believes the news media have a liberal bias. The proportion has been quite stable, ranging from 45 percent to 48 percent over the last few years. However, there has also been an increase in the share of people who think the media have a conservative bias. In 2001 only 11 percent of the public viewed the press as too conservative. By 2007, 18 percent made that claim. This trend is worth noting, but the important point is that Americans generally perceive a liberal tilt to the press's coverage of politics.[82]

The debate over whether the news media are too liberal or too conservative misses the central point about the news today. With so many sources of information, it is easy to find news with a liberal spin and news with a conservative spin. In fact, in the second decade of the twenty-first century, much news reporting is partisan, more like the party-dominated press of the nineteenth century than the objective and neutral press of the twentieth century. Media choice and multiple outlets mean that a Democrat can find a Democratic-leaning source for news and a Republican can find a Republican-leaning source. It is fair to conclude that individual news outlets are biased, but collectively the media provide a full range of ideological viewpoints.

Christopher Morris/VII/AP Photo

Quality of Information

The idea that people are getting news from Oprah rather than from Cronkite is disconcerting to political observers. The general worry is that people are getting less hard news and instead are relying on what we earlier called soft news—feature stores that are more personal and less policy focused, more sensationalized and less objective, than the political facts of hard news.[83] News about crime or natural disasters can fit the soft news category when the focus is about the drama surrounding the event (such as loss of life or homes) rather than a discussion of public policy that could reduce crime or perhaps provide quicker government response to disasters.[84]

Part of this underlying concern is the emphasis on image as opposed to substance. The assumption here is that visuals (television and Internet news, in contrast to print news) appeal to the emotions more than to the intellect, so visual news formats are in themselves less "hard" and more superficial. It is true that visual images convey impressions that go beyond the facts, but that does not mean that such information is not valuable. In the 1950s, for example, televised congressional hearings gave the public a chance to see Senator Joseph McCarthy in action and undid his credibility (see Chapter 4). While newspapers had covered the excesses of his charges about Communist infiltration of the government, his actions on camera were much more harmful to his reputation.[85] There is a great deal to be learned from visual images.

All media of communication shape how information is shared and digested. Radio, for example, puts a premium on the quality of people's voices. Franklin Roosevelt probably made the most famous use of radio with his compelling and reassuring voice. He was the

News coverage of Hurricane Katrina was at once "hard" and "soft." Hard news accounts focused on the government's lack of preparation and inadequate response to this Category 5 hurricane, which flooded the city of New Orleans and left more than 1,800 people dead. Soft news focused on the some of the millions of personal tragedies wrought by this natural disaster.

Are the people smarter than the news media think we are?

During the Great Depression, President Franklin Roosevelt used radio to speak directly to the American people. His first fireside chat was broadcast on March 12, 1933, a week after he took office. Addressing the banking crisis, he explained government's response in clear terms: "We have provided the machinery to restore our financial system," he said, "and it is up to you to support and make it work. . . . Together we cannot fail."

fireside chats: *Radio addresses by President Franklin Delano Roosevelt that were the first regular communications from a president to a large portion of the American public.*

sound bites: *Brief snippets of information that stress the short, catchy statement over substantive analysis.*

What kinds of news do you seek? What should the American people seek?

first president to use radio to communicate directly with the people, broadcasting **fireside chats** from the White House in which he explained what he was doing to end the Great Depression.[86] Other politicians with less appealing voices would not have been able to put radio to such good use. Consider politics prior to the invention of the microphone. Who were the most effective politicians? Perhaps it was individuals with deep voices that could project to a large audience. A soft-spoken politician would have been at a real disadvantage.

It is also important to realize that images did not begin with the advent of television. Although it may be easier to engage in "image" politics in an era of video, politicians have always wanted to convey a favorable image and have done so using the media of their time. Abraham Lincoln sought to project himself as the self-made man that he was, so his 1860 campaign distributed pictures depicting him working with his hands as a rail-splitter.[87] Andrew Jackson (1829–37) built a successful run to the White House in part on his reputation as a tough military leader. Image has always been important to politicians.

In the same way, **sound bites**—very brief snippets of information—did not begin with the advent of television. Many observers fear that by stressing short catchy statements rather than more detailed substantive statements, sound bites undermine the quality of information. Campaigns, however, have always made effective use of simple slogans. In 1900, for example, President William McKinley (1897–1901) sought reelection with the slogan "A full dinner pail," reminding voters about the economic prosperity enjoyed during his first term.[88]

The purpose of this discussion is to urge caution in making hasty judgments about differences in the kinds of information available via the news media over the last 230 years. Soft news may be more informative than hard news because people find it easier to understand and more enjoyable. It is important, therefore, not to let the definition of what counts as news shape judgment of the press. That news reporting is no longer filtered by Walter Cronkite but instead by Bill O'Reilly does not mean the news media are no longer doing their job. They are just doing it differently.

Despite recent changes in the mass media, evidence suggests that Americans have as much information about politics as they did before the arrival of the Internet and the 24-7 news cycle. According to a 2007 survey released by the Pew Research Center for the People and the Press, "the coaxial and digital revolutions and attendant changes in the news audience behaviors have had *little* impact on how much Americans know of about national and international affairs."[89] Patterns from the 2008 presidential campaign provide further evidence. Americans were not less informed about the two candidates than in previous elections; they simply secured information in new ways.[90]

Implications of the Internet

There is evidence that the arrival of the Internet has not changed the overall amount of information the public possesses, but it is important to acknowledge that the Internet is not equally available to all Americans. Only about 35 percent of Americans making less than $20,000 a year in 2009 have access to the Internet; for those making $75,000 or more, the proportion climbs to 85 percent.[91] Older Americans also have less access to the Internet than do younger Americans.

These data suggest a further inequality—that those with Internet access may be much better informed than the public generally just twenty years ago, whereas those without access may be even less informed. Variations among groups buried in discussions of the public as a whole are significant. These variations will likely decrease as more people secure access to the Internet. Figure 7.1 on page 222, which shows the many options people have for information, suggests that Americans will move toward universal access. There will always be a gap between the well informed and the poorly informed, but in time the Internet will give older and less wealthy Americans a better chance to become informed about politics than they currently are.

The Era of Media Choice

Perhaps the best word to describe today's media environment is *choice*.[92] The spread of cable television, the Internet, and satellite radio means that people have many possible sources for political information, as well as a huge array of entertainment programming that may lead them to opt out of political news altogether. In the mid-twentieth century, when the network evening news was the source of information, viewers had fewer choices and less opportunity to opt out. They might change channels at dinnertime, but they would get similar news from a different network. The evening news was the only show available during the dinner hour. The lack of choice may have given people more exposure to politics than they wanted.[93]

The TV network news standardized the information that many Americans had access to. With the wide array of choices now available, information is more polarized today. Viewers who choose a conservative TV network such as Fox and listen to Rush Limbaugh on the radio will have different information from those who watch MSNBC and tune in to National Public Radio. Those who lack interest in politics can avoid political news altogether. In other words, media choice cuts two ways: polarizing the type of information available, and making it possible to receive no political information at all.

The consequences of media choice are complex and are only beginning to be understood. New technologies in the future could further fragment what Americans as a people know. Efforts to make political news more interesting may mean a further "softening" of the news. The main point is that Americans have access to a vast amount of information, but the availability of more information does not necessarily mean that the public as a whole is better informed. Lurking beneath the general patterns is the real prospect that media choice will further fuel polarization.

Granger Collection, New York

During the presidential campaign of 1860, Republican candidate Abraham Lincoln sought to portray himself as a common man with a humble background who understood the needs of the people. To develop this image, Lincoln's campaign stressed that as a young man he split rails to build a fence around his home. The image became part of campaign lore.

What are the consequences of media choice?

The Mass Media and Public Policy: Censorship

Any effort by government to control the media or to curtail the freedom of the press faces an immediate debate and often strong protest. When the courts decide between national security concerns and press freedoms, they usually support the press. Libel suits rarely result in convictions. Yet the advent of radio and television and the recent proliferation of electronic media have brought new challenges to determining what kinds of content should be restrained and what kinds should be allowed to flow freely. No government agency regulates the print media, but the Federal Communications Commission has the authority to regulate the content and ownership of radio, television, the Internet, and all electronic media. One area of special concern has been what might be considered obscene or offensive material.

Obscene Content in Broadcast Media

The landmark Supreme Court decision in *FCC v. Pacifica Foundation* (1978) established the precedent that the FCC has the legal authority to fine any media outlet that knowingly allows the expression of obscene content, under certain circumstances. The background of the case was that in 1973 a New York radio station aired George Carlin's monologue "Filthy Words," which included seven words that could not be said on the public airwaves. The station had prefaced the monologue with a warning to listeners that it included "sensitive language which might be regarded as offensive to some." A listener who was in the car with his young son when he heard the broadcast filed a complaint with the FCC.

Should the government censor language on the air?

The underlying question in this case was whether the First Amendment inhibits the power of the government to restrict the public broadcast of indecent language under any circumstances. The Supreme Court ruled in a 5–4 decision that the government could invoke limited civil sanctions against the radio broadcast of patently offensive words dealing with sex and excretion without violating the First Amendment. The Court also said that the words did not have to be obscene to warrant sanction and that, in decisions on whether sanctions on media content are fair and justified, other factors such as audience type, the time that the broadcast was aired, and how it was transmitted are relevant.[94]

In today's television, music, and video climate, the boundaries for socially acceptable visual and verbal content are constantly evolving. Two recent cases reflect the ongoing policy discussion about acceptable restrictions on media expression. In *FCC v. Fox Television Stations*, Fox Broadcasting Company appealed fines that the FCC imposed for its 2002 and 2003 broadcasts of the Billboard Music Awards, during which participants uttered expletives. Fox claimed that participants on previous broadcasts had used similar language and that the FCC had ruled that the use was "fleeting" and was not seriously harmful, so it objected to a change in FCC enforcement with no warning. In a 5–4 decision, the Supreme Court ruled that the FCC only needed to prove that its new policy was justifiable and reasonable.[95] In response to what has been viewed as a stricter crackdown on language content, network television and radio stations have taken to "bleeping" or "buzzing" over words that might be viewed as harmful by the FCC. In live broadcasts, networks typically use a five-second delay in sending their signals over the airways to make sure they have time to bleep out offensive language. Cable television outlets are not under this same type of restriction because they broadcast to paid subscribers who thus have more control over the content they choose to view.

Using similar reasoning, the Supreme Court also ruled in support of the FCC in *CBS Inc. v. FCC*, which dealt with an incident during the halftime show for the 2004 Super Bowl. During a performance by Justin Timberlake and Janet Jackson, part of Jackson's costume was ripped off, and her breast was momentarily exposed. The FCC fined CBS $550,000 for allowing the viewing of indecent images, and CBS sued to appeal the fine. The Court of Appeals for the Third Circuit ruled that the fine was illegal because the FCC had changed its policy on indecent images without notifying CBS and other broadcast networks. The FCC then appealed that ruling, and in 2009 the Supreme Court sent the case back to the court of appeals for reconsideration in light of its decision in the *Fox Television* case.[96]

These three Supreme Court cases exert a significant impact on the way government restricts expression of speech and visual images through the media. Current policy distinguishes between media outlets that are free to the public and those that audiences subscribe to and pay for. Supporters of expanded FCC powers argue that the government has a compelling interest in keeping airways and television "clean" or at least in promoting content that does not contain language or behavior deemed socially undesirable. Opponents of a strong FCC believe that media content should be restricted only when it can be shown to be seriously and deeply damaging to the social fabric of the democracy. Given advances in the technical delivery of media content, such as the delivery of print and video to cell phone converters, further controversies involving FCC restrictions are likely to occur.

Safety, Social Networking, and the Internet

The Internet is not exactly a broadcast medium, but given its wide availability to the general public, Congress has sought to restrict its content. In 1996 Congress passed the Communications Decency Act, which established broadcast-style content regulations for the Internet. The act banned the posting of "indecent" or "patently offensive" materials in a public forum on the Internet, including in newsgroups, chat rooms, web pages, and online discussion lists. The American Civil Liberties Union (ACLU) challenged the law, and in 1997 the Supreme Court ruled unanimously that it was unconstitutional because it imposed sweeping restrictions that violated the free speech protections of the First Amendment.[97]

In 1998 Congress tried for a second time to limit content on the Internet when it passed the Child Online Protection Act (COPA).[98] The act made it a crime for anyone using an Internet site or e-mail over the Internet to make any communication for commercial reasons considered "harmful to minors" unless the person had prohibited access by minors by requiring a credit card number to access the material. In addition, the act imposed fines of up to $50,000 a day. Again, the legislation was ultimately struck down, this time by the Court of Appeals for the Third Circuit. The court ruled that COPA, like the Communications Decency Act before it, violated the First Amendment in that it "effectively suppresses a large amount of speech that adults have a constitutional right to receive and to address one another" and thus was too broad.[99] Further, in 2009 the U.S. Supreme Court refused to hear the government's appeal of this decision.

Congress subsequently responded by passing the Children's Online Privacy Protection Act (COPPA), which requires sites directed to children under the age of 13 to gain parental

What should the government do about pornography on the Internet? If you think there should be a restriction of freedom of expression or access, what is the justification?

consent before collecting, maintaining, or using children's information. Parents can review their children's online activity under COPPA. The act also requires such a site to post a privacy policy on its home page and a link to the privacy policy on every page where personal information is collected.[100] In addition, in 2003 Congress passed a law designed to prevent the exploitation of children by prohibiting pornographic websites from showing sexually explicit material involving children on their home pages.[101]

In a related move, the government has acted to shield consumers from receiving unsolicited e-mail. The CAN-SPAM Act (2003) requires all commercial e-mailers to provide Internet users with the opportunity to opt out of getting further messages, restricts them from sending e-mail with false header information, and sets civil penalties for misleading subject lines on commercial e-mail.[102]

Given the vastness of the Internet and the speed at which technology evolves, it becomes fundamentally harder to keep the Internet "safe" for users of all ages as well as to preserve the security of information that is passed over it. Because the Internet is an engine of commerce as well as a media outlet, it is also regulated by the Federal Trade Commission (FTC).[103] The FTC's Bureau of Consumer Protection offers detailed information to consumers about what information they should never release on the Internet, what websites are not secure, how to determine secure websites, and how to report wrongdoing. Citizens who fail to read privacy policies or are not careful about the information they release are vulnerable, and the FTC is the government agency responsible for helping to prevent Internet abuse and fraud.

What, if anything, should the government do to make the Internet secure and safe? Under the Constitution, what could be the justification?

Although society has a legitimate interest in censoring explicit sexual and violent images on the Internet, the Supreme Court has repeatedly ruled that using broad or vague language to create blanket restrictions jeopardizes the right to free speech guaranteed by the First Amendment. Now that the Internet has created a global community, balancing the individual right to public expression and upholding community standards of behavior will continue to be a challenge in the twenty-first century.

The Mass Media and Democracy

The news media, as watchdogs, are a central player in democratic politics. In the twenty-first century the mass media are far more open than they were just a few decades ago, providing additional chances to forge accountability, responsiveness, and equality. But these are only chances because the media are in the midst of a transformation whose repercussions are not yet known.

For example, nearly all public appearances and statements of political figures can now be caught on video or audiotape. As a result, politicians have a tougher time ducking responsibility; they are more easily held accountable for their actions and words. However, the threat of being caught on tape in an embarrassing moment may encourage politicians to stay in the **bubble**, sheltered from public scrutiny and shielded from assertive journalists or potentially harmful situations. Politicians build staffs and organizations designed to keep them from making mistakes and from interacting with journalists and citizens. They want to appear at staged events where they can control the message.

bubble: *State in which politicians are sheltered from public scrutiny and uncontrolled situations.*

The more open and more democratic new media thus have the potential to let citizens know more about the politicians who lead them; they also give people more opportunities to express opinions for politicians to consider as they develop and enact laws. Thus blogs and other new media may help forge responsiveness. But these gateways have potential costs: The opinions may come from people who are not representative of the American mainstream. Information offered as fact in these settings has not been checked and is potentially filled with errors.

The many changes in the news media have also led to a decline in the number of professional journalists who are covering politics. With fewer professional journalists, the press may be less able to investigate stories that might unearth corruption or provide a more complete account of some politicians' backgrounds.

The decline in investigative reporting could, in short, undermine accountability. But there is some reason for optimism. For example, Paul Steiger, former editor of the *Wall Street Journal*, has formed a nonprofit organization called ProPublica that pursues investigations, offering the findings to newspapers and magazines. By taking advantage of funding from private sources, the organization offers a way to compensate for the decline of investigative journalism.[104] In a sense, the rise of the Internet has lessened the need for professional journalists, but the power of the Internet has also provided a way to pool resources and undertake important investigations. It is far too early to know whether ProPublica will work. But innovative uses of the Internet demonstrate the dynamic nature of the mass media.

Concern about the media's ability to advance democratic government come mostly from people who favor a top-down approach for providing political information. For those who see the merit and appeal in a bottom-up approach, the changes seem far less worrisome. On average, the Millennial generation will not be so worried; these young people have grown up with the transformed mass media. They see the potential that the Internet and other media have for promoting equality—and for providing more chances to be part of the process. But until access to the Internet becomes universal, these changes offer more hope than reality.

FOCUS QUESTIONS

- How do the mass media help make government accountable to the people?

- How has the rise of the Internet increased or decreased the ability of the public to hold government accountable?

- How does the bottom-up approach of twenty-first-century mass media affect citizen participation and equality? What are its other effects?

- When, and under what conditions, should government regulate the media?

- In what ways do the mass media offer gateways to American democracy? In what ways do the modern media establish new gates?

GATEWAYS TO LEARNING

Top Ten to Take Away

1. In a democracy, the people rely on the mass media for the information they need in order to hold government accountable and make it responsive. The press plays the role of watchdog, and the First Amendment protects the freedom of the press. (pp. 210–11, 212–15)

2. The mass media perform three important tasks: informing, investigating, and interpreting the news. (pp. 211–12)

3. When the government attempts to constrain the press, the Supreme Court generally sides with the press, believing that it is better to protect press freedoms than to permit government censorship. (pp. 213–15)

4. Unlike the press, radio, television, and electronic media are heavily regulated by the Federal Communications Commission. (pp. 213, 215, 237–40)

5. The history of the press in American is dynamic, developing from occasional pamphlets to comprehensive daily publications and online enterprises with a mix of news and entertainment. The profession of journalism has developed over time as well, with a commitment to objectivity. In the 1950s television began to replace newspapers as the source of news. (pp. 215–21)

6. In the twenty-first century technological advances are changing the media environment once again. The rise of cable television, satellite TV, and the Internet make news available day and night. Soft news, with personal stories and emotional content, is replacing hard news. Blogs are evidence of a new bottom-up journalism by citizens. (pp. 221–30)

7. Political scientists describe the impact of the news media on the public as agenda setting, priming, and framing. (pp. 230–33)

8. Although the public has lost faith in the media and generally think the media are too liberal, media choice and multiple outlets ensure a full range of ideological viewpoints. The sources of information are changing, but the public has as much information about politics as ever. (pp. 233–37)

9. The decline of newspapers is a real concern. The decreasing number of journalists means that newspapers have less ability to inform and investigate. If the press cannot perform its watchdog role, the public loses a means by which it holds government accountable. (pp. 223–24, 240–41)

10. Technology has changed the media and the way Americans receive the news since before the nation was founded. Americans quickly adopt new technologies, and they have always sought the news. Increasing Internet access will eventually even out inequalities, giving all Americans a chance to be informed about politics. (pp. 221–23, 241)

Ten to Test Yourself

1. Describe the contributions of Zenger, Franklin, Day, Pulitzer, and Ochs to the role of the press in American democracy.

2. What caused partisan newspapers to decline in the middle of the nineteenth century?

Timeline to Keep Things in Order

1734	1776	1788	1833	1898
Trial of John Peter Zenger establishes the press's right to criticize the government.	Tom Paine's *Common Sense* promotes the idea of American independence.	*Federalist Papers* argue for ratification of the Constitution.	*New York Sun* initiates the era of the circulation-based penny press.	Sensational stories (yellow journalism) incite the Spanish-American War.

3. Compare and contrast freedom of the press and regulation of radio and electronic media.

4. What can the FCC regulate? How is the FCC regulated?

5. Describe the rise of professional journalism.

6. Describe the role of the citizen journalist.

7. What evidence is there that the press is declining?

8. What evidence is there of media bias?

9. What does "media choice" mean, and what are its effects?

10. Why is the press so important to democratic politics?

Terms to Know and Use

actual malice (p. 213)
agenda setting (p. 231)
authoritarianism (p. 215)
background (p. 220)
blog (pp. 226, 227)
blogosphere (p. 227)
bubble (p. 240)
citizen journalists (p. 227)
Federal Communications Commission (p. 213)
Federalist Papers (p. 217)

fireside chats (p. 236)
framing (p. 232)
hard news (p. 223)
infotainment (p. 225)
libel (p. 213)
mass media (p. 211)
media environment (p. 221)
Millennials (p. 211)
minimal effects model (p. 231)
muckraking (p. 219)
Near v. Minnesota (p. 213)

news media (p. 211)
New York Times v. Sullivan (p. 213)
not-so-minimal effects model (p. 231)
off the record (p. 220)
penny press (p. 218)
Pentagon Papers case (p. 213)
political talk radio (p. 224)
press (p. 211)
priming (p. 232)
prior restraint (p. 213)

propaganda model (p. 230)
Sedition Act (p. 218)
seditious libel (p. 217)
selective exposure (p. 231)
selective perception (p. 231)
soft news (p. 225)
sound bites (p. 236)
the scoop (p. 220)
watchdog (p. 211)
Watergate scandal (p. 212)
yellow journalism (p. 219)

Learning That Works

WHAT YOU NEED . . .

TO KNOW

Why the Constitution protects press freedom

What the press does

What motivates journalists

The full range of news sources

What media choice is

The purpose and limits of government control of the media

TO DO

Understand the role of the press in a democracy

Determine whether the press is still doing its job

Assess media bias

Decide which source for news you trust

Evaluate whether citizens are well informed

Distinguish between what should and should not be censored on the Internet

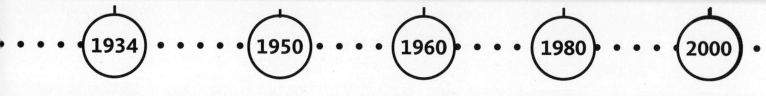

1934 — Federal Communications Commission is established to regulate radio in the public interest.

1950 — Television news begins to replace newspapers.

1960 — First presidential debate is televised.

1980 — Cable news begins its rise.

2000 — Cable TV and the Internet make news available 24-7.

8 INTEREST GROUPS

▲ University of Idaho, Moscow

> *Citizens are the engineers of their own destiny. They have to be proactive in order to achieve the goals they set for themselves and for the nation as a whole.*

At the University of Idaho, Al Baker is a mechanical engineering student and a gun rights activist. As both the Idaho state director for Students for Concealed Carry on Campus (SCCC) and the organization's Rocky Mountain regional director, he works with college students, parents, teachers, and other educators to persuade state legislators and college administrators "to grant concealed handgun license holders the same rights on college campuses that those licensees currently enjoy in most other unsecured locations." This is the group's mission statement. The group is student led—Baker is also on the national board of directors and serves as the organization's vice president—and student founded. In April 2007, in response to the tragic loss of life in the shooting deaths on the Virginia Tech campus, Chris Brown, a political science major at the University of Texas, organized SCCC from his dorm room. Beginning with a website and Facebook, the organization now has more than 350 chapters on college campuses and universities and some 43,000 members. Although the group has the core principle of gun rights, it is not officially associated with the National Rifle Association or with any political party.

Baker has always lived in Idaho and enjoys its opportunities for outdoors activities. He is a wilderness hiker and is also interested in motorcycling, automobile restoration, and recreational shooting. As a sportsman and a responsible firearms owner, he has been a campus leader in SCCC since its inception. He wants colleges and universities to allow members of their communities to legally carry licensed concealed weapons because, he points out, students are citizens and they have an actual need for self-defense in light of the crimes common on college campuses, including assault, robbery, and rape. On February 13, 2008, Baker testified before the Idaho state legislature in favor of a bill that would prevent localities from banning guns. He made the point that the tragedy at Virginia Tech and other campus shootings have made students afraid of being attacked on campus.

Al Baker

CourseMate

Visit http://www.cengagebrain.com/shop/ISBN/0618906959 for interactive tools including:

- Quizzes
- Flashcards
- Videos and more

© www.JayBeeStock.com

DianeRicePhotos.com

Students need to be able to protect themselves, he argued. Challenged that the risk of violence from armed students in the classroom would outweigh any potential protection guns on campus might provide, Baker disagreed. Students are at the mercy of crazed gunmen, he countered. "We sit there as sitting ducks waiting and hoping some madman doesn't come and kill us." For Baker and the members of SCCC, it is better to have the opportunity to fight off an attacker off with a gun than to be a victim. As an interest group, the SCCC serves as a gateway to influence that allows students to make their views about gun rights known throughout the nation.

Currently Utah is the only state that allows concealed carry at all public colleges and universities. In other states, SCCC students offer testimony in defense of their position on campus and in the halls of state legislators. Members sign petitions, write letters and op-ed pieces, organize e-mail drives, and plan Empty Holster protests, during which they wear empty holsters to class "as an act of silent protest," says the SCCC website, "against laws and policies that discriminate against legally armed citizens." The group also offers information packets, fliers, posters, tip sheets, and form letters that can help members get out its message, and it is considering starting a magazine. One member has initiated a lawsuit. Whether one agrees or disagrees with SCCC's perspective, its grassroots origins and current activities are examples of students engaging in collective action to generate change and using university and political resources to raise awareness and support for a cause.[1]

Small or large, student-run or established national organizations more than a century old, interest groups are a mechanism of representation in a democracy because they help translate individual opinions and interests into outcomes in the political system. Interest groups form for many reasons: to advance economic status, express an ideological viewpoint, influence public policy, or promote activism on international affairs. In a democracy, the most crucial role of interest groups is their attempt to influence public policy. In this chapter we examine the history of interest groups, why they form, what they do, and their impact on democratic processes. We also identify how and why some groups are more influential than others. Throughout the chapter we focus on interest groups as gateways to citizen participation and, at the same time, point out how they can erect gates when they pursue narrow policy interests.

FOCUS QUESTIONS

- How do interest groups influence economic and social policy?

- How do interest groups help or hinder government responsiveness to all citizens in an equal and fair way?

- Are interest groups themselves democratic organizations? Are their leaders accountable to their members? Explain.

- Do interest groups balance each other out across income levels, regions, and ethnic backgrounds? Explain and give examples.

- Are interest groups gates or gateways to democracy?

Interest Groups and Politics

In 1831 the French political theorist Alexis de Tocqueville came to the United States to observe American social and political behavior. He stayed for more than nine months and later published his study as *Demcracy in America,* a classic of political literature. He wrote, "The most natural right of man, after that of acting on his own, is that of combining his efforts with those of his fellows and acting together. Therefore the right of association seems to me by nature almost as inalienable as individual liberty."[2] Tocqueville noticed that Americans in particular liked to form groups and join associations as a way of participating in community and political life. To Tocqueville, the formation of group life was an important element of the success of the American democracy.

Why do you think Americans like to join organizations? How does this tendency relate to American political culture?

What Are Interest Groups?

Tocqueville used the term *association* to describe the groups he observed throughout his travels in America; today we call them interest groups. An **interest group** is a group of citizens who share a common interest, whether a political opinion, religious affiliation, ideological belief, social goal, or economic objective, and try to influence public policy to benefit members. Other types of groups form for purely social or community reasons, but this chapter focuses on the groups that form to exert political influence.

Most interest groups arise from conditions in public life. A **proactive group** arises when an enterprising individual sees an opening or opportunity to create the group for social, political, or economic purposes. A **reactive group** forms to protect the interests of members in response to a perceived threat from another group, or to fight a government policy the members believe will adversely affect them, or to respond to an unexpected external event. Groups whose members share a number of common characteristics are described as homogeneous, whereas groups whose members come from varied backgrounds are described as heterogeneous. All interest groups are based on the idea that members joining together in a group can secure a shared benefit that would not be available to them if they acted alone.

Citizens most often join groups to advance their personal economic well-being, to get their voices heard as part of a larger group's efforts on an issue, or to meet like-minded citizens who share their views. There is no legal restriction on the number of groups that people can join, and citizens are frequently members of a number of organizations. On the large scale, citizens join groups as a way of participating in democratic society.

The Right to Assemble and to Petition

The First Amendment states that Congress cannot prohibit "the right of the people peaceably to assemble, and to petition the Government for a redress of grievances." This right to assemble is the **right of association**. The Framers understood that human beings naturally seek out others who are similar to them, and they believed that the opportunity to form groups was a fundamental right that government may not legitimately take away. At the same time, however, they were fearful that such groups, which Madison called **factions**, might divide the young nation. In *Federalist* 10 Madison wrote, "By a faction I understand a number of citizens, whether amounting to a majority or minority of the whole, who are united and actuated by some common impulse of passion, or of interest, adverse to the rights of other citizens, or to the permanent and aggregate interests of the community." Although he recognized that such groups could not be suppressed without abolishing liberty, he also argued in *Federalist* 51 that, in a large and diverse republic, narrow interests would balance each other out and be checked by majority rule. (See *Federalist* 10 and *Federalist* 51 in the Appendix.) Factions are not exactly the same as political parties, which form explicitly to win elections and which we examine in Chapter 9 (Political Parties), but Madison feared they could have the same divisive or polarizing effect in a democracy. Nevertheless, the Bill of Rights contains protections

interest group: *Group of citizens who share a common interest—a political opinion, religious or ideological belief, social goal, or economic objective—and try to influence public policy to benefit themselves.*

proactive group: *Group that forms when an enterprising individual sees an opening or opportunity to create the group for social, political, or economic purposes.*

reactive group: *Group that forms in response to a perceived threat from another group, or to fight a government policy those who join believe will adversely affect them, or in response to an unexpected external event.*

right of association: *Right to freely associate with others and form groups, protected by the First Amendment.*

faction: *Defined by Madison as any group that places its own interests above the aggregate interests of society.*

Do you think interest groups are divisive and polarizing? Or do you think they bring citizens together? Can you give examples to support your opinion?

right of petition: *Right to ask the government for assistance with a problem or to express opposition to a government policy, protected by the First Amendment.*

lobbying: *Act of trying to persuade elected officials to adopt a specific policy change or maintain the status quo.*

Have you ever signed a petition? What was it for?

for the rights of association and petition because these rights are essential for citizens to be able to hold their government accountable, ensure the responsiveness of elected officials, and participate equally in self-government.

The **right of petition** gives individuals with a claim against the government the right to ask for compensation, and it also includes the right to petition to ask for a policy change or to express opposition to a policy. It was the earliest and most basic gateway for citizens seeking to make government respond to them, and it has been used from the beginning of government under the Constitution. For example, in the First Congress, cotton growers asked the government for direct payment of subsidies to allow them to keep their farms in years with low crop yields. Owners of shipping companies petitioned Congress to limit the amount of goods that foreign ships could deliver to the United States so they could maximize their share of the carrying trade. Even the makers of molasses got together to ask the government to impose higher taxes on imported molasses so they would face less competition.[3] In the nineteenth century petitions were used for broader and more sweeping issues such as appeals to end slavery, to ban alcoholic beverages, and to secure the right to vote for women. In the twenty-first century the Internet has made it possible for individuals to directly "ask" Congress for a benefit via e-mail or to sign onto a "virtual" petition that can be presented to Congress. Interest groups also use their high membership numbers as a proxy for the direct expression of support that once came from petitioners' personal visits to lawmakers.

Granger Collection, New York

Citizens have been using their right to petition to influence government since the earliest days of the democracy. Here female lobbyists in the late nineteenth century are trying to persuade members of Congress in the Marble Room of the U.S. Capitol. Even though women did not yet have the right to vote, they still went to Washington to make their voices heard on issues that were important to them.

Today the rights of association and petition most often take the form of **lobbying**, or trying to persuade elected officials to adopt or reject a specific policy change. Lobbying is a legitimate form of petitioning, and interest groups of all sizes and purposes engage in it, from Students for Concealed Carry on Campus, to big corporations such as Microsoft and Google, to large-scale grassroots groups such as the Sierra Club. The term *lobbying* was coined over three hundred years ago when individuals seeking favors from the British government would pace the halls, or lobbies, of the Parliament building, waiting for a chance to speak with members. The practice was immediately adopted in the new United States. "Lobbyists have been at work from the earliest days of the Congress," explained the late Senator Robert C. Byrd (D-W.Va.), citing a 1795 Philadelphia newspaper describing lobbyists waiting outside Congress Hall to "give a hint to a Member, teaze or advise as may best suit."[4] Lobbying is well established as a means of political participation in America.

Interest groups lobby the legislative, executive, and even judicial branches of government at the state and federal levels. For example, when groups lobby Congress or state legislatures, they typically meet with members' staff aides to make the case for their policy goals. Lobbyists may also try to influence the executive branch by meeting personally with key bureaucrats and policy makers. Lobbying of the judicial branch takes the form of lawsuits against government policies that interest groups see as fundamentally unconstitutional or that go against the original intent of law. Such lawsuits can be high profile and are initiated by groups of all political ideologies. For example, cases orchestrated by the National Association for the Advancement of Colored People (NAACP) and other liberal interest groups ended school segregation (see Chapter 5, Civil Rights), and cases led by the Center for Individual Rights and other conservative interest groups challenged affirmative action (see Chapter 15, The Judiciary). For other cases, interest groups can also submit **amicus curiae briefs** ("friends of the court") that record their opinions even if they are not the primary legal participants in a case. Interest groups also lobby for and against judicial nominees, especially Supreme Court appointments. Lobbying strategies and tactics differ according to the branch of government at the state and federal levels, but no government entity is outside the scope of lobbyists' efforts.[5]

amicus curiae briefs: *Briefs filed by outside parties ("friends of the court") who have an interest in the outcome of a case.*

How did interest groups work to end slavery? How long did it take women's suffrage groups to accomplish their goal?

The History of Interest Groups

As the nation expanded its geographic borders, its population, and its economic base, government took on more responsibilities that affected individual lives. Issues that were once considered local became nationally important, and improvements in travel and communications enabled citizens with a national concern to band together. Slavery was the most divisive of these national issues, and citizens who opposed slavery formed the American Anti-Slavery Society in 1833. Soon many other groups were urging the abolition of slavery, creating the abolitionist movement. Abolitionists held rallies, distributed pamphlets, and collected signatures on petitions to persuade Americans, specifically members of Congress, to abolish slavery.

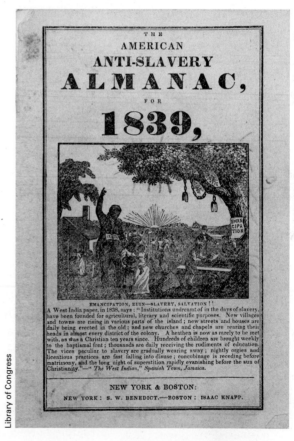

Library of Congress

Advocates for women's suffrage (the right to vote) paid close attention to antislavery efforts, seeing in them an example of the power of organization. In 1848 the women's suffrage movement was officially launched at Seneca Falls, New York, with a "Declaration of Sentiments" that used the language of the Declaration of Independence to state that all men and women were created equal and to argue that women should have the vote.[6] To the members of this group, the refusal to allow women to vote was a gate that stood in the way of true political equality among all citizens. The abolitionist and the women's movements paralleled each other in relying on the principle of equality as a rationale for supporting their policy goals.

Abolitionists used stark imagery and words to rally citizens against slavery. In 1843 Lydia Maria Child compiled *The American Anti-Slavery Almanac.* Its cover alone makes the case for abolition. Child was a writer and editor who was also active in the women's suffrage movement.

Later in the nineteenth century, as America industrialized, the business community began to strengthen its efforts to influence policy. Large trade associations formed, both regional and national. For example, the National Association of Wool Manufacturers was established in 1864 with approximately 123 wool-manufacturing firms as members. At its annual meeting in 1867 the group took credit for collecting vital information about its industry that could be used to influence trade policy: "a list of all persons known or believed to be engaged in the woolen manufacture," "statistics of the woolen machinery," "the amount and description of wool consumed, and the quantity and character of goods manufactured." This information, the wool manufacturers claimed, was "indispensable for wise and just legislation in matters affecting our own interests."[7] Previously, major wool manufacturers had tried individually to influence trade policy through their members of Congress, but they now recognized that consolidating their efforts would make them more powerful. Other large businesses, including sugar manufacturers, mining companies, and railroad owners, combined to form interest groups based on their common economic interests, and these groups gave wealthy owners of corporations a disproportionate influence over public policy.

Are groups representing manufacturers and corporations more or less powerful than citizens' interest groups? Do groups balance each other out?

By the mid-1880s other groups also organized to seek benefits from the government. Improvements in communication and transportation made it easier for large numbers of citizens who lived in different areas to become members of the same group. The Grand Army of the Republic (GAR), the first large-scale veterans' advocacy interest group,[8] successfully lobbied for pensions for those who had served in the Union Army in the Civil War, and those pension programs became the foundation of modern programs such as veterans' health care and educational benefits. The Anti-Saloon League of America, founded in 1895, sought **Prohibition**—the outlawing of the manufacture, sale, and consumption of alcoholic beverages. The league used a variety of tactics: It sought out candidates for elected office and asked them to sign petitions supporting Prohibition.[9] It set up a publishing company to print and distribute thousands of pamphlets. It collected signatures on petitions in support of Prohibition and organized marches in Washington, D.C., to publicly pressure Congress to support its cause. Largely in response to these efforts, Congress passed and the states ratified the Eighteenth Amendment, which banned the manufacture, sale, transportation, importation, or export of "intoxicating liquors." Enforcement proved difficult, however, and in light of widespread noncompliance and increased crime, groups such as the Association against the Prohibition Amendment and the Women's Moderation Union formed to lobby for repeal of Prohibition, which was accomplished by the Twenty-First Amendment in 1933.

Prohibition: *The Eighteenth Amendment, enacted in 1919, that banned the manufacture, sale, consumption, importation, and export of alcoholic beverages; repealed by the Twenty-First Amendment in 1933; also used to identify the time period the amendment was in effect.*

Evaluate Prohibition as an interest group–led reform. Did it represent a special interest or the people's interest?

To counteract the power of wealthy business corporations, workers organized to protect their interests, which were different from the interests of the people who owned industries but at the same time were interconnected with them. The International Ladies' Garment Workers' Union (ILGWU) is an instructive example. It was formed in 1900 by workers (mostly women) who assembled women's clothing. By 1910 workers in this industry had staged several strikes against employers to secure better working conditions. The turning point for the union came in 1911, when 141 workers died in a fire at the Triangle Shirtwaist Factory in New York City because they were trapped on the factory's upper floors. The fire escapes were inadequate, and the elevator was broken. Most of the victims were young immigrant women who needed this kind of work because it did not require English reading or writing skills.[10] Leaders of the union saw a chance to turn tragedy into accomplishment by expanding their membership and lobbying the government to force manufacturers to improve worker safety. In part due to their efforts, the Department of Labor was created as a separate cabinet-level department in 1913. It enforces mandatory standards for worker safety and oversees bargaining agreements between management and labor unions.[11]

Today business and trade associations, unions, citizens' organizations, and **grassroots movements** are a familiar part of the landscape of interest group politics. With the growth in the economy and in the size and scope of government in the American democracy, citizens have responded by forming more groups. The Chamber of Congress, the National Rifle Association (NRA), AARP (formerly known as the American Association of Retired Persons), and the Sierra Club have existed for more than fifty years. Each claims to have millions of members, and each has different policy goals. However, not all modern interest groups are national in scope, and some are newly formed, so it is difficult to know how many groups are in existence at any one time. In 2005 scholars estimated that approximately seven thousand groups were operating in the American political system.[12] Their methods of communication and persuasion may differ from those of the very first petitioners of Congress, but they share the common role of serving as a gateway through which the opinions of ordinary citizens are expressed to their elected officials.

Fotosearch/Getty Images

On March 25, 1911, New York City's worst factory fire took the lives of 141 workers. The workers, mostly young immigrant women, had been trapped on the top floors of a ten-story building on the city's Lower East Side. Afterward, family members came to the New York City morgue to identify the bodies.

Types of Interest Groups

Because the universe of interest groups is so large and diverse, it can be helpful to categorize groups by their core organizing purposes and the arenas in which they seek to influence public policy. In this section, we survey three types of interest groups—economic, ideological, and foreign policy–focused—to illustrate and explain differences in interest group policy goals and strategies.

Economic Interest Groups

Economic interest groups form to advance the economic status of their members and are defined by a specific set of financial or business concerns. Their membership bases tend to be exclusive because their purpose is to secure tangible economic benefits for themselves; if they grow too large or too inclusive, members' benefits are necessarily diluted. However, if the underlying industries represented by these groups disappear or merge with others, the groups have to adapt in order to attract new members.

grassroots movement: *Group that forms in response to an economic or political event, but does not focus on only one issue.*

economic interest group: *Group formed to advance the economic status of its members.*

What are the professional associations in the career field you are thinking of now? Are they worth joining?

Trade and Professional Associations.

Trade associations focus on particular businesses or industries and make up a subcategory of economic interest groups. Examples include the National Association of Manufacturers, the Chamber of Commerce, the National Retail Federation, and the Semiconductor Industry Association. Trade associations form because business owners believe that they will have more influence on the policy process collectively than they would individually.

Professional associations are formed by individuals who share similar jobs. Examples include the American Bar Association (lawyers), the American Medical Association (doctors), and the American International Automobile Dealers Association (car dealers). These associations are frequently responsible for setting guidelines for professional conduct—from business practices to personal ethics—and for collectively representing the members in the policy process.

Corporations.

Large corporations are a type of economic interest group in that they try to influence policy on their own as well as by joining trade associations comprising businesses with similar goals. Corporations such as Wal-Mart, Comcast, and Boeing have thousands of employees, and that alone encourages politicians to listen to their concerns.

Unions.

Unions are a type of economic interest group. A union comprises people who share a common type of employment. Unions seek safer working conditions and better wages for their members, and they are traditionally organized as local chapters that are part of a national organization. For example, autoworkers might join the United Auto Workers (UAW), truck drivers the International Brotherhood of Teamsters, television script writers the Screen Writers Guild, health care workers the Service Employees International Union, and high school teachers the National Educational Association.

The strength of a union as an economic group rests on the fact that workers who agree to unionize are agreeing to allow union leaders to bargain for them with their employers over wages and working conditions. This is known as collective bargaining, and it is protected by the **National Labor Relations Act**, passed by Congress in 1935. The act also provides that only one union can be selected to represent workers in a specific location, so that once a union successfully organizes a work location, those workers have to abide by that union's decisions.[13] The persuasive power of unions rests in their ability to call strikes, work stoppages that always decrease employers' profits. The mere threat of a strike is frequently enough to win benefits for workers who are represented by a union.

The biggest weakness that unions face is that when the industry they represent loses jobs, union membership shrinks, and the smaller the union, the less power it can exert on both manufacturers and elected officials. Following the Triangle fire, the ILGWU grew very powerful, but as the manufacture of women's clothing shifted overseas, thousands of jobs disappeared. By 1976 the union existed in name only and merged with the Amalgamated Clothing and Textile Workers Union (ACTWU), but even that merger could not save it. By 1996 it was officially extinct. The remaining workers in the garment industry joined with the larger group of hotel and service industry employees in the United States and Canada as part of the Union of Needletrades, Industrial, and Textile Employees (UNITE).[14] The once large and

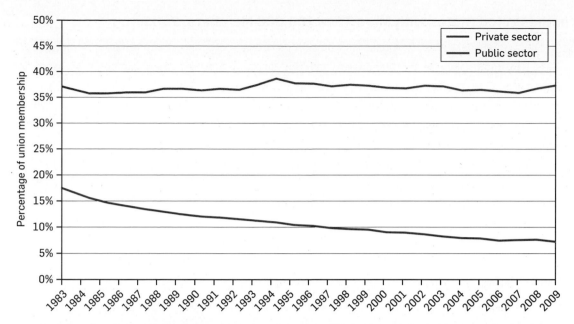

Note: Data refer to the sole or principal job of full- and part-time workers. All self-employed workers are excluded, regardless of whether or not their businesses are incorporated. Data for 1990–93 have been revised to reflect population controls from the 1990 census. Beginning in 2000 data reflect population controls from census 2000 and new industry and occupational classification systems. Beginning in 2000 private sector data refer to private sector wage and salary workers; private sector data for earlier years refer to private nonagricultural wage and salary workers.

FIGURE 8.1 Percentage of Wage and Salary Workers with Union Membership, 1983–2009. Private union membership has been declining over time, while public union membership has increased.
Source: Bureau of Labor Statistics based on Current Population Survey, www.bls.gov.

powerful United Steelworkers Union has suffered a similar decline as a result of financial difficulties in the American auto industry.

Overall, private sector union membership has been declining (see Figure 8.1). One effective response by unions to a declining traditional membership base is to seek to represent workers in other types of industries. For example, the UAW now represents cafeteria and janitorial staffs on campuses all over the nation. As do other interest groups, unions try to respond and adapt to changing external conditions.

Despite the recent downturn in membership in large industrial and manufacturing unions, unions representing teachers, health service workers, communications workers, and government employees have all made large gains over the past two decades. Table 8.1 lists the top thirty-eight unions in the country. Together, the top five unions have over 8 million members and, in total, the top thirty-eight unions, each with at least one hundred thousand members, have a combined membership of more than 17 million workers. Today, unions represent 12.3 percent of the overall workforce in the United States.[15]

Do you know any union members? Are you a union member, or would you join a union?

American unions are both economically and politically powerful because they can mobilize their members to vote for candidates they see as favorable on issues such as higher minimum wages, standards for overtime pay, better access to health care insurance, worker safety, and international trade agreements. In other nations, unions play important economic and political roles (see Other Places: Trade Unions in South Africa).

TABLE 8.1 Unions in the United States with More Than 100,000 Members, 2003

NEA—National Education Association	2,679,396
SEIU—Service Employees International Union	1,464,007
UFCW—United Food and Commercial Workers International Union	1,380,507
IBT—International Brotherhood of Teamsters	1,350,000
AFSCME—American Federation of State, County and Municipal Employees	1,350,000
LIUNA—Laborers' International Union of North America	840,180
AFT—American Federation of Teachers	770,090
IBEW—International Brotherhood of Electrical Workers	700,548
IAM—International Association of Machinists and Aerospace Workers	673,095
UAW—United Automobile, Aerospace and Agricultural Implement Workers of America	638,722
CWA—Communications Workers of America	557,136
USWA—United Steelworkers of America	532,234
UBC—United Brotherhood of Carpenters and Joiners of America	531,839
IUOE—International Union of Operating Engineers	390,388
NPMHU—National Postal Mail Handlers Union	388,480
UA—United Association of Journeymen and Apprentices of the Plumbing and Pipe Fitting Industry of the United States and Canada	325,914
NALC—National Association of Letter Carriers	294,315
APWU—American Postal Workers Union	292,901
PACE—Paper, Allied-Industrial, Chemical and Energy Workers International Union	274,464
IAFF—International Association of Fire Fighters	261,551
HERE—Hotel Employees and Restaurant Employees International Union	249,151
UNITE—Union of Needletrades, Industrial and Textile Employees	209,876
AFGE—American Federation of Government Employees	200,600
AGVA—American Guild of Variety Artists	182,597
UAN—United American Nurses	152,000
OPEIU—Office and Professional Employees International Union	150,882
SMW—Sheet Metal Workers International Association	148,378
BSORIW—International Association of Bridge, Structural, Ornamental and Reinforcing Iron Workers	130,928
IUPAT—International Union of Painters and Allied Trades	115,511
BCTGM—Bakery, Confectionery, Tobacco Workers, and Grain Millers International Union	114,618
TWU—Transportation Workers Union of America	110,000
AACSE—American Association of Classified School Employees	109,188
IATSE—International Alliance of Theatrical Stage Employees, Moving Picture Technicians, Artists and Allied Crafts of the United States and Canada	104,102
AFM—American Federation of Musicians of the United States and Canada	102,000
NRLCA—National Rural Letter Carriers' Association	101,810
BAC—International Union of Bricklayers and Allied Craftworkers	101,499
TCU—Transportation Communications International Union	101,228
UMWA—United Mine Workers of America	100,570

Source: Bureau of National Affairs, Directory of U.S. Labor Organizations, 2004 ed., www.workinglife.org.

⬤otherplaces

Trade Unions in South Africa

Unions play an important role in countries outside the United States. For example, in South Africa, a nation with a population of about 49 million, there are three major union federations: the Congress of South African Trade Unions (COSATU), the Federation of Unions of South Africa (FEDUSA), and the National Council of Trade Unions (NACTU). These three federations represent a total of 2.7 million workers, about 15.6 percent of the total workforce, in a varied set of industries.

Although unions have been active in South Africa for nearly sixty years, they were segregated under apartheid, a policy of oppression and racial segregation that governed the nation from 1948 to 1994. Under apartheid, union membership was restricted to whites, Indians, and colored (non-black). Consequently millions of black South Africans were not granted the same protections for working conditions as white workers.

As the political resistance to apartheid grew stronger in the 1980s, the international community pressured white South African leaders to eliminate racist policies and allow broader political participation. Union leaders and local organizers arranged protests and mini-strikes to undermine support for the apartheid regime. In 1994 the first free elections were established, and political and economic rights were granted to black South Africans. Nelson Mandela was elected president, the first black to hold the position, and his political party, the African National Congress, won control of the legislature. New laws were enacted that gave more bargaining power to unions, and the National Economic Development and Labour Council (NEDLAC) was created to negotiate labor disputes between management and workers.

The development of unions in South Africa shows how they can be powerful economically and politically. In advocating on behalf of their members, unions implicitly make the case for full political equality and participation. These arguments are advantageous for unions because their capacity for influence grows stronger with more members who can vote.

- **What two things did unions do to overturn apartheid in South Africa?**

- **How is political freedom connected to union power in South Africa?**

Sources: South Africa Info: Gateway to the Nation, "Trade Unions in South Africa," www.southafrica.info; Central Intelligence Agency, *The World Factbook: South Africa*, www.cia.gov. See also *Africana: The Encyclopedia of the African and African American Experience*, ed. Kwame Anthony Appiah and Henry Louis Gates Jr. (New York: Perseus Books, 1999), www.africanaencyclopedia.com.

© STR/Reuters/Corbis

Unions provide solidarity for workers and an opportunity to join together to encourage economic fairness and political participation. Here South African workers in the Congress of South Africa Trade Unions (COSATU) march together to celebrate Labor Day, wearing T-shirts to express their support for candidates from a specific political party.

Ideological and Issue-Oriented Groups

ideological interest groups: *Groups that form among citizens with the same beliefs about a specific issue.*

citizens' groups: *Groups that form to draw attention to purely public issues that affect all citizens equally.*

single-issue groups: *Groups that form to present one view on a highly salient issue that is intensely important to members, such as gun control or abortion.*

polarization: *Condition in which differences between parties and/or the public are so stark that disagreement breaks out, fueling attacks and controversy.*

How do ideological interest groups contribute to polarization?

Ideological interest groups form among citizens with the same beliefs about specific issues. We describe these groups as ideological rather than economic because economic benefits are not the primary basis for their existence. This category can include **citizens' groups** (Common Cause, Public Citizen), **single-issue groups** (National Rifle Association, Right to Life), and grassroots movement groups (MoveOn.org, National Organization for Women). Citizens' groups, sometimes called public interest groups, are typically formed to draw attention to public issues that affect all citizens equally, such as environmental protection, transparency in government, consumer product safety, ethics reform, and campaign finance reform. Single-issue groups form to present one view about a highly salient issue that is intensely important to its members, such as the right to carry a concealed weapon for members of Students for Concealed Carry on Campus. In contrast, broader organizations typically emerge in response to an economic or political event but do not focus solely on one issue. For example, MoveOn.org was founded by two wealthy men who were angry that President William Jefferson (Bill) Clinton (1993–2001) was impeached even though most people opposed the proceedings. MoveOn.org advocated for more responsive government and called for an end to the Iraq War during the George W. Bush administration (2001–2009).

Ideological groups provide a way for individual members to express their opinions on issues more forcefully than would be possible for any one person alone. Members of ideological groups benefit from knowing that others share their views and from feeling empowered. In this way, ideological groups can encourage political participation in a democratic society. At the same time, these groups contribute to the **polarization** of the American public. Because a group of this type gets its power from agreement within its ranks on a highly salient issue, it discourages debate and disagreement within the group and any type of compromise outside the group.

For example, on the controversial matter of third-trimester abortion, also called partial-birth abortion, which most Americans consider acceptable only if the mother's life or health is endangered, NARAL (formerly known as the National Abortion Rights Action League) takes the position that a woman has the right to terminate a pregnancy without limitations, whereas the Right to Life organization holds that all third-trimester abortions should be forbidden, regardless of the circumstances. Individual members in each group may hold more moderate views, but the leadership believes that any public compromise will alienate core members and diminish the group's status on the issue within the media and government. In this case, ideological groups not only balance each other out but also block the way forward. The intensity with which each side holds its position discourages cross-group dialogue and makes it harder for elected officials to achieve a reasonable and widely acceptable resolution of the issue. Because an interest group seeks a favorable government response on a narrowly defined issue important to it, the group can also create imbalances that verge on inequalities.

Foreign Policy Groups

foreign policy groups: *Groups founded to create support for favorable U.S. policies toward one or several foreign countries.*

Foreign policy groups form to generate support for favorable U.S. policies toward one or several foreign countries. One of the best-known organizations of this type is the American Israel Public Affairs Committee (AIPAC). This group seeks a strongly pro-Israel American foreign policy and uses public advocacy and member mobilization to influence members of Congress to support its goals. AIPAC first formed in the early 1950s, and it claims credit for getting the first aid package to Israel, $65 million dollars to help relocate Holocaust refugees, passed by Congress in 1951.[16] Today, AIPAC has more than one hundred thousand active members and is widely considered to be one of the most influential groups of its kind in Washington.

Other foreign policy groups focus attention on human rights violations or starvation in certain areas of the world. For example, the Coalition to Save Darfur was founded in 2004 in response to intense violence and famine in Darfur, a rural part of the African nation of Somalia. It was started by a small number of human rights groups that believed U.S. and U.N. intervention was necessary. In January 2006 the group launched a grassroots effort, using personal contact and the Internet, to have people send President George W. Bush 1 million postcards urging the United States to join with other countries to intervene in the region. In June 2006 the group reached its goal with the millionth postcard signed by then-Senator Hillary Rodham Clinton (D-N.Y.), who was appointed secretary of state in 2009.[17] Their efforts helped focus the attention of lawmakers and the media on the situation in Darfur. By the end of 2009 the situation in Darfur had stabilized, and the violence had ebbed; in response, the group changed its focus from stopping the violence to supporting "a vision for peace."[18] The Coalition to Save Darfur illustrates the power of an interest group to draw attention to a situation occurring in a foreign land and to solicit a powerful response from average citizens and elected officials alike.[19]

Should foreign countries or corporations be allowed to lobby the U.S. government? Why?

What Interest Groups Do

Interest groups perform a number of functions in the political process. They collect information about the implications of policy changes and convey that information to lawmakers and other policy makers. Their lobbying efforts aim to construct policies in ways that will most benefit their members. This section examines the tactics of lobbying, from providing information, to contributing to campaigns, to orchestrating grassroots movements that increase political participation on an issue. Lobbying is one of the fundamental gateways for expressing views and securing a favorable response from government officials.

Inform

All interest groups provide information to their members, the media, government officials, and the general public. The type of interest group dictates the kind of information it disseminates. For example, the Semiconductor Industry Association keeps its members up to date on the latest advances in technology in the United States and other countries. Before the Internet, groups provided members with this sort of information through newsletters and sessions at annual conventions. Today they disseminate information on their websites and try to limit access by requiring members to register and sign in to the websites.

Interest groups do more than merely report on current policy developments; they also provide members with interpretations of how the developments will affect their mission

When interest groups gather and disseminate information, are they performing a public service? Or do they do it just to advance their own causes? If so, is there anything wrong with that?

and goals. For example, when President Barack Obama's (2009–) climate change bill passed the House of Representatives on June 26, 2009, the executive director of the Sierra Club posted a letter to members on the group's website explaining the impact of the bill.[20] Even though Sierra Club members might be able to find information about how the bill's passage would affect environmental policy from other sources, it would take more time and effort to gather a complete picture. Interest groups see it as their responsibility to effectively package information to members in the most efficient and complete way possible.

Interest groups also work hard to inform government officials about the impact of specific public policies. Most of the time, lobbyists have pro or con positions on a policy proposal, and their goal is to persuade government officials to agree with their perspective. Legislators and government officials are generally knowledgeable in their areas of expertise, but the vast size of the federal and state governments makes it hard to know the impact of policies on every citizen. Economic and ideological groups constantly monitor policies that might affect their members in a positive or negative way and strive to make legislators and government officials aware of the impact of policy proposals. As the scholar Jeffrey Berry explains, groups and lobbyists must maintain their credibility by providing policy makers with accurate information about their members' opinions as well as accurate assessments of policy impacts.[21]

Groups convey information via e-mail, telephone, and personal meetings with staff, elected officials, and bureaucrats. For example, if a major elementary and secondary educational reauthorization bill, such as the No Child Left Behind bill, is before Congress, the National Education Association (NEA), a teachers' union, will want to make its position known by testifying at hearings. At the same time, the NEA will alert teachers across the country to contact their members of Congress about the specific ways the bill might impact their schools and school systems. The information that interest groups can provide is especially important when a policy has a narrow or regional impact; there is little chance that legislators who are not from the region will be aware of negative consequences for it unless interest groups inform them.

Lobby

Almost every kind of group with every kind of economic interest or political opinion—including business firms, trade and professional organizations, citizens' groups, labor unions, and universities and colleges—engages in one form of lobbying or another.[22] State, county, and city government officials maintain lobbying offices in Washington, D.C., both separately and as part of larger national groups like the National Governors Association, the United States Conference of Mayors, and the National Conference of State Legislatures. Lobbyists for these government entities frequently visit with the state's congressional delegation to keep the representatives informed about how federal programs are operating back home and to ask for legislation that will benefit their states. Mayors and county executives do the same thing, trying to influence their state legislators and governor by keeping them informed about how policies affect their constituents.

The Lobbyists. Groups can use their own employees as lobbyists or contract with firms that specialize in lobbying. According to the Center for Responsive Politics, in 2009

Because unions represent large numbers of workers, they can effectively stage marches and protests to get the attention of private companies, the public, and elected officials. Here nursing home workers from Ohio in the Service Employees International Union (SEIU) stage a protest at the Washington, D.C., headquarters of the company that owned their facility.

there were 13,739 individuals registered as active lobbyists in Washington, D.C. That amounts to nearly 26 lobbyists for each member of the House and Senate.[23] The offices of many of these lobbyists are concentrated in an area of northwest Washington known as the K Street corridor; when people say they work on K Street, it is safe to assume that they are lobbyists.

Although lobbyists are frequently stereotyped as representing only the narrow interests of their clients, they are typically individuals who have held public service jobs at some point in their careers. There are three common pathways to becoming a Washington lobbyist: working on Capitol Hill, working in the executive branch, or working on a political campaign. Lobbyists may start out on a political campaign for a congressional candidate, work in congressional office, and then leave to join a corporation, lobbying firm, or a law firm with a branch that lobbies on specific legal matters. Or lobbyists may start out as practicing attorneys, then go to work in Congress or the executive branch, and subsequently join a company or lobbying firm.

Why is the public perception of lobbyists so negative?

In 2009 interest groups and lobbying firms spent nearly $2.5 billion on a wide range of expenses associated with lobbying, including salaries for in-house lobbyists, consulting fees charged by lobbying firms, overhead for office space, and travel costs of staff (see Table 8.2).[24] In the past, the costs of lobbying also included paid trips for members of Congress and their staffs (known as junkets), as well as expensive meals. Lobbyists justified these expenses as a way of getting to know members of Congress in a smaller and more relaxed setting, which they claimed would enable them to enhance their or their client's influence in the policy process. In 2007 congressional ethics reforms prohibited paid trips and meals for members and

TABLE 8.2 Top Spenders on Lobbying, 2009

Large corporations and trade associations tend to be the biggest spenders for lobbying the federal government. The amount of money they spend varies based on the legislation being considered by Congress and the president.

Lobbying Client	Issues	Total Dollars Spent
U.S. Chamber of Commerce	Product liability, taxes, health care	$144,496,000
Exxon Mobil	Energy regulation, oil and gas drilling, gasoline taxes	$27,430,000
Pharmaceutical Research and Manufacturers of America	Prescription drug costs, health care research	$26,150,520
General Electric	Offshore production, taxes, environmental policy	$25,520,000
Pfizer	Prescription drug regulation, health care research	$24,619,268
Blue Cross/Blue Shield	Health insurance premiums, coverage	$23,225,439
AARP	Social Security and Medicare benefits	$21,010,000
American Medical Association	Health care reform, doctors' payments	$20,830,000

Source: Center for Responsive Politics, "Lobbying: Top Spenders, 2009", www.opensecrets.org.

staff.[25] Still, lobbyists can use money to maintain their influence in other ways. For example, their salaries typically include allocations to make strategic campaign contributions to members of Congress who preside over issues that are important to their companies or clients.[26]

During a typical day, lobbyists phone, e-mail, or meet with congressional staffers, their clients, and possibly members of the media to gather information about relevant issues for their clients or to promote their clients' policy positions. Lobbyists also attend congressional hearings, executive branch briefings, and even committee markups in which members of Congress write legislation. Interest groups, businesses, and industries do not survive by lobbying only, but lobbying is a natural outgrowth of their purpose, because members expect their leaders to advocate for them when it is necessary to do so.

Lobbying Strategies. Lobbying frequently involves a multipronged strategy. Groups usually try an inside lobbying strategy first, in which they deal directly with legislators and their staff to ask for a specific policy benefit or to try to stop a policy that they oppose. These insider meetings require access to policy makers, which typically comes about as a result of longtime interactions that build mutual trust. The key aspect of the inside strategy is to keep the policy request narrowly tailored to the group's needs because the broader the policy request, the more likely other groups will become involved in the negotiations, and complications can ensue. Either the policy request has to expand, so that each group gets a high level of benefits, or each group has to be satisfied with less, and few groups are ever satisfied with less. Nevertheless, if several groups share the same policy goals, they may form a temporary coalition, working together to improve their chances of success.

When an inside strategy does not work, groups adopt a more public or outside lobbying strategy by getting the press and their members more directly involved. A group may go straight to the press to provide details about the adverse effects of the proposal, hoping that the journalists will inform the general public. In this way, interest groups try to make use of the press's **watchdog** role over the government. For example, a nonprofit group called Citizens for Responsibility and Ethics in Washington consistently tries to get the press to focus on whether government officials are obeying ethics laws.[27] Early in 2009 this group was successful in launching an examination of President Obama's ethics rules for executive branch employees.

Michael Brown/Getty Images

The Coalition to Save Darfur is an interest group that mobilizes people to e-mail, call, or send letters to their legislators on behalf of its effort to end violence and famine in the Darfur region of the African nation of Somalia. In 2006 thousands joined a grassroots rally in New York City to express their support for sending United Nations troops to Darfur to help stop the violence there.

watchdog: *Role of the press in monitoring government actions.*

Through publicity and coordinated activities, groups also try to promote grassroots lobbying by encouraging action by their own members and the larger public. Energizing constituents in congressional districts used to be the work of regional offices. Today interest groups can generate citizen involvement through the Internet, asking that a message be sent by e-mail, text messaging, or cell phone. The Coalition to Save Darfur, for example, gets grassroots support by asking members to e-mail, call, or send letters to their local legislator as well as to others who might be sympathetic to their cause. In addition, marches and rallies show strength in numbers to elected officials and also generate publicity that can attract new people to join advocacy efforts. In these ways, groups directly give their membership a stronger voice in the policy-making process.

The core organizational purpose also helps shape a group's lobbying strategy. For example, economic groups typically adopt an insider lobbying strategy and limit their activity to key actors in Congress and the executive branch. The more specific a policy goal is, the less likely another group will rise in opposition, especially if efforts are kept very quiet. In contrast, citizens' groups typically adopt the outsider strategy to take advantage of the strength that comes from their large memberships. If they can mobilize their members to communicate to elected officials and simultaneously use the media to spread their message, they believe they will be successful.

Campaign Activities

Interest groups also promote their views by engaging in campaign activities, though federal law regulates their participation. Groups with tax-exempt status are prohibited from engaging in any activity on behalf of a candidate or party in an election campaign. These groups, commonly referred to as **501(c)(3) organizations**, after the section of the Internal Revenue

501(c)(3) organizations: *Tax-exempt groups that are prohibited from lobbying or campaigning for a party or candidate.*

Code that governs their activities, are likely to be charities, religious organizations, public service organizations, employee benefit groups, and fraternal societies, which are exempt from paying federal tax. Although they cannot engage in lobbying in any significant way, they can produce voter education guides or other nonpartisan educational materials that explain issues brought up during a political campaign and keep the public informed.[28]

Groups that fall outside the tax-exempt category are free to engage in lobbying and campaign activities. But to set boundaries between the group's core mission and politics, they generally create parallel organizations that make campaign contributions to legislators. These **political action committees (PACs)** raise funds to support electoral candidates and are subject to campaign finance laws (see Chapter 10, Elections and Campaigns). In one sense, PACs serve as gateways for expanding interest groups' political influence through financial involvement in campaigns.

PACs began growing in number and force after the Supreme Court's landmark decision *Buckley v. Valeo* (1976) upheld congressional limits on donations to campaigns.[29] As the costs of campaign spending rose over time, groups realized that creating or expanding an affiliated PAC to make campaign contributions could increase their influence over elected officials. Unaffiliated PACs, groups that make campaign contributions but are not associated with specific interest groups, also grew in size as a means of coordinating campaign contributions from individual citizens who wanted to express their campaign support as part of a larger group. All PACs make campaign contributions to the candidates whom they believe will be supportive of their policy goals (see Table 8.3). Thus PACs expand the reach of interest groups well beyond lobbying to include active engagement in the electoral arena.

Given the amount of money that PACs spend on campaign support, many observers have expressed concern that PACs exert a disproportionate influence over legislators, which creates an imbalance in government responsiveness toward some groups. However, scholars have had difficulty establishing exactly what PACs are getting for their money. Although campaign contributions can make it easier for groups to get access to legislators, they generally do not buy results. Interest groups tend to lobby and contribute to members of Congress who are leaning in their direction, so it is difficult to prove the impact of a campaign contribution.[30]

More generally, campaign finance laws impose limits on what interest groups can do in terms of **issue advocacy**, the practice of running advertisements or distributing literature on a policy issue rather than for a specific candidate. In general, the Supreme Court has ruled that campaign spending is a form of speech and that, as with other forms of speech, Congress must show a compelling interest before it can pass laws to regulate it. The McCain-Feingold Bipartisan Campaign Reform Act (2002) restricted corporations and unions from using television and radio ads for "electioneering communications"—commercials that refer to a candidate by name—within thirty days of a primary and sixty days of a general election. Since 2002 many groups have run ads that could be interpreted as issue advocacy or as outright campaigning. In 2007 in *Federal Election Commission v. Wisconsin Right to Life, Inc.*, the Supreme Court ruled that if a campaign advertisement could be reasonably viewed as issue based, it was protected under the guarantee of free speech and could not be prohibited under the McCain-Feingold Act.[31]

Running issue ads has become a regular feature of interest group activity, even in nonelection years. In the summer of 2009 a wide range of interest and industry groups, including the pharmaceutical industry, health care providers, and unions, began running ads in support of President Obama's health care reform proposals.[32] These ads were legal; they did not advocate

political action committees (PACs): *Groups formed to raise and contribute funds to support electoral candidates and that are subject to campaign finance laws.*

Should there be limits on how much money interest groups can contribute to campaigns? Why or why not?

issue advocacy: *Sponsoring advertisements (issue ads) or distributing literature on a policy issue, rather than for a specific candidate.*

TABLE 8.3 Top Twenty PAC Contributors, 2009-2010

PAC Name*	Total Amount	Percentage to Democrats	Percentage to Republicans
Honeywell International	$2,760,600	55%	45%
AT&T Inc.	$2,597,375	50%	50%
International Brotherhood of Electrical Workers	$2,561,123	98%	2%
National Beer Wholesalers Association	$2,244,500	56%	44%
American Association for Justice	$2,202,500	97%	3%
Operating Engineers Union	$2,109,300	89%	11%
American Bankers Association	$1,981,430	39%	61%
American Federation of State/County/Municipal Employees	$1,869,500	100%	0%
International Association of Fire Fighters	$1,843,500	83%	17%
National Association of Realtors	$1,818,298	58%	41%
Boeing Co.	$1,765,000	59%	41%
Teamsters Union	$1,732,910	98%	2%
American Crystal Sugar	$1,729,500	68%	32%
American Federation of Teachers	$1,682,250	100%	0%
Laborers Union	$1,670,000	96%	4%
Lockheed Martin	$1,657,950	58%	42%
Machinists/Aerospace Workers Union	$1,646,500	98%	2%
Credit Union National Association	$1,598,446	58%	42%
National Air Traffic Controllers Association	$1,594,900	83%	17%
Plumbers/Pipefitters Union	$1,554,075	96%	3%

Totals include subsidiaries and affiliated PACs, if any.

* For ease of identification, the names of the organizations connected with the PACs are listed, rather than the official PAC names.

Source: Center for Responsive Politics, www.opensecrets.org, based on data released by the Federal Election Commission, August 22, 2010.

the election or reelection of specific candidates, and they fell outside the time limit imposed by the McCain-Feingold Act. Although they served the purposes of interest groups, they also encouraged elected officials to be more responsive to constituents' needs because they focused attention on issues of importance to constituents. In 2010 the Supreme Court further extended protections to issue ads (see Supreme Court Cases: *Citizens United v. Federal Election Commission*).

Are issue ads fair or unfair? Are they informative or "disinformative"?

supremecourtcases

Citizens United v. Federal Election Commission (2010)

QUESTION: Can the government limit campaign spending by corporations and unions without violating First Amendment rights?

ORAL ARGUMENT: March 24, 2009, reargued September 9, 2009 (listen at www.oyez.org/cases/)

DECISION: January 21, 2010 (read at www.findlaw .com/casecode/supreme.html)

OUTCOME: No, governmental restrictions on corporate speech violate First Amendment rights (5–4).

In an attempt to equalize finances in political campaigns, Congress passed the Bipartisan Campaign Reform Act of 2002, also called the McCain-Feingold Act after its two leading sponsors. In 1976 the Supreme Court had upheld limits on what congressional campaigns could spend but struck down limits on what independent groups unaffiliated with the campaign could spend. In response, McCain-Feingold restricted corporations and unions from using television or radio ads for "electioneering communications"—commercials that refer to a candidate by name—within thirty days of a primary or sixty days of a general election.

While corporations are often for-profit operations, such as General Motors or Microsoft, nonprofit and political entities such as the NAACP also organize as corporations under the tax code. One such political organization is Citizens United, a conservative interest group "dedicated to restoring our government to citizen control." During the 2008 Democratic primary campaign, it released a documentary called

Hillary: The Movie, which was severely critical of Senator Clinton (D-N.Y.). Citizens United planned to show the documentary on pay-per-view television and to market it in advertisements on broadcast television. Concerned about violating McCain-Feingold, Citizens United sued the FEC, seeking an injunction prohibiting enforcement of the act as a violation of the First Amendment rights of corporations.

In a break with past decisions, the Supreme Court declared that corporations and unions had the same First Amendment rights as U.S. citizens. Using the compelling interest test (see Chapter 4, Civil Liberties), the Court ruled that Congress cannot disfavor certain subjects or different speakers. While recognizing that corporations may have more money to spend than individual citizens, the Court ruled that First Amendment protections do not depend on the speaker's "financial ability to engage in public discussion." Such limitations violate the marketplace of ideas that the First Amendment is designed to protect. The ruling left open the question of whether Congress could limit the speech rights of foreign corporations operating within the United States.

The dissenters claimed that money is not equivalent to speech and that the law was a reasonable attempt to level the playing field in campaigns. President Barack Obama attacked the decision in his State of the Union Address in February 2010.

- **Why is campaign spending a form of speech?**
- **Should corporations receive the same free speech protections as ordinary citizens?**

The Impact of Interest Groups on Democratic Processes

"I have often admired the extreme skill," wrote Tocqueville, "with which the inhabitants of the United States succeed in proposing a common object to the exertions of a great many men, and in inducing them voluntarily to pursue it."[33] Both Tocqueville and James Madison assumed that voluntary association or the forming of factions was a natural process of citizens interacting in a free society. Scholars have been interested in the same process, examining why interest groups form and what effects they have in a democratic society. In this section, we survey various perspectives on interest groups that relate to government responsiveness and citizen equality.

Natural Balance or Disproportionate Power

Over the last sixty years scholarly debate has centered on the process of interest group formation and its consequences. In the 1950s David Truman agreed with Tocqueville and Madison, describing interest group formation as natural. He observed that when individuals have interests in common, they naturally gravitate toward each other and form a group. So long as those individuals share a characteristic, opinion, or interest, the group continues to exist, but if the commonality disappears, the group disappears.[34] But Mancur Olson, writing in the mid-1960s, argued that merely having something in common with other people was not enough to give a group life and keep it going as an effective organization.[35] Olson focused on the costs of organizing and maintaining a group, and noted that costs increase as a group grows in size and reach. The people who pay membership dues expect benefits in return. To Olson, the cost-benefit structure that underlies group formation contradicts Truman's claim that all groups naturally form and sustain themselves.

The debate between Truman and Olson raises the fundamental issue of whether interest groups are natural and can compete on an equal basis, or artificial because they distort public policy in favor of some citizens over others. Other scholars have addressed this question in different ways. Robert Dahl argued that in a **pluralist** society, the battles over public policy by the varied interest groups that emerge to represent their members will produce a consensus that serves the public's common interest.[36] As noted in Chapter 1, scholars such as C. Wright Mills worried that a power elite controlled power in the American democracy.[37] His concerns were echoed by Theodore Lowi, who argued that in a democracy some voices are louder than others and that government is more responsive to louder voices and will consistently serve such groups at the expense of those who cannot make their voices heard. This kind of policy making is, according to Lowi, **elitist** and fundamentally antidemocratic.[38]

Traditionally, the narrow focus of interest groups has engendered a sense of illegitimacy. Interest groups form and survive by appealing to a particular segment of society (economic, ideological, or social), so they are inherently exclusive. Exclusive groups act only in the best interests of their members, even if nonmembers thereby lose out. E. E. Schattschneider described this aspect of interest groups as an actual threat to democracy. He argued that if interest groups are given legitimacy because they claim to represent citizens' interests, but in fact they seek narrow benefits for their members at the expense of nonmembers, there is an inherent unfairness to them. Moreover, citizens will be lulled into a false sense of security

pluralist: *View of democratic society in which interest groups compete over policy goals and elected officials are mediators of group conflict.*

Do you think interest groups form from the bottom up or from the top down?

elitist: *View of democratic society in which a select few interest groups shape policies in favor of a small group of wealthy or powerful citizens.*

What distinguishes a legitimate interest from an illegitimate interest?

about living in an "interest group society" because they believe that every interest group has an equal opportunity to be influential.[39]

There is a middle ground between these contrasting views. Given the approximately seven thousand registered groups in America today, it is clear that group formation is a natural outgrowth of the freedom to associate and of community life in which human beings share social, economic, and political goals. For example, citizens who care about environmental issues can form a local community group to plant public gardens or argue for energy efficiency at their workplace. On a larger scale, individuals can also join the Sierra Club, a multi-million-member organization that lobbies for domestic and global environmental protection. The interest group system provides multiple gateways through which individuals can see their views represented. Theoretically, because there are so many different interest groups, they balance each other, as Madison hoped they would.

special interests: *Set of groups seeking a particular benefit for themselves in the policy process.*

Do interest groups balance each other the way that Madison thought they would?

But if Olson is right and successful cost-benefit strategies determine whether a group can survive or grow, groups led by individuals with sufficient time and money stand a greater chance of winning a policy fight than do groups without such resources. In this view, interests become **special interests**, a term with negative connotations suggesting that some groups exert a disproportionate amount of power in interest group competition. To the extent that a well-funded interest group can more easily pressure the government to produce policies that are beneficial to its members, government responds unequally across all citizens. In this view, financial advantage creates an artificial imbalance of influence that acts as a gate against equality.

FLOW

FLOW is a non-profit organization dedicated to keeping the Olentangy River and its tributaries clean and safe for all to enjoy, through public education, volunteer activities, and coordination with local decision makers.

Northern End of Whetstone Island (at confluence of Adena Brook and the Olentangy) Fall 2002 © George C. Anderson

Take the Clean Water Pledge
Winter Newsletter: Looking Back on 2009 and Ahead to 2010

Take the example of MoveOn.org, which describes itself as a grassroots interest group but, as noted earlier, was founded by two very wealthy Internet entrepreneurs. MoveOn.org is a nonprofit, progressive, but nonpartisan organization that organizes a wide range of activities designed to inform average citizens and motivate them to participate more in the governing process. Its goals and mission sound very democratic, and joining the group requires little more than a click of a button on the Internet. For those who debate the merit of interest groups, the question is whether the public service mission of a group outweighs the fact that it is founded and run by a small, elite set of citizens.

Friends of the Lower Olentangy Watershed (FLOW) is a nonprofit organization in Columbus, Ohio. Many interest groups are local rather than national in focus.

Self-Service or Public Service

In assessing the relative power of interest groups in a democratic political system, it is essential to remember that interest groups do not pass or implement laws; they try to influence state and federal governments to enact their policy goals. To do so, they constantly interact with political parties, members of Congress, executive branch bureaucrats, and even the judicial system. The question of legitimacy of an interest group's activities comes when a victory for one group means a loss for another, or more broadly a loss for the general public.

For example, during most of the 1990s and 2000s, car manufacturers—acting alone and as part of their larger trade association, the American Association of Automobile Manufacturers—successfully lobbied to block efforts by environmental groups to secure an increase in government-mandated fuel efficiency standards. These standards, known by the general term *corporate average fuel economy* (CAFE), are designed to ensure that automobiles use as little fuel as possible to run efficiently. The government has an interest in requiring such efficiency in order to promote energy conservation more generally. However, automobile manufacturers argued that increased fuel efficiency is more expensive to produce and that CAFE standards would cut into their profits and might even decrease sales. In other words, the auto manufactures would pay the price for accomplishing the public goal of promoting energy conservation. On this issue, the self-interest of the auto manufacturers conflicted with that of the general public.

But by 2007, with high increases in fuel prices and a general increased awareness of global warming, President George W. Bush agreed to a modest increase in fuel efficiency standards. When President Obama took office in 2009, he reiterated support for those standards and put in a speedier timetable for their implementation. In 2010 the Environmental Protection Agency issued final regulations putting those tougher standards in place.[40] At the same time, an economic crisis hit the American automobile industry, undermining its financial and organizational ability to fight the increases. The case of CAFE standards is one example of how time and circumstances almost always shift the playing field and the balance of power in the interest group arena.

The frustrating aspect of the role that interest groups play in a democracy is that groups contesting a single issue frequently talk over each other, not with each other. As in the example of NARAL and Right to Life on abortion, compromise is difficult to achieve. It is often left to members of Congress and the executive branch to balance their own responses to interest group requests and still maintain responsiveness to constituents and the nation at large. Over time, most interest groups experience wins and losses in the policy system; the necessary condition for a democracy is that every group has a chance to make its case.

Open or Closed Routes of Influence

While it may be true that interests ultimately balance each other and that changing conditions ultimately level the playing field, the fact that a tightly knit group of specialists often controls policy areas raises concern about fairness both inside and outside interest group organizations. For example, lobbyists work to build good relationships with legislators and officials in the bureaucracy. Given their knowledge of particular policy areas, many of them move in and out of government. Are they always thinking of their groups' members when they engage in their activities, or are they thinking about their next job? Do they constitute an insider group that is ultimately self-serving rather than serving the public?

Scholars have long used the phrase **iron triangle** to describe the relationship among interest groups, members of Congress, and federal agencies. In essence, an iron triangle is a network forged by members in three categories that works to seal off access to public

Name two or three interest groups that you think have a lot of power in American politics. Do you agree or disagree with their positions?

iron triangle: *Insular and closed relationship among interest groups, members of Congress, and federal agencies.*

policy making. Lobbyists and interest groups want to maximize their benefits from federal programs; members of Congress want to maximize their power to shape the programs; and federal bureaucrats want to maximize their longevity as administrators of these programs.

Critics of the influence of interest groups in a democracy often describe iron triangles as unbreakable and argue that they contribute to the inefficiency of the federal government because they sustain programs that should be eliminated, or enlarge programs beyond what is necessary to meet their intended purposes. The criticism is not limited to scholars. In his farewell address in 1961, President Dwight D. Eisenhower (1953–61) warned of what he called the **military-industrial complex**, a self-serving interconnection among the U.S. military, the defense manufacturing industry, and federal agencies overseeing scientific research. Eisenhower was greatly concerned that the defense industry had undue influence that would be used to unnecessarily increase spending on defense programs. "This conjunction of an immense military establishment and a large arms industry is new in the American experience," he said. "The total influence—economic, political, even spiritual—is felt in every city, every State house, every office of the Federal government. We recognize the imperative need for this development. Yet we must not fail to comprehend its grave implications. Our toil, resources, and livelihood are all involved; so is the very structure of our society."[41] President Eisenhower's stature as a decorated general who commanded U.S. and Allied forces in World War II gave him credibility on the issue of defense spending, and his depiction of the military-industrial complex as a type of iron triangle drew a great deal of notice. By the 1970s the term *iron triangle* was applied to a wide range of issue areas beyond defense policy.[42] Forty years later it can be seen as operative in issues related to health care and prescription drugs (see Figure 8.2).

Yet the well-known interest group scholar Hugh Heclo claims that the interconnection of interest groups and the government is more benign, suggesting that the term **issue networks** is better than *iron triangle* to describe the relationship.[43] Heclo argues that interest groups, members of Congress, and bureaucrats all share information constantly, and that their interactions are open and transparent, not closed. Heclo wrote thirty years ago, before the advent of the 24-7 news cycle, Twitter messaging, and other telecommunications innovations, so it stands to reason that it is harder than ever for self-serving interconnections to go unnoticed. In addition, citizens' watchdog groups, such as Common Cause, and policy institutes, such as the Center for Responsive Politics, monitor interest group influence on government activities and policies. When these groups find evidence of wrongdoing in government, they loudly blow a whistle by issuing reports and holding press conferences to inform the media and the general public.

What remains true is that lobbyists, members of Congress and their staffs, and members of the executive branch do pass through what scholars describe as a **revolving door** of paid positions in one another's organizations, with knowledge and experience on a specific issue the valued commodity. The term *revolving door* has a negative connotation, suggesting that an iron triangle

military-industrial complex: *Self-serving interconnection among the U.S. military, the defense manufacturing industry, and federal agencies overseeing scientific research.*

Do you think the military-industrial complex exists today?

issue network: *View of the relationship among interest groups, members of Congress, and federal agencies as more fluid, open, and transparent than that described by the term iron triangle.*

How does government prevent corruption among government officials?

revolving door: *Movement of members of Congress, lobbyists, and executive branch employees into paid positions in each other's organizations.*

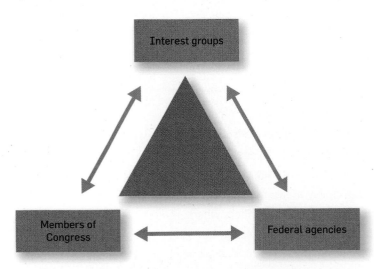

FIGURE 8.2 Iron Triangle. The iron triangle is a policy-making structure that includes congressional committees, federal agencies, and interest groups.

of influence consists of the same set of people moving from one branch of government to another and then to the private sector. The image of a revolving door also suggests that the system does not stop to include outsiders with new perspectives; in other words, it can act as a gate against wider political participation.

Take, for example, Representative Billy Tauzin (R-La.), who as chair of the Energy and Commerce Committee was instrumental in passing the Medicare Prescription Drug, Improvement, and Modernization Act in 2003. In 2005 Representative Tauzin left the House of Representatives to be named president of the Pharmaceutical Research and Manufacturers of America (PhRMA), a major beneficiary of that Medicare Prescription Drug bill. At the time, government watchdog groups were concerned about Representative Tauzin's behavior because he was in a position to provide disproportionate benefits to PhRMA in the Medicare bill, and PhRMA might have rewarded him for these benefits with a job when he left Congress. In 2009 Representative Tauzin led the negotiations on behalf of PhRMA with Democrats in Congress and President Barack Obama on health care reform, but the deal they worked out was subsequently abandoned. The board of PhRMA was displeased, and Tauzin resigned his position in June 2010. Although it was never proven that Tauzin was "bought" by the pharmaceutical industries, at the very least the revolving door creates the perception that members of Congress and the bureaucracy are improperly influenced by industries seeking preferential treatment in an issue area.

It is also essential to remember that not all relationships among lobbyists, members of Congress, and federal officials are tainted or suspicious. Congress and the federal bureaucracy each have elaborate rules governing their behavior with respect to interest groups and lobbyists, and most members and bureaucrats follow them closely.

AP Photo/Matt Slocum

Billy Tauzin
PhRMA President and CEO

In the iron triangle, a member of Congress can serve as chair of a key committee, write legislation, and then leave to head an organization that directly benefits from the legislation. For example, Billy Tauzin (R-La.) chaired a key House committee that wrote legislation for the Medicare Prescription Drug Improvement and Modernization Act, and then left Congress to head PhRMA, the interest group that represents drug manufacturers.

Characteristics of Successful Interest Groups

The measure of a successful interest group is how well it accomplishes its goals. Some groups want to stay in existence forever, but other groups form temporarily for a specific purpose, as did the Students for Concealed Carry on Campus, and disband once they accomplish their goal. For the groups that want to establish an enduring voice in a democracy, success can be measured in four ways: leadership accountability, membership stability, financial stability, and public influence.

Identify two interest groups with an enduring voice in American democracy.

Leadership Accountability

As anyone who has tried to get a group of students together to perform a task, lodge a protest, or plan an event knows, coordination can be difficult. It typically takes an individual who acts as an **interest group entrepreneur** to organize citizens into a formal group that agrees on a united purpose. In return for organizing the group, the interest group entrepreneur typically takes a leadership role in directing the group's activities.

interest group entrepreneurs: *Individuals who expend their own time, energy, and resources to form an interest group.*

There are benefits that come from being a group leader, ranging from salary as a paid staff member to prestige and extra influence over the group's goals and strategies. The well-known interest group scholar Robert Salisbury calls the trade-off between the work and the benefits of being a leader the "exchange theory of interest groups," and he argues that no one would rationally expend the energy and time to start a group if he or she could not take a prominent role in directing it.[44] Members are willing to pay their group leaders and give them power in the group in return for accomplishing the group's collective goals.

iron law of oligarchy: *Theory that leaders in any organization eventually behave in their own self-interest, even at the expense of rank-and-file members; the larger the organization, the greater the likelihood that the leader will behave this way.*

How do groups perpetuate themselves at the expense of their mission? Can you give an example?

Transparency about the group's political and financial activities in pursuit of its goals is an important democratic element of an interest group; without it, there is a risk that the leaders could act in ways that do not properly serve the members. Internally, an interest group owes it to the members to stay true to the mission. However, leaders do sometimes act in their own self-interest, by misusing group finances, for example, or they may take the group in an ideological direction that does not mirror the majority opinion in the group. More than a hundred years ago, Robert Michels coined the phrase **iron law of oligarchy** to describe this scenario, and he argued that larger interest groups were especially susceptible to unresponsive or abusive leadership. When leaders take such actions at the expense of rank-and-file members, the internal governance of the interest group breaks down. Flaws in interest group management can be a major problem for a democracy if citizens join a group with the expectation that the group will accurately represent their opinions and interests, and it does not.

Members must be able to register satisfaction or dissatisfaction with the group's leadership. Yet it is difficult for the average member to hold an interest group internally accountable. Some groups elect their leaders at annual conventions, but in order to vote, members have to spend time and money to attend those conventions, and few do. Other groups send ballots by mail or use the Internet, but casting a ballot takes time, as does obtaining information. A member can read about the group's activities on the group's website, but the group's leaders provide the content of that website, so it is not purely objective. All in all, the larger the organization, the more difficult it is for members to be sure they are being represented actively and honestly.

If interest group leaders do not act in good faith on behalf of their members, the legitimacy of the policies they promote can be called into question. Legitimacy is established by accountability. Interest groups must represent their members' needs and opinions accurately to encourage government officials to respond. Citizens have a right to expect accountability both from government officials and from interest group leaders.

Membership Stability

Whether a group is small or large, attracting members and keeping them over time are essential to its survival. People join groups because they share similar interests or political viewpoints or because they want to protect their economic livelihoods. For the leaders of groups, the challenge is to find the right balance between membership size and the organization's purpose. Too many members may create internal disagreements about policy goals, but too few may weaken the group's ability to exert influence in the policy system.

selective benefits: *Benefits offered exclusively to members of an interest group.*

material benefits: *Tangible benefits available only to members of a group, such as discounts and monthly magazines.*

Selective Benefits.   One way to attract and keep members is to provide benefits exclusive to members, which Olson labels **selective benefits**.[45] These can include **material benefits**, such as direct monetary benefits from policies that the group advocates, discounts on travel or prescriptions, and even monthly magazines. **Solidary benefits** are less tangible. They range from the simple pleasure of being surrounded by people with similar interests and perspectives to the networking benefits of interacting with people who share professional or personal concerns. **Expressive benefits** are the least tangible in that they consist of having a specific opinion expressed in the larger social or political sphere. When individuals join a group, they know that their viewpoint is being actively represented in the policy system, and that knowledge can be gratifying all by itself.

The Free Rider Problem.

Many of the benefits that large interest groups seek on behalf of their members—clean air by the Sierra Club, or gun rights by the National Rifle Association—are **public goods**. That is, they are available to all people, whether they have contributed toward the provision of that good or not. Public goods are typically the spillover effects of public policies that affect all citizens. If a group lobbies for public goods or collective benefits that are so widespread that members and nonmembers alike receive them, incentives to join the group disappear. Olson addressed this collective action dilemma, calling it the **free rider problem**.[46] Why pay to join a group if one can get the benefits for free? Why join if the group is so large that it does not actually need an additional member?

Tangible Benefits.

There is no easy answer to this question, so large interest groups take no chances with maintaining their members. The Sierra Club, for example, makes membership more attractive by providing material benefits like knapsacks and calendars. Additionally, by wearing a knapsack, a T-shirt, or a button with the name of the Sierra Club on it, a member is providing free advertising for the group. Similarly, the National Rifle Association provides members with magazine subscriptions and small life insurance policies. Whether a group is on the left side or right side of the political spectrum, as it grows larger and the public benefits it seeks become more widespread, it turns to providing tangible benefits as a necessary part of organizational maintenance.

Economic and Political Changes.

Changes in both the economy and the political environment can affect the stability of a group's membership. For economic groups, the size and number of people in a particular occupation can ebb and flow, affecting membership potential. The decline and disappearance of the ILGWU is an example of what can happen to union membership when an entire industry disappears. From a political standpoint, groups can "succeed" their way out of existence. The NAACP is an example: In the course of its hundred-year history it successfully fought discrimination and secured civil rights, and today it seems less urgently needed than it was in the past. In a sense, the election of Barack Obama as the first African American president and the selection of Eric Holder as the first African American attorney general are mixed blessings in that they are both the culmination of everything the organization has worked for and the undermining of its reason to exist. In recent years, the group has experienced leadership turmoil and a decline in membership, and it is currently reformulating its core mission to focus on multiracial human rights.[47]

The concern for interest group survival in an increasingly crowded interest group society can sometimes bring an interest group into conflict with its core principles. Groups can try to counteract declining membership by creating new issues to rally members around, or by portraying serious threats to the issues most important to members. These information campaigns

solidary benefits: *Benefits to members of a group that are intangible but come from interacting with people who share similar professional or personal interests.*

expressive benefits: *Benefits to interest group members of having a specific opinion expressed in the larger social or political sphere.*

Would you join an interest group for its material benefits? Its solidary benefits? Its expressive benefits? What would make you decide to join?

public goods: *Goods or benefits provided by government from which everyone benefits and from which no one can be excluded.*

free rider problem: *Problem faced by interest groups when a collective benefit they provide is so widespread and diffuse that members and nonmembers alike receive it, reducing the incentive for joining the group.*

Do you belong to a group in which some people do far more work than others to accomplish the group's goals?

Interest groups offer tangible benefits to individuals to encourage them to join. Some interest groups offer informational and networking benefits in addition to advocating for shared goals.

(sometimes called "disinformation campaigns") can activate members to contact their elected officials while reinforcing members' perceptions that they need the organization to protect their interests.

Financial Stability

Together with keeping a membership base, a group must also establish financial stability. Groups of all types require money to sustain their organizations, and they collect it from various sources, including membership dues, royalties on magazines and other publications, contributions from corporations and foundations, and outside contributions from nonmembers. Membership dues are funds that individuals or businesses pay to join the group. The price of membership in a group is typically tied to the group's organizing purpose. For example, a grassroots group that seeks to attract as many members as possible to support its cause, such as the National Rifle Association, keeps it dues relatively modest, between $25 to $150 a year. A smaller professional organization, such as the American Political Science Association (APSA), scales its membership fees according to salary and academic position; full professors, for example, contribute more than assistant professors, who usually earn less.

Second, groups find ways to make money by creating not-for-profit businesses within the organization. AARP is a classic example of a large interest group that wears two hats: a politically powerful lobby on policies that affect senior citizens, and a multimillion-dollar business that provides health insurance, life insurance, and discounts on movies, travel, and prescriptions to members, who have to be at least 50 years old to join. A basic AARP membership costs only $16 a year, and it provides the opportunity to purchase the other services at discounted rates. In turn, AARP receives payments from businesses that it contracts with to provide services to its members.[48] AARP is among the most successful large-scale interest groups in American history; in 2008 it claimed a membership of 40 million and took in over $249 million in membership dues.[49] Its size alone gives it power and influence; it ranks seventh out of all groups in the amount of money spent on lobbying in 2009 (see Table 8.2).

The financial challenge for many groups is to keep their operating costs in line with their expected income. For the very largest interest groups, such as AARP, a single year's operating budget can be over $1 billion.[50] For most other groups, the operating budget ranges from thousands to millions of dollars per year.[51] Groups can experience financial difficulty as a result of financial mismanagement by group leaders, or, in some cases, they may simply outlive their usefulness and members cease paying dues. In such cases, they may be forced to scale back their activities and close local chapter offices.

Imagine an AAYP, an American Association for Young People. What would it lobby for? What benefits would it offer?

Influence in the Public Sphere

The extent to which an interest group appears to influence public debate on an issue of concern to its members is another characteristic of success. There are several indicators of influence: being quoted in the press when a bill in the group's policy area is considered in Congress; being asked to testify before House and Senate committees during hearings on such a bill; drawing a comment from a member of Congress about a policy paper or issue brief that the group has written; being quoted during final debate on the bill on the chamber floor. Another public sign of influence occurs when the president or members of his cabinet meet with representatives of the group, and either the press or the group informs the public about the meeting. Each of these actions signals to the interest group's membership, as well as to the public at large, that the group has a significant role in policy formation on the issues that it is most concerned about.

Interest Groups and Public Policy: Immigration

Among the most contentious issues in the public policy sphere is the question of immigration reform. Immigration has fueled U.S. population growth since the nation's founding, and the United States now comprises citizens with ancestries from many different foreign lands. In 2008 there were 37,264,000 foreign-born people in the United States—12 percent of the total population. The largest percentage of foreign-born people come from Latin America (mostly Mexico), followed by people from Asia and then Europe.[52] Immigration laws serve simultaneously as gates to entry into the United States and as gateways to eventual citizenship.

The Legal Immigration Process

The legal immigration process is jointly administered by the U.S. Department of State and the U.S. Citizenship and Immigration Services (USCIS), an agency of the Department of Homeland Security. Immigrants seeking to come to the United States apply for visas, which are granted by the Department of State; once they arrive, their journey toward citizenship is overseen by USCIS.[53] To come to the United States with the intention of staying on a permanent basis, individuals can apply for a general immigration visa, a family relations visa, or an employment visa. The Immigration and Nationality Act of 1990 sets an annual limit of between 416,000 and 675,000 on these types of visas.[54] In addition, 50,000 visas are set aside for people born in countries that have recently had the lowest numbers of immigrants to the United States.[55]

green card: *Permanent resident card issued to eligible immigrants.*

To become a naturalized citizen, an immigrant must first apply to be a legal permanent resident (LPR) of the United States, a step known as getting a **green card**, which is the permanent resident card issued to those who are eligible. (The green card is no longer green, but the name has remained.) To get a green card, an individual must secure a sponsor who will attest that the individual has some means of financial support. The individual must also take a medical exam and secure proof of employment if he or she intends to hold a job in the United States. This last criterion can present a significant barrier to permanent residency: The federal government requires an individual seeking permanent residence to have talents or skills for a particular job that a current U.S. citizen could not provide. To become a fully naturalized U.S. citizen, a green card holder must reside in the United States continuously for at least five years; be able to read, write, and speak English; pass a citizenship test on the history and government of the United States (see Chapter 5); and pledge support for the United States.[56]

Because the number of immigration visas is limited, there is significant competition among interest groups representing people of various ethnic origins who seek to come to the United States. There is also competition between "old" and "new" immigrant groups. For example, the Ancient Order of Hibernians represents Irish Americans, who began large-scale immigration to the United States in the 1840s. In contrast, South Asian Americans Leading Together (SAALT) represents a newer immigrant group that includes Indians, Pakistanis, and Sri Lankans who came to the United States after 1965. In any battle over legal immigration policy, each group tries to construct grassroots lobbying campaigns that might give it an edge in influence. For example, in 2009 SAALT held a national summit that brought together students, professionals, and politicians to address issues of importance to South Asians living in the United States and abroad.[57] The purpose of the summit was to draw attention to immigration, civil rights, and housing issues that affect the South Asian community.

In contrast, groups such as NumbersUSA, founded in 1996 by Roy Beck, seek to limit legal immigration to the United States. NumbersUSA claims that the United States does not have the natural resources to sustain increased domestic population growth and increased immigration. Its organization makes it easy for likeminded individuals to e-mail or fax letters to a state or federal official directly through its website. All people have to do to join the group is register their name and address; there is no membership fee. The group relies on voluntary donations and foundation money to maintain its activities.[58]

The Debate over Illegal Immigration

Chapter 5 described the reasons for historical restrictions on immigration from certain countries. Today the drive to reform immigration laws stems from the number of individuals who enter the country illegally. The last major piece of legislation to deal specifically with illegal immigration was the 1986 Immigration Reform and Control Act, which granted amnesty, or forgiveness, to almost 2.8 million individuals who had entered the country illegally and wished to stay as legal residents.[59] Since then amnesty has been extended to specific groups of illegal residents from Latin America and Haiti, and amnesty is still available to anyone who was eligible under the 1986 law but has not yet filed for legal residence.

In the immigration debate, would you side with NumbersUSA or with interest groups representing immigrants?

Nevertheless, in the past two decades, an estimated 12 million more people have entered the United States illegally. In 2007 President George W. Bush and the Democratic Congress tried to produce a new immigration reform bill that would give illegal immigrants who are already in the United States an opportunity to become citizens but would, at the same time, discourage future illegal immigration. They failed to reach agreement, and the issue was featured prominently in the 2008 presidential election campaign. In 2010 President Obama signaled his intention to work with Congress to revisit immigration reform, but he and Congress failed to make significant progress on the issue.

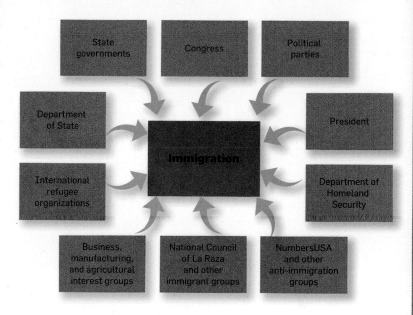

One position toward immigration reform holds that individuals who broke the law to enter the United States must be forced to return to their country of origin and apply for legal immigration status. Another position argues that individuals who arrived illegally but have since established productive lives should be legally incorporated into society and have the opportunity to be full and active citizens.

Interest groups align along both sides of the debate. Proponents of amnesty argue that giving illegal residents legal status would make it possible for them to earn fair wages, participate in politics, and pay taxes on their earnings. Without amnesty, proponents argue, families would be torn apart when parents whose children who were born in the United States and therefore are citizens are forced to leave the United States and might leave the children behind. One of the most vocal proponents of illegal immigration reform has been the National Council of La Raza (NCLR), founded in 1968. The largest Hispanic civil rights and advocacy organization in the nation, NCLR comprises local chapters as well as three hundred affiliated community-based organizations, and it claims to speak for millions of Hispanic residents in the United States. During the immigration reform debate, the group has relied on local chapters to organize marches and rallies across the country to express support for immigration reform legislation.[60]

Opponents of immigration reform argue that the previous amnesty program encouraged more people to enter the United States illegally and that a new bill would do the same. They also contend that illegal immigrants take away jobs from the legal resident population, because illegal immigrants are willing to work for lower wages and their employers do not pay Social Security tax on their earnings. During the most recent debate, NumbersUSA launched a campaign to stop immigration reform that generated close to a million faxed messages to members of Congress, though it had just 447,000 members at the time.[61]

What is your position on immigration reform?

There are strong sentiments on both sides of this debate. One could side with the National Council of La Raza and point out that this country was literally built by waves of immigrants from foreign lands, so to close the door on immigration is to reject one of the founding principles of the American democracy. Or one could side with NumbersUSA's policy positions holding that the laws of the land must be respected and that the modern United States cannot economically support a large influx of new immigrants every year. No matter which position one takes, actions by each group illustrate how grassroots movements enable individuals to get their opinions heard in the policy process. Ultimately it will be a major challenge for policy makers to construct a holistic immigration policy that is both fair and practical.

Why do so many people want to immigrate to the United States? Why do so few people decide to leave the United States?

Refugees and Political Asylum

The Department of State has two categories of special immigration status for individuals whose lives are at great risk in their homelands: refugee status and political asylum. Refugee status is granted when the U.S. government determines that individuals are at risk because of their race, religion, political views, or social, ethnic, or tribal group; refugees apply to enter the United States from their homeland or from another foreign nation.[62] Political asylum status is a narrower category involving individuals who are already in the United States and would face persecution if they returned to their homeland. After individuals are granted political asylum, they are treated like people with refugee status. In 2009 the United States resettled 74,654 refugees across forty-nine states and the District of Columbia.[63]

Interest groups, religious organizations, and charity groups play important roles in making the case that individuals deserve refugee status because of conditions in their homelands, and they subsequently assist refugees when they arrive in the United States. For example, the U.S. Committee for Refugees and Immigrants (USCRI) has worked for nearly a hundred years to help refugees navigate their new lives in the United States.[64] Such private organizations coordinate with the Office of Refugee Resettlement, an agency of the Department of Health and Human Services, to implement programs in local communities that assist with language, job training, health care, and other resettlement issues. Government efforts to grapple with legal and illegal patterns of immigration, as well as to deal with the millions of refugees caught up in foreign conflicts, have created an environment in which groups have worked harder than ever to elicit the political participation of their members on a grassroots level.

Through the use of mass media and advanced technology, groups can organize protest marches on a much larger scale than ever before. On March 21, 2010, Reform America staged a huge march on the National Mall in Washington, D.C., calling for immigration reform that includes a secure border strategy, expansion of the number of legal immigration visas, and amnesty for illegal immigrants currently in the United States.

Interest Groups and Democracy

Interest groups are a powerful instrument of democracy because they crystallize the opinions and interests of average citizens and present those views to elected officials during the policy-making process. It was precisely this power to influence policy that Madison feared so much, and why he hoped that in a large republic competition among interest groups would prevent any one of them from gaining too much influence. Interest groups contribute to a democracy by holding the government accountable for its actions, pressuring elected officials to be responsive to their constituents, and serving as a vehicle to equalize the influence of different groups of citizens in the policy process.

A group can channel the power of separate individuals into a single collective voice that is more likely to be heard throughout the policy system. Moreover, the very existence of an interest group can keep citizens informed about the direct impact of policy on their lives; with that information, constituents can better hold their elected officials accountable for those policies.

Interest groups engage in several methods to influence economic and social policy, including direct lobbying, media campaigns, legal challenges, and grassroots organizing. For example, when Congress was considering the health care reform bill in 2009–2010, groups such as the American Medical Association, the Health Insurance Association of America, and the Chamber of Commerce conveyed their opinions about regulation of doctors' fees, insurance coverage, and small business insurance premiums to members of Congress (see Chapter 12, Congress, for more details on health care reform).

In today's democracy, elected officials, bureaucrats, and even the judiciary often act as intermediaries in interest group conflict. In Congress, political parties adopt positions that are favored or opposed by specific interest groups and thus create alliances between parties and interest groups. Although there are more interest groups today than ever before, political parties serve as a counterweight to the influence of interest groups. As partisanship has grown stronger in the House, the Senate, and even the White House, members who are asked to choose between an interest group and a political party choose the party. However, given that political parties tend to align very closely with supportive interest groups, members do not have to make that choice very often. To the extent that interest groups can influence politicians to address narrow or exclusive interests to the detriment of what is best for all citizens, they can be viewed as a negative aspect of the U.S. democracy.

Yet interest groups also represent a positive aspect of democracy when they serve to express wide-ranging viewpoints, and they continue to be an effective way of giving voice to citizens' needs and concerns. Interest groups continuously win and lose within the American policy-making system, and they reinvent their lobbying strategies in response to changing political and economic conditions. However, sole reliance on interest groups as a means of citizen participation is dangerous, because some groups have more resources—time, money, and membership—than others and consequently win more often. In this way, interest groups can be both gateways and gates to citizen equality and the securing of policy benefits. Ultimately, citizens must hold both their interest group leaders and their elected officials accountable for public policy outcomes.

FOCUS QUESTIONS

- How do interest groups influence economic and social policy?

- How do interest groups help or hinder government responsiveness to all citizens in an equal and fair way?

- Are interest groups themselves democratic organizations? Are their leaders accountable to their members? Explain.

- Do interest groups balance each other out across income levels, regions, and ethnic backgrounds? Explain and give examples.

- Are interest groups gates or gateways to democracy?

GATEWAYS TO LEARNING

Top Ten to Take Away

1. Interest groups are groups of citizens who share a common interest—political opinions, religious affiliations, ideological beliefs, social goals, or economic objectives—that try to influence public policy to benefit their members. (pp. 246–47)

2. The constitutional basis for interest groups lies in the First Amendment, which guarantees both the right to assemble and the right to petition the government for redress of grievances. (pp. 247–49)

3. Individuals and interest groups have lobbied legislators from the nation's earliest days, and their numbers have vastly increased. Today groups also lobby executive branch officials and attempt to influence judicial appointments and the courts through lawsuits and *amicus curiae* briefs. (pp. 249–51)

4. Interest groups can be categorized as economic, ideological, and foreign policy, and each has different policy goals and strategies. (pp. 251–57)

5. Generally, interest groups gather and disseminate information in their issue areas, lobby using various strategies, and contribute to political campaigns and advertising to the extent that federal law allows. (pp. 257–64)

6. Scholars who study why interest groups form and their effects in a democratic society debate whether the wealthy have disproportionate power to use interest groups to their advantage, and so to the disadvantage of others. Scholars also debate whether interest groups balance each other out. (pp. 265–67)

7. Lobbyists, federal regulators, and members of Congress form networks that some describe as "iron" and closed to citizen influence, and some describe as transparent and open to citizen influence. (pp. 267–69)

8. Issue networks can tend or appear to be self-serving when members of Congress and federal agency employees leave their jobs to become lobbyists in the issue area of their specialty. (pp. 266–69)

9. The success of interest groups can be measured in four ways: leadership accountability, membership stability, financial stability, and public influence. (pp. 269–273)

10. In today's democracy, elected officials, bureaucrats, and even the judiciary often act as intermediaries in interest group conflict. (pp. 276–77)

A full narrative summary of the chapter is on the book's website.

Ten to Test Yourself

1. What is an interest group?

2. What is an interest group entrepreneur?

3. What is the role of interest groups in American government and society?

4. Compare and contrast interest groups, factions, political parties, special interests, and movements.

5. Identify the three types of interest groups in terms of their core organizational purpose.

6. What do lobbyists do?

7. What campaign activities can interest groups engage in? What are the limits?

8. What is the free rider problem, and how do interest groups solve it?

9. Compare and contrast iron triangles and issue networks.

10. Describe interest group pressures on immigration policy.

More review questions and answers and chapter quizzes are on the book's website.

Timeline to Keep Things in Order

First Amendment protects the right to assemble and to petition government.

American Anti-Slavery Society is the first of many groups opposing slavery.

Women's rights meeting in Seneca Falls, New York, initiates a movement for women's suffrage.

Anti-Saloon League begins its campaign to outlaw liquor.

International Ladies' Garment Workers' Union represents workers who sew and assemble women's clothing.

1791   1833   1848   1895   1900

Terms to Know and Use

amicus curiae briefs (p. 249)

citizens' groups (p. 256)

economic interest group (p. 251)

elitist (p. 265)

expressive benefits (p. 271)

faction (p. 247)

501(c)(3) organizations (p. 261)

foreign policy groups (p. 256)

free rider problem (p. 271)

grassroots movement (p. 251)

green card (p. 274)

ideological interest groups (p. 256)

interest group (p. 247)

interest group entrepreneurs (p. 269)

iron law of oligarchy (p. 270)

iron triangle (p. 267)

issue advocacy (p. 262)

issue network (p. 268)

lobbying (p. 248)

material benefits (p. 270)

military-industrial complex (p. 268)

National Labor Relations Act (p. 252)

pluralist (p. 265)

polarization (p. 256)

political action committees (PACs) (p. 262)

proactive group (p. 247)

professional associations (p. 252)

Prohibition (p. 250)

public goods (p. 271)

reactive group (p. 247)

revolving door (p. 268)

right of association (p. 247)

right of petition (p. 248)

selective benefits (p. 270)

single-issue groups (p. 256)

solidarity benefits (p. 271)

special interests (p. 266)

trade associations (p. 252)

unions (p. 252)

watchdog (p. 261)

Use the vocabulary flash cards on the book's website.

Learning That Works

WHAT YOU NEED . . .

TO KNOW

What interest groups are

Why interest groups form

What interest groups do

How interest groups work

How much interest groups spend

How interest groups influence policy

TO DO

Choose to join one, or recognize that a group you already belong to is an interest group

Assess whether they distort or amplify citizen participation

Decide whether their effect on democracy is positive, negative, or both

Evaluate whether lobbying is legitimate in a democracy

Begin to judge whether money has too much influence in policy making

Understand why it has been difficult to develop a coherent immigration policy

1911 — Deaths in Triangle Shirtwaist Factory fire in New York prompt government to issue standards for worker safety.

1935 — National Labor Relations Act recognizes the right of unions to engage in collective bargaining.

2002 — McCain-Feingold reform limits certain interest group activities in campaigns.

2007 — Supreme Court strikes down some limits on interest group issue ads in campaigns in *FEC v. Wisconsin Right to Life*.

2010 — Supreme Court strikes down remaining limits on interest group issue ads in campaigns in *Citizens United v. FEC*.

9 POLITICAL PARTIES

Furman University, Greenville,
South Carolina

> *Self-government is not an easy thing to do. It requires a lot from citizens. . . . I believe it is my obligation, not a choice, to be informed about my local, state, and national government.*

Josh McKoon, elected to the Georgia Senate in 2010, credits his experience at Furman University in Greenville, South Carolina, for launching "his lifetime commitment to conservative politics." As a political science and communications major, he volunteered on Republican Bob Dole's 1996 presidential campaign and worked for both a state representative running for Congress and a U.S. congressman running for the Senate. His wealth of campaign experience was one reason he was elected president of the College Republicans chapter at Furman. McKoon maintains that his time at Furman allowed him to become plugged into the Republican network. "I learned very early," he said in a phone interview, "that it is 90 percent about who you know, and making those contacts with the right individuals."

In 1999 McKoon met George W. Bush, the governor of Texas who was running for president. By making contacts with Bush's campaign team, McKoon landed a job as a director of field operations on Bush's primary campaign in South Carolina. As a field director, he coordinated campaign activities with Bush supporters at Clemson and Furman universities and built volunteer networks that facilitated Bush's get-out-the-vote efforts. When Bush won the primary, McKoon organized the victory rally on Furman's campus.

After completing law school, McKoon headed back to Columbus, the Georgia city where he was born, and reconnected with the Muscogee County Republican Party. Using his networking and leadership skills, he started a Young Republicans chapter, and by 2007 he had risen to party chair.

Because the goal of any party chair is to get more party members elected to public office, McKoon sought to get more Republicans involved in state and local government using a three-pronged approach. First, he worked to expand grassroots campaign operations throughout Muscogee County to give Republican challengers

Josh McKoon ▶

Courtesy of Josh McKoon

© Nathan Guim Photography

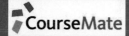 **Course**Mate

Visit http://www.cengagebrain.com/shop/ISBN/0618906959 for interactive tools including:

- Quizzes
- Flashcards
- Videos
- Animated PowerPoint slides, Podcast summaries, and more

the capacity to wage better campaigns. To that end, he created an executive director position to lead Republican committee outreach efforts. Second, he tried to recruit more viable Republican candidates with the talent and qualifications to challenge incumbent Democrats in the Georgia statehouse. Third, he used his fundraising skills to fill the party coffers to support local races. As it turned out, McKoon became one of the Republican candidates himself, running to represent the 29th district in the state senate. His fundraising skills came in handy; as early as April 2010 he had raised nearly $200,000 for his state senate campaign. He had also generated a great deal of volunteer support from college students. One of them, Theresa Garcia, was quoted in a local newspaper as saying that she got involved "because of Josh's concerns about issues folks my age are concerned about. . . . Josh is concerned about jobs—and jobs are on everybody's minds. Will there be jobs when we graduate? . . . . We want to see Josh in the state Senate because he is not far removed from us." Josh McKoon's campaign provided an opportunity for students to participate in politics and to support someone young enough to relate to and respond to their needs.

McKoon calls the Republican Party his "gateway." "In Columbus as a high school student and as an attorney," he says, "in Tuscaloosa as a law student, and in Greenville as a college student, the Republican Party offered me an access point to candidates, campaigns, and political experiences." At age 31, he built on these experiences and put them to the test by taking a successful leap into electoral politics.[1]

Political parties offer every citizen in America the opportunity to participate in politics and even to run for elected office. In this chapter, we look at the role of political parties in the American constitutional system by examining what they do, how they formed and evolved over time, and what role they play in shaping electoral choices for candidates and voters alike.

FOCUS QUESTIONS

- How do political parties shape the choices voters face in local, state, and federal elections?

- In what ways do political parties allow voters to hold their elected officials accountable for the policies they produce?

- How do political parties respond to changes in public opinion on key issues?

- Do political parties enable all citizens to participate equally in self-government, or do they help give more power to some people, and less to others? Explain.

- Are political parties a gate or a gateway to democracy?

The Role of Political Parties in American Democracy

A democratic government must be responsive to its citizens, and for government to be equally responsive, every citizen must have an equal opportunity to influence it. But mobilizing the more than 308 million people in the United States to take an active role in monitoring their government is a truly momentous challenge. In the United States, political parties fill an essential need by shaping the choices that voters face in elections, which serve as the key mechanism by which voters hold their government accountable. With so many public offices to fill, voters need some sort of road map to compare candidates and make the choices that will serve their best interests. The potential danger of relying on parties to shape these choices is that parties become interested only in winning office, not in serving the interests of the people. It takes action and vigilance on the part of voters to ensure that parties do not go in this direction.

In this section, we look at the role that parties play in the American democratic system, specifically at the way they organize the electorate, shape the elections that determine whether their candidates win office, and guide the actions of elected officials.

What Are Political Parties?

A **political party** is a group of individuals who join together to choose candidates for elected office—whether by informal group voting or a formal nominating process. These candidates agree to abide by the **party platform**, a document that lays out the party's core beliefs and policy proposals. Parties operate through national, state, and county committees; members include party activists, citizen volunteers, and elected officials. A party's main purpose is to win elections in order to control governmental power and implement its policies.

At the national level, the party issues its platform during presidential election years (see Table 9.1). In their 2008 platforms, for example, the Republican Party and the Democratic Party stated their positions on national security, health care, environment, and taxes. These platforms not only define the positions of the presidential and vice presidential candidates but also serve as a general guide to the policy positions of all the candidates running under the party label. From time to time, individual candidates may disagree with elements of the party's platform, but in general, candidates who choose to run under a party label are defined by it. Using party labels as a shortcut for the party platform, voters can hold the elected officials accountable for their policy successes, and blame them for policy failures.

Citizens tend to vote for one party over the other in somewhat predictable patterns. Classic political scientists, such as V. O. Key, use the term **party in the electorate** to describe the general patterns of voters' party identification and their behavior on election day. A main goal of any political party is to maximize party affiliation among voters so that it translates into a solid majority of the party in the electorate, which can in turn translate to a solid majority of the **party in government**. To accomplish this goal, the **party as an organization** is created, with internal structures that guide how the party functions. [2] The modern American political party is multilevel, with committees at the federal, state, and local levels.

political parties: *Broad coalitions of individuals organized to win elections in order to enact a commonly supported set of public policies.*

party platform: *Document that lays out a party's core beliefs and policy proposals for each presidential election.*

party in the electorate: *Percentage of voters who are likely to choose a party's candidates in an election.*

party in government: *Members of government who share the same party affiliation and work together to accomplish the party's electoral and policy goals.*

party as an organization: *Internal structure of a political party at the county, city, state, and federal levels.*

What Political Parties Do

In this section, we move from theoretical ideas about political parties to what they actually do in the American political system.

Parties in the Electorate. Parties offer several layers of opportunity for political participation. Most simply, a person can claim to be a member of a party simply by stating that he or she identifies with it, for example, by saying "I am a Republican." That statement is an acknowledgment of **party identification**—an attachment or allegiance to a political party. Voters identify with parties for several reasons. The simplest is the belief that the policies put forth by one party will serve their interests better than the policies proposed by other parties in the political arena. Another reason to join a party stems from family or social environment, in which being a member of a party is similar to other personal characteristics. As Chapter 6 (Public Opinion) explains, many young people adopt the party identification of their parents. Although parties always ask for contributions, there are no membership fees. For this reason, parties provide the broadest and most open gateway to participation in American politics.

Which political party do you identify with?

party identification: *Attachment or allegiance to a political party; partisanship.*

In what ways are parties gateways for citizen participation? As you read this chapter, look for evidence.

TABLE 9.1 Democratic Party Platform Meetings, 2008

The Democratic Party's 2008 platform was named "Listening to America: The Democratic Platform for Change," and it was put together at 1,645 platform meetings held in all fifty states, plus the District of Columbia, Puerto Rico, and the Virgin Islands. Between July 15 and August 8 more than thirty thousand Democrats assembled to present and discuss ideas. The list below is a sampling of the places and the topics.

State and City	Date	Platform Meeting
Alabama, Toney	July 18	Small-town Alabama issues
Arizona, Phoenix	July 15	LGBTQ community Democratic Party platform
Colorado, Colorado Springs	July 21	Planks for environment and climate change policy
Florida, Jacksonville	July 12	Health care, an American crisis
Hawaii, Honolulu	July 26	Native Hawaiian and Democratic Party of Hawaii platform input to platform for change
Illinois, Chicago	July 24	Urban policy in America
Kansas, Stilwell	July 19	Opportunity to be part of change
Maine, Vinalhaven	July 26	For islanders
Maryland, Baltimore	July 24	Platform meeting: at-risk and homeless youth
Michigan, Sault Sainte Marie	July 16	Peacenik tree-huggers for Obama
Mississippi, Jackson	July 25	Praying for Godly leadership
Nebraska, Lincoln	July 27	Women's issues: platform meeting for change
Nevada, Las Vegas	July 20	Armenians for Obama
New Jersey, Paterson	July 21	Artists-4-Obama
New Mexico, Albuquerque	July 26	Law and science for the future
New York, Brooklyn	July 23	Educators for Obama
North Carolina, Wilson	July 22	Wilson Labor Council platform meeting
Ohio, Brooklyn	July 25	Pro-life Democrats
Oregon, Myrtle Point	July 18	Rural retirees for Obama
Pennsylvania, Levittown	July 16	The economy and the national debt
South Carolina, Columbia	July 22	Mental health care
Texas, Austin	July 18	Space policy platform meeting
Virgin Islands, Christiansted	July 26	Virgin Islands platform for change: bringing in the sunlight
West Virginia, Charleston	July 24	Focus on social issues
Wisconsin, Fond du Lac	July 28	Veteran's for Obama platform meeting

Source: Democratic National Committee and the Obama for America presidential campaign, www.democrats.org.

voter registration: *Enrollment required prior to voting to establish eligibility.*

A more formal step of party identification is stating party affiliation when registering to vote. **Voter registration** rules vary by state, but they typically require a citizen to show proof of identity and address to an official government office. In some places voters can register by mail or when they get their driver's licenses, but in others they must fill out the forms in person at a local board of elections.

At the next level of participation, voters can become active in the party at the town, county, state, and federal level. Parties encourage people to volunteer on campaigns at every level—making phone calls to prospective voters, passing out bumper stickers, or maintaining e-mail contact through the campaign website. Of course, political parties expect their members to vote on election day, and to bring their friends, coworkers, and family members to the polls with them. Parties also rely on supporters to build up the organization and candidates by making financial contributions.

Political parties also serve as a gateway to elected office. Josh McKoon, for example, got his start in politics through volunteer work with a local party on a campaign, and then he ran for the Georgia Senate. Many candidates who seek public office start out by affiliating with a party in college and rise through the ranks of party organizations, as McKoon did. Parties also actively recruit individuals in their county, district, or state to run for elected office. Candidate recruitment involves party leaders at all levels trying to identify people who will make good candidates for elected office, because they are well known in the community, have personal wealth, or have a professional record that speaks to current issues and would appeal to voters. For example, during a period of intense discussion of health care reform, a doctor might be a good candidate for office. Finding good candidates to run for office takes up a great deal of party leaders' time because it involves meeting with potential candidates repeatedly and vetting their backgrounds.

Parties in Government.

Parties also serve to organize members of Congress and state legislatures into cohesive groups, known as **party caucuses**, that consistently vote, year after year, for the policies that the parties promise in their platforms. The party in government is made up of the elected officials who share the same party affiliation and work together to accomplish the party's electoral and policy goals. Elected officials often hold positions in party organizations as well. For example, Tim Kaine, Democratic governor of Virginia from 2006 to 2010, served as chair of the national Democratic Party during his last two years in office. Even the president, whose primary responsibility is to govern, is expected to serve as leader of his political party by setting the agenda according to party policy goals. The president is also increasingly expected to engage in political support for party candidates, from campaign appearances to party fundraisers.

Party Organization.

The modern political party is structured as a multilevel organization with units at the federal, state, and local levels. **National committees** are at the top of the party organization, and their members are chosen by each state party organization (see Figure 9.1). A new president can select the national committee chair; in the case of the presidential "out" party, the national committee itself elects the party chair. The national committee is responsible for running the party's presidential nominating convention every four years. Key to that effort is overseeing the states' primary delegate selection process and officially recognizing a state's delegation at the convention.

The main job of the national committee is to do everything possible to elect the party's presidential nominee every four years, and that requires strengthening all party organizations, from the national down to the local levels. The national committee runs training

Have you formally affiliated with a political party? What are the advantages and the disadvantages of doing so?

party caucus: *Group of party members in a legislature.*

national committee: *Top level of national political parties; coordinates national presidential campaigns.*

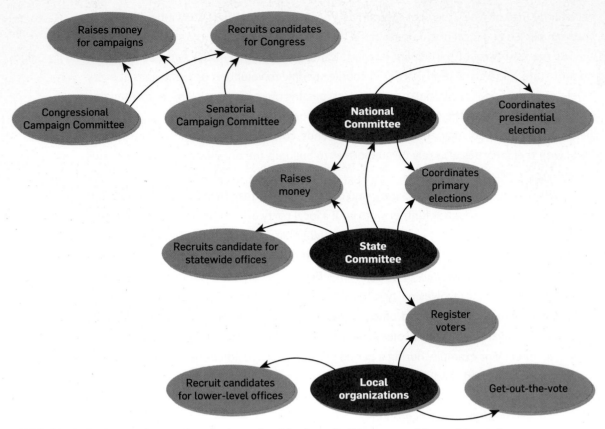

FIGURE 9.1 Party Organization at the National, State, and Local Levels.

workshops on party-centered activities like candidate recruitment and fundraising. It has to raise money; for example, in the 2008 presidential campaign the Democratic National Committee raised $260 million and the Republican National Committee raised $428 million.[3] The national party can spend its money on coordinated expenditures, that is, in cooperation with the presidential campaign, and it can make independent expenditures, which are funds spent separately on general efforts to increase voter turnout for the party's nominee.

Each major political party has a committee dedicated to raising money for **incumbent** House and Senate members. For the Democrats it is the Democratic Congressional Campaign Committee and the Democratic Senatorial Campaign Committee, and for the Republicans, the National Republican Congressional Committee and the National Republican Senatorial Committee. These congressional party committees are also responsible for recruiting qualified challengers to run for seats held by the opposing party and helping to fund their campaigns. The four congressional party organizations raised a combined $529.7 million in the 2005–2006 electoral cycle, and $551 million in the 2007–2008 electoral cycle.[4]

State political parties are the next level of party organization, and they are regulated by state law, so their responsibilities can vary by state. Typically a political party has a **state central committee** that tries to elect candidates to statewide office and also works with local organizations to recruit new voters and raise money. Each state party organization has its own website, which displays the structure of the state party organization and provides information about how to become involved with the party.

incumbent: *Occupant of elected office.*

state central committee: *Top level of state political parties; helps recruit and raise money for statewide candidates and drafts state party policies.*

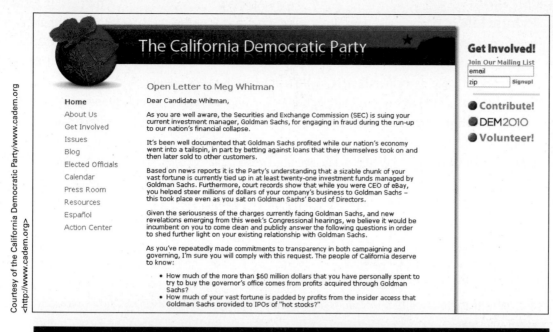

The California Democratic Party

Get Involved!

Join Our Mailing List
email
zip   Signup!

● Contribute!
● DEM2010
● Volunteer!

Home
About Us
Get Involved
Issues
Blog
Elected Officials
Calendar
Press Room
Resources
Español
Action Center

Open Letter to Meg Whitman

Dear Candidate Whitman,

As you are well aware, the Securities and Exchange Commission (SEC) is suing your current investment manager, Goldman Sachs, for engaging in fraud during the run-up to our nation's financial collapse.

It's been well documented that Goldman Sachs profited while our nation's economy went into a tailspin, in part by betting against loans that they themselves took on and then later sold to other customers.

Based on news reports it is the Party's understanding that a sizable chunk of your vast fortune is currently tied up in at least twenty-one investment funds managed by Goldman Sachs. Furthermore, court records show that while you were CEO of eBay, you helped steer millions of dollars of your company's business to Goldman Sachs – this took place even as you sat on Goldman Sachs' Board of Directors.

Given the seriousness of the charges currently facing Goldman Sachs, and new revelations emerging from this week's Congressional hearings, we believe it would be incumbent on you to come clean and publicly answer the following questions in order to shed further light on your existing relationship with Goldman Sachs.

As you've repeatedly made commitments to transparency in both campaigning and governing, I'm sure you will comply with this request. The people of California deserve to know:

- How much of the more than $60 million dollars that you have personally spent to try to buy the governor's office comes from profits acquired through Goldman Sachs?
- How much of your vast fortune is padded by profits from the insider access that Goldman Sachs provided to IPOs of "hot stocks?"

CALIFORNIA REPUBLICAN PARTY   Search

HOME   NEWSROOM   ABOUT   YOUR GOP   CALENDAR   CANDIDATES   PROGRAMS   > Sign-Up

FEATURES   ISSUES   VIDEO   AUDIO

Jobs & The Economy

We believe in the power and opportunity of American's free-market economy. We believe in the importance of sensible business regulations that promote confidence in our economy among consumers, entrepreneurs and businesses alike. We oppose interventionist policies that put the ...

» View Full Story

1 2 3 4

Receive alerts via email or SMS

Name

Latest News

Apr 30   Garrick Talks About High Wage Job Creation in Assembly Republican Weekly Radio Address

DONATE

THE CALIFORNIA

State political parties can be powerful in shaping state politics. They help recruit candidates for the state legislatures; after the primaries they work hard to elect their party's nominees to statewide office. Here the websites of the California Democratic Party and the California Republican Party announce news, activities, and opinions on issues. California is so large that its statewide elections are considered indicative of national trends.

Local party organizations exist at the county, town, and precinct or ward levels. The Muscogee County Republican Party, which Josh McKoon chaired, is an example of a local party organization. The essential functions of local party organizations are to recruit candidates for lower-level elected offices, register voters, and, most important, ensure that voters get to the polls on election day.[5]

The Party Nomination Process

One of the most important functions of parties is to nominate candidates for office and then elect them, a process accomplished in two stages. In elections with more than one candidate seeking the party's nomination, parties hold **primary elections**, in which voters determine the party's choice to run in the next stage, the **general election**.

local party organization: First level of political parties; recruits candidates for lower-level elected office, registers voters, and ensures that its voters get to the polls on election day.

primary election: Election in which voters select the candidates who will run on the party label in the general election; also called direct primary.

general election: Election in which voters choose their elected officials.

Primaries.   Primary elections are a very important way that each voter can have an equal voice in nominating his or her party's candidates for elected office. Although most states rely heavily on the primary, some states authorize both the primary and a nominating convention of state party members to approve the party's set of nominees.[6]

As noted, state laws regarding elections vary, and there are several types of primaries. A **closed primary** is one in which voters must affiliate with a party before casting a vote (either by registering prior to the election or on primary election day). A **semi-closed primary** is one in which party-affiliated voters cast votes in their party's primary, and nonaffiliated voters can choose which party's primary to vote in. In an **open primary** voters do not have to affiliate with a party before voting. Instead, they are given **ballots** with each party's list of candidates, and they can choose which ballot to use but are restricted to voting for only one party's nominees. A final type of primary, no longer used, is called a **blanket primary**. In this type, voters were given the ballots from all parties and were allowed to cast votes for any party's candidates as long as they cast only one vote per elected office. But in 2000, in *California Democratic Party v. Jones*, the U.S. Supreme Court ruled that blanket primaries were unconstitutional because they violated the First Amendment's guarantee of right of association (see Supreme Court Cases: *California Democratic Party v. Jones*).

Primary elections are a fact of political life, but insofar as they create competition within a political party and encourage candidates to reveal negative aspects of each other's professional or personal lives, they can weaken the party's eventual nominee when he or she faces opponents in the general election. Because party organizations always want the candidate who is most likely to win the election nominated under the party banner, they try to exert control over the primary election process in several ways. First, state laws govern party ballot access—literally, who can actually get on the primary election ballot. The relationship between elite state party members and state legislators is very close, so the party controls the gate by determining how open or restrictive ballot access is for candidates seeking to run for office on the party label. Second, although party organizations remain technically neutral during the primary election season, they can steer donors toward their preferred candidates, and away from candidates who do not agree with their goals. As a consequence, individuals who are perceived as weak or as not loyal to the party may run into major roadblocks set up by the party organization.

In 2010 voters in California passed Proposition 14, which eliminates party-based primaries as a means of choosing candidates to run in the general election. The proposition creates a single nominating election in which all candidates—Democrats, Republicans, and independents—compete against each other. The top two candidates then face each other in the general election.[7] It is clear that the voters in California want a system that bypasses the parties' hold on the candidate selection process.

The Presidential Nomination.
The process by which each party nominates its presidential candidate has evolved from one that was concentrated in the hands of a small group of elites to the modern process that allows millions of voters to participate directly in choosing the party's presidential nominee (see Figure 9.2).

In a presidential primary, voters cast a vote for a particular candidate, but what they are really doing is choosing **delegates** who will support that nominee at the party's national nominating convention. In a presidential **caucus**, which serves the same nominating purpose,

---

closed primary: *Primary election in which the voter must affiliate with a party before casting a vote.*

semi-closed primary: *Primary election in which party-affiliated voters cast votes and nonaffiliated voters can choose which party's primary to vote in.*

open primary: *Primary election in which voters do not have to affiliate with a party before voting.*

ballot: *List of candidates who are running for elected office; used by voters to make their choice.*

blanket primary: *Primary election in which voters are allowed to cast votes for any party's candidates as long as they cast only one vote per elected office.*

Have you voted in a primary election? What kind of primary was it? Did you have to identify your party affiliation?

Think back to the presidential election of 2008. Was the presidential nomination process fair?

delegate: *Individual selected by party voters in a primary or caucus election who is committed to supporting a particular presidential nominee at the party's national nominating convention.*

caucus: *Meeting of party members in town halls, schools, and private homes to select a presidential nominee.*

supremecourtcases

California Democratic Party v. Jones (2000)

QUESTION: Do blanket primaries, in which voters can vote for any party's candidate regardless of their own party affiliation, violate the right of association of political parties that wish to limit their primaries to those who belong to the party?

ORAL ARGUMENT: April 24, 2000 (listen at www .oyez.org/cases)

DECISION: June 26, 2000 (read at www.findlaw.com/ casecode/supreme.html)

OUTCOME: Yes, the right of association means that states cannot force parties to open their primaries to voters who are not party members (7–2).

In 1996 voters in California approved Proposition 198, which established a blanket primary in which each voter can vote in any primary election, regardless of party affiliation. In 2000, to prevent Republicans from voting in its primary, the California Democratic Party went to court, claiming that California's blanket primary law violated the state Democratic Party's right to freedom of association as guaranteed by the First Amendment.

Ultimately, the case reached the Supreme Court, where Justice Antonin Scalia wrote the majority opinion in favor of the California Democratic Party. The Court ruled blanket primaries to be unconstitutional because they violated the First Amendment. The majority argued that a blanket primary violated a political party's right to associate exclusively with its members, which can be extended to mean that political parties have the right to allow only registered party members to choose their party's nominees in a primary. Scalia wrote that "Proposition 198 forces political parties to associate with—to have their nominees, and hence their positions, determined by—those who, at best, have refused to affiliate with the party, and, at worst, have expressly affiliated with a rival."

- **Should a political party be forced to give voters who are not members the same privileges that party members have?**

- **Why might a political party want to be responsive to voters who are not members?**

EQUAL JUSTICE UNDER LAW

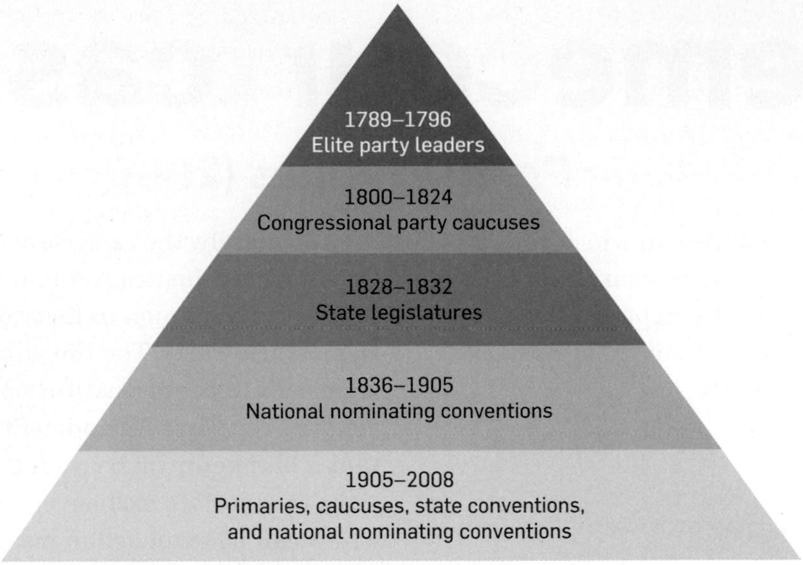

1789–1796
Elite party leaders
1800–1824
Congressional party caucuses
1828–1832
State legislatures
1836–1905
National nominating conventions
1905–2008
Primaries, caucuses, state conventions, and national nominating conventions

FIGURE 9.2 The Evolution of the Presidential Nominating Process, 1789–2008.

the process is less formal and more personal in that party members meet together in town halls, schools, and even private homes to choose a nominee. Each state is awarded a number of delegates to the convention by the national party organization based largely on the number of Electoral College votes the state has, but also on the size of party support in that state. The candidate who wins a majority of the delegates from the primary and caucus elections is selected at the national convention as the party's nominee for president.

winner-take-all system: *Electoral system in which whoever wins the most votes in an election wins the election.*

McGovern-Fraser Commission: *Democratic Party commission whose reforms of the party's presidential nominating system increased access by underrepresented groups.*

proportional representation: *Used by the Framers to signify a system of legislative districting in which larger states receive more representatives than smaller states; today an electoral system that assigns party delegates according to vote share in a presidential primary election or that assigns seats in the legislature according to vote share in a general election.*

What difference does proportional representation make for the Democratic Party?

The Democratic Party and Republican Party allocate their delegates within the primaries and caucuses differently. The Democratic Party has had a more tumultuous nominating process due in large part to some key rules changes in the 1970s and 1980s. In the 1960s members of underrepresented groups, such as women and African Americans, began calling for a change in the presidential nominating procedures for the Democratic Party. Specifically, they objected to the use of the unit rule, or **winner-take-all system**, which meant that whoever won the majority of primary or state nominating convention votes would win the entire state's delegates. Activists believed that the unit rule allowed conservative white men to dominate the nominating process. In response to this grassroots movement, the Democrats formed the **McGovern-Fraser Commission**, which recommended changes in the way that delegates were chosen and awarded to candidates during the primary season. In 1972 the Democratic Party instituted requirements that states' delegations accurately reflect the distribution of preferences for presidential candidates in the state. For the 1976 election the Democrats formally instituted **proportional representation**, that is, the number of delegates that a candidate receives is based on the percentage of the vote received in the primary or caucus, either at the state level or in each congressional district. In most states, delegates are committed to a candidate before the primary election takes place.

To further address the activists' concern that the nominating process was dominated by white men, the 1972 reforms required a certain percentage of each state's delegates to be women, African Americans, and other underrepresented groups based on their proportion in each state's population. If states did not comply with this requirement, the national party reserved the right not to "seat" or count their delegates in the final nominating vote held at the party's national convention. Although the party stated the goal of increasing delegates from underrepresented groups, it did not really increase African American convention participation until the presidential election of 1984, when Jesse Jackson, an African American, ran for the Democratic nomination. Although the nomination went to former Vice President Walter

Mondale, Jackson was successful enough to insist that more people of color be delegates to the convention. The cumulative effect of these reforms was to create a gateway for members of underrepresented groups to exert influence in determining the Democratic Party presidential nominee.

In 1981 the Democratic Party made several other changes, including requiring that each state's delegation comprise an equal number of men and women, and creating a category of delegates known as **superdelegates**. The superdelegates are not chosen through the pri-

Chip Somodevilla/Getty Images

mary voting process but rather are active members of the party who will be instrumental in turning out party voters in the general election. Most superdelegates are elected officials in the party, such as governors and members of Congress from each state, as well as state party committee chairs and key activists in interest groups that are loyal to the Democrats. They are uncommitted and free to choose whomever they wish to support at the convention.

In the 2008 Democratic nomination contest between Senator Barack Obama (D-Ill.) and Senator Hillary Clinton (D-N.Y.), superdelegates played the most important role since their creation. By the end of the regular primary season, Obama led in the primary and caucus delegate count, but not by enough to win the nomination outright. The nomination would be determined by the 823 superdelegates, only about half of whom had committed to one or the other candidate early in the process. As it became clear that Obama had more support among party members generally, many of the remaining superdelegates swung their support to him. In the end, Obama won 463 superdelegates, for a final delegate count of 2,229.5; Clinton won 257 superdelegates, for a total of 1,896.5 delegates.[8] The 2008 contest for the Democratic nomination

Senator Hillary Clinton closely competed with Barack Obama for the presidential nomination in 2008 and was the most successful female candidate for president in history. The reform of the Democratic Party nomination process in the 1970s was one factor in making her candidacy viable. Here Clinton is shown giving a victory speech after winning the West Virginia primary on May 13, 2008. She ultimately fell short of the number of delegates required to win the nomination and later was chosen to be secretary of state in President Obama's administration.

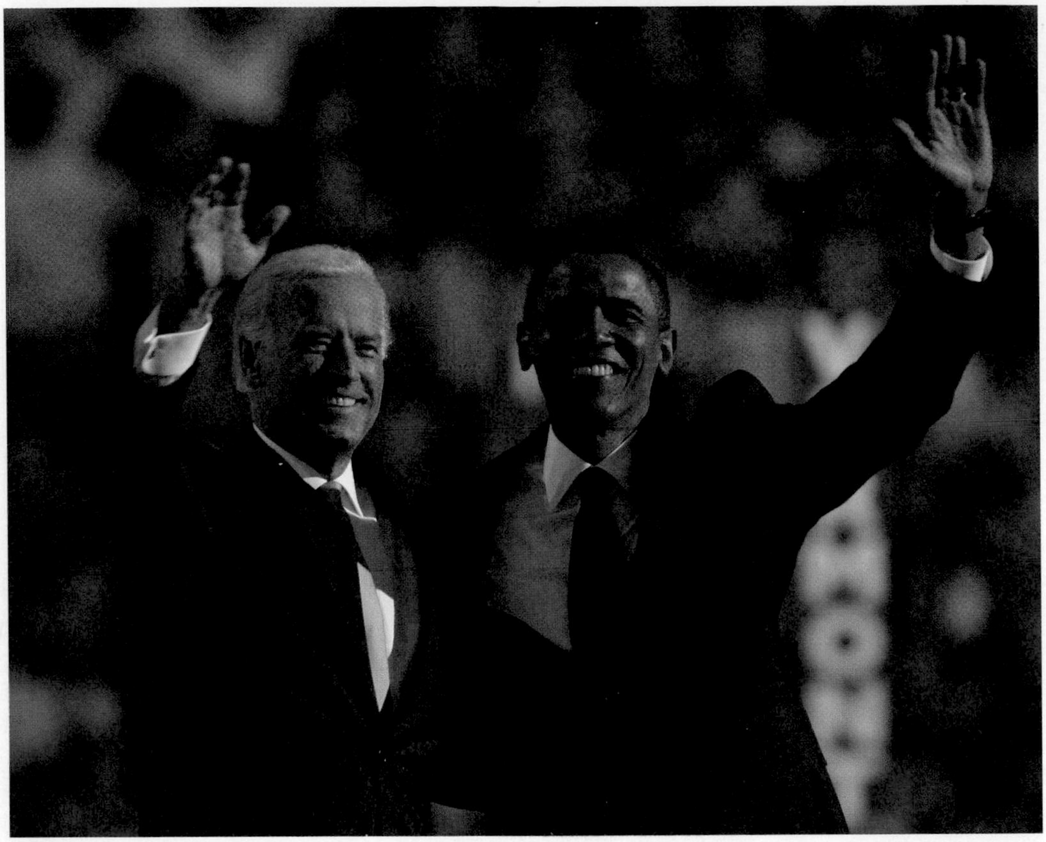

AP Photo/Paul Sancya

Senator Barack Obama made history as the first African American presidential nominee of any party, and then as the first African American president. Senator Joe Biden was an early candidate for the 2008 nomination but quickly dropped out; he was later chosen by Obama as his vice presidential running mate. Here they are together at the Democratic National Convention on August 27, 2008, after Biden accepted the nomination to be the party's vice presidential candidate.

was one of the closest ever. Very often, close nominating contests encourage the nominee to choose one of his opponents as a running mate or, if he wins the election, as a member of his cabinet. In this case, Obama chose Senator Joe Biden (D-Del.), who had briefly run for the 2008 nomination, as his running mate, and he later appointed Hillary Clinton to be secretary of state.

Unlike the Democratic Party, the Republican Party has rarely faced an internal demand for more diverse representation, so it has not significantly changed its nominating system. Republicans use the unit rule to award their delegates, and the only modification is that some states award delegates by vote totals in congressional districts rather than by the entire state. In addition, the Republicans have no requirements as to the racial or gender composition of a state's delegates, and they have no superdelegates.

With a winner-take-all nomination system, the Republican Party tends to resolve its nomination process more quickly than the Democratic Party.[9] In 2008 John McCain (R-Ariz.), who started out with less campaign money than his competitors, effectively secured the nomination in February, while the Democrats did not determine their nominee until June. McCain made history in the Republican Party by choosing a female vice presidential candidate, Governor Sarah Palin of Alaska. The shorter nomination process typically gives Republicans an advantage in the general election because their nominee can develop the strategy for the general election far sooner than the Democratic nominee can. Although the Democratic candidate ultimately won the presidential election in 2008, the Democrats have begun discussions on how to simplify and shorten their nomination process.

Should the Republicans adopt proportional representation? Should the Democrats give it up?

The timing of primaries has become an integral part of the presidential nomination strategy. Larry Bartels's work demonstrates that states that hold primaries early in the process exert disproportional influence by giving one or another candidate an early stamp of approval and momentum.[10] Candidates who win in the early primaries can solicit more campaign money and garner more endorsements from key constituent groups than those who lose. It also literally pays off economically to be a state with an early presidential primary because candidates, their staff, and members of the media spend a disproportionate amount of time in the state prior to the primary, generating income for local businesses. Traditionally, the two earliest presidential contests have been the New Hampshire primary and the Iowa caucus; in 2008 both were held in

January. Even though these are relatively small states, the fact that they have the first two presidential contests for each major party makes them disproportionately influential in generating publicity and momentum for the winners.[11] For the 2008 elections other states moved their primary dates closer to those of Iowa and New Hampshire to elevate their own importance in the nomination contest. Ultimately, such **frontloading**, holding many primaries simultaneously early in the year, creates an imbalance of influence across states in determining the party's nominee; a candidate who manages to do well in early primary states diminishes the chances for other candidates and reduces the influence of the voters in later primary states.

Chip Somodevilla/Getty Images

Senator John McCain was the Republican presidential nominee in 2008, and he chose Sarah Palin, governor of Alaska, as his running mate. Palin was the first female vice presidential candidate in Republican Party history, and she proved to be very popular. Here the two candidates campaign together at a rally at the Virginia Beach Convention Center on October 13, 2008.

frontloading: *Moving a state primary or caucus earlier in the year to increase its influence.*

Explain how frontloading affects voter equality.

The Dynamics of Early Party Development

Political parties in 2011 seem very well organized, as if they have existed as long as the nation itself. But parties were not intended to be part of the original fabric of the political system. They emerged from disagreements among the Framers, who were able to compromise just enough to adopt the Constitution but not enough to suppress different perspectives on the role of government. Today, rather than the narrow organizations that the Framers feared, there are two large parties that each include a broad swath of the electorate and must make internal compromises to stay unified. In this section, we trace the background to these developments.

Political Factions: Federalist versus Antifederalist

James Madison, writing in *Federalist Papers* 10 and 51 (see the Appendix), predicted the rise of **factions**, groups of individuals who share a common political goal and ally with each other on a temporary basis to accomplish that goal. Madison recognized that factions would be a natural outgrowth of different interests among citizens and that there

faction: *Defined by Madison as any group that places its own interests above the aggregate interests of society.*

Chris Hondros/Getty Images

As the state with the earliest party primary in the presidential nomination process, New Hampshire has a disproportionate influence on which candidates are considered viable for the nomination. Here a voter requests a ballot to vote in the 2008 primary on January 8. Across the nation, young people turned out in record high numbers to vote in primaries that year.

Given the Framers' views on factions and political parties, do you think the development of parties has been good or bad for American democracy?

Federalists: *Initially, those who supported the Constitution during the ratification period; later, the name of the political party established by supporters of Alexander Hamilton.*

Antifederalists: *Those who opposed the new proposed Constitution during the ratification period.*

was little government could do to stop them without denying citizens important civil liberties. Although factions were not considered the same thing as political parties of the kind that had emerged in Britain, the Framers also feared that both factions and parties might encourage divisions in the young democracy that could threaten its existence.

Yet factions emerged even before the Constitution was adopted. In the debate over ratification (see Chapter 2, The Constitution), those who argued for the Constitution called themselves **Federalists**. They believed that a stable federal government that could collect tax revenue, fund and regulate a national army, regulate foreign and domestic trade, and stabilize currency would make the American democratic experiment a success. Opponents of a strong national government, however, viewed the future of the United States in terms of loosely affiliated but sovereign states that governed themselves, managing their own tax policies and internal security. These were the **Antifederalists**. In their view, the United States had just fought a war to overturn a strong monarch, and they did not want to put themselves under the rule of an oppressive new centralized government that would govern from the top down (see Table 9.2).

Ultimately, the Federalist viewpoint triumphed, and the Constitution was ratified. But the debate did not end there. The nation's first president, George Washington (1789–97), formed a government that included proponents of a strong national government (led by

TABLE 9.2 Federalist and Antifederalist Policies

Federalist	Antifederalist
Ratify the Constitution	Oppose ratification of the Constitution
Establish central bank	Oppose central bank
Protect commercial interests	Support agricultural interests
Assert federal supremacy	Preserve state power
See no need for Bill of Rights	Pass Bill of Rights

Source: John H. Aldrich and Ruth Grant, "The Antifederalists, the First Congress, and the First Parties," *Journal of Politics* 55 (1993): 295–326.

Alexander Hamilton and John Adams) and strong state governments (led by Thomas Jefferson). Washington worried that opposing views could lead to organized political parties that would cause conflict in the new nation.[12] Tensions between the factions accelerated after John Adams's (1797–1801) election as president, especially following passage of the Sedition Act, which severely restricted freedom of the press and freedom of speech critical of the government, in 1798 (see Chapter 4, Civil Liberties). Jefferson opposed this law and in 1800 mounted a campaign against Adams for the presidency, arguing that the Federalists were too heavy-handed in their approach to governing.

Try to relate the modern Democratic and Republican Parties to the viewpoints of the Federalists and the Antifederalists. Which party comes closest to which viewpoint?

Thomas Jefferson, Andrew Jackson, and the Emergence of the Democratic Party

Thomas Jefferson won the election of 1800, and his election marked the beginning of established partisan politics. The new president used his victory to transform his fledgling political party into a viable long-term organization known as the **Democratic-Republicans** (most candidates shortened the name to Republican).[13] The Democratic-Republicans occu-

Democratic-Republicans: *Political party formed by Thomas Jefferson to oppose the strong central government policies of the Federalists.*

pied the White House for the next twenty-eight years with the terms of Jefferson (1801–1809), James Madison (1809–17), James Monroe (1817–25), and John Quincy Adams (1825–29). The Federalists diminished in number and faded away as a force in politics.

Despite their electoral success and lack of opposition, the Democratic-Republicans themselves grew divided. The conflict was led by Andrew Jackson, an ambitious politician who wanted to take the party to a new level of inclusiveness and use that wider reach to become president. Jackson, from Tennessee, had served

Granger Collection, New York

in both the House and the Senate, but he made his national reputation during the War of 1812, especially as the hero of the Battle of New Orleans. After his military service ended, Jackson returned to Congress and attempted to win the presidential nomination of the Democratic-Republicans in 1824.[14] At that time, presidential nominations were decided by party caucuses in Congress, and Jackson was challenging John Quincy Adams, the son of President John Adams. Although the congressional party caucus nominated William H. Crawford of Georgia, fewer than a third of the members of the party showed up to cast their votes, reflecting a lack of consensus around a majority candidate. Consequently, there was no clear choice among

Andrew Jackson (1767–1845) originated the modern political party by encouraging grassroots participation by voters and party organizations in his election campaigns and by building the Democratic Party while he served as president from 1829 to 1837.

the Democratic-Republicans in the election of 1824, and no one won a majority in the Electoral College. The outcome then had to be determined by the House of Representatives, which selected Adams (for an explanation of this process, see Chapter 10, Elections and Campaigns).

By 1828 the nomination process had been taken over by party members in state legislatures who voted for their preferred nominees either in the legislature or at state party conventions. By locating the nomination process in the states instead of in Congress, parties were enlarging the number of people involved in making the decision about who could run for president. As we note in Chapter 11 (Voting and Participation), Jackson wanted states to open up the voting process to as many people as possible by eliminating such barriers to voting as property ownership requirements. In 1828, using a grassroots state-level strategy to attract both the support of state legislators and the voters themselves, Jackson worked closely with Martin Van Buren, a powerful New York politician, to again challenge Adams for the nomination of the Democratic-Republicans; this time, he won the nomination and the presidential election.

As president, Jackson worked closely with Van Buren to knock down the gates that stood in the way of public access to party decisions, to make their political party more accessible to the general public, and to attract the votes of an ever-expanding nation. They recognized that parties could be more than mere coalitions of politicians who agreed on policy; they could be full-fledged organizations.[15] To accomplish that goal, they had to offer incentives to individuals to join the party organization and run it; they even shortened the name of the party to Democrat to signal that they were building a new kind of political party organization.

By 1832, the end of Jackson's first term in office, politics had changed in fundamental ways because of the nation's rapid geographic and population growth.[16] The Jackson-led Democrats emerged as a large grassroots majority political party, and Jackson used all the powers of the presidency to strengthen his political party around the country. In the meantime, the anti-Jackson wing of the old Democratic-Republicans had taken the name National Republicans. In the presidential election of 1832, the National Republicans nominated Henry Clay, a U.S. senator from Kentucky, to run against Jackson, but Jackson was victorious.

Although Henry Clay lost that election to Jackson, he returned to the Senate and started laying the groundwork for a new political party that would oppose Jackson's policies. He encouraged members of the National Republicans to join forces with others who opposed Jackson and to form the **Whig Party**, which objected to what they viewed as Jackson's abuse of presidential power for partisan gains. As Clay put it, "The Whigs of the present day are opposing Executive encroachments, and a most alarming extension of Executive power and prerogative."[17] From 1832 to 1856 the Democrats and the Whigs dominated American politics and presidential elections. However, the issue of slavery soon emerged to shake up the party balance.

The Antislavery Movement and the Formation of the Republican Party

The Democratic Party's general strategy for opening up a larger gateway for citizen participation in politics inadvertently encouraged alternate groups and political parties to emerge on the political scene. In 1833 William Lloyd Garrison, a white journalist, formed the American Anti-Slavery Society to press for the abolition of slavery. Several years later Frederick Douglass, an African American, began organizing free blacks in the North for the same purpose.

How did Jackson open gateways to citizen participation?

Whig Party: *Political party formed to oppose the Jackson Democrats.*

Over time, groups that opposed slavery combined under the umbrella of the **abolitionist movement**. Although the movement was not a political party per se, it grew large and vocal enough to pressure the Democrats and Whigs to take a formal position on slavery, especially the extension of slavery into western territories.

Northern and southern Democrats were united against the abolitionist movement, but for different reasons. Northern Democrats recognized that if the slavery question came to the forefront of politics, the nationally dominant Democratic Party would be split between the North and the South. Southern Democrats opposed abolishing slavery outright or limiting its expansion because the plantation economy of the South was heavily dependent on slave labor. The Whig Party was also divided along northern and southern lines on the question of slavery.

Further complicating party politics were smaller **third parties** that arose in the North, some explicitly antislavery. Third parties are minor political parties that present an alternative to the two dominant political parties in the American political system. Typically, third parties focus on a single issue, as in the case of the Liberty Party, which focused on slavery; but as frequently happens in American politics, this smaller party was absorbed into a larger coalition of groups, led by the Free Soilers, that opposed the expansion of slavery in the territories. Meeting in Ripon, Wisconsin, in 1854, these groups were also joined by some antislavery northern Democrats, and the modern Republican Party was born. In the words of one activist, Alvan E. Bovay, "We went into the little meeting held in a schoolhouse Whigs, Free Soilers, and Democrats. We came out of it Republicans."[18] Six years later, the Republican Party had consolidated its support and elected Abraham Lincoln (1861–65) to the presidency.

Shortly after Lincoln's election, seven southern states seceded from the union, and on April 12, 1861, the Confederates fired on the federal government's fort in Charleston Harbor, and the Civil War began. Four more southern states seceded, leaving the Republicans in complete control of Congress. On January 1, 1863, in issuing the Emancipation Proclamation (see Chapter 5, Civil Rights), Lincoln publicly affirmed that ending slavery was a fundamental aim of the war. The Confederacy dissolved after the war ended in 1865, but southerners resented northerners and the Republican Party because of both the South's physical and economic losses and the continued occupation of the South by northern troops. Since then, the Democrats and the Republicans have been the nation's two major political parties.

Party Loyalty and Patronage

Andrew Jackson set an example of how to build a political party organization using government resources. Just as Jackson worked to expand the electorate, he sought to expand the size of the federal government in order to increase the number of federally funded jobs his party could control. The Jacksonian era provided many opportunities to bring the federal government into the state and local arena by the building of forts, post roads (for mail delivery), customhouses, and lighthouses. Whoever controlled the jobs associated with these programs could also demand political allegiance from those who filled them. By the late nineteenth century a system emerged whereby the politician became the "patron" of the businessmen and workers who were on the payrolls of the federal or the state governments. Jobs built party loyalty, and those hired often had to declare their political allegiance to the politician who arranged for the job, and promise to vote for him. Such a system is commonly referred to as a **patronage system**.

abolitionist movement: *Grassroots movement to abolish slavery.*

third parties: *Minor political parties that present a third alternative to the two dominant political parties in the American political system.*

patronage system: *Political system in which government programs and benefits are awarded based on political loyalty to a party or politician.*

Do you see the patronage system still at work today in American politics? Explain.

As the government expanded, so did the party organization. At each level—federal, state, and local—there were parallel party committees. Parties became the top-down organizations they are today, with a national committee, state committees, and local chapters at the county, ward, town, or precinct level. At each level, leaders who had power within the party acted as **party bosses**, controlling the distribution of public funds by rewarding supporters and withholding them from opponents. The key element in this system was the loyalty of supporters, who on election day voted for the boss's preferred set of candidates. Voter support in this kind of system was so reliable and predictable that it became known as **machine politics**; it ran like a well-oiled machine.

The expansion of party machines was fueled by a huge influx of new immigrants in the late nineteenth century who mostly settled in large cities of the North and Midwest. Democratic bosses in these cities recognized that immigrants, once naturalized, would be a major source of new voters, and courted their loyalty through patronage. In turn, parties served as a type of gateway for immigrants to become integrated into American political life. As city populations increased at a much faster rate than rural populations, Democrats gained political power in cities, while Republican power in the North and Midwest tended to be concentrated in rural areas.

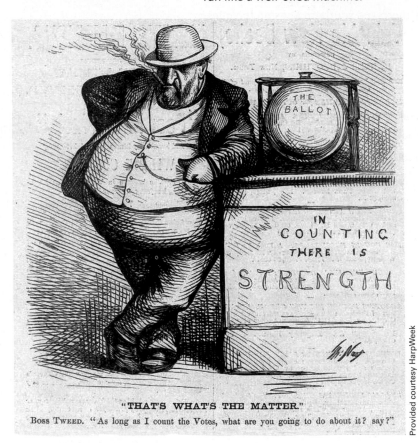

"THAT'S WHAT'S THE MATTER."

Boss Tweed. "As long as I count the Votes, what are you going to do about it? say?"

Provided courtesy HarpWeek

Reform and the Erosion of Party Control

A critical factor in the success of machine politics was party control of voting. In contrast to today's system—in which states manage most aspects of elections, including ballot design and ballot counting—local parties in the late nineteenth century printed their own ballots, called party strip ballots, which listed only their candidates, and gave them to voters on their way into the polling places. In many places, party officials counted the votes as well, further manipulating the voting process to their advantage.

However, three developments in the late nineteenth and early twentieth centuries eroded party organizations' control over government jobs and elections: the creation of a merit-based system of government employment, the introduction of ballot reforms, and a change in the way nominees for elected office were selected. All three reforms were led by **Progressives**, coalitions of Democrats and Republicans who believed that government had been captured by corrupt elites who were using government resources to enrich themselves rather than to serve citizens.

Since Andrew Jackson's day, bosses in the old patronage system had taken for granted the right to distribute government jobs to their supporters. But in 1883 the Pendleton Act reformed the **civil service** by requiring that government jobs be filled based on merit, not

William Marcy "Boss" Tweed was the head of the Democratic Party machine in New York City in the 1850s and 1860s. He was notorious for using political office to hand out favors and benefits to loyal party members and to accumulate personal wealth. The editorial cartoons of Thomas Nast helped expose the graft and corruption of the "Tweed Ring."

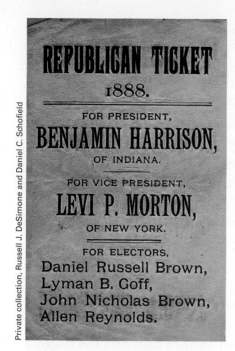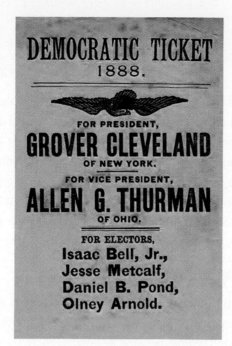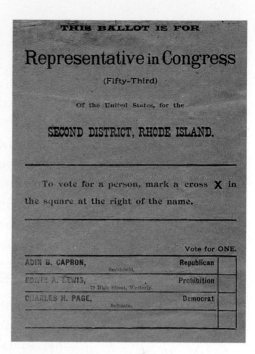

FIGURE 9.3 Ballot Reform. On the left are examples of party strip ballots used in Rhode Island in 1888. These types of ballots were printed by political parties and handed to voters on election day. They gave a voter no opportunity to split the vote among different parties. On the right is an example of the so-called Australian ballot. Like this ballot used in Rhode Island in 1892, Australian ballots were printed by state governments rather than by political parties. They listed all candidates for elected office, not just candidates from a single party, and therefore allowed a voter to split the vote among different parties.
Source: Russell J. DeSimone and Daniel C. Schofield, "Rhode Island Election Tickets: A Survey," Technical Services Department Faculty Publications (Kingston: University of Rhode Island, 2007),

on political connections (see Chapter 14, The Bureaucracy, for more on the civil service). This was the first of several laws that slowly transformed the federal bureaucracy from a corrupt insider organization to a neutral, policy-based organization.[19]

Voting procedures were also reformed between 1888 and 1911 as states adopted the so-called **Australian ballot** system, which originated in Australia in 1858, to replace the party strip ballots (see Figure 9.3).[20] When parties had printed the ballots and had given them to voters, who then put them in the ballot box, there was no privacy, and party officials monitored citizens' votes. The Australian ballot system introduced the secret ballot; each ballot listed all the candidates from all the parties who were running for office, and voters marked their choices in private. In addition, poll watchers and ballot counters were expected to perform their tasks without favoring a specific party and without intimidating voters. This reform greatly reduced party boss control over election outcomes.[21]

Lastly, Progressives launched grassroots campaigns for direct primaries run by the state for nominating party candidates. These primaries aimed to replace the nomination of candidates in local and state party conventions, which were typically dominated by party bosses. Although states were relatively slow to adopt direct primaries, eventually this system became the dominant means of choosing party candidates. The effect of direct primaries was to greatly reduce the control that party bosses and machines had over the choices offered in elections. As party bases broadened, leaders turned their attention to finding ways to keep coalitions of voters together.

civil service: *System of employment in the federal bureaucracy under which employees are chosen and promoted based on merit.*

Australian ballot: *Voting system in which state governments run elections and provide voters the option of choosing candidates from multiple parties; also called the secret ballot.*

The Effects of a Two-Party System

Following the Civil War, party divisions ran largely along geographic lines, with Republicans dominant in the Northeast and West, and Democrats dominant in the South and increasingly in the nation's largest cities. Today, the Democratic and Republican parties have reversed their geographic strongholds, but the two-party system remains intact. In this section we examine the effects of a two-party system not only on citizens' choices but also on the ways that government can respond. We also examine the reasons why the United States, even before the Civil War, never had more than two major parties, and we explore the role of the third parties that have occasionally arisen to challenge two-party dominance.

Limited Political Choice

Surely there are more than two views on how to solve important policy problems. If a group of students has a conversation about a political issue, whether it is war, civil liberties, education, crime, or same-sex marriage, there will likely be more than two opinions expressed. It might seem logical, therefore, that a large democracy like the United States should have as many political parties as there are diverse viewpoints. But the United States has only two major parties, and they stand in stark contrast to each other. Scholars have debated whether this two-party system adequately reflects the range of views among citizens.

In 1957 the scholar Anthony Downs argued that voters whose views fall between the two parties were actually represented in a two-party system. His **median voter theorem** proposed that, in a two-party race, if voters select candidates on the basis of ideology and everyone participates equally, the party closer to the middle will win. As candidates from each party seek to attract a majority of votes, and because most voters fall in the middle of the ideological spectrum, both parties move toward a compromise, or middle position. In this way **moderates** have a great deal of potential political influence in a two-party system.[22]

Nevertheless, the impact of ideologically extreme campaign activists and interest groups that align with a party can pressure parties and candidates to move away from the center.[23] In today's highly partisan atmosphere, it seems as though the political center has almost entirely disappeared. Each party appears to be so dominated by its more extreme wing that there is little opportunity within each to make moderate views known or to compromise. The current two-party system increasingly appears to contradict Downs's expectations about convergence to the middle. In regions where one party is very dominant, elected officials may not be responsive to voters from the other party.

The Structural Limits

Despite its limitations, the two-party system is built into the American electoral system, as the political scientist Maurice Duverger explains. The American electoral system is a **single-member plurality system**, in which one legislative seat (on a city council, in a state assembly, in the House of Representatives) represents citizens who live in a geographically defined district.[24] To win that seat, a candidate usually needs only a **plurality** of votes, not a pure

median voter theorem: *Theory that, in a two-party race, if voters select candidates on the basis of ideology and everyone participates equally, the party closer to the middle will win.*

moderates: *Individuals who are in the middle of the ideological spectrum and do not hold consistently strong views about whether government should be involved in people's lives.*

Do you think the major political parties reflect the views of citizens? If not, what can be done to change that?

single-member plurality system: *Electoral system that assigns one seat in a legislative body to represent citizens who live in a defined area (a district) based on which candidate wins the most votes.*

plurality vote: *Vote in which the winner needs to win more votes than any other candidate.*

majority, that is, more votes than any other candidate, but not necessarily 50 percent plus 1. Because there is only one seat to be won in a district, voters have become accustomed to choosing between candidates from the two major parties.

Other electoral systems work differently. Many democracies assign the number of seats a party wins according to proportional representation, based on the percentage of votes it receives in a particular election. This type of electoral system encourages smaller parties to form around specific issues and to field candidates for office. Voters are likewise encouraged to support smaller parties. With so many parties fielding candidates, no single party is likely to receive a majority, and parties govern by forming coalitions (see Other Places: Proportional Representation Electoral Systems).

In the United States, however, the single-member plurality system encourages a two-party system, and the two-party system in turn encourages political debates that ask Americans to take a "for" or an "against" position on an issue. There is little effort during an election to arrive at the middle ground, although there is often debate within a party as to what its position will be. In fact, the two-party system works to transfer the battleground from between parties to within parties. Each party—rather than government itself—is a coalition.

The Role of Third Parties

In one sense, a two-party system stands as a gate that blocks the emergence of alternative viewpoints and reduces the choices available to voters in terms of perspectives on how to govern. On the other hand, when the two parties together do not offer policy proposals that a significant number of voters want to see enacted, third parties form. These third parties can mount challenges so significant that the major parties are compelled to act, often by incorporating the third party's policy proposal into their platforms.

We have already seen how the antislavery ideas of the Liberty Party and the Free Soil Party were absorbed into the Republican Party when it was founded in 1854. A second example occurred in the late nineteenth century, when farmers were in an uproar about declining crop prices, the lack of available credit, and the constricting use of gold rather than silver as the collateral for U.S. currency. Splinter parties rose up around these issues. Of these, the Populist Party was the largest and most viable; its presidential candidate in the 1892 presidential election, James Weaver, won four states outright and split the vote in two other states.[25] In the 1896 election, the Democrats thought they saw an opportunity to win votes by incorporating the Populist demand for free and unlimited coinage of silver into their party platform. They even nominated the Populist candidate, William Jennings Bryan, as their own. Bryan lost the election, and with that defeat the "free silver" movement, which had been strong in the West, rapidly declined.

The next strongest showing for a third party at the presidential level came in 1912, when Theodore "Teddy" Roosevelt ran for president as the Progressive Party candidate. Roosevelt, a Republican, had served as president from 1901 to 1909. He decided to run for president again in 1912 because he felt that a different political option should be offered to the voters. As is often the case with third-party candidates, Roosevelt's campaign helped mobilize voters around a host of issues supported by Progressive reformers, most notably the idea of popular elections for U.S. senators. At that time, U.S. senators were elected in state legislatures rather than directly by the voters. Although Roosevelt lost, the Progressives were successful

majority vote: *Vote in which the winner needs to win 50 percent plus 1 of the votes cast.*

Do the political parties provide citizens with opportunities for debate on the issues? Do the political parties reflect citizens' views?

Proportional Representation Electoral Systems

In contrast to the U.S. single-member plurality system, many nations in Europe and in Central and Latin America have proportional representation electoral systems. This system assigns multiple seats to a geographic district according to the proportion of votes a political party receives in an election. In this system, there are rewards for forming more than two parties because parties that receive even a small percent of the vote, for example 10 percent, are likely to be awarded seats in the legislature. The legislatures typically have coalition majorities, where members from different parties agree on policies and form a working majority. In this way, proportional representation grants multiple parties the power to make policy and deliver benefits to voters.

There are trade-offs in terms of participation, responsiveness, and accountability in each type of electoral system. Single-member plurality electoral systems tend to produce fewer political parties, which reduces the number of opinions that can be actively represented in a political system. Two-party systems also encourage strict partisanship among officeholders and discourage bipartisanship. On the other hand, this stark contrast allows voters to more easily hold their elected officials accountable.

Proportional representation systems produce multiple parties and greater diversity of representation. However, this system tends to produce coalition government because no party can gain a straight majority. Coalitions encourage compromise among parties, but it is also true that the parties that make up the coalition can withdraw at any time, which makes the ruling government potentially unstable.* Moreover, voters cannot easily identify which party in the coalition should be rewarded or blamed for government policies, so accountability is more difficult than in single-member plurality systems.

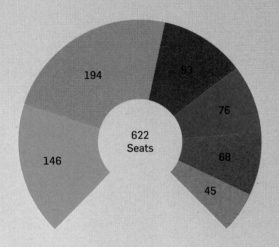

- Sozialdemokratische Partei Deutschlands (Socialist Party of Germany)
- Christlich Demokratische Union (Christian Democratic Union)
- Freie Demokratische Partei (Free Democratic Party)
- Die Linke (The Left)
- Die Grünen (The Green)
- Christlich-Soziale Union (Christian Social Union)

Seats Allocated by Party in the German Bundestag, 2009.

The German Bundestag, which is equivalent to the U.S. House of Representatives, awards a percentage of seats to each party depending on its vote share in the election (each citizen votes for a district representative and for a party). Following an election in 2008, the Christian Democrats and their Bavarian ally, the Christian Social Union, formed a coalition government with the Free Democrats.

Source: The Federal Returning Officer, www.bundeswahlleiter.de.

- **How does a proportional representation electoral system translate votes into legislative power in the government?**

- **Why are governments established under proportional representation systems inherently unstable?**

* Ko Maeda and Misa Nishikawa, "Duration of Party Control in Parliamentary and Presidential Governments," *Comparative Political Studies* 39 (2006): 352–74.

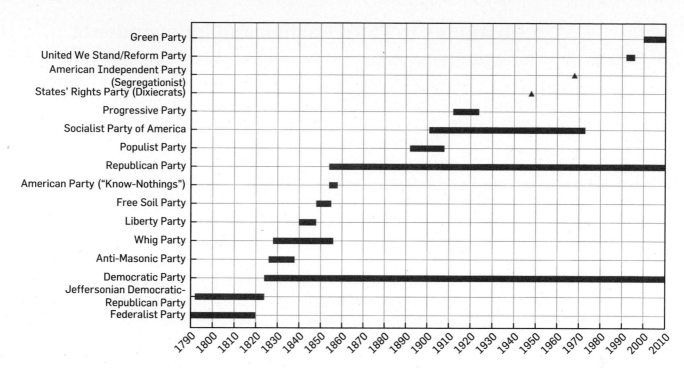

FIGURE 9.4 American Political Parties, 1789–2010. Note that the Democratic Party is the nation's oldest political party. The graph shows it beginning under President Andrew Jackson, but some argue that it actually began with President Thomas Jefferson's Democratic-Republicans.

in getting Congress to pass and the states to ratify the Seventeenth Amendment on April 8, 1913, which allowed for the direct election of U.S. senators.

Since Teddy Roosevelt's run, five contenders representing significant third parties have entered presidential elections, but none has been unable to build a sustained organization over time. Two of these candidates, Strom Thurmond (Dixiecrats) and George Wallace (American Independent Party), ran on segregationist platforms of parties that were splinter groups of the Democratic Party. John Anderson (National Unity Party) and Ross Perot (United We Stand) each ran on a platform that favored moderate social policy and strict fiscal discipline. Ross Perot was given credit for forcing the two major party candidates in 1992, President George H. W. Bush (1989–93) and William Jefferson (Bill) Clinton (1993–2001), to address the federal deficit, the amount by which annual government spending exceeds incoming revenue. During the 2000 election Ralph Nader ran for president on the Green Party ticket, promoting a platform that called for stronger environmental and consumer protections. In addition, both the Libertarian Party and the Constitution Party have put forth presidential candidates in recent elections. For a compact list of significant parties in American politics, see Figure 9.4.

Third parties thus present an alternative to the two dominant political parties. Today's Green Party is one example. However, an alternative party can also act as a spoiler for major party candidates and can, as a consequence, alienate potential voters. Some Democratic Party activists argued that if Ralph Nader had not run for president on the Green Party ticket in 2000 and had not received 97,488 votes in the state of Florida, Albert Gore Jr. would have been elected president instead of George W. Bush.[26] Although Nader did not win in 2000, 2004, or 2008, his messages of change and open government were clearly echoed by the mainstream Democratic candidate, Barack Obama (2009–), in his successful 2008 presidential campaign. A third-party platform can ultimately be brought into the political mainstream if a major party candidate adopts part or all of it and is elected.

What are the benefits and the risks of voting for a third-party candidate?

Obstacles to Third Parties and Independents

Because third-party candidates can act as spoilers, the two major parties do everything they can to discourage them. The Democrats and Republicans have controlled state legislatures and Congress for so long that they have successfully established gates within state electoral laws that favor a two-party system over a multiple-party system. For example, state laws typically require a candidate to collect thousands of signatures to get on the ballot, and the names and addresses of the signers have to be exactly right for the signatures to count. To prevent a third-party candidate or an **Independent** not affiliated with any political party from getting on the ballot, state and local political parties frequently challenge the signatures on ballot petitions in court to try to get them invalidated. Moreover, without the backing of a major party to get out the vote, collect campaign contributions, and arrange for media coverage, most third-party and Independent candidates do not stand much chance of being elected. Consequently, voters who consider themselves Independents do not have the opportunity to vote for candidates who might be closest to them in terms of policy preferences.

Parties also directly influence the policy agendas of state legislature and the U.S. Congress. The party that wins the majority of seats in the legislature becomes the majority party and consequently controls the legislative process. Once the legislative session begins, members are asked to express their opinions in subcommittees, committees, and on the floor by voting with or against their party's proposed legislation, and it is rare that an alternative to the major party proposal is considered (see Chapter 12, Congress).

Even if a candidate wins elected office as an Independent, as did Senator Bernie Sanders (I-Vt.) and Senator Joe Lieberman (I-Conn.), there is no party organization for them to join in the legislature. Independents must pledge to support one of the two major parties in order to sit on committees and perform their other responsibilities as legislators. In 2009 both Sanders and Lieberman chose to caucus with the Democrats in the Senate.

Independents: *Individuals who do not affiliate with either of the major political parties.*

Should laws that discourage third parties be changed? What would be the effects in terms of government responsiveness?

What are the advantages and disadvantages of being an Independent?

Challenges to Party Power from Interest Groups

In addition to challenges from third parties, the two major parties face challenges from established interest groups and from broader social groups formed at the grassroots of American politics (see Chapter 8, Interest Groups). These groups and movements, such as the Tea Party movement in 2010, draw attention to each party's failings in specific issue areas and engage in activities from staging protest rallies to nominating alternative candidates to run in primaries in order to get parties to move closer to the policy positions the group or movement advocates. They are important in a democracy because they can force the political parties to be more responsive to the policy concerns of voters generally, even if they are not party members. Interest groups and grassroots movements can also force a party to be accountable to its own members on issues that the members feel should be included in the party's platform. When they are large enough, these groups have the potential to move the party platform in new directions and, in turn, to change federal laws.[27]

Over the past two decades, interest and social movement groups have become more tightly aligned with specific political parties, and that alignment has undermined their capacity to serve as independent checks on—or competitors with—political parties. For example, unions such as the American Federation of Labor and Congress of Industrial Organizations (AFL-CIO) and environmental groups such as the Sierra Club are generally supportive of the Democratic Party, whereas business groups such as the Chamber of Commerce and the National Rifle Association are supportive of the Republican Party. For interest groups, the risk in continuously supporting one party is that the party will take their support for granted. In fact, parties are most responsive to interest groups when they threaten to withdraw their support or start their own party organizations. Consequently, interest groups maintain their influence with political parties by constantly expressing their preferences on policies to party leaders and providing support only when the party is responsive to their concerns.

How do interest groups encourage citizen participation in political parties? How do they limit it?

Party Alignment and Ideology

Throughout U.S. history, there have been long stretches of time during which the party affiliations of voters remained stable, but there have also been key elections in which parties lost or gained significant blocs of voters. Scholars have tried to identify the factors that explain why voters make large, permanent shifts from one party to another. Shifts in party allegiance can occur when there is an external shock to the nation, such as an economic depression or a foreign military attack. Shifts can also occur when public attitudes change considerably and one party appears to respond more quickly to those changes than another.

The Parties after the Civil War

Following the Civil War, as we have seen, the Republicans were dominant in the Northeast and West, and the Democrats were dominant in the South and increasingly in large cities with big immigrant populations. This **party alignment**—voters identifying with a party in repeated elections—was relatively stable until 1896, when a number of smaller parties challenged the Republican and Democratic Parties. The Republican Party emerged from that election with a victory, and the smaller parties faded from the national political scene.

party alignment: *Voter identification with a political party in repeated elections.*

From 1896 to 1932 the basic geographic pattern of party alignment stayed the same, but the combination of the stock market crash of October 24, 1929, a global depression that followed, and a drop in worldwide agricultural prices brought political trouble to the Republican Party. By 1932 voters in every part of the country were ready for a change not only in political leadership but also in the entire approach to government.

The New Deal and the Role of Ideology in Party Politics

During the election of 1932 voters were exposed to a new **political ideology**, or set of consistent political views, about the way that the federal government could work. Today's voters might describe themselves as liberal or conservative, but voters before 1932 typically identified themselves with a political party. In that election year, Franklin Delano Roosevelt (1933–45), governor of New York State, ran for president on a platform designed to reverse the effects of the Great Depression. The idea that the federal government would help individuals to help themselves was transformative in American politics. The Democratic Party platform resonated with voters, and Roosevelt won the election.

political ideology: *Set of consistent political beliefs.*

Should the federal government help individuals to help themselves?

New Deal: *Franklin Delano Roosevelt's program for ending the Great Depression through government intervention in the economy and development of a set of safety-net programs for individuals.*

After he took office, Roosevelt championed a vast array of new government programs that are commonly referred to as the **New Deal**. These programs were designed to help individuals who were jobless, homeless, or otherwise in financial need. Essentially the New

AP Photo

In his acceptance speech at the Democratic National Convention in 1932, Franklin Delano Roosevelt introduced an innovative campaign platform. "I pledge you," he said, "I pledge myself, to a new deal for the American people." The term "New Deal" came to describe federal programs that took an active role in helping individual citizens find jobs, save for retirement, and benefit from fair working conditions.

liberals: *Individuals who have faith in government to improve people's lives, believing that private efforts are insufficient. In the social sphere, liberals usually support diverse lifestyles and tend to oppose any government action that seeks to shape personal choices.*

conservatives: *Individuals who distrust government, believing that private efforts are more likely to improve people's lives. In the social sphere, conservatives usually support traditional lifestyles and tend to believe that government can play a valuable role in shaping personal choices.*

Deal was a promise by the federal government to provide a safety net for workers and their families who fell on hard times. Following his electoral victory in 1932, Roosevelt built a coalition of white southerners, working-class ethnic northerners, liberal advocates for socialist policies, and northern African Americans who had previously been Republicans. This was a radical shift for African Americans, who since the Civil War had followed the party of Abraham Lincoln and shunned the Democrats, whom they associated with racism and slavery. This electoral coalition was large but fragile, and to maintain it Roosevelt engaged in a great deal of political balancing and a wide distribution of government benefits.

In supporting the New Deal, voters came to accept the ideological viewpoint that government involvement in the economic aspects of individuals' lives was legitimate and, on balance, a good thing. As we noted in Chapter 1, this perspective on government serves as a foundation for the modern definition of a **liberal**. Today the liberal viewpoint builds on the New Deal perspective by favoring government redistribution of income through higher taxes on the wealthy to provide social benefits, such as health care, unemployment insurance, and welfare payments to the poor. Those who opposed the New Deal are the forefathers of the modern **conservatives**, who believe in lower taxes and less government involvement in economic life.

In response to Roosevelt's big government approach, the Republicans seized what they saw as the main weakness of the New Deal, which was the high cost of all these newly created programs. To pay for them, the federal and state governments would have to raise taxes on businesses and workers alike. The Republicans recognized that they had an opportunity to reshape their party platform to exploit the Democrats' weakness.

In the aftermath of 1932, the two parties transformed; it was almost as if they had switched places. The Democrats changed from a party that believed in state's rights, low taxes, and little government intervention in individuals' lives to the party that created a large social safety net that relied on the federal government to ensure personal economic stability. The Republicans changed from a party that believed in a strong central federal government and in intervention in the economy when necessary to the party of a strictly limited federal government and fiscal responsibility. Alongside these opposing economic viewpoints, modern liberals and conservatives also differ on social issues, including abortion, gun control, affirmative action, prayer in school, and same-sex marriage.

Voters responded to these partisan and ideological changes by changing their own party allegiances over time, essentially producing a **realignment** of the electorate. In the broadest sense, Democrats today support expanding the size of government to accomplish specific policy goals, even if it means raising taxes, and support liberal social values. In contrast, Republicans support limiting the size of government by keeping taxation and regulation of the economy to a minimum and support preserving conservative social values.

realignment: *Long-term shift in voter allegiance from one party to another.*

How does the realignment that followed the election of 1932 echo the divisions between the Federalists and the Antifederalists? Or is the political ideology of the modern era entirely different?

Civil Rights, the Great Society, and Nixon's Southern Strategy

The Democratic and Republican Parties remained divided mainly along this economic dimension until the early 1960s, when the Democratic Party established itself as the party of civil rights for African Americans. During the presidency of Lyndon Baines Johnson (1963–69), the Civil Rights Act of 1964, the Voting Rights Act of 1965, the Department of Housing and Urban Development Act of 1965, and the Fair Housing Act of 1966 were all signed into law. These acts gave the federal government strong enforcement powers to guarantee African Americans the fullest extent of the civil rights afforded to every American and served as a key gateway for full political participation by African Americans. Johnson's policies brought a second dimension to liberal ideology: Now the federal government was granted the power not only to help individuals in need economically, but also to take affirmative steps to overrule state and local governments to prevent discrimination on all levels. As noted in Chapter 5, the government's role evolved from preventing unequal treatment under the law to ensuring equality in all walks of life, from education to employment to housing.

Which perspective comes closest to your own views—liberal or conservative?

By putting the stamp of the Democratic Party on the pledge to preserve civil rights, Johnson began the process of stripping the party of the last vestiges of its reputation for racism and segregation. Today African Americans remain the most loyal of any demographic constituency in the Democratic Party. In 2004, 88 percent of African American voters chose the Democratic candidate, John Kerry, over President George W. Bush, and that number held firm in the 2006 midterm congressional elections.[28] In 2008, 95 percent of African Americans voted for the Democratic candidate, Barack Obama, who was elected as the nation's first African American president.[29]

The Johnson administration also expanded federal programs that granted aid to individuals and to state and local governments in the areas of health care, education, housing, job training, and welfare to families with children (see Chapter 13, The Presidency, for an extensive discussion of Johnson's programs). This set of policies was called the **Great Society** and was founded on the idea that federal expansion would strengthen American society by helping all citizens reach their potential. By expanding the reach of the federal government this way, Johnson reinforced the liberal ideological underpinnings of the Democratic Party.

Great Society: *Lyndon Johnson's program for expanding the federal social welfare programs in health care, education, and housing and for ending poverty.*

As this shift in Democratic policies occurred, Republicans saw a new opportunity to attract support from voters who opposed the expansion of the federal government into race relations or the regulation of the economy. Beginning with the campaign of Barry Goldwater in 1964, and continuing with the campaign of Richard M. Nixon (1969–74) in 1968, the Republicans employed a so-called southern strategy, presenting themselves to southern white voters as holding opposite views on civil rights and race from the Democrats.

What would the Federalists think of the federal government today? What would the Antifederalists think?

Although Republicans did not sanction racism and discrimination, they made it clear that they would not take the same strong steps as the Democrats to impose federal law on states to remedy these problems. Republicans extended their philosophy of limited government intervention by asserting that each state was responsible for enforcing civil rights and that the federal government was overstepping its bounds by interfering at the state and local levels. At the same time, Republicans opposed the Great Society policies as too expensive, and they were philosophically opposed to the federal government giving so much aid directly to individuals without asking for something in return. In this way, the Republican Party continued to move toward a more conservative ideology that sought to limit the powers and programs of the federal government.

The Reagan Revolution and Conservative Party Politics

In 1980 Ronald Reagan (1981–89), former Republican governor of California, defeated the incumbent President Jimmy Carter (1977–81), a Democrat, partly by appealing to those who opposed the Supreme Court's legalization of abortion in *Roe v. Wade* (1973). Following the ruling, the national stance of the parties diverged, with the Democratic Party publicly supporting the decision and the Republican Party split on the issue. When Reagan won the Republican Party's presidential nomination, he moved the Republicans more firmly into the anti-abortion camp. In the general election, Reagan's campaign offered a consistent conservative ideology that focused on limiting the size of the federal government, opposing abortion, and allowing religious prayer in public schools, which had been prohibited by the Supreme Court ruling in *Engel v. Vitale* in 1962 (see Chapter 4 for further discussion of prayer in school).[30] Reagan's campaign strategy was designed to attract conservative Democrats who were alienated by their party's official position on abortion and to attract the growing numbers of active evangelical Christian voters, especially in the South.

Reagan also took advantage of the instability in foreign relations that marked Jimmy Carter's four years in office. Although Carter had increased defense spending for the military while in office, he focused on protecting human rights. For Reagan, protecting individual political freedom was a moral obligation for the United States. Reagan campaigned on a strong defense and tough foreign policy that actively promoted freedom, and he made it clear that, under his administration, the United States would work to undermine the Communist political and economic system that was dominant in the Soviet Union, eastern Europe, and Cuba.

The combination of these issues brought Reagan the support of many working-class, ethnic, northern voters and southern white voters. These voters were subsequently referred to as **Reagan Democrats**, and it was in large part due to them that Ronald Reagan won the presidential election of 1980.

Although the Republicans dominated the presidency for the next twelve years, many of the voters who supported Republicans at the national level stayed loyal to the Democrats in congressional, state, and local elections. This **split-ticket voting** made it hard for parties to sustain complete voter allegiance at all levels of elected office.

Reagan Democrats: *Voters traditionally affiliated with the Democratic Party based on their working-class status who voted for Ronald Reagan in the 1980s because of his conservative message on social issues, emphasis on national security, and call for limited government.*

split-ticket voting: *Practice of voting for candidates from different parties for different elected offices in a single election.*

What are the advantages and disadvantages of split-ticket voting? Is it best to be an Independent?

Reagan's vice president, George H. W. Bush (1989–93), elected president in 1988, had to work with a Democratic-controlled House and Senate. While in office, President Bush was confronted with a very large budget deficit and subsequently approved deficit reduction legislation that raised some taxes and also raised voter anger, particularly among Republican voters who had supported him in 1988. Not only did the Republican Party have a central belief that taxes should be as low as possible, but Bush had promised that he would not raise taxes in his nomination acceptance speech at the Republican National Convention, where he said, "Read my lips: No new taxes." When Ross Perot entered the race as a third-party candidate to emphasize fiscal responsibility, he took voter support away from Bush, who lost his reelection bid to Clinton.

© Robert Maass/CORBIS

In his acceptance speech at the Republican National Convention in 1988, George H. W. Bush promised not to raise taxes. "Read my lips," he famously said, "No new taxes." It was a campaign promise he came to regret when in 1990 he agreed with Congress to raise taxes and decrease government spending to reduce the federal budget deficit.

The Modern Partisan Landscape

Bill Clinton was governor of Arkansas when he successfully ran for president in 1992. As had Reagan, Clinton changed his party's direction with a campaign platform that advocated dropping opposition to the death penalty, being more open to free trade, and promising a middle-class tax cut. These policies moved the Democrats away from liberal policies, but even though Clinton appeared more moderate than previous Democratic presidential candidates, he still ran under the established Democratic Party label. Clinton thus appealed to a wider range of voters, and he was able to recapture some electoral territory the Democrats had lost in the southern states.

In office, however, Clinton lost popularity by veering away from core issues such as the middle-class tax cut and economic growth to address socially liberal policies on abortion and gays in the military, which he had given far less emphasis on the campaign trail. Clinton also proposed a stimulus package of government spending and the creation of a major federal health care program for the uninsured. At the time, voters perceived these policies as too liberal, and they caused conflict among liberal, moderate, and conservative members of the Democratic Party. The conflict grew intense enough that it prevented the Democratic majority in Congress from passing key legislative measures, and the public nature of the infighting made it appear as if the Democrats were not capable of governing efficiently. These political missteps, and the erosion of Democratic Party unity in Congress, set the stage for a Republican Party resurgence.

In the 1994 midterm congressional elections, Republicans took control of both the House and the Senate for the first time since 1954. Led by Newt Gingrich, a Republican House member from Georgia, the Republicans put forth a party platform called the **Contract with America**, which promised ten major policy initiatives, such as a balanced federal budget and less federal regulation (for more on the Contract with America, see Chapter 12, Congress). Every Republican candidate for the House signed it, and by coordinating candidates this way, the Republican Party presented a single national message to voters about what it would do if it won control of Congress. In addition, Gingrich strategically targeted seats in the South that were held by conservative Democrats, trying to appeal to the same set of southern voters who elected Ronald Reagan. Republican efforts were successful, finally overcoming the split-ticket voting of southern voters who had previously voted Democratic in congressional elections.[31]

At the presidential level, George W. Bush, the son of former President George H. W. Bush and a conservative Republican governor of Texas, built on the momentum of the Republicans to launch a bid for the presidency in 1999. Josh McKoon's first paid job on a presidential campaign was working for Bush in South Carolina to get out the college-age vote. The presidential election of 2000 was highly controversial because there were irregularities in the vote count in several states, including Florida, which were ultimately resolved by the Supreme Court. It was also an election in which the candidate with the greatest number of popular votes, the Democrat Al Gore, was defeated by the candidate with the greatest number of Electoral College delegates (see the discussion of the operation of the Electoral College in Chapter 10).

In 2004 the Democratic Party had to try to regroup and present a viable alternative to lure back the voters it had seemingly lost. At that time, nearly 50 percent of voters identified themselves as Democrats or leaning Democratic, 40 percent identified themselves as Republicans or leaning Republican, and 10 percent did not identify with either party.[32] Despite the Democrat's seeming partisan edge, Bush was reelected in 2004 by a much greater margin than in 2000; his victory was in large part viewed as a result of his strong stance on terrorism after the September 11, 2001, terrorist attacks and his successful tax cut politics.

In 2006 the Democrats began to regain electoral momentum with voters who self-identified as Democrats but had not been voting that way in recent elections, as well as with Independent voters. In the congressional and gubernatorial elections held that year, the Democrats made sufficient gains in districts and states that had been narrowly or moderately leaning Republican to regain control of the House of Representatives and Senate. But one election does not constitute voter realignment. That year, there were powerful short-term forces, such as corruption scandals and the Iraq War, that put voters in a particularly sour mood toward incumbent Republicans.

The results of the 2008 elections were a sign that the party landscape was shifting again (see Figure 9.5).[33] Clearly the election of an African American president is a significant turning point in race relations; Barack Obama received 43 percent of the white vote in 2008, 2 percentage points higher than white candidate John Kerry received in 2004. Obama won five states that had been considered solidly Republican in previous presidential elections: Florida, Indiana, North Carolina, Ohio, and Virginia. In addition, Democrats won an additional twenty-two seats in the House of Representatives and nine seats in the Senate from states that had also been considered traditional Republican strongholds.

Contract with America:
Campaign proposal containing ten legislative initiatives used by all Republicans running for the House of Representatives in 1994.

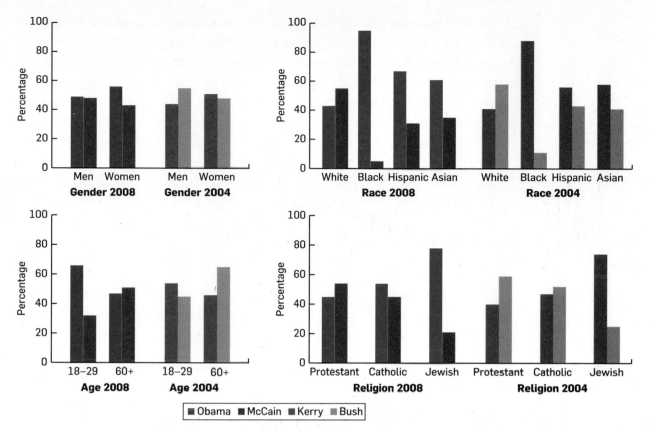

FIGURE 9.5 Votes for President in 2004 and 2008, by Demographic Group. Patterns of support among voters can change from one election to the next depending on the candidate the party chooses as its nominee.

Source: New York Times, elections.nytimes.com.

However, when voters give one party majority party control of the White House and Congress, they have high expectations for a strong governing track record. In one way, that is what political scientists mean by **responsible parties**; if the parties offer voters clear choices, voters can hold the party in charge responsible for policy outcomes. When President Obama and the Democrats took charge of government in 2009, they faced some of the greatest economic challenges since the Great Depression, ongoing wars in Iraq and Afghanistan, and the task of trying to make health insurance available to all Americans. The 2010 congressional midterm elections were the first opportunity that voters had to register their satisfaction or dissatisfaction with the president and his party. The Democratic losses and Republican gains showed the responsible party system in action because voters held the incumbent majority party accountable for its performance on the economy, health care, and the ongoing wars.

There is a trade-off between responsible party government and bipartisan cooperation; where there is one, there is almost never the other. Although the divisions between Democrats and Republicans are clearer than ever, this same divide is causing the greatest level of disagreement between the parties in Congress since the Civil War.[34] In the past two decades, parties have taken on starker opposing positions and have ramped up their rhetoric to the point that it has become difficult for members of opposing parties to communicate at all. Elected officials from each party draw such sharp distinctions between themselves and their partisan opponents that voters sometimes wonder whether partisanship is taking precedence over policy making.

responsible parties: *Parties that take responsibility for offering the electorate a distinct range of policies and programs, thus providing a clear choice.*

What are the advantages and disadvantages of responsible parties?

Do you think partisanship is taking precedence over policy making? What can be done about that?

When a new issue arises or opinion changes, each party has to update its positions and present a united front. The highest-ranking elected officials from the party—from the president down to governors and members of Congress—must consult with their state and local party organizations. This process takes time, and consequently parties appear slow to respond. When there is internal disagreement, they may be unable to respond at all. In addition, the current level of partisanship has reduced the incentive for the parties to cooperate to solve problems. As a result, government is less responsive to overall public needs.

Are consensus and compromise good or bad for American democracy? Give examples.

Political Parties and Public Policy: The Environment

Political parties lay out their platforms during the campaign season, and elections serve as a key link between parties and policy outcomes. The extent to which candidates honor their party's platform can differ depending on external conditions and the opportunities available to them. Not every element of a party platform can be enacted into law, but lawmakers, from the president to state legislators, recognize that they must try to address the issues raised in their campaign platforms to retain the trust of voters.

Party Platforms on Environmental Policy

In the 2008 presidential election, the platforms of both parties addressed environmental protection and energy conservation. The Democratic Party platform centered on creating green jobs and renewable energy sources and on reducing greenhouse emissions.[35] As the Democratic Party nominee, Barack Obama made this approach to environmental problems a key part of his presidential campaign. The Republican Party platform focused on promoting clean and reliable sources of energy in America, funding an energy trust fund, and increasing emphasis on energy conservation and efficiency. The Republican Party nominee John McCain promoted this approach in his presidential campaign, with a special emphasis on tax incentives for energy innovators.[36]

As is typically the case, the political party that wins control of the White House tries to implement its policy platform. One of President Obama's first environmental initiatives was to ask Congress to pass a bill to reduce carbon emissions. H.R. 2454, originally known as the "cap and trade bill," establishes a system whereby the government establishes a maximum amount of carbon emissions for the entire country, with a goal of reducing these emissions by 17 percent by 2020. Within the maximum, each company that produces carbon gases is granted a permit for a set amount of emissions. Companies can buy, sell, and trade permits with one another if they expect their emissions to exceed or fall below expectations. Over time, the government will reduce the maximum to reduce pollution.[37] The policy, if enacted into law, would implement the Democratic Party's agenda for reducing emissions, creating new energy resources, and making the United States more energy independent in the future.[38]

H.R. 2454 passed the House of Representatives in a close vote (219–212) on June 26, 2009. Many House Republicans opposed the bill, arguing that it would increase energy costs for companies, which would result in higher costs for consumers as well as potential job losses as companies cut back on hiring.[39] This opposition is consistent with the Republican Party platform of trying to use tax credits, which reduce taxes, to decrease energy use rather than adopting tax increases or requiring the purchase of government permits. Republicans also argued that any real decrease in carbon emissions would take too long to accomplish, at too great a cost.[40]

Competing Constituent and Interest Group Pressures

The vote on the climate change bill in the House of Representatives was not a straight **party-line vote**; members of both parties voted against their party's official position. Eight Republican members of Congress, predominantly from the East and West Coasts, voted for the bill, saying that their local constituents supported it. Even more surprising, forty-four Democratic members of Congress—from the Southeast, northern tier, and western states— voted against the bill.[41] These Democrats cited concerns over job displacement, increased taxation, and disproportionate costs imposed on oil-, gas-, and coal-producing states. The voting patterns on the bill suggest that the members weighed the local interests of their regions and constituents more heavily than national party platforms.[42]

party-line vote: *Voting in Congress according to party position, so that a majority of one party votes against a majority of the other party.*

Should members of Congress always vote the party line? Why?

In addition, organized interest groups expressed their support or opposition to the bill. Some liberal environmental groups, such as Friends of the Earth and Greenpeace, were dissatisfied because they believed that the bill did not go far enough in limiting carbon emissions. Agriculture groups feared that limits on emissions would reduce their capacity to produce crops by raising the cost of fertilizer and of the electricity used to power machines on their farms. Also, farm animals produce waste that emits methane gas, which could be categorized as a greenhouse gas emission.[43] On the other hand, major energy companies, such as Shell Oil and General Electric, supported the bill because it took a gradual approach to transforming energy consumption that would give all businesses time to adapt their energy use to new circumstances.[44]

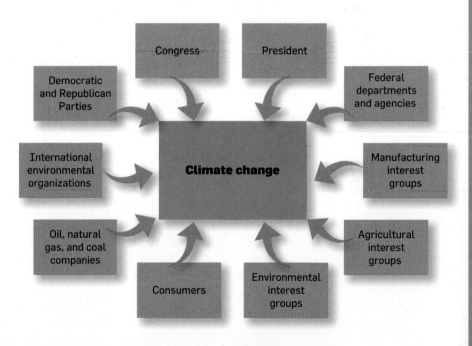

In the Senate, the bipartisan trio of Senators John Kerry (D-Mass.), Joseph Lieberman (I-Conn.), and Lindsay Graham (R-S.C.) worked together to produce a version of the bill that could pass the Senate. One of the first things they did was to remove the "cap and trade" label and use the less controversial name of "climate change" to describe the bill. They were set to introduce the bill to the full Senate in April 2010, but their efforts were interrupted when immigration replaced climate change as a priority for the Obama administration and Senator Graham withdrew his support for their bill. Because the Senate relies so heavily on bipartisan cooperation to consider legislation (see Chapter 12), the bill could not proceed successfully without his support. The same month, a massive oil spill in the Gulf of Mexico brought additional scrutiny to energy policy more generally and detracted from any momentum the bill might have had earlier in the year (see Chapter 14 for discussion of the oil spill).

The stakes for both major political parties remain high when it comes to environmental policy because voters will hold them responsible for their promises. The Democratic Party, under the leadership of President Obama, promised to use its electoral victory in 2008 to accomplish real policy change in this area. If the Democrats succeed in enacting a climate change bill before the presidential election in 2012, they meet their short-term platform goal and appear credible in their campaign promises. But if the bill imposes high costs on consumers, the consumers may blame the Democrats in the 2012 elections. The Republican Party promised to maintain its vigilance against higher taxes on businesses and consumers, as well as to present incentives for alternative energy development. If Republicans oppose the bill outright, they too maintain their electoral credibility, but they also risk appearing unproductive, for which they may also be held accountable by voters in the 2012 elections. The case of the climate change bill illustrates how party platforms and the policy-making process can intersect to produce conflicting incentives for elected officials.

Do political parties help voters hold government responsible? Why?

Political Parties and Democracy

Political parties, which emerged in the nation's first decade, now play a major role in American democracy. The Democrats and the Republicans together claim the allegiance of over 80 percent of voters. Political parties determine the choices voters have at the polls by crafting the laws that allow candidates to be on the ballot and overseeing the primaries that allow voters to choose candidates. Parties also recruit candidates for elected office, raise funds for campaigns, register voters, and organize get-out-the-vote drives. In sum, parties shape the selection of candidates who seek, run for, and win elected office.

Do political parties make it easier for voters to hold elected officials accountable? Party platforms tell voters what candidates intend to do if elected, and voters can compare their actions against their campaign pledges. If pledges and policies match up, voters typically reelect the officials; if they do not, voters can vote for the opponents in the next election. One advantage of clear dividing lines between the parties is that it makes the job of monitoring the government easier for the average voter. However, such clear divisions also bring the disadvantages of conflict and stalemate that make bipartisan policy making difficult.

Parties do a mixed job of promoting equal political participation among all citizens. On the one hand, they are a gateway to participation because membership in a political party is free and citizens can work a little or a lot on behalf of the party. Primaries and caucuses give every party member a say in determining who will represent the party in elected office, and they force candidates who seek the party's endorsement to shape their campaign platforms according to party voters' preferences. Because voters are free to join and leave political parties as frequently as they wish, parties are always seeking to represent their members' viewpoints.

On the other hand, parties can discourage political participation by putting obstacles in the way of third-party formation. The U.S. party system is structured around two major parties, and even though third parties have arisen at various times, they are quickly subsumed or defeated by one of the two major

- How do political parties shape the choices voters face in local, state, and federal elections?

- In what ways do political parties allow voters to hold their elected officials accountable for the policies they produce?

- How do political parties respond to changes in public opinion on key issues?

- Do political parties enable all citizens to participate equally in self-government, or do they help give more power to some people, and less to others? Explain.

- Are political parties a gate or a gateway to democracy?

parties. The two-party system reduces major policy issues to two-sided questions, when in fact the complexity of these issues warrants multiple perspectives. The problem for democracy is that there is no formal venue for presenting multiple perspectives in elections or in the governing institutions.

The larger question is whether the twenty-first-century U.S. party system fulfills the role of enabling widespread participation in the governing process. In terms of responding to changes in public opinion, political parties fall short of meeting their responsibilities as agents of democratic government. They are large, entrenched organizations with multiple layers—federal, state, and local—that can differ in their viewpoints on specific issues. The breadth of the national parties makes it difficult to reach internal consensus on issues at every level of government.

The combination of intra-party divisions with interparty polarization and conflict has produced a party-dominated democracy that is not consistently responsive to voters' interests and opinions. However, in a democracy, power rests on winning elections, and for that parties will always depend on voters like you, who hold the power to change them by staying loyal or switching your allegiance.

GATEWAYS TO LEARNING

Top Ten to Take Away

1. Political parties are the broadest and most open gateway to participation in American politics. (pp. 282–83)
2. They have one primary purpose: to win elections in order to control government power and implement their policies. (p. 283)
3. Parties organize the electorate by giving them choices of policies and candidates, and they also organize Congress and state legislatures into cohesive groups that consistently vote for the policies that they promise in their platforms. (pp. 283–85)
4. Parties nominate candidates for office in primary elections, which are open to all voters, although in some states voters must affiliate with a party before voting. (pp. 284–93)
5. The basic division between the Federalists and the Antifederalists over the ratification of the Constitution survived into the Washington administration to become factions; by the time of Jefferson's election in 1800, the factions had become political parties. (pp. 293–95)
6. Between 1800 and the Civil War, various parties rose and fell, but since the end of the war the two major parties—the Democratic Party and the Republican Party—have dominated the American political system. (pp. 295–99)
7. The effects of the two-party system are to limit voter choices to "for" and "against" and to discourage third parties, although the issues third parties arise to address are frequently adopted by one of the major political parties. (pp. 300–305)
8. Voter realignments occur when the parties readjust the focus of their policies, typically as a result of a major event such as an economic depression or a military conflict. (p. 305)
9. Since Franklin D. Roosevelt's New Deal of the 1930s, liberals have generally aligned with the Democratic Party and conservatives with the Republican Party. (pp. 305–9)
10. The modern political landscape is marked by a partisan divide, with the parties taking on starker opposing positions and ramping up the rhetoric to the point that voters sometimes wonder if partisanship is taking precedence over policy making. (pp. 309–12)

A full narrative summary of the chapter is on the book's website.

Ten to Test Yourself

1. What is a faction? What is a political party? How are they different?
2. When and how did the first nationally organized political party emerge?
3. How is the presidential nomination system organized?
4. How do the rules for and practices of nominating presidents and members of Congress influence who runs and who can win?
5. What was the Australian ballot, and how did it transform the American political party system?
6. What is the difference between party identification and political ideology?
7. How did the New Deal change the party balance among voters between Republicans and Democrats?
8. What was the Reagan revolution, and how does it help explain the balance of partisan power today?
9. How do the Democratic and Republican Parties differ from what they were a century ago in terms of voter base, geography, and party policy?
10. How do the Democrats and Republicans differ on environmental policy?

More review questions and answers and chapter quizzes are on the book's website.

Timeline to Keep Things in Order

Factions emerge over the ratification of the Constitution, and they form the foundations for political parties.

Thomas Jefferson uses his electoral victory to turn his Democratic-Republicans into a full-fledged political party.

Andrew Jackson broadens the base of the Democratic Party and initiates party patronage.

The Republican Party forms by absorbing various antislavery factions and third parties.

After the Civil War the Republican Party dominates the North and West, and the Democratic Party dominates the South and, increasingly, big cities.

1787　　1800　　1828　　1854　　1865

Terms to Know and Use

abolitionist movement (p. 297)
Antifederalists (p. 294)
Australian ballot (p. 299)
ballot (p. 288)
blanket primary (p. 288)
caucus (p. 288)
civil service (pp. 298, 299)
closed primary (p. 288)
conservatives (p. 306)
Contract with America (p. 310)
delegate (p. 288)
Democratic-Republicans (p. 295)
faction (p. 293)
Federalists (p. 294)
frontloading (p. 293)

general election (p. 287)
Great Society (p. 307)
incumbent (p. 286)
Independent (p. 304)
liberals (p. 306)
local party organization (p. 287)
machine politics (p. 298)
majority vote (p. 301)
McGovern-Fraser
  Commission (p. 290)
median voter theorem (p. 300)
moderates (p. 300)
national committee (p. 285)
New Deal (p. 305)
open primary (p. 288)

party alignment (p. 305)
party as an organization (p. 283)
party boss (p. 298)
party caucus (p. 285)
party identification (p. 283)
party in government (p. 283)
party in the electorate (p. 283)
party-line vote (p. 313)
party platform (p. 283)
patronage system (p. 297)
plurality vote (p. 300)
political ideology (p. 305)
political parties (p. 283)
primary election (p. 287)
Progressives (p. 298)

proportional representation
  (p. 290)
Reagan Democrats (p. 308)
realignment (p. 307)
responsible parties (p. 311)
semi-closed primary (p. 288)
single-member plurality
  system (p. 300)
split-ticket voting (p. 308)
state central committee (p. 286)
superdelegates (p. 291)
third parties (p. 297)
voter registration (p. 284)
Whig Party (p. 296)
winner-take-all system (p. 290)

Use the vocabulary flash cards on the book's website.

Learning That Works

WHAT YOU NEED . . .

TO KNOW	TO DO
What political parties do	Choose to join one
What primaries are	Decide whether you will take the time to vote in one
Why political parties formed	Evaluate whether they are gateways or obstacles to representation
The viewpoints of the Federalists and the Antifederalists	Consider whether these views have survived to explain the differences between Democrats and Republicans today
The advantages and disadvantages of a two-party system	Assess whether the parties reflect your views
What third parties offer	Determine whether a third party better reflects your views, and join it
Democratic and Republican policies on the environment	Debate the strategy that is most likely to achieve environmental protection

The Pendleton Act is the first of a series of reforms that end party patronage and curtail corruption.

The election of Franklin Roosevelt and the passage of New Deal programs begin to realign the electorate and set up modern political ideology.

The election of Ronald Reagan marks a conservative resurgence and realigns the electorate once again.

Republicans win control of the House and Senate for the first time since 1954.

Democrats win back control of the House and Senate.

The midterm elections mark the renewed strength of the Republican Party.

 1883
 1932
1980
1994
2006
 2010

10 ELECTIONS AND CAMPAIGNS

> *As far as this generation, I think we're a very involved and engaged demographic. I think you saw that in the last election.*

Aaron Schock, Republican member of the House from Illinois, was voted the "hottest congressional freshman" in a 2009 reader's poll. There is no question that Schock is good-looking, single, and barely over 30, but he is also a near-perfect example of what dedication and hard work can accomplish in the American political system. He has always been on a fast track. It took him just two years to graduate from Bradley University in Peoria, Illinois, with a degree in finance. He was already a successful businessman. As a child he had grown strawberries on his father's farm, and then harvested and sold them. In his teens he worked after-school jobs in sales; later he earned up to $18,000 a year working in a gravel pit. He saved it all. He began contributing to an IRA at age 14. At age 18 he bought his first piece of real estate. After graduation from college, he and a partner started a small business that employed three people.

The next year Schock entered politics. Running as a write-in candidate for the Peoria school board, he knocked on enough doors to introduce himself and win with 60 percent of the vote. As a school board member, he worked hard to research issues and information. Four years later his fellow board members unanimously elected him president. He was 23 years old. But by this time he was already a member of the Illinois House of Representatives, having run, and won, a difficult campaign in a traditionally Democratic district. In the Illinois House he was appointed to five committees, including one on school appropriations and one on financial services. In 2007 he shared with Barack Obama (then a U.S. senator) an award for "outstanding legislative and constituency service" from the Illinois Committee for Honest Government. The next year Schock entered national politics, campaigning and winning election to the U.S. House of Representatives from the 18th Congressional District in Illinois. This young Republican was the youngest member of the 111th Congress and the first person born in the 1980s to serve in Congress.

Aaron Schock ▶

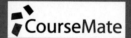

AP Photo/Seth Perlman

- In what ways do elections encourage accountability and responsiveness in government?

- How does citizen equality work, or not work, in elections and campaigns? Are elections and campaigns fair?

- How well do campaigns work to inform the public so as to allow voters to hold candidates accountable?

- Do laws that regulate the financing of campaigns impede or advance equality and accountability in elections?

- In what ways are elections and campaigns gateways to American democracy? What are the gates?

Schock's gateway to American politics and influence was through elections and campaigns. From a write-in candidate for a local school board to a representative in the U.S. Congress, he challenged the odds. He defeated incumbents through hard campaigning and won reelection through hard work. His interests in finance and education were manifest in his committee assignments and legislative proposals. Early in his first term in the U.S. House he proposed a successful amendment mandating a website to track TARP (Troubled Asset Relief Program) "bailout" funds. In 2010 he was easily reelected.[1]

Elections and campaigns, as the experience of Aaron Schock demonstrates, offer a gateway into the American political system. They provide many opportunities for participation, not only running for office but also volunteering and working at the polls. During campaigns, candidates offer competing visions of the role of government and promise to enact specific policies. The people decide to support a candidate and a campaign program when they go to the polls. Elections provide the most common (and easiest) gateway for the people to express their opinions and to hold elected officials accountable. Together, elections and campaigns offer the public a chance to shape the course of government. In this chapter, we examine how elections and campaigns work, asking whether, and how, these institutions promote government responsiveness and equality for citizens.

The Constitutional Requirements for Elections

Given the importance of elections to the democratic process, it is surprising that the Constitution says so little about them. The requirements the Constitution does lay out for elections indicate that the Framers wanted to set up barriers against direct democracy. Only the House of Representatives was to be elected directly by the people. In elections for the president and for the Senate, the public's role was indirect and complex. Today, senators are elected directly by the people. Presidential elections also give citizens more say in the process, but these contests continue to be shaped by constitutional requirements that serve as a gate between the people and the presidency. In this section, we explain the constitutional requirements for American elections as background for understanding the ways in which presidential and congressional campaigns are run.

Why did the Framers set up gates against popular participation in elections?

Presidential Elections

The constitutional rules governing the selection of the president reflect three fundamental themes that guided the Framers' thinking. First, the states were given broad discretion on key matters regarding presidential elections to ensure their importance and to counterbalance the power of the national government. Second, the Framers designed the presidency with George Washington in mind and did not spell out all aspects in great detail, including

Why did the Framers give so much authority over elections to the states?

elections. Over time, the details were filled in. Third, the presidency was envisioned as being above party politics, doing what was right for the nation rather than supporting one faction over another. That assumption went awry early on, and parties formed almost from the start.

The Electoral College.

The means by which the president of the United States is elected was born of compromise between the interests of the states and the interests of the people, yielding a system that even today is indirect and confusing. Like the Connecticut Compromise that produced a legislature with an upper chamber to represent the states and a lower chamber to represent the people, the system for electing the president was intended to be similarly balanced. The formal selection of the president is in the hands of **electors**, who collectively constitute the **Electoral College**.

The selection of electors was originally the responsibility of state legislatures, whose members were, for the most part, elected by the people. This arrangement gave the public an indirect say in the choice. The idea was that the state legislatures would serve as gatekeepers against rash or ignorant voters. There was little support among the Framers for letting the people pick the president directly. In fact, during the debates at the Constitutional Convention, George Mason said that allowing the people to select the president would be like referring "a trial of colors to a blind man."[2] Today the people of each state, not the members of state legislatures, choose the electors, in an arrangement that has given citizens a new gateway for influence (see Figure 10.1).

electors: *The individuals who serve in the Electoral College and cast votes for president and vice president.*

Electoral College: *The 538 presidential electors, elected to represent the votes of their respective states, who meet every four years to cast the electoral votes for president and vice president of the United States.*

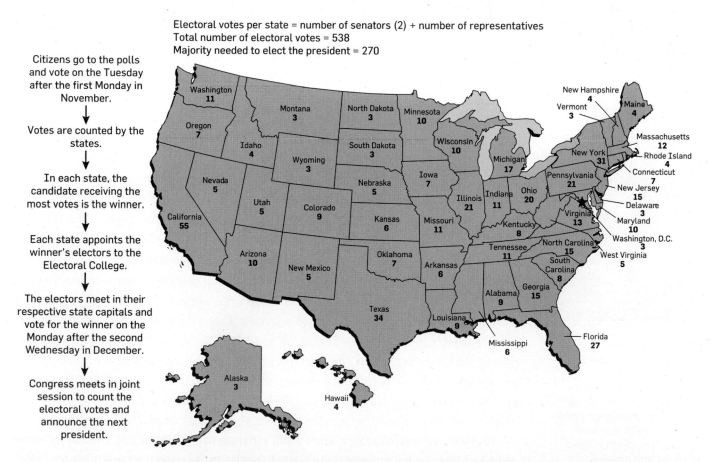

Electoral votes per state = number of senators (2) + number of representatives
Total number of electoral votes = 538
Majority needed to elect the president = 270

Citizens go to the polls and vote on the Tuesday after the first Monday in November.

Votes are counted by the states.

In each state, the candidate receiving the most votes is the winner.

Each state appoints the winner's electors to the Electoral College.

The electors meet in their respective state capitals and vote for the winner on the Monday after the second Wednesday in December.

Congress meets in joint session to count the electoral votes and announce the next president.

Each state's number of electors for the 2004 and 2008 elections, allocated on the basis of the 2000 census.

Note: In every state but two the winner of the popular vote takes all of the electoral votes. Maine and Nebraska allocate votes by congressional district and so can split their electoral votes.

FIGURE 10.1 How the Electoral College Works.

The electors, however, remain the formal decision makers for choosing the president. They are selected in a variety of ways in the fifty states. Each party lines up electors for its candidate prior to the election. In the 2008 presidential elections, when Barack Obama won the most votes in the state of California, his electors were chosen to serve in the Electoral College. John McCain had different electors ready to serve if he had won. Both McCain and Obama chose people they could trust to be loyal to them. This is important because many states allow electors to vote their conscience; they are not bound by the results of the election in their state. However, electors who deviate from the candidate to whom they are pledged are rare.

Each state receives a number of electoral votes equal to its number of senators and members of the House of Representatives. The minimum is three, because every state has at least one House member and two senators. In 2008 seven states (Alaska, Delaware, Montana, North Dakota, South Dakota, Vermont, and Wyoming) and the District of Columbia had only three votes in the Electoral College. With fifty-five electoral votes, California had the most. In all but two states, all the state's electoral votes are allocated to the candidate who finishes first in the voting. This **winner-take-all system** means that if a candidate wins California by just a single vote, that candidate gets all fifty-five of the state's electoral votes. The two exceptions are Nebraska and Maine, which allocate votes by congressional district and so can split their electoral votes. In 2008 Obama won one congressional district in Nebraska, securing one of Nebraska's five electoral votes. This was the first time either state split its votes.

To win the presidency, a candidate needs to win a majority (270) of the 538 electoral votes (538 is the total of 435 representatives and 100 senators plus 3 votes from the District of Columbia, which can vote for president but does not have representation in Congress). If no one wins a majority of electoral votes, the election is thrown into the House of Representatives. At this point, each state delegation gets a single vote, and the candidate who wins a majority of the states becomes the next president. That last happened in 1824.

Problems with the Electoral College.

The Electoral College has never worked as the Framers envisioned, as an institution that would allow a group of independent decision makers to get together in the many states and deliberate over who would make the best president. The Framers viewed the presidency as a contest between individuals, not between political parties, and in the first four presidential elections (1789, 1792, 1796, and 1800), electors cast ballots for their top two choices; the winner became president, and the second-place finisher became vice president. The process ignored the parties of the candidates; the goal was to select the most qualified person. In 1796 the process yielded John Adams (1797–1801) as president and his chief rival, Thomas Jefferson, as vice president. Just imagine John McCain as Barack Obama's vice president!

Problems increased in 1800, when political parties had fully emerged. Thomas Jefferson and Aaron Burr, both running as Democratic-Republicans, received the same number of Electoral College votes, even though everyone knew that Jefferson was seeking the presidency and Burr the vice presidency. Adams, who was also running again as a Federalist, finished

winner-take-all system: *Electoral system in which the candidate who wins the most votes in an election wins the election.*

Is the winner-take-all system fair?

How did the emergence of political parties change the way the Framers hoped elections would work?

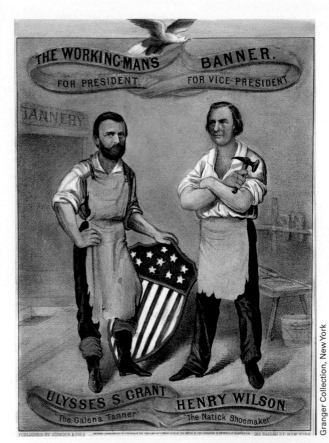

Granger Collection, New York

Following passage of the Twelfth Amendment, presidential and vice presidential candidates campaigned on the same ticket. This campaign poster from the 1872 election shows President Ulysses S. Grant and his vice presidential candidate using their humble beginnings to appeal to workingmen.

third. Because there was no outright majority in the Electoral College and Burr would not concede, a lengthy battle in the House ensued, lasting thirty-seven ballots before Thomas Jefferson (1801–1809) won the presidency. The Twelfth Amendment, adopted in 1804, fixed this problem by combining the vote for president and vice president into one ballot, with the person running for each office named.

Another source of problems in the system was that states were free to set their own rules for selecting electors. In the first presidential election in 1789, four states (Delaware, Maryland, Pennsylvania, and Virginia) held direct popular elections to choose electors.[3] Others had state legislatures select electors. Further, there was no agreed-upon time for holding these elections. In 1800 voting took place any time between April and November. New York selected its electors in April, and Pennsylvania and South Carolina did not even have rules for selecting theirs until November. States also frequently changed their methods of selecting electors. Only Maryland used a **popular vote** for selecting electors in the first four presidential contests.

Because of this odd hodgepodge of frequently changing rules, the presidential contest in the early nineteenth century was very different from the campaigns of today. Now states hold elections all on the same day—the first Tuesday after the first Monday in November—and electors meet in December to choose the next president. The outcome in December is now largely a formality, a historic relic of the Framers' constitutional design.

Electoral College Reform.

The biggest problem with the Electoral College occurs when winning the nation's popular vote does not automatically translate into a win in the Electoral College, meaning that the individual who received fewer votes could become the president. This happened in the 1824, 1876, 1888, and 2000 presidential elections. There is also some evidence suggesting that John F. Kennedy (1961–63) may have received fewer votes than Richard Nixon in 1960.[4] Such outcomes raise questions about equality; because of the Electoral College, votes in some states matter more than votes in others. The votes citizens cast in Alaska have more than twice the influence of those cast in California.[5] If a democracy rests on the idea of majority rule—that is, the candidate with the most support in the public wins the election—then four or five presidential elections (about 10 percent) have been undemocratic.

Some may wonder why the country does not just change the rules to select the president through the popular vote. This method would appear more democratic because all votes would be treated equally. But the current system has some advantages. For example, the Electoral College system encourages candidates to secure support in all corners of the country, not just in areas with dense populations. A system of popular votes would privilege Los Angeles over New Hampshire. In America's federal system, the states do matter. Eliminating the Electoral College would decrease the role of the states, dampening the significance of state interests. There are also practical problems. Doing away with the Electoral College through a constitutional amendment would be difficult, because it is unlikely that three-quarters of the states, needed to ratify an amendment, would support such a reform. Small states see merit in the system.

What inequalities does state control of elections introduce?

popular vote: *Tally of total votes from individual citizens, as opposed to the electoral vote.*

Rutherford B. Hayes Presidential Center

The 1876 election was contested, and its outcome determined by an electoral commission. Some feared public disturbances at the inauguration, so Rutherford B. Hayes, who had won the Electoral College but not the popular vote, took the oath of office privately in the White House. The formal ceremony at the Capitol, two days later, was peaceful.

Should the Electoral College be eliminated? What would be the consequences?

The 2000 Presidential Election.

Because elections are a centerpiece of democracy, it is important for them to be viewed as fair. The events surrounding the 2000 presidential election tested the credibility of the American electoral process. The margin between Vice President Albert Gore Jr. and George W. Bush (2001–2009) was razor thin. In the popular vote, Gore received nearly 600,000 more votes than Bush—just a 0.5 percentage point difference (48.4 percent to 47.9 percent). The number of electoral votes did not identify a winner on election night because the state of Florida was too close to call, and without that state's electoral votes, neither candidate had the necessary 270 votes. Bush led in Florida by 537 votes out of 5.8 million votes cast—a 0.0001 percent difference. Demands for a recount ensued, and the Florida recount revealed how difficult it is to produce an accurate vote count. A series of court cases resulted in a Supreme Court decision that determined the outcome of the election (see Supreme Court Cases: *Bush v. Gore*).

Many votes had not been counted in Florida, and some had been counted for the wrong candidate. Citizens across the country lost faith in American elections. Nearly one in five voters had doubts about whether his or her vote had been counted.[6] Only 32 percent thought there was "a fair and accurate vote count in Florida."[7] In January 2001, just a few days before George W. Bush was to be sworn in as president, only 51 percent of the public felt he had won the presidency "legitimately."[8] More than 60 percent wanted to do away with the Electoral College.[9]

Since that time, the public's confidence has been restored. By 2008 only one in twenty Americans had doubts about whether his or her vote had been counted.[10] Few people had any doubt that Senator Obama had beaten Senator McCain.[11] The 2000 election raised distrust in the short run, but did little lasting damage to the nation's electoral institutions.

Election workers in Miami manually recount votes while representatives of both parties observe. The 2000 Florida recount was fraught with difficulty, and a series of court cases regarding the election culminated in a Supreme Court decision on December 12 that halted the recount and essentially made George W. Bush the winner of the election.

Was the outcome of the 2000 presidential election fair? Does it matter if it was fair?

Congressional Elections

The constitutional guidelines for congressional elections also reflect the compromise between the interests of the states and the interests of the people. The Senate was intended by the Framers to bring state interests to bear on the legislative process, while the House was intended to represent the people. Each state, regardless of size, has two senators, while representatives are elected from congressional districts within states whose boundaries are adjusted to accommodate changes in population. Senators serve staggered six-year terms, while House members serve two-year terms.

Progressives: *Reformers who sought to end corruption in government; also a third party in the early twentieth century.*

How do differences in term lengths and constituencies affect how senators and House members behave?

Senate Elections. Like the choice of electors, the Constitution originally gave the choice of senators to state legislatures. Again the Framers inserted a gate between the people and those who were to serve their interests in the Senate. In the late nineteenth century, however, **Progressive** reformers called for elimination of this gate, arguing that the people ought to have a direct say in the election of senators. This reform became a reality with the adoption of the Seventeenth Amendment in 1913. Even with this change, however, there are barriers against overwhelming change in the composition of the Senate because Senate elections are staggered; only one-third of senators are up for election at a time. This arrangement ensures that the Senate is insulated from large shifts in public sentiment.

supremecourtcases

Bush v. Gore (2000)

QUESTION: Does Florida's subjective recount mechanism violate equal protection of the law? If so, should there be a recount using more objective standards?

ORAL ARGUMENT: December 11, 2000 (listen at www.oyez.org/cases)

DECISION: December 12, 2000 (read at /www.findlaw .com/casecode/supreme.html)

OUTCOME: Yes, Florida's recount procedures violate the equal protection clause (7–2), and no, there is insufficient time to conduct a recount (5–4).

The presidential election of 2000 came down to Florida's electoral votes. The candidate who won the state—Republican Governor George W. Bush of Texas or Democratic Vice President Al Gore—would win the election. The early counts were excruciatingly close, with the networks first calling the election for Gore, then declaring it undecided, then declaring Bush the winner, and then putting it back in the undecided column.

Due to the closeness of the race, an automatic machine recount took place. Bush led Gore by 537 votes out of nearly 6 million cast. Because elections, even for federal office, are administered under state law, Gore went to state court in Florida, asking for a hand recount in four counties that would require election officials in those counties to determine, from each ballot, the intent of the voter. In punch card ballots, the machine will not read a ballot unless the chad—the area that is to be punched out by the voter—is completely removed. But a hand count might be able to determine the voter's intent from a "hanging" or "dimpled" or "pregnant" chad—indented but not sufficiently punched out so as to break off or even break the corners.

The Florida Supreme Court ruled for Gore by a 4–3 vote on December 8. Bush then filed suit in federal court, claiming that the standard of the intent of the voter that Florida used, which could mean different standards by different officials, was so arbitrary as to violate the equal protection clause. The Bush legal team asked for an injunction, an order blocking further recount. Both the U.S. District Court and the U.S. Court of Appeals rejected Bush's request. Bush then appealed to the Supreme Court.

The Supreme Court agreed to hear the case, and on December 9, it decided, by a 5–4 vote, to halt the recount prior to the Court's decision. The Court heard oral arguments on December 11 and announced its decision at 10:00 P.M. on December 12.

The Supreme Court ruled by a 7–2 vote that the absence of specific standards for gauging the intent of the voter was so arbitrary as to violate the equal protection clause. The Court also declared by a 5–4 vote that Florida's legislature intended all recounts to be completed by December 12, thus making a recount impossible.

The dissenters declared that the machinery of running elections is a state question that should not involve the federal courts; that the Court's prior interpretation of the equal protection clause has allowed differential treatment as long as there is no intent to discriminate against certain groups; and that the Court's December 12 deadline was never stated in Florida law.

Vice President Gore conceded the election the next day.

- **Why was the Supreme Court so rushed in its decision?**
- **In what way did Florida's recount plan violate equality?**

House Elections and Redistricting.

In contrast to the Senate, the entire House of Representatives is up for election every two years. Also in contrast to the Senate, House members have always been elected directly by the people.

The Constitution requires that representatives be apportioned, within each state, according to population, which is counted every ten years in a **census**. Originally each member was to represent no more than 30,000 people. As the population grew, the House of Representatives grew as well, from 65 members in 1789 to 237 members in 1857. The House continued to grow until 1911, and in 1929 the number was capped at 435. A member now represents nearly 650,000 people, and the 2010 census will surely increase the population size of congressional districts. Every ten years, new district lines are drawn following a census. Depending on patterns of population growth or decline, states win or lose congressional seats with each new census. Currently seven states have populations so small that they qualify for only one member of the House of Representatives (Alaska, Delaware, Montana, North Dakota, South Dakota, Vermont, and Wyoming). These states do not need to worry about drawing new congressional districts.

State legislatures are responsible for drawing the district lines in a process known as **redistricting**. While the official aim of redistricting is to try to keep districts equal in terms of population, the majority party in the state legislature tries to construct each district in such a way as to make it easier for its candidates to win congressional seats. Although citizens are not required to disclose party affiliation in the census, past voting patterns give parties a strong indication of where they have the advantage. A main limitation of this redistricting process is that the boundaries of the district must be contiguous (uninterrupted).

Redistricting has also been used as a tool to achieve greater minority representation in the House of Representatives. Following passage of the Voting Rights Act in 1965, some states sought

census: *Constitutionally mandated count of the population every ten years.*

Do majority-minority districts help advance equality or introduce inequalities?

redistricting: *Process whereby state legislatures redraw the boundaries of congressional districts in the state to make them equal in population size.*

© Bettmann/CORBIS

The term *gerrymander* comes from this salamander-shaped district in Massachusetts, which Governor Elbridge Gerry approved following the census of 1810. Political rivals denounced the blatant seeking of political advantage that had produced such an oddly shaped congressional district, and the taunt stuck, passing into common usage in politics.

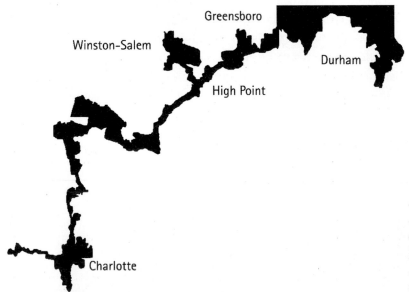

Election Data Services Inc.

Gerrymandered districts never go out of style. This one, from North Carolina in 1991, was designed to create a district with African Americans in the majority. Federal courts later ruled that North Carolina had to revise these district lines so that the congressional district was more compact. *Source:* Elecion Data Services Inc.

to dilute the effect of minority voters by drawing district lines so as to split their voting strength. In 1982 amendments to the Voting Rights Act forbade this practice, and in response state legislatures created majority-minority districts, in which African Americans or Hispanics would constitute a majority of the voters in the district, thereby increasing the possibility of their electing African American or Hispanic candidates. In 1992, for example, Nydia Velázquez won election to the House from a newly created congressional district in New York that was designed to give Latinos a majority (see Chapter 12, Congress). In the past decade, however, the federal courts have ruled that state legislatures overemphasized the racial composition of these districts to the point that the districts made no geographic sense. As a result, current guidelines on redistricting call for the consideration of race in drawing district lines, but not to the extreme that it has been employed in the past.[12]

Any change to the size and shape of a district can have political implications because shifts in its partisan makeup alter which party might be able to capture the seat. For these reasons, there are major battles over the composition of districts. The politicization of drawing districts is called **gerrymandering**. Chapter 12 provides more details about this process and explains how different compositions of districts can alter the kind of gateway congressional elections offer.

gerrymandering: *Redistricting that blatantly benefits one political party over the other or concentrates (or dilutes) the voting impact of racial and ethnic groups.*

Other Elections

The only type of election mentioned in the Constitution in which the people could directly participate is the election of members of the U.S. House of Representatives. Today, however, U.S. citizens elect the president (through electors), members of Congress, governors, state legislators, and a range of local officials, including at the city, town, or village level. In some states, voters can cast ballots on specific policies through **initiatives** and **referenda**[13] (see Chapter 3, Federalism). Further, in thirty-nine of the fifty states some sort of election is involved in the selection or the retention of judges.[14] No other developed country has as many elections as the United States (see Other Places: The Number of Elections).[15]

There are three reasons for this heavy reliance on the ballot. First, the public views elections as legitimate devices for making political choices.[16] Second, the Constitution was vague about rules surrounding the choice of presidents and members of Congress, allowing states to make greater use of elections, and many have done so. Third, the federal system created layers of government and multiple political offices to fill them, most of which are elected. At the local level, the people generally elect school board members and commissions that deal with various public tasks, such as water and road construction.

initiative: *Process by which citizens place proposed laws on the ballot for public approval.*

referendum: *Process by which public approval is required before a state can pass certain laws.*

The Presidential Campaign

Presidential campaigns capture the interest of nearly all Americans. In October 2008, 95 percent of the electorate paid at least some attention to the presidential contest between John McCain and Barack Obama.[17] Every move a presidential candidate makes is watched and assessed. This focus on the presidency would have surprised the Framers, who expected the legislative branch to be the center of attention. But as the executive branch has gained power, so has the importance of the contest to fill the office of president.

The course of the modern presidential campaign is long and difficult. From the decision to run to the final victory and concession speeches, the road to the White House is shaped by constitutional requirements, interparty struggles, and strategies for attracting votes that highlight the many gates and gateways along the way.

Do presidential campaigns ensure that the best person for the office wins?

otherplaces

The Number of Elections

Holding free elections is a hallmark of any democracy, and the United States holds more national elections than other democracies. Since World War II this nation has held three times as many national elections as India and more than twice as many as Mexico. These data actually understate the use of elections in America for, with the federal system, there are a great many state elections—for governor, for the state legislature, and for other statewide offices—as well as local elections for mayors and school boards and sheriffs. Aaron Schock, for example, began his career on the Peoria School Board.

In short, the United States places great faith in elections. Elections hold officials accountable and help make sure government is responsive to voters' preferences and opinions. But some critics say that too many elections may cause citizens to tire

of the electoral process. Further, countries like the United Kingdom hold elections in response to the current political situation, so even though the U.K. has fewer elections than the United States, these contests may provide more opportunity for encouraging responsiveness and accountability. It is also true that many elections in the United States are low-stimulus, leading to low turnout and limited interest by the public. In short, elections are important, but increasing the frequency and number does not necessarily make a country more democratic.

- **Do you think more elections mean more democracy?**

- **Should the United States increase the number of elections held?**

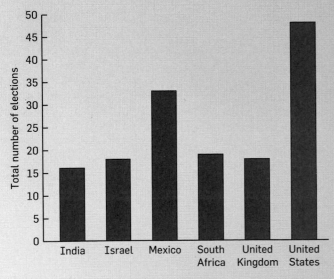

The Number of National Elections since World War II.
Source: The authors and Randy Stevenson, www.randystevenson.com

Evolution of the Modern Campaign

As in so many matters of custom and protocol, George Washington shaped the way future presidential aspirants would campaign for president. Like others at the Constitutional Convention, he worried that a chief executive could morph into a monarch, so he deliberately avoided doing anything to advance his candidacy. He took these steps even though he and all the Framers knew that the office of president was created with him in mind. He stayed at Mount Vernon, his Virginia estate on the Potomac River, and let others work on his behalf. The electors met on February 4, 1789, and the vote for Washington was unanimous. Only then did Washington make preparations to proceed to New York City, then the capital, where he took the oath of office on April 30.

Washington's conduct continued to influence presidential campaigns until the start of the twentieth century. Candidates allowed their political parties to campaign on their behalf but avoided looking too ambitious. In 1896 William McKinley (1897–1901) stayed home in Canton, Ohio, speaking to well-wishers from his front porch. This **front porch campaign** strategy proved successful, but only because his campaign manager, Mark Hanna, and the Republican Party were raising funds and securing votes behind the scenes.

Although candidates in the early nineteenth century sought to appear aloof and above the fray, their supporters took every opportunity to advance their candidacies. Buttons and slogans promoted favorites, and parades and barbeques sought to convince the undecided. Participation had much more of a social component than it does now. Many observers argue that the high rate of voting in the late nineteenth century reflected the fact that campaigns were often fun.[18]

By the early twentieth century presidential contenders began to campaign actively, too, and campaigning started earlier and earlier. The 2008 presidential campaign began in January 2007, when Hillary Clinton announced her candidacy. Barack Obama announced the very next month. Not long after Obama was inaugurated in 2009, potential contenders for the 2012 election began **jockeying for position**.

Many have expressed concern over what has been called the **permanent campaign**,[19] a worry that politicians, especially presidents, spend too much time working toward reelection and not enough time governing. During the debate over health care reform in 2009, for example, the Republican consultant Karl Rove, a former adviser to President George W. Bush, contended that Obama needed to realize he was no longer campaigning for office and that, as president, he should show more leadership on this pressing issue facing the American public.[20] Rove is hardly unbiased, but his comments reflect the long-standing worry about the influence of the never-ending campaign.

The Decision to Run and the Invisible Primary

The decision to seek the presidency is a serious one. The presidency is the highest elective office in the land and a position that offers a chance both to influence the course of the nation and to leave a legacy that no other job in the world offers. It is perhaps for these reasons that

Granger Collection, New York

In 1896 William McKinley, former House member and governor of Ohio, ran for president from his front porch in Canton, Ohio. Visitors arrived by train, and he spoke to groups of them, sometimes several times a day. In contrast, his opponent, William Jennings Bryan, traveled all over the country by train, speaking to crowds from the back of train cars. McKinley won.

front porch campaign:
Nineteenth-century campaign style in which the candidate stays home and does not actively campaign.

jockeying for position:
Opening stages of the presidential campaign when candidates compete for financial support and credibility to demonstrate their viability for the party's nomination.

permanent campaign: *Charge that presidents and members of Congress focus more on winning the next election than on governing.*

Who are the potential candidates for the 2012 presidential race? Are you satisfied with these options?

so many of the nation's political leaders consider running for this great office. The decision is not, however, an easy one to make, and potential candidates must ask themselves many difficult questions:

How will a presidential campaign affect my family?

Will my indiscretions in college come back to haunt me?

Can I build a team of advisers that will allow me to win the presidency?

Can I raise enough money to be competitive?

Who else might run for the office?

What do I want to accomplish if elected?

Am I prepared to campaign eighteen hours a day for nearly two years straight?

Am I capable of handling the pressure that comes with being in the Oval Office?

Can I win?

What happens if I lose?

These are some of the questions that swirl in potential candidates' minds when they are thinking about "throwing their hat in the ring," a phrase from the sport of boxing that Theodore Roosevelt used to announce his candidacy in 1912. It is no wonder that prominent political figures, such as former Secretary of State Colin Powell, decide against running.

The campaign for president is unlike that for any other office. The demands are intense. Every move a major candidate makes is discussed and analyzed by the press and political pundits. Presidential campaigns are pressure cookers—perhaps appropriately, because the office is demanding. The American public wants to know whether a candidate has the toughness to serve as commander-in-chief and the wisdom to sort out the best policies. Candidates describe the process as being put through a meat grinder. For an overview of the two-year-long ordeal, see Table 10.1.

invisible primary: *Period just before the primaries begin during which candidates attempt to capture party support and media coverage.*

Once a candidate decides to run for president, he or she enters what is has been called the **invisible primary**. No votes are cast, but candidates are jockeying for position so they can be ready to do well in the initial primaries and caucuses. They must line up party support,

TABLE 10.1 The Road to the White House

Beginning in January of year before election year	**Decision to run**, in which candidates weigh their options and make formal announcements
	Invisible primary, in which candidates jockey for position and try to build momentum
Beginning in January of election year	**Caucuses and primaries**, in which the people vote and one candidate in each party emerges as the front-runner
Summer of election year	**National party conventions**, in which the front-runner in each party is formally nominated and gives an acceptance speech
Fall of election year	**National campaign**, during which televised presidential debates are a highlight
November of election year	**Election day**, in which the people vote
December of election year	**Electoral College**, in which electors meet in their state capitals and vote the people's choice
January after election year	**Inauguration day**

AP Photo/J. Scott Applewhite

financial backing, and credibility with journalists in the news media. Candidates who can get attention from the news media can raise more money and secure more endorsements from party leaders. Running for election is a game that relies heavily on **momentum**.

Incumbent presidents usually win their party's nomination for a second term. If that part of the contest is a struggle, as it was in 1980 for President Jimmy Carter (1977–81), it is a sign that the incumbent is in trouble, and he usually goes on to lose the general election. But when the seat is open—when an incumbent is in his second term or decides not to run again, as Lyndon Baines Johnson (1963–69) did in 1968—a battle unfolds. These struggles tend to be multicandidate affairs, often with seven or eight serious contenders seeking the nomination. The 2008 election was unusual because both nominations were open, meaning that neither the sitting president nor the sitting vice president was seeking the nomination of his party—a situation that had last occurred in 1952. As a result, twelve major candidates were competing for nomination by the two major parties. Hillary Clinton, senator from New York and wife of former president William Jefferson (Bill) Clinton (1993–2001), gathered impressive support from the start. She was always a major contender on the Democratic side. Mike Huckabee, on the Republican side, was not. As the little-known governor of Arkansas, he was ignored at first by the news media and the public, but he got the attention of evangelical Christians. By December 2007 he was ahead in the polls in Iowa, where the first caucuses would take place. This surge recast his campaign. His campaign events were now well attended, and the media began covering his every move. He appeared on the covers of major magazines and newspapers.[21] He had momentum. While Huckabee won the Iowa caucuses, his appeal was largely confined to southern evangelicals, and his campaign struggled in states outside the South.

Over the last thirty years this phase of the campaign has tended to favor **party insiders**, candidates with deep ties to major party leaders who are not challenging the existing party leadership. Of the nomination contests in which there was no incumbent, the party insider won all but one time. The sole exception was Hillary Clinton's loss to Barack Obama. Because Clinton had nearly all the insider support, it was widely assumed that she would win the nomination. Obama had substantial support, but few thought he had a chance against the power of the Clintons.[22]

NBC's Brian Williams, right, moderates the first Democratic presidential primary debate of the 2008 election at South Carolina State University in Orangeburg on April 26, 2007. The candidates are, left to right, New Mexico Governor Bill Richardson, Senator Christopher Dodd of Connecticut, former North Carolina Senator John Edwards, Senator Joe Biden of Delaware, Senator Barack Obama of Illinois, Senator Hillary Rodham Clinton of New York, Representative Dennis Kucinich of Ohio, and former Alaska Senator Mike Gravel.

momentum: *Campaign visibility that builds on itself to gain press coverage, financial backing, and political support.*

party insiders: *Candidates with deep ties to party leaders and views that comport well with their political viewpoints.*

The Caucuses and Primaries

What inequalities are imposed by the primary system?

primary election: *Election in which voters select the candidates who will run on the party label in the general election; also called direct primary.*

caucus: *Meeting of party members in town halls, schools, and private homes to select a presidential nominee.*

frontloading: *Moving a state primary or caucus earlier to increase its influence.*

To win a party's nomination, a candidate must secure a majority of delegates to the national party convention. The national party allocates delegates to each of the fifty states (plus the District of Columbia, Guam, and Puerto Rico) and sets guidelines on how the states may choose their delegates. If a state does not follow the guidelines, the party can refuse to accept its delegates at the national convention. This situation arose in 2008 when both Florida and Michigan failed to follow the rules set by the Democratic National Committee. Only a compromise allowed these two states to seat delegates at the Democratic National Convention in Denver.

About 70 percent of the states use some form of **primary election** in which citizens go to the polling booths and vote for their favorite party candidates. The other 30 percent use **caucuses**, which are something like town meetings. The Iowa caucus, the nation's first and most famous caucus, requires people to attend a meeting of about two hours in which they indicate their preferences and then try to convince those who are undecided to join their candidate's group. Because caucuses demand more time from voters, participation is usually low.

Caucuses and primaries take place over six months, from January through June of the election year. Some states hold these events earlier than others, and the first states to hold primaries and caucuses wield tremendous influence; in most election years the early primaries quickly build momentum for a front-runner and yield a likely nominee. Iowa and the first state to hold a primary, New Hampshire, get a great deal of attention from candidates and the media. In a process called **frontloading**, other states have been moving their dates earlier to avoid the possibility of holding a primary after the winner has already been determined. A stark exception to the usual pattern was the Democratic primary season in 2008, in which Clinton and Obama battled to the very last primary in one of the closest contests in recent memory.

AP Photo/Mark Hirsch

On January 3, 2008, the day of the Iowa caucuses, the Jackson County Democratic Precinct 2 caucus gets under way with a count of the participants. The caucus met at Kalmes, a combination gas station, restaurant, and general store in St. Donatus.

acceptance speech: *Important and heavily scrutinized speech given by the party's candidate at its national convention, laying out his vision for the country.*

party platform: *Document that lays out a party's core beliefs and policy proposals for each presidential election.*

What is the purpose of the national conventions?

The National Convention

Following the primary season, each party meets in a national convention. Before the 1960s conventions were often exciting because it was far from clear who would be the nominee. In 1924, for example, it took the Democrats 124 ballots to decide on their nominee. But by the 1960s conventions began to be televised, so the parties wanted to ensure that they were orderly. To avoid projecting an image that would lose votes in the upcoming election, party leaders instituted rule changes designed to increase the odds that the likely nominee would be known well in advance of the convention. Convention planners could then stage the event to emphasize party unity, rather than discord, to impress television viewers.

Today party conventions usually last for four days and provide a chance for activists and party leaders to get together to discuss strategy and policy behind the scenes. The highlight of these four days is the **acceptance speech**, in which the party's nominee has a chance to speak directly to the nation, laying out a vision for the country. Also in front of the cameras, the **party platform** is formally adopted, laying out its plan for government. There is much excitement surrounding these events. Because one party dominates the news for these four days, the convention is both an advertisement for the party and its candidate and an important springboard for the fall campaign.

The Presidential Debates

With the party ostensibly unified behind its nominee, campaigning gets even more intense after the convention. One significant event in the fall is the series of televised **presidential debates**. In 2008 more than 50 million people watched Obama and McCain address the issues in a debate format.[23] Today these events, as well as a vice presidential debate, are managed by the nonpartisan, non-profit Commission on Presidential Debates, which was established in 1987. The commission chooses the locations and sets the rules.

The first presidential debate was between John Kennedy and Richard Nixon in 1960, and many felt that Kennedy's performance was critical to his narrow win.[24] Thereafter, incumbent candidates were reluctant to participate in televised debates, fearing that they might have more to lose than to win. But in 1976 President Gerald R. Ford (1974–77), behind in the polls, viewed the debates as a chance to narrow Jimmy Carter's lead. Since that time, the presidential debates have been a regular feature of the fall campaign.

The debates draw tremendous amounts of attention from the news media. Any mistake by a candidate generates scrutiny. In 1992 President George H. W. Bush (1989–93) was caught looking at his watch during one of the debates, giving the impression that he was bored. That perception fueled the belief that Bush was out of touch, causing him problems in his reelection bid against Arkansas Governor Bill Clinton. In 2000 Al Gore, who was supposed to be off camera, was caught sighing while his opponent, George W. Bush, was speaking, giving the impression that Gore had little respect for Bush. The incident made Gore look pompous and not someone the public could relate to. Debates have much more risk than reward, and campaign insiders usually hope for an error-free performance by their candidate.

AP Photo/David J. Phillip

Vice President Al Gore kisses his wife, Tipper, just prior to his acceptance speech at the 2000 Democratic National Convention in Los Angeles. This display of emotion by Gore was thought by many observers to make him a more appealing candidate. In 2010 the couple—thought to have an ideal political marriage—announced they were separating.

Issues in Presidential Campaigns

Citizen participation in American politics peaks during presidential campaigns. Supporters and people who are undecided have the chance to attend rallies, hear speeches, read commentary, and watch the never-ending advertisements on television. There seems to be almost no way for the public not to be involved. Because the campaigns are important gateways for public participation, we look in particular at fundraising and campaign strategies that make public engagement possible but may also introduce inequalities.

Fundraising and Money

Of course, no one could run for president without funding. Spending by presidential candidates has risen sharply in recent years, despite passage of legislation to control it. In 1971 Congress tried to put candidates on an equal financial footing and make them less beholden to special interests with the Federal Election Campaign Act (FECA). Under the rules, candidates seeking

presidential debates: *Official televised debates between presidential nominees that are highly important to the campaign.*

Have you watched any presidential debates? Did they help you make up your mind about which candidate to support?

The stakes in presidential debates are huge. In 2008 John McCain needed to score points against Barack Obama in order to close in on Obama's lead, but was never able to do so. Here McCain listens to Obama talk to the audience in a town hall–style debate at Belmont University in Nashville, Tennessee, on October 7, 2008.

matching funds: *Public funding given to a presidential candidate equaling the dollar amount the candidate raises from private contributors, with a limit of $250 per individual contributor.*

bundling: *Influencing others to donate to a political campaign and collecting their donations so as to raise more money than the $2,300 contribution per individual permitted by FEC rules.*

political action committees (PACs): *Groups formed to raise and contribute funds to support electoral candidates that are subject to campaign finance laws.*

What are the pros and cons of laws that regulate campaign finance?

their party's nomination are given public funds for the campaign in the form of **matching funds:** a dollar amount equal to the amount the candidates raise from private contributors, with a limit per individual contributor and an overall cap. In 2008 the limit per contributor was $2,300 in the primary and $2,300 in the general campaign; the cap was $42 million for the primary and $84 million for the general election. Some contributors try to amplify their impact by **bundling**—amassing individual contributions. **Political action committees (PACs)**, groups formed with the express purpose of donating money to candidates who agree with their policy agenda, can also give money to candidates—in some cases as much as $5,000 per candidate.[25]

The rules for the public financing of presidential nomination campaigns are complicated and are designed to ensure that candidates are serious contenders before subsidizing them. The Federal Election Commission (FEC), which monitors campaign finance, does not want to subsidize candidates who have no chance of winning the nomination or to encourage people to run just because the government makes it possible. First, candidates must raise at least $5,000 in twenty states from donations that are less than $500 each. Most candidates can meet this standard, but staying eligible for funds is much harder. A candidate who does not get at least 10 percent of the vote in two consecutive primaries loses eligibility; to reestablish it, he or she must get 20 percent of the vote in a subsequent primary. These standards are hard to meet when four or five other serious candidates are also seeking votes. They also discourage third-party candidates from running.

Even if candidates remain eligible, matching funds place additional constraints on them. In addition to the overall cap, a candidate can spend only a certain amount of money per state. This constraint produces odd behavior. For example, because the New Hampshire primary is the first and perhaps the most important primary, candidates want to invest heavily in it. Yet under matching funds, they face a spending limit in the state, so they might spend the night in a hotel in an adjoining state, Vermont or Maine, to avoid having to charge that expense against the New Hampshire limit.

Increasingly, candidates have decided to forego matching funds in their quest for the nomination. One reason is to be able to spend money in states important to the contest without regard to FEC limits. But primarily they believe they can raise (and spend) more money if they do not accept federal matching funds. In 2000 George W. Bush believed he could raise much more than the $40 million allowed and, foregoing matching funds, raised $70 million prior to the first primary.[26] Steve Forbes joined Bush in rejecting federal funds, funding his campaign from his personal wealth. In 2004 Howard Dean had been so successful in raising money over the Internet that he, too, decided to reject matching funds. John Kerry joined him, as did President Bush, who was running unopposed for renomination.

During the 2008 presidential campaign, John McCain used public funds, receiving about $80 million from the government, but Barack Obama opted out of general election funding for the first time since the system began in

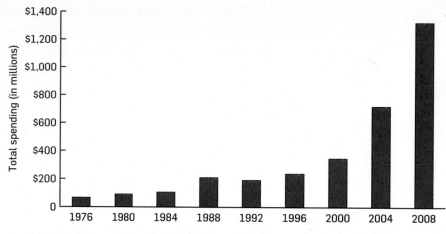

FIGURE 10.2 **Total Spending by Presidential Candidates, 1976–2008.**
Source: Center for Responsive Politics, www.opensecrets.org.

1976. By so doing, he had access to far more money than did McCain. In September 2008 alone Obama raised nearly $90 million.[27] Over the course of the yearlong campaign, he spent $730 million, breaking all previous fundraising records. McCain spent $333 million dollars during that same period, a huge amount by historical standards, but dwarfed by Obama's spending (see Figure 10.2 for total spending).

Obama's record fundraising will change how presidential campaigns are funded, starting with the 2012 presidential election. Serious candidates and the eventual nominees will almost surely not use federal funds, raising and spending their own money instead. The key constraint will be the approximate $2,500 limit an individual can contribute to a campaign in 2012.[28] Given the amounts Obama raised in 2008, the total amount spent on the next presidential campaign can be expected to approach $2 billion.

Many observers worry that these huge amounts raise questions about fairness and equality, that people who have money will have more gateways than those who do not. But even with bundling, the $4,600 total limit does offer some important constraints. It is impossible to "buy" a candidate with $4,600. Moreover, the money is being spent on getting candidates' messages out to the public and building organizations to get out the vote. In many ways, it is being used to stimulate interest in the election, and that is a public benefit. Further, the rise of Internet fundraising has made it worthwhile for candidates to pursue small contributions—as small as $15—instead of only large contributions. The Internet has made small donations cost-effective, encouraging candidates to broaden their base of contributors. By setting up websites that permit online donations, candidates do not need to pay people to call potential voters or knock on doors. They just need to maintain the websites and ensure that lots of people know about them. The Internet has given more people a gateway to be part of the electoral process by contributing small amounts of money.

Swing States

Even though partisanship is extremely high, **swing voters** still exist—people who do not fall into either the Republican or Democratic camp—and so do **swing states** that might vote either Democratic or Republican in an election. Parties avidly pursue swing

Should FEC rules work to encourage third parties? Why?

Are campaigns too expensive?

swing voters: *Voters who are neither reliably Republican nor reliably Democratic and who are pursued by each party during an election, as they can determine which candidate wins.*

swing states: *States that are not clearly pro-Republican or pro-Democrat and therefore are of vital interest to presidential candidates, as they can determine election outcomes.*

voters during a presidential election, as they can swing the results one way or the other. Though the number of swing voters varies from year to year, it is usually about 20 percent of the electorate. In 2004 the share of swing voters was just 13 percent, the lowest in four decades, as the public had strong opinions—negative and positive—about President George W. Bush.

More important for campaign strategy are the swing states, which can mean the difference between victory and defeat. Because of the Electoral College's winner-take-all system, presidential candidates invest time and effort only in states that they can win. In 2008, for example, it would have made no sense for John McCain to campaign in Massachusetts, a reliably Democratic state that he could not win. But both McCain and Barack Obama campaigned hard in Pennsylvania—a **battleground state** that each thought he had a chance to win. Other key battleground states in 2008 were Florida, Ohio, North Carolina, and Virginia.

Citizens in these states got lots of attention (see Figure 10.3). Nearly 90 percent of campaign visits were to battleground states. TV viewers were deluged with campaign ads, and party-based get-out-the-vote organizations were active in even the smallest towns. This flurry of activity filtered down to the public. Citizens in these states were well informed and increasingly interested in the campaign. But the strategy of pursuing votes in swing states yields an important inequality, for citizens in non–swing states do not get such attention, and interest in the campaign lags, especially among the poor. According to one estimate, "the seven battleground states targeted by both major parties contained only 18% of the nation's population" in 2004, "with another 24% residing in states that were classified as leaning, but not quite safe."[29] That means that about 60 percent of the public did not get the benefits of a campaign in 2004. Much the same was true in 2008, as candidates again paid close attention to a handful of states, although Obama did try to run a national campaign. Nevertheless, nearly 25 percent of all visits by McCain and Obama were to Ohio and Pennsylvania.[30]

Microtargeting

Since the 1960s, when consumer behavior became a popular field of study, direct marketers have refined the practice of gathering detailed information about different cross-sections of consumers to sell their products.[31] Today, the technique of **microtargeting** (also called narrowcasting) has become a boon to political parties and electoral campaigns. By identifying and tracking potential supporters, campaign strategists can design specific political messages tailored for each of the voting profiles developed from the data. In 1996, for example, President Bill Clinton's reelection campaign sought to reach so-called soccer moms—"busy suburban women devoted to their jobs and kids, who had real concerns about real presidential politics."[32] Polls and other information suggested that these voters could be moved into the Clinton camp, although men, for the most part, seemed to have already made up their minds. In 2004 the focus

battleground state: *State in which the outcome of the presidential election is uncertain and in which both candidates invest much time and money, especially if its votes are vital for a victory in the Electoral College.*

Do you live in a swing or a battleground state? What is the impact on you?

microtargeting: *Gathering detailed information on cross-sections of the electorate to track potential supporters and tailor political messages for them; also called narrowcasting.*

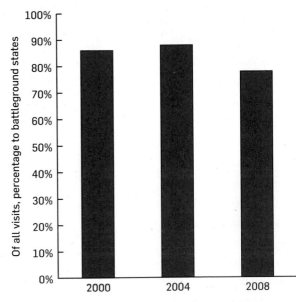

FIGURE 10.3 Visits by Presidential Candidates, 2000–2008.
Source: Daron R. Shaw, *The Race to 270: The Electoral College and the Campaign Strategies of 2000 and 2004* (Chicago: University of Chicago Press, 2006); figures for 2008 provided by Daron R. Shaw.

was on "NASCAR dads"—working-class white males who lived mostly in the South. Many thought the Democrats had to win this group to capture the presidency.

As a campaign strategy, microtargeting has begun to replace traditional polling techniques and precinct-by-precinct get-out-the-vote drives (see Chapter 6, Public Opinion). By combining information from polling surveys with political participation and consumer information obtained from data-gathering companies like Acxiom and InfoUSA, political parties and campaigns can establish profiles of the many different types of voters and the issues they support. The resulting database can then be "mapped" to get a geographic depiction of the trends in voting habits and political interests of different voters. Each party works with its own large database: The Democrats have "Vote-Builder," and the Republicans have "Voter Vault."[33]

Rather than a general political message sent through a specific medium, campaigns are now able to send dozens of versions of the message using various methods—mail, phone calls, e-mail, home visits—to reach targeted audiences. This strategy takes a person-by-person view of the electorate rather than a view of the electorate en masse. So, instead of targeting a broad category like women, campaigns can now focus on categories like "married iPhone owners in their 40s with a master's degree who shop at Costco."[34]

The strategy is not entirely new. A crude form was used by Jimmy Carter in the 1976 election when advisers adjusted his stump speech to emphasize different issues as he traveled to different parts of the country.[35] But with more and more information becoming available about voters, microtargeting became easier and more cost-effective. In Florida, for example, Republicans were able to extend their reach to 84 percent of eventual Bush voters in 2004, up from 33 percent in 2000. This 51 percentage point increase in contact allowed Republicans to reach voters in traditional Democratic neighborhoods and precincts. In Ohio, Republican microtargeting found that blacks wanted candidates to talk more about education and health care, so the Bush campaign contacted these voters through direct mailings and phone calls and emphasized Bush's accomplishments on these topics rather than the campaign's broader message of Iraq and terrorism. Bush improved his share of the black vote in Ohio from 9 percent in 2000 to 16 percent in 2004.[36]

Since 2004 the Democrats have responded with their own microtargeting strategy, employing it for dozens of races in 2006. Barack Obama's campaign built on previous Democratic data by adding its own information culled from the campaign's online efforts. The goal was not only to contact potential voters but also to expand the electorate as a whole, because the campaign believed it would receive the support of a larger portion of newly registered voters. Existing evidence, although limited, suggests that this strategy worked. Even so, the keys to Obama's win were much more tied to the economy and the unpopularity of the Iraq War than to successful efforts to increase turnout through microtargeting.

What is your microtargeting profile? Can the category predict how you will vote?

Gilles Mingasson/Getty Images

Fans follow the NASCAR race in Las Vegas on March 7, 2004, from the top of a motor home parked in the track's infield and outfitted with a television to catch the replays. The 37 million NASCAR fans were targeted by the Bush campaign in 2004. Male, overwhelmingly white, religious, and patriotic, this demographic group—the so-called NASCAR dads (in contrast to soccer moms)—generally votes Republican.

Campaign Issues

Campaigns are very much shaped by issues. Many observers think that the personalities of the candidates dictate the race, but that view is not consistent with the evidence. Between 1960 and 2000, for example, 56 percent of the content of advertising in presidential campaigns involved policy, with 26 percent concerning the personal traits of the candidates, and the remaining 18 percent focusing on general values such as freedom, hard work, and patriotism.[37] In 2008 the economy dominated the discussion between John McCain and Barack Obama. According to one estimate, over 50 percent of the appeals made by these contenders dealt with the economy alone.[38]

For greater understanding of how issues influence campaigns, political scientists have drawn a distinction between **valence issues** and **position issues**.[39] A valence issue is a vague claim to a goal, such as "a strong economy," "improved education," or "greater national security." These are goals all candidates talk about and voters seek: No candidate has ever opposed a strong economy or called for less national security. Valence issues provide limited insight into the policies a candidate might pursue once in office. A position issue is different. Here candidates adopt views that allow voters to understand specific plans for government. Two examples from the 2008 campaign are Obama's favoring pulling troops out of Iraq within eighteen months of taking office and McCain's opposing gay marriage. Because views on position issues may drive some votes away, presidential candidates rely more heavily on valence issues than on position issues. According to one study, about three-quarters of their TV ads highlight valence issues.[40]

Candidates use issues strategically to win votes. In 2008 the economy as a campaign issue favored Obama over McCain. Obama wanted to talk about the economic downturn because public concern about it was helping his candidacy. McCain, on the other hand, wanted to change the subject. He could have tried **matching** Obama's positions on economic policy to bring his views in line with Obama's. But if McCain did this, he would have been accused of **flip-flopping**. Charges of flip-flopping are common during campaigns, and they resonate with voters, so matching is not a common strategy. McCain could have tried **pushing** Obama away from his positions on economic policy through attacks, and he often did so. For example, Obama's claim that he favored lower taxes was, according to McCain, not consistent with his record. A final possibility is **ducking** the issue and raising a new issue to change the subject. In 2008 McCain tried to move the campaign away from the economy and to focus instead on Obama's lack of experience, while Obama sought to keep the discussion on the economy. Campaigns are often not just about the positions candidates adopt on issues but also about what issues define the campaign. Control of the agenda is very important.

Because campaigns are competitive struggles for votes, candidates look for ways to secure extra votes while maintaining existing support. This dynamic is especially true for candidates who trail because they need to find some way to break up the support for the candidate in the lead. One strategy is to use a **wedge issue** that has the potential to break up the opposition's coalition.[41] Wedges usually involve controversial policy concerns, such as abortion and gay marriage, that divide people rather than build consensus. In 2004 the Republicans used gay marriage as a wedge issue that alarmed social conservatives and helped ensure their support for President George W. Bush despite their unhappiness with the Iraq War and concerns about the economy.[42]

What should shape a presidential campaign—issues or character?

valence issues: *Noncontroversial or widely supported campaign issues that are unlikely to differ among candidates.*

position issues: *Political issues that offer specific policy choices and often differentiate candidates' views and plans of action.*

matching: *Campaign strategy of closely aligning one's views to the opponent's position, making it more difficult for the public to differentiate the two.*

flip-flopping: *Changing position on an issue for reasons of political expediency.*

pushing: *Campaign strategy of attacking opponents to move them to a less favorable position on the issue in question.*

ducking: *Campaign strategy of avoiding discussion of one issue and introducing a new or different issue.*

wedge issue: *Divisive issue focused on a particular group of the electorate that candidates use to gain more support by taking votes away from their opponents.*

Identify three wedge issues that are important to you. Do they determine your vote?

Negativity

Candidates are very good at telling voters why they should vote for them, but they are also good at telling the public why they should not vote for their opponents. These reasons often involve issues. A candidate might, for example, remind voters that his or her opponent raised taxes. But other times, a campaign releases an array of information about a candidate that raises doubts and concerns about fitness for office. Because the public does need to know both the good and the bad, **negativity** plays an important, and usually underappreciated, role in campaigns.

One of the most famous negative ads was the "Daisy spot," aired only once by President Lyndon B. Johnson in his 1964 campaign against the Republican nominee, Arizona Senator Barry Goldwater. The implication was that if Goldwater was elected president, he would start a nuclear war. It was a very hard-hitting claim that many thought unfair.[43] But was it? Goldwater had called for the tactical use of nuclear weapons and made some loose statements about attacking the Soviet Union with nuclear weapons. This issue was among the most important facing the nation—much like terrorism is now. The public needed to know Goldwater's views, and this negative ad helped generate a debate.

In recent years, the amount of negativity has been on the rise (see Figure 10.4). In the 2008 campaign, about two-thirds of all statements were negative. Many observers worry about this trend, viewing attacks on the opposition as weakening the fabric of democracy. Nearly 80 percent of the public dislikes negative ads.[44] But they serve a purpose. To ensure accountability, candidates need to be able to critique the other side. So, in 2008 Barack Obama reminded the public of the problems brought on by Republican policies during President

LBJ Library Photo by the Democratic National Committee

The "Daisy spot" is perhaps the most famous negative ad in American history. It was aired only once by President Lyndon Johnson in the 1964 campaign, and it never explicitly mentioned his opponent, Senator Barry Goldwater. But Goldwater had made statements about the possible use of nuclear weapons, and they made the meaning of this ad clear and emotionally resonant.

negativity: *Campaign strategy of telling voters why they should not vote for the opponent and of highlighting information that raises doubts about the opponent.*

What is your response to negative ads?

FIGURE 10.4 Share of Negativity in Presidential Campaigns, 1960–2008. Negativity in presidential campaigns is clearly on the rise. Between 1965 and 1984 about 25 percent of the messages in presidential campaign ads were negative. Starting in 1988 the proportion increased until it stood at 50 percent in 2004. In 2008 it jumped to 64 percent. *Source:* Authors.

UNION AND LIBERTY!   AND   UNION AND SLAVERY!

Published by M. W. Siebert, Printer, 28 Centre Street, Corn.' Reade.

The Granger Collection New York

Negative campaigning is not new. This poster from the 1864 election shows Abraham Lincoln defining his opponent, General George McClellan, as the ally of Confederate President Jefferson Davis and perpetuator of the slave system. Lincoln, on the other hand, is for the working-man and freedom. Notice the integrated school with happy children.

George W. Bush's two terms. At the same time, John McCain questioned whether Obama had enough experience to be president. After hearing both sides, the public would decide. It is also important to know that although negativity is on the rise, it is not new. In 1948 President Harry S. Truman (1945–53) equated the Republicans with the Nazi leadership in Germany during World War II.[45] In 1800 the Federalist Party claimed that Thomas Jefferson was the Antichrist.[46] These attacks make McCain's claims about Obama's inexperience look tame.

Polls and Prediction Models

Given Barack Obama's victory in 2008, it is easy to overestimate his skill and John McCain's lack of skill. The winners always look brilliant and the losers misguided. But such judgments are not very useful. To look beyond a single case, political scientists have developed **prediction models** that yield specific estimates of the vote share in presidential elections. The goal is to provide a general understanding of who wins and why. In 2008 eight of the nine models predicted an Obama win.[47] Some thought he would win narrowly (predicting 50.1 percent); others anticipated a major landslide (predicting 58.2 percent). Nate Silver (see Chapter 6) called it right, too, predicting the outcomes in 49 of the 50 states correctly.[48] Only one model predicted a McCain win, and it relied on the public's judgment about the candidates immediately after the Republican National Convention. McCain was riding high in the polls with the excitement that surrounded Sarah Palin's nomination as vice president—too high, as it turned out, leading this model astray.

The best prediction models use some combination of the following key structural factors:

1. *The economy.* What is the condition of the economy? A strong economy leads voters to support the incumbent party. A struggling economy gives an edge to the challenger.
2. *Presidential popularity.* How popular is the sitting president? An unpopular president will hurt the chances for his party's candidate.
3. *The incumbent party's time in office.* How long has the incumbent party controlled the presidency? The American public has shown a consistent preference for change. A party that has been in power for a long time usually has made enough mistakes to lead citizens to vote for the other side.

prediction models: *Formulas that take into account an array of factors, such as a candidate's popularity or the state of the national economy, to project a winner.*

Apply these three factors to the upcoming presidential campaign.

Considering these three factors, it becomes clear that McCain faced a tough road. The economy was struggling. With the stock market and banking sector in turmoil, President Bush's popularity was the lowest of any president since such measurements began in the 1930s. And the Republicans had controlled the White House for eight years.

McCain could have won the election, but only if Obama had made major mistakes. That is, the conditions that favored Obama still required him to run an effective campaign. He had to show the public that he was ready to deal with the economic challenges—in effect, ready to be president. He did not make many mistakes and so was able to take advantage of the favorable context of the election.

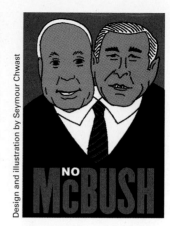

Design and illustration by Seymour Chwast

One strategy developed by the Obama campaign in the 2008 presidential contest was to associate John McCain with President George W. Bush, whose popularity had plummeted during his second term in office.

Congressional Campaigns

Nearly all congressional campaigns start with a primary election at which the party's official candidate is selected. The general election then follows. These campaigns occur every two years. In the Senate, one-third of all seats are contested every two years. For the House of Representatives, every member faces reelection every two years.

The Decision to Run and the Primaries

People who chose to run for Congress are usually visible residents of their district or state. Often they already hold local or state-level elected offices. They might, like Aaron Schock, be school board members, city council members, or state legislators. Many grew up in the district or state and can claim long-standing ties to it. This was certainly true of Schock. Contenders with strong local roots can organize core supporters who volunteer time, and often money, to advance their candidacies.

Although candidates do not have to declare their intention to run for Congress until about a year before the election, both **incumbents**—those already holding the office—and **challengers** generally begin campaigning nearly two years before election day. For House members, that means that the campaign never stops—yet another manifestation of the permanent campaign. The contests that occur in between the four-year presidential election cycles are called **midterm elections**.

Party primaries nearly always determine which candidate will gain the party endorsement for a House or Senate seat, although a handful of states, such as Colorado, Connecticut, New Mexico, New York, and Utah, hold preprimary conventions to determine who can compete in the primary. To win the primary election, a candidate generally shapes campaign messages to please core party members in the district or state. For Democrats, that typically means slanting toward a more liberal set of policies, and for Republicans, toward a more conservative set of policies. But the message also depends on the number and type of candidates in the primary contest. If there are more than two candidates, each has to take competitors into account when crafting the slant of the campaign message.

The Fall Campaign

Following the primaries, the two winning candidates often revise their campaign messages to attract more moderate voters. Anthony Downs explained this shift in message with the **theorem of the median voter**, which argues that candidates in their quest for votes should adopt

What is the personal background of your representative? Of your senators?

incumbent: *Occupant of elected office.*

challengers: *Candidates seeking to unseat current officeholders.*

midterm elections: *Congressional elections held between the presidential elections.*

median voter theorem: *Theory that, in a two-party race, if voters select candidates on the basis of ideology and everyone participates equally, the party closer to the middle will win.*

Congressman Aaron Schock (R-Ill.) campaigns for reelection in May 2010 in Burns, Illinois.

moderate positions on issues. If one candidate fails to do so, the other candidate can move to the center, winning a majority of votes and the election.[49] To win the general election, candidates usually need votes from party members as well as from Independents and members of the opposing party. It is for these reasons that elections are often battles over the so-called middle.

Running for Congress requires attending local gatherings such as town meetings, parades, festivals, and high school sporting events. Candidates meet with as many key business people, members of the press, and local interest groups as possible. They give speeches, and their campaigns develop slogans and TV ads. Elections to the House of Representatives typically focus more on local issues intrinsic to the district, and less on national programs and issues. Senate elections pay more attention to national issues because the Senate is viewed as more nationally focused. In elections where an incumbent is running, the contest becomes an evaluation of his or her performance in office compared to what the challenger promises to do if elected.

The geographic size of a congressional district or state can affect campaign strategy. Some candidates have far less territory to cover than others. Crisscrossing California to meet voters is a much larger task than driving across Delaware. Because it is so difficult to establish a personal relationship with constituents in large districts and states, congressional campaigns in these areas are typically less about the personal characteristics of the candidates and more about issues and party policies.[50]

Issues in Congressional Campaigns

Congressional elections do not draw as much attention as presidential elections, but they involve many of the same issues. Money and fundraising are concerns, and again the FEC sets limits. Political parties attempt to work within—or get around—these limits to help their candidates. Voters almost always reelect House and Senate members, so whether congressional elections actually serve to hold Congress accountable is a question for American democracy. Voters know less about these candidates than about the candidates in presidential elections, suggesting perhaps that there is not much accountability. Nevertheless, the composition of Congress changes in response to conditions in the country. If times are good, the party in power is rewarded. In general, the pattern of Republican and Democratic gains and losses indicates that voters hold members of Congress accountable and that Congress is, therefore, a responsive institution.

Fundraising and Money

A key element in launching and running a congressional campaign is fundraising. Every campaign needs an office, staff members, computers, posters and pamphlets, a website, and money for television and radio ads. Senate campaigns generally cost more than House campaigns because they seek to reach voters across an entire state rather than just a district.

Did you vote in the 2010 midterm election? Why or why not?

Federal campaign finance laws set the same limits on congressional elections as on presidential elections: An individual can contribute up to $2,400 to a candidate for the primary election in 2010, and the same amount for the general election. Individuals can contribute to candidates in different races, up to a total of $45,600 for primaries and the same amount for general election campaigns. Candidates also raise money from PACs, which are limited to donating $5,000 for a primary election, and $5,000 for a general election, to a single candidate.[51] In the 2006 midterm elections, on average, a challenger had to raise at least $1.5 million to win a seat in the House of Representatives, and an incumbent had to raise at least $1.2 million to keep his or her seat. For Senate races, on average a challenger had to raise $8.2 million, and an incumbent $9 million.[52]

The amount of money required to wage a competitive contest for a seat in Congress is formidable, and it gives an advantage to people who are personally wealthy and able to make good use of personal or business connections. Name recognition also helps in fundraising. A local sports hero or decorated war veteran, for example, who chooses to run for office gets enough free publicity to attract interest. Curt Schilling, the former pitcher for the Boston Red Sox, generated a lot of attention in 2009 when he considered running for the Senate from Massachusetts in a special election to fill Ted Kennedy's seat following Kennedy's death.[53] Translating fame into credibility for officeholding is not always easy (Schilling decided against running), but name recognition is clearly an advantage.

The cost of TV and radio advertising time affects the price of running for office and the eventual success of the campaign. Media costs are frequently a function of the population density of a district or state. For example, even though Manhattan is geographically very small, a candidate running there faces a large hurdle because television and radio time is very expensive, and he or she is competing for attention with many other elected officials who are also running for office. In contrast, a candidate in Montana, who has a large state to cover, has a much less expensive media market, and less competition for attention from other elected officials.

Hillary Rodham Clinton, running to return to the Senate in 2006, is presented with a birthday cake in honor of her 59th birthday at a fundraiser in New York. Equally pleased is her husband, former President Bill Clinton.

The Role of Political Parties

Of the other sources of financial support available to candidates, the most important is the political party. Parties are forbidden by campaign finance laws from actively coordinating a specific individual's congressional or senatorial campaign, but local parties can engage in general activities, such as voter registration drives, partisan rallies, and get-out-the-vote efforts on election day that help party-endorsed candidates at every level.

The role of national political parties in congressional elections is more complex. National parties are also forbidden from directly coordinating with individual campaigns, but there is much they can do to help their candidates win. They can pay for campaign training for candidates and their staff members, hold general party fundraisers, and buy campaign advertisements that attack the opposing candidate so long as they do not mention their party's candidate. They can also share lists of campaign donors and party members who are likely to volunteer their time to candidates' campaigns.

Both the Democratic and Republican Parties have congressional campaign organizations designed to recruit and support candidates for the House and Senate. For the Democrats, they are the Democratic Senatorial Campaign Committee and the Democratic Congressional Campaign Committee. On the Republican side, they are the National Republican Congressional Committee and the National Republican Senatorial Committee (see Figure 9.1, Party Organization at the National, State, and Local Levels, in Chapter 9). These committees are arms of the congressional party leadership, and they can choose to be more or less supportive of incumbents seeking reelection, depending on how loyal the incumbents have been to the party. Individuals can contribute to these congressional committees in addition to making donations to the candidates themselves, although an individual is limited to $25,000 in donations to a single party campaign committee.[54] In 2006 these national party committees spent more than $230 million overall, with about $150 million devoted to House races and $80 million to Senate races.[55]

Incumbency Advantage

Incumbents almost always win.[56] In House races, they are reelected about 95 percent of the time, and in Senate races, at least 80 percent of the time (see Figure 10.5). In the last two decades, more than 70 percent of House incumbents received 60 percent or more of the vote. Since the 1960s the number of competitive races has been in decline, a trend called **vanishing marginals**. The idea here is that fewer and fewer congressional elections are competitive. Noncompetitive districts are often referred to as **safe seats**. The high rates of incumbent reelection may indicate that incumbents are doing a good job, especially with constituent services that build support with voters (see also Chapter 12, Congress). Or they might raise concerns about whether elections really foster accountability. Concerns about the lack of accountability are extensive enough that some observers call for **term limits**, which would force members to retire after serving a maximum number of terms. Presidents, for example, can serve only two terms, and most governors are similarly constrained.

Chief executives have more concentrated power than do legislators, so ensuring turnover in the executive branch does keep gateways to responsive government open. Further, more turnover actually occurs in the House than the data in Figure 10.5 suggest. Members often engage in **strategic retirement**, deciding against reelection when the outcome is likely to be unfavorable. It is also unclear what reelection rates exactly mean. For example, the lower reelection rates of senators do not imply that the Senate is more responsive than the House. Instead, the gap may be a function of differences between the two

vanishing marginals: *Trend marking the decline of competitive congressional elections.*

safe seat: *Seat in Congress considered to be reliably held by one party or the other.*

term limits: *Rule restricting the number of terms an elected official can serve in a given office.*

Why do incumbents usually win reelection?

Are term limits for Congress a good idea? What are the pros and the cons?

strategic retirement: *Decision to retire from Congress based on the unlikelihood of winning the next election.*

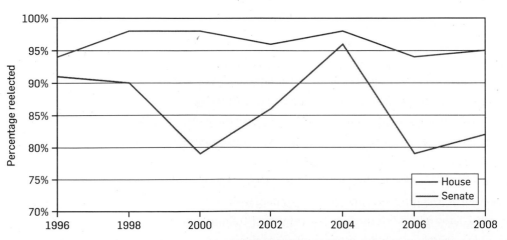

FIGURE 10.5 Reelection Rates of Incumbents in Congress, 1996–2008.
Source: Center for Responsive Politics; Bruce Oppenheimer.

chambers. A seat in the Senate, the upper house, is a more coveted position than a seat in the House, and Senate races generally attract higher-quality challengers than do House races. Better challengers yield more competitive elections and more defeats for incumbents. The ability of challengers to do better in Senate races than in House races is also related to the additional media attention these races receive; quite simply, voters learn more about the challengers. Finally, the difference in terms—six years as opposed to two—may indicate that House members stay in closer touch with constituents than do senators, and their constituents reelect them.[57]

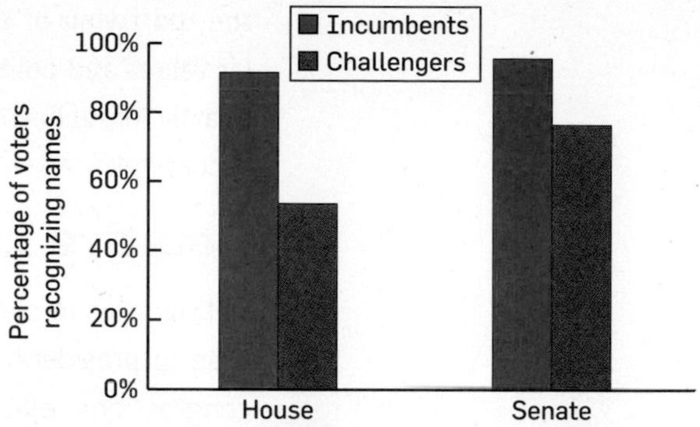

Incumbents also win reelection at high rates because they are known commodities to their constituents. Figure 10.6 indicates that name recognition for House and Senate incumbents is over 80 percent. Senate challengers do better than House challengers, but still about a quarter of the electorate does not recognize their names. Compare these percentages to the recent presidential election, in which only 1 percent of the public claimed not to know the name of John McCain or Barack Obama.[58]

Being an incumbent can be a disadvantage, however, if one's party falls out of favor with voters. This was the case in 1994, 2006, and 2010, when a large number of incumbents of the party in power lost seats in the House and the Senate. In 1994 and 2006 Congress changed hands, becoming Republican in 1994 and Democratic in 2006. In 2010, voters handed the Republicans major victories that allowed them to take control of the House and significantly reduce the Democratic majority in the Senate. Usually such a strong tide would have swept both chambers, but the Democrats held fifty-nine seats prior to the election, enough of a cushion for them to sustain losses but maintain control.

Additional explanations have been advanced to explain incumbency advantage. For example, with the bureaucracy growing in size and reach, people expect more from their government. Citizens, as a result, need a mediator to handle issues that arise with the bureaucracy. Members of Congress serve as a conduit to help connect people with government services. Thus a citizen who fails to receive a Social Security check or has trouble with a passport calls his or her member of Congress for help. The result is constituent loyalty and an increased willingness to support that official's reelection. Other scholars have offered a more sinister interpretation. Members of Congress, in this view, design bureaucratic agencies and programs in ways that assure their inability to carry out the tasks that constituents demand. In a sense, the bureaucracy is built to fail, so constituents have to contact their representative or senator to make it work; when help arrives, loyalty to the incumbent is built.[59] There is also a simple explanation for why reelection rates of incumbents are so high: Candidates who win once obviously have the skills to be elected, and these serve them well in reelection campaigns.[60]

Moreover, recent evidence suggests that members of Congress may be the beneficiaries of the migration of Americans. That is, incumbency advantage appears to be increasing because districts are becoming "deep red" (Republican) and "deep blue" (Democrat) due to people's decisions about where to live. The assumption is that a Republican who has a choice to live, for example, in San Francisco or Dallas, will tend to choose Dallas because it offers a political culture more in line with his or her preferences. In this sense, because of

FIGURE 10.6 Average Share of Voters Recognizing Congressional Candidates' Names, 1980–2004.
Source: Gary C. Jacobson, *The Politics of Congressional Elections*, 7th ed. (Boston: Pearson Longman, 2009), 124.

the redrawing of district lines and the desire of individuals to live near people with similar values and political leanings, congressional districts are becoming heavily Democratic or heavily Republican. The result is that fewer races are competitive and incumbents are more successful.[61]

Relative Lack of Interest

Voting rates in congressional elections, particularly in midterm elections, are always lower than in presidential elections. Presidential elections are high-stimulus elections, whereas congressional elections are low-stimulus. The attention and excitement of a presidential election means that voters are bombarded with information about the contest. Congressional elections generate far less attention. Even high-profile Senate races, such as Hillary Clinton's campaign for the Senate in New York in 2000, or *Saturday Night Live* star Al Franken's campaign for the Senate in Minnesota in 2008, have a lower profile than the battle for the presidency. A major consequence of these differences is that voters in congressional elections often do not know much about the candidates.

As a result, voting is driven largely by two major forces: partisanship and incumbency. Voters follow **party identification** and vote for their party's candidates. And, as we have seen, voters also tend to vote for incumbents. There is also the effect of **presidential coattails**— that is, a popular president running for reelection brings additional party candidates into office. Voters going to the polls in high-stimulus elections to vote for president cast ballots for other members of the party for lower-level offices. While scholars debate this effect, it is clear that the partisan makeup of Congress reflects the popularity of the president or presidential candidate.[62]

Is voting in congressional elections a means by which citizens in a democracy hold government responsible? Does voting in congressional elections yield the will of the majority? Figure 10.7 shows how many additional seats the Republicans have gained and lost (and by implication how many Democrats have lost and gained) in the House of Representatives for the last 108 years. In many years, the changes have been small, but there have been some big shifts as well. In 1932 the Democrats gained 101 seats. In 1946 the Republicans picked up 56 seats. In 1994 the Republicans gained 54 seats and captured the majority in the House for the first time in forty years. In 2006 and 2008 the Democrats picked up more than 50 total seats. In 2010 the pendulum swung back and the Republicans captured more than 60 seats, giving them control of the House.

Such shifts are often attributed to the state of the

If Congress is supposed to be the branch closest to the people, why do congressional campaigns generate less interest than presidential campaigns?

party identification:
Attachment or allegiance to a political party; partisanship.

presidential coattails:
Effect of a popular president or presidential candidate on congressional elections, boosting votes for members of his party.

What was the basis for your vote in the 2010 congressional elections?

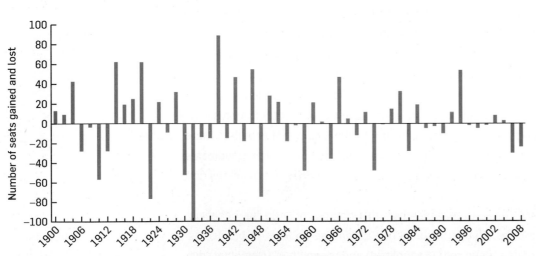

FIGURE 10.7 Republican Gains and Losses in the House of Representatives, 1900–2008. As this graph shows, elections have brought big gains and losses for both parties. In 2010, the Republicans made major gains.
Source: Congressional Quarterly.

economy and the popularity of the incumbent president. The huge gain the Democrats made in 1932 reflects the terrible economic conditions that gripped the nation after the Great Depression began during the term of Republican President Herbert Hoover (1929–33). According to estimates from political scientists, a party can lose up to forty-six seats when its president is highly unpopular. At the same time, a gain of 2 percent in people's income can produce eleven more seats in Congress for the incumbent party.[63]

Because of these aggregate shifts in midterm congressional elections, many scholars have viewed midterm elections as referenda on the sitting president. But given the fact that the president's party has just come off a victory in the previous election, winning seats that might often go to the other party, the normal occurrence is that the president's party loses seats in the midterm election. Only three times in the last twenty-one midterm elections (1930–2010) has the president's party gained seats. The average seat loss for the president's party in midterm elections is about twenty-five. The extent of these losses, or whether they can even be turned into gains, depends on the approval rating of the president. So in 1994 the sweep by Republicans was interpreted as a repudiation of President Bill Clinton's policies, and the Republican success in the midterm elections in 2002 as a vindication of President George W. Bush. In 2010, voters were unhappy with President Obama, whose approval ratings had slipped throughout the year. To signal their discontent, voters handed the Republicans control of the House of Representatives.

Economic conditions and presidential popularity indirectly influence voters in another way. Because politicians are ambitious and want to run for office when the prospects for success are high, they survey conditions when deciding whether to run. In December 2001, with President George W. Bush's sky-high popularity, conditions looked good for Republicans in the 2002 midterm elections, and many high-quality Republican candidates decided to run. In contrast, in December 2007 President Bush was unpopular, the economy was sagging, and the Iraq War was dragging on, so many high-quality Republican contenders decided not to run in 2008, waiting for a more favorable time. The aggregate effect of these decisions produces an outcome for congressional elections that correlates with economic conditions and presidential popularity. Political scientists call this influence the **strategic politician hypothesis**.[64]

Much has been written on the exact mechanisms that drive voters and congressional elections. While there is disagreement over the specifics, it is clear that the composition of Congress changes in response to economic conditions. When there are good times, the president's party benefits. When times are bad, the president's party suffers.

strategic politician hypothesis: *Effect that the strength of the economy and the popularity of the sitting president have on the decision to run for Congress.*

Elections and Campaigns and Public Policy: Campaign Finance and Campaign Promises

Elections and campaigns are the key instruments of American democracy because they allow voters to judge their elected officials and replace them if enough voters disapprove of their job performance. The playing field of elections has to be fair, and the rules have to be enforced equally across all candidates, parties, and interest groups. The federal government

Should elections be read as signals on the direction of public policy?

has sought to enact rules with these goals in mind. Moreover, elections are intrinsically connected to public policy outcomes because politicians take them as indicators of which policies voters want the government to pursue. In this section we detail how the rules of campaigns are enforced and how closely policy follows from the promises that elected officials make to voters on the campaign trail.

Campaign Finance Laws

The 1971 Federal Election Campaign Act (FECA) transformed the way campaigns are conducted and monitored, as it requires candidates, political parties, and political action committees to disclose their campaign financial records. In 1974 Congress amended the law to set strict limits on how much money could be contributed by individuals, parties, and PACs to campaigns and, more important, created the Federal Election Commission as an independent agency to closely monitor campaign finance.[65] When Senator James Buckley (R-N.Y.) challenged the rules on contributions on the grounds that they interfered with freedom of speech (see also Chapter 4, Civil Liberties), the Supreme Court's decision in *Buckley v. Valeo* (1976) declared that limits on contributions and enforcement of those limitations were constitutional, but that limits on how much money candidates spent were not constitutional.[66] In 2002 the Bipartisan Campaign Reform Act (BCRA) raised the legal contribution allowances for campaigns; prohibited political parties from accepting and spending unlimited amounts of money directly on campaigns; restricted the ability of interest groups to run campaign ads without fully identifying themselves; and prohibited them from running such ads within thirty days of a primary and sixty days of the general election.[67] The 2010 Supreme Court ruling in *Citizens United v. Federal Election Commission* (see Supreme Court Cases in Chapter 8, Interest Groups) undoes many of these restrictions, allowing unions and businesses to spend money on campaigns.

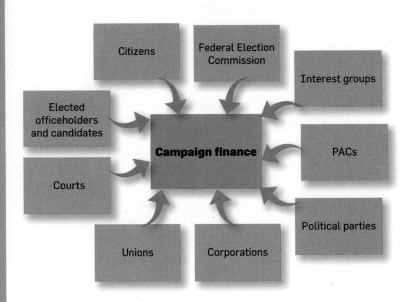

The FEC takes its job seriously. If an individual citizen makes a complaint against a candidate, group, or political party for violating campaign finance laws, the FEC investigates. In 2006, for example, in response to complaints about campaign-related behavior in the 2004 presidential election, the FEC assigned stark penalties to three prominent advocacy groups—MoveOn.org Voter Fund ($150,000), League of Conservation Voters ($180,000), and the Swift Boat Veterans and POWs for Truth ($299,500)—for violations of campaign finance laws. According to the FEC, these groups behaved like PACs but did not follow the PAC contribution and reporting requirements. The FEC indicated that the sole purpose of the Swift Boat Veterans was to defeat John Kerry, which the organization sought to do by airing ads on television and sending direct mail calling for his defeat.[68]

Note that the FEC's enforcement decisions were evenhanded, not favoring or targeting groups representing one ideology or the other. The FEC continues to serve as a tool whereby citizens can help ensure a fair playing field in elections.

Campaign Promises and Electoral Mandates

Elections are supposed to send signals to politicians about which policies should be pursued, and winning candidates like to claim that their elections constitute **mandates**, clear signals from the public about the policies government should pursue. The bigger a candidate's win, the stronger the belief in a mandate. In 1964, when Lyndon Johnson received a **landslide** 62 percent of the vote, a reporter from the *New York Times* asked, "How will [Johnson] use the mandate to lead and govern that has been so overwhelmingly tendered by the American people?"[69] In 1980 Ronald Reagan (1981–89) claimed that his presidential victory was a mandate for enacting his campaign promises of limiting the size and scope of the federal government.

How can an election result, even a lopsided one, be viewed as evidence of a mandate? The key link between a campaign and a policy outcome is the extent to which candidates are specific in their campaign promises. Vague promises do not translate well into public policy because they fail to provide a blueprint for Congress and the public. Moreover, claiming a mandate presupposes that the candidates' policies were sufficiently distinct or that voters' decisions can be read as a real choice between two different plans for federal policies.

For example, in the 2008 presidential election Barack Obama promised that he would change the priorities of the federal government, be more cautious in the use of military power, and make government more accessible to the average citizen. John McCain promised to limit the size of government, protect national security, and reduce taxes. But when voters went to the polls on election day 2008, no one really knew why they cast their votes the way they did; with the secret ballot and 120 million people voting for president in 2008, there is no way to use elections to detect mandates.[70] The only thing the election indicated for sure was that about 53 percent of the public liked Obama better than McCain. Such information is hardly evidence that Obama received a mandate from the public to institute his platform. It seems clear the election was a rejection of President George W. Bush. The public wanted change, but the specifics of the kind of change were not registered in the vote.

If it is not possible to connect campaign promises to voters' decisions, why do successful candidates claim mandates? Mandates serve a political purpose for the winners of campaigns in American politics in that they help persuade Congress, the media, and interest groups that the president has majority public support for his program. Even without the specifics, when voters choose a president by a large percentage over the opposition candidate, they are sending a strong message that they have trust and confidence in him to run the country. So long as the president does not stray too far from his campaign promises, he can use the idea of a mandate to successfully accomplish his goals.

Party Platforms and Campaign Promises

Campaign promises are not made solely by presidential candidates. They are also made by the party in the form of the party platform, which lays out its vision for government. Party platforms are adopted at the national conventions. Overall, one study has concluded that about 66 percent of campaign promises have been enacted, only about 10 percent were ignored, and the remaining 20 percent or so were blocked in Congress.[71] A study comparing campaign

mandate: *Political power the president claims after a decisive electoral victory.*

landslide: *Overwhelming victory by a presidential candidate that demonstrates his political support and increases his ability to govern.*

Do you take campaign promises seriously?

Are election outcomes a good indicator of what the people think about specific issues?

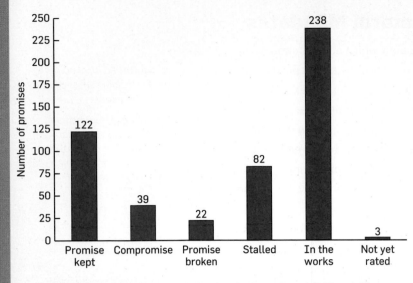

PolitiFact compiled more than five hundred promises that Barack Obama made during the campaign and has tracked their progress, rating those that are completed as "promise kept," "compromise," or "promise broken," and the others as "not yet rated," "in the works," or "stalled."

FIGURE 10.8 Obama's Campaign Promises Kept and Broken, as of October 1, 2010. Despite the common perception that politicians do not keep their campaign promises, these data suggest that President Barack Obama has at least tried to keep his. This pattern applies for politicians in general, including recent presidents George W. Bush and Bill Clinton.
Source: PolitiFact, "The Obameter: Tracking Obama's Campaign Practices," *St. Petersburg Times*, PolitiFact.com.

Should presidents who change their minds be accused of flip-flopping? Under what circumstances is a change of mind a bad thing? A good thing?

appeals in House elections to subsequent introduction and cosponsorship of legislation finds that House members also keep their promises.[72] It appears that even images in television advertisements aired in congressional elections, which are usually thought of as vague and empty, serve to guide the policies House members support.[73]

Has President Obama kept his promises? The data in Figure 10.8 suggest that he has done a pretty good job of doing what he said he would do during the campaign. Of the more than five hundred promises he made during the campaign, nearly halfway through his term he had broken only twenty-two. A great many are still in the works and not yet tackled.[74]

Perhaps the most famous breaking of a promise occurred in 1991, when President George H. W. Bush agreed to a tax increase as part of a budget deal with congressional Democrats. In his acceptance speech at the 1988 Republican National Convention, Bush had pledged he would not raise taxes, saying, "Read my lips, no new taxes." This emphatic statement was his best-known line, and it came back to haunt him. Although he regretted that he broke his promise, it is not clear that his actions were wrong. Many people assume that a truly responsive political system would demonstrate a perfect correspondence between campaign promises and government performance. But situations change, and elected officials need to change with them. In other words, there are times when breaking a promise is not a violation of the public's trust. In response to external events, such as a foreign policy crisis or a downturn in the economy, the people may want to change course, and responsive politicians act accordingly.

Consider that prior to the terrorist attacks of September 11, 2001, President George W. Bush had promised not to engage in nation building. But after the attacks, he ordered the military to invade Afghanistan, overthrow the Taliban, and institute a new government. This move was almost universally applauded. Had Bush refused to respond in this fashion, citing previous campaign promises, there would have been an outcry against him.

Every democratic government that rests on regularly scheduled campaigns and elections requires the contests to be fair and as open to the public as possible. Elections serve an important public policy purpose because they allow voters to declare their approval or disapproval of government actions. Politicians recognize that they have to offer voters some blueprints for their future actions in office, and that is the purpose of campaign promises. Campaigns themselves are the selling of contrasting political products, and voters choose the one they think they will like the best. The policies that are produced after every election are the products that are sold to the public by candidates and political parties during each election cycle. But just as citizens require truth in advertising about consumer goods, they also require politicians to live up to their promises. In the end, it is up to each citizen to judge the public policies that are enacted after every election to ensure that the electoral connection between campaigns and policy is strong.

Elections, Campaigns, and Democracy

American elections and the campaigns that precede them are the means by which citizens participate in selecting those who will govern them. It is inevitable that they are at the center of concerns about American democracy. Many observers worry that campaigns are too long, that candidates spend too much money, and the voters are not very well informed. These concerns often focus on the fairness of the process and of the outcome. In the long term, the process has worked reasonably well. In the short term, it is those who lose who see the process as unfair.

In any assessment of the American political system, partisanship needs to be set aside. In 1980, for example, many Americans were unhappy with the state of the economy and foreign affairs. Over 70 percent of the electorate felt that the nation was on the wrong track.[75] The 1980 campaign offered the public a chance to correct course by changing presidents, and the public did so by electing Ronald Reagan. Reagan promised to end the era of big government, slashing taxes and domestic spending. Four years later, only 26 percent of the electorate felt that America was on the wrong track,[76] and President Reagan won the 1984 election in a landslide, losing only one state. In 2008 the public again was very dissatisfied with the direction of the country—only 14 percent felt the nation was on the right track.[77] The Republicans lost control of the White House, giving Barack Obama a chance to correct course. If things do not improve, President Obama can expect to serve only one term.

The general lesson is that elections and campaigns, although imperfect, provide a real chance to ensure government responsiveness. Candidates seek the support of the public through speeches, ads, press releases, and other methods of campaigning. The public digests that information and chooses a candidate. People's votes are a blunt instrument, but they help to forge accountability. If elected officials want to stay in office, they need to act in a way that will increase the chances of continued support. Of course, the party out of office would like to get back in, and it, too, seeks the support of the public. It is through this competitive struggle that American democracy works. Critics worry that the public does not know many of the details of candidates and their platforms, and that is clearly true. But the American public should not be underestimated. That the country has not only survived for the last 230 years but has thrived suggests just the opposite. The fact that the public collectively seems to act in reasonably coherent ways is testimony to political scientist V. O. Key's classic observation that "voters are not fools."[78]

FOCUS QUESTIONS

- In what ways do elections encourage accountability and responsiveness in government?

- How does citizen equality work, or not work, in elections and campaigns? Are elections and campaigns fair?

- How well do campaigns work to inform the public so as to allow voters to hold candidates accountable?

- Do laws that regulate the financing of campaigns impede or advance equality and accountability in elections?

- In what ways are elections and campaigns gateways to American democracy? What are the gates?

GATEWAYS TO LEARNING

Top Ten to Take Away

1. The constitutional requirements for elections set up gates against direct democracy by allowing only the House of Representatives to be elected by the people. State legislatures chose both senators and the electors who would elect the president. (p. 320)

2. Today senators are elected directly by the people, and presidential elections give the people more influence, but the Electoral College enhances the influence of small states over states with large populations and affects the strategy of presidential campaigns. (pp. 320, 335–36)

3. Because of the structure of the Electoral College, the candidate with the highest number of popular votes sometimes does not win the presidency. (pp. 323–24)

4. Each state has two senators. House members represent state congressional districts whose lines are redrawn every ten years following the census to make the population represented roughly equal. (pp. 324–27)

5. Presidential campaigns are demanding on the candidates and are shaped by constitutional requirements, interparty struggles, and strategies for attracting votes. (pp. 327–33)

6. Campaigns make public engagement possible but are very expensive. Strategies for winning states crucial to winning the electoral vote introduce inequalities, as does the shaping of appeals to voters. (pp. 333–41)

7. Congressional elections take place every two years, when terms end for one-third of senators and all members of the House. Congressional incumbents almost always win. Congressional campaigns do not draw as much attention as presidential elections. (pp. 341–47)

8. The federal government regulates the financing of campaigns to help equalize opportunities to run for federal office. (pp. 347–49)

9. Campaign promises, including those in party platforms, are the measure against which citizens can evaluate the performance of the president and Congress. (pp. 349–51)

10. The presidency and the composition of Congress change in response to economic conditions and foreign relations, and the pattern of party gains and losses indicates that voters use elections to hold officials accountable and that the presidency and Congress are responsive institutions. (pp. 346–47, 350–51)

A full narrative summary of the chapter is on the book's website.

Ten to Test Yourself

1. How has campaigning for president changed since George Washington's time?
2. How did the 1965 Voting Rights Act affect redistricting in states?
3. What is the difference between a primary election and the general election?
4. What is the role of money in campaigns, and how is it regulated?
5. What are the roles of issues and advertising in campaigns?
6. What are the primary factors in determining who wins a presidential campaign?
7. What kinds of advantages, as well as disadvantages, do incumbents usually have over their challengers?
8. Was the outcome of the 2008 election more about the success of Barack Obama or the failure of John McCain?
9. Why do congressional incumbents almost always win?
10. What is the relationship between campaign promises and policy making?

More review questions and answers and chapter quizzes are on the book's website.

Timeline to Keep Things in Order

 Twelfth Amendment combines the vote for president and vice president. **1804**

 House of Representatives determines the outcome of the 1824 presidential election. **1825**

 An electoral commission determines the outcome of the 1876 presidential election. **1877**

 Seventeenth Amendment provides for direct election of senators. **1913**

Terms to Know and Use

acceptance speech (p. 332)
battleground state (p. 336)
bundling (p. 334)
caucus (p. 332)
census (p. 326)
challengers (p. 341)
ducking (p. 338)
Electoral College (p. 321)
electors (p. 321)
flip-flopping (p. 338)
frontloading (p. 332)
front porch campaign (p. 329)
gerrymandering (p. 327)
incumbent (p. 341)

initiatives (p. 327)
invisible primary (p. 330)
jockeying for position (p. 329)
landslide (p. 349)
mandate (p. 349)
matching (p. 338)
matching funds (p. 334)
microtargeting (p. 336)
median voter theorem
 (p. 341)
midterm elections (p. 341)
momentum (p. 331)
negativity (p. 339)
party identification (p. 346)

party insiders (p. 331)
party platform (p. 332)
permanent campaign
 (p. 329)
political action committees
 (PACs) (p. 334)
popular vote (p. 323)
position issues (p. 338)
prediction models (p. 340)
presidential coattails (p. 346)
presidential debates (p. 333)
primary election (p. 332)
Progressives (p. 324)
pushing (p. 338)

redistricting (p. 326)
referenda (p. 327)
safe seat (p. 344)
strategic politician
 hypothesis (p. 347)
strategic retirement
 (p. 344)
swing states (p. 335)
swing voters (p. 335)
term limits (p. 344)
valence issues (p. 338)
vanishing marginal (p. 344)
wedge issue (p. 338)
winner-take-all system (p. 322)

Use the vocabulary flash cards on the book's website.

Learning That Works

WHAT YOU NEED . . .

TO KNOW

How winner-take-all works

How the Electoral College works

The steps in presidential elections

Strategies in elections

The rules regarding campaign finance

Promises made in the 2008 and 2010
 elections

TO DO

Understand campaign strategies

Evaluate potential inequalities in American elections

Determine whether voters have a fair chance to pick and influence
 candidates

Assess whether voters have enough solid information to cast votes

Decide whether money distorts campaign outcomes

Consider whether those elected should be reelected

John F. Kennedy and Richard M. Nixon are the first presidential candidates to debate each other on television.

Voting Rights Act authorizes federal supervision to ensure voting rights.

Federal Election Campaign Act establishes federal oversight of campaign funding.

Bush v. Gore decides the outcome of the 2000 presidential election.

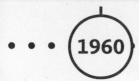 **1960**   **1965**   **1971**  **2000**

11 VOTING AND PARTICIPATION

▲ **University of Science and Arts of Oklahoma, Chickasha**

> *It's within your power to change the system. Don't ever feel that you're not capable of leading in our democracy.*

As a senior political science major at the University of Science and Arts of Oklahoma in Chickasha, Maya Torralba might have focused, like many seniors, on grades and a job search, but she instead turned her efforts to helping her community. As a Native American—a member of the Kiowa tribe and also of Comanche and Wichita descent—she was less worried about her personal prospects than about the prospects for young women in her hometown of Anadarko, a city in central Oklahoma where Native Americans form a near majority. She knew that these teenagers were battling drug abuse, teen pregnancy, and a general lack of hope. "They feel like they don't fit into society," Torralba explains. Through the Community Esteem Project that she established in 2008 as a fellow with Young People For, a leadership initiative of the People for the American Way Foundation, Torralba has sought to empower these young women. "I want to show the ladies the power that Native women have had within themselves throughout history," she explains.

The program has taught teenagers how to make traditional regalia and has brought them together with elder women who talk about their life experiences and overcoming obstacles associated with the loss of Native culture. "What I found," says Torralba, "is that the girls have a defeatist mentality in their education and academic work. They don't feel like they can achieve good grades or finish school." Through the Community Esteem Project, the young women of Anadarko are reconnecting with their heritage. They are learning that "they don't have to 'fit' anywhere," says Torralba. "They make their own spot by going back to their traditions."

Native empowerment has been a theme of Torralba's life. She helps with the Anadarko UNITY Council, does research for the Celebrate Native Health Grant, and volunteers for an Indians for Indians radio program. She and her brother started an online radio station, Radio Kiowa, to help Native American children learn their indigenous languages. Torralba believes that voting

Maya Torralba ▶

CourseMate

Visit http://www.cengagebrain
.com/shop/ISBN/0618906959
for interactive tools including:

- Quizzes
- Flashcards
- Videos
- Animated PowerPoint slides,
Podcast summaries, and more

- Why is voting such an important gateway for any democracy?

- Is more participation always a good thing?

- How does citizen participation in the political system affect the prospects for accountability and equality?

- Do young citizens participate enough to make the system responsive to their preferences? What about other groups?

- How do other forms of participation, besides voting, serve as gateways to democracy? Are they more or less effective than voting?

is a gateway to Native empowerment. In the summer of 2006 she led voter registration drives at Native events in western Oklahoma and made sure that registered voters got to the polls in November. She was also active in the 2008 get-out-the-vote drive.

Torralba's commitment to helping her community demonstrates that the gateways to participation at the local level are wide open. As a student, she balanced schoolwork, family life (she and her husband have three young children), and community service. She also recognized the gates that seemed to stand in the way of a strong civic life, especially for Native Americans. But she knew, too, that if people voted, their voices would be heard, and that if young women believed in themselves, they would invest in their communities. Self-esteem, she believes, builds community esteem.[1]

Democracy rests on a citizenry that is prepared to be involved in ways that advance both self-interest and civic interest. Participation is essential to making the system responsive. Voting is the most important gateway to participation, but as Torralba's community-focused work attests, it is only one of the ways that active citizens can make their communities better. In this chapter we examine how Americans participate in the political process. We give the most attention to voting, with an examination of the history of voting, the rules of voting, and the reasons for voting. The chapter also addresses other forms of participation that help hold government accountable, including protests and the rise of e-participation. Finally, we look at recent and future public policy concerning participation and voting.

The Practice and Theory of Voting

Americans enjoy near universal opportunities to vote. Even so, no one should assume that such opportunities have always existed or that they are permanent. Despite the widespread belief in the importance of elections for democratic institutions, some Americans have argued that voting rights should not be universal. Who votes shapes the outcome of elections and the conduct of government. Voting, in short, is a gateway to power, so there are always battles over who gets access to the ballot.

Why does the Constitution say so little about voting?

The Constitution and Voting

The Constitution is nearly silent on the rules about voting in elections, leaving such choices to the states. As Article I, Section 4 of the Constitution states, "The Times, Places and Manner of holding Elections for Senators and Representatives, shall be prescribed in each State by the Legislature thereof." The Constitution does spell out in some detail the workings of the **Electoral College**, which chooses the president (see Chapter 10, Elections and Campaigns). But states were given latitude about how to choose their members to the College.

Electoral College: *The 538 presidential electors, elected to represent the votes of their respective states, who meet every four years to cast the electoral votes for president and vice president of the United States.*

The consequence of this delegation of authority is a system of voting that is very complicated because state rules vary considerably. The differing rules also lead to inequalities among the states. It is, for example, easier to vote in some states than in others. We explore some of these issues in this chapter and in Chapter 10 as well.

Competing Views of Participation

Debates about voting and the removal of obstacles to voting have often centered on whether potential voters would be qualified to cast ballots. For example, in the nineteenth century, many lawmakers did not think women would make wise political choices and were therefore reluctant to consider granting them **suffrage**.[2] Others worried that too much participation yields too many demands on government, making government less able to respond. It seems that those opposed to removing obstacles to voting feared that too much democracy could be bad for democracy.[3]

We label these ideas the **Hamiltonian model of participation**. Alexander Hamilton represents a perspective that sees risks in greater participation and, thus, favors a larger role for **elites**. In this model, not only would the quality of the decision be diluted by more participation, but government would be less able to advance the national interest because it would be responding to uninformed voters. The Hamiltonian model stands in stark contrast to the **Jeffersonian model**, which holds that more participation yields a more involved and engaged public and that, in turn, produces better outcomes.[4] In other words, democracy thrives with more democracy. Thomas Jefferson had more faith than Hamilton in the people's ability and worried that excessive reliance on elites would make government less responsive to its citizens.

Figure 11.1 offers a summary of these competing views. Proponents of the Hamiltonian model do seek accountability, but they place much more faith in the ability of elites than in ability of the general public to make the right decisions. The people, they contend, are often uninformed and cannot make the best choices. In contrast, proponents of the Jeffersonian model want to see more participation, believing that the people can be trusted and that getting more people involved will push government to be more responsive to the people's interests. They contend that if certain groups of people are disenfranchised, government will be less responsive. People may not be well informed about politics, but if they have a chance to be involved, they will become better informed. An informed citizenry that actively participates in politics will ensure that government is both accountable and responsive.

Obviously the Jeffersonian model holds equality as an important political value, whereas the Hamiltonian model places more emphasis on efficient and effective outcomes. These competing visions of citizen involvement have played out in nearly all debates about expanding the opportunity for more citizens to cast ballots. In the course of the nation's history, proponents and opponents of expanding the right to vote have each achieved

suffrage: *Right to vote; also called* franchise.

Can you think of any reason why a citizen should not be allowed to vote?

Hamiltonian model of participation: *View of participation that suggests that too much participation is a bad thing and that many people are not well-enough informed to cast votes.*

elites: *Group of people who may lead public opinion, such as journalists, politicians, and policy makers.*

Jeffersonian model of participation: *View of participation that suggests that more is better. That is, as people get involved more, they learn more about politics and want to get even more involved.*

Do you lean toward the Hamiltonian or the Jeffersonian model of participation?

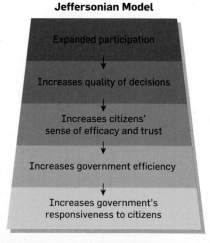

FIGURE 11.1 Hamiltonian and Jeffersonian Models of Participation.

victories. Although the overall trend has been constant expansion, the contest has been fraught with conflict—not only debate in Congress and the courts but also violence in the streets, as the following section will attest.

The History of Voting in America

The history of voting in America falls into three general eras.[5] First, from the 1790s to 1870, voting rights expanded, and by 1860 universal white male suffrage had been achieved. After the Civil War, voting rights were extended to African American males by means of the Fifteenth Amendment. But states, localities, and political parties sought by various means to block African Americans, Asian immigrants, and others from voting. From the 1870s until 1920 the barriers to voting often increased. Reforms were underway as well, and beginning with the Nineteenth Amendment in 1920, which granted women the right to vote, voting rights began to expand again. The civil rights movement of the 1950s and 1960s culminated in the passage of laws protecting voting rights for African Americans, and an amendment in 1971 extended the right to vote to 18-year-olds. Citizens of the District of Columbia were given the opportunity to vote in presidential elections starting in 1961 (see Figure 11.2). Thus, in the twentieth century, there was a second wave of expansion of voting rights.

These three eras suggest that voting and the electorate have expanded in the long run, though not consistently and with contractions that have violated civil rights (see Chapter 5, Civil Rights). In this section, we survey these developments by looking at the first era of expanding voting rights, women's suffrage, the denial and then protection of voting rights for African Americans, and voting restrictions and opportunities for other minorities and immigrants.

Expansion of Voting, 1790s to 1870

George Washington (1789–97) was elected to the presidency twice, unanimously both times.[6] By all accounts, he was a popular president and the overwhelming choice of the public. Yet a close look at the first presidential elections shows that very few citizens actually voted for Washington. In fact, for the first nine presidential elections (1789–1820), **popular votes** were not even recorded. Most states did not allow the public to cast ballots for president; state legislators chose the electors who voted in the Electoral College. State legislators also chose U.S. senators. The people could vote for representatives

popular vote: *Tally of total votes from individual citizens, as opposed to the electoral vote.*

FIGURE 11.2 Amendments That Pertain to the Right to Vote.

Color Code :
Participation Equality

Fifteenth (1870): Prohibits states from denying the right to vote on account of race

Seventeenth (1913): Gives the people (instead of state legislatures) the right to choose U.S. senators

Nineteenth (1920): Guarantees women the right to vote

Twenty-Third (1961): Grants residents of the District of Columbia votes in the Electoral College

Twenty-Fourth (1964): Prohibits poll taxes

Twenty-Sixth (1971): Guarantees 18-year-olds the right to vote to the House of Representatives, but eligibility to vote was limited to white males who owned a certain amount of property or paid a certain amount of taxes. Slaves could not vote, and free black males often did not have the right to vote. South Carolina, Georgia, and Virginia blocked free blacks from voting when the Constitution was first adopted. In New Jersey, women who owned property could vote from 1776 until 1807, when the right was repealed.[7]

Library of Congress

Not until the rise of **Jacksonian democracy** in the 1820s did the **franchise** (the right to vote) begin to expand significantly. In the 1824 presidential election only about 366,000 votes were cast, representing just over 25 percent of eligible voters.[8] None of the four candidates won a majority in the Electoral College, though Andrew Jackson won the most popular votes (41 percent), so the election was decided by the House of Representatives. In one of the most controversial deals in American politics, Henry Clay, who had come in third, threw his support to John Quincy Adams, who had come in second, thereby enabling Adams to win the presidency. Once in office, President Adams (1825–29) named Clay secretary of state.

Jackson's supporters charged that Adams and Clay had made a "corrupt bargain," generating widespread outrage over the "deal."[9] Determined to get Jackson elected to office the next time, they pursued a number of strategies (see also Chapter 9, Political Parties). Among them, Jackson's supporters pressed states to remove property requirements for voting and to allow citizens, instead of state legislatures, to vote for president. Their efforts paid off. In the presidential election of 1828, turnout tripled to over 1.1 million votes cast and produced a landslide for Jackson (1829–37), who won 56 percent of the popular vote and two-thirds of the Electoral College vote. By the time of the Civil War, property and tax qualifications had been largely eliminated, but the franchise was still limited largely to white males. Women could not vote, nor could many free blacks. Those who voted for president in 1860, consequently, were almost exclusively white males.

Following the Civil War, the Fifteenth Amendment gave African American males the right to vote. Efforts by southern states to deny that right (covered later in this chapter) have shaped American politics into the present.

The Road to Women's Suffrage, 1848 to 1920

In 1848 in Seneca Falls, New York, the first women's rights meeting initiated a movement for **women's suffrage**. The movement gained energy after the Civil War, as women individually and through suffrage organizations pressured state legislatures to change state laws to allow women to vote. Susan B. Anthony, a leader in the National Woman Suffrage Association,

When the 1824 presidential election produced no majority in the Electoral College, the House of Representatives selected John Quincy Adams, who had received fewer votes than Andrew Jackson. Jackson's supporters, angered at this outcome, worked to expand the right to vote before the next election. In 1828 Jackson beat Adams in the popular vote and in the Electoral College. Following Jackson's inauguration on March 4, 1829, crowds of supporters celebrated at the White House.

Jacksonian democracy: *Political philosophy of President Andrew Jackson and his supporters that sought greater influence for the common man on the policies and actions of government.*

franchise: *Right to vote; also called* suffrage.

Why has Jackson been called "the people's president"?

women's suffrage: *Movement to grant women the right to vote.*

The Granger Collection, New York

In the early 1870s suffragists such as Susan B. Anthony tried to exercise the right to vote. When Virginia Minor was blocked from registering to vote in Missouri, she sued. Her case, decided by the Supreme Court in 1875, determined that women were citizens but that the Constitution does not confer a right to vote. In this drawing Victoria Claflin Woodhull points to the Constitution as she tries to vote in a local New York City election; her sister Tennessee Claflin stands behind her.

Describe theories of representation that could have been used to justify denying women the right to vote.

Why were women able to vote in some states but not in others?

How did suffrage for women affect the responsiveness of government?

turnout: *Share of all eligible voters who actually cast ballots.*

worked tirelessly for most of her life to secure women the right to vote. In 1872, for example, she went to the polls in her hometown of Rochester, New York, and cast a ballot, claiming that the Fourteenth Amendment's statement that "all persons [not just men] born or naturalized in the United States . . . are citizens" gave women the right to vote. Later, she was arrested (as she hoped she would be), and her trial gave the issue of suffrage for women much attention. She was found guilty of breaking the law, but not before she had used the trial as a platform for her cause.[10]

The efforts of the suffrage movement were gradually successful. In 1869 the territory of Wyoming granted the right to women, and that right was retained when Wyoming became a state in 1890. By 1916 eleven states, all in the West, allowed women to vote (see Figure 5.2, Women's Suffrage by States, 1890, 1919, in Chapter 5). The piecemeal approach of statewide campaigns came to an end on August 26, 1920, when the Tennessee legislature ratified the Nineteenth Amendment by a single vote. With Tennessee, three-quarters of the states had ratified the amendment, giving constitutional protection to women's suffrage. The amendment states, "The right of citizens of the United States to vote shall not be denied or abridged by the United States or by any State on account of sex." Some southern states used the late date of the Tennessee ratification, only ten weeks before the presidential election, to deny women's access to the ballot until the next election cycle.[11]

The effect of women's vote was debated and even feared at the time. There was speculation that women were not well suited to be active participants in the political process and that allowing them to vote would provide "an unpredictable or volatile addition to the electorate."[12] Others were concerned about nearly doubling the voting electorate and the additional demands that would place on government. Such views are closely associated with the Hamiltonian model of voting. But evidence gathered by political scientists suggests that these worries were unfounded. Women in the 1920s voted in ways that suggested that reflected their interests just as much as men's did.[13] The adoption of the Nineteenth Amendment did not, in other words, undermine the basic stability of electoral politics—a finding supportive of those who favor the Jeffersonian approach to participation.

With women able to vote, overall **turnout** did drop in the short term. From 1904 to 1916 the average rate of turnout in presidential elections was about 63 percent. With the inclusion of women as eligible voters, turnout fell to 49 percent in both 1920 and 1924. But then it started to climb as women increasingly exercised their right to vote, reaching 57 percent in both 1928 and 1932. By 1940 the turnout rate was 62 percent—essentially at the pre-1920 level. These data strongly suggest that women quickly became involved in the political process. By 1984 women voted at a slightly higher rate than men—a trend that continues today. In the 2008 elections, for instance, 66 percent of women and 62 percent of men voted.[14]

The Denial of African American Suffrage, 1870 to 1965

The story of gates against African American participation is long and agonizing. Following the Civil War, Congress and the states ratified the Fifteenth Amendment, which reads: "The right of citizens of the United States to vote shall not be denied or abridged by the United States or by any State on account of race, color, or previous condition of servitude." With such constitutional protection, African Americans should have been able to exercise their right to vote. During **Reconstruction** (1865–77), the period when the federal government effectively controlled the state governments in the South, southern blacks were able vote. Their votes made it possible for South Carolina—the first state to secede and the first to fire on federal troops—to elect the first African American member of the House of Representatives, Joseph Rainey, in 1870.

© Corbis

Joseph Rainey had been born a slave in South Carolina, but his father purchased his freedom. After the Civil War, Rainey quickly became active in Republican Party politics. He was a delegate to the South Carolina constitutional convention and a member of the South Carolina Senate before being elected, in 1870, to the U.S. House of Representatives, where he served until 1879.

The presidential election of 1876 ended any hope of integrating blacks into American political life. Neither the Democrat Samuel Tilden nor the Republican Rutherford B. Hayes won a majority in the Electoral College. Contested votes in three southern states and Oregon, with charges of fraud, led Congress to appoint an Electoral Commission to resolve the matter of who should count the votes of the electors (the Constitution does not say who should resolve disputed votes). In an unofficial bargain, all the disputed votes went to Hayes (1877–81) in return for his promise that federal troops would be removed from the South and the region would return to self-governance. With this agreement, Reconstruction was effectively over, and so was African American participation in the political process.

In an era known as **Jim Crow**, Southern state legislatures, no longer under federal authority, started to pass laws that denied African Americans basic political rights. State and local laws systematically undermined the political, economic, and social standing of African Americans by requiring segregation of the races in public schools, parks, accommodations, and transportation. Those who disobeyed segregation laws were subject not only to fines and jailing but also to lynching and other acts of brutal violence. Between 1889 and 1930 more than 3,700 lynchings were reported, most of them of southern blacks, and many other lynchings and mob actions were not reported in the press.[15]

The law-based means of denying African Americans the right to vote included the following strategies.

Reconstruction: *The period from 1865 to 1877 in which the former Confederate states gained readmission to the Union and the federal government passed laws to help the emancipated slaves.*

Jim Crow laws: *Southern laws that established strict segregation of the races.*

What was the justification for denying African Americans the right to vote?

literacy tests: *Tests requiring reading and interpretation skills in order to vote.*

Should people have to be able to read before they can vote? Should people have to be able to read English before they can vote?

Literacy Tests.
Literacy tests, which required potential voters to prove they could read, were applied differently to whites and blacks. African Americans were often given harder tests to ensure they would not pass. In some cases, the tests were set up to guarantee failure, as there were no correct answers. Figure 11.3 reproduces some questions from the Louisiana literacy test, a test that is impossible to pass.

FIGURE 11.3 Louisiana Literacy Test. These questions, excerpted from a three-page test, make it clear that the test was not intended to test literacy but to deny African Americans the right to vote.

The State of Louisiana

Literacy Test (This test is to be given to anyone who cannot prove a fifth grade education.)

Do what you are told to do in each statement, nothing more, nothing less. Be careful as one wrong answer denotes failure of the test. You have 10 minutes to complete the test.

1. Draw a line around the number or letter of this sentence.

2. Draw a line under the last word in this line.

3. Cross out the longest word in this line.

4. Draw a line around the shortest word in this line.

5. Circle the first, first letter of the alphabet in this line.

6. In the space below draw three circles, one inside (engulfed by) the other.

7. Above the letter X make a small cross.

8. Draw a line through the letter below that comes earliest in the alphabet.

ZVSBDMKITPHC

9. Draw a line through the two letters below that come last in the alphabet.

ZVBDMKTPHSYC

10. In the first circle below write the last letter of the first word beginning with "L".

11. Cross out the number necessary, when making the number below one million.

10000000000

12. Draw a line from circle 2 to circle 5 that will pass below circle 2 and above circle 4.

①②③④⑤

13. In the line below cross out each number that is more than 20 but less than 30.

31 16 48 29 53 47 22 37 98 26 20 25

Source: Rethinking Schools, www.rethinkingschools.org/.

Poll Taxes. **Poll taxes** were another means of discouraging blacks from voting. In the 1890s an individual had to pay $1 in Mississippi and $2 in South Carolina to vote, an amount that may seem small today but was huge in the poverty-stricken postwar South, where the average annual income was equivalent to $86 in today's dollars; the South Carolina poll tax would be equivalent to about $1,000 today.[16] For most blacks, almost all poor farmers, this tax made voting impossible.[17]

Grandfather Clauses. To help keep literacy tests and poll taxes from discouraging white voters, exemptions were allowed for those whose grandfathers had voted. Because the grandfathers of most African Americans had been slaves with no voting rights, these **grandfather clauses** never benefited them.

poll taxes: *Tax on voting; prohibited by the Twenty-Fourth Amendment (1964).*

grandfather clauses: *Election rules that exempted people from difficult literacy and interpretation tests for voting if their grandfathers had been eligible to vote.*

The White Primary. Following the Civil War, the Democratic Party dominated in the South. By restricting its primary to white voters, it kept black voters—even if they could exercise the right to vote—from having any influence, because whoever won the Democratic primary always won the general election. In 1944 the U.S. Supreme Court, in *Smith v. Allwright*, ruled the **white primary** unconstitutional.[18]

white primary: *Election rules that prohibited blacks from voting in Democratic primaries.*

The Civil Rights Movement and African American Voting, 1950s and 1960s

The era of Jim Crow lasted for decades because, despite the guarantee of the Fifteenth Amendment, states retained authority over voting laws, and these laws were not challenged. Moreover, Democratic Party dominance ensured the continuation of the so-called **Solid South**, a voting bloc critical to all Democratic presidential candidates from Woodrow Wilson (1913–21) to Franklin Delano Roosevelt (1933–45) to John F. Kennedy (1961–63), who therefore did not push for civil rights. Southern senators had the power to block efforts to end Jim Crow laws, given their seniority and the option (or threat) of using the **filibuster** (see Chapter 12, Congress).[19]

Solid South: *Tendency of southern voters to vote Democratic that started after the Civil War and ended in the 1960s.*

filibuster: *Tactic of extended speech designed to delay or block passage of a bill in the Senate.*

Beginning in the 1950s the **civil rights movement** challenged the denial of basic political rights. Boycotts, sit-ins, and marches called attention to the lack of equal treatment for African Americans in the South (see Chapter 5), and public support for ending the legal barriers grew. For instance, in October 1963, 86 percent of the American public approved of "a federal law that requires negroes be given equal rights in voting."[20] In 1964 support by the public helped give Congress the impetus to pass the **Civil Rights Act**, which protected voting rights and put severe restrictions on the administration of literacy tests. To strengthen protections of voting rights, in 1965 Congress passed the **Voting Rights Act**, which effectively ended literacy tests and other strategies that had discriminated against African Americans at the polls and gave the Justice Department the authority to supervise **voter registration** in locales that had discriminated (see also Chapter 5). The Twenty-Fourth Amendment, ratified in 1964, banned poll taxes.

civil rights movement: *Movement after World War II to gain equal rights for African Americans, later expanded to end discrimination on account of race, gender, sexual preference, and disability status.*

Civil Rights Act: *Prohibits discrimination in employment, education, and places of public accommodation (1964).*

Voting Rights Act: *Gives the federal government the power to prevent discrimination in voting rights (1965).*

voter registration: *Enrollment required prior to voting to establish eligibility.*

One consequence of these measures was a huge upswing of voter participation in the South. From 1920 to 1960 the turnout rate in southern states averaged 23 percent in presidential elections, whereas in the rest of the country it was 65 percent. The low turnout in the South was due not only to the exclusion of blacks; the South was also poorer than much of the rest of the country, and poverty generally depresses turnout. Moreover, Democratic Party dominance meant that elections were not competitive and generated little public interest. But **voter apathy** in the South has declined as wealth has risen, and Democratic Party dominance has ended as well. In 2008, 62 percent of southerners reported voting, whereas the figure for the rest of the country was about 64 percent.[21]

voter apathy: *Lack of interest in voting and in politics generally.*

Using African Americans as an example, describe how voting affects government responsiveness.

Those with the Hamiltonian model mind-set worried that African Americans would not have the necessary education and skills to recognize how their interests could be best served at the polls. But, as in the case of women, the worries were unfounded. The political revival of African Americans gave them reason to become more attentive, more informed, and better citizens overall. As one study reports, "African-Americans developed the attitudes and skills necessary to 'learn the trade' of politics in a remarkably short period of time."[22] The fact that blacks overcame informational and educational disadvantages imposed on them in the Jim

Crow era casts doubts on the Hamiltonian theory of participation, giving advocates of the Jeffersonian school reason for optimism.

As African Americans increasingly exercised their right to vote, politicians who wanted to win office needed the votes and adjusted their views to court the new voters. One of the most striking examples is Alabama Governor George Wallace, an outspoken segregationist in the early 1960s, who personally "stood in the schoolhouse door" to keep black students from registering at the University of Alabama. Twenty years later, running for governor once again, Wallace won because of the votes of African Americans. He had changed his views on race and apologized for his earlier racist statements and behavior.[23] Wallace's change of position is indicative of the power of the ballot box to generate responsiveness.

In 1963, as governor of Alabama, George Wallace literally "stood in the schoolhouse door" to prevent black students from registering at the University of Alabama. His stand for segregation and state's rights won him nearly 10 million popular votes and five states in the 1968 presidential election. Campaigning for president again in 1972, he was shot and partly paralyzed. When he ran for governor again in 1982, he admitted that he had been wrong about race, and he was elected with unprecedented black support. As governor he made it a point to meet with civil rights leaders and apologize. In the bottom photo, taken in 1973, he congratulates Terry Points, Alabama's first black homecoming queen.

The Vote for Eighteen-Year-Olds, 1971

Until 1971 nearly all states set the minimum age for voting at 21,[24] but with the adoption of the Twenty-Sixth Amendment that year, the federal government mandated that states could not deny the right to vote to anyone age 18 or over. The impetus for this extension of the franchise was the Vietnam War, which heightened awareness of the fact that young men were being sent off to fight at age 18 but could not participate in elections. The call for the 18-year-old vote also took place in the context of campus antiwar protests and student demands for greater rights, and in the wake of African American achievements in civil and voting rights—protests that had achieved protection of the right to vote. At that moment in the country's history people were receptive to arguments in favor of greater participation. Unlike the extension of the franchise to women and African Americans, the amendment was not controversial. Even President Richard M. Nixon (1969–74) supported it, although he knew from polling data that the young voters were not likely to support him in the upcoming 1972 presidential election.

How did the votes of 18-year-olds affect the responsiveness of government?

Voting by Minorities and Immigrants

Other minority groups, such as Native Americans, and immigrants have at times been denied the right to vote because citizenship was denied to them. A person must be a citizen to vote. American Indians were first extended citizenship in 1924 by an act of Congress. Chinese immigrants were denied citizenship by the **Chinese Exclusion Act** of 1882. A steep rise in immigration from China beginning in the 1850s had fueled the effort to restrict their rights.

Chinese Exclusion Act: *1882 act barring immigration of Chinese to America.*

Understanding how these minority groups participate is complicated by two factors. First, the labels are broad, placing people with very different backgrounds in the same group. The 2 million people described as American Indians, for instance, include Eskimos, Navajos, Sioux, and members of more than 550 other tribes, each with different histories, cultures, and traditions. In the category of Asian Americans are people from Korea, China, Japan, the Philippines, and other nations. Arab Americans also have diverse cultural backgrounds. Latinos come from such different places as Mexico, Cuba, and the many countries of Latin America. The second problem involves a lack of data about many of these groups. Until recently, there has not been much study of Latino, Asian, and especially Native American voting in comparison to the study of African American voting. This gap is closing as these important groups draw more and more attention.[25]

Who Votes?

Voting is an important gateway to influence, but not everyone has the inclination or the desire to participate. Failure to vote has real implications for the political process; it affects which representatives govern and make laws, which has policy consequences that affect everyone in the United States. Low turnout raises questions about government's responsiveness, and unequal turnout by various demographic groups suggests that government's response is unequal, too. Low turnout among young people, for example, in contrast to older Americans, means that elected officials may give more attention to issues affecting senior voters, such as Social Security, than to issues affecting younger voters, such as the costs of education (see Figure 11.4). In this section, we examine turnout rates generally, and then look at turnout rates by various demographic groups.

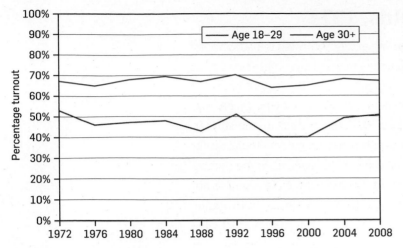

FIGURE 11.4 Gap in Voter Turnout by Age in Presidential Elections, 1972–2008. Young voters between the ages of 18 and 29 have turned out in greater numbers in the last two presidential elections, but their rate of turnout is still lower than that of people over 30, decreasing the likelihood that government will be responsive to their interests.
Source: Nonprofit Voter Engagement Network, America Goes to the Polls, "Voting Gaps in the 2008 Election," October 2009.

Turnout

Even with widespread opportunity to cast ballots and shape the course of government, Americans often choose not to vote. In 1996 fewer than half of eligible voters (about 48 percent) took the time to vote in the presidential contest between William Jefferson (Bill) Clinton (1993–2001) and Senator Robert Dole (R-Kans.). In 2008 the rate of participation improved to over 57 percent. But presidential elections are high-stimulus events (see Chapter 10). In midterm congressional elections, which are low-stimulus elections, turnout is usually less than 40 percent. For primary elections during presidential nominations, turnout is even lower. In the all-important New Hampshire presidential primary, turnout is often less than 40 percent, and that represents the high end in the primaries and caucuses that decide party nominees. In New York, often a critical primary for candidates, the rate of participation in 2008 was less than 20 percent.[26] If we consider local school board elections, we find an even smaller electorate: Often fewer than 10 percent of eligible citizens vote in such contests. A general assessment of turnout in the United States is offered later in the chapter. Here, we turn to the demographics of turnout (see Figure 11.5).

When some groups vote less frequently than other groups, what is the effect on government?

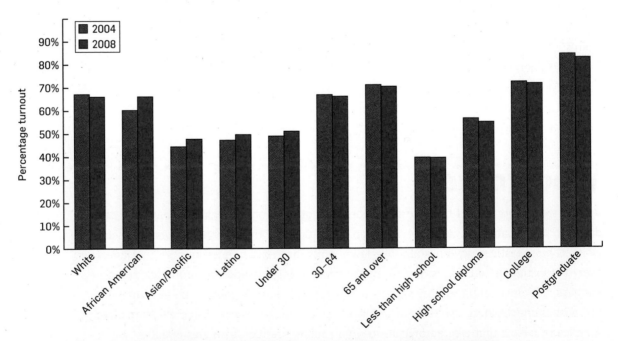

FIGURE 11.5 Turnout Rates in Presidential Elections, 2004 and 2008.
Source: Michael P. McDonald, "2008 Current Population Survey Voting and Registration Supplement," United States Elections Project, April 6, 2009, elections.gmu.edu; Doug Hess, "Analysis of the 2008 Current Population Survey (CPS) Voter and Registration Supplement," Project Vote, April 8, 2009, www.projectvote.org/.

The Demographics of Turnout

Given the important power that voting brings in a democracy, a central question becomes, Who votes? Do various demographic groups vote in equal proportions? If not, what are the consequences for government responsiveness?

The following sections use statistics to answer these questions. The data suggest that people who are most likely to vote tend to be better educated, better paid, and older than those who are unlikely to vote. There are some modest race and gender differences, but when scholars control for differences in education and income, differences in race pretty much disappear.[27] The key lesson is that the driving force of participation is the development in young people of the kinds of skills and habits that prepare an individual for active citizenship.

Race and Ethnicity. Whites have a slightly higher rate of participation than blacks. In the 1960s this gap was substantial, but it has declined dramatically. In 2004, 60 percent of blacks and 67 percent of whites voted. By 2008 the gap had disappeared: 66 percent of whites and 65 percent of African Americans reported voting. Barack Obama's (2009–) campaign clearly engaged the African American community. Whether this engagement is permanent is not yet known.

Other minority groups participate less frequently. About 47 percent of Asian Americans vote.[28] Native Americans appear to have the lowest rate of turnout, although precise estimates have been difficult to gather.[29] Latinos vote less frequently than whites or blacks, at about 50 percent, but Latino voting rates are increasing and will become a more significant force in U.S. elections. In 1988 Latinos constituted less than 4 percent of voters. Twenty years later, the proportion had more than doubled to nearly 8 percent.[30]

In general, turnout rates among ethnic minorities tend to be below the average for the entire country. Part of the reason is that members of minority groups often are not well off, and lower income generally means lower turnout. Many are not eligible to vote because they are not citizens. This is especially true for Asians and Latinos.

Sex. Women turn out at a slightly higher rate than men, by perhaps 3 to 5 percentage points. In 2008, 68 percent of women reported voting, and 62 percent of men claimed to have cast ballots.[31] The **gender gap** is important in American politics. But the gap is mostly a factor in political preferences, such as the greater tendency of women than men to identify themselves as Democrats. The gap in turnout is far less consequential.

Age. Age affects rates of participation. Turnout peaks once voters are about 45 years old and continues at that rate until advanced age sets in (80 years or older). Even when differences in education and income are controlled for, participation remains higher for older Americans. In 2004 around 70 percent of citizens over 65 years old claimed to have voted. The proportion is just 47 percent for those under 24 years of age, and it is even lower for those 21 and younger. Such findings are tied to the fact that younger citizens are often more mobile and less integrated into the community than are older citizens.[32]

It is worth noting that participation by the very youngest voting-age citizens (18–29) climbed to over 51 percent in 2008, from 49 percent in 2004. Nearly all this gain was among young blacks, whose rate of participation jumped 9 percentage points between 2004 and

Why do better-educated, better-paid, and older people vote at higher rates than less-educated, more poorly paid, and younger people? What is the effect on government?

gender gap: *Differences in the political attitudes and behavior of men and women.*

What can you do to get young people in your community to vote? Why is it important?

2008 (from 49 percent to 58 percent). Just a decade earlier, turnout among youths had hovered around 30 percent. One has to be cautious in making too much of this surge, but it does suggest that younger people become more active in politics in certain contests. In 2008 the increase in voting by youths was probably tied to concerns about the war in Iraq and the appeal of Barack Obama. According to one poll, 66 percent of 18- to 29-year-olds voted for Obama, which is an overwhelming share, given that Obama won just 53 percent of the vote nationally.[33] In general, these data speak to some of the early patterns of greater participation that have been found among the Millennials—the youngest cohort of voting-age citizens.

Income.   The higher one's income, the more likely one is to vote. More income generally means that the person has more at stake and thus more reason to vote. People with higher incomes are also likely to be in environments in which politics is frequently discussed, and that provide greater opportunities for learning about the political process. Political knowledge is strongly correlated with the propensity to vote. Further, individuals with higher incomes are more likely to be able to arrange to vote than are those with low-paying jobs, who may be less able to take time off from work.

Data from the Census Bureau strongly document this pattern. In 2004 over 80 percent of people with total family incomes of more than $100,000 reported that they went to the polls. For people whose incomes fell in the range that represents the annual median family income in America—$40,000 to $50,000—turnout was 69 percent. For the least well off (those earning less than $20,000), the proportion who claimed to have voted was 48 percent. As we show later in this chapter (see Figure 11.7, page 376), this pattern is consistent.

Education.   Although race and ethnicity, sex, age, and income have some effects on the propensity of people to vote, the number of years of formal education seems to be the most important influence. Social science research has documented the connection between education and voting.[34] The youngest voting-eligible citizens (18- to 24-year-olds) who have college degrees are 14 percentage points more likely to vote than are older citizens (65 and above) who do not have a high school education.[35] Table 11.1 shows the propensity to vote by educational level from 1988 to 2008. The gap between people with the least education and those with the most is 50 percentage points in 2008, a huge difference. Nearly three-fourths of college-educated people vote, whereas less than a quarter of those with just a grade school education do so.

TABLE 11.1 Rates of Turnout in Presidential Elections by Education, 1988–2008

	1988	1992	1996	2000	2004	2008
Years of Education	**Turnout Rate**					
8 years or fewer	37%	35%	30%	27%	24%	23%
Less than high school	41%	41%	34%	34%	34%	27%
High school	55%	58%	49%	49%	50%	50%
Less than college	65%	69%	61%	60%	66%	65%
College or more	78%	81%	73%	72%	74%	73%

Source: Harold Stanley and Richard Niemi, *Vital Statistics on American Politics* (Washington, D.C.: CQ Press, 2009).

The relationship between education and voting may not be as simple as these data suggest, however. New evidence indicates that going to college does not matter as much as childhood **socialization**, which imbues the values of citizenship and similarly affects the decision to attend college. It is not, therefore, spending four years in college that makes college graduates more likely to vote; rather, it is having been raised in an environment that stresses the importance of education that shapes willingness to vote.[36]

The gap in turnout between people who are more educated and those with little education has increased over the last forty or so years. The increase can be explained by increased access to education. Individuals who lack a high school education are at a much bigger disadvantage than in the past. These patterns suggest that inequalities may result as government responds more effectively to those who vote than to those who do not.

Why Vote?

With the right to vote guaranteed and widely available, why do some people choose not to vote, and why are some groups more likely to vote than others? Perhaps we can start to answer that question by reversing it, that is, by looking at why people vote. Political scientists have developed three approaches to explain why eligible voters choose to cast ballots. One model draws from the field of economics, the second draws from psychology, and the third focuses on the rules and context of the election. In this section we present these explanations as well as some new ideas about the relationship of genetics and voting. Finally, we briefly discuss the impact of weather on voting.

An Economic Model of Voting

The economic model of voting starts with the assumption that all choices involve calculations about **self-interest** that balance costs and benefits. In choosing a college, students consider the price of tuition, the location of the school and its reputation, the quality of the education, and the potential social life. The decision to vote is no different. According to the economic model, citizens consider the costs and benefits of voting; when the benefits exceed the costs, they turn out to vote. So, according to this model, if voting becomes less costly to all citizens, there should be an increase in participation. If it becomes more costly, fewer people will turn out. Voters, under this model, act in a rational, self-interested fashion.

However, economic voting is not straightforward. In *An Economic Theory of Democracy* (1957), Anthony Downs describes **rational voting** as a puzzle. He points out that there are some costs tied to voting, such as the time it takes to become informed and to go to the polls.[37] Costs could also involve lost work time and the cost of gas to drive to the local polling place. These costs are not huge, but they are real.

The benefits of voting are less clear. If benefits are defined in a narrow, self-interested fashion, there are no tangible benefits to be had from voting. A voter may favor a candidate (or party) because of a specific policy, such as the promise of a tax cut that would provide a big financial benefit. But a tax cut is a **public good** that is shared by all in society, including those who do not vote. Moreover, and perhaps most important, the chance that one vote will alter the outcome of the election is very small—so small, in fact, that there is a greater chance of being killed in an accident on the way to the polls than of changing the outcome of the

socialization: *Impact and influence of one's social environment on the views and attitudes one carries in life, a primary source of political attitudes.*

self-interest: *Concern for one's own advantage and well-being.*

Did you vote in the 2010 midterm elections? Why or why not?

rational voting: *Economic model of voting wherein citizens weigh the benefits of voting against the costs in order to take the most personally beneficial course of action.*

public goods: *Goods or benefits provided by government from which everyone benefits and from which no one can be excluded.*

What can, or should, government do to lower the cost of voting?

civic duty: *Social force that binds a person to actively participate in public and political life.*

Do you feel like you have a civic duty to vote? If so, where did you get that sense of duty?

civic interest: *Concern for the well-being of society and the nation as a whole.*

election. Even in the razor-thin contest in Florida in the 2000 presidential election, the margin was 537 votes.[38] One vote did not make the difference. Thus, given that there are some financial costs to voting, why should a self-interested person participate?

In short, the conclusion of the economic model is that voting is not in one's self-interest and in fact is irrational. If the decision to vote is driven by a self-interested assessment of costs and benefits, people should not take the time to vote. That is a troubling conclusion for the workings of democratic government. Obviously, if citizens do not bother to vote, government cannot be responsive, and public officials will not be held accountable.

Downs understood the troubling implications of his model and claimed that people voted because they knew that the system would collapse if no one voted. To save the system from collapse, it was rational to vote. This observation has appeal at first glance, but the logic is flawed:. One vote will not save the system from collapsing. So even if the system is about to crumble, it remains rational to abstain from voting.

Downs's model has drawn much attention from scholars. William Riker and Peter Ordeshook have argued that the model is incomplete because it does not calculate **civic duty** as a benefit of voting. The notion of civic duty is important, but it is not economic in nature. Instead, civic duty describes a psychological attitude voters might have.[39] Thus Riker and Ordeshook's argument does not solve the problem in Downs's model; the act of voting remains irrational from a narrow, self-interested point of view.[40] Yet many people do cast ballots, so the economic model of voting has clear weaknesses. Political scientists instead tend to think of voting as more of a psychological process than as a narrow economic or self-interested process.

AP Photo/Phil Coale

Kids Voting USA is a national organization that promotes civic learning in schools and communities. In 2008 more than 1.8 million children participated by "voting" in the presidential election and chose Barack Obama over John McCain by almost 2 to 1. Votes were also cast for libertarians and socialists running for various small parties, as well as for Independents and the Green Party. Here an 8-year-old "votes" in Tallahassee, Florida.

A Psychological Model of Voting

The psychological model views voting as a product of citizens' attitudes about the political system. These attitudes are often a product of socialization and early political experiences. People who are raised in households in which voting is important are likely to think that participation matters. Those who have a strong sense of trust in government or believe that their votes matter are more likely to participate. The focus here is on what we called **civic interest** in Chapter 1.

Riker and Ordeshook's concept of civic duty fits well in this psychological model of voting. Many people who vote recognize that being a citizen in a democracy carries the obligation to vote. In 2006, for example, 88 percent of repeat voters claimed that it was their "duty as a citizen to always vote."[41] The act of voting makes citizens feel good and feel that they are part of the political system. Surveys have found a strong correlation between civic-mindedness and the propensity to vote. In fact, there is often guilt associated with not voting, so much so that people tend to overreport the frequency with which they go to the polls.[42]

Another psychological component tied to the act of voting is **partisanship**. Citizens who align themselves with the Democratic or the Republican Party are more likely to vote. Being a partisan implies an engagement in politics, and partisans see importance in the outcomes of elections. Partisanship increases the prospects that an individual will vote.

Both civic duty and partisanship are attitudes formed in childhood. One survey found that a person's attitude about citizenship expressed in 1965 was a powerful predictor of his or her voting in the 1980 presidential election.[43] The relationship between socialization and voting holds even after education and other important variables that drive participation are taken into account. Moreover, parents' electoral activism in 1965 also explains their children's willingness to vote in 1980. Much has changed since 1980, but socialization continues to have a long and powerful reach. For these reasons, some states have "Kids Voting"—a program designed to instill the habit of voting in grade school children.[44]

It is also clear that citizens who express greater trust in government are more willing to participate. In addition, people who think they have a voice in government are more likely to vote. Political scientists call this attitude **efficacy**—the belief that one's involvement influences the course of government.

An Institutional Model of Voting

A third explanation of voting looks at political context. In the **institutional model**, voting is understood to be shaped by the rules of the system, by political party behavior, by the ways candidates run their campaigns, and by the context of the election.[45] This model does not ignore individuals' personal resources or psychological attitudes; it simply points out that the political environment is a factor that shapes participation.

It is clear, for example, that the popularity and appeal of the candidates affect turnout.[46] Contenders who are viewed as unexciting, even boring, offer voters few reasons to participate. But both very popular and very unpopular candidates might spur turnout. A highly controversial candidate might lead people who are strongly opposed to show up in great numbers on election day. A highly popular candidate likewise brings out supporters.

The competitiveness of an election also influences motivation. Elections that look to be close draw voters' interest and attention, especially if they think their votes might influence the outcome. A close race is exciting, and people like to be part of it. But elections often are not competitive, lessening citizens' incentive to make time to cast their ballots.

Because voting takes time, efforts by parties, interest groups, and civic organizations to bring people to the polls can make a difference. Get-out-the-vote drives, such as those Maya Torralba has participated in, seem to pay big dividends, especially at the local level. For example, direct personal contact, such as going door to door, may increase the rate of voting by 7 to 10 percentage points

partisanship: *Attachment or allegiance to a political party; party identification.*

efficacy: *Extent to which people believe their actions can affect public affairs and the actions of government.*

institutional model: *Model of voting that focuses on the context of the election, including whether it is close and whether the rules encourage or discourage participation.*

Joey Foley/FilmMagic

Campaigns to encourage Americans to vote have many supporters. In Dayton, Ohio, the Beastie Boys perform at a get-out-the-vote concert on October 30, 2008.

Have you participated in or been contacted by a get-out-the-vote program? How did it affect you?

in local elections.[47] The size of these effects is not likely to apply to presidential elections because many people are already inclined to vote in these high-stimulus elections. Parties, too, can increase turnout by mobilizing their base to participate.[48] Canvassing by telephone or in person not only may lower information costs but also may activate citizens' sense of civic duty. In some cases, parties or other organizations pick up people and bring them to the polls, lowering the costs of voting. In the 2008 Nevada presidential caucuses, former President Bill Clinton, whose wife, Hillary, was a candidate, personally took a number of voters to the polls.[49] This case is highly unusual, but it underscores the fact that efforts to help people vote can alter their decisions to vote.

Is Voting in Your Genes?

It makes sense that voting is a product of psychological forces or perhaps of the costs and benefit of participating. But might the choice to be active in politics have a deeper cause? Might it be in your genes? Over two thousand years ago, Aristotle contended that "man is by nature a political animal." Political scientists have tended to believe that citizens are "blank slates," nurtured by socialization, education, and environment. Recent evidence, however, has suggested a genetic component to participation. In 2007 James Fowler and his colleagues found a strong relationship between genes and turnout.[50] Another study in 2008 reported "that two extensively studied genes are significant predictors of voter turnout."[51] These new data are important because they suggest that scholars may need to move beyond looking at the nurture side of the equation and start to consider the role nature plays in shaping individuals politically. Even so, much more evidence is needed before a genetic model of participation is accepted. Still, the idea is intriguing and worth mentioning as a new way of thinking about voting.

Weather

There has been a long-standing view that weather affects why some people vote and others do not. With bad weather, potential voters may ask, Why bother voting? Is it worth dealing with the unpleasant weather? People who would have to travel through an ice storm in Oklahoma may have less incentive to turn out than those in Oregon on a day with sunny skies and pleasant temperatures.

The impact of weather has produced much speculation. People deal with varying weather conditions all the time, and perhaps bad weather has little effect on them. Recently, three political scientists have undertaken a comprehensive examination of this question using data "from over 22,000 weather stations to provide election day estimates of rain and snow for each U.S. County." The results are clear: Rain significantly reduces voter participation by a rate of just less than 1 percent per inch, and an inch of snowfall decreases turnout by almost 0.5 percent. These scholars go on to show that bad weather benefits Republicans slightly by discouraging less-well-off voters from participating, giving weather a potential partisan bias.[52]

Assessing Turnout

As this chapter has established, most Americans do not vote in most elections. Even in presidential elections, for which turnout is highest, only slightly more than half of eligible voters go to the polls. In this section we assess turnout in the United States. Is it too low for responsive and responsible government? Even more important, does turnout increase the prospects of governmental action that ensures equality?

Is Turnout Low?

There is a widespread belief among political scientists, political observers, and journalists that turnout in American elections is low. Consider the titles of some recent books on the topic of voting in the United States: *Why Americans Still Don't Vote* (2000), *Where Have All the Voters Gone?* (2002), and *The Vanishing Voter* (2003).[53] When less than 40 percent of the American public took the time to vote in the 2006 congressional elections, the concern about low turnout expressed in these books seems justified. Even with all the attention and interest surrounding the 2008 presidential elections, turnout of the voting-age population was about 57 percent.[54] Such data strike many as disappointing. But further investigation of turnout can offer a different way to interpret the situation.

What does it mean for democracy when only 40 percent of Americans vote in midterm elections?

The United States Compared to Other Democracies.
Compared to other democracies, turnout in the United States is near the bottom. The average rate of turnout in U.S. presidential elections between 1945 and 2008 was 56 percent. In Australia turnout is 95 percent; in Malta it is 98 percent. The only nation where turnout is significantly lower than the United States is Afghanistan at 48 percent. A survey of twenty-five nations reveals that a typical rate of participation is about 71 percent—15 percentage points higher than in the United States (see Other Places: Turnout). These numbers compel an assessment of why U.S. turnout is so low.

One reason has to do with the rules for voting. Australia has **compulsory voting**— citizens are required by law to vote. Those who do not vote must pay a $20 fine, and the fine increases to $50 if the nonvoter does not answer the Australian Election Commission's inquiry about why he or she did not vote. New Zealand requires all citizens to register to vote. In most of the countries of western Europe, the government is responsible for registering citizens to vote. In the United States, by contrast, both voting and registering are voluntary, and only about 70 percent of the public is registered. That means that nearly one-third of potentially eligible voters cannot cast votes on election day even if they want to do so.

compulsory voting: *Practice that requires citizens to vote in elections or face punitive measures such as community service, fines, or imprisonment.*

Should the United States adopt compulsory voting?

Another reason has to do with the convenience of voting. Most European countries lessen the costs of voting by allowing it to take place on Sunday. In the United States voting takes place on Tuesday, a workday for most people. Federal law stipulates that the first Tuesday after the first Monday in November is the day on which voting for president and members of Congress will take place, and most states have also selected Tuesdays as the day for voting in primaries and in state and local elections. The costs of voting are increased because people may be at work and may have difficulty finding the time to vote. With more costs to voting, turnout is lower in the United States than in many European democracies. This discussion highlights the importance of considering the context of each election, which is the theoretical focus of the institutional model of voting.

Should the United States vote on Saturday or Sunday instead of a weekday?

According to one estimate, turnout in the United States would be 27 percentage points higher (or more than 80 percent) if the nation had laws and rules that foster voting.[55] At the least, this figure suggests that comparisons of turnout in various democracies require a careful accounting of the rules and institutions that shape the willingness of citizens to go to the polls.

Trends in Turnout.
A second way turnout in American elections looks problematic is the trend over the last fifty years. One of the lines in Figure 11.6 (see page 376) represents the percentage of turnout in presidential elections measured against the

⊕otherplaces

Turnout

Percentage of Turnout in Twenty-Five Nations

Nation	Percentage
Malta	98%
Australia	95%
Belgium	86%
Brazil	84%
Denmark	83%
Sweden	81%
Uzbekistan	81%
Italy	79%
Netherlands	78%
Norway	77%
Germany	72%
Israel	71%
Ireland	69%
Belarus	68%
Finland	68%
Chile	67%
Japan	67%
Iraq	64%
Mexico	64%
India	61%
United Kingdom	58%
United States	57%
South Africa	56%
France	55%
Afghanistan	48%
Average	71%

Source: International IDEA, Voter Turnout, www.idea.int.

The wide range of turnout shown in the table underscores the importance of understanding the rules and context of each election. That Australia has 95 percent turnout is a consequence of its voting laws, which require that each citizen vote or pay a fine. That Afghanistan has half that turnout rate (48 percent) is a consequence of its being a poor, embattled country that has just recently begun to hold elections.

Any judgment that concludes that differences in turnout result from differences in the types of citizens is hasty. Instead, it appears that the rules and context of voting drive the differences. European nations have higher rates of voting than the United States not because Europeans are more interested in politics than Americans but because the rules for participation make it easier to cast ballots. This general pattern is true across nations.

- **Why are higher rates of turnout a murky indicator of a country's democratic leanings?**

- **If you wanted to increase turnout in the United States, what reforms would produce a jump in participation?**

voting-age population (VAP): *Used to calculate the rate of participation by dividing the number of voters by the number of people in the country who are 18 and over.*

voting-age population (VAP), the number of those eligible to vote. In the United States all citizens over 18 years old constitute the VAP. The graph shows that there has been an overall decline in voting since 1960, despite a recent upswing. This pattern is much the same for midterm elections. In 1962 turnout for congressional elections was 48 percent. It fell to a low of 38 percent in 1986, with a slight rebound to about 40 percent in 2006.

This downward trend becomes more worrisome in light of rising levels of education since 1960, as education is one of the strongest predictors of turnout. Even though education levels have increased over the last fifty years (see Table 11.1 on page 369), the rate of participation in elections has not increased.

These data have led political scientists to study why fewer Americans seem to be voting.[56] Explanations have varied. One explanation looks at the difference between those who enter the electorate and those who leave. The concept of **generational replacement** describes a trend in which older voters who pass away are replaced in the electorate by less reliable young voters.[57] It is very difficult, however, to sort out generational differences from changes in self-interest. That is, do older voters turn out to vote because of the generation they were part of, or because they are older and have more experience in dealing with politics, or because they want to protect their interests or expand the benefits that directly affect them, such as Medicare and low payments for prescription drugs?

A second explanation has been the decline of party organizations.[58] Local parties have been less able to turn out the vote on election day than they were in the late nineteenth and early twentieth centuries, and therefore the voting rate has declined. Some scholars have estimated that half of the decline in turnout can be attributed to the drop in mobilization efforts.[59] This explanation has appeal, but parties in many ways are stronger today than they were in the past, although the days of big city bosses and urban **political machines** are gone (see Chapter 9, Political Parties). The Republican Party was successful in turning out the vote in 2004, especially in key states like Ohio,[60] and citizens are voting along party lines more than any time since scientific surveys began in the 1950s. So a decline in party strength (perceived or real) is not an adequate explanation for low turnout.

A third explanation for declining turnout is the increasingly harsh tone of political campaigns. Some argue that negative campaigns have fueled voter apathy. It is clear that negative advertising on TV often fosters voters' disgust with politics. About 80 percent of people say they do not like these campaign tactics.[61] Initial studies suggested that negative campaigns could decrease turnout by about 5 percentage points.[62] Moreover, there is clear evidence that negativity in campaigns has been on the rise since the 1960s (see Figure 10.4, Share of Negativity in Presidential Campaigns, 1960–2008, in Chapter 10), so there has been an apparent correlation between the two trends.[63] Scholars and pundits rushed to endorse this hypothesis. But subsequent studies have called the hypothesis into question.[64] A harsh campaign is likely to be competitive, and competitive campaigns draw interest and therefore increase turnout. Further, negative attacks can activate partisanship, which also increases turnout. People often choose to affiliate with a party in part because they do not like members of the opposite party. An attack ad by the Republicans can remind their supporters why they oppose the Democrats, giving them more reason to participate. A recent comprehensive study of all research on this topic shows clearly that negativity is not responsible for lowering turnout.[65]

The Voting Eligible Population Measure.

Two political scientists, Michael McDonald and Samuel Popkin, offer a fourth explanation by arguing that turnout has not declined over the last thirty years: The VAP measure has been in error because it does not take into account increases in the number of convicted felons and immigrants who are ineligible to vote. Over the last thirty years, there has been a steep increase in the number of illegal immigrants. With the sagging economy of the last few years, the numbers have declined, but

generational replacement: *Cycle whereby younger generations replace older generations in the electorate.*

political machines: *Disciplined political parties that command support by providing benefits, such as jobs, to voters.*

What effect do negative ads have on you?

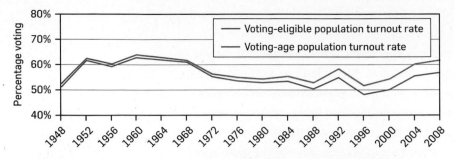

FIGURE 11.6 Presidential Turnout Rates, 1948–2008. The VAP measure is the traditional approach to assessing turnout, dividing the number of voters by the voting-age population. The VEP seeks to correct for overcounting in the voting-age population by removing illegal immigrants and people in jail who are not eligible to vote. Until 1972 this correction made only a modest difference. But given the surge of immigration and the growth in the number of convicted felons since then, the VEP measure is more accurate. Turnout in the 2004 and 2008 elections is actually comparable to turnout in the 1950s and 1960s. *Source:* United States Elections Project, elections.gmu.edu.

voting-eligible population (VEP): *Used to calculate the rate of participation by dividing the number of voters by the number of people in the country who are eligible to vote rather than just of voting age.*

even so, the number of illegal immigrants is estimated to be about 12 million (or about 4 percent of the population).[66] Over the last twenty years there has also been nearly a threefold increase in the number of people in prison (from 585,000 to 1.6 million), reflecting tougher sentencing in American courts of law.[67]

McDonald and Popkin correct for these trends by introducing a new measure called the **voting-eligible population (VEP)**. The top line in Figure 11.6 presents the VEP estimates for turnout. It indicates that turnout in the 2008 presidential election was actually about 62 percent. By this measure, turnout has not declined over the last thirty years. In fact, turnout is now a full 10 percentage points higher than in the presidential election of 1948, when it was 52 percent. These revised estimates put a new spin on what has been perceived as a problem with U.S. elections, suggesting that Americans are not less willing to vote than in the past or than citizens in other democracies.[68]

Do Turnout Rates Promote Inequality?

Voting is a hallmark of democratic politics and is certainly a cherished American value. The idea is simple. Each person has one vote, and each vote should be equal. The fact that those who are better educated or better off participate at a greater rate is a potential source of concern. The income gap between the rich and the poor is increasing,[69] and because the rich are becoming richer, they are better able to contribute money to parties and candidates.[70] Such donations only further advance their potential influence.

The data in Figure 11.7 indicate that individuals making more than $50,000 a year are much more likely to vote than those making less than $50,000 a year. The pattern is consistent. For instance, 76 percent of people with incomes above $50,000 participated in the 2008 elections, while the proportion of those making less than $50,000 was 59 percent.[71] The 2000 and 2004 elections tell the same story.

Do Americans have equality in voting? Explain.

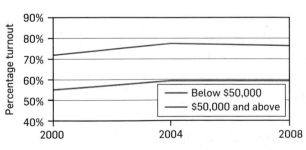

FIGURE 11.7 Voter Turnout by Income, 2000–2008.
Source: Nonprofit Voter Engagement Network, America Goes to the Polls, "Voting Gaps in the 2008 Election," October 2009.

That individuals with more resources participate more is not a new idea. Its implications have fueled much speculation, but were supported by little evidence until recently. Research reported in 2008 by Larry Bartels has provided a systematic account of the impact of these differences.[72] Focusing on the behavior of U.S. senators, Bartels has shown that they respond more to the rich, less to people of middle income, and not at all to the poor. It makes sense that politicians respond to people who participate and do not respond to those who do not. That is why it is so important for people to get involved in politics. It is also why the increasing rate of participation in the last decade or so is good news.

Participation beyond Voting

Voting is by far the most common form of participation. But in a democracy, citizens have opportunities to express their views in other ways. In fact, voting is a very constrained form of participation: Voters select one person from a limited set of candidates. There is no way to tell from a single vote whether the citizen agrees or disagrees with the candidate on the key issues of the day. But the American political system gives individuals the opportunity to express their preferences and the intensity of those preferences in other ways. Although far fewer Americans join political campaigns or protest movements, both are important gateways for the expression of political views.

Aside from voting, how have you participated in politics and civic life?

Involvement in Political Campaigns

Campaigns give citizens a chance to talk about politics, volunteer, promote issues they care about, and make financial donations to candidates and causes. The weeks leading up to an election allow candidates and interest groups to connect with the public. The campaign is an important gateway that allows the public to influence politics and politicians to influence the public.

As a result, political scientists try to understand the motivations for people's involvement in campaigns and the nature of their involvement. Do Americans try to influence other citizens? Over the last few decades, about 40 percent of Americans have reported that they talk about presidential politics with their fellow citizens.[73] Table 11.2 reports that 28 percent of Americans claimed in 1996 that they tried to influence others to vote a certain way. This was the lowest rate over the last seven presidential elections and probably reflects the fact that few doubted that President Bill Clinton would beat the Republican nominee, Robert Dole. In 2008, 45 percent of Americans said they tried to influence others' votes, a greater than 50 percent jump from 1996. The 2008 contest between Democrat Barack Obama and Republican John McCain captured the public's interest: 62 percent of Americans were "very interested" in the election, compared to just 36 percent in 2000.[74] In another poll, nearly two-thirds of Americans claimed to be "more excited and interested in voting" in the 2008 campaign than in previous contests.[75]

By contrast, as shown in Table 11.2, the proportion of people who work in a campaign has been small and very stable over the last three decades, hovering around 3 percent. Nearly 10 percent of citizens attended a political meeting during the course of the 2008 campaign. Willingness to give money to a campaign was a bit higher, reaching 14 percent in 2008. More citizens also claimed to display a bumper sticker or wear a button than to have engaged in campaign activities other than trying to influence other people's votes.

Have you ever contributed time or money to a political campaign? Why or why not?

This body of evidence about political participation suggests some important conclusions. First, if active citizens are defined as individuals who vote and engage in at least one of the activities reported in Table 11.2, nearly 40 percent have met the standard over this twenty-eight-year period. More than 15 percent of the public voted and engaged in two of the activities. Second, recent presidential elections have shown a real jump in these kinds of political activities. More people were willing to give money, wear campaign buttons, and try to influence others' votes. Such increases underscore the importance of the contest to many

TABLE 11.2 Nonvoting Measures of Political Participation, 1980–2008

	Tried to Influence Others' Votes	Attended a Political Meeting	Worked for a Party or a Candidate	Wore a Button or Displayed a Bumper Sticker	Gave Money to a Campaign
1980	36%	8%	4%	7%	8%
1984	32%	8%	4%	9%	8%
1988	29%	7%	3%	9%	9%
1992	37%	8%	3%	11%	7%
1996	28%	5%	2%	10%	8%
2000	34%	5%	3%	10%	9%
2004	48%	7%	3%	21%	13%
2008	45%	9%	4%	18%	14%

Source: American National Election Study, 1948–2008.

voters and indicate the American public's willingness to engage in politics when elections matter to them.

Some might wonder whether 15 percent is an impressive number. A comparison to other countries can put it in perspective. While in recent years nearly 50 percent of Americans have tried to persuade others about how to cast their ballots, in 2004 the proportion in Brazil was 37 percent; in France it was 29 percent; and in Sweden it was just 13 percent.[76] The same pattern holds for attending meetings and displaying bumper stickers. Americans are far more engaged in campaigns than citizens in other democracies.

Protest Politics

Boston Tea Party: *Protest in 1773 in which colonists dressed as Indians boarded vessels in Boston Harbor and threw chests of tea overboard to express anger at Britain's tax policies and commercial regulations.*

Political protests are an important means of expressing opinions and bringing about change. The **Boston Tea Party**, where protesters dumped tea into Boston Harbor rather than support the British government-backed monopoly, is perhaps the first and most famous American protest. This protest was not about taxes, but rather about the fact that the British were undermining local merchants. Throughout American history, abolitionists seeking an end to slavery, women seeking the vote, working people seeking the right to strike and organize unions, civil rights activists calling for an end to segregation and discrimination, antiwar activists seeking to end the wars in Vietnam and Iraq, and many others have called attention to their causes though marches, street demonstrations, petitions, and advertising campaigns. Recently, people protesting the 2009 stimulus package and 2010 health care reform have sought to recall the spirit of the Boston Tea Party by calling their gatherings Tea Parties.[77] This movement for small government and reduced federal spending caught fire during the 2010 midterm campaigns, leading to the election of a number of Tea Party candidates, including Senator Rand Paul in Kentucky.

Why is the right to protest important for democracy?

What do the Tea Party protests that began in 2009 have in common with the Boston Tea Party?

Protests sometimes backfire. In 1932, in the midst of the Great Depression, army veterans seeking early payment of their World War I bonuses descended on Washington, D.C. Thousands camped out in tents and shacks. The House of Representatives agreed to early payment, but the Senate refused, and the protesters were ordered to go home. When some

THE DESTRUCTION OF TEA AT BOSTON HARBOR.

Library of Congress

The American colonists hated the British tax on tea, but the famous Boston Tea Party that took place on December 16, 1773, was also a protest against the monopoly over the tea trade that the British had given the struggling East India Company. This 1846 lithograph has become a classic image of the event.

HALEY/SIPA/AP Images

In 2009–2010 critics of taxes, big government generally, and government spending in the stimulus bill and the health care reform act came together to label their protests Tea Parties. On April 17, 2010, Tea Party supporters take part in the second annual tea-throwing event at the Choptank River Fisher Pier in Trappe, Maryland.

did not, President Herbert Hoover (1929–33) called out federal troops. Using tanks, cavalry, and tear gas, General Douglas MacArthur sought to disperse the veterans in an action that led to the death of one veteran.[78]

Protests can become so controversial and stir up such strong emotions that the government takes steps to limit them. Such action, one could argue, constrains First Amendment rights of speech and assembly. But do protesters have the right to undermine the freedoms of others? This is not an easy question to answer. The courts have weighed in on such debates, seeking to balance competing rights. One of the most controversial cases concerns the right

Jack Benton/Getty Images

of anti-abortion protesters to protest outside of abortion clinics and in particular to try to convince women coming to the clinics for services to change their minds (see Supreme Court Cases: *Hill v. Colorado*).

In general, very few Americans participate in protests. In March 2003 only 3 percent of the public claimed to have joined any of the "recent antiwar protests."[79] Overall, only about 5 percent of Americans claim to have participated in a "protest, march, or demonstration" over the last five years. Australians report a three times greater willingness to engage in such activities, and in Spain and France about 25 percent of the citizenry claim to have done so.[80] High rates of protest activities in other democracies can be attributed to strong labor parties—some of them socialist and Communist—that make protests common and symbolic. One expert on European protests comments that they are "more fun in Europe than [in the United States], having the feel of attending the county fair."[81]

Although the right to assemble and express political opinions is protected by the First Amendment, protests occasionally lead to violence. In 1932, when World War I army veterans assembled in Washington, D.C., to ask for early payment of bonuses, President Herbert Hoover ordered them to leave, and when some did not, he sent federal troops to disperse them.

What does the fact that few Americans participate in protests mean? That they are satisfied with government?

What is the effect of new technologies on voting and participation?

E-Participation

In the past decade, many Americans have engaged in politics through e-mail and the Internet. It is easier and cheaper to send an e-mail message to a member of Congress than to write a letter, and Americans do so with increasing frequency. In 1998 members of Congress received over 23 million e-mails; two years later that number had doubled to 48 million.[82] Recent figures are not available, but the use of e-mail to contact members of Congress has surely exploded over the last decade, underscoring the ease and convenience of e-mail, and transforming the way voters communicate with politicians.

Beyond e-mail, people express their opinions through blogs. As Chapter 7 (The News Media and the Internet) demonstrates, blogs have become an important way to share information and to influence the political process. Candidates now hire their own bloggers in an effort to influence the direction of these exchanges. Most recently, politicians have started to use Twitter to share information with people. When the 2008 Republican vice presidential candidate Sarah Palin decided to resign as governor of Alaska in July 2009, she used Twitter to announce her decision and also to react to negative reports about it.[83]

Participating by writing a blog or responding in writing to one and by using other e-communications will continue to rise. As of May 2008 about 75 percent of the public made at least occasional use of e-mail or the Internet.[84] Of those who have access to e-information, as many as 20 percent claim to participate in blogs, online discussions, or e-mail lists on political issues of interest.[85] These data suggest that, overall, about 14 percent of the public may be participating in politics through blogs.

The Internet has also transformed fundraising and campaign involvement. Former Vermont Governor Howard Dean's 2004 campaign for the Democratic presidential nomination was the first to tap successfully into the power of the Internet. Since then, other candidates have made use of the Internet and have developed websites and various outreach programs. The Internet is a means to gather small contributions cheaply, as Barack Obama's

supremecourtcases

Hill v. Colorado (2000)

QUESTION: May Colorado prohibit antiabortion activists from protesting within one hundred feet of a health care facility?

ORAL ARGUMENT: January 19, 2000 (listen at www .oyez.org/cases)

DECISION: June 28, 2000 (read at www.findlaw.com/ casecode/supreme.html)

OUTCOME: Yes, antiabortion protests can be limited (6–3).

The right to protest the laws and practices of government is a fundamental right of American citizens, so long as the protests are peaceful and legal—that is, so long as the proper permits have been obtained. In 1985 Leila Hill, an obstetrics nurse opposed to abortion, formed a group named Sidewalk Counselors for Life. Police arrested Hill for protests outside of abortion clinics in 1987 and 1988, but charges were dropped both times.

Nationally, the anti-abortion group Operation Rescue began hostile protests outside of abortion clinics. In response, the state of Colorado required protesters to obtain consent from people within one hundred feet of any health care facility before displaying signs, speaking to them, or handing them pamphlets. Hill sued Colorado, claiming that she engaged in sidewalk counseling about abortion and its alternatives and that the area outside of abortion clinics was the most natural place to engage in such counseling. She claimed that the law violated her First Amendment rights of speech, press, and assembly. Court records showed that although other abortion protesters had been abusive toward patients, Hill had never been abusive or confrontational.

The state of Colorado claimed that the law in question was not a restriction on speech, but merely a restriction on where speech may take place. Although the Supreme Court generally does not allow restrictions on speech, it does allow restrictions on the "time, place and manner" of speech. States may impose time, place, and manner restrictions on speech, for example, by prohibiting demonstrations in residential neighborhoods at night or limiting the decibel levels of sound equipment. The key to such regulations is that they must be content-neutral. That is, the regulation cannot be aimed at limiting a particular viewpoint.

In the *Hill* case, the Supreme Court ruled that the Colorado law restricted the First Amendment interests of Hill, but also noted the legitimate interest of Colorado in trying to protect the health and safety of people entering health care facilities, including the right to be left alone. Given these competing interests, the Court upheld the statute on the grounds that it was a neutral regulation of where speech may take place, and that it did not favor one side or another in public debate. Alternatively, the dissenters argued that although the law did apply to all protesters outside of health care facilities regardless of their message, the law was clearly aimed at the only group that actually protests outside of health care facilities: anti-abortion protesters.

- **Why might elected officials respond to some forms of participation more than others?**

- **Does the Court treat anti-abortion protesters equally to other protesters?**

2008 campaign for president exemplified. Obama broke all records for fundraising during the primary, raising $32 million in January 2008, $28 million of it via the Internet.[86] As the campaign progressed, Obama started to rely more on fundraising in person, but his campaign still made extensive use of the Internet.[87] In fact, David Plouffe, Obama's campaign manager, argued in 2009 that the ability to raise money through the Internet was a key ingredient in Obama's winning the election.[88] Formerly, it cost more to secure a $25 donation than it was worth, but now campaigns solicit contributions as small as $5. Ron Paul, who ran for the Republican nomination for president in 2008, raised $4 million on the Internet in a single day.[89]

Voting and Participation and Public Policy: Voting Laws and Regulations

The rules surrounding voting alter participation rates. Policy making regarding voting is undertaken at both the federal and state levels. State governments continue to manage most voting laws and procedures, although the federal government steps in to prevent discrimination at the polls. Both state and federal governments are committed to increasing participation by making voting as easy as possible. At the same time, both work to prevent voter fraud. Thus, policy making regarding voting has the effect of both expanding and potentially contracting turnout. This section reviews policies that have altered the way voting works in the United States.

Reforms to Voting Laws in the 1890s

Rules matter, as the institutional model of voting suggests. Any change in the laws governing voting (or any process related to voting) will alter how that process works. A classic example of the power of rules can be found in the late nineteenth century, when the **Progressives** called for a series of reforms to the voting process to end corrupt practices. The reforms affected who was eligible to vote and the way people actually voted. In other words, they altered who participated in elections.

Progressives: *Reformers who sought to end corruption in government; also a third party in the early twentieth century.*

Corrupt voting practices did need to be ended. Big-city political machines routinely "stuffed" the ballot box,[90] and party members manipulated the results to ensure victory. Turnout in some cities exceeded 100 percent, meaning that not only were some people voting who should not have been, but also that some were voting multiple times. Party members often rounded up people and brought them, in sequence, to various polling precincts around the city, making sure they voted in each one. Someone who had died would remain on the rolls, and the party machine would "allow" that person to vote. This corrupt practice has been referred to as **graveyard voting**.[91]

graveyard voting: *Corrupt practice of using a dead person's name to cast a ballot in an election.*

In response to these excesses, Progressives called for voter registration.[92] The idea was that voters would have to preregister with a government official to be placed on an official list of voters. The list would be updated when someone died, and it would be used at the polls on election day to ensure that a potential voter had the right to vote and had not already voted.

This reform spread rapidly. Today, all states except North Dakota require voter registration. The specific rules of registration vary a great deal among the states. For example, only in Idaho, Iowa, Maine, Minnesota, Montana, North Carolina, New Hampshire, Wisconsin, and Wyoming can a person register and vote on election day.[93] All other states require registration prior to the actual voting.

Voter registration laws prevented outright fraud at the polls. An additional consequence was that they prevented immigrants from voting. Party machines had benefited greatly from the support of immigrants in city elections, and many of the newcomers to America who came in great numbers in the late nineteenth and early twentieth centuries were among those who were encouraged by parties to vote multiple times. Some states, such as Wisconsin, allowed white immigrants to vote, providing they declared their intention to become citizens.[94] But the new registration laws made voting a two-step process, requiring potential voters to document, prior to the election, that they met the conditions for voting. Voter registration added a new gate to the system. While it reduced fraud, decreased the strength of the party machines, and pleased Americans who were worried about the impact of immigrants, it caused an overall decline in turnout. In 1888 turnout in presidential elections stood at 81 percent. By 1912 it had fallen to 59 percent. It is surely true that the 81 percent turnout was inflated due to corrupt voting practices, but the introduction of voter registration had negative effects for participation.[95]

Another important change in voting rules in the 1890s was the adoption of the **Australian ballot**, also known as the secret ballot (see Figure 9.3, Ballot Reform, in Chapter 9). Like voter registration, it was adopted as a reform intended to prevent the corrupt practices of political machines. In the early nineteenth century voting was public, and was often done by "party strips." That is, voters would enter a polling precinct and ask for a ballot from one party or the other, thereby indicating their preferences.

If you are a registered voter, what was your experience with registration? Was it a gate or a gateway?

How can government prevent fraud and still encourage citizens to vote?

Australian ballot: *Voting system in which state governments run elections and provide voters the option of choosing candidates from multiple parties; also called the secret ballot.*

The Granger Collection, New York

The County Election (1852), by American artist George Caleb Bingham, portrays election day in Missouri. In the mid-nineteenth century, voting was public and a social event, marked by alcohol and games as much as by debate. One of the voters pictured here writes his vote on a piece of paper, and another, on the porch, gives his written ballet to an official.

It was easy to cast and count such ballots, but voters were also subjected to pressure from party bosses. Those who operated the polling precincts would know how voters planned to vote by observing which party strip they requested. The introduction of the secret ballot meant that voters faced less intimidation. But voting also became more complicated. Voters now could choose candidates for each office separately; they no longer had automatic access to party line voting as they did with the strip ballot. With a more complicated process, once again turnout declined. Despite decreasing turnout, the secret ballot has become a cornerstone of American democracy.

The National Voter Registration Act and Voter Identification

In 1993 Congress sought to streamline voter registration procedures so that more Americans would exercise their right to vote, at least in federal elections. The National Voter Registration Act, commonly known as the "Motor Voter" law, requires states to allow citizens to register to vote at the same time they apply for or renew their driver's licenses. This law also requires states to inform citizens who are removed from the approved voter rolls and limits removal to a change of address, conviction for a felony, and, of course, death. These requirements responded to charges that local governments, controlled by political parties, improperly removed voters from the voter rolls without their knowledge; under the guise of updating voter registration lists, officials of one party were disqualifying voters who would tend to vote for the other party's candidates. The 1993 law imposes criminal penalties on anyone who tries to coerce or intimidate voters on their way to the polling place or tries to prevent registered voters from casting their ballots.[96]

Should government take steps to increase voting? Why?

To avoid voter fraud, many states have instituted voter identification requirements (see Figure 11.8). Their implementation on election day has been controversial, and in the case of Indiana's photo identification law, opponents sued in federal court to strike it down. The fundamental issue in this case was whether state laws that were intended to prevent voter fraud had the result of preventing citizens who were legally entitled to vote from doing so because they lacked proper identification. Indiana argued that the requirement of a photo ID was not unduly burdensome because the state provided voter identification cards to citizens who had no other photo IDs. But the opponents argued that the process of getting such a card was too complicated and that the overall effect of the law would be to disenfranchise thousands of citizens. In 2008 the Supreme Court upheld the Indiana law by a 6–3 vote. Justice John Paul Stevens wrote on behalf of the majority, "The state interests identified as justifications for [the law] are both neutral and sufficiently strong to require us to reject" the lawsuit. However, Justice David Souter wrote in dissent that "Indiana has made no such justification [for the statute] and as to some aspects of its law, it hardly even tried." Further, Souter said that the law "threatens to impose nontrivial burdens on the voting right of tens of thousands of the state's citizens."[97]

Is it a good idea or a bad idea to require voters to show photo IDs before voting?

With the Hamiltonian and Jeffersonian views of voting in mind, it is important to decide what standards should be imposed for citizens to vote. Clearly, the federal government has taken steps to make the voting process easier and more convenient. But ultimately states and localities administer and oversee elections, and states have responded inconsistently

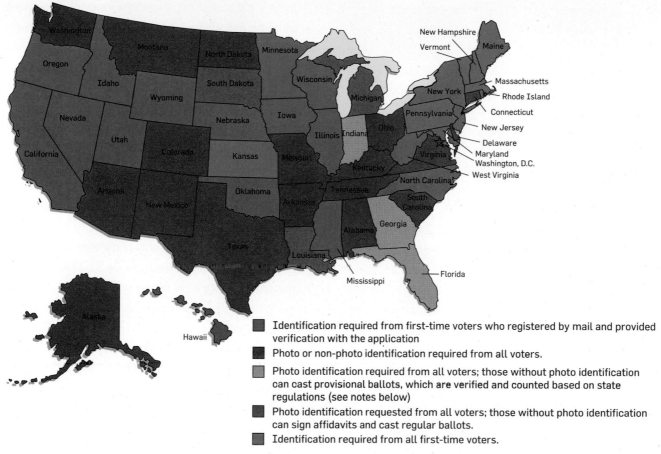

Identification required from first-time voters who registered by mail and provided verification with the application

Photo or non-photo identification required from all voters.

Photo identification required from all voters; those without photo identification can cast provisional ballots, which are verified and counted based on state regulations (see notes below)

Photo identification requested from all voters; those without photo identification can sign affidavits and cast regular ballots.

Identification required from all first-time voters.

Notes: Florida voters lacking required ID must cast provisional ballots. The canvassing board determines the validity of the ballot. In Indiana, if voters are unable or unwilling to present photo ID on Election Day, they may cast a provisional ballot. The have until noon 10 days after the election to follow up with the county election board and either provide photo ID or affirm one of the law's exemptions applies.

FIGURE 11.8 Voter Identification Requirements.

Source: Pew Center on the States, www.pewcenteronthestates.org.

to the federal efforts. Some appear to have made it easier to vote, but others, such as Indiana, have made it harder by requiring photo identification at the polling place. It would seem that, in a democracy, all citizens should have an equal opportunity to cast their votes because voting is the fundamental mechanism by which we hold government accountable. As states introduce more laws regarding identification, disparities in the opportunity to vote may be growing.

New Forms of Voting

As indicated above, some states are experimenting with laws that make voting easier. Some have instituted early voting, allowing voters to cast ballots prior to the Tuesday on which a general election is held. This flexibility helps working people, who might find it hard to find time to vote on a Tuesday. It also provides more than a single day for voting, so that schedule conflicts (such as a dental appointment or a sick child) do not interfere. In Texas, for example, citizens can vote any time between seventeen and four days prior to election day so "you don't have to stand in long lines on election day."[98] Other states, such as Oregon, have started to make use of a **vote-by-mail (VBM) system**. Voters get ballots in the mail two weeks before the election, giving them a chance to research the candidates

vote-by-mail (VBM) system:
Method of voting in an election whereby ballots are distributed to voters by mail, completed, and returned by mail.

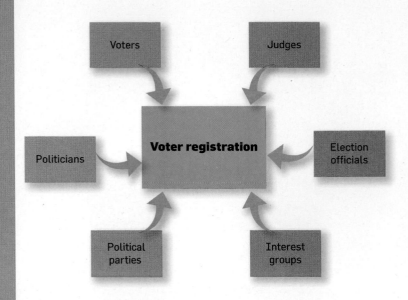

```
         Voters              Judges

Politicians  →  Voter registration  ←  Election
                                         officials

      Political                Interest
      parties                  groups
```

What are the risks and benefits of early voting? Of voting by mail?

and cast their ballots. They can make their choices at home and avoid the often long lines at the polling booth. This innovation lowers the cost of voting, and it has increased participation. In 2004, 87 percent of registered voters in Oregon voted—the highest rate in the nation.[99]

In the future, other forms of voting may be used, including the Internet and cell phones. A study conducted in 2008 sent text messages to 3,600 young mobile phone users chosen at random from a pool of 5,400 people who had registered to vote in the Super Tuesday presidential primary on February 5, 2008. The researchers found that simply reminding the voters to go to the polls increased turnout by 4.6 percent. When the text message was delivered the day before election day, turnout increased by 2.6 percent. To verify the effect of the text message reminders, the researchers matched the mobile phone users with voting records to see if they voted.[100]

The study suggests that cell phone technology could increase voter turnout, implying that if citizens could vote via their cell phones or the Internet, voting rates might also rise, especially among elderly and disabled people who find it physically challenging to get to a polling place. However, opponents of using this technology argue that it would be too susceptible to voter fraud for two reasons: First, there would be no way to identify the person who is casting the vote, unless citizens are given individual pin codes or use their Social Security numbers. Given the number of Internet security breaches, opponents argue that such a system would not guard personal privacy. Second, votes are counted by election officials, but Internet and cell voting data would likely be collected and counted by computer servers, which are vulnerable to hacking and other security breaches.

In considering the effects of voting by Internet or cell phone, the beneficial effects on community and civic life of having everyone vote on a single day should also be considered. The act of standing in line and talking with fellow voters, or discussing the act of voting with friends and family at the end of the day, can reinforce the sense of political efficacy and provide a foundation for the democratic process. Voting by mail, cell phone, or the Internet may detract from this shared experience, and that cost must be weighed against the added benefits of increased voter participation.

Voting and Participation and Democracy

The United States government has lasted more than 230 years. This longevity is not an accident. It is attributable in large part to the fact that Americans have, collectively, taken the time to participate. There have been many barriers, from limited suffrage to rules that discourage voting. But the long-term trend has been increased participation, and that speaks to the health of American democracy. Now suffrage—the right to vote—is available to all citizens except some convicted felons (see Chapter 5).[101] The rate of voting in the United States is not as low as many observers tend to assert. Further, looking at participation more broadly, Americans do more than just vote in elections. They are engaged in political campaigns and in making their communities better at the local level. The Internet offers a world of possibilities for greater amounts and different forms of participation. The future has many bright spots.

There is one danger to a democracy from a distortion in turnout; the rich participate more than the poor, and this gap seems to be growing. With nonvoters being poorer and less educated, their failure to participate may help explain why government is not as responsive to their needs. Put another way, the government may be overly responsive to the needs of the well-off. This disparity in responsiveness threatens the underpinnings of a democratic and egalitarian society. If the political system responds to one segment of the population and systematically ignores other segments, general support for democracy, based on principles of fairness, could drop significantly.

With the Internet's growing influence, there may be other dangers to democracy. Wealthier citizens have more access to the information and resources on the Internet and therefore become even more informed and better able to make government responsive to their needs. The rich have always had advantages, but their advantages may be growing. At the same time, the Internet might be used to extend participation. As Howard Dean's presidential campaign showed, this technology can be used to expand the number of contributors to include people who have only a few dollars to contribute or who might want to show up at a local meeting to learn about an issue of relevance to them.

Let us now return to Figure 11.1 (page 357), which offered two models of participation. The Hamiltonian model argued that more participation is not always a good thing, and that government works best with limited involvement from the public. The Jeffersonian model contended that greater participation improves both the quality of the input and the lives of citizens. Within our book's gateway approach, the participatory model of voting has more appeal than the elite model. Democracy becomes more responsive, more accountable, and more equal if more people participate. The cycle is reinforcing. Citizens themselves need to do all they can to encourage participation; doing so is in their self-interest and their civic interest. Democracy rests on the active and healthy participation of the citizenry. In other words, as the number of gateways increase, so does the quality of American civic life.

FOCUS QUESTIONS

• Why is voting such an important gateway for any democracy?

• Is more participation always a good thing?

• How does citizen participation in the political system affect the prospects for accountability and equality?

• Do young citizens participate enough to make the system responsive to their preferences? What about other groups?

• How do other forms of participation, besides voting, serve as gateways to democracy? Are they more or less effective than voting?

Top Ten to Take Away

1. Participation is essential to the functioning of democracy, and voting is the most common means by which people get involved. (p. 356)

2. The Constitution gives states authority over the "Times, Places and Manner of holding Elections." State rules vary, introducing some inequalities in access. (pp. 356–57)

3. Today Americans enjoy almost universal opportunities to vote, but in the past the vote was denied to African Americans, women, Native Americans, and immigrant groups denied citizenship. (pp. 356, 358–65)

4. Because voting shapes the outcome of elections and the conduct of government, there have always been debates over who gets access to the ballot. The Hamiltonian model of participation sees risks in the extension of the franchise to groups that may be uninformed and favors a larger role for elites. The Jeffersonian model of participation maintains that greater participation produces better outcomes and encourages citizens to get more involved in self-government. (pp. 356–58)

5. From the 1790s to the 1870s voting rights expanded. From the 1870s to 1920 barriers to voting, especially for African Americans, increased. After 1920 voting rights expanded again and were increasingly protected by the federal government. The overall trend has been toward constant expansion of the right to vote. (pp. 358–65, 386–87)

6. Unequal turnout by various demographic groups suggests that government's response is unequal. Most troubling for democracy is the tendency for people with higher incomes to vote at higher rates than the poor. Older people and those with more education also tend to vote at higher rates than younger people and those with less education. (pp. 365–69, 387)

7. Political scientists explain why people vote (and choose not to vote) using theoretical models. The economic model examines the costs and benefits of voting. The psychological model examines attitudes, including the idea of civic duty and the influence of partisanship. The institutional model examines the rules and regulations surrounding voting, including political party behavior, campaign strategy, and the context of the election. Genetic factors are a new consideration, and the weather is often considered a factor as well. (pp. 369–72)

8. Turnout in the United States is lower than in many other democracies, but it can be explained by the institutional model. (pp. 372–76)

9. Americans participate in the political system in other ways, including being involved in political campaigns, participating in protests that call attention to causes, and, with the rise of the Internet and other new technologies, engaging in political debates, fundraising, and political campaigns on the web. (pp. 377–82)

10. Voter registration helps prevent fraud in elections but also poses a gate that decreases turnout. (pp. 382–86)

A full narrative summary of the chapter is on the book's website.

Ten to Test Yourself

1. What are the differences between the Hamiltonian and Jeffersonian models of participation?

2. How would you characterize the history of voting in the United States?

3. What are the demographic characteristics of a typical voter? A typical nonvoter?

4. How does turnout in the United States compare to turnout in other nations?

Timeline to Keep Things in Order

1787	1824	1825	1870	1920
Constitution grants authority over elections to the states.	Popular votes are counted in a presidential election for the first time.	Andrew Jackson and his supporters begin to promote an end to property qualifications for voting.	Fifteenth Amendment extends the right to vote to African American males.	Nineteenth Amendment extends the right to vote to women.

5. What is the relationship between turnout and government responsiveness?
6. What is the trend in turnout in U.S. presidential elections?
7. How do political scientists explain voters' decisions to vote and not to vote?

8. What rules of American elections serve as gates against voting? What rules are gateways to voting?
9. In what other ways do Americans participate in politics and civic life, aside from voting?
10. How are the Internet and other new technologies affecting participation?

More review questions and answers and quizzes are on the book's website.

Terms to Know and Use

Australian ballot (p. 383)
Boston Tea Party (p. 378)
Chinese Exclusion Act (p. 365)
civic duty (p. 370)
civic interest (p. 370)
Civil Rights Act (p. 363)
civil rights movement (p. 363)
compulsory voting (p. 373)
efficacy (p. 371)
Electoral College (p. 356)
elites (p. 357)
filibuster (p. 363)
franchise (p. 359)

gender gap (p. 367)
generational replacement (p. 375)
grandfather clauses (p. 362)
graveyard voting (p. 382)
Hamiltonian model of participation (p. 357)
institutional model (p. 371)
Jacksonian democracy (p. 359)
Jeffersonian model of participation (p. 357)
Jim Crow laws (p. 361)

literacy tests (p. 361)
partisanship (p. 371)
political machines (p. 375)
poll taxes (p. 362)
popular vote (p. 358)
Progressives (p. 382)
public good (p. 369)
rational voting (p. 369)
Reconstruction (p. 361)
self-interest (p. 369)
socialization (p. 369)
Solid South (p. 363)
suffrage (p. 357)

turnout (p. 360)
vote-by-mail (VBM) system (p. 385)
voter apathy (p. 363)
voter registration (p. 363)
voting-age population (VAEP) (p. 374)
voting-eligible population (VEP) (p. 376)
Voting Rights Act (p. 363)
white primary (p. 363)
women's suffrage (p. 359)

Use the vocabulary flash cards on the book's website.

Learning That Works

WHAT YOU NEED . . .

TO KNOW

The history of the right to vote in America

Theories of voting

The consequences of not voting

The rules regarding voting in your state

The meaning of participation

TO DO

Appreciate the importance of voting

Distinguish between self-interest and civic interest

Determine whether you should vote

Make sure you can vote on election day

Recognize small ways you can make your community better

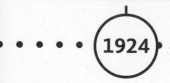
Congress extends citizenship to Native Americans.
1924

Twenty-Fourth Amendment bans poll taxes.
1964

Voting Rights Act gives the federal government the authority to prevent discrimination in voting.
1965

Twenty-Sixth Amendment extends the right to vote to 18-year-olds.
1971

12 CONGRESS

University of Puerto Rico, Río Piedras,
San Juan

> *The future of our nation is held in the hands of our youth, and we must do all we can to prepare them for the competitive, international job market they will enter.*

As a young girl, Nydia Velázquez had to convince her family to let her start school early. By age 16 she was already a student at the University of Puerto Rico. Her major—political science—was no surprise to her family, because her father, a sugarcane cutter, had long been a political activist. He founded a political party in Yabucoa, where the family lived; and, Nydia remembered, dinner conversations were full of talk about workers' rights. She credits him with passing on to her a strong social conscience. "I always wanted by be like my father," she told the *New York Times.*

After graduating with honors in 1974, Velázquez pursued a master's degree in political science at New York University and went on to serve as a legislative aide to African American Congressman Ed Towns, from New York. She also worked as the director of the Department of Puerto Rican Community Affairs for the governor of Puerto Rico and, like her father, was a community activist on behalf of Latinos, organizing massive voter registration drives in the New York City area.

But the key element in Velázquez's story is how she won a seat in the U.S. House of Representatives in 1992. Running in a newly created congressional district that was designed to include a majority of Latino voters, she faced challenges from other Latino candidates and from a white former congressman seeking to reclaim his seat. During her campaign, she and her volunteers went door to door in the district's poorest neighborhoods to register voters and ask for their support. On election day she emerged victorious with the help of thousands of Latino voters, and she has never forgotten them. "Her biggest commitment," reports an observer, "is to her district and her 'pueblo'—the Latino community she says has historically been shut off from access to power and information." With her election, Nydia Velázquez did not just win a seat in Congress; she gave the Latino residents of her district a voice in national policy making that they never had before.[1]

Nydia Velázquez

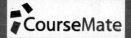
CourseMate

Visit http://www.cengagebrain
 .com/shop/ISBN/0618906959
 for interactive tools including:

• Quizzes

• Flashcards

• Videos

• Animated PowerPoint slides,
  Podcast summaries, and more

In the House, Congresswoman Velázquez has been a strong advocate on behalf of Latinos, especially Latino women, as well as of the Chinese and African American residents in her district. She has focused on immigration issues and on strengthening ties with Latin America. She has spoken out against English-only laws because, she argues, Latinos need both Spanish and English in their early years of education to overcome language barriers and become full citizens. In 2007 Congresswoman Velázquez became chair of the House Committee on Small Business, and in 2009 she became chair of the Congressional Hispanic Caucus. She believes that economic empowerment for the working poor is her district's chief challenge, and her position in Congress gives her the opportunity to bring home federal dollars, in the form of projects and grants, to provide economic and political opportunities for her constituents.

As a protector of her constituents who never forgets her roots, Velázquez has been reelected nine times. Her very presence in Congress helps advance the cause of equality; she represents a series of firsts: first in her family to graduate from college, first Puerto Rican woman elected to Congress, first Latina to chair a House committee. She believes her background as a Puerto Rican woman helps her to better address the needs and concerns of people of all ethnicities because she shares their experiences.

In this chapter, we explain how members of Congress navigate the gates and gateways embedded in the legislative branch to best serve the interests of their constituents. The fact that members of Congress must repeatedly return home to ask the voters to reelect them helps to keep them responsive to their constituents, who hold them accountable for the policies they enact into law. But the process of congressional representation—that is, of putting good ideas into practice as law—is difficult and complex. There are structural gates embedded in a separation of powers system of government and in a democratic legislative process that encourages competition among groups with conflicting interests. Navigating this terrain is not easy, but Nydia Velázquez's efforts on behalf of her district show how an individual member of Congress can be an advocate as well as a legislator.

FOCUS QUESTIONS

- How are members of Congress held accountable, both individually and for the collective output of Congress as a whole?

- In what ways is Congress responsive as a decision-making body? How does Congress address the pressing needs of the American people?

- What opportunities are there for the average person to influence the policy process in Congress? Is Congress accessible to citizens equally?

- How do the institutional structures in the House of Representatives and those in the Senate work as gates blocking the enactment of legislation? Are there any gateways in these chambers that can help overcome these obstacles? Why did the Framers set up the legislative branch this way?

- Is Congress a gate or a gateway to democracy?

Congress as the Legislative Branch

In Chapter 2 (The Constitution) we discussed the ideas of representation that shaped the Framers' thinking. They believed that a democratic government had to be responsive and accountable to the people. In such a government, leaders would not inherit power; rather, they would be elected by the people at regular intervals, and these elections would be the key way that voters would hold government officials accountable for their actions. The

Framers of the Constitution designed Congress to be the legislative branch of the federal government, and they gave it broad powers to enact laws. At the same time, they wanted the process of lawmaking to be complex and deliberative so that members of Congress would not succumb to impulsive actions that might harm constituents or violate fundamental constitutional rights. Over time, Congress has increased the scope and range of its powers, but the added responsibilities have added a layer of complexity that makes it harder than ever to pass laws.

Representation and Bicameralism

In Chapter 1 (Gateways to American Democracy), we asked whether the people's representatives in the legislature should act as **trustees** who exercise independent judgment about what they believe is best for the people or act as **delegates** who do exactly as the people wish. In Chapter 6 (Public Opinion), we examined the polls and other means by which legislators try to determine what the people wish. We also learned that citizens do not have informed views on every issue. Thus, members of Congress have to act as both trustees and delegates.

Essential to understanding how Congress facilitates **representation** in the American democracy is to recognize that it is **bicameral**, that is, it is divided into two separate chambers: the House of Representatives and the Senate. This structure reflects the Framers' fear that the power of the legislative branch might grow to the point where it could not be controlled by the other two branches. Because the legislative branch is closest to the people—its members represent specific population groups, by region, and can be removed by election—the Framers believed that Congress would have a democratic legitimacy that neither the executive nor the judicial branches would possess.

The solution, according to James Madison, was to divide the legislature into two parts that would check each other. In *Federalist* 51 he explained that this would "render them . . . as little connected with each other, as the nature of their common functions, and their common dependence on the society, will admit." The House of Representatives would be a large body that reflected population size within states and was directly elected frequently (every two years), and the Senate would be an elite chamber, with two senators for every state

trustee: *Idea of representation that says elected officials should do what they think best, even if the public disagrees, and that elections allow the public to render a judgment on their decisions.*

delegate: *Idea of representation that says elected officials should do what the public wants and not exercise independent judgment.*

Who are your representatives and senators? Do you want them to be trustees or delegates?

representation: *Idea that government officeholders are elected by the people to act on their behalf.*

bicameral: *Two-chamber legislature, as the U.S. House of Representatives and Senate.*

istockphoto

The Framers created the House of Representatives and the Senate as separate chambers of Congress, but both are located in the U.S. Capitol. In this view from the National Mall, the Senate chamber is on the left, and the House chamber is on the right. There are six office buildings for members of Congress and their staff members, three on each side of the Capitol.

regardless of population size elected by state legislatures for six-year terms. In that way, both the popular opinions of average voters and the elite opinions of the well educated and the wealthy would be represented in Congress. This arrangement also guaranteed that large states could not overwhelm smaller states in determining the content of laws. The specific differences between the two parts of Congress are discussed in the next section.

Constitutional Differences between the House and Senate

To accomplish Madison's goal, the Constitution establishes four key differences between the two chambers of Congress: qualifications for office, mode of election, terms of office, and constituencies (see Table 12.1).

Qualifications for Office.   To serve as a member of the House of Representatives, an individual must be at least 25 years old, reside in the state that he or she represents, and have been a U.S. citizen for seven years before running for office. The qualifications for the Senate are that an individual must be at least 30 years old, reside in the state he or she represents, and have been a U.S. citizen for nine years before running for office. Senators are expected to be older and to have lived in the United States for a longer period of time than House members because the Framers believed those characteristics would make the Senate the more stable partner in the legislative process.

Although the members of the First Congress (1789–91) were all white men, no provision in the Constitution delineates a specific race, gender, income level, or religion as a prerequisite for serving in Congress. Twenty-first-century Congresses have been much more diverse, with female, African American, Hispanic, Pacific Islander, and Native American members in the House (see Figure 12.1). The average House and Senate member is older than 55. House members tend to serve an average of five terms (ten years) and Senators an average of two terms (twelve years).[2] The twenty-first-century House has included members from the Protestant, Catholic, Jewish, Greek Orthodox, Mormon, Buddhist, Quaker, and—for the first time—Muslim faiths. The religious background of senators has been slightly less varied, but has also included members from the Protestant, Roman Catholic, Mormon, and Jewish faiths.[3]

House members have more varied prior experience than their Senate colleagues. A majority of House members served in their state legislatures before coming to Congress;

TABLE 12.1 Comparison of House and Senate Service

	House	Senate
Minimum age	25 years old	30 years old
Citizenship	7 years	9 years
Term of office	2 years	6 years
Geographic constituency	District	State
Redistricting	Every 10 years	—
Mode of election until 1914	Direct	Indirect through state legislatures
Mode of election after 1914	Direct	Direct

others were mayors, law enforcement officers, doctors, ministers, radio talk show hosts, accountants, business owners, and even an airline pilot. Just as House members use state legislatures as stepping-stones, senators use the House of Representatives to launch their bids for the Senate. In the 111th Congress, forty-nine senators had previously served in the House of Representatives, and others had been mayors, governors, and attorneys general or had held executive branch positions.

Mode of Election.

House members are elected directly by citizens. Senators are elected directly as well, but that is a more recent development. From 1789 to 1914, the mode of election for

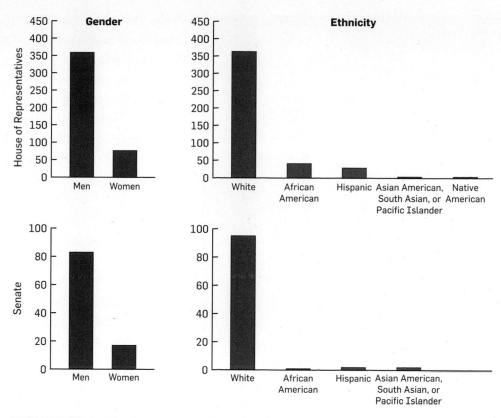

FIGURE 12.1 The Demographics of the 111th Congress.

the Senate was indirect: Citizens voted for members of their state legislatures, who then selected the U.S. senators. The mode of election for the House and Senate was different on purpose. The House was supposed to be more immediately responsive to the opinions of the people, but the Framers designed the Senate to insulate senators from the direct voice of the people, in other words, to make them less directly responsive to the people.

The mode of election for the Senate was changed from indirect to direct with the ratification of the Seventeenth Amendment in 1913. At the end of the nineteenth century, in response to charges of deadlock and corruption during the election of U.S. senators in state legislatures, Progressives led a movement to allow voters to directly elect their senators. Gradually, this movement for popular elections gained support. The U.S. Senate passed the amendment in 1911, the House passed it in 1912, and on May 31, 1913, the thirty-sixth state (making three-fourths of the states) ratified it.[4] The change to direct elections opened up a much more direct gateway of influence for constituents over their U.S. senators.

Terms of Office.

A term of office is the length of time that an elected official serves before facing the voters again in an election. The term of office for House members is two years, and the term of office for U.S. senators is six years. The difference in term of office leads to key differences in how each chamber operates. House members have a shorter amount of time to demonstrate their effectiveness before they face reelection, so the House of Representatives as a whole is usually in a greater hurry to pass legislation than is the Senate. Senators know they have six years before they have to face their voters, so they have a bit more flexibility in working out disagreements among their constituents and balancing constituents' interests against the interests of the nation as a whole. Because senators know they

have a longer time in which to establish a good reputation among their home state voters, the Senate takes more time to deliberate over legislation.

In any given election year, the entire membership of the House of Representatives must face the voters, but only one-third of senators stand for reelection. To guarantee that the whole Senate would never stand for reelection all at once, the Constitution divided the first Senate, which met in 1789, into three classes of senators who would be elected at different six-year intervals.[5] To this day, the maximum number of senators who stand for regularly scheduled reelection in the same year is thirty-four (out of a possible 100), thereby ensuring that a majority of the Senate is never up for reelection at the same time as the entire House of Representatives.[6] This electoral condition reinforces the stability of the Senate's membership; it also limits the electoral incentives for House and Senate members to cooperate with one another to pass legislation.

The late Senator Robert C. Byrd (D-W.Va.), who passed away in June 2010, was the oldest and longest serving member of Congress. He served as Senate majority leader and chair of the Senate Appropriations Committee, and he was pivotal in modifying and interpreting the rules that govern Senate floor procedure. On January 29, 2003, he proposed a measure requiring President George W. Bush to obtain United Nations approval before going to war with Iraq.

constituency: *Defined group of citizens officially designated to elect a legislative representative.*

census: *Constitutionally mandated count of the population every ten years.*

Constituencies.   A constituency is the set of people that officially elects the House or Senate member; in the United States, **constituency** is defined geographically. Each member of the House of Representatives represents a congressional district with established geographic boundaries within the state. Each U.S. senator represents an entire state, and two U.S. senators are elected from each state. The Framers wanted to have two senators for each state to make sure there was always at least one senator actively representing a state in the Senate.[7] At various times, deaths, resignations, and political disputes have reduced a state's representation to a single senator or no senator.[8] As recently as 2009, Minnesota had just one senator for six months due to legal conflict over the outcome of the 2008 Senate election there.

In 1789 the average size of a congressional district was about 30,000 people, and the average size of a state was about 300,000 people; today, a congressional district has about 640,000 people, and the nation's largest state, California, has approximately 37 million residents.[9] Because the Framers knew that the country would grow, they required a count, or **census**, of the population every ten years. Following the census, the number of congressional districts in each state would be adjusted to reflect population changes. The House started with 65 members and, when capped at 435 in 1929, had increased by 670 percent.[10] That year, Congress passed a law that limited the size of the House to 435, concerned that if the House grew any larger it would not be possible to conduct legislative business.[11] Today, because there is an absolute limit on the total number of House members, population growth or decline has a direct bearing on a state's representation, increasing or decreasing the state's number of representatives and thus its relative influence in the House.

Geographic boundaries on constituencies have a direct impact on congressional representation. A member of the House is responsive to the needs of the residents of a district, but a U.S. senator is responsive to the needs of the residents of an entire state. As a result, members of the House and Senate from the same state can react differently to the same issue. For example, in 1999 Congresswoman Velázquez supported President

William Jefferson (Bill) Clinton's (1993–2001) proposal to grant clemency to members of the FALN, a Puerto Rican opposition group, who were convicted of and serving prison sentences for a series of violent protests, including a bombing in the U.S. Capitol Building. In contrast, the senior Democratic senator from New York, Daniel Patrick Moynihan, opposed the measure because he believed it was inconsistent with a tough stand on terrorism. Congresswoman Velázquez felt a duty to her own heritage, as well as the heritage of many of the residents of her district, to support clemency for the FALN members, but Moynihan, who was elected by the entire state of New York, did not feel the same obligation to respond to the opinions of the residents of Congresswoman Velázquez's district on this issue. In this case, the House and Senate were checking and balancing each other, as the Framers had envisioned.

Redistricting.

Only the House of Representatives is subject to **redistricting**, which is the redrawing of the boundaries of congressional districts in a state to make them approximately equal in population size. Because the size of the House is limited to 435, the overall number of congressional seats per state must be adjusted following a census if there have been population changes. Based on the state's allocation of congressional districts, the state legislature redraws the districts, and the only real limitation on redistricting is that the boundaries of the district must be contiguous (uninterrupted). During redistricting, the majority party in the state legislature tries to influence the process to construct each district in such a way that a majority of voters favors its party, thereby making it easier for its candidates to win, in a process known as **gerrymandering**. Sometimes the majority party will combine two existing districts that have House members from the other party, forcing them to run against each other.

Redistricting has also been used as a tool to achieve greater minority representation in the House of Representatives. The Voting Rights Act of 1965 prohibits states and political subdivisions from denying or abridging "the right of any citizen of the United States to vote on account of race or color"; it was later amended to protect the voting rights of non-English-speaking minorities—referring to Latinos—as well. This act is discussed in detail in Chapters 5 (Civil Rights), 10 (Elections and Campaigns), and 11 (Voting and Participation); here we focus on the fact that many states initially responded to the law by redrawing congressional districts to group minority voters in a way that would deny them the voting strength to elect a minority member of Congress. In 1982 Congress amended the Voting Rights Act to prevent this kind of manipulation. In response, some state legislatures created so-called majority-minority districts in which African Americans or Latinos would constitute a majority of the voters and would have enough votes to elect an African American or Latino candidate.[12] The New York district from which Congresswoman Velázquez was first elected was one of them. Since then, the federal courts have ruled that state legislatures overemphasized the racial composition of these districts to the point that the districts made no geographic sense. Current guidelines on redistricting call for the consideration of race in drawing district lines, but not to the extreme that it was employed in the past.[13]

Because representation in the Senate is related to state boundaries, not to population size, some scholars have argued that the Senate is less responsive than the House. It is true that there are vast differences in population size among the states

Which congressional district do you live in? Which congressional district is your college in?

redistricting: *Process whereby state legislatures redraw the boundaries of congressional districts in the state to make them equal in population size.*

gerrymandering: *Redistricting that blatantly benefits one political party over the other or concentrates (or dilutes) the voting impact of racial or ethnic groups.*

How do majority-minority districts provide a gateway for better representation of minority interests?

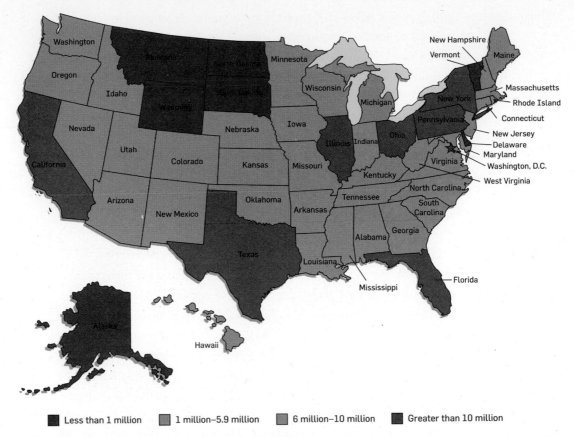

| ■ Less than 1 million | ■ 1 million–5.9 million | ■ 6 million–10 million | ■ Greater than 10 million |

FIGURE 12.2 States by Population, 2009. The U.S. Senate has two senators for every state, regardless of state population size. This arrangement makes states equal in Senate votes: Wyoming has the same number of votes as California. But it also means that the 1 million citizens of Wyoming have the same voice in the Senate as the 37 million citizens of California. Equal representation in the Senate did not seem as imbalanced when states had more similar population sizes, but today, with such huge differences among states, some observers think representation in the Senate is inherently unfair. *Source:* U.S. Census Bureau.

With each state having the same number of senators, what are the consequences for citizen equality across small and large states?

(see Figure 12.2).[14] As we explore later in this chapter, the rules of the Senate amplify this imbalance of influence by granting each senator equal power to block legislation. As a result, a senator who represents a state like Wyoming, with fewer than 1 million people, can block a policy that might benefit a state like California, with 37 million people.

The Powers of Congress

As Chapter 2 describes, the Framers granted Congress powers that were necessary to construct a coherent and forceful federal government. Some of these, such as the power to tax and to regulate commerce among the states, had been denied to Congress under the Articles of Confederation, and their absence had weakened the new republic. At the same time, the Framers worried that the legislative branch would grow too powerful. So they limited the powers of Congress to a list in Article I, Section 8 of the Constitution, together with a few stated responsibilities in other sections. The following discussion highlights the most important powers of Congress. It also examines the ways that Congress has used its constitutional powers to expand its role in the policy-making system, and ways that Congress, as the legislative branch, is balanced and checked by the executive and judicial branches.

How have the powers of Congress increased? Why did they increase?

Taxation and Appropriation

Congress has the power "To lay and Collect Taxes." In a division of this important power, the Constitution states that all bills for raising revenue should originate in the House of Representatives, but the Senate "may propose or concur with Amendments, as on other Bills." Initially, the Framers thought that tax revenue would come primarily from levies placed on imported goods. As the industrial economy grew, so did the need for government services and programs that cost money. With the Sixteenth Amendment, ratified in 1913, Congress gained the power "to lay and collect taxes on incomes," whatever the source. This amendment overturned prohibitions on certain types of income taxes.

Why do you think the Framers gave the House, rather than the Senate, the authority to originate revenue bills?

Paralleling the power to tax, Congress also has the power to spend—"to pay the Debts and to provide for the common Defence and general Welfare." The **general welfare clause** has proven to be a major means by which Congress's power has expanded. Congress **appropriates** (or allocates) federal monies on programs it **authorizes** (or creates) through its lawmaking power. This "power of the purse" has been instrumental in the expansion of Congress's relative strength among the branches of government.[15] The Constitution also gives Congress the authority to borrow money, to coin money, and to regulate its value, and it requires a regular accounting of revenue and expenditures of public money.

general welfare clause: *Gives Congress the power to tax to provide for the general welfare (Article I, Section 8).*

appropriate: *Congress's power to allocate a set amount of federal dollars for a specific program or agency.*

authorize: *Congress's power to create a federal program or agency and set levels of federal funds to support that program or agency.*

War Powers

The Constitution gives Congress authority to "provide for the common Defence." In reality, the war powers are shared with the president. For example, Congress has the sole power to declare war, but this power is typically used only after the president has requested a declaration of war. In many cases, the president may ask Congress for specific authorization to take military action; under its power of taxation and appropriation, Congress has the authority to fund or refuse to fund military operations. Generally, Congress also has the power "to raise and support Armies," "to provide and maintain a Navy," "to provide for calling forth the Militia," and to make rules and regulations regarding the armed forces and their organizations. Relations between Congress and the president over war powers have sometimes been harmonious, but in recent decades they have become contentious. The struggle between the president and Congress over the war powers is examined in detail in Chapter 13, The Presidency.

Regulation of Commerce

The Constitution gave Congress an important power that it did not have under the Articles of Confederation: the power "to regulate Commerce with foreign Nations, and among the several States, and with the Indian Tribes." Using the power in this **commerce clause**, Congress established a national set of laws regulating commerce that are applicable to all states equally.[16] In time, the authority to regulate interstate commerce has allowed Congress to expand its power to the point that almost no economic activity is beyond its reach. For example, in 1942 the Supreme Court upheld Congress's power to regulate wheat production even when that wheat is not sold or transported in interstate commerce but is consumed on the farm where it was planted and harvested (see Supreme Court Cases: *Wickard v. Filburn*). In the name of regulating interstate commerce, Congress has passed laws that permit the federal government to break up monopolies,

commerce clause: *Gives Congress the power to regulate commerce with foreign nations, with Indian tribes, and among the various states (Article I, Section 8).*

supremecourtcases

Wickard v. Filburn (1942)

QUESTION: Does the commerce clause allow Congress to regulate wheat production on a farm when the wheat is consumed on that farm?

ORAL ARGUMENT: October 13, 1942

DECISION: November 9, 1942 (read at www.findlaw.com/casecode/supreme.html)

OUTCOME: Yes, Congress has the authority to regulate such production (9–0).

To raise farm prices for struggling farmers, the Agricultural Adjustment Act of 1938 established quotas for how much wheat farmers could grow. Farmer Roscoe Filburn owned a small dairy farm in Ohio where he also grew wheat, some of it for sale, but most of it for use on his farm. Overall, Filburn planted twenty-three acres of wheat, substantially beyond the eleven acres he was allotted. The United States charged him a penalty on the wheat he grew over his allotment regardless of whether it was intended for market or home consumption. Filburn refused to pay a $117.11 fine on his excess wheat, so the government refused to grant him a marketing card that would allow him to sell any of the wheat. Filburn sued the government. The district court ruled in favor of Filburn, and Secretary of Agriculture Claude Wickard appealed the case to the Supreme Court, which granted review.

Farmer Filburn argued that wheat grown on his farm for consumption on his farm was local in character and that any impact of such wheat on the interstate market for wheat was indirect at best. The Court, however, ruled that by growing the excess wheat, he was not purchasing that amount of extra wheat on the market. Although the effect of Filburn's wheat not purchased on the market might be trivial, there were thousands of other farmers similarly situated. If all of them grew excess wheat rather than purchasing it on the market, the cumulative effect on the market for wheat would be substantial.

The *Filburn* case greatly expanded the scope of Congress's authority under the commerce clause. Virtually any economic activity, when multiplied by all similarly situated activities, can be said to have an impact on interstate commerce. Thus there is very little economic activity that is beyond the reach of congressional regulation.

- **In the attempt to limit wheat production, is it fair to treat the wheat that *Filburn* used only on his own farm equally to wheat for sale? Why?**

- **How does the *Filburn* case reflect the challenges for Congress in balancing individual needs against the common good?**

EQUAL JUSTICE UNDER LAW

The Senate exercises its advice and consent powers when it holds hearings on presidential nominees and then votes to approve or reject them. In the summer of 2009 senators questioned President Barack Obama's first Supreme Court nominee, Sonia Sotomayor, an appeals court judge from New York. She was confirmed on August 6, 2009, by a vote of 68 to 31.

Ryan Kelly/Congressional Quarterly/Getty Images

protect labor unions, set a minimum wage, and outlaw racial discrimination by businesses and commercial enterprises.

Appointments and Treaties

advice and consent: *Power of the Senate to approve or reject presidential appointments, such as cabinet secretaries, ambassadors, and judges, as well as international treaties.*

In recognition of the Senate's perceived wisdom and stability, the Framers gave the Senate, and not the House, the power of **advice and consent**. In the appointment of high-level executive branch appointees, such as cabinet secretaries and ambassadors, this power allows the Senate to evaluate the qualifications of a presidential nominee and, by majority vote, to approve or reject the nominee. Similarly, the appointment of all federal judges, from district courts to the Supreme Court, is subject to the approval of the Senate (see Chapter 15, The Judiciary, for more details on this process). Additionally, the Senate acts as a check on the president's power to make treaties with foreign nations: Treaties must be approved by a two-thirds vote or they fail to take effect (see Chapter 13 for more on treaty negotiation and ratification). The advice and consent role of the Senate acts as a gateway for citizen influence over presidential appointments and treaties because senators are more likely to block appointments and treaties that they believe are unpopular with their constituents.

Why did the Framers give the Senate the power of advice and consent?

Impeachment and Removal from Office

impeachment: *Process whereby the House brings charges against the president or another federal official that will, upon conviction by the Senate, remove him or her from office.*

Congress's ultimate check on the executive and judicial branches is its power to remove officials and judges from office by **impeachment**. The president, vice president, and high officials are subject to impeachment for "Treason, Bribery, or other high Crimes and Misdemeanors." This power is rarely used. In Chapter 13 we examine the two cases where presidents have been impeached, but not removed from office. In the case of President

Richard Nixon (1969–74), the threat of impeachment was credible enough that he resigned from office.

The process of impeachment and removal from office takes place in two steps. First, a majority of the House of Representatives votes to bring formal charges against the president or other federal official, an action called impeachment. Then the Senate conducts the trial, with the chief justice of the United States presiding in the case of the president's impeachment, and votes to convict or acquit. If two-thirds of the senators present vote to convict, the president or the federal official will be removed from office.

Lawmaking

enumerated powers: *Powers of Congress listed in Article I, Section 8 of the Constitution, such as regulating commerce and coining money.*

necessary and proper clause: *Gives Congress the power to pass all laws necessary and proper to the powers enumerated in Section 8 (Article I, Section 8).*

implied powers: *Powers not explicitly granted to Congress but added through the necessary and proper clause.*

Congress, as the legislative branch, is responsible for lawmaking. Unlike the **enumerated powers** listed at the beginning of Article I, Section 8 and explained above, the final paragraph of Section 8 gives Congress broad authority "to make all Laws which shall be necessary and proper for carrying into Execution the foregoing Powers." In combination with the general welfare clause and the commerce clause, this **necessary and proper clause** allows Congress a great deal of leeway to carry out its responsibilities under the assumption that additional powers are **implied** in these clauses, although not explicitly stated in the Constitution. Over time, Congress has made full use of this flexibility to expand its authority in a wide range of areas, such as regulating interstate railroads, establishing civil rights protections, funding school lunch programs, limiting greenhouse gases, and providing student loans. Essentially, if an argument can be made that a service or program is important for the nation, Congress has used its powers to create it.

Authorization of Courts

Judiciary Act: *1789 act that created the lower federal judiciary, district courts, and circuit courts of appeal.*

Marbury v. Madison: *An 1803 Supreme Court decision that established the Supreme Court's power of judicial review.*

judicial review: *Authority of courts to declare laws passed by Congress and acts of the executive branch to be unconstitutional.*

In Article I the Constitution also gave Congress the power to "constitute Tribunals inferior to the Supreme Court." Article III, the section on the judiciary, reiterates congressional control by saying that Congress may "ordain and establish" courts at levels lower than the Supreme Court. In 1789 Congress used this power to pass the **Judiciary Act**, which established federal district courts and circuit courts of appeal. Today, there are ninety-four district courts and thirteen appellate circuits.[17]

The federal judicial branch asserted more authority over the other two branches in the Supreme Court case of *Marbury v. Madison* (1803; see Chapter 2). This case established **judicial review**, which is the federal judiciary's power to declare laws passed by Congress as unconstitutional. The *Marbury* decision gave the courts the power to interpret the Constitution and determine how congressional laws (and even executive branch actions) conform to its explicit language and its intent (see Chapter 15 for further explanation of this decision).

In recent years the Senate has tried to reassert its influence over the federal courts through the nomination process.[18] As we discuss later in the chapter, individual senators can try to stall or block presidential nominees for federal judgeships with whom they disagree on key constitutional questions.

Oversight

Once a bill becomes a law, the executive branch, headed by the president, is supposed to carry out the law according to Congress's wishes. But the executive branch is a bureaucracy with many departments and agencies that have authority to implement laws. The sheer size and complexity of the federal bureaucracy make it difficult for Congress to determine whether laws are being administered according to their intent (see Chapter 14, The Bureaucracy, for more details). Over time, Congress has asserted its **oversight** authority to monitor the ways in which the executive branch implements law. This authority stems from Congress's responsibility to appropriate money to provide for the general welfare of the nation. Congress constantly exercises this authority, but less so under **unified government**, when the same party controls Congress and the White House, than under **divided government**, when the party that controls Congress is not the party of the president. Under unified government, members of Congress assume that because they share the same partisan affiliation as the president, his administration is more likely to implement laws according to congressional intent.

In contrast, legislatures in countries that have parliamentary systems typically choose their executives from among the members of the majority party so that the executive and legislative branches always share the same policy goals. Consequently, legislative oversight is not a fundamental element of those political systems (see Other Places: The Parliamentary System of the United Kingdom).

Members of Congress engage in oversight activities in several ways. They hold **hearings** with cabinet officials and bureaucrats to analyze how well programs are working, and they frequently invite members of the public to describe how federal programs operate in their communities. Members of Congress regularly write letters to executive branch agency heads to inquire about specific programs, and they keep careful track of the responses they receive. In cases of special investigations or suspected wrongdoing by members of the executive branch, Congress can legally require members of the administration to testify. In some instances, Congress convenes special committees, such as the Iran-Contra Committee (see Chapter 13 for more details), to investigate actions involving members of the president's staff or even the president himself. In these ways, members of Congress provide a gateway for the people to constantly monitor and hold the federal government accountable for how it implements the law.

oversight: *Power of Congress to monitor how the executive branch implements laws.*

unified government: *Situation when the same party controls the executive and legislative branches.*

divided government: *Situation when one party controls the executive branch and the other party controls the legislative branch.*

hearings: *Congressional committee meetings to gather information or hear testimony on bills, issues, or appointments.*

Think about the power to investigate. Which branch should have this power?

The Organization of Congress

The House and the Senate have evolved into very different institutions by virtue of their differences in size, rules, structure, and responsibilities. The Constitution establishes few guidelines for how the House and Senate should operate, so it was left to the members to determine how to choose their leaders and how much power to give them. Some aspects of leadership are shared by the House and Senate, but there are important differences in the amount of power each grants to its leaders. Notably, the power of political parties to shape policy is vastly different in each chamber.

The Role of Political Parties

In today's political world, political parties seem natural and intrinsic to the organization of Congress. But it was not always so. The House did not organize itself along strict partisan lines until well into the nineteenth century. As scholars Sarah Binder and Eric Schickler each show, not until after the Civil War did the House change its internal rules to give the majority party the ability to get its preferred policies passed over the objections of the minority

otherplaces

The Parliamentary System of the United Kingdom

All democracies have a legislature and an executive, but their relationship to each other produces differences in the way people are represented. The United States has separate legislative and executive branches. In the United Kingdom the executive and the legislative branches are intertwined. The United Kingdom is a limited monarchy democracy, with a queen as the head of state and a parliament for its legislature. The British Parliament is bicameral; the House of Commons has 650 members, and elections are held in single-member districts, as they are in the United States. The party that wins the most seats wins control of the chamber. The House of Lords has 783 members, some of whom inherit their seats and others of whom are appointed by the queen. The approval of both branches of the legislature is necessary to pass legislation.

In the British system, the prime minister, who is the chief executive of the government, is an elected member of the House of Commons chosen by the majority party and officially recognized by the queen. He appoints ministers and advisers to his cabinet without the formal approval of the legislature. Because the prime minister comes from the majority party in the legislature, the executive and the legislature typically agree on the legislation that needs to be passed to accomplish the party's goals. As party leader, the prime minister is responsive to the party's voting base. There are no regularly scheduled parliamentary elections, but elections must be held at least once every five years, and the campaigns last for less than three weeks. The prime minister calls for elections either when the majority party is very popular, so that it can retain power, or when it is so unpopular that the public calls for a change.

In 2010 Prime Minister Gordon Brown, a member of the Labour Party, had lost popularity, and in the May 6 election the Conservatives, led by David Cameron, won more seats than the Labour Party, but fell short of a working majority. As a result, the Conservatives joined with members of a third party, the Liberal Democrats, to form a working majority party in Parliament. The end result of the elections was a complete change of majority party control.

THE HOUSE OF COMMONS

1. Speaker
2. Pages
3. Government Members
4. Opposition Members
5. Prime Minister
6. Leader of the Official Opposition
7. Leader of Second Largest Party in Opposition
8. Clerk and Table Officers
9. Mace
10. Hansard Reporters
11. Sergeant-at-Arms
12. The Bar
13. Interpreters
14. Press Gallery
15. Public Gallery
16. Official Gallery
17. Leader of the Opposition's Gallery
18. Members' Gallery
19. Members' Gallery
20. Members' Gallery
21. Speaker's Gallery
22. Senate Gallery
23. T.V. Cameras

In the House of Commons, members of the two major parties sit on opposite sides, as in the U.S. Congress, but they are identified as "government" and "opposition."

- **How does the British parliamentary system differ from the U.S. separation of powers system?**
- **Compare citizen control in elections that are regularly scheduled and in elections that are scheduled by the majority party in power.**

Source: UK Parliament Website, www.parliament.uk.

party.[19] Since then, party affiliation and party loyalty have become the defining features of how policy is made in the House of Representatives.

Are political parties in the House too powerful? Are they a gate or a gateway to passing legislation?

The reason parties could become so powerful inside the House chamber was that they were important outside Washington, back home in local districts. Being identified with a political party became an essential stepping-stone to political office. Political parties controlled the nomination process for Congress, and anyone who wanted to run on a party ticket had to pledge support for the party's policies. Consequently, each individual member had a strong incentive to align with a political party both at home in the district and in Washington (see Chapter 9, Political Parties, for more on party affiliations).

With the rise in party strength at the district level, House members were increasingly judged on the performance of their party in office, and elections became centered on gaining majority control of the chamber. If the majority party could pass policies that it favored and prevent those who disagreed with them (the minority party) from gaining any power, majority party members could return to their districts and claim credit for being effective legislators.

Although the Senate also became more party-oriented at the end of the nineteenth century, its members never changed the rules of the chamber to give the majority party complete dominance. Because the number of senators has remained small, it is still possible to conduct legislative business in a personal manner, and each senator exerts individual influence over policy outcomes. Senators also have the chance to make individual impressions on voters over a longer time (six years) and from a more visible vantage point, as they represent entire states rather than just one district. Voters still consider a senator's party affiliation in their voting decision, but it is not as important as in House elections. Consequently, senators have had fewer incentives to hand over their individual powers to a single party leader to accomplish party goals.

The Senate has remained small enough that each individual senator can wield relatively equal amounts of power. As a result, members of the minority party in the Senate have far more power in the policy-making process than do their counterparts in the House.[20] In essence, getting any legislation passed in the Senate usually requires compromise and cooperation among all senators—majority and minority party members—in one way or another.

What evidence of compromise and cooperation do you see in the Senate today?

The House of Representatives

As is the case with any large organization, success requires leadership. To maximize party cohesion, members of the House meet in a **party caucus** ("to caucus" literally means "to gather") of the members of their political party. Each party's caucus chooses its party leaders: For the majority party, the top party leader is the Speaker of the House, and for the minority party, it is the minority leader.

party caucus: *Group of party members in a legislature.*

The Speaker of the House.   **Speaker of the House** is the only formal leadership position written into the Constitution. Article I, Section 2 states that "the House of Representatives shall chuse their Speaker and other Officers," but there the official description ends. The Speaker is elected by a majority of House members every two years, on the first day of the first session of each new Congress. The position first became organizationally powerful under the tenure of Thomas Brackett Reed (R-Maine), who served as Speaker from 1889 to

Speaker of the House: *Constitutional and political leader of the House.*

Why is the Speaker of the House so powerful? Why is the person who holds this position third in line in presidential succession, after the vice president?

Reed's Rules: *Procedural changes proposed by Speaker Thomas Reed to strengthen the power of the majority party over the minority party in the House.*

Contract with America: *Campaign proposal containing ten legislative initiatives used by all Republicans running for the House of Representatives in 1994.*

1891 and again from 1895 to 1899.[21] Reed was elected to the House in 1876, and by the early 1880s he was already displaying political ambition.

As Speaker, Reed implemented a set of procedural changes known as **Reed's Rules** that strengthened the power of the majority party over the minority party. Because the House ran on majority rule, the party that had the most votes could pass a bill outright. Reed's party granted him the power to appoint all committee chairmen, approve all members' committee assignments, refer bills to committee, bring bills that reflect the majority party's ideas to the House floor, and refuse to allow the minority party to delay legislation.[22] The former Speaker of the House, Nancy Pelosi (D-Calif.), used many of the same powers to run the House, although she presided over a more complex decision-making environment than did Reed (we discuss decision making later in the chapter).

In the century following Reed, the leadership styles of Speakers varied according to how much power the rank-and-file party members wanted to give to their leaders. The scholar David Rohde and others argue that the variation in leadership style can be explained by the underlying coherence of the majority party during these years. When the rank-and-file membership of the majority party is unified in its policy goals, it hands power to party leaders, especially the Speaker, to accomplish those goals under what Rohde called conditional party government.[23]

The tenure of Newt Gingrich (R-Ga.) as Speaker (1995–98) is an example of conditional party government in action. After forty straight years in power, the Democrats lost control of the House of Representatives when Republicans swept in under a campaign platform called the **Contract with America**. The Contract with America presented ten legislative proposals, and every Republican who ran for the House in the 1994 election signed it and pledged to honor it if elected. Once the Republicans won control of the House, they elected Newt Gingrich as Speaker and gave him control over almost every aspect of legislative work; he became the public face of the party. Although he was initially very successful in passing most of the Contract with America in the House, few of the proposals managed to pass the Senate and get enacted. By 1998 Gingrich had experienced a number of political problems, ranging from a government shutdown over budget disputes with President Bill Clinton, to disagreements with moderate Republican members over environmental and farm programs, and finally to unpopular impeachment proceeding against President Clinton. That year, the Republicans lost seats in the midterm elections, and Gingrich—as party leader—took responsibility for them and resigned from office.

Thomas Brackett Reed (R-Maine) served as Speaker of the House from 1889 to 1891 and again from 1895 to 1899. He changed the rules of the House to give the majority party the advantage in setting the policy agenda and passing bills that accomplished its goals.

Library of Congress

After Gingrich, the Republicans chose a less powerful Speaker, Dennis Hastert (R-Ill.) and moved from a conditional party government system to what scholars call a party cartel system. According to Gary Cox and Mathew McCubbins, in this system, the power of party leaders rests on their ability to set the legislative agenda and provide services, such as campaign finance funds, and organizational positions, such as committee positions, to party members in exchange for their loyalty.[24] This type of system worked better for the Republicans after 2001, when a Republican was elected to the White House and set the policy agenda for members of the party. Typically under unified government, members of the majority party in the House use the president's agenda as a starting point. As a result, the Speaker can lose independence in setting the policy direction for the House.

After the Democrats won control of the House in the 2006 elections, Nancy Pelosi was elected the first female Speaker of the House. She retained many of the powers that the Republicans had given their party leaders and tried to use a combination of the conditional party government and cartel system to run the House. Whether she works with a

JOSHUA ROBERTS/AFP/Getty Images

same- or an opposite-party president, the Speaker's most important responsibility is to maintain power in the House for the majority party, and that means getting the members of the majority party reelected. To do so, the Speaker supports a set of policies that she believes are popular with voters, and she tries to get those policies enacted into law. For example, during the consideration of health care reform in the House, the Democrats shared the goal of passing a health care reform bill, so they allowed the Speaker to use all the tools at her disposal to get the bill passed. The Democrats suffered big losses in the 2010 elections in part due to voter backlash on this issue.

House Party Leaders.

The **House majority leader**, as second in command, works with the Speaker to decide which issues the party will consider. He or she also coordinates with committee leaders on holding hearings and reporting bills to the House floor for a vote. The House majority leader must strike a compromise among many competing forces, including committee chairs and external interest groups. He or she is also expected to raise a significant amount of campaign contributions for party members, and that role produces more pressure to appease as many interest groups as possible. The majority leader also has nine majority whips to help "whip up" support for the party's preferred policies and keep lines of communication open between the party leadership and the rank-and-file membership. The majority leader and **whips** work hard to track members' intended votes—in a process called the whip count—because they want to bring to the floor only those bills that will pass; any defeat on the floor could weaken voter confidence in the majority party.[25]

The minority party in the House is the party that has the largest number of House members who are not in the majority party. The highest-ranking member of the minority party is the **House minority leader**, and his or her main responsibility is crafting the minority party's

Newt Gingrich (R-Ga.) served as Speaker of the House from 1995 to 1998, during a resurgence of Republican power. He was first elected to the House in 1978 after a career as a history professor, and he worked his way up the political ladder of the Republican Party. In 1994 he led the Republicans to majority power in the House by promising to enact a set of policy proposals set forth in the Contract with America. The Republicans retained majority control of Congress for the next twelve years.

House majority leader: *Leader of the majority party in the House and second in command to the Speaker.*

whips: *Legislators designated to count votes within the majority party or the minority party.*

House minority leader: *Leader of the minority party in the House.*

KEVIN DIETSCH/UPI /Landov

Nancy Pelosi (D-Calif.) was elected the first female Speaker of the House of Representatives in 2007. She was generally considered a strong Speaker because she exerted control over committee chairs and the conditions under which bills were considered on the House floor. Here she carries a large gavel to symbolize the accomplishment of enacting major health care reform in 2010.

Does the institutional structure of the House promote party dominance? Responsible lawmaking? What can be done about the structure of Congress?

president pro tempore: *Constitutional leader of the Senate.*

position on an issue and serving as the public spokesperson for the party. If the minority party is the same as the president's party, the House minority leader is also expected to garner support for the president's policies among minority party members. The House minority leader works with minority whips, who are responsible for keeping all the minority members in line with the party's public positions.

The challenge for the minority party in the House of Representatives is that it has very little institutional power; the majority party uses its numerical advantage to control committee and floor actions. Because of its institutional disadvantages, the minority party in the modern House of Representatives rarely has the power to stop majority party proposals from passing. Minority party members can vote no, but their real power lies in making speeches, issuing press releases, and stirring up grassroots opposition to majority party proposals.

The Senate

The Senate has always been a smaller chamber than the House because it is based on the number of states in the union and does not adjust according to population growth. Since 1959, when Hawaii and Alaska joined the union, the Senate has had one hundred members, and the magic number to secure majority control in the Senate has been fifty-one senators. Not until the 1910s did senators formally appoint individual senators to speak for them as majority and minority party leaders. However, the Senate majority leader has fewer formal powers to advance the party's agenda compared to the Speaker of the House. Because the Senate never grew to be as large and unwieldy as the House, the individual members have rarely seen the benefit of giving up power to party leaders to make the Senate run efficiently or enact the party's agenda.

President Pro Tempore.   Article 1, Section 3 of the Constitution states that the vice president shall be the president of the Senate, but that in his absence the Senate may appoint a **president pro tempore** (temporary president) to preside over the Senate. For most of the Senate's history, the vice president presided over the Senate, and his main functions were to recognize individual senators who wished to speak and to rule on which procedural motions were in order on the Senate floor. The vice president can also break a tie vote in the Senate, a power that can give the president's party control of the outcome on the floor. But in the 1950s the vice president became more active in executive branch business and less active in the Senate. Subsequently, the Senate began appointing the oldest serving member from the majority party as the president pro tempore to serve as the temporary presiding officer. The president pro tempore is closely advised by the **Senate parliamentarian**, who is responsible for administering the rules of the Senate.

Senate parliamentarian: *Official in charge of interpreting the rules of the Senate.*

Senate Party Leaders.

The majority party elects the **Senate majority leader**, but unlike the Speaker of the House, this position is not written into the Constitution. The job of the Senate majority leader is to make sure the Senate functions well enough to pass legislation. To accomplish that goal, the Senate majority leader tries to craft legislation as close to the preferred policies of his or her party as possible, necessitating a great deal of compromise. As the scholar Ralph Huitt describes it, the power of the Senate majority leader is predominantly the "power of persuasion."[26]

Senate majority leader: *Leader of the majority party in the Senate.*

Still, the Senate majority leader does have several formal powers. For instance, he or she is the official scheduler of Senate business and is always recognized first to speak on the Senate floor. Every senator has the right to speak on the Senate floor, but senators must speak one at a time. Being recognized first, before any other senator, gives the majority leader the power to control the floor and prevent any other senator from speaking. But because the Senate majority leader relies on the senators' voluntary cooperation to conduct the business of the Senate, there are limits on how tough he or she can be on Senate colleagues. If a Senate majority leader tries to bully senators, they might retaliate by constantly using their individual floor powers to delay or block key legislation.

Does the institutional structure of the Senate promote party dominance? Responsible lawmaking? Individual careers? What can be done about the structure of Congress?

The **Senate minority leader** is the leader of the minority party in the Senate and is expected to represent minority party senators in negotiations with the majority leader on which bills are brought to the Senate floor and under what circumstances. Similar to the House counterpart, the Senate minority leader's job is to organize minority party senators into a coherent group that can present viable alternatives to the majority party's proposals.

Senate minority leader: *Leader of the minority party in the Senate.*

The extended leadership structure of the Senate looks similar to that of the House (see Figure 12.3). It consists of an assistant majority leader, majority and minority whips, and conference chairs, all of whom are responsible for uniting the senators in their respective parties and crafting legislative proposals that can garner enough support to pass the Senate.

The Committee System

Almost all legislation that passes the House or Senate goes through a committee. The House and Senate are organized into separate committees to deal with the different issues that fall under the purview of the federal government. The party that has the majority in the entire House or Senate also has the majority of seats on each committee, and the **committee chair** is chosen from the majority party, with the approval of the party caucus. Typically, each House member or senator gives the party leadership a list of desired committee assignments, and the leadership assigns committee seats according to seniority and the availability of seats on specific committees.

committee chair: *Majority party member of a House or Senate committee who has been chosen to lead the committee and determine which issues the committee considers.*

The House and Senate each have several types of committees. A **standing committee** is a permanent committee with the power to write legislation and report it to the full chamber.

standing committee: *Permanent committee in the House or Senate.*

FIGURE 12.3 The Structure of Party Leadership in Congress. Each chamber of Congress has its own separate party leadership structure designed to help party leaders keep rank-and-file members united and accomplish the party's policy goals.

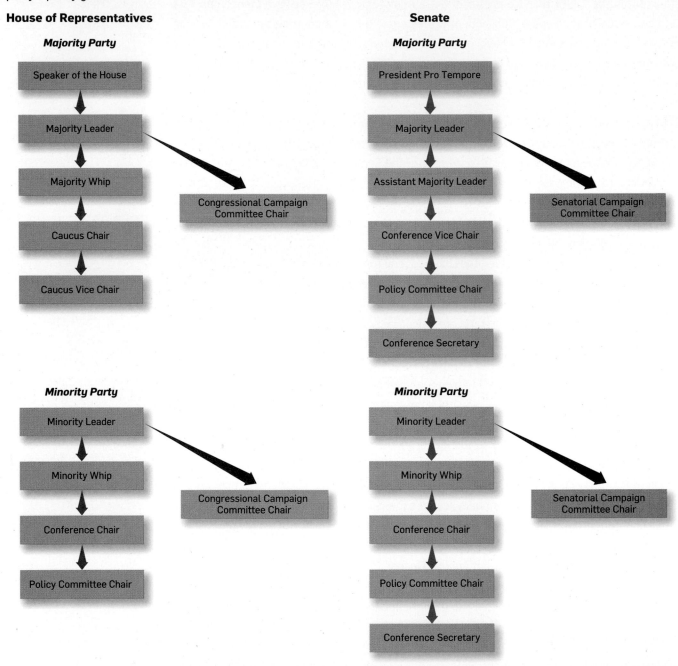

House of Representatives

Majority Party

Speaker of the House → Majority Leader → Majority Whip → Caucus Chair → Caucus Vice Chair

Majority Leader → Congressional Campaign Committee Chair

Minority Party

Minority Leader → Minority Whip → Conference Chair → Policy Committee Chair

Minority Leader → Congressional Campaign Committee Chair

Senate

Majority Party

President Pro Tempore → Majority Leader → Assistant Majority Leader → Conference Vice Chair → Policy Committee Chair → Conference Secretary

Majority Leader → Senatorial Campaign Committee Chair

Minority Party

Minority Leader → Minority Whip → Conference Chair → Policy Committee Chair → Conference Secretary

Minority Leader → Senatorial Campaign Committee Chair

---

select committee: *Committee in the House or Senate that has very limited powers over a specific issue.*

joint committee: *Committee that includes members of both the House and Senate.*

special committee: *Committee formed to address a specific issue area or controversy, typically for a defined period of time.*

Select committees, **joint committees**, and **special committees** are usually focused on a more narrow set of issues, such as aging or tax policy, but none has the same legislative clout and authority as a standing committee. In the House, there are twenty standing committees, and the average House committee has forty-three members. In the Senate, there are sixteen standing committees, and the average Senate committee has twenty members.[27] The committee system is the central hub of legislative activity in Congress. Committees hold hearings to consider members' bills, to conduct oversight of the executive branch, or to draw attention to a pressing issue. Committees also write the legislation that is eventually

TABLE 12.2 Standing Committees in Congress

House of Representatives (20 committees)	Senate (16 committees)
Agriculture	Agriculture, Nutrition, and Forestry
Appropriations	Appropriations
Armed Services	Armed Services
Financial Services	Banking, Housing, and Urban Affairs
Budget	Budget
Education and Labor	Health, Education, Labor, and Pensions
Energy and Commerce	Commerce, Science, and Transportation
	Energy and Natural Resources
	Environment and Public Works
Foreign Affairs	Foreign Relations
Homeland Security	Homeland Security and Governmental Affairs
Oversight and Government Reform	
House Administration	Rules and Administration Committee
Judiciary	Judiciary
Natural Resources	
Transportation and Infrastructure	
Rules	
Science and Technology	
Small Business	Small Business and Entrepreneurship
Standards of Official Conduct	
Veterans' Affairs	Veterans' Affairs
Ways and Means	Finance

Source: U.S. House of Representatives, www.house.gov; and Senate, www.senate.gov. See the committee membership lists.

considered on the House and Senate floors. Table 12.2 lists the standing committees in each chamber.

During committee hearings, committee members literally hear testimony on the content and impact of a bill from other members of Congress, executive branch officials, interest groups, businesses, state and local government officials, and citizens' groups. For the public, hearings are a direct gateway for influence on members of Congress because important information is conveyed in a public setting. Committee hearings serve five basic functions for members of Congress: They draw attention to a current problem or issue that needs public attention, inform committee members about the consequences of passing a specific bill, convey constituents' questions and concerns about an issue, exert oversight of the executive branch to determine whether congressional intent is being honored, and provide an arena in which individual members make speeches to attract media attention that is often used later in a campaign as evidence that the member is

markup: *Process where bills are literally marked up, or written by the members of the committee.*

Identify the functions of hearings. How do they serve as gateways?

ranking member: *Leader of the minority party members of the committee.*

doing his or her job. Committee chairs decide which bills receive hearings and which go on to **markup**, a meeting in which committee members write the version of the bill that they may send to the entire chamber for a vote. In both the hearing and markup process, the committee chair gives preference to the views of the majority party members of the committee.

Committee chairs have powerful roles. The chair is typically the majority party member who has the most seniority (longest time) on the committee. However, the Speaker or the Senate majority leader reserves the right to suggest a less senior member as chair if he or she believes that person will better serve the party's interests. In 2008 House Democrats replaced moderate John Dingell (D-Mich.) as chair of the House Energy and Commerce Committee with the more liberal Henry Waxman (D-Calif.), believing that Waxman more closely shared their views on a number of issues. The minority party leader on a committee is called the **ranking member** and is the member of the committee from the minority party with the greatest seniority.

Until 1994 there was no limit on the number of terms that committee chairs could serve. However, in 1995 the Republican majorities in the House and the Senate adopted six-year term limits on chairs. Limiting the tenure of committee chairs makes it harder for them to amass long-term individual power, so the Speaker retains more control over the committees' legislative agendas. In 2007, when the Democrats took the majority in the House and Senate, House Democrats retained term limits, but Senate Democrats did not; in January 2009 House Democrats eliminated term limits on committee chairs.[28]

When Congresswoman Velázquez became chair of the House Committee on Small Business, she scheduled hearings to draw attention to budget cuts in key programs that provided loans to owners of small businesses in low-income areas and helped minorities start their own businesses.[29] These types of federal programs are essential to Congresswoman Velázquez's constituents, and she used her position as committee chair to draw attention to their needs.

In general, when a bill is referred to a committee, it is assigned to a subcommittee, a smaller group of committee members who focus on a specific subset of the committee's issues. Subcommittees can consider legislation, but only the full committee can report a bill

Chairs of House and Senate committees hold hearings to explore key issues of concern to their constituents and to the nation as a whole. They also use their position to advance legislation they believe will accomplish their own and their party's policy goals. Here Nydia Velázquez chairs the House Committee on Small Business during a hearing on October 28, 2008.

AP Photo/Susan Walsh

to the chamber floor for consideration. In 1973 the House expanded the number of subcommittees and subcommittee chairs, largely as a result of the efforts of young representatives who wanted to enact policies that older committee chairs opposed. By creating more subcommittees, the House created smaller centers of power in which individual members could exert influence over the content of legislation.[30] The Senate did not make similar changes; each senator already had individual power and did not see the need to make changes in the committee structure.

Advocacy Caucuses

In addition to committees in the House and Senate, there are also **advocacy caucuses**, groups whose members have a common interest and work together to promote it. Members might have similar industries located in their districts and states, such as coal mining; or share a background, such as the Congressional Black Caucus or the Hispanic Caucus; or hold similar opinions on issues, such as abortion or land conservation. Members join an advocacy caucus because it gives them an opportunity to work closely with colleagues to represent specific interests and to draw attention to issues of concern to them and to their constituents. Many advocacy caucuses are bipartisan, that is, both Democrats and Republicans join as members. Advocacy caucuses are important to the interactions of Congress because they bring together members from different parties and regions who might not otherwise work closely with each other.[31]

How do advocacy caucuses counteract the role of parties in Congress? How can they be a gateway for citizen influence?

Nearly three hundred advocacy caucuses are registered with the Committee on House Administration. In contrast, the Senate has only one official caucus, on International Narcotics Control. However, the Senate has a number of informal caucuses, such as the Senate Air Force Caucus and the Senate Steel Caucus, with members from both parties. The latter is a counterpart to the Congressional Steel Caucus in the House, a long-standing and large bipartisan caucus.

Advocacy caucuses have no formal legislative power, but they can be influential on a bill, especially in the House, because they represent a bloc of members who could vote together in support or opposition. As an alternative to joining a caucus, senators can join together in a temporary coalition and call a press conference to draw attention to the group, industry, or issue that unites them. Senators can also join a congressional caucus even though it is lodged in the House. When he was a senator from Illinois (2005–2008), Barack Obama joined the Congressional Black Caucus.

The Lawmaking Process

In this section, we examine the lawmaking process. The process by which a policy proposal becomes a bill and then a law is long and winding, and the Framers designed it deliberately to ensure that laws were reasonable and well thought out. The gates against passage are almost too successful. In the 110th Congress (2007–2008), for example, members introduced 7,271 public bills in the House of Representatives and 3,676 public bills in the Senate. Of the total of 10,947 public bills, Congress enacted only 334—or 3 percent—into law.[32] It requires compromise and cooperation for a bill to become a law. For an overview of the process, see Figure 12.4.

FIGURE 12.4 How a Bill Becomes a Law.

When the president signs the bill or allows it to become law without his signature, or if Congress overrides a presidential veto, the bill becomes law.

The House and Senate bills are reconciled to produce one bill, which is sent to the president.

House of Representatives

12. House votes to pass or defeat the bill.

11. If the House accepts the rule, the bill is debated, and amendments may be offered.

10. Members of the House vote to adopt or reject the rule.

9. Rules Committee writes the rule on the bill, which determines what amendments, if any, can be offered when the bill is considered on the House floor.

8. Committee votes to recommend the bill to the full House, and the bill is sent to the House Rules Committee (the gatekeeper).

7. Full committee marks up the bill.

6. Full committee may hold hearings on the bill.

5. Subcommittee reports the bill to the full committee.

4. Subcommittee holds a markup session on the bill.

3. Subcommittee holds hearings on the bill.

2. Bill is referred by the Speaker of the House to a committee and subcommittee.

1. Bill is introduced by a House member on the House floor.

Senate

11. Senate votes to pass or defeat the bill.

10. Senators may offer amendments to the bill and debate the bill.

9. Majority leader crafts a unanimous consent agreement outlining which amendments will be offered and how long debate will continue; if unanimous consent is not achieved, there is unlimited debate on the bill unless cloture is invoked.

8. Majority leader brings up the bill on the Senate floor.

7. Bill is placed on the Senate legislative calendar.

6. Full committee holds a markup session and recommends the bill to the Senate.

5. Full committee may hold hearings on the bill.

4. Subcommittee may hold hearings on the bill; depending on the committee, the subcommittee may or may not mark up the bill.

3. Committee may refer the bill to a subcommittee.

2. Bill is referred to a committee by the Senate parliamentarian.

1. Bill is introduced by a senator on the Senate floor.

Do the procedural rules of the House and Senate serve as gates or gateways to legislation? Why would there be gates that prevent Congress from fulfilling its fundamental responsibility to pass laws?

The Procedural Rules of the House and Senate

Just as the roles of political parties and leaders differ in the House and Senate, so do the internal rules of these chambers. Over time, House and Senate members have adopted different procedures for considering legislation, and these procedures can make compromise between the two chambers more difficult.

The House Committee on Rules.

To proceed from committee to the House floor, all bills must pass through the **House Rules Committee**. Because the House is so large, bills cannot proceed to the floor from committee unprotected; otherwise, the number of **legislative amendments** that could be offered by the 435 members of the House would overwhelm lawmaking.

The Rules Committee maintains control before the bill goes to the floor by issuing a **rule** dictating how many amendments may be considered. A closed rule means that no amendments may be offered; a modified closed rule allows a few amendments; and an open rule, as its name suggests, allows any number of amendments. The most typical rule is a modified closed rule, which allows the minority party to offer at least one alternative to the bill supported by the majority party. The rule is voted on by all members of the House; if it is approved, debate on the bill begins. If the rule is defeated, the bill is returned to the House Rules Committee or the originating committee for further consideration.

The majority party has learned over time how to use the Rules Committee to maintain policy advantages over the minority party. The majority party uses its numerical advantage on the Rules Committee (9–4 in the 111th Congress) to structure floor debate to limit the minority party's opportunity to amend or change a bill. The Speaker appoints all the majority party members to the Rules Committee, and they are expected to use their powers to advance the party's preferred version of a bill.

Agenda-Setting Tools in the Senate.

The Senate does not have a gatekeeper committee like the Committee on Rules in the House, and all senators have the power to try to amend legislation on the floor. The tool that they use is Rule XIX of the Standing Rules of the Senate, which grants senators the right to speak on the Senate floor. Over time, senators have used this right to make speeches, offer amendments to bills, object to consideration of a bill on the floor, or engage in filibusters, extended debates whose purpose is to delay or even prevent the passage of bills.[33] All senators in the majority and the minority parties can use the **filibuster**. Throughout Senate history, a wide range of bills, from civil rights legislation to product liability legislation, have been delayed or defeated by filibusters.[34]

The only way to stop a filibuster is by invoking **cloture**, a motion to end debate that requires a supermajority of sixty votes to pass. As the Democrats in the 111th Congress realized, this supermajority is hard to achieve, even when the majority party technically has sixty members. Once cloture has been invoked on a bill, no more than thirty additional hours of debate are permitted. All amendments must be germane to the bill's issues, and a time for a final vote is set. Figure 12.5 illustrates the variation in the number of cloture motions in the Senate over time.

In addition, Senate rules no longer require those seeking to block a bill to speak continuously on the floor. Senators who oppose a bill can merely state their intention to filibuster,

House Rules Committee: *Gatekeeping committee that sets the guidelines for debating, changing, and voting on a bill on the floor.*

legislative amendment: *In Congress, a proposed change to a bill.*

rule: *Guidelines issued by the House Rules Committee that determine how many amendments may be considered for each bill.*

filibuster: *Tactic of extended speech designed to delay or block passage of a bill in the Senate.*

Is the filibuster a legitimate means of protecting minority rights?

cloture: *Vote that can stop a filibuster and bring debate on a bill to end.*

Strom Thurmond Collection, Clemson University

On August 29, 1957, Strom Thurmond (D.-S.C.; later became a Republican) set the record for the longest individual filibuster in Senate history—twenty-four hours and eighteen minutes. Despite the effort, his filibuster served only to delay, not to kill, the Civil Rights Act of 1957, which ultimately passed.

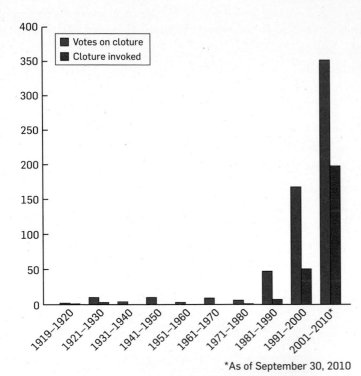

*As of September 30, 2010

FIGURE 12.5 Senate Action on Cloture Motions, 1919–2010.
Source: United States Senate, www.senate.gov.

unanimous consent agreement: *Agreement among all one hundred senators on how a bill or presidential nomination will be debated, changed, and voted on in the Senate.*

hold: *Power available to a senator to prevent the unanimous consent that allows a bill or presidential nomination to come to the Senate floor, which can be broken by invoking cloture (sixty votes).*

and that will be sufficient to block the bill from consideration on the floor. Senators also use the threat of a filibuster to block the president's judicial nominations at all levels, a practice that has come under increasing scrutiny. Filibusters of this type are an expression of partisanship or ideology, and they can disrupt the operation of the federal courts.[35] To counteract the filibuster in recent years, the Senate has resorted to a two-track system in which a bill that is being filibustered can be set aside to allow the Senate to proceed to other bills. But even with this two-track system, the filibuster has imposed substantial costs on the Senate, both in terms of the legislation that has failed to pass and the legislation that could not be brought to the floor.

Some scholars have argued that the filibuster has been used too frequently as a way of blocking action on important public policies and is not a legitimate democratic instrument of power.[36] Others argue that filibustering is a responsive and effective means of representation in Congress; if there is intense opposition to a bill in a senator's state, or from a minority of voters nationwide, the senator may consider it a responsibility to block the bill's passage.[37]

Without a gatekeeper like the House Committee on Rules and with the constant threat of a filibuster, there are few restrictions on a bill when it comes to the Senate floor. When the Senate majority leader wishes to bring a bill up for consideration, he or she must ask unanimous consent of every senator. Consequently, the Senate typically operates under **unanimous consent agreements** to establish guidelines for debating a bill. Senators strike a deal about how a bill will be debated on the Senate floor, how and when amendments will be offered, how much time will be allocated to debate and vote on amendments, and at what time on what date the final vote on the complete bill will take place. Senators have accepted this form of limitation on their rights to amend or block a bill because it requires their consent and enables the Senate to move forward and pass key legislation.

Nevertheless, a senator can object to a unanimous consent request to bring a bill to the Senate floor in a practice known as a **hold**. A hold is a less drastic measure than a filibuster, but it can be used by any senator to delay a bill for a minimum of twenty-four hours. The majority leader can circumvent a hold by requesting a vote on cloture; if sixty senators agree, the Senate proceeds to consider the bill. Typically, senators hold up bills to extract concessions from Senate leaders or from the administration on the legislation being considered. They also use the hold to draw increased attention to a bill or to delay a presidential nominee whom they oppose, in the hope that public opposition will develop. Twenty-four hours may not seem like a long time, but in an age of 24-7 media and the Internet, public impressions can form quickly. In March 2010, Senator Jim Bunning (R-Ky.) used his power to object to unanimous consent to delay a bill that would have extended benefits to unemployed workers. Although he explained that he was doing so to avoid increased deficit spending, the bill was perceived by members of both parties to be vital; Senate leaders managed to bring sufficient public pressure to bear on Bunning, and he dropped his objection.

Legislative Proposals

The lawmaking process starts with an idea. Ideas for legislation can come from a number of sources, including constituents, interest groups, local or national newspaper stories, state or local governments, staff members, and the members' own personal interests.[38] When an idea is agreed upon, the House or Senate member's staff consults with the Office of Legislative Counsel, which turns the general outlines of a bill into the technical language that will alter the U.S. Code, the set of federal laws that governs the United States. After approving the final legal language of a bill, the member introduces the bill into the respective chamber (House or Senate), an action known as **bill sponsorship**. Once a bill is introduced, other members can sign on to be cosponsors (sponsorship of legislation is discussed in more detail later in this chapter). In reality, many freestanding bills that are introduced separately are later incorporated into larger **omnibus bills** that are passed by Congress. Combining bills into omnibus legislation can be useful, especially in periods of divided government. These big bills allow Congress to pass numerous provisions that might not pass if each was presented separately.[39]

Committee Action

After a member introduces a bill, it is referred to one or more committees or subcommittees that have jurisdiction over its subject matter. The first step in getting the bill enacted into law is to secure a hearing on a bill in subcommittee or full committee. In general, a committee tends to act first on bills that are sponsored by the chair of the committee, then on those sponsored by the subcommittee chairs, and last on bills sponsored by regular members of the committee. If the sponsor is not on the committee to which the bill is assigned, it is much harder to get action on the bill. This arrangement also makes sense because committee members are more likely to have expertise on the issues covered by the committee than are other legislators, so their bills are taken more seriously by their fellow committee members.[40] In rare cases, however, as a result of intense interest group lobbying or media pressure, a committee might hold a hearing on a bill sponsored by someone who is not a committee member, but the committee typically drafts its own bill to address the same issue.

After the hearings, the committee may move to the markup. At this point, the stakes intensify in terms of what the bill will ultimately look like, so the stakeholders in the policy process try to exert influence. Once the full committee approves a bill, it and an accompanying committee report are sent to the full House or Senate for consideration by all members.

Floor Action and the Vote

When a bill is sent to the full House or Senate—commonly known as "going to the floor"—all the members of the chamber gather to debate and vote on it. Debate takes different forms in each chamber. In the House, it is heavily structured, and most members are allowed no more than five minutes to speak on a measure, leaving almost no time for actual deliberation among members. But in the Senate, as noted earlier, there are few limits on the time allowed for members to speak on an issue on the floor. If the Senate is operating under a unanimous consent agreement or cloture, time is limited; otherwise, senators can make speeches and even engage in active debate on an issue for much longer than their House counterparts. Unfortunately for the current political system, real debate rarely occurs on the floor; instead,

How can you as a citizen influence legislation in Congress?

How do omnibus bills make accountability more difficult?

bill sponsorship: *Act of introducing a bill on the House or Senate floor.*

omnibus bill: *One very large bill that encompasses many separate bills.*

What is the purpose of floor debate? Does it change minds and votes?

roll call vote: *Vote that a House or Senate member casts on a bill or amendment when his or her name is called.*

party-line votes: *Voting in Congress according to party position, so that a majority of one party votes against a majority of the other party.*

message politics: *Strategy of framing choices on legislation so as to push members into casting votes that can later be used against them in campaigns.*

conference committee: *Temporary committee created after a bill passes the House and the Senate to resolve any differences in the provisions of the bills so a single bill can be sent to the president.*

representatives and senators use their opportunity to speak to make partisan speeches or to direct their remarks to their constituents back home.

During a **roll call vote**, the clerks of the House or Senate call the name of each member, who registers his or her vote electronically. Members cast up or down votes on legislation (to pass or reject), to table (set aside) legislation, or to approve a motion to recommit (send it back to committee with instructions to rewrite it). In addition to individually recorded votes, general voice votes can be taken when a consensus exists and there is no perceived need to record each member's vote. A roll call vote is the most fundamental way that a member of Congress represents his or her constituents and is therefore a key gateway for citizen influence in the legislative process.

Scholars have long characterized roll call voting by partisan dimension and by ideological or spatial dimension, because in the past both the Democratic and Republican parties contained both liberals and conservatives.[41] Currently, the vast majority of Democratic members are liberal, and the vast majority of Republican members are conservative. Consequently, scholars now can examine roll call voting through both the partisan and ideological lens simultaneously. They confirm that most votes in the House and Senate are **party-line votes**, in which a majority of one party votes yes on a bill and a majority of the other party votes no. In the 110th Congress, for example, 89 percent of House votes and 84 percent of Senate votes were party-line votes.[42] In today's Congress, leaders frame the content of bills and the choices for roll call votes along the lines of party platforms and ideology. Essentially, they are engaging in **message politics**, designing legislation to push members into casting votes that may later be used in campaigns against them.[43] This framework reflects a responsible parties system (see Chapters 6 and 9) in which voters can clearly distinguish Democratic and Republican legislative policy goals. Although the increased emphasis on partisanship makes it easier for citizens to more clearly hold Congress accountable, it decreases the likelihood of bipartisan cooperation and makes it more difficult to pass legislation that addresses pressing needs of citizens on an equal basis.

Conference Committee

For a bill to become law, the House and Senate have to pass an identically worded version of it to send to the president for signature. The last stage in the congressional legislative process takes place when the House and Senate meet in **conference committee** to resolve any differences in the versions that passed each chamber. The Speaker of the House and the Senate majority leader typically appoint the chairs and ranking members from the committees that originated the bills, plus other members who have been active on the bill. If the bill is very important to the party leaders, they also have the power to appoint themselves to the committee, though this does not happen often. If the conferees are successful, the conference committee issues a conference report that must be voted on by the entire House and Senate. Because the conference report represents the end of the negotiation process between the two chambers, members cannot offer amendments to change it. However, if a majority of members of the House or Senate are displeased with the final results of the conference, they can defeat the report outright or vote to instruct the conference committee to revise the agreement.

In the past two decades, Congress has also used alternative ways of constructing a compromise between versions of House and Senate bills. When a bill involves the work of several

TABLE 12.3 Federal Deficits and the National Debt (in billions of dollars), 1970–2009

Year	Revenues	Outlays	Total Deficit	National Debt
1970	192.8	195.6	−2.8	283.2
1975	279.1	332.3	−53.2	394.7
1980	517.1	590.9	−73.8	711.9
1985	734.0	946.3	−212.3	1,507.3
1990	1,032.0	1,253.0	−221.0	2,411.6
1995	1,351.8	1,515.8	−164.0	3,604.4
2000	2,025.2	1,789.0	236.2	3,409.8
2005	2,153.6	2,472.0	−318.3	4,592.2
2009	2,104.6	3,518.2	−1,413.6	7,544.0

Source: Congressional Budget Office, January 24, 2010, www.cbo.gov.

committees, party leaders have sometimes chosen not to form an official conference committee but instead take on the responsibility of producing a final bill themselves. In choosing this path, they concentrate power in the hands of fewer members of Congress than in the traditional conference committee system.[44] Although this alternative provides a more streamlined way of legislating, it also acts as a gate against input from committee members who wish to represent their constituents' views on the final version of the bill.

The Budget Process and Reconciliation

Although the federal government tries to spend about as much money as it takes in from revenues, it does not typically succeed. Instead, the federal government usually runs a budget **deficit**, which requires it to borrow money to meet all its obligations (see Table 12.3 and Figure 12.6). Although the process is complex, essentially this means that the federal government pays interest on outstanding loans, and the loans and interest that accumulate over time constitute the **national debt**.

The modern Congress operates under a budget process created in the Congressional Budget and Impoundment Control Act of 1974, which was enacted to give Congress more power over the federal budget.[45] It was passed at time of relatively low deficits, but many new government programs were being implemented

federal deficit: *Difference between the amount of money the federal government spends in outlays and the amount of money it receives from revenues.*

national debt: *Sum of loans and interest that the federal government has accrued over time to pay for the federal deficit.*

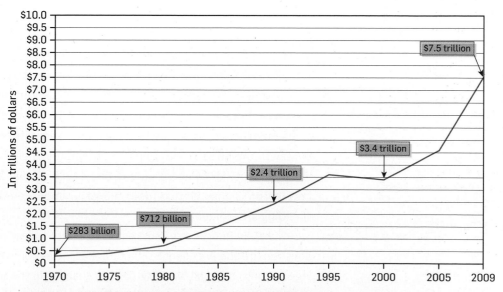

FIGURE 12.6 The National Debt, 1970–2009. Since 1970 the federal government has operated under a budget deficit in most years, except between 1998 and 2000, when it ran a surplus. The U.S. government borrows money, for which it pays interest, to fill the gap between what it takes in and what it spends. The total outstanding loan balance is the national debt.
Source: Congressional Budget Office.

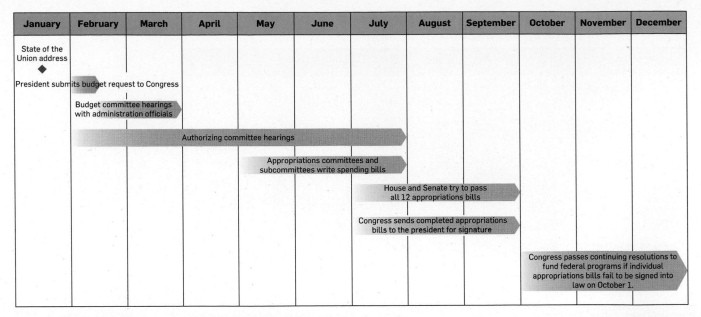

January	February	March	April	May	June	July	August	September	October	November	December

State of the Union address ◆

President submits budget request to Congress

Budget committee hearings with administration officials

Authorizing committee hearings

Appropriations committees and subcommittees write spending bills

House and Senate try to pass all 12 appropriations bills

Congress sends completed appropriations bills to the president for signature

Congress passes continuing resolutions to fund federal programs if individual appropriations bills fail to be signed into law on October 1.

FIGURE 12.7 The Congressional Budget Timeline. Congress produces its own blueprint for the federal budget to serve as an alternative to the president's budget and to guide the appropriations process. If necessary, Congress also produces a reconciliation bill to make changes to tax and entitlement programs.
Source: Based on the Budget and Impoundment Control Act of 1974, Title III, Section 300 (Washington D.C.: Government Printing Office, 1987), 72.

Congressional Budget Office: *Estimates the cost of policy proposals for Congress.*

concurrent budget resolution: *Congressional blueprint outlining general amounts of funds that can be spent on federal program.*

continuing resolution: *Measure passed to fund federal programs when the appropriations process has not been completed by September 30, the end of the fiscal year.*

Does the congressional budget process help or hurt deficit reduction efforts?

reconciliation: *A measure used to bring all bills that contain changes in the tax code or entitlement programs in line with the congressional budget.*

entitlement programs: *Federal programs, such as Social Security, Medicare, and Medicaid, that pay out benefits to individuals based on a specified set of eligibility criteria.*

and government financial obligations were steadily rising. The act created the House and Senate Budget Committees and the **Congressional Budget Office** so that Congress could construct its own budget blueprint as an alternative to the president's annual budget.

The federal government's fiscal year begins on October 1 and ends on September 30, and the key aspect of the budget process (see Figure 12.7) is that the congressional budget, known as the **concurrent budget resolution**, is supposed to be approved by both chambers by April 15. Because the budget resolution does not have the force of law, it is not sent to the president for his signature. Rather it serves as general instructions to congressional committees about how much money can be allocated for federal programs in the fiscal year. The authorizing committees take this blueprint into account when they reauthorize existing programs or create new ones, and the appropriations committees in the House and Senate use it to allocate funds in twelve separate bills. They typically begin their work in May in the hope of enacting all appropriations bills by September 30. If Congress and the president fail to agree on any one of the twelve appropriations bills, a **continuing resolution** is enacted that funds the government temporarily while disagreements about spending are worked out.

The 1974 Budget Act also created a parallel budget bill, known as **reconciliation**, which does require the president's signature. Reconciliation was specifically designed as umbrella legislation to bring all bills that contain changes in the tax code or entitlement programs in line with the congressional budget. **Entitlement programs**, such as Social Security, Medicare, and Medicaid, are considered mandatory because they are federal programs that pay out benefits to individuals based on a specified set of eligibility criteria. When Congress wishes to make a change to one of these programs, it must pass a reconciliation bill. The reconciliation bill has special procedural protections in the Senate: It cannot be filibustered, and it can be debated for no more than twenty hours. A bill that cannot be filibustered was a tempting target for those who wanted to add non-budget-related provisions. Consequently, in 1985 the budget process was modified to include the Byrd rule, which required that reconciliation be used only to reduce the federal deficit, which at the time was $212.3 billion.[46] In subsequent years, the Byrd rule has been interpreted to mean that all provisions of reconciliation must be directly related to the budget.[47]

Despite the Byrd rule, Congress has found ways to use the reconciliation process to pass controversial legislation. Most recently, the Democratic majority in Congress used it to pass part of its comprehensive health care reform, which we discuss below. Both Democrats and Republicans have used the reconciliation process to go beyond changes in the tax code, or to balance the budget, on issues ranging from welfare reform to children's health insurance.[48]

Presidential Signature or Veto, and the Veto Override

In the last step in the legislative process, the bill is sent to the president for his approval or rejection. A president can actively reject, or **veto**, a bill. If Congress will be going out of session within ten days, the president can wait for the session to end and simply not sign the bill, a practice known as a **pocket veto**. If Congress remains in session and the president neither vetoes the bill nor signs it, the bill becomes law (see Chapter 13 for more discussion of the presidential use of the veto power).

The veto is a powerful balancing tool for the president against the overreach of Congress; but the Framers also gave Congress the **override**, the power to overturn a presidential veto with a two-thirds vote in each chamber. When the president vetoes a bill, it is returned to the chamber from which it originated; if two-thirds of the members of that chamber vote to override the veto, it is sent to the other chamber for a vote. A two-thirds vote by each chamber, rather than just a majority vote, is required for an override because the Framers wanted to enable the president to block a bill passed by Congress if he does not believe that it is in the best interest of the nation as a whole. The president can use the veto either to prevent a bill from becoming law or to pressure Congress into making changes that are closer to his policies.[49] In the 110th Congress (2007–2008), President George W. Bush (2001–2009) vetoed nine bills, and Congress overrode four of them.[50]

veto: *Authority of the president to block legislation passed by Congress. Congress can override a veto by a two-thirds majority in each chamber.*

pocket veto: *Automatic veto that occurs when Congress goes out of session within ten days of submitting a bill to the president and the president has not signed it.*

override: *Congress's power to overturn a presidential veto with a two-thirds vote in each chamber.*

Why did the Framers give Congress the final say in whether a bill should become a law?

The Member of Congress at Work

The cardinal rule of succeeding in the House or Senate is simple: Never forget where you came from. Representative Nydia Velázquez has shown how a member tries to balance the competing demands of legislating with the core responsibility of serving constituents. The following sections describe exactly what the job of a House or Senate member entails.

Offices and Staff

For all newly elected members in the House and Senate, the first steps are to set up an office and hire staff members. In the House, each representative receives about the same amount of money for office operations. In the Senate, the office budget is determined by the population size of the senator's home state, based on the reasoning that senators from larger states have more constituents and more issues to deal with than their smaller-state colleagues. Most members bring some of their campaign workers to Washington to work on their staffs and try to hire people from their districts or states. New members of Congress also seek out individuals with prior Capitol Hill experience to help orient them to their new surroundings and provide specific issue expertise.

Generally, a member of Congress's Washington office has a chief of staff who oversees the entire office, a scheduler who makes the member's appointments, a press secretary who handles all interactions with the media, and a legislative director who oversees the member's legislative work. In addition, legislative assistants handle specific issues, and legislative correspondents are responsible for answering constituent mail.

House and Senate members aim to be responsive to constituents, and that means providing prompt and extensive **constituent services**. To do so, they establish district offices in the congressional district for representatives, and around the state for senators. These offices help constituents navigate federal agencies if they have difficulty, for example, getting a Social Security check or a passport, and advise constituents on how to win federal contracts. Specific requests for help are assigned to caseworkers. These local offices serve as direct and important links between voters and members of Congress and affect both accountability and responsiveness.[51]

constituent services:
Individualized services performed by a member of Congress for a constituent, such as help with a passport, a Social Security problem, or any other issue that requires federal government involvement.

Have you ever contacted your representative or senators? If so, was it to express an opinion or to ask for help?

Legislative Responsibilities

A successful legislator typically fulfills four responsibilities: securing desired committee assignments and performing committee work, sponsoring and cosponsoring bills, casting votes, and obtaining federal funds for the district or state.

Committee Work. Just before the start of each new Congress, members are asked which committees they would like to join, and party leaders try to accommodate their wishes, although freshman members rarely get their most favored committees immediately. Freshman members choose committee assignments based on the needs of their district or state, their professional background, and their personal experience. A House member from Oregon might seek a seat on the House Natural Resources Committee because that committee oversees logging and other land use issues that are important to constituents. A senator from Iowa might seek membership on the Senate Agriculture, Nutrition, and Forestry Committee because farming is a key economic interest in that state. However, a new senator has to accommodate his or her committee assignment wish list to the reality of the existing committee assignments of the senior senator from the state. All members of the House and Senate try to put themselves in the best possible institutional position to address issues that matter to their constituents.

Committee work consists of attending hearings and participating in markups as well as initiating ideas for legislation for consideration by the committee. Committee members also meet with interest groups, businesses, and citizens' groups that are specifically concerned about bills to be considered in the committee. The extent to which members participate actively in committee business varies according to the local concerns of their constituents, their personal interests, and whether the committee might provide an opportunity for political advancement.[52]

Committees themselves provide different gateways for members to serve their constituents and advance their careers. For example, the Appropriations Committee and the Environment and Public Works Committee distribute federal funds for a wide range of programs and projects, and thereby provide an opportunity for members to influence how these funds are spent. Serving on other committees, such as the Armed Services Committee, can provide members with credentials in the area of defense policy, which can be useful if they represent areas with high military employment or envision themselves running for president one day.

Bill Sponsorship. Members can sponsor a bill by themselves, or they can ask colleagues to cosponsor bills with them; the higher the number of cosponsors, the greater the show of support for the bill. Members sponsor and cosponsor bills for three important reasons: First, bill sponsorship is an effective tool for giving voters in a district or state a voice in the federal policy-making system. Second, it is a means of staking out specific territory that members can claim as their area of expertise and can be a means of fulfilling campaign promises.[53] Third, it attracts the attention of the media, relevant interest groups, and the press, and thereby can help House and Senate members build their reputations as legislators.

One bill that accomplishes all three goals is H.R. 44, the Stabilizing Affordable Housing for the Future Act, which Congresswoman Velázquez sponsored and introduced on January 4, 2007. This bill proposed an increase in the amount of federally sponsored affordable housing available to citizens with low incomes; it would have directly benefited Velázquez's constituents by equalizing the opportunity for finding affordable housing. The bill fell directly under the jurisdiction of the Committee on Small Business that Velázquez chaired. Although it did not pass, it drew media attention to the national problem of a shortage of affordable housing.

Roll Call Votes. Each representative and senator is expected to cast a roll call vote on the bills and amendments that reach the floor of the House and Senate. In the House alone, members cast 1,876 roll call votes during the 110th Congress.[54] Given the large number of roll call votes, voters have difficulty identifying how their members of Congress voted on bills that affect them directly. Because most members of Congress vote the party line, party identification can be helpful in holding members accountable for their roll call votes. If members do not vote the party line, they risk losing the support of party voters in their district or state. However, most members will not vote for a measure that goes against their constituents' opinion or interests. For this reason, majority party leaders try to construct bills that will benefit the constituents of the members of their party.

Federal Funds. Most members of Congress try to secure federal funds for their districts and states. The effort to carve out some piece of the federal financial pie is typically referred to as "bringing home the bacon" or pork barrel spending, and it can work through **funding formulas** for federal programs or **earmarks**, which are narrowly defined federally funded projects.[55] Federal funds can be used to rebuild a highway, build a fairground, fund a local orchestra, construct a research center on the effects of pig odor, and even support a water taxi service in Connecticut.[56] Over the past decade, spending on earmarks has

funding formula: *Formula written into law by Congress that determines how funds will be distributed in a federal program.*

earmark: *Federal dollars devoted specifically to a local project in a congressional district or state.*

Federal funds for local projects are often denounced as "pork." How does pork figure in your decision to vote for or against an incumbent?

franking privilege: *Special free mail that a House or Senate member can use to send letters to constituents.*

What communications have you received from your representative and senators? Have they arrived in the mail or via the Internet?

home style: *The way incumbents portray themselves to constituents.*

increased tenfold. Although the Democrats promised to cut spending on earmarks when they won control of Congress in 2007, two years later, $19.1 billion was authorized to fund 10,160 earmarks.[57] Simply put, spending on these programs has not declined in the dramatic way that the Democrats claimed it would under their watch.

Although the purposes of earmarks always sound useful, they can range in price from $100,000 to $200 million and can prove to be wasteful. One of the most infamous earmarks in recent years was the so-called bridge to nowhere in Alaska championed by the late Senator Theodore (Ted) Stevens (R-Alaska), when he was chair of the Senate Appropriations Committee. A combination of conservative members of Congress and public watchdog groups raised media awareness about the enormous cost of this bridge, and pointed to the fact that it would have served a few thousand people at most. In response, the House and Senate backtracked and directed the state of Alaska to spend the money that was allocated for the bridge on other, more necessary transportation projects.[58]

Despite the conflict over the earmark and federal funding process generally, one could argue that obtaining federal dollars for the district is a form of responsiveness to the local needs of voters. Voters are taxpayers, and members of Congress are simply seeking to bring some of that tax money back home in a directed fashion. On the other hand, many of the projects are not necessary to most voters, and they create waste and inefficiency that can make the federal government less effective.

Carl Oberman www.TexPic.net

Pete Sessions is a Republican congressman from Texas representing the 32nd District, which includes Dallas. Sessions was elected in 1996 and has become influential in the House Republican Party organization. He has continued to balance his district work with his Washington work. Here he meets with his constituents back home in a town meeting, August 2009.

Communication with Constituents

Congressional representation depends on good communication between constituents and their representatives and senators. It is important to remember that members of Congress have two distinct places of work: Washington D.C., and their home district or state.

In Washington, members take advantage of technological innovations, such as e-mail and the Internet, to stay in touch with their constituents. Before e-mail and the Internet, members used the **franking privilege**, which is free mail service, to respond to constituent letters and to send quarterly newsletters as updates on their activities. Much of that hard-mail correspondence has disappeared, and today members of Congress e-mail their newsletters and use Facebook and Twitter to transmit information about their activities to constituents.

To help members stay in touch with their constituents, the federal government pays for House and Senate members to return home to their districts or states approximately thirty-three times a year. These trips home are crucial for building bonds with voters, and members make sure to meet with individuals, speak to local interest groups, attend local parades and business openings, and attract local media coverage.

Cultivating direct links with constituents and making a good impression on them is what the political scientist Richard Fenno calls **home style**, or the way members portray themselves to constituents.[59] Members can choose to emphasize their local work for constituents, or they can emphasize their influence on national policy; some try to do both. Members can be very good at giving charismatic speeches, or they can be quiet, unassuming workers; successful members adapt their home style to the expectations and customs of constituents.

The Next Election

As political scientist David Mayhew explains, members of Congress look to the next election.[60] Elections are the means by which constituents express approval or disapproval of the job members of Congress are doing, and they are the fundamental tool that voters use to hold their members accountable for individual legislative work and the collective performance of their party in office. House members have only two years to show that they can manage to gain influence in the House and be responsive to local concerns at the same time. Senators have six years, but a senator has to share the job with another senator from the same state and compete for voter support, media attention, committee assignments, and the chance to be the go-to senator on key issues affecting the state. Because Senate elections are staggered, voters in a state elect each senator separately, at different times. A newly elected senator almost always finds that the senior colleague is established on key committees and well positioned on issues that are important to the state. Junior senators, therefore, are left to scramble for the leftovers and to establish good reputations among constituents in the shadows of their senior colleagues.[61]

The fact is that most **incumbents** in the House and Senate win reelection; in 2008, 94 percent of all House incumbents and 84 percent of all Senate incumbents won reelection.[62] Most of this textbook's discussion of congressional elections is contained in Chapter 10 (Elections and Campaigns); in this section, we focus on the incumbency advantage and reelection. Congressional campaigns are typically divided into two categories: those with an incumbent seeking reelection, and those with open seats, where no incumbent is seeking reelection. In elections in which an incumbent is running, the contest becomes an evaluation of the job he or she has done in office compared to what the **challenger** promises to do if elected. Incumbents have major advantages because they have already won at least one election in the district, they are likely to have moderate name recognition, and they have the power of their congressional office to provide services to constituents.

Reelection is far from automatic, however. Part of the incumbent advantage rests on incumbents' efforts to use all their resources to serve their constituents responsively; successful incumbents have a strong motivation to perform well so that they will be reelected. Many members come from areas in which they grew up or have lived a long time, so they have a genuine desire to help constituents, who could be their neighbors or former schoolmates. Incumbents also have an electoral incentive to work on behalf of constituents to earn high approval ratings. Moreover, if incumbents have any ambition to run for another political office in their state, such as governor, they want to make sure constituents have a good impression of them.

Members' concern for their local districts or states can be one of the biggest gates standing in the way of a productive Congress, and frequently the party works to overcome division among its members. Parties provide a collective set of policy goals that will benefit or appeal to party members at the local level. For a member of Congress, however, tying electoral fortunes to the political party can be risky if the majority party falls out of favor with voters

incumbent: *Occupant of elected office.*

challenger: *Candidate who runs against an incumbent.*

In 2010 did you vote for the incumbent or challenger in your district? What was the basis for your decision?

who can hold it accountable for policy outcomes. In 1994 and 2006 large numbers of incumbents from both major parties lost their seats in the House and Senate, and party control of the chambers changed hands as a result; in 2010 the Democrats lost more than sixty seats and majority control of the House but retained a slim majority in the Senate. Although elections with such significant changes are infrequent, they are powerful reminders that incumbents must constantly balance the needs of their constituents with the ideas of their party and stay responsive, or risk losing their bids for reelection.

Congress and Public Policy: Health Care

A central challenge to the institution of Congress in carrying out its fundamental responsibility of lawmaking is to find a way to balance the individual interests of its members with the collective need of the nation. The party leaders and committee chairs in each chamber try to write legislation that will attract the support of enough rank-and-file members to pass. At the same time, Congress considers opinions from organized interest groups and, of course, the president, whose approval is necessary to enact laws. The heath care reform efforts in the 111th Congress reflect the challenges of congressional policy making precisely because the proposal was national in scope but faced opposition from members' constituencies all over the country.

The American Health Care System

Essentially, the United States has a mixture of private and public health care insurance systems. Most Americans receive health insurance through their employment or purchase it independently from private insurance companies. People over the age of 65 are covered by Medicare, a federally funded health insurance program, and very-low-income people are covered by Medicaid, a jointly funded health insurance program offered by the federal, state, and local governments.[63] However, in 2008 approximately 45 million Americans did not have access to health insurance because their employer did not offer it or they were self-employed and could not afford to purchase it, they were unemployed but not poor or old enough for a government program, or they were deemed ineligible by private insurance companies because they had health conditions that made them high risk and expensive to cover (see Figure 12.8).[64]

The health care reform process has a very long history in American politics, dating back to the New Deal, and it always attracts intense support and opposition from various sectors of the policy-making arena. Two central issues have been the availability of health insurance coverage and the cost of health care programs. President Bill Clinton tried to reform health care in 1993–94 but did not succeed. President Barack Obama (2009–) promised to address health care reform during his 2008 presidential campaign and followed through by asking Congress to write legislation in the summer of 2009. Although Congress did not meet that deadline, it passed the Patient Protection and Affordable Care Act in 2010. The process by which health care policy moved from proposal to bill to law was long and winding, as lawmaking always is, and it was especially

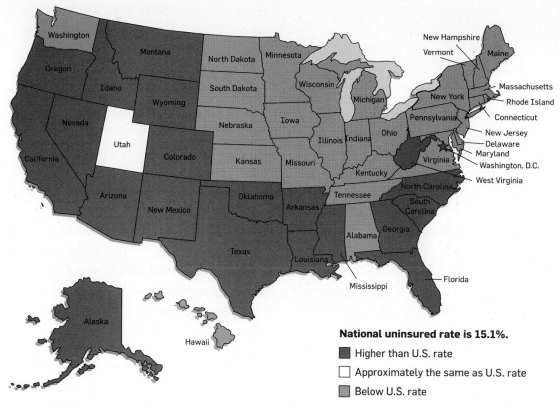

National uninsured rate is 15.1%.

■ Higher than U.S. rate
□ Approximately the same as U.S. rate
▨ Below U.S. rate

FIGURE 12.8 Percentage of Individuals without Health Insurance by State, 2008.
Inequalities in access to health care, and especially the problem of 45 million uninsured Americans, made health care reform an issue in the 2008 presidential campaign. Even so, it took until 2010 for health care reform to become law, and implementation of the law will occur over several years. Health care reform illustrates the complexities of the policy process, from internal congressional rules and procedures to external involvement by the president and various interest groups.
Source: Joanna Turner, Michael Boudreaux, and Victoria Lynch, "A Preliminary Evaluation of Health Insurance Coverage in the 2008 American Community Survey," U.S. Census Bureau, Health Insurance Coverage Working Paper: 2008 American Community Survey, September 22, 2008, www.census.gov.

complicated because of the nature of America's health care system, party politics and partisanship, and the heightened political rhetoric that surrounded the effort.

How has health care reform affected you?

Committee Action

The complication for Congress in beginning the task of addressing health care reform was committee jurisdiction. Normally, a bill might be referred to one or two committees at most, but multiple committees claimed jurisdiction over the vast number of programs that constitute the American health care system: the publicly funded Medicare, Medicaid, and related public health service programs, as well as a large private sector component that includes insurance companies and medical professionals. Because of the vast scope of the health care system, there are many different viewpoints on how to reform it, and many organizations have major stakes in the outcome of reform efforts.

In the House, Representative John Dingell (D-Mich.) introduced the America's Affordable Health Choices Act of 2009 (H.R. 3200) on July 14, 2009. Importantly, the chairs of three committees with primary jurisdiction for health care—Energy and Commerce, Ways and Means, and Education and Labor—were cosponsors of the bill, and the House leadership simultaneously referred the bill to those committees. The three committees

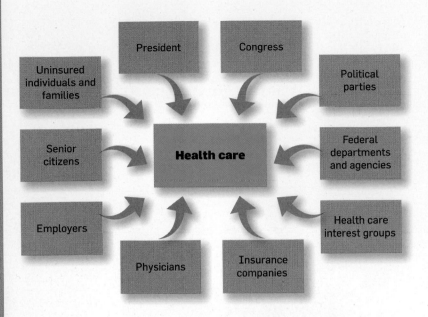

produced separate bills that dealt with their sections of health care policy. Henry Waxman (D-Calif.), chair of Energy and Commerce who had a long history of legislative involvement in health care policy, led the coordination effort. Despite the efforts of House leadership, this bill did not pass the House. On October 29, 2009, Representative Dingell introduced the Affordable Health Care for America Act (H.R. 3962), a merged version of bills proposed by the committee chairs and the House Democratic Party leadership. On November 7, 2009, the House passed this bill by a vote of 220–215 and sent its version of the bill to the Senate. Key to the House bill was the inclusion of a so-called public option that would authorize the creation of a federal health insurance program to create competition with private health insurance providers.[65] This sequence demonstrates the complexity of policy reform: Reforming a policy requires the cooperation and approval of many players, and even when a bill passes one chamber of Congress, it still must pass the other.

In the Senate, the Health, Education, Labor, and Pensions Committee (HELP) and the Finance Committee had primary jurisdiction. Each worked on drafting a separate version of health care reform, and the HELP committee reported its bill, the Affordable Health Choices Act of 2009 (S. 1679), to the full Senate on September 17, 2009. The Senate Finance Committee could not come to agreement on a version of health care reform, and because it has jurisdiction over key components of the health care system, no single bill could be brought to the Senate floor without it. On October 20, 2009, Senator Max Baucus (D-Mont.) introduced America's Healthy Future Act of 2009 (S. 1796), which was amended and approved by the Senate Finance Committee.[66] Although reaching consensus in the Senate Finance Committee was a great leap forward for health care reform, Senate leaders still had to reconcile this bill with the HELP committee's bill in order for health care reform legislation to pass the Senate. On Christmas Eve 2009 the Senate stayed in session for a roll call vote on a compromise version of health care reform entitled America's Healthy Future Act of 2009. The bill passed with a vote of 60–39; voting was strictly along party lines.[67] Senate leaders believed they had made great progress, but the bill differed substantially from that passed by the House, notably because it did not contain the public option. For legislation to be enacted, each chamber has to agree on the same version of the bill and send it to the president for his consideration.

Party Politics

Blue Dog Democrats:
Democratic House members from conservative-leaning districts who care deeply about fiscal discipline.

The strongest opposition to the bill in the Democratic caucus in the House came from **Blue Dog Democrats**, fifty-two Democratic members from conservative-leaning districts who care deeply about fiscal discipline.[68] They were concerned that the health care bill was too costly and would contribute to an unacceptable level of deficit spending. At the same time, they expressed concern that any cuts made in other federal services to pay for the bill would fall disproportionately on services in rural areas, whose residents constitute a large base of constituents for the Blue Dog Democrats. The debate over health care reform within the Democratic caucus in the House reflects the constant tension between party goals and local concerns involved in congressional policy making.

For their part, the Republicans in the House opposed the bill's provisions on the grounds that they were too costly and would introduce government interference into individual choice on health care decisions. The minority party, which is outnumbered in committees and on the House floor, has few procedural tools to obstruct the majority in the House, so the Republicans did not have the power to stop the bill.

Sarah L. Voisin/The Washington Post/Getty Images

Policy discussion occurs in a number of different places in Congress, including in members' offices, in committee rooms, on the House and Senate floors, and among staff members. Such discussion plays an important internal and external role in shaping legislation. Here senators consider health care legislation in committee, with their aides sitting behind them to provide additional information if they need it.

In contrast, the Senate Republicans, despite being the minority party, had the power to filibuster the health care bill on the Senate floor, and the Democrats needed sixty votes to invoke cloture to shut down a filibuster. Democrats technically had a coalition of sixty senators, including two independent senators, Joseph Lieberman (I-Conn.) and Bernie Sanders (I-Vt.), for all of 2009. However, in January 2010 Scott Brown, a Republican, was elected to fill the Massachusetts Senate seat held by the late Senator Edward Kennedy, a Democrat, so the Democrats lost their sixtieth vote.

Without the necessary sixty votes to invoke cloture, the Democrats feared they could not pass a new or revised version of health care. So Democratic leaders in the House and Senate, working with President Obama, decided that the House would have to approve the version of the bill that had already passed in the Senate so that the Senate would not have to vote on it again. Democratic House members who supported a more liberal version of the bill were not happy about this compromise, especially about the loss of the public option, and they insisted that in addition to approving the Senate bill, a second bill would have to be passed to include changes that would expand the group of people covered by the bill. Senate Democrats turned to the reconciliation procedure to make these changes in order to avoid a new filibuster by the bill's opponents in the Senate. As noted earlier, reconciliation bills cannot be filibustered and only require a majority (fifty-one votes) to pass. The House passed the Senate version of health care, the Patient Protection and Affordable Care Act, by a vote of 219–212 on March 21, 2010, and President Obama signed it on March 23, 2010. The second bill, the Health Care and Education Reconciliation Act of 2010, was passed by the Senate by a vote of 56–43 on March 25, 2010, passed by the House by a vote of 220–207 on March 25, 2010, and signed by President Obama on March 30, 2010. The education part of this bill was included because federal student loan programs have budgetary implications and using the reconciliation process was necessary to revamp the program.

The health care reform act establishes a number of new programs, the most notable of which extends health insurance coverage to approximately 32 million uninsured citizens and legal immigrants through an expansion of Medicaid and the provision of federal subsidies to workers to purchase private health insurance.[69] The act provides for increased regulation of private insurance company practices, mandates that young adults under the age of 26 be able to stay on a parent's insurance policy, and bans the denial of health insurance based on a preexisting condition. The bill also increases payment levels to doctors who participate in the Medicaid program and helps senior citizens by closing a loophole in Medicare coverage for prescription drugs.

The process of health care reform in the House and Senate starkly illustrates the differences between the two chambers, especially the procedures by which each considers a bill. The House of Representatives uses majority rules and does not give members the opportunity to individually block or delay legislation, so compromise occurs within the majority party more than it does between the majority and minority parties. But in the Senate, the power of the minority party to filibuster makes compromise essential to successful legislating; without it the majority party must resort to invoking cloture and other procedural maneuvers to pass a bill.

In 2010 the media and public debated this question: Is government broken? Do you think Congress is broken? Defend your answer.

Interest Group Involvement

Because of the vast scope of the health care reform effort, hundreds of organizations became involved in lobbying efforts both on Capitol Hill and back home in members' districts and states. These organizations included large employers such as Wal-Mart, large medical associations such as the Federation of American Hospitals, and spending watchdog groups such as the Club for Growth. In fact, 1,026 different organizations reported lobbying on this bill in 2009 alone.[70] Interest group participation was so strong that members of Congress, and even President Obama, spent the second half of 2009 and early 2010 trying to clarify the reform effort and build public support for it.[71]

Political Rhetoric

Intensifying the struggle to pass health care reform legislation in 2009 was commotion from politicians outside of Washington, D.C. In August 2009 Sarah Palin, the 2008 Republican vice presidential candidate, attacked the efforts of congressional Democrats and President Obama on her Facebook page. She wrote that Democrats intended to include a "death panel" in their health care bill, creating a system that is "downright evil."[72] President Obama responded that rumors of a death panel were "simply not true."[73] Nonetheless, the accusation by the former vice presidential candidate provoked a backlash from concerned citizens. Congressional offices took many calls from angered constituents who demanded that their representatives vote against any legislation with a death panel. To dispel this rumor and others, the White House set up a website to "push back on the misinformation about health care reform."[74] As these events show, although Congress has control of passing legislation, politicians outside of Washington can influence the legislative process, and Congress and the president must try to counter that influence by making what they hope will be persuasive arguments on behalf of their policies.

As this brief account of health care policy and reform demonstrates, the internal structure of Congress, the intensity of partisan politics, and the role of citizens and the president all present gates and gateways for legislative policy making.

Congress and Democracy

The composition of Congress has changed considerably over the nation's 230 years. The lawmaking body has tripled in size and now includes men and women from a wide range of ethnic, racial, and religious backgrounds. From the standpoint of equality of opportunity to serve in Congress, the increased diversity is a positive step.

Is Congress a responsive decision-making body? Individual members clearly work hard to address the concerns of their constituents, both at home in the district or state and in their Washington offices. But Congress as a whole is not always capable of addressing the immediate needs of the nation in a timely fashion. The bicameral nature of the institution, with each chamber's separate rules of operation, makes the legislative process time-consuming and complex. In the House, the majority party almost always succeeds in passing legislation that reflects the party's policy goals. In the Senate, the minority has much greater power to block the majority through the threat of a filibuster, so minority party views are typically incorporated into legislation. These differences offer advantages and disadvantages; if Congress acts too hastily, it can pass harmful legislation, but if it acts too slowly, it can fail to meet its fundamental responsibilities to address issues that citizens care about.

Are individual members of Congress accountable for the collective output of Congress as a whole? Not always. The fundamental difficulty with the representative structure of Congress is that each member is elected separately, so that voters may reelect their own representative or senator but still be unhappy with Congress as a whole. It is too easy for one member of Congress to say to constituents, "I am working hard to help you; it is all those other men and women who are not doing their jobs." Only in the rarest of election years do voters actually hold all the members of the Congress accountable for their collective performance. This lack of collective accountability can be a significant obstacle or gate to Congress's productivity and responsiveness to important policy needs.

Is Congress equal in its treatment of each citizen relative to all others? Because each state has the same number of senators regardless of population size, are the citizens of small states more powerful in the Senate than citizens who live in large states? Are the laws that Congress passes fair and balanced, or do they benefit one group more consistently than another? There are no simple answers to these questions. Some voices in society are louder and more prominent than others, and members of Congress tend to respond to citizens whom they perceive to be supportive, who donate more money, and who vote regularly. In some issue areas, the more prominent members of society win out over citizens who are less active and less visible. It is not clear that Congress sets out to give some people greater advantages than others, but the process of balancing the different individual and regional interests in national policy making produces winners and losers. The fundamental challenge to Congress is to make sure that there are no permanent winners or losers, and the challenge to all citizens is to monitor their members of Congress to be sure they are performing their legislative responsibilities.

FOCUS QUESTIONS

- How are members of Congress held accountable, both individually and for the collective output of Congress as a whole?

- In what ways is Congress responsive as a decision-making body? How does Congress address the pressing needs of the American people?

- What opportunities are there for the average person to influence the policy process in Congress? Is Congress accessible to citizens equally?

- How do the institutional structures in the House of Representatives and those in the Senate work as gates blocking the enactment of legislation? Are there any gateways in these chambers that can help overcome these obstacles? Why did the Framers set up the legislative branch this way?

- Is Congress a gate or a gateway to democracy?

GATEWAYS TO LEARNING

Top Ten to Take Away

1. The Framers designed Congress as a bicameral legislature so that the House of Representatives and the Senate—with different qualifications for office, modes of election, terms of office, and constituencies—would check and balance each other. (pp. 392–98)

2. Although its enumerated powers are limited, Congress has built on its implied powers to become the powerful legislative branch that it is today. (pp. 398–403)

3. Differences in size, rules, structure, and responsibility have molded the House and the Senate into very different institutions. (pp. 403–13)

4. Political parties play a stronger role in the organization and operation of the House than of the Senate. (pp. 403–408)

5. In the Senate, each member has relatively equal power, and passing legislation requires compromise and cooperation. (pp. 408–9)

6. The procedures through which a bill becomes a law are different in the House and Senate, but each chamber engages in committee work, hearings, floor debate, and voting. Following passage by each chamber individually, a formal conference committee or an informal group

of party leaders resolves differences between the two bills to produce a single bill that is presented to the president for signature. (pp. 409–21)

7. If the president vetoes a bill, Congress can override the veto with a two-thirds majority in each house. (p. 421)

8. The process of lawmaking is not smooth or efficient, and there are structural gates against a bill's passage. Only a very small percentage of bills introduced are enacted into law. Lawmaking requires balancing competing interests through cooperation, compromise, and deal-making. (pp. 413–21)

9. In recent years, intense partisanship, including party-line voting and message politics, has decreased the likelihood of bipartisan cooperation and made it more difficult for Congress to pass legislation. (pp. 415–16, 426–30)

10. Members of Congress try to balance the competing demands of legislation and constituent service, and they are always anticipating the next election. A successful legislator seeks to be responsive to constituents by engaging in committee work, sponsoring and voting on bills, and securing federal funds for his or her district or state. (pp. 421–26)

A full narrative summary of the chapter is on the book's website.

Ten to Test Yourself

1. Compare and contrast the constitutional differences between the House and the Senate.

2. How do these differences explain the different paths of development of the House and the Senate?

3. What are two key differences in the ways bills are considered in the House and the Senate?

4. What is committee markup?

5. Compare and contrast the power of political parties to shape policy in the House and in the Senate.

6. Who is more powerful, the Speaker of the House or the Senate majority leader?

7. Describe the rules and procedures in the House and Senate that make passage of legislation difficult.

8. Identify and describe three ways that a member of Congress builds a bond with constituents.

9. Why do representatives and senators vote with their party leaders on legislation?

10. Describe the various factors that complicated consideration of health care reform in 2009–2010.

More review questions and answers and chapter quizzes are on the book's website.

Timeline to Keep Things in Order

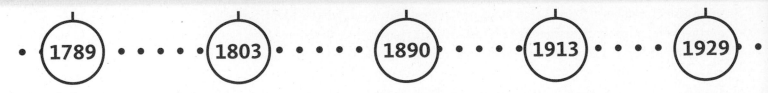

First Congress, with sixty-five members, convenes.

Marbury v. Madison establishes that the federal judiciary has the power to declare laws passed by Congress unconstitutional.

Reed's Rules strengthen the power of the majority party in the House.

Seventeenth Amendment provides for the direct election of senators.

Size of the House is capped at 435 members.

1789   1803   1890   1913   1929

Terms to Know and Use

advice and consent (p. 401)
advocacy caucus (p. 413)
appropriate (p. 399)
authorize (p. 399)
bicameral (p. 393)
bill sponsorship (p. 417)
Blue Dog Democrats (p. 428)
census (p. 396)
challenger (p. 425)
cloture (p. 415)
commerce clause (p. 399)
committee chair (p. 409)
concurrent budget
  resolution (p. 420)
conference committee (p. 418)
Congressional Budget Office
  (p. 420)
constituency (p. 396)
constituent services (p. 422)
continuing resolution (p. 420)

Contract with America (p. 406)
delegate (p. 393)
divided government (p. 403)
earmark (p. 423)
entitlement programs (p. 420)
enumerated powers (p. 402)
federal deficit (p. 419)
filibuster (p. 415)
franking privilege (p. 424)
funding formula (p. 423)
general welfare clause (p. 399)
gerrymandering (p. 397)
hearings (p. 403)
hold (p. 416)
home style (p. 424)
House majority leader (p. 407)
House minority leader (p. 407)
House Rules Committee (p. 415)
impeachment (p. 401)
implied powers (p. 402)

incumbent (p. 425)
joint committee (p. 410)
judicial review (p. 402)
Judiciary Act (p. 402)
legislative amendment (p. 415)
Marbury v. Madison (p. 402)
markup (p. 412)
message politics (p. 418)
national debt (p. 419)
necessary and proper
  clause (p. 402)
omnibus bill (p. 417)
override (p. 421)
oversight (p. 403)
party caucus (p. 405)
party-line votes (p. 418)
pocket veto (p. 421)
president pro tempore (p. 408)
ranking member (p. 412)
reconciliation (p. 420)

redistricting (p. 397)
Reed's Rules (p. 406)
representation (p. 393)
roll call vote (p. 418)
rule (p. 415)
select committee (p. 410)
Senate majority leader (p. 409)
Senate minority leader (p. 409)
Senate parliamentarian (p. 409)
Speaker of the House (p. 405)
special committee (p. 410)
standing committee (p. 409)
trustee (p. 393)
unanimous consent
  agreement (p. 416)
unified government (p. 403)
veto (p. 421)
whips (p. 407)

Use the vocabulary flash cards on the book's website.

Learning That Works

WHAT YOU NEED . . .

TO KNOW	TO DO
What the Framers feared about Congress	Understand why they made passing legislation so difficult
The role of parties in Congress	Recognize why passing legislation continues to be difficult
What the constitutional powers of Congress are	Understand how Congress has become so powerful
Who your representative and senators are	Determine whether you are being well represented in Congress
How to track votes in Congress	Decide how you will vote in the next election and whether you will hold your representative and senators accountable for the performance of Congress as a whole
What happened in the health care reform debate	Evaluate whether the public interest has been served by Congress's action and what would have been the consequence of inaction
What happened in the 2010 election	Judge whether the electorate holds Congress accountable

1959	1973	1994	2006	2010
Admission of Alaska and Hawaii increases Senate membership to one hundred.	House expands the number of subcommittees to decentralize power and open opportunities for influence to young members.	Republicans take the House for the first time in forty years, using the Contract for America as their campaign platform.	Democrats regain majority control of the House and Senate.	The Republicans regain majority control of the House, and Democrats hold the Senate.

13 THE PRESIDENCY

▲ Smith College, Northampton, Massachusetts

> *I can't stress how important it is to simply get involved. Get into the fight. Do everything you can to get hands-on experience.*

As a government and economics major at Smith College, Stephanie Cutter enjoyed politics, but it was her adviser's encouragement that turned interest into involvement. Her work on the 1988 presidential campaign of Michael Dukakis opened a whole new world and, it turned out, a career. After college, she took a job as a receptionist in the Washington office of New York Governor Mario Cuomo, but she shortly returned to presidential campaign work, serving as a staff member on the campaigns of Bill Clinton, John Kerry, and Barack Obama. Campaign work led, in turn, to White House work. For Clinton, Cutter was communications director. For Obama, she has served as chief spokesperson for his transition team, head of communications at the Department of the Treasury, and coordinator of press strategy for the nomination of Sonia Sotomayor to the Supreme Court. In May 2010 she became an assistant to the president for special projects and was given the task of coordinating public outreach on the implementation of health care reform. Over the past years, between White House assignments, Cutter got a law degree and worked for Senator Edward Kennedy, First Lady Michele Obama, and the Democratic National Committee.

Stephanie Cutter's career exemplifies the gateways that open when one gets involved in politics. It also reveals the political networks that talented and hard-working volunteers establish on presidential campaigns and how they use them to secure influential positions in the executive branch. Cutter's specialty is communications. She describes handling the press for political leaders as "a game of Ping-Pong," planning press briefings and fielding questions from the news media, in an effort to get the president's message out. Her skills at this game offer insight into the management of the modern presidency and into the importance of presidential agendas and citizen response.[1]

In this chapter we examine how the president governs and how responsive he can be to the people. We look at his constitutional powers and the way he

CourseMate

Visit http://www.cengagebrain.com/shop/ISBN/0618906959 for interactive tools including:

- Quizzes
- Flashcards
- Videos
- Animated PowerPoint slides, Podcast summaries, and more

Stephanie Cutter

- In what ways is the president held accountable both individually and for the collective economic, military, and social condition of the nation?

- How responsive is the presidency as a democratic office? How can the president address the vital public policy concerns of the American people?

- What opportunities are there for the average citizen to influence the decisions of the president?

- What powers does the president have to ensure equality across all citizens?

- Is the modern presidency a gate or a gateway to democracy?

uses the executive power to achieve his policy goals. We also look at the limits on presidential power. As presidential scholar Charles Jones has argued, successful presidents work within a separation of powers system and alongside the legislative and judicial branches.[2] The most successful presidents are strong leaders with clear policy visions and excellent communication and negotiation skills. In the twenty-first century the American president has to implement existing law and, equally important, leads the effort to turn his policy goals into law and achieve his vision for the nation.

Presidential Qualifications

The American presidency was invented at the Constitutional Convention in 1787. The Framers had no definitive models to help them determine what sort of person should serve as a democratically elected head of state because nations were still ruled by monarchs whose power to rule was hereditary. But the Framers had George Washington, the hero of the Revolutionary War, in mind for the office, and he helped shape the idea of what a president should be. Still, they left the qualifications as open as possible, and men with diverse experiences have served as president.

Constitutional Eligibility and Presidential Succession

Article II, Section 1 of the Constitution states that the president must be a **natural-born citizen** (or a citizen at the time the Constitution was adopted), at least 35 years old, and a resident of the United States for at least fourteen years. The original Constitution did not specify eligibility for the vice presidency, as the person who came in second in the vote for president would be vice president. But in 1800 Thomas Jefferson (1801–1809) and Aaron Burr ended up in a tie in the Electoral College when in fact supporters wanted to elect them as a team, with Jefferson as president and Burr as vice president. The Twelfth Amendment, ratified in 1804, changed the process so that candidates are elected for president and vice president separately. The amendment also directs that the vice president must meet the same eligibility requirements as the president and that electors cannot vote for both a president and a vice president from the elector's home state. This requirement makes it difficult for parties to nominate presidents and vice presidents from the same state.

The Constitution also states that when the president is removed from office by death, resignation, or inability to perform the duties of the office, the vice president becomes president. It stipulates that if neither the president nor the vice president is able to complete the elected term, Congress should designate a successor by law. In 1792 Congress passed the Presidential Succession Act, which designated the **president pro tempore** of the Senate as next in line, and then the **Speaker of the House**. John Tyler (1841–45) was the first elected vice president to succeed a president who died in office, replacing William Henry Harrison who died a month after his inauguration in 1841. In 1886 Congress changed the order of succession to include only **cabinet secretaries** in the sequence in which the **cabinet departments** were created, starting with the State Department, Treasury Department, War Department, and attorney general, who is the head of the Justice Department (for more on cabinet departments, see Chapter 14, The Bureaucracy). In 1947 Congress changed presidential succession once again, putting the order

natural-born citizens: *People who are citizens in a nation from birth, usually by being born there.*

president pro tempore: *Constitutional leader of the Senate.*

Speaker of the House: *Constitutional and political leader of the House.*

cabinet secretaries: *Heads of cabinet departments and chief advisers to the president on the issues under their jurisdiction.*

cabinet departments: *Executive branch organizations responsible for carrying out federal policy in a specific set of issue areas.*

of succession as vice president, Speaker of the House, and president pro tempore, followed by the cabinet secretaries, starting with the secretary of state and again following in order the dates of the departments' creation.

There was no constitutional provision for replacement of the vice president, and in the course of the nation's history the office has occasionally been vacant, as it was after Vice President Andrew Johnson (1865–69) assumed the presidency in 1865, following Abraham Lincoln's (1861–65) death. Eventually, the Twenty-Fifth Amendment, ratified in 1967, required the president to nominate a replacement vice president, who must be approved by a majority vote of the House and the Senate. The first vice president to assume office in this manner was Gerald R. Ford, nominated by President Richard M. Nixon (1969–74) in 1973, following the indictment and subsequent resignation of Vice President Spiro T. Agnew. The amendment also allows for a temporary transfer of power from the president to the vice president in cases of incapacity when invoked by either the president or vice president and a majority of the cabinet. To date only the president has invoked this clause and then only when he has had to have surgery that would require sedation. For example, in 1985, when President Ronald Reagan (1981–89) had a colonoscopy, Vice President George H. W. Bush was **acting president** for eight hours.[3] In contrast, no one invoked the clause when President Reagan was shot in a failed assassination attempt in 1981; Vice President Bush stood in for him at official functions and meetings for approximately two weeks but did not serve as the official acting president during this time.

Today another constitutional amendment, the Twenty-Second (1951), limits the president to two elected terms. For a century and a half, presidents followed the precedent established by George Washington (1789–1797) when he stepped down after two terms. But in 1940 President Franklin Delano Roosevelt (1933–45) chose to run for a third term and won, and also won election to a fourth term in 1944. Though the dangers of World War II were a factor in his staying in office, many Americans, especially Republicans, worried that a long-standing president could expand executive branch power too much, so they sought a way to limit presidential terms of service. In 1946 Republicans captured a majority in the House and Senate, and on the very first day the new Congress met, they proposed a constitutional amendment limiting the president to two full terms in office.[4] For a list of constitutional amendments that pertain to the presidency, see Figure 13.1.

The Granger Collection, New York

George Washington was a successful military general who led American troops in the Revolutionary War. He was widely admired and was chosen to be the first president of the United States because it was believed that his experience and personal characteristics would be a model for the future. He took the oath of office on April 30, 1789, on the balcony of Federal Hall in New York City, then the nation's capital.

acting president: *Status given to the person who assumes the presidency when the president is unable to carry out his duties.*

FIGURE 13.1 Constitutional Amendments That Pertain to the Presidency.

Color Code :
Structure

Twelfth (1804): Requires that electors cast separate votes for president and vice president and specifies requirements for vice presidential candidates

Twentieth (1933): Declares that presidential term begins on January 20 (instead of March 4)

Twenty-Second (1951): Limits presidents to two terms

Twenty-Fifth (1967): Specifies replacement of the vice president and establishes the position of acting president during a president's disability.

term limits: *Rule restricting the number of terms an elected official can serve in a given office.*

lame duck: *Term-limited official in his or her last term of office.*

How do term limits make the president less responsive to public opinion?

Being born in a log cabin was an asset for presidential hopefuls in the nineteenth century, and candidates liked to portray their humble origins and demonstrate that they were men of the people. In 1840 William Henry Harrison cultivated the connection with campaign images such as this one, although he was born in an elegant plantation manor house. But the claims of other presidents, such as Abraham Lincoln, were legitimate. The log cabin birthplaces of James Buchanan and James A. Garfield still stand.

Term limits enforce turnover and open opportunity for new leadership, but they also act as a gate that prevents voters from reelecting a popular president whom they want to keep in office. Because a president in his second term cannot seek reelection, he is commonly referred to as a **lame duck**. Lawmakers know that the president's time in office is limited, so they are less likely to cooperate or compromise with him. On the other hand, a president who wants to chart a policy course that is unpopular may be more likely to do so when he does not have to face the voters. Lame duck status therefore has the advantage of giving the president more political freedom, but the disadvantage of making him less directly responsive to public opinion. George W. Bush (2001–2009) is an example. By 2007, during his second term, public opinion was unfavorable toward continuing the Iraq War, but President Bush maintained U.S. commitments in that conflict. Some critics believe he should have heeded the public and withdrawn troops, but others argue that he was taking the unpopular but correct course of action for the nation. Absent the pressure of seeking reelection to a third term, Bush had the flexibility to pursue a policy on what he perceived to be its merits.

Background and Experience

In keeping with the democratic spirit of the founding of the United States, the Framers did not specify qualifications for the presidency beyond age and citizenship, and in the ensuing 230 years, men of varying backgrounds have served in the office. Presidents have come from all walks of life and from almost all regions (see Figure 13.2). There is no single gateway profession that leads to the presidency. Harry S. Truman (1945–53), born in Missouri, was a farmer and owner of a men's clothing store. Ronald Reagan, born in Illinois, was a radio sports announcer and actor. Barack Obama (2009–), born in Hawaii, was a community organizer and constitutional law professor.[5] Until John F. Kennedy (1961–63), a Catholic, was elected in 1960, all presidents were from Protestant backgrounds. Until Obama, an African American, was elected in 2008, all presidents were white. All presidents have been male, but in 1984 Walter Mondale made history by selecting Geraldine Ferraro as the first woman to run for vice president. In 2008 Hillary Clinton made a serious run for the Democratic nomination, and the Republican nominee John McCain selected Sarah Palin as his vice presidential candidate.

The Granger Collection, New York

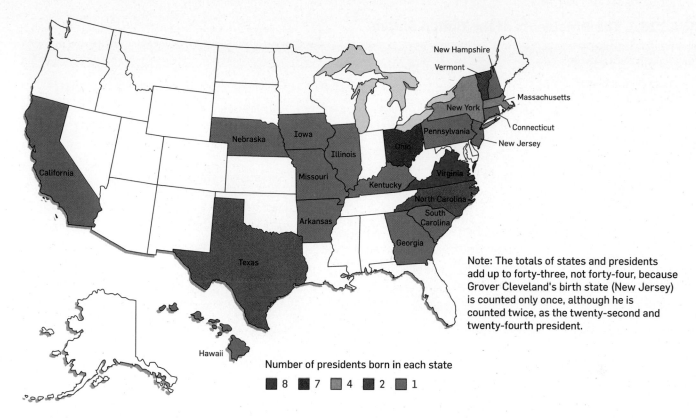

Note: The totals of states and presidents add up to forty-three, not forty-four, because Grover Cleveland's birth state (New Jersey) is counted only once, although he is counted twice, as the twenty-second and twenty-fourth president.

Number of presidents born in each state

■ 8 ■ 7 ■ 4 ■ 2 ■ 1

FIGURE 13.2 The States Where Presidents Were Born.

The clearest path to the White House is through the office of the vice president, but most presidents have some combination of service in the military, in a state legislature or as governor, in the U.S. House of Representatives and Senate, and in a prior presidential administration. For example, James Monroe (1817–25) was a soldier in the Revolutionary War, a U.S. senator, minister to France, secretary of state, and secretary of war. Herbert Hoover (1929–33) was an international food relief worker and secretary of commerce.[6]

There are advantages and disadvantages to specific types of experience prior to becoming president. Lyndon Baines Johnson (1963–69) was very successful in passing his domestic policy agenda in large part due to his experience as a House member, U.S. senator, and Senate majority leader. His prior experience taught him crucial negotiating skills with members of Congress, and he used his skills to their fullest extent. In contrast, Jimmy Carter (1977–81) was generally considered to have failed in getting his domestic policy agenda enacted because of his lack of experience in Washington. He came to the White House from the governor's mansion in Georgia, and he was used to exercising executive power with little challenge from the legislature. When he faced a Congress that did not embrace his agenda, he lacked the negotiating skills to be successful. Of course, there is no single set of qualifications or experiences that will guarantee success as a president. When voters cast their ballots for president, they take a leap of faith that the person who wins will be trustworthy, accountable, and responsive to their needs and will implement the laws equally for every citizen. For a full list of the men who have been president of the United States, see Table 13.1.

Unlike members of Congress, presidents represent all the people of the United States. How can a president represent all the people?

TABLE 13.1 The Presidents of the United States

	President	Term Dates	Party	Prior Experience
1	George Washington	1789–97		General
2	John Adams	1797–1801	Federalist	Vice president
3	Thomas Jefferson	1801–1809	Democratic-Republican	Vice president, secretary of state
4	James Madison	1809–17	Democratic-Republican	Secretary of state, state legislator
5	James Monroe	1817–25	Democratic-Republican	Minister to France, U.S. Senate
6	John Quincy Adams	1825–29	Democratic-Republican	Secretary of state, U.S. Senate
7	Andrew Jackson	1829–37	Democrat	U.S. House, U.S. Senate, general
8	Martin Van Buren	1837–41	Democrat	Vice president, U.S. Senate
9	William Henry Harrison	1841 (died in office)	Whig	General, governor
10	John Tyler	1841–45	Whig	Vice president, governor, U.S. Senate, U.S. House
11	James K. Polk	1845–49	Democrat	Governor, U.S. House
12	Zachary Taylor	1849–50 (died in office)	Whig	General
13	Millard Fillmore	1850–53	Whig	U.S. House, Vice president
14	Franklin Pierce	1853–57	Democrat	State legislator, U.S. Senate, U.S. House
15	James Buchanan	1857–61	Democrat	U.S. House, U.S. Senate, secretary of state
16	Abraham Lincoln	1861–65 (died in office)	Republican; National Union	State legislator
17	Andrew Johnson	1865–69	Democrat; National Union	U.S. House, U.S. Senate, vice president
18	Ulysses S. Grant	1869–77	Republican	General
19	Rutherford B. Hayes	1877–81	Republican	Governor, U.S. House, general
20	James A. Garfield	1881 (died in office)	Republican	U.S. House, general, state legislator
21	Chester A. Arthur	1881–85	Republican	Vice president, collector of the Port of New York
22	Grover Cleveland	1885–89	Democrat	Governor, mayor
23	Benjamin Harrison	1889–93	Republican	U.S. Senate
24	Grover Cleveland	1893–97	Democrat	President, governor, mayor
25	William McKinley	1897–1901 (died in office)	Republican	Governor, U.S. House

TABLE 13.1 (Continued)

	President	Term Dates	Party	Prior Experience
26	Theodore Roosevelt	1901–1909	Republican	Governor, lieutenant colonel
27	William Howard Taft	1909–13	Republican	Secretary of war, federal judge
28	Woodrow Wilson	1913–21	Democrat	Governor, university president
29	Warren G. Harding	1921–23 (died in office)	Republican	State legislator, lieutenant-governor, U.S. Senate
30	Calvin Coolidge	1923–29	Republican	Vice president, governor
31	Herbert Hoover	1929–33	Republican	Secretary of commerce
32	Franklin Delano Roosevelt	1933–45 (died in office)	Democrat	Governor, assistant secretary of the Navy, state legislator
33	Harry S. Truman	1945–53	Democrat	Vice president, U.S. Senate
34	Dwight D. Eisenhower	1953–61	Republican	General
35	John F. Kennedy	1961–63 (died in office)	Democrat	U.S. Senate, U.S. House
36	Lyndon Baines Johnson	1963–69	Democrat	Vice president, U.S. Senate, U.S. House
37	Richard M. Nixon	1969–74 (resigned)	Republican	Vice president, U.S. Senate, U.S. House
38	Gerald R. Ford	1974–77	Republican	Vice president, U.S. House
39	Jimmy Carter	1977–81	Democrat	Governor
40	Ronald Reagan	1981–89	Republican	Governor, actor
41	George H. W. Bush	1989–93	Republican	Vice president, CIA director, U.S. House
42	William J. Clinton	1993–2001	Democrat	Governor, state attorney general
43	George W. Bush	2001–2009	Republican	Governor
44	Barack Obama	2009–	Democrat	U.S. Senate, state senator

The Expansion of the Presidency

President George Washington had the enormous responsibility of setting the standard for how a president should govern in a democracy, and he was very careful not to infuse the office with airs of royalty or privilege. The Framers anticipated that the executive branch would be led by one person whose primary responsibility would be the defense of the United States. As commander of the Continental Army during the Revolutionary War, Washington had military experience, but he was also a cautious and thoughtful statesman who wanted to establish a precedent for how the chief executive should operate.

In the course of the nineteenth century, from the presidencies of Thomas Jefferson, to Andrew Jackson (1829–37), to Abraham Lincoln, and finally to William McKinley (1897–1901), the nation grew in size, population, and economic power. The job of the chief executive grew accordingly, but though increasingly demanding and complex, it remained essentially focused on internal security. In the twentieth century, however, the United States became a leading international military and economic power. Its role in World War II and the subsequent **Cold War** against the Soviet Union expanded the authority of the presidency. Historian and presidential adviser Arthur Schlesinger Jr. used the term **imperial presidency** to describe the power of the president to speak for the nation on the world stage and to set the policy agenda at home.[7] Schlesinger's view suggests that as long as the United States is engaged in military conflicts all over the world to promote and protect its interests, the president will be considered the most important figure in American politics.

Presidential Power: Constitutional Grants and Limits

As we saw in Chapter 12 (Congress), the Framers enumerated Congress's powers, both to assert powers that were missing under the Articles of Confederation, such as the powers to collect taxes and to regulate commerce, and to constrain the branch they anticipated would be the most powerful. The Framers expected the executive branch to be smaller and less powerful and did not believe it necessary to enumerate the executive powers as they did the legislative powers (see Table 13.2). Instead, in the very first sentence of Article II, they "vested" the president with a general grant of "executive Power" and then, later in the article, stated certain additional powers and responsibilities. The general grant of executive power has allowed the presidency to become the powerful office it is today. In this section, we look at the constitutional sources of the president's powers, the ways in which presidents have sought to expand their constitutional powers, and the ways in which the other branches, especially Congress, act to check and balance the president.

Commander in Chief

The president is the commander in chief of the armed forces of the United States, which includes the Army, Navy, Air Force, Marine Corps, and Coast Guard, plus their Reserve and National Guard units. An elected commander in chief, rather than an appointed military officer, is a distinctly important element of American democracy. The president directs all war efforts and military conflict. Congress, however, has the power to officially declare war and to authorize funding for the war effort. Because the war powers that are divided between the president and Congress are so contentious, we examine them later in the chapter.

TABLE 13.2 A Comparison of Legislative and Executive Authority under the Constitution

While the Constitution grants specific legislative authority to Congress, it provides a general grant of authority to the president that does not require specific enumerated grants of power. Nor is there an executive equivalent of Article I, Section 9, which specifically limits congressional authority.

	Legislative	Executive
Authority	"All legislative Powers herein granted shall be vested in a Congress of the United States"	"The executive Power shall be vested in a President of the United States"
Specific Powers	Article I, Section 8, including: • lay and collect taxes • provide for the common defense • regulate interstate and foreign commerce • authorize courts • set uniform rules for naturalization and bankruptcy • establish post offices • make all laws that are "necessary and proper" for carrying out the listed powers	Article II, Section 2, including: • act as commander in chief of armed forces • grant pardons • make treaties • receive foreign ministers • appoint ambassadors, judges, cabinet-level officials Article II, Section 3: • ensure that the laws are faithfully executed Article I, Section 7: • veto legislation
Limits on Power	Explicit limits on powers: Article I, Section 9, including: • no bills of attainder • no ex post facto laws • no titles of nobility. Bill of Rights: • substantive limits of the First through Eighth Amendments Ninth Amendment: • enumeration of rights does not grant general authority Tenth Amendment: • people and states retain reserved powers not granted to Congress	Mostly through checks and balances: • veto override • Senate confirmation on appointments • removal by impeachment

Power to Pardon

The president has the power to grant **clemency**, or mercy, for crimes against the United States, except in the case of impeachment from federal office. Clemency is a broad designation that includes a **pardon**, which is forgiving an offense altogether, and a **commutation**,

clemency: *General power of the president to grant mercy for a federal criminal offense.*

pardon: *Full forgiveness for a crime.*

commutation: *Decision to shorten a federal prison sentence.*

Should the president have the power to pardon? What impact does this power have on citizen equality?

which is shortening a federal prison sentence; in general, pardoning someone is considered a more sweeping act of clemency than commuting a sentence. For example, in his last year in office, President George W. Bush issued seventy-six pardons and commuted seven sentences, including one for a former White House staff member, I. Lewis Libby, who had been convicted of lying and **obstruction of justice** in a federal investigation about a leak of confidential information. President Bush commuted his prison sentence but did not grant him a pardon.[8]

Treaties and Recognition of Foreign Nations

The president or his designated representative has the power to negotiate and sign treaties with foreign nations, but he must do so with the "Advice and Consent of the Senate," as specified by the Constitution. For a treaty to be valid, two-thirds "of the Senators present" must approve. Historically, the Senate has refused to approve some notable treaties, ranging from the Treaty of Versailles ending World War I signed by President Woodrow Wilson (1913–21), to the Kyoto Protocol on climate change signed by Vice President Albert Gore Jr. who was representing President William Jefferson (Bill) Clinton (1993–2001). These examples illustrate how the requirement that the Senate approve treaties serves as a gateway for public input into presidential actions, and how it can be a gate that blocks a president's attempt to reach agreements with foreign nations. Today, with the expansion of globalization, the president's representatives negotiate treaties over a wide range of areas, such as military alliances, human rights accords, environmental regulations, and trade policies.

The president's authority in foreign affairs includes the power to "receive Ambassadors and other public Ministers," which allows the president to recognize the legitimacy of foreign regimes. Such decisions are frequently based on the internal political system of the foreign nation. For example, revolutionaries overthrew Russia's czarist regime in 1917, but the new Soviet Union, a Communist nation, was not recognized by the United States until 1933, through the action of President Franklin Delano Roosevelt. In contrast, in 2008, when the young democracy of Kosovo declared its independence from Serbia, President George W. Bush immediately recognized it as an independent nation.[9]

Appointments and Judicial Nominations

The president has the power to appoint all federal officers, including cabinet secretaries, heads of independent agencies, and ambassadors. The presidential appointment process has two steps: nomination, and subsequent approval by a majority of the Senate. The appointed officers are typically referred to as **political appointees**, and they are expected to carry out the president's political and policy agenda (in contrast to **civil servants**, who are hired through a merit-based system and are politically neutral; see Chapter 14, The Bureaucracy). During Senate recesses, the president can make appointments that will expire when the Senate officially adjourns at the close of a Congress (adjourns *sine die*), unless the appointee is subsequently confirmed. Presidents have sometimes used recess appointments to bypass the Senate. In 2005 George W. Bush

political appointees: *Federal employees appointed by the president with the explicit task of carrying out his political and partisan agenda.*

civil servants: *Federal employees hired through a merit-based system to implement federal programs, who are expected to be neutral in their political affiliation.*

appointed John Bolton as United Nations ambassador in a recess appointment, but Bolton resigned at the end of 2006, when it was clear he would not win Senate approval. The president also nominates judges in the federal judicial system, from district court level to the Supreme Court, and they too must receive majority approval in the Senate. In recent years, this process has become more ideological and contentious; rather than considering only qualifications for the job, presidents and members of the Senate also consider a nominee's ideological views on key issues such as abortion (see Chapter 15, The Judiciary, for more information on the nomination process). As with the treaty process, the Senate's advice and consent role in appointments and nominations is a gateway for citizen influence.

The president has the power to fire federal officers, but not to remove judges, who can be removed only by impeachment. Even though they have the formal power to do so, presidents rarely remove cabinet members because that would entail an admission of error in making the appointment in the first place. Some cabinet secretaries who disagreed with presidents about policies or, worse, committed acts of corruption were subsequently fired or were asked to resign. In an example we discuss later in the chapter, President Andrew Johnson fired his secretary of war who disagreed with Johnson about the policy of **Reconstruction** in the South after the Civil War.

Veto and the Veto Override

The president has an important role in the enactment of legislation. He has the power to **veto** bills passed by Congress before they become law by refusing to sign them and sending them back to the chamber in which they originated with his objections. If Congress will be going out of session within ten days, he can simply not sign the bill, a practice known as a **pocket veto**. In cases where the president refuses to sign the bill and Congress remains in session, the bill is enacted into law.

To counter the power of the veto, the Framers gave Congress the veto **override**, the power to overturn a presidential veto with a two-thirds vote in each chamber. Because the two-thirds threshold is higher than the majority vote needed to pass a bill in the first place, it is difficult for Congress to overcome presidential opposition to a bill. The high threshold reinforces the power of the president in blocking congressional action and so serves as a gateway for presidential influence in the legislative process. One could also see the veto as a gate that legislation must pass through to become law, which can be unlocked only with a congressional supermajority.

The veto is the most direct way that the president checks the power of Congress. Presidents use the veto power either to prevent a bill from becoming law or to pressure Congress into making changes to bring the bill closer to his policies and his view of the national interest (see Table 13.3). For most of the twentieth century, Congress sent the president a large number of single-issue or narrowly drawn bills each year. In recent decades, however, Congress has learned to get around the threat of a presidential veto by passing **omnibus bills** that include provisions affecting a number of issue areas. These bills are costly to veto because they affect a wide range of voters and generate a lot of public support, so they give Congress an advantage in negotiating with the president.[10]

Consider the Senate's power to check the president in making treaties and appointments. What are the costs and benefits of this power sharing in terms of government efficiency and responsiveness?

Reconstruction: *The period from 1865 to 1877 in which the former Confederate states gained readmission to the Union and the federal government passed laws to help the emancipated slaves.*

veto: *Authority of the president to block legislation passed by Congress. Congress can override a veto by a two-thirds majority vote in each chamber.*

pocket veto: *Automatic veto that occurs when Congress goes out of session within ten days of submitting a bill to the president and the president has not signed it.*

override: *Congress's power to overturn a presidential veto with a two-thirds vote in each chamber.*

omnibus bills: *One very large bill that encompasses many separate bills.*

TABLE 13.3 Presidential Vetoes, 1789–2010

President	Congresses	Regular Vetoes	Pocket Vetoes	Total Vetoes	Vetoes Overridden
George Washington	1st–4th	2	0	2	0
John Adams	5th–6th	0	0	0	0
Thomas Jefferson	7th–10th	0	0	0	0
James Madison	11th–14th	5	2	7	0
James Monroe	15th–18th	1	0	1	0
John Quincy Adams	19th–20th	0	0	0	0
Andrew Jackson	21st–24th	5	7	12	0
Martin Van Buren	25th–26th	0	1	1	0
William Henry Harrison	27th	0	0	0	0
John Tyler	27th–28th	6	4	10	1
James K. Polk	29th–30th	2	1	3	0
Zachary Taylor	31st	0	0	0	0
Millard Fillmore	31st–32nd	0	0	0	0
Franklin Pierce	33rd–34th	9	0	9	5
James Buchanan	35th–36th	4	3	7	0
Abraham Lincoln	37th–39th	2	5	7	0
Andrew Johnson	39th–40th	21	8	29	15
Ulysses S. Grant	41st–44th	45	48	93	4
Rutherford B. Hayes	45th–46th	12	1	13	1
James A. Garfield	47th	0	0	0	0
Chester A. Arthur	47th–48th	4	8	12	1
Grover Cleveland	49th–50th	304	110	414	2
Benjamin Harrison	51st–52nd	19	25	44	1
Grover Cleveland	53rd–54th	42	128	170	5
William McKinley	55th–57th	6	36	42	0
Theodore Roosevelt	57th–60th	42	40	82	1
William Howard Taft	61st–62nd	30	9	39	1
Woodrow Wilson	63rd–66th	33	11	44	6
Warren G. Harding	67th	5	1	6	0
Calvin Coolidge	68th–70th	20	30	50	4
Herbert Hoover	71st–72nd	21	16	37	3
Franklin Delano Roosevelt	73rd–79th	372	263	635	9
Harry S. Truman	79th–82nd	180	70	250	12
Dwight D. Eisenhower	83rd–86th	73	108	181	2

TABLE 13.3 (Continued)

President	Congresses	Regular Vetoes	Pocket Vetoes	Total Vetoes	Vetoes Overridden
John F. Kennedy	87th–88th	12	9	21	0
Lyndon Baines Johnson	88th–90th	16	14	30	0
Richard M. Nixon	91st–93rd	26	17	43	7
Gerald R. Ford	93rd–94th	48	18	66	12
Jimmy Carter	95th–96th	13	18	31	2
Ronald Reagan	97th–100th	39	39	78	9
George H. W. Bush	101st–102nd	29	15*	44	1
William Jefferson Clinton	103rd–106th	36	1	37	2
George W. Bush	107th–110th	12	0	12	4
Barack Obama	111th	1	1	0	0
Total		**1,497**	**1,067**	**2,563**	**110**

* President George H. W. Bush attempted to pocket veto two bills during intra-session recess periods. Congress considered the two bills enacted into law because of Bush's failure to return the legislation. The bills are not counted as pocket vetoes in this table.

Source: Kevin R. Kosar, "Regular Vetoes and Pocket Vetoes: An Overview," January 5, 2010, 3–4, Congressional Research Service.

Presidents naturally tend to veto more bills when Congress is controlled by the opposite party, a condition known as **divided government**. One of the most dramatic veto battles occurred in the fall of 1995 and early winter of 1996 between Democratic President Bill Clinton and the Republican-controlled Congress led by Speaker Newt Gingrich (see Chapter 3, Federalism). President Clinton and Congress differed over the size of cuts in **entitlement programs** such as Medicare, the health care program for the elderly. Clinton vetoed two omnibus funding bills that Congress sent him, resulting in the shutdown of the entire government both times. The second shutdown lasted several weeks and affected veterans' hospitals, all national parks and monuments, and other government-run services. The public blamed the Republican Congress, not the president, for the impasse, and many of the voters who generally supported the Republicans lived in areas that were hard hit by the shutdown. In January 1996 Congress compromised by agreeing to a funding bill that was closer to President Clinton's position. For the rest of 1996 President Clinton and the Republican majority in Congress worked to produce key legislation on welfare reform, health insurance portability, and the minimum wage. In each case, the president used the threat of more vetoes to get members of Congress to produce legislation closer to his policy positions.[11]

divided government:
Situation when one party controls the executive branch and the other party controls the legislative branch.

entitlement programs:
Federal programs, such as Social Security, Medicare, or Medicaid, that pay out benefits to individuals based on a specified set of eligibility criteria.

How does the veto power give the president influence in the legislative process?

Other Powers

The president works within this framework of formal powers and constraints to lead the nation, and in doing so becomes the chief agenda setter for domestic and foreign policy. In a later section of this chapter, we discuss agenda setting in more detail; here it is important to note that, over time, smaller tasks assigned to the president in the Constitution have evolved into powerful tools for influencing legislation. One tool is the **State of the Union address**, which is authorized in Article II, Section 3: The president "shall from time to time give to the Congress Information of the State of the Union, and recommend to their Consideration such Measures as he shall judge necessary and expedient." Nothing in this passage requires the president to inform Congress on a yearly basis or to do so in person. Presidents George Washington and John Adams (1797–1801) delivered the State of the Union address in person, but subsequent presidents began sending a written message instead, a tradition that lasted until 1913, when President Woodrow Wilson went to Congress once again to give the report as an address.[12] Over the last century, presidents have turned this obligation into an opportunity to outline a broad policy agenda for the nation. That same passage also says that the president "may, on extraordinary Occasions convene both Houses, or either of them." Thus the president can call Congress into a special session to consider legislation or to hear him deliver an important speech.[13]

Have you watched a State of the Union address? What do you think its purpose was? What did you learn from it?

Congress's Ultimate Check on the Executive: Impeachment

Congress's ultimate check on the president is its power to remove him from office. Article II, Section 4 of the Constitution stipulates that the president, vice president, and all civil officers (including cabinet secretaries and federal judges) are subject to removal for "Treason, Bribery, or other high Crimes and Misdemeanors." Should these officers be removed from office, they may be subject to normal criminal charges and proceedings, where applicable.

impeachment: *Process whereby the House brings charges against the president or another federal official that will, upon conviction by the Senate, remove him or her from office.*

The process of removal begins with **impeachment** in the House of Representatives. Typically, the House Judiciary Committee investigates charges and recommends to the full House whether to impeach or not. If the House votes to impeach a federal officer, the Senate holds a trial, with the chief justice of the Supreme Court presiding. If two-thirds of the senators vote to convict, the official is removed from office.

At the highest level of federal office, two presidents—Andrew Johnson and Bill Clinton—have been impeached, but neither was convicted by the Senate, and both remained in office. Impeachment resolutions have been introduced by individual members of the House of Representatives against other presidents, but they were not acted on. The case of Richard M. Nixon shows that the threat of impeachment can be enough to remove a president from office. Knowing he was about to be impeached, Nixon resigned instead. In addition to charges of wrongdoing, partisan disagreements can influence some members of Congress in their votes to move forward with impeachment proceedings.

Think about the impeachments and the near-impeachment described here. What was the basis for impeachment in each case?

As the following discussion of these cases will show, impeachment is a rarely used but powerful instrument that makes it possible for Congress to hold the president accountable for his actions. In a democratic nation guided by the rule of law, all citizens are equally obligated to obey the laws of the land, including the president.

Andrew Johnson. The first presidential impeachment case was against President Andrew Johnson. A Democratic senator from Tennessee who had remained loyal to the Union, Johnson was elected as Lincoln's vice president in 1864 and succeeded to the presidency following Lincoln's assassination in 1865. Johnson opposed the Reconstruction policies of the Republican-dominated Congress, which included military occupation of the South. A standoff ensued in which Johnson vetoed Reconstruction acts and Congress overrode his vetoes.[14] Johnson's secretary of war, Edwin Stanton, stood with the Republicans, and Johnson would have dismissed him, but in 1867 Congress had passed, over Johnson's veto, the Tenure of Office Act, which prevented a president from firing a cabinet member without the Senate's approval. When Johnson took advantage of a loophole in the act to suspend Stanton, the Senate responded by refusing to confirm the suspension. Finally, on February 21, 1868, Johnson fired Stanton outright, contending that the Tenure of Office Act was unconstitutional.[15]

Impeachment proceedings against Johnson had already begun based on charges of usurpation of power; and when Johnson violated the Tenure of Office Act, the full House moved to approve eleven **articles of impeachment** against him by a vote of 126–47. The trial in the Senate began on March 30, and on May 16 the Senate voted 35 to convict (and 19 to acquit), one vote short of the two-thirds necessary to remove Johnson from office.[16] On May 26 the Senate voted on two more articles of impeachment but again failed to get the 36 votes necessary to convict, so it dropped all remaining charges, and the trial ended. President Johnson served out his term until March 1869, when he was succeeded by Ulysses S. Grant (1869–77). In 1887 Congress officially repealed the Tenure of Office Act.

Richard M. Nixon.

President Richard M. Nixon was embroiled in a serious scandal known as Watergate, after the name of a complex in Washington where the Democratic National Committee had its headquarters. It was there that the scandal began with a break-in on June 17, 1972 (see Figure 13.3). In August the *Washington Post* reported that the bank account of one of the five men caught in the act and arrested had $25,000 in funds originally given to the Nixon 1972 reelection campaign.[17]

Nixon denied any connection and was reelected in the fall, but all the while he and his aides were working to cover up the fact that his reelection committee had ordered the break-in to install listening devices on Democratic Party phones. Two *Washington Post* reporters, Bob Woodward and Carl Bernstein, continued to investigate the story. As connections between Nixon and the break-in were revealed, several of his aides were convicted of conspiracy, burglary, and wiretapping, and others resigned. In May 1973 the Senate's newly formed Watergate Committee began televised hearings on the Watergate break-in and cover-up, and the Justice Department appointed Archibald Cox as the **special prosecutor** in charge of the Watergate investigation.

In the months that followed, a Nixon staffer revealed that the president had tape-recorded all his White House conversations, and both the Senate Watergate Committee and the House Judiciary Committee formally issued **subpoenas** demanding that Nixon turn over the recordings. The turning point in what became known as the **Watergate scandal** came on Saturday, October 20, 1973, when President Nixon asked his attorney general, Elliott Richardson, to fire Archibald Cox and abolish the office of special prosecutor entirely. Richardson refused, as did the deputy attorney general. Both resigned. Solicitor General Robert Bork, next in command, then carried out the president's wishes. What had been a struggle for information became a question of obstruction of justice by the president.

President Nixon turned over a limited number of tapes, but there was an eighteen-and-a-half-minute gap on one tape, and Congress wanted to know what was discussed during that time and why it was erased. The administration claimed that the tape was erased by mistake. During the next months, Nixon released only partial transcripts and said that others were protected by **executive privilege**—the president's right to engage in communications with his advisers that he does not have to reveal. The justification for this privilege is that

What should happen when the president breaks the law?

articles of impeachment: *List of charges against the president in an impeachment proceeding.*

special prosecutor: *Attorney appointed by the Justice Department to investigate wrongdoing associated with the executive branch.*

subpoena: *Order issued by a legal authority demanding that an individual appear to testify at, or turn over documents relevant to, a legal proceeding.*

Watergate scandal: *Scandal uncovered by Washington Post reporters that led to the resignation of President Richard M. Nixon in 1974.*

executive privilege: *President's right to engage in confidential communications with his advisers.*

FIGURE 13.3 Watergate Chronology. The Watergate scandal undermined American confidence in the office of the presidency. In large part due to reporting by the *Washington Post*, evidence was uncovered that President Richard M. Nixon abused the powers of the office and lied about his role in covering up those abuses. He resigned the presidency rather than face impeachment.

June 17, 1972: Five men, one of whom says he used to work for the CIA, are arrested trying to bug the offices of the Democratic National Committee at the Watergate complex.

June 19, 1972: A GOP security aide is among the Watergate burglars. Former Attorney General John Mitchell, head of the Nixon reelection campaign, denies any link to the operation.

August 1, 1972: A $25,000 cashier's check, apparently earmarked for the Nixon campaign, is found in the bank account of a Watergate burglar.

October 10, 1972: FBI agents establish that the Watergate break-in stems from a massive campaign of political spying and sabotage conducted on behalf of the Nixon reelection effort.

November 7, 1972: Nixon is reelected in one of the largest landslides in American political history, taking more than 60 percent of the vote and crushing the Democratic nominee, Senator George McGovern of South Dakota.

January 30, 1973: Former Nixon aides G. Gordon Liddy and James W. McCord Jr. are convicted of conspiracy, burglary, and wiretapping in the Watergate incident.

April 30, 1973: Nixon's top White House staffers, H. R. Haldeman and John Ehrlichman, and Attorney General Richard Kleindienst resign over the scandal. White House counsel John Dean is fired.

May 18, 1973: The Senate Watergate Committee begins its nationally televised hearings. Attorney General–designate Elliot Richardson taps former Solicitor General Archibald Cox as the Justice Department's special prosecutor for Watergate.

June 13, 1973: Watergate prosecutors find a memo addressed to John Ehrlichman describing in detail the plans to burglarize the office of *Pentagon Papers* defendant Daniel Ellsberg's psychiatrist.

July 13, 1973: Alexander Butterfield, former presidential appointments secretary, reveals in congressional testimony that Nixon has recorded all conversations and telephone calls in his offices since 1971.

July 23, 1973: Nixon refuses to turn over the presidential tape recordings to the Senate Watergate Committee or the special prosecutor.

October 20, 1973: Nixon fires Archibald Cox and abolishes the office of the special prosecutor. Attorney General Richardson and Deputy Attorney General William D. Ruckelshaus resign in what is called the Saturday Night Massacre. Pressure for impeachment mounts in Congress.

November 17, 1973: Nixon declares, "I'm not a crook," maintaining his innocence in the Watergate case.

December 7, 1973: The White House is unable to explain an eighteen-and-one-half-minute gap in one of the subpoenaed tapes.

July 24, 1974: The Supreme Court rules unanimously that Nixon must turn over the tape recordings of sixty-four White House conversations, rejecting the president's claims of executive privilege.

July 27, 1974: The House Judiciary Committee passes the first of three articles of impeachment, charging obstruction of justice.

August 8, 1974: Richard Nixon becomes the first U.S. president to resign. Vice President Gerald R. Ford assumes the country's highest office. He will later pardon Nixon of all charges related to the Watergate case.

Source: Washington Post history of Watergate, www.washingtonpost.com.

Should the president have executive privilege?

the president must make difficult choices and, without the guarantee of privilege, may not receive or deliver the fullest information in the course of his deliberations.

The Supreme Court created an exception to this privilege in *United States v. Nixon* when on July 24, 1974, it unanimously ruled that executive privilege is not absolute and must give way when the government needs the information for a trial. The tapes showed that Nixon and his aides had conspired to cover up the Watergate break-in. Three days later the House Judiciary Committee approved three articles of impeachment against Nixon.[18] With the full House of Representatives ready to vote on the articles, President Nixon resigned on August 8, 1974.

In 1975 Nixon's successor, former Vice President Gerald R. Ford (1974–77), pardoned Nixon of all federal offenses he might have committed. The Watergate scandal had a negative impact on the American presidency, raising public mistrust of the office and of the federal government more generally.

William Jefferson Clinton.

The most recent case of impeachment involved President Bill Clinton.[19] In 1979 then Arkansas Governor Clinton and his wife Hillary formed a real estate company called Whitewater with some business associates. After Clinton was elected president in 1992, his foes pushed for an investigation into the Whitewater dealings, and in January 1994 public pressure led the attorney general to authorize an investigation by an independent counsel into these dealings. The first independent counsel was Robert Fiske, but he was perceived to be less than vigorous in pursuit of the investigation, and in August 1994 he was replaced by Kenneth Starr.[20]

Meanwhile, in an unrelated event, a woman named Paula Jones, who had met with then Governor Clinton in an Arkansas hotel room in 1991, had filed a sexual harassment suit against him. President Clinton's lawyers moved to prevent the lawsuit from proceeding while he was still in office.[21] That case, *Jones v. Clinton,* made its way to the Supreme Court, which on May 27, 1997, ruled that a sitting president has no immunity from a civil suit arising from

perjury: *Lying under sworn oath.*

Should the president be subjected to civil lawsuits while he is in office? State the reasons for your answer.

AP Photo/U.S. Senate

acts occurring before he took office and that Jones's lawsuit could proceed. In the course of their work, Jones's lawyers uncovered information alleging that Clinton had engaged in a sexual affair with a White House intern named Monica Lewinsky. Independent counsel Kenneth Starr found out about Lewinsky and her possible testimony in the Jones case, and he won permission to question the president about the affair. In essence, he was trying to secure evidence about whether President Clinton had committed **perjury** (lied under oath) about his relationship with Lewinsky during his deposition in the Jones trial.

Starr concluded that there was sufficient evidence that Clinton had committed perjury, and on September 9, 1998, he released his report to members of the House of Representatives.

Stemming from charges that he lied under oath in his testimony in the Paula Jones case, President Bill Clinton was impeached by the House of Representatives on December 19, 1998. In a trial that began the following month in the Senate, presided over by Chief Justice William Rehnquist, the president was acquitted.

In the impeachment process, what evidence do you see of checks and balances?

On October 8 the House approved an impeachment inquiry, and on December 19 the House debated four articles of impeachment against President Clinton for two counts of perjury, one count of obstruction of justice, and one count of **abuse of power**, subsequently voting to impeach Clinton on one count each of perjury and obstruction of justice.[22] The formal phase of the trial began in the Senate on January 7, 1999, and lasted until February 8, when voting fell far short of the two-thirds (sixty-seven) vote necessary to convict President Clinton of the two charges against him. He was acquitted and served out the remainder of his second term. Ironically, the original Whitewater investigation that had led to the impeachment proceedings failed to unearth solid evidence that President Clinton or his wife Hillary committed any crime.

Impeachment is not a power to be used lightly, but it does serve as a gateway for the public, through its elected officials in Congress, to hold the president, cabinet officials, and federal judges accountable for abuses of power.

The Growth of Executive Influence

What should be done about the growth of executive power? Is it a problem for checks and balances among the separate branches?

With all the formal constitutional restrictions on the president, one has to wonder how the modern presidency became so powerful. The answer lies in the general grant of executive power discussed earlier in the chapter. In addition to vesting this power in the president at the beginning of Article II, the Constitution also requires the president to "take Care that the Laws be faithfully executed," which he promises to do when he takes the oath of office. Presidents have found ways to unlock the enormous powers inherent in the general grant of power and in the **take care clause** to expand their role and authority by means not explicitly granted in the Constitution, and they draw on these powers to help them get their preferred policies enacted into law. The president's veto power and Congress's power to override and to impeach the president counteract each other and help ensure that each branch remains responsive to its governing responsibilities. However, Congress has no formal means to balance and check the president's growing executive power, though at times the judicial branch has been able to do so.

Presidential Directives and Signing Statements

Presidents use the executive power to issue **presidential directives** that give specific instructions on a federal policy that do not require congressional approval. Recent presidents have used this unilateral power much more frequently than previous presidents, especially under conditions of divided government or interbranch policy conflict.[23] Presidential directives might take the form of executive orders, proclamations, or military orders. They are the primary way that presidents shape policy implementation, and the instrument they use to act quickly in case of national emergencies.[24]

The best-known type of directive is the **executive order**, which can be used for a wide range of purposes. Typically, executive orders instruct federal employees to take a specific action or implement a policy in a particular way. Some scholars argue that executive orders are an important source of "independent authority" that is used solely at the discretion of the president.[25] Even though presidents since Washington have issued executive orders, the orders were not officially numbered until 1862 and not published in the *Federal Register* until 1935.[26] In 1948 President Harry Truman integrated the armed forces with Executive Order 9981, stating "there shall be equality of treatment and opportunity for all persons in the armed forces, without regard to race, color, religion, or national origin."[27] Truman used the power of executive order to bypass congressional and some military opposition to integration of the armed forces because he believed it was the right thing for the country.

Walter McNamee/CORBIS

The power of the presidency is symbolized by the unique presidential seal, which is emblazoned on the rug used in the Oval Office during the George W. Bush administration. The Oval Office, located in the West Wing of the White House, evokes the enormous power vested in a single elected official.

Similarly, in 1957 President Dwight D. Eisenhower (1953–61) used a combination of executive orders, **proclamations**, and **military orders** to enforce school integration in Little Rock, Arkansas. Following the 1954 and 1955 *Brown v. Board of Education* Supreme Court rulings that struck down the practice of segregation in public schools, the governor of Arkansas, Orval Faubus, called up the Arkansas National Guard to block nine African Americans from attending Central High School in Little Rock. President Eisenhower responded by issuing a proclamation calling on the governor to cease and desist, and when the governor ignored the proclamation Eisenhower issued Executive Order 10730 to send the 101st Airborne Division to Little Rock to ensure that the students would be allowed into the school. He also used his authority as commander in chief to take command of the Arkansas National Guard and order it to assist in the school's integration. Eisenhower intervened because he believed it was his obligation as president to enforce the laws of the land as set forth by the rulings of the Supreme Court.[28]

Still, a presidential directive is not completely immune from scrutiny or accountability. In 1952, during the Korean War, the United Steelworkers union threatened to stop work at steel mills. In response, President Truman used his executive powers to order the seizure of steel mills and put them under the control of the United States government. Although the steel workers were willing to put off the strike and work in the newly government-controlled mills, the steel mill owners sued to challenge the legality of the seizure. In *Youngstown Sheet and Tube Co. v. Sawyer,* better known as the *Steel Seizure* case, the Supreme Court ruled against the president, claiming he had no statutory authority from Congress to seize the mills and that his commander in chief status did not allow him to seize domestic property when the United States was at war in a foreign land (see Supreme Court Cases: *Youngstown Sheet and Tube Co. v. Sawyer*).

Federal Register: *Official published record of all executive branch rules, regulations, and orders.*

proclamation: *Presidential directive usually issued to declare a change in federal policy.*

military orders: *Presidential directive that gives instructions to a branch of the armed forces.*

supremecourtcases

Youngstown Sheet and Tube Co. v. Sawyer
(Steel Seizure Case, 1952)

QUESTION: Can the president seize steel mills to prevent a strike during wartime?

ORAL ARGUMENT: May 12, 1952

DECISION: June 2, 1952 (read at www.findlaw.com/casecode/supreme.html)

OUTCOME: No, the seizure was overturned (6–3).

After North Korea's invasion of South Korea in June 1950, President Harry Truman sought and received a United Nations resolution permitting intervention on behalf of South Korea. In 1952, with the Korean War still raging, the United Steelworkers announced plans for an April strike. President Truman feared that the strike would severely harm America's war effort. One alternative for putting off the strike was to seek a temporary court order prohibiting a strike when national security is at stake, a provision allowed under the Taft-Hartley Labor Act.

Uncomfortable with what was perceived to be an antilabor policy, Truman instead ordered Secretary of Commerce Charles Sawyer to seize the steel mills and run them under the flag of the United States. Because the steelworkers preferred working at the steel mills under the government to the Taft-Hartley alternatives, they agreed to come back to work after the seizure.

The steel mill owners then brought suit challenging the seizure. Truman claimed the authority to do this under his power to make sure that the laws were faithfully executed and his power as commander in chief of the armed forces. The Court's decision rejected the president's authority to seize the steel mills, noting that Congress had not passed a law allowing the seizure, so there were no laws involving the seizure to be faithfully executed. The Court also ruled that the president's authority to rule as commander in chief did not extend to domestic seizures during foreign wars. Without congressional authorization, the president could not seize the steel mills. A separate concurring opinion, since treated as the heart of the case, noted that the president's authority is at its peak when he acts under the express authority of Congress, is in a middle category when Congress has not acted, and is at its lowest when the president acts contrary to congressional will. As Congress had rejected granting the president the authority to seize property in labor disputes, Truman was acting under the lowest level of authority. Without congressional authorization, the president could not seize the steel mills.

The *Steel Seizure* case still stands as the leading decision on presidential authority. The Supreme Court relied heavily on it in deciding that President George W. Bush did not have the authority to hold enemy combatants from the war in Afghanistan at the U.S. naval base at Guantanamo Bay, Cuba, without a hearing, since Congress had not authorized the action.*

- **Why did the Court block President Truman's seizure of the steel mills?**
- **Did the decision place the president above Congress, below Congress, or equal to Congress in terms of making policy?**

* *Hamdan v. Rumsfeld,* 548 U.S. 557 (2006).

In foreign and military affairs, presidents can issue **presidential directives on national security**, which have a similar purpose to executive orders but are not published in the *Federal Register*. These directives can announce specific sanctions against individuals who are considered enemies of the United States or make larger statements about U.S. policy toward a foreign country. President George W. Bush used this power frequently in what he described as a war on terror and in the conduct of the wars in Afghanistan and Iraq. For example, he issued an order in 2001 to create

© Bettmann/CORBIS

military tribunals that would try suspected enemy combatants and terrorists, rather than allowing them to be tried in a regular military court. He also created a special subcategory called Homeland Security Presidential Directives, which are not as widely publicized as other directives and deal only with homeland security policy.

When a president signs a bill into law, he can issue **signing statements**, written remarks that reflect his interpretation of the law that are not required or authorized by the Constitution. Signing statements can be classified as nonconstitutional and constitutional (see Table 13.4). Nonconstitutional statements are typically symbolic, celebrating the passage of the law or providing technical instructions for implementing a bill. Constitutional statements are more serious in that the president uses them to indicate a disagreement with Congress on specific provisions in the bill. In constitutional signing statements, the president may go so far as to refuse to implement specific provisions of bills. This kind of statement is a challenge to Congress's constitutional authority to legislate.[29] Even when the presidency and the Congress are controlled by the same party, signing statements can be used to shift the implementation of policy toward presidential preferences. President Barack Obama recognized the controversy over signing statements, and he issued a memorandum early in his administration stating that he would use signing statements "to address constitutional concerns only when it is appropriate to do so as a means of discharging my constitutional responsibilities."[30] In issuing this memorandum, President Obama was trying to alleviate concerns about abusing executive power but at the same time preserving the presidential power to interpret legislation that is inherent in signing statements. In his first twenty months in office President Obama issued twelve signing statements and seventy executive orders.[31]

Presidential directives and signing statements create tension between the president and Congress and between the president and the judiciary because they are an expansion

In September 1957, in a move that demonstrated federal power over state power as well as the authority of the commander in chief, President Dwight D. Eisenhower sent the 101st Airborne Division to Little Rock, Arkansas, to protect nine African American students attempting to attend previously all-white Central High School. He also nationalized the Arkansas National Guard for the same purpose.

presidential directive on national security: *Presidential directive that deals with government action in the area of foreign policy and is not publicly released.*

military tribunal: *Specially authorized court that determines the innocence or guilt of enemy combatants.*

What limits can Congress, the courts, and/or the American people place on the president?

signing statements: *Written remarks issued by the president when signing a bill into law that often reflect his interpretation of how the law should be implemented.*

TABLE 13.4 Presidential Signing Statements, 1969–2008

President	Nonconstitutional	Constitutional	Total
Richard M. Nixon	111 (94.9%)	6 (5.1%)	117
Gerald R. Ford	123 (89.8%)	14 (10.2%)	137
Jimmy Carter	198 (86.8%)	30 (13.2%)	228
Ronald Reagan	165 (66.3%)	84 (33.7%)	249
George H. W. Bush	106 (46.5%)	122 (53.5%)	228
William Jefferson Clinton	294 (77.4%)	86 (22.6%)	380
George W. Bush	32 (19.9%)	129 (80.1%)	161
Total	**1,029 (68.6%)**	**471 (31.4%)**	**1,500**

Source: Michael J. Berry, "Controversially Executing the Law: George W. Bush and the Constitutional Signing Statement," *Congress and the Presidency* 36 (2009): 252.

bully pulpit: *Nickname for the power of the president to use the attention associated with the office to persuade the media, Congress, and the public to support his policy positions.*

President Theodore Roosevelt was a larger-than-life figure who challenged corporate monopolies, sought to strengthen U.S. international power, and increased federal efforts at land conservation. He was known for using the office of the president as a bully pulpit to persuade the public to support his policies.

of presidential power. At times they have been deemed illegal.[32] Many presidents, from Lincoln to Franklin Delano Roosevelt to George W. Bush, have taken temporary actions that have violated constitutional rights in the name of national security, from suspending *habeas corpus* to interning Japanese Americans to eavesdropping on U.S. citizens (see Chapter 4, Civil Liberties, and Chapter 5, Civil Rights, for expanded discussions of these actions). Judging the merit of such actions is difficult because citizens have to decide whether the president is acting in good faith on behalf of the country or seeking to expand his own power and agenda.

Power to Persuade

Presidents understand that communicating well with the public is essential to building support for their policies. President Theodore Roosevelt (1901–1909) described the office of the president as a **bully pulpit**, where presidents could use the attention associated with the office to make a public argument in favor of or against a policy.[33] The key to using the bully pulpit effectively is to explain a policy in simple and accessible terms, to get the public's attention, and to frame an issue in a way that is favorable to the president's policy position. Using the bully pulpit can accomplish the president's goals only If he already has a receptive audience. In today's highly partisan and divided political climate, there is no guarantee that the president's detractors will listen to his message.[34]

A president's relationship with the members of the news media is a crucial factor in successful communication, and it has evolved dramatically over time. Samuel Kernell, a presidential media scholar, argues that over the last seventy years, presidents have increased the extent to which they control their interactions with the press. Press conferences are one important way of sustaining a relationship with the news media, and presidents have tried to use them to their advantage. Some presidents are more comfortable with the press than others. Franklin Delano Roosevelt held an average of eighteen solo press conferences per year, Lyndon Baines Johnson held twenty-five, Ronald Reagan held six, Bill Clinton held six, and George W. Bush held five. In his first twenty months in office, Barack Obama held ten.[35] Press conferences are somewhat risky because, unlike speeches, presidents do not control the content of the questions that are asked, and they can sometimes make unrehearsed statements that have political consequences. For this reason, Barack Obama has also used new technologies to bypass the media and speak directly to the people: creating a blog on the White House website, posting videos of his speeches, and sending mass e-mails to citizens who inquire about specific proposals.[36]

Political scientist Richard Neustadt has argued that the real power of the presidency can be measured in how successfully a president persuades members of Congress and other policy makers to support his policies. Several factors affect a president's power to persuade, notably his professional reputation and his **approval ratings**.[37] A presidential approval rating is usually expressed as the percentage of the American people who say the president is doing a good job. A president's professional reputation is a combination of his prior experience and the steps he takes throughout his term. When a president comes to the Oval Office with executive experience or a strong reputation as a productive legislator, he is likely to have a reservoir of respect from members of Congress, the public, and the media. That reservoir can become depleted if the president makes missteps and is not successful with his legislative agenda.

Lawmakers are more likely to pass a president's policy proposals when his approval rating is high, and they are less cooperative when the president is unpopular. Members of Congress pay attention to presidential approval ratings because national polls are a barometer of public opinion. Members of Congress from districts or states in which a majority of voters chose the incumbent president generally want to support the president. It follows, then, a large presidential electoral victory will yield a greater number of supportive members of Congress. Even members of Congress from districts that did not support the incumbent president want to be careful in the way that they oppose a popular president for fear of looking unpatriotic or unresponsive to majority public opinion. Public approval can be essential to presidential policy success, which is why the president tries to maintain public support throughout his years in the White House (see Chapter 6, Public Opinion, for more on presidential approval ratings and presidential effectiveness).[38]

To be persuasive, a president has to balance his own policy preferences with those of members of Congress to and convince the American public that he is leading the country in the right direction.[39] The stakes can be very high for presidents as they navigate the legislative process. The president's need to be responsive to public opinion serves as a gateway for influence by the public on his decision making. As discussed in Chapter 12, Congress, President Obama successfully pushed for a reform of the nation's health care system in his first two years in office and simultaneously had to negotiate with Congress

AP Photo

President John F. Kennedy was completely at ease with the press and held sixty-four press conferences during his time in office. They were televised, and not only White House reporters, but also the American public, looked forward to the lively exchanges between the press and the president, who was known for his sense of humor and ready wit.

How does the current president use the bully pulpit to generate public support for his ideas?

approval rating: *Job performance evaluation for the president, Congress, or other public official or institution that is generated by public opinion polls and is typically reported as a percentage.*

Does the bully pulpit serve as a communication gateway between the president and citizens?

Has the increased emphasis on job approval ratings strengthened the power of the public to hold the president accountable?

and appeal for support from the American public. The president traveled the country to give speeches at health care–focused events, gave a nationally televised presidential address to Congress, and met personally with members of Congress, efforts that were designed to simultaneously persuade Congress and the public that health care reform was necessary. His efforts yielded legislative success, and he signed health care reform legislation into law in March 2010.

Agenda Setting

As the chief executive officer of the entire federal government, the president has an obligation and an opportunity to work with Congress to set the foreign and domestic policy agenda for the nation, from determining how to configure military strength, to overseeing economic growth, to ensuring the health and safety of individual citizens. The president has formal and informal advantages over Congress in directing the federal agenda toward his policy preferences, starting with the fact that he is the sole occupant of his elected office, as compared with 535 members of the House and Senate. Consequently, the president has the power to focus the nation's attention on his ideas and policy proposals.

head of state: *Title given to the president as national leader.*

In dealing with foreign powers, the president is **head of state** and commander in chief of the military. As head of state, the president oversees a vast organization of employees in the State Department and the office of the U.S. Trade Representative who lay the groundwork for negotiations with foreign leaders on issues ranging from nuclear weapons control to trade policy. Upon their recommendation, the president proposes new treaties or revisions to existing agreements as needed. Ultimately, the president is the public face of and the authority behind U.S. foreign policy decisions. He must establish working relationships with foreign leaders and demonstrate an understanding of how other nations' political systems operate, especially the extent to which the executive power is placed in one person or shared, as it is in parliamentary systems (see Other Places: The Executive Power in India).

Because the president is presumed to serve the best interest of the entire nation, the American public frequently supports most of his foreign policies—at least initially. The main congressional counterweights to the president's powers in these areas are the power of the Senate to ratify treaties and the power of Congress to appropriate money for federal programs, including foreign aid and diplomatic programs. These congressional powers come in the form of responses to the president's proposals. Congress can have some influence on the president's foreign policy agenda through hearings and press statements, but if the president is able to persuade the public to support his positions, he is typically able to forge his own path on foreign policy.

federal budget: *Budget of all federal programs, typically released by the president in early February.*

In the area of domestic policy, the president uses the State of the Union address, the **federal budget**, the power to make executive appointments, the bully pulpit, the executive power to implement laws, and the veto power as his agenda-setting tools. He issues his federal budget in early February, shortly after he delivers the State of the Union address. The budget is a blueprint that indicates his spending priorities for all areas of the federal government. Congress does not have to abide by this budget, and Congress frequently ignores it and constructs its own federal budget (see Chapter 12 for a discussion of the budget). All measures that raise taxes and spend federal money can be vetoed by the president, and, as we have seen, the veto or the threat of a veto gives the president a means of exerting pressure on Congress to follow his budget priorities.

Identify two of the president's agenda-setting tools.

⬤otherplaces

The Executive Power in India

The Indian political system is a democracy with elements of the U.S. system of separated powers. The president is elected by the members of the federal and state legislatures and serves a five-year term. There is also a vice president who serves for the same number of years. The president is the head of state and commander in chief of the armed forces, appoints federal officers and judges, and selects the prime minister from among the members of the majority party in the legislature or, if there is no clear majority, from the party with the largest share of seats in the legislature.

The presidency in India is largely a ceremonial office. President Pratibha Devisingh Patil encourages unity and uses her visibility to draw attention to national issues such as education, the arts, and health care. On March 8, 2010, International Women's Day, she presented awards to eminent Indian women in recognition of their personal courage and integrity.

Unlike the unitary executive in the United States, the president and the prime minister of India share executive responsibilities. The president focuses more on symbolic activities, and the prime minister leads the policy-making process. The prime minister oversees all the ministers who run government departments, proposes changes to domestic and foreign policy, and works directly with the Ministry of External Affairs to negotiate treaties and international agreements with foreign countries.

However, the president can be an important figure in Indian politics by encouraging national unity and cooperation across different political and religious groups. The president does this by promoting issues that all citizens can agree on, such as the availability of education, health care, and immunizations. President Pratibha Devisingh Patil was elected the first female president of India in 2007 as a member of the United Progressive Alliance. President Patil has been especially persuasive in encouraging greater female participation in the Indian parliament and in promoting the cause of women's rights. She also represents the nation at domestic and international events in an effort to promote Indian accomplishments in the economic, intellectual, and artistic arenas.

- **How do the president and the prime minister of India share executive power?**

- **What powers do the president of India and the president of the United States have in common?**

Sources: The President of India, www.presidentofindia .nic.in; Prime Minister of India, www.pmindia.nic.in/pmo .htm; PressTV, "Indian President Calls for Empowerment of Women," March 9, 2010, www.presstv.ir.

The president engages in domestic policy agenda setting in other ways as well. For example, as in the case of President Obama and health care, presidents can propose legislation that changes existing programs or creates new ones, and ask Congress to consider his suggestions. He can also be even more proactive by issuing presidential directives that direct the bureaucracy to implement laws as he sees fit. The president's major speeches, press conferences, interviews, and travels always command media attention, so he has a constantly open forum to try to persuade voters to support his proposals.[40]

AP Photo/Pablo Martinez Monsivais

The president, as head of state, engages in direct diplomacy with foreign leaders in a number of different settings. On November 24, 2009, President Barack Obama received the Indian Prime Minister Dr. Manmohan Singh and his wife at a state dinner in Washington. Such formal functions expose world leaders to elite members of the American political and economic arenas.

What powers should the president have during wartime?

The President in Wartime

As executive branch powers have grown, presidents have increasingly come into conflict with the other two branches of government, especially in times of national crisis and war. As Chapter 4 (Civil Liberties) and Chapter 7 (The News Media and the Internet) demonstrate, the judicial branch frequently protects the right of the free press to exercise its watchdog role, even in reports related to national security. In this section, we examine the power struggle between the president and Congress over war powers, which the Constitution divides between the two branches, and the power struggle between the president and the judiciary on the scope of presidential powers and civil liberties.

Power Struggles between the President and Congress

The Constitution gives Congress the power to declare war, but it has been the practice for presidents to first formally ask Congress for a declaration of war. Once Congress declares war, the president as commander in chief has the authority to direct the conflict. Through its constitutional powers in Article I, Section 8 to "to raise and support Armies" and "to provide and maintain a Navy," Congress retains the power to cut off the flow of money for the war effort. Generally, the president and Congress have worked together in times of military conflict, but in the late 1960s opposition to the Vietnam War brought about significant divisions between the executive and legislative branches over war powers.

Vietnam and the War Powers Act.
Vietnam had been a divided nation since 1954, with Communist forces controlling North Vietnam and anti-Communists controlling South Vietnam, and a civil war had erupted between them. President Dwight D. Eisenhower and then Presidents John F. Kennedy and Lyndon Baines Johnson believed that containing Communism and keeping the North Vietnamese Communists from taking over South

Vietnam were important, but the U.S. troop buildup was slow at first. In 1964, however, President Johnson presented evidence to Congress that the North Vietnamese were attacking U.S. ships on patrol duty in international waters in the Gulf of Tonkin off the shore of North Vietnam. Johnson asked Congress for the authority to fight back, and Congress responded with the Tonkin Gulf Resolution, stating that "The Congress approves and supports the determination of the President, as Commander in Chief, to take all necessary measures to repel any armed attack against the forces of the United States and to prevent further aggression."[41] Congress passed the resolution with only two dissenting votes, few restrictions, and no time limit on how long the United States would stay involved in the conflict.[42]

By 1968 the United States had more than five hundred thousand troops in Vietnam, and the conflict was commonly referred to as the Vietnam War, although there was never a formal declaration of war by Congress. The conflict had become highly unpopular, and President Johnson was forced to give up his bid for reelection. That year, Richard M. Nixon was elected president and promised to end the Vietnam War; however, he actually broadened the conflict to the neighboring countries of Cambodia and Laos in his efforts to win the war.

By 1971 Congress had repealed the Tonkin Gulf Resolution, and, following the Paris Peace Accords signed in January 1973, U.S. troops were withdrawn from Vietnam. In October 1973 Congress passed a more formal proposal to limit presidential authority to engage in military conflict. This **War Powers Act** states that the president cannot send troops into military conflict for more than a total of ninety days without seeking a formal declaration of war, or authorization for continued military action, from Congress. President Nixon vetoed the act, but Congress overrode the veto.

The War Powers Act was ostensibly a gate that would stand in the way of a president's decision to launch a war without first gauging congressional support. Although the act tried to clarify presidential authority and limits, the scholar Louis Fisher argues that it is flawed because the ninety-day limit does not begin until the president has officially reported the troop engagement to Congress. A president could send troops into a conflict and not report it to Congress, thereby avoiding a trigger of the War Powers Act.[43] Moreover, the act did not really give Congress the power to end a military conflict except by denying all funding for it, as it ultimately did with Vietnam. However, if there is considerable public support for an ongoing military engagement, the president can make the case that it is too dangerous to cut off all funding, and Congress would be reluctant to cut off funding when troops were still in the field and could be harmed. The irony of the War Powers Act is that it gives presidents an incentive to seek a declaration of war or authorization to use military force, after which time Congress loses much of its control of the operation of the conflict.[44] In other words, once Congress gives the president permission to go to war, it is next to impossible for Congress to stop the war.[45]

The Iraq War.

The most recent struggle between the president and Congress over a military conflict has been the Iraq War that began in 2003. Its origins date back to August 1990, when Iraq invaded Kuwait. This act of aggression caused a worldwide outcry, and in late January 1991 the United States led a United Nations–sanctioned multilateral effort to push Iraq out of Kuwait, a conflict known as the Gulf War. The Gulf War was short-lived and successful; as part of the peace settlement, Iraq was prohibited from developing weapons of mass destruction and was required to submit to constant UN monitoring.

War Powers Act: *1973 act that provides that the president cannot send troops into military conflict for more than a total of ninety days without seeking a formal declaration of war, or authorization for continued military action, from Congress.*

Think about the conduct of war. Who should be in charge? The president? Congress? The military?

By 2002 it had become increasingly difficult for UN inspectors to accurately assess Iraq's capabilities for producing weapons of mass destruction. Although there had been no concrete evidence of such weapons, President George W. Bush argued that a preemptive strike against Iraq was necessary to preserve the security of the United States. In accordance with the War Powers Act, President Bush asked Congress for a resolution authorizing military action. On October 10, 2002, the House of Representatives approved a joint resolution that gave the president the authority to use all military force to "defend the national security of the United States" and to ensure that Saddam Hussein, the Iraqi leader, complied with a UN resolution allowing inspectors into Iraq to search for weapons of mass destruction.[46] The Senate approved the resolution the next day by a vote of 77–23.

President George W. Bush, in his role as commander in chief, requested and was granted authority from Congress to use all military force necessary to enforce UN requirements for inspection for weapons of mass destruction in Iraq. The United States launched a military action in 2003, with no declaration of war issued by Congress.

The Iraq War was launched on March 19, 2003. The initial phase was over quickly. Saddam Hussein was captured in December 2003 and was eventually tried and hanged for war crimes. Nevertheless, instability in Iraq continued. By 2006, with violence in Iraq at a high level, the Democrats in Congress—many of whom had initially supported the war—withdrew their support and called for the return of all U.S. troops and an end to the war. During the midterm congressional elections that year, Democrats made ending the war a campaign issue, and they won majority control of the House and the Senate. However, they were unable to make significant progress in bringing U.S. involvement in the Iraq War to an end. Instead, in January 2007 President Bush increased the number of troops in Iraq in an effort known as the "surge," which was designed to reduce the violence there.

In January 2009, when President Obama was inaugurated, the three dominant groups in Iraq—the Sunnis, the Shiites, and the Kurds—operated under a parliamentary system of government. In March 2010 the Iraqis held their second round of national elections. Although a great deal of instability remains, the Iraqis are making progress toward a legitimate democracy. President Obama announced that he would keep his campaign promise to initiate the return of the majority of U.S. troops within sixteen months. He worked with the secretary of defense and the Iraqi army to safely withdraw U.S. troops, and on August 31, 2010, he announced the end of the nation's formal combat involvement in Iraq.

The Afghanistan War.

At the time the Iraq War seemed to be coming to a close, the ongoing war in Afghanistan flared up considerably. This conflict began after the September 11, 2001, terrorist attacks were traced back to al Qaeda operatives harbored by the Afghan Taliban regime. President George W. Bush addressed Congress on September 20, 2001, indicating that the Taliban would be held responsible for the attacks, and in early October the United States and its allies launched a military action on Afghanistan designed to find those responsible for the 9/11 attacks and bring down the Taliban regime. Although the Taliban

How much responsibility should Presidents Bush and Obama assume for the Iraq and Afghanistan Wars, respectively? Does Congress have shared responsibility in those conflicts?

regime was subsequently toppled and a new leader, Hamid Karzai, was elected and later reelected, the Taliban mounted a resurgence in Afghanistan. In 2009 President Obama, as commander in chief, responded to resurgent Taliban-sponsored attacks on U.S. troops and civilian Afghanis by ordering 30,000 additional troops to Afghanistan; by September 2010 there were 98,000 American troops there.[47]

The tension between the presidency and Congress over war powers compels the president to make the case to Congress and the American people that military action is necessary. When President Obama made his decision to increase troop levels in Afghanistan, he gave a speech at West Point on December 1, 2009, to outline his rationale.[48] His speech was met with general but reserved support from Congress; Republicans were more vocally supportive of the increase than were their

AP Photo/Charles Dharapak

Democratic counterparts, who were skeptical but refrained from outright criticism of a Democratic president.[49] A problem arises for presidents when congressional and public support starts to erode and the original rationale for the war is questioned. After President Obama outlined his Afghanistan strategy, public opinion was narrowly supportive of the effort (51 percent to 40 percent, with 9 percent undecided).[50] With such limited support, and growing casualties, maintaining U.S. involvement there might become difficult, and, as President George W. Bush learned in Iraq, an unpopular war can erode a president's popularity and effectiveness, as discussed in Chapter 6.

After the September 11, 2001, attacks, the United States held the Taliban government in Afghanistan responsible for harboring members of al Qaeda, including its leader, Osama bin Laden, who claimed responsibility for the attacks. President George W. Bush requested and was granted authority from Congress to attack Afghanistan to capture those responsible. Here President Barack Obama pays a surprise visit to troops in Afghanistan on March 28, 2010.

Power Struggles between the President and the Judiciary

Power struggles between the president and the judiciary in wartime generally focus on civil liberties. In Chapter 4 we examined the Court's rejection of Abraham Lincoln's argument about the suspension of *habeas corpus*, and in Chapter 5 we discussed the Court's acquiescence in President Franklin Delano Roosevelt's executive order on the internment of Japanese Americans.

As noted earlier, the leading case on presidential authority in wartime is the *Steel Seizure* case, which ruled that the Constitution grants "all legislative Powers" to Congress. Because Congress had enacted no law authorizing the seizure of the steel mills and, indeed, had explicitly rejected giving the president such power, the president did not have any constitutional authority for the seizure. Nor did the president's role as commander in chief of the armed forces authorize the action because the steel mills were not part of the theater of war. Supreme Court Justice Robert H. Jackson's concurring opinion agreed with the result but set out a separate rationale, which is now widely cited as precedent. Jackson argued that the president's authority is at its peak when his actions are consistent with the express or implied will of Congress, is in a middle territory in the absence of a congressional grant or denial of power, and is at its lowest when he acts, as he did in seizing the mills, contrary to the express or implied will of Congress.[51]

What limits should the judiciary impose on presidential actions in wartime? Give examples.

The most recent clashes between the president and the judiciary over wartime powers arose during President George W. Bush's declared war on terror. Following the terrorist attacks of September 11, 2001, President Bush greatly expanded the powers of the executive branch of government. Specifically, he created separate military tribunals to try captured terrorists, claimed exemption from the **Geneva Convention** rules on the treatment and detainment of prisoners, and authorized the National Security Agency to monitor conversations of suspected terrorists with residents of the United States without obtaining warrants. President Bush's justification was that, as commander in chief, he had the foremost responsibility to protect American citizens and that actions taken for that purpose should be not be subject to the approval of Congress or the courts.

A combination of congressional action and Supreme Court decisions following the guidelines of the *Steel Seizure* case constrained most of these presidential actions. In 2004 the Supreme Court's *Hamdi v. Rumsfeld* decision rejected Bush administration attempts to deny *habeas corpus* protections to an enemy combatant who was a U.S. citizen because federal law prohibits such denial to U.S. citizens.[52] That same day the Court also rejected the administration's authority to deny *habeas corpus* to an enemy combatant who was not a U.S. citizen.[53] The Bush administration then established special military tribunals to review the detention of enemy combatants at Guantanamo Bay, but the Court rejected the authority of the tribunals because Congress had not authorized them.[54] The Court rejected congressional and presidential efforts to limit the Court's jurisdiction to hear such appeals, claiming that those limits did not apply to cases that had been filed before Congress passed the law. Even when Congress and the president authorized tribunals, the Supreme Court declared that neither Congress nor the president has the authority to suspend *habeas corpus*, which the Constitution allows only during "Cases of Rebellion or Invasion."[55] Thus, in cases involving terrorism, the Court has put gates in the way of Congress and the president in their efforts to restrict civil liberties in the name of national security. (For a broader discussion of the balance between laws against terrorism and civil liberties, see Chapter 4.)

How are acts of terrorism different from or the same as acts of war? How should the president, Congress, and the judiciary respond to terrorist attacks?

Two days after President Obama was inaugurated, he issued three executive orders requiring a complete evaluation of all policies related to interrogation, detention, and military tribunals for military prisoners, and he ordered an immediate stop to practices that constituted torture under international law.[56] At the same time, he declared his intent to close the detention center at Guantanamo Bay, but not in a way that would put U.S. citizens at risk from terrorism threats. Because of security concerns about sending prisoners back to their home countries, that process has taken longer than expected. In May 2009 President Obama decided that the United States would continue the use of military tribunals to prosecute terrorism suspects so long as they were guaranteed fundamental constitutional rights in the process.

The Organization of the Modern White House

The way that a president organizes the Executive Office and the cabinet reveals a great deal about his management style as well as his policy preferences. The president relies on his White House advisers for policy recommendations. The modern president has the challenge of encouraging cooperation between political appointees and members of the civil service and making sure that employees in each category are held accountable for their decisions.

The Executive Office of the President

The president runs a large organization known as the **Executive Office of the President (EOP)**, a loosely knit unit of several key organizations that report directly to him. These include the **White House Office**, the **Office of Management and Budget (OMB)**, the **National Security Council** (NSC), and the **Council of Economic Advisers** (CEA). Each office has influence over budgetary, military, and economic policies. Stephanie Cutter worked in the EOP when she served on the communications staff for Presidents Clinton and Obama.

The growth of the president's staff in the past seventy-five years is stunning. At the start of his term, President Franklin Delano Roosevelt had only sixty employees; President George W. Bush had more than five thousand people working directly or indirectly for him, and the Obama administration is expected to equal that number.[57] Roosevelt established the Executive Office of the President, and his decision in 1939 to move the Bureau of the Budget from the Treasury Department to the EOP gave the president more direct control over the federal budget. But the EOP really grew during the administration of Dwight D. Eisenhower, a highly decorated army general who was accustomed to a formal chain of command. He instituted a more formal staff structure in the White House, starting with the appointment of the first **chief of staff**, Sherman Adams. Eisenhower also raised the status of the National Security Council and the Bureau of the Budget to full advisory roles reporting directly to his office.

Staff organizations can have a real impact on the success of a presidential administration. For many presidents, the choice of how to organize their staffs rests with their own personalities and operating styles. These personal characteristics can make a president more or less likely to take advice from one adviser, or balance the advice from several advisers and come to a final decision on his own; how much presidents rely on their advisers often depends on how much they trust their own judgment.[58]

In general, a tightly organized White House staff organization yields a productive presidency, and the chief of staff is central to that effort in several ways. He serves as a gatekeeper by controlling the flow of staff and paperwork and focuses the president's attention on key issues. The chief of staff also monitors the coherence of presidential policies across cabinet departments and can serve as a referee for disagreements among members of the president's senior staff. Lastly, he can be important in forming bridges between the president and Congress; President Obama acknowledged that this was a major reason why he chose Rahm Emanuel, a former congressman from Illinois, as his chief of staff. When Emanuel left in October 2010, President Obama replaced him with a longtime Capitol Hill staff member, Pete Rouse.

When a president fails to get his agenda approved, he may respond by changing his senior staff. In its first two years, Bill Clinton's administration was viewed as chaotic and inefficient, and not adept at dealing with Congress. In November 1994 Republicans took control of the House and Senate largely by portraying Democratic Party government (the Democrats controlled Congress as well as the presidency) as a failure. Clinton's response to the electoral losses of his own party was to replace his chief of staff, Thomas McLarty, his childhood friend from Arkansas, with Leon Panetta, a former congressman with considerable legislative experience. Panetta brought order and discipline to the White House, and Clinton was able to produce enough popular policies to win reelection to a second term.

Executive Office of the President (EOP): *Organization that houses all staff members who work directly for the president.*

White House Office: *President's personal staff organization.*

Office of Management and Budget (OMB): *Federal agency that oversees the federal budget and all federal regulations.*

National Security Council: *President's personal set of advisers on international security.*

Council of Economic Advisers: *President's personal set of advisers on the economy.*

How have presidents chosen to manage all the responsibilities of the Executive Office?

chief of staff: *Person who coordinates and oversees interactions among the president, his personal staff, and his cabinet secretaries.*

President Harry S. Truman had a sign on his desk that read "The Buck Stops Here." What did it mean?

Another important element in presidential productivity is staff continuity, and new presidents often bring former executive branch personnel into their administrations. These staff members bring personal experience to a new president's organization. They also bring policy expertise that will help bolster the president in dealing with members of Congress who specialize in specific policy areas. Some prominent individuals who have served in multiple administrations include Patrick Buchanan, Donald Rumsfeld, Colin Powell, Condoleezza Rice, and Leon Panetta, who was brought back into the executive branch by President Obama to be the director of the Central Intelligence Agency.

The Office of the Vice President

Traditionally, the office of the vice president has not had many important responsibilities. It was not until the twentieth century that vice presidents were chosen by presidential candidates to enhance their electoral prospects, and even then, once they were in office, they were given little more than ceremonial tasks. However, with the increasing complexity and international significance of the presidential role following World War II, President Dwight D. Eisenhower assigned his vice president, Richard M. Nixon, the task of traveling around the world to meet with foreign leaders. Twenty years later Walter Mondale, President Jimmy Carter's vice president, expanded the role of the office by serving as a close adviser to the president on issues ranging from national security to domestic policy.[59] More recently, Al Gore , vice president to President Clinton, took on responsibility for specific issues, including federal efficiency, science and technology, and global warming.

Each vice president tries to carve out a role that he is most comfortable with and that the president finds acceptable. During the eight years of the George W. Bush administration, for example, Vice President Richard Cheney assumed a prominent role in the nation's military and foreign policy. He had been secretary of defense under Bush's father, George H. W. Bush (1989–93), and oversaw the Gulf War. Cheney was widely perceived to be highly influential on such issues as the Iraq War, antiterrorism policies, and energy development. The fact that George W. Bush relied so heavily on Cheney to make key decisions elevated the power, visibility, and even controversy of the role of the vice president. Cheney's successor, Joseph Biden, who serves as vice president under President Obama, has also been given considerable responsibility for foreign affairs. Ultimately, the people hold the president accountable for the actions and policies of his administration; even if a vice president exerts influence, it is the president who bears responsibilities for the outcomes.

What constitutional responsibilities does the vice president have? What authority should he have?

The Office of the First Lady

The role of the first lady has evolved over the history of the presidency, paralleling in some ways the increasing public roles available to women over the past century. Although the wife of the president has always been seen as an important partner in the president's social and diplomatic activities, such as planning receptions and dinners, her role as a public advocate on policy issues emerged in the twentieth century. Eleanor Roosevelt, the wife of Franklin Delano Roosevelt, was widely believed to hold considerable sway over her husband's views, but her most public moment as first lady came in 1939 when she came to the defense of Marian Anderson, a famous African American opera singer. When the Daughters of the American Revolution canceled a performance by Anderson at Constitution Hall on account of her race, Eleanor Roosevelt arranged for Anderson to perform on the steps of the Lincoln Memorial in

What do Americans expect from the first lady? Does her office serve as a gateway for the expression of views on women's issues?

front of thousands of cheering listeners.[60] Her action was interpreted as a strong stand for civil rights, despite the fact that her husband's administration was not actively pursuing civil rights as part of the domestic agenda.

The modern office of the first lady has no formally stated responsibilities, but the first lady has a staff that includes a press secretary, a scheduler, and speechwriters. Since Eleanor Roosevelt, first ladies have often taken on single issues to champion, such as Lady Bird Johnson on nature conservation, Betty Ford on alcoholism, Rosalynn Carter on mental health, Nancy Reagan on drug addiction, Barbara Bush on literacy, Hillary Clinton on health care and child welfare, and Laura Bush on reading and education. As first lady, Michelle Obama has taken a broad approach to her role by emphasizing the contribution each individual can make in his or her community on a range of issues from homelessness, to education, to childhood nutrition.

Michelle Obama is the first African American first lady, and like Hillary Clinton, she came to the White House from a career as a practicing attorney. She is also the mother of two daughters. The first lady has a wide range of duties as the wife of the president, including hosting dignitaries, overseeing White House events, and advancing important social causes. On May 25, 2010, Michelle Obama, kicked off a series of events to promote physical activity and engage children in Let's Move, a campaign to combat the epidemic of childhood obesity.

Presidential Greatness

President Obama is the forty-fourth president of the United States. The men who came before him served with varying degrees of success as leaders in foreign and domestic policy. Presidential leadership is judged by whether a president is able to get his preferred policies passed by Congress and enacted into law and by how well he oversees the bureaucracy to make the government run effectively and efficiently (for more on the bureaucracy, see Chapter 14).

The American people like to rank their presidents, and scholars also assess presidential greatness, looking at the clarity of a president's vision for policy, his communication and negotiation skills, and the effectiveness of his use of presidential powers, especially the general grant of executive power (see Figure 13.4). Good presidents do not have to excel in every one of these categories, but they have to compensate for a weakness in one area with greater strength in another. Stephen Skowronek argues that presidents have opportunities to continue the policies of their predecessors or forge new paths, and that the decisions they make in this regard affect their presidential greatness factor. He also points out that a president's success is often determined by external events, such as a terrorist attack or a global economic downturn.[61] The scholar Aaron Wildavsky suggests that there are actually "two presidencies": a foreign policy presidency and a domestic policy presidency.[62] On foreign policy, the president often must work quickly and in private, as negotiations must be conducted discretely. Domestic politics rarely require immediate action and usually entail open debate, with many citizens and interest groups vested in the outcome.[63]

The following discussion focuses on three presidents who are frequently singled out for their impact on public policy: Franklin Delano Roosevelt, a Democrat from a wealthy, elite New York family; Lyndon Baines Johnson, a Democrat from a very poor Texas family; and Ronald Reagan, a Republican from a middle-class family in Illinois. Each had a major impact on domestic and foreign policies during the twentieth century.[64] Each had strengths and

Name two presidents you think should be called great.

FIGURE 13.4 Presidential Leadership Survey, 2009.

C-SPAN 2009 Historians Presidential Leadership Survey

HISTORIANS SURVEY RESULTS CATEGORY

TOTAL SCORES/OVERALL RANKING

President's Name	2009 Final Score	Overall Ranking 2009	Overall Ranking 2000
Abraham Lincoln	902	1	1
George Washington	854	2	3
Franklin D. Roosevelt	837	3	2
Theodore Roosevelt	781	4	4
Harry S. Truman	708	5	5
John F. Kennedy	701	6	8
Thomas Jefferson	698	7	7
Dwight D. Eisenhower	689	8	9
Woodrow Wilson	683	9	6
Ronald Reagan	671	10	11
Lyndon B. Johnson	641	11	10
James K. Polk	606	12	12
Andrew Jackson	606	13	13
James Monroe	605	14	14
Bill Clinton	605	15	21
William McKinley	599	16	15
John Adams	545	17	16
George H. W. Bush	542	18	20
John Quincy Adams	542	19	19
James Madison	535	20	18
Grover Cleveland	523	21	17
Gerald R. Ford	509	22	23
Ulysses S. Grant	490	23	33
William Howard Taft	485	24	24
Jimmy Carter	474	25	22
Calvin Coolidge	469	26	27
Richard M. Nixon	450	27	25
James A. Garfield	445	28	29
Zachary Taylor	443	29	28
Benjamin Harrison	442	30	31
Martin Van Buren	435	31	30
Chester A. Arthur	420	32	32
Rutherford B. Hayes	409	33	26
Herbert Hoover	389	34	34
John Tyler	372	35	36
George W. Bush	362	36	NA
Millard Fillmore	351	37	35
Warren G. Harding	327	38	38

SURVEY LINKS

Index

Total Scores/Overall Ranking

Survey Participants

INDIVIDUAL LEADERSHIP CHARACTERISTICS

Public Persuasion

Crisis Leadership

Economic Management

Moral Authority

International Relations

Administrative Skills

Relations with Congress

Vision/Setting An Agenda

Pursued Equal Justice For All

Performance Within Context of Times

Source: C-SPAN Historians Presidential Leadership Survey, www.c-span.org.

weaknesses, and each knew how to maximize his greatest asset—intellect, negotiating skills, public communications—to try to accomplish his goals.

Franklin Delano Roosevelt (1933–45): The New Deal and World War II

When Franklin Delano Roosevelt (FDR) took office in 1933, the nation was experiencing the Great Depression. Unemployment had reached 25 percent, and Americans, many of them homeless and hungry, were suffering. To combat the effects of the depression, FDR had a clear policy vision, which he called the **New Deal**. In the first three years of his presidency he succeeded in getting Congress to pass legislation that radically altered the size and shape of the federal government. His immediate need was to find a way to get cash into the hands of individual citizens, but he opposed handouts. Instead, he created job programs, including the Conservation Corps, the Works Progress Administration, and the Tennessee Valley Authority, all of which both employed and trained workers.

New Deal: *Franklin Delano Roosevelt's program for ending the Great Depression through government intervention in the economy and development of a set of safety-net programs for individuals.*

Identify one of Franklin Roosevelt's successes and one of his failures.

FDR also expanded the government's role in regulating the economy. The creation of the Securities and Exchange Commission and other laws relating to banking and finance helped restore confidence in banks and the stock market. The National Labor Relations Act established federal oversight of working conditions, labor standards, and labor disputes. This legislation brought the government and the business and labor sectors closer together. The Social Security program, a pension program to which workers contributed through a payroll tax that was also paid by employers, further entwined business and government.

As had his distant cousin, former President Theodore Roosevelt, Franklin Roosevelt used the bully pulpit and advanced the use of communication technology in the office of the president. He invented the **fireside chat**, a radio address to voters explaining the reasoning behind his governing decisions. Because fewer than half of all Americans owned radios at this time, FDR also turned the chats into newsreels that were shown in movie theaters. Ever since, presidents have found direct communications with voters to be an effective governing device.[65] President Roosevelt was also open and available to the Washington press corps, and his very first press conference in 1933 was a success. As a media-savvy president, FDR created the formal position of White House press secretary.[66]

The White House Historical Association (White House Collection)

Franklin Delano Roosevelt

Roosevelt took a personal role in negotiating legislative deals with members of the House and Senate, which were controlled by the Democrats. He allowed his staff to lay out the conditions for a compromise, but Roosevelt would finish the negotiations himself.[67] During his first five years in office, Roosevelt had great success in getting legislation through Congress. But in 1937 he overstepped by proposing to expand the size of the Supreme Court. The Court had struck down several of Roosevelt's favored policies, often by closely divided votes, and his so-called **Court-packing plan** would have allowed him to appoint additional justices and secure a majority favorable to him. Congress rejected Roosevelt's attempt to circumvent the checks and balances, and after that his relationship with Congress began to falter.

fireside chat: *Radio addresses by President Franklin D. Roosevelt that were the first regular communications from the president to a large portion of the American public.*

Court-packing plan: *President Franklin Roosevelt's proposal to add new justices to the Supreme Court so that the Court would uphold his policies.*

On December 7, 1941, Japan attacked the United States at Pearl Harbor in Hawaii, drawing the United States into World War II. From that point on, foreign affairs dominated Roosevelt's presidency, but the New Deal legislation of the previous decade laid the groundwork for the modern structure of domestic programs in the United States.

Lyndon Baines Johnson (1963–69): The Great Society and Vietnam

President Lyndon B. Johnson (LBJ) focused his mission on improving race relations and ending poverty because he believed they stood in the way of social, political, and economic progress. Most of his programs, which he called the **Great Society**, built on the infrastructure of FDR's New Deal, but they went much further in connecting the individual to the federal government. In the area of race relations, Johnson believed it was the obligation of the federal government to guarantee civil rights to all Americans. He persuaded Congress to pass the Civil Rights Act of 1964, the Voting Rights Act of 1965, and the Fair Housing Act of 1968, which together formed a powerful set of laws protecting the rights of African Americans and subsequently the rights of other minority groups as well (see Chapter 5).

LBJ believed that it was possible for people to work very hard but still remain poor, and that poor people were severely disadvantaged in terms of education, access to jobs, and affordable housing. He transformed the contract between the individual and the federal government into one that included pure need, rather than merit based on work. He created two major federal health insurance programs: Medicaid, a health insurance program for the poor, and Medicare, a health insurance program for the elderly. He was also responsible for creating the Food Stamp Program, the School Lunch Program, Head Start, the Job Corps, and the Elementary and Secondary Education Act.

Johnson was not a skilled communicator or comfortable giving speeches, and he did not come across well on television, which by this time had succeeded radio as the dominant form of political communication. He compensated for his lack of communication skills by relying more heavily on his very strong negotiation skills. From his prior experience as a member of Congress and Senate majority leader, Johnson understood how to convince members of Congress that it was in their best interests to pass legislation. Johnson made sure that his programs would benefit all poor people, white and black, rural and urban. By creating wide eligibility criteria, Johnson almost guaranteed that every congressional district in the country would receive some benefit from the programs. For example, both Medicaid and Medicare legislation included subsidies to rural hospitals and to big inner-city hospitals for services and capital expenditures such as improving facilities and building new ones. School lunch programs benefited schoolchildren as well as farmers, who sold the federal government their meat, milk, cheese, and grains at a guaranteed price, so they always had a market.

Great Society: *Lyndon Johnson's program for expanding the federal social welfare programs in health care, education, and housing and for ending poverty.*

Identify one of Lyndon Johnson's successes and one of his failures.

The White House Historical Association (White House Collection)

Lyndon Baines Johnson

Johnson also used his presidential powers to distribute and award federal contracts and federal funds to key members of Congress and key state officials in return for their support of his programs. He understood that if a member of Congress needed to explain his vote in support of a liberal bill, he could do so more easily if he could point to some other federal benefit he had secured, such as a bridge, a Navy or Army base, or a new hospital wing.

Although Johnson's personal relationship with the press and the public started out reasonably well, as U.S. involvement in the Vietnam War escalated the press began to distrust him, and many journalists believed he was not being candid about the war with them and the American people. By the end of his presidency, Johnson's relationship with the press was downright hostile, and the press gave the president much negative publicity. In fact, negative reporting on the progress of the Vietnam War and its unfavorable impact on Johnson's approval ratings are widely believed to be the reasons Johnson decided not to seek reelection in 1968.

Ronald Reagan (1981–89): The Reagan Revolution and the End of the Cold War

President Ronald Reagan's vision of the relationship between the individual and the federal government was different from the views of Roosevelt and Johnson. Reagan believed that the New Deal and the Great Society had combined to sap individual initiative and responsibility. When he took office, he mounted an aggressive campaign to scale back federal programs that provided benefits to individuals.

Tax cuts were the first thing on Reagan's agenda for two reasons. First, he believed that if taxes went down, the economy would flourish. Second, he knew that if tax revenue went down and spending increased, **federal deficits** would be created. These deficits would serve as justification for proposing cuts in entitlement programs, such as Social Security, Medicaid, and Aid to Families with Dependent Children (replaced in 1996 by the Temporary Aid to Needy Families program). Entitlement programs put a strain on the federal budget, especially as the number of people living in poverty grew and the elderly lived longer. Reagan managed to make cuts in the programs for the poor and elderly by restricting eligibility for benefits, but he did not succeed in dismantling them.

At the same time Reagan was implementing his domestic policy vision, he was also implementing his foreign policy vision. He took a firm stand against the Soviet Union, which he perceived as a direct threat to the United States and as a major promoter of Communism throughout the world. The defense buildup he ordered set off a military spending race that strained the Soviets' state-controlled economy to the breaking point. By the end of Reagan's second term, it was clear that the Soviet Union was moving toward collapse and could no longer control its satellite nations in Eastern Europe. Reagan's foreign policy was arguably an important factor in the end of Communism and the Cold War.

federal deficit: *Difference between the amount of money the federal government spends in outlays and the amount of money it receives from revenues.*

Identify one of Ronald Reagan's successes and one of his failures.

The White House Historical Association (White House Collection)

Ronald Reagan

Ronald Reagan is referred to as the "Great Communicator" because he came across very well on television; as a former actor, he was able to give engaging, persuasive, and even comforting speeches. In January 1986, when the space shuttle *Challenger* blew up shortly after takeoff as millions of Americans watched their TVs in horror, Reagan's words eased the national pain: "The crew of the space shuttle *Challenger* honored us by the manner in which they lived their lives. We will never forget them, nor the last time we saw them, this morning, as they prepared for their journey and waved goodbye and slipped the surly bonds of earth to touch the face of God."[68] In any analysis of presidential success, the power of speech cannot be overestimated because it is the most basic way that the president tries to connect with the people.

Reagan did not hesitate to use his formal presidential powers to their fullest. Early in his presidency, when the Federal Air Traffic Controllers Union went on strike in 1981, he ordered the controllers back to work. When they refused, he fired all of them and replaced them with Air Force and civilian (private) air traffic controllers. Eventually, the union relented, and most of the air traffic controllers were hired back, but with fewer benefits and at lower salaries. This action sent a clear signal to members of Congress and to interest groups that Reagan was not afraid to take a potentially unpopular stand to accomplish his goals.

President Reagan delegated much of the actual negotiating over policy to staff members. He also enhanced the power of the director of the Office of Management and Budget to negotiate with Congress on budgetary matters. He and his staff knew how to position themselves in a favorable way on most issues, but on issues on which they were at a public disadvantage, Reagan knew when to compromise. During his last two years in office, he had considerable success in working with a Democratic-controlled Congress to pass trade legislation, welfare reform, and the first comprehensive AIDS funding and treatment bill.

Reagan's presidency was not without controversy, however. In late 1986, the **Iran-contra scandal** erupted when it was revealed that members of the National Security Council were selling U.S. weapons to Iran for cash, which was then given to the contra resistance movement in Nicaragua that was fighting the Communist-leaning Sandinista regime. Congress had passed a law expressly prohibiting aid to the contras and held hearings to investigate the administration's actions. President Reagan himself was never directly implicated, but the scandal raised questions about the accountability of the president for his staff's actions, and it tarnished the last two years of his presidency. Although Reagan enjoyed relatively consistent popularity and was perceived as highly responsive to his base of supporters, his record came under greater scrutiny after he left office because his policies resulted in higher federal budget deficits and lower spending programs for the disadvantaged.

The example of Reagan, in the context of Roosevelt and Johnson, shows how the office of the presidency can shape domestic and foreign policy for future generations. Reagan ran for president thirty-five years after Roosevelt died and eleven years after Johnson left office on a campaign platform of scaling back the New Deal and the Great Society. In turn, Reagan left a conservative political legacy about the limited role of the federal government that remains a powerful rallying cry for Republicans today.

Iran-contra scandal: *Covert operation in violation of congressional intent that was designed to sell U.S. weapons to fund military resistance by the contras against the Sandinista regime in Nicaragua.*

Describe the legacy of Franklin Roosevelt, of Lyndon Johnson, and of Ronald Reagan. How did each change the presidency?

The President and Public Policy: Taxing and Spending

All presidents confront a vast policy landscape, but their performance with regard to the nation's economy is a primary point on which they are judged. Despite the fact that presidents cannot actually control the economy, they are generally held accountable for it. As chief executive, the president oversees a large economic infrastructure related to taxation and government spending. In the section that follows we describe his direct and indirect roles in implementing economic policy.

Tax Policy

Beginning with Theodore Roosevelt and accelerating under Franklin Roosevelt, presidents have led federal intervention in the economy—regulating business practices, ensuring workplace safety, overseeing banking and finance, and constructing a safety net of unemployment and disability benefits, among many other programs. When the economy is weak, there is pressure on the president to take extraordinary steps to address it. This is what Franklin Roosevelt did during the Great Depression and what Barack Obama did in 2009 in response to a deep recession. A **recession** is typically defined as a downturn in economic activity, with declines in employment levels, income, retail spending, and industrial production. The recession that began in 2008 was largely attributed to inflated housing prices, irresponsible lending by banks, and excessive borrowing by consumers, all of which led to widespread foreclosures and the collapse of major sectors of the financial and construction industries. The U.S. economy has long been driven by consumer spending. When people lose jobs, consumer spending declines, forcing business and industry to cut back production and lay off workers.

recession: *Downturn in economic activity, with declines in employment levels, income, retail spending, and industrial production.*

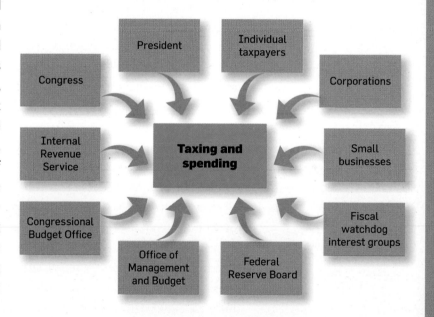

Government can use **fiscal policy** to intervene in the economy by manipulating the money supply through taxing and spending. Increasing spending or decreasing taxes increases the money supply. Decreasing spending or increasing taxes decreases the money supply. In times of severe economic crises, the president may support a policy of increasing the money supply to ward off a recession. Alternatively, an increase in prices can cause workers to demand raises. Higher wages will lead to even larger increases in prices, setting off **inflation**. In this case, the president may support a decrease in the money supply to ward off or reduce the extent of inflation.

The Constitution grants Congress the explicit power to raise or lower federal taxes, but the executive branch has always been responsible for collecting the taxes. The

fiscal policy: *Means of controlling the money supply through taxing and spending.*

inflation: *Condition in which money supply and higher wages lead to large increases in prices.*

Should the government intervene in the economy to ward off recession and prevent inflation?

Internal Revenue Service, a unit in the Department of the Treasury, monitors the payment of federal taxes. Americans pay a wide range of federal taxes to support federal programs, including income tax and taxes supporting Medicare, Social Security, disability benefits, and unemployment compensation. There are also corporate taxes and customs fees. The federal government collects taxes on goods and services, such as gasoline, cigarettes, and cell phones.

As chief executive of the federal government, the president must make decisions about fiscal policy in terms of taxes and federal spending. Republican presidents have typically wanted to lower all taxes, a policy that provides less revenue to the federal government and subsequently decreases federal spending. Democratic presidents have typically wanted to cut taxes for individuals with lower incomes and to raise taxes on wealthier citizens to support federal programs. In 2009 President Obama responded to the severe economic crisis by asking Congress to pass a nearly $800 billion stimulus bill—a combination of spending increases favored by Democrats and tax credits (which amount to tax cuts) favored by Republicans to increase the money supply.

The problem that modern presidents face is the complexity of the tax code itself, with thousands of pages of rules and regulations. That complexity means that hundreds of groups and businesses lobby Congress for provisions that will help them. Some economists argue that business decisions and job growth are too tied to tax incentives rather than to the marketplace. In 1986 Congress passed and President Reagan signed the Tax Reform Act, which tried to simplify the tax code and make it work for citizens at all income levels. However, the changes did not last because the Reagan administration produced large federal budget deficits, and the next two presidents, George H. W. Bush and Bill Clinton, raised taxes to balance the budget. President George W. Bush cut taxes in the early years of his administration, but by the end of his second term, the federal budget deficit and the **national debt** had increased dramatically (see Chapter 12 for further explanation). President Obama's federal stimulus package added to the deficit, and his administration now bears the responsibility of bringing the federal budget back into balance.

The constant revisiting of the tax code and the changing levels of spending in the federal budget create an unpredictable economic environment for the country. With tax policy so complicated and vast, it becomes increasingly difficult for the president to be equally responsive to all citizens and, in turn, for citizens to hold the president accountable for spending their tax dollars. Even more frustrating for the president is the fact that he might propose a tax plan, but Congress has the power to accept it, alter it, or reject it. In this way, Congress checks presidential influence in the management of the federal budget.

Monetary Policy

The president is limited in his power to directly influence the nation's economic condition because **monetary policy** is in reality under the control of the **Federal Reserve Board**, an independent agency (see Chapter 14). Monetary policy, enacted by a nation's central bank, increases or decreases the money supply by changing the reserve requirements—the amount of cash reserves that banks must keep on hand (see Table 13.5). Congress created the Federal Reserve in 1913 as a system of twelve regional banks that all belong to one national banking system in an effort to stabilize American currency and control the flow of money in the economy.

TABLE 13.5 Comparison of Tax and Monetary Policy

Actions by Congress and the president affect fiscal policy, while actions by the Federal Reserve Board affect monetary policy.

Type of Policy	Policy Maker	Action	Direct Effect	Effect on Money Supply
Fiscal	Congress, president	Increase spending or cut taxes	Consumers have more money to spend.	Increases
	Congress, president	Decrease spending or increase taxes	Consumers have less money to spend.	Decreases
Monetary	Federal Reserve Board	Increase reserve requirement	Banks have less money to loan.	Decreases
	Federal Reserve Board	Decrease reserve requirement	Banks have more money to loan.	Increases
	Federal Reserve Board	Increase the discount rate	Loans are more expensive.	Decreases
	Federal Reserve Board	Decrease the discount rate	Loans are less expensive.	Increases

The Federal Reserve System is led by a seven-member board of governors. Each member is nominated by the president and confirmed by the Senate. Members serve fourteen-year terms, and the president selects the board chair, who serves a four-year term. The chair of the Federal Reserve is typically a public figure who testifies before Congress frequently and also goes before banking and investment firms to explain federal monetary policy. Alan Greenspan, who served as chair from 1987 to 2006, rose to such prominence that many economic analysts paid greater attention to him than to the presidents he served under.[69] The current chair of the Federal Reserve is Ben Bernanke, who was nominated by George W. Bush. In 2009 President Obama nominated Bernanke to a second term, making it clear that Bernanke's views and policies were in line with his own; Bernanke was subsequently confirmed by the U.S. Senate.

AP Photo/Evan Vucci, file

The chair of the Federal Reserve is a public figure who is often called to testify before Congress about the state of the nation's economy and finances. The current chair, Ben Bernanke, taught economics at Princeton and served on George W. Bush's Council of Economic Advisers. Bush first appointed him to the Federal Reserve Board, and President Obama renewed the appointment in 2009.

The Federal Reserve Board can increase or decrease the money supply using monetary policy. When the Federal Reserve increases reserve requirements, banks have less money to lend, and the money supply decreases. When the Federal Reserve decreases reserve requirements, banks have more money to lend, and thus the money supply increases. The Federal Reserve Board also controls the money supply through the discount rate, or the interest rate that the Federal Reserve charges other banks on loans. When the Federal Reserve lowers the discount rates, member banks can loan money out at lower rates, increasing the amount of money borrowed and thus the money supply. When the Federal Reserve increases the discount rate, member banks have to charge higher interest on loans, lowering the amount of money borrowed and thus reducing the money supply. To address the effects of the recent recession, the Federal Reserve dropped the discount rate to nearly zero in an effort to increase borrowing.

Although the president can name people to the Federal Reserve, he cannot fire them if they push monetary policy in a direction different from the one he wants. His only real power over the Federal Reserve comes with the nomination process, especially in choosing the chair. Despite the fact that the president has very limited control over the actions of the Federal Reserve, he is ultimately held accountable for whether its actions improve or worsen economic conditions.

The Presidency and Democracy

From George Washington to Barack Obama, the presidency has evolved from an institution with strictly limited responsibilities to the large and powerful institution it is today. Certainly the Framers would be surprised by the growth of the presidency, and they might wonder whether the executive branch is too focused on serving the president individually, and not focused enough on the needs of citizens more generally.

FOCUS QUESTIONS

- In what ways is the president held accountable both individually and for the collective economic, military, and social condition of the nation?

- How responsive is the presidency as a democratic office? How can the president address the vital public policy concerns of the American people?

- What opportunities are there for the average citizen to influence the decisions of the president?

- What powers does the president have to ensure equality across all citizens?

- Is the modern presidency a gate or a gateway to democracy?

Is the president held accountable for the performance and policies of the federal government? Probably much more than he deserves to be. The president operates in a separation of powers system, and laws must be passed with the cooperation of Congress, so the president cannot be rewarded or blamed entirely for the federal government's policies.[70] Voters can render their direct verdict on the president's job performance when they choose whether to reelect him, provided he runs for a second term. Voters also indirectly register their opinions in congressional midterm elections, which focus on members of the House and Senate but are also interpreted as judgments on the president's record. Because there is no possibility of a third term in office, presidents in their second term are typically freer from public accountability. In cases of very serious wrongdoing, Congress has the power to impeach and convict the president, but the threshold for impeachment is extremely high, and it happens very rarely. No president has ever been convicted and removed from office after being impeached.

Overall, it is difficult for the average citizen to hold the president personally accountable for his actions. Surrounded by so many staff members, a president does not give ordinary citizens much chance to influence him, nor does he often make himself available to be responsive to citizen needs. Given the vast size of the nation and security concerns for the president's safety, it is not easy for citizens to convey their opinions directly to the president. In the course of the nation's history, presidents have grown less accessible to the average voter. However, technological innovations as simple as fast airplane travel and, more recently, e-mail, texting, and social networking websites provide many more modes of communication between voters and the president or the president's staff. Although the president will not meet most of the people he represents, each town meeting he holds and public speech he gives is an opportunity for an exchange of views. And the job of presidential staff is to keep him as well informed on public opinion as possible.

Despite the limited opportunities for accountability, presidents do tend to be responsive to public opinion over the course of their time in office, although less so in the second term. However, each president strives for success and wants to leave behind a legacy that is respected and honored. In the modern age, presidents are considered their political party's leaders, and they want their records to reflect well on other elected officials from their party. All presidents see it as their responsibility to do what they believe to be best for the country, even in the face of opposition from the media, the public, and Congress. At times, this opposition can result in a less effective president than some might want, but the operation of checks and balances on presidential power accords with the Framers' vision of presidential leadership.

In terms of equality under the law, there is no question that the president's professional and moral obligation is to enforce all laws equally, with no bias or prejudice against any one type or group of citizen. Until the Civil Rights Act of 1964, one might argue that past presidents failed this test of presidential duty. However, presidents cannot enact laws individually, and if Congress refuses to cooperate, they are forced to use their executive powers to do what they believe to be right. Lincoln did so with the Emancipation Proclamation, Truman did so with the executive order to integrate the armed forces, and Eisenhower did so when he sent the army to Little Rock. Ultimately, as the single occupant of the most powerful office in America, the president is first in line to uphold the principle of equality. The president is also equal to every other citizen in that he is subject to the law.

Overall, the modern presidency acts as both a gate and a gateway to democracy at the same time. It is a gate in that the president oversees a very large federal government that can be complex and difficult to change in response to public needs. It is a gateway in that any natural-born citizen can run for the most powerful office in the land, and although wealth, education, and connections are extremely helpful in winning, they are not prerequisites for victory. The men who have been elected president have come from a wide range of economic, educational, and professional backgrounds. After the 2008 presidential election, when both racial and gender barriers were broken, one can argue that the path to the White House is more open than ever before.

Top Ten to Take Away

1. The American presidency was an innovation in governance. As the nation grew, the presidency grew accordingly. Today the president speaks for the nation on the world stage and sets the policy agenda at home. (pp. 436–38, 441–42)

2. Presidents have come from a wide range of backgrounds. All have been male, although a woman was a serious contender in 2008. (pp. 438–41)

3. Among the president's constitutional powers are those associated with being commander in chief. The president also has the power to pardon, to negotiate and sign treaties and recognize foreign nations, to veto bills passed by Congress, and to appoint federal officers. (pp. 442–48)

4. Congress's ultimate check on the executive is the power to impeach and remove from office. (pp. 448–52)

5. The Constitution vests the president with a general grant of executive power and requires that he "take Care that the Laws be faithfully executed." These responsibilities have been used by presidents to vastly increase presidential power. (pp. 452–60)

6. The president uses his executive power to issue presidential directives. He also uses the office to persuade the people and Congress and to set the agenda for domestic and foreign policy. (pp. 452–60)

7. As presidential power has grown, the president has come into increasing conflict with the other two branches of government, particularly during wartime. (pp. 460–64)

8. The Executive Office of the President has great influence over budgetary, military, and economic policies. The roles of vice president and first lady have grown in recent years. (pp. 464–67)

9. Presidential leadership is generally judged on how successful a president is in getting his preferred policies passed into law and in getting the bureaucracy to be effective and efficient. Americans also judge their presidents on their communication and negotiation skills. (pp. 467–72)

10. Presidents' performance with regard to the nation's economy is a primary point on which they are judged. (pp. 473–76)

A full narrative summary of the chapter appears on the book's website.

Ten to Test Yourself

1. How did the Executive Office of the President change from Roosevelt to Obama?

2. How does a president's prior experience shape his leadership style?

3. What is the president's most powerful bargaining chip with Congress?

4. How does the power of impeachment restrict presidential abuse of power?

5. What was the relationship between the Vietnam War and the War Powers Act?

6. Give one example of an executive order that changed U.S. history, and explain why it did.

7. What are the roles of the chief of staff and vice president in helping to carry out the president's agenda?

8. How do presidents use the bully pulpit to accomplish their policy goals?

9. Compare Franklin Roosevelt's and Ronald Reagan's visions of the federal government's responsibilities toward individual citizens.

10. What role does the president play in the economy?

More review questions and answers and chapter quizzes are on the book's website.

Timeline to Keep Things in Order

Twelfth Amendment specifies requirements for the vice presidency.

John Tyler is the first vice president to succeed a president who dies in office.

Franklin Delano Roosevelt increases presidential power over the budget.

Twenty-Second Amendment limits the president to two elected terms.

Steel Seizure case is the leading decision on presidential authority.

 **1804** · · · ·  **1841** · · · ·  **1939** · · · ·  **1951** · · · · **1952** · · ·

Terms to Know and Use

abuse of power (p. 452)
acting president (p. 437)
approval rating (p. 457)
articles of impeachment (p. 449)
bully pulpit (p. 456)
cabinet departments (p. 436)
cabinet secretaries (p. 436)
chief of staff (p. 465)
civil servants (p. 444)
clemency (p. 443)
Cold War (p. 442)
commutation (p. 443)
Council of Economic Advisers (p. 465)
Court-packing plan (p. 469)
divided government (p. 447)
entitlement programs (p. 447)

Executive Office of the President (EOP) (p. 465)
executive order (p. 452)
executive privilege (p. 449)
federal budget (p. 458)
federal deficit (p. 471)
Federal Register (p. 453)
Federal Reserve Board (p. 474)
fireside chat (p. 469)
fiscal policy (p. 473)
Geneva Conventions (p. 464)
Great Society (p. 470)
head of state (p. 458)
Impeachment (p. 448)
imperial presidency (p. 442)
inflation (p. 473)
Internal Revenue Service (p. 474)

Iran-contra scandal (p. 472)
lame duck (p. 438)
military orders (p. 453)
military tribunals (p. 455)
monetary policy (p. 474)
national debt (p. 474)
National Security Council (p. 465)
natural-born citizens (p. 436)
New Deal (p. 469)
obstruction of justice (p. 444)
Office of Management and Budget (p. 465)
omnibus bills (p. 445)
override (p. 445)
pardon (p. 443)
perjury (p. 451)
pocket veto (p. 445)
political appointees (p. 444)

presidential directive (p. 452)
presidential directive on national security (p. 455)
president pro tempore (p. 436)
proclamation (p. 453)
recession (p. 473)
Reconstruction (p. 445)
signing statements (p. 455)
Speaker of the House (p. 436)
special prosecutor (p. 449)
State of the Union address (p. 448)
subpoena (p. 449)
take care clause (p. 452)
term limits (p. 438)
veto (p. 445)
War Powers Act (p. 461)
Watergate scandal (p. 449)
White House Office (p. 465)

Use the vocabulary flash cards on the book's website.

Learning That Works

WHAT YOU NEED . . .

TO KNOW

The constitutional powers of the president

How presidents have used the office to increase their power

The many different leadership roles a president plays

How Congress and the Supreme Court can limit the president's power

Ways presidential leadership has been evaluated

The president's role in the economy

TO DO

Recognize how the powers of the presidency have grown

Judge whether the president has become too powerful

Understand the requirements and duties of the office

Determine whether these limits are effective

Evaluate the current president

Consider whether the president's economic policy preferences meet the needs of the nation

---

| 1953 | 1967 | 1973 | 1974 | 1980 | 2008 |

Dwight D. Eisenhower appoints the first chief of staff.

Twenty-Fifth Amendment addresses vice presidential replacement and presidential disability.

War Powers Act clarifies presidential authority and limits.

Richard M. Nixon resigns the office of the presidency.

Ronald Reagan is elected on platform of limited federal government.

Barack Obama becomes the first African American to be elected president.

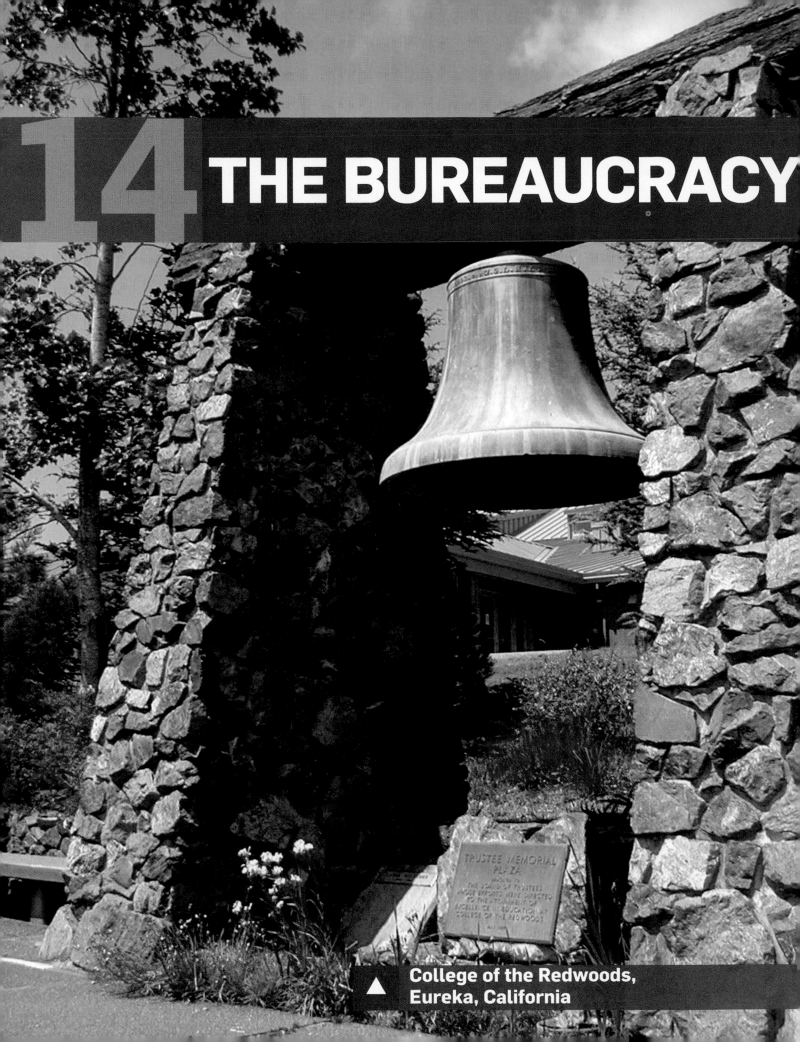

14 THE BUREAUCRACY

College of the Redwoods,
Eureka, California

> *Get involved. You have no idea what you can accomplish until you become unstoppable. . . . If I had a nickel for every time someone said we would fail I would never have to work again.*

When Kate Hanni was a student at the College of the Redwoods, she was a theater arts major who dreamed of being a rock star—"to be in front of a gazillion people with their lighters on," as she put it. Today she is a different kind of rock star, founder and head of the Coalition for an Airline Passengers' Bill of Rights (FlyersRights.org), which claimed a major victory in December 2009 when the Department of Transportation ruled that airlines must allow passengers stuck on stranded planes to get off.

Hanni had not planned to be a political activist. For years, she was a successful real estate broker in Napa County, California, who enjoyed family and friends and still sang on occasion with her rock band, the Toasted Heads. But on December 29, 2006, her life took a new direction. With 134 other passengers, she and her family were stranded for nine hours and sixteen minutes in a jet parked at the Austin, Texas, airport. There was little food or water, and the lavatories reeked. "People got so angry they were talking about busting through the emergency exits," Hanni recalled. "I was fuming. It was imprisonment."

When Hanni got home, she drafted an online petition demanding legal rights for airline passengers. The following month, when an ice storm at New York's Kennedy International Airport stranded thousands of passengers in planes for up to eleven hours, her cause took off. She gave up her real estate business, and she and her husband took out a line of credit on their house to build a website. Soon her petition had eighteen thousand signatures, and people in her e-mail network wrote to Congress and the Federal Aviation Administration and posted videos of the stranded flight experience on YouTube. Hanni got media attention, promoting passengers' rights in radio and TV interviews. Her coalition gained support from airline labor unions, air traffic controller unions, and consumer groups. She talked her congressman, Mike Thompson (D-Calif.), into

Kate Hanni ▶

Chapter Topics

 CourseMate

Visit http://www.cengagebrain
.com/shop/ISBN/0618906959
for interactive tools including:

- Quizzes
- Flashcards
- Videos and more

introducing legislation. In September 2007 Hanni staged a "strand-in" near the Capitol in Washington, with a tent outfitted to resemble the interior of an airplane and invitations to members of Congress to see what it felt like to be trapped. As the movement's theme song, she got the Toasted Heads to rewrite the Animals' 1965 hit, "We've Gotta Get Out of This Place."

As the movement grew, the airlines fought back, claiming that conditions were not as bad as Hanni reported. The Air Transport Association argued that deplaning would only cause delays and cancellations and might compromise passenger safety. A version of Congressman Thompson's bill passed the House, but a similar bill introduced by Barbara Boxer (D-Calif.) did not pass the Senate. New York and California passed airline passenger laws, but a federal court of appeals struck down New York's law on the grounds that only the federal government has the authority to regulate airline service.

In the end, that's exactly what happened. On December 21, 2009, Transportation Secretary Ray LaHood announced new airline regulations. After two hours on the tarmac, airlines must give passengers food and water. After three hours, they must let them off or face stiff fines—$27,500 per passenger. In an e-mail to supporters, an elated Hanni called the regulations "an early Christmas present," but reminded them that "we're not done yet!" Citing fees for checked bags and chronically delayed or canceled flights, she will continue to push for passenger rights legislation. Already, she has jumped into the debate over body scanners.[1]

The story of Kate Hanni is remarkable because she, as an ordinary citizen, demanded that the federal government live up to its responsibility of ensuring the safe travel of passengers. She took matters into her own hands and used the gateways of citizen influence on policy making to draw attention to the issue. Her activism got the Federal Aviation Administration, a subdivision of the Department of Transportation, to respond.

In this chapter we examine the cabinet-level departments, agencies, and other organizations that constitute the executive branch. We look at their structure, characteristics, rationale, procedures, accountability, and responsiveness to citizens' concerns. A fundamental question for students of American government is whether the sprawling nature of the bureaucracy makes it a gate or a gateway to effectively serving the people.

FOCUS QUESTIONS

- How does the federal bureaucracy play a role in responding to the individual needs of ordinary citizens?

- How does the structure of the federal bureaucracy shape the way policies are implemented?

- What powers does the bureaucracy have to ensure that federal policies are administered equally across all citizens?

- How can the average citizen influence the decisions of the bureaucracy?

- Is the bureaucracy a gate or a gateway to democracy? Explain.

The American Bureaucracy

What federal employees have you come in contact with in the past? What was the most recent experience like?

Just mention the word *bureaucracy*, and most people roll their eyes and utter phrases like "red tape" or "slow as molasses." Of all the components of American government, the bureaucracy is most likely to be perceived as annoying and daunting, as a gate against getting things done. Of all the components of American government, the bureaucracy is also the most likely to have a direct impact on citizens' lives. Most Americans have never met a president or a member of Congress or a federal judge, but every American has likely interacted with an employee of the government. Whether the interaction involves showing identification to a TSA agent in the airport or waiting in line at the post office, the rules and regulations of the federal bureaucracy present numerous opportunities for frustration.

Bureaucracies generally are not afforded much respect because they seem so complicated and impenetrable, and bureaucrats are often portrayed as faceless robots who merely enforce the rules. Yet enforcing the rules is the bureaucracy's job; as an extension of the presidency, bureaucratic implementation is how the president executes the law. Rules must be enforced equally across all citizens. In the most obvious example, a first-class stamp costs the same in every state and will get a letter to any place in the nation, just across town or from Houston to Honolulu.

Despite the well-known problems associated with bureaucracies, organization is essential to modern government. In the late nineteenth-century the German sociologist Max Weber described bureaucracies as highly rational organizations that enabled large numbers of people to get difficult jobs done efficiently.[2] If the federal bureaucracy does not seem efficient today, that may be because of the enormous responsibilities it bears not only to implement complex policy and law established by the president and Congress, but also to do so in a way that is orderly, predictable, fair, equal for all citizens, and transparent. The formal aspects of bureaucratic structure promote accountability, while the informal operations—the bureaucratic culture—determine how well the organization carries out its own mission and how well it interacts with other organizations. We discuss these elements in detail to draw a practical road map not only to understanding the federal government but to actually make it work better for ordinary citizens.

© Chip East/Reuters/Corbis

The federal bureaucracy has a direct impact on your life. Most Americans are familiar with waiting in line at the post office, but not everyone is aware that the quality of the grains in breakfast cereal they eat in the morning, the safety of the highways they drive during the day, and the purity of the water they drink are also regulated by government agencies.

bureaucracy: *Executive branch departments, agencies, boards, and commissions that carry out the responsibilities of the federal government.*

What Is the Bureaucracy?

The **bureaucracy** is the large collection of executive branch departments, agencies, boards, commissions, and other government organizations that carry out the responsibilities of the federal government. At first, the nation did not require many employees to fulfill the government's duties, which

Chris Slane/CartoonStock

CHRIS

What is your impression of the federal bureaucracy? Which branch of government do you think works best? Which works least well?

regulations: *Guidelines issued by federal agencies for administering federal programs and implementing federal law.*

cabinet: *Set of executive departments responsible for carrying out federal policy in specific issue areas.*

cabinet secretaries: *Heads of cabinet departments and chief advisers to the president on the issues under their jurisdiction.*

were limited to large national issues such as defense, tariffs on imported goods, and settling western lands. As the nation's lands and economy grew, so did the need for a more complex structure at the federal level to oversee government activities. These responsibilities are established by laws passed by Congress and signed by the president, but for execution they often entail expertise, so the legislature relies on specialists—the bureaucrats—to write the **regulations** that implement the law.

In 2010 the number of federal employees, including the armed services, totaled almost 4.5 million people.[3] The jobs of federal employees vary widely. A national park ranger is a federal employee, as is a border patrol officer, a bridge designer with the Army Corps of Engineers, an accountant with the Securities and Exchange Commission, and a lawyer with the Department of Justice. For every federal job classified as "professional," there are also staff jobs, including clerks, office managers, janitors, mechanics, and delivery personnel who keep the bureaucracy running. Skills and specialties in almost any type of work can be a gateway to employment in the federal government, which we discuss in more detail later in the chapter.

One simple way to understand the basic structure of the bureaucracy is to imagine a piece of furniture called a cabinet that stores different types of items in different drawers. It is no accident that the term *bureaucracy* has "bureau" at its base, an old-fashioned term for a cabinet. President Thomas Jefferson (1801–1809) had a separate room in the White House that he called his cabinet, and the centerpiece of the room was a long table with drawers on each side that served as his desk, in which he stored all important federal papers according to issue area.[4] President Barack Obama (2009–) could not fit all the paperwork of the federal bureaucracy in a single desk, but the idea of compartmentalizing federal responsibilities has endured over time. Today, a president builds a **cabinet**—his set of key advisers who are responsible for the areas under their jurisdiction. For example, President Obama appointed Janet Napolitano as secretary of the Department of Homeland Security based on her experience with border control as governor of Arizona, and Senator Ken Salazar (D-Colo.) as secretary of the interior based on his experience with land management policy in Colorado. Most cabinet members are **cabinet secretaries** and head executive departments, but presidents may select additional advisers for cabinet-rank status.

On April 20, 2009, President Obama posed in the East Room of the White House with Vice President Joe Biden and other members of his cabinet.

Official White House Photo by Chuck Kennedy

In the Obama administration, these include the vice president, the chief of staff, the heads of the Environmental Protection Agency and of the Office of Management and Budget, the U.S. trade representative, the U.S. ambassador to the United Nations, and the chair of the Council of Economic Advisers.[5]

Constitutional Foundations

The word *bureaucracy* does not appear in the U.S. Constitution, but the foundations of the federal bureaucracy can be traced to a few key sentences in Article II that relate to the powers of the president.

Appointments. Article II, Section 2 gives the president the power to "nominate, and by and with the Advice and Consent of the Senate, . . . appoint . . . all other Officers of the United States, whose Appointments are not herein otherwise provided for, and which shall be established by Law." This section goes on to state that Congress can "by Law vest the Appointment of such inferior Officers, as they think proper, in the President alone, in the Courts of Law, or in the Heads of Departments." Thus the discussion of the president's appointment power implies the existence of executive departments.

Opinions on Federal Policies. Article II, Section 2 references the executive branch more directly when it authorizes the president to "require the Opinion, in writing, of the principal Officer in each of the executive Departments, upon any subject relating to the Duties of their respective Offices." The Framers envisioned that the president would manage a staff of federal officers who would oversee executive departments managing the operations of government, although it is doubtful that they expected the president's staff to be as large as it is today.

Execution of the Laws. Article II, Section 3 gives the president broad powers to "take Care that the Laws be faithfully executed." At the same time that the Framers wanted to make sure that the president would follow the intent of Congress, they also gave him wide discretion in how he carried out the laws. This broad executive power is the foundation for the growth of the federal bureaucracy as well as for the growth of the presidency, as we saw in Chapter 13 (The Presidency).

The Structure of the Bureaucracy

For more than two centuries the federal bureaucracy has been changing, growing, and developing into today's interlinked set of organizations that implement federal policy. Some organizations are vast, such as the executive departments, and some are small advisory boards and commissions. Coordinating the authority and operations of these different types of organizations is a significant challenge for the executive branch as it carries out its constitutional duties. The structure of the U.S. bureaucracy is not unique, nor are the challenges it faces. Bureaucratic organization is essential for the operation of modern governments, as a look at the bureaucracy in France indicates (see Other Places: The French Bureaucracy).

Why do you think the Constitution provides so little direction for the bureaucracy?

⬤otherplaces

The French Bureaucracy

The French bureaucracy operates within a parliamentary system with a separately elected president, a prime minister, and a bicameral legislature consisting of the National Assembly, whose 577 members are directly elected, and the Senate, whose 343 members are chosen by locally elected officials. The president chooses the prime minister with the approval of the National Assembly, so the prime minister is usually a member of the largest political party or coalition of parties in the National Assembly. The president also chooses the ministers who constitute the federal executive branch and carry out policies that are favored by the majority party in the legislature. Laws can be proposed by ministers in the executive branch or members of the legislature, and they must be approved by the legislature before being sent to the president for his signature. If the majority party in the legislature becomes dissatisfied with the government, it has the power to require that one or all of the ministers, including the prime minister, be replaced.

The French bureaucracy consists of sixteen important ministries, with multiple sublayers within each ministry. Each ministry employs civil service members and political appointees. Although control over federal programs is generally centralized in Paris, the nation's capital, regional departments distribute government benefits and oversee government services at the local level. France has a wide-reaching set of federal programs administered through its bureaucracy, and its control over labor and business regulation has led some to suggest that the bureaucracy stands as a gate in the way of creativity and equality of economic opportunity. French President Nicolas Sarkozy proposed reducing the size of the French bureaucracy and eliminating unnecessary paperwork, but he was unable to enact major changes to the system.

- **Is there separation of powers between the executive and the legislature in France?**

- **How does the National Assembly exert control over the federal bureaucracy?**

All modern governments use bureaucratic organizations to implement the laws. In France, there are sixteen executive departments are called ministries, each headed by a minister appointed by the French president. The Ministry of Health and Sports in Paris is pictured here. In addition to centralized offices, branches of the federal ministries are located in different regions in France. The French bureaucracy has both political appointees and career civil service employees.

Sources: Legifrance, www.legifrance.gouv.fr; Parlement Français, www.parlement.fr; and Service-Public, http://service-public.fr (accessed using Google Translate, http://translate.google.com). Also see John Tagliabue, "Pace of Change Too Slow in France to Keep Entrepreneurs in France," *New York Times*, March 11, 2008.

Executive Departments. Today there are fifteen executive, or cabinet-level, departments in the federal bureaucracy. A cabinet department is an executive branch organization led by a cabinet secretary appointed by the president. Cabinet departments are responsible for implementing laws and policies in specific areas, and the job of the secretary is to oversee implementation, provide advice to the president about the issues under the department's control, and develop an annual budget for the department. Congress has the authority to create a cabinet department, but once it is created, it is under the control and supervision of the president as head of the executive branch. Table 14.1 lists each department, the year it was created, its website, and its number of employees.

Each cabinet department consists of subdivisions arranged in a hierarchical form to divide up its tasks and theoretically maximize efficiency and responsiveness. Figure 14.1 shows how the Department of Health and Human Services (HHS) is organized. This organizational chart makes it clear that each department has many subdivisions, or layers, each assigned a specific federal policy to implement. HHS is one of the largest cabinet departments. It oversees three hundred programs, with 65,100 employees and a budget of $868.2 billion.[6] This massive and complex organization is necessary to respond to the needs of all the individuals affected by the programs that HHS manages.

TABLE 14.1 Cabinet Departments of the Federal Government, 2010

Department	Year Established	Website	Employees (in thousands)
State	1789	www.state.gov	35.0
Defense (originally, War)	1789	www.dod.gov	720.2
Treasury	1789	www.treasury.gov	113.5
Interior	1849	www.interior.gov	70.6
Agriculture	1862	www.usda.gov	101.0
Justice	1870	www.justice.gov	119.3
Commerce	1903	www.commerce.gov	141.5
Labor	1913	www.labor.gov	17.9
Housing and Urban Development	1965	www.hud.gov	9.7
Transportation	1966	www.transportation.gov	57.9
Energy	1977	www.energy.gov	16.6
Education	1979	www.education.gov	4.3
Health and Human Services	1980	www.hhs.gov	65.1
Veterans Affairs	1989	www.va.gov	284.3
Homeland Security	2003	www.dhs.gov	177.0

Source: White House, www.whitehouse.gov; Office of Management and Budget, *Analytical Perspectives Budget of the U.S. Government FY 2011,* "Table 10-1 Federal Civilian Employment in the Executive Branch," p. 107, www.whitehouse.gov/omb. For the history of each department, see the websites listed above.

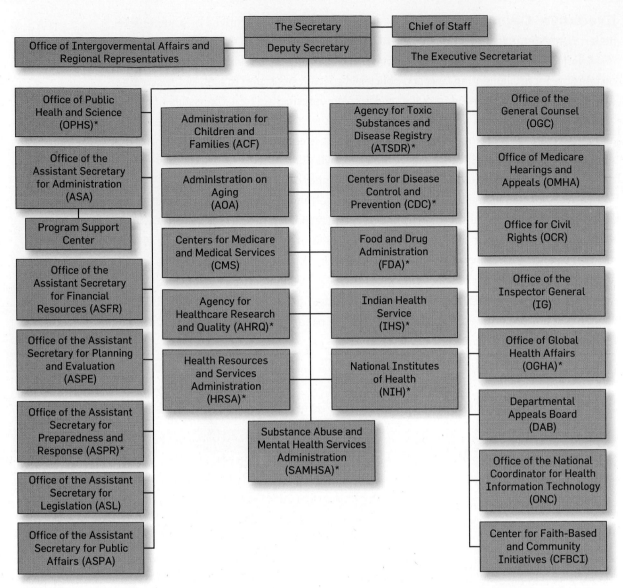

The Secretary

Chief of Staff

Deputy Secretary

The Executive Secretariat

Office of Intergovernmental Affairs and Regional Representatives

Office of Public Health and Science (OPHS)*

Office of the Assistant Secretary for Administration (ASA)

Program Support Center

Office of the Assistant Secretary for Financial Resources (ASFR)

Office of the Assistant Secretary for Planning and Evaluation (ASPE)

Office of the Assistant Secretary for Preparedness and Response (ASPR)*

Office of the Assistant Secretary for Legislation (ASL)

Office of the Assistant Secretary for Public Affairs (ASPA)

Administration for Children and Families (ACF)

Administration on Aging (AOA)

Centers for Medicare and Medical Services (CMS)

Agency for Healthcare Research and Quality (AHRQ)*

Health Resources and Services Administration (HRSA)*

Agency for Toxic Substances and Disease Registry (ATSDR)*

Centers for Disease Control and Prevention (CDC)*

Food and Drug Administration (FDA)*

Indian Health Service (IHS)*

National Institutes of Health (NIH)*

Substance Abuse and Mental Health Services Administration (SAMHSA)*

Office of the General Counsel (OGC)

Office of Medicare Hearings and Appeals (OMHA)

Office for Civil Rights (OCR)

Office of the Inspector General (IG)

Office of Global Health Affairs (OGHA)*

Departmental Appeals Board (DAB)

Office of the National Coordinator for Health Information Technology (ONC)

Center for Faith-Based and Community Initiatives (CFBCI)

*Designates components of the Public Health Service

FIGURE 14.1 Organizational Chart of the Department of Health and Human Services.
Cabinet departments are complex hierarchical organizations with layers of authority and sublevel agencies that have jurisdiction over specific federal programs and policies. This organizational chart of the Department of Health and Human Services shows sublevel agencies with lines of responsibility.
Source: U.S. Department of Health and Human Services, Organizational Chart, www.hhs.gov/about/orgchart/index.

Medicaid: *Government health insurance program for the poor.*

For example, HHS is responsible for administering the Supplemental Children's Health Insurance Program (SCHIP), which provides funding to state governments to provide health insurance coverage for children living in working families that are not able to afford private health insurance and are also not poor enough to receive benefits through the **Medicaid** program. Medicaid is a government-provided health insurance program for individuals in poverty created in 1965, and it falls under the jurisdiction of the Centers for Medicaid and Medicare Services (www.cms.hhs.gov), a division of HHS. Medicaid is strictly limited to people at specific income levels, and millions of children are not eligible for health care insurance under this program. To care for the health of these children, Congress created SCHIP in 1997, but it expired in 2007, and President George W. Bush (2001–2009) could not agree on a reauthorization plan with the Democratic-controlled Congress. Consequently, states were limited in the coverage they could offer to children in 2007–2008. Without continued permission and federal funds to offer medical services to eligible children, the states had no choice but to pull back. On February 3, 2009, Congress passed the State Children's Health Insurance Program Reauthorization, and President Barack Obama signed the legislation the next day, extending this program to 11 million children.[7]

The responsibilities of HHS grew even broader when President Obama signed the Patient Protection and Affordable Care Act into law on March 23, 2010. Because HHS oversees Medicaid, Medicare, and other federal health-related programs, it bears the bulk of the responsibility to implement the new programs associated with this legislation. For example, HHS will try to remedy deficiencies in the Medicare prescription drug program for senior citizens, inform citizens about expanded eligibility for health insurance through Medicaid, coordinate health insurance exchanges, work with states to enhance existing state-based insurance programs, and join with other federal agencies to encourage wellness and disease prevention programs.[8] SCHIP and health care reform are two examples of federal policy that are implemented by a cabinet department, in conjunction with state governments.

Other Types of Federal Organizations   In addition to cabinet-level departments, there are numerous independent organizations that constitute the federal government, including agencies, commissions, administrations, boards, corporations, and endowments (see Table 14.2). These organizations vary by structure, mission, and degree of independence from the president. For example, the **Office of Management and Budget (OMB)** has final authority over the entire federal budget, and each agency and department must submit its proposed budget to OMB for approval before it is included in the president's official proposed budget. The director of OMB is part of the president's cabinet, although OMB is not a cabinet department. Additionally, all regulations must go through OMB before they take effect.

The **Environmental Protection Agency (EPA)** is an **independent agency**, a type of federal organization established by Congress with authority to regulate an aspect of the economy or a sector of the federal government. Independent agencies do not operate within a cabinet department. Congress designs such agencies to operate with their own authority. The EPA has a unique role in the federal government, with responsibility for preserving the quality of the air, water, and land. It can issue regulations and create policy—as it did on greenhouse gas emissions in January 2010; its regulations are subject to OMB approval, just like regulations from any cabinet department. We discuss the regulatory process, and environmental policy making more specifically, in further detail later in this chapter.

A **federal regulatory commission** is an agency typically run by a small number of officials, known as commissioners, who are appointed by the president for fixed terms and are responsible for overseeing a sector of the economic or political arena. One example is the **Securities and Exchange Commission (SEC)**, which is responsible for monitoring all business practices involving the stock market. The SEC has five commissioners who serve staggered five-year terms and manage 3,800 employees.[9] The SEC oversees the work of accountants, stockbrokers, hedge fund managers, financial advisers, and small business owners. It has legal

TABLE 14.2 Selected Independent Agencies and Commissions, 2010

Department	Year Established	Website	Employees (in thousands)
Environmental Protection Agency (EPA)	1970	www.epa.gov	17.4
Equal Employment Opportunity Commission (EEOC)	1965	www.eeoc.gov	2.5
Federal Deposit Insurance Corporation (FDIC)	1933	www.fdic.gov	7.6
General Services Administration (GSA)	1949	www.gsa.gov	13.0
International Broadcasting Bureau (IBB)	1999	www.bbg.gov	2.1
National Aeronautics and Space Administration (NASA)	1958	www.nasa.gov	18.6
National Archives and Records Administration (NARA)	1934	www.archives.gov	3.2
National Labor Relations Board (NLRB)	1935	www.nlrb.gov	1.7
National Science Foundation (NSF)	1950	www.nsf.gov	1.4
Nuclear Regulatory Commission (NRC)	1974	www.nrc.gov	4.0
Office of Personnel Management	1978	www.opm.gov	4.9
Peace Corps	1961	www.peacecorps.gov	1.3
Railroad Retirement Board	1935	www.rrb.gov	1.0
Securities and Exchange Commission (SEC)	1935	www.sec.gov	3.8
Small Business Administration (SBA)	1953	www.sba.gov	3.5
Social Security Administration (SSA)	1935	www.socialsecurity.gov	67.6
Tennessee Valley Authority	1933	www.tva.gov	13.0
U.S. Agency for International Development	1961	www.usaid.gov	2.8

Source: White House, www.whitehouse.gov; Office of Management and Budget; *Analytical Perspectives: Budget of the U.S. Government FY 2011,* "Table 10-1, Federal Civilian Employment in the Executive Branch," p. 107 (Washington D.C.: Government Printing Office, 2010), www.whitehouse.gov/omb.

authority to demand information from these professionals, impose fines for bypassing investment rules, and even bring formal charges for serious violations of the law.

A **federal administration** is responsible for running a federal program or overseeing specific areas of federal responsibility. The Federal Aviation Administration (FAA), as we saw at the beginning of this chapter, is located within the Department of Transportation and is responsible for overseeing the entire airline industry and setting the requirements and guidelines for safe travel. It has approximately forty-eight thousand employees, including air traffic controllers and safety inspectors.[10] Its stated mission is "to provide the safest, most efficient aerospace system in the world."[11] This is a huge responsibility, and the internal complexity of the FAA makes it difficult for air travelers such as Kate Hanni to find the right office to contact

federal administration: *Federal organization responsible for running or administering a federal program.*

federal board: *Federal organization with a narrow scope of authority over a specific area of jurisdiction.*

about a problem. Her efforts to get the FAA to respond to travelers' needs are therefore all the more inspiring.

A **federal board** typically has a more narrow scope of authority but can possess the power to require changes in operating procedures and to suggest fines. It usually consists of individuals appointed for a specific term and who, ideally, have expertise in the area of the board's jurisdiction. For example, the **National Transportation Safety Board (NTSB)** is responsible for investigating transportation-related accidents such as the "Miracle on the Hudson" emergency airplane landing in January 2009, after a US Airways jetliner lost power because geese flew into its engines. There were no fatalities in that water landing, and only a few injuries. Whenever an accident involves any form of transportation, one of the five board members is appointed to oversee an investigation. Ultimately the NTSB issues a report on the accident to try to keep it from happening again. The NTSB can issue recommendations for safe transportation practices, but it does not have the power to issue federal regulations.

A **federal corporation** is a type of federal organization similar to a private business in that it provides a service or commodity for a price to the public, but it also receives federal funding. For example, the **National Railroad Passenger Corporation**, better known as **Amtrak**, is essentially a for-profit railroad, but it receives federal funding and is subject to federal restrictions and controls.

A **national endowment** is also a type of federal organization that uses funds specifically allocated to promote a public good or service. The **National Endowment for the Arts**, for example, was created to support scholarship and art that would be available to the general public, but it does not have any formal responsibility to monitor private- and public-sector activities in a specific set of issue areas. Because endowments are funded by the federal government, they are expected to serve as gateways for the expression of a wide range of viewpoints and perspectives in the work that they support.

National Transportation Safety Board (NTSB): *Federal organization responsible for investigating transportation-related accidents and recommending safety standards.*

federal corporation: *Federal organization that is similar to a private business in that it provides a service or commodity for a price to the public but that also receives federal funding.*

National Railroad Passenger Corporation (Amtrak): *Railroad that receives federal funding.*

Why would the government fund a for-profit railroad?

national endowment: *Federal organization that distributes funds to promote a public good or service.*

National Endowment for the Arts: *Federal organization that funds scholarships and art made available to the general public.*

AP Photo/Steven Day

The National Transportation Safety Board investigates the causes of transportation accidents, such as the bird strike that forced US Airways Flight 1549 to land in the Hudson River on January 15, 2009. Not all accidents have such fortunate outcomes, and the NTSB makes recommmendations for preventing similar accidents in the future.

Core Components of the Bureaucracy

All these bureaucratic organizations share four core components that determine how government implements policy and, more immediately, how government responds to the individual needs of citizens. These components are a mission, a hierarchical decision-making process, expertise, and a bureaucratic culture.

Mission

mission: *Federal organization's defined role and set of responsibilities.*

Each federal agency has a stated **mission** that defines its role and responsibilities within the federal bureaucracy. For example, the mission of the Department of Health and Human Services is stated on its website:

> The Department of Health and Human Services (HHS) is the United States government's principal agency for protecting the health of all Americans and providing essential human services, especially for those who are least able to help themselves.[12]

How has the Internet made it easier to interact with, and influence, the bureaucracy?

A mission statement is important as the public face of the department, and it is the measure by which members of Congress and the general public can hold the department accountable for the success or failure of its efforts.

Hierarchical Decision-Making Process

To carry out its mission, every federal organization has a hierarchical decision-making process that structures the way policy is implemented. The hierarchy of authority in a bureaucracy means that an employee's decision on the implementation of policy is reviewed at each higher level in the organization. For example, HHS contains the following levels of authority, in ascending order: bureau chief, assistant secretary, deputy secretary, secretary. Each of these officials puts his or her expert input into policy implementation and then sends the decision up to the next level for approval. Not every department uses these levels of authority in the same way, but each leads up to the secretary, who is responsible for all the policy decisions that come out of a department, and ultimately to the president.

How important is a hierarchical decision-making process to government responsiveness and citizen equality?

The hierarchical decision-making process has advantages and disadvantages. It ensures that the unit responds consistently and predictably. The process also requires careful consideration of a policy before it is implemented. These two structural characteristics, taken together, are designed to ensure that policies are administered equally across citizens. However, this same hierarchical structure can present an obstacle to speedy decision making. Despite efforts to streamline the process, the step-by-step review of decision making inevitably slows down the implementation of federal laws.

Expertise

expertise: *Specialized knowledge and experience in an issue area.*

Fundamental to the core of the federal bureaucracy is the presumption that the people who hold bureaucratic positions have **expertise** in the issue areas they oversee and implement. This expertise can come from a number of sources. Individuals can enter the bureaucracy at the lowest possible levels and stay in their jobs long enough to acquire knowledge about federal programs. An employee might have worked in a particular industry, such as nuclear energy, and then have brought his or her preexisting knowledge to the bureaucracy as a mid-level employee. Other bureaucrats may have studied a federal policy area in academia or at policy think tanks and then have been offered government positions. Congress, with members who chaired or served on relevant congressional committees, is a major source of cabinet secretary appointments.

Bureaucratic Culture

bureaucratic culture: *Set of beliefs and behaviors that governs how a federal agency operates.*

The fourth core component of a bureaucracy is **bureaucratic culture**. As one political scientist explained, "Every organization has a culture, that is, a persistent, patterned way of thinking about the central tasks of and human relationships within an organization. Culture is to an organization what personality is to an individual. Like human culture it is passed on from one generation to the next."[13] Fundamental to bureaucratic culture is the constant drive to self-perpetuate; employees in a bureaucratic organization want to preserve their jobs and their influence in the policy-making system. For this reason, bureaucratic culture can act as a gate that prevents efficiency and responsiveness in government because it can create situations in which employees in different organizations duplicate tasks, counterbalance each others' efforts, and ultimately fail to accomplish their agency's or department's mission.

What are the causes of bureaucratic failure?

At its worst, bureaucratic failure can result in a terrible loss of life, as in the case of the terrorist attacks of September 11, 2001. Many politicians, members of the media, and citizens blamed the federal agencies that oversee intelligence gathering—the Federal Bureau of Investigation (FBI), the Central Intelligence Agency (CIA), and the National Security Agency (NSA)—for failing to uncover and prevent the attacks. Each agency detected warning signs of such an attack, but the agencies did not work together. The bureaucratic culture of each agency was insular and distrustful, and lack of coordination among them resulted in an intelligence failure.[14]

To remedy the lack of coordination among the nation's national security and disaster relief agencies, Congress created the cabinet-level Department of Homeland Security in 2003. The hope was that a single large federal organization, presumably with one culture and one overarching mission, would be more effective. The new department consolidated several key units that had been operating independently, including the Coast Guard, U.S. Citizenship and Immigration Services, Customs Service, Secret Service, and Federal Emergency Management Agency, and also created new intelligence offices that would try to serve as bridges between the FBI and the CIA. However, the department was not functioning well enough to coordinate the government's response to Hurricane Katrina in 2005, where, once again, warnings of possible catastrophe—from the National Weather Service and the Army Corps of Engineers that the levees might break and flood New Orleans—went unheeded. As in the case of the 9/11 attacks, key federal emergency agencies failed to coordinate with one another. In particular, the inexperience of the director and top aides of the Federal Emergency Management Agency was blamed for the loss of life and property that occurred during and after Hurricane Katrina.[15]

Other types of disasters do not involve as large a loss of life but still reflect mismanagement of risk by the government. In 2010 the Deepwater Horizon oil rig exploded in the Gulf of Mexico near Louisiana, killing eleven workers and unleashing millions of gallons of oil into Gulf waters. The oil rig was leased by the British-owned company BP. At first it appeared that the oil spill would be contained, but the rig sank, creating complications in the cleanup effort, and the oil spill grew larger and approached U.S. shores from Florida to Texas. This bureaucratic failure began in the office of the Minerals Management Service, the agency in the Department of the Interior that gave BP permission to drill without first requiring assessments from other federal agencies, specifically the National Oceanic and Atmospheric Administration, about the risks to endangered species in the area, as well as the overall probability of an accident similar to the one that occurred.[16] This lack of coordination has proved costly to the environment and to the people who live along the shores of the Gulf of Mexico. As a result of the disaster, the chief federal bureaucrat responsible for overseeing offshore drilling resigned, as did the head of the Mineral Managements Agency. President Barack

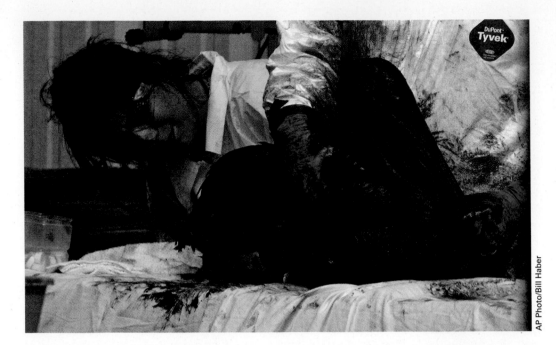

On April 20, 2010, the Deepwater Horizon oil rig, leased by the BP oil company, exploded in the Gulf of Mexico, killing eleven workers and unleashing millions of gallons of oil into Gulf waters. Controversy surrounded this massive environmental disaster, with the Obama administration, BP, and government officials in the Gulf Coast states asking how such an event could have been allowed to occur. Here emergency responders clean pelicans at a Louisiana facility.

AP Photo/Bill Haber

Obama responded by issuing an executive order to form a commission to investigate the failure, instituted a temporary ban on all offshore drilling projects, and addressed the nation to explain how the federal government was addressing the crisis.

Although each of the disasters discussed above was brought about by entirely different circumstances, a common lack of communication and expert direction exposed the inherent dangers of a flawed bureaucratic culture. If such failings are serious enough, the president may ultimately be held accountable for them.

A lack of communication and cooperation among key agencies remains a serious concern for national security. The FBI, CIA, and NSA continue to be independent agencies, outside the authority of the Department of Homeland Security. In addition, these agencies may continue to resist change, not wanting to give up any authority. The danger of their lack of cooperation was on display again in late December 2009, when an alleged al Qaeda operative managed to smuggle explosives aboard an international flight bound for Detroit. Fortunately, he failed to set off the explosives, but it was later revealed that both the CIA and the State Department had ample warning of this terrorist plot, yet did not communicate with each other about it. Change in any long-standing organization is difficult to achieve and generally happens only when the people at the top of the chain of command tear down the barriers to cooperation.

Bureaucratic culture can be shaped by the type of person drawn to work in a government bureaucracy. Bureaucrats are often depicted as narrow-minded and resistant to innovation. But many different types of people seek jobs in the bureaucracy.[17] A person who works in a long-standing government division may seek job security and stability, but someone who joins a newly formed department or agency might seek opportunities for creativity. Moreover, policies evolve over time in response to changing external conditions. For example, twenty years ago, the Department of Energy might have focused on more efficient ways of drilling for oil and subsequently hired geologists; today, with the emphasis on reducing national dependence on fossil fuels, the Department of Energy seeks to hire individuals with expertise in new energy technologies. There is no single personality type in the bureaucracy.

The bureaucracy is so complex and diverse that individuals with a wide range of skills and interests choose to work within it.

What are the advantages of a government job? What are the disadvantages?

One counteracting force to the drawbacks of bureaucratic culture and its tendency to block cooperation among agencies is **bureaucratic reputation**. Federal agencies want to develop good reputations for their effective implementation of federal policy. Most people take pride in the jobs they do, and bureaucrats are no different. Moreover, good reputations are important to the political process because they enhance an agency's ability to prevent interference in its decision making from outside forces, such as interest groups, Congress, and the media.[18] Where bureaucratic culture impedes cooperation, bureaucratic reputation can be the element that overcomes disagreement and produces a more coherent federal policy. Bureaucrats know that when an agency becomes viewed as incompetent, it risks budget and personnel cuts, being rolled into a larger agency, or being dissolved altogether.

bureaucratic reputation:
Perceived quality and status of a federal agency among the federal government, the media, Congress, and the general public.

The Historical Evolution of the Bureaucracy

The federal bureaucracy is as old as the nation itself, but it has evolved in ways that the Framers would barely recognize. Although they understood that the population would increase and the country's borders would expand, they could never have imagined that the federal government would have so many responsibilities and be so integral to citizens' daily lives. Over time, in tandem with economic, social, and technological developments, Congress passed laws creating new executive departments and other bureaucratic organizations. Here we trace the growth of the federal bureaucracy and the development of professional staff positions to implement federal policy.

What made the bureaucracy grow? Is it too big?

The Expansion of Executive Branch Departments

The first departments created by Congress in 1789 were State, War, and Treasury. The attorney general also sat on the president's cabinet, though he did not yet head a department. In addition, the Post Office, first created in 1775 by the Continental Congress to serve the vital function of establishing communication routes among the colonies, became a permanent government organization in 1794.[19] Through these organizations, Congress intended to fulfill the constitutional responsibilities set forth in Article I, Section 8—to regulate commerce among the states and with foreign nations, to provide for defense, to collect taxes and borrow money, and to establish post offices and post roads.

Why was the Post Office so important in the early days of the United States?

In 1849 Congress created the Department of the Interior, consolidating under its direction several organizations that regulated the sale and development of federal lands and the management of Indian affairs. The Department of Agriculture came into existence in 1889 in response to the importance of the agricultural sector in the nation's economy and to the hardships caused by crop and price fluctuations. To address these hardships, Congress created crop subsidies that remain in place today. In 1870 the Office of the Attorney General, first set up in 1793, was transformed into the Department of Justice, which employed lawyers to handle the legal business of the nation and managed all prosecutions and suits in which the United States had an interest.

As with the Departments of the Interior and Agriculture, the next two departments, Commerce and Labor, represented economic concerns. Congress addressed them by creating a single department in 1903, but within a decade the issues of child safety and workers' standards became so important that Congress divided the department, giving Labor its own cabinet status. This sequence was paralleled later in the twentieth century by the creation of the Department of Health, Education, and Welfare in 1953 and its subsequent division into two departments— the Department of Education, created in 1979 to coordinate programs dealing with elementary, secondary, and postsecondary education, and the Department of Health and Human Services in 1980 to oversee health care and welfare programs, such as Medicare and Medicaid. Legislation enacted in 1947 and expanded on in 1949 transformed the War Department into the Department of Defense, coordinating the Army, Navy, and Air Force. In 1965 Congress created the Department of Housing and Urban Development to oversee federal programs designed to build more affordable housing for people with low incomes and to help restore inner cities that were losing residents. The Department of Transportation was created in 1966, following a decade of interstate highway building authorized by the Highway Act of 1956. Increases in trucking also put pressure on the federal government to maintain highways and regulate business and labor practices in trucking and the air travel industry. As a direct response to the energy crisis of the early 1970s, the Department of Energy was created in 1977 to promote fuel conservation as well as the development of alternatives to fossil fuels, including nuclear, ethanol, and solar power.

In 1989 the Department of Veterans Affairs was created with the support of President George H. W. Bush (1989–93). It elevated the Veterans Administration, which oversaw a separate federally funded health care system for veterans, to a cabinet-level department intended to give visibility and support to veterans' critical needs. Finally, as noted earlier, Congress created the Department of Homeland Security in 2003 in a direct response to the widely perceived intelligence failures associated with the terrorist attacks of September 11, 2001.

The Growth of Regulatory Agencies and Other Organizations

In addition to the formal cabinet departments, the executive branch contains numerous regulatory agencies and other organizations that are responsible for administering the details of laws in specific areas, as well as for overseeing the practices of businesses and individuals involved in all facets of economic and political life. These agencies serve as gateways for the federal government to respond to citizens in targeted ways and on a localized level, and they are especially important in ensuring safety and economic fairness for citizens in daily life. Among the concerns these agencies address are highway and air travel, food inspection and product labeling, and the practices of banks and the stock market.

The first regulatory agency, the **Interstate Commerce Commission**, was created in 1887 specifically to monitor the business practices of large railroad companies and their owners to make sure that consumers were given fair and equal access to rail services. More than a hundred years later, this agency still exists, but it is now known as the Surface Transportation Board and has a portfolio that includes railroads, trucking companies, bus companies, and moving companies.[20]

Perhaps a more familiar type of regulatory agency is the **Food and Drug Administration** (FDA), which monitors food safety and handling practices as well as pharmaceutical drug

---

The expansion of executive departments reflects the growth of the nation. What do you think will be the next executive department created?

Interstate Commerce Commission: *First regulatory agency, created in 1887 to monitor and prevent unfair business practices by interstate railroads.*

How did it happen that the government went from monitoring railroads to funding them? How does this change illustrate the increased role of government in private industry?

Food and Drug Administration: *Federal organization that monitors food safety and handling as well as pharmaceutical drug development.*

development and approval procedures. The motto of the FDA summarizes its mission, "Protecting and Promoting *Your* Health." The agency fulfills its mission by issuing guidelines and standards for companies to follow. Well-publicized cases of *E. coli* contamination in ground beef in 2007, 2008, and 2009 and salmonella in eggs in 2010, which resulted in illness and even death, illustrate just how difficult it is for the FDA to monitor food safety. Americans consume billions of pounds of ground beef each year, most of it processed by private companies that are subject to FDA inspection but are expected to do most of the food quality and safety monitoring themselves.[21]

Is protecting people from food poisoning the government's job? Why?

As the nation's economy has grown, so has the number of industries, products, and services that may warrant government regulation. This growth has expanded the workload of existing agencies and may require the creation of new ones. For example, Congress established the Federal Trade Commission to protect consumers from unfair financial and marketplace practices and the Consumer Product Safety Commission to ensure that basic goods purchased by consumers are safe.[22] In 2010 President Barack Obama and Congress worked together to create a new regulatory agency—the Consumer Financial Protection Bureau—that would help consumers navigate mortgage and other housing loans as well as real estate investments.[23] This new government agency was included in the Wall Street Reform and Consumer Protection Act, which overhauled the banking and investment industries; it is discussed later in this chapter.

There are limits to the effectiveness of regulatory agencies. They have government authority to monitor practices, issue fines, and even shut down businesses, but the government must rely on voluntary cooperation by the vast majority of private businesses in following agency guidelines. The

Provided courtesy HarpWeek

176　　　　　　　　　HARPER'S WEEKLY.　　　　　　　　[MARCH 16, 1861.

OFFICE-SEEKERS AT WASHINGTON DURING THE INAUGURATION.

These Gentlemen, who are ready, like good Patriots, to serve their Country, are all ORIGINAL LINCOLN MEN. 'Tis true, they voted for PIERCE and BUCHANAN; but this was a deep game to insure the Election of LINCOLN in 1860.

distinct separation between the government and private businesses that is the hallmark of the American economy can also stand as a gate against effective government regulation and oversight. Nevertheless, regulatory agencies are gateways through which citizens can ask government to protect them from fraudulent and unsafe products sold in the marketplace.

From Patronage to the Civil Service

For the nation's first forty years, jobs in the executive branch were filled by wealthy elites who had personal political and social connections to members of Congress and the president.[24] But President Andrew Jackson (1829–37) used the executive powers of the president

Nineteenth-century presidents complained of being besieged by office seekers, men who hoped their connections with members of Congress or the president could help them land lucrative or powerful positions in the executive departments. In this engraving, office seekers wait to see Abraham Lincoln.

to appoint people from wider social and economic backgrounds to federal positions. He also demanded political loyalty from federal employees; to get a job in the Jackson administration, one had to be an active political supporter of Jackson and the Democratic Party. This arrangement, in which the politician appoints employees who pledge loyalty to him, is generally referred to as the **patronage system**. Jackson's political enemies called it the **spoils system**, charging Jackson with awarding jobs to political friends in the manner of the saying "To the victor belong the spoils."

For most of the nineteenth century, Congress and the president shared the patronage power; the president allowed members of Congress to recommend individuals for government posts. With each election in which a different party assumed office, there was a large turnover in staff. The federal patronage system allowed politicians to manipulate federal programs and positions for political and private gain.[25] For example, the Republican-controlled Congress created programs to provide pensions for Civil War veterans who had fought for the North, which was heavily Republican.

As the nation grew larger and the economy more complex, the federal bureaucracy needed more expertise and stability. The assassination of President James A. Garfield in 1881 by an individual who had sought, but had not received, a federal job caused a public outcry against patronage in government employment. Although the assassin had had no direct contact with Garfield, he evidently held the president responsible for his failure to secure a federal job. In response, Congress passed the **Pendleton Act**, which was signed into law by President Chester A. Arthur (1881–85) on January 16, 1883. It was the first of the reforms that slowly changed the federal bureaucracy from a corrupt and partisan insider organization to a neutral, policy-based organization.[26]

The Pendleton Act created the **Civil Service Commission** to administer entrance exams for the federal civil service and set job requirements and promotion standards based on merit and performance, not political affiliation. At first the civil service covered only a small fraction of federal jobs; the rest were controlled primarily by powerful members of Congress who used their influence to direct federal jobs to loyal supporters. But over time, successive presidents wrested more control over the federal bureaucracy from Congress by issuing executive orders to classify a greater percentage of jobs as merit-based and as part of the **civil service**. By 1897, 50 percent of federal jobs were covered by the civil service, and by 1951, 88 percent of federal jobs were civil service jobs.[27] The remaining federal employees are **political appointees** appointed by the president to carry out his political and partisan agenda within the federal policy-making system.

Career Civil Service

Career civil servants are nonpolitical personnel who must pass an exam to secure their jobs and compete on an equal playing field with anyone else who has the same credentials. For the number of executive branch employees, and other members of the federal workforce, see Figure 14.2. The vast majority of executive branch employees are located in the metropolitan Washington, D.C., area.[28] In general, federal civil service employees fall into three categories: blue-collar, white-collar, and senior executive positions. Blue-collar jobs consist of "craft, repair, operator, and laborer jobs," and employees in this category are under the Federal Wage System, which sets pay levels associated with specific jobs.[29] White-collar workers fill a wide range of professional positions ranging from clerks and administrative assistants

patronage system: *Political system in which government programs and benefits are awarded based on political loyalty to a party or politician.*

spoils system: *Term used by Jackson's critics to describe his brand of the patronage system.*

Pendleton Act: *1883 act that established a merit- and performance-based system for federal employment.*

Civil Service Commission: *Created by the Pendleton Act to administer entrance exams for the federal civil service and set standards for promotion based on merit.*

civil service: *System of employment in the federal bureaucracy under which employees are chosen and promoted based on merit.*

political appointees: *Federal employees appointed by the president with the explicit task of carrying out his political and partisan agenda.*

Compare the patronage system to the merit-based civil service system. Which is more efficient?

career civil servants: *Federal employees who are hired through a merit-based system to implement federal programs and who are expected to be neutral in their political affiliations.*

to engineers, informational technology specialists, and lawyers. These types of jobs are governed by the General Schedule (GS), which has fifteen grades or levels of pay assigned according to level of responsibility and work experience. In 2010, for example, the entry-level pay was $17,803 for GS 1 and $99,628 for GS 15.[30] Executive-level management employees are governed by the Senior Executive Service guidelines, which generally follow the GS pay scale. All federal employees are subject to performance evaluations and may receive gradual raises, promotions up the career ladder, and incentive and merit bonuses for outstanding job performance.

Some departments and agencies are staffed by career employees who are not in the civil service but nonetheless operate under similar structures. For example, the State Department oversees a corps of diplomats known as Foreign Service officers who are sent all over the world to manage U.S. embassies and consulates. To join the Foreign Service, one must meet certain qualifications and pass an entrance exam, similar to the procedure for entering the civil service generally. However, the Foreign Service has its own pay scale and promotion criteria. As mentioned earlier in the chapter, there are a wide range of areas in which the federal government offers employment opportunities, and each department and agency tries to recruit qualified young people. Figure 14.3 illustrates some of the ways that federal departments and agencies use their websites to recruit new employees.

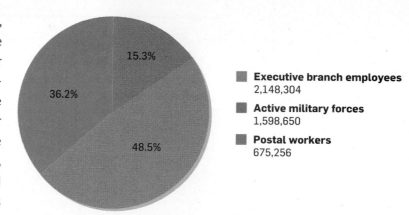

FIGURE 14.2 Distribution of Federal Government Workforce, 2010. Federal employment is divided into several categories: executive branch, active military forces, and the U.S. Postal Service.
Source: Office of Management and Budget, "The Budget for Fiscal Year 2011," www.omb.gov; United States Postal Service, "Postal Facts 2010," www.usps.com.

- **Executive branch employees** 2,148,304
- **Active military forces** 1,598,650
- **Postal workers** 675,256

AP Photo/Atlanta Journal-Constitution, Rich Addicks

Federal civil service employment begins with a standardized test, progresses to personal interviews, and involves background checks that can be complex and far reaching, depending on the position.

Due to the specific nature of their responsibilities, the CIA and the FBI also have their own career tracks with separate requirements. So do the Library of Congress, the Smithsonian Institution, and the National Institutes of Health. These personnel work under merit systems; they are hired, retained, and promoted through a standardized system of performance review, and politics are not officially considered. Although politics may permeate any workplace, the civil service is designed to protect employees from partisanship, and employees are expected to be objective as they carry out their job responsibilities. Civil servants remain

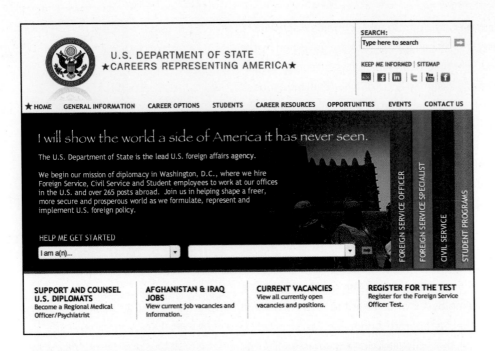

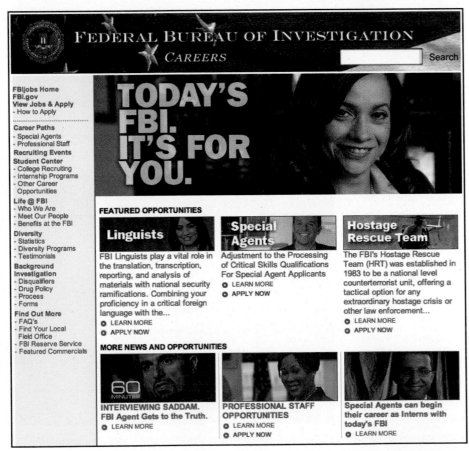

FIGURE 14.3 Careers at the U.S. Department of State and the Federal Bureau of Investigation. Federal departments and agencies present career opportunities for individuals and make that information known on their websites. The websites of the U.S. Department of State and the Federal Bureau of Investigation display various routes for employment and different types of jobs.
Source: U.S. Department of State, Careers Representing America, www.careers.state.gov; Federal Bureau of Investigation, Careers, www.fbijobs.gov.

in their positions from one administration to the next, and they cannot be asked to resign for partisan reasons.

Political Appointees

Political appointees, unlike civil servants, get their jobs because they are members of the same party that controls the executive branch, they have connections to politically powerful people, or they have served in a prior presidential administration. Political appointees can occupy a wide range of positions, from cabinet secretary to commissioner to administrator. Although it is uncommon, political appointees can also come from the opposition party, especially when they have particular expertise in a policy area or a president wants continuity in department leadership early in his administration. This was the case with Secretary of Defense Robert Gates, who served in the George W. Bush administration and was asked to stay on by President Barack Obama. No matter their personal views, political appointees are expected to carry out the president's policy agenda.[31]

Political appointees can come from a variety of backgrounds. Typically they are members of the president's inner circle or campaign team, have served as congressional committee chairs, or have served in former presidential administrations. In some cases, they come from the private sector. There are advantages and disadvantages to the president in choosing people from any of these backgrounds. Sometimes a president's trusted campaign advisers are not talented administrators; sometimes members of the private sector find government work too frustrating. Presidents try to make the best choices possible, but occasionally a cabinet secretary is replaced during a presidential term, especially if he or she has become a lightning rod for a broader controversy or an unpopular position. When a president is reelected for a second term, he customarily requests the resignations of

AP Photo/Gerald Herbert

his entire cabinet and then chooses which resignations to accept and which to reject. This custom gives presidents the opportunity to change policy direction and bring fresh perspectives into the executive branch at the start of a second term.

Top-level political appointees require Senate confirmation, and that number has risen from 73 under Franklin Delano Roosevelt (1933–45) to 521 for President Obama.[32] But there are hundreds of other jobs that are considered political appointments. For example, President Dwight D. Eisenhower (1953–61) appointed a layer of federal employees, known

How much authority should the president have over executive branch employees?

What are two gateways to becoming a presidential appointee?

In large part due to the unpopularity of the Iraq War, which he oversaw, Secretary of Defense Donald Rumsfeld announced his resignation on November 8, 2006, after large Republican losses in the congressional midterm election. The announcement took place in the Oval Office.

as **Schedule C appointees**, to oversee civil service employees. By some accounts, in creating this category Eisenhower was able to add approximately a thousand politically appointed positions to the bureaucracy over the course of his administration.[33] Subsequently, Presidents John F. Kennedy (1961–63), Lyndon Baines Johnson (1963–69), and Richard M. Nixon (1969–74) added more political appointees.

In 1978 President Jimmy Carter (1977–81) created the **Senior Executive Service (SES)**, experienced personnel who can be assigned by the president to senior management positions throughout the federal bureaucracy. For SES positions, the president generally chooses career civil service employees who have shown expertise in their jobs, but he also has the authority to bring individuals in from the private sector. The SES provides a layer of administration over federal programs that is directed by the president, infusing the federal bureaucracy with political perspectives that can clash with the goal of objective implementation of federal policy. Since 1980 the total number of political appointees has averaged about three thousand.[34] Although that may not seem like a high number compared to the total federal workforce, the category of political appointee has been used successfully by many presidents to expand their direct influence within the bureaucracy.

Private-Sector Contract Workers

In addition to civil service employees and political appointees, the federal government hires thousands of individuals and companies from the private sector to administer programs and carry out tasks associated with specific policies. These companies can range from nonprofit community organizations, to midsize security firms, to large health care conglomerates. They are not under the direct control of the federal bureaucracy, but they carry out crucial tasks for it. During the administration of William Jefferson (Bill) Clinton (1993–2001), Vice President Albert Gore Jr. took on the job of revamping the bureaucracy. His Reinventing Government plan sought to reduce the complexity and size of the federal bureaucracy by contracting out the provision of key services and administration of federal programs. Other presidents had made similar efforts, but President Clinton was the first Democrat since the 1930s to suggest that some of the services provided by the federal government could be more efficiently done by the private sector. In addition, incentive programs were put in place to reward federal civil servants for efficiency, in the same way that employees in the private sector receive bonuses.

Should government services be contracted out to the private sector? Why?

President George W. Bush continued this trend of contracting out the performance of government tasks to private companies. For example, during the Iraq War, the federal government contracted with major construction companies to work with the Army Corps of Engineers to rebuild war-torn areas of Iraq. It also contracted with private security firms to provide additional security for U.S. diplomatic and civilian personnel. At home, much of the actual administration and provision of benefits under the Medicare and Medicaid programs is carried out by large private health maintenance organizations (HMOs).

There are costs and benefits to the privatization of federal services. One concern is that the federal government does not have close oversight over the quality, experience, or job performance of the employees who work in the private companies. Although company employees have an incentive to do their jobs well, fraud, waste, and abuse can go undetected for years because of the lack of direct federal oversight. Sometimes the federal government ends up paying more for the provision of services through private contractors than it would if federal employees administered the program directly. The benefit of using private firms is that they do not technically count as additional federal employees, so when they are used, the overall size of the federal workforce appears smaller. In some cases, it is more efficient to use a private firm that has expertise in an area to provide a service at a lower cost than to use permanent employees and achieve the same outcome.

Bureaucrats and Politics

The civil service was created to protect federal employees from partisan politics, but by 1939 it had become clear that political influence was still rampant throughout the bureaucracy, not only at the federal level but at state and local levels as well. In response, Congress passed the **Hatch Act**, which prohibited government employees from working on political campaigns, using their positions to solicit campaign donations, or promoting candidates for elected office. This mandated separation of politics from the bureaucracy was designed to eliminate the last vestiges of patronage. It took pressure off bureaucrats, who could tell campaigning politicians that they were prohibited from engaging in certain political activities. In 1993 the **Hatch Act Reform Amendments (HARA)** significantly loosened restrictions on political activities by government employees as long as the activities occurred while they were off duty. Now political appointees are explicitly allowed to engage in political activities on behalf of the president so long as the costs for these activities are not paid with tax dollars. However, bans on political activities remain in force for employees in law enforcement and intelligence agencies as well as for employees of the Federal Election Commission, which monitors federal campaign activities.[35]

By 1977, when President Jimmy Carter took office, the civil service was demoralized by the increasing number of political appointees and by the general public's perception that the merit-based branch of the federal government was not working well. Civil servants remain in the government even when presidential administrations change parties, so they outlast almost every political appointee. These two factors—neutrality and longevity—frequently bring about conflict between political appointees who want to accomplish the president's partisan policy agenda and civil servants who take a programmatic approach, aiming instead to do what is necessary to make the program work efficiently. To encourage cooperation between political appointees and civil servants, and to make sure that each was held accountable for decision making, President Carter proposed the **Civil Service Reform Act** of 1978. The act created the Office of Personnel Management (OPM) to oversee both categories of federal employees. The OPM, under the direct control of the Executive Office of the President, can expand the number of political appointees and reduce the number of career civil servants. With more politically appointed personnel in the bureaucracy, presidents assert greater control over how federal policy is formulated and implemented. To preserve the essential political neutrality of the career civil service, the act also created the Merit Systems Protection Board, which ensures that the protections afforded to career civil servants through the merit system remain in place.

Nevertheless, bureaucrats do face conflicting pressures when Congress is controlled by one political party and the executive branch is controlled by the other political party, a condition known as **divided government**. Under divided government, federal bureaucrats are frequently caught in the middle because they are pressured by Congress to implement policy one way and by political appointees in their agencies to implement policy in a different way.

Hatch Act: *1939 act that limits the political activities of federal, state, and local government employees.*

Hatch Act Reform Amendments (HARA): *1993 amendments to the Hatch Act that permit political activity by government employees as long as the activities are not conducted during business hours.*

Should there be a gate blocking government employees from engaging in certain kinds of political activities? Are these prohibitions more important than compromising citizen equality?

Civil Service Reform Act: *1978 act that replaced the Civil Service Commission with the Office of Personnel Management, which oversees both civil servants and political appointees.*

divided government: *Situation when one party controls the executive branch and the other party controls the legislative branch.*

Why was the civil service designed so that employees remain in place despite turnover in the presidency and in Congress?

iron triangle: *Insular and closed relationship among interest groups, members of Congress, and federal agencies.*

issue networks: *View of the relationship among interest groups, members of Congress, and federal agencies as more fluid, open, and transparent than that described by the term iron triangle.*

Objectively, policy is supposed to be implemented in a manner that will produce the most efficient and responsive results, but trying to please two powerful bosses can result in inefficient and ineffective policy. Fortunately, the career nature of the civil service, with its built-in protections against political pressure, helps mitigate the negative consequences of divided government. Moreover, because career civil servants frequently outlast presidents and some members of Congress, they have a longer-term perspective on the impact of their decisions.

At the same time, bureaucrats tend to form long-term working relationships with members of Congress and even with interest group lobbyists in the policy areas in which they specialize. In Chapter 8 (Interest Groups), we explored the concepts of **iron triangle** (see Figure 8.2 on page 268) and **issue networks**, both of which are used to describe these relationships. Bureaucrats want to maximize their longevity as administrators of federal programs, so they try to be as responsive as possible to the other members of the network, and each member constantly shares information with the others.[36] Critics of iron triangles and issue networks argue that they contribute to the inefficiency of the federal government because they sustain programs that may be duplicative or outdated, and they may encourage corruption within the government. However, given the 24-7 news cycle and the amount of government information available on the Internet, the public, the media, and watchdog groups are able to monitor such relationships, and they are now more transparent than ever before. Nevertheless, iron triangles are another indication that, despite the protections of a merit-based civil service, politics will always influence, to some degree, the bureaucrats who implement federal policy.

The Bureaucracy and Public Policy: The Regulatory Process and Financial Oversight

For a law to be implemented, there must be rules on how to follow it to instruct policy makers, government officials, and businesses in the private sector. The bureaucracy makes the rules. In this section, we examine the regulatory process—from issuing regulations to congressional oversight and judicial interpretation—focusing on environmental policy because of its widespread reach into citizens' daily lives. In the last part of this section we look at what happens when the regulatory process fails to prevent fraud and abuse in private financial markets.

The Regulatory Process and the Role of the Executive Branch

regulatory process: *System of rules that govern how a law is implemented; also called the rule-making process.*

The formal responsibility for policy implementation falls to the bureaucracy in what is commonly called the **regulatory process**. In Chapter 1, we provided a broad overview of this process, from policy proposals, to implementation, to evaluation and updating of existing programs. We identified key stakeholders in the policy process, including the president,

Congress, political parties, interest groups, and of course the voters. Here, we get more specific by tracking how an idea that is enacted into law is put into practice.

The current framework for the regulatory process has its foundation in the **Administrative Procedures Act (APA)** that Congress passed in 1946 to provide a consistent blueprint for all federal agencies in the issuing of regulations. In 1947 the *Attorney General's Manual on the Administrative Procedure Act* was issued to explain APA guidelines.[37] Although it has been modified over the years, the APA is still the predominant blueprint for the federal regulatory process.

The federal government typically issues regulations when a law is first enacted and when a new circumstance or policy need arises that requires updates to the way the law is implemented. One such circumstance might be a change in the political control of the White House. Frequently, an incoming president of a different party issues new regulations to reverse the previous administration's policies. This reversal can be accomplished in an expedited form through a **presidential memorandum**. For example, President Obama used a presidential memorandum to reverse an EPA decision issued in 2008 that denied California the right to set stricter motor vehicle emission standards than those set forth by the EPA (see Figure 14.4). Obama's memorandum instructed the EPA to reconsider its denial in light

MEMORANDUM FOR	THE ADMINISTRATOR OF THE ENVIRONMENTAL PROTECTION AGENCY

SUBJECT: State of California Request for Waiver Under 42 U.S.C. 7543(b), the Clean Air Act

Under the Clean Air Act (42 U.S.C. 7401-7671q), the Environmental Protection Agency (EPA) sets emissions standards for new motor vehicles. California may also adopt standards for new motor vehicles if the Administrator of the EPA, based on criteria set out in the statute, waives the general statutory prohibition on State adoption or enforcement of emissions standards. Other States may adopt emissions standards for new motor vehicles if they are identical to the California standards for which a waiver has been granted and comply with other statutory criteria.

For decades, the EPA has granted the State of California such waivers. The EPA's final decision to deny California's application for a waiver permitting the State to adopt limitations on greenhouse gas emissions from motor vehicles was published in the *Federal Register* on March 6, 2008.

In order to ensure that the EPA carries out its responsibilities for improving air quality, you are hereby requested to assess whether the EPA's decision to deny a waiver based on California's application was appropriate in light of the Clean Air Act. I further request that, based on that assessment, the EPA initiate any appropriate action.

This memorandum is not intended to, and does not, create any right or benefit, substantive or procedural, enforceable at law or in equity by any party against the United States, its departments, agencies, or entities, its officers, employees, or agents, or any other person.

You are hereby authorized and directed to publish this memorandum in the *Federal Register*.
BARACK OBAMA
THE WHITE HOUSE, January 26, 2009

FIGURE 14.4 Presidential Memorandum on Motor Vehicle Emissions Standards. Presidents use their executive power to issue presidential directives, including memorandums and executive orders, that direct the bureaucracy to implement the laws in specific ways.
Source: White House, www.whitehouse.gov.

of the fact that administrations previous to George W. Bush's had granted California such authority.[38] Subsequently the EPA granted California's request to set stricter motor vehicle emission standards.

More commonly, a new president instructs federal agencies and the OMB to revise existing regulations to better reflect his policy preferences. The president can also influence policy, when he signs a congressional bill into law, by issuing a **signing statement** that reflects his interpretation of what the law should accomplish (see Chapter 13, The Presidency, for a fuller discussion of signing statements).

signing statements: *Written remarks issued by the president when signing a bill into law that often reflect his interpretation of how the law should be implemented.*

Issuing Regulations.

The primary means by which the bureaucracy implements the law is by issuing regulations. In 1963 Congress passed the Clean Air Act to reduce pollution, in response to growing public concerns and calls for stricter government controls.[39] The first step in implementing the law was to identify the agency with jurisdiction over air pollution. In this case, administration of the **Clean Air Act** was ultimately assigned to the Environmental Protection Agency, which was created in 1970 in part to administer the act.

Clean Air Act: *1963 act, with amendments, that allows the government to monitor and limit the levels of air pollution.*

Once an agency has been created, it is responsible for policy implementation within its jurisdiction. When the federal government proposes a policy change, whether independently or as a response to a new law passed by Congress, the agency in charge of that policy issues **preliminary regulations**, the draft instructions for following or implementing a law. Since 1970 the EPA has been the primary source for regulations on environmental issues. After the policy experts at the EPA draft preliminary regulations, the political appointees at the EPA review these preliminary regulations to determine whether they are in line with the president's policy views. Although the bureaucracy is theoretically supposed to be insulated from direct political pressure, the reality is that the president's policies are considered during this process.

preliminary regulations: *Draft instructions for implementing a law.*

When there is some agreement on the content of the preliminary regulations, they are submitted to the Office of Information and Regulatory Affairs (OIRA) within the OMB for approval to be printed in the *Federal Register*, the official published record of all executive branch rules, regulations, and orders. As noted previously, the OMB must review all regulations before they take effect. The OMB, created by President Richard M. Nixon in 1970 from the old Bureau of the Budget, is now an important gatekeeper in the implementation of federal policy. President Ronald Reagan (1981–89) expanded its power by issuing executive orders to specify the types of considerations that agencies should take into account in issuing regulations, including cost-benefit analysis and risk assessment. President Bill Clinton also expanded the control of the president over the regulatory process by issuing an executive order that required all agencies to submit proposed regulations to the OIRA for approval.[40] As his first OMB director, President Barack Obama chose Peter Orszag, former head of the **Congressional Budget Office**, which estimates the cost of policy proposals for Congress, and Orszag played an integral role in negotiations with Congress over the cost of implementing federal policy. By increasing OMB's role in the regulatory process, each of these presidents further consolidated presidential power over the bureaucratic policy-making process.

Federal Register: *Official published record of all executive branch rules, regulations, and orders.*

Congressional Budget Office: *Estimates the cost of policy proposals for Congress.*

When preliminary regulations appear in the *Federal Register*, there is a defined period of time for public comment (typically outlined in the originating legislation), ranging from thirty to ninety days. During this period, ordinary citizens, interest groups, and relevant industries and businesses can submit their opinions to the agency about the regulations. In addition,

**FIGURE 14.5
The Regulatory Process.**

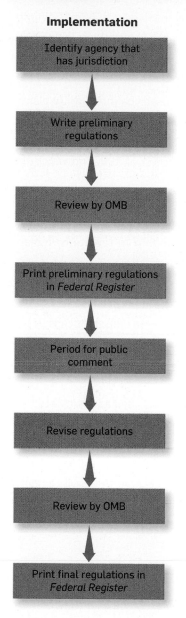

the agency or its local affiliate can hold public hearings in locations across the country to solicit opinions on the regulations.

Based on all the responses it receives, the responsible agency—in this case, the EPA—revises the preliminary draft regulations and issues **final regulations**. These are once again sent to the OMB and then are published in the *Federal Register* thirty days in advance of taking formal effect. Once the final regulations are issued, the program is officially ready to be implemented (see Figure 14.5).

final regulations: *Final version of the instructions for implementing a law.*

Revising Regulations. Since 1963 the Clean Air Act has generated an enormous number of regulations, in part because pollution standards constantly change as new technologies for manufacturing are introduced. Moreover, Congress has amended the act several times to give more specific direction about ways to control and reverse air pollution. The 1990 Clean Air Act Amendments imposed stricter standards on, among other things, the toxic gases that are responsible for acid rain.[41]

The complexity of implementing the Clean Air Act and its amendments is that the act affects every citizen who wants to breathe clean air and every industry or business, such as coal mining, that releases chemicals into the air as part of its operations. Individuals with jobs in these industries are also affected. The standards issued by the EPA to implement the law have tried to balance competing interests, but, because of changing partisan control of the legislative and executive branches, environmental policy has not been consistent over time.

Should the industries being regulated be permitted to influence public policy?

An example of the challenge of implementing environmental regulations concerns the Clean Air Interstate Rule (CAIR). In 2005 the EPA issued the CAIR regulation in response to the 1990 Clean Air Act Amendments that set significant targets for reducing pollution around coal-fired power plants, which contribute to acid rain. The intent of the regulation was to improve the air quality in the downwind states that are affected by the emissions.[42] A summary of the final regulation was printed in the *Federal Register:*

> On March 10, 2005, EPA issued the Clean Air Interstate Rule (CAIR), requiring reductions in emissions of sulfur dioxide (SO_2) and nitrogen oxides (NO_x) in 28 eastern States and the District of Columbia. When fully implemented, CAIR will reduce SO_2 emissions in these states by over 70 percent and NO_x emissions by over 60 percent from 2003 levels. The CAIR imposes specified emissions reduction requirements on each affected State, and establishes an EPA-administered cap and trade program for EGUs [electric generating units] in which States may participate as a means to meet these requirements.[43]

The regulation was issued in final form, but it was not immediately implemented. What happened next exemplifies not only how a gateway for one interest can set up a gate against another interest, but also how the courts can become directly involved in the policy implementation process.

Lawsuits and the Role of the Judicial Branch

In response to CAIR, Duke Energy, a major utility company that used coal-fired utility plants, sued to prevent the regulation from taking effect. The case reached the Court of Appeals for the District of Columbia, which struck down CAIR in July 2008, saying that the EPA exceeded its authority and was going beyond the intent of the Clean Air Act of 1990, on which the regulation was based.[44]

In response, members of Congress, environmental activists, and the George W. Bush administration united to get this judicial ruling reversed so that the regulation could be implemented. Environmental groups quickly asked Congress and the EPA to rewrite or replace the regulation. Even electric companies were in favor of the regulation. William Bumpers, an attorney representing Entergy Corp., was quoted by MSNBC as saying that few electric companies flatly opposed the regulation and most generally favored it because it included cap and trade provisions. Such provisions allow companies that exceed emissions caps to buy credits from companies that do not. "The power-generating industry had already invested billions and billions of dollars in anticipation of the trading market," Bumpers said. "They're not happy with this development."[45]

On December 23, 2008, the same federal appeals court reversed itself and reinstated the regulation in response to further arguments made by the EPA, industries, and environmental interest groups. The court said it was persuaded by arguments by the EPA and others, including environmental advocates, that "allowing CAIR to remain in effect until it is replaced by a rule consistent with our opinion would at least temporarily preserve the environmental values covered by CAIR."[46] In other words, the appeals court ruling affirmed that the bureaucracy issued a regulation that followed the intent of Congress and that it should therefore be upheld.

How do the courts provide access for citizens to influence the regulatory process?

The CAIR case offers insights into the context of policy making in a separation of powers system. First, the CAIR ruling and subsequent reversal illustrates how and why policy implementation is complex and time-consuming; it is this complexity and balancing of interests that can make the bureaucracy seem slow and impenetrable. Second, this case highlights the potential for judicial interference in the regulatory process. The courts can serve as effective monitors of executive implementation of congressional legislation because they are a gateway for groups adversely affected by a federal regulation to argue their case against it. Typically, the courts intervene when there is a dispute between Congress and the executive on the interpretation of a law, and not when the two branches agree. In fact, an earlier Supreme Court ruling declared that when the intent of Congress was not explicit, agencies should have considerable discretion in implementing rules, so long as they are reasonable (see Supreme Court Cases: *Chevron U.S.A. v. National Resources Defense Council*).

In the CAIR case, the court initially reversed a regulation that was agreed upon by Congress and the president. Eventually the court reversed its own ruling, illustrating that when Congress and the president strongly agree on how a law should be implemented, the judiciary generally limits its role in the regulatory process.

supremecourtcases

Chevron U.S.A. v. Natural Resources Defense Council (1984)

QUESTION: Can the Environmental Protection Agency (EPA) allow pollution-producing plants to update equipment at some sources of pollution at a plant without requiring that it update all equipment at the plant?

ORAL ARGUMENT: February 29, 1984 (listen at www.oyez.org/cases/)

DECISION: June 25, 1984 (read at www.findlaw.com/casecode/supreme.html)

OUTCOME: Yes, the EPA can adjust regulations because courts recognize a responsibility to defer to agency decisions in the absence of specific congressional instructions to administer the law differently (6–0; three justices did not participate).

Congress establishes agencies to handle both routine administrative chores and highly technical decisions. Because Congress cannot foresee all questions that may arise, it delegates rule-making authority to agencies. These rules are subject to review by the federal judiciary to ensure that they are consistent with the intent of Congress.

Under the Carter administration, the EPA made rules governing the emission of air pollution from sources such as plants and factories. Under those rules, replacing any equipment at a source would mean that all equipment at the source would have to meet the stringent standards of the 1977 amendments to the Clean Air Act. During the Reagan administration, the EPA subsequently loosened the rules so that plants with multiple sources of pollution could update some of the sources at a plant as long as total pollution from the plant did not increase.

The National Resources Defense Council sued Chevron U.S.A., claiming that the EPA's decision to loosen the rules violated congressional intent. The Court of Appeals for the District of Columbia agreed, striking the new EPA rule and restoring the older rule. Chevron appealed the court of appeals decision to the Supreme Court.

The Supreme Court reversed the decision of the court of appeals. Although the decision allowed looser regulations of pollution control, it also stated that federal courts should grant a great deal of deference to the decisions and rules made by federal agencies. Specifically, the Court declared that if Congress has explicitly expressed a preference on an issue, the agency must follow that intent. If, however, as is often the case, Congress has not explicitly expressed a preference on the issue, courts must accept the agency's rule as long as the rule is reasonable. In the *Chevron* suit, the Supreme Court declared that it was reasonable for the EPA to allow plants to replace equipment at some sources without having to replace equipment at all sources. Otherwise, plants might simply put off any improvements in equipment. Reasonableness is a very broad standard, so this decision grants federal agencies a great deal of flexibility in how to implement federal law.

- **Why would the Supreme Court generally want to defer to the judgment of bureaucracies on a rule?**

- **How might responsiveness suffer when Congress and the Court delegate authority to the bureaucracy?**

President Obama's administration faces similar legal challenges to a series of EPA final regulations on limiting emissions to reduce pollution. The challenges come from affected industries as well as state governments, which either have their own standards in place or fear that imposing strict standards on industry will thwart economic growth.[47] The substance of these challenges ranges from requesting a longer timeline for implementation to questioning the scientific basis for the regulations. It may be possible for the administration to work with the opponents of the regulations to reach some sort of agreement, but judicial involvement may once again end up playing a major role in policy implementation.

Oversight, Funding, and the Role of the Legislative Branch

Congress also contributes to the regulatory process through its oversight of bureaucratic agencies and through its so-called power of the purse.

oversight: *Power of Congress to monitor how the executive branch implements laws.*

Congressional Oversight.   Congressional **oversight** is a powerful legislative check on the executive. It can occur in two phases: before a bill is passed into law, and as the law is being implemented.

As a bill is debated and voted on in both houses of Congress, the legislative process allows members of Congress to make their views known as to how they and their constituents would like to see a law implemented. The official record comprises their remarks during hearings and bill **markups**, and a separate committee report is issued when the bill is reported to the House and Senate floors. Once the **conference committee** agrees on the final version of the bill, it issues an explanation of the bill's provisions.

markup: *Process whereby bills are literally "marked up," or written by the members of the committee.*

conference committee: *Temporary committee created after a bill passes the House and the Senate to resolve any differences in the provisions of the bills so a single bill can be sent to the president.*

In the second phase of congressional oversight, congressional committees with jurisdiction in a set of issue areas can request that agency and cabinet officials testify before them to explain the way they implement programs under their jurisdiction.[48] This phase can get complicated because both the House and the Senate have oversight committees, namely the House Committee on Oversight and Government Reform and the Senate Committee on Homeland Security and Governmental Affairs, but any congressional committee with jurisdiction over an issue area can request information from a federal agency. In addition, at the individual level, members of Congress can write to agencies and request information about a program or offer their opinion as to how it should be run. Consequently, when the time comes to write new regulations for a federal program, the relevant agency is typically well aware of the opinions of the key members of Congress who oversee their agency.

authorize: *Congress's power to create a federal program or agency and set levels of federal funds to support that program or agency.*

appropriate: *Congress's power to allocate a set amount of federal dollars for a specific program or agency.*

Agency Funding.   Another way Congress tries to exert its influence over the federal bureaucracy and policy making is through its powers to **authorize** and **appropriate**. When Congress authorizes, it grants the power to create a federal program or agency and spend federal funds to support that program or agency, as it did when it created the SCHIP program discussed earlier in the chapter. When Congress appropriates, it allocates a set amount of federal dollars for a specific program or agency. When the president believes a need exists that is not being met by existing federal agencies, he may seek to create a new one, like the Consumer Financial Services Protection Bureau discussed earlier in the chapter. However, creating a new agency requires approval and funding by Congress, which then has a great deal of influence over the agency's mission and policy goals. Thereafter, because Congress sets funding levels for all federal programs on a yearly basis, it has the opportunity to evaluate federal agencies. If members of Congress are unhappy with the way a federal agency or a specific federal program has been run,

AP Photo/Harry Hamburg

its funding levels may be reduced. Agency heads are fully aware of this congressional power, and it is a key reason that they take congressional opinion into account when they implement federal programs. Congressional influence of this type serves as a gateway for the public—which elects members of Congress—to hold the bureaucracy accountable for its actions.

Financial Oversight and Failure to Act

The bureaucracy has grown because Congress has continually responded to changes in the economy and society that have required government action. What happens if Congress fails to respond adequately to developments in a policy area? The absence of regulation of an industry or policy area is itself a type of policy; the government is essentially allowing activity in this area to continue without oversight, and there can be severe consequences. For example, the deep recession that began in 2008 revealed the consequences of Congress's failure to properly regulate banks and financial markets.

The primary organization responsible for controlling the flow of money is the **Federal Reserve**, which is discussed at length in Chapter 13.[49] From 1998 to 2007, as a result of a combination of deregulation in the banking and investment industries, the Federal Reserve's decisions to lower interest rates, and Congress's priority of making loans available to low-income families to purchase homes, large numbers of individuals could no longer meet their mortgage payments. Compounding the problem was that the banks that made "subprime" loans to riskier individuals began packaging these loans and selling them as investment opportunities. In other words, instead of holding onto the loans and receiving the interest, the banks sold groups of them to investors who hoped to receive the interest on the loans as return on their investments.

This type of investment was a new invention, and Congress, not recognizing its importance, failed to take active steps to regulate it. When so many people defaulted on their mortgages, investors' returns on investment disappeared. As defaults grew in number, so did foreclosures on properties whose worth declined rapidly. As a result, major banking

Congressional committees with jurisdiction in a set of issue areas can ask agency and cabinet officials to testify before them to explain the way they implement programs under their jurisdiction. Here Postmaster General John Potter is sworn in before testifying before a House Committee on Oversight and Government Reform hearing on the U.S. Postal Service on April 15, 2010.

Identify two ways that Congress oversees the federal bureaucracy.

Federal Reserve: *National banking system created in 1913 to control the flow of money in the economy.*

What caused the recession that began in 2008? Who or what was to blame?

institutions lost billions of dollars and became less willing to make loans for housing, businesses, and consumer purchases, including automobile loans.

In late fall 2008 President George W. Bush and Congress responded by enacting the Troubled Asset Relief Program (TARP), commonly referred to as the "banking bailout bill." The TARP program authorized $700 billion to subsidize banks by purchasing packaged loans that had lost their value because of consumer defaults. The condition that the government imposed on this rescue was that banks had to resume lending to businesses and individuals. When President Barack Obama took office in January 2009, more than $300 billion of TARP money had been distributed to banks, but lending had not loosened up and members of Congress and voters began to wonder how their taxpayer money had been spent. When the public learned that several of the companies receiving bailout money had distributed multimillion-dollar bonuses to their employees and continued to plan lavish retreats and purchase corporate jets, anger at Wall Street intensified.

Public pressure built quickly on Congress and the president to hold the banks accountable, and Congress reacted by holding oversight hearings in both the House and Senate Banking Committees. On February 11, 2009, the House Banking Committee asked the chief executive officers of eight of the nation's largest banks that received TARP money to come together and explain how they had used the funds to increase lending and dispose of bad assets. It is this type of forum that Congress uses to exercise its oversight function, and it was all the more important to do so at this time because the government was on the brink of distributing more funds to the same banks.

The factors that led up to this dramatic intervention in the nation's economy raise serious questions about the effectiveness of congressional oversight of the bureaucracy. Ultimately, Congress and the president will be held accountable for the long-term success of the TARP program. Two years after the TARP program was enacted, most of the major banks that participated in it had repaid part or all of the loans, significantly lowering the overall cost of the program for taxpayers, but lending to consumers and businesses had not reached the same levels as before the crisis began.[50] In this case, congressional failure to act imposed hardships on millions of homeowners, investors, and banks, and on the executive branch itself.

In 2010 Congress and President Obama worked to pass comprehensive financial reform and passed the Wall Street Reform and Consumer Protection Act. This legislation made a number of important changes designed to place the banking industry under greater federal supervision and protect against future financial crises. As noted earlier, it creates a new consumer protection bureau under the authority of the Federal Reserve, which prohibits banks and other companies from engaging in unethical lending practices, such as offering high-interest mortgages and credit cards to individuals who do not have incomes to afford them. It forces banks to set aside large sums of money to guard against losses from risky or highly unprofitable investments. It also forces large banks to organize their investment practices as separate entities apart from their more traditional banking functions, so if investments, such as derivatives and credit-default swaps, go bad, the entire bank will not be put at risk.[51] All these provisions illustrate the way the president and Congress try to adapt to the invention of new products, services, and economic practices.

Accountability and Responsiveness in the Bureaucracy

Typically, the power of the vote in regularly scheduled elections is used to monitor elected officials, but there are no ways for the average voter to register an opinion about the collective job performance of employees of the federal bureaucracy. Because the bureaucracy varies by type of agency, size of agency, and type of employee, it is difficult for citizens to evaluate job performance and hold bureaucrats collectively accountable for their actions. At the individual level, the job performance of civil servants is reviewed by supervisors at regular intervals, and political appointees can be removed by the president if he is unhappy with their work. But democracy requires that citizens be able to hold their entire government accountable for the policies it implements, and there is no readily available mechanism for the public to hold civil servants accountable for their job performance. There are, however, certain standards and procedures that Congress has put in place to hold the bureaucracy accountable and encourage responsiveness.

Is it easy or hard for citizens to hold the bureaucracy accountable for its actions? Why?

Efficiency and Transparency

One of the biggest challenges a bureaucratic organization faces is carrying out its mission efficiently while maintaining transparency to the American public. A chronic complaint about the bureaucracy is that it is slow. Yet issuing rules and regulations takes so long because the process solicits input from all sectors, including members of Congress, businesses and industries that are being regulated, and average citizens with a stake in the issue. The government can justify the slowness of the decision-making process on the grounds that it considers many points of view in implementing policy. Unfortunately, inclusiveness comes at the expense of efficiency.

Moreover, the issues related to food and drug safety, transportation safety, working conditions, and antiterrorism measures can be matters of life and death. Citizens expect the federal government to act in their best interests, but such issues require caution, and caution can lead to delay. On the other hand, if the government fails to make its practices transparent and does not consider all the implications of its decisions, citizens may lose trust in government.

These concerns were part of the rationale behind a series of bills designed to open up the workings of the federal bureaucracy to the general public. In 1966 the **Freedom of Information Act** established a procedure by which ordinary citizens can directly request documents and reports from the federal government by paying a nominal fee, so long as the documents are not classified. Access to a classified document or report is automatically restricted to federal employees who hold security clearances and have a legitimate need to see the document. In times of military conflict, such as during the Vietnam and Iraq Wars, presidents typically restrict access to public documents relating to war efforts. In response to the mistrust of the federal government that grew out of the Vietnam War and the Watergate scandal, in 1976 Congress enacted the **Government in the Sunshine Act**, which tried to

Freedom of Information Act: *1966 act that established procedures by which citizens can request documents from the federal government about its operations.*

Government in the Sunshine Act: *1976 act that requires government agencies to hold open forums to allow the public to comment on their decisions.*

Why is transparency important in a democracy?

increase transparency by requiring government agencies to hold open forums to allow the public to comment on their decisions, regulations, and performance.

To highlight the tension between efficiency and transparency, let us return to the Food and Drug Administration, discussed earlier in the chapter. One of the agency's most important responsibilities is monitoring pharmaceutical development from the initial testing of drugs to final approval for widespread use. Even before a drug is submitted to the FDA for approval, pharmaceutical companies have conducted three phases of clinical trials—experiments and applications on human subjects that measure the efficacy and safety of the drug. If the drug shows promise, the company submits a New Drug Application to the FDA. If agency employees agree that the clinical trial results are reliable, the FDA forms a review panel whose members have different types of expertise about the potential effects of the drug. The panel serves as a gateway for nonemployees of the agency to participate in the drug approval process. Members of the panel consider all the results of the trials and offer opinions as to whether the drug can be approved for sale. Ultimately, the FDA makes the final decision.

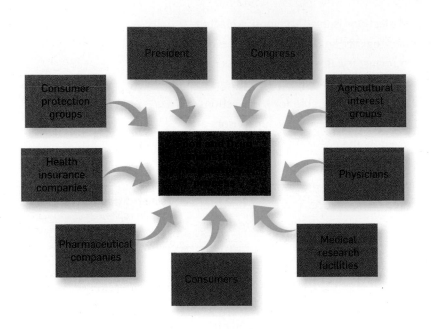

This process illustrates the trade-off between efficiency and transparency.[52] When a new drug is effective against disease, the public wants access to that drug as soon as possible. However, every new drug has unforeseen side effects, some of which may not be visible in the short term, so the more information the FDA has, the more likely the drugs it approves for the market will be safe. Forming review committees with members from outside the agency is one way of collecting a wide range of information about the possible impacts of the drug. Yet this process is time-consuming; the more participants, the more slowly it moves. Like many federal agencies, then, the FDA must weigh the cost of efficient decision making against the cost of approving a drug before it has been thoroughly tested.

At times the FDA has approved a drug that has later proved to have unacceptably dangerous side effects. The agency has then reversed the approval and issued a public health advisory warning of the side effects. When the FDA issues such an advisory to the public, the manufacturer usually withdraws the drug from the market. Such was the case with Vioxx, a strong pain reliever that was shown to increase the risk of cardiac problems with extended use.[53]

The issue of transparency is especially highlighted when the federal government enacts large spending bills, like the TARP plan or the American Recovery and Reinvestment Act, usually called the stimulus bill, that was signed into law in February 2009. The nearly $800 billion stimulus bill authorized a combination of spending and tax cuts, including funds for infrastructure, education, extension of unemployment benefits, and tax breaks for homeowners and businesses. The challenge confronting the federal bureaucracy in implementing this bill was getting the funds to recipients as quickly as possible while at the same time enforcing federal program rules and being clear about where the money was going.[54] Critics of the bill pointed to the huge amount of money involved and questioned the practical effect that the stimulus funds could have on the economy because of the length of time it would take to distribute the money according to standard federal practices. President Barack Obama responded by saying that he would consider revamping standard bureaucratic practices to streamline the process of distributing the funds. However, such streamlining could reduce accountability and transparency. President Obama, aware of the importance of transparency to voters, created a website (www.recovery.gov) that pinpointed how and where the funds were distributed, down to a block on a street.

What is more important, transparency or efficiency?

Whistleblowing

Most federal employees are careful, dedicated, and hardworking. However, as in all organizations run by human beings, there can be inefficiency, error, abuse of power, and corruption. Each federal agency has an **Office of Inspector General (IG)** that monitors the activities of the agency's employees. But unless a wrongdoing is identified and brought to the IG's attention, it frequently goes unpunished.

Office of Inspector General (IG): *Office within federal organizations that monitors the activities of employees in the organization to ensure they are doing their jobs properly.*

To encourage more candid disclosure of wrongdoing in federal agencies, Congress passed the Whistleblower Protection Act in 1989 to protect government employees, known as **whistleblowers**, who report mismanagement, corruption, or illegal activity within their agencies.[55] Prior to the passage of this act, whistleblowers had no real protection against reprisals from their colleagues, especially from those at higher levels of authority. The act established grievance and appeal procedures for employees who believe they have been retaliated against for reporting wrongdoing in their agencies. However, it is important to note that employees in law enforcement and national security are not currently covered by this act. In 2010, as part of the comprehensive financial services reform legislation described earlier, Congress extended protections to employees in the financial services industry who act as whistleblowers.

whistleblowers: *Employees who report mismanagement, corruption, or illegal activity within their agencies.*

Are private contractors working for the government likely to be whistleblowers? Why or why not?

Bureaucratic Failure

Whether whistleblowers come from inside or outside the federal government, it is up to the federal government to respond to them in an effective fashion. Unfortunately, there are serious cases in which a government agency has failed to respond. What happens when an entire agency fails to accomplish its mission? The Securities and Exchange Commission (SEC) did just that in the case of the fraudulent activities of investor and financial manager Bernard Madoff.

One of the realities of federal management and oversight is that a federal agency or a congressional committee needs to be aware of a problem in order to address it. The Madoff scandal is an example of bureaucratic and congressional oversight after the fact. In December 2008 Madoff confessed to engaging in fraudulent investment practices over the span of thirty years, costing individual investors (many of whom were retirees who lost their life savings), financial management firms, and charitable foundations an estimated $50 billion. Simply put, Madoff collected money, known as principal, from the investors, but at some point he stopped investing the money in real companies. Although he paid dividends (profits from investments) to his clients, the money came from new clients, not

What can be done about lack of responsiveness by the bureaucracy?

from investments; to maintain the scheme, he had to continue to recruit wealthy investors. When the financial crisis hit in 2008, some of his wealthy investors demanded large sums of their principal back, but Madoff did not have the money so could not return it to them. Madoff confessed his scheme to his sons, who reported him to the authorities; he was subsequently tried and convicted of financial fraud and sentenced to 150 years in prison.

Mario Tama/Getty Images

In June 2009, 71-year old financial investment manager Bernard Madoff was sentenced to 150 years in prison for fraud. His financial scam was estimated to have cost investors close to $50 billion.

Madoff's investments activities should have been more closely monitored by the SEC, which was accused of not doing its job properly. The SEC had been warned about Madoff repeatedly over a ten-year period by Harry Markopolos, an investment fund manager. Markopolos contacted a Boston regional SEC officer about Madoff's scheme in 2000, after he tried to replicate Madoff's stated earnings and could not find any sound way to do so. Over the next six years Markopolos actively tried to get the SEC to act, but not until 2006 did it start an inquiry into Madoff's dealings. Even then, following interviews of Madoff and some of his business associates, SEC lawyers found no wrongdoing and dropped the case.[56]

When the House Banking Committee questioned SEC commissioners about why they had acted as a gate against investigating Madoff and, more important, why they found no wrongdoing, they had little to say. As a general explanation, they said that the SEC was understaffed and ill-equipped to investigate such a massive fraud. In a hearing held on February 4, 2009, Congressman Gary Ackerman (D-N.Y.) said the following to the SEC commissioners:

Your mission you said was to protect investors and detect fraud quickly. How'd that work out? What went wrong? . . . You have single handedly diffused the American public of any sense of confidence in our financial markets if you are the watchdogs. You have totally and thoroughly failed in your mission. Don't you get it? . . . You forfeited your right to investigate by not doing it. Certainly not doing it properly or adequately. . . . What happened here? That's a question.[57]

Mark Wilson/Getty Images

A private citizen turned whistleblower, Harry Markopolos tried to inform the SEC that Bernard Madoff was a fraud and that his financial dealings were unsound, but the agency did not act on his warnings. On February 4, 2009, Markopolos testified during a House Financial Services Committee hearing.

How could such major financial dealings go unnoticed, even with information provided over time by a very determined private citizen? The SEC's failure to monitor and prevent such fraud and the lack of congressional intervention until it was too late illustrate the limits of the federal bureaucracy as well as of congressional oversight.

The dual responsibilities of accountability and responsiveness in the federal bureaucracy require the bureaucracy to do its job well enough to protect citizens from physical and financial harm. Unfortunately, the American people are so familiar with the failures of the federal bureaucracy that its successes are overlooked. The fact that 308 million people live in relative peace and security; experience safe and reasonable working conditions; trust that the medications they take are well tested; travel on trains, buses, and planes without incident; drink clean water; and receive their mail every day is a testament to the ways in which the federal bureaucracy meets its obligations. It is up to the voters to hold their elected officials—in Congress as well as the president—accountable for the performance of the federal bureaucracy.

The Bureaucracy and Democracy

The federal government that started with three cabinet departments has grown to include fifteen cabinet departments and many powerful independent agencies. The federal bureaucracy, including the armed services, employs nearly 4.5 million people. Their jobs affect the lives of every citizen, from the quality of the food they eat, to the safety of the highways they drive, to the purity of the water they drink.

In some important ways, the federal bureaucracy has become far more responsive to the needs of average individuals in the course of the nation's history, especially in the areas of social benefits, health care, environmental protection, and civil rights enforcement. The federal bureaucracy has tried to be more transparent in its operations by placing comprehensive information on the Internet for the public to access at any time. However, as the responses to Hurricane Katrina in 2005 and the Gulf Oil Spill of 2010 show, there have been notable and serious failures in the government's responses to disaster, especially in areas with higher concentrations of poor and rural residents.

The structure of the bureaucracy includes many gates against speedy implementation of federal policy. The fact that there are so many layers of authority even within one agency, much less an entire cabinet department, adds considerable delay to the process of policy implementation. Multiple agencies can have jurisdiction over the same federal program or share responsibility for responding to natural disasters such as hurricanes. Such overlap can lead to miscommunication and to competition over authority and power. The hierarchy and procedural barriers that come with a large federal bureaucracy can stand in the way of efficient government.

At the same time, the rules and guidelines governing decision making in the bureaucracy are designed to ensure equal implementation of the law, which is a crucial element of a democracy. Americans expect federal laws to be applied in a consistent manner, with openness and vigilant congressional and public oversight. Understanding how laws are implemented, especially the gateways through which federal regulations are issued and enforced, gives citizens the power to hold the government accountable.

Citizens like Kate Hanni and Harry Markopolos have the opportunity, in a democracy, to pressure the government to be responsible and implement the laws with vigor in all areas. But one might also argue that advocates should not be needed to ensure that the bureaucracy works with efficiency and transparency. Hanni and Markopolos both experienced frustration in trying to navigate the gateways of the bureaucracy. Fortunately, they were persistent in their efforts to overcome obstacles. Their experiences are indicative of both the gates and gateways that the bureaucracy presents for citizen involvement in policy implementation.

FOCUS QUESTIONS

- How does the federal bureaucracy play a role in responding to the individual needs of ordinary citizens?

- How does the structure of the federal bureaucracy shape the way policies are implemented?

- What powers does the bureaucracy have to ensure that federal policies are administered equally across all citizens?

- How can the average citizen influence the decisions of the bureaucracy?

- Is the bureaucracy a gate or a gateway to democracy? Explain.

GATEWAYS TO LEARNING

Top Ten to Take Away

1. The bureaucracy is the collection of executive branch departments, regulatory agencies, and other organizations that carry out the responsibilities of the federal government. Today nearly 4.5 million people, including those in the armed services, work for the federal government. (pp. 482–85)

2. Each bureaucratic organization has a clear mission, a hierarchical decision-making process, an area of expertise, and a bureaucratic culture. Aside from cabinet departments, there are various types of organizations within the bureaucracy, some designed to be more or less independent of the president. (pp. 485–95)

3. The constitutional foundations for the bureaucracy include the president's power to nominate and appoint officers of executive departments, from whom he may request advice. The bureaucracy is also based in the president's broad grant of executive power. (p. 485)

4. Since 1789 the bureaucracy has grown from three to fifteen executive departments as government's responsibilities have grown, primarily in the area of the economy. The first regulatory agency was established in 1887 to regulate railroad practices. (pp. 495–97)

5. Federal employment has developed from a corps of wealthy elites with political connections to members

of the Congress and the president into a merit- and performance-based civil service designed to be protected from political influence. (pp. 497–501, 503–4)

6. The president appoints cabinet secretaries and other high-level political appointees who are expected to carry out the president's agenda. (pp. 501–2)

7. Following a consistent regulatory process, agencies draft regulations, which are open to comment by citizens, members of Congress, interest groups, and relevant businesses and industries before they are finalized. (pp. 504–8)

8. Lawsuits can involve the judicial branch in the interpretation of public policy. Congress exercises influence over policy through its oversight responsibilities and power to authorize and allocate funds. (pp. 508–12)

9. The bureaucracy is subject to criticism for acting slowly, but in a democracy the need for efficiency is counterbalanced by the need for transparency. Reform efforts have improved transparency by providing protections for whistleblowers. (pp. 513–17)

10. Media attention also puts pressure on the bureaucracy to be more responsive to citizens and to administer the laws equally. (pp. 495, 504)

A full narrative summary of the chapter is on the book's website.

Ten to Test Yourself

1. What is the role of a cabinet department in the bureaucracy?

2. What explains the growth in the number of cabinet departments over time?

3. What is the difference between a federal commission and a federal corporation?

4. What are the four core components of a bureaucracy?

5. What is the relationship between bureaucratic culture and bureaucratic reputation?

6. What is the difference between a civil servant and a political appointee?

7. What do the Pendleton Act and the Civil Service Reform Act have in common?

8. Describe the steps involved in the federal regulatory process.

9. What are the two phases of congressional oversight of the bureaucracy?

10. Who are the stakeholders in food and drug oversight?

More review questions and answers and chapter quizzes are on the book's website.

Timeline to Keep Things in Order

Government under the Constitution begins with three executive departments.

1789

Andrew Jackson initiates patronage-based federal employment that his critics call a spoils system.

1829

Pendleton Act establishes a merit- and performance-based civil service.

1883

Interstate Commerce Commission is established to monitor railroad practices.

1887

Terms to Know and Use

Administrative Procedures Act (APA) (p. 505)

appropriate (p. 510)

authorize (p. 510)

bureaucracy (p. 483)

bureaucratic culture (p. 492)

bureaucratic reputation (p. 495)

cabinet (p. 484)

cabinet secretaries (p. 484)

career civil servants (p. 498)

civil service (p. 498)

Civil Service Commission (p. 498)

Civil Service Reform Act (p. 503)

Clean Air Act (p. 506)

conference committee (p. 510)

Congressional Budget Office (p. 506)

divided government (p. 503)

Environmental Protection Agency (EPA) (p. 489)

expertise (p. 492)

federal administration (p. 490)

federal board (pp. 490, 491)

federal regulatory commission (p. 489)

federal corporation (p. 491)

Federal Register (p. 506)

Federal Reserve (p. 511)

final regulations (p. 507)

Food and Drug Administration (p. 496)

Freedom of Information Act (p. 513)

Government in the Sunshine Act (p. 513)

Hatch Act (p. 503)

Hatch Act Reform Amendments (HARA) (p. 503)

independent agency (p. 489)

Interstate Commerce Commission (p. 496)

iron triangle (p. 504)

issue networks (p. 504)

markup (p. 510)

Medicaid (p. 488)

mission (p. 492)

national endowment (p. 491)

National Endowment for the Arts (p. 491)

National Railroad Passenger Corporation (Amtrack) (p. 491)

National Transportation Safety Board (NTSB) (p. 491)

Office of Inspector General (IG) (p. 515)

Office of Management and Budget (OMB) (p. 489)

oversight (p. 510)

patronage system (p. 498)

Pendleton Act (p. 498)

political appointees (p. 498)

preliminary regulations (p. 506)

presidential memorandum (p. 505)

regulations (p. 484)

regulatory process (p. 504)

Schedule C appointees (p. 502)

Securities and Exchange Commission (SEC) (p. 489)

Senior Executive Service (SES) (p. 502)

signing statements (p. 506)

spoils system (p. 498)

whistleblowers (p. 515)

Use the vocabulary flash cards on the book's website.

Learning That Works

WHAT YOU NEED . . .

TO KNOW	TO DO
The role of the bureaucracy	Determine whether it is a gate or gateway for representation
Competing demands on the bureaucracy	Understand why it seems slow and inefficient
Complex responsibility of the bureaucracy	Evaluate how inclusiveness causes inefficiency
The scope of federal regulations	Comprehend how the federal government affects your daily life
The conditions of federal employment	Consider whether you would like to work for the government
How the bureaucracy works	Recognize how you can influence public policy
The stakeholders in food and drug policy	Assess government responsiveness on consumer food and drug safety

1939	1946	1978	1989	2003
Hatch Act attempts to protect civil servants from politics.	Administrative Procedures Act provides for consistency in the issuing of regulations.	Civil Service Reform Act creates the Office of Personnel Management.	Whistleblower Protection Act protects federal employees who identify fraud and abuse in government agencies.	Department of Homeland Security becomes the fifteenth executive department.

15 THE JUDICIARY

▲ University of Michigan—Dearborn

> *In 1997, I read an article . . . about a possible lawsuit against the University of Michigan. . . . I knew I wanted to be involved. . . . I thought I'd be stuffing envelopes . . . even at that moment I never thought I'd become a plaintiff in a historic lawsuit.*

CourseMate

Visit http://www.cengagebrain .com/shop/ISBN/0618906959 for interactive tools including:

- Quizzes
- Flashcards
- Videos
- Animated PowerPoint slides, Podcast summaries, and more

"The envelope was way too thin," thought Jennifer Gratz, a high school senior in the class of 1995 at Southgate Anderson High School, in Southgate, Michigan. Despite graduating in the top 5 percent of her class, having a 3.8 (out of 4.0) GPA, and receiving a score of 25 out of 36 (83rd percentile) on her ACT, she had received a wait-list letter and ultimately a rejection letter from her first choice for college, the University of Michigan.

Elsewhere in Michigan, Barbara Grutter, a mother of two in her mid-40s who had decided to attend law school, did not get admitted to her first and only school choice. Despite a 3.8 undergraduate GPA and a score of 161 out of 180 (86th percentile) on her LSAT, she, too, was wait-listed and ultimately denied admission to the law school at the University of Michigan.

Gratz and Grutter then took a step that most students do not take; they chose to sue the school that rejected them. Each challenged the university's affirmative action policies, which gave underrepresented minority students preferential advantages in admissions compared to whites with similar GPAs and standardized test scores. The preference at the undergraduate college, for example, was equivalent to a full point on a 4-point GPA scale. That is, a student from an underrepresented minority group with a 2.8 GPA would have the same chance of admissions as a middle-class white student with a 3.8 GPA. Gratz and Grutter claimed that these policies denied them "equal protection of the laws" as guaranteed by the Fourteenth Amendment. Instead of an equal opportunity to gain admission to the university of their choice, they were, as individuals, disadvantaged. Supporters of affirmative action, on the other hand, claim that affirmative action policies enhance equality generally by increasing the chances that the university student body as a whole better represents the population as a whole. The consequence is a greater equality of outcome.

Jennifer Gratz

Sandy Huffaker/Detroit Free Press/Newscom

Gratz and Grutter received legal assistance from the Center for Individual Rights, a conservative legal group that actively sought students looking to fight affirmative action. Both lawsuits named Lee Bollinger, the president of the University of Michigan, as the respondent. They sought admission to the respective colleges (the undergraduate college for Gratz, and the law school for Grutter) and an end to the colleges' use of race as a criterion for admission. Meanwhile Gratz, although disappointed not to attend Michigan's flagship Ann Arbor campus, had enrolled in one of the school's regional campuses, the University of Michigan–Dearborn.[1]

In this chapter, we track the *Gratz* and *Grutter* cases all the way to the Supreme Court. Lawsuits such as these provide a gateway for one individual to have an enormous impact on the political system of the United States. The Supreme Court ultimately delivered a set of decisions that upheld the affirmative action plan of the law school, but found constitutional violation in the plan of the undergraduate college. As these cases help show, the judicial system of the United States, because of its authority to rule on the constitutionality of federal and state laws and policies, has an extraordinary amount of power in the American political system. The Supreme Court, as the highest court in the land, decides not only whether affirmative action may be allowed, but also decides other issues, such as whether abortion can be prohibited or the death penalty inflicted. The justices on the Court make important decisions that affect the lives of individuals and the policies of the nation at large despite the fact that they are not elected by the people and cannot be removed from office if the people disagree with the decisions that they make. Thus we examine, too, the controversial role and power of the judiciary in a democracy.

FOCUS QUESTIONS

- Why is the apparently simple requirement of providing "equal protection of the laws" more difficult than it seems?

- In what ways do the federal courts lack traditional means of accountability?

- How are courts, nevertheless, responsive?

- Do citizens have equal access to the justice system? Does the justice system treat them equally?

- Is the judiciary a gate or a gateway to democracy?

The Role and Powers of the Judiciary

The job of courts is to resolve legal disputes. The American legal system is based largely on the English system, which is the system that the colonists were familiar with. The legal system under the Constitution kept many of the same practices, but added some innovations.

English Legal Traditions

adversary process:
Confrontational legal process under which each party presents its version of events.

Do courts produce the fairest decision possible? Can you give examples?

trial by jury: *Method of placing the determination of issues of fact in a trial into the hands of fellow citizens.*

Resolution of legal disputes follows an **adversary process**. In an adversarial system, each party, usually represented by an attorney, presents its version of events, with virtually all attempts to slant information short of lying under oath deemed acceptable. According to a noted Supreme Court scholar, "The underlying assumption is that two persons arguing, as partisanly as possible, will produce the fairest decision."[2]

While in some cases a judge decides which side in such legal battles is correct, a group of ordinary citizens more usually determines the outcome. The right to **trial by jury** dates back in England to the Magna Carta (1215), where it replaced trial by ordeal, the practice of subjecting people to drowning or burning to see if they were innocent. Trial by jury is crucial to liberty, for it inserts a gate of citizen judgment between the accused person and the government that protects the accused from arbitrary detention and unjust punishment.

Trials involve questions of fact (for example, did the University of Michigan set different standards for white and minority students?) and questions of law (for example, do such differing standards violate the Fourteenth Amendment?). Trial court decisions about questions of fact are presumed to be valid because the trial judge or the jury directly hears the evidence in the case. But because trial courts sometimes make mistakes about questions of law, the American legal system has followed the British practice by allowing **appeals** from trial court rulings of law. Appeals are heard by appeals courts and by the Supreme Court.

Trials resolve two distinct types of disputes. In a **criminal case**, the government prosecutes an individual for breaking the law. Criminal cases are based almost exclusively on prohibitions on behavior written into statutes (laws) passed by federal, state, or local legislatures. In a **civil suit**, a plaintiff, such as Jennifer Gratz, sues a defendant, such as the University of Michigan, to enforce a right or to win monetary damages. The U.S. Constitution guarantees jury trials in all criminal cases and in all civil suits over $20. Today, Congress limits access to the federal courts in monetary civil suits to claims of $75,000 or more. Suits for lesser amounts must go to state courts.

Criminal law is based on statutory authority, but statutory authority cannot cover all possible civil disputes between individuals. Many disputes are actions that no legislative authority could have ever imagined. When there are gaps in statutory law, courts rely on judge-made law known as **common law**. Common law requires judges to accept and rely on previous decisions (if each judge makes his or her own decisions on each case, there can be no common law). Thus, British royal judges developed the practice of reaching decisions based on **precedents**, or the previous decisions of other royal judges. Deciding cases based on precedents means that similar cases are decided similarly. Precedent is perhaps the most fundamental feature of English and American law. Because similar cases get decided similarly, following precedent promotes greater equality, predictability, and stability in law.

Constitutional Grants of Power

Article III of the Constitution establishes the judicial branch of government. It briefly refers to a Supreme Court of the United States and grants Congress the authority to create lower courts at its discretion. The Constitution grants the federal courts the authority to hear "cases or controversies," which the Supreme Court has interpreted to require that people who initiate lawsuits have **standing**, that is, have suffered a harm that the law arguably protects. Standing is a gate that limits access to the judicial system by requiring real disputes involving legally recognized harms, not hypothetical cases.

Because the Constitution says so little about the judicial branch, one of the early acts of the First Congress, the **Judiciary Act** of 1789, established 13 **district (trial) courts** and 3 circuit courts with both trial and appellate authority and serve at an intermediate level between the district courts and the Supreme Court. Today, there are 665 district court judges serving in 94 separate district courts and 179 **court of appeals** judges serving in 13 intermediate appellate circuits.[3]

appeal: *Legal proceeding whereby the decision of a lower court on a question of law can be challenged and reviewed by a higher court.*

criminal case: *Government prosecution of an individual for breaking the law.*

civil suit: *Lawsuit by a person, organization, or government against another person, organization, or government.*

common law: *Judge-made law in England and the United States that results from gaps in statutory law.*

precedent: *Practice of reaching decisions based on the previous decisions of other judges.*

standing: *Requirement that a party bringing a lawsuit has suffered a harm that the law arguably protects.*

If you recognize an injustice but have not been harmed by it, how can you get government to respond?

Judiciary Act: *1789 act creating the lower federal judiciary, district courts, and circuit courts of appeal.*

district courts: *Federal trial courts at the bottom of the federal judicial hierarchy.*

courts of appeals: *Intermediate federal courts that are above the district courts and below the Supreme Court.*

The lawful authority of a court to hear a case is its **jurisdiction**. In general, jurisdiction for any federal court requires either that the case involve federal law (including the Constitution and treaties); that the parties include the United States, ambassadors, or other public ministers; or that the parties are residents of different states. These latter suits are called diversity suits. As for the Supreme Court, the Constitution further divides its jurisdiction into **original jurisdiction**, that is, authority to hear a case directly from a petitioning party (as in a trial), and **appellate jurisdiction**, authority to hear cases on appeals from lower courts. Specifically, the Supreme Court has original jurisdiction in "all Cases affecting Ambassadors, other public Ministers and Consuls, and those in which a State shall be Party" (Article III, Section 2). The Constitution then declares that "in all the other Cases" properly before the Court, it would have appellate jurisdiction subject to such exceptions and regulations that Congress shall make.

The Constitution grants the president the authority to nominate judges, but these nominations are subject to the advice and consent of the Senate. Judges confirmed by the Senate serve during "good behavior," which, short of impeachment, essentially means a life term. The House has impeached only one Supreme Court justice, Samuel Chase (1805), in an attempt by the Democratic-Republicans to remove an ardent Federalist from the bench. The Senate rejected every charge against Chase, establishing a custom crucial to **judicial independence** that judges would not be removed due to partisan disagreements with their decisions.

The Constitution grants the federal courts the authority to hear cases of law and **equity**. These cases can involve (1) the common law when there are gaps in legislative authority; (2) **statutory interpretation**, where the courts have to determine what Congress meant by a statute (for example, is discrimination on the grounds of pregnancy included in the prohibition on sex discrimination in the Civil Rights Act of 1964?), and (3) **constitutional interpretation**, where the courts must decide whether a law or practice violates a provision of the Constitution, such as the Fourteenth Amendment's guarantee of **equal protection of the laws**.

Constitutional interpretation brings forth the greatest power of the federal judiciary, **judicial review**. This power is not explicitly in the Constitution, but it is a power that Alexander Hamilton, the author of *Federalist* 78, expected would belong to the courts.[4] Judicial review is the power of courts to declare actions of Congress, the president, or state officials unconstitutional and therefore void. The Supreme Court used this extraordinary power to

The Supreme Court's first chambers were on the ground floor of the U.S. Capitol Building. The Court continued to meet in the Capitol until 1935, when the current Supreme Court Building was completed. Following the Judiciary Act of 1789, President George Washington appointed six justices. By 1863 the number of justices had grown to ten. In 1869 Congress set the number at nine, where it has remained ever since.

jurisdiction: *Lawful authority of a court to hear a case.*

original jurisdiction: *Authority to hear a case directly from a petitioning party, as in a trial.*

appellate jurisdiction: *Authority of a court to hear cases on appeal from lower courts.*

judicial independence: *Ability of judges to reach decisions without fear of political retribution.*

equity: *Doctrines of fairness followed in countries that follow the English common law.*

Franz Jantzen, Collection of the Supreme Court of the United States strike down segregated schools in *Brown v. Board of Education* (1954) and the anti-abortion laws of forty-seven states in *Roe v. Wade* (1973), as well as to rule on the Michigan **affirmative action** cases in 2003. The Supreme Court granted itself the power of judicial review in the case of ***Marbury v. Madison*** (1803).

Marbury v. Madison

The *Marbury* case arose out of the election of 1800, which resulted in the defeat of President John Adams (1797–1801) by Thomas Jefferson (1801–1809). It also resulted in the defeat in Congress of Adams's Federalist Party by Jefferson's Democratic-Republicans (see Chapter 9, Political Parties). In the days before the Jeffersonians took control of government, the defeated Federalists, seeking to maintain some bit of power, passed the Judiciary Act of 1801. This act created many new judgeships that presumably would be filled by Federalists nominated by outgoing President Adams and confirmed by the outgoing Federalist Senate.

One of the judges nominated by Adams and confirmed by the Senate was William Marbury. In the hectic final hours of the Adams administration, Secretary of State John Marshall, who had recently been confirmed as chief justice of the Supreme Court, failed to deliver Marbury's judicial commission, thus preventing Marbury from assuming his position. After Jefferson's presidential term began, Marbury requested that Jefferson's secretary of state, James Madison, deliver the commission, but Madison refused. Marbury then took his case directly to the Supreme Court, seeking a writ of *mandamus,* an order compelling Madison to deliver the commission. Marbury believed that the Judiciary Act of 1789 gave the Supreme Court original jurisdiction to hear cases involving writs of *mandamus.*

The decision of the Supreme Court, written by Chief Justice John Marshall, unanimously decreed that Marbury had a legal right to his commission, but the Supreme Court could not order Madison to provide it because the Court did not have jurisdiction to hear the case. The Court did not have jurisdiction, Marshall wrote, because the section of the Judiciary Act of 1789 that expanded the Court's original jurisdiction to cover writs of *mandamus* was unconstitutional. The decision was brilliant. In declaring that the Court did not have jurisdiction to hear the case, Marshall established that the Court has the power to decide whether a law passed by Congress is valid under the Constitution.

In declaring the authority to declare acts of Congress to be unconstitutional, the Court noted that if Congress passes a law that violates a provision of the Constitution, either that law is valid or the constitutional provision is valid, but not both. So, argued the Court, if the Constitution specifically limits the Supreme Court's original jurisdiction to certain types of cases, but Congress passes legislation to expand it beyond those cases, either the legislation expanding jurisdiction is valid or the constitutional limit on jurisdiction is valid. Which is it? And who gets to decide?

Although it is obvious to us today that the Constitution is supreme over regular legislation, that relationship was not as clear in 1803. In *Marbury v. Madison,* Chief Justice Marshall clarified that the Constitution must be supreme and that regular laws cannot overrule constitutional requirements. Which branch gets to decide whether a law violates the Constitution? Marshall answered simply: "It is emphatically the province of the judicial department to say what the law is."[5] In short, Marshall was interpreting the Constitution to say that the Court has the power to interpret the meaning of the rules laid down by the Constitution's

statutory interpretation: *Cases in which the courts have to determine what Congress meant by a statute.*

constitutional interpretation: *Decisions by a Court defining the meaning of a constitutional provision, often to determine whether a law or practice violates a provision of the Constitution.*

equal protection of the laws: *Guarantee in the Fourteenth Amendment that no state shall deny any person equal treatment.*

judicial review: *Authority of courts to declare laws passed by Congress and acts of the executive branch to be unconstitutional.*

affirmative action: *Policies that grant racial or gender preferences in hiring, education, or contracting.*

Marbury v. Madison: *An 1803 Supreme Court decision that established the Supreme Court's power of judicial review.*

How does "less is more" apply to the decision in *Marbury*?

John Marshall was the nation's fourth chief justice and the first one to make an impact. His decisions, starting with *Marbury v. Madison* (1803), strengthened the judiciary branch specifically and the federal government generally. Not only did he set forth the power of judicial review, but in a series of decisions during thirty-four years on the Court he crafted a broad interpretation of the Constitution that expanded the scope of national power and ensured the uniformity of federal law.

Marshall Court: *Named after Chief Justice John Marshall, the Court that greatly expanded national power (1801–35).*

In *Marbury*, the Court established its power over laws made by Congress. Why, then, did the Marshall Court also expand Congress's power?

necessary and proper clause: *Gives Congress the power to pass all laws necessary and proper to the powers enumerated in Section 8 (Article I, Section 8).*

commerce clause: *Gives Congress the power to regulate commerce with foreign nations, with Indian tribes, and among the various states (Article I, Section 8).*

Framers and to hold those rules supreme over legislative acts passed by Congress. More than two hundred years later, this decision stands as the foundation of judicial power in the United States (see Supreme Court Cases: *Marbury v. Madison* in Chapter 2, The Constitution). Since that time, approximately 120 nations have adopted this constitutional arrangement, but in 1803 it was an innovative departure even from the British system of justice (see Other Places: Judicial Review).

Historical Trends in Supreme Court Rulings

In *Federalist* 78, Alexander Hamilton described the judiciary as "the least dangerous branch" because it has no power over the sword or the purse. But due to the power of judicial review, the Supreme Court has actually played a major role in dividing authority between the nation and state, between Congress and the president, and between government, whether state or local, and the people. Through the Court's history, its interpretations have expanded, then contracted, and once again expanded national powers. After a long and slow start, it has also moved, fairly consistently, toward greater protections of equality.

Expansion of National Power under the Marshall Court

During George Washington's administration (1789–97), the Supreme Court had so little power or status that its first chief justice, John Jay, resigned to become governor of New York. Not until the fourth chief justice, John Marshall, did the Court begin to establish itself as a major player in national politics. The **Marshall Court** (1801–1835; Courts are often named after the sitting chief justice) did so not only by affirming its power of judicial review in the *Marbury* case, but also by setting forth a broad interpretation to the scope of national power in the cases of *McCulloch v. Maryland* (1819) and *Gibbons v. Ogden* (1824) and by limiting the authority of state judiciaries in a series of decisions culminating in *Cohens v. Virginia* (1821; see Supreme Court Cases: *McCulloch v. Maryland* in Chapter 3, Federalism).[6]

The decision in *McCulloch v. Maryland* expanded national power in two ways: by granting the national government the right to create a bank through the **necessary and proper clause**, and by limiting state power by denying the states the authority to tax activities of the national government. Similarly, in *Gibbons v. Ogden*, the Court took an expansive view of national power, declaring that the **commerce clause**, which granted the national government the authority to regulate commerce "among the several States," would be broadly defined to include not just the shipping of goods across state lines but also the economic activities within a state that concern other states. As in *McCulloch*, what the Constitution grants as a legitimate object of national authority (here, interstate commerce) could not be regulated by a state.

⬤otherplaces

Judicial Review

The notion of judicial review arguably began in England in 1610 when Lord Coke declared in Dr. Bonham's Case that "when an act of parliament is against common right and reason, or repugnant, or impossible to be performed, the common law will control it, and adjudge such act to be void." The case, though, involved an unlawful imprisonment, not an unconstitutional law, so Lord Coke was only speaking hypothetically.

Judicial review did not catch on in Great Britain for two reasons. First, unlike the United States, where Congress's powers are limited, Parliament is supreme. Second, Great Britain does not have a written constitution, thus depriving courts of a basis to declare that a law is unconstitutional.

The United States thus became the first modern nation to establish judicial review, but until recently few countries followed this practice. In recent years, with greater attention to human rights around the world, most countries have moved toward some form of judicial review.

The United Kingdom still does not have a system of judicial review, but it has shown some movement in that direction. The British Human Rights Act, which went into effect in 2000, allows British courts to declare that laws are not compatible with the European Convention on Human Rights, a European treaty that protects certain rights and liberties. Such a declaration does not void the law, but it can be used to embarrass Parliament into changing the law.

Great Britain also has power-sharing agreements with Scotland and Northern Ireland. If Parliament passes laws that violate these agreements, British courts may be unwilling to enforce them.

- **Why might more countries be accepting judicial review?**

- **How are rights protected in countries without judicial review?**

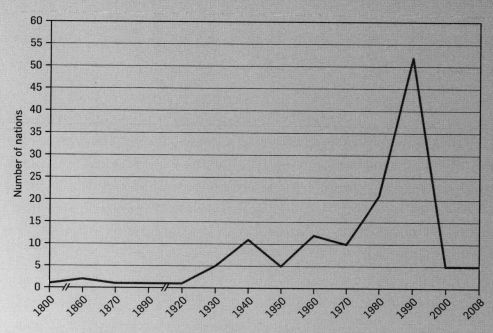

Number of Nations Adopting Judicial Review, 1800–2008.
Source: Tom Ginsberg, *Judicial Review in New Democracies: Constitutional Courts in Asian Cases* (Cambridge, U.K.: Cambridge University Press, 2003); Robert Maddex, *Constitutions of the World* (Washington, D.C.: Congressional Quarterly, 1995); CIA World Factbook; various national supreme court websites; *Dr. Bonham's Case*, 8 Co. Rep. 114 (Court of Common Pleas [1610]).

supremacy clause: *Makes federal law supreme over state laws (Article VI).*

This supremacy of federal law over state law is explicitly stated in the Constitution's **supremacy clause**. But the fact that federal law is supreme over state law does not necessarily answer whether the national courts or the state courts get the final say over what federal law means. In decisions made necessary by state court refusals to abide by its initial decisions, the Supreme Court declared that federal courts have the final say over what federal law means, establishing the federal judiciary as supreme over state judiciaries on questions of national law. These cases, culminating in *Cohens v. Virginia*, are not as famous as *Marbury* and *McCulloch*, but they have been essential in preventing the sort of divisions that would arise if state judges had the final say on what federal tax laws, or any other federal laws, meant in their home states.

By establishing judicial review, expanding national power, and ensuring the uniformity of federal law, the Marshall Court set the United States on the path to a strong and unified nation.

Limits on National Power, 1830s to 1930s

Starting in the 1830s the Supreme Court began limiting national power over slavery and, later, civil rights and over governmental efforts to regulate the economy. Although the Constitution permitted slavery, the justices did not address the issue until the case of *Dred Scott v. Sandford* (1857).[7] As noted in Chapter 5 (Civil Rights), the Supreme Court declared that no black person could be an American citizen and that Congress did not have the authority to regulate slavery in the territories. The decision inflamed the tensions over slavery that soon led to the outbreak of the Civil War.

Following the war, Congress proposed and the states ratified the Fourteenth Amendment, which overturned the *Scott* case by making "all persons born in the United States . . . citizens of the United States." The amendment further prevented states from denying any person due process of law or the equal protection of the laws and from abridging the privileges or immunities of citizens of the United States. The amendment granted Congress the means to enforce the amendment's commands by appropriate legislation, thus adding to Congress's enumerated powers.

On what basis did the Court say, in *Dred Scott v. Sandford*, that Congress did not have the authority to regulate slavery in the territories?

The Supreme Court interpreted these clauses narrowly, thus limiting national power. For example, the *Slaughterhouse Cases* gave a restricted interpretation of the privileges or immunities that states could not abridge, holding that the clause protects the right of access to the seat of government, the right to pass freely from state to state, and the right to demand the protection of the federal government on the high seas or abroad, but little more.[8] Through precedent, the limited reading of the clause largely remains in effect today.

Why did the Court reduce or limit federal power in this era?

In *United States v. Cruikshank*, the Supreme Court reversed federal charges against the perpetrators of the Colfax massacre (see Chapter 5), arguing that the right to enforce the due process clause gave Congress the authority to act only against states, not against individuals.[9] Similarly, in the *Civil Rights Cases*, the Court refused to grant Congress the authority to prohibit discrimination by private individuals under the equal protection clause, declaring that state-sponsored inequality was all that the amendment prohibited.[10] But when the states actively discriminated against blacks by mandating segregated facilities, the Court allowed this too, under the **separate-but-equal doctrine** (see Chapter 5), which the Court established in the 1896 case *Plessy v. Ferguson*.[11] Moreover, for more than fifty years, neither the Court nor the segregated states paid attention to whether separate facilities were actually equal.

separate-but-equal doctrine: *Supreme Court doctrine that upheld segregation as long as there were equivalent facilities for blacks.*

The Supreme Court limited national authority in the economy, too. Following the Civil War, as the shift in the American economy from agriculture to industry accelerated, powerful business and industrial interests sought to limit attempts by Congress and the states to regulate economic activity and labor. The Supreme Court generally backed business and industrial interests by setting up barriers to regulation. It promoted laissez faire, the belief that the government should not intervene in the economy, through two constitutional doctrines. First, when Congress attempted to regulate the economy, the Court narrowly read the commerce clause, declaring that economic regulation was to be left to the states. But when states tried to regulate the economy, the Court, siding with business interests, prohibited them from doing so under its reading of the Fourteenth Amendment's due process clause.

For example, Congress attempted to control business monopolies by passing the Sherman Antitrust Act of 1890, which made "every contract, combination . . . or conspiracy in restraint of trade or commerce among the several states, or with foreign nations . . . illegal." Responding to this law, the Justice Department sought to break up the Sugar Trust, a company that had acquired control of 98 percent of the nation's sugar refining. In 1895, in what is known as the *Sugar Trust Case,* the Court conceded that the Sugar Trust was an illegal monopoly but stated that Congress had no power to suppress monopolies.[12] These issues were a matter for state regulation. Manufacturing, according to the Court, precedes commerce and thus cannot be regulated by the federal government. In this way the Court established that it would determine what constituted interstate commerce.

But when the states attempted to regulate economic activity by setting maximum hours and minimum wages, the Court ruled such laws invalid because they violated the Fourteenth Amendment clause that prohibits states from depriving individuals of "life, liberty, or property, without due process of law." Such limits on the conditions of labor deprived individuals of liberty, said the Court, specifically of a judicially created **right to contract**, a right not explicitly in the Constitution. According to the Court, individuals must have the right to contract their labor for more than the allowable number of hours or less than the minimum allowable wage, free of interference from state regulations.[13]

right to contract: *Court-created right not explicitly in the Constitution that prohibited restrictions on labor contracts, such as minimum wages or maximum hours.*

If a right is not explicitly stated in the Constitution, should it be protected?

Strengthened National Power, 1930s to the Present

Following the onset of the Great Depression in 1929, citizens called on the states and the national government to try to regulate the economy and to assist workers, but the Supreme Court held firm in creating a constitutional gate that declared much economic legislation passed in the early years of the Franklin Delano Roosevelt administration (1933–45) unconstitutional. Under pressure from Congress and Roosevelt, the Court eventually opened a gateway by allowing the federal and state governments greater leeway in regulating the economy. During this same period, the Court began restricting state government limits on civil rights and liberties, while strengthening national power to protect civil rights.

Economic Regulation.   Franklin Roosevelt, elected president in 1932 on a platform of economic recovery and reform, saw several pieces of his New Deal legislation—which aimed to alleviate the nation's economic hardships—struck down by the Court, often by closely divided votes. After his 1936 reelection Roosevelt struck back at the Court, proposing a so-called **Court-packing plan** that would have allowed him to appoint a new justice for every justice over 70 who failed to resign. This scheme would have increased the Court's size to fifteen and guaranteed judicial support for his economic plans.

In the historic "switch in time that saved nine," two of the moderate backers of the Court's laissez-faire policies proved themselves responsive to the hostile political environment facing the Court. They began to change their votes, providing majorities for both national and state plans to regulate the economy, thereby removing the need for Roosevelt's controversial Court-packing plan. In a series of cases decided in 1937, the Court upheld minimum wage laws and the right of unions to organize and bargain collectively as within the powers of Congress to regulate under the commerce clause. In one case (see Supreme Court Cases: *Wickard v. Filburn*, in Chapter 12), the Court went so far as to declare that wheat grown by a farmer on his own farm for consumption on his own farm was produced in interstate commerce, because of the effect that the wheat, and all similarly grown wheat, would have on the marketplace.[14] The implication of this decision was clear: If such wheat was involved in interstate commerce, then virtually all economic activity involves interstate commerce and thus falls within the regulatory powers of Congress.

Increased Protections for Civil Liberties and Civil Rights.

With the government's authority over the economy established, cases before the Court dealt increasingly with questions of civil rights and civil liberties, topics discussed more fully in Chapters 4 (Civil Liberties) and 5. As noted in Chapter 4, paving the way for closer scrutiny of these rights were Court decisions incorporating various provisions of the Bill of Rights, making them binding on the states. This **incorporation doctrine** began slowly, with First Amendment rights among the few incorporated before the 1950s. The doctrine expanded during the liberal **Warren Court** (1953–69), which made most of the criminal procedure guarantees of the Bill of Rights binding on the states.

Outside of incorporation, the Warren Court greatly expanded the interpretation of liberties involving the First Amendment, equal protection, the right to privacy, and criminal procedure. In First Amendment cases, the Court protected the speech rights of those advocating violence against religious and racial minorities, the press rights of newspapers against libel suits by public figures, and the right to publish allegedly obscene materials as long as they had even the slightest amount of redeeming social value. It also limited prayer and Bible readings in the schools.[15] Regarding equal protection, beyond the momentous *Brown v. Board of Education* decision striking at segregation, the Court launched a **reapportionment** revolution, striking down arrangements in which some congressional or state legislative districts had ten or twenty times the population of other districts. Setting forth a "one person, one vote" requirement, the Court demanded equality in the number of citizens represented in each legislative district.[16] The Warren Court also created a **right to privacy** that is not explicitly in the Constitution, striking down a Connecticut statute that prohibited any person—including married couples—from using birth control and any person—including doctors—from counseling people or patients on such use.[17] Finally, regarding criminal justice, the Warren Court demanded

Court-packing plan: *President Franklin Roosevelt's proposal to add new justices to the Supreme Court so that the Court would uphold his policies.*

Do you think justices over the age of 70 should be allowed to stay on the Supreme Court? Is appointment for life a good or a bad idea?

incorporation doctrine: *Process by which the Supreme Court made some provisions of the Bill of Rights binding on the states.*

Warren Court: *Liberal Supreme Court that made landmark decisions on equal protection, criminal procedure, and the right to privacy (1953–69).*

reapportionment: *Redistricting to achieve equal numbers in legislative districts.*

right to privacy: *Constitutional right inferred by the Court that has been used to protect unlisted rights such as sexual privacy, reproductive rights, plus the right to end life-sustaining medical treatment.*

Is there a right to privacy? Where should the line be drawn against government intrusion in private life?

that evidence obtained by police in violation of the Fourth Amendment's protection against unreasonable searches or seizures should be excluded at trial (the exclusionary rule) and that subjects in custody not be interrogated without being informed of their right to remain silent and have an attorney (the so-called *Miranda* warnings, after the plaintiff in the case).[18]

Conservatives decried liberal Warren Court decisions on civil rights, school prayer, and criminal procedure, and this opposition led to unsuccessful grassroots attempts to impeach Earl Warren. In 1968 Republican presidential candidate Richard M. Nixon attacked the Supreme Court for "hamstringing the peace forces in our society and strengthening the criminal forces."[19] Nixon (1969–74) won the election and was able to appoint four new justices to the Court, including Chief Justice Warren Burger. But with greater social acceptance of racial integration and police acceptance of the *Miranda* warnings, neither the more conservative Burger Court (1969–86) nor the Rehnquist Court (1986–2005) undid what the liberal Warren Court had done.

While school desegregation originally meant allowing children to go to their neighborhood school regardless of race, such desegregation did little in places where whites and blacks lived in separate areas. In such areas, neighborhood schools would still be segregated. To remedy this situation, the Burger Court allowed children to be bused away from their neighborhood schools to increase integration. The Burger Court also established abortion rights, limited the death penalty, protected women's rights under the equal protection clause of the Fourteenth Amendment, and, in a precursor to the *Gratz* and *Grutter* lawsuits, first allowed affirmative action at colleges and universities.[20] On the other hand, the Burger Court chose not to extend equal protection rights to the unequal funding of school districts and, in the criminal justice area, limited the reach of the exclusionary rule and the *Miranda* warnings.[21] It also limited presidential authority in *United States v. Nixon*, declaring that the Nixon administration could not withhold tapes related to the Watergate scandal.[22] This decision and the evidence from the tapes led directly to Nixon's resignation (see Chapter 13, The Presidency).

Although conservative, the Rehnquist Court, over Chief Justice William Rehnquist's dissent, first extended privacy rights to homosexual conduct.[23] On the other hand, the Rehnquist Court limited, however slightly, the scope of abortion rights and cut back, again only slightly, the scope of congressional authority under the commerce clause and sovereign immunity (see Chapter 3, Federalism). It also issued split decisions in the *Gratz* and *Grutter* cases.[24] And perhaps most important, as noted in Chapter 10 (Elections and Campaigns), it ended the dispute over the 2000 presidential election with its decision in *Bush v. Gore*.[25]

The Appointment Process for Federal Judges and Justices

Among the important consequences of the George W. Bush presidency (2001–2009) was his nomination of two Supreme Court justices who share his conservative ideology, John Roberts and Samuel Alito. Given the importance of John Marshall, Earl Warren, and other justices to the nation, Supreme Court nominations may be among the most important decisions a president makes.[26] Article III of the Constitution, however, says no more about appointments of judges and justices than that the president shall nominate federal judges "with the Advice and Consent of the Senate." As procedures have evolved, the president and the Senate accommodate each other on district court appointments, but there is some Senate resistance at the appeals court level. At the Supreme Court level, presidential nominees face intense scrutiny by the Senate, which often reflects concerns by citizens and interest groups.

The District Courts

When a vacancy occurs in a district court, the president selects a nominee, but with awareness of how the senators from the state in which the court is located might react. Before the nomination is announced, presidential staff members consult with the state's senators if they are members of the president's party; if one of them is opposed to the nomination, he or she can invoke the norm of **senatorial courtesy** and receive the support of other members of the Senate in blocking that nominee. When the two senators are from different parties, the senator from the president's party sometimes offers the other senator a percentage of the appointments, hoping the favor will be returned if the other party wins the presidency. For example, Sonia Sotomayor, who would go on to become President Barack Obama's (2009–) first Supreme Court nominee, received her district court nomination during the presidency of Republican George H. W. Bush (1989–1993) due to an appointment-sharing deal between New York's two senators, Republican Alfonse D'Amato and Democrat Daniel Patrick Moynihan. Like the president, senators use a variety of criteria in naming district court judges, including ideology, qualifications, and the rewarding of party loyalty.[27]

Patrick Duggan, the district court judge in the *Gratz* case, and Bernard Friedman, the judge in the *Grutter* case, had fairly similar backgrounds. Both parlayed campaign work for the Republican Party into state court judgeships, and both received federal court nominations from President Ronald Reagan (1981–89).

Confirmation of district court judges is generally routine, with nearly 90 percent of nominees since the administration of Jimmy Carter (1977–81) approved.[28] Following the nomination, the **Senate Judiciary Committee** conducts hearings on nominees. At the hearings, the American Bar Association (ABA), an organized interest group representing the nation's attorneys, evaluates the merits of nominees. District court nominees may also be requested to testify. If the Judiciary Committee approves the nomination, it moves to the Senate floor for a vote. Unless the vote is blocked by a filibuster, a majority is all that is needed for approval.[29]

The Courts of Appeals

The formal process of appointment of court of appeals judges is the same as that of district court judges, but the greater authority of court of appeals judges means that the Senate and outside interest groups pay much closer attention to the president's nominees. While court of appeals judges formally represent multiple states, seats are informally considered to belong to particular states. Thus, senatorial courtesy still applies. This norm is enhanced by the practice of the chair of the Judiciary Committee of sending "blue slips," so-called because of the color of the paper, to the senators of the president's party of a nominee's home state, asking whether they approve of the choice.[30] Without a positive response, the Judiciary Committee generally will not hold a hearing on the nominee; with no hearing, there is no vote. Even with a positive response to the blue slip, the Judiciary chair may choose not to hold a hearing, particularly if the chair is of the opposite party of the president.

For example, Senate Democrats twice blocked the nomination of future Chief Justice John Roberts, a conservative Republican, to the U.S. Court of Appeals. President George H. W. Bush first nominated Roberts in 1991, but the Democrats never gave Roberts a hearing, thereby killing the nomination. Ten years later, President George W. Bush renominated Roberts to the court of appeals, and again the Democrats in charge of the Judiciary Committee did not provide a hearing. Only after a third nomination in 2003, at which point Republicans controlled the Senate (and thus the Judiciary Committee), did Roberts receive a hearing and a vote. Of course, Republicans withheld hearings from many of President William J. Clinton's nominees when they controlled the Senate during his administration, including Elena Kagan after Clinton nominated her to the D.C. Court of Appeals in 1999. Overall, the Senate has failed to confirm more than 20 percent of court of appeals nominees since Jimmy Carter's administration, with the overwhelming majority being blocked at the Judiciary Committee.[31] With a short-lived filibuster-proof majority in the Senate, President Barack Obama had little trouble appointing lower court judges in 2009, but overall he has been slow in making such nominations.[32] In 2010 Senate Republicans began extensive use of **holds**, a process by which a single senator can block the **unanimous consent agreements** by which the Senate operates, to prevent or delay votes on many of President Obama's nominees.[33]

The Supreme Court

Given the Supreme Court's authority, the appointment of a Supreme Court justice is a high-stakes affair with extensive media coverage, interest group mobilization, public opinion polls, and the occasional scandal. As President Richard M. Nixon correctly noted, "The most important appointments a President makes are those to the Supreme Court of the United States."[34] While Nixon was no doubt referring to the ideological and policy implications of such appointments, presidents also use Supreme Court appointments for electoral advantage and even to reward loyal friends.

Given the increased scrutiny that nominees face in the Senate, the nomination of close friends is less prevalent than it once was. Harry S. Truman (1945–53) nominated four of his close friends to Supreme Court seats, and Lyndon Johnson was able to appoint his closest friend, Abe Fortas, to the Supreme Court in 1965. Nevertheless, the Senate balked when Johnson tried to promote Fortas to chief justice in 1968 and place another crony in Fortas's associate justice seat. George W. Bush's close friendship and professional relationship with Harriet Miers was one of the factors that led to the outcry against her failed 2005 nomination.

Often, presidents choose nominees in part because of perceived electoral advantages. This was undoubtedly the case in October 1956, a month before the general election, when Republican President Dwight D. Eisenhower (1953–61), burnishing his above-politics credentials, nominated Democrat William Brennan to the Court. It also helped that Brennan was a Catholic and Cardinal Spellman of New York had been lobbying hard for a Catholic nominee.[35] Presidential candidate Ronald Reagan promised to nominate the first woman to the Court and did so with his 1981 appointment of Sandra Day O'Connor. Fear that George W. Bush would get credit for nominating the first Latino to the Supreme Court was one of the factors that led Democratic interest groups to oppose Miguel Estrada's court of appeals nomination.[36] Keeping him off the court of appeals denied him the judicial experience that would be important for a Supreme Court nomination. President Obama received credit for nominating the first Hispanic to the Supreme Court with Sonia Sotomayor's appointment in 2009.

hold: *Power available to a senator to prevent the unanimous consent that allows a bill or presidential nomination to come to the Senate floor, which can be broken by invoking cloture (sixty votes).*

unanimous consent agreement: *Agreement among all one hundred senators on how a bill or presidential nomination will be debated, changed, and voted on in the Senate.*

Should judicial appointments be subject to partisanship?

Should judges be appointed without regard to race, ethnic background, gender, or religion?

© Bettmann/CORBIS

In 1987 the Supreme Court nomination of Robert Bork, a prominent conservative whose opposition to the right to privacy was well known, drew strong opposition from civil rights and women's rights groups. The hearings were heated, and ultimately the Senate rejected the nomination. Since that time Supreme Court nominees have been guarded in responding to senators' questions about contentious issues, causing 2010 Court nominee Elena Kagan, before her own nomination to the Court, to describe confirmation hearings as "a vapid and hollow charade."

What are the effects of televising congressional hearings?

Though electoral advantage certainly influences presidential decisions, presidents also try to choose nominees who are close to them ideologically, hoping to shape the direction of the Court for years to come. Ronald Reagan had this in mind when he nominated the conservatives Robert Bork (whom a Democratic-controlled Senate rejected) and Antonin Scalia (whom a Republican-controlled Senate approved), and George W. Bush did when he named conservatives John Roberts and Samuel Alito. Abe Fortas, while a friend of President Johnson, also shared Johnson's liberal philosophy. Considerations of ideology are not new. George Washington named eleven consecutive Federalists to the first Supreme Court, and Franklin Roosevelt appointed only supporters of his New Deal programs, most of whom were Democrats.

In recent times, nominees for the Supreme Court always receive hearings from the Senate Judiciary Committee. These hearings include testimony by the ABA on the qualifications of the nominee, comments by organized interests for and against the nominee, and testimony by the nominee. Every nominee since 1986 has received a unanimous vote of "well qualified" from the ABA except Robert Bork (of the fifteen members of the ABA Standing Committee on Federal Judiciary, ten voted that he was well qualified, one voted not opposed, and four voted that he was not qualified), Clarence Thomas (twelve voted qualified, two not qualified, and there was one recusal), and Harriet Miers, who withdrew her nomination in the face of substantial opposition to her ties to the president and her lack of qualifications.

Other interest groups mobilize for and against nominees, too. When in 1987 Ronald Reagan nominated Robert Bork, who was outspoken in opposing the constitutional right to privacy, Planned Parenthood released an ad stating: "State controlled pregnancy? It's not as far-fetched as it sounds. Carrying Bork's position to its logical end, states could ban or require any method of birth control, impose family quotas for population purposes, make abortion a crime, or sterilize anyone they choose."[37]

Figure 15.1 presents the number of interest groups supporting and opposing nominees at Judiciary Committee hearings since 1969. As can readily be seen, there has been a substantial growth in interest group involvement in Supreme Court nominations, largely due to the crucial role that the Court plays in so-called values issues such as abortion, the death penalty, and affirmative action. Lobbying by interest groups can substantially influence senators' votes for and against nominations.[38]

While the Judiciary Committee can kill a nomination by refusing to report it to the Senate floor, the committee has reported every recent Supreme Court nominee, even when the recommendation is negative, as it was in 1987 for Robert Bork (9–5 against) and in 1991 for Clarence Thomas (13–1 to forward without recommendation). Bork's hearings changed the nature of testimony by nominees. An outspoken conservative, Bork answered questions about his legal beliefs directly, openly discussing his opposition to the right to privacy. The result was a 58–42 vote against him by the full Senate. Since the Bork rejection, nominees have dodged questions about their beliefs. Recently, they have stated that it would be improper to answer any questions about any issue that might conceivably come before the Court. With testimony from the nominees carefully scripted, hearings have become less informative and

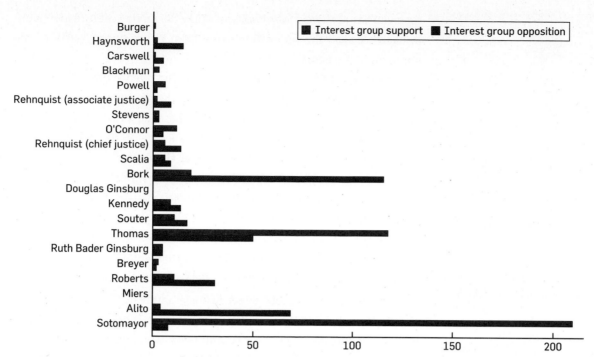

FIGURE 15.1 Number of Interest Groups Supporting and Opposing Supreme Court Nominees in Senate Judiciary Committee Hearings, 1970–2009.
Source: Derived from GPO Access, "Senate Committee on the Judiciary: Supreme Court Nomination Hearings."

more of a showcase for senators. Former Senator Joseph Biden (D-Del., now vice president) once took more than twenty minutes to ask a single question of Samuel Alito.[39]

Once the nomination is on the floor, senators debate the pros and cons of the nominee until the vote is set. Floor votes can be postponed indefinitely through a filibuster, a tactic used on occasion for court of appeals nominees, but Abe Fortas's chief justice nomination (1968) is the only Supreme Court nomination to be defeated by a filibuster.

Overall, the votes by senators largely depend on two crucial factors about the nominees: their perceived ideology and their perceived qualifications.[40] Figure 15.2 shows the relationship for senators' votes and nominees' ideology. Senators are much more likely to vote for nominees who are ideologically close to them, as either liberals or conservatives. Virtually all the opposition to the conservative John Roberts (2005) came from ideologically distant liberal Democrats, whereas virtually all the opposition to the liberal Abe Fortas (1968) came from both Republican and Democratic Party conservatives. The opposition to Sotomayor came exclusively from Republicans, who voted 31–9 against her. Constituent preferences matter: Six of the nine Republicans who represented states that voted for Obama supported Sotomayor. In contrast, only three of the thirty-one Republicans who represented states that voted for McCain supported her.

The nominees' perceived qualifications are no less important. Figure 15.3 shows the likelihood that a senator will vote for a nominee given high, medium, and low levels of perceived qualifications. Until recently, highly qualified nominees typically received overwhelming support even if they were very conservative (such as Antonin Scalia in 1986, who passed unanimously) or very liberal (such as Ruth Bader Ginsburg in 1993, who received only three no votes). But increased partisanship since the 1990s has meant that John Roberts (2005), Samuel Alito (2006), and Elena Kagan (2010), all highly qualified,

Should public opinion affect judicial appointments?

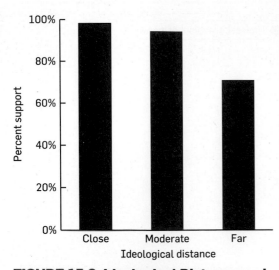

FIGURE 15.2 Ideological Distance and Voting for Supreme Court Nominees, 1937–2009. U.S. senators overwhelmingly (98.2 percent) vote for Supreme Court nominees who are ideologically close to them—liberal senators for liberal nominees and conservative senators for conservative nominees. When senators are moderately close to nominees (moderates and liberals, or moderates and conservatives), the approval rate drops to 94.2 percent. But senators who are ideologically distant from nominees vote for the nominees only 70.9 percent of the time. *Source:* Updated by authors from Lee Epstein and Jeffrey A. Segal, *Advice and Consent: The Politics of Judicial Appointments* (New York: Oxford University Press, 2005).

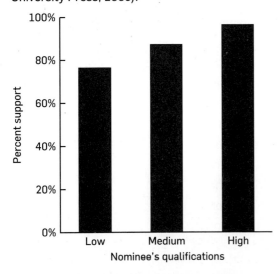

FIGURE 15.3 Qualifications and Voting for Supreme Court Nominees, 1937–2009. U.S. senators are much more likely to support Supreme Court nominees perceived to be high in qualifications (96.6 percent favorable) than nominees perceived to be low in qualifications (76.5 percent favorable). *Source:* Updated by authors from Lee Epstein and Jeffrey A. Segal, *Advice and Consent: The Politics of Judicial Appointments* (New York: Oxford University Press, 2005).

received twenty-two, forty-two, and thirty-seven no votes, respectively. In each case, all the opposition came from the opposing party of the nominating president.

Lower-qualified nominees have long faced even more trouble, with G. Harrold Carswell, a little-known federal judge whom Richard Nixon nominated to the Supreme Court in 1970, a case in point. Generally, lower-qualified nominees are confirmed with an average of 76.5 percent of the Senate, still enough to pass under normal circumstances, particularly if the president's party controls the Senate. But as with Carswell, when the president's party does not control the Senate, the Senate often rejects a poorly qualified nominee.

The question of qualifications includes not just ability, but also ethics. The Senate derailed Nixon's nomination of Clement Haynsworth in 1970, in part because Haynsworth, while on the court of appeals, voted on cases in which he had a small but direct financial interest. Much larger ethical questions surrounded the nomination of Clarence Thomas in 1991. During the televised hearings for Thomas, Anita Hill, who had worked for him at the Department of Education and later at the Equal Employment Opportunity Commission (EEOC), charged Thomas with sexual harassment. Thomas vociferously denied the charges. The senators acted the way elected officials of both parties normally do in such circumstances: Those who were ideologically close to the nominee—in this case, conservatives—believed him, whereas those who were ideologically distant did not.[41] The end result was that the Senate approved Thomas by a 52–48 vote.

In a Court long dominated by white males, Thomas was only the second African American to serve; Thurgood Marshall (1967), a distinguished litigator for the National Association for the Advancement of Colored People (NAACP) who argued *Brown v. Board of Education* (1954) before the Court, was the first. The Senate has confirmed 112 justices to seats on the Supreme Court. Of those 112, only 4—Sandra Day O'Connor (1981), Ruth Bader Ginsburg, Sonia Sotomayor (2009), and Elena Kagan (2010)—have been female. Sotomayor is the first and only Hispanic. By some measures, the current Supreme Court, with three women, one African American, and one Hispanic, is the most diverse ever.

It is also the case that the first thirty-two nominations went to Protestants, long the dominant religious group in American politics. The first Roman Catholic was Roger Taney in 1836; the first Jew was Louis Brandeis in 1916. Today, in a sign that the gateways to prominent positions have opened dramatically, the Court has six Roman Catholic justices, three Jewish justices, and no Protestants.

This diversity matters in a number of ways. Sandra Day O'Connor, for example, understood sex discrimination well. After graduating second in her class from Stanford Law School, no law firm in California offered her a job as an attorney, but one did offer her a secretarial position. Given that the Court has tremendous discretion about which cases to hear, greater diversity means that the Court may be more responsive to the issues that matter most to an increasingly diverse national population.

On the other hand, for the first time in history, not one member of the Supreme Court held elective office prior to service on the Court. The background of the current justices is fairly narrow. Every one of them attended either Harvard or Yale Law School, only Sotomayor served as a trial judge, and all the justices except Kagan came to the Supreme Court from federal appeals courts. This narrowness of background has not always been the case. In the past, many Supreme Court nominees graduated from modestly ranked law schools, and the justices often came to the Court from governorships, cabinet positions, the Senate, and private practice. To people who believe that the justices simply make decisions that are commanded by the Constitution, this narrowness does not matter. But to those who believe that just as experience with discrimination helps judges understand civil rights complaints, experience in the executive or legislative branches helps judges understand the constraints operating on those branches, the lack of this form of diversity hurts both the Court and the nation.

Brad Markel/Liaison

In 1991 President George H. W. Bush nominated Clarence Thomas to the Supreme Court, to replace the retiring Thurgood Marshall. Thomas was not a supporter of affirmative action, and civil rights and feminist groups objected to his nomination. Then Anita Hill, who had worked for Thomas at the Department of Education and the Equal Employment Opportunity Commission, accused him of sexual harassment. Despite her testimony, the Senate confirmed Thomas by a narrow margin.

Does diversity on the Court matter? Should the Supreme Court be age diverse?

State and Lower Federal Courts

While the Supreme Court is the highest court in the United States, it hears only a small percentage of the cases filed in federal court. Litigants might insist that they will take a case all the way to the Supreme Court, but the overwhelming majority of federal cases are resolved in the district courts, which conduct civil and criminal trials. Cases appealed from the district courts go to one of the U.S. Courts of Appeals, in which three-judge panels usually decide cases. From those panels, losing litigants can appeal cases to the entire circuit for an *en banc* ("by the full court") hearing, or they can appeal directly to the U.S. Supreme Court (see Figure 15.4).

State Courts in the Federal Judicial System

Each state has its own judicial system, and unless a case involves federal law or the type of parties that create federal jurisdiction, cases get resolved in state courts, each of which has its own hierarchy of trial and appellate courts. Cases that involve federal issues that begin in one of the fifty separate state court systems can be appealed to the federal court system in one of two ways. First, criminal defendants who have exhausted their state appeals, that is, have gone through their last appeal at the state level, can file a **writ of *habeas corpus*** with a U.S. District Court, which then allows the court to determine whether one or more of the defendant's federal legal rights have been violated. Second, any parties who have exhausted their state appeals can file a request for review, known as a **petition for a writ of *certiorari***, directly with the Supreme Court.

writ of *habeas corpus*: *Right of individuals who have been arrested and jailed to go before a judge, who determines whether their detention is legal.*

petition for a writ of *certiorari*: *Request to the Supreme Court that it review a lower court case.*

The District Courts

The Judiciary Act of 1789 established thirteen district courts for the thirteen states. Today, there are ninety-four districts. Many states have more than one district, but no district covers more than one state. Districts that cover only part of a state receive geographical names, such as the Northern District of Illinois. Altogether there are 665 district judgeships. Many districts have only one judge, but the Southern District of New York has twenty-eight, and

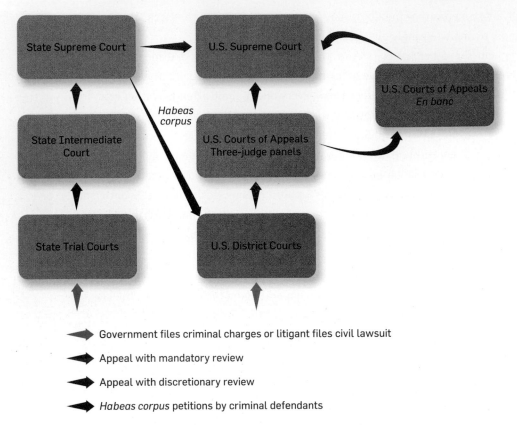

Government files criminal charges or litigant files civil lawsuit

Appeal with mandatory review

Appeal with discretionary review

Habeas corpus petitions by criminal defendants

FIGURE 15.4 Judicial Organization in the United States.
Source: Adapted from Lee Epstein, Jeffrey A. Segal, Harold J. Spaeth, and Thomas G. Walker, *The Supreme Court Compendium*, 4th ed. (Washington, D.C.: CQ Press, 2007), Figure 7-3.

the Central District of California has twenty-seven. Nevertheless, with rare exceptions, district judges oversee trials alone, not in panels.

Trials in the district courts are either criminal or civil. In civil suits the plaintiffs (the parties bringing the suit) often request monetary damages to compensate for harm done to them, such as by a broken contract or a defective product. When rights are alleged to have been violated, they may ask that the practice be stopped. Litigants filed over 267,000 civil suits in the district courts in 2008, and the government commenced nearly 71,000 criminal prosecutions.[42]

When Gratz and Grutter sued the University of Michigan over its admissions policies, the first stop for each was the U.S. District Court. Both had standing to sue, as their rejections by the university were real injuries, and because they claimed that their rights to equal protection under the Fourteenth Amendment had been violated, their cases raised a constitutional issue and entered the federal court system. Gratz and Grutter sought not only their own admission to the University of Michigan, but also an end to the university's use of race in admissions decisions. The district courts allowed both suits to move forward as **class action** lawsuits, meaning that Gratz and Grutter were suing not only on behalf of themselves but also on behalf of all people denied admission at Michigan on account of their race. Class action lawsuits can open the gateways of access to groups of citizens in the same circumstances, thus broadening the impact over the possible result of an individual lawsuit.

class action: *Lawsuit filed by one person on behalf of that person plus all similarly situated people.*

Civil Procedure. The overwhelming majority of lawsuits filed in federal court settle out of court with a negotiated agreement between the plaintiff and the defendant. In 2005 plaintiffs filed suit in federal court in over 250,000 cases, but the district courts commenced only 5,000 civil trials. Of these, slightly more than half, including the *Grutter* and *Gratz* cases, were bench (nonjury) trials.

Once a case is assigned to a judge, the next step in a civil suit is **discovery**. Discovery grants each side access to information relevant to its suit held by the other side. Crucial to the *Gratz* and *Grutter* suits were University of Michigan documents showing differential admission rates for whites and minorities who had similar grades and standardized test scores. During discovery, the attorneys for each side can also question witnesses for the other side in a process known as **deposition**. Following discovery, litigants file briefs with the court, laying out their arguments.

Outside interests can file *amicus curiae* ("friend of the court") **briefs**, stating their concerns in a case.[43] The most influential *amicus* briefs are those filed in the name of the United States, as represented by the Office of the **Solicitor General** in the Justice Department.[44] In the *Gratz* and *Grutter* cases, the Clinton administration filed briefs in favor of the University of Michigan, which argued that affirmative action was necessary to obtain a diverse student body. General Motors also filed a brief in favor of the university's affirmative action program, stating that it needed a diverse pool of highly qualified attorneys, managers, and the like. Eventually, Microsoft and nineteen other Fortune 500 companies signed briefs supporting the university.[45]

Civil trials begin with opening statements by the plaintiff and respondent. The plaintiff then calls its witnesses, who can be cross-examined by the respondent's attorney. Once the plaintiff rests the case, the respondent calls its witnesses, who can be cross-examined by the plaintiff's attorney.

Trial courts make determinations as to fact and as to law, whereas appellate courts generally make determinations only as to law, applying the facts as determined by the trial court. That would normally mean that it would be up to the district court to determine factually whether race played a role in admissions at Michigan and how much of a role it played. Then it would decide as a matter of law whether that role was allowable or not. The parties in the *Gratz* and *Grutter* cases made the decision a bit easier for the judges, for the University of Michigan readily admitted—indeed, strongly defended—its use of race in admissions. Therefore, the question for the trial judge was not a question of fact, but a question of law: Does the equal protection clause of the Fourteenth Amendment prohibit the use of race as a factor in university admissions?

While trial judges or juries have nearly complete discretion in deciding questions of fact, they are constrained by the courts above them on questions of law. In affirmative action, the key precedent was the 1978 Supreme Court decision in *Regents of the University of California v. Bakke*.[46] A divided Court ruled in *Bakke* that the University of California's quota system of reserving a certain number of seats for minorities was unconstitutional, but that a system in which race was a "plus" in admissions could be justified due to the benefits that a diverse student body provides all the students (see Chapter 5).

Barbara Grutter was in her 40s when she applied to law school. The mother of two children, she also ran a consulting business. In this photo, Jennifer Gratz listens on the right.

discovery: *Process in lawsuit prior to trial in which each side receives relevant information held by the other side.*

deposition: *Process in a lawsuit prior to trial in which each side gets to interview witnesses from the other side.*

***amicus curiae* briefs:** *Briefs filed by outside parties ("friends of the court") who have an interest in the outcome of a case.*

solicitor general: *Official in the Justice Department who represents the president in federal court.*

How important is a diverse student body? How important is a diverse workforce? What is your experience?

Should race be a factor in university admissions?

In December 2000 Judge Duggan ruled in the *Gratz* case that the point system used by the university—in which each applicant could receive up to 150 points including 20 for being from an underrepresented minority group—was a valid and necessary means of obtaining a diverse student body. On the other hand, Judge Friedman ruled in March 2001 that the law school's use of race in admissions violated the Constitution, finding that it was an "enormously important factor" in admissions, and not the mere plus approved by the Supreme Court in *Bakke*. The University of Michigan appealed Friedman's decision to the Sixth Circuit Court of Appeals, while the Center for Individual Rights backed Gratz's appeal to the same circuit.

Criminal Procedure.   Beyond civil cases like the Michigan affirmative action suits, trial courts also conduct criminal trials. A criminal prosecution begins with an alleged violation of federal criminal law. In the U.S. federal system, states have primary authority over law enforcement, but the federal government frequently prosecutes drug, weapons, and immigration cases, plus other crimes that involve interstate commerce or the instrumentalities of the federal government, such as the post office and government buildings.

The clearance rate for state and federal crimes—that is, the percentage of reported crimes in which someone is arrested, charged, and turned over for prosecution—is highest for violent crimes (over 45 percent in 2002) but much lower for property crimes such as burglary (16.5 percent).[47] Under the Constitution, an accused criminal in a federal court has a right to indictment by a **grand jury**, a specially empanelled jury consisting of between sixteen and twenty-three citizens who determine whether the government has sufficient evidence to charge the suspect with a crime. In the rare occasions in which a grand jury chooses not to indict, the suspect is freed.

Following indictment, the accused is arraigned, or informed of the charges against him or her, and asked to enter an initial plea of guilty or not guilty. About 90 percent of federal criminal cases are resolved through **plea bargains**, in which the accused plead guilty, usually in exchange for reduced charges or lesser sentences.[48]

In the small number of cases that proceed to trial, the accused has the right to a trial by jury, but is free to request a bench trial, in which the judge decides guilt or innocence. A jury in a federal felony case consists of twelve individuals who must reach a verdict unanimously. (Neither twelve people nor unanimity is required in a state court.) The accused can appeal a guilty verdict, but the double jeopardy clause of the Constitution prohibits the government from appealing a verdict of not guilty. If the accused is found guilty, the judge determines the sentence based on guidelines that depend on the nature of the offense, the number of prior convictions, and other factors as recommended by the U.S. Sentencing Commission. In death penalty cases, the decision on the punishment is left to the jury. That is, following a guilty verdict, the jury hears new testimony by the prosecutor and defense attorney about whether death is the appropriate punishment.

The Courts of Appeals

Sitting hierarchically above the ninety-four district courts are the U.S. Courts of Appeals. They are divided geographically into eleven numbered circuits plus a circuit for the District of Columbia and a "federal circuit" that hears appeals from specialized lower courts that deal with patents and customs (see Figure 15.5). Each of the numbered courts of appeals

grand jury: *Special jury charged with determining whether people should be put on trial.*

plea bargain: *Agreement by a criminal defendant to plead guilty in return for a reduced sentence.*

Do plea bargains make efficiency more important than justice?

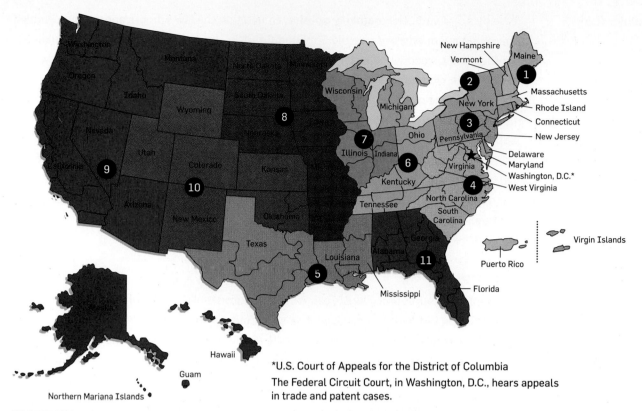

FIGURE 15.5 **U.S. Courts of Appeals and U.S. District Courts.**
Source: United States Courts, Court Locator, www.uscourts.gov/.

*U.S. Court of Appeals for the District of Columbia
The Federal Circuit Court, in Washington, D.C., hears appeals
in trade and patent cases.

has jurisdiction over several states. For example, the Sixth Circuit Court of Appeals, which sits in Cincinnati, hears appeals from district courts in Kentucky, Michigan, Ohio, and Tennessee.

The number of judgeships in each circuit ranges from six in the First Circuit, which covers the New England states, to twenty-nine in the Ninth Circuit, which covers California and eight other western states. Regardless of the number of judgeships, three-judge panels usually hear appeals from the district courts.

The courts have mandatory jurisdiction over cases appealed to them. That is, if a losing party from the district court appeals to the appropriate court of appeals, the court must hear the case. Because the circuit courts are in the middle of the federal judicial hierarchy, cases can be both appealed to the court of appeals and appealed from the court of appeals (see Figure 15.4 on page 538). Appeals from the Court of Appeals can happen in two ways. First, losing litigants at the court of appeals who believe that the three-judge panel that heard their case did not represent the judgment of the circuit as a whole can request an *en banc* review. Alternatively, losing litigants can request review by the Supreme Court. In both cases, further review is at the discretion of the court that is being appealed to.

Given the importance of the *Grutter* and *Gratz* cases, they made it through the U.S. Court of Appeals in anything but a normal manner. Rather than a hearing with a three-judge panel, possibly followed by *en banc* and/or Supreme Court review, the Center for Individual Rights, which represented Gratz and Grutter, requested and was granted an immediate *en banc* review. On May 14, 2002, the Sixth Circuit ruled in favor of the university in the law school

majority opinion: *Opinion of a court laying out the official position of the court in the case.*

equality of outcome: *Expectation that equality is achieved if results are comparable for all citizens regardless of race, gender, or national background, or that such groups are proportionally represented in measures of success in life.*

equality of opportunity: *Expectation that citizens may not be discriminated against on account of race, gender, or national background, and that every citizen should have an equal chance to succeed in life.*

case by a 5–4 vote. The **majority opinion** argued that the law school's approach resembled the plus system approved by the Supreme Court in the *Bakke* case. All three Republicans on the circuit sided with Grutter; five of the six Democrats sided with the university, consistent both with generally greater support among Democrats than Republicans for **equality of outcome** over **equality of opportunity** and with evidence that such attitudes often influence judicial decisions. Not surprisingly, Barbara Grutter appealed the decision to the Supreme Court.

On October 1, 2002, ten months after oral arguments, the court of appeals still had not issued its ruling in the undergraduate case. In an unusual step, Gratz's attorneys asked the Supreme Court to bypass the court of appeals and rule directly on their appeal. On December 1 the Supreme Court accepted review in both cases.

The Supreme Court

The Supreme Court's procedure in handling cases consists of deciding whether to grant review and, if review is granted, of receiving briefs, hearing oral arguments, deciding who wins, and writing the majority opinion.[49] If desired, justices who do not agree with the majority opinion can write concurring and dissenting opinions. The majority opinion, however, stands as the precedent for lower court judges to apply in similar cases dealing with the same issue.

Granting Review

Each year about eight thousand losing litigants ask the Supreme Court to review their cases. Most have lost in one of the U.S. Courts of Appeals or one of the fifty state supreme courts. The vast majority of appeals to the Supreme Court come in the form of petitions for writs of *certiorari*, often shortened to "cert." The Supreme Court's decision to grant cert is purely discretionary, but its rules suggest that a grant of cert is more likely when a lower court resolves issues of law differently from the way other lower courts have or issues a decision that conflicts with decisions of the Supreme Court. The Supreme Court is also more likely to grant review when the government of the United States, represented by the solicitor general's office, requests it, either as a petitioning party or as an *amicus curiae*. The filing of *amicus* briefs by other parties can also be important to the Court, as it signals that the case involves important questions of public policy.[50]

The large number of petitions for cert prevents the justices from fully reviewing each one. Instead, they rely on their clerks, who are usually recent law school graduates, to write summaries. Most of the justices' chambers have joined the "cert pool," which splits the cert petitions among the justices in the pool.

The large number of petitions also prevents the justices from fully discussing each one. Rather, the chief justice passes around a "discuss list," a set of cases he thinks worthy of discussion. Any justice can add any other case to the list if he or she wishes. Cases not on the discuss list are automatically denied cert, leaving the lower court's decision as final. The justices then meet in conference to consider each of the cases on the discuss list. The Court grants cert through a **rule of four**. That is, although five votes constitute a majority, the Court will agree to hear a case if any four justices vote to grant cert. Overall, the Court grants only about 1 percent of cert petitions, leaving the lower court decision as final in the remaining 99 percent of the cases.

rule of four: *Supreme Court rule that grants review to a case if as few as four of the justices support review.*

In 1929 Chief Justice William Howard Taft—the only chief justice who was also a president—convinced Congress to move the Supreme Court out of the U.S. Capitol to "a building of dignity and importance suitable for its use as the permanent home of the Supreme Court of the United States." The new building, across the street from the Capitol, was completed in 1935.

The justices' votes on *certiorari* remain secret unless a justice leaves his or her papers to the public, as justices sometimes do after they retire. To date, the justices' votes in the *Gratz* and *Grutter* cases are unavailable, but the importance of the issue plus a split between the Sixth Circuit Court upholding affirmative action and an earlier Fifth Circuit decision striking it down at the University of Texas made a grant of *certiorari* highly likely.[51] On December 2, 2002, the Court granted review to both cases.

Oral Arguments

Following a grant of cert, the justices receive written briefs from the litigants explaining why their position should win. Other parties may file *amicus curiae* briefs urging the Court to affirm or reverse the lower court decision. Again, the most influential of these briefs come from the solicitor general's office, which represents the current presidential administration at the Supreme Court. Thus, while the Clinton administration sided with the university at the district court level in the *Gratz* and *Grutter* cases, the George W. Bush administration switched sides and asked the Supreme Court to strike down the law school and undergraduate admissions programs. On the other hand, seventy-four organizations filed *amicus* briefs supporting the university, the most ever in a Supreme Court case. One of these came from a group of high-ranking military officers, who wrote about the need for a diversified officer corps and thus the need for diversified service academies. Critically, they argued that without affirmative action, the service academies would be overwhelmingly white.

Parties normally receive thirty minutes each for oral argument, although the justices frequently interrupt with questions. The quality of oral argument varies enormously, and one justice, Harry Blackmun, actually graded the quality of such arguments in his notes.

Should the federal government be allowed to try to influence a court decision?

A tough grader, he gave Ruth Bader Ginsburg, a world-class litigator who revolutionized sex-discrimination law and later joined Blackmun on the Supreme Court, grades between C and B on her oral arguments.[52] The quality of these arguments, not surprisingly, can influence which party wins.[53]

The Supreme Court heard oral arguments in the *Gratz* and *Grutter* cases on April 1, 2003, hearing the *Grutter* case first. Grutter's attorney, Kirk Kolbo from the Center for Individual Rights, spoke first, arguing that the Constitution prohibits distinctions based on race. Justice O'Connor immediately interrupted, asking the attorney about Court precedents holding that race could be used if the government had a compelling interest in doing so. Kolbo responded that the school could legally achieve a diverse student body without using racial preferences by using factors that are not explicitly racial, such as economic status. U.S. Solicitor General Theodore Olson spoke next, opposing Michigan's use of affirmative action but, under President Bush's directive, not calling for a complete ban on the use of race. Olson chose not to answer questions about the military's use of affirmative action, stating that he had not examined military policies. Michigan's attorney, Maureen Mahoney, a former law clerk for Chief Justice Rehnquist, tried to distinguish between the university's attempt to obtain a diverse student body and the type of quota system declared unconstitutional in the *Bakke* case. "She's very good," Justice Ginsburg whispered to Justice David Souter after the arguments ended. "She's fabulous," replied Souter.[54] Her ability, of course, would help Michigan's chances.

Kolbo represented Gratz as well as Grutter, arguing in Gratz's case that the use of race as a factor must be extraordinary and rare, and that diversity does not meet that extraordinary standard. Michigan's attorney in the undergraduate case defended the need for a "critical mass" of minority students, so that those students would not feel like tokens. (Oral arguments in the *Gratz* and *Grutter* cases, as well as in hundreds of other cases, are available at www.oyez.org.)

The Decision

Within a few days of oral argument, the justices meet in conference to vote on the merits of the case, that is, to decide which side wins, and to assign a justice to write the Opinion of the Court in the case. If the chief justice is in the majority, he determines who will write the opinion. If the chief justice is not in the majority, the assignment is made by the senior justice who is in the majority.

The opinion is the heart of the Court's legal and policy-making power. It explains the Court's justification for its decision and sets guidelines for other courts to follow in subsequent cases. To have this authority, it must become a majority opinion by gaining the assent of a majority of the justices.

concurring opinion: *Opinion by a judge that agrees with the Court majority's result (that is, which party wins) but sets out a separate rationale.*

dissenting opinion: *Opinion written by a judge who disagrees with the result reached by the majority as to who should win a case.*

Assigning the writing of the Opinion of the Court to a justice does not mean that a majority opinion will result. If a justice writes an opinion siding with one side, and other justices agree with the result (that is, agree on who wins) but not with the reasoning, they can concur in the judgment. That means that they are not joining the Opinion of the Court. Such justices will typically write a **concurring opinion** that explains their reasoning or join the concurring opinion of another justice. Justices who disagree with the result reached by the majority can write a **dissenting opinion** explaining why they believe the Court's decision was in error. If, due to a combination of concurring and dissenting

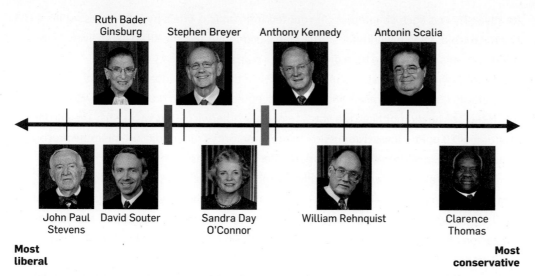

Ruth Bader Ginsburg   Stephen Breyer   Anthony Kennedy   Antonin Scalia

John Paul Stevens   David Souter   Sandra Day O'Connor   William Rehnquist   Clarence Thomas

Most liberal   **Most conservative**

FIGURE 15.6 Ideology and Votes of Supreme Court Justices in the *Gratz* and *Grutter* Cases. The justices are aligned from most liberal to most conservative. The six justices to the right of the blue line voted with Gratz to strike the undergraduate affirmative action program at the University of Michigan. The five justices to the left of the brown line voted with the University of Michigan in upholding the law school's affirmative action program. *Source for justices' ideology:* Martin-Quinn Scores, http://mqscores.wustl.edu/. *Photos:* Ginsburg, Breyer, Kennedy, Scalia, Stevens, and Thomas by Steve Petteway, Collection of the Supreme Court of the United States; Souter by Joseph Bailey, National Geographic Society, Courtesy of the Collection of the Supreme Court of the United States; O'Connor by Dane Pennland, Smithsonian Institution, Collection of the Supreme Court of the United States; Rehnquist by Dane Pennland, Smithsonian Institution, Collection of the Supreme Court of the United States.

justices, fewer than five justices join the opinion of the court, that opinion becomes a **plurality judgment** rather than a majority opinion. Plurality judgments have less value as precedents than majority opinions.

The conference on the affirmative action cases revealed a split in the justices' preferences: 5–4 in favor of the law school program, but 6–3 against the undergraduate program. As Figure 15.6 shows, four conservative justices thought that both the undergraduate and the law school affirmative programs violated the Fourteenth Amendment and were unconstitutional, whereas the three most liberal justices thought that both programs were acceptable because of the university's compelling interest in creating a diverse student body and the narrow tailoring of the affirmative action programs to meet that interest. Justices Sandra Day O'Connor and Stephen Breyer were the swing justices. They agreed that diversity constituted a compelling interest but did not believe that the undergraduate program, which automatically gave a set number of points to minority applicants, was narrowly tailored to meet that interest. They thus voted with the more conservative justices to strike the undergraduate program. But O'Connor and Breyer voted with the liberals to uphold the law school program, which overall gave strong preferences to underrepresented minorities but was more careful in considering the importance of race in each individual's application.

Because Chief Justice Rehnquist dissented in the law school case, Justice Stevens, the senior justice in the majority, assigned the opinion. Given Justice O'Connor's role as the swing justice in the case, he assigned the opinion to her. O'Connor declared that while racial categorizations could be used only if the state had a compelling interest in doing so, the need

plurality judgment: *Opinion of the Court that results when a majority of the justices cannot agree on the rationale for a decision.*

Should Gratz have won her case? Should Grutter?

for diversity was such an interest. She quoted from *amicus* briefs by businesses, which cited the need for a diverse workforce in the global economy, and she cited extensively from the military brief's stated need for a diverse officer corps.

Chief Justice Rehnquist was in the majority in the undergraduate case, and he assigned the majority opinion to himself. His opinion accepted the notion that diversity was a compelling interest—he did not have the votes to declare otherwise—but wrote that the automatic granting of 20 points toward admission to every minority student did not meet the precedent required in *Bakke* of considering each particular applicant as an individual.

Though Gratz won her case, she had by this point graduated from a different Michigan campus, the University of Michigan—Dearborn. The University of Michigan changed its admissions procedures to be more like the law school's: Race would still be used as an admissions factor, but there would be no automatic point total added just because of an applicant's race.

Impact

The fact that the Supreme Court issues a decision does not necessarily mean that government officials charged with implementing it will comply. The courts have no power of enforcement. The Court's school desegregation decision in *Brown*, for example, met with massive resistance from supporters of segregation: Elected officials urged disobedience, local boards of education ignored the decision, and lower courts complied with the decision half-heartedly at best. All the while, citizens rallied in the streets in opposition (see Supreme Court Cases: *Cooper v. Aaron*; see also Chapter 13, The Presidency). In part because of these reactions, very few schools desegregated in the ten years following *Brown*.[55] And the fact that a decision might be complied with does not necessarily mean that it will have the impact that the Court intended. The advances in school desegregation over time have not meant that educational equality has been achieved in the United States.

Additionally, many types of court decisions can be overturned by Congress, state legislatures, or other legislative mechanisms such as state-level referenda. When a court's decision is based on the meaning of a statute (for example, is carbon dioxide considered a pollutant under the Clean Air Act?), Congress can simply overturn the court's decision if it disagrees with the Court's conclusion.

In the constitutional realm, if the Court declares that a practice is not unconstitutional, as in the affirmative action case, that practice can still be prohibited through the legislature or, if the state allows, through a referendum. So when the Supreme Court rules that affirmative action is not prohibited by the Constitution, that does not mean that the university is required to implement an affirmative action program or that the state is required to allow such a program. Following the Supreme Court decision in her case, Jennifer Gratz used the gateway provided by Michigan's **initiative** procedure, organizing a Michigan statewide proposal that banned the use of race, gender, or ethnicity for admissions or hiring in higher education. The initiative passed decisively in November 2006 by a 58 percent to 42 percent margin. Thus, despite the Supreme Court's decision in the affirmative action cases, affirmative action in admissions is illegal at all public colleges in Michigan, including the University of Michigan.

On the other hand, when the Supreme Court declares that the Constitution prohibits an activity, legislatures find that prohibition difficult to overturn. For example, when the

How are court decisions enforced? Would government work better if the courts had the power of enforcement?

initiative: *Process by which citizens place proposed laws on the ballot for public approval.*

Did the Michigan ballot initiative undermine justice or help ensure it?

supremecourtcases

Cooper v. Aaron (1958)

QUESTION: Does the threat of violence negate a school district's obligation to desegregate?

ORAL ARGUMENT: September 11, 1958 (listen at www.oyez.org/cases)

DECISION: September 12, 1958 (read at www.findlaw.com/casecode/supreme.html)

OUTCOME: No, desegregation is required, even when mobs threaten violence (9–0).

Perhaps the most violent reaction to the Supreme Court's school desegregation decision came in Little Rock, Arkansas, in 1957. Despite substantial opposition in the South to the 1954 *Brown* desegregation decision, the Little Rock school board approved a plan in May 1955 that would begin to integrate its schools as of September 1957. In response, the state legislature declared that no student could be required to attend an integrated school. Nevertheless, the NAACP, an interest group that sponsored litigation promoting integration, selected nine African American students, based on their grades, attendance, and fortitude, to attempt to integrate Central High School.

As September 1957 approached, Governor Orval Faubus called out the Arkansas National Guard to physically prevent the students from entering the school.* For three weeks the Guard kept the school off limits to the nine students. This action encouraged the segregationists, who took to the streets around the school to protest integration.

On September 20, 1957, a federal district court issued an order prohibiting the Arkansas Guard from interfering with desegregation efforts. In response, Faubus withdrew the Guard, leaving the streets under the control of the dangerous and angry mobs that had gathered.

On September 23 the African American students entered school under police protection, but the police were unable to control the mob and quickly removed the students. Two days later President Dwight D. Eisenhower sent the 101st Airborne Division to Little Rock to disperse the mobs and protect the students. Eight of the nine black students remained at the school for the remainder of the school year.

Given the unrest, the Little Rock school board sought to postpone its desegregation plan. In June 1958 the district court upheld its request. In August the court of appeals reversed the district court. The Supreme Court granted the board's request for a writ of *certiorari* and heard the case in a special session.

In an unusual opinion signed the day after oral argument by all nine justices, the Supreme Court refused to allow the board to back out of its desegregation plan due to the threat of violence. The Court declared that the Constitution of the United States and the Supreme Court's interpretation of the Constitution are the supreme law of the land. In response, Governor Faubus closed the school for the year, but it reopened as an integrated school in 1959. Beyond the battle over desegregation, this expansion of the Court's authority—adding the Court's interpretation of the Constitution to those items that are the "supreme law of the land"—has drawn criticism of judicial overreaching from people on the right and the left.

- **Why is the judiciary the branch of government best able to make decisions that a majority of citizens strongly oppose?**
- **Can the Supreme Court be effective in guaranteeing equality when the majority of citizens actively oppose equality?**

*Accounts of the battle from the school newspaper, including student editorials supporting integration, are at www.centralhigh57.org/the_tiger.htm.

TABLE 15.1 Constitutional Amendments Overturning Supreme Court Decisions

Supreme Court Decision	Amendment
Chisolm v. Georgia (1793) allowed citizens to sue other states in federal court.	Eleventh Amendment (1795) establishes sovereign immunity for states.
Dred Scott v. Sandford (1857) denied citizenship to African Americans.	Fourteenth Amendment (1868) makes all people born in the United States citizens of the United States.
Minor v. Happersett (1874) denied voting rights to women.	Nineteenth Amendment (1920) guarantees women the right to vote.
Pollock v. Farmers' Loan and Trust (1895) limited Congress's authority to tax income.	Sixteenth Amendment (1913) grants Congress the authority to tax income from whatever source derived.
Oregon v. Mitchell (1970) prompted Congress to set the voting age at 18 for all elections. The case struck the law as applied to state elections.	Twenty-Sixth Amendment (1971) sets the voting age at 18 for all elections.

Court declared that Congress did not have the authority to set the voting age at 18 for state elections, the only recourse was for Congress and the states to pass a constitutional amendment overturning that decision. Only five of the Supreme Court's constitutional decisions have ever been overturned via amendment (see Table 15.1). Most Supreme Court decisions and virtually all of its constitutional decisions are not overturned by Congress or by amendment.

Moreover, most Supreme Court decisions are complied with, even when the consequences for the losing litigants are serious. Following the Supreme Court's Watergate decision, President Richard M. Nixon turned over the Watergate tapes, even though doing so meant the end of his presidency.[56] Following the Supreme Court's decision in reapportionment cases, state legislatures reapportioned their states, even though it meant that many of the legislators would be reapportioned out of their seats.[57] Similarly, states stopped prosecuting doctors for providing abortions following *Roe v. Wade*.[58]

The Judiciary and Public Policy: Affirmative Action and Judicial Activism and Restraint

An overly simple view of American politics holds that the legislative branch makes the law, the judicial branch interprets the law, and the executive branch enforces the law. But the president can issue executive orders, and executive branch agencies can issue regulations that often are indistinguishable from legislation. The legislative branch holds hearings on executive branch agencies that often focus on how those agencies enforce the law. The job of the courts is to interpret the law, but in doing so they often appear to go beyond mere interpretation and get actively involved in policy making. Supporters and critics of the *Roe* abortion decision often agree that the decision, which established different degrees of abortion rights depending on the trimester of the pregnancy (see Chapter 4), reads more like the making of policy than the interpretation of law.

Consider affirmative action. We have noted throughout this book that representative democracy requires the government to treat people equally. Does the government do so when, to make up for past discrimination and current inequalities that exist in society, it provides preferences to some groups over others? The Supreme Court's answer was a tentative yes. But how did the Court come to that decision? We now consider two broad approaches to understanding judicial policy making: a legal approach, which suggests that courts rely on legally relevant factors, and an extralegal approach, which suggests that courts rely on legally irrelevant factors. We look at affirmative action policy in particular and then examine the consequences for a democracy of the reliance on extralegal factors by an unelected judiciary.

The Legal Approach

According to the legal approach, justices base their decisions on legally relevant materials, such as prior court precedents, the **plain meaning** of the text of the law under consideration, and the **intent of the Framers** of the law.

As we explained earlier in the chapter, precedent means a reliance on the prior decisions of the Court. In the *Grutter* case the Court accepted the arguments from the *Bakke* case that the government had a compelling interest in achieving a diverse student body but concluded that systems that establish racial quotas go too far. Reliance on precedent creates stability in law: Decisions change gradually rather than abruptly. Reliance on precedent also generates a degree of equality and fairness. If you slip on your neighbor's walkway, it is not necessarily clear whether your neighbor is at fault for a slippery surface or you are at fault for not being careful. It is hard to say in advance that ruling one way is just and ruling the other way is unjust. But if the judge rules that the owner is not liable and the next week under similar conditions the neighbor slips on your walkway, fairness demands that the judge should again rule that the owner is not liable. That is what ruling based on precedent accomplishes. Lower courts are bound by Supreme Court precedents, but the Supreme Court does not necessarily consider itself strictly bound to its own precedents. Otherwise there would be no growth in the law, and, for example, the United States might still have the separate-but-equal school systems that were declared unconstitutional in *Brown v. Board of Education*.

Beyond precedent, legal-based approaches consider the plain meaning of the law being interpreted. Justice Antonin Scalia is the Court's foremost proponent of this approach. If there is no right to privacy written in the Constitution, he claims, then the Supreme Court should not be creating privacy rights. According to Scalia, if such rights are to be protected, they should be granted by democratically elected legislatures, not by life-appointed judges. But while a textual approach makes some issues perfectly clear, for example that a 34-year-old cannot be president, it does not necessarily answer whether affirmative action plans designed to increase diversity or fair representation in an unequal society violate equal protection of the law.

Similarly, Justice Clarence Thomas often argues for decision making based on the intent of the Framers. This approach places the meaning of the Framers ahead of the literal meaning

In the *Gratz* and *Grutter* cases, was government responsive? Did the decisions help ensure equality?

plain meaning: *Interpretation of laws or constitutional provisions based on the literal meaning of what the law says.*

intent of the Framers: *Interpretation of a law or constitutional provision based on what the Framers of the law intended.*

What should judges and justices base their decisions on?

of the words that they wrote. Thus, while dissenting in a case that upheld federal prohibitions on medicinal marijuana under Congress's authority to regulate interstate commerce, Thomas ignored more than seventy years of precedent that had expanded the scope of the commerce clause. He argued that local activities such as the medical use of homegrown marijuana were not what the Framers meant by commerce.[59] This may well be true, but in many circumstances it is difficult to know what the Framers meant or what they would have thought if they could have envisioned modern American society. Does the Fourth Amendment's protection of one's person, houses, papers, and effects against unreasonable searches and seizures include telephone wires, cell phones, and wireless e-mail?

The Extralegal Approach

Legal approaches often fail to provide a good indicator of what the Supreme Court will do. While some precedents, notably the 1978 *Bakke* decision, supported affirmative action, more recent cases prior to *Grutter* had pushed in the opposite direction. The text of the Fourteenth Amendment guarantees equality, but there is no evidence that the Framers of the amendment intended it to prohibit policies that tried to help disadvantaged groups.

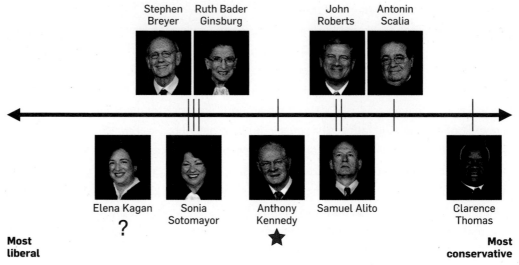

★ = Median (swing) justice
? = Ideology on the Court not yet determined

FIGURE 15.7 Ideology of the Supreme Court Justices, 2010. Although liberalism and conservatism mean different things at different times, liberalism on the Supreme Court is usually associated with support for women and minorities in civil rights cases, support for governmental authority in economic cases, support for defendants and convicts in criminal cases, and support for individuals claiming abridgment of rights in First Amendment and privacy cases. Conservatism is associated with the opposite values. The figure shows the ideology of the Court in June 2010, after the resignation of Justice John Paul Stevens and before the voting record of replacement Elena Kagan was available. Assuming that Kagan votes more liberally than Kennedy, Kennedy will remain the swing justice. In other words, when he votes liberally, the four more liberal colleagues probably will also vote liberally, and when he votes conservatively, the four more conservative colleagues probably will vote conservatively as well.
Source: Judicial liberalism: Lee Epstein, Jeffrey A. Segal, Harold J. Spaeth, and Thomas G. Walker, *The Supreme Court Compendium*, 4th ed. (Washington, D.C.: CQ Press, 2007), Table 6-4. The justices' ideology: Martin-Quinn Scores, http://mqscores.wustl.edu/. *Photos:* Steve Petteway, Collection of the Supreme Court of the United States.

Alternatively, we can consider extralegal approaches to Supreme Court decision making. Extralegal factors go beyond the legal factors that courts are supposed to consider. The most important extralegal considerations include the justices' own preferences and strategic considerations based on the preferences of others.

The Justices' Preferences. Recall from the affirmative action cases that the four most conservative justices voted to strike both the undergraduate and the law school plans, the three most liberal justices voted to uphold both, and two justices in the middle voted to uphold the law school program but to strike the undergraduate program. (For the ideology of the justices currently on the Court, see Figure 15.7.)

This sort of relationship between the justices' ideology and their votes is fairly common. But because Supreme Court scholars cannot obtain information from the justices themselves about their ideology, they use indirect measures. As Figure 15.8 shows, there exists a very strong relationship between the justices' ideology and their votes once on the Court.[60]

What role should ideology play in judicial decisions? What role does it play?

Strategic Considerations. Justices cannot behave solely on the basis of their ideological preferences. Justice Rehnquist, while writing the *Gratz* opinion, may have preferred

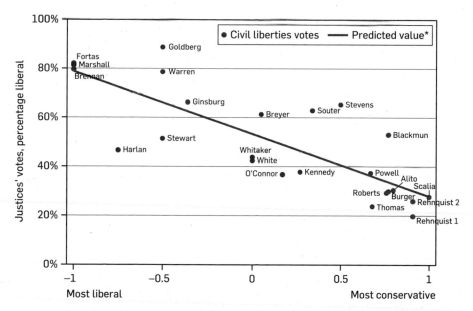

*Predicted value is the percent of time the justice is predicted to vote liberally given his or her ideology.

Note: Rehnquist 1 indicates his term as an associate justice; Rehnquist 2 indicates his term as chief justice.

FIGURE 15.8 Justices' Votes by Their Ideology, 1953–2009. The graph shows that, as justices line up from the left (most liberal) to the right (most conservative), the percentage of the time they vote liberally drops substantially. Generally speaking, the most liberal justices, those farthest to the left on the graph (Fortas, Marshall, and Brennan), vote in the liberal direction (toward the top of the graph), whereas the most conservative justices (Rehnquist and Scalia) vote conservatively most of the time.

Source: Justices' ideology: Data updated and backdated by Jeffrey Segal from Jeffrey Segal and Albert Cover, "Ideological Values and the Votes of Supreme Court Justices," *American Political Science Review* 83 (1989): 557–65. Justices' votes: Lee Epstein, Jeffrey A. Segal, Harold J. Spaeth, and Thomas G. Walker, *The Supreme Court Compendium*, 4th ed. (Washington, D.C.: CQ Press, 2007).

When oral arguments in the *Gratz* and *Grutter* cases were being heard before the Court on April 3, 2010, the National Association for the Advancement of Colored People (NAACP) and other interest groups rallied in support of affirmative action. While Supreme Court justices are not directly responsive to public opinion, the same factors that influence the public (war, crime, the economy) also influence the justices, leading to a general congruence between public opinion and the justices' decisions.

Is affirmative action fair?

Which is more important, equality of opportunity or equality of outcome?

to declare that virtually all affirmative action plans are unconstitutional, but if he had done so he might have lost the support of Justices O'Connor, Breyer, and Kennedy. So he compromised and accepted diversity as a rationale but nevertheless was able to strike down the undergraduate program. Negotiations over the content of the majority opinion are a routine part of Supreme Court decision making.[61]

A justice may need to consider not only the preferences of other justices but also the preferences of other actors in the political environment. The efforts of President Franklin Delano Roosevelt to pack the Court in the face of the Court's rejection of his New Deal programs assuredly played a role in the Court's about-face and subsequent approval of such programs. Similarly, the Court backed down from efforts to limit congressional investigations into Communism in the 1950s when Congress threatened to remove the Court's jurisdiction from such cases.

Affirmative Action

The term *affirmative action* first made its way into federal policy through Executive Order 10925, signed by President John F. Kennedy (1961–63) in 1961. The order required federal contractors to "take affirmative action to ensure that applicants are employed, and that employees are treated during employment, without regard to their race, creed, color, or national origin."[62] In 1964 the Civil Rights Act, while generally prohibiting discrimination on account of race or sex, specifically allowed preferential treatment for Native Americans living on or near reservations. Today federal funding acts for education, defense, and transportation routinely grant contracting preferences for minority- and female-owned business. The Department of Education interprets the nondiscrimination provisions of the Civil Rights Act to encourage voluntary affirmative action plans that help achieve a diverse student population.[63]

As the *Gratz* and *Grutter* cases show, the courts have a major role in this process, balancing equality of opportunity against affirmative action policies aimed at providing greater equality of outcome. Given the play of extralegal factors in such decisions, are judges, in fact, policy makers?[64] When the Supreme Court decides for the nation that affirmative action programs are allowed as long as they provide individualized assessments of students' records, they are making policy. The fact that this is not merely interpretation of the law is supported by the fact that the justices' ideological preferences overwhelmingly explain their votes on the Court.

But we might reach a different conclusion regarding the lower courts. Consider a district court judge faced with a suit by a white student to gain admission to a university that has an affirmative action program similar to the Michigan law school program. The judge applies the precedent from *Grutter* and rejects the student's challenge. Although that judge has made a decision that is crucial to the student, both the scope of the decision (which applies only to that student) and the low level of discretion involved in reaching it (the judge felt bound by the Supreme Court precedent in *Grutter*) make this sort of behavior distinct from policy making.

Activism and Restraint

Because judges are unelected and serve for life, they are not accountable to the people in the same way that presidents and members of Congress are. Nevertheless, they have an extraordinary power— the power of judicial review. Judicial review allows an unelected branch of government to strike the laws and actions of the elected branches of government—Congress and the president. This authority by the judicial branch is questionable in a democracy, where the people are supposed to have the final say. Therefore, along with judicial review comes what law professor Alexander Bickel has labeled the **countermajoritarian difficulty**.[65] We expect the judiciary to enforce limits on governmental power, but when it does so it acts in a countermajoritarian manner, because unelected judges are using this power to strike the actions of democratically elected executives and legislatures.

The Supreme Court first held an act of Congress unconstitutional in 1803, and then did not hold another one unconstitutional until 1857. Since that time, however, the Court has struck down 165 congressional laws, slightly more than one per year, with seven laws struck down in 1935 during the height of the Court's battle with the New Deal (see Figure 15.9).

Is the judicial branch, as Hamilton said, "the least dangerous branch"? Defend your answer.

countermajoritarian difficulty: *Alexander Bickel's phrase for the tension that exists for representative government when unelected judges have the power to strike laws passed by elected representatives.*

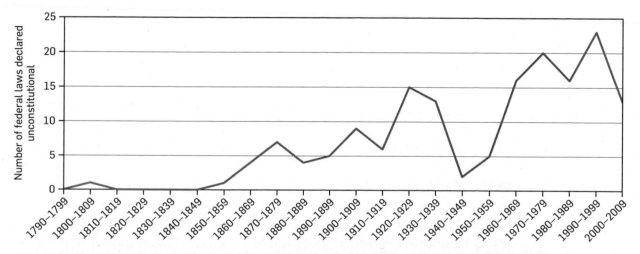

FIGURE 15.9 Number of Federal Laws Declared Unconstitutional, 1790–2009.
Source: Harold W. Stanley and Richard G. Niemi, eds., *Vital Statistics on American Politics*, 3rd ed. (Washington, D.C.: CQ Press, 1992); Lawrence Baum, *The Supreme Court*, 8th ed. (Washington, D.C.: CQ Press, 2004), 170, 173; Harold J. Spaeth, Lee Epstein, Andrew D. Martin, Jeffrey A. Segal, and Thomas W. Walker, United States Supreme Court Database, scdb.wustl.edu.

Since 1986 the Court has struck down nearly three times as many state and municipal laws (97) as federal laws (36).[66]

Given the undemocratic nature of judicial review, politicians frequently decry **judicial activists**, judges who go beyond what the law requires and seek to impose their own policy preferences on society through their decisions. These critics insist that judges should act with **judicial restraint**, that is, judges should respect the decisions of other branches or, through the concept of precedent, the decisions of earlier judges.

Contemporary research suggests that justices respect the decisions of legislatures and earlier judges when those decisions are consistent with the justices' ideology. Thus, for example, liberal justices such as Ginsburg and Breyer overwhelmingly vote to uphold liberal precedents[67] or federal laws favored by liberals.[68] But when conservative precedents or laws favored by conservatives are under consideration, liberal justices are more than willing to strike them. Similarly, conservative justices such as Scalia and Thomas overwhelmingly vote to uphold conservative precedents or the constitutionality of federal laws favored by conservatives. But when precedents are liberal in direction or when liberals favor the laws under review, conservative justices are more than willing to strike them.

Is judicial review a problem for democracy?

The Senate debated the topic of judicial activism during the nomination process for Judge Sonia Sotomayor, President Obama's first Supreme Court appointment, focusing squarely on a statement Sotomayor made in 2005 that the "Court of Appeals is where policy is made."[69] Opponents of judicial activism, holding that policy making is the responsibility of Congress and not the courts, objected that Sotomayor would be an activist justice who would use her position on the Supreme Court to make public policy rather than interpret the law. Senator Jeff Sessions (R-Ala.), the ranking Republican member of the Senate Judiciary Committee, was not convinced that Sotomayor would judge with restraint rather than activism. He opposed her nomination, stating, "In speech after speech, year after year, Judge Sotomayor set forth a fully formed judicial philosophy that conflicts with American philosophy of blind justice to the law."[70]

How do elections affect judicial decisions? Should they?

The vast majority of justices are restrained toward laws and precedents that they agree with ideologically, but are quite willing to overturn laws and precedents that they are distant from ideologically. Justice Kagan, confirmed with unanimous support by Democrats and a small number of Republicans, is unlikely to differ from this trend. Elections have consequences, and one of the consequences of presidential elections is that the president gets to choose which judges will make judicial policy in the United States.

The Judiciary and Democracy

The judicial system of the United States promotes the equal right of participation by allowing a single individual who has been harmed by a law to challenge its constitutionality. People who have financial resources or who can find support from organized interests may fare better than those who have to act on their own. The action may not be successful. Nevertheless, the judiciary provides a separate gateway to the political system, one that is different in kind from the gateway to the legislative or executive branch. By filing a suit through the judiciary, a single individual—such as Oliver Brown (in the *Brown v. Board* school desegregation case) or Jane Roe (in the *Roe v. Wade* abortion decision)—can have an enormous influence on the American political system.

Representative democracy requires government to be accountable and responsive to the public. Yet the judicial branch is not accountable in any meaningful way: Even if the public is dissatisfied with judges' decisions, judges cannot be removed from office, given the historical practice following Justice Chase's impeachment. Yet this does not mean that the Court is not responsive to the public or to the public's representatives. Responsiveness can happen through four different gateways.

The first gateway is through the electoral process.[71] During the 1960s the Warren Court made a series of decisions on contentious issues such as criminal procedure and religious freedom that were significantly more liberal than many Americans might have preferred. Richard M. Nixon campaigned for president in 1968 with promises to appoint justices who were significantly more pro-police and significantly less pro-defendant. Nixon won the election and, in the course of his first term, appointed four justices, all of whom were considerably more conservative on criminal procedure than the rest of the Court. The result was a conservative shift in Supreme Court decisions in criminal cases that mirrored public preferences.

Second, in cases where the Court is unresponsive to congressional preferences, Congress can threaten the Court's institutional authority. During the Civil War Congress took away the Court's appellate jurisdiction over *habeas corpus* appeals. In the 1930s Franklin Roosevelt threatened to dilute the Court by adding six new members. In both cases, the Court backed down and responded favorably to congressional (and thus, presumably, public) preferences.

The third gateway is through current events, which can move public opinion and judges' behavior in the same direction. Immediately after the attacks of September 11, 2001, Americans were increasingly willing to allow the government to examine personal mail, Internet activity, and the like (see Chapter 6, Public Opinion), and judges moved in the same direction. During the Vietnam War, as events in Southeast Asia led American citizens to oppose the war in greater numbers, those same events led federal judges to impose shorter sentences on draft dodgers.[72] As society became more progressive on women's rights and other issues, judges, who themselves are members of society, became more progressive on those issues, too.

Fourth, judges might believe that they have an obligation to rule consistently with public opinion, even if they are not subject to electoral sanctions. It is probably no accident that the Supreme Court's split decision in the Michigan affirmative action cases reflected America's ambivalence about whether equality meant treating everybody exactly the same or whether, to promote equality of outcomes, underrepresented groups should be given advantages in admissions. Justice O'Connor, who split the difference over what can be done in the name of equal protection in the *Gratz* and *Grutter* cases, has spoken often about the need of the Supreme Court not to vary too far from public preferences.

That argument cuts both ways. As Justice Robert Jackson declared in a case striking down mandatory flag salutes, "The very purpose of a Bill of Rights was to withdraw certain subjects from the vicissitudes of political controversy, to place them beyond the reach of majorities and officials and to establish them as legal principles to be applied by the courts. One's right to life, liberty, and property, to free speech, a free press, freedom of worship and assembly, and other fundamental rights may not be submitted to vote; they depend on the outcome of no elections."[73] If justices are responsive, it is not because the Constitution's framework encourages it; it is because they choose to be.

FOCUS QUESTIONS

- Why is the apparently simple requirement of providing "equal protection of the laws" more difficult than it seems?

- In what ways do the federal courts lack traditional means of accountability?

- How are courts, nevertheless, responsive?

- Do citizens have equal access to the Justice system? Does the justice system treat them equally?

- Is the judiciary a gate or a gateway to democracy?

Top Ten to Take Away

1. The American legal system is based on the English system, following an adversary process, guaranteeing a right to trial by jury, and depending on common law in the absence of statuary authority. (pp. 522–23)

2. The Constitution established the Supreme Court. Congress has created federal district courts and courts of appeal. The Supreme Court has both original jurisdiction and appellate jurisdiction. (pp. 523–24)

3. Through the power of judicial review established in *Marbury v. Madison,* the Supreme Court has the authority to declare laws and executive actions unconstitutional and thus void. In this decision and others, the Marshall court set the United States on the path to a strong and unified nation. (pp. 524–26)

4. Through the Court's history, its interpretations have expanded, then contracted, and once again expanded national powers, especially with regard to economic regulation. After a long and slow start the Court has also moved, fairly consistently, toward greater protections of equality. (pp. 526–31)

5. The president appoints federal judges with the advice and consent of the Senate. The higher the court, the more likely the Senate is to scrutinize nominees and refuse consent on the basis of nominees' ideology and/or qualifications. (pp. 531–37)

6. The Supreme Court, which once contained only white, male Protestants, has increasingly diversified with respect to religion, race, and gender. This more-equal access to the Supreme Court may also make the Court more responsive to an increasingly diverse nation. (pp. 536–37)

7. District courts conduct civil and criminal trials, while courts of appeal hear appeals from district courts. Cases from the courts of appeal can be appealed to the Supreme Court. (pp. 537–42)

8. Supreme Court decisions are made by a majority, though the justices sometimes write concurring opinions that agree with the majority but give a different rationale. The minority who disagree may write dissents. (pp. 542–48)

9. Judicial policy making can be explained by both legal and extralegal approaches, with legal approaches having more sway at lower levels and extralegal approaches at higher levels, where judicial activism can be problematic for a democracy. (pp. 548–54)

10. Although the Supreme Court is not directly accountable to the public, it is to some degree responsive to public opinion. (pp. 554–55)

A full narrative summary of the chapter is on the book's website.

Ten to Test Yourself

1. Why does common law require a system of precedent?
2. What is the federal courts' jurisdiction?
3. What is judicial review?
4. Describe the broad trends and eras in Supreme Court rulings over the nation's history.
5. Describe the current federal judicial system.
6. Why was the Supreme Court's ruling in *Cohens v. Virginia* crucial to national unity?
7. What are the most important determinants of a senator's vote for or against a Supreme Court nominee?
8. In what way is judicial review problematic for a representative government?
9. How has the Supreme Court acted in response to attacks on it by Congress and the president?
10. What guidance has the Court provided on affirmative action?

More review questions and answers and chapter quizzes are on the book's website.

Timeline to Keep Things in Order

1789	1803	1819	1821	1868
Judiciary Act establishes district courts and courts of appeal.	*Marbury v. Madison* establishes the power of judicial review.	*McCulloch v. Maryland* expands federal power under the necessary and proper clause.	*Cohens v. Virginia* establishes that the Supreme Court has final say over what federal law means.	The Fourteenth Amendment guarantees equal protection of the laws.

Terms to Know and Use

adversary process (p. 522)
affirmative action (p. 525)
amicus curiae briefs (p. 539)
appeal (p. 523)
appellate jurisdiction (p. 524)
civil suit (p. 523)
class action (p. 538)
commerce clause (p. 526)
common law (p. 523)
concurring opinion (p. 544)
constitutional interpretation (pp. 524, 525)
countermajoritarian difficulty (pp. 553)
Court-packing plan (p. 530)
courts of appeals (p. 523)
criminal case (p. 523)

deposition (p. 539)
discovery (p. 539)
dissenting opinion (p. 544)
district courts (p. 523)
equality of opportunity (p. 542)
equality of outcome (p. 542)
equal protection of the laws (pp. 524, 525)
equity (p. 524)
grand jury (p. 540)
hold (p. 533)
incorporation doctrine (p. 530)
initiative (p. 546)
intent of the Framers (p. 549)
judicial activists (pp. 554)
judicial independence (p. 524)
judicial restraint (p. 554)

judicial review (pp. 524, 525)
Judiciary Act (p. 523)
jurisdiction (p. 524)
majority opinion (p. 542)
Marbury v. Madison (p. 525)
Marshall Court (p. 526)
necessary and proper clause (p. 526)
original jurisdiction (p. 524)
plain meaning (p. 549)
plea bargain (p. 540)
plurality judgment (p. 545)
precedent (p. 523)
reapportionment (p. 530)
right to contract (p. 529)
right to privacy (p. 530)
rule of four (p. 542)

Senate Judiciary Committee (p. 532)
senatorial courtesy (p. 532)
separate-but-equal doctrine (p. 528)
solicitor general (p. 539)
standing (p. 523)
statutory interpretation (pp. 524, 525)
supremacy clause (p. 528)
trial by jury (p. 522)
unanimous consent agreement (p. 533)
Warren Court (p. 530)
writ of *certiorari* (p. 537)
writ of *habeas corpus* (p. 537)

Use the vocabulary flash cards on the book's website.

Learning That Works

WHAT YOU NEED . . .

TO KNOW

How the court system works

What standing is

The responsibilities of the judicial branch

The limits on the judicial branch

How judges and justices are appointed

How judges and justices make decisions

The arguments for and against affirmative action

TO DO

Assess whether courts are gateways to citizen influence and to justice

Recognize when a lawsuit may be a remedy for an injustice

Determine whether the judicial branch is responsive to the people

Evaluate whether the judiciary is dangerous to democracy

Consider the merits of diversity in the courts

Conclude whether the courts ensure equality

Decide whether you think equality of opportunity or equality of outcome is more important

Franklin Delano Roosevelt threatens to expand the Court, and the Court begins to approve his New Deal programs.

1937

The Warren Court begins to reshape judicial decisions in a liberal direction.

1954

Thurgood Marshall is the first African American appointed to the Supreme Court.

1967

Sandra Day O'Connor is the first woman appointed to the Supreme Court.

1981

Sonia Sotomayor is the first Hispanic appointed to the Supreme Court.

2009

16

THE UNITED STATES AS A GLOBAL PARTNER

▲ University of North Carolina—
Chapel Hill

> *The essence of democracy is voluntary participation, civic engagement, and taking a stand for issues that you believe in.*

In 2007 Emma Lawrence, Elliott Miller, and Lauren Slive, three students at the University of North Carolina—Chapel Hill, went on a community service trip to Ghana, where they saw a health care system in need of better access to basic health knowledge, higher quality of care, and vital medical supplies. When they returned to campus, they determined to do something to help and, through Campus Y, UNC's center for social justice, founded Project HEAL. This student-run organization aims to engage undergraduates in international service projects in Ghana and connect them with local health officials there to build community-based initiatives. According to Slive, "As college students and American citizens, we recognized the medical, educational and financial resources that we had, and we worked to use these resources to empower Ghanaian health professionals to provide better care."

Project HEAL is ongoing and continues to offer UNC students opportunities for service today, though its founders have graduated. Before they graduated, however, Lawrence and Slive knew they wanted to take their commitment to the next level, so they developed a business plan for MedPLUS Connect. The "Connect" part of the name points to their gateway for global involvement. Lawrence and Slive were public policy majors; Miller was a biology major. They joined with Emily Nix, a mathematics and economics major, and Philip Gennett, an economics major. Pooling their classroom knowledge and campus leadership skills, they designed an organization modeled after a nonprofit in Cleveland called MedWish International that sends surplus medical supplies from the United States to developing countries throughout the world. The students wanted to replicate the program but to direct medical supplies specifically to Ghana and to give the hospital medical staff there more input into the process. They sought ideas from workers in

Lauren Slive ▶

CourseMate

Visit http://www.cengagebrain .com/shop/ISBN/0618906959 for interactive tools including:

- Quizzes
- Flashcards
- Videos
- Animated PowerPoint slides, Podcast summaries, and more

courtesy Lauren Slive

health-related fields and cooperated with community organizations to consolidate their efforts. The students entered their business plan in the Carolina Challenge Entrepreneurial Competition and in 2009 won two awards, for a total of $16,000, to implement their program. "We are very passionate about making this happen," said Slive at the time. "We eventually hope to be able to help any hospital in a developing country with a significant budget."

Two months later, MedPLUS Connect was a reality, delivering more than twenty-two thousand pounds of surplus medical supplies—sutures, gloves, even hospital beds—to the Lawra District Hospital in Ghana. For the doctors and nurses in this rural hospital, the supplies meant that other funding could go to improving facilities and expanding the children's ward.

Today, as executive director of MedPLUS Connect, Emily Nix continues to work with underserved health care systems in developing countries. For her, what began as a student activity has become a career. Lauren Slive is on the MedPLUS board, and, as an Emory University law student focusing on health law, she is preparing herself for a related career.[1] In the interconnected world of the twenty-first century, these UNC students exemplify how to establish partnerships with people on their campus, in their country, and on continents far away. The Millennial generation has opportunities to learn of and serve worldwide humanitarian needs that would not have been possible in the pre-Internet era. Their work is evidence of the gateways that exist for U.S. citizens to make global connections and the opportunities for the nation to play a new world role.

In this chapter we examine the nature of the United States as a global partner. As a world leader in pursuit of its national interest, the United States also has the opportunity to represent democracy and to encourage democratic institutions, responsive government, and citizen equality through foreign policy, trade policy, and humanitarian programs. U.S. participation in international organizations provides an opportunity for citizens to connect to people in other countries. Improvements in communications and technology bring information and images of foreign nations straight to the cell phones of average citizens, and that raises awareness of the ways in which they can provide assistance even to people living thousands of miles away. At the same time, the United States as a sovereign nation must structure its foreign involvement to protect its strategic interests, and agreements with other nations can often entangle the United States in a web of commitments that do not always serve those interests well. The checks and balances written into an eighteenth-century idea of how democratic government should work can be gates to efficiency and the swift response necessary in a world in which information travels in seconds. This chapter provides an overview of how and why the United States participates in global life, and at the same time poses questions about the

FOCUS QUESTIONS

• What are the opportunities and constraints facing the United States as it seeks to lead the world on political, economic, military, and humanitarian dimensions in the twenty-first century?

• What role should the United States take in preserving or promoting democracy around the world? In promoting worldwide government responsiveness and citizen equality? Does the United States hold itself to equal or higher democratic standards as compared with the rest of the world?

• What are the benefits and costs for the United States in international collective action?

• What should be the aims of U.S. foreign and trade policy in the twenty-first century?

• Does the United States, by its example, serve as a gateway to democracy for citizens of other nations?

appropriate range of U.S. influence. In some ways, we are casting an even broader net when it comes to understanding gateways and gates. The combination of the U.S. position in the world and the many technological changes suggests that we should break beyond the normal boundaries of American politics and consider these new realities.

Background to the U.S. Global Position

The international arena in which the United States is positioned today is nothing like the world in which the Framers wrote the Constitution. Travel to Europe is now a matter of hours instead of months; communication with all parts of the world is instantaneous. Conflict, disease, and poverty are not just localized problems but are global in scope. In this section, we examine how the United States came to its position as world leader and discuss the constitutional gates and international conditions that constrain its actions.

Traditional Foreign Policy

When the Framers wrote the Constitution, the United States, as a democracy, stood virtually alone in a world ruled by monarchs. Though independent and isolated by geography, the new nation was still vulnerable, and in its first years it was caught up in European rivalries. In 1796, when he was leaving the presidency, George Washington (1789–97) warned against foreign entanglements: "The great rule of conduct for us in regard to foreign nations," he wrote in his farewell address, "is in extending our commercial relations, to have with them as little political connection as possible."[2] The two themes of increasing trade and avoiding Europe's conflicts guided American foreign policy for more than a century. Today maximizing trade with other nations is still a guiding principle of U.S. foreign and economic policy, but the **isolationist** foreign policy Washington set in motion was reversed in the twentieth century. In this chapter, we discuss foreign policy first, and then explain how trade policy has evolved over time.

In 1914, when World War I began in Europe, President Woodrow Wilson (1913–21) proclaimed neutrality, but German attacks on U.S. commercial shipping in international waters convinced him to change course. In asking for a declaration of war from Congress on April 2, 1917, Wilson argued, "The world must be made safe for democracy. Its peace must be planted upon the tested foundations of political liberty."[3] Wilson had a vision for peace that inspired Americans and Europeans alike, and he took a leading role in writing the treaty that ended the war. One provision of the treaty created an international organization that would help preserve the political independence of its members against aggressor nations. But the Senate voted to reject the treaty twice, in 1919 and in 1920, and, with it, Wilson's vision of a role for America in the world. Politicians and voters alike feared that membership in the **League of Nations** would compromise the nation's **sovereignty**.

World War I overturned old empires and established new nations. Despite President Wilson's efforts to engage the United States in international democracy building, the United States once again turned inward and adopted a policy of isolationism. In Russia a **Communist** revolution installed a political and economic system that used government management

How has the U.S. government adapted to the many changes in international affairs from George Washington's time to today?

isolationism: *Foreign policy approach that avoids international alliances and involvements in foreign wars.*

League of Nations: *International organization formed after World War I to promote peace and mediate disputes between nations; the United States never joined (1919–46).*

sovereignty: *Essential condition of a nation-state, with independent and complete control over domestic and foreign policy.*

Communism: *Economic and political system in which key industries and economic sectors are owned and run by the government and political life is structured around a single political party.*

© Bettmann/CORBIS

of the economy to prevent large concentrations of private wealth. A long-term goal of this system was economic security and equality for all citizens. The Communist Party was the only political party in the new Soviet Union, stifling virtually all dissent. In Germany the new democracy struggled until the Great Depression so weakened its legitimacy that a takeover by Adolf Hitler and the Nazi Party could not be prevented. Under Hitler's dictatorship, Germany became an aggressor once again, and in 1939 its invasion of Poland triggered the Second World War. In Asia Japan had launched a similar course of action, and its air assault on Pearl Harbor on December 7, 1941, led President Franklin Delano Roosevelt (1933–45) to ask Congress for a declaration of war against Japan the next day (and against Germany and Italy on December 11, 1941).

When World War II ended in 1945, America was the leading world power and could no longer sustain its isolationist policies. New weapons technology, especially airpower, expanded the reach and level of destruction that one nation could impose on another. Like Wilson, Roosevelt envisioned a peace in which an international organization, stronger than the League of Nations, could prevent aggression and meet humanitarian needs. The **United Nations** (UN) was founded in April 1945, and Congress ratified U.S. membership in December. Its headquarters was built along the East River in New York City, and it became a gateway for nations to interact with each other and try to resolve disputes in a neutral environment. The supporters of the United Nations also believed it could act as an effective gate to block violence among nations. Although he did not live to see it, more than sixty-five years later, Roosevelt's vision has become a reality.

The Legacy of the Cold War

Hopes for a peaceful world were shortly shattered, however, as a rivalry between the United States and the Soviet Union became a **Cold War** that seemed to divide the world between "free" and Communist nations. As new nations emerged from the aftermath of the war, they were in essence asked to choose democracy or Communism. In 1947 President Harry S. Truman (1945–53) described the stark difference between the two:

> *At the present moment in world history nearly every nation must choose between alternative ways of life. The choice is too often not a free one. One way of life is based upon the will of the majority, and is distinguished by free institutions, representative government,*

When he attended the Versailles Peace Conference following World War I, Woodrow Wilson (left) became the first president to travel to Europe in an official capacity. For America's role in the Allies' victory and for his role in promoting peace, Wilson was cheered by the British and French. But at home his plan for an international organization to preserve the peace was rejected by the U.S. Senate.

United Nations: *International organization formed after World War II to mediate conflicts, protect human rights, prevent worldwide hunger, and assist developing nations; the United States is a leader.*

Cold War: *Economic competition and political conflict between Communist and democratic nations from 1945 to 1991.*

Compare and contrast American attitudes toward the League of Nations and the United Nations.

Following World War II, the United States helped found the United Nations, a new organization dedicated to the preservation of peace, security, and the protection of human rights around the world. For its headquarters, a team of prominent architects designed a thirty-nine-story building along New York City's East River. Completed in 1953, the UN Secretariat Building houses the General Assembly Hall and institutional offices.

free elections, guarantees of individual liberty, freedom of speech and religion, and freedom from political oppression. The second way of life is based upon the will of a minority forcibly imposed upon the majority. It relies upon terror and oppression, a controlled press and radio, fixed elections, and the suppression of personal freedoms. I believe that it must be the policy of the United States to support free peoples who are resisting attempted subjugation by armed minorities or by outside pressures.[4]

Truman's belief that the United States must actively try to stop the spread of Communism became known as the **Truman Doctrine**, and Congress quickly endorsed this new foreign policy aim by authorizing aid to Greece and Turkey. Within a month, Truman sent military missions to these nations to help prevent Communist takeovers. For the next decades, U.S. efforts to "contain" Communism involved the nation in **military interventions**, most notably in Korea and Vietnam but also in the Middle East and Latin America. As we saw in Chapter 13 (The Presidency), these military interventions were undertaken by the president in his role as commander in chief. No president since Franklin Roosevelt has asked Congress for a declaration of war. Presidential power grew in accord with America's commitment to world leadership. In an age when atomic bomb capabilities called for split-second decisions, the president's authority to command military response went mostly unchallenged.

One year after the announcement of the Truman Doctrine, the United States began a program of economic and humanitarian aid that also aimed to contain Communism. The **Marshall Plan** provided billions of dollars to rebuild the infrastructure of European nations, including defeated Germany. Secretary of State George Marshall, its architect, declared its purpose to be "the revival of a working economy in the world so as to permit the emergence of political and social conditions in which free institutions can exist."[5] In 1949 Truman initiated a formal collective defense pact with the democratic nations of western Europe. According to the terms of the **North Atlantic Treaty Organization (NATO)**, an attack on any one of the member nations would be considered an attack on them all: NATO is exactly the type of entangling alliance that George Washington sought to avoid. The Soviet Union

What powers does Congress have regarding military interventions?

Truman Doctrine: *Policy set forth by President Harry Truman that the United States would actively try to stop the spread of Communism.*

military interventions: *Military actions short of declarations of war ordered by the president.*

Marshall Plan: *U.S.-sponsored program to rebuild the economies of Europe after World War II so that democratic institutions could thrive.*

North Atlantic Treaty Organization (NATO): *Military alliance formed in 1949 by the United States and the democratic nations of western Europe.*

Do you think the motivation behind the Marshall Plan was humanitarian, strategic, or military?

On March 12, 1947, President Harry Truman spoke to a joint session of Congress convened to consider a growing economic crisis in Greece. He clearly stated his belief that the economic stability of Greece was essential to keeping it from falling to the Communists. During this speech Truman set forth the policy that the United States would take active steps to preserve democracy and contain Communism throughout the world, a policy that became known as the Truman Doctrine.

Harry S. Truman Library

Warsaw Pact: *Military alliance formed in 1955 by the Soviet Union and the Communist nations of eastern Europe.*

nuclear proliferation: *Spread of nuclear technology and weapons.*

Young people in the 1950s and 1960s feared nuclear annihilation. Is that something you think about? Is it a continuing threat?

human rights: *Right to life free from physical threat or abuse, plus protections for freedom of belief, freedom of religious worship, and freedom of speech.*

responded by initiating its own programs of economic and humanitarian aid and, in 1955, forming a mutual defense treaty with the Communist nations of Eastern Europe called the **Warsaw Pact** (see Figure 16.1). Both sides engaged in an arms race, which, after the Soviets achieved nuclear capability in 1949, threatened the future of human life on the planet. One legacy of the Cold War are the nuclear stockpiles amassed by the superpowers and their allies and the fear of **nuclear proliferation**—the spread of nuclear weapons technology to even more nations.

Another legacy for the United States is the anti-American sentiment that its military interventions often generated. U.S. efforts to contain Communism sometimes put it in the position of supporting dictators whose regimes suppressed dissent and denied **human rights**, broadly defined as the right to life free from physical threat or abuse, plus protections for freedom of belief, freedom of religious worship, and freedom of speech. Such was the case in Vietnam, where the United States shored up the regime of a corrupt dictator and viewed a nationalist movement seeking to unite a divided Vietnam as Communist aggression. It was also the case in Iran, where in 1953 **covert action** by the United States brought down a nationalist leader and installed a monarch—the shah—whose autocratic and oppressive regime was friendly to U.S. and Western oil interests. In 1979, after the exiled religious leader Ayatollah Ruhollah Khomeini returned to lead a revolution against the shah, Iranian militants seized the U.S. embassy in Tehran and held fifty-two Americas hostage for 444 days.[6] Too often nations such as Vietnam and Iran, which became independent as Europe decolonized, were pawns in the superpower standoff.

Beginning in 1989, facing enormous economic difficulties and organized political dissent, the Communist regimes of eastern Europe began to fall, and in 1991 the Soviet Union itself disintegrated into separate states. Thus the United States could declare victory in the Cold War but now faced the challenge of winning and keeping the peace.

Globalization

The context for international relations at the end of the Cold War was vastly different from earlier eras. After that struggle ended, the old bipolar world of the two superpowers became **multipolar**, with numerous centers of power competing for regional dominance and with numerous regional conflicts. Since the end of World War II many nations in addition to Vietnam and Iran had gained independence from such former colonial powers as France and the United Kingdom. Some of these nations—India and Indonesia, for example—had risen to prominence by attempting to remain neutral in the superpower struggle, forming the nonaligned movement (NAM). Modernization in China gave that huge nation new international stature. In the Middle East, tensions between Israel and the Arab states went unresolved. In Africa, decolonization had created a patchwork of new states struggling against

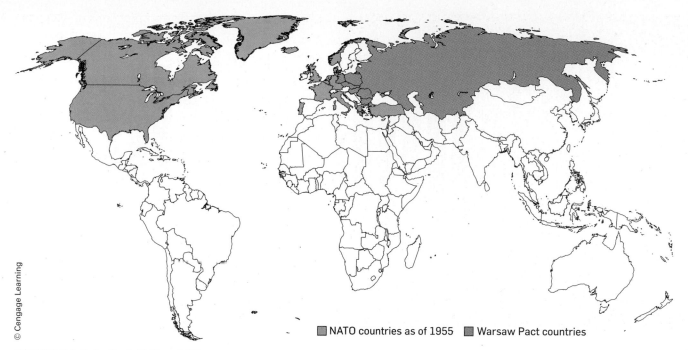

FIGURE 16.1 Cold War Alliances. During the Cold War the world was divided into two hostile camps. The United States led the NATO alliance, and the Soviet Union led the Warsaw Pact. Most nations were asked or forced to align with either the democratic or the Communist system.

◼ NATO countries as of 1955   ◼ Warsaw Pact countries

© Cengage Learning

corruption, poverty, and disease. And in the old Soviet bloc, especially in central Asia, new states struggled to suppress regional, religious, and ethnic hostilities and to resist Russian dominance.

For the United States as the only remaining superpower, this new world order presented much uncertainty. U.S. foreign and humanitarian aid programs were challenged by the enormity of the need, yet newly independent nations questioned the motivations for U.S. intervention both past and present. The United States professed support for human rights, but its strategic support for nondemocratic regimes contradicted its claims. Nevertheless, because the United States was the world's leading economic and military power, it seemed to have a stake in hostilities, health crises and epidemics, and natural disasters and environmental degradation wherever they occurred.

At the same time, in a process now described as **globalization**, regional economies, societies, and cultures had become increasingly integrated through trade, capital investment, labor flows, migration, travel, and, most strikingly, the World Wide Web and instantaneous communication (see Figures 16.2 and 16.3). In one sense, these changes opened the economic and political gates that long kept nations apart. People are today interconnected on multiple levels. Citizens of China drink Coke and eat McDonald's hamburgers, and Americans wear clothing with "made in China" on the label. Globalization proceeded at the intersection of economics and politics. Developed nations found it cheaper to manufacture goods in developing countries, and free trade was thought to promote peace and stability among nations whose economies were closely intertwined, even serving as a gateway to more open and democratic societies in nations previously closed to outside influences.

covert action: *Undercover actions taken by one nation against another to destabilize it or bring about regime change.*

multipolar: *Having numerous centers of power competing for regional dominance and marked by numerous regional conflicts.*

What have been the threats to the United States since the end of the Cold War?

Why should the promotion of human rights be important for a democracy?

globalization: *Process whereby nations become interconnected in their economies, military actions, health and disease concerns, and environmental impacts, notably through trade, business and industry, and technological advances in transportation and communication.*

What can or should national governments do about economic globalization?

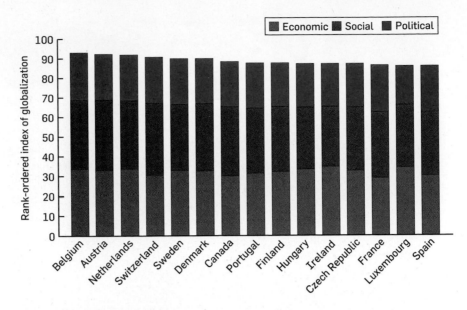

FIGURE 16.2 The Fifteen Most Globalized Nations, 2010.
Although globalization is difficult to measure, economists have computed an index of globalization that includes how much trade a nation conducts with other nations, how much it cooperates politically with other nations, and how freely its citizens work with citizens of other nations on social and economic issues. For the fifteen least globalized nations, there are almost no data on such matters.
Source: KOF Swiss Economic Institute, "KOF Index of Globalization 2010," Chart 2, p. 2, January 22, 2010, www.kof.ethz.ch.

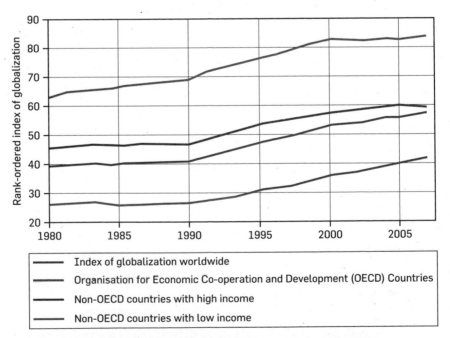

FIGURE 16.3 Globalization by Income across Regions, 1980–2008. Richer nations are more likely to be highly integrated into the global economy, while poorer nations still lag behind.
Source: KOF Swiss Economic Institute, "KOF Index of Globalization 2010," Dreher, Axel, "Does Globalization Affect Growth? Evidence from a new Index of Globalization," *Applied Economics* 38, 10: 1091-1110 (2006). Reprinted by permission.

Humanitarian Concerns and Conflict Resolution

The interdependence of the new globalized world might sound like a formula for peace, but in fact the connections are complex. Being connected does not mean sharing political systems and religions, or even cultures below the level of popular culture. The differences that do exist have intensified in the new global age and have produced political, social, and military conflict. America has objective strategic interests that it must protect, but it also has a strong commitment to human rights and democratic principles of government, and sometimes these guiding principles clash.[7] As a leading military and economic power, the United States has to balance the need to preserve its own interests against the benefits that arise from working with other nations under an international framework of laws and policies. In this section, we look at U.S. humanitarian and military interventions since the 1990s, and at the international treaties and organizations that work toward resolving international conflict but can cause political disagreement at home.

AP Photo

While he was president, Jimmy Carter made human rights a fundamental part of America's foreign policy agenda. Speaking at graduation ceremonies at the University of Notre Dame in South Bend, Indiana, Carter asserted, "We can no longer separate the traditional issues of war and peace from the new global questions of justice, equity, and human rights" and affirmed "America's commitment to human rights as a fundamental tenet of our foreign policy."

How does globalization affect society?

Nuclear Proliferation and International Arms Control

The fear of nuclear proliferation that was a legacy of the Cold War intensified as the Cold War ended. Russia emerged as the largest and most powerful former Soviet state and the only one with nuclear missiles, but there were concerns about the security of its nuclear stockpiles, especially with the rise of terrorism. In addition to the United States, the United Kingdom, France, China, and Israel had nuclear capabilities by this time, and by the end of the 1990s so did India and Pakistan. Because India and Pakistan have experienced border clashes and are generally unfriendly toward each other, their possession of nuclear weapons poses a threat to the stability of Southeast Asia. Most recently, concerns about nuclear weapons development have focused on Iran and North Korea.

As the preeminent international peacekeeping organization, the United Nations (discussed in depth later in the chapter) has long led efforts to curb nuclear proliferation through treaties that would ban the testing of nuclear weapons and set up an official verification system whereby countries would be regularly inspected to make sure they were not

In 2010 President Barack Obama took several important steps in reducing the number of nuclear weapons in the U.S. military arsenal, and he continued to work with other nations to prevent the spread of nuclear weapons capability. Here he discusses nuclear weapons proliferation with South Korean President Lee Myung-bak at the April 2010 Nuclear Security Summit in Washington, D.C.

Nuclear Non-Proliferation Treaty: *International treaty with 190 signatories designed to discourage nations from developing nuclear weapons technology that went into effect in 1970.*

Comprehensive Nuclear Test Ban Treaty: *International treaty that bans the testing and development of nuclear weapons (1996).*

The checks and balances between the executive and legislative branches can slow down or stall progress in foreign relations. Is this eighteenth-century system of divided powers a good idea for the twenty-first century?

developing nuclear capabilities. The **Nuclear Non-Proliferation Treaty** that went into effect in 1970 was designed to discourage nations from developing nuclear weapons technology; currently, 190 nations are signatories.[8] The key element of this treaty is the use of the International Atomic Energy Commission to monitor and inspect nations' weapons capability.

In 1996 the United Nations sought to build on the effort to stem nuclear proliferation by proposing a second treaty, the **Comprehensive Nuclear Test Ban Treaty**. President William Jefferson (Bill) Clinton (1993–2001) signed the treaty,[9] but it met with strong resistance from senators who believed it was too invasive in permitting the monitoring of U.S. weapons capabilities. Senator Jesse Helms (R-N.C.), chair of the Senate Committee on Foreign Relations, which had jurisdiction over the treaty, refused to hold hearings on it for two years. Finally, in 1999, with the end of his presidency approaching, Clinton pressured the Senate to get the treaty out of committee to be considered by the full Senate. In the final vote, the treaty was rejected 48 to 51, well below the necessary two-thirds for ratification.[10]

During the next eight years, President George W. Bush (2001–2009) did not resubmit the treaty to the Senate for ratification. By 2009, 195 nations had signed the treaty, but it could not go into effect until all 44 nations that possessed nuclear weapons capability when the treaty was written in 1996 ratified it, and 9 nations, including the United States, have failed to do so.[11] The fate of this treaty exemplifies the way the Senate can be a gate blocking the exercise of the president's power to negotiate and enforce international treaties, even when the treaties are in the interest of promoting international security and peace. The failure to ratify this treaty also makes it more difficult for the United States to object to other nations' development of nuclear weapons capability.

Nevertheless, in the past decade the United States has put pressure on Iran, which appears to be developing nuclear capability, and on North Korea, which is widely believed to possess this capability, although the UN has not been able to confirm it.[12] In April 2010 President Barack Obama (2009–) took two significant steps to renew the U.S. commitment to reducing the development and use of nuclear weapons. First, as part of U.S. participation in the international Nuclear Security Summit, he issued a Nuclear Posture Review, which took steps to reassure nonnuclear nations that the United States would not use its own nuclear weapons arsenal against them provided they did not actively seek to develop nuclear weapons of their own. Second, he signed a new Strategic Arms Reduction (START) Treaty with Russia in which both countries agreed to dismantle a significant number of their nuclear weapons. On May 13, 2010, President Obama submitted the treaty to the Senate for ratification.[13]

It remains to be seen whether he will be more successful than his predecessors in securing Senate approval for nuclear weapons reduction treaties.

Humanitarian Intervention

With the disintegration of the Soviet Union came a major rise in ethnic violence, even **genocide**—the eradication of one group by another based on race, political belief, religion, or culture—in regions that had formerly been under Soviet control or Communist influence. For example, in the late 1980s the Communist nation of Yugoslavia began breaking apart into regions dominated by hostile ethnic and religious groups. Between 1991 and 1995 Serbs and Croats, in particular, engaged in intense conflict over which group would control which territory and dominate the political system. In a program of **ethnic cleansing**, thousands were killed and tortured based on their ethnic and religious affiliations. Neighboring countries in Europe did not intervene to stop the violence, nor did the United States. Fairly or not, the inaction was likened to international inaction that had allowed genocide in the Holocaust and raised questions about the U.S. role as the protector of democracy and human rights. Despite its position as a world leader, American citizens were still hesitant about foreign entanglements, especially in the aftermath of the Vietnam War (see Chapter 13).

Ultimately, however, international outcry about the conflict in the former Yugoslavia pushed the United States to the forefront of **humanitarian intervention**, military action to stop crimes against humanity including murder, forced starvation, and the use of rape and torture on a mass level. President George H. W. Bush (1989–93) and President Bill Clinton supported United Nations efforts to bring peace to the region but were initially reluctant to commit U.S. air and ground forces. An underlying issue in U.S. military involvement was the proposal to send troops into an operation led by NATO. In effect, U.S. troops would be under the command of NATO, not their own military leaders, and the prospect of the loss of military command made many in Congress uneasy. By 1995, however, revelations of mass murder changed public opinion to favor the use of U.S. military power to intervene in the conflict. In August 1995 President Clinton agreed to U.S. participation with its European NATO allies in a wide-scale air assault on several key positions, but committed no ground troops in active military operations. The bombings were effective, and shortly thereafter the leaders of Croatia, Serbia, and Bosnia agreed to end the fighting.[14]

Rogue States and Failed States

The atrocities committed in the former Yugoslavia were not isolated incidents; similar ethnic conflict occurred in developing nations around the world. Some of these nations came to be seen as **rogue states**, nations that do not comply with international law and norms, and **failed states**, nations that lack working governments and are unstable. In the case of rogue states, U.S. strategy has been to impose political and economic sanctions to pressure their leaders to come under the umbrella of international law. Such is the case with Libya, a North African state led by Muammar el-Qaddafi. Under Qaddafi's dictatorship, Libya funded a wide range of terrorist acts around the world in the 1980s, culminating in the bombing of Pan Am Flight 103, a civilian airliner, in 1988. After a retaliatory bombing of Qaddafi's palace by the United States and the imposition of harsh sanctions, the Qaddafi regime has, in the past two decades, slowly reformed its activities to observe international law. Today, Libya is no longer perceived as a rogue state that supports terrorism, but it has not yet been fully accepted into the international community.[15]

genocide: *Eradication of a group based on race, political belief, religion, or culture.*

ethnic cleansing: *Use of mass murder to remove residents from a territory.*

To what extent should the United States engage in humanitarian interventions? What if American lives are lost?

humanitarian intervention: *Military actions undertaken to stop crimes against humanity, including mass murder, forced starvation, and mass rape and torture.*

rogue states: *Nations that do not observe international law.*

failed states: *Nations that lack a working government and are therefore unstable.*

Scott Peterson/Liaison/Getty Images

Somalia is a stark example of a failed state. As part of a UN peacekeeping mission designed to resolve conflict between warring factions that erupted after a dictatorship was toppled, the United States sent troops to Somalia in 1992 to minimize civilian casualties and provide security for the provision of humanitarian aid. In late 1993 eighteen U.S. soldiers were killed and eighty-four were wounded when a battle broke out in Somalia's capital city of Mogadishu.[16] As a result of public dismay at the loss of life in a peacekeeping mission, President Clinton severely scaled back U.S. involvement in Somalia and became reluctant to commit U.S. troops to intervene in foreign conflicts. In fact, the failed mission in Somalia was one of the reasons the United States stayed out of the conflict in the former Yugoslavia for as long as it did, and it is often cited as the primary reason for U.S. refusal to directly intervene in conflicts in Rwanda and, more recently, Sudan.

A civil war in Somalia led the United Nations to send peacekeeping troops, and U.S. soldiers also participated in a humanitarian mission to provide food and supplies. In October 1993, following fighting in the city of Mogadishu, the bodies of dead U.S. soldiers were dragged through the streets. As a result, U.S. public opinion turned against interventions in foreign conflicts.

What should the United States do about the Somali pirates?

Can military intervention be a gateway to peace? Under what circumstances?

Somalia continues to be a chaotic, war-torn, and famine-stricken nation. Most recently, Somali pirates have emerged as a major economic and military threat to international shipping along the Somali coast, waging attacks against U.S. citizens in the process.[17] Such distant and relatively small-scale attacks may not seem to pose a direct threat to the United States, but given the nature of the global economy, the violent disruption of international commerce can be regarded as harming U.S. interests. More broadly, Somali piracy is an outgrowth of Somalia's instability, and it illustrates how failed states can pose a danger to the international community at large.

The Promotion of Democracy

Bush Doctrine: *Policy set forth by President George W. Bush that the United States would take military action to promote democratic principles and protect its security and interests.*

For the United States, the questions of whether, how, and when to intervene in foreign conflicts come up over and over again. Until the terrorist attacks on the United States on September 11, 2001, the nation maintained a limited interventionist policy. Thereafter, under President George W. Bush, U.S. policy became more directly interventionist. Bush argued, in what became known as the **Bush Doctrine**, that the United States has the responsibility and obligation to promote democratic principles around the world and that it should and would take any actions necessary to protect its own security and interests.[18] The global war on terror initiated under Bush was a sweeping policy change in which the United States justified military actions, such as the capture of suspected terrorists in a foreign nation, that could be seen as violations of other nations' sovereignty (see Chapter 4, Civil Liberties, for more on the war on terror).

In one sense the Bush Doctrine served as a gateway for the United States to take a role in foreign conflicts; it took Wilson's idea that the United States should make the world "safe for democracy" and Truman's idea that the United States should intervene militarily to promote and defend against Communist takeovers to a new level. The program accorded with the democratic peace theory, which holds that the world is a safer place if nations are democratic, because democratic nations almost never go to war against other democracies.[19] But unlike Wilson, who believed in international cooperation, and Truman, who built a defensive alliance system, Bush adopted the perspective of **unilateralism** and was willing for the United States to act alone. Unilateralism stood in contrast to the **multilateralism** of previous administrations, which worked with other nations to resolve international conflicts.

President George W. Bush argued that the United States had to have the capacity and flexibility to respond swiftly to a whole range of threats and that doing so sometimes required unilateral action. The twenty-first century had ushered in new weaponry and new levels of violence committed by nations and **nonstate actors**, terrorist groups who took up violence against civilians as a means of attacking the United States and other Western nations. The Bush administration used this new reality to justify military action against the Taliban regime in Afghanistan and to defend the detention and torture of suspected terrorists. The president went one step further to launch a **preemptive attack** against Iraq to remove Saddam Hussein from power and dismantle alleged weapons of mass destruction that might be used against the United States and its allies (see Chapter 13 for more on the Iraq War). Although Hussein did not in fact have such weapons, the Bush administration maintained that Hussein's aggressive behavior and posturing threatened the security and interests of the United States.

Opponents of the Bush Doctrine argue that attacking Iraq without world approval alienated foreign nations and diminished the credibility of the United States. Supporters point out that removing Hussein's dictatorial regime has allowed Iraq to make some progress toward being a democracy with free elections and an independent government.

Today, the question of what is justified in the name of preserving and promoting the American form of democracy remains unresolved, and it is one of the major tasks facing President Barack Obama as he charts a new course for the nation's foreign policy. Making the case to the American people that direct U.S. intervention is necessary in distant regions with long histories of conflict, such as the Middle East, is difficult to do (see Chapter 6, Public Opinion). America's international reputation was tarnished by its unilateralism in the Iraq War, making it more difficult for the United States to gain cooperation from the international community for intervention. For this reason, the United States may become more reliant on working through international organizations like the United Nations to settle conflicts in foreign lands.

The United Nations

The United States is a participating member in several important **international governmental organizations (IGOs)**, institutions set up to mediate conflicts between two or more nations as well as to help combat world hunger, poverty, and disease. The most important of these is the United Nations, which, as noted earlier, was founded at the end of World War II.

What responsibility should the United States assume for international peacekeeping?

Should the United States engage in military actions to promote democracy?

unilateralism: *Military action or economic policy undertaken alone, without a cooperative agreement among a group of nations.*

multilateralism: *Military action or economic policy undertaken through cooperation of a group of nations.*

nonstate actors: *Individuals or groups that take military or political actions outside the framework of a nation-state.*

preemptive attack: *Attack intended to prevent an anticipated attack.*

What is your position on the wars in Iraq and Afghanistan?

international governmental organizations (IGOs): *Organizations formed to develop solutions to military and economic problems through cooperation among member nations.*

The UN is an international gateway for peace because nations can turn to it to resolve conflicts before resorting to violence.

The United Nations is neutral, meaning that it does not explicitly endorse one form of government over another. The wide range of political and economic systems represented in the UN requires compromises that leave some members dissatisfied or produce responses to conflict that are so weak that they are ineffective and easily ignored by member nations. The support of major powers such as the United States has a large impact on how well UN decisions are implemented, but even the United States does not abide by all UN decisions and takes unilateral action when it believes its interests are at stake.

What role should the United States play in the United Nations?

As of 2010 the United Nations had 192 member nations and, with a budget of nearly $5 billion, operated five major programs in the areas of peace and security, development, human rights, humanitarian affairs, and international law.[20] Each member nation is expected to pay dues, based generally on the nation's wealth, measured as per capita income, to support UN efforts. Collecting the dues can be problematic; some nations are unable to pay them, and others, including the United States, at times refuse to pay to signal displeasure with UN actions. All member nations participate in the UN General Assembly, where each is accorded equal power. The Security Council, which is a small subset of member nations, was mandated by the founders of the UN to keep international peace and security. The five permanent members of the Security Council (the United States, Russia, the United Kingdom, China, and France) along with ten rotating members choose the leader of the UN, who serves a five-year term that is renewable; Ban Ki-moon is the current secretary general. The Security Council nations make key decisions about whether to impose sanctions or authorize peacekeeping and peace enforcement missions, and are thus more powerful than other member nations. The United States wields considerable influence in the Security Council, but since any one of the five permanent member nations can veto a proposal, each of these nations can stand as a gate to block actions it opposes.

The UN relies on the cooperation of member nations to send their countries' military personnel to accomplish its missions. In general, troops on UN missions are deployed to act as a buffer between opposing forces. They are not allowed to fire on other forces unless they are fired upon or are acting in defense of others who might be attacked.[21] Since its founding, the UN Security Council has authorized the dispatch of troops or "peacekeepers" on more than sixty missions to countries all over the world, including Angola, Bosnia, Darfur, Ethiopia, Haiti, India, Iraq, Lebanon, Rwanda, Sierra Leone, and Somalia.[22] It is crucial for the UN to maintain neutrality during these peacekeeping missions to build trust among the forces involved in the conflict and to preserve the safety and security of the troops. In recent years, the UN Security Council has moved the focus of such missions beyond military intervention by coordinating the provision of medical, educational, and humanitarian services alongside the peacekeeping troops. Because UN missions underscore the humane and fair treatment of all citizens in a country, especially of religious and ethnic minorities, they also work to promote democratic ideals of equality.

In 1948 the UN adopted a Universal Declaration of Human Rights, affirming that the organization would try to prevent or mediate conflicts around the world, protect human rights, prevent worldwide hunger, and assist developing nations. Its preamble (see Figure 16.4) includes parallels with the U.S. Declaration of Independence, particularly the commitment to equality and the preservation of individual freedom. Ironically, at the time the United States was voting

FIGURE 16.4 Preamble to the United Nations Universal Declaration of Human Rights.

Whereas recognition of the inherent dignity and of the equal and inalienable rights of all members of the human family is the foundation of freedom, justice and peace in the world,

Whereas disregard and contempt for human rights have resulted in barbarous acts which have outraged the conscience of mankind, and the advent of a world in which human beings shall enjoy freedom of speech and belief and freedom from fear and want has been proclaimed as the highest aspiration of the common people,

Whereas it is essential, if man is not to be compelled to have recourse, as a last resort, to rebellion against tyranny and oppression, that human rights should be protected by the rule of law,

Whereas it is essential to promote the development of friendly relations between nations,

Whereas the peoples of the United Nations have in the Charter reaffirmed their faith in fundamental human rights, in the dignity and worth of the human person and in the equal rights of men and women and have determined to promote social progress and better standards of life in larger freedom,

Whereas Member States have pledged themselves to achieve, in co-operation with the United Nations, the promotion of universal respect for and observance of human rights and fundamental freedoms,

Whereas a common understanding of these rights and freedoms is of the greatest importance for the full realization of this pledge,

Now, Therefore THE GENERAL ASSEMBLY proclaims THIS UNIVERSAL DECLARATION OF HUMAN RIGHTS as a common standard of achievement for all peoples and all nations, to the end that every individual and every organ of society, keeping this Declaration constantly in mind, shall strive by teaching and education to promote respect for these rights and freedoms and by progressive measures, national and international, to secure their universal and effective recognition and observance, both among the peoples of Member States themselves and among the peoples of territories under their jurisdiction.

Source: United Nations, www.un.org/.

to approve this declaration, it was still a segregated nation that denied fundamental human rights to African Americans.

The Geneva Conventions

In keeping with the idea of peacekeeping and universal human rights, the United Nations abides by the **Geneva Conventions**, standards for the treatment of civilians and prisoners of war that were adopted by the international community in the nineteenth century and were updated in 1949 in the aftermath of the genocide of World War II. All 192 nations that

Geneva Conventions: *Set of treaties that define lawful military combat and protect the rights of prisoners of war.*

Should the United States abide by the Geneva Conventions? What are the reasons for doing so? What are the reasons for not doing so?

belong to the UN have ratified the Geneva Conventions. That means that the nations agree in principle to a uniform standard about how civilians should be treated during wartime and, equally important, that individuals who surrender or who are captured during a conflict cannot be subject to physical or emotional abuse that might be tantamount to torture.[23]

Unfortunately, not all nations observe the Geneva Conventions in practice, and the conventions have not succeeded as well as their authors hoped in preventing or stopping genocide. Even the United States was accused of violating the Geneva Conventions in its treatment of Iraqi prisoners of war at the Abu Ghraib prison, and the individual soldiers involved have been charged, but so far no formal charges have been brought against the U.S. government. When President Barack Obama took office in 2009, he reiterated the U.S. commitment to respecting the Geneva Conventions. In recent decisions, the Supreme Court has also reinforced the applicability of U.S. constitutional protections to the treatment of individuals in U.S. custody (see Supreme Court Cases: *Boumediene v. Bush*).

The International Court of Justice and the International Criminal Court

Another mechanism for resolving international conflicts is the International Court of Justice (ICJ), which is the legal wing of the United Nations. The court was included in the founding charter of the United Nations, and its role is to hear cases involving disputes between nations or groups of nations, give its legal opinions on the extent of wrongdoing, and establish a settlement.[24] It consists of fifteen judges who serve nine years and are selected by the UN with approval by the Security Council.

Although the United States recognizes the legitimacy of the court, the nation cedes authority to it over selected cases only. In other words, when the United States believes that international law does not apply to its actions or that its own laws supersede international law, it will not submit to the court's authority.[25] Arguments can be made in favor of and against the U.S. position toward the ICJ. On the one hand, this policy sets a bad precedent for the power of international law because if one country can ignore the ICJ, other countries might take the same action. On the other hand, the U.S. Constitution explicitly delineates the powers of the president and Congress over U.S. citizens but makes no provision for any government body to give up sovereignty to international law. It is unclear that the president or Congress can agree to abide by rulings that violate the Constitution.

Should the United States submit to the authority of the International Court of Justice? Why or why not?

The International Criminal Court (ICC) was formally established in 1998 to try individuals who are accused of international crimes against humanity and who are not tried by a home country. One hundred ten nations have agreed to participate in the ICC, but the United States is not one of them. In refusing to actively participate in the ICC, the United States reserves the right to capture and try any person who is suspected of planning and/or committing a crime against a U.S. citizen. U.S. policy with respect to this international organization is consistent with its other policies; cooperation in the international community is strategically important and useful so long as it does not reduce or impede U.S. sovereignty over its own economic, political, judicial, or military affairs. Because the United States believes it has one of the fairest judicial systems in the world, protected by the U.S. Constitution, it does not cede its authority to bring accused individuals to justice within that system.

supremecourtcases

Boumediene v. Bush (2008)

QUESTION: Does the U.S. constitutional right of *habeas corpus* apply to foreign enemy combatants held by the United States at Guantanamo Bay, Cuba?

ORAL ARGUMENT: December 15, 2007 (listen at http://www.oyez.org/cases)

DECISION: June 12, 2008 (Read at http://www.findlaw.com/casecode/supreme.html)

OUTCOME: Yes, enemy combatants at Guantanamo Bay have the right to *habeas corpus* (5–4).

In October 2001 Bosnian police arrested Lakhdar Boumediene, an Algerian national, on charges of supporting al Qaeda and planning an attack on the U.S. embassy. Finding no evidence to hold Boumediene, the Bosnian Supreme Court ordered his release. American troops in Bosnia then arrested Boumediene and transported him to the U.S. Naval Base at Guantanamo Bay, Cuba. While the naval base remains under Cuban sovereignty, a 1903 treaty with Cuba gave the United States complete control over the territory. The treaty can only be broken by mutual consent.

In the aftermath of the terrorist attacks on the United States on September 11, 2001, the Bush administration decided to keep captured enemy combatants at Guantanamo, as U.S. constitutional rights had not previously been applied overseas and the administration thought it would be too dangerous to grant constitutional rights to terrorists captured in the "fog of war." Congress agreed, passing the Military Commissions Act of 2006, which removed the *habeas corpus* rights of detainees at Guantanamo and provided for trials by military tribunals, which allow far fewer rights to the accused than do regular criminal trials.

At Guantanamo, Boumediene sought a writ of *habeas corpus*, which would grant him access to the federal courts so that the legality of his detention could be determined. Though Congress had seemingly restricted such rights, it is still up to the courts to determine the validity of such restrictions.

By a 5–4 vote, the Supreme Court declared that the writ of *habeas corpus* applies to enemy combatants held at Guantanamo. Though such rights do not usually apply overseas, Guantanamo was a special case because the United States exercises absolute and indefinite control over it. As to the dangers of granting procedural rights to alleged terrorists in the difficult times facing the nation following 9/11, Justice Anthony M. Kennedy wrote, "The laws and Constitution are designed to survive, and remain in force, in extraordinary times."

Upon taking office in January 2009, President Barack Obama declared that he would close the Guantanamo detention facility within a year, freeing some of the detainees, putting others on trial in criminal courts in the United States, and holding those deemed most dangerous for whom usable evidence might be lacking in indefinite detention. As of 2010 the detention facility remains open.

- **Which branches of government should have responsibility for overseeing the treatment of prisoners of war?**

- **What constitutional rights should the United States abide by when it acts overseas?**

Public and Private International Organizations

In addition to being an active member of the UN, the United States supports organizations that send individuals to foreign nations for peacekeeping, educational, and cultural purposes. The **Peace Corps** is perhaps the best known of these organizations. President John F. Kennedy (1961–63) established the Peace Corps in 1961 by executive order; since then, almost 200,000 U.S. citizens, called volunteers, have lived and worked in seventy-six countries all over the world.[26] The mission of the Peace Corps is to help train citizens of other nations in essential skills, establish communication about Americans with other nations, and bring more knowledge about foreign peoples back to America through the volunteers. When the organization was first established, communication between ordinary Americans and people elsewhere in the world was limited. Kennedy believed that if people got to know each other, they could be friends, and if impoverished nations could view the United States as supporting them, democratic values would have a better chance of flourishing. Although the Peace Corps was primarily an aid organization, it also served a strategic purpose for the United States in the battle against Communism.

Kennedy designed the Peace Corps to attract recent college graduates, and he first promoted the idea in a 1960 campaign speech at the University of Michigan. Today the Peace Corps still attracts recent college graduates and others who work in seventy-six countries in wide-ranging fields, including teaching, agriculture, HIV/AIDS prevention, medicine, engineering, communications, environmental conservation, and construction. The model of the Peace Corps has spurred the creation of domestic volunteer organizations like AmeriCorps and Teach for America, which operate within the United States but pursue similar goals of education and economic development in underserved areas.

In addition to the Peace Corps, many religious organizations and foundations provide international humanitarian aid and disaster relief. For example, the Catholic Relief Services sponsors a Global Solidarity Network for college students to communicate with people living in small villages or towns in developing countries. The National Council of Churches USA provides funding and coordinates religious and humanitarian missions to foreign countries.[27] Since September 11, 2001, Muslim organizations have been hampered by restrictions on fundraising and distribution of funds to Muslims in other nations, especially in the Arab world.[28]

Major private foundations, such as the Ford Foundation, serve as gateways for America's participation in addressing key global concerns such as poverty, disease, ethnic conflict, climate change, and human rights. Some foundations seek to promote democracy as an explicit part of their mission, but others aim more generally to improve living conditions. For example, the Bill and Melinda Gates Foundation, which was established in 1994 by the founder of the Microsoft software company, has close to $33 billion in assets. It focuses its efforts on

Peace Corps: *Agency created by President John F. Kennedy that sends U.S. citizen volunteers to poor nations to provide education, medical care, and infrastructure support.*

Is the Peace Corps still appealing to college students? Why or why not?

© Chor Sokunthea/Reuters/Corbis

Since its founding in 1961 by President John F. Kennedy, the Peace Corps has promoted world peace and friendship. Volunteers help with housing, education, nutrition, and medical care around the world, and people in other countries learn about America firsthand, often from enthusiastic young people. Here volunteers in Cambodia to teach English meet a Buddhist monk.

Courtesy Lauren Slive

Courtesy Lauren Slive.

eradicating poverty and improving health care around the world and on supporting education within the United States.[29] In 2001 former President Bill Clinton established the William J. Clinton Foundation, which works to address global poverty, HIV/AIDS, childhood obesity, and climate change. The foundation does not make grants to organizations and individuals; instead, its staff members coordinate private donors, government entities, and nonprofit organizations to provide services and resources to communities.

Finally, **nongovernmental organizations (NGOs)** monitor and improve political, economic, and social conditions in the United States and around the world. Human Rights Watch, for example, tries to protect Individuals from discrimination, persecution, and physical harm.[30] Such organizations are not affiliated with any government and work hard to preserve their neutrality so that they can operate in as many parts of the world as possible. NGOs typically rely on foundation grants and donations from supporters to fund their activities, and they try to use the media to get out their message. Nongovernmental organizations play an important role in global affairs because they promote equal treatment of people throughout the world while taking into account the enormous political, social, and cultural variations that exist.

As we saw with Project HEAL and MedPLUS, private organizations, foundations, and NGOs allow people from many nations to connect directly with one another. Governments are finding that committed and active citizens working together in private capacities can bring significant improvements in living conditions and in economic and social life, and they can help promote peace.

College students can make a global contribution, as the founders of MedPLUS did with their idea to match surplus medical supplies in the United States with the specific needs of the hospitals and people of Ghana.

Should governments seek to solve hunger, disease, and other worldwide social problems? Or should private charities play this role?

nongovernmental organizations (NGOs):
Organizations independent of governments that monitor and improve political, economic, and social conditions throughout the world.

Global Partnership and Public Policy: International Trade

Washington's Farewell Address in 1796 acknowledged the importance of international commerce to the new nation, and the Framers knew that trade with foreign nations was integral to its economic success and stability. At the time, Britain and France had well-established shipping and manufacturing interests, while the United States could offer only agricultural products and natural resources. Over the course of the nineteenth century, however, the United States grew economically strong through innovation, vast natural resources, and an increasing population that expanded both its workforce and its consumer base. In the twentieth century the United States built on its economic strength by becoming an innovator in intellectual and technical services. In the twenty-first century trade remains an important gateway to economic, political, and cultural relationships with other nations, though in recent years the nation has begun to import more goods than it exports.

Traditional and Twenty-First Century Trade Policy

Trade policy has long been aligned with foreign policy and has been used by the United States to export both capitalism and democracy. In a bold move, President Richard M. Nixon (1969–74) sought to open trade with Communist China in 1972, hoping not only to drive a wedge between China and the Soviet Union, two huge Communist nations that competed with each other, but also to open China as a market for American goods. The vast movement of goods across international boundaries affects a nation's power and its stature in the international arena.

Protectionism versus Free Trade.   International trade policy is complex because each nation wants to negotiate deals that give its industries the greatest advantages either to sell their goods abroad or to be protected from cheaper imports from foreign nations. A policy that protects against foreign imported goods more than it promotes exports is known as **protectionist**, and a policy that strikes down barriers on imported foreign goods is known as **free trade**. A third and relatively recent policy, **fair trade**, encourages foreign trade as long as there are comparable working conditions and wages within the industries in the trading nations. If one nation exploits its workers with long hours, unsafe conditions, and low pay to produce and sell goods more cheaply than another, it violates fair trade practices. When a nation violates fair trade practices, individuals may boycott its products, or, more significantly, other nations may refuse to trade with it.

The president takes the lead in negotiating international trade agreements, either bilaterally (with one other country) or multilaterally through the office of the **United States Trade Representative (USTR)**, an office created within the Executive Office of the President by President Kennedy in 1963. The U.S. trade representative and staff are responsible for negotiating the terms of international trade agreements. To present a balanced position on behalf of the U.S. government, the USTR solicits information and feedback about the potential impact of the trade agreement from import- and export-related industries, cabinet departments, and members of Congress. Gathering such information is helpful not only in crafting an agreement that benefits U.S. industries but also in building the necessary support to get the treaty ratified by the U.S. Senate.

During the twentieth century, protectionist trade policies enabled U.S. industries to corner the consumer market and make huge profits. Businesses reinvested those profits in developing technology and in expanding so that the United States became the major supplier of manufactured goods throughout the world. It did not face strong competition in the world marketplace until the late 1980s, when Japan, China, and India developed their industrial capacity sufficiently to become competitive in a number of economic sectors. They replicated

How does trade policy promote capitalism and democracy?

protectionism: *Trade policy that protects against foreign imported goods more than it promotes exports.*

free trade: *Trade policy that strikes down barriers on imported foreign goods.*

fair trade: *Trade policy that encourages foreign trade as long as there are equivalent working conditions and wages within the industries in trading nations.*

United States Trade Representative (USTR): *Office in the Executive Office of the President responsible for negotiating the terms of international trade agreements.*

the U.S. policy of exporting their goods while maintaining trade barriers against the import of U.S. goods.

In the early 1990s, to shore up production in the Western Hemisphere and create an effective trading bloc to compete with these nations, the United States negotiated a free trade agreement with Canada and Mexico. Called **NAFTA**, the **North American Free Trade Agreement** was approved by Congress in 1993. It had a major impact on the United States. It created a free trade zone of goods and services across the northern and southern borders of the United States, which created jobs nationwide, but some industries, such as the domestic textile industry, were affected negatively and lost jobs. Owners of businesses and industries moved their production facilities to Mexico, where it was less expensive to produce goods. These goods could then be sold cheaply in the United States because, under the free trade agreement, no import duties could be charged. The impact of NAFTA is an example of the unintended consequences of policies that are designed to integrate the U.S. economy into the global world of trade.

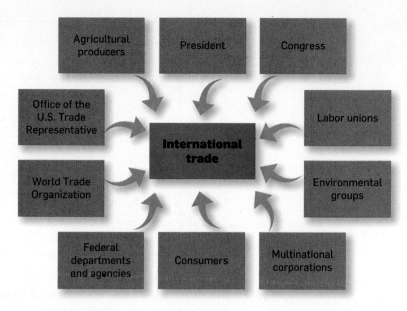

Most Favored Nation Status.

By the end of the 1990s, other nations wanted to have similar agreements with the United States whereby they could sell goods in U.S. markets with few trade barriers in exchange for opening their markets to U.S. goods. The United States uses an instrument called **most favored nation status**, which reduces trade barriers for countries that are awarded the designation, to strike unilateral trade deals. More important, the United States also uses the designation as an economic incentive to encourage nations to become more democratic in their political practices. In 2000, for example, Congress voted to award China most favored nation status in return for China's agreement to abide by international human rights standards and to improve labor conditions and environmental protection. Although this agreement is credited with opening up Chinese markets to U.S. goods and for some progress toward greater freedoms for the Chinese, it also encouraged American producers of goods such as textiles, apparel, steel, and electronics to relocate their production facilities to China. Ten years later, the United States has a large trade imbalance with China; for example, in the first seven months of 2010, U.S. imports exceeded exports to China by nearly $145 billion.[31] The increase in the number of economically developed nations as producers and consumers of goods, combined with the presence of U.S.-owned industries in these nations, has created a strong incentive for the United States to be a supportive partner in the international economy (see Figure 16.5).

Trade and International Economic Organizations

In addition to the unilateral trade agreements that it has struck with other nations, the United States also participated in the **General Agreement on Tariffs and Trade (GATT)**, which governed multinational trade agreements between 1948 and 1994. The complicated set of rules and regulations embedded in the GATT grew out of many separate deals struck among

North American Free Trade Agreement (NAFTA): *1993 agreement that created a free trade zone of goods and services among the United States, Canada, and Mexico.*

How has NAFTA affected you or your community?

most favored nation status: *Trade status that reduces trade barriers.*

Should Americans "buy American"? Why or why not?

General Agreement on Tariffs and Trade (GATT): *Set of agreements that governed world trade between 1948 and 1994.*

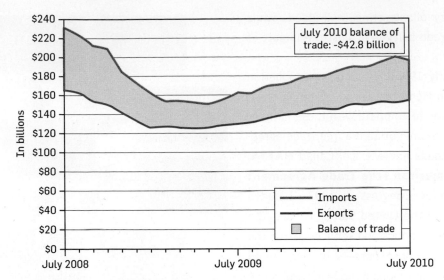

FIGURE 16.5 U.S. Balance of Trade, 2008–2010. The United States currently imports more goods and services than it exports. *Source:* U.S. Census Bureau, Foreign Trade Statistics, www.census.gov/.

Why is it important for the United States to participate in international trade agreements and organizations?

World Trade Organization (WTO): *International organization created in 1995 with the authority to resolve trade disputes among nations.*

European Union (EU): *Organization of twenty-seven nations that cooperate on economic and political issues such as monetary policy, trade subsidies, immigration, and international criminal justice.*

nations.[32] Each time nations wanted to revise trade rules, they held negotiation meetings, called "rounds," which took several years to complete. Twenty-three nations were involved in the first round of the GATT in Geneva, Switzerland, in 1947–48; by 1994 the eighth round of negotiations included 123 nations.

World Trade Organization.

During the eighth round of GATT negotiations, the **World Trade Organization (WTO)** was created to deal with the explosive expansion of the global trade community and to establish a single international organization with the authority to resolve trade disputes.[33] If one country claims that another country is engaged in unfair trading practices, it can bring its case to the WTO; each party to the dispute must abide by the WTO's ruling or face monetary fines and trade limitations. For example, in 2009 Congress placed a temporary ban on all poultry products from China; in response China lodged a formal complaint with the WTO, which formed a panel to resolve the issue. The ban stemmed from concerns about food safety, but it also helped U.S. domestic poultry producers by making it unnecessary for them to compete with Chinese poultry. The issue at stake is not limited to poultry imports; China might retaliate by raising import taxes on other U.S. goods like wheat. The inherent problem with solving trade disputes is that protection for one industry can frequently mean putting another industry at a disadvantage.

More than a year after China lodged the complaint, the WTO panel had not yet returned a decision on the case.[34] The slow pace of the WTO deliberation illustrates how an international organization can serve as a gate or obstacle to efficient resolution of economic disputes. Entering the WTO was a major change in U.S. trade policy because it required the United States to relinquish its right to act unilaterally in trade disputes. At the same time, by agreeing to abide by WTO rulings, the United States gave assurance to foreign nations that it would respect international rules and would be a fair and reliable trading partner.

European Union.

Another significant development in international trade relations was the creation of the **European Union (EU)**, a major expansion of a preexisting

European economic organization known as the European Community.[35] The European Union consists of twenty-seven member nations that cooperate on economic and political issues such as monetary policy, trade subsidies, immigration, and international criminal justice. Although each EU member nation retains its own separate government and control over its military, all member nations agree to abide by the decisions of the European Union. In joining

JOHN G. MABANGLO/AFP/Getty Images

together under a single formal institution, these nations now constitute a powerful trading partner. For example, an EU ban on American beef because of the use of certain hormones might persuade U.S. cattle farmers to change their practices. Many of the EU nations also share a common currency, the euro, although the United Kingdom, Sweden, and Denmark are among those that have retained their own currencies.[36] By adopting a common currency that is not tied to a single nation's economy, the EU has achieved a greater role in shaping international monetary policy and the value of the U.S. dollar. However, when one EU member nation suffers a major financial crisis, as Greece did in 2010, there can be widespread negative effects on financial markets across the globe. For the United States, the expansion of the EU means that it must now consider the effects of its trade and monetary policies on a number of countries simultaneously, rather than working out agreements with each nation separately or in smaller groups.

As many as 100,000 protesters showed up when the World Trade Organization met in Seattle in November 1999. Groups promoting human rights and environmental protection joined religious and labor leaders who sought fair trade policies, not just free trade, while protectionists objected to free trade altogether. Some of the protests turned violent.

The World Bank and the International Monetary Fund.

In addition to unilaterally promoting economic development, the United States is also a member of the World Bank and the International Monetary Fund, two global economic organizations. The **World Bank** was founded in 1944 as an international aid and reconstruction organization to help rebuild nations that had been badly damaged during World War II.[37] Today it has 187 members, known as shareholders, and five divisions that work together to provide low-interest loans, grants, and investment capital to build and improve infrastructure and alleviate poverty. The United States is the largest shareholder in the World Bank and consequently has leadership responsibilities; the president nominates the head of the bank, who serves a five-year renewable term.[38] The World Bank funds specific projects to improve transportation, provide clean water, build energy utilities, modernize medical care, initiate crop development programs, and provide start-up money for new businesses in poor and developing countries. In fiscal year 2009 the World Bank provided $58.8 billion in grants, loans, and investment capital to nations around the world.[39]

World Bank: *International aid and reconstruction organization, founded in 1944, that provides loans, grants, and investment capital to poor nations.*

What responsibility does the United States have for economic development and fiscal stability throughout the world?

International Monetary Fund: *Agency founded in 1944 to preserve international economic stability, including currency values, and to provide short-term loans to poor nations.*

The **International Monetary Fund (IMF)** was created alongside the World Bank in 1944 with a different mission. The IMF focuses on preserving economic stability, including currency values, among nations and makes short-term loans to nations that cannot balance their budgets or are in need of immediate funds.[40] The IMF also works with nations to try to reduce their government debt by renegotiating loans or by providing loans on better terms. The IMF has the same set of members as the World Bank, and each member makes a financial contribution to the fund based on its share of the global economy. The IMF has a board of governors, which includes a governor from each member nation, but the daily operations of the fund are overseen by a managing director and a twenty-four-member executive board. In contrast to its role in the World Bank, the United States does not play a prominent role in directing IMF operations and does not nominate the managing director. However, the United States pays the largest single share (17 percent) of the IMF's fund, so it wields significant influence over lending decisions. In 2009 the IMF had $35.8 billion in outstanding loans to sixty-five countries, all of which is expected to be repaid.

U.S. Agency for International Development (USAID): *Independent agency that promotes democracy and free market economics around the world.*

USAID.   Within the U.S. federal government, the **U.S. Agency for International Development (USAID)** is an independent agency with the mission of providing gateways for the provision of training, education, and materials to developing nations and of promoting democracy.[41] It is led by an administrator appointed by the president who works closely with other federal departments, including the Department of State, on international aid issues. USAID was created by President John Kennedy in 1961 as part of the Foreign Assistance Act, and it was originally conceived as reinforcing the positive aspects of democratic political systems among poor nations that might have otherwise turned to Communism. Today its activities have expanded to include disaster relief, child health and nutrition, and disease treatment and prevention, in addition to more general economic assistance. In fiscal year 2010 it had an operating budget of $2.7 billion.[42]

If the United States were to sponsor a Marshall Plan today, what would the plan do? To which countries would it be directed?

Global Health Concerns and Shared Resources

Navigating the international organizations that attempt to regulate trade and finance reveals the complexities of an interconnected world. The issues of health and the world's natural resources have also become an increasingly large part of global interactions. Although concerns such as famine and child nutrition have been on the international agenda for some time, the spread of disease across borders has become an increasingly important issue, especially with increased travel and trade among a wider range of nations. The development of industrial production in countries like India and China has also put greater pressure on the world's energy reserves; there are more people consuming higher amounts of energy than ever before. This new global level of production has also produced higher levels of air and water pollution as well as increased consumption of land-based natural resources. The modern industrial world presents new challenges to the United States as it seeks to accomplish policy goals in these areas.

What can nations do about problems, such as pollution, that cross international borders?

World Health

Just as the United States has participated in international organizations to promote economic development, it has also increased its role in improving world health, eradicating disease, and preventing famine. Domestically, the **Centers for Disease Control and Prevention (CDC)** is the federal agency charged with monitoring disease and prevention efforts, but it is also responsible for issuing travel warnings about health conditions abroad and, in cases of epidemics such as H1N1 (swine flu), for recommending measures to prevent or control outbreaks in the United States.[43] The Obama administration spent $1.6 billion to develop a supply of 229 million vaccine doses for immunization against swine flu under the auspices of a partnership between the CDC and pharmaceutical companies.[44] Because of the tremendous amount of international business and travel, protecting U.S. citizens domestically is not always sufficient to address a global health threat. Consequently, the United States worked with other nations in the effort to develop an effective vaccine.[45]

The United States also works closely with the **World Health Organization (WHO)**, which was founded as part of the United Nations in 1948.[46] The primary responsibilities of the WHO include improving health care around the world through vaccinations, better sanitary conditions, and access to medicines and preventing the spread of diseases like HIV/AIDS, cholera, malaria, and influenza. The WHO is controlled by the World Health Assembly, which comprises representatives from UN member nations and meets once a year. The operations of the WHO are overseen by a director general who is nominated by a thirty-four-member executive board and approved by the World Health Assembly and who has no set term of office.

The WHO can serve as a crucial source of information and guidance in the prevention or containment of a global epidemic. Its representatives travel around the world demonstrating safe medical practices and distributing vaccines and other medicines designed to combat disease. For example, during the H1N1 flu outbreak, the World Health Organization tracked the spread of the disease, recorded successful treatments, and tried to reach population segments that were most susceptible to it. More than 65 million doses of H1N1 vaccine were distributed to seventy-four nations.[47] As a member of the WHO, the United States plays an important role in sharing its medical advances with member nations that do not ordinarily have access to methods or treatments that are effective in saving lives.

In addition to working with the WHO, the United States works with domestic foundations, charities, and pharmaceutical companies to encourage the funding of international medical care. President George W. Bush put the HIV/AIDS crisis in Africa on the world agenda during his 2003 State of the Union address, announcing the **President's Emergency Plan for AIDS Relief (PEPFAR)**, which allocated $15 billion to purchase medicines for treatment and to assist in AIDS education and prevention.[48] PEPFAR focused its efforts on thirty-two

Centers for Disease Control and Prevention (CDC): *Federal agency that monitors disease and prevention efforts.*

World Health Organization (WHO): *UN organization that aims to improve health care and prevent the spread of disease.*

President's Emergency Plan for AIDS Relief (PEPFAR): *U.S. program that allocates funds to purchase medicines for treatment of HIV/AIDS and assist in education and prevention.*

Courtesy of The World Health Organization

The World Health Organization is responsible for reaching remote nations to ensure access to health care and disease prevention. Here the H1N1 vaccine is received by health care workers in the remote nation of Mongolia.

nations, mostly in Africa, that were either the hardest hit by AIDS or were facing a grow-ing threat, and the United States coordinated its efforts with international AIDS programs directed by the United Nations.[49] As part of the PEPFAR program, antiretroviral AIDS treat-ments are made available to heavily afflicted countries at a discounted cost. In 2008, the last year of the Bush administration, PEPFAR was renewed for five years as part of a larger health effort to combat HIV/AIDS, tuberculosis, and malaria, with a total budget of $48 billion. Presi-dent Obama continues the U.S. commitment in this area and has increased the budget for PEPFAR.[50]

International Environmental and Energy Policy

Concern for environmental protection and energy conservation has risen dramatically since the 1990s. The United States is one of the largest consumers of energy in the world, based on energy use per capita (per each resident), but nations such as India and China have also become major consumers of energy in their efforts to develop industrialized economies.[51] The United States is the world's largest emitter of greenhouse gases, which, some have argued, contribute to climate change. There is an inherent tension between industrialized nations that have used the world's energy resources freely for more than a hundred years and more recently developed nations that are seeking to industrialize their economies. Now that more advanced nations are concerned about the environment, they want to encourage, even require, all nations to use energy-efficient technology. Developing nations argue, however, that energy-efficient technology is expensive and that using it will increase their costs and slow down economic growth. The matter of fairness among nations in terms of consumption and pollution is not easily solved (see Other Places: The U.S. Global Footprint).

The United States holds a contradictory position in the debate over global energy consump-tion and environmental protection. The **Kyoto Protocol** is the central international agreement negotiated through the UN Framework Convention on Climate Change. It seeks to reduce the percentage of carbon emissions globally to 5 percent lower than 1990 levels by 2012.[52] The agreement also pledges to develop alternative energy sources and energy-efficient technology.

The Kyoto Protocol was signed on December 11, 1997, and it officially went into effect in 2005. The United States was an original signatory.[53] As of 2010, 190 nations had ratified or approved the agreement, but the United States is not among them.[54] Even before the treaty was signed by Vice President Albert Gore Jr. on behalf of the Clinton administration, the Senate had passed a resolution rejecting its terms. Senators expressed concerns that restric-tions on carbon dioxide emissions would put the United States at an economic disadvantage because developing nations were not subject to the same limitations. By signing the agree-ment in spite of the Senate's explicit opposition, the Clinton administration was putting the United States on record as supporting the goals all the while knowing that it would not be ratified. The Kyoto Protocol is an example of how the Senate's power of advice and consent (for ratification, two-thirds of the Senate must concur) limits the president's ability to carry through on international agreements. President Clinton's successor, George W. Bush, did not submit the Kyoto Protocol to the Senate for consideration during his administration.

The Kyoto Protocol can be viewed as both a gate and a gateway for the United States to be a productive environmental partner in the world. It serves as a gate in that the United States refuses to fully abide by the agreement and, by setting the example of opting out, encourages

As one of the largest per capita consumers of energy, what can the United States do to compensate for its depletion of natural resources? When it comes to consumption, does equality among nations matter?

Kyoto Protocol: *1997 international agreement that seeks to reduce carbon emissions.*

Should the Senate have ratified the Kyoto Protocol? Why or why not?

otherplaces

The U.S. Global Footprint

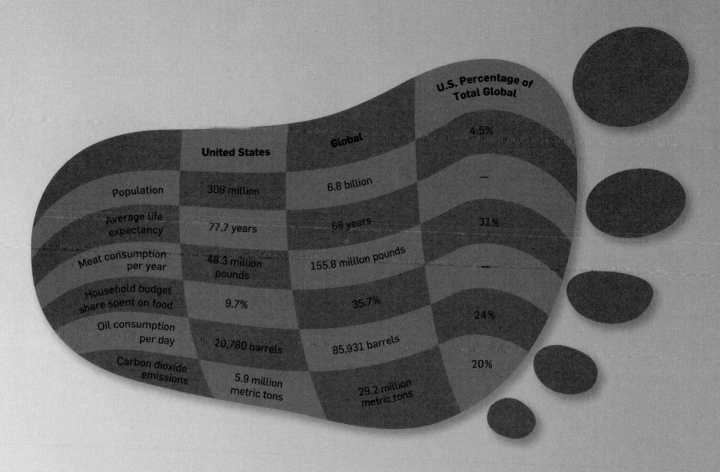

	United States	Global	U.S. Percentage of Total Global
Population	308 million	6.8 billion	4.5%
Average life expectancy	77.7 years	68 years	—
Meat consumption per year	48.3 million pounds	155.8 million pounds	31%
Household budget share spent on food	9.7%	35.7%	—
Oil consumption per day	20,780 barrels	85,931 barrels	24%
Carbon dioxide emissions	5.9 million metric tons	29.2 million metric tons	20%

- **What should the U.S. government do to actively reduce energy consumption?**

- **How could you personally reduce your carbon footprint?**

Sources: Centers for Disease Control, www.cdc.gov; United Nations, "World Population to Exceed 9 Billion by 2050," March 11, 2009, www.un.org; Anita Regmi and James L. Seale Jr., *Cross-Price Elasticities of Demand across 114 Countries*, TB-1925, U.S. Department of Agriculture, Economic Research Service, March 2010, www.ers.usda.gov; United States Department of Agriculture, Foreign Agricultural Service, Production, Supply, and Distribution Database, "Table 23, World Supply and Utilization of Major Crops, Livestock, and Products," www.usda.gov; United States Department of Agriculture, Economic Research Service: Agricultural Outlook, April 2010, "Table 10, U.S. Meat Supply and Use," www.ers.usda.gov; Energy Information Administration, U.S. Department of Energy, "United States Energy Profile," www.doe.gov.

other nations to disregard it as well. On the other hand, by agreeing to the terms of the Kyoto Protocol, the Clinton administration put the United States on record as supporting the general principle of limiting worldwide carbon emissions. President George W. Bush took some steps in this direction, and under President Obama, the United States has undertaken more concrete actions to limit carbon emissions (see Chapter 12, Congress, and Chapter 14, The Bureaucracy).

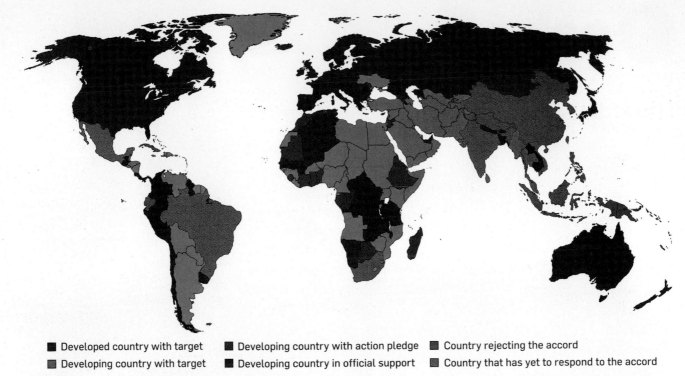

■ Developed country with target   ■ Developing country with action pledge   ■ Country rejecting the accord

■ Developing country with target   ■ Developing country in official support   ■ Country that has yet to respond to the accord

FIGURE 16.6 The Copenhagen Accord at Three Months. The Copenhagen Accord was negotiated in December 2009. By March 2010, 110 nations had agreed to abide by its goals of cutting greenhouse gas emissions and reducing the probability of climate change. The different categories sort nations by their levels of economic development (which is directly related to the amount and type of energy they consume) and their level of commitment to the agreement. *Source:* Andrew Light and Sean Pool, "The Copenhagen Accord at Three Months" 110 Countries Now Support a New Global Effort to Achieve Climate Safety," March 29, 2010. This material was created by the Center for American Progress, www.americanprogress.org. Reprinted by permission.

Copenhagen Accord: *2009 international agreement to encourage a speedier effort to reduce carbon emissions in accordance with the Kyoto Protocol.*

What are the costs to the United States of reducing its carbon footprint? What are the benefits, domestically and internationally?

Overall, the UN has had difficulty in getting all the nations that signed the Kyoto Protocol to comply with the agreement's goals; to date, only 21 nations submitted formal plans for carbon emission reductions.[55] In December 2009 the UN sponsored another conference on global warming in Copenhagen, where representatives from 190 countries met to encourage a speedier effort, through the **Copenhagen Accord**, to reduce carbon emissions.[56] President Obama attended the conference and tentatively agreed to try to reduce U.S. greenhouse gas emissions by 17 percent before 2020. He also asked Congress to consider a major climate change bill that would help the United States meet that goal, but the bill stalled in the Senate. By attending the Copenhagen conference, Obama tried to send a strong signal that the United States will be a more willing participant in international efforts to reduce carbon emissions (see Figure 16.6).

Global Politics and Democracy

As the second decade of the twenty-first century unfolds, the international profile of the United States is changing across all dimensions of life, both within the United States and around the world. The individual actions of Americans who participate in politics, at home or internationally, add up to a very large global footprint.

The modern world provides an opportunity for Americans, from the average citizen to the president, to participate on a wider level and improve living conditions everywhere. A world with more stable nations that treat their citizens equally and with dignity benefits the United States because it means that fewer military and humanitarian interventions will be required. Nongovernmental organizations, such as charities and foundations, provide an avenue for U.S. citizens personally to take an active role in international life.

Still, the question that opened this chapter lingers: Should the United States take advantage of a more open global society—a gateway—to impart the principles of participation, governmental responsiveness and accountability, and citizen equality to a wider audience? Indications are that the administration of President Barack Obama will encourage these principles in dealing with foreign nations. On a visit to Kenya in 2009, Hillary Clinton, Obama's secretary of state, observed that "true economic progress in Africa will depend on responsible governments that reject corruption, enforce the rule of law and deliver results for their people."[57] This statement reflects a broad set of guidelines that the United States might set for nations that are still developing their political and economic systems and demonstrates a commitment to building lasting relationships with them.[58]

Enforcing such a policy carries the risk of alienating nations that do not wish to be told how to run their governments. However, failing to insist on democratic reforms may leave the United States open to charges of supporting repressive governments that deny their citizens basic human rights. Some level of engagement with such governments might be necessary to keep avenues of communication open. For example, in sending former President Bill Clinton to North Korea to negotiate the release of two American journalists in 2009, the United States was agreeing to meet with a dictator who was trying to develop nuclear weapons in violation of international law. Still, the journalists were released unharmed. Where the line should be drawn in international relations is decided by each presidential administration, and every four years the presidential election is a gateway through which the American voters have the opportunity to render their opinions on whether to reset the boundaries of engagement.

FOCUS QUESTIONS

- What are the opportunities and constraints facing the United States as it seeks to lead the world on political, economic, military, and humanitarian dimensions in the twenty-first century?

- What role should the United States take in preserving or promoting democracy around the world? In promoting worldwide government responsiveness and citizen equality? Does the United States hold itself to equal or higher democratic standards as compared with the rest of the world?

- What are the benefits and costs for the United States in international collective action?

- What should be the aims of U.S. foreign and trade policy in the twenty-first century?

- Does the United States, by its example, serve as a gateway to democracy for citizens of other nations?

GATEWAYS TO LEARNING

Top Ten to Take Away

1. As a global leader in the twenty-first century, the United States has multiple responsibilities and complex constraints imposed by constitutional requirements and by the process of globalization. (pp. 560–61)

2. George Washington set the course of American foreign policy, advising that commercial relations be extended but foreign entanglements be avoided. The United States pursued an isolationist foreign policy until 1941, when it entered World War II. (pp. 561–62)

3. Following the war, the United States led the world's democracies in a contest against Communist nations led by the Soviet Union. (pp. 562–64)

4. By the 1990s the Soviet bloc had collapsed, and the bipolar world became multipolar, with numerous centers of power and regional conflicts. At the same time, the world's economies, societies, and cultures became integrated as never before. (pp. 564–66)

5. Current foreign policy has the goal of protecting strategic interests and a strong commitment to human rights and democratic principles of government. (pp. 567, 570–71)

6. A dilemma for the United States is how to resolve conflicts, promote democracy, and protect its strategic interests. (pp. 567–77)

7. The United States seeks to mediate conflicts and combat world hunger, poverty, and disease through intergovernmental and international organizations. (pp. 571–77, 582–86)

8. U.S. trade policies seek not only commercial advantages but also political and humanitarian goals. (pp. 577–82)

9. On issues of health and natural resources, the United States works through international organizations as well as its own initiatives. (pp. 582–86)

10. In today's globalized world, and particularly through the Internet, the individual actions of American citizens who participate in humanitarian programs or work to change U.S. policy have effects that influence people everywhere. (pp. 577, 586–87)

A full narrative summary of the chapter is on the book's website.

Ten to Test Yourself

1. What was President Wilson's justification for the League of Nations?

2. Describe the impact of the Cold War on international relations.

3. Why was NATO established, and what does it do today?

4. What is the main purpose of the United Nations?

5. What is nuclear proliferation, and what steps has the international community taken to stop it?

6. What is the difference between humanitarian and military intervention, and under what circumstances would one be justified without the other?

7. Identify a nongovernmental organization, and explain the purpose it can serve in the global arena.

8. What role does the World Trade Organization play in regulating international trade?

9. What is the Kyoto Protocol's relationship to international policy on climate change?

10. How does USAID serve as a gateway for U.S. participation in international economic development?

More review questions and answers and chapter quizzes are on the book's website.

Timeline to Keep Things in Order

George Washington warns against foreign entanglements.	The Senate rejects membership in the League of Nations.	The United States enters World War II.	World War II ends; the United States helps create the United Nations; the Cold War begins.	The Communist Soviet bloc collapses, and the Cold War ends.
1796	**1919–20**	**1941**	**1945**	**1989–91**

Terms to Know and Use

Bush Doctrine (p. 570)

Centers for Disease Control and Prevention (CDC) (p. 583)

Cold War (p. 562)

Communism (p. 561)

Comprehensive Nuclear Test Ban Treaty (p. 568)

Copenhagen Accord (p. 586)

covert action (pp. 564, 565)

ethnic cleansing (p. 569)

European Union (EU) (p. 580)

failed states (p. 569)

fair trade (p. 578)

free trade (p. 578)

General Agreement on Tariffs and Trade (GATT) (p. 579)

Geneva Conventions (p. 573)

genocide (p. 569)

globalization (p. 565)

humanitarian intervention (p. 569)

human rights (p. 564)

international governmental organizations (IGOs) (p. 571)

International Monetary Fund (IMF) (p. 582)

isolationism (p. 561)

Kyoto Protocol (p. 584)

League of Nations (p. 561)

Marshall Plan (p. 563)

military interventions (p. 563)

most favored nation status (p. 579)

multilateralism (p. 571)

multipolar (pp. 564, 565)

nongovernmental organizations (NGOs) (p. 577)

nonstate actors (p. 571)

North American Free Trade Agreement (NAFTA) (p. 579)

North Atlantic Treaty Organization (NATO) (p. 563)

Nuclear Non-Proliferation Treaty (p. 568)

nuclear proliferation (p. 564)

Peace Corps (p. 576)

preemptive attack (p. 571)

President's Emergency Plan for AIDS Relief (PEPFAR) (p. 583)

protectionism (p. 578)

rogue states (p. 569)

sovereignty (p. 561)

Truman Doctrine (p. 563)

unilateralism (p. 571)

United Nations (p. 562)

United States Trade Representative (USTR) (p. 578)

U.S. Agency for International Development (USAID) (p. 582)

Warsaw Pact (p. 564)

World Bank (p. 581)

World Health Organization (WHO) (p. 583)

World Trade Organization (WTO) (p. 580)

Use the vocabulary flash cards on the book's website.

Learning That Works

WHAT YOU NEED...

TO KNOW

The background to the current U.S. global position

The checks and balances on foreign and trade policy

The terms of international agreements

What globalization is

What the threats to the United States are

Ways you can participate in global concerns

TO DO

Reflect on the course and purpose of the nation's foreign policy

Understand internal constraints on U.S. actions

Recognize the external constraints on U.S. actions

Decide whether U.S. sovereignty is compromised by international cooperation

Determine what actions you think the nation should take

Become an active citizen of the United States and the world

The Senate ratifies the North American Free Trade Agreement.

The United States joins European allies to end conflict and genocide in the former Yugoslavia.

Terrorist attacks on the United States begin an era of U.S. interventionism.

The United States participates in the UN climate change conference in Copenhagen.

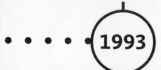
1993

1995

2001

2009

17 JUDGING THE DEMOCRATIC EXPERIMENT

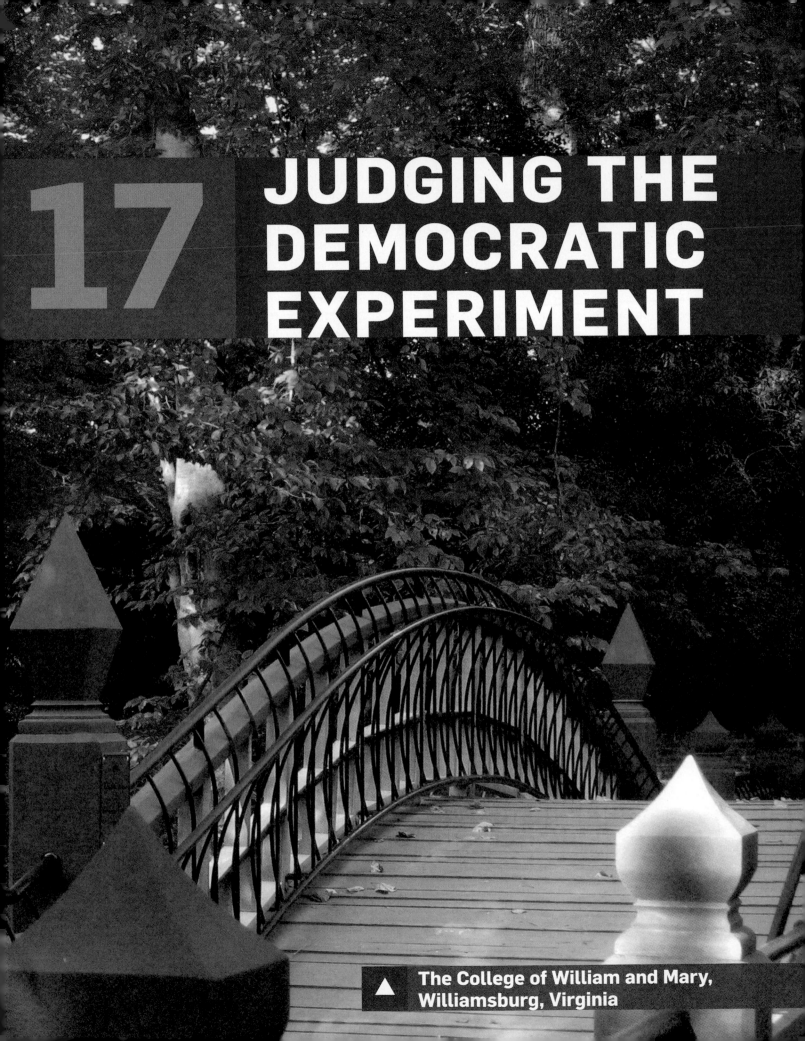

▲ The College of William and Mary,
Williamsburg, Virginia

> *Educate and inform the whole mass of the people. . . .*
> *They are the only sure reliance for the preservation of*
> *our liberty.*

CourseMate

Visit http://www.cengagebrain
.com/shop/ISBN/0618906959 for
interactive tools including:

- Quizzes
- Flashcards
- Videos
- Animated PowerPoint slides,
  Podcast summaries, and more

In 1760 Thomas Jefferson left his boyhood home in the hills of Piedmont Virginia to attend the College of William and Mary in the colonial capital of Williamsburg. There were only six colleges in the American colonies, and Jefferson was fortunate to have the opportunity to pursue his education. From the time he was a young boy, he had been interested in books and reading. At William and Mary, he studied mathematics, physics, ethics, and the law. He described himself as a "hard student," and, according to family tradition, he studied fifteen hours a day, rising at dawn and reading far past midnight. "Determine never to be idle," he later told his daughter. "It is wonderful how much may be done if we are always doing." Although Jefferson did well in college, there was little indication of the greatness that lay ahead. But his family's position in Virginia gave rise to expectations. Jefferson's father, Peter Jefferson, owned a considerable amount of land and, like his grandfather and great-grandfather, was involved in colonial politics. Jefferson's family background suggested that he, too, might be influential at the local level.

Despite his family's wealth, however, Jefferson faced personal hardships. His father died unexpectedly in 1757, making him the head of the family at age 14. Once he reached 21, he would inherit most of his father's wealth and land, but until then he had to pursue his education while assisting his one brother and six sisters. He managed to fulfill his family responsibilities and complete his studies, staying in Williamsburg after graduating from William and Mary in 1762 to study law with one of the colony's leading lawyers. In 1769, at age 26, he won election to the House of Burgesses—the legislative assembly for the colony of Virginia.[1]

Thomas Jefferson ▶

Thomas Jefferson, attributed to Thomas Sully.
U.S. Senate Collection

Thomas Jefferson entered politics at a time of great upheaval in America. Discontent with British rule was rising, and Virginia was a hotbed of opposition. When the House of Burgesses began considering various measures in opposition to British rule, the colonial governor—a representative of the British Crown—dissolved it. This act closed a gateway. With no legitimate way to express grievances, the colonists began to talk of independence.

Independence was a radical step; it meant revolution, and revolution would mean the end of colonial government and the creation of new institutions of government that would, Jefferson and his fellow patriots hoped, be more responsive to the goals and needs of the colonists. Jefferson understood the connection between the people and their government as a social contract; if a government did not serve the people, the people should end it. He speaks of revolution as a right of self-governing men in the Declaration of Independence:

> We hold these truths to be self-evident, that all men are created equal, that they are endowed by their Creator with certain unalienable rights, that among these are life, liberty and the pursuit of happiness; that to secure these rights, governments are instituted among men, deriving their just powers from the consent of the governed; that whenever any form of government becomes destructive of these ends, it is the right of the people to alter or to abolish it, and to institute new government, laying its foundation on such principles, and organizing its powers in such form, as to them shall seem most likely to effect their safety and happiness.

This passage from the Declaration of Independence is famous. Most Americans know the ringing statement on equality with which it begins, and in this course you have studied what it means to have a government that derives its power "from the consent of the governed." Immediately, Jefferson goes on to say that if government is not responsive to the governed, the people have the right "to alter or to abolish it." In other words, it is the people's right—and responsibility—to ensure that the gateways to democracy are always open and available to them in their pursuit of life, liberty, and happiness. Jefferson and the other Founders in effect sought to replace the British Crown and build effective and meaningful gateways whereby the people of the new nation could enjoy a responsive government while retaining their individual freedoms. These themes of the Declaration of Independence—*equality* and *responsiveness*—were present at the creation of the new government. They continue to shape our government as each generation of Americans has sought to make them a reality.

The questions we put before you throughout the book and in this final chapter are these: Does American democracy work? Is the American government really democratic? Does it foster equality and responsiveness?

We are not answering these questions for you; instead, we first ask you to reflect on what you have learned so far. Look at the Review Questions on page 594 to reflect on what you have absorbed. Then continue reading, as we offer some perspectives for you to consider as you develop your own answers to the big questions.

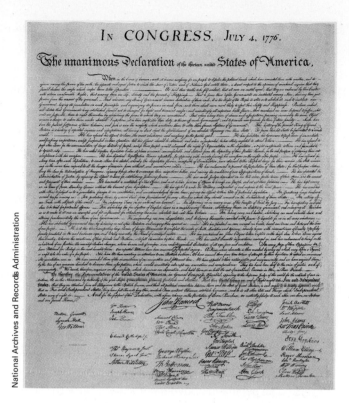

National Archives and Records Administration

© Richard T. Nowitz/Corbis

Writing the Declaration of Independence was one of Thomas Jefferson's proudest accomplishments. The document the Continental Congress approved and signed, dated July 4, is exhibited in the rotunda of the National Archives in Washington, D.C. It is badly faded, but every day people stand in long lines to look at the nation's most cherished symbol of liberty and equality.

We will highlight ways to assess the operation of the government, suggest some standards for making these assessments, and summarize the changes in the gateways to political influence that have occurred in the course of the nation's history. It is your responsibility to draw your own conclusions. It has been a central aim of this book to give you the information and the analytical tools you will need to judge the Founders' democratic experiment for yourself.

What Would the Founders Say?

We begin by bringing the Founders back into the modern conversation about American democracy. If we brought them and the Framers (the people who wrote the Constitution) back to life, what might they think about the American political system today? Did they anticipate the changes that have unfolded? Would they approve or disapprove?

The Founders risked their lives and their fortunes in pursuit of a new and radical form of government that would provide, they hoped, greater freedom and prosperity for Americans. When they signed the Declaration of Independence in 1776, they did not know what the outcome would be. Would the colonists be able to defeat the British? The answer was far from clear. If they did not, the men who signed the Declaration would surely be hanged as traitors to the British Crown. They took courage from believing that their cause was just. The gateways to self-government under the British had closed. Only a new and democratic government could open new gateways so as to preserve individual liberties and rights.

When the Founders and Framers embarked on this risky path, they did not yet have a vision of what the new government or the new nation could become. They had hopes and

Review Questions

In Chapter 1 we posed these questions to help guide your reading of this textbook and your learning in this course. Did you try to answer them? How would you answer them now? We hope the information and perspectives this textbook has provided will help you. For review, turn back to the chapters noted in parentheses. The questions get at the heart of the successes and the challenges of American democracy. As you reflect on them in an informed and meaningful way, and as you discuss them with your classmates and other citizens, you are engaging in a civic discourse that is one of the nation's many gateways to democracy.

1. Does American democracy work? How can you evaluate it? (Chapter 1)

2. How democratic was the constitutional system of 1787? How democratic is the United States today? (Chapter 2)

3. What are the pros and cons of a system in which state governments and a national government share power? (Chapter 3)

4. What should be the balance between liberty and order? How has the U.S. government balanced the two? What liberty versus order questions do citizens face today? (Chapter 4)

5. Why is equality important in a democracy? What role does, or should, government play in ensuring equality? What kinds of equality can, or should, government ensure? What should be the balance between equality and liberty? (Chapter 5)

6. What role does public opinion play in government responsiveness? How responsive should government officials be to public opinion? (Chapter 6)

7. Describe the role of the press, or more generally the media, in a democracy. Are the media today working to make government better or to make governing more difficult? (Chapter 7)

8. What is the role of interest groups in a democracy? How do interest groups serve citizens? Are they working today to make government better or to make governing more difficult? (Chapter 8)

9. What is the role of political parties in the American electorate? In government? Are they working today to make government better or to make governing more difficult? (Chapter 9)

10. Why are elections important? Are they fair? Do political campaigns ensure that voters' ideas and wishes are represented? (Chapter 10)

11. Voting is the most fundamental action a citizen can take. Does voting matter? Is voting fair? What ways other than by voting can citizens influence public policy? (Chapter 11)

12. The Framers thought that Congress would be the most powerful branch of government. Is it? How effective is Congress as a legislative body? What gates limit its effectiveness? (Chapter 12)

13. The presidency grew in power over the last one hundred years. Is it too powerful now? What are the checks on presidential power? What are the necessities for presidential power? (Chapter 13)

14. The bureaucracy is often under attack for inefficiency and unresponsiveness. Describe the purpose of the bureaucracy. Which parts of it function well? Which do not? Why? (Chapter 14)

15. The pediment above the main entrance to the Supreme Court proclaims "Equal Justice under Law." What does that mean? How do the courts ensure equality? Is the judiciary responsive? (Chapter 15)

16. How has the U.S. role in the world changed in your lifetime? What are the prospects for global partnerships? For global conflict? (Chapter 16)

17. How do you judge the American democratic experiment? (Chapter 17)

18. What are the dangers to democratic government in the twenty-first century?

19. Why do you think the United States has survived as a representative democracy for more than two centuries? What has been the experience of other democracies?

20. How easy or hard is it to influence public policy? What types of people have had the greatest influence—politicians, corporate executives, military leaders, grassroots organizers?

21. How do cultural similarity and diversity work to help or impede the operations of American democracy?

22. How can you get yourself and your opinions represented in government?

23. How can you make government more responsive and responsible to its citizens?

24. How equal are America's citizens? How equal should they be? What kinds of opportunities do American citizens have? Are the outcomes equitable?

25. What can you do, as an active citizen, to make American democracy better?

FIGURE 17.1 Amendments That Opened Gateways to Participation.

Thirteenth (1865): Prohibits slavery in the United States

Fourteenth (1868): Makes all persons born in the United States citizens of the United States, and prohibits states from denying persons within its jurisdiction the privileges or immunities of citizens, the due process of law, or equal protection of the laws; apportionment by whole persons

Fifteenth (1870): Prohibits states from denying the right to vote on account of race

Seventeenth (1913): Gives the people (instead of state legislatures) the right to choose U.S. senators directly

Nineteenth (1920): Guarantees women the right to vote

Twenty-Third (1961): Grants residents of the District of Columbia Electoral College votes

Twenty-Fourth (1964): Prohibits poll taxes

Twenty-Sixth (1971): Guarantees 18-year-olds the right to vote

dreams, but it would be fair to say that few envisioned the United States as a major player on the world stage. They did not even know if the governmental system they instituted would work. Their first attempt, under the Articles of Confederation, did not go very well. Many worried that their second effort, under the Constitution of 1787, might not work either.

Yet today, after more than 220 years, the Constitution and the government it established are largely intact. There are still three branches of government. Though the power of each has expanded enormously, they still check and balance each other, as the Framers had hoped they would. There have been just twenty-seven amendments to the Constitution, most of which have expanded liberties, such as freedom of speech, or opened gateways to participation—by African Americans (the Thirteenth, Fourteenth, and Fifteenth Amendments), by women (the Nineteenth Amendment), by poor people (the Twenty-Fourth Amendment), and by young adults (the Twenty-Sixth Amendment) (see Figure 17.1). The Seventeenth Amendment further enhanced democracy by providing for the direct election of senators. Arguably, the only amendment to restrict rights was the Eighteenth Amendment, which prohibited the manufacture, sale, and transportation of alcohol within the United States, but the Twenty-First Amendment repealed it.

With the Constitution and its amendments, the nation has not only survived but has prospered. The success of the United States would surely be welcome news to any of the Founders and Framers. But has the nation met their expectations? As we address this question, it is important to point out that these early leaders were not of one mind. They were talented individuals with a range of perspectives about what constituted good government. A useful way to organize their many perspectives is to consider again two perspectives that first battled during the administration of George Washington: the Jeffersonian view and the Hamiltonian view.

The Jeffersonian view had the following major tenets:

1. Jeffersonians believed in the fundamental equality of all people and held that the American Revolution set into motion forces that would give rise to greater equality. Even though the rights of African Americans and women were not recognized in the 1787 Constitution, the system was set up to be flexible enough to incorporate future generations of citizens into political life.

2. They worried that any form of government could be corrupted and feared a strong executive in particular.

3. They wanted the states, not the federal government, to have power in the belief that citizens could keep better watch over the government that was closest to them.

4. They assumed that the United States would be an agrarian nation not involved in world affairs and argued that the closer the people were to their own land, the stronger would be their interest in preserving their political and social way of life.

5. They regarded expanding gateways of influence as a good thing, confident that the people would check the power of government and ensure individual liberty.

The Hamiltonian view had the following major tenets:

1. Hamiltonians preferred having elites govern the nation, especially at its inception, and they took some degree of inequality as inevitable because some people have more ability and motivation than others.

2. They believed that a successful government demanded a strong executive.

3. They viewed a strong national government as a way to unify the many competing interests of the thirteen former colonies.

4. They hoped that the United States would become both more industrial and a military power that would play a major role in international affairs.

5. They regarded restrictions on the gateways to influence as a good thing because educated and experienced elites would be better at governing than common citizens.

These two schools of thought anticipated some of the many changes that have unfolded over more than 230 years. The Jeffersonians correctly recognized that the American Revolution would give rise to greater demands for equality. In terms of political equality, those demands have been largely met, as all citizens over age 18 (except some convicted felons) now have a gateway to political power through the ballot box. In terms of economic equality, the Hamiltonian assumption that there would always be inequality among citizens, even in a democracy, has also proven true, given the nation's income disparities.[2]

The Jeffersonian assumption that the United States would remain an agrarian nation with limited involvement in world affairs has proved incorrect. Although farming expanded with the nation's boundaries, the Hamiltonians correctly foresaw that the United States would be an industrial power with significant influence in world affairs. Yet, that both agriculture and industry have flourished is evidence of just how strongly these two views reflected the fundamentals of the U.S. economy from the beginning.

Some of the other differences in the two schools of thought reflect competing political values. The Jeffersonians wanted strong states, a limited national government, and a weak chief executive. The Hamiltonians held no loyalty to states and viewed the national government, under a strong leader, as best able to bring prosperity and military power. Commerce rather than agriculture would assure the continuity and stability in government essential for success. It is clear, again, that the Hamiltonian view more closely resembles the modern United States, but there is still a deep strain among the American people that favors the Jeffersonian ideal of limited government and an isolationist international posture.

All in all, the Hamiltonians had a clearer understanding of America's future than the Jeffersonians, and they probably would be happier with the outcome. Even so, the Jeffersonian faith in equality and in the capabilities of the people has been vindicated. Jefferson himself would be stunned by the size of twenty-first-century government, the trappings of the American presidency, and the military might of the nation. But he would be pleased to see the expansion of fundamental rights and the increase in the number of gateways to influence. Hamilton would be worried by the amount of power held by average people. Perhaps today's wide access to education would ease his concerns, but Jefferson was, by nature, more optimistic about the ability of citizens to govern themselves.

Evaluating the American Political System

The views of the Founders and Framers provide some context for judging the American political system, but the central question is whether most Americans are satisfied with the core institutions of government. Individuals may be unhappy with particular leaders, such as Barack Obama or George W. Bush, but these opinions reflect partisan assessments, not assessments of the overall political system. If you ask Americans whether they are proud of the country, or patriotic, there is near consensus. In January 2009 over 95 percent of the public claimed to be proud to be an American, with just 1 percent claiming they are "not at all" proud.[3] Pollsters do not even ask people if they favor replacing the Constitution. Why bother? Almost no one holds such an opinion. It is not a subject for discussion, except on extreme blogs that provide an outlet, even a gateway, for views far outside the mainstream of America.

How you judge American politics depends in large part on where you sit. If you are financially well off, you are likely to see the merits of the American system. But what if you are poor? Homeless? Out of work? Context and perspective are critical. To make this point, we offer an analogy.

Nearly 100 million Americans watch the Super Bowl each year. It is the most popular event in sports. Let's assume we assign two reporters to cover the game for Moldavia—a country that has little familiarity with American football. One reporter roams the sidelines, looking at the game at ground level along the line of scrimmage. The other reporter flies overhead in a blimp, assigned to provide aerial shots of the game. The task of each journalist is to report on the game. They will produce very different stories.

The reporter in the blimp might write about the size of the crowd, the back and forth on the field between the two teams, and perhaps the occasional stoppage of play. The game's grace and strategy are likely to be central to the story. By stark contrast, the reporter on the sidelines will surely discuss the violence of the game, the size of the players, their speed, the yelling between the teams. It will be a story about the bruising, physical battle between the combatants on the field.

Each reporter offers a valuable perspective on the game, but the perspectives are different. Whether you see professional football as a violent sport or as a game with strategy and grace depends very much on where you sit. Neither perspective is wrong, although they share very few of the same conclusions.

Jim Watson/AFP/Getty Images

Americans, whether natural-born citizens or naturalized, are a patriotic people. Those taking the oath of citizenship often carry small American flags. This 2006 naturalization ceremony took place at Mount Vernon, George Washington's home in Virginia.

The same is true for American politics; your interpretation will be shaped by where you sit. Consider the American Recovery and Reinvestment Act of 2009. This stimulus bill authorized $787 billion of spending and tax cuts to revitalize the sagging economy in 2009. If you sit in the committee rooms and on the floor of Congress as the legislation is drafted, your story would be about contest and compromise—the hallmark of legislative policy making in the American political system. Legislators try to get advantages for their constituents that will help them get reelected. At the same time, there are cross-pressures on the legislative process, from competition among staffers, to the influence of lobbyists representing competing interests, to the urgency for quick action expressed by the president. A close-up view of this process would not be pretty and would not necessarily build faith in the political system. There is an old saying: "Two things that shouldn't be observed: the sausage being made and a bill becoming law." From an up-close and personal look at the political process, it is not easy to see how the views of ordinary citizens are represented; the process does not seem to be coherent, organized, or even democratic.

With a bit more distance, one can see that the compromises bring progress, and the process looks more democratic. When the political parties disagree on how best to write a bill, it is in large part because they are reflecting the concerns of their members, the rank-and-file voters. Citizens disagree fundamentally on whether there should be more tax cuts or more federal spending, and Congress typically reflects those concerns. On top of that, the nation's separation of powers system gives the president an important say in the content of legislation. In early 2009 the Democratic majorities in each house along with a Democratic president made passage of the stimulus bill possible. The Democrats had just won the 2008 elections in which the public was calling for change. The Democrats were trying to institute that change. So, from this vantage point, Congress and the president were striving to be responsive to the wishes of the public. It may not be democratic in the sense that the people directly rule (see Chapter 1, Gateways to American Democracy), but it looks more democratic than what was reported from the political trenches in Congress.

What is clear is that whether we live in times of unified or divided party government, policy making forges on, and the members of the nation's elected institutions are forced to tackle the pressing problems of the moment, from the economy, to terrorism, to health care. No elected politician can long escape responsibility for dealing with these problems, and that is where we see the fundamental mechanism of democratic accountability emerge.

The real lessons here are twofold. First, we always need to remember that the accuracy of any interpretation of the American political process depends on where you sit. So if there is disagreement about an interpretation, it is owing, in part, to differences in perspective. Second, there is no single or correct interpretation of the American political system. So if you disagree with someone about the policy outcomes that the American system produces, look to see if one of you sits on the sidelines while the other rides in the blimp. If so, then you may be able to better understand each other. It is not that you will agree about things, but at least you will see where the other person is coming from.

But there is more than just perspective. The standards you bring to bear on your judgment of the American system matter a great deal. We turn to them next.

Defining Standards of Evaluation

When deciding whether the United States is democratic or not, we must, as this book's first chapter makes clear, grapple with the very definition of *democracy*, and the definition itself is contested. For some, a democracy is simply majority rule. As we wrote in Chapter 1, "In a democracy, the citizens hold political authority, and they develop the means to govern themselves. In practice, that means rule by the majority." But not all people subscribe to this definition because if the majority can make all the decisions, it can also block minority rights. Thus democracy also has to ensure liberty for all citizens, and it does so through the rule of law: "all people are equal before the law, all are subject to the law, and no one is above it," as we explained in Chapter 1. In some sense, the Constitution sought to balance these competing views by giving the majority a chance to have its say while ensuring that the minority, too, could advance its interests.

If one adopts the "pure" definition that democracy is "rule by the people," it is difficult to conclude that America is democratic. There are many gateways in the American constitutional system, but there are gates, too. The Electoral College is one example of a gate where majority rule can be thwarted, as it was in the 2000 presidential election in which the candidate with the most votes, Albert Gore Jr., lost the election. The U.S. Senate, where the 550,000 citizens of Wyoming have the same number of senators as the 24.8 million citizens of Texas, is another example.[4] These two examples underscore the facts that the American system is complicated and that it does not have rules consistent with a direct democracy. That might lead you to question the fairness of the American government's responsiveness to its citizens and even the equality of its citizens, given their differing opportunities for influence.

Hill Street Studios/Blend Images

Students in America are free to discuss and evaluate the U.S. government. Active citizenship requires engagement, and engagement requires knowledge. Such opportunities for discourse and learning in college are not available in many parts of the world.

The standard of equality is indeed contested. If we focus on equality of outcome, there is reason to think that America comes up short. The nation tolerates huge income inequalities: Some people have multiple homes and private jets; others have no place to sleep and not enough to eat. If we focus on equality of opportunity, the United States fares better. One reason many people celebrated President Obama's election, even if they did not vote for him, was that it validated the idea of equal opportunity. The nation still faces problems with racial, ethnic, and religious discrimination (to name only a few). Even so, Americans do enjoy equality in civil liberties (Chapter 4, Civil Liberties), including rights such as freedom of expression, of association, of religion, and of speech. These are not absolutes, but the United States fares well by these measures. Compared to the rest of the world on these matters of freedom, it is in the very top tier.[5]

The conversation about whether the United States is democratic or not is a good thing in and of itself. The chance to discuss and evaluate the nation openly underscores the freedom Americans have. Moreover, it is a powerful reminder that when evaluating whether a political system is democratic, standards of judgment are not fixed. They are dynamic, and they evolve over time. The Founders, for example, were revolutionary for their day, asserting that "all men are created equal" and daring to create a government based on "the consent of the governed" at a time when all other nations were monarchies or authoritarian regimes. Democracy was not yet a credible form of government. Yet, by today's standards the Founders can be thought of as racist, sexist, and antidemocratic. They allowed slavery to continue. They made no provision for the rights of women. Under the 1787 Constitution, the people directly elected only members of the House of Representatives.

It is important to understand that there will always be a gap between the people's ideals and the institutional response. When Americans reform their institutions to bring them closer to their ideals, there is progress. But ideals are not static; they are constantly reshaped. New standards for equality evolve all the time. In the early 1900s the debate was about women's right to vote, and there was little discussion about the rights of homosexuals. Today, the right of homosexuals to marry is debated. Sometimes technology forces new debates. Right-to-die issues are current today because people live longer and there are technological ways to keep people alive that were not possible in the nineteenth century.

The gap between ideals and institutions, or ideals and the law, may be frustrating for some, but it is the constant motivator of reform. In this way, the gap fuels progress. Life does not stand still, and people's concerns change over time. It is for these reasons that gateways are so important. Access to government means that citizens have a chance to push institutions in new directions. The process is often messy, but in the course of the nation's history there has been a slow and steady march toward more rights and more opportunities for all Americans.

In short, you can be pessimistic or optimistic about the future of the American political system. We encourage you to make use of the information we have provided to make your own judgment. As authors of this textbook, we do not have a stake in the direction you take or the conclusion you reach, so long as you reach one. The nation as a whole benefits when more people weigh in. The more people participate, the better the policy outcomes. Chances for equality increase, and government's responsiveness is more likely.

Gates and Gateways in American Politics

From the vantage point of that blimp, the gateways to American democracy have opened wider over the last 230 years. For example:

- Citizens, not state legislatures, now vote for the president and U.S. senators.
- Initiatives and referenda allow many citizens a direct say in policy making in the states.
- Equal suffrage has been extended to all Americans.

- New media have opened new avenues of communication between citizens and elected leaders.
- Scientific polling has deepened the understanding of public opinion.
- Increased educational opportunities have made it possible for more citizens to be better informed about government and policy debates.

Have any new gates arisen? Are there new hurdles that block access to the American political system? The answers are less clear. Some changes in American politics have proved to be both gateways and gates, depending on where one sits.

Consider the size of the federal government. The vast bureaucracy in Washington serves as a gateway for people to secure responsiveness on some matters of interest to them. But sheer size can impede efficiency. Regulations and red tape can inhibit fast action. But whenever a major disaster occurs, such as 9/11 or Hurricane Katrina or the BP oil spill in the Gulf of Mexico, people immediately turn to the government for relief.

The population of the country has also increased, and here again size may prove to be a gate. With the 2000 census, each congressional district served roughly 650,000 people, and that figure will likely increase to over 700,000 after the 2010 census. In 1789 the typical congressional district held around 30,000 people. That means that today a member of the House represents more than twenty times as many people as did representatives in the First Congress. To deal with this population increase, the size of the congressional staff has grown. Additional staff should make it possible for House members to continue to be responsive to the needs of their constituents, but it also creates a gate between constituents and their member of Congress or senator. In the nineteenth century each senator had just one clerk and much more time to meet voters in his home state because Congress was less frequently in session. Perhaps today's longer sessions make it possible for members to be responsive to constituents, or perhaps the longer sessions keep members away from their constituents and allow gates to develop.

Technology has, of course, advanced beyond anything the Founders could have imagined. E-mail, blogs, and cell phones can serve as gateways for increased participation. But what is the nature of that participation? Technology often reduces direct human interaction. If people do not have to gather in the same room to communicate, do the bonds of civic association decrease? Can the new modes of communication fuel disassociation and apathy? Here is another recent development that can be both a gateway and a gate.

The growth of interest groups has the same dual outcome. Interest groups increase the number of voices in the political system, but they can also create inequality among those new voices. If the voices of the less powerful cannot be heard as well as the voices of those with more power and money, what are the consequences for equality? Moreover, interest groups interpose themselves between elected officials and citizens, serving as gates against direct citizen influence even as they operate as gateways. Again, the assessment of the impact of interest groups depends on one's vantage point. The contradictory consequences of all reforms and changes in the American political system need to be considered in any evaluation of it.

The case for an overall increase in the number of gateways to American democracy is clear. There are many new gateways—that is a certainty. Whether there are also new gates is less clear, but any judgment of the American democratic experiment will have to take the possibility into account.

Gateway to the Future

We have sought to make this textbook a complete, fair, and nonpartisan account of American politics, relying on the most recent scholarship and thinking. In this era of polarized political parties, it is especially important not to interject partisanship into the study of American government. Both parties have important things to say about policy and the best way to run the U.S. government. If only one party were always right, the "wrong" party would lose elections, never gain power, and eventually cease to exist. Further, the hold that parties have on power is tenuous because no one side has all the answers. The in-party makes mistakes, and the out-party rebounds. The Democrats may control the Senate and the presidency now, but that will not last forever. In fact, the chances are good that the Republicans will be back in the White House by 2017. The country tends to change ruling parties every eight years.[6]

It is the competition between candidates and parties that is so important to the process. The struggle for power provides the incentive to put forward and enact legislation that will respond to the needs and interests of Americans and improve their lives. This struggle is what allows the nation to move toward its goals of greater equality and responsiveness. That struggle may be ugly at times, but the process is essential for progress. In general, the more engaged citizens are in this process, the better the outcomes.

As we bring this book to a close, we want to emphasize that in America each individual is important and full of potential. Although the American political system has gates, it has even more gateways. But gateways have little value unless someone travels through them. We started each chapter with a story about an individual who took advantage of a gateway to have an impact on American politics. Having read this book, you now know a good deal about the gates and gateways to participation. Think of this information as a kind of GPS that will allow you to navigate the American political system. Take advantage of the gateways.

Not all of you will be able to recast an election, as S. R. Sidarth did, or help end discrimation, as Diane Nash did, or create an influential blog, as Kos did, or influence a Supreme Court ruling, as Jennifer Gratz did, or get elected to Congress, as Nydia Velázquez and Aaron Schock did. But every time one person gets involved, the nation is better off. Participation matters. America is more equal and more responsive than it was in the days of the Founders because individual citizens made it so. Only with citizen involvement can democracies endure and thrive. Much work remains. But it is the acts of everyday citizens that have helped America reach the promise set forth in the Declaration of Independence that all have a right to "life, liberty, and the pursuit of happiness." We urge you to live that promise by moving forward through the gateways to American democracy.

THE DECLARATION OF INDEPENDENCE

In Congress, July 4, 1776

The Unanimous Declaration of the Thirteen United States of America

When, in the course of human events, it becomes necessary for one people to dissolve the political bands which have connected them with another, and to assume, among the powers of the earth, the separate and equal station to which the laws of nature and of nature's God entitle them, a decent respect to the opinions of mankind requires that they should declare the causes which impel them to the separation.

We hold these truths to be self-evident: That all men are created equal; that they are endowed by their Creator with certain unalienable rights; that among these are life, liberty, and the pursuit of happiness; that, to secure these rights, governments are instituted among men, deriving their just powers from the consent of the governed; that whenever any form of government becomes destructive of these ends, it is the right of the people to alter or to abolish it, and to institute new government, laying its foundation on such principles, and organizing its powers in such form, as to them shall seem most likely to effect their safety and happiness. Prudence, indeed, will dictate that governments long established should not be changed for light and transient causes; and accordingly all experience hath shown that mankind are more disposed to suffer, while evils are sufferable, than to right themselves by abolishing the forms to which they are accustomed. But when a long train of abuses and usurpations, pursuing invariably the same object, evinces a design to reduce them under absolute despotism, it is their right, it is their duty, to throw off such government, and to provide new guards for their future security. Such has been the patient sufferance of these colonies; and such is now the necessity which constrains them to alter their former systems of government. The history of the present King of Great Britain is a history of repeated injuries and usurpations, all having in direct object the establishment of an absolute tyranny over these states. To prove this, let facts be submitted to a candid world.

He has refused to assent to laws, the most wholesome and necessary for the public good.

He has forbidden his governors to pass laws of immediate and pressing importance, unless suspended in their operation till his assent should be obtained; and, when so suspended, he has utterly neglected to attend to them.

He has refused to pass other laws for the accommodation of large districts of people, unless those people would relinquish the right of representation in the legislature, a right inestimable to them, and formidable to tyrants only.

He has called together legislative bodies at places unusual, uncomfortable, and distant from the depository of their public records, for the sole purpose of fatiguing them into compliance with his measures.

He has dissolved representative houses repeatedly, for opposing, with manly firmness, his invasions on the rights of the people.

He has refused for a long time, after such dissolutions, to cause others to be elected; whereby the legislative powers, incapable of annihilation, have returned to the people at large for their exercise; the state remaining, in the mean time, exposed to all dangers of invasions from without and convulsions within.

He has endeavored to prevent the population of these states; for that purpose obstructing the laws for naturalization of foreigners; refusing to pass others to encourage their migration hither, and raising the conditions of new appropriations of lands.

He has obstructed the administration of justice, by refusing his assent to laws for establishing judiciary powers.

He has made judges dependent on his will alone, for the tenure of their offices, and the amount and payment of their salaries.

He has erected a multitude of new offices, and sent hither swarms of officers to harass our people and eat out their substance.

He has kept among us, in times of peace, standing armies, without the consent of our legislatures.

He has affected to render the military independent of, and superior to, the civil power.

He has combined with others to subject us to a jurisdiction foreign to our constitution, and unacknowledged by our laws, giving his assent to their acts of pretended legislation:

For quartering large bodies of armed troops among us:

For protecting them, by a mock trial, from punishment for any murders which they should commit on the inhabitants of these states;

For cutting off our trade with all parts of the world;

For imposing taxes on us without our consent;

For depriving us, in many cases, of the benefits of trial by jury;

For transporting us beyond seas, to be tried for pretended offenses;

For abolishing the free system of English laws in a neighboring province, establishing therein an arbitrary government, and enlarging its boundaries, so as to render it at once an example and fit instrument for introducing the same absolute rule into these colonies;

For taking away our charters, abolishing our more valuable laws, and altering fundamentally the forms of our governments;

For suspending our own legislatures, and declaring themselves invested with power to legislate for us in all cases whatsoever.

He has abdicated government here, by declaring us out of his protection and waging war against us.

He has plundered our seas, ravaged our coasts, burned our towns, and destroyed the lives of our people.

He is at this time transporting large armies of foreign mercenaries to complete the works of death, desolation, and tyranny already begun with circumstances of cruelty and perfidy scarcely paralleled in the most barbarous ages, and totally unworthy the head of a civilized nation.

He has constrained our fellow-citizens, taken captive on the high seas, to bear arms against their country, to become the executioners of their friends and brethren, or to fall themselves by their hands.

He has excited domestic insurrections among us, and has endeavored to bring on the inhabitants of our frontiers the merciless Indian savages, whose known rule of warfare is an undistinguished destruction of all ages, sexes, and conditions.

In every stage of these oppressions we have petitioned for redress in the most humble terms; our repeated petitions have been answered only by repeated injury. A prince, whose character is thus marked by every act which may define a tyrant, is unfit to be the ruler of a free people.

Nor have we been wanting in our attentions to our British brethren. We have warned them, from time to time, of attempts by their legislature to extend an unwarrantable jurisdiction over us. We have reminded them of the circumstances of our emigration and settlement here. We have appealed to their native justice and magnanimity; and we have conjured them, by the ties of our common kindred, to disavow these usurpations, which would inevitably interrupt our connections and correspondence. They, too, have been deaf to the voice of justice and of consanguinity. We must, therefore, acquiesce in the necessity which denounces our separation, and hold them, as we hold the rest of mankind, enemies in war, in peace friends.

We, therefore, the representatives of the United States of America, in General Congress assembled, appealing to the Supreme Judge of the world for the rectitude of our intentions, do, in the name and by the authority of the good people of these colonies, solemnly publish and declare, that these United Colonies are, and of right ought to be, FREE AND INDEPENDENT STATES; that they are absolved from all allegiance to the British crown, and that all political connection between them and the state of Great Britain is, and ought to be, totally dissolved; and that, as free and independent states, they have full power to levy war, conclude peace, contract alliances, establish commerce, and do all other acts and things which independent states may of right do. And for the support of this declaration, with a firm reliance on the protection of Divine Providence, we mutually pledge to each other our lives, our fortunes, and our sacred honor.

John Hancock, *President and delegate from Massachusetts*

Georgia
  Button Gwinnett
  Lyman Hall
  George Walton

North Carolina
  William Hooper
  Joseph Hewes
  John Penn

South Carolina
  Edward Rutledge
  Thomas Heyward Jr.
  Thomas Lynch Jr.
  Arthur Middleton

Maryland
  Samuel Chase
  William Paca
  Thomas Stone
  Charles Carroll of Carrollton

Virginia
  George Wythe
  RIchard Henry Lee
  Thomas Jefferson
  Benjamin Harrison
  Thomas Nelson Jr.
  Francis Lightfoot Lee
  Carter Braxton

Pennsylvania
  Robert Morris
  Benjamin Rush
  Benjamin Franklin
  John Morton
  George Clymer
  James Smith
  George Taylor

James Wilson
George Ross

Delaware
  Caesar Rodney
  George Read
  Thomas McKean

New York
  William Floyd
  Philip Livingston
  Francis Lewis
  Lewis Morris

New Jersey
  Richard Stockton
  John Witherspoon
  Francis Hopkinson
  John Hart
  Abraham Clark

New Hampshire
  Josiah Bartlett
  William Whipple
  Matthew Thornton

Massachusetts
  Samuel Adams
  John Adams
  Robert Treat Paine
  Elbridge Gerry

Rhode Island
  Stephen Hopkins
  William Ellery

Connecticut
  Roger Sherman
  Samuel Huntington
  William Williams
  Oliver Wolcott

THE CONSTITUTION
OF THE UNITED STATES

We the People of the United States, in Order to form a more perfect Union, establish Justice, insure domestic Tranquility, provide for the common defence, promote the general Welfare, and secure the Blessings of Liberty to ourselves and our Posterity, do ordain and establish this Constitution for the United States of America.

Article I.

Section 1. All legislative Powers herein granted shall be vested in a Congress of the United States, which shall consist of a Senate and House of Representatives.

Section 2. The House of Representatives shall be composed of Members chosen every second Year by the People of the several States, and the Electors in each State shall have the Qualifications requisite for Electors of the most numerous Branch of the State Legislature.

No Person shall be a Representative who shall not have attained to the age of twenty five Years, and been seven Years a Citizen of the United States, and who shall not, when elected, be an Inhabitant of that State in which he shall be chosen.

Changed by the Fourteenth Amendment, Section 2.

Representatives and direct Taxes shall be apportioned among the several States which may be included within this Union, according to their respective Numbers, which shall be determined by adding to the whole Number of free Persons, including those bound to Service for a Term of Years, and excluding Indians not taxed, three fifths of all other Persons. The actual Enumeration shall be made within three Years after the first Meeting of the Congress of the United States, and within every subsequent Term of ten Years, in such Manner as they shall by Law direct. The Number of Representatives shall not exceed one for every thirty Thousand, but each State shall have at Least one Representative; and until such enumeration shall be made, the State of New Hampshire shall be entitled to chuse three, Massachusetts eight, Rhode-Island and Providence Plantations one, Connecticut five, New-York six, New Jersey four, Pennsylvania eight, Delaware one, Maryland six, Virginia ten, North Carolina five, South Carolina five, and Georgia three.

When vacancies happen in the Representation from any State, the Executive Authority thereof shall issue Writs of Election to fill such Vacancies.

The House of Representatives shall chuse their Speaker and other Officers; and shall have the sole Power of Impeachment.

Section 3. The Senate of the United States shall be composed of two Senators from each State, chosen by the Legislature thereof, for six Years; and each Senator shall have one Vote.

Changed by the Seventeenth Amendment

Immediately after they shall be assembled in Consequence of the first Election, they shall be divided as equally as may be into three Classes. The Seats of the Senators of the first class shall be vacated at the Expiration of the second Year, of the second Class at the Expiration of the fourth Year, and of the third Class at the Expiration of the sixth Year, so that one third may be chosen every second Year; and if Vacancies happen by Resignation, or otherwise, during the Recess of the Legislature of any State, the Executive thereof may make temporary Appointments until the next Meeting of the Legislature, which shall then fill such Vacancies.

Changed by the Seventeenth Amendment.

No Person shall be a Senator who shall not have attained to the Age of thirty Years, and been nine Years a Citizen of the United States, and who shall not, when elected, be an Inhabitant of that State for which he shall be chosen.

The Vice President of the United States shall be President of the Senate, but shall have no Vote, unless they be equally divided.

The Senate shall chuse their other Officers, and also a President pro tempore, in the Absence of the Vice President, or when he shall exercise the Office of President of the United States.

The Senate shall have the sole Power to try all Impeachments. When sitting for that Purpose, they shall be on Oath or Affirmation. When the President of the United States is tried the Chief Justice shall preside: And no Person shall be convicted without the Concurrence of two thirds of the Members present.

Judgment in Cases of Impeachment shall not exceed further than to removal from Office, and disqualification to hold and enjoy any Office of honor, Trust or Profit under the United States: but the Party convicted shall nevertheless be liable and subject to Indictment, Trial, Judgment and Punishment, according to Law.

Section 4. The Times, Places and Manner of holding Elections for Senators and Representatives, shall be prescribed in each State by the Legislature thereof; but the Congress may at any time by Law make or alter such Regulations, except as to the Places of chusing Senators.

The Congress shall assemble at least once in every Year, and such Meeting shall be on the first Monday in December, unless they shall by Law appoint a different Day.

Changed by the Twentieth Amendment, Section 2.

Section 5. Each House shall be the Judge of the Elections, Returns and Qualifications of its own Members, and a Majority of each shall constitute a Quorum to do Business; but a smaller number may adjourn from day to day, and may be authorized to compel the Attendance of absent Members, in such Manner, and under such Penalties as each House may provide.

Each House may determine the Rules of its Proceedings, punish its Members for disorderly Behaviour, and, with the Concurrence of two thirds, expel a Member.

Each House shall keep a Journal of its Proceedings, and from time to time publish the same, excepting such Parts as may in their Judgment require Secrecy; and the Yeas and Nays of the Members of either House on any question shall, at the Desire of one fifth of those Present, be entered on the Journal.

Neither House, during the Session of Congress, shall, without the Consent of the other, adjourn for more than three days, nor to any other Place than that in which the two Houses shall be sitting.

Section 6. The Senators and Representatives shall receive a Compensation for their Services, to be ascertained by Law, and paid out of the Treasury of the United States. They shall in all Cases, except Treason, Felony and Breach of the Peace, be privileged from Arrest during their Attendance at the Session of their respective Houses, and in going to and returning from the same; and for any Speech or Debate in either House, they shall not be questioned in any other Place.

Amplified by the Twenty-Seventh Amendment.

No Senator or Representative shall, during the Time for which he was elected, be appointed to any civil Office under the Authority of the United States, which shall have been created, or the Emoluments whereof shall have been encreased during such time; and no Person holding any Office under the United States, shall be a Member of either House during his Continuance in Office.

Section 7.   All Bills for raising Revenue shall originate in the House of Representatives; but the Senate may propose or concur with Amendments as on other Bills.

Every Bill which shall have passed the House of Representatives and the Senate, shall, before it become a Law, be presented to the President of the United States; If he approve he shall assign it, but if not he shall return it, with his Objections to that House in which it shall have originated, who shall enter the Objections at large on their Journal, and proceed to reconsider it. If after such Reconsideration two thirds of that House shall agree to pass the Bill, it shall be sent, together with the Objections, to the other House, by which it shall likewise be reconsidered, and if approved by two thirds of that House, it shall become a Law. But in all such Cases the Votes of both Houses shall be determined by yeas and Nays, and the Names of the Persons voting for and against the Bill shall be entered on the Journal of each House respectively. If any Bill shall not be returned by the President within ten Days (Sundays excepted) after it shall have been presented to him, the Same shall be a Law, in like Manner, as if he had signed it, unless the Congress by their Adjournment prevent its Return, in which Case it shall not be a Law.

Every Order, Resolution, or Vote to which the Concurrence of the Senate and House of Representatives may be necessary (except on a question of Adjournment) shall be presented to the President of the United States; and before the Same shall take Effect, shall be approved by him, or being disapproved by him, shall be repassed by two thirds of the Senate and House of Representatives, according to the Rules and Limitations prescribed in the Case of a Bill.

Section 8.   The Congress shall have Power To lay and Collect Taxes, Duties, Imposts and Excises, to pay the Debts and provide for the common Defence and general Welfare of the United States; but all Duties, Imposts and Excises shall be uniform throughout the United States.

To borrow Money on the credit of the United States;

To regulate Commerce with foreign Nations, and among the several States, and with the Indian Tribes;

To establish an uniform Rule of Naturalization, and uniform Laws on the subject of Bankruptcies throughout the United States;

To coin Money, regulate the Value thereof, and of foreign Coin, and fix the Standard of Weights and Measures;

To provide for the Punishment of counterfeiting the Securities and current Coin of the United States;

To establish Post Offices and post Roads;

To promote the Progress of Science and useful Arts, by securing for limited Times to Authors and Inventors the exclusive Right to their respective Writings and Discoveries;

To constitute Tribunals inferior to the Supreme Court;

To define and punish Piracies and Felonies committed on the high Seas, and Offences against the Law of Nations;

General welfare clause gives Congress the power to tax to provide for the general welfare.

Commerce clause gives Congress the power to regulate commerce with foreign nations, with Indian tribes, and among the various states.

To declare War, grant Letters of Marque and Reprisal, and make Rules concerning Captures on Land and Water;

To raise and support Armies, but no Appropriation of Money to that Use shall be for a longer Term than two Years;

To provide and maintain a Navy;

To make Rules for the Government and Regulation of the land and naval Forces;

To provide for calling forth the Militia to execute the Laws of the Union, suppress Insurrections and repel Invasions;

To provide for organizing, arming, and disciplining, the Militia, and for governing such Part of them as may be employed in the Service of the United States, reserving to the States respectively, the Appointment of the Officers, and the Authority of training the Militia according to the discipline prescribed by Congress;

To exercise exclusive Legislation in all Cases whatsoever, over such District (not exceeding ten Miles square) as may, by Cession of Particular States, and the Acceptance of Congress, become the Seat of the Government of the United States, and to exercise like Authority over all Places purchased by the Consent of the Legislature of the State in which the Same shall be, for the Erection of Forts, Magazines, Arsenals, dock-Yards and other needful Buildings;—And

To make all Laws which shall be necessary and proper for carrying into Execution the foregoing Powers, and all other Powers vested by this Constitution in the Government of the United States, or in any Department or Officer thereof.

Necessary and proper clause gives Congress the power to pass all laws necessary and proper to the powers enumerated in Section 8.

Section 9.   The Migration or Importation of such Persons as any of the States now existing shall think proper to admit, shall not be prohibited by the Congress prior to the Year one thousand eight hundred and eight, but a Tax or duty may be imposed on such Importation, not exceeding ten dollars for each Person.

The Privilege of the Writ of Habeas Corpus shall not be suspended, unless when in Cases of Rebellion or Invasion the public Safety may require it.

No bill of Attainder or ex post facto Law shall be passed.

No Capitation, or other direct, Tax shall be laid, unless in Proportion to the Census or Enumeration herein before directed to be taken.

Changed by the Sixteenth Amendment.

No Tax or Duty shall be laid on Articles exported from any State.

No Preference shall be given by any Regulation of Commerce or Revenue to the Ports of one State over those of another; nor shall Vessels bound to, or from, one State, be obliged to enter, clear or pay Duties in another.

No Money shall be drawn from the Treasury, but in Consequence of Appropriations made by Law; and a regular Statement and Account of the Receipts and Expenditures of all public Money shall be published from time to time.

No Title of Nobility shall be granted by the United States: And no Person holding any Office of Profit or Trust under them, shall, without the Consent of the Congress, accept of any present, Emolument, Office, or Title, of any kind whatever, from any King, Prince, or foreign State.

Section 10.   No State shall enter into any Treaty, Alliance, or Confederation; grant Letters of Marque and Reprisal; coin Money; emit Bills of Credit; make any Thing but gold and silver Coin a Tender in Payment of Debts; pass any Bill of Attainder, ex post facto Law, or Law impairing the Obligation of Contracts, or grant any Title of Nobility.

No State shall, without the Consent of the Congress, lay any Imposts or Duties on Imports or Exports, except what may be absolutely necessary for executing its inspection Laws; and the net Produce of all Duties and Imposts, laid by any State on Imports or Exports, shall be for the Use of the Treasury of the United States; and all such Laws shall be subject to the Revision and Control of the Congress.

No State shall, without the Consent of Congress, lay any Duty of Tonnage, keep Troops, or Ships of War in time of Peace, enter into any Agreement or Compact with another State, or with a foreign Power, or engage in War, unless actually invaded, or in such imminent Danger as will not admit of delay.

Article II.

Section 1.   The executive Power shall be vested in a President of the United States of America. He shall hold his Office during the term of four Years, and, together with the Vice President, chosen for the same Term, be elected, as follows

Vesting clause gives the president the executive power.

Each State shall appoint, in such Manner as the Legislature thereof may direct, a Number of Electors, equal to the whole Number of Senators and Representatives to which the State may be entitled in the Congress: but no Senator or Representative, or Person holding an Office of Trust or Profit under the United States, shall be appointed an Elector.

Changed by the Twelfth Amendment.

The Electors shall meet in their respective States, and vote by Ballot for two Persons, of whom one at least shall not be an Inhabitant of the same State with them-selves. And they shall make a List of all the Persons voted for, and of the Number of Votes for each; which List they shall sign and certify, and transmit sealed to the Seat of the Government of the United States, directed to the President of the Senate. The President of the Senate shall, in the Presence of the Senate and House of Representatives, open all the Certificates, and the Votes shall then be counted. The Person having the greatest Number of Votes shall be the President, if such Number be a Majority of the whole Number of Electors appointed; and if there be more than one who have such Majority, and have an equal Number of Votes, then the House of Representatives shall immediately chuse by Ballot one of them for President; and if no Person have a Majority, then from the five highest on the List the said House shall in like Manner chuse the President. But in chusing the President, the Votes shall be taken by States, the Representation from each State having one Vote; a quorum for this Purpose shall consist of a Member or Members from two thirds of the States, and a Majority of all the States shall be necessary to a Choice. In every Case, after the Choice of the President, the Person having the greatest Number of Votes of the Electors shall be the Vice President. But if there should remain two or more who have equal Votes, the Senate shall chuse from them by Ballot the Vice President.

The Congress may determine the Time of chusing the Electors, and the Day on which they shall give their Votes, which Day shall be the same throughout the United States.

No Person except a natural born Citizen, or a Citizen of the United States, at the time of the Adoption of this Constitution, shall be eligible to the Office of President; neither shall any person be eligible to that Office who shall not have attained to the Age of thirty five Years, and been fourteen Years a Resident within the United States.

Changed by the Twenty-Fifth Amendment.

In Case of the Removal of the President from Office, or of his Death, Resignation, or Inability to discharge the Powers and Duties of the said Office, the Same shall devolve on the Vice President, and the Congress may by Law provide for the Case of Removal, Death,

Resignation or Inability, both of the President and Vice President, declaring what Officer shall then act as President, and such Officer shall act accordingly, until the Disability be removed, or a President shall be elected.

The President shall, at stated Times, receive for his Services, a Compensation, which shall neither be encreased nor diminished during the Period for which he shall have been elected, and he shall not receive within that Period any other Emolument from the United States, or any of them.

Before he enter on the Execution of his Office, he shall take the following Oath or Affirmation:—"I do solemnly swear (or affirm) that I will faithfully execute the Office of President of the United States, and will to the best of my Ability, preserve, protect and defend the Constitution of the United States."

Section 2.   The President shall be Commander in Chief of the Army and Navy of the United States, and of the Militia of the several States, when called into the actual Service of the United States; he may require the Opinion, in writing, of the principal Officer in each of the executive Departments, upon any Subject relating to the Duties of their respective Offices, and he shall have Power to grant Reprieves and Pardons for Offences against the United States, except in Cases of Impeachment.

He shall have Power, by and with the Advice and Consent of the Senate, to make Treaties, provided two thirds of the Senators present concur; and he shall nominate, and by and with the Advice and Consent of the Senate, shall appoint Ambassadors, other public Ministers and Consuls, Judges of the supreme Court, and all other Officers of the United States, whose Appointments are not herein otherwise provided for, and which shall be established by Law: but the Congress may by Law vest the Appointment of such inferior Officers, as they think proper, in the President alone, in the Courts of Law, or in the Heads of Departments.

The President shall have Power to fill up all Vacancies that may happen during the Recess of the Senate, by granting Commissions which shall expire at the End of their next Session.

Section 3.   He shall from time to time give to the Congress Information of the State of the Union, and recommend to their Consideration such Measures as he shall judge necessary and expedient; he may, on extraordinary Occasions, convene both Houses, or either of them, and in Case of Disagreement between them, with Respect to the Time of Adjournment, he may adjourn them to such Time as he shall think proper; he shall receive Ambassadors and other public Ministers; he shall take Care that the Laws be faithfully executed, and shall Commission all the Officers of the United States.

Take care clause requires the president to make sure that the laws are "faithfully executed."

Section 4.   The President, Vice President and all civil Officers of the United States, shall be removed from Office on Impeachment for, and Conviction of, Treason, Bribery, or other high Crimes and Misdemeanors.

Article III.

Section 1.   The judicial Power of the United States, shall be vested in one supreme Court, and in such inferior Courts as the Congress may from time to time ordain and establish. The Judges, both of the supreme and inferior Courts, shall hold their Offices during good Behaviour, and shall, at stated Times, receive for their Services, a Compensation, which shall not be diminished during their Continuance in Office.

Section 2.   The judicial Power shall extend to all Cases, in Law and Equity, arising under this Constitution, the Laws of the United States, and Treaties made, or which shall be made, under their Authority;—to all Cases affecting Ambassadors, other public Ministers and Consuls;—to all Cases of admiralty and maritime Jurisdiction;—to Controversies to which the United States shall be a Party;—to Controversies between two or more States;—between a State and Citizens of another State;—between Citizens of different States;—between Citizens of the same State claiming Lands under Grants of different States, and between a State, or the Citizens thereof, and foreign States, Citizens or Subjects.

In all Cases affecting Ambassadors, other public Ministers and Consuls, and those in which a State shall be Party, the supreme Court shall have original Jurisdiction. In all the other Cases before mentioned, the supreme Court shall have appellate Jurisdiction, both as to Law and Fact, with such Exceptions, and under such Regulations as the Congress shall make.

The Trial of all Crimes, except in Cases of Impeachment, shall be by Jury; and such Trial shall be held in the State where the said Crimes shall have been committed; but when not committed within any State, the Trial shall be at such Place or Places as the Congress may by Law have directed.

Section 3.   Treason against the United States, shall consist only in levying War against them, or in adhering to their Enemies, giving them Aid and Comfort. No Person shall be convicted of Treason unless on the Testimony of two Witnesses to the same overt Act, or on Confession in open Court.

The Congress shall have Power to declare the Punishment of Treason, but no Attainder of Treason shall work Corruption of Blood, or Forfeiture except during the Life of the Person attainted.

Article IV.

Section 1.   Full Faith and Credit shall be given in each State to the public Acts, Records, and judicial Proceedings of every other State. And the Congress may by general Laws prescribe the Manner in which such Acts, Records and Proceedings shall be proved, and the Effect thereof.

Section 2.   The Citizens of each State shall be entitled to all Privileges and Immunities of Citizens in the several States.

A person charged in any State with Treason, Felony, or other Crime, who shall flee from Justice, and be found in another State, shall on Demand of the executive Authority of the State from which he fled, be delivered up, to be removed to the State having Jurisdiction of the Crime.

No Person held to Service or Labour in one State, under the Laws thereof, escaping into another, shall, in Consequence of any Law or Regulation therein, be discharged from such Service or Labour, but shall be delivered up on Claim of the Party to whom such Service or Labour may be due.

Section 3.   New States may be admitted by the Congress into this Union; but no new State shall be formed or erected within the Jurisdiction of any other State; nor any State be formed by the Junction of two or more States, or Parts of States, without the Consent of the Legislatures of the States concerned as well as of the Congress.

Changed by the Eleventh Amendment.

Full faith and credit clause requires states to accept civil proceedings from other states.

Privileges and immunities clause requires states to treat nonresidents equally to residents.

Fugitive slave clause required states to return runaway slaves; negated by the Thirteenth Amendment.

The Congress shall have Power to dispose of and make all needful Rules and Regulations respecting the Territory or other Property belonging to the United States; and nothing in this Constitution shall be so construed as to Prejudice any Claims of the United States, or of any particular State.

Section 4. The United States shall guarantee to every State in this Union a Republican Form of Government, and shall protect each of them against Invasion; and on Application of the Legislature, or of the Executive (when the Legislature cannot be convened) against domestic Violence.

Guarantee clause provides a federal government guarantee that the states will have a republican form of government.

Article V.

The Congress, whenever two thirds of both Houses shall deem it necessary, shall propose Amendments to this Constitution, or, on the Application of the Legislatures of two thirds of the several States, shall call a Convention for proposing Amendments, which, in either Case, shall be valid to all Intents and Purposes, as Part of this Constitution, when ratified by the Legislatures of three fourths of the several States, or by Conventions in three fourths thereof, as the one or the other Mode of Ratification may be proposed by the Congress; Provided that no Amendment which may be made prior to the Year One thousand eight hundred and eight shall in any Manner after the first and fourth Clauses in the Ninth Section of the first Article; and that no State, without its Consent, shall be deprived of its equal Suffrage In the Senate.

Article VI.

All Debts contracted and Engagements entered into, before the Adoption of this Constitution, shall be as valid against the United States under this Constitution, as under the Confederation.

This Constitution, and the Laws of the United States which shall be made in Pursuance thereof; and all Treaties made, or which shall be made, under the Authority of the United States, shall be the Supreme Law of the Land; and the Judges in every State shall be bound thereby, any Thing in the Constitution or Laws of any State to the Contrary notwithstanding.

Supremacy clause makes federal law supreme over state laws.

The Senators and Representatives before mentioned, and the Members of the several State Legislatures, and all executive and judicial Officers, both of the United States and of the several States, shall be bound by Oath or Affirmation, to support this Constitution; but no religious Test shall ever be required as a Qualification to any Office or public Trust under the United States.

Article VII.

The Ratification of the Conventions of nine States, shall be sufficient for the Establishment of this Constitution between the States so ratifying the Same.

Done in Convention by the Unanimous Consent of the States present the Seventeenth Day of September in the Year of our Lord one thousand seven hundred and Eighty seven and of the Independence of the United States of America the Twelfth In witness whereof We have hereunto subscribed our Names,

George Washington, *President and deputy from Virginia*

Delaware

George Read

Gunning Bedford Jr.

John Dickinson

Richard Bassett

Jacob Broom

Maryland

James McHenry

Daniel of St. Thomas Jenifer

Daniel Carroll

Virginia

John Blair

James Madison Jr.

North Carolina

William Blount

Richard Dobbs Spaight

Hugh Williamson

South Carolina

John Rutledge

Charles Cotesworth Pinckney

Charles Pinckney

Pierce Butler

Georgia

William Few

Abraham Baldwin

New Hampshire

John Langdon

Nicholas Gilman

Massachusetts

Nathaniel Gorham

Rufus King

Connecticut

William Samuel Johnson

Roger Sherman

New York

Alexander Hamilton

New Jersey

William Livingston

David Brearley

William Paterson

Jonathan Dayton

Pennsylvania

Benjamin Franklin

Thomas Mifflin

Robert Morris

George Clymer

Thomas FitzSimons

Jared Ingersoll

James Wilson

Gouverneur Morris

[The first ten amendments, known as the Bill of Rights, were ratified in 1791.]

First Amendment

Establishment clause prohibits governmental establishment of religion.

Free exercise clause protects the free exercise of religion.

Congress shall make no law respecting an establishment of religion, or prohibiting the free exercise thereof; or abridging the freedom of speech, or of the press; or the right of the people peaceably to assemble, and to petition the Government for a redress of grievances.

Second Amendment

A well regulated Militia, being necessary to the security of a free State, the right of the people to keep and bear Arms, shall not be infringed.

Third Amendment

No Soldier shall, in time of peace be quartered in any house, without the consent of the Owner, nor in time of war, but in a manner prescribed by law.

Fourth Amendment

The right of the people to be secure in their persons, houses, papers, and effects, against unreasonable searches and seizures, shall not be violated, and no Warrants shall issue, but upon probable cause, supported by Oath or affirmation, and particularly describing the place to be searched, and the persons or things to be seized.

Fifth Amendment

No person shall be held to answer for a capital, or otherwise infamous crime, unless on a presentment or indictment of a Grand Jury, except in cases arising in the land or naval forces, or in the Militia, when in actual service in time of War or public danger; nor shall any person be subject for the same offence to be twice put in jeopardy of life or limb; nor shall be compelled in any criminal case to be a witness against himself, nor be deprived of life, liberty, or property, without due process of law, nor shall private property be taken for public use, without just compensation.

Double jeopardy clause prevents the government from retrying someone for a crime after an initial acquittal.

Self-incrimination clause protects people from having to testify against themselves at trial.

Due process clause prevents the federal government from denying any person due process of law.

Takings clause requires just compensation when the government seizes private property for a public purpose.

Sixth Amendment

In all criminal prosecutions, the accused shall enjoy the right to a speedy and public trial, by an impartial jury of the State and district wherein the crime shall have been committed, which district shall have been previously ascertained by law, and to be informed of the nature and cause of the accusation; to be confronted with the witnesses against him; to have compulsory process for obtaining witnesses in his favor, and to have Assistance of Counsel for his defence.

Seventh Amendment

In Suits at common law, where the value in controversy shall exceed twenty dollars, the right of trial by jury shall be preserved, and no fact tried by a jury, shall be otherwise reexamined in any Court of the United States, than according to the rules of the common law.

Eighth Amendment

Excessive bail shall not be required, nor excessive fines imposed, nor cruel and unusual punishments inflicted.

Cruel and unusual punishment clause prohibits cruel and unusual punishments.

Ninth Amendment

The enumeration in the Constitution, of certain rights, shall not be construed to deny or disparage others retained by the people.

Tenth Amendment

The powers not delegated to the United States by the Constitution, nor prohibited by it to the States, are reserved to the States respectively, or to the people.

Reserve powers clause reserves to the states or to the people those powers not delegated to United States.

Eleventh Amendment (1798)

The Judicial power of the United States shall not be construed to extend to any suit in law or equity, commenced or prosecuted against one of the United States by Citizens of another State, or by Citizens or Subjects of any Foreign State.

Twelfth Amendment (1804)

The Electors shall meet in their respective states and vote by ballot for President and Vice President, one of whom, at least, shall not be an inhabitant of the same state with themselves; they shall name in their ballots the person voted for as President, and in distinct ballots the person voted for as Vice President, and they shall make distinct lists of all persons voted for as President, and of all persons voted for as Vice President, and of the number of votes for each, which lists they shall sign and certify, and transmit sealed to the seat of the government of the United States, directed to the President of the Senate;—The President of the Senate shall, in the presence of the Senate and House of Representatives, open all the certificates and the votes shall then be counted;—The person having the greatest number of votes for President, shall be the President, if such number be a majority of the whole number of Electors appointed; and if no person have such majority, then from the persons having the highest numbers not exceeding three on the list of those voted for as President, the House of Representatives shall choose immediately, by ballot, the President. But in choosing the President, the votes shall be taken by states, the representation from each state having one vote; a quorum for this purpose shall consist of a member or members from two-thirds of the states, and a majority of all the states shall be necessary to a choice. And if the House of Representatives shall not choose a President whenever the right of choice shall devolve upon them, before the fourth day of March next following, then the Vice President shall act as President, as in the case of the death or other constitutional disability of the President.—The person having the greatest number of votes as Vice President, shall be the Vice President, if such number be a majority of the whole number of Electors appointed, and if no person have a majority, then from the two highest numbers on the list, the Senate shall choose the Vice President; a quorum for the purpose shall consist of two-thirds of the whole number of Senators, and a majority of the whole number shall be necessary to a choice. But no person constitutionally ineligible to the office of President shall be eligible to that of Vice President of the United States.

Changed by the Twentieth Amendment, Section 3.

Thirteenth Amendment (1865)

Section 1. Neither slavery nor involuntary servitude, except as a punishment for crime whereof the party shall have been duly convicted, shall exist within the United States, or any place subject to their jurisdiction.

Section 2. Congress shall have power to enforce this article by appropriate legislation.

Fourteenth Amendment (1868)

Section 1. All persons born or naturalized in the United States and subject to the jurisdiction thereof, are citizens of the United States and of the State wherein they reside. No State shall make or enforce any law which shall abridge the privileges or immunities of citizens of the United States; nor shall any State deprive any person of life, liberty, or property, without due process of law; nor deny to any person within its jurisdiction the equal protection of the laws.

Citizenship clause makes all persons born in the United States citizens of the United States and of the state in which they reside.

Privileges or immunities clause prohibits states from abridging certain fundamental rights.

Due process clause prevents state governments from denying any person due process of law.

Equal protection clause prevents states from denying any person the equal protection of the laws.

Section 2. Representatives shall be apportioned among the several States according to their respective numbers, counting the whole number of persons in each State, excluding Indians not taxed. But when the right to vote at any election for the choice of electors for President and Vice President of the United States, Representatives in Congress, the Executive and Judicial officers of a State, or the members of the Legislature thereof, is denied to any of the male inhabitants of such State, being twenty-one years of age, and citizens of the United States, or in any way abridged, except for participation in rebellion, or other crime, the basis of representation therein shall be reduced in the proportion which the number of such male citizens shall bear to the whole number of male citizens twenty-one years of age in such State.

Changed by the Nineteenth and Twenty-Sixth Amendments.

Section 3. No person shall be a Senator or Representative in Congress, or elector of President and Vice President, or hold any office, civil or military, under the United States, or under any State, who, having previously taken an oath, as a member of Congress, or as an officer of the United States, or as a member of any State legislature, or as an executive or judicial officer of any State, to support the Constitution of the United States, shall have engaged in insurrection or rebellion against the same, or given aid or comfort to the enemies thereof. But Congress may by a vote of two-thirds of each House, remove such disability.

Section 4. The validity of the public debt of the United States, authorized by law, including debts incurred for payment of pensions and bounties for services in suppressing insurrection or rebellion, shall not be questioned. But neither the United States nor any State shall assume or pay any debt or obligation incurred in aid of insurrection or rebellion against the United States, or any claim for the loss or emancipation of any slave; but all such debts, obligations and claims shall be held illegal and void.

Section 5. The Congress shall have power to enforce, by appropriate legislation, the provisions of this article.

Fifteenth Amendment (1870)

Section 1. The right of citizens of the United States to vote shall not be denied or abridged by the United States or by any State on account of race, color, or previous condition of servitude.

Section 2. The Congress shall have power to enforce this article by appropriate legislation.

Sixteenth Amendment (1913)

The Congress shall have power to lay and collect taxes on incomes, from whatever source derived, without apportionment among the several States, and without regard to any census or enumeration.

Seventeenth Amendment (1913)

The Senate of the United States shall be composed of two Senators from each State, elected by the people thereof, for six years; and each Senator shall have one vote. The electors in each State shall have the qualifications requisite for electors of the most numerous branch of the State legislatures.

When vacancies happen in the representation of any State in the Senate, the executive authority of such State shall issue writs of election to fill such vacancies: *Provided*, That the legislature of any State may empower the executive thereof to make temporary appointments until the people fill the vacancies by election as the legislature may direct.

This amendment shall not be so construed as to affect the election or term of any Senator chosen before it becomes valid as part of the Constitution.

Eighteenth Amendment (1919)

Section 1. After one year from the ratification of this article the manufacture, sale, or transportation of intoxicating liquors within, the importation thereof into, or the exportation thereof from the United States and all territory subject to the jurisdiction thereof for beverage purposes is hereby prohibited.

Repealed by the Twenty-First Amendment.

Section 2. The Congress and the several States shall have concurrent power to enforce this article by appropriate legislation.

Section 3. This article shall be inoperative unless it shall have been ratified as an amendment to the Constitution by the legislatures of the several States, as provided in the Constitution, within seven years from the date of the submission hereof to the States by the Congress.

Nineteenth Amendment (1920)

The right of citizens of the United States to vote shall not be denied or abridged by the United States or by any State on account of sex.

Congress shall have power to enforce this article by appropriate legislation.

Twentieth Amendment (1933)

Section 1.   The terms of the President and Vice President shall end at noon on the 20th day of January, and the terms of Senators and Representatives at noon on the 3rd day of January, of the years in which such terms would have ended if this article had not been ratified; and the terms of their successors shall then begin.

Section 2.   The Congress shall assemble at least once in every year, and such meeting shall begin at noon on the 3d day of January, unless they shall by law appoint a different day.

Section 3.   If, at the time fixed for the beginning of the term of the President, the President elect shall have died, the Vice President elect shall become President. If a President shall not have been chosen before the time fixed for the beginning of his term, or if the President elect shall have failed to qualify, then the Vice President elect shall act as President until a President shall have qualified; and the Congress may by law provide for the case wherein neither a President elect nor a Vice President elect shall have qualified, declaring who shall then act as President, or the manner in which one who is to act shall be selected, and such person shall act accordingly until a President or Vice President shall have qualified.

Section 4.   The Congress may by law provide for the case of the death of any of the persons from whom the House of Representatives may choose a President whenever the right of choice shall have devolved upon them, and for the case of the death of any of the persons from whom the Senate may choose a Vice President whenever the right of choice shall have devolved upon them.

Section 5.   Sections 1 and 2 shall take effect on the 15th day of October following the ratification of this article.

Section 6.   This article shall be inoperative unless it shall have been ratified as an amendment to the Constitution by the legislatures of three-fourths of the several States within seven years from the date of its submission.

Twenty-First Amendment (1933)

Section 1.   The eighteenth article of amendment to the Constitution of the United States is hereby repealed.

Section 2.   The transportation or importation into any State, Territory, or possession of the United States for delivery or use therein of intoxicating liquors, in violation of the laws thereof, is hereby prohibited.

Section 3.   This article shall be inoperative unless it shall have been ratified as an amendment to the Constitution by conventions in the several States, as provided in the Constitution, within seven years from the date of the submission hereof to the States by the Congress.

Twenty-Second Amendment (1951)

Section 1.   No person shall be elected to the office of the President more than twice, and no person who has held the office of President, or acted as President, for more than two years of a term to which some other person was elected President shall be elected to the office of the President more than once. But this Article shall not apply to any person holding the office of President when this Article was proposed by the Congress, and shall not prevent any person who may be holding the office of President, or acting as President, during the term within which this Article becomes operative from holding the office of President or acting as President during the remainder of such term.

Section 2.   This Article shall be inoperative unless it shall have been ratified as an amendment to the Constitution by the legislatures of three-fourths of the several States within seven years from the date of its submission to the States by the Congress.

Twenty-Third Amendment (1961)

Section 1.   The District constituting the seat of Government of the United States shall appoint in such manner as the Congress may direct:

A number of electors of President and Vice President equal to the whole number of Senators and Representatives in Congress to which the District would be entitled if it were a State, but in no event more than the least populous State; they shall be in addition to those appointed by the States, but they shall be considered, for the purposes of the election of President and Vice President, to be electors appointed by a State; and they shall meet in the District and perform such duties as provided by the twelfth article of amendment.

Section 2.   The Congress shall have power to enforce this article by appropriate legislation.

Twenty-Fourth Amendment (1964)

Section 1.   The right of citizens of the United States to vote in any primary or other election for President or Vice President, for electors for President or Vice President, or for Senator or Representative in Congress, shall not be denied or abridged by the United States or any State by reason of failure to pay any poll tax or other tax.

Section 2.   Congress shall have power to enforce this article by appropriate legislation.

Twenty-Fifth Amendment (1967)

Section 1.   In case of the removal of the President from office or of his death or resignation, the Vice President shall become President.

Section 2.   Whenever there is a vacancy in the office of the Vice President, the President shall nominate a Vice President who shall take office upon confirmation by a majority vote of both Houses of Congress.

Section 3.   Whenever the President transmits to the President pro tempore of the Senate and the Speaker of the House of Representatives his written declaration that he is unable to discharge the powers and duties of his office, and until he transmits to them a written declaration to the contrary, such powers and duties shall be discharged by the Vice President as Acting President.

Section 4.   Whenever the Vice President and a majority of either the principal officers of the executive departments or of such other body as Congress may by law provide, transmit to the President pro tempore of the Senate and the Speaker of the House of Representatives their written declaration that the President is unable to discharge the powers and duties of his office, the Vice President shall immediately assume the powers and duties of the office as Acting President.

Thereafter, when the President transmits to the President pro tempore of the Senate and the Speaker of the House of Representatives his written declaration that no inability exists, he shall resume the powers and duties of his office unless the Vice President and a majority of either the principal officers of the executive department[s] or of such other body as Congress may by law provide, transmit within four days to the President pro tempore of the Senate and the Speaker of the House of Representatives their written declaration that the President is unable to discharge the powers and duties of his office. Thereupon Congress shall decide the issue, assembling within forty-eight hours for that purpose if not in session. If the Congress, within twenty-one days after receipt of the latter written declaration, or, if Congress is not in session, within twenty-one days after Congress is required to assemble, determines by two-thirds vote of both Houses that the President is unable to discharge the powers and duties of his office, the Vice President shall continue to discharge the same as Acting President; otherwise, the President shall resume the powers and duties of his office.

Twenty-Sixth Amendment (1971)

Section 1.   The right of citizens of the United States, who are eighteen years of age or older, to vote shall not be denied or abridged by the United States or by any State on account of age.

Section 2.   The Congress shall have power to enforce this article by appropriate legislation.

Twenty-Seventh Amendment (1992)

No law varying the compensation for the services of the Senators and Representatives shall take effect, until an election of Representatives shall have intervened.

10

James Madison

November 22, 1787

To the People of the State of New York

Among the numerous advantages promised by a well constructed Union, none deserves to be more accurately developed than its tendency to break and control the violence of faction. The friend of popular governments, never finds himself so much alarmed for their character and fate, as when he contemplates their propensity to this dangerous vice. He will not fail therefore to set a due value on any plan which, without violating the principles to which he is attached, provides a proper cure for it. The instability, injustice and confusion introduced into the public councils, have in truth been the mortal diseases under which popular governments have every where perished; as they continue to be the favorite and fruitful topics from which the adversaries to liberty derive their most specious declamations. The valuable improvements made by the American Constitutions on the popular models, both ancient and modern, cannot certainly be too much admired; but it would be an unwarrantable partiality, to contend that they have as effectually obviated the danger on this side as was wished and expected. Complaints are every where heard from our most considerate and virtuous citizens, equally the friends of public and private faith, and of public and personal liberty; that our governments are too unstable; that the public good is disregarded in the conflicts of rival parties; and that measures are too often decided, not according to the rules of justice, and the rights of the minor party; but by the superior force of an interested and over-bearing majority. However anxiously we may wish that these complaints had no foundation, the evidence of known facts will not permit us to deny that they are in some degree true. It will be found indeed, on a candid review of our situation, that some of the distresses under which we labor, have been erroneously charged on the operation of our governments; but it will be found, at the same time, that other causes will not alone account for many of our heaviest misfortunes; and particularly, for that prevailing and increasing distrust of public engagements, and alarm for private rights, which are echoed from one end of the continent to the other. These must be chiefly, if not wholly, effects of the unsteadiness and injustice, with which a factious spirit has tainted our public administrations.

By a faction I understand a number of citizens, whether amounting to a majority or minority of the whole, who are united and actuated by some common impulse of passion, or of interest, adverse to the rights of other citizens, or to the permanent and aggregate interests of the community.

There are two methods of curing the mischiefs of faction: the one, by removing its causes; the other, by controlling its effects.

There are again two methods of removing the causes of faction: the one by destroying the liberty which is essential to its existence; the other, by giving to every citizen the same opinions, the same passions, and the same interests.

It could never be more truly said than of the first remedy, that it is worse than the disease. Liberty is to faction, what air is to fire, an aliment without which it instantly expires. But it could not be a less folly to abolish liberty, which is essential to political life, because it nourishes faction, than it would be to wish the annihilation of air, which is essential to animal life, because it imparts to fire its destructive agency.

The second expedient is as impracticable, as the first would be unwise. As long as the reason of man continues fallible, and he is at liberty to exercise it, different opinions will be formed. As long as the connection subsists between his reason and his self-love, his opinions and his passions will have a reciprocal influence on each other; and the former will be objects to which the latter will attach themselves. The diversity in the faculties of men from which the rights of property originate, is not less an insuperable obstacle to a uniformity of interests. The protection of these faculties is the first object of Government. From the protection of different and unequal faculties of acquiring property, the possession of different degrees and kinds of property immediately results: and from the influence of these on the sentiments and views of the respective proprietors, ensues a division of the society into different interests and parties.

The latent causes of faction are thus sown in the nature of man; and we see them every where brought into different degrees of activity, according to the different circumstances of civil society. A zeal for different opinions concerning religion, concerning Government and many other points, as well of speculation as of practice; an attachment to different leaders ambitiously contending for pre-eminence and power; or to persons of other descriptions whose fortunes have been interesting to the human passions, have in turn divided mankind into parties, inflamed them with mutual animosity, and rendered them much more disposed to vex and oppress each other, than to co-operate for their common good. So strong is this propensity of mankind to fall into mutual animosities, that where no substantial occasion presents itself, the most frivolous and fanciful distinctions have been sufficient to kindle their unfriendly passions, and excite their most violent conflicts. But the most common and durable source of factions, has been the various and unequal distribution of property. Those who hold, and those who are without property, have ever formed distinct interests in society. Those who are creditors, and those who are debtors, fall under a like discrimination. A landed interest, a manufacturing interest, a mercantile interest, a monied interest, with many lesser interests, grow up of necessity in civilized nations, and divide them into different classes, actuated by different sentiments and views. The regulation of these various and interfering interests forms the principal task of modern Legislation, and involves the spirit of party and faction in the necessary and ordinary operations of Government.

No man is allowed to be a judge in his own cause; because his interest would certainly bias his judgment, and, not improbably, corrupt his integrity. With equal, nay with greater reason, a body of men, are unfit to be both judges and parties, at the same time; yet, what are many of the most important acts of legislation, but so many judicial determinations, not indeed concerning the rights of single persons, but concerning the rights of large bodies of citizens; and what are the different classes of legislators, but advocates and parties to the causes which they determine? Is a law proposed concerning private debts? It is a question to which the creditors are parties on one side, and the debtors on the other. Justice ought to hold the balance between them. Yet the parties are and must be themselves the judges; and the most numerous party, or, in other words, the most powerful faction must be expected to prevail. Shall domestic manufactures be encouraged, and in what degree, by restrictions on foreign manufactures? are questions which would be differently decided by the landed and the manufacturing classes; and probably by neither, with a sole regard to justice and the public good. The apportionment of taxes on the various descriptions of property, is an act which seems to require the most exact impartiality; yet, there is perhaps no legislative act in which greater opportunity and temptation are given to a predominant party, to trample on the rules of justice. Every shilling with which they over-burden the inferior number, is a shilling saved to their own pockets.

It is in vain to say, that enlightened statesmen will be able to adjust these clashing interests, and render them all subservient to the public good. Enlightened statesmen will not always be at the helm: Nor, in many cases, can such an adjustment be made at all, without taking into view indirect and remote considerations, which will rarely prevail over the immediate interest which one party may find in disregarding the rights of another, or the good of the whole.

The inference to which we are brought, is, that the *causes* of faction cannot be removed; and that relief is only to be sought in the means of controlling its *effects*.

If a faction consists of less than a majority, relief is supplied by the republican principle, which enables the majority to defeat its sinister views by regular vote: It may clog the administration, it may convulse the society; but it will be unable to execute and mask its violence under the forms of the Constitution. When a majority is included in a faction, the form of popular government on the other hand enables it to sacrifice to its ruling passion or interest, both the public good and the rights of other citizens. To secure the public good, and private rights, against the danger of such a faction, and at the same time to preserve the spirit and the form of popular government, is then the great object to which our enquiries are directed: Let me add that it is the great desideratum, by which alone this form of government can be rescued from the opprobrium under which it has so long labored, and be recommended to the esteem and adoption of mankind.

By what means is this object attainable? Evidently by one of two only. Either the existence of the same passion or interest in a majority at the same time, must be prevented; or the majority, having such co-existent passion or interest, must be rendered, by their number and local situation, unable to concert and carry into effect schemes of oppression. If the impulse and the opportunity be suffered to coincide, we well know that neither moral nor religious motives can be relied on as an adequate control. They are not found to be such on the injustice and violence of individuals, and lose their efficacy in proportion to the number combined together; that is, in proportion as their efficacy becomes needful.

From this view of the subject, it may be concluded, that a pure Democracy, by which I mean, a Society, consisting of a small number of citizens, who assemble and administer the Government in person, can admit of no cure for the mischiefs of faction. A common passion or interest will, in almost every case, be felt by a majority of the whole; a communication and concert results from the form of Government itself; and there is nothing to check the inducements to sacrifice the weaker party, or an obnoxious individual. Hence it is, that such Democracies have ever been spectacles of turbulence and contention; have ever been found incompatible with personal security, or the rights of property; and have in general been as short in their lives, as they have been violent in their deaths. Theoretic politicians, who have patronized this species of Government, have erroneously supposed, that by reducing mankind to a perfect equality in their political rights, they would, at the same time, be perfectly equalized and assimilated in their possessions, their opinions, and their passions.

A republic, by which I mean a government in which the scheme of representation takes place, opens a different prospect, and promises the cure for which we are seeking. Let us examine the points in which it varies from pure democracy, and we shall comprehend both the nature of the cure and the efficacy which it must derive from the union.

The two great points of difference, between a democracy and a republic, are, first, the delegation of the government, in the latter, to a small number of citizens, elected by the rest; secondly, the greater number of citizens, and greater sphere of country, over which the latter may be extended.

The effect of the first difference is, on the one hand, to refine and enlarge the public views, by passing them through the medium of a chosen body of citizens, whose wisdom may best discern the true interest of their country, and whose patriotism and love of justice, will be least likely to sacrifice it to temporary or partial considerations. Under such a regulation, it may well happen, that the public voice, pronounced by the representatives of the people, will be more consonant to the public good, than if pronounced by the people themselves, convened for the purpose. On the other hand the effect may be inverted. Men of factious tempers, of local prejudices, or of sinister designs, may by intrigue, by corruption, or by other means, first obtain the suffrages, and then betray the interest of the people. The question resulting is, whether small or extensive republics are most favorable to the election of proper guardians of the public weal, and it is clearly decided in favor of the latter by two obvious considerations.

In the first place, it is to be remarked that, however small the republic may be, the representatives must be raised to a certain number, in order to guard against the cabals of a few; and that however large it may be, they must be limited to a certain number, in order to guard against the confusion of a multitude. Hence, the number of representatives in the two cases not being in proportion to that of the constituents, and being proportionally greatest in the small republic, it follows, that if the proportion of fit characters be not less in the large than in the small republic, the former will present a greater option, and consequently a greater probability of a fit choice.

In the next place, as each Representative will be chosen by a greater number of citizens in the large than in the small Republic, it will be more difficult for unworthy candidates to practise with success the vicious arts, by which elections are too often carried; and the suffrages of the people being more free, will be more likely to center on men who possess the most attractive merit, and the most diffusive and established characters.

It must be confessed, that in this, as in most other cases, there is a mean, on both sides of which inconveniences will be found to lie. By enlarging too much the number of electors, you render the representatives too little acquainted with all their local circumstances and lesser interests; as by reducing it too much, you render him unduly attached to these, and too little fit to comprehend and pursue great and national objects. The Federal Constitution forms a happy combination in this respect; the great and aggregate interests being referred to the national, the local and particular, to the state legislatures.

The other point of difference is, the greater number of citizens and extent of territory which may be brought within the compass of Republican, than of Democratic Government; and it is this circumstance principally which renders factious combinations less to be dreaded in the former, than in the latter. The smaller the society, the fewer probably will be the distinct parties and interests composing it; the fewer the distinct parties and interests, the more frequently will a majority be found of the same party; and the smaller the number of individuals composing a majority, and the smaller the compass within which they are placed, the more easily will they concert and execute their plans of oppression. Extend the sphere, and you take in a greater variety of parties and interests; you make it less probable that a majority of the whole will have a common motive to invade the rights of other citizens; or if such a common motive exists, it will be more difficult for all who feel it to discover their own strength, and to act in unison with each other. Besides other impediments, it may be remarked, that where there is a consciousness of unjust or dishonorable purposes, communication is always checked by distrust, in proportion to the number whose concurrence is necessary.

Hence it clearly appears, that the same advantage, which a Republic has over a Democracy, in controlling the effects of factions, is enjoyed by a large over a small Republic—is enjoyed by the Union over the States composing it. Does this advantage consist in the substitution of Representatives, whose enlightened views and virtuous sentiments render them superior to local prejudices, and to schemes of injustice? It will not be denied, that the Representation of the Union will be most likely to possess these requisite endowments. Does it consist in the greater security afforded by a greater variety of parties, against the event of any one party being able to outnumber and oppress the rest? In an equal degree does the increased variety of parties, comprised within the Union, increase this security? Does it, in fine, consist in the greater obstacles opposed to the concert and accomplishment of the secret wishes of an unjust and interested majority? Here, again, the extent of the Union gives it the most palpable advantage.

The influence of factious leaders may kindle a flame within their particular States, but will be unable to spread a general conflagration through the other States: a religious sect, may degenerate into a political faction in a part of the Confederacy but the variety of sects dispersed over the entire face of it, must secure the national Councils against any danger from that source: a rage for paper money, for an abolition of debts, for an equal division of property, or for any other improper or wicked project, will be less apt to pervade the whole body of the Union, than a particular member of it; in the same proportion as such a malady is more likely to taint a particular county or district, than an entire State.

In the extent and proper structure of the Union, therefore, we behold a Republican remedy for the diseases most incident to Republican Government. And according to the degree of pleasure and pride, we feel in being Republicans, ought to be our zeal in cherishing the spirit, and supporting the character of Federalists.

PUBLIUS

51

James Madison

February 6, 1788

To the People of the State of New York

To what expedient then shall we finally resort for maintaining in practice the necessary partition of power among the several departments, as laid down in the constitution? The only answer that can be given is, that as all these exterior provisions are found to be inadequate, the defect must be supplied, by so contriving the interior structure of the government, as that its several constituent parts may, by their mutual relations, be the means of keeping each other in their proper places. Without presuming to undertake a full development of this important idea, I will hazard a few general observations, which may perhaps place it in a clearer light, and enable us to form a more correct judgment of the principles and structure of the government planned by the convention.

In order to lay a due foundation for that separate and distinct exercise of the different powers of government, which to a certain extent, is admitted on all hands to be essential to the preservation of liberty, it is evident that each department should have a will of its own; and consequently should be so constituted, that the members of each should have as little agency as possible in the appointment of the members of the others. Were this principle rigorously adhered to, it would require that all the appointments for the supreme executive, legislative, and judiciary magistracies, should be drawn from the same fountain of authority, the people, through channels, having no communication whatever with one another. Perhaps such a plan of constructing the several departments would be less difficult in practice than it may in contemplation appear. Some difficulties however, and some additional expense, would attend the execution of it. Some deviations therefore from the principle must be admitted. In the constitution of the judiciary department in particular, it might be inexpedient to insist rigorously on the principle; first, because peculiar qualifications being essential in the members, the primary consideration ought to be to select that mode of choice, which best secures these qualifications; secondly, because the permanent tenure by which the appointments are held in that department, must soon destroy all sense of dependence on the authority conferring them.

It is equally evident that the members of each department should be as little dependent as possible on those of the others, for the emoluments annexed to their offices. Were the executive magistrate, or the judges, not independent of the legislature in this particular, their independence in every other would be merely nominal.

But the great security against a gradual concentration of the several powers in the same department, consists in giving to those who administer each department, the necessary constitutional means, and personal motives, to resist encroachments of the others. The provision for defense must in this, as in all other cases, be made commensurate to the danger of attack. Ambition must be made to counteract ambition. The interest of the man must be connected with the constitutional rights of the place. It may be a reflection on human nature, that such devices should be necessary to control the abuses of government. But what is government itself but the greatest of all reflections on human nature? If men were angels, no government would be necessary. If angels were to govern men, neither external nor internal controls on government would be necessary. In framing a government which is to be administered by men over men, the great difficulty lies in this: You must first enable the government to control the governed; and in the next place, oblige it to control itself. A dependence on the people is no doubt the primary control on the government; but experience has taught mankind the necessity of auxiliary precautions.

This policy of supplying by opposite and rival interests, the defect of better motives, might be traced through the whole system of human affairs, private as well as public. We see it particularly displayed in all the subordinate distributions of power; where the constant aim is to divide and arrange the several offices in such a manner as that each may be a check on the other; that the private interest of every individual, may be a sentinel over the public rights. These inventions of prudence cannot be less requisite in the distribution of the supreme powers of the state.

But it is not possible to give each department an equal power of self defense. In republican government the legislative authority, necessarily, predominates. The remedy for this inconveniency is, to divide the legislature into different branches; and to render them by different modes of election, and different principles of action, as little connected with each other, as the nature of their common functions, and their common dependence on the society, will admit. It may even be necessary to guard against dangerous encroachments by still further precautions. As the weight of the legislative authority requires that it should be thus divided, the weakness of the executive may require, on the other hand, that it should be fortified. An absolute negative, on the legislature, appears at first view to be the natural defense with which the executive magistrate should be armed. But perhaps it would be neither altogether safe, nor alone sufficient. On ordinary occasions, it might not be exerted with the requisite firmness; and on extraordinary occasions, it might be prefidiously abused. May not this defect of an absolute negative be supplied, by some qualified connection between this weaker department, and the weaker branch of the stronger department, by which the latter may be led to support the constitutional rights of the former, without being too much detached from the rights of its own department?

If the principles on which these observations are founded be just, as I persuade myself they are, and they be applied as a criterion, to the several state constitutions, and to the federal constitution, it will be found, that if the latter does not perfectly correspond with them, the former are infinitely less able to bear such a test.

There are moreover two considerations particularly applicable to the federal system of America, which place that system in a very interesting point of view.

First. In a single republic, all the power surrendered by the people, is submitted to the administration of a single government; and usurpations are guarded against by a division of the government into distinct and separate departments. In the compound republic of America, the power surrendered by the people, is first divided between two distinct governments, and then the portion allotted to each, subdivided among distinct and separate departments. Hence a double security arises to the rights of the people. The different governments will control each other; at the same time that each will be controlled by itself.

Second. It is of great importance in a republic, not only to guard the society against the oppression of its rulers; but to guard one part of the society against the injustice of the other part. Different interests necessarily exist in different classes of citizens. If a majority be united by a common interest, the rights of the minority will be insecure. There are but two methods of providing against this evil: The one by creating a will in the community independent of the majority, that is, of the society itself, the other by comprehending in the society so many separate descriptions of citizens, as will render an unjust combination of a majority of the whole, very improbable, if not impracticable. The first method prevails in all governments possessing an hereditary or self appointed authority. This at best is but a precarious security; because a power independent of the society may as well espouse the unjust views of the major, as the rightful interests, of the minor party, and may possibly be turned against both parties. The second method will be exemplified in the federal republic of the United States. While all authority in it will be derived from and dependent on the society, the society itself will be broken into so many parts, interests and classes of citizens, that the rights of individuals or of the minority, will be in little danger from interested combinations of the majority. In a free government, the security for civil rights must be the same as for religious rights. It consists in the one case in the multiplicity of interests, and in the other, in the multiplicity of sects. The degree of security in both cases will depend on the number of interests and sects; and this may be presumed to depend on the extent of country and number of people comprehended under the same government. This view of the subject must particularly recommend a proper federal system to all the sincere and considerate friends of republican government: Since it shows that in exact proportion as the territory of the union may be formed into more circumscribed confederacies or states, oppressive combinations of a majority will be facilitated, the best security under the republican form, for the rights of every class of citizens, will be diminished; and consequently, the stability and independence of some member of the government, the only other security, must be proportionally increased. Justice is the end of government. It is the end of civil society. It ever has been, and ever will be pursued, until it be obtained, or until liberty be lost in the pursuit. In a society under the forms of which the stronger faction can readily unite and oppress the weaker, anarchy may as truly be said to reign, as in a state of nature where the weaker individual is not secured against the violence of the stronger: And as in the latter state even the stronger individuals are prompted by the uncertainty of their condition, to submit to a government which may protect the weak as well as themselves: So in the former state, will the more powerful factions or parties be gradually induced by a like motive, to wish for a government which will protect all parties, the weaker as well as the more powerful. It can be little doubted, that if the state of Rhode Island was separated from the confederacy, and left to itself, the insecurity of rights under the popular form of government within such narrow limits, would be displayed by such reiterated oppressions of factious majorities, that some power altogether independent of the people would soon be called for by the voice of the very factions whose misrule had proved the necessity of it. In the extended republic of the United States, and among the great variety of interests, parties and sects which it embraces, a coalition of a majority of the whole society could seldom take place on any other principles than those of justice and the general good; and there being thus less danger to a minor from the will of the major party, there must be less pretext also, to provide for the security of the former, by introducing into the government a will not dependent on the latter; or in other words, a will independent of the society itself. It is no less certain than it is important, notwithstanding the contrary opinions which have been entertained, that the larger the society, provided it lie within a practicable sphere, the more duly capable will be of self government. And happily for the *republican cause,* the practicable sphere may be carried to a very great extent, by a judicious modification and mixture of the *federal principle.*

PUBLIUS

ENDNOTES

Chapter 1

1. This story was compiled from Tim Craig and Michael D. Shear, "Allen Quip Provokes Outrage, Apology," *Washington Post,* August 15, 2006, A1; Fredrick Kunkle, "Fairfax Native Says Allen's Words Stung," *Washington Post,* August 25, 2006, B1; S. R. Sidarth, "I Am Macaca," *Washington Post,* November 12, 2006, B2; and telephone and e-mail interviews with S. R. Sidarth, December 25, 28, 2009, conducted for this textbook; chapter-opening quotation from December 25, 2009, interview.

2. International Social Survey Program, as cited in Russell Dalton, *The Good Citizen* (Washington, D.C.: CQ Press, 2007), 144; Morley Winograd and Michael D. Hais, *Millennial Makeover: MySpace, YouTube and the Future of American Politics* (New Brunswick, N.J.: Rutgers University Press, 2008), 260–63. The caption for the photo on page 5 is drawn from this source.

3. Dalton, *Good Citizen,* 153.

4. Larry Bartels, *Unequal Democracy* (Princeton, N.J.: Princeton University Press, 2008); David Cay Johnston, "The Gap between Rich and Poor Grows in the United States," *New York Times,* March 29, 2007. The caption for the photo on page 6 is drawn from these sources and from U.S. census data.

5. Marc Hetherington, *Why Trust Matters* (Princeton, N.J.: Princeton University Press, 2005).

6. Kerem Ozan Kalkan, Geoffrey C. Layman, and Eric M. Uslaner, "Attitudes toward Muslims in Contemporary American Society," *Journal of Politics* 69 (2009): 847–62.

7. Charles Beard, *American Government and Politics* (New York: Macmillan Company, 1915), 18.

8. Edmund Burke, *Reflections on the Revolution in France,* in *The Portable Edmund Burke,* ed. Isaac Kramnick (New York: Viking, 1999), 32.

9. John Adams to John Taylor, April 15, 1814, in *The Political Writings of John Adams: Representative Selections,* ed. George Peek Jr. (New York: Hackett Publishing, 2003), 67.

10. Quoted in David McCullough, *John Adams* (New York: Simon and Schuster, 2001), 68.

11. See Josiah Ober, *Mass and Elite in Democratic Athens* (Princeton, N.J.: Princeton University Press, 1991).

12. Harold Laswell, *Politics: Who Gets What, When, How* (New York: McGraw-Hill, 1936).

13. Bryan D. Jones and Frank M. Baumgartner, *The Politics of Attention* (Chicago: University of Chicago Press, 2005).

14. Poll conducted by CBS News, February 2–4, 2009, based on telephone interviews with a national adult sample of 864.

15. Michael Grabell and Jennifer La Fleur, "Stimulus Spending Fails to Follow Unemployment, Poverty," August 6, 2009, Huffington Post, www.huffingtonpost.com.

16. David Remnick, "The President's Hero," *New Yorker,* February 2, 2009.

17. Winograd and Haas, *Millennial Makeover;* Morley Winograd and Michael D. Hais, "The Boomers Had Their Day: Make Way for the Millennials," *Washington Post,* February 3, 2008, B1, B5.

18. Social Security Administration, "A Summary of the 2009 Annual Reports," www.ssa.gov. In 2008 the annual cost of Social Security benefits represented 4.4 percent of the gross domestic product (GDP); by 2034 the cost is projected to increase to 6.2 percent of GDP—nearly a 50 percent jump.

19. *USA Today,* "Our View on the Cost of Education: Colleges Duck Tough Cuts, Keep Hiking Pay and Tuition," March 30, 2009, http://blogs.usa today.com/.

20. Darrell West et al., "Invisible: 1.4 Percent Coverage for Education Is Not Enough," December 2, 2009, Brookings Institution, www.brookings.edu/.

21. James Madison, "Epilogue: Securing the Republic," August 4, 1822, in *The Founder's Constitution,* University of Chicago Press, http://press-pubs.uchicago.edu/founders/documents.

Chapter 2

1. This story was compiled from *USA Today,* May 8, 1992; and an e-mail interview with Gregory Watson on January 29, 2010, conducted for this textbook; chapter-opening quotation from interview.

2. Gordon S. Wood, *The American Revolution* (New York: Modern Library Chronicles, 2002), 39.

3. Edmund Burke, "Speech to the Electors of Bristol," in *The Founders' Constitution,* University of Chicago Press, http://press-pubs.uchicago.edu/.

4. Robert Middlekauff, *The Glorious Cause* (New York: Oxford University Press, 1982), 231.

5. Thomas Paine, *Common Sense,* www.ushistory.org/.

6. Articles of Confederation, Article IX, paragraph 5, www.usconstitution.net/.

7. Thomas Jefferson, "Notes on the State of Virginia," 245, http://etext.virginia.edu/.

8. University of Virginia Library, Historical Census Browser, http://fisher.lib.virginia.edu/.

9. Middlekauff, *Glorious Cause,* 624.

10. William Riker, "The Heresthetics of Constitution Making," *American Political Science Review* 78 (1984): 1–16.

11. William Patterson, "New Jersey Plan," http://avalon.law.yale.edu/.

12. "1790 Census of Slave and Free Population," U.S. Census of Population and Housing, University of Virginia, http://fisher.lib.virginia.edu/.

13. Quoted in Max Farrand, *The Framing of the Constitution of the United States* (New Haven, Conn.: Yale University Press, 1913), 1:486–87.

14. Garry Wills, *Negro President: Jefferson and the Slave Power* (Boston: Houghton Mifflin, 2003).

15. James Madison, *Letters and Other Writings of James Madison: 1769–1793* (New York: Worthington, 1884), 1:186.

16. Quoted in *The Records of the Federal Convention of 1787*, ed. Max Farrand (New Haven, Conn.: Yale University Press, 1911), 3:359.

17. See Allison M. Martens, "Reconsidering Judicial Supremacy: From the Counter-Majoritarian Difficulty to Constitutional Transformations," *Perspectives on Politics* 5 (2007): 447–59.

18. James Madison, *Federalist 47*, in *The Federalist Papers*, www.constitution.org/.

19. James Madison, *Federalist 39*, in *The Federalist Papers*, http://press-pubs.uchicago.edu/.

20. Brutus, "Antifederalist 5," www.constitution.org/.

21. Virginia ratification debates, www.constitution.org/.

22. James Madison, *Federalist 41*, in *The Federalist Papers*, www.constitution.org/.

23. Virginia ratification debates, www.constitution.org/.

24. Brian Gaines, "Popular Myths about Popular Vote–Electoral College Splits," *PS* 34 (March 2001): 70–75.

25. Daryl J. Levinson and Richard H. Pildes, "Separation of Parties, Not Powers," *Harvard Law Review* 119 (2006): 2311.

26. *Furman v. Georgia*, 408 U.S. 238 (1972).

27. *Gregg v. Georgia*, 428 U.S. 153 (1976).

28. Death Penalty Information Center, "States with and without the Death Penalty," www.deathpenaltyinfo.org/.

29. Death Penalty Information Center, "The Federal Death Penalty," www.deathpenaltyinfo.org/.

30. David Baldus, Charles A. Pulaski Jr., and George Woodworth, *Equal Justice and the Death Penalty* (Boston: Northeastern University Press, 1990).

31. *McCleskey v. Kemp*, 481 U.S. 279 (1987).

32. *Roper v. Simmons*, 543 U.S. 551 (2005); *Kennedy v. Louisiana*, 171 L. Ed. 2d 525 (2008).

33. The Innocence Project, "27 Years Later, Donald Gates Is Declared Innocent," www.innocenceproject.org/.

34. *District Attorney's Office v. Osborne*, 174 L. Ed. 2d 38 (2009).

35. See Alexander Keyssar, *The Right to Vote* (New York: Basic Books, 2000).

Chapter 3

1. This story was compiled from Stephanie Grace, "Bobby Goes Home," *Brown Alumni Magazine*, November/December 2003, www.brownalumnimagazine.com/; "Transcript of Gov. Jindal's GOP Response to Obama Speech," CNN, February 24, 2009, which is also the source of the chapter-opening quotation.

2. Colin Bonwick, *The American Revolution* (Charlottesville: University of Virginia Press, 1991).

3. Archiving Early America, The First Political Cartoons in America, www.earlyamerica.com/.

4. William Riker, *Federalism: Origin, Operation, Significance* (Boston: Little Brown, 1964), 5.

5. James Madison, *Federalist 39*, "Conformity of the Plan to Republican Principles," www.constitution.org/.

6. *Luther v. Borden*, 7 Howard 1 (1849).

7. *Cohens v. Virginia*, 19 U.S. 264 (1821).

8. *Pennsylvania v. Nelson*, 350 U.S. 497 (1956).

9. *Chisolm v. Georgia*, 2 U.S. 419 (1793).

10. Elinor Ostrom, *Governing the Commons: The Evolution of Institutions for Collective Action* (New York: Cambridge University Press, 1990).

11. *McCulloch v. Maryland*, 17 U.S. 316 (1819).

12. *Gibbons v. Ogden*, 22 U.S. 1 (1824).

13. Daniel Webster's statement is from his Senate debate with Robert Y. Hayne of South Carolina, January 27, 1830. The Jefferson Day dinner took place on April 13, 1830. See Richard B. Morris and Jeffrey B. Morris, eds., *Encyclopedia of American History*, 7th ed. (New York: HarperCollins, 1996), 189–90.

14. Scott Basinger, "Regulating Slavery: Deck-Stacking and Credible Commitment in the Fugitive Slave Act of 1850," *Journal of Law, Economics, and Organization* 19 (2003): 307.

15. *Dred Scott v. Sandford*, 19 Howard 393 (1857).

16. South Carolina Declaration of Succession, "States' Rights," www.civilwarhome.com/.

17. Teaching American History, Veto of the Civil Rights Bill, http://teachingamericanhistory.org/library/.

18. Morton Grodzins, *The American System: A New View of the Government of the United States* (New York: Rand McNally, 1966).

19. *United States v. E.C. Knight Co.*, 156 U.S. 1 (1895).

20. Wendy J. Schiller, "Building Careers and Courting Constituents: U.S. Senate Representation, 1889–1924," *Studies in American Political Development* 20 (2006): 1.

21. *Carter v. Carter Coal Co.*, 298 U.S. 238 (1936).

22. *United States v. Butler*, 297 U.S. 1 (1936).

23. *National Labor Relations Board v. Jones and Laughlin Steel Corporation*, 301 U.S. 1 (1937).

24. *United States v. Darby Lumber Company*, 312 U.S. 100 (1941).

25. Grodzins, *American System*.

26. *Brown v. Board of Education*, 347 U.S. 484 (1954).

27. The American Presidency Project, "American Independent Party Platform of 1968," www.presidency.ucsb.edu/ws/.

28. Sean Nicholson-Crotty, "Rational Election Cycles and the Intermittent Political Safeguards of Federalism," *Publius: The Journal of Federalism* 38 (2008): 295–314.

29. Timothy Conlon, *New Federalism: Intergovernmental Reform from Nixon to Reagan* (Washington D.C.: Brookings Institution, 1988).

30. American Rhetoric, "Ronald Reagan, First Inaugural Address," www.americanrhetoric.com/speeches/.

31. CBS News/*New York Times* poll conducted February 1995.

32. President Clinton Radio Address, CNN, "The Era of Big Government Is Over," www.cnn.com/.

33. Tim Conlan and John Dinan, "Federalism, the Bush Administration, and the Transformation of American Conservatism," *Publius: The Journal of Federalism* 37 (2007): 279–303.

34. Scott F. Abernathy, *No Child Left Behind and the Public Schools* (Ann Arbor: University of Michigan Press, 2007).

35. Clifford Rechtschaffen, "Sidestepping Regulations: On Environment, Bush Ignores Federalism," *San Francisco Chronicle*, August 18, 2003, www.sfgate.com/.

36. Conlan and Dinan, "Federalism, the Bush Administration, and the Transformation of American Conservatism," 280.

37. John Schwartz, "Obama Seems to Be Open to a Broader Role for States," *New York Times*, January 29, 2009, www.nytimes.com/; Stephen Dinan and Ben Conery, "DEA Continues Pot Raids Obama Opposes," February 5, 2009, www.mpp.org/.

38. David M. Herszenhorn, "Recovery Bill Gets Final Approval," *New York Times,* February 13, 2009, www.nytimes.com/.

39. *Younger v. Harris,* 403 U.S. 37 (1971).

40. *United States v. Lopez,* 514 U.S. 549 (1995).

41. *United States v. Morrison,* 529 U.S. 598 (2000).

42. *Alden v. Maine,* 527 U.S. 706 (1999).

43. *College Savings Bank Florida v. Prepaid,* 527 U.S. 627 (1999).

44. *Board of Trustees v. Garrett,* 531 U.S. 356 (2001).

45. *Gonzalez v. Raich,* 545 U.S. 1 (2005).

46. State of Wisconsin Legislative Reform Bureau, "The Partial Veto in Wisconsin," www.legis.state.wi.us/.

47. Wisconsin Legislative Reference Bureau, "Wisconsin Briefs: Constitutional Amendment to Be Considered by Wisconsin Voters," April 1, 2008, www.legis.state.wi.us/.

48. Michael Cooper, "Budget Is Job of Governor, Judges Rule," *New York Times,* December 17, 2004.

49. Charles Barrilleaux and Michael Berkman, "Do Governors Matter? Budgeting Rules and the Politics of State Policymaking," *Political Research Quarterly* 56 (2003): 409–17.

50. Melinda Gann Hall, "Constituent Influence in State Supreme Courts: Conceptual Notes and a Case Study," *Journal of Politics* 49 (1987): 1117–24; Gregory A. Huber and Sanford C. Gordon, "Accountability and Coercion: Is Justice Blind When It Runs for Office?" *American Journal of Political Science* 48 (2004): 247–63.

51. *Republican Party of Minnesota v. White,* 536 U.S. 765 (2002).

52. Texans for Public Justice, "Pay to Play: How Big Money Buys Access to the Texas Supreme Court," http://info.tpj.org/.

53. *Caperton v. Massey Coal Co.* 173 L. Ed. 2d 1208 (2009).

54. "Local Government," www.america.gov/.

55. Frank M. Bryan, *Real Democracy: The New England Town Meeting and How It Works* (Chicago: University of Chicago Press, 2003).

56. National Conference of State Legislatures, "Initiative, Referendum, and Recall," www.ncsl.org/.

57. University of Southern California, Initiative and Referendum Institute, www.iandrinstitute.org/.

58. Frances E. Lee, "Bicameralism and Geographic Politics: Allocating Funds in the House and Senate," *Legislative Studies Quarterly* 29 (2004): 185–213.

59. U.S. Census Bureau, "Federal Aid to States for Fiscal Year 2007," www.census.gov/.

60. Eric Lipton, "New Rules for Giving Out Antiterror Aid," *New York Times,* January 3, 2006.

61. Valentino Larcinese, Leonzio Rizzo, and Cecilia Testa, "Allocating the U.S. Federal Budget to the States: The Impact of the President," *Journal of Politics* 68 (2006): 447–56.

62. *New State Ice Co. v. Liebmann,* 76 L Ed. 311 (1932). See Andrew Karch, *Democratic Laboratories: Policy Diffusion among the American States* (Ann Arbor: University of Michigan Press, 2007).

63. Craig Volden, "States as Policy Laboratories: Emulating Success in the Children's Health Insurance Program," *American Journal of Political Science* 50 (2006): 294–312.

64. Michael Mintron and Sandra Vergari, "Policy Networks and Innovations Diffusion: The Case of State Education Reforms," *Journal of Politics* 60 (1998): 126–48.

65. Christopher Stream, "Health Reform in the States: A Model of State Small Group Health Insurance Market Reforms," *Political Research Quarterly* 52 (1999): 499–525.

66. Frederick J. Boehmke and Richard Witmer, "Disentangling Diffusion: The Effects of Social Learning and Economic Competition on State Policy Innovation and Expansion," *Political Research Quarterly* 57 (2004): 39–51.

67. Charles R. Shipan and Craig Volden, "Bottom-Up Federalism: The Diffusion of Antismoking Policies from U.S. Cities to States," *American Journal of Political Science* 50 (2006): 825–43.

68. Robert R. Preuhs, "State Policy Components of Interstate Migration in the United States," *Political Research Quarterly* 52 (1999): 527–47.

69. David M. Konisky, "Regulatory Competition and Environmental Enforcement: Is There a Race to the Bottom?" *American Journal of Political Science* 51 (2003): 853.

70. *Shapiro v. Thompson,* 394 U.S. 618 (1969); *Saenz v. Roe,* 526 U.S. 489 (1999).

71. Craig Volden, "The Politics of Competitive Federalism: A Race to the Bottom in Welfare Benefits?" *American Journal of Political Science* 46 (2006): 352–63.

72. John Adams, "Dissertation on Canon and Feudal Law," in *The Political Writings of John Adams,* ed. George A. Peek Jr. (Indianapolis: Hackett Publishing, 2003), 4.

73. U.S. Department of Education, "The Federal Role in Education," www.ed.gov/.

74. Michael B. Berkman and Eric Plutzer, *Ten Thousand Democracies* (Washington D.C.: Georgetown University Press, 2005).

75. U.S. Department of Education, "1957–1960 Eisenhower Administration," www.archives.nysed.gov/; "1965–1968 Johnson Administration," www.archives.nysed.gov/.

76. *Plessy v. Ferguson,* 163 U.S. 537 (1896).

77. *Brown v. Board of Education,* 349 U.S. 294 (1955).

78. Michael W. Giles, "HEW versus the Federal Courts: A Comparison of School Desegregation Enforcement," *American Politics Quarterly* 3 (1975): 81–90.

79. Zero to Three: National Center for Infants, Toddlers, and Families, *Federal Agencies Responsible for Implementing Programs Affecting Infants and Toddlers,* www.zerotothree.org/.

80. Maria Gold, "Obama to Rebrand 'No Child Left Behind,'" *Washington Post,* June 23, 2009, www.cbsnews.com/.

81. *Peterson's College Money Handbook* (Lawrenceville, N.J.: Nelnet, 2008).

82. Mark Kantrowitz, "Congress Passes Legislation Ending the Federally Guaranteed Student Loan Program," September 22, 2009, www.fastweb.com; The Library of Congress, http://thomas.loc.gov/.

83. Statements by Dr. Jill Biden and President Barack Obama at the signing of the Health Care and Education Reconciliation Act of 2010, March 30, 2020, www.whitehouse.gov. Also see The White House, Issues: Higher Education, "Making College More Affordable." www.whitehouse.gov.

Chapter 4

1. *Tinker v. Des Moines,* 393 U.S. 503 (1969).

2. This story was compiled from Peter Irons, *The Courage of Their Convictions* (New York: Penguin Books, 1988); John W. Johnson, "The Overlooked Litigant in *Tinker v. Des Moines,*" in *Constitutionalism and American Culture,* ed. Sandra F. VanBurkleo, Kermit L. Hall, and Robert J. Kaczorowski (Lawrence: University Press of Kansas, 2002); John Tinker, "*Tinker v. Des Moines:* Frequently Asked Questions," http://schema-root.org/; Diana Hadley, "Mary Beth Tinker: An 'Ordinary' Woman with Extraordinary Courage," Indiana High School Press Association, http://ihspa.blogspot.com/; and an e-mail interview with Mary Beth Tinker, January 27, 2010, conducted for this

textbook; chapter-opening quotation is from this interview. Theodore Roosevelt High School, illustrated at the beginning of the chapter, is where Chris Eckhardt went to school. Mary Beth Tinker attended Warren Harding Junior High School.

3. *Guiles v. Marineau,* 349 F. Supp. 2d 871 (2004); *Hansen v. Ann Arbor Public Schools,* 293 F. Supp. 2d 780 (2003); *Lowry v. Watson Chapel School District,* 540 F.3d 752 (2008).

4. "Brutus," *Antifederalist* 2, "To the Citizens of the State of New-York," www.constitution.org/.

5. *West Virginia State Board of Education v. Barnette,* 319 U.S. 624 (1943).

6. *Congressional Record,* June 8, 1789, http://press-pubs.uchicago.edu/.

7. *Schenck v. United States,* 249 U.S. 47 (1919).

8. *Barron v. Baltimore,* 32 U.S. 243 (1833); Zechariah Chafee Jr., *Free Speech in the United States* (Cambridge, Mass.: Harvard University Press, 1967); *Gilbert v. Minnesota,* 254 U.S. 325 (1920).

9. *Ex Parte Starr,* 263 F. 145 (1920).

10. Judith A. Baer, *Equality under the Constitution* (Ithaca, N.Y.: Cornell University Press, 1983).

11. *Chicago B & Q Railway Company v. Chicago,* 166 U.S. 226 (1897).

12. *Gitlow v. New York,* 268 U.S. 652 (1925).

13. *Palko v. Connecticut,* 302 U.S. 319 (1937).

14. Abraham Lincoln, Speech to Congress, July 4, 1861, http://facweb.furman.edu/.

15. *Ex Parte Milligan,* 71 U.S. 2 (1866).

16. *Ex parte McCardle,* 74 U.S. 506 (1868).

17. *Schenck v. United States,* 249 U.S. 47 (1919); *Debs v. United States,* 249 U.S. 211 (1919).

18. *Abrams v. United States,* 250 U.S. 616 (1919).

19. David Cole, "Enemy Aliens," *Stanford Law Review* 54 (2002): 953.

20. Bernard A. Weisberger, "Terrorism Revisited," *American Heritage Magazine* 44 (November 1993), www.americanheritage.com/.

21. Tony Mauro, "The Quirin Ruling," www.counterpunch.org/.

22. John Earl Haynes and Harvey Klehr, *Venona: Decoding Soviet Espionage in America* (New Haven, Conn.: Yale University Press, 1999).

23. *Watkins v. United States,* 354 U.S. 178 (1957).

24. *Barenblatt v. United States,* 360 U.S. 109 (1959).

25. Ellen Schrecker, *Many Are the Crimes: McCarthyism in America* (Boston: Little, Brown, 1998), xiii.

26. Select Committee to Study Governmental Operations, "Intelligence Activities and the Rights of Americans," Book II, final report, www.icdc.com/.

27. *Hirota v. MacArthur,* 338 U.S. 197 (1948).

28. *Hamdan v. Rumsfeld,* 548 U.S. 557 (2006).

29. Robert McMillan, "Obama Administration Defends Bush Wiretapping," *PC World,* www.pcworld.com/.

30. *Chaplinsky v. New Hampshire,* 315 U.S. 568 (1942).

31. David L. Hudson Jr., "Hate Speech and Campus Speech Codes," First Amendment Center, www.firstamendmentcenter.org/.

32. *UWM Post v. Board of Regents of the University of Wisconsin,* 774 F. Supp. 1163 (1991).

33. Kermit Hall, "Free Speech on Public College Campuses," First Amendment Center, www.firstamendmentcenter.org/.

34. Alan Charles Kors and Harvey Silvergate, *The Shadow University: The Betrayal of Liberty on America's Campuses* (New York: Free Press, 1998).

35. *John Doe. v. University of Michigan,* 721 F. Supp. 852 (1989).

36. Ibid.

37. *UWM Post v. Board of Regents of the University of Wisconsin,* 774 F. Supp. 1163 (1991).

38. *United States v. O'Brien,* 391 U.S. 367 (1968).

39. *Virginia v. Black,* 538 U.S. 343 (2003).

40. *West Virginia Board of Education v. Barnette,* 319 U.S. 624 (1943).

41. *Texas v. Johnson,* 491 U.S. 397 (1989).

42. *Morse v. Frederick,* 551 U.S. 393 (2007).

43. *Grayned v. City of Rockford,* 408 U.S. 104 (1972).

44. *National Socialist Party of America v. Village of Skokie,* 432 U.S. 43 (1977).

45. *Hill v. Colorado,* 530 U.S. 703 (2000).

46. William Blackstone, *Commentaries on the Laws of England,* 1769 (Chicago: University of Chicago Press, 2002), 4:151–53.

47. *New York Times v. United States,* 403 U.S. 713 (1971).

48. *United States v. Progressive,* 467 F. Supp. 990 (1979).

49. See www.wikileaks.org.

50. Adam Liptak and Brad Stone, "Judge Shuts Down Web Site Specializing in Leaks," *New York Times,* February 20, 2008.

51. *Hustler Magazine v. Falwell,* 485 U.S. 46 (1988).

52. Anna Badkhen, "Web Can Ruin Reputation with Stroke of a Key," *San Francisco Chronicle,* May 6, 2007.

53. *Miller v. California,* 413 U.S. 15 (1973).

54. *Jenkins v. Georgia,* 418 U.S. 153 (1974).

55. *New York v. Ferber,* 458 U.S. 747 (1982).

56. *Ashcroft v. Free Speech Coalition,* 535 U.S. 234 (2002).

57. *Reno v. American Civil Liberties Union,* 521 U.S. 844 (1997).

58. *Roberts v. United States Jaycees,* 468 U.S. 609 (1984).

59. *Boy Scouts v. Dale,* 530 U.S. 640 (2000).

60. Edward Hart, "Remonstrance of the Inhabitants of the Town of Flushing to Governor Stuyvesant," December 27, 1657, www.nyym.org/.

61. Henry J. Abraham and Barbara A. Perry, *Freedom and the Court,* 6th ed. (New York: Oxford University Press, 1994), 223.

62. Ontario Consultants on Religious Tolerance, "Religious Laws," www.religioustolerance.org/.

63. *Church of Lakumi Babalu Aye v. City of Hialeah,* 508 U.S. 520 (1993).

64. *Reynolds v. United States,* 98 U.S. 145 (1878).

65. *Clay, aka, Ali v. United States,* 403 U.S. 698 (1971). Also cited, in the next paragraph, are *Employment Division v. Smith,* 494 U.S. 872 (1990), and *Boerne v. Flores,* 521 U.S. 507 (1997), at 536.

66. See "Rethinking the Incorporation of the Establishment Clause: A Federalist View," *Harvard Law Review* 105 (1992): 1700.

67. *Everson v. Board of Education,* 330 U.S. 1 (1947).

68. *Lemon v. Kurtzman,* 403 U.S. 602 (1971).

69. *Engel v. Vitale,* 370 U.S. 421 (1962); *Abington School District v. Schempp,* 374 U.S. 203 (1963).

70. *Epperson v. Arkansas,* 393 U.S. 97 (1968).

71. *Edwards v. Aguillard,* 482 U.S. 578 (1987).

72. *Lee v. Weisman*, 505 U.S. 577 (1992).

73. *Santa Fe Independent School District v. Doe*, 530 U.S. 290 (2000).

74. *Board of Education v. Allen*, 392 U.S. 236 (1968).

75. *Meek v. Pittinger*, 421 U.S. 349 (1975).

76. *District of Columbia v. Heller*, 171 L. Ed. 2d 637 (2008).

77. *McDonald v. Chicago*, 2010, www.supremecourtus.gov/opinions/.

78. *Schneckloth v. Bustamonte*, 412 U.S. 218 (1973).

79. See Jeffrey A. Segal, "Predicting Supreme Court Decisions Probabilistically: The Search and Seizure Cases, 1962–1981," *American Political Science Review* 78 (1984): 801.

80. *California v. Ciraolo*, 476 U.S. 207 (1986).

81. *Kyllo v. United States*, 533 U.S. 27 (2001).

82. *Virginia v. Moore*, 553 U.S. 164 (2008).

83. *Vernonia School District 47J v. Acton*, 515 U.S. 646 (1995); *National Treasury Union v. Von Raab*, 489 U.S. 656 (1989); *Chandler v. Miller*, 520 U.S. 305 (1997).

84. *Mapp v. Ohio*, 367 U.S. 643 (1961).

85. Priscilla H. Machado Zotti, *Injustice for All: Mapp v. Ohio and the Fourth Amendment* (New York: Peter Lang, 2005).

86. *Miranda v. Arizona*, 384 U.S. 436 (1966).

87. *Dickerson v. United States*, 530 U.S. 428 (2000).

88. *Powell v. Alabama*, 287 U.S. 45 (1932).

89. *Betts v. Brady*, 316 U.S. 455 (1942).

90. *Gideon v. Wainwright*, 372 U.S. 335 (1963).

91. *Argersinger v. Hamlin*, 407 U.S. 25 (1972).

92. *Williams v. Florida*, 399 U.S. 78 (1970); *Johnson v. Louisiana*, 406 U.S. 356 (1972).

93. *Georgia v. McCollum*, 505 U.S. 42 (1992); *J. E. B. v. Alabama*, 511 U.S. 127 (1994).

94. Akhil Amar, *The Bill of Rights* (New Haven, Conn.: Yale University Press, 1998), 82.

95. *Rummel v. Estelle*, 445 U.S. 263 (1980).

96. *Furman v. Georgia*, 408 U.S. 238 (1972).

97. *Gregg v. Georgia*, 428 U.S. 153 (1976).

98. *Griswold v. Connecticut*, 381 U.S. 479 (1965).

99. *Eisenstadt v. Baird*, 405 U.S. 438 (1972).

100. Gerald Rosenberg, *The Hollow Hope* (Chicago: University of Chicago Press, 1991), 262.

101. *Roe v. Wade*, 410 U.S. 113 (1973).

102. *Planned Parenthood of Southeastern Pennsylvania v. Casey*, 505 U.S. 833 (1992). Also cited, in the next paragraph, are *Stenberg v. Carhart*, 530 U.S. 914 (2000), and *Gonzalez v. Carhart*, 550 U.S. 124 (2007).

103. Lori Ringhand, "Supreme Court Confirmation Dataset," www.uga.edu/.

104. *Bowers v. Hardwick*, 478 U.S. 186 (1986).

105. National Opinion Research Center, General Social Survey, University of Chicago.

106. *Lawrence v. Texas*, 539 U.S. 558 (2003).

107. *Cruzan v. Director, Missouri Department of Health*, 497 U.S. 261 (1990), at 278.

108. *Washington v. Glucksberg*, 521 U.S. 702; *Vacco v. Quill*, 521 U.S. 793 (1997).

109. *Village of Belle Terre v. Boraas*, 416 U.S. 1 (1974).

110. *Lucas v. South Carolina Coastal Council*, 505 U.S. 1003 (1992).

111. *Old Dominion Land Co. v. United States*, 269 U.S. 55 (1925).

112. *Kelo v. City of New London*, 545 U.S. 469 (2005).

113. Patrick McGeehan, "Pfizer to Leave City That Won Land Use Case," *New York Times*, November 12, 2009, www.nytimes.com/.

114. *West Virginia State Board of Education v. Barnette*, 319 U.S. 624 (1943).

115. Robert Dahl, "Decision-Making in a Democracy: The Supreme Court as a National Policy-Maker," *Journal of Public Law* 6 (1957): 279–295.

116. Anthony Lewis, *Freedom for the Thought That We Hate* (New York: Basic Books, 2007).

117. John L. Sullivan, James Pierson, and George Marcus, *Political Tolerance and American Democracy* (Chicago: University of Chicago Press, 1973); James L. Gibson, "Enigmas of Intolerance: Fifty Years after Stouffer's *Communism, Conformity, and Civil Liberties*," *Perspectives on Politics* 21, no. 4 (2006): 22.

118. August 2007 Freedom Forum Survey, accessed via Roper Center for Public Opinion Research, University of Connecticut.

Chapter 5

1. This story has been compiled from Juan Williams, *Eyes on the Prize: America's Civil Rights Years, 1954–1965* (New York: Penguin Books, 1987), 130–31, also, generally, 122–61; Michael Westmoreland-White, "Diane Nash (1938–): Unsung Heroine of the Civil Rights Movement," October 20, 2002, www.ecapc.org/articles/; Linda T. Wynn, "Diane Judith Nash (1938–): A Mission for Equality, Justice, and Social Change," in *Tennessee Women: Their Lives and Times*, ed. Sarah Wilkerson Freeman and Beverly Greene Bond (Athens: University of Georgia Press, 2009), 281–304; interview with Diane Nash, November 12, 1985, www.teachersdomain.org; chapter-opening quotation is from this interview.

2. See Alexander Keyssar, *The Right to Vote* (New York: Basic Books, 2000).

3. Senator Lyman Trumbull, quoted in Judith Baer, *Equality under the Constitution* (Ithaca, N.Y.: Cornell University Press, 1983), 96.

4. Ronald Dworkin, *Taking Rights Seriously* (Cambridge, Mass.: Harvard University Press, 1978).

5. Quoted in Steven M. Gillon and Cathy D. Matson, *The American Experiment*, 2nd ed. (Boston: Houghton Mifflin, 2006), 61.

6. *Dred Scott v. Sandford*, 60 U.S. 393 (1857).

7. *United States v. Cruikshank*, 92 U.S. 542 (1875).

8. Ronald Walters, "'The Association Is for the Direct Attack': The Militant Context of the NAACP Challenge *Plessy*," *Washburn Law Journal* 43 (2003): 329.

9. *Plessy v. Ferguson*, 163 U.S. 537 (1896).

10. California Alien Land Law (1913).

11. Vicki L. Ruiz, "South by Southwest: Mexican Americans and Segregated Schooling, 1900–1950," *Magazine of History* 15 (Winter 2001), www.oah.org/pubs/.

12. *Westminster School District v. Mendez.*, 161 F.2d 774 (1947).

13. Ruiz, "South by Southwest."

14. Quoted in Renata Fengler, "Abigail and John Adams Discuss Women and Republican Government: 1776," University of Wisconsin–Green Bay, www.historytools.org/sources/.

15. Keyssar, *Right to Vote*.

16. *Minor v. Happersett*, 88 U.S. 162 (1874).

17. Justice Bradley, concurring in *Bradwell v. Illinois*, 83 U.S. 130 (1872), at 142.

18. Judith A. Baer, *The Chains of Protection* (Westport, Conn.: Greenwood Press, 1978).

19. The Women's History Project of Lexington Area National Organization for Women, "Timeline of Women's Suffrage in the United States," www.dpsinfo.com/women/history/.

20. Survey by the Office of Public Opinion Research, July 1945.

21. "The Law: Up from Coverture," *Time Magazine,* March 20, 1972, www.time.com/.

22. *Kirchberg v. Feenstra*, 450 U.S. 455 (1981), at 456.

23. Richard Kluger, *Simple Justice* (New York: Knopf, 1975), 376.

24. See Laurence H. Tribe, *American Constitutional Law* (Mineola, N.Y.: Foundation Press, 1988), 1561–65.

25. Ibid.

26. Baer, *Chains of Protection.*

27. *Hoyt v. Florida*, 368 U.S. 57 (1961).

28. Peter H. Schuck and Rogers M. Smith, *Citizenship without Consent* (New Haven, Conn.: Yale University Press, 1985), 1–2.

29. *Johnson v. M'Intosh*, 21 U.S. 543 (1823), at 569.

30. *Elk v. Wilkins*, 112 U.S. 94 (1884).

31. Immigration Act of 1907, www.multied.com/documents/.

32. Rogers M. Smith, *Civic Ideals* (New Haven, Conn.: Yale University Press, 1997), 16.

33. Richard Wormser, "The Rise and Fall of Jim Crow," PBS, www.pbs.org/.

34. Smith, *Civic Ideals*, 17.

35. "Immigration Act of 1924," Documents of American History II, http://tucnak.fsv.cuni.cz/~calda/Documents/.

36. *Korematsu v. United States*, 323 U.S. 214 (1944).

37. Ann McDermott, "Orphans Tell of World War II Internment," www.cnn.com/.

38. David Cole, "No More Roundups," *Washington Post*, www.washingtonpost.com/.

39. *Civil Rights Cases*, 109 U.S. 3 (1883); *Shelley v. Kraemer*, 334 U.S. 1 (1948).

40. *Missouri ex rel. Gaines v. Canada*, 305 U.S. 337 (1938); *Sipuel v. Board of Regents of University of Oklahoma*, 332 U.S. 631 (1948); *Sweatt v. Painter*, 339 U.S. 629 (1950).

41. *Bolling v. Sharpe*, 347 U.S. 497 (1954).

42. *Brown v. Board of Education*, 349 U.S. 294 (1955).

43. *Cooper v. Aaron*, 358 U.S. 1 (1958).

44. Gerald N. Rosenberg, *The Hollow Hope: Can Courts Bring about Social Change* (Chicago: University of Chicago Press, 1991).

45. *Alexander v. Holmes County Board of Education*, 396 U.S. 1218 (1969).

46. *Browder v. Gayle*, 352 U.S. 903 (1956).

47. *Jackson v. Alabama*, 348 U.S. 888 (1954).

48. Quoted in Walter F. Murphy, *Elements of Judicial Strategy* (Chicago: University of Chicago Press, 1964), 193.

49. *Loving v. Virginia,* 388 U.S. 1 (1967).

50. Henry Abraham and Barbara Perry, *Freedom and the Court*, 6th ed. (New York: Oxford University Press, 1994), 380. See also David Halberstam, *The Children* (New York: Fawcett Books, 1998), 230–34. The caption for the photo on page 156 was drawn from this source.

51. David Fankhauser, "Freedom Rides: Recollections by David Fankhauser," http://biology.clc.uc.edu/fankhauser/.

52. Martin Luther King Jr., "Letter from Birmingham Jail," The King Center, http://coursesa.matrix.msu.edu/.

53. Martin Luther King Jr., "I Have a Dream," www.usconstitution.net/.

54. *Heart of Atlanta Motel v. United States*, 379 U.S. 241 (1964); *Katzenbach v. McClung*, 379 U.S. 294 (1964).

55. *Griggs v. Duke Power Co.*, 401 U.S. 424 (1971).

56. *Wards Cove Packing Co. v. Antonio*, 490 U.S. 642 (1989).

57. *Ricci v. DeStefano* 174 L. Ed. 2d 490 (2009).

58. *Guinn v. United States*, 238 U.S. 347 (1915); *Smith v. Allwright*, 321 U.S. 649 (1944).

59. Martin Luther King Jr., "Civil Right No. 1" *New York Times Magazine*, March 14, 1965, p. 26.

60. Lyndon B. Johnson, "We Shall Overcome," The History Place, www.historyplace.com/.

61. Mark Hugo Lopez and Paul Taylor, "Dissecting the 2008 Electorate: Most Diverse in U.S. History," Pew Research Center, http://pewresearch.org/.

62. *Northwest Austin Municipal Utility District No. One v. Holder* 174 L. Ed. 2d 140 (2009).

63. *Bowers v. Hardwick*, 478 U.S. 186 (1986).

64. *Romer v. Evans*, 517 U.S. 620 (1996).

65. *Lawrence v. Texas*, 539 U.S. 558 (2003).

66. General Social Survey, April 2008, Roper Center for Public Opinion Research, University of Connecticut.

67. A CBS *New York Times* poll in April 2010 asked, "Which comes closest to your view? . . . Gay couples should be allowed to legally marry. Gay couples should be allowed to form civil unions but not legally marry. There should be no legal recognition of a gay couple's relationship." Of those polled, 39 percent said gay couples should be allowed to legally marry; 24 percent said they should be allowed to form civil unions; 30 percent said there should be no legal recognition; and 7 percent didn't know or did not answer.

68. Lyndon Johnson, Commencement Address at Howard University, "To Fulfill These Rights," June 4, 1965, www.lbjlib.utexas.edu/johnson/.

69. Martin Luther King Jr., quoted in Stephen B. Oates, *Let the Trumpet Sound* (New York: HarperCollins, 1994), 426.

70. *Steelworkers v. Weber*, 443 U.S. 193 (1979).

71. *Firefighters Local Union No. 1784 v. Stotts*, 467 U.S. 561 (1984).

72. *Johnson v. Transportation Agency*, 480 U.S. 616 (1987).

73. *Fullilove v. Klutznick*, 448 U.S. 448 (1980).

74. *Richmond v. J. A. Croson Co.*, 488 U.S. 469 (1989).

75. *Metro Broadcasting, Inc. v. FCC*, 497 U.S. 547 (1990); *Adarand Constructors, Inc. v. Pena*, 515 U.S. 200 (1995).

76. *Bakke v. California*, 438 U.S. 265 (1978).

77. *Grutter v. Bollinger*, 539 U.S. 306 (2003).

78. *Gratz v. Bollinger*, 539 U.S. 244 (2003).

79. "Employing and Accommodating Individuals with Histories of Alcohol or Drug Abuse," National Council on Alcoholism and Drug Dependence of the San Fernando Valley, Inc., www.ncadd-sfv.org/.

80. David A. Harris, "Driving While Black: Racial Profiling on Our Nation's Highways," American Civil Liberties Union, www.aclu.org/.

81. Ibid.

82. *United States v. Travis,* 837 F. Supp. 1386 (1993); *State of New Jersey v. Patterson* 270 N. J. Super. 550 (1994); *Derricott v. State of Maryland* 611 A.2d 592 (1992).

83. ProCon. State Felon Voting Laws. http://felonvoting.procon.org/.

84. Jeff Manza and Christopher Uggen, "Punishment and Democracy: Disenfranchisement of Nonincarcerated Felons in the United States," *Perspectives on Politics* 2 (2004): 491–505.

85. Fox News poll, April 2006, Roper Center for Public Opinion Research, University of Connecticut.

86. *Plyler v. Doe,* 457 U.S. 202 (1982).

87. Remus Ilies, Nancy Hauserman, Susan Schwochau, and John Stibal, "Reported Incidence Rates of Work-Related Sexual Harassment in the United States," *Personnel Psychology* 56 (2003): 607–31.

88. U.S. Equal Employment Opportunity Commission, "Sexual Harassment Charges EEOC and FEPAs Combined: FY 1997–FY 2008," www.eeoc.gov/eeoc/.

89. *Meritor Savings Bank v. Vinson,* 477 U.S. 57 (1986).

90. National Committee on Pay Equity, "Ledbetter Bill Becomes Law," February 28, 2009, www.pay-equity.org/.

91. *Burlington Northern and Sante Fe Railway Co. v. White,* 548 U.S. 53 (2006).

92. *Ledbetter v. Goodyear Tire and Rubber Co.,* 550 U.S. 618 (2007).

93. Ibid., 645.

94. House of Representatives, Lilly Ledbetter Fair Pay Act, http://edlabor.house.gov/.

95. Martin Luther King Jr., "Civil Right No. 1" *New York Times Magazine,* March 14, 1965, 26.

96. M. V. Hood, Quentin Kidd, and Irwin L. Morris, "The Key Issue: Constituency Effects and Southern Senators' Roll-Call Voting on Civil Rights," *Legislative Studies Quarterly* 26 (2001): 599–621.

97. See the Poole and Rosenthal Common Space scores, www.voteview.com.

Chapter 6

1. This story was compiled from Stephanie Clifford, "Finding Fame with a Prescient Call for Obama," *New York Times,* November 10, 2008; Adam Sternbergh, "The Spreadsheet Psychic," *New York Magazine,* October 12, 2008; James Wolcott, "The Good, the Bad, and Joe Lieberman," *Vanity Fair,* February 2009, 76; and Nate Silver, "Will Young Voters Turn Out for Obama?" *New York Post,* August 10, 2008, http://www.nypost.com/p/news/opinion/opedcolumnists/; opening quotation from Silver, "Will Young Voters Turn Out for Obama?"

2. Quoted in Harry Jaffa, *The Crisis of the House Divided,* 2nd ed. (Chicago: University of Chicago Press, 1959), 10.

3. See James Bryce, *The American Commonwealth* (New York: MacMillan, 1895), 239.

4. The first scholar to discuss how the public rallies to support the president in time of trouble was John Mueller, *War, Presidents, and Public Opinion* (New York: Wiley, 1970).

5. Quoted in Ted Barrett and Steve Brusk, "Bush: Immigration Bill Will Enforce Borders, Workplaces," CNN, June 12, 2007, http://www.cnn.com/.

6. A CBS/*New York Times* poll conducted October 31–November 2, 2008, indicated that only 20 percent of the public approved of Bush's job as president. Prior to that, Harry Truman (23 percent) and Richard Nixon (24 percent) had been the least popular presidents. Both Truman and Nixon rebounded a bit from those low points as they left office.

7. Brian Montopoli, "Obama Approval Rating Falls to 50 Percent," *CBS News,* December 9, 2009, http://www.cbsnews.com/.

8. Poll conducted by CBS News/*New York Times,* February 5–10, 2010, based on 1,084 telephone interviews.

9. See Marc Hetherington, *Why Trust Matters* (Princeton, N.J.: Princeton University Press, 2005).

10. Survey by Eric Liu and Nick Hanaver conducted by Greenberg Quinlan Rosner Research, August 12–14, 2008, based on telephone interviews with a national adult sample of one thousand.

11. It is hard to know the exact share of people who would support overthrowing the American government because pollsters almost never ask that question. We say "almost never," but in our search of questions asked over the last seventy-five years we have not found one such question. A database at the Roper Center at the University of Connecticut contains nearly five hundred thousand questions, so we are able to do a detailed search.

12. Quoted in Francis B. Carpenter, *Six Months at the White House: The Story of a Picture* (New York: Hurd and Houghton, 1866), 218. See also Mario Cuomo, *Lincoln on Democracy* (New York: Harper, 1990).

13. Robert Hilderbrand, *Power and the People* (Chapel Hill: University of North Carolina Press, 1981).

14. Eli Saslow, "Obama, Reaching Outside the Bubble," *Washington Post,* March 1, 2009, A1; Ashley Parker, "Picking Letters, 10 a Day, That Reach Obama," *Washington Post,* April 21, 2009.

15. Quoted in John Geer, *From Tea Leaves to Opinion Polls* (New York: Columbia University Press, 1996), 50–51.

16. Benjamin Ginsberg, *The Captive Public* (New York: Basic Books, 1986).

17. Robert Erikson and Kent Tedin, *American Public Opinion,* 6th ed. (New York: Longman, 2003), 7.

18. V. O. Key, *Public Opinion and American Democracy* (New York: Knopf, 1961), 536.

19. George Gallup, *The Pulse of Democracy* (New York: Simon and Schuster, 1940).

20. Seymour Sudman and Norman M. Bradburn, "The Organizational Growth of Public Opinion Research in the United States," *Public Opinion Quarterly* 51, pt. 2, Supplement: 50th Anniversary Issue (1987): S67–S78.

21. Franklin Roosevelt did make some use of polls, but it was sporadic. Truman had no use for polls, but Eisenhower's advisers clearly paid attention to them. For the best scholarly account of the presidential use of polls, see Robert Eisinger, *The Evolution of Presidential Polling* (New York: Cambridge University Press, 2003).

22. Survey by Pew Research Center for the People & the Press. Conducted by Opinion Research Corporation, December 4–7, 2009, and based on telephone interviews with a national adult sample of 1,003.

23. Erikson and Tedin, *American Public Opinion,* 26.

24. "Miss America," February 25, 2010, in Wikipedia, the Free Encyclopedia.

25. Alicia C. Shepard, "How They Blew It," *American Journalism Review,* January/February 2001.

26. Kathy Frankovic, "The Truth about Push Polls," *CBS News,* 2000, http://www.cbsnews.com/.

27. Scott Keeter, "Cell Phones and the 2008 Election: An Update," *Pew Research Center,* July 17, 2008, http://pewresearch.org/.

28. Herbert Asher, *Polling and the Public,* 7th ed. (Washington D.C.: CQ Press, 2007), 93.

29. Pew Research Center for the People and the Press, "Polls Face Growing Resistance, but Still Representative," April 20, 2004, http://people-press.org/.

30. Erikson and Tedin, *American Public Opinion,* 121.

31. M. Kent Jennings, Laura Stoker, and Jake Bowers, "Politics across Generations," *Journal of Politics* 71 (July 2009): 782–99.

32. John Alford and John Hibbing, "Biology and Rational Choice," *Political Economy Newsletter,* Fall 2005.

33. Amy Lavoie, "The Genes in Your Congeniality: Researchers Identify Genetic Influence in Social Networks," *Harvard Science: Culture + Society,* January 26, 2009.

34. Peter Hatemi, Nathan A Gillespie, Lindon J. Eaves, Brion S. Maher, Sarah E. Medland, David C. Smyth, Harry N. Beeby, Scott D. Gordon, Grant W. Montgomery, Ghu Zhu Enda Byrne, Bradley T. Webb, Andrew C. Heath, and Nicholas G. Martin, "A Genome-Wide Analysis of Liberal and Conservative Political Attitudes," *Journal of Politics* (2010): forthcoming.

35. John R. Alford, John Hibbing, and Carolyn L. Funk, "Twin Studies, Molecular Genetics, Politics, and Tolerance," *Perspectives on Politics* 6 (December 2008); John Hibbing, John R. Alford, and Carolyn L. Funk, "Beyond Liberals and Conservatives to Political Genotypes and Phenotypes," *Perspectives on Politics* 6 (June 2008): 321–28.

36. Scott Keeter, "Young Voters in the 2008 Election," *Pew Research Center,* November 12, 2008, http://pewresearch.org/.

37. Scott Keeter and Paul Taylor, "The Millennials," *Pew Research Center,* December 11, 2009, http://pewresearch.org/.

38. Jason Barabas, "Rational Exuberance," *Journal of Politics* 68 (2006): 50–61.

39. This theory comes out of the work of John Zaller, *Nature of Mass Beliefs* (New York: Cambridge University Press, 1992).

40. NBC News/*Wall Street Journal* poll, October 25–28, 1997, and January 17–20, 2007.

41. The classic book that lays out the argument about party identification is Angus Campbell, Philip Converse, Warren Miller, and Donald Stokes, *The American Voter* (New York: Wiley, 1960).

42. Poll conducted by CBS News/*New York Times,* February 5–10, 2010, based on 1,084 telephone interviews.

43. Poll conducted by CBS News/*New York Times,* September 20–23, 2001, based on 1,216 telephone interviews.

44. See "Party Identification 7-Point Scale: 1952–2004," *The ANES Guide to Public Opinion and Electoral Behavior,* http://www.electionstudies.org/.

45. David Brooks, "What Independents Want," *New York Times,* November 5, 2009, A31.

46. John Sides, "Three Myths about Political Independents," December 17, 2009, www.monkeycage.org/.

47. Data from an NBC News/*Wall Street Journal* poll conducted in December 2008. The same pattern exists for 2009.

48. This way of thinking about the public comes from Philip Converse, "Nature of Belief Systems in Mass Publics," in *Ideology and Discontent,* ed. David Apter (New York: Free Press, 1964).

49. Data from William Jacoby "The Formation of Issue Concepts and Partisan Change," paper presented at the 2007 annual meeting of the Southern Political Science Association.

50. The exact percentage of the public that was literate at the time of the founding is unclear. This percentage reflects the best guess of some historians.

51. *CIA World Factbook,* February 4, 2010, https://www.cia.gov/.

52. Paul Lazarsfeld, Bernard Berelson, and Helen Gaudet, *The People's Choice* (New York: Duell, Sloane, Pearce, 1944).

53. Bernard Berelson, Paul F. Lazarsfeld, and William N. McPhee, *Voting: A Study of Opinion Formation in a Presidential Campaign* (Chicago: University of Chicago Press, 1954).

54. Converse, "Nature of Belief Systems in Mass Publics."

55. These data all come from Erikson and Tedin, *American Public Opinion,* 62.

56. See John Zaller, "Monica Lewinsky and the Mainsprings of American Politics," in *Mediated Politics: Communication in the Future of Democracy,* ed. W. Lance Bennett and Robert M. Entman (Cambridge, U.K.: Cambridge University Press, 2001).

57. Stanley Kelley, *Interpreting Elections* (Princeton, N.J.: Princeton University Press, 1983).

58. Christopher Achen, "Mass Political Attitudes and the Survey Response," *American Political Science Review* 69 (1975): 1218–31.

59. Jennifer Hochschild, *What's Fair* (New Haven, Conn.: Yale University Press, 1980).

60. Sam Popkin developed this concept in his book *The Reasoning Voter* (Chicago: University of Chicago Press, 1991).

61. Nolan McCarty, Keith Poole, and Howard Rosenthal, "Party Polarization: 1879–2009," Polarized America website, January 4, 2006, http://polarizedamerica.com/.

62. For a comprehensive account of these data, see Alan Abramowitz and Kyle Saunders, "Is Polarization a Myth?" *Journal of Politics* 70 (2008): 542–55.

63. See Morris Fiorina, *Culture War?* (New York: Longman, 2008).

64. Morris Fiorina, Samuel Abrams, and Jeremy Pope, "Polarization in the American Public," *Journal of Politics* 70 (2008): 556–60.

65. See Alan Abramowitz, *The Disappearing Center* (New Haven, Conn.: Yale University Press, 2010).

66. These data are from the CBS/*New York Times* polls conducted during the presidential campaigns and available through the Roper Center.

67. Erikson and Tedin, *American Public Opinion,* 193.

68. Ibid., 208.

69. "Muslim Americans: Mostly Middle Class and Mostly Mainstream," *Pew Research Center,* May 22, 2007, http://pewresearch.org/.

70. Erikson and Tedin, *American Public Opinion,* 215.

71. Center for the American Woman and Politics, "The Gender Gap: Voting Choices in Presidential Elections," December 2008, http://www.cawp.rutgers.edu/.

72. "Support for Abortion Slips: Issue Ranks Lower on the Agenda," *Pew Research Center,* October 1, 2009, http://pewresearch.org/.

73. Data from National Election Studies, http://www.electionstudies.org/.

74. Data from the 2004 General Social Survey conducted by the National Opinion Research Center (NORC) at the University of Chicago.

75. Carole Jean Uhlaner and F. Chris Garcia, "Latino Public Opinion," in *Understanding Public Opinion,* ed. Barbara Norrander and Clyde Wilcox (Washington, D.C.: CQ Press, 2002).

76. Rodolfo De la Garza, Louis DeSipio, F. Chris Garcia, John Garcia, and Angelo Falcon, *Latino Voices: Mexican, Puerto Rican, and Cuban Perspectives on American Politics* (Boulder, Colo.: Westview Press, 1992).

77. David Leal, "Latino Public Opinion," Texas A&M Department of Political Science: Project for Equity, Representation, and Justice, http://perg.tamu.edu/lpc/Leal.pdf.

78. Marisa Abrajano, R. Michael Alvarez, and Jonathan Nagler, "The Hispanic Vote in the 2004 Presidential Election," *Journal of Politics* 70 (2008): 368–82.

79. Scott Keeter, "Where the Public Stands on Immigration Reform," *Pew Research Center,* November 23, 2009, http://pewresearch.org/.

80. See Norman H. Nie, Jane Junn, and Kenneth Stehlik-Barry, *Education and Democratic Citizenship in America* (Chicago: University of Chicago Press, 1996).

81. Ellen C. Collier, "Instances of Use of United States Forces Abroad, 1798–1993," *Naval Historical Center*, http://www.history.navy.mil/.

82. John Mueller, *War, Presidents, and Public Opinion* (New York: Wiley, 1970).

83. Presidential Approval Ratings, Gallup Historical Statistics, http://www.gallup.com/.

84. Presidential Approval Ratings, George W. Bush, http://www.gallup.com/.

85. Christian Grose and Bruce Oppenheimer, "The Iraq War, Partisanship, and Candidate Attributes: Explaining Variation in Partisan Swing in the 2006 U.S. House Elections," *Legislative Studies Quarterly* 32 (2007): 4.

86. Scott Sigmund Gartner, "The Multiple Effects of Casualties on Public Support for War: An Experimental Approach," *American Political Science Review* 102 (2008): 96–106.

87. Helene Cooper, "Fearing Another Quagmire in Afghanistan," *New York Times,* January 24, 2009.

88. "The Abu Ghraib Files," *Salon*, March 14, 2006, http://www.salon.com/.

89. Sarah Mendelson, "The Guantanamo Countdown," *Foreign Affairs*, October 1, 2009.

90. V. O. Key, *The Responsible Electorate* (Cambridge, Mass.: Harvard University Press, 1966), 1.

91. Robert S. Erikson, Michael B. MacKuen, and James A. Stimson, *The Macro Polity* (Cambridge, U.K.: Cambridge University Press, 2002).

92. See Key, *Public Opinion and American Democracy*, and Douglas Arnold, *Logic of Congressional Action* (New Haven, Conn.: Yale University Press, 1991).

Chapter 7

1. This story was compiled from the Daily Kos website, http://www.dailykos.com/; Christopher Null, "The 50 Most Important People on the Web," *PC World,* March 5, 2007, http://www.pcworld.com/; David M. Ewalt, "The Web Celeb 25," *Forbes,* January 23, 2007, http://www.forbes.com/; eBizMBA, "Top 25 Most Popular Blogs," http://www.ebizmba.com/, Daily Kos website's ranking as reported on January 2, 2010; Markos ("Kos") Moulitsas Zúniga, foreword to Lowell Feld and Nate Wilcox, *Netroots Rising: How a Citizen Army of Bloggers and Online Activists Is Changing American Politics* (Westport, Conn: Praeger, 2008), viii, which is the source of the chapter-opening quotation.

2. Herbert Gans, *Democracy and the News* (New York: Oxford University Press, 2003), 1.

3. Thomas Jefferson, "The Founders' Constitution, Volume 5, Amendment I (Speech and Press), Document 8," University of Chicago Press, January 16, 1787, http://press-pubs.uchicago.edu/founders/documents/.

4. Pew Research Center's Project for Excellence in Journalism, "The State of the News Media 2009: The Economy Emerges as a Major Story," Pew Research Center's Project for Excellence in Journalism, journalism.org, 2009.

5. Bob Woodward and Carl Bernstein, *All the President's Men* (New York: Simon and Schuster, 1994).

6. Thomas E. Patterson, *Out of Order* (New York: Knopf, 1993), 82.

7. Pew Research Center's Project for Excellence in Journalism, "The State of the News Media 2009: Clear Channel," Pew Research Center's Project for Excellence in Journalism, journalism.org, 2009.

8. Pew Research Center's Project for Excellence in Journalism, "The State of the News Media 2004: Newspapers," Pew Research Center's Project for Excellence in Journalism, journalism.org, 2004.

9. Jeremy D. Mayer, *American Media Politics in Transition* (New York: McGraw Hill, 2007), 76.

10. Benjamin Franklin, "An Apology for Printers," *Pennsylvania Gazette,* May 27, 1731, reprinted as *An Apology for Printers* (Washington, D.C.: Acropolis Books, 1973).

11. Mayer, *American Media Politics in Transition*, 81.

12. Michael Schudson and Susan Tifft, "American Journalism in Historical Perspective," in *The Press,* ed. Geneva Overholser and Kathleen Hall Jamieson (New York: Oxford University Press, 2005), 19.

13. Michael Schudson, *Discovering the News: A Social History of American Newspapers* (New York: Basic Books, 1978).

14. William Riker, *The Strategy of Rhetoric: Campaigning for the American Constitution* (New Haven, Conn.: Yale University Press, 1996).

15. David McCullough, *John Adams* (New York: Simon and Schuster, 2001).

16. John Geer, *In Defense of Negativity: Attack Ads in Presidential Campaigns* (Chicago: University of Chicago Press, 2006).

17. See Michael Schudson, *The Sociology of News* (New York: W.W. Norton, 2003), 75.

18. Melvin Laracey, "Who Listened? Political Media Communications by 'Pre-Modern' Presidents," paper presented at the annual meeting of the Midwest Political Science Association, Chicago, Ill., 2004.

19. James Hamilton, *All the News That's Fit to Sell: How the Market Transforms Information into News* (Princeton, N.J.: Princeton University Press, 2006).

20. Ibid., 53.

21. See PBS, "Yellow Journalism," www.pbs.org/.

22. As quoted by Matt Drudge in "Anyone with A Modem Can Report on the World," address before the National Press Club, June 2, 1998.

23. Mayer, *American Media Politics in Transition,* 98.

24. Jon Blackwell, "1906: Rumble over 'The Jungle,'" *The Trentonian,* www.capitalcentury.com/.

25. Schudson and Tifft, "American Journalism in Historical Perspective," 17–46.

26. Rose McDermott, *Presidential Leadership, Illness, and Decision Making* (New York: Cambridge University Press, 2007).

27. Roper Center for Public Opinion Research poll, www.azpbs.org/.

28. "The ANES Guide to Election Behavior and Public Opinion," American National Elections Studies, www.electionstudies.org/.

29. Theodore H. White, *The Making of the President, 1960* (New York: Atheneum Publishers, 1961).

30. Sidney Krause, *The Great Debates: Kennedy v. Nixon, 1960* (Bloomington: Indiana University Press, 1977). The quotation in the caption on page 222 is from Kennedy's telegram to the NBC board chair, accepting the invitation to debate, quoted in the *Tri City Herald,* July 28, 1960.

31. Schudson and Tifft, "American Journalism in Historical Perspective," 26.

32. Data from the October 2007 Current Population Survey.

33. Data provided by Fenn Communications Group; also http://www.wired.com/gadgetlab/2010/06/apples-ipad-sales-accelerate-three-million-sold-in-80-days.

34. Pew Research Center's Project for Excellence in Journalism, "The State of the News Media 2009," Pew Research Center's Project for Excellence in Journalism, journalism.org, 2009.

35. Alex Jones, *Losing the News* (New York: Oxford University Press, 2009).

36. "Nielsen Online: Newspaper Websites," Newspaper Association of America, June 2009.

37. Bill Mitchell, "Clues in the Rubble: Finding a Framework to Sustain Local News," Discussion Paper Series, Joan Shorenstein Center, Harvard University, 2010.

38. Geoffrey Cowan, "Leading the Way to Better News," Discussion Paper Series, Joan Shorenstein Center, Harvard University, 2008, 7.

39. Ibid.

40. See Jones, *Losing the News*.

41. See Mitchell, "Clues in the Rubble."

42. Quoted in Cowan, "Leading the Way to Better News," 7.

43. Pew Research Center's Project for Excellence in Journalism, "The State of the News Media 2009: Audio," Pew Research Center's Project for Excellence in Journalism, journalism.org, 2009.

44. Pew Research Center's Project for Excellence in Journalism, "The State of the News Media 2009: Talk Radio," Pew Research Center's Project for Excellence in Journalism, journalism.org, 2009.

45. Lee Sigelman, "Conservative Dominance of Political Talk Radio," The Monkey Cage, February 16, 2008.

46. No one has studied why liberal talk radio has failed; we are offering some hypotheses here. I want to thank Markus Prior of Princeton University for brainstorming with us on this topic.

47. These data divide the number of viewers by the number of Americans at the time: 226 million in 1980 and 309 million in 2010.

48. Pew Research Center's Project for Excellence in Journalism, "The State of the News Media 2009: Digital Trends," Pew Research Center's Project for Excellence in Journalism, journalism.org, 2009.

49. Thomas Goetz, "Reinventing Television," *Wired*, September 2009.

50. Most of the data presented here came from "Journalism, Satire or Just Laughs? 'The Daily Show with Jon Stewart,' Examined," May 8, 2008, www.journalism.org/.

51. eBizMBA, "Top 25 Most Popular Blogs," January 2, 2010, www.ebizmba.com/.

52. Eric Lawrence, John Sides, and Henry Farrell, "Self-Segregation or Deliberation? Blog Readership, Participation, and Polarization in American Politics," *Perspectives on Politics* 8, no. 1 (2010): 146.

53. See www.huffingtonpost.com.

54. See www.drudgereport.com; http://rush-limbaugh-speaks.blogspot.com/.

55. See http://blog.wired.com/business/2007/05/controlled_chao.html.

56. Ben Rigby, *Mobilizing Generation 2.0* (San Francisco: Jossey-Bass, 2008), 17–18.

57. Katharine Seelye, "Blogger Is Surprised by Uproar over Obama Story, but Not Bitter," *New York Times,* April 14, 2008, www.nytimes.com/.

58. Data collected by Peter Fenn, president of Fenn Communications Group.

59. Mike Snider, "iPods Knock Over Beer Mugs," *USA Today,* June 7, 2006, www.usatoday.com/.

60. Christine Williams and Jeff Gulati, "Social Networks in Political Campaigns: Facebook and the 2006 Midterm Elections," paper presented at Annual Meeting of the American Political Science Association, Chicago, August 30–September 2, 2007.

61. ABC News, "ABC News Joins Forces with Facebook," http://abcnews.go.com/, 2007.

62. Noam Cohen, "Twitter on the Barricades: Six Lessons Learned," *New York Times,* June 21, 2009, www.nytimes.com/.

63. John Palfrey, Robert Faris, and Bruce Etling, "In Washington Post Op-Ed, Berkman Center Directors Discuss Twitter Revolution in Iran," Harvard Law School, www.law.harvard.edu/ June 22, 2009.

64. Rigby, *Mobilizing Generation 2.0,* 130.

65. Pew Research Center's Internet and American Life Project, press release, June 15, 2008, from a survey conducted April 8–May 11, 2008.

66. Pew Research Center, "The Millennials: Confident, Connected, Open to Change," February 2010.

67. Data from "Young People and News," Harvard University, July 2007.

68. Morley Winograd and Michael D. Hais, *Millennial Makeover: MySpace, YouTube and the Future of American Politics* (New Brunswick, N.J.: Rutgers University Press, 2008).

69. Paul Lazarsfeld, Bernard Berelson, and Hazel Gaudet, *The People's Choice* (New York: Columbia University Press, 1944). It is worth noting that the 1940 campaign was probably the worst campaign in which to look for possible media effects. It was the only presidential election in U.S. history in which a sitting president was running for a third term. The stability of preference surely reflected the fact that people had opinions about Roosevelt and that not much would change them one way or the other. In contrast, Senator Obama was not a well-known figure in the 2008 presidential campaign.

70. Angus Campbell et al., *The American Voter* (New York: Wiley, 1960).

71. Lydia Saad, "Public Support for Stimulus Package Unchanged at 52%," Gallup, February 5, 2009, www.gallup.com/.

72. In political science, the most important book to reshape the field was Shanto Iyengar and Donald R. Kinder, *News That Matters: Television and American Opinion* (Chicago: University of Chicago Press, 1987). Also see the work on communication of Maxwell McCombs.

73. Bernard Cohen, *The Press and Foreign Policy* (Princeton, N.J.: Princeton University Press, 1963), 13.

74. Darrell West et al., "Invisible: 1.4 Percent Coverage for Education Is Not Enough," December 2, 2009, Brookings Institution, www.brookings.edu/.

75. Shanto Iyengar and Jennifer A. McGrady, *Media Politics: A Citizen's Guide* (New York: W.W. Norton, 2007), 216.

76. These scholars have reshaped how we think about framing. In fact, Kahneman won a Nobel Prize for this work in 2003. See www.psych.stanford.edu/~knutson/bad/tversky81.pdf for one example of their scholarship.

77. W. Lance Bennett, Regina C. Lawrence, and Steven Livingston, *When the Press Fails: Political Power and the News Media from Iraq to Katrina* (Chicago: University of Chicago Press, 2007).

78. Stephen Farnsworth and Robert Lichter, *The Nightly News Nightmare* (Lanham, Md.: Roman and Littlefield, 2003); James Fallows, *Breaking the News: How the Media Undermine American Democracy* (New York: Vintage Press, 1996); Patterson, *Out of Order.*

79. Pew Research Center's Project for Excellence in Journalism, "The State of the News Media 2009: Public Attitudes," Pew Research Center's Project for Excellence in Journalism, journalism.org, 2009.

80. Schudson, *Sociology of News,* 33.

81. See Accuracy in Media, www.aim.org.

82. The data in this paragraph come from Gallup polls made available through the Roper Center and its IPOLL search engine.

83. Thomas Patterson, "Political Roles of the Journalist," in *The Politics of the News,* ed. Doris Graber, Denis McQuail, and Pippa Norris (Washington, D.C.: CQ Press, 2000), 3.

84. For a thoughtful discussion of soft news, see Matthew Baum, *Soft News Goes to War: Public Opinion and American Foreign Policy in the New Media Age* (Princeton, N.J.: Princeton University Press, 2003), 6–7.

85. Schudson and Tifft, "American Journalism in Historical Perspective," 28.

86. Information for the caption for the photo on page 236 is from American Rhetoric, www.Americanrhetoric.com.

87. Gary Bunker, *From Rail-Splitter to Icon: Lincoln's Image in Illustrated Periodicals, 1860–1865* (Kent, Ohio: Kent State University Press, 2001).

88. Presidential Campaign Slogans, CB Presidential Research Services, 2009, http://www.presidentsusa.net/.

89. The Pew Research Center for the People and the Press, "Public Knowledge of Current Affairs Little Change by News and Information Revolutions," 2007, http://people-press.org/.

90. Pew Research Center, "High Marks for Campaign, High Bar for Obama," November 13, 2008, http://pewresearch.org/.

91. Pew Internet, "Home Broadband Adoption 2009," www.pewinternet.org/.

92. The argument presented over the next few paragraphs is inspired by the work of Markus Prior, *Post Broadcast Democracy* (New York: Cambridge University Press, 2007).

93. Ibid.

94. *Federal Communications Commission v. Pacifica Foundation*, 438 U.S. 726 (1978); the Oyez Project, www.oyez.org/.

95. *FCC v. Fox Television Stations*, 556 U.S. (2009); the Oyez Project, www.oyez.org/.

96. Matthew Lasar, "Supreme Court Remands FCC 'Nipplegate' Case to Lower Court," Ars Technica, http://arstechnica.com/.

97. The Center for Democracy and Technology, "Communications Decency Act," http://cdt.org/; the Oyez Project, www.oyez.org/.

98. The Center for Democracy and Technology, "Legislative History of COPA," http://cdt.org/.

99. U.S. Court of Appeals for the 3rd Circuit, *Mukasey v. American Civil Liberties Union*, www.cdt.org/.

100. The Federal Trade Commission, "Facts for Consumers," 2007.

101. Library of Congress, "An Act to Prevent Child Abduction and the Sexual Exploitation of Children," http://thomas.loc.gov/.

102. The Center for Democracy and Technology, "CAN-SPAM Signed into Law," http://cdt.org/, 2003.

103. Federal Trade Commission, "Computers and the Internet: Privacy and Security," www.ftc.gov.

104. Richard Pérez-Peña, "Group Plans to Provide Investigative Journalism," *New York Times*, October 15, 2007, www.nytimes.com/.

Chapter 8

1. This story was compiled from the Students for Concealed Carry on Campus website, www.concealedcampus.org; Dean A. Ferguson, "Campus Gun Ban Bill Disarmed," *Lewiston Tribune*, February 14, 2008, www.lmtribune.com; Suzanne Smalley, "More Guns on Campus?" *Newsweek*, February 15, 2008, and an e-mail interview with Al Baker, April 6, 2010, conducted for this textbook, which is the source of the chapter-opening quotation.

2. Alexis de Tocqueville, *Democracy in America*, trans. George Lawrence and ed. J. P. Mayer (New York: Doubleday & Company, 1969), 193.

3. William C. DiGiacomantonio, "Petitioners and Their Grievances," in *The House and Senate in the 1790s: Petitioning, Lobbying, and Institutional Development*, ed. Kenneth R. Bowling and Donald R. Kennon (Columbus: Ohio University Press, 2002).

4. Robert C. Byrd. "Speech to the United States Senate: Lobbyists" September 27, 1987, www.senate.gov.

5. Interest groups at the state level have even been involved in elections for state judges. See Clive S. Thomas, Michael L. Boyer, and Ronald J. Hrebenar, "Interest Groups and State Court Elections: A New Era and Its Challenges." *Judicature* 87 (2003): 135–49.

6. Elizabeth Cady Stanton, Susan B. Anthony, and Matilda J. Gage, eds., *History of Woman Suffrage*, vol. 1 (Rochester, N.Y.: Charles Mann Publishers, 1887), 70.

7. Notes of the National Association of Wool Manufacturers, Annual Meetings, 1867, 24–25.

8. Theda Skocpol, *Protecting Soldiers and Mothers* (Cambridge, Mass.: Harvard University Press, 1992), 111–12.

9. Westerville Public Library, "Anti-Saloon League, 1893–1933: Purley Baker," www.wpl.lib.oh.us; Ohio History Central: An Online Encyclopedia of Ohio History, "Anti-Saloon League of America," www.ohiohistorycentral.org.

10. "141 Men and Girls Die in Waist Factory Fire; Trapped High Up in Washington Place Building; Street Strewn with Bodies; Piles of Dead Inside," *New York Times*, March 26, 1911, p. 1.

11. Office of the Secretary, United States Department of Labor. "Our Mission." www.dol.gov.

12. Beth L. Leech, Frank R. Baumgartner, Timothy M. La Pira, and Nicholas A. Semanko, "Drawing Lobbyists to Washington: Government Activity and the Demand for Advocacy," *Political Research Quarterly* 58, no. 1 (2005): 19–30.

13. National Labor Relations Board, "National Labor Relations Act, www.nlrb.gov.

14. UNITE HERE, "UNITE HERE Historical Timeline," www.unitehere.org.

15. U.S. Bureau of Labor Statistics, *Current Population Survey*, www.bls.gov.

16. American Israel Public Affairs Committee, "About AIPAC," www.aipac.org.

17. Coalition to Save Darfur, Press Releases, "Senators Frist and Clinton Sign One Millionth Postcard Urging President Bush to Advocate Multinational Peacekeeping Force to Stop Darfur Genocide," June 29, 2006, www.savedarfur.org. Senator Clinton became the U.S. secretary of state in 2009.

18. Jeffrey Gettleman, "After Years of Mass Killings, Fragile Calm Holds in Darfur," *New York Times*, January 2, 2010, A1; Coalition to Save Darfur, "Sudan 365: A Beat for Peace," www.savedarfur.org.

19. For a broader discussion of the impact of the Internet on interest group power, see Bruce Bimber, *Information and American Democracy: Technology in the Evolution of Political Power* (New York: Cambridge University Press, 2003).

20. Carl Pope, "Not the End, Not the Beginning of the End, Perhaps the End of the Beginning," June 26, 2009, www.sierraclub.org.

21. Jeffrey M. Berry, *The Interest Group Society*, 3rd ed. (New York: Longman, 1997), Chapter 5.

22. Anthony J. Nownes, *Total Lobbying* (New York: Cambridge University Press, 2006).

23. Center for Responsive Politics, "Lobbying Database," www.opensecrets.org.

24. Center for Responsive Politics, www.opensecrets.org.

25. Bart Jansen, "Legislative Summary: Congressional Affairs: Lobbying Practices and Disclosures," *CQ Weekly Online*, January 7, 2008, 39.

26. Gregory Koger and Jennifer N. Victor, "Polarized Agendas: Campaign Contributions by Lobbyists," *PS: Political Science and Politics* 42 (2009): 485–88.

27. Citizens for Responsibility and Ethics in Washington, "About CREW," www.citizensforethics.org.

28. U.S. Internal Revenue Service, "Exemption Requirements—Section 501(c)(3) Organizations," www.irs.ustreas.gov.

29. *Buckley v. Valeo,* 424 U.S. 1 (1976).

30. See John R. Wright, *Interest Groups and Congress: Lobbying, Contributions, and Influence* (Boston: Allyn & Bacon, 1995, reprinted in Longman Classics Series, 2009); Michelle L. Chin, Jon R. Bond, and Nehemia Geva, "A Foot in the Door: An Experimental Study of PAC and Constituency Effects on Access," *Journal of Politics* 62 (2000): 534–49.

31. *Federal Election Commission v. Wisconsin Right to Life, Inc.,* 551 U.S. 449 (2007).

32. Kate Ackley, "Health Care Ads Could Pick Up after the Break," *Roll Call,* June 29, 2009.

33. Alexis de Tocqueville, *Democracy in America,* ed. Richard D. Heffner (New York: Mentor Books, 1956), 198.

34. David Truman, *The Governmental Process: Political Interests and Public Opinion* (New York: Alfred Knopf, 1971).

35. Mancur Olson, *The Logic of Collective Action* (Cambridge, Mass.: Harvard University Press, 1971).

36. Robert Dahl, *A Preface to Democratic Theory* (Chicago: University of Chicago Press, 1956). Also see Robert Dahl, *Who Governs?* 2nd ed. (New Haven, Conn.: Yale University Press, 2005).

37. C. Wright Mills, *The Power Elite* (New York: Oxford University Press, 1956).

38. Theodore J. Lowi, *The End of Liberalism: Ideology, Policy, and the End of Public Authority* (New York: Norton, 1969).

39. E. E. Schattschneider, *The Semi-Sovereign People* (New York: Holt, Rinehart, and Winston, 1960). Also see E. E. Schattschneider, *Politics, Pressures, and the Tariff* (New York: Prentice-Hall, 1935).

40. On April 1, 2010, the EPA and the Department of Transportation jointly issued the final regulations. See Environmental Protection Agency 40 CFR Parts 85, 86, and 600, Department of Transportation National Highway Traffic Safety Administration. 49 CFR Parts 531, 533, 537 and 538 Light-Duty Vehicle Greenhouse Gas Emission Standards and Corporate Average Fuel Economy Standards; Final Rule.

41. Dwight D. Eisenhower, Farewell Address, January 17, 1961, www.millercenter.virginia.edu.

42. William Safire, "The Way We Live Now: 3-12-00: On Language; Iron Triangle," *New York Times,* March 12, 2000, www.nytimes.com.

43. Hugh Heclo, "Issue Networks and the Executive Establishment," in *The New American Political System,* ed. Anthony King (Washington, D.C.: American Enterprise Institute, 1978), 87–124.

44. Robert H. Salisbury, "An Exchange Theory of Interest Groups," *Midwest Journal of Political Science* 13 (1969): 1–32.

45. Olson, *Logic of Collective Action.*

46. Ibid.

47. DeWayne Wickham, "Group Loses Another Leader, and More Luster," *USA Today,* March 6, 2007, A13; Krissah Thompson, "100 Years Old, NAACP Debates Its Current Role," *Washington Post,* July 12, 2009, www.washingtonpost.com.

48. AARP Consolidated Financial Statements, December 31, 2008 and 2007, www.aarp.org.

49. AARP Summary of 2008 AARP Consolidated Financial Statements, www.aarp.org.

50. AARP's 2008 operating budget was $1.14 billion (ibid.).

51. "The Numbers," February 16, 2008, *National Journal,* www.nationaljournal.com.

52. U.S. Census Bureau, "Table 3.1 Foreign-Born Population by Sex, Age, and World Region of Birth: 2008," www.census.gov.

53. U.S. Citizenship and Immigration Services, "About Us," www.uscis.gov.

54. Randall Monger, "Annual Flow Report: U.S. Legal Permanent Residents: 2009," 1, Office of Immigration Statistics, Department of Homeland Security, April 2010, www.dhs.gov.

55. Ibid., 2.

56. U.S. Citizenship and Immigration Services, "A Guide to Naturalization," www.uscis.gov/natzguide.

57. South Asian Americans Leading Together, www.saalt.org.

58. NumbersUSA: For Lower Immigration Levels, www.numbersusa.com.

59. US Immigration Support: Your Online Guide to U.S. Visas, Green Cards and Citizenship, www.usimmigrationsupport.org.

60. National Council of La Raza, www.nclr.org/.

61. Robert Pear, "A Million Faxes Later, a Little-Known Group Claims a Victory on Immigration," *New York Times,* July 14, 2007, A17.

62. U.S. Department of Health and Human Services, Administration for Children and Families, Office of Refugee Resettlement, "Who We Serve," www.acf.hhs.gov.

63. U.S. Department of Health and Human Services, Office of Refugee Resettlement, "Fiscal Year 2009 Refugee Arrivals," www.acf.hhs.gov.

64. U.S. Committee for Refugees and Immigrants (USCRI), "About USCRI," www.refugees.org.

Chapter 9

1. This story has been compiled from Josh McKoon, McKoon State Senate 29, www.joshmckoon.com; Larry Gierer, "Local GOP Elects New Chairman, Officers: Attorney Josh McKoon to Take Helm of Party," *Columbus Ledger-Enquirer,* March 31, 2007; Brian McDearmon, "Attorney to Run for GOP Chair: McKoon Seeks Top Post Vacated by Rob Doll," *Columbus Ledger-Enquirer,* February 26, 2007; Chuck Williams, "Republican Josh McKoon Running for Senate District 29 Seat with Abandon, Even with No Opposition Yet," *Columbus Ledger-Enquirer,* March 28, 2010; phone interview with Josh McKoon, January 28, 2008, and e-mail interview with Josh McKoon, April 29, 2010, both conducted for this textbook. The chapter-opening quotation is from the April 29 e-mail interview.

2. V. O. Key Jr., *Politics, Parties, and Pressure Groups,* 5th ed. (New York: Thomas Y. Crowell Company, 1964).

3. Center for Responsive Politics, "Political Parties Overview," 2009, www.opensecrets.org.

4. Ibid.

5. For more on the informal networking that occurs among party activists, see Gregory Koger, Seth Masket, and Hans Noel, "Partisan Webs: Information Exchange and Party Networks," *British Journal of Political Science* 39 (2009): 633–53.

6. Marjorie Hershey, *Party Politics in America,* 12th ed. (New York: Pearson-Longman, 2007), 159.

7. Jesse McKinley, "A Revolution on the Ballot," *New York Times,* June 10, 2010, A1, www.nytimes.com.

8. Not all the superdelegates used their right to vote. See www.realclearpolitics.com.

9. John M. Broder, "Show Me the Delegate Rules, and I'll Show You the Party," *New York Times,* February 17, 2008, www.nytimes.com.

10. Larry M. Bartels, *Presidential Primaries and the Dynamics of Public Choice* (Princeton, N.J.: Princeton University Press, 1988).

11. Brian G. Knight and Nathan Schiff, "Momentum and Social Learning in Presidential Primaries," Working Paper W13637, National Bureau of Economic Research, November 2007.

12. George Washington, "Washington's Farewell Address," reprinted in Randall E. Adkins, *The Evolution of Political Parties, Campaigns, and Elections* (Washington, D.C.: CQ Press, 2008), 47–50.

13. John F. Bibby and Brian F. Schaffner, *Politics, Parties and Elections in America,* 6th ed. (Boston: Thomson-Wadsworth, 2008), 24.

14. United States Senate, Office of the Historian, *Biographical Directory of the United States Congress,* http://bioguide.congress.gov.

15. Martin Van Buren, "Letter to Thomas Ritchie," 1827, reprinted in *The Evolution of Political Parties, Campaigns, and Elections: Landmark Documents, 1787–2007,* ed. Randall E. Adkins (Washington, D.C.: CQ Press, 2008), 65–69.

16. United States Census Bureau, "1990 Population and Housing Unit Counts: United States," Table 2, www.census.org.

17. Henry Clay, speech to the United States Senate on the Whig Party, April 14, 1834, in *The Evolution of Political Parties, Campaigns, and Elections: Landmark Documents, 1787–2007,* ed. Randall E. Adkins, (Washington, D.C.: CQ Press, 2008), 73.

18. Quoted in James L. Sundquist, *Dynamics of the Party System* (Washington, D.C.: Brookings Institution Press, 1973), 65.

19. Sean M. Theriault, *The Power of the People* (Columbus: Ohio State University Press, 2005), Chapter 3.

20. Douglas W. Jones, "The Australian Paper Ballot," in "A Brief Illustrated History of Voting," University of Iowa Department of Computer Science, http://www.cs.uiowa.edu/.

21. Erik J. Engstrom and Samuel Kernell, "Manufactured Responsiveness: The Impact of State Electoral Laws on Unified Party Control of the Presidency and the House of Representatives, 1840–1940," *American Journal of Political Science* 49 (July 2005): 531–49, see 535.

22. Anthony Downs, *An Economic Theory of Democracy* (New York: Harper, 1957).

23. Stuart Elaine Macdonald and George Rabinowitz, "Solving the Paradox of Nonconvergence: Valence, Position, and Direction in Democratic Politics," *Electoral Studies* 17, no. 3 (1998): 281–300.

24. Maurice Duverger, "Public Opinion and Political Parties in France," *American Political Science Review* 46, no. 4 (1952): 1069–78, especially 1071.

25. James R. Whitson, "President Elect: The Unofficial Homepage of the Electoral College," www.presidentelect.org.

26. Presidential Vote Statistics, 2000, Popular Votes for Ralph Nader, www.statemaster.com.

27. For a detailed discussion of how interest groups interact with parties in campaigning, see Matthew J. Burbank, Ronald J. Hrebenar, and Robert C. Benedict, *Parties, Interest Groups, and Political Campaigns* (Boulder, Colo.: Paradigm Publishers. 2008).

28. Cornell Belcher and Donna Brazile, "The Black and Hispanic Vote in 2006," *Democratic Strategist,* 2007, www.thedemocraticstrategist.org.

29. *New York Times,* Election Results 2008, www.elections.nytimes.com/.

30. *Engel v. Vitale,* 370 U.S. 421 (1962).

31. For a broad discussion of the resurgence of Republican conservatives, see Mark A. Smith, *The Right Talk: How Conservatives Transformed the Great Society into the Economic Society* (Princeton, N.J.: Princeton University Press, 2007).

32. Data from the Inter-university Consortium for Political and Social Research (ICPSR) National Election Study 2004, as cited in Hershey, *Party Politics in America,* 32.

33. Scholar Tasha Philpot pointed to underlying shifts as early as 2004. See Tasha S. Philpot, "A Party of a Different Color? Race, Campaign Communication, and Party Politics," *Political Behavior* 26 (2004): 249–70.

34. Nolan McCarty, Keith T. Poole, and Howard Rosenthal, "Party Polarization: 1879–2009," www.polarizedamerica.com.

35. The Democratic Party, "Renewing America's Promise," Democratic Party Platform 2008, www.democrats.org.

36. Republicans in Congress, "Offering Smart Solutions: Energy," www.gop.gov.

37. "The Cap and Tax Fiction," *Wall Street Journal,* www.wsj.com.

38. Library of Congress, H.R. 2454, thomas.loc.gov.

39. Steve Musfon, David A. Farenthold, and Paul Kane, "In Close Vote, House Passes Climate Bill," *Washington Post,* June 27, 2009, www.washingtonpost.com.

40. Republicans in Congress, "G.O.P American," www.gop.gov.

41. "House Vote 477-H.R.2454: On Passage American Clean Energy Act," *New York Times,* www.politics.nytimes.com.

42. Ibid.

43. Elizabeth Wasserman, "Greenhouse Gas Admissions," *CQ Weekly Online,* October 19, 2009, 2385–2404, www.cqpress.com.

44. John Carey, "House Passes Carbon Cap-and-Trade Bill," *Business Week,* June 26, 2009, www.businessweek.com.

Chapter 10

1. This story has been compiled from Huffington Post poll with 10,000 respondents reported on February 4, 2009; Aaron Schock's House of Representatives website, www.schock.house.gov; "Aaron Schock in GQ: The Hill's Hottest Freshman Models Conservative Suits," September 16, 2009, www.huffingtonpost.com/; and Randy James, "The First Gen Y Congressman," *Time,* January 8, 2009, www.time.com, which is the source of the chapter-opening quotation. The election Schock refers to in the quotation is 2008.

2. Quoted in Jeff Broadwater, *George Mason, Forgotten Founder* (Chapel Hill: University of North Carolina Press, 2006), 178.

3. *Presidential Elections, 1789–2004* (Washington, D.C.: Congressional Quarterly Press, 2005), 179.

4. Brian Gaines, "Popular Myths about Popular Vote-Electoral College Splits," *PS* 34 (March 2001): 70–75.

5. This claim arises from dividing the number of electoral votes by the total number of voters. Alaska had 3 electoral votes and about 317,000 voters in 2008. California had 55 electoral votes and more than 13.2 million voters.

6. CBS News polls, December 9–10, 2000.

7. CBS News polls, December 14–16, 2000.

8. CBS News polls, January 15–17, 2001.

9. Cable News Network/*USA Today* poll conducted by Gallup Organization, November 11–12, 2000.

10. These data come from surveys done by the Pew Research Center for the People and the Press.

11. These data were collected by using the iPOLL search engine from the Roper Center.

12. For a longer discussion of redistricting, see Bernard Grofman, Lisa Handley, and Richard G. Niemi, *Minority Representation and the Quest for Voting Equality* (New York: Cambridge University Press, 1992).

13. Stephen Nicholson, *Voting by Agenda* (Princeton, N.J.: Princeton University Press, 2005).

14. Chris W. Bonneau and Melinda Gann Hall, *In Defense of Judicial Elections* (New York: Routledge, 2009).

15. Susan Hyde and Nikola Marinov, "National Elections across Democracy and Autocracy," http://hyde.research.yale.edu/research.

16. Robert A. Dahl, "What Political Institutions Does Large-Scale Democracy Require," *Political Science Quarterly* 120 (2005): 187–98.

17. CBS News/*New York Times* poll, October 19–22, 2008, based on telephone interviews with a national adult sample of 1,152.

18. Michael McGerr, *The Decline of Popular Politics* (New York: Oxford University Press, 1986).

19. Sidney Blumenthal, *The Permanent Campaign* (New York: Simon and Schuster, 1982).

20. Karl Rove, "Obama and the Permanent Campaign," *Wall Street Journal*, August 13, 2009.

21. See, for example, *New York Times Magazine*, December 12, 2007.

22. Marty Cohen, David Karol, Hans Noel, and John Zaller, *The Party Decides: Presidential Nominations before and after Reform* (Chicago: University of Chicago Press, 2008).

23. Associated Press, "52.4 Million Watch U.S. Presidential Debate, Far from Record," *The Canadian Press*, September 29, 2008.

24. Sidney Krause, *The Great Debates: Kennedy v. Nixon 1960* (Bloomington: Indiana University Press, 1977).

25. Federal Election Commission, "The FEC and Federal Campaign Finance Law," February 2004.

26. Jim Drinkard, "Let the Fundraising Begin—Again," *USA Today*, March 10, 2000, 14a.

27. Center for Responsive Politics, www.opensecrets.org.

28. The maximum an individual can contribute to a candidate in 2009–10 is $4,800, which was adjusted for inflation from the $4,600 in 2008. The $5,000 estimate reflects a guess about future inflation.

29. James G. Gimpel, Karen M. Kaufmann, and Shanna Pearson-Merkowitz, "Battleground States versus Blackout States," *Journal of Politics* 69 (2007): 786–97.

30. Taofang Huang and Daron Shaw, "Beyond Battlegrounds?" paper presented at the University of Texas—Austin, 2009.

31. Chris Cillizza, "Romney's Data Cruncher," *Washington Post*, September 7, 2007, A1.

32. Mark Penn with E. Kinney Zalesne, *Microtrends: The Small Forces behind Tomorrow's Big Changes* (New York: Twelve, Hatchett Book Group USA, 2007), xiii.

33. Aaron Blake, "DNC Holds National Training As It Rolls Out New Voter File," *The Hill*, August 15, 2007.

34. Mike Madden, "Barack Obama's Super Marketing Machine," July 16, 2008, www.salon.com/.

35. Cillizza, "Romney's Data Cruncher."

36. Ibid.

37. John G. Geer, *In Defense of Negativity* (Chicago: University of Chicago Press, 2006), 59–60.

38. Lynn Vavreck, *The Message Matters* (Princeton, N.J.: Princeton University Press, 2009).

39. Donald Stokes, "Spatial Models of Party Competition," *American Political Science Review* 57 (1963): 368–77.

40. Geer, *In Defense of Negativity*, 105.

41. Sunshine Hillygus and Todd Shields, *The Persuadable Voter* (Princeton, N.J.: Princeton University Press, 2008), 36.

42. Ibid.

43. Kathleen Jamieson, *Dirty Politics* (New York: Oxford University Press, 1992).

44. Geer, *In Defense of Negativity*.

45. Zachary Karabell, *The Last Campaign* (New York: Vintage, 2001).

46. Geer, *In Defense of Negativity*.

47. APSA Press Release, "6 of 9 Presidential Election Forecasts Predict Obama Will Win Popular Vote," *APSA*, October 16, 2008.

48. See www.fivethirtyeight.com for Silver's predictions in the 2008 election.

49. Anthony Downs, *An Economic Theory of Democracy* (New York: Harper, 1957).

50. Mark Westlye, *Senate Elections and Campaign Intensity* (Baltimore: Johns Hopkins University Press, 1991).

51. Federal Election Commission, "Federal Election Campaign Laws," 2005, 56–60, www.fec.gov. Note that the contribution levels have been increased slightly to adjust for inflation.

52. Campaign Finance Institute, "Candidates' Money Was Up, but Party Spending Was Way Up," November 11, 2006.

53. Bernie Becker, "From Pitcher's Mound to Senate?" *New York Times*, September 2, 2009, http://thecaucus.blogs.nytimes.com/.

54. Federal Election Commission, "Federal Election Campaign Laws," 2005, 56–60, www.fec.gov. Note that the contribution levels have been increased slightly to adjust for inflation.

55. Campaign Finance Institute, "Candidates' Money Was Up, " Tables 2 and 4.

56. Albert Cover, "One Good Term Deserves Another: The Advantage of Incumbency in Congressional Elections," *American Journal of Political Science* 21, no. 3 (August 1977): 523–41.

57. Richard Fenno, *Home Style* (Boston: Little and Brown, 1978).

58. NBC News/*Wall Street Journal* poll, conducted by Hart and Newhouse Research companies, November 1–2, 2008.

59. Morris Fiorina, *Congress: Keystone to the Washington Establishment* (New Haven, Conn.: Yale University Press, 1977).

60. John Zaller, "Politicians as Prize Fighters," in *Politicians and Party Politics*, ed. John G. Geer (Baltimore: Johns Hopkins University Press, 1998), 128–85.

61. Bruce Oppenheimer, "Deep Red and Blue Congressional Districts: The Causes and Consequences of Declining Party Competitiveness," in *Congress Reconsidered*, 8th ed., ed. Lawrence Dodd and Bruce Oppenheimer (Washington, D.C.: CQ Press, 2005), 135–58.

62. Gary C. Jacobson, *The Politics of Congressional Elections*, 7th ed. (Boston: Pearson Longman, 2009), 168.

63. Ibid., 160.

64. See Gary Jacobson and Samuel Kernell, *Strategy and Choice in Congressional Elections* (New Haven, Conn.: Yale University Press, 1983).

65. Federal Election Commission, "The FEC and Federal Campaign Finance Law: Historical Background," February 2004.

66. *Buckley v. Valeo*, 424 U.S. 1 (1976); Federal Election Commission, "Court Case Abstracts: *Buckley v. Valeo*."

67. Federal Election Commission, "Bipartisan Campaign Reform Act of 2002."

68. Federal Election Commission, "FEC Collects $630,000 in Civil Penalties from Three 527 Organizations," December 13, 2006, www.fec.gov/.

69. Quoted in Lawrence J. Grossman, David A. M. Peterson, and James A. Stimson, *Mandate Politics* (New York: Cambridge University Press, 2007).

70. This discussion draws heavily on Stanley Kelley's *Interpreting Elections* (Princeton, N.J.: Princeton University Press, 1983).

71. Gerald M. Pomper, *Elections in American* (New York: Longman, 1980), 161.

72. Tracy Sulkin, "Promises Made and Promises Kept," in *Congress Reconsidered*, ed. Lawrence Dodd and Bruce Oppenheimer (Washington, D.C.: CQ Press, 2009), 119–40.

73. Tracy Sulkin and Nathaniel Swigger, "Is There Truth in Advertising?" *Journal of Politics* 70 (2008): 232–44.

74. Politifact, "The Obameter: Tracking Obama's Campaign Practices," *St. Petersburg Times*, Politifact.com, updated as of October 1, 2010.

75. Roper Poll, February 9–23, 1980.

76. Poll conducted by Penn and Schoen Associates, October 10–12, 1984.

77. Poll conducted by Greenberg Quinlan Rosner Research, October 30–November 2, 2008.

78. V. O. Key, *The Responsible Electorate* (Cambridge, Mass.: Harvard University Press, 1966).

Chapter 11

1. This story has been compiled from "USAO Student Reaches Out to Anadarko Youth," University of Science and Arts of Oklahoma press release, December 17, 2008, www.usao.edu; Dan Klein, "Featured Fellow: Maya Torralba," interview with Maya Torralba, July 2008, www.yp4.org; "Student Reaches Out to Anadarko Youth," *Native Times*, January 5, 2009; a biography of Torralba on the Indigenous Democratic Network website, www.indsnlist.org; and an e-mail interview with Maya Torralba, March 23, 2010, conducted for this textbook, which is the source for the chapter-opening quotation.

2. Kevin Corder and Christina Wolbrecht, "Political Context and the Turnout of New Women Voters after Suffrage," *Journal of Politics* 68 (2006): 34–49.

3. Samuel Huntington, "The United States," in *The Crisis of Democracy*, ed. Michael Crozier, Samuel Huntington, and Joji Watanuki (New York: NYU Press, 1975), 59–115.

4. Steve Finkel "Reciprocal Effects of Participation and Political Efficacy: A Panel Analysis," *American Journal of Political Science* 29, no. 4 (1985): 891–913; Steve Finkel, "The Effects of Participation on Political Efficacy and Political Support: Evidence from a West German Panel," *Journal of Politics* 49, no. 2 (1987): 441–64. These articles provide empirical evidence that supports the arguments of Carol Pateman, *Participation and Democratic Theory* (New York: Cambridge University Press, 1970).

5. This section draws heavily on Alexander Keyssar, *The Right to Vote: The Contested History of Democracy in the United States* (New York: Basic Books, 2001).

6. Washington actually won 132 of the 135 Electoral College votes in 1792. Three electors—one from Vermont and two from Maryland—did not cast ballots.

7. Keyssar, *Right to Vote*, 10–21.

8. The exact percentage was 26.7 percent. See www.presidency.ucsb.edu/data/turnout.

9. Some now question the claims of a "corrupt bargain." See Jeffrey A. Jenkins and Brian R. Sala, "The Spatial Theory of Voting and the Presidential Election of 1824," *American Journal of Political Science* 42, no. 4 (October 1998): 1157–79.

10. See Elisabeth Griffith, *In Her Own Right: The Life of Elizabeth Cady Stanton* (New York: Oxford University Press, 1984), 153–54. See also www.law.umkc.edu/faculty/projects/ftrials/anthony/sbaaccount.html.

11. Harold Gosnell, *Getting Out the Vote* (Chicago: University of Chicago Press, 1927).

12. Kevin Corder and Christina Wolbrecht, "Political Context and the Turnout of New Women Voters after Suffrage," *Journal of Politics* 68 (2006): 34–49, especially 46.

13. Ibid., 46.

14. Data from U.S. Census Bureau, "Voting and Registration in the Election of November 2008."

15. Ronald Davis, "Creating Jim Crow: In-Depth Essay," *The History of Jim Crow*, www.jimcrowhistory.org/.

16. This figure underestimates the true cost of the poll tax in today's dollars. We divided $2 by $86 to arrive at 2.3 percent. We then multiplied the 2.3 percent by $43,000, the median income in the United States in 2000. The precise dollar estimate is $989. But the average income of blacks in the South was surely less than $86, and that ignores the issue that African Americans would rarely have that much cash available to them.

17. Morgan J. Kousser, "Poll Tax," in Congressional Quarterly, *The International Encyclopedia of Elections* (Washington, D.C.: CQ, 1999), 208–209.

18. *Smith v. Allwright*, 321 U.S. 649 (1944).

19. Sarah A. Binder and Steven S. Smith, *Political or Principle: Filibustering in the United States Senate* (Washington, D.C.: Brookings Institution Press, 1996).

20. The term *negroes* was commonly used at the time. Polling conducted by Opinion Research Corporation, October 15–November 15, 1963, based on personal interviews with a national adult sample of 1,506.

21. U.S. Census Bureau, Voting and Registration, www.census.gov/.

22. Thomas Rochon and Ikuo Kabashima, "Movement and Aftermath," in *Politicians and Party Politics*, ed. John G. Geer (Baltimore: Johns Hopkins University Press, 1998), 102–21.

23. Steven Lasher, *George Wallace* (Cambridge, Mass.: Da Capo Press, 1995). The information in the caption for the photos on page 364 is from Howell Raines, "George Wallace, Segregation Symbol, Dies at 79," *New York Times*, September 14, 1998; Richard Pearson, "Former Ala. Gov. George C. Wallace Dies," *Washington Post*, September 14, 1998.

24. There were four exceptions: the voting age was 18 in Georgia and Kentucky, 19 in Alaska, and 20 in Hawaii.

25. See Marisa Abrajano and Michael Alvarez, *New Faces, New Voices: The Hispanic Electorate in America* (Princeton, N.J.: Princeton University Press, 2010); and Matt A. Barreto, Gary M. Segura, and Nathan D. Woods, "The Mobilizing Effect of Majority-Minority Districts on Latino Turnout," *American Political Science Review* 98, no. 1 (2004): 65–75.

26. United States Election Project, "2008 Presidential Nomination Contest Turnout Rates," http://elections.gmu.edu/.

27. See Jan Leighley, "Attitudes, Opportunities, and Incentives," *Political Research Quarterly* 48 (1995): 184.

28. Mark Hugo Lopez and Paul Taylor, "Dissecting the Electorate: Most Diverse in U.S. History," April 30, 2009, Pew Research Center.

29. Mark Hugo Lopez, Emily Kirby, and Jared Sagoff, "The Youth Vote 2004," CIRCLE: The Center for Information and Research on Civic Learning and Engagement, July 2005.

30. Lopez and Taylor, "Dissecting the Electorate."

31. Ibid.

32. See Leighley, "Attitudes, Opportunities, and Incentives," 181–209.

33. Scott Keeter, Juliana Horowitz, and Alec Tyson, "Young Voters in the 2008 Election," Pew Research Center, November 12, 2008.

34. See, for instance, Raymond Wolfinger and Steven Rosenstone, *Who Votes?* (New Haven, Conn.: Yale University Press, 1980). There has been much research since the publication of this book, but it is the best known.

35. U.S. Census Bureau report on the 2004 presidential election.

36. Cindy Kam and Carl Palmer, "Education as a Cause or Proxy? Unpacking the Effects of Education on Political Participation," *Journal of Politics* 70, no. 3 (2008): 612–31.

37. Anthony Downs, *An Economic Theory of Democracy* (New York: Harper, 1957).

38. Howard Gillman, *The Votes That Counted* (Chicago: University of Chicago Press, 2001), 77.

39. William Riker and Peter Ordeshook, "A Theory of the Calculus of Voting," *American Political Science Review* 62 (1968): 25–42.

40. For other efforts to solve this problem, see John Aldrich, "*Turnout and Rational Choice*," *American Journal of Political Science* 37, no. 1 (1993): 246–78; Robert Grafstein, "An Evidential Decision Theory of Turnout," *American Journal of Political Science* 35 (1991): 989–1010.

41. These data are from a Pew Research Center report released on October 18, 2006.

42. Allyson Holbrook and Jon Krosnick, "Vote Over-Reporting: Testing the Social Desirability Hypothesis in Telephone and Internet Surveys," paper presented at the annual meeting of the American Association for Public Opinion Research, Miami Beach, Florida, 2009.

43. David Campbell, *Why We Vote* (Princeton, N.J.: Princeton University Press, 2006).

44. Kids Voting USA: A Community Commitment to Democracy, www.kidsvotingusa.org/. The information in the caption for the photo on page 370 is drawn from this website.

45. Henry Brady, Sidney Verba, and Kay Schlozman, "Beyond SES: A Resource Model of Political Participation," *American Political Science Review* 89 (June 1995): 271–94.

46. John Zipp, "Perceived Representativeness and Voting: An Assessment of the Impact of 'Choices' vs. 'Echoes,'" *American Political Science Review* 79 (1985): 50–61.

47. Alan Gerber, Donald Green, and David Nickerson, "Getting Out the Vote in Local Elections: Results from Six Door-to-Door Canvassing Experiments," *Journal of Politics* 65 (2003): 4.

48. Steven J. Rosenstone and Mark Hansen, *Mobilization, Participation, and Democracy in America* (New York: Macmillan Publishing Co., 1993).

49. "Clinton Wins Nevada," *Las Vegas Sun,* January 19, 2008.

50. James H. Fowler, Laura A. Baker, and Christopher T. Dawes, "The Genetic Basis of Political Participation," *American Political Science Review* 102, no. 2 (2008): 233–48.

51. James Fowler and Christopher Dawes, "Two Genes Predict Voter Turnout," *Journal of Politics* 70 (July 2008): 579–94.

52. Brad Gomez, Thomas Hansford, and George Krause, "Republicans Should Pray for Rain," *Journal of Politics* 69 (2007): 649–63.

53. Frances Fox Piven and Richard Cloward, *Why Americans Still Don't Vote* (Boston: Beacon Press, 2000); Martin Wattenberg, *Where Have All the Voters Gone?* (Boston: Harvard University Press, 2002); Thomas Patterson, *The Vanishing Voter* (New York: Alfred A. Knopf, 2002).

54. United States Election Project, "2008 Presidential Nomination Contest Turnout Rates," October 8, 2008, http://elections.gmu.edu/.

55. G. Bingham Powell, "American Voter Turnout in Comparative Perspective," *American Political Science Review* 80 (1986): 17–37.

56. This "puzzle of participation" was first discussed by Richard Brody in *The New American Political System,* ed. Anthony King (Washington, D.C.: American Enterprise Institute for Public Policy Research, 1978).

57. Warren Miller, "Puzzle Transformed," *Political Behavior* 14 (1992): 1–43.

58. Rosenstone and Hansen, *Mobilization, Participation, and Democracy in America.*

59. Ibid.

60. Matt Bai, "Who Lost Ohio?" *New York Times Magazine,* November 21, 2004.

61. Keena Lipsitz, Christine Trost, Matthew Grossman, and John Sides, "What Voters Want from Campaign Communication," *Political Communication* 22 (2005): 337–54.

62. Steven Ansolabehere and Shanto Iyengar, *Going Negative* (New York: Free Press, 1995).

63. John G. Geer, *In Defense of Negativity* (Chicago: University of Chicago Press, 2006).

64. See, for example, Joshua Clinton and John Lapinski, "'Targeted' Advertising and Voter Turnout: An Experimental Study of the 2000 Presidential Election," *Journal of Politics* 66 (2004): 1.

65. Richard Lau, Lee Sigelman, and Ivy Brown Rovner, "A New Meta-Analysis," *Journal of Politics* 69 (2007): 1176–1209.

66. Estimate from the Pew Hispanic Research Center.

67. Jenifer Warren, "One in 100 behind Bars in America 2008," Pew Center on the States, February 2008.

68. Michael P. McDonald and Samuel Popkin, "The Myth of the Vanishing Voter," *American Political Science Review* 95 (2001): 963–74.

69. See Larry Bartels, *Unequal Democracy* (Princeton, N.J.: Princeton University Press, 2008).

70. Task Force on American Inequality, "American Democracy in an Age of Rising Inequality," American Political Science Association, 2004.

71. Nonprofit Voter Engagement Network press release, October 2009.

72. Bartels, *Unequal Democracy.*

73. Survey data available through the Roper Center's iPoll search engine.

74. Data from *Los Angeles Times* polls conducted in fall 2008 available on iPoll through the Roper Center.

75. Poll conducted for McClatchy, October 30–November 2, 2008.

76. Jeffrey A. Karp and Susan A. Banducci, "Party Mobilization and Political Participation in New and Old Democracies," *Party Politics* 13, no. 2 (2007): 217–34.

77. For more information on the new "Boston tea parties," see the Independent Political Report website at www.independentpoliticalreport.com/.

78. "The Sad Tale of the Bonus Marchers," Doughboy Center, www.worldwar1.com/.

79. Fox News, March 2003, available through the Roper Center.

80. Data from Russell Dalton, "The Myth of the Disengaged American," 2005, www.umich.edu/.

81. Thomas R. Rochon, *Mobilizing for Peace* (Princeton, N.J.: Princeton University Press, 1988).

82. Dennis Johnson, in *Congress and the Internet,* ed. James Thurber and Colton Campbell (New York: Prentice Hall, 2003).

83. See Sarah Palin's Twitter page at http://twitter.com/AKGOVSarahPalin.

84. Sydney Jones and Susannah Fox, "Generational Differences in Online Activities," Pew Internet and American Life Project, January 2009.

85. The percentage comes from a Pew Center survey conducted in November 2006 about whether people were participating in blogs, online discussions, or e-mail lists about the November elections. The data are available through the Roper Center.

86. Matthew A. Mosk, "Internet Donors Fuel Obama," *Washington Post,* February 7, 2008.

87. Matthew A. Mosk, "In Obama Fundraising, Signs of a Shift from Online to in-Person," *Washington Post,* July 18, 2008.

88. David Plouffe, *The Audacity to Win* (New York: Viking Press, 2009).

89. Katherine Q. Seelye and Leslie Wayne, "The Web Takes Ron Paul for a Ride," *New York Times*, November 11, 2007.

90. See Dayton McKean, *The Boss: The Hague Machine in Action* (New York: Russell and Russell Publishers, 1967) for an account of the corrupt practices of machine politicians.

91. See James Bryce, *The American Commonwealth* (New York: MacMillan, 1895).

92. For the best account of the importance and impact of registration, see Benjamin Highton, "Voter Registration and Turnout in the United States," *Perspectives on Politics* 2 (2004): 507–15.

93. See NonProfitVote.Org.

94. Karyn Rotker, "State History and Immigrant Voting," *Milwaukee Journal Sentinel*, October 29, 2006.

95. See Highton, "Voter Registration and Turnout."

96. Library of Congress Thomas, H.R. 2, www.thomas.gov/.

97. *Crawford v. Marion County Election Board*, 553 U.S. (2008). See also Bill Mears, "High Court Upholds Indiana's Voter ID Law," www.cnn.com/; Linda Greenhouse, "In a 6-to-3 Vote, Justices Uphold a Voter ID Law," *New York Times*, April 29, 2008.

98. Texas Secretary of State Hope Andrade, www.sos.state.tx.us/.

99. Bill Bradbury, "Vote-by-Mail: The Real Winner Is Democracy," *Washington Post*, January 1, 2005.

100. Michael Connery, "New Study: Text Message Reminders Increase Voter Turnout by 4.6 Percent," http://futuremajority.com/.

101. See Jeff Manza and Christopher Ugge, *Locked Out: Felon Disenfranchisement and American Democracy* (Oxford, U.K.: Oxford University Press, 2007).

Chapter 12

1. This story has been compiled from Answers.com, Nydia Velázquez, www.answers.com; U.S. House of Representatives, www.house.gov; Sally Friedman, *Dilemmas of Representation: Local Politics, National Factors, and the Home Styles of Modern U.S. Congress Members* (Albany: State University of New York Press, 2007), 164; and Congresswoman Nydia Velázquez, "Velázquez: President Determined to Lay Foundation for Future Growth," February 25, 2009, www.house.gov/, which is the source of the chapter-opening quotation.

2. Mildred Amer and Jennifer E. Manning, "CRS Report for Congress, Membership of the 111th Congress: A Profile," Congressional Research Service, Washington, D.C., 2009.

3. Ibid. For a broader discussion of the careers of women legislators in the House, see Jennifer Lawless and Sean Theriault, "Will She Stay or Will She Go? Career Ceilings and Women's Retirement from the US Congress," *Legislative Studies Quarterly* 30 (2005): 581–96.

4. See Lana R. Slack, *Senate Manual: Standing Rules, Orders, Laws, and Resolutions Affecting the Business of the United State Senate* (Washington, D.C.: Government Printing Office, 1988), 684–85.

5. United States Senate, www.senate.gov.

6. In rare cases where a senator dies or resigns, an interim replacement is chosen by the governor of the state until an election is held to fill the seat.

7. Wendy J. Schiller, *Partners and Rivals: Representation in U.S. Senate Delegations* (Princeton, N.J.: Princeton University Press, 2000).

8. This was the case for Delaware, whose state legislature would not agree on electing either senator during the years 1901–1903. Slack, *Senate Manual*, 737.

9. U.S. Census Bureau, www.census.gov.

10. After the first census of the new federal government under the Constitution, Congress grew to 105 members in 1792. See Brian Frederick, *Congressional Representation and Constituents: The Case for Increasing the Size of the U.S. House of Representatives* (New York: Routledge, 2010), 23–24.

11. U.S. House of Representatives, www.clerk.house.gov.

12. For a discussion of representation by Latino members, see Jason P. Casellas, "The Institutional and Demographic Determinants of Latino Representation," *Legislative Studies Quarterly* 34, no. 3 (2009): 399–426; see also David Leal and Frederick M. Hess, "Who Chooses Experience? Examining the Use of Veteran Staff by House Freshman," *Polity* 36 (2004).

13. See *Shaw v. Reno*, 509 U.S. 630 (1993), *Miller v. Johnson*, 515 U.S. 900 (1995), and *Easley v. Cromartie*, 532 US 234 (2001). *Thornburg v. Gingles*, 478 U.S. 30 (1986) provides plaintiffs with a right to force a state to create a majority-minority district if the minority community is large and concentrated enough to form a majority in the district, the minority community votes cohesively, and white voting prevents the minority community from electing its preferred candidate. For a longer discussion of redistricting, see Bernard Grofman, Lisa Handley, and Richard G. Niemi, *Minority Representation and the Quest for Voting Equality* (New York: Cambridge University Press, 1992).

14. Frances E. Lee and Bruce I. Oppenheimer, *Sizing up the Senate: The Unequal Consequences of Equal Representation* (Chicago: University of Chicago Press, 1999).

15. Two prominent works on this point are Richard F. Fenno, *The Power of the Purse: Appropriations Politics in Congress* (Boston: Little, Brown, 1966), and Aaron B. Wildavsky, *The New Politics of the Budgetary Process* (Boston: Addison-Wesley Educational, 1992).

16. Fiona McGillivray, "Trading Free and Opening Markets" in *International Trade and Political Institutions*, ed. Fiona McGillivray, Iain McLean, Robert Pahre, and Cheryl Schonhardt-Bailey (Cheltenham, U.K.: Edward Elgar, 2001), 80–98.

17. U.S. Courts: The Federal Judiciary, www.uscourts.gov.

18. Sarah A. Binder and Forrest Maltzman, "Senatorial Delay in Confirming Federal Judges, 1947–1998," *American Journal of Political Science* 46, no. 1 (2002): 190–99.

19. Sarah A. Binder, *Majority Rights, Minority Rule* (New York: Cambridge University Press, 1997); Eric Schickler, *Disjointed Pluralism: Institutional Innovation and the Development of the U.S. Congress* (Princeton, N.J.: Princeton University Press, 2001).

20. Sean Gailmard and Jeffery A. Jenkins, "Minority-Party Power in the Senate and the House of Representatives," in *Why Not Parties? Party Effects in the United States Senate*, ed. Nathan W. Monroe, Jason M. Roberts, and David W. Rohde (Chicago: University of Chicago Press, 2008).

21. Randall Strahan, *Leading Representatives: The Agency of Leaders in the Politics of the U.S. House.* (Baltimore: Johns Hopkins University Press, 2007).

22. Ibid., 79–126.

23. David W. Rohde, *Parties and Leaders in the Postreform House* (Chicago: University of Chicago Press, 1991).

24. Gary W. Cox and Mathew D. McCubbins, *Legislative Leviathan: Party Government in the House* (Berkeley: University of California Press, 1993).

25. Barry C. Burden and Tammy M. Frisbee, "Preferences, Partisanship, and Whip Activity in the U.S. House of Representatives," *Legislative Studies Quarterly* 29 (2004): 569–90.

26. Ralph Huitt, "Democratic Party Leadership in the Senate," *American Political Science Review* 55 (1961): 333–44.

27. E. Scott Adler and John Wilkerson, "Intended Consequences: Jurisdictional Reform and Issue Control in the U.S. House of

Representatives," *Legislative Studies Quarterly* 33, no. 1 (2008): 85–112.

28. Richard E. Cohen, "Dems May Repeal Term Limits for House Chairs," *National Journal Online,* December 31, 2008, www.nationaljournal .com; Sara Burrows, "House Term Limits Repealed, Rangel to Retain Committee Chairmanship," Cybercast News Service, January 8, 2009, www.cns.com.

29. Ron Nixon, "House Committee to Examine Recent Performance of S.B.A.," *New York Times*, February 7, 2007, C7.

30. David W. Rohde, "Committee Reform in the House of Representatives and the Subcommittee Bill of Rights," *Annals of the American Academy of Political and Social Science* 411, no. 1 (1974): 39–47.

31. For a list of current caucuses, see www.cha.house.gov.

32. Daily Digest, *Congressional Record D1675*, December 31, 2007; Daily Digest, *Congressional Record D1675*, November 17, 2008, http:// thomas.loc.gov.

33. For an extended discussion of the right of recognition and the powers it affords senators, see Floyd Riddick, *Senate Procedure*, ed. Alan Frumin (Washington D.C.: U.S. Government Printing Office, 1992), 1091–99.

34. Sarah A. Binder and Steven S. Smith, *Politics or Principle: Filibustering in the U.S. Senate* (Washington, D.C.: Brookings Institution Press, 1997). For a discussion of the use of the filibuster by retiring senators, see Martin Overby, L. Overby, and Lauren Bell, "Rational Behavior or the Norm of Cooperation? Filibustering among Retiring Senators," *Journal of Politics* 66 (2004): 906–24.

35. David Stout, Carl Hulse, and Sheryl Gay Stolberg, "Senate Backs Disputed Judicial Nomination," *New York Times*, October 27, 2007, A21.

36. Ibid.

37. Wendy J. Schiller, "Resolved the Filibuster Should Be Abolished—Con," in *Debating Reform*, ed. Richard J. Ellis and Michael Nelson (Washington D.C.: CQ Press, 2010).

38. Wendy J. Schiller, "Senators as Political Entrepreneurs: Using Bill Sponsorship to Shape Legislative Agendas," *American Journal of Political Science* 1 (1995): 186–203.

39. Glen Krutz, *Hitching a Ride: Omnibus Legislating in the U.S. Congress* (Columbus: Ohio State University Press, 2001).

40. Keith R. Krehbiel, *Information and Legislative Organization* (Ann Arbor: University of Michigan Press, 1991).

41. For a few examples of this work, see Aage Clausen, *How Congressmen Decide* (New York: St. Martin's Press, 1973); John Kingdon, *Congressmen's Voting Decisions* (New York: Harper & Row, 1989); David W. Brady, *Critical Elections and Congressional Policy Making* (Stanford, Calif.: Stanford University Press, 1988); Stanley Bach and Steven S. Smith, *Managing Uncertainty in the U.S. House of Representatives* (Washington, D.C.: Brookings Institution, 1989). For examples of the ideological examination of roll call voting, see Keith T. Poole and Howard Rosenthal, *Ideology and Congress* (New Brunswick, N.J.: Transaction Publishers, 2009).

42. "U.S. Congress Votes Database," *Washington Post*, www .washingtonpost.com.

43. C. Lawrence Evans and Walter J. Oleszek, "Message Politics and Senate Procedure," in *The Contentious Senate: Partisanship, Ideology and the Myth of Cool Judgment,* ed. Colton C. Campbell and Nicol C. Rae (Lanham, Md.: Rowman and Littlefield, 2000).

44. Barbara Sinclair, *Unorthodox Lawmaking: New Legislative Processes in the U.S. Congress,* 3rd ed. (Washington, D.C.: CQ Press, 2007).

45. Congressional Budget and Impoundment Control Act of 1974 (Public Law 93-344). For additional background on budget history, see the Senate Committee on the Budget, www.budget .senate.gov.

46. Balanced Budget and Emergency Deficit Control Act of 1985 (Public Law 99-177). For historical tables on the U.S. federal budget, see Congressional Budget Office, "The Budget and Economic Outlook Fiscal Years 2010 to 2020," January 26, 2010. Fiscal 1985 budget deficit number are taken from Table F-1, www.cbo.gov.

47. See Walter J. Oleszek, *Congressional Procedures and the Policy Process,* 6th ed. (Washington, D.C: CQ Press, 2004), especially 63–69. For a more comprehensive look at the history of budget politics and deficits, see Jasmine Farrier, *Passing the Buck: Congress, Budgets, and Deficits* (Lexington: University of Kentucky Press, 2004).

48. Kathleen Hunter, "GOP Readies Procedural Salvo against Reconciliation Play," *CQ Weekly Online,* March 8, 2010, 568.

49. Charles M. Cameron, *Veto Bargaining: Presidents and the Politics of Negative Power* (New York: Cambridge University Press, 2000).

50. Daily Digest, *Congressional Record D1675* (December 31, 2007); Daily Digest, *Congressional Record D1675* (November 17, 2008).

51. Albert D. Cover and Bruce S. Brumberg, "Baby Books and Ballots: The Impact of Congressional Mail on Constituent Opinion," *American Political Science Review* 76 (1982): 347–59.

52. Richard L. Hall, *Participation in Congress* (New Haven, Conn.: Yale University Press, 1998).

53. Tracy Sulkin, *Issue Politics in Congress* (New York: Cambridge University Press, 2005).

54. Office of the Clerk of the House of Representatives, www.clerk .house.gov.

55. For a comprehensive look at this congressional activity, see Diana Evans, *Greasing the Wheels: Using Pork Barrel Projects to Build Majority Coalitions in Congress* (New York: Cambridge University Press, 2004).

56. Citizens against Taxpayer Waste, *2009 Congressional Pig Book,* www .cagw.org.

57. Ibid.

58. Jennifer A. Diouhy, "Alaska 'Bridge to Nowhere' Funding Gets Nowhere; Lawmakers Delete Project after Critics Bestow Derisive Moniker," *San Francisco Chronicle*, November 17, 2005, A7.

59. Richard F. Fenno Jr., *Home Style: Representatives in Their Districts* (Boston: Little, Brown, 1978).

60. David R. Mayhew, *Congress: The Electoral Connection.* (New Haven, Conn.: Yale University Press, 1974).

61. For an extended discussion of how senators from the same state interact, see Schiller, *Partners and Rivals.*

62. Center for Responsive Politics, www.opensecrets.com.

63. For details on these programs, see the U.S. Department of Health and Human Services, Centers for Medicare and Medicaid Services (CMS), www.cms.hhs.gov.

64. Joanna Turner, Michael Boudreaux, and Victoria Lynch, "A Preliminary Evaluation of Health Insurance Coverage in the 2008 American Community Survey," U.S. Census Bureau: Health Insurance Coverage Working Paper: 2008 American Community Survey, September 22, 2008, www.census.gov.

65. Open Congress, "H.R. 3962—Affordable Health Care for America Act," Participatory Politics Foundation and Sunlight Foundation, www.opencongress.org.

66. Open Congress, "S. 1796—America's Healthy Future Act of 2009," Participatory Politics Foundation and Sunlight Foundation, www .opencongress.org.

67. Patricia Murphy, "Senate Passes Sweeping Health Care Reform, but Trouble Lies Ahead," *Capitolist*, December 24, 2009, www .politicsdaily.com.

68. Naftali Bendavid, "'Blue Dog' Democrats Hold Health-Care Overhaul at Bay," *Wall Street Journal*, July 27, 2009, www.wsj.com.

69. Henry J. Kaiser Family Foundation, "Summary of Coverage Provisions in the Patient Protection and Affordable Care Act and the Health Care and Education Reconciliation Act of 2010," March 23, 2010, www.kff.org.

70. Center for Responsive Politics, Influence and Lobbying: Clients Lobbying on HR 3200, www.opensecrets.org.

71. Jonathan Weisman, "Under Pressure, Obama Defends Health Care Plan," *Wall Street Journal*, August 12, 2009, www.wsj.com; John Amick, "Recess Doesn't Slow Health Care Rhetoric," *Washington Post*, August 9, 2009.

72. Sarah Palin, "Statement on the Current Health Care Debate," Facebook, August 7, 2009, www.facebook.com.

73. Celeste Katz, "President Obama Fires Back at Sarah Palin Post Claiming His Health Plan Would Create a 'Death Panel,'" *New York Daily News*, August 8, 2009, www.nydailynews.com.

74. Macon Phillips, "Facts Are Stubborn Things," White House Blog, August 4, 2009, www.whitehouse.gov.

Chapter 13

1. This story was compiled from Meena Dev, "Alumna Hits Campaign Trail with Kerry," *Sophian* (Smith College), September 30, 2004, www.media.www.smithsophian.com; "Stephanie Cutter," www.WhoRunsGov.com; White House Office of the Press Secretary, "President Obama Names Stephanie Cutter Assistant to the President for Special Projects," April 22, 2010; the chapter-opening quotation is from the article about Cutter in *Sophian*.

2. Charles Jones, *The President in a Separated System* (Washington, D.C.: Brookings Institution Press, 2005).

3. See Hedrick Smith, "Bush Says He Sought to Avoid Acting Like Surrogate President," *New York Times*, April 12, 1981, www.nytimes.com.

4. Bruce G. Peabody and Scott E. Grant, "The Twice and Future President: Constitutional Interstices and the Twenty-Second Amendment," *Minnesota Law Review* 83 (1999): 565–94.

5. Ibid.

6. The White House, "The Presidents," www.whitehouse.gov.

7. Arthur Schlesinger Jr., *The Imperial Presidency* (New York: Mariner Books, 2004; first published 1973).

8. "I. Lewis Libby, Jr.," Times Topics, www.nytimes.com.

9. Robert Wielaard, "Kosovo Recognition Irritates Russia and China," *Herald-Tribune*, February 19, 2009, A11, www.heraldtribune.com.

10. Glenn S. Krutz, *Hitching a Ride: Omnibus Legislating in the U.S. Congress* (Columbus: Ohio State University Press, 2001). Also see Charles M. Cameron, *Veto Bargaining: Presidents and the Politics of Negative Bargaining* (New York: Cambridge University Press, 2000).

11. William W. Lammers and Michael A. Genovese, *The Presidency and Domestic Policy* (Washington, D.C.: CQ Press, 2000), 315–24.

12. Wilson delivered the speech on December 2, 1913. See John Woolley and Gerhard Peters, "The American Presidency Project: Length of State of the Union Messages and Addresses (in words) Washington–Obama," www.presidency.ucsb.edu. See also Jeff Cummins, "State of the Union Addresses and the President's Legislative Success," *Congress and the Presidency* 37 (2010): 176–99.

13. Ibid.

14. Douglas Linder, "The Andrew Johnson Impeachment Trial of 1868: A Trial Account," Famous American Trials, 1999, www.law.umkc.edu.

15. Ibid.

16. Douglas Linder, "Map Showing Impeachment Vote in the Trial of Andrew Johnson," Famous American Trials, 1999, www.law.umkc.edu.

17. The chronology that follows is taken from the *Washington Post*'s history of Watergate, www.washingtonpost.com.

18. Ibid.

19. Douglas Linder, "The Impeachment Trial of William Clinton," Famous American Trials, 2005, www.law.umkc.edu.

20. "A Whitewater Chronology: What Really Happened during the Clinton Years," *Wall Street Journal*, May 28, 2003, www.wsj.com.

21. Ibid.

22. The Library of Congress, Legislative Information, http//thomas.loc.gov.

23. William G. Howell, *Power without Persuasion: The Politics of Direct Presidential Action* (Princeton, N.J.: Princeton University Press, 2003).

24. Harold C. Relyea, "Presidential Directives: Background and Overview," Washington, D.C. Congressional Research Service Report for Congress 98-611, 2007.

25. Kenneth R. Mayer, "Executive Orders and Presidential Power," *Journal of Politics* 61 (1999): 445–66, especially 448.

26. Ibid.

27. Papers of Harry S. Truman, "Memorandum concerning the Interpretation of the President's Order 9981, January 1948," www.trumanlibrary.org.

28. "Press Release, Executive Order 10730, Providing for the Removal of an Obstruction of Justice within the State of Arkansas, September 24, 1957," www.eisenhower.archives.gov.

29. Christopher S. Kelley and Bryan W. Marshall, "The Last Word: Presidential Power and the Role of Signing Statements," *Presidential Studies Quarterly* 38 (2008): 248–67; Michael J. Berry, "Controversially Executing the Law: George W. Bush and the Constitutional Signing Statement," *Congress and the Presidency* 36 (2009): 244–71.

30. White House, "Memorandum for the Heads of Executive Departments and Agencies: Subject: Presidential Signing Statement," March 9, 2009, www.whitehouse.gov.

31. John Woolley and Gerhard Peters, "The American Presidency Project," www.presidency.ucsb.edu.

32. Joseph A. Pika and John Anthony Maltese, *The Politics of the Presidency* (Washington, D.C.: CQ Press, 2008), 15–17.

33. C-SPAN Congressional Glossary, www.c-span.org.

34. George C. Edwards III, *On Deaf Ears: The Limits of the Bully Pulpit* (New Haven, Conn.: Yale University Press, 2006).

35. All data are from John Woolley and Gerhard Peters, "The American Presidency Project: Presidential News Conferences," www.presidency.ucsb.edu.

36. Also see Melvin C. Laracey, *Presidents and People: The Partisan Story of Going Public* (College Station, Tex.: Texas A&M University Press, 2002); Reed L. Welch, "Presidential Success in Communicating with the Public through Televised Addresses," *Presidential Studies Quarterly* 33 (2003): 347–65.

37. Richard E. Neustadt, *Presidential Power and the Modern Presidents* (New York: Free Press, 1990).

38. Jon R. Bond, Richard Fleisher, and B. Dan Wood, "The Marginal and Time Varying Effect of Public Approval on Presidential Success in Congress," *Journal of Politics* 65 (2003): 92–110.

39. Andrew Barrett and Matthew Eshbaugh-Soha, "Presidential Success on the Substance of Legislation," *Political Research Quarterly* 60 (2007): 100–112.

40. Emily Jane Charnock, James A. McCann, and Kathryn D. Tenpas, "Presidential Travel from Eisenhower to George W. Bush: An Electoral College Strategy," *Political Science Quarterly* 124 (2009): 323–39.

41. Joint Resolution of Congress, House Joint Resolution 1145, August 7, 1964, *Department of State Bulletin*, August 24, 1964, reprinted in Henry Steele Commager and Milton Cantor, eds., *Documents of American History*, 10th ed. (Englewood Cliffs, N.J.: Prentice Hall, 1988), 2: 690.

42. Louis Fisher, *Presidential War Power*, 2nd ed. (Lawrence: University Press of Kansas, 2004), 128–33.

43. Ibid., 144–51.

44. For a longer discussion of this struggle for power over the conduct of war, see William G. Howell and Jon C. Pevenhouse, *Congressional Checks on Presidential War Powers* (Princeton, N.J.: Princeton University Press, 2007).

45. For more on presidential decisions to engage in military conflicts, see James Meernick, "Domestic Politics and the Political Use of Military Force by the United States," *Political Research Quarterly* 54 (2001): 889–904.

46. U.S. House of Representatives, House Joint Resolution, 114 Section 3 (a) 1, http://thomas.loc.gov.

47. John J. Kruzel.. "Afghanistan Troop Level to Eclipse Iraq by Midyear." American Forces Press Service, United States Army, March 25, 2010, www.army.mil.

48. Barack Obama, "Remarks by the President in Address to the Nation on the Way Forward in Afghanistan and Pakistan," West Point, December 1, 2009, www.whitehouse.gov.

49. Paul Kane, "Lawmakers Split over Obama's Troop Plan for Afghanistan," *Washington Post*, December 1, 2009, www.washingtonpost.com.

50. Garance Franke-Ruta, "USA Today/Gallup Poll: Majority Support Obama's Afghan Strategy," *Washington Post*, December 3, 2009, www.washingtonpost.com.

51. *Youngstown Sheet and Tube Co. v. Sawyer*, 343 U.S. 579 (1952).

52. *Hamdi v. United States*, 542 U.S. 507 (2004).

53. *Rasul v. Bush*, 542 U.S. 466 (2004).

54. *Hamdan v. Rumsfeld*, 548 U.S. 557 (2006).

55. *Boumediene v. Bush*, 553 U.S. 723 (2008).

56. White House, Executive Order Nos. 13491, 13492, 13493, January 22, 2009, Washington, D.C.: Government Printing Office, www.docket.access.gpo.gov.

57. James P. Pfiffner, *The Modern Presidency*, 6th ed. (Boston: Wadsworth Cengage Learning, 2011), 99.

58. Fred I. Greenstein, *Presidential Difference*, 3rd ed. (Princeton, N.J.: Princeton University Press, 2009).

59. Mondale wrote a detailed memorandum to President Carter outlining his views of the office of vice president. For a broader discussion of Mondale's vice presidential tenure, see Richard Moe, "The Making of the Modern Vice Presidency: A Personal Reflection," *Minnesota History* 60 (2006): 88–99.

60. Women in History, "Marian Anderson," www.womeinhistoryohio.com.

61. Stephen Skowronek, *The Politics Presidents Make: Leadership from John Adams to Bill Clinton* (Cambridge, Mass.: Harvard University Press, 1997). Also see Stephen Skowronek, *Presidential Leadership in Political Time: Reprise and Reappraisal* (Lawrence: University Press of Kansas, 2008).

62. Aaron Wildavsky, "The Two Presidencies" in *The Presidency*, ed. Aaron Wildavsky (Boston: Little, Brown, and Company, 1969), 231–43.

63. For a more recent test of this theory, see Brandes Canes-Wrone, William G. Howell, and David E. Lewis, "Toward a Broader Understanding of Presidential Power: A Reevaluation of the Two Presidencies Thesis," *Journal of Politics* 69 (2007): 1–16.

64. Lammers and Genovese, *Presidency and Domestic Policy*. See also Neustadt, *Presidential Power and the Modern Presidents*.

65. Samuel Kernell, *Going Public*, 4th ed. (Washington, D.C.: CQ Press, 2007), 131.

66. Ibid., 87–88.

67. Lammers and Genovese, *Presidency and Domestic Policy*.

68. American Rhetoric, "Top 100 Speeches," www.americanrhetoric.com.

69. See "Alan Greenspan," Times Topics: People, www.topics.nytimes.com.

70. Hank C. Jenkins-Smith, Carol L. Silva, and Richard W. Waterman, "Micro- and Macrolevel Models of the Presidential Expectations Gap," *Journal of Politics* 67 (2005): 690–715.

Chapter 14

1. This story has been compiled from Marilyn Adams, "Pair of Flier Advocates Fight for Airline Passengers' Rights," *USA Today*, May 19, 2008; Joan Lowy, "Government Asking Why Passengers Were Stranded," August 12, 2009, www.abcnews.go.com; Jeff Bailey, "An Air Travel Activist Is Born," *New York Times*, September 20, 2007; Matthew L. Wald, "Stiff Fines Are Set for Long Wait on the Tarmac," *New York Times*, December 21, 2009; Coalition for an Airline Passengers' Bill of Rights, "An Early Christmas Present for the Flying Public," e-mail, December 23, 2009, http://FlyersRights.org; and an e-mail interview with Kate Hanni, January 22, 2010, conducted for this textbook, from which the chapter-opening quotation is taken.

2. Max Weber, *Economy and Society*, ed. Guenther Roth and Claus Wittich (Berkeley, Calif.: University of California Press, 1978).

3. Office of Management and Budget; *Analytical Perspectives Budget of the U.S. Government FY 2011* (Washington, D.C.: Government Printing Office, 2010), Table 10-2, Total Federal Employment, p. 108, www.whitehouse.gov/omb/; United States Postal Service, "Postal Facts 2010," www.usps.com. Note that the total number of federal employees cited above does not include active and reserve members of the National Guard.

4. EyeWitness to History, "President Jefferson in the White House," www.eyewitnesstohistory.com.

5. White House, "The Cabinet," www.whitehouse.gov.

6. Office of Management and Budget, *Analytical Perspectives Budget of the U.S. Government Fiscal Year 2011*, Table 26-11, Outlays by Agency in the Baseline Projection of Current Policy, p. 413, www.whitehouse.gov/omb.

7. National Council of State Legislatures, Summary of the State Children's Health Insurance Program (SCHIP), www.ncsl.org.

8. Department of Health and Human Services, "Health Reform and the Department of Health and Human Services," www.healthreform.gov.

9. Office of Management and Budget, *Analytical Perspectives Budget of the U.S. Government Fiscal Year 2011*, Table 10-1, Federal Civilian Employment in the Executive Branch, p. 107.

10. U.S. Department of Transportation, "Budget Estimates Fiscal Year 2011, Federal Aviation Administration, Exhibit I," www.dot.gov.

11. Federal Aviation Administration, www.faa.gov.

12. Department of Health and Human Services, www.hhs.gov.

13. James Q. Wilson, *Bureaucracy* (New York: Basic Books, 1989), 91.

14. Donald F. Kettl, *System under Stress: Homeland Security and American Politics*, 2nd ed. (Washington, D.C.: CQ Press, 2007), 37–39.

15. Kettl, *System under Stress*. Also see David E. Lewis, *The Politics of Presidential Appointments: Political Control and Bureaucratic Performance* (Princeton, N.J.: Princeton University Press, 2008), 141–71.

16. Ian Urbina, "U.S. Said to Allow Drilling without Needed Permits," *New York Times*, May 13, 2010, www.nytimes.com.

17. Wilson, *Bureaucracy*, 69–70.

18. Daniel P. Carpenter, *The Forging of Bureaucratic Autonomy: Reputations, Networks, and Policy Innovation in Executive Agencies, 1862–1928* (Princeton, N.J.: Princeton University Press, 2001).

19. United States Postal Service, Office of the Postmaster, *The United States Postal Service: An American History, 1775–2006* (Washington, D.C.: Office of Government Relations, United States Postal Service, 2007), 6–7, www.usps.com.

20. Surface Transportation Board, "About STB Overview," www.stb.dot.gov.

21. Michael Moss, "E. Coli Path Shows Flaws in Beef Inspection," *New York Times*, October 3, 2009, A1, www.nytimes.com; Michael Moss, "E. Coli Outbreak Traced to Company That Halted Testing of Ground Beef Trimmings," *New York Times*, November 12, 2009, A16, www.nytimes.com.

22. U.S. Consumer Product Safety Commission, www.cpsc.gov.

23. White House, "Remarks by the President on the Consumer Financial Protection Bureau," September 17, 2010, www.whitehouse.gov.

24. Lewis, *Politics of Presidential Appointments*, 12–13.

25. Theda Skocpol, *Protecting Soldiers and Mothers* (Cambridge, Mass.: Harvard University Press, 1992).

26. Sean M. Theriault, *The Power of the People* (Columbus: Ohio State University Press, 2005), Chapter 3.

27. Lewis, *Politics of Presidential Appointments*, 19–20, especially Figure 2.1.

28. U.S. Office of Personnel Management, "Federal Employment Statistics: Distribution of Federal Employment by Major Geographic Area for November 2008," www.opm.gov.

29. Bureau of Labor Statistics, U.S. Department of Labor, *Career Guide to Industries, 2010–11 Edition*, Federal Government, www.bls.gov.

30. U.S. Office of Personnel Management, "Salaries and Wages: 2010 General Schedules (Base)," www.opm.gov.

31. For more on political appointees, see Jeff Gill and Richard Waterman, "Solidary and Functional Costs: Explaining the Presidential Appointment Contradiction," *Journal of Public Administration Research and Theory* 14 (2004): 547–69.

32. Lewis, *Politics of Presidential Appointments*, 97; "Head Count Tracking Obama's Appointments," www.washingtonpost.com.

33. Lewis, *Politics of Presidential Appointments*, 11.

34. Ibid., p. 100, Figure 4.3.

35. U.S. Office of Special Counsel, "Political Activity and the Federal Employee," 2000, www.oklahoma.feb.gov.

36. For more on the relationship between bureaucrats, members of Congress, and interest groups, see Anthony M. Bertelli and Christian R. Grose, "Secretaries of Pork? A New Theory of Distributive Public Policy," *Journal of Politics* 71 (2009): 926–45; and Sanford C. Gordon and Catherine Hafer, "Corporate Influence and the Regulatory Mandate," *Journal of Politics* 69 (2007): 300–319.

37. OMB Watch, www.ombwatch.org.

38. Barack Obama, "Memorandum for the Director of the Environmental Protection Agency on State of California Request for Waiver Under 42 U.S.C. 7543(b), the Clean Air Act," January 26, 2009, www.whitehouse.gov.

39. Jack Lewis, "The Birth of the EPA," *EPA Journal* (Washington, D.C.: U.S. Environmental Protection Agency, 1985), www.epa.gov.

40. OMB Watch, "Executive Order 12866," February 12, 2002, www.ombwatch.org. President Clinton issued the order in 1993.

41. U.S. Environmental Protection Agency, www.epa.gov.

42. Felicity Barringer, "In Reversal, Court Allows a Bush Plan on Pollution," *New York Times*, December 24, 2008, A13.

43. From the *Federal Register* 70, no. 128 (July 6, 2005): 39103–72; accessed via GPO Access, wais.access.gpo.gov.

44. "Editorial: A Major Setback for Clean Air," *New York Times*, July 16, 2008.

45. Power-Gen Worldwide, "Court Tosses Out CAIR Emissions Rule," July 11, 2008, www.pepei.pennnet.com.

46. Deborah Zaranbeko, "Court Reinstates EPA Power Plant Pollution Rule," Reuters, December 23, 2006, www.reuters.com.

47. Stephen Power and Ian Talley, "States Want Delay on Emission Rules," *Wall Street Journal*, January 11, 2010, A1.

48. For in-depth studies of congressional oversight, see Charles R. Shipan, "Regulatory Regimes, Agency Actions, and the Conditional Nature of Congressional Influence," *American Political Science Review* 9 (2004): 467–80; and Keith W. Smith, "Congressional Use of Authorization and Oversight." *Congress and the Presidency* 37 (2010): 45–63.

49. Federal Reserve Education, "History of the Federal Reserve," www.federalreserveeducation.org; Board of Governors of the Federal Reserve System, www.federalreserve.gov.

50. Rebecca Christie, "Geithner Says TARP Repayments Don't Hurt Bank Lending Ability," Bloomberg.Com/News, December 19, 2009, www.bloomberg.com.

51. Rachelle Younglai and Jon Paschal, "Factbox: Winners and Losers in the Senate's Financial Bill," May 19, 2010, www. Reuters.com.

52. Daniel P. Carpenter, "Groups, the Media, Agency Waiting Costs, and FDA Drug Approval," *American Journal of Political Science* 46, no. 3 (2002): 490–505. Also see Susan L. Moffitt, "Promoting Agency Reputation through Public Advice: Advisory Committee Use in the FDA," *Journal of Politics* 72, no. 3 (2010): 1–14. For a longer discussion of the history and effectiveness of the FDA, see Daniel P. Carpenter, *Reputation and Power: Organizational Image and Pharmaceutical Regulation at the FDA* (Princeton, N.J.: Princeton University Press, 2010).

53. U.S. Food and Drug Administration, "Vioxx (Rofecoxib) Questions and Answers," September 30, 2004, www.fda.gov.

54. Stephen Power and Neal King Jr., "Next Challenge on Stimulus: Spending all that Money," *Wall Street Journal*, February 13, 2009, A1.

55. L. Paige Whitaker, *The Whistleblower Protection Act: An Overview*, CRS Report for Congress, 2007.

56. Gregory Zuckerman and Kara Scannell, "Madoff Misled SEC in '06, Got Off," *Wall Street Journal*, December 18, 2008.

57. Nancy Pelosi's Channel, "Rep. Ackerman on Madoff Fraud," February 4, 2009, www.youtube.com. Ackerman spoke at the House Financial Services Subcommittee on Capital Markets, Insurance, and Government Sponsored Enterprises hearing on the Madoff scandal. He was speaking to members of the Securities and Exchange Commission who were testifying at the hearing.

Chapter 15

1. This story was compiled from Greg Stohr, *A Black and White Case* (Princeton, N.J.: Bloomberg Press, 2004). Documents related to the cases are available at http://supreme.lp.findlaw.com/. The chapter-opening quotation is from Jennifer Gratz, "MSU Speech, Part 1," November 14, 2008, http://www.youtube.com/watch?v=fD5kpuNCBZs.

2. Harold J. Spaeth, *Supreme Court Policy Making* (San Francisco: W. H. Freeman and Company, 1979), 38.

3. Administrative Office of the U.S. Courts, www.uscourts.gov/.

4. Alexander Hamilton, *Federalist 78*, in the *Federalist Papers*, www.constitution.org/.

5. *Marbury v. Madison*, 5 U.S. 137, 177 (1803).

6. *McCulloch v. Maryland*, 4 Wheaton 316 (1819); *Gibbons v. Ogden*, 9 Wheaton 1 (1824); and *Cohens v. Virginia*, 6 Wheaton 264 (1821).

7. *Dred Scott v. Sandford*, 60 U.S. (19 How.) 393 (1857).

8. *Slaughterhouse Cases*, 83 U.S. 36 (1873).

9. *United States v. Cruikshank*, 92 U.S. 542 (1876).

10. *Civil Rights Cases*, 109 U.S. 3 (1883).

11. *Plessy v. Ferguson*, 163 U.S. 537 (1896).

12. *United States v. E.C. Knight Co.*, 156 U.S. 1 (1895).

13. *Lochner v. New York*, 198 U.S. 45 (1905); *Adkins v. Children's Hospital*, 261 U.S. 525 (1923).

14. *Wickard v. Filburn*, 317 U.S. 111 (1942).

15. *Brandenburg v. Ohio*, 395 U.S. 444 (1969) (speech rights); *New York Times v. Sullivan*, 376 U.S. 254 (1964) (press rights); *Memoirs v. Massachusetts*, 383 U.S. 413 (1966) (obscenity); and *Engel v. Vitale*, 370 U.S. 421 (1962); *Abington Township School District v. Schempp*, 374 U.S. 203 (1963) (prayer and Bible reading).

16. *Brown v. Board of Education*, 347 U.S. 484 (1954); *Wesberry v. Sanders*, 376 U.S. 1 (1964); *Reynolds v. Sims*, 377 U.S. 533 (1964).

17. *Griswold v. Connecticut*, 381 U.S. 479 (1965) (birth control); *Roe v. Wade*, 410 U.S. 113 (1973).

18. *Mapp v. Ohio*, 367 U.S. 643 (1961); *Miranda v. Arizona*, 384 U.S. 436 (1966).

19. "The Law: The Nixon Radicals," June 5, 1972, www.time.com/time/.

20. *Swann v. Charlotte-Mecklenburg Board of Education*, 402 U.S. 1 (1971) (busing); *Roe v. Wade*, 410 U.S. 113 (1973) (abortion); *Furman v. Georgia*, 408 U.S. 238 (1972) (death penalty); *Reed v. Reed*, 404 U.S. 71 (1971) (sex discrimination); and *Regents of the University of California v. Bakke* 438 U.S. 265 (1978) (affirmative action).

21. *San Antonio Independent School District v. Rodriguez*, 411 U.S. 1 (1973) (school funding); *United States v. Leon*, 468 U.S. 897 (1984) (limiting the exclusionary rule); and *New York v. Quarles*, 467 U.S. 649 (1984) (limiting *Miranda*).

22. *United States v. Nixon*, 418 U.S. 683 (1974).

23. *Lawrence v. Texas*, 539 U.S. 558 (2003).

24. *Planned Parenthood v. Casey*, 505 U.S. 833 (1992); *United States v. Lopez*, 514 U.S. 549 (1995); *Gratz v. Bollinger*, 539 U.S. 244 (2003); and *Grutter v. Bollinger*, 539 U.S. 306 (2003).

25. *Bush v. Gore*, 531 U.S. 98 (2000).

26. Jeffrey A. Segal and Harold J. Spaeth, *The Supreme Court and the Attitudinal Model Revisited* (New York: Cambridge University Press, 2002), 179.

27. Lee Epstein and Jeffrey A. Segal, *Advice and Consent: The Politics of Judicial Appointments* (New York: Oxford University Press, 2006).

28. Denis Steven Rutkus, CRS Report for Congress: Judicial Nomination Statistics, 1977–2003, www.senate.gov/, Table 2(b).

29. David W. Rohde and Kenneth A. Shepsle, "Advising and Consenting in the 60-Vote Senate: Strategic Appointments to the Supreme Court," *Journal of Politics* 69 (2007): 664–77.

30. Mitchel A. Sollenberger, "The Blue Slip: A Theory of Unified and Divided Government, 1979–2009," *Congress and the Presidency* 37, no. 2 (2010): 125–56.

31. Rutkus, CRS Report for Congress: Judicial Nomination Statistics, Table 2(b).

32. Michael A. Fletcher, "Obama Criticized as Too Cautious, Slow on Judicial Posts," *Washington Post*, October 16, 2009, www.washingtonpost.com/.

33. Bernie Becker and David Herszenhorn, "Democrats Lash Out at Secret Holds," May 6, 2010, http://thecaucusblogs.nytimes.com.

34. Richard Nixon, "Transcript of President's Announcement," *New York Times*, October 22, 1971.

35. David Yalof, *Pursuit of Justices* (Chicago: University of Chicago Press, 1999).

36. Information is from Democratic strategy memos obtained and reprinted by the *Wall Street Journal*. See "'He Is Latino': Why Dems Borked Estrada, in Their Own Words," www.opinionjournal.com/.

37. "Robert Bork's Position on Reproductive Rights," *New York Times*, September 13, 1987, B9. The remarks by Elena Kagan quoted in the caption for the photo on page 534 are from her article "Confirmation Messes, Old and New," *University of Chicago Law Review* 62, no. 2 (Spring 1995): 941.

38. Gregory Caldeira and Jack Wright, "Lobbying for Justice: Organized Interests, Supreme Court Nominations, and the United States Senate," *American Journal of Political Science* 42 (1998): 499.

39. Elisabeth Bumiller, "Court in Transition: The Committee; but Enough about You, Judge; Let's Hear What I Have to Say," *New York Times*, January 11, 2006.

40. Data here follow Jeffrey A. Segal and Albert D. Cover, "Ideological Values and the Votes of U.S. Supreme Court Justices," *American Political Science Review* 83 (1989): 557–65, updated at http://ws.cc.stonybrook.edu/polsci/jsegal/qualtable.pdf. Perceived ideology and perceived qualifications of the nominees are derived from content analysis of newspaper editorials at the time of each candidate's nomination.

41. Charles M. Cameron, Albert D. Cover, and Jeffrey A. Segal, "Senate Voting on Supreme Court Nominees: A Neoinstitutional Model," *American Political Science Review* 84 (1990): 525–34.

42. Federal litigation data can be found at www.uscourts.gov/.

43. Paul M. Collins Jr., "Friends of the Court: Examining the Influence of *Amicus Curiae* Participation in U.S. Supreme Court Litigation," *Law and Society Review* 38 (2004): 807–32.

44. Rebecca Salokar, *The Solicitor General: The Politics of Law* (Philadelphia: Temple University Press, 1992).

45. Lisa Solowiej and Paul Collins Jr., "Counteractive Lobbying in the US Supreme Court," *American Politics Research* 37 (2009): 670–99.

46. *Regents of the University of California v. Bakke*, 438 U.S. 265 (1978).

47. Federal Bureau of Investigation, Crime in the United States 2002, www.fbi.gov/.

48. United States Sentencing Commission, *2003 Sourcebook of Federal Sentencing Statistics*, 2004, 91.

49. The quotation in the caption on page 543 is from Supreme Court of the United States, Court Building, www.supremecourt.gov/.

50. Gregory Caldeira and John R. Wright, "Organized Interests and Agenda Setting in the U.S. Supreme Court," *American Political Science Review* 82 (1988): 1109–28.

51. *Hopwood v. Texas*, 78 F.3d 932 (1996).

52. Linda Greenhouse, *Becoming Justice Blackmun* (New York: Times Books, 2005).

53. Timothy Johnson, Paul Wahlbeck, and James Spriggs, "The Influence of Oral Arguments on the U.S. Supreme Court," *American Political Science Review* 100 (2006): 99.

54. Stohr, *A Black and White Case,* 277.

55. Gerald Rosenberg, *The Hollow Hope* (Chicago: University of Chicago Press, 1991).

56. *United States v. Nixon,* 418 U.S. 683 (1974).

57. *Reynolds v. Sims*, 377 U.S. 533 (1964).

58. *Roe v. Wade*, 410 U.S. 113 (1973).

59. *Gonzalez v. Raich* 545 U.S. 1 (2005).

60. Segal and Spaeth, *Supreme Court and the Attitudinal Model*.

61. Lee Epstein and Jackl Knight, *The Choices Justices Make* (Washington, D.C.: CQ Press, 1998); Forrest Maltzman, James F. Spriggs II, and Paul J. Wahlbeck, *Crafting Law on the Supreme Court: The Collegial Game* (New York: Cambridge University Press, 2000).

62. EEOC, Executive Order 10925, www.eeoc.gov/.

63. Charles V. Dale, CRS Report for Congress, Federal Affirmative Action Law: A Brief History, http://k20.internet2.edu/.

64. See Lawrence Baum, *The Puzzle of Judicial Behavior* (Ann Arbor: University of Michigan Press, 1997).

65. Alexander Bickel, *The Least Dangerous Branch: The Supreme Court at the Bar of Politics* (Indianapolis: Bobbs-Merrill, 1963).

66. Supreme Court Database, http://scdb.wustl.edu/.

67. Jeffrey A. Segal and Robert M. Howard, "How Supreme Court Justices Respond to Litigant Requests to Overturn Precedent," *Judicature* 85 (2001): 148–57.

68. Jeffrey A. Segal and Robert M. Howard, "A Preference for Deference? The Supreme Court and Judicial Review," *Political Research Quarterly* 57 (2004): 131–43. See also Lori Ringhand, "The Changing Face of Judicial Activism: An Empirical Examination of Voting Behavior on the Rehnquist Natural Court," *Constitutional Commentary* 24 (2007): 43.

69. Charlie Savage, "A Judge's View of Judging Is on the Record," *New York Times*, May 14, 2009, http://www.nytimes.com/.

70. Manu Raju, "Sonia Sotomayor Clears the Senate Judiciary Committee," Politico, July 29, 2009, http://www.politico.com/.

71. Robert Dahl, "Decision Making in a Democracy: The Supreme Court as a National Policy-Maker," *Journal of Public Law* 6 (1957): 179–295.

72. Herbert M. Kritzer, "Federal Judges and Their Political Environments: The Influence of Public Opinion," *American Journal of Political Science* 23 (1979): 194–207.

73. *West Virginia State Board of Education v. Barnette*, 319 U.S. 624 (1943), 638.

Chapter 16

1. This story is compiled from information on the websites of Campus Y at the University of North Carolina—Chapel Hill, MedPLUS Connect, and MedWish International, and from an e-mail interview with Lauren Slive, February 2, 2010, conducted for this textbook. The chapter-opening quotation is from the interview.

2. Washington's Farewell Address, 1796, Yale Law School Avalon Project, avalon.law.yale.edu.

3. Woodrow Wilson, "Address to Congress Requesting a Declaration of War against Germany," April 2, 1917, www.millercenter.org.

4. Harry S. Truman, "Speech before a Joint Session of Congress," March 12, 1947, www.millercenter.org.

5. U.S. Agency for International Development, "George C. Marshall: Commencement Address at Harvard University, June 5, 1947," www.usaid.gov.

6. Of the sixty-six hostages taken in November 1979, thirteen were released quickly, one was released In the summer of 1980, and the remaining fifty-two were held for 444 days. See the Jimmy Carter Library and Museum, "The Hostages and Casualties," www.jimmycarterlibrary.gov.

7. The quotation from Jimmy Carter in the caption for the photo on page 567 is from Miller Center of Public Affairs at the University of Virginia, http://millercenter.org/scripps/archive/speeches.

8. United Nations Office for Disarmament Affairs (UNODA), Treaty on the Non-Proliferation of Nuclear Weapons (NPT), www.un.org.

9. Glen S. Krutz and Jeffrey S. Peake, *Treaty Politics and the Rise of Executive Agreements* (Ann Arbor: University of Michigan Press, 2009), 129–34. Also see United Nations Office for Disarmament Affairs, Comprehensive Nuclear Test Ban Treaty (CTBT), www.un.org.

10. Krutz and Peake, *Treaty Politics and the Rise of Executive Agreements,* 129–34.

11. CTBTO Preparatory Commission, "CTBTO Fact Sheet," www.ctbto.org.

12. Federation of American Scientists, "Status of World Nuclear Forces," www.fas.org.

13. White House, "The President's Message to the Senate (on the Submission of the New START Treaty)," www.whitehouse.gov.

14. Douglas C. Foyle, "Public Opinion and Bosnia: Anticipating Disaster," in *Contemporary Cases in U.S. Foreign Policy,* ed. Ralph Carter (Washington, D.C.: CQ Press, 2002), 31–58.

15. Michael Slackman, "Chafing after 40 Years, Qaddafi Battles the West," *New York Times,* August 25, 2009, A11, www.nytimes.com.

16. Chester A. Crocker, "The Lessons of Somalia: Not Everything Went Wrong," *Foreign Affairs* 74 (1995): 2–8; for a chronology of U.S. involvement in Somalia, see "Ambush in Mogadishu," *Frontline*, www.pbs.org.

17. Mark McDonald, "Record Number of Somali Pirate Attacks in 2009," *New York Times*, December 30, 2009, A9, www.nytimes.com.

18. Thomas Donnelly, "The Underpinnings of the Bush Doctrine," American Enterprise Institute for Public Policy Research Outlook Series, 2003, www.aei.org; also see Jeffrey S. Lantis and Eric Moskowitz, "The Return of the Imperial Presidency? The Bush Doctrine and U.S. Intervention in Iraq," in *Contemporary Cases in U.S. Foreign Policy,* 2nd ed., ed. Ralph G. Carter (Washington, D.C.: CQ Press, 2005), 89–122.

19. Michael W. Doyle, "Liberalism and World Politics," *American Political Science Review* 80 (1986): 1151–69.

20. Information in this and the following paragraphs is from United Nations, www.un.org. See also http://www.un.org/News/Press/docs/2009/gaab3925.doc.htm.

21. United Nations, "United Nations Peacekeeping Operations: Principles and Guidelines," 2008, 31, www.pbpu.unlb.org.

22. Ibid.; United Nations Peacekeeping, "List of Operations, 1948–2009," www.un.org.

23. Society of Professional Journalists, "Geneva Conventions: A Reference Guide," www.genevaconventions.org. For a list of the nations, see International Committee of the Red Cross, "Geneva Conventions of 12 August 1949," www.icrc.org.

24. International Court of Justice, www.icj-cij.org.

25. Sean D. Murphy, "The United States and the International Court of Justice: Coping with Antimonies," *The United States Courts and Tribunals*, ed. Cesare Romano, George Washington Law School Legal Research Studies Paper 291 (2008).

26. Information in this and subsequent paragraphs is from Peace Corps, www.peacecorps.gov.

27. Mark R. Amstutz, "Faith-Based NGOs and U.S. Foreign Policy," in *The Influence of Faith: Religious Groups and Foreign Policy,* ed. Elliot Abrams (Lanham, Md.: Rowman and Littlefield Publishers, 2001), 175–87; National Council of Churches USA, www.ncccusa.org.

28. ACLU, "Blocking Faith, Chilling Charity," June 16, 2009, www.aclu.org.

29. Bill and Melinda Gates Foundation, www.gatesfoundation.org.

30. Human Rights Watch, www.hrw.org.

31. U.S. Census Bureau, "Foreign Trade Statistics," www.census.gov. For a longer discussion of U.S.-China trade, see Keith Bradsher, "China-U.S. Trade Dispute Has Broad Implications," *New York Times*, September 15, 2009, www.nytimes.com.

32. World Trade Organization, www.wto.org.

33. Information in this paragraph is from World Trade Organization, www.wto.org.

34. World Trade Organization, "Communication from the Chairman of the Panel on United States—Certain Measures Affecting Imports of Poultry from China," March 24, 2010, www.wto.org.

35. Europa: Gateway to the European Union, http://europa.eu/.

36. European Central Bank, www.ecb.int/.

37. World Bank, www.worldbank.org.

38. World Bank, Archives, www.worldbank.org.

39. World Bank, News and Broadcast, www.worldbank.org.

40. Information in this and the next paragraphs is from International Monetary Fund, www.imf.org.

41. United States Agency for International Development, www.usaid.gov.

42. White House, Office of Management and Budget, *The Budget for Fiscal Year 2011*, 870, www.whitehouse.gov.

43. Centers for Disease Control and Prevention, www.cdc.gov.

44. Amanda Gardner, "Only 1 in 4 Americans Got H1N1 Vaccine," *Business Week*, April 1, 2010, www.businessweek.com.

45. Daniel DeNoon, "Swine Flu Vaccine: When?" CBS News, July 21, 2009, www.cbsnews.com.

46. Information in this and the next paragraph from World Health Organization, www.who.int/.

47. World Health Organization, "Pandemic (H1N1) 2009 Vaccine Deployment Update—May 31, 2010," www.who.int/.

48. Raymond W. Copson, "AIDS in Africa," in *Politics and Economics in Africa*, vol. 6, ed. Olefumi Wusu (Hauppauge, N.Y.: Nova Science Publishers, 2006), www.pepfar.gov/.

49. The United States President's Emergency Plan for AIDS Relief, "Obligation and Outlay Reports," May 15, 2009, www.pepfar.gov/.

50. For an update on PEPFAR, see "The United States President's Emergency Plan for AIDS Relief: Making a Difference: Funding," www.pepfar.gov. Also see "60 Minutes Reports on PEPFAR, a U.S. Program That Has Helped Provide Treatment to Thousands," April 4, 2010, www.cbsnews.com/.

51. U.S. Energy Information Administration, "International Energy Outlook 2009," May 27, 2009, www.eia.doe.gov/.

52. United Nations Framework Convention on Climate Change, "Kyoto Protocol to the United Nations Framework Convention on Climate Change," http://unfccc.int/.

53. United Nations Framework Convention on Climate Change, "Status of Ratification of the Kyoto Protocol," http://unfccc.int/.

54. Ibid.

55. UNFCCC, "Status of Ratification, Amendment to Annex B of the Kyoto Protocol," January 6, 2010, http://unfccc.int/.

56. United Nations, "Copenhagen United Nations Climate Change Conference Ends with Political Agreements to Cap Temperature Rise, Reduce Emissions, and Raise Finance," December 19, 2009, http://unfccc.int/.

57. Jeffrey Gettlemen, "Kenya's Volatile Politics Shadow Clinton," *New York Times*, August 6, 2009, www.nytimes.com.

58. For a broader discussion of Hillary Clinton's role in shaping foreign policy, see David Rothkopf, "It's 3 AM. Do You Know Where Hillary Clinton Is?" *Washington Post*, August 23, 2009, www.washingtonpost.com.

Chapter 17

1. This story has been compiled from from The College of William and Mary, www/wm.edu; Dumas Malone, *Jefferson and His Time,* Vol. 1, *Jefferson the Virginian* (Boston: Little, Brown, 1948), 56; and *The Writings of Thomas Jefferson,* ed. Andrew Adgate Lipscomb and Albert Ellery Bergh (Washington, D.C.: Thomas Jefferson Memorial Association of the United States, 1903–05), 6:392, which is the source of the 1787 letter from Jefferson to James Madison from which the chapter-opening quotation is excerpted. The six American colleges were Harvard (1636), William and Mary (1693), Yale (1701), Princeton (then called the College of New Jersey; 1746), Columbia (1754), and University of Pennsylvania (then called the College of Philadelphia; 1757).

2. See Larry Bartels, *Unequal Democracy* (Princeton, N.J.: Princeton University Press, 2008).

3. Survey by Cable News Network conducted by Opinion Research Corporation, January 12–15, 2009.

4. U.S. Census Bureau. "State and Country Quick Facts," www.census.gov.

5. See Freedom House, www.freedomhouse.org.

6. Larry Bartels made this point in a presentation at Princeton University in November 2009.

Sources for Endpapers

Front: The United States in the Twenty-First Century

Bottled water: New York State Department of Environmental Conservation, www.nyrecycles.org; Watershed, reported in Petz Scholtus, "The U.S. Consumes 1500 Water Bottles Every Second," www.treehugger.com; Bottled Water Facts, buzzle.com.

Marriage: U.S. Census Bureau, reported in Conor Dougherty, "New Vow: I Don't Take Thee," *Wall Street Journal*, September 29, 2010, A3.

Life expectancy: U.S. Census Bureau, 2010 Statistical Abstract, www.census.gov.

Racial/ethnic groups: U.S. Census Bureau, United States Population Projections, 2000 to 2050, www.census.gov.

Schooling: UNESCO Education Statistics, www.nationmaster.com; U.S. Census Bureau, www.census.gov; National Center for Public Policy and Higher Education, www.highereducation.org; National Center for Education Statistics, U.S. Department of Education, http://nces.ed.gov.

Population: U.S. Census Bureau, www.census.gov.

Jobs: "Business 2.0: The Next Job Boom," CNN Money, http://money.cnn.com; Gallup, "Gallup Finds U.S. Unemployment at 10.0% in Mid-October," October 18, 2010, www.gallup.com.

Work: CIA World Factbook, United States, Economy, GDP, Labor Force—By Occupation, www.cia.gov.

Gap between the rich and the poor: U.S. Census Bureau, reported in Hope Yen, "Income Gap Widens: Census Finds Record Gap between Rich and Poor," Huffington Post, September 28, 2010, http://huffingtonpost.com; U.S. Internal Revenue Service, reported in Mark Robyn and Gerald Prante, "Summary of Latest Federal Individual Income Tax Data," Fiscal Fact No. 2049, October 6, 2010, www.taxfoundation.org; U.S. Census Bureau, Current Population Survey, 1968–2010, www.census.gov.

Poverty rate: U.S. Census Bureau, People and Households, Poverty Data, www.census.gov.

Money spent on campaigns: Center for Responsive Politics, www.opensecrets.org.

Growth rate and GDP: CIA World Factbook, United States, Economy, GDP—Real Growth Rate, GDP—Per Capita, and GDP—Composition by Sector, www.cia.gov.

Back: The United States in the World

Internet connections: John D. Sutter, "Why Internet Connections Are Fastest in South Korea," March 31, 2010, CNN, www.cnn.com.

Internet users: CIA World Factbook, Country Comparison, Internet Users, www.cia.gov.

Mobile phones: CIA World Factbook, Country Comparison, Telephone—Mobile Cellular, www.cia.gov.

Warmest decade: "2009: Second Warmest Year on Record; End of Warmest Decade," January 21, 2010, National Aeronautics and Space Administration, www.nasa.gov; also National Oceanic and Atmospheric Administration, Climatic Data Center, www.noaa.gov.

World population: CIA World Factbook, World, Population, www.cia.gov; UN, Department of Economic and Social Affairs, Population Division, *World Population to 2300* (New York: United Nations, 2004).

Most populous nation: CIA World Factbook, Country Comparison—Population, www.cia.gov; UN, Department of Economic and Social Affairs, Population Division, *World Population to 2300* (New York: United Nations, 2004).

Population growth rate: CIA World Factbook, Country Comparison—Population Growth Rate, www.cia.gov.

Most college degrees: College Board, reported in Jamaal Abdul-Alim, "College Board Releases 'Scorecard' Report on U.S. Degree Completion Progress," July 23, 2010, http://diverseeducation.com; Tamar Levin, "Once a Leader, U.S. Lags in College Degrees," *New York Times*, July 23, 2010.

Nobel Laureates: Nobel Foundation, nobelprize.org.

Carbon-monoxide emissions: Union of Concerned Scientists, "Each Country's Share of CO2 Emissions," www.ucsusa.org.

Infant mortality: CIA World Factbook, Country Comparison—Infant Mortality Rate, www.cia.gov.

Gap between the rich and the poor: U.S. Census Bureau, reported in Hope Yen, "Census Finds Record Gap between Rich and Poor," September 28, 2010, www.salon.com.

Military expenditures: CIA World Factbook, Country Comparison—Military Expenditures, www.cia.gov.

Obesity: OECD Health Data, reported in "Fat of the Lands: The Bulging Problem of Obesity," September 23, 2010, *The Economist*, www.economist.com; Organisation for Economic Co-operation and Development, oecd.org.

INDEX

Note: Page numbers followed by an "f" indicate figures. Page numbers followed by a "t" indicate tables.